Financial Management:
Principles and Applications

TENTH EDITION

Financial Management: Principles and Applications

ARTHUR J. KEOWN

Virginia Polytechnic Institute and State University
R.B. Pamplin Professor of Finance

JOHN D. MARTIN

Baylor University
Carr P. Collins Chair in Finance

J. WILLIAM PETTY

Baylor University
Professor of Finance
W. W. Caruth Chair in Entrepreneurship

DAVID F. SCOTT, JR.

University of Central Florida
Holder, Phillips-Schenck Chair in American Private Enterprise
Executive Director, Dr. Phillips Institute for the Study of American Business Activity
Professor of Finance

Pearson Education International

Senior Acquisitions Editor: Jackie Aaron
Editorial Director: Jeff Shelstad
Managing Editor (Editorial): Gladys Soto
Assistant Editor: Francesca Calogero
Media Project Manager: Victoria Anderson
Executive Marketing Manager: Debbie Clare
Marketing Assistant: Amanda Fisher
Managing Editor (Production): Cynthia Regan
Production Editor: Denise Culhane
Production Assistant: Joe DeProspero
Production Manager: Arnold Vila
Manufacturing Buyer: Diane Peirano
Design Manager: Maria Lange
Art Director: Janet Slowik
Interior Design: Liz Harasymczuk
Cover Design: Liz Harasymczuk
Cover Photo: Daniel Bailey/Index Stock Imagery
Illustrator (Interior): ElectraGraphics, Inc.
Photo Researcher: Kathy Ringrose
Image Permission Coordinator: Nancy Seise
Print Production Manager: Christy Mahon
Composition/Full-Service Project Management: Carlisle Communications, Ltd.
Printer/Binder: R.R. Donnelley/Willard

Credits and acknowledgments borrowed from other sources and reproduced, with permission, in this textbook appear on appropriate page within text.

Photo Credits
Front cover: Daniel Bailey/Index Stock Imagery; inset photos (left to right): 1. Photograph courtesy of Harley-Davidson Photography & Imaging; 2. AP/Wide World Photos; 3. Photograph courtesy of Harley-Davidson Photography & Imaging; 4. Omni-Photo Communications, Inc. **Back cover:** (photos left to right): 1. Getty Images Inc. – Stone Allstock; 2. Photograph courtesy of Harley-Davidson Photography & Imaging; 3. Getty Images Inc. – Stone Allstock; 4. Photograph courtesy of Harley-Davidson Photography & Imaging. **Pages 2, 30, 106, 180, 222, 254, 326, 370, 434, 550, 672,** and **704** Photographs courtesy of Harley-Davidson Photography & Imaging; **Page 70** Getty Images Inc. – Stone Allstock; **Page 136** Getty Images Inc. – Stone Allstock; **Page 288** AP/Wide World Photos; **Page 404** AP/Wide World Photos; **Page 468** Stock Boston; **Page 504** Getty Images Inc. – Image Bank; **Page 604** Omni-Photo Communications, Inc.; **Page 644** AP/Wide World Photos; **Page 738** Getty Images Inc. – Stone Allstock; **Page 772** Corbis/Bettmann.

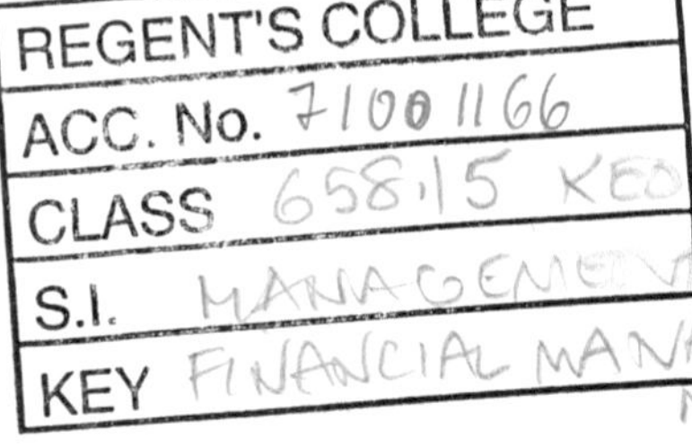

Pearson Education LTD.
Pearson Education Singapore, Pte. Ltd
Pearson Education, Canada, Ltd
Pearson Education-Japan
Pearson Education Australia PTY, Limited
Pearson Education North Asia Ltd
Pearson Educación de Mexico, S.A. de C.V.
Pearson Education Malaysia, Pte. Ltd
Pearson Education Upper Saddle River, New Jersey

10 9
ISBN 0-13-127318-3

The tenth edition of *Financial Management: Principles and Applications* is dedicated to our families—the ones who love us the most.

Barb, Emily, and Artie
Arthur J. Keown

Sally, Dave and Mel, and Jess
John D. Martin

To the future of four wonderful grandchildren: Ashley, Cameron, John, and MacKenzie
J. William Petty

To my dear late wife Peggy. Thank you for 36 marvelous, irreplaceable years.
David F. Scott, Jr.

BRIEF CONTENTS

PART 4: CAPITAL STRUCTURE AND DIVIDEND POLICY

PART 5: WORKING-CAPITAL MANAGEMENT AND SPECIAL TOPICS IN FINANCE

PART 6: SPECIAL TOPICS IN FINANCE

*Chapters 23 and 24 can be found at **www.prenhall.com/keown**

CONTENTS

*Chapters 23 and 24 can be found at **www.prenhall.com/keown**

PREFACE

In many ways, Harley-Davidson embodies the American experience. Its beginnings date back to 1903 and the start of America's Industrial Revolution. The company has survived two world wars, the Great Depression, and competition from countless competitors from both home and abroad. However, Harley-Davidson came close to becoming a part of history in 1985 as it teetered on the verge of bankruptcy. Since then, Harley-Davidson has reinvented itself, becoming one of the most successful companies in America and, as President Ronald Reagan once proclaimed, "an American success story."

In many ways, the evolution of Harley-Davidson illustrates the enormous challenges faced by any company that wishes to survive and prosper in today's world. In this text, we will focus on how a firm can create wealth for its shareholders. How did Harley do it? Since 1986, when Harley-Davidson returned to public ownership with a successful stock offering, the company has delivered 17 consecutive years of record revenues and earnings. In 2002, shareholders realized a five-year total return of 242 percent. This was all done through outstanding financial management. The company made good decisions. That is what we are going to look at in this book. We will examine what it took to turn Harley-Davidson, as well as other companies around, and what it takes to keep a company like Harley alive and well.

OUR APPROACH TO FINANCIAL MANAGEMENT

The first-time student of finance will find that corporate finance builds upon both economics and accounting. Economics provides much of the theory that underlies our techniques, whereas accounting provides the input or data on which decision making is based. Unfortunately, it is all too easy for students to lose sight of the logic that drives finance and to focus instead on memorizing formulas and procedures. As a result, students have a difficult time understanding the interrelationships between the topics covered. Moreover, later in life when the problems encountered do not fit neatly into the textbook presentation, the student may have problems abstracting from what was learned. To overcome this problem, the opening chapter presents 10 basic principles of finance that are woven throughout the book. What results is a text tightly bound around these guiding principles. In essence, the student is presented with a cohesive, interrelated subject from which future, as yet unknown, problems can be approached.

Teaching an introductory finance class while faced with an ever-expanding discipline puts additional pressures on the instructor. What to cover, what to omit, and how to make these decisions while maintaining a cohesive presentation are inescapable questions. In dealing with these questions, we have attempted to present the chapters in a stand-alone fashion so that they can easily be rearranged to fit almost any desired course structure and course length. Because the principles are woven into every chapter, the presentation of the text remains tight regardless of whether or not the chapters are rearranged. Again, our goal is to provide an enduring understanding of the basic tools and fundamental principles upon which finance is based. This foundation will give a student beginning his or her studies in finance a strong base on which to build future studies and give the student who will only take one finance class a lasting understanding of the basics of finance.

Although historical circumstances continue to serve as the driving force behind the development and practice of finance, the underlying principles that guide our discipline remain the same. These principles are presented in an intuitively appealing manner in Chapter 1 and thereafter are tied to all that follows. With a focus upon the big picture, we provide an introduction to financial decision making rooted in current financial theory and the current state of world economic conditions. This focus can be seen in a number of ways, perhaps most obvious being the attention paid both to valuation and to the capital markets, as well as their influence on corporate financial decisions. What results is an introductory treatment of a discipline rather than the treatment of a series of isolated finance problems. The goal of this text is to go beyond teaching the tools of a discipline or a trade, and help students gain a complete understanding of the subject. This will give them the ability to apply what they have learned to new and yet unforeseen problems—in short, to educate students in finance.

A TOTAL LEARNING PACKAGE

Financial Management is not simply another introductory finance text. It is a total learning package that reflects the vitality and ever-expanding nature of the discipline. Finance has grown too complex not to teach it with an eye on the big picture, focusing on the interrelationships between the covered materials. The following distinctive pedagogical features will assist the student in understanding how concepts in finance link to the big picture of finance.

Learning Aids in the Text

TEN PRINCIPLES OF FINANCE The fundamental principles that drive the practice of corporate finance are presented in the form of 10 principles. These principles first appear in Chapter 1 and thereafter appear through in-text inserts called "Back to the Principles." These inserts serve to refocus the student's attention on the underlying principles behind what is being done. In effect, they serve to keep the student from becoming so wrapped up in specific calculations that the interrelationships and overall scheme are lost.

CHAPTER INTRODUCTIONS FEATURING HARLEY-DAVIDSON Each chapter opens with an introductory example, many involving Harley-Davidson, that sets the stage for what is to follow. In this way, the student can easily understand the relevance, use, and importance of the material to be presented. Moreover, by having most of the features focus on the challenges facing a single company, the student can better understand the interrelationships between the different financial topics that are presented.

FINANCE MATTERS Strong emphasis is also placed upon practice, where practice is used to demonstrate both the relevance of the topics discussed and the implementation of theory. Moreover, to add life to the discussion, "Finance Matters" boxed inserts are provided throughout the text. These boxes are largely taken from the popular press, with analysis and implications provided following each box. In this way, the subject matter comes to life with added relevance to the student.

NEW! EXPANDED COVERAGE OF ETHICS Extensive coverage of ethics is provided through new **Finance Matters—Ethics** boxes. Ethics even has its own principle—*Principle 10: Ethical Behavior Is Doing the Right Thing, and Ethical Dilemmas Are Everywhere in Finance.* There are also ethics boxes throughout the text; for example, Chapter 1 includes one titled "Is It Wrong to Tell a Lie?" along with three boxes that deal with Enron: "The Enron Lessons," "The Enron Lessons: Maximizing Shareholder Wealth," and "The Enron Lessons: Trust." Several other Enron boxes appear in Chapters 2, 6, and 12.

NEW! BEST PRACTICES Notable topics of the day will be highlighted through the use of "Best Practices" boxes. For example, the best practices related to boards of directors, stock options, and executive pay will be highlighted in "Best Practices: Governance" boxes, while "Best Practices: Value-Based Management" boxes will be used to point out value drivers throughout the book. These value drivers will be linked to the discussion of the creation of shareholder wealth using EVA®, which is presented in detail in Chapter 13. In addition, "Best Practices: Financial Reporting" boxes will look at issues related to auditing, as well as recent financial scandals.

NEW! FINANCE: AN ENTREPRENEUR'S PERSPECTIVE Through the use of "An Entrepreneur's Perspective" boxes, the student is introduced to how finance relates to the entrepreneurial journey.

During the past decade, starting and growing companies has caught the interest of a lot of individuals. Many people want to own their own business. In fact, while many of the large companies are reducing the number of employees, smaller companies are creating new jobs.

Entrepreneurship has been defined as a relentless pursuit of opportunity. The process involves recognizing a good opportunity, gaining access to the needed resources, launching the venture, growing the business, and finally capturing the value created by successfully exiting the business.

Entrepreneurial Finance boxes titled, "An Entrepreneur's Perspective," highlight issues faced by small and medium-sized firms. These boxes look at finance from the point of view of someone who would like to start his or her own successful business.

NEW! WEB WORKS The web work end-of-chapter exercises introduce the student to useful information on the Internet, guiding the student to information and data that make financial topics and concepts come alive. Most chapters contain two to three new "Web Works" problems. Check them out at the end of Chapter 5.

NEW! UNIQUE TREATMENT OF MANAGERIAL COMPENSATION AND MANAGING FOR SHAREHOLDER VALUE The Tenth Edition of *Financial Management* provides an entire chapter on managing for shareholder value which will be tied to the "Best Practices: Value-Based Management" boxes that point out value drivers throughout the book. In Chapter 13, Managing for Shareholder Value, we focus on the use of economic value added or EVA® to measure firm and divisional performance along with how that value is created. This measure of performance has been found to be an effective tool for managing shareholder value by a large number of firms both in the United States and abroad. In fact, even the U.S. Postal Service has implemented a variant of the model to better control its internal operations.

Traditionally, the finance profession has had little to say about performance appraisal of the firm beyond a cursory discussion of financial ratios. By focusing on value-based management, we discuss value creation first in terms of how the market accords value to the firm in the context of market value added. Next we connect value creation to the individual contributions that the firm makes year-to-year in the form of EVA®. However, measuring value creation is not enough. The proponents of shareholder value creation point out, quite appropriately, that to assure the continued focus of the firm's employees on value creation the firm must reward them for doing the things that lead to value creation. Thus, the second half of this new chapter focuses on managerial compensation. This is the first corporate finance text to undertake a synthesis of both the measurement (EVA®) and reward (compensation) systems that are commonplace among the top value creators in corporate America.

INTERNATIONAL FINANCIAL MANAGEMENT In view of the continued globalization of world markets, we have integrated examples of international finance throughout the text. In addition, at the close of most chapters a new section has been added dealing with how the material in that chapter relates to the multinational firm. Finally, recognizing the fact that many of us approach the teaching of international finance in different ways, a separate chapter on international financial management also is provided.

CHAPTER LEARNING OBJECTIVES AND KEY TERMS Each chapter begins by setting out the learning objectives for that chapter, and setting in mind what that chapter will enable the student to do. In addition, at the end of each chapter, key terms and their locations in the text are identified, creating an easy review for the student.

THE EVA® TRAINING TUTOR The Tenth Edition of *Financial Management* also includes the EVA® Training Tutor by Stern Stewart & Co. The EVA® Training Tutor is a computer training program incorporating the latest interactive, multimedia techniques. It instills business and financial literacy by teaching the EVA® decision-making framework that Stern Stewart has been using for years to help many of the world's best-known companies succeed.

EVA® ties more closely to the creation of shareholder wealth than any other measure of business performance. That is why companies that manage with EVA® usually perform better for shareholders. Employees who work in EVA® companies tend to have higher levels of business literacy and earn bigger bonuses.

FINANCIAL SPREADSHEETS AND CALCULATORS The use of financial spreadsheets and calculators has been integrated throughout this text. This provides the student with access to both methods of problem solving and introduces them to the advantages of each. In addition, we provide the student with hints and strategies for the use of financial spreadsheets directly in the text, while providing an Appendix in the back of the book that guides them through the use of a financial calculator.

EXPANDED USE OF REAL-WORLD EXAMPLES OTHER THAN HARLEY-DAVIDSON In addition to the focus on Harley-Davidson, we have greatly expanded the illustrative use of examples of problems facing other real-world firms. This adds to student interest both by showing the relevance of the subjects covered and by providing an exciting framework within which to discuss financial concepts.

HOW FINANCIAL MANAGERS USE THIS MATERIAL Each chapter closes with a section entitled "How Financial Managers Use This Material." This section ties the material presented in the chapter both to the student's future job setting and to real-world companies, thereby enhancing the student's interest and displaying the relevance of the material covered.

FUNCTIONAL INTEGRATION TO BUSINESS Where appropriate, we have pointed out the relevance of the material covered to those students who are not finance majors—such as information technology, accounting, marketing, and management majors. In this way, students who are not finance majors are brought more fully into the subject matter.

NEW TO THIS EDITION

In addition to an updating and streamlining of the material, the following list includes the major additions that are new to *Financial Management*:

- **Chapter 1:** The treatment of ethics in finance has been substantially upgraded with the addition of three boxes that deal with Enron and the ethical lessons that were learned. In addition, a new "Entrepreneurial Finance" box dealing with the keys to entrepreneurial success appears in Chapter 1.
- **Chapter 2:** A new, intuitive presentation of the basics of computing free cash flows is introduced in Chapter 2. In addition, the treatment of ethics in finance is presented in a new "Finance Matters" box that discusses the recent scandals related to integrity in financial reporting and their impact on the firms involved.
- **Chapter 3:** Starbucks was added as an additional illustration in evaluating a firm's financial performance.
- **Chapter 4:** This chapter was thoroughly updated with the addition of new company examples.
- **Chapter 5:** The problem set was dramatically expanded with more problems directed at students using financial calculators.
- **Chapter 6:** The revision of Chapter 6 centered on the incorporation of more timely examples and graphs illustrating the term structure of interest.
- **Chapter 7:** This chapter introduced a discussion on behavioral finance relating to efficient markets.
- **Chapter 8:** The revision of Chapter 8 included a discussion of Warren Buffet and his philosophies of investing.
- **Chapter 9:** Chapter 9 was thoroughly updated with the addition of new company examples. In addition, a new "Finance Matters" box deals with companies such as Heinz, Quaker, Frito-Lay, and others that have introduced brightly colored food products aimed at the young consumer.
- **Chapter 10:** In response to reviewers' comments, the calculation of operating cash flows was dramatically revised and simplified so that the student can easily gain an intuitive grasp of these calculations. In addition, operating cash flows are calculated using four different methods, with each producing the same result. Since each of these methods is used in practice, it is important to demonstrate their equivalence.
- **Chapter 11:** This chapter was revised with the addition of new examples demonstrating the high degree of risk for projects in areas where the technology is constantly changing, such as the wireless technology field.
- **Chapter 12:** The update in this chapter focused on the addition of new company examples to make the discussion more real.
- **Chapter 13:** This chapter's update included the addition of three new "Best Practices" boxes: "How Are Executives Paid?," "Employee Compensation Policies," and "Executive Stock Options."
- **Chapter 14:** Several changes are spread throughout this chapter in response to suggestions from reviewers. The section on *The Private Placement Market and Venture Capital* is both deepened and lengthened. Venture capital activity and risk taking is related to the stage of the domestic business cycle with discourse, tabular presentation, and graphic presentation. The venture capital section includes a new example of *Finance and the Entrepreneur* which focuses on the venture capitalist's approach to "financing the deal." This new section is complete with a numerical example where the student learns how to solve for the internal rate of return on the amount of venture capital at risk. Two other new sections are prominent in this chapter. A *Best Practices* section uses an actual document from an Atlanta, Georgia-based firm to

illustrate that firm's selection criteria for an investment banker. In addition, the *Public Company Accounting Reform and Investor Protection Act* (Sarbanes-Oxley Act of 2002) is thoroughly reviewed along with the creation of the Public Company Accounting Oversight Board. In short, this is a much more lively chapter.

- **Chapter 15:** This chapter adds more actual company examples and discussions. For example, students are directed to Harley-Davidson's annual report to verify financial performance numbers that are discussed in the introduction to the chapter. The Walt Disney Company's Web site is used to allow the student to calculate the degree of combined leverage for this firm.
- **Chapter 16:** More real-world discussions were added including the Coca-Cola Company, Harley-Davidson, Georgia-Pacific, and The Walt Disney Company. The student is directed to Coca-Cola's Web site and the specific location called the "Investor Center." The student can then review Coke's debt policy, bond ratings, and various measures of financial leverage use, including the interest coverage ratio. Further, target bond ratings are discussed as a practical method used by financial managers for implementing the debt-capacity concept. This also involves the Federal Reserves' Web site and its important H.15 report on "Selected Interest Rates."
- **Chapter 17:** Examples have been added that utilize policies from both Starbucks Corporation and Home Depot. A thorough example of the actual dividend policy from Harley-Davidson also is included. Implications of the "Jobs and Growth Tax Reconciliation Act of 2003" for corporate dividend policy also are presented.
- **Chapter 18:** The update in this chapter focused on the addition of new company examples to make the discussion more real.
- **Chapter 19:** In addition to an update of the figures and numbers in this chapter, new company examples were added throughout.
- **Chapter 20:** The discussion of accounts receivables and inventory management was updated and new examples were added to help focus attention to the importance of this decision.
- **Chapter 21:** This chapter was updated to reflect the incredible increase in the use of options and futures (for example, on a typical day, over $25 billion in option contract value is traded).
- **Chapter 22:** This chapter was updated to reflect the increasing importance of the Euro and the impact of swings in the Euro on U.S. companies.
- **Chapter 23:** A new "Best Practices" box titled "Corporate Boards of Directors" was added along with a discussion of Enron's corporate governance and how it failed the stockholder.
- **Chapter 24:** In addition to an update of the figures and numbers in this chapter, new company examples were added throughout the chapter.

LEARNING AIDS SUPPLEMENTAL TO THE TEXT

Financial Management integrates the most advanced technology available to assist the student and the instructor. Not only does it make their financial management come alive with the most current information, but it also enhances a total understanding of all tools and concepts necessary in mastering the course.

THE SUPPORT PACKAGE

STUDENT STUDY GUIDE Written by the authors, the Study Guide contains several innovative features to help the student of *Financial Management*. Each chapter begins with an overview of the key points, which can serve as a preview and quick survey of the chapter content, as well as a review. There are problems (with detailed solutions) and self-tests that can be used to aid in the preparation of outside assignments and to study for examinations. The problems are keyed to the end-of-chapter problems in the text in order to provide direct and meaningful student aid. Multiple-choice and true/false questions are also included to provide a self-test over the descriptive chapter material.

INSTRUCTOR'S MANUAL WITH SOLUTIONS The Instructor's Manual, prepared by the authors, contains these four key elements for each chapter:

1. A chapter orientation, which offers the instructor a simple statement of the authors' intent for the chapter, and a useful point of departure for in-class lecture;
2. A chapter outline for easy reference to key issues;
3. Answers to all end-of-chapter questions in the text;
4. A second set of alternative problems with answers.

TEST BANK The Test Bank, revised for this edition by Jennifer Frazier, James Madison University, provides multiple-choice, true/false, and short-answer questions with complete and detailed answers.

NEW TESTGEN-EQ SOFTWARE The print Test Banks are designed for use with the TestGen-EQ test-generating software. This computerized package allows instructors to custom design, save, and generate classroom tests. The test program permits instructors to edit, add, or delete questions from the test banks; edit existing graphics and create new graphics; analyze test results; and organize a database of tests and student results. This new software allows for greater flexibility and ease of use. It provides many options for organizing and displaying tests, along with a search and sort feature.

POWERPOINT PRESENTATION Lecture notes have been prepared by Professor Anthony Byrd of the University of Central Florida. These electronic slides exhibit full-color presentations of chapter overviews and examples coordinated with *Financial Management*, 10th Edition. The PowerPoint slides are available from the Prentice Hall Web site—**www.prenhall.com/keown.**

SPREADSHEET TEMPLATES AND SOLUTIONS In addition to the solutions being provided in the Instructor's Manual, the authors have also developed Spreadsheet Solutions for virtually all of the end-of-chapter problems. These solutions have been prepared in Excel.

The user can change the assumptions in the problem and thereby generate new solutions. Student templates consist of select end-of-chapter problems that are meant to be worked out off the Prentice Hall Web site—**www.prenhall.com/keown.**

COMPANION WEB SITE: www.prenhall.com/keown

The Companion Web Site is a content-rich, multidisciplinary Web site with exercises, activities, and resources related specifically to *Financial Management*, Tenth Edition.

The Online Study Guide offers students another opportunity to sharpen their problem-solving skills and to assess their understanding of the text material. The Online Study Guide for Keown/Martin/Petty/Scott contains quizzes that are made up of multiple-choice, true/false, and essay questions for each chapter. The Online Study Guide grades each question submitted by the student, provides immediate feedback for correct and incorrect answers, and allows students to e-mail results to up to four e-mail addresses.

For Instructors

- **Syllabus Manager** This feature allows instructors to enhance their lectures with all the resources available with this text. Instructors can post their own syllabus and link to any of the material on the site.
- **Downloadable Supplements** These features allow instructors to access the book's PowerPoint presentations and Instructor's Manual.

ACKNOWLEDGMENTS

We gratefully acknowledge the assistance, support, and encouragement of those individuals who have contributed to *Financial Management.* Specifically, we wish to recognize the very helpful insights provided by many of our colleagues. For their careful comments and helpful reviews of this edition of the text, we are indebted to:

Kenneth Beller, Washington State University–Tri-Cities
Douglas O. Cook, University of Mississippi
Brad Johnson, Eastern Oregon University
Chet Lakhani, Pepperdine University
John Stansfield, University of Missouri–Columbia
Herbert Witt, University of San Francisco
Kermit C. Zieg, Jr., Florida Institute of Technology

We would also like to thank those who have provided helpful insights in past editions. For their comments and reviews, we would like to thank:

Kamal Abouzeid, V. T. Alaganan, Michael T. Alderson, Dwight C. Anderson, Nasser Arshadi, Sung C. Bea, Gary Benesh, Laura Berk, Sam G. Berry, Randy Billingsley, Eric Blazer, Laurence E. Blouse, Russell P. Boisjoly, Robert Boldin, Michael Bond, Waldo L. Born, Virgil L. Brewer, Jozelle Brister, Paul Burzik, John Byrd, Michael W. Carter, Don M. Chance, Perikolam Raman Chandy, K. C. Chen, Santosh Choudhury, Jeffrey S. Christensen, M. C. Chung, Albert H. Clark, David W. Cole, Steven M. Dawson, Yashwant S. Dhatt, Bernard C. Dill, Mark Dorfman, John W. Ellis, Suzanne Erickson, Marjorie Evert, Slim Feriani, Greg Filbeck, Sidney R. Finkel, Fredrick G. Floss, Lyn Fraser, John Glister, Sharon S. Graham, Jack Griggs, Nancy Lee Halford, Ken Halsey, James D. Harris, William R. Henry, Dr. Linda C. Hittle, Stephen M. Horan, Keith Howe, Charles R. Idol, Vahan Janjigian, Nancy Jay, Jeff Jenkins, William Jens, Steve A. Johnson, Ravi Kamath, Djavad Kashefinejad, Terry Keele, James D. Keys, Robert Kleiman, David R. Klock, Reinhold P. Lamb, Larry Lang, George B. F. Lanigan, William R. Lasher, Howard C. Launstein, David E. Letourneau, Leonard T. Long, Richard MacMinn, Judy E. Maese, Abbas Mamoozadeh, Terry S. Maness, Balasundram Maniam, Surendra K. Mansinghka, James A. Miller, Naval Modani, Eric J. Moon, Scott Moore, M. P. Narayan, Willliam E. O'Connell, Jr., Shalini Perumpral, Jeffrey H. Peterson, Mario Picconi, Ted R. Pilger, John M. Pinkerton, Stuart Rosenstein, Ivan C. Roten, Marjorie A. Rubash, Jack H. Rubens, Todd Schank, Peter A. Sharp, Jackie Shu, Michael Solt, Raymond F. Spudeck, Suresh Srivastava, Joseph Stanford, Edward Stendardi, Donald L. Stevens, Glenn L. Stevens, David Suk, Elizabeth Sun, L. E. Sweeney, Philip R. Swensen, R. Bruce Swensen, Amir Tavakkol, Lee Tenpao, John G. Thatcher, Gary L. Trennepohl, Ronald Tsang, Paul A. Vanderheiden, K. G. Viswananthan, Al Webster, Patricia Webster, Herbert Weintraub, Kenneth L. Westby, Sandra Williams, Lawrence C. Wolken, Kevin Woods, Steve B. Wyatt, Wold Zemedkun, and Marc Zenner.

We also thank our friends at Prentice Hall. They are a great group of folks. We offer our personal expression of appreciation to our editor, Jackie Aaron, who provided leadership and direction to this project. She is the best. In addition, Jackie is just a great person—thanks, Jackie. We would also like to thank Francesca Calogero for her administrative deftness. She was superb. With Francesca watching over us, there was no way the ball could be dropped. We would also like to extend our thanks to Gladys Soto, who, once again, played a major role in this revision. Gladys oversaw this project, continuously offered insights and direction, and often served as a sounding board for revisions and new ideas. Unfortunately, this may be the last time we work with Gladys, as she is moving to the economics area. We will miss her. She is a wonderful person and a true friend. Our thanks also go to Debbie Clare for her marketing prowess. Debbie has an amazing understanding of the market, coupled with an intuitive understanding of what the market is looking for. In addition to being a joy to work with, she is also the hardest working person in America. We also thank Torie Anderson, our media manager, who did a great job of making sure this project is on the cutting edge in terms of Web applications and offerings. Erika Rusnak, our supplements project manager, did an excellent job of ensuring that our supplements would be the best in the marketplace. Erika did an outstanding job of enlisting Jennifer Frazier of James Madison University, in our opinion one of the best instructors in the country, to work on the test item file. We express a very special thank you to Denise Culhane, the production editor, for seeing the book through a very complex production process and keeping it all on schedule while maintaining extremely high quality.

As a final word, we express our sincere thanks to those using *Financial Management* in the classroom for making us a part of your team. Always feel free to give any of us a call or contact us through the Internet when you have questions or needs.

PART 1

The Scope and Environment of Financial Management

LEARNING OBJECTIVES

After reading this chapter, you should be able to

1. Describe what the subject of financial management is about.
2. Explain the goal of the firm.
3. Compare the various legal forms of business and explain why the corporate form of business is the most logical choice for a firm that is large or growing.
4. Explain the 10 principles that form the basics of financial management.
5. Explain what has led to the era of the multinational corporation.

CHAPTER 1

An Introduction to Financial Management

In 1985, Harley-Davidson teetered only hours away from bankruptcy as one of Harley's largest lenders, Citicorp Industrial Credit, was considering bailing out on its loan. Since its beginning in 1903, the company survived two world wars, the Great Depression, and competition from countless competitors, but by the early 1980s, Harley had become known for questionable reliability and leaving oil stains on people's driveways. It looked for a while like the future was set, and Harley wouldn't be there. It looked like the future of motorcycles in America would feature only Japanese names like Honda, Yamaha, Kawasaki, and Suzuki. But none of that happened, and today Harley-Davidson stands, as President Reagan once proclaimed, as "an American success story." For a company in today's world, surviving one scare is not enough—Today the business world involves a continuous series of challenges. As for Harley, it was a major accomplishment to make it through the 1980s, allowing it to face another challenge in the 1990s: a market that looked like it might disappear within a few years. How did Harley do against what looked like a shrinking market? It increased its motorcycle shipments from just over 60,000 in 1990 to over 260,000 in 2002 with expected sales in 2003 of around 290,000! How have the shareholders done? Between 1986, when Harley-Davidson returned to public ownership with a successful stock offering, and Spring 2003, Harley's stock price rose approximately 125-fold. How did Harley-Davidson, a company whose name grown men and women have tattooed on their arms and elsewhere, a company that conjures up images of burly bad boys and Easy Rider hippies in black leather jackets riding down the road, pull off one of the biggest business turnarounds of all time? Harley made good decisions. That's what we're going to look at in this book. We'll look at what it takes to turn Harley or any other company around. We'll look at how a company goes about making decisions to introduce new product lines. For example, in 2003, Harley-Davidson introduced the Buell Lightning Low XB95, a low-cost, lightweight bike with a lower seat height aimed at bringing shorter riders into the sport. How did it make this decision? We'll also follow Harley-Davidson throughout this book, examining how its experience fits in with the topics we are examining. In doing so, we will see that there are countless interactions among finance, marketing, management, and accounting. Because finance deals with decision making, it takes on importance, regardless of your major. Moreover, the tools, techniques, and understanding you will gain from finance will not only help you in your business career, but will also help you make educated personal investment decisions in the future.

CHAPTER PREVIEW

In this chapter, we will lay a foundation for the entire book. We will explain what finance is, and then we will explain the key goal that guides financial decision making: maximization of shareholder wealth. We will examine the legal environment of financial decisions. Then, we will describe the golden thread that ties everything together: the 10 basic principles of finance. Finally, we will look at the importance of looking beyond our geographic boundaries.

Objective 1

WHAT IS FINANCE?

Financial management is concerned with the maintenance and creation of economic value or wealth. Consequently, this course focuses on decision making with an eye toward creating wealth. As such, we will deal with financial decisions such as when to introduce a new product, when to invest in new assets, when to replace existing assets, when to borrow from banks, when to issue stocks or bonds, when to extend credit to a customer, and how much cash to maintain.

To illustrate, consider two firms, Merck and General Motors (GM). At the end of 2003, the total market value of Merck, a large pharmaceutical company, was $103 billion. Over the life of the business, Merck's investors had invested about $30 billion in the business. In other words, management created $73 billion in additional wealth for the shareholders. GM, on the other hand, was valued at $30 billion at the end of 2003; but over the years, GM's investors had actually invested $85 billion—a loss in value of $55 billion. Therefore, Merck created wealth for its shareholders, while GM lost shareholder wealth.

In introducing decision-making techniques, we will emphasize the logic behind those techniques, thereby ensuring that we do not lose sight of the concepts when dealing with the calculations. To the first-time student of finance, this may sound a bit overwhelming. However, as we will see, the techniques and tools introduced in this text are all motivated by 10 underlying principles or axioms that will guide us through the decision-making process.

Objective 2

GOAL OF THE FIRM

We believe that the preferable goal of the firm should be *maximization of shareholder wealth*, by which we mean maximization of the price of the existing common stock. Not only will this goal be in the best interest of the shareholders, but it will also provide the most benefits to society. This will come about as scarce resources are directed to their most productive use by businesses competing to create wealth.

To better understand this goal, we will first discuss profit maximization as a possible goal for the firm. Then we will compare it to maximization of shareholder wealth to see why, in financial management, the latter is the more appropriate goal for the firm.

PROFIT MAXIMIZATION

In microeconomics courses, profit maximization is frequently given as the goal of the firm. Profit maximization stresses the efficient use of capital resources, but it is not specific with respect to the time frame over which profits are to be measured. Do we maximize profits over the current year, or do we maximize profits over some longer period? A financial manager could easily increase current profits by eliminating research and development expenditures and cutting down on routine maintenance. In the short run, this might result in increased profits, but this clearly is not in the best long-run interests of the firm. If we are to base financial decisions on a goal, that goal must be precise, not allow for misinterpretation, and deal with all the complexities of the real world.

In microeconomics, profit maximization functions largely as a theoretical goal, with economists using it to prove how firms behave rationally to increase profit. Unfortunately, it ignores many real-world complexities that financial managers must address in their decisions. In the more applied discipline of financial management, firms must deal every day with two major factors not considered by the goal of profit maximization: uncertainty and timing.

Microeconomics courses ignore uncertainty and risk to present theory more easily. Projects and investment alternatives are compared by examining their expected values or weighted average profits. Whether one project is riskier than another does not enter into these calculations; economists do discuss risk, but only tangentially.[1] In reality, projects differ a great deal with respect to risk characteristics, and to disregard these differences in the practice of financial management can result in incorrect decisions. As we will discover later in this chapter, there is a very definite relationship between risk and expected return—that is, investors demand a higher expected return for taking on added risk—and to ignore this relationship would lead to improper decisions.

Another problem with the goal of profit maximization is that it ignores the timing of the project's returns. If this goal is only concerned with this year's profits, we know it inappropriately ignores profit in future years. If we interpret it to maximize the average of future profits, it is also incorrect. Inasmuch as investment opportunities are available for money in hand, we are not indifferent to the timing of the returns. Given equivalent cash flows from profits, we want those cash flows sooner rather than later. Thus the real-world factors of uncertainty and timing force us to look beyond a simple goal of profit maximization as a decision criterion.

Finally, and possibly most important, accounting profits fail to recognize one of the most important costs of doing business. When we calculate accounting profits, we consider interest expense as a cost of borrowing money, but we ignore the cost of the funds provided by the firm's shareholders (owners). If a company could earn 8 percent on a new investment, that would surely increase the firm's profits. However, what if the firm's shareholders could earn 12 percent with that same money in another investment of similar risk? Should the company's managers accept the investment because it will increase the firm's profits? Not if they want to act in the best interest of the firm's owners (shareholders). Now look at what happened with Burlington Northern.

Burlington Northern is a perfect example of erroneous thinking. In 1980, Richard Bressler was appointed as Chief Executive Officer (CEO) of the company. Bressler, unlike his predecessor, was not a "railroad man." He was an "outsider" who was hired for the express purpose of improving the value of the shareholders' stock. The reason for the change was that Burlington Northern had been earning about 4 percent on the shareholders' equity, when Certificates of Deposit (CDs) with no risk were paying 6 percent. Management was certainly increasing the firm's profits, but they were destroying shareholder wealth by investing in railroad lines that were not even earning a rate of return equal to that paid on government securities. We will turn now to an examination of a more robust goal for the firm: maximization of shareholder wealth.

Maximization of Shareholder Wealth

In formulating the goal of maximization of shareholder wealth, we are doing nothing more than modifying the goal of profit maximization to deal with the complexities of the operating environment. We have chosen maximization of shareholder wealth—that is, maximization of the market value of the existing shareholders' common stock—because the effects of all financial decisions are thereby included. Investors react to poor investment or dividend decisions by causing the total value of the firm's stock to fall, and they react to good decisions by pushing up the price of the stock. In effect, under this goal, good decisions are those that create wealth for the shareholder.

Obviously, there are some serious practical problems in implementing this goal and in using changes in the firm's stock to evaluate financial decisions. We know the price of a firm's stock fluctuates, often for no apparent reason. However, over the long run, price equals value. We will keep this long-run balancing in mind and focus on the effect that

[1] See, for example, Robert S. Pindyck and Daniel Rubenfield, *Microeconomics*, 2d ed. (New York: Macmillan, 1992), 244–46.

FINANCE MATTERS ETHICS

THE ENRON LESSONS

On December 2, 2001 the Enron Corporation (Houston, TX) declared bankruptcy. Enron's failure shocked the business community because of the size and prominence of the firm. Perhaps most telling is the fact that Enron Corp. had been named the most innovative company in America by *Fortune Magazine* for six straight years, with the most recent award being made in January 2001. The Enron failure dominated the financial press for months thereafter and also resulted in a series of high profile congressional hearings. Throughout this book we will be presenting the lessons learned from Enron in a series of boxes, but first, here is an assessment of why there was so much public concern over the event.

In a capitalistic economy firms are formed by entrepreneurs—some grow to be large, publicly traded firms like Enron, and many of them eventually fail. So why is the failure of Enron so important? After all, failure is just evidence of the Darwinian survival of the fittest principle at work, right? However, the Enron situation seems to be different. Let's consider some of the reasons why the Enron case might be special and see if they can explain the public rancor over the firm's failure.

This Was the Largest Bankruptcy Ever[a]

True, Enron's bankruptcy is the largest such bankruptcy ever with a total of $63 billion in equity value vaporized in a 12-month period. But this loss of shareholder value is far from the largest such loss of value ever. Consider the fact that the following list of firms have lost more than twice the shareholder value that Enron lost: AOL Time Warner, Cisco, EMC, Intel, JDS Uniphase, Lucent, Microsoft, Nortel, Sun Microsystems, and Worldcom. In fact, the value of Cisco's equity fell a mind boggling $423 billion compared to Enron's meager $63 billion. But since Enron lost everything, that's different, right? Global Crossings also lost everything (more than $48 billion), and there was not nearly the public outcry over this bankruptcy.

Failure of the Public Reporting Process

What we've learned about the deep seeded problems at Enron after the firm's failure has led many investors to question the adequateness of public reporting. For example, where were the analysts and credit rating agencies, since no early warning was sounded? Where were the firm's auditors and why were they not reporting what appear in hindsight to be a blatant disregard for standard reporting practice to the board of director's auditor committee? Speaking of which, where was the firm's board of directors and why were they not questioning some of Enron's related party transactions?

It would appear that an important source of the public outcry associated with the failure of Enron comes from the fact that this failure provides a clear warning as to just what can happen. Investor confidence in the system of public reporting has been shaken. If the most innovative company in America for six straight years and the darling of Wall Street can be this close to bankruptcy and no one seems to notice, what about less notable firms?

Political Influence, Fraud, and Scandal

Even the *National Enquirer* devoted its cover story to Enron.[b] Add the prospect of criminal wrongdoing by Enron's executives to the fact that Enron was a major contributor to both political parties (although its ties to the Republican party are better known) and you have the stuff of which good soap opera plots are made.

[a]From "More Reasons to Get Riled Up," Geoffrey Colvin, *Fortune* (3/4/02). © 2002 Time, Inc. All Rights Reserved.

[b]Kevin Lynch, Michael Hanrahan, and David Wright, "Enron: The Untold Story," *The National Enquirer* (February 26, 2002).

our decision *should* have on the stock price if everything else were held constant. The market price of the firm's stock reflects the value of the firm as seen by its owners and takes into account the complexities and complications of the real-world risk. As we follow this goal throughout our discussions, we must keep in mind that the shareholders are the legal owners of the firm. See the Finance Matters box, "Ethics: The Enron Lessons."

CONCEPT CHECK

1. What are the problems with the goal of profit maximization?
2. What is the goal of the firm?

LEGAL FORMS OF BUSINESS ORGANIZATION

Objective 3

In the chapters ahead, we will focus on financial decisions for corporations. Although the corporation is not the only legal form of business available, it is the most logical choice for a firm that is large or growing. It is also the dominant business form in terms of sales in this country. In this section, we will explain why this is so. This will in turn allow us to simplify the remainder of the text, as we will assume that the proper tax code to follow is the corporate tax code, rather than examine different tax codes for different legal forms of businesses. Keep in mind that our primary purpose is to develop an understanding of the logic of financial decision making. Taxes will become important only when they affect our decisions, and our discussion of the choice of the legal form of the business is directed at understanding why we will limit our discussion of taxes to the corporate form.

Legal forms of business organization are diverse and numerous. However, there are three categories: the sole proprietorship, the partnership, and the corporation. To understand the basic differences between each form, we need to define each form and understand its advantages and disadvantages. As we will see, as the firm grows, the advantages of the corporation begin to dominate. As a result, most large firms take on the corporate form.

SOLE PROPRIETORSHIP

The **sole proprietorship** is a business owned by a single individual. The owner maintains title to the assets and is personally responsible, generally without limitation, for the liabilities incurred. The proprietor is entitled to the profits from the business but must also absorb any losses. This form of business is initiated by the mere act of beginning the business operations. Typically, no legal requirement must be met in starting the operation, particularly if the proprietor is conducting the business in his or her own name. If a special name is used, an assumed-name certificate should be filed, requiring a small registration fee. Termination occurs on the owner's death or by the owner's choice. Briefly stated, the sole proprietorship is, for all practical purposes, the absence of any formal *legal* business structure.

Sole proprietorship
A business owned by a single individual.

PARTNERSHIP

The primary difference between a **partnership** and a sole proprietorship is that the partnership has more than one owner. A partnership is an association of two or more persons coming together as co-owners for the purpose of operating a business for profit. Partnerships fall into two types: (1) general partnerships and (2) limited partnerships.

Partnership
An association of two or more individuals joining together as co-owners to operate a business for profit.

GENERAL PARTNERSHIP In a general partnership, each partner is fully responsible for the liabilities incurred by the partnership. Thus, any partner's faulty conduct even having the appearance of relating to the firm's business renders the remaining partners liable as well. The relationship among partners is dictated entirely by the partnership agreement, which may be an oral commitment or a formal document.

LIMITED PARTNERSHIP AND LIMITED LIABILITY COMPANY In addition to the general partnership, in which all partners are jointly liable without limitation, many states provide for a limited partnership. The state statutes permit one or more of the partners to have limited liability, restricted to the amount of capital invested in the partnership. Several conditions must be met to qualify as a limited partner. First, at least one general partner must remain in the association for whom the privilege of limited liability does not apply. Second, the names of the limited partners may not appear in the name of the firm. Third, the limited partners may not participate in the management of the business. If one of these restrictions is violated, all partners forfeit their right to limited liability. In essence, the intent of the statutes creating the limited partnership is to provide limited liability for a person whose interest in the partnership is purely as an investor. That individual may not assume a management function within the organization.

Limited liability company (LLC)
An organizational form that is a cross between a partnership and a corporation.

A **limited liability company (LLC)** is a cross between a partnership and a corporation. It retains limited liability for its owners, but is run and taxed like a partnership. Both states and the IRS have rules for what qualifies as an LLC, but the bottom line is that it must not look too much like a corporation or it will be taxed as one.

Corporation

Corporation
An entity that *legally* functions separate and apart from its owners.

The **corporation** has been a significant factor in the economic development of the United States. As early as 1819, Chief Justice John Marshall set forth the legal definition of a corporation as "an artificial being, invisible, intangible, and existing only in the contemplation of law."[2] This entity *legally* functions separate and apart from its owners. As such, the corporation can individually sue and be sued, and purchase, sell, or own property; and its personnel are subject to criminal punishment for crimes. However, despite this legal separation, the corporation is composed of owners who dictate its direction and policies. The owners elect a board of directors, whose members in turn select individuals to serve as corporate officers, including president, vice president, secretary, and treasurer. Ownership is reflected in common stock certificates, designating the number of shares owned by its holder. The number of shares owned relative to the total number of shares outstanding determines the stockholder's proportionate ownership in the business. Because the shares are transferable, ownership in a corporation may be changed by a shareholder simply remitting the shares to a new shareholder. The investor's liability is confined to the amount of the investment in the company, thereby preventing creditors from confiscating stockholders' personal assets in settlement of unresolved claims. This is an extremely important advantage of a corporation. After all, would you be willing to invest in General Electric if you would be liable in the event that one of their airplane engines malfunctions and people die in a crash? Finally, the life of a corporation is not dependent on the status of the investors. The death or withdrawal of an investor does not affect the continuity of the corporation. The management continues to run the corporation when stock is sold or when it is passed on through inheritance. See the Finance Matters box, "Ethics: The Enron Lessons."

Comparison of Organizational Forms

Owners of new businesses have some important decisions to make in choosing an organizational form. Whereas each business form seems to have some advantages over the others, we will see that, as the firm grows and needs access to the capital markets to raise funds, the advantages of the corporation begin to dominate.

Large and growing firms choose the corporate form for one reason: ease in raising capital. Because of the limited liability, the ease of transferring ownership through the sale of common shares, and the flexibility in dividing the shares, the corporation is the ideal business entity in terms of attracting new capital. In contrast, the unlimited liabilities of the sole proprietorship and the general partnership are deterrents to raising equity capital. Between the extremes, the limited partnership does provide limited liability for limited partners, which has a tendency to attract wealthy investors. However, the imprac-

[2] *The Trustees of Dartmouth College v. Woodward*, 4 Wheaton 636 (1819).

FINANCE MATTERS

ETHICS

THE ENRON LESSONS

The bankruptcy and failure of the Enron Corporation on December 2, 2001 shook the investment community to its very core and resulted in congressional hearings that could lead to new regulations with far reaching implications. Enron's failure provides a sober warning to employees and investors and a valuable set of lessons for students of business. The lessons we offer below reach far beyond corporate finance and touch on fundamental principles that have always been true, but that are sometimes forgotten.

Lesson: Maximizing Share Value Is Not Always the Best Thing to Do

If there is a disconnect between current market prices and the intrinsic worth of a firm then attempts to manipulate share value may appear to be possible over the short run. Under these circumstances problems can arise if firms use equity-based compensation based on performance benchmarks using stock price or returns. These circumstances can lead to a type of managerial short-sightedness or myopia that focuses managerial attention on "hyping" the firm's potential to investors in an effort to reach higher market valuations of the firm's stock.

From the shareholder's perspective one might ask what is wrong with achieving a higher stock price? The problem is that this can lead to a situation where investor expectations become detached from what is feasible for the firm. Ultimately, when investors realize that the valuation of the firm's shares is unwarranted, there is a day of reckoning that can bring catastrophic consequences as it did with Enron. Thus, maximizing share value where the firm's underlying fundamentals do not support such valuations is dangerous business. In fact, it is not clear which is worse, having an over- or an undervalued stock price.

The problems associated with managing for shareholder value in a capital market that is less than omniscient (perfectly efficient) is largely uncharted territory for financial economists.

ticality of having a large number of partners and the restricted marketability of an interest in a partnership prevent this form of organization from competing effectively with the corporation. Therefore, when developing our decision models, we will assume that we are dealing with the corporate form. The taxes incorporated in these models will deal only with the corporate tax codes. Because our goal is to develop an understanding of the management, measurement, and creation of wealth, and not to become tax experts, in the following chapter we will only focus on those characteristics of the corporate tax code that will affect our financial decisions.

The Role of the Financial Manager in a Corporation

Although a firm can assume many different organizational structures, Figure 1-1 presents a typical representation of how the finance area fits into a corporation. The Vice President for Finance, also called the Chief Financial Officer (CFO), serves under the corporation's Chief Executive Officer (CEO) and is responsible for overseeing financial planning, corporate strategic planning, and controlling the firm's cash flow. Typically, a Treasurer and Controller serve under the CFO. In a smaller firm, the same person may fill both roles, with just one office handling all the duties. The Treasurer generally handles the firm's financial activities, including cash and credit management, making capital expenditure decisions, raising funds, financial planning, and managing any foreign currency received by the firm. The Controller is responsible for managing the firm's accounting duties, including producing financial statements, cost accounting, paying taxes, and gathering and monitoring the data necessary to oversee the firm's financial well-being. In this class, we focus on the duties generally associated with the Treasurer and on how investment decisions are made.

FIGURE 1-1 How the Finance Area Fits into a Corporation

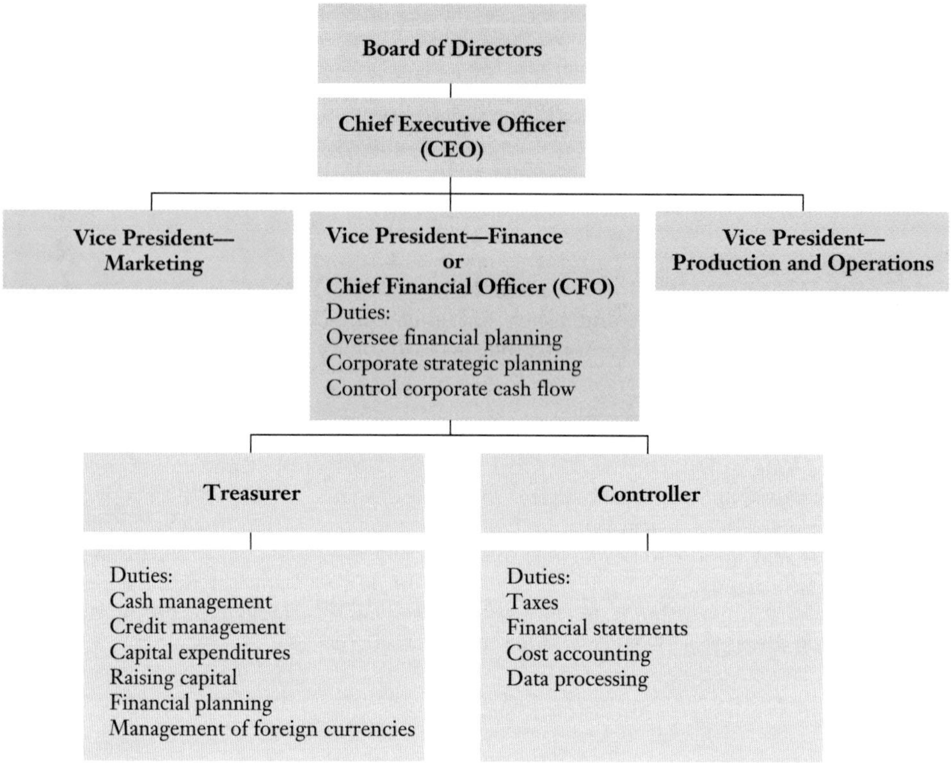

Board of Directors

Chief Executive Officer (CEO)

Vice President—Marketing

Vice President—Finance or Chief Financial Officer (CFO)
Duties:
Oversee financial planning
Corporate strategic planning
Control corporate cash flow

Vice President—Production and Operations

Treasurer
Duties:
Cash management
Credit management
Capital expenditures
Raising capital
Financial planning
Management of foreign currencies

Controller
Duties:
Taxes
Financial statements
Cost accounting
Data processing

CONCEPT CHECK

1. What are the primary differences among a sole proprietorship, a partnership, and a corporation?
2. Explain why large and growing firms tend to choose the corporate form.
3. What are the duties of the Corporate Treasurer? Of the Corporate Controller?

The Corporation and the Financial Markets: The Interaction

Without question, the ease of raising capital is the major reason for the popularity of the corporate form. While we will look at the process of raising capital in some detail in Chapter 14, let's spend a moment looking at the flow of capital through the financial markets among the corporation, individuals, and the government.

Figure 1-2 examines these flows. (1) Initially, the corporation raises funds in the financial markets by selling securities. The corporation receives cash in return for securities—stocks and debt. (2) The corporation then invests this cash in return-generating assets—new projects for example—and (3) the cash flow from those assets is then either reinvested

FIGURE 1-2 The Corporation and the Financial Markets: The Interaction

1. Initially, the corporation raises funds in the financial markets by selling securities—stocks and bonds; 2. The corporation then invests this cash in return-generating assets—new project; 3. The cash flow from those assets is either reinvested in the corporation, given back to the investors, or paid to the government in the form of taxes.

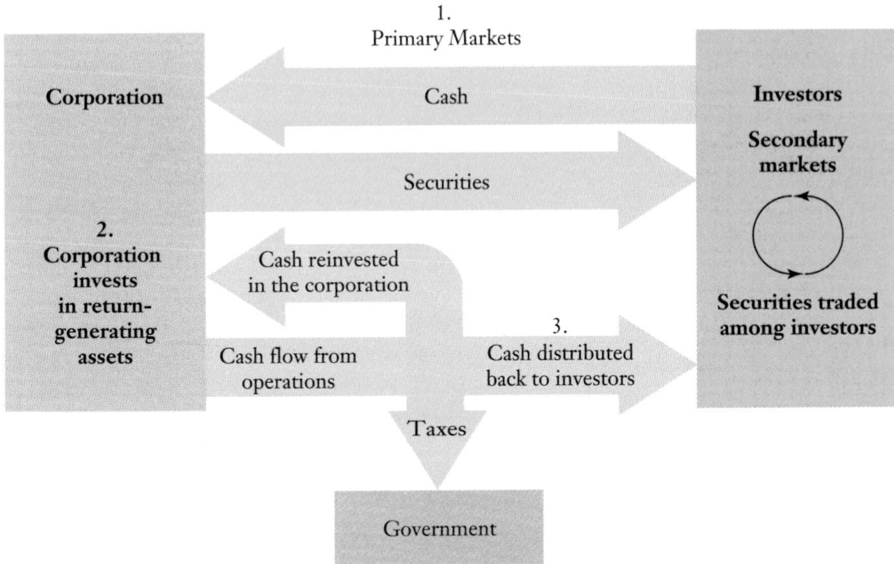

in the corporation; given back to the investors in the form of dividends or interest payments, or used to repurchase stock, which should cause the stock price to rise; or given to the government in the form of tax payments.

One distinction that is important to understand is the difference between primary and secondary markets. Again, we will reexamine raising capital and the difference between primary and secondary markets in some detail in Chapter 14. To begin with, a securities market is simply a place where you can buy or sell securities. These markets can take the form of anything from an actual building on Wall Street in New York City to an electronic hookup among security dealers all over the world. Securities markets are divided into primary and secondary markets. Let's take a look at what these terms mean.

A **primary market** is a market in which new, as opposed to previously issued, securities are traded. This is the only time that the issuing firm actually receives money for its stock. For example, if Nike issues a new batch of stock, this issue would be considered a primary market transaction. In this case, Nike would issue new shares of stock and receive money from investors. Actually, there are two different types of offerings in the primary markets: initial public offerings and seasoned new issues or primary offerings. An **initial public offering (IPO)** is the first time the company's stock is sold to the general public, whereas a **seasoned new issue** refers to stock offerings by companies that already have common stock traded in the secondary market. Once the newly issued stock is in the public's hands, it then begins trading in the **secondary market**. Securities that have previously been issued and bought are traded in the secondary market. For example, if you bought 100 shares of stock in an IPO and then wanted to resell them, you would be reselling them in the secondary markets. The proceeds from the sale of a share of IBM stock in the secondary market go to the previous owner of the stock, not to IBM. That is because the only time IBM ever receives money from the sale of one of its securities is in the primary markets.

Primary market
A market in which new, as opposed to previously issued, securities are traded.

Initial public offering (IPO)
The first time the company's stock is sold to the public.

Seasoned new issue
Stock offerings by companies that already have common stock traded.

Secondary market
The market in which stock previously issued by the firm trades.

A FOCUS ON HARLEY-DAVIDSON

ROAD RULES

AN INTERVIEW WITH JEFF BLEUSTEIN, HARLEY-DAVIDSON'S CEO

Jeff Bleustein is the Chief Executive Officer at Harley-Davidson Company, Inc. In our interview with Mr. Bleustein, he highlighted a number of milestones that he believes have greatly influenced the company's success over the past two decades. Much of what he had to say related directly to the main topics of this book. Specifically, he talked about the company's strategies in the areas of investment decisions, working-capital management, financing decisions, marketing strategies, and global expansion. He also emphasized the importance of the people who implement these decisions. He insists that there is more to business than crunching the numbers; it is people that make the difference. Mr. Bleustein's remarks can be summarized as follows:

- In 1981, the management of Harley-Davidson bought the company from its parent company, AMF, in a leveraged buyout. The extremely high level of debt incurred to finance the purchase placed the company in a very frail financial condition. The downturn in the economy, combined with the debt load, created a powerful incentive to improve operations to conserve cash. To add to the problems, the firm's principal lender, Citibank, announced in 1985 that it wanted out of its creditor position for the firm. Last-minute refinancing was arranged on December 31, 1985 to save the company from bankruptcy. Then, within a few short months the company's financial picture had improved to the point where we were able to take the company public in an initial public offering.
- During the past two decades, the company has made significant capital investments in new product lines, such as the Evolution engine, the Softail motorcycle, and most recently, the Twin Cam 88 engine, one of our current engine designs. Also, in 1998 we invested in new manufacturing facilities in Kansas City, Missouri, and Menominee Falls, Wisconsin.
- To improve the firm's management of its working capital, we introduced the use of just-in-time inventory control. We called our program MAN, which stands for Materials As Needed. This program allowed us to remove $51 million from our work-in-process inventory and provided much-needed capital to support our operations while we paid on the firm's large amounts of debt.
- In 1983, we established our Harley Owner's Group (HOG) to encourage our customers to use their bikes and stay involved with the company. At the end of 2000, we had nearly 600,000 members. We also began a program of carefully managing the licensing of the Harley-Davidson name.
- In the 1980s, we began a program to empower our employees. We needed to let everyone in the organization know what was expected of him or her, which led us to the development of our corporate vision and statement of values.[a] I strongly believe that the only sustainable corporate advantage a company can have is its people.
- In 1994, we began fostering a partnership with our unions to enable them to participate fully in the business. Today our two unions participate fully with the firm's management in a wide range of decision making, including the firm's strategies.
- We also initiated our circle organization, which involves the use of a team structure at our vice president level of management to make the decisions. As a result, we eliminated a whole layer from top management.
- Beginning in the 1990s, we entered into a serious effort to globalize the company. We established a management team in Europe, and over time we acquired our independent distributors in major markets, such as the Benelufx, and Italy.

All of these decisions have significant financial implications that are tied to our study of finance. Specifically, they reflect financing choices, investment decisions, and working-capital management. So, we invite you to join us in our study of finance and, in the process, learn about a company that has accomplished in real terms what few others have been able to do.

[a]Harley-Davidson Motor Company's mission statement is, "We fulfill dreams through the experiences of motorcycling by providing to motorcyclists and the general public an expanding line of motorcycles, branded products and services in selected market segments. The firm's value statement is expressed as, 'Tell the truth, be fair, keep your promises, respect the individual, and encourage intellectual curiosity.'"

Objective 4

TEN PRINCIPLES THAT FORM THE BASICS OF FINANCIAL MANAGEMENT

We will now look at the *finance* foundations that lie behind the decisions made by financial managers. To the first-time student of finance, the subject matter may seem like a collection of unrelated decision rules. This could not be further from the truth. In fact, our decision rules, and the logic that underlies them, spring from 10 simple principles that do not require knowledge of finance to understand. *However, while it is not necessary to understand finance in order to understand these principles, it is necessary to understand these principles in order to understand finance.* Keep in mind that although these principles may at first appear simple or even trivial, they will provide the driving force behind all that follows. These principles will weave together concepts and techniques presented in this text, thereby allowing us to focus on the logic underlying the practice of financial management. In order to make the learning process easier for you as a student, we will keep returning to these principles throughout the book in the form of "Back to the Principles" boxes—tying the material together and letting you sort the "forest from the trees."

PRINCIPLE 1 ***The Risk-Return Trade-Off—We won't take on additional risk unless we expect to be compensated with additional return***

At some point, we have all saved some money. Why have we done this? The answer is simple: to expand our future consumption opportunities—for example, save for a house, a car, or retirement. We are able to invest those savings and earn a return on our dollars because some people would rather forgo future consumption opportunities to consume more now—maybe they're borrowing money to open a new business or a company is borrowing money to build a new plant. Assuming there are a lot of different people that would like to use our savings, how do we decide where to put our money?

First, investors demand a minimum return for delaying consumption that must be greater than the anticipated rate of inflation. If they didn't receive enough to compensate for anticipated inflation, investors would purchase whatever goods they desired ahead of time or invest in assets that were subject to inflation and earn the rate of inflation on those assets. There isn't much incentive to postpone consumption if your savings are going to decline in terms of purchasing power.

Investment alternatives have different amounts of risk and expected returns. Investors sometimes choose to put their money in risky investments because these investments offer higher expected returns. The more risk an investment has, the higher will be its expected return. This relationship between risk and expected return is shown in Figure 1-3.

FIGURE 1-3 The Risk-Return Relationship

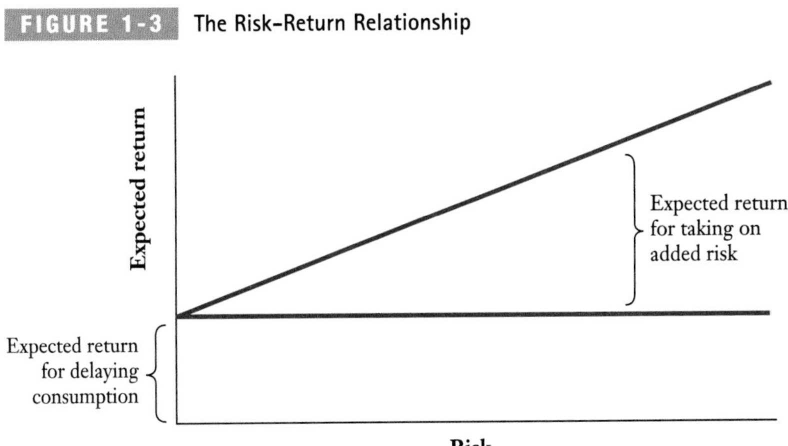

Notice that we keep referring to *expected* return rather than *actual* return. We may have expectations of what the returns from investing will be, but we can't peer into the future and see what those returns are actually going to be. If investors could see into the future, no one would have invested money in the software maker Citrix, whose stock dropped 46 percent on June 13, 2000. Citrix's stock dropped when it announced that unexpected problems in its sales channels would cause second-quarter profits to be about half what Wall Street expected. Until after the fact, you are never sure what the return on an investment will be. That is why General Motors bonds pay more interest than U.S. Treasury bonds of the same maturity. The additional interest convinces some investors to take on the added risk of purchasing a General Motors bond.

This risk-return relationship will be a key concept as we value stocks, bonds, and proposed new projects throughout this text. We will also spend some time determining how to measure risk. Interestingly, much of the work for which the 1990 Nobel Prize for Economics was awarded centered on the graph in Figure 1-3 and how to measure risk. Both the graph and the risk-return relationship it depicts will reappear often in this text.

PRINCIPLE 2 *The Time Value of Money—A dollar received today is worth more than a dollar received in the future*

A fundamental concept in finance is that money has a time value associated with it: A dollar received today is worth more than a dollar received a year from now. Because we can earn interest on money received today, it is better to receive money earlier rather than later. In your economics courses, this concept of the time value of money is referred to as the opportunity cost of passing up the earning potential of a dollar today.

In this text, we focus on the creation and measurement of wealth. To measure wealth or value, we will use the concept of the time value of money to bring the future benefits and costs of a project back to the present. Then, if the benefits outweigh the costs, the project creates wealth and should be accepted; if the costs outweigh the benefits, the project does not create wealth and should be rejected. Without recognizing the existence of the time value of money, it is impossible to evaluate projects with future benefits and costs in a meaningful way.

To bring future benefits and costs of a project back to the present, we must assume a specific opportunity cost of money, or interest rate. Exactly what interest rate to use is determined by **Principle 1: The Risk-Return Trade-Off**, which states investors demand higher returns for taking on more risky projects. Thus, when we determine the present value of future benefits and costs, we take into account that investors demand a higher return for taking on added risk.

PRINCIPLE 3 *Cash—Not Profits—Is King*

In measuring wealth or value, we will use cash flows, not accounting profits, as our measurement tool. That is, we will be concerned with when the money hits our hand, when we can invest it and start earning interest on it, and when we can give it back to the shareholders in the form of dividends. Remember, it is the cash flows, not profits, that are actually received by the firm and can be reinvested. Accounting profits, however, appear when they are earned rather than when the money is actually in hand. As a result, a firm's cash flows and accounting profits may not be the same. For example, a capital expense, such as the purchase of new equipment or a building, is depreciated over several years, with the annual depreciation subtracted from profits. However, the cash flow, or actual dollars, associated with this expense generally occurs immediately. Therefore cash inflows and outflows involve the actual receiving and payout of money—when the money hits or leaves your hands. As a result, cash flows correctly reflect the timing of the benefits and costs.

PRINCIPLE 4 *Incremental Cash Flows—It's only what changes that counts*

In 2000, Post, the maker of Cocoa Pebbles and Fruity Pebbles, introduced Cinna Crunch Pebbles, "Cinnamon sweet taste that goes crunch." There is no doubt that Cinna Crunch Pebbles competed directly with Post's other cereals and, in particular, its Pebbles products. Certainly some of the sales dollars that ended up with Cinna Crunch Pebbles would have been spent on other Pebbles and Post products if Cinna Crunch Pebbles had not been available. Although Post was targeting younger consumers with this sweetened cereal, there is no question that Post sales bit into—actually cannibalized—sales from Pebbles and other Post lines. Realistically, there's only so much cereal anyone can eat. The *difference* between revenues Post generated after introducing Cinna Crunch Pebbles versus simply maintaining its existing line of cereals is the incremental cash flows. This difference reflects the true impact of the decision.

In making business decisions, we are concerned with the results of those decisions: What happens if we say yes versus what happens if we say no? **Principle 3** states that we should use cash flows to measure the benefits that accrue from taking on a new project. We are now fine tuning our evaluation process so that we only consider *incremental* cash flows. The incremental cash flow is the difference between the cash flows if the project is taken on versus what they will be if the project is not taken on.

What is important is that we *think* incrementally. Our guiding rule in deciding whether a cash flow is incremental is to look at the company with and without the new product. In fact, we will take this incremental concept beyond cash flows and look at all consequences from all decisions on an incremental basis.

PRINCIPLE 5 *The Curse of Competitive Markets—Why it's hard to find exceptionally profitable projects*

Our job as financial managers is to create wealth. Therefore, we will look closely at the mechanics of valuation and decision making. We will focus on estimating cash flows, determining what the investment earns, and valuing assets and new projects. But it will be easy to get caught up in the mechanics of valuation and lose sight of the process of creating wealth. Why is it so hard to find projects and investments that are exceptionally profitable? Where do profitable projects come from? The answers to these questions tell us a lot about how competitive markets operate and where to look for profitable projects.

In reality, it is much easier evaluating profitable projects than finding them. If an industry is generating large profits, new entrants are usually attracted. The additional competition and added capacity can result in profits being driven down to the required rate of return. Conversely, if an industry is returning profits below the required rate of return, then some participants in the market drop out, reducing capacity and competition. In turn, prices are driven back up. This is precisely what happened in the VCR video rental market in the mid-1980s. This market developed suddenly with the opportunity for extremely large profits. Because there were no barriers to entry, the market quickly was flooded with new entries. By 1987, the competition and price cutting produced losses for many firms in the industry, forcing them to flee the market. As the competition lessened with firms moving out of the video rental industry, profits again rose to the point where the required rate of return could be earned on invested capital.

In competitive markets, extremely large profits simply cannot exist for very long. Given that somewhat bleak scenario, how can we find good projects—that is, projects that return more than their expected rate of return given their risk level (remember Principle 1). Although competition makes them difficult to find, we have to invest in markets that are not perfectly competitive. The two most common ways of making markets less competitive are to differentiate the product in some key way or to achieve a cost advantage over competitors.

Product differentiation insulates a product from competition, thereby allowing a company to charge a premium price. If products are differentiated, consumer choice is no longer made by price alone. For example, many people are willing to pay a premium for Starbucks coffee. They simply want Starbucks and price is not important. In the pharmaceutical industry, patents create competitive barriers. Schering-Plough's Claritin, an allergy relief medicine, and Hoffman-La Roche's Valium, a tranquilizer, are protected from direct competition by patents.

Service and quality are also used to differentiate products. For example, Levi's has long prided itself on the quality of its jeans. As a result, it has been able to maintain its market share. Similarly, much of Toyota and Honda's brand loyalty is based on quality. Service can also create product differentiation, as shown by McDonald's fast service, cleanliness, and consistency of product that brings customers back.

Whether product differentiation occurs because of advertising, patents, service, or quality, the more the product is differentiated from competing products, the less competition it will face and the greater the possibility of large profits.

Economies of scale and the ability to produce at a cost below competition can effectively deter new entrants to the market and thereby reduce competition. Wal-Mart is one such case. For Wal-Mart, the fixed costs are largely independent of the store's size. For example, inventory costs, advertising expenses, and managerial salaries are essentially the same regardless of annual sales. Therefore, the more sales that can be built up, the lower the per-sale dollar cost of inventory, advertising, and management. Restocking from warehouses also becomes more efficient as delivery trucks can be used to full potential.

Regardless of how the cost advantage is created—by economies of scale, proprietary technology, or monopolistic control of raw materials—the cost advantage deters new market entrants while allowing production at below industry cost. This cost advantage has the potential of creating large profits.

The key to locating profitable investment projects is to first understand how and where they exist in competitive markets. Then the corporate philosophy must be aimed at creating or taking advantage of some imperfection in these markets, either through product differentiation or creation of a cost advantage, rather than looking to new markets or industries that appear to provide large profits. Any perfectly competitive industry that looks too good to be true won't be for long. It is necessary to understand this to know where to look for good projects and to accurately measure the project's cash flows. We can do this better if we recognize how wealth is created and how difficult it is to create it.

Efficient Capital Markets—The markets are quick and the prices are right

Efficient market
A market in which the values of all assets and securities at any instant in time fully reflect all available public information.

Our goal as financial managers is the maximization of shareholder wealth. How do we measure shareholder wealth? It is the value of the shares that the shareholders hold. To understand what causes stocks to change in price, as well as how securities such as bonds and stocks are valued or priced in the financial markets, it is necessary to have an understanding of the concept of **efficient markets**.

Whether a market is efficient or not has to do with the speed with which information is impounded into security prices. An efficient market is characterized by a large number of profit-driven individuals who act independently. In addition, new information regarding securities arrives in the market in a random manner. Given this setting, investors adjust to new information immediately and buy and sell the security until they feel the market price correctly reflects the new information. Under the efficient market hypothesis, information is reflected in security prices with such speed that there are no opportunities for investors to profit from publicly available information. Investors competing for profits ensure that security prices appropriately reflect the expected earnings and risks involved and thus the true value of the firm.

What are the implications of efficient markets for us? First, the price is right. Stock prices reflect all publicly available information regarding the value of the company. This means we can implement our goal of maximization of shareholder wealth by focusing on the effect each decision *should* have on the stock price if everything else were held constant. That is, over time good decisions will result in higher stock prices and bad ones, lower stock prices. Second, earnings manipulations through accounting changes will not result in price changes. Stock splits and other changes in accounting methods that do not affect cash flows are not reflected in prices. Market prices reflect expected cash flows available to shareholders. Thus, our preoccupation with cash flows to measure the timing of the benefits is justified.

As we will see, it is indeed reassuring that prices reflect value. It allows us to look at prices and see value reflected in them. While it may make investing a bit less exciting, it makes corporate finance much less uncertain.

PRINCIPLE 7 *The Agency Problem—Managers won't work for owners unless it's in their best interest*

Although the goal of the firm is the maximization of shareholder wealth, in reality, the agency problem may interfere with the implementation of this goal. The **agency problem** results from the separation of management and the ownership of the firm. For example, a large firm may be run by professional managers who have little or no ownership in the firm. Because of this separation of the decision makers and owners, managers may make decisions that are not in line with the goal of maximization of shareholder wealth. They may approach work less energetically and attempt to benefit themselves in terms of salary and perquisites at the expense of shareholders.

Agency problem
Problem resulting from conflicts of interest between the manager (the stockholder's agent) and the stockholders.

To begin with, an agent is someone who is given the authority to act on behalf of another, referred to as the principal. In the corporate setting, the shareholders are the principals, because they are the actual owners of the firm. The board of directors, the CEO, the corporate executives, and all others with decision-making power are agents of the shareholders. Unfortunately, the board of directors, the CEO, and the other corporate executives don't always do what's in the best interest of the shareholders. Instead, they act many times in their own best interest. Not only might they benefit themselves in terms of salary and perquisites, but they might also avoid any projects that have risk associated with them—even if they're great projects with huge potential returns and a small chance of failure. Why is this so? Because if the project doesn't turn out, these agents of the shareholders may lose their jobs.

The costs associated with the agency problem are difficult to measure, but occasionally we see the problem's effect in the marketplace. For example, if the market feels management of a firm is damaging shareholder wealth, we might see a positive reaction in stock price to the removal of that management. In 1989, on the day following the death of John Dorrance, Jr., chairman of Campbell Soup, Campbell's stock price rose about 15 percent.

Some investors felt that Campbell's relatively small growth in earnings might be improved with the departure of Dorrance. There was also speculation that Dorrance was the major obstacle to a possible positive reorganization.

If the management of the firm works for the owners, who are the shareholders, why doesn't the management get fired if it doesn't act in the shareholders' best interest? *In theory*, the shareholders pick the corporate board of directors and the board of directors in turn picks the management. Unfortunately, *in reality* the system frequently works the other way around. Management selects the board of director nominees and then distributes the ballots. In effect, shareholders are offered a slate of nominees selected by the management. The end result is management effectively selects the directors, who then may have more allegiance to managers than to shareholders. This in turn sets up the potential for agency problems with the board of directors not monitoring managers on behalf of the shareholders as they should.

We will spend considerable time monitoring managers and trying to align their interests with shareholders. Managers can be monitored by auditing financial statements and managers' compensation packages. The interests of managers and shareholders can be aligned by establishing management stock options, bonuses, and perquisites that are directly tied to how closely their decisions coincide with the interest of shareholders. The agency problem will persist unless an incentive structure is set up that aligns the interests of managers and shareholders. In other words, what's good for shareholders must also be good for managers. If that is not the case, managers will make decisions in their best interests rather than maximizing shareholder wealth.

PRINCIPLE 8 *Taxes Bias Business Decisions*

Hardly any decision is made by the financial manager without considering the impact of taxes. When we introduced **Principle 4**, we said that only incremental cash flows should be considered in the evaluation process. More specifically, the cash flows we will consider will be *after-tax incremental cash flows to the firm as a whole.*

When we evaluate new projects, we will see income taxes playing a significant role. When the company is analyzing the possible acquisition of a plant or equipment, the returns from the investment should be measured on an after-tax basis. Otherwise, the company will not truly be evaluating the true incremental cash flows generated by the project.

The government also realizes taxes can bias business decisions and uses taxes to encourage spending in certain ways. If the government wanted to encourage spending on research and development projects it might offer an *investment tax credit* for such investments. This would have the effect of reducing taxes on research and development projects, which would in turn increase the after-tax cash flows from those projects. The increased cash flow would turn some otherwise unprofitable research and development projects into profitable projects. In effect, the government can use taxes as a tool to direct business investment to research and development projects, to the inner cities, and to projects that create jobs.

All Risk Is Not Equal—Some risk can be diversified away, and some cannot

Much of finance centers around **Principle 1: The Risk-Return Trade-Off**. But before we can fully use **Principle 1**, we must decide how to measure risk. As we will see, risk is difficult to measure. **Principle 9** introduces you to the process of diversification and demonstrates how it can reduce risk. We will also provide you with an understanding of how diversification makes it difficult to measure a project's or an asset's risk.

You are probably already familiar with the concept of diversification. There is an old saying, "don't put all of your eggs in one basket." Diversification allows good and bad events or observations to cancel each other out, thereby reducing total variability without affecting expected return.

To see how diversification complicates the measurement of risk, let us look at the difficulty Louisiana Gas has in determining the level of risk associated with a new natural gas well drilling project. Each year, Louisiana Gas might drill several hundred wells, with each well having only a 1 in 10 chance of success. If the well produces, the profits are quite large, but if it comes up dry, the investment is lost. Thus, with a 90 percent chance of losing everything, we would view the project as being extremely risky. However, if Louisiana Gas each year drills 2,000 wells, all with a 10 percent, independent chance of success, then they would typically have 200 successful wells. Moreover, a bad year may result in only 190 successful wells, and a good year may result in 210 successful wells. If we look at all the wells together, the extreme good and bad results tend to cancel each other out and the well drilling projects taken together do not appear to have much risk or variability of possible outcome.

The amount of risk in a gas well project depends upon our perspective. Looking at the well standing alone, it looks like a lot; however, if we consider the risk that each well contributes to the overall firm risk, it is quite small. This is because much of the risk associated with each individual well is diversified away within the firm. The point is: We can't look at a project in isolation. Later, we will see that some of this risk can be further diversified away within the shareholder's portfolio.

Perhaps the easiest way to understand the concept of diversification is to look at it graphically. Consider what happens when we combine two projects, as depicted in Figure 1-4. In this case, the cash flows from these projects move in opposite directions, and when they are combined, the variability of their combination is totally eliminated. Notice that the return has not changed—each individual project's and their combination's return averages 10 percent. In this case, the extreme good and bad observations cancel each other out. The degree to which the total risk is reduced is a function of how the two sets of cash flows or returns move together.

As we will see for most projects and assets, some risk can be eliminated through diversification, whereas some risk cannot. This will become an important distinction later in our studies. *For now, we should realize that the process of diversification can reduce risk, and as a result, measuring a project's or an asset's risk is very difficult.* A project's risk changes depending on whether you measure it standing alone or together with other projects the company may take on. See the Finance Matters box, "Ethics: The Enron Lessons."

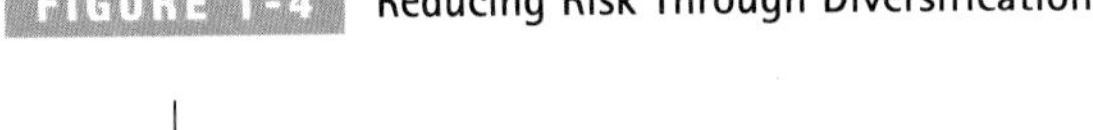

Reducing Risk Through Diversification

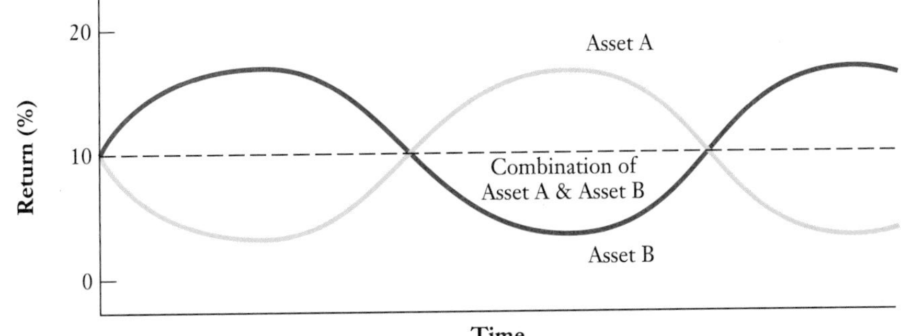

FINANCE MATTERS — ETHICS

THE ENRON LESSONS

The bankruptcy and failure of the Enron Corporation on December 2, 2001 shook the investment community to its very core and resulted in congressional hearings that could lead to new regulations with far reaching implications. Enron's failure provides a sober warning to employees and investors and a valuable set of lessons for students of business. The lessons we offer below reach far beyond corporate finance and touch on fundamental principles that have always been true, but that are sometimes forgotten.

Lesson: Trust and Credibility Are Essential to Business Success

The viability of any firm hinges critically on the firm's credibility with its customers, employees, regulators, investors, and even to some degree, its competitors. This is particularly critical for a trading company such as Enron whose primary business rests on the willingness of the firm's counter parties with whom it trades to "trust" in Enron's ability to "be there" when the time to settle up arrives. When the faith of the investment community was tested with the revelation of losses from some of its largest investments and the subsequent revelation of Enron's off-balance sheet liabilities, Enron's trading business evaporated.

In addition, we were reminded of the fact that investors must believe that the firm's published financial reports are a fair representation of the firm's financial condition. Without this trust outside investors would refuse to invest in the shares of publicly traded firms and financial markets would collapse.[a]

Trust between two entities is hard to sustain when one of the parties to the relationship has dual and conflicting motives. We refer to the presence of multiple motives as a conflict of interest and the potential for conflict of interest problems were in abundance as Enron fell to earth. Some of the following sources of conflict apply only to Enron while others are applicable to many firms:

- Enron's chief financial officer (CFO) attempted to serve two masters when he was both the general partner for a series of limited partnerships used by Enron to finance its investments and hedge certain investment returns, as well as serving as Enron's CFO. There were times when he represented the interests of Enron in circumstances that were in direct conflict with the interests of the partners to the partnerships. It is still not clear how he handled these circumstances, but the source of concern to Enron shareholders is obvious.
- Were corporate insiders (executives) selling their stock based on their privileged knowledge of the firm's true financial condition during the months prior to the firm's failure while outside investors were being duped into holding their shares? Allegations abound that top corporate executives at Enron were selling their shares long before other employees and outside investors knew how serious the firm's problems were. Regardless of the outcome in the Enron case, this raises a serious dilemma for investors who cannot know as much about the financial condition of the firms in which they invest as the managers do.
- Can auditing firms that accept consulting engagements with their audit clients be truly independent or is that independence compromised? The Enron failure has called into question the wisdom of relying on external auditing firms who are beholden to the firms they audit both for their continued employment as an auditor and also for consulting fees that can sometimes dwarf their auditor fees.
- Finally, can investors rely on the opinions of equity analysts whom they believe are basing those opinions on their independent research? Investors make the assumption that the analysts are offering unfettered, independent opinions of the company's financial prospects. However, in many cases the analysts work for investment banks that, in turn, rely on investment banking fees from the very companies the analysts cover. The potential conflict of interest is obvious.

[a]This is simply a recasting of the famous result from microeconomics stating that where informational asymmetry problems between buyers and sellers are extreme, markets will collapse (George Akerlof, "The Market for Lemons: Qualitative Uncertainty and the Market Mechanism," *Quarterly Journal of Economics*, 84 (1970), 488–500).

PRINCIPLE 10 *Ethical behavior is doing the right thing, and ethical dilemmas are everywhere in finance*

Ethics, or rather a lack of ethics, in finance is a recurring theme in the news. During the late 1980s and early 1990s, the fall of Ivan Boesky and Drexel, Burnham, Lambert, and the near collapse of Salomon Brothers seemed to make continuous headlines.

Meanwhile, the movie *Wall Street* was a hit at the box office and the book *Liar's Poker*, by Michael Lewis, chronicling unethical behavior in the bond markets, became a best seller. Unfortunately, ethics, or the lack of them, continued to make the front page in the early 2000s, with Enron, Worldcom, and Arthur Anderson all serving to illustrate that ethical errors are not forgiven in the business world. Not only is acting in an ethical manner morally correct, it is congruent with our goal of maximization of shareholder wealth.

Ethical behavior means "doing the right thing." A difficulty arises, however, in attempting to define "doing the right thing." The problem is that each of us has his or her own set of values, which forms the basis for our personal judgments about what is the right thing to do. However, every society adopts a set of rules or laws that prescribe what it believes to be "doing the right thing." In a sense, we can think of laws as a set of rules that reflect the values of the society as a whole, as they have evolved. For purposes of this text, we recognize that individuals have a right to disagree about what constitutes "doing the right thing," and we will seldom venture beyond the basic notion that ethical conduct involves abiding by society's rules. However, we will point out some of the ethical dilemmas that have arisen in recent years with regard to the practice of financial management. So as we embark on our study of finance and encounter ethical dilemmas, we encourage you to consider the issues and form your own opinions.

Many students ask, "Is ethics really relevant?" This is a good question and deserves an answer. First, although business errors can be forgiven, ethical errors tend to end careers and terminate future opportunities. Why? Because *unethical behavior eliminates trust, and without trust, businesses cannot interact*. Second, *the most damaging event a business can experience is a loss of the public's confidence in its ethical standards*. In finance, we have seen several recent examples of such events. It was the ethical lapses at Arthur Anderson and its work with Enron that brought down that once-great accounting firm. See the Finance Matters box, "The Wall Street Journal Workplace-Ethics Quiz."

Beyond the question of ethics is the question of social responsibility. In general, corporate social responsibility means that a corporation has responsibilities to society beyond the maximization of shareholder wealth. It asserts that a corporation answers to a broader constituency than shareholders alone. As with most debates that center on ethical and moral questions, there is no definitive answer. One opinion is that because financial managers are employees of the corporation, and the corporation is owned by the shareholders, the financial managers should run the corporation in such a way that shareholder wealth is maximized and then allow the shareholders to decide if they would like to fulfill a sense of social responsibility by passing on any of the profits to deserving causes. Very few corporations consistently act in this way. For example, Bristol-Myers Squibb Co. gives away heart medication to those who cannot pay for it. This decision to give away heart medication came in the wake of an American Heart Association report showing that many of the nation's working poor face severe health risks because they cannot afford heart drugs. Clearly, Bristol-Myers Squibb felt it had a social responsibility to provide this medicine to the poor at no cost.

How do you feel about this decision?

A Final Note on the Principles

Hopefully, these principles are as much statements of common sense as they are theoretical statements. These principles provide the logic behind what is to follow. We will build on them and attempt to draw out their implications for decision making. As we continue, try to keep in mind that although the topics being treated may change from chapter to chapter, the logic driving our treatment of them is constant and is rooted in these 10 principles. See the Entrepreneur's Perspective box, "The Entrepreneur and Finance."

THE WALL STREET JOURNAL WORKPLACE-ETHICS QUIZ

Without question, when you enter the workforce you will be faced with a number of ethical dilemmas that you have never considered. The spread of technology into the workplace has raised a variety of new ethical questions, and many old ones still linger. The following is a quiz dealing with ethical questions that will both give you some questions to think about, and also allow you to compare your answers with those of other Americans surveyed.

Office Technology

1. Is it wrong to use company e-mail for personal reasons?
   Yes No
2. Is it wrong to play computer games on office equipment during the workday?
   Yes No
3. Is it unethical to blame an error you made on a technological glitch?
   Yes No

Gifts and Entertainment

4. Is a $50 gift to a boss unacceptable?
   Yes No
5. Is a $50 gift from the boss unacceptable?
   Yes No
6. Of gifts from suppliers: Is it OK to take a $200 pair of football tickets?
   Yes No
7. Is it OK to take a $100 holiday food basket?
   Yes No
8. Can you accept a $75 prize won at a raffle at a supplier's conference?
   Yes No

Truth and Lies

9. Due to on-the-job pressure, have you ever abused or lied about sick days?
   Yes No
10. Due to on-the-job pressure, have you ever taken credit for someone else's work or idea?
    Yes No

Ethics-Quiz Answers

1. 34% said personal e-mail on company computers is wrong
2. 49% said playing computer games at work is wrong
3. 61% said it's unethical to blame your error on technology
4. 35% said a $50 gift to the boss is unacceptable
5. 12% said a $50 gift from the boss is unacceptable
6. 70% said it's unacceptable to take the $200 football tickets
7. 35% said it's unacceptable to take the $100 food basket
8. 40% said it's unacceptable to take the $75 raffle prize
9. 11% reported they lie about sick days
10. 4% reported they take credit for the work or ideas of others

Sources: Ethics Officer Association, Belmont, Mass.; Ethical Leadership Group, Wilmette, Ill.; surveys sampled a cross-section of workers at large companies and nationwide; Reprinted by permission of *The Wall Street Journal*, Copyright © 1999 Dow Jones & Company, Inc. All Rights Reserved Worldwide. License number 880500341261.

CONCEPT CHECK

1. According to Principle 1, how do investors decide where to invest their money?
2. Why is it so hard to find extremely profitable projects?
3. Why is ethics relevant?

OVERVIEW OF THE TEXT

In this text, we will focus on the maintenance and creation of wealth. Although this will involve attention to decision-making techniques, we will emphasize the logic behind those techniques to ensure that you do not lose sight of the concepts driving finance and the creation of wealth. The text begins by discussing the goal of maximization of shareholder wealth, a goal that is to be used in financial decision making, and presents the legal

AN ENTREPRENEUR'S PERSPECTIVE

THE ENTREPRENEUR AND FINANCE

Do you ever think about wanting to someday own your own business? Does being an entrepreneur have any appeal to you? Well, it does for a lot of people. During the past decade, starting and growing companies have been the preferred avenue many have chosen for careers. In fact, while many of the large companies are reducing the number of employees, smaller companies are creating new jobs by the thousands. A lot of individuals have thought that there was greater security in working with a big company, only to be disillusioned in the end when they were informed that "Friday is your last day."

Defining an entrepreneur is not an easy thing to do. But we can say with some clarity what *entrepreneurship* is about. Entrepreneurship has been defined as a relentless pursuit of opportunity for the purpose of creating value, without concern for the resources owned.

To be successful, the entrepreneurial process requires that the entrepreneur be able to:

- ***Identify a good opportunity.*** Oftentimes we may have a "good idea," but it may not be a "good opportunity." Opportunities are market driven. There must be enough customers who want to buy our product or service at a price that covers our expenses and leaves an attractive profit—no matter how much we may like the idea.
- ***Gain access to the resources needed.*** For any venture, there are critical resources—human, financial, and physical—that must be available. The entrepreneur usually does not have the capital to own all the resources that are needed. So she must have access to resources, but usually cannot afford to own them. It's what we call *bootstrapping*. The goal is to do more with less.
- ***Launch the venture.*** All the planning in the world is not enough. The entrepreneur must be action oriented. It requires a "can do" spirit.
- ***Grow the business.*** A business has to grow if it is to be successful. Frequently, the firm will not break even for several years, which means that we will be burning up cash each month. Being able to survive during the time that cash flows are negative is no easy task. If we grow too slow, we lose, but also if we grow too fast, we may lose as well. During this time, additional capital will be needed, which requires that we know how to value the firm and how to structure financing.
- ***Exit the business.*** If a venture has been successful, the entrepreneur will have created economic value that is locked up in the business. At some point in time, the entrepreneur will want to capture the value that has been created by the business. It will be time to *harvest*.

To be successful as an entrepreneur requires an understanding of finance. At the appropriate places in *Financial Management*, we will be presenting how finance relates to the entrepreneurial journey. It is an interesting topic that we think you will enjoy.

and tax environment in which these decisions are to be made. Since this environment sets the ground rules, it is necessary to understand it before decision rules can be formulated. The 10 guiding principles that provide the underpinnings for what is to follow are then presented. Chapters 2 through 4 introduce the basic financial tools the financial manager uses to maintain control over the firm and its operations. These tools enable the financial manager to locate potential problem areas and plan for the future.

Chapter 5 explores how the firm and its assets are valued. It begins with an examination of the mathematics of finance and the concept of the time value of money. An understanding of this topic allows us to compare benefits and costs that occur in different time periods. We move on in Chapter 6 to develop an understanding of the meaning and measurement of risk. Valuation of fixed income securities is examined in Chapter 7, and Chapter 8 looks at valuation models that attempt to explain how different financial decisions affect the firm's stock price.

Using the valuation principles just developed, Chapter 9 discusses the capital-budgeting decision, which involves the financial evaluation of investment proposals in fixed assets. We then examine the measurement of cash flows in Chapter 10, and introduce methods to incorporate risk in the analysis in Chapter 11. In Chapter 12, we will examine the financing of a firm's chosen projects, looking at what costs are associated with alternative ways of raising new funds. Then, in Chapter 13, we look at managing the firm for shareholder value.

Chapter 14 examines the financial markets and the act of raising funds. Chapter 15 examines the firm's capital structure along with the impact of leverage on returns to the enterprise. Once these relationships between leverage and valuation are developed, we move on to the process of planning the firm's financing mix in Chapter 16. This is followed in Chapter 17 with a discussion of the determination of the dividend-retained earnings decision.

Chapters 18 through 20 deal with working-capital management, the management of current assets. We will discuss methods for determining the appropriate investment in cash, marketable securities, inventory, and accounts receivable, as well as the risks associated with these investments and the control of these risks.

Chapter 21 presents discussion of the use of futures, options, and swaps by financial managers to reduce risk. The final chapter in the text, Chapter 22, deals with international financial management, focusing on how financial decisions are affected by the international environment. In addition, Chapter 23, an introduction to corporate restructuring including mergers, spinoffs, and leveraged buyouts, is provided on the Internet. Similarly, Chapter 24, Loans and Leases, is also provided on the Internet.

Objective 5

FINANCE AND THE MULTINATIONAL FIRM: THE NEW ROLE

In the search for profits, U.S. corporations have been forced to look beyond our country's borders. This movement has been spurred on by the collapse of communism and the acceptance of the free market system in Third World countries. All of this has taken place at a time when information technology has experienced a revolution brought on by the personal computer (PC). Concurrently, the United States went through an unprecedented period of deregulation of industries. These changes resulted in the opening of new international markets, and U.S. firms experienced a period of price competition here at home that made it imperative that businesses look across borders for investment opportunities. The end result is that many U.S. companies, including General Electric, IBM, Walt Disney, American Express, and General Motors, have restructured their operations in order to expand internationally. However, not only do U.S. firms have a freer access to international markets, but also foreign firms have an easier job of entering the U.S. markets and competing with U.S. firms on their own turf.

The bottom line is that what you think of as a U.S. firm may be much more of a multinational firm than you would expect. For example, Coca-Cola earns over 80 percent of its profits from overseas sales. Moreover, Coca-Cola earns more money from its sales in Japan than it does from all its domestic sales, and this is not uncommon. In fact, Dow Chemical, Colgate-Palmolive, 3M, Compaq, Hewlett-Packard, and Gillette make over half their sales overseas and earn over half of their profits from international sales. In addition to U.S. firms venturing abroad, foreign firms have also made their mark in the United States. You need only look to the auto industry to see what changes the entrance of Toyota, Honda, Nissan, BMW, and other foreign car manufacturers have made in the auto industry. In addition, foreigners have bought and now own such companies as Brooks Brothers, RCA, Pillsbury, A&P, 20th Century Fox, Columbia Pictures, and Firestone Tire & Rubber. Consequently, even if we wanted to, we couldn't keep all our attention focused on the United States, and even more important, we wouldn't want to ignore the opportunities that are available across international borders.

CONCEPT CHECK

1. What has brought on the era of the multinational corporation?
2. Has looking beyond U.S. borders been a profitable experience for U.S. corporations?

HOW FINANCIAL MANAGERS USE THIS MATERIAL

As the chapter title states, this chapter provides you with an introduction to financial management. The principles presented in this chapter provide you with some clues as to the types of questions that will be dealt with by financial managers. As you will find out over the course of your studies, financial questions abound. In the Spring of 2003, headlines in *The Wall Street Journal* were full of financial decisions, including the giant drug makers Pfizer and Pharmacia winning final approval for their merger, Disney nearing a deal to sell its Anaheim Angels baseball team for $160 to $180 million, and AOL Time Warner Inc. reporting a 2002 net loss of $98.7 billion after taking a fourth-quarter charge of $45.5 billion, mostly to write down the value of its troubled America Online unit while it tried to sell its Atlanta-based teams—baseball's Atlanta Braves, basketball's Atlanta Hawks, and hockey's Atlanta Thrashers. But financial questions and decisions also appeared in the headlines in the sports section when the Washington Redskins signed Lavernues Coles to a $35 million contract and basketball coach Ben Howland took the UCLA coaching job at a salary of $900,000 per year.

What do all of these financial decisions have in common? They are all based on the 10 principles presented in this chapter, and they all deal with decision making. They are all financial decisions, because the focus of finance is how to raise and spend or invest money. Your goal as a financial manager is to manage the firm in such a way that shareholder wealth is maximized. As you will see, there are few, if any, major decisions that a manager makes that don't have financial implications.

SUMMARY

This chapter outlines a framework for the maintenance and creation of wealth. In introducing decision-making techniques aimed at creating wealth, we will emphasize the logic behind those techniques. This chapter begins with an examination of the goal of the firm. The commonly accepted goal of profit maximization is contrasted with the more complete goal of maximization of shareholder wealth. Because it deals well with uncertainty and time in a real-world environment, the goal of maximization of shareholder wealth is found to be the proper goal for the firm. *Objective 1* *Objective 2*

The sole proprietorship is a business operation owned and managed by a single individual. Initiating this form of business is simple and generally does not involve any substantial organizational costs. The proprietor has complete control of the firm, but must be willing to assume full responsibility for its outcomes. *Objective 3*

The general partnership, which is simply a coming together of two or more individuals, is similar to the sole proprietorship. The limited partnership is another form of partnership sanctioned by states to permit all but one of the partners to have limited liability if this is agreeable to all partners.

The corporation increases the flow of capital from public investors to the business community. Although larger organizational costs and regulations are imposed on this legal entity, the corporation is more conducive to raising large amounts of capital. Limited liability, continuity of life, and ease of transfer in ownership, which increase the marketability of the investment, have contributed greatly in attracting large numbers of investors to the corporate environment. The formal control of the corporation is vested in the parties who own the greatest number of shares. However, day-to-day operations are managed by the corporate officers, who theoretically serve on behalf of the common stockholders.

Objective 4

This chapter closes with an examination of the 10 principles on which finance is built that motivate the techniques and tools introduced in this text:

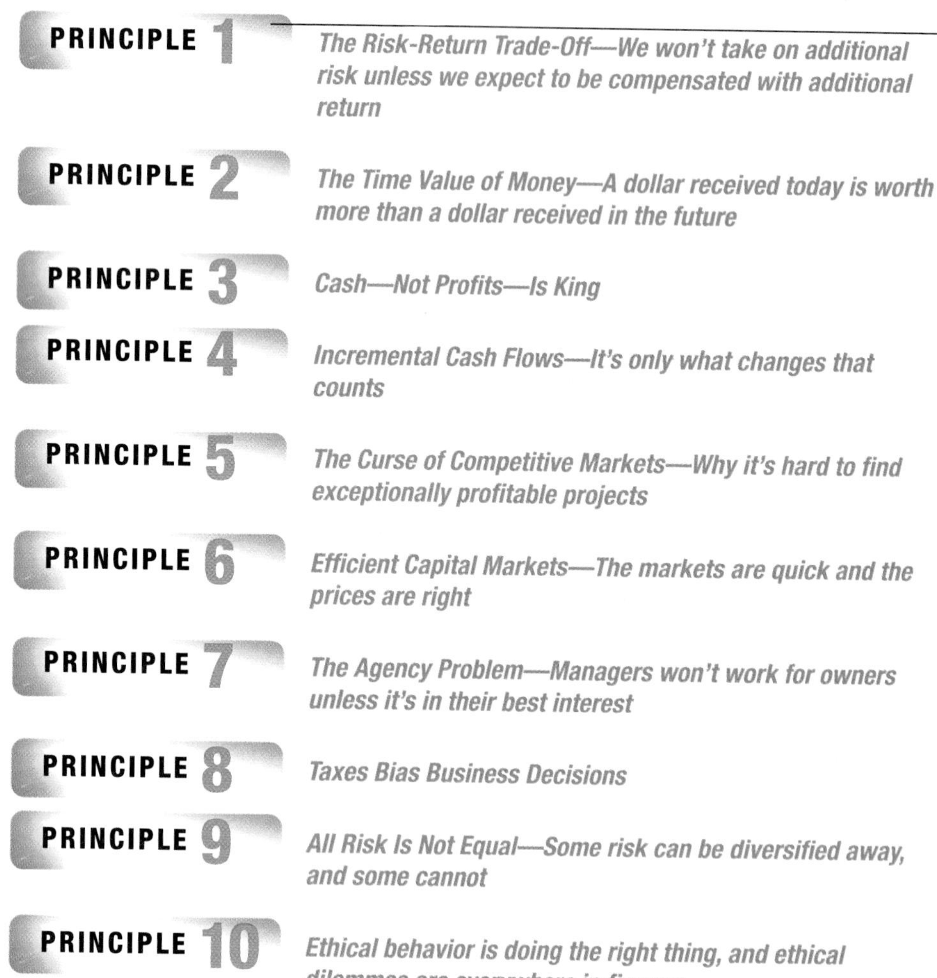

Objective 5

With the collapse of communism and the acceptance of the free market system in Third World countries, U.S. firms have been spurred on to look beyond our own boundaries for new business. The end result has been that it is not uncommon for major U.S. companies to earn over half their income from sales abroad.

KEY TERMS

Agency problem, 17
Corporation, 8
Efficient market, 16
Initial public offering (IPO), 11
Limited liability company (LLC), 8
Partnership, 7
Primary market, 11
Seasoned new issue, 11
Secondary market, 11
Sole proprietorship, 7

Go To:
www.prenhall.com/keown
for downloads and current events associated with this chapter

STUDY QUESTIONS

1-1. What are some of the problems involved in the use of profit maximization as the goal of the firm? How does the goal of maximization of shareholder wealth deal with those problems?

1-2. Compare and contrast the goals of profit maximization and maximization of shareholder wealth.

1-3. Firms often involve themselves in projects that do not result directly in profits; for example, IBM and Mobil Oil frequently support public television broadcasts. Do these projects contradict the goal of maximization of shareholder wealth? Why or why not?

1-4. What is the relationship between financial decision making and risk and return? Would all financial managers view risk-return trade-offs similarly?

1-5. Define (a) sole proprietorship, (b) partnership, and (c) corporation.

1-6. Identify the primary characteristics of each form of legal organization.

1-7. Using the following criteria, specify the legal form of business that is favored: (a) organizational requirements and costs, (b) liability of the owners, (c) continuity of business, (d) transferability of ownership, (e) management control and regulations, (f) ability to raise capital, and (g) income taxes.

INTEGRATIVE PROBLEM

The final stage in the interview process for an Assistant Financial Analyst at Caledonia Products involves a test of your understanding of basic financial concepts. You are given the following memorandum and asked to respond to the questions. Whether or not you are offered a position at Caledonia will depend on the accuracy of your response.

To: Applicants for the position of Financial Analyst

From: Mr. V. Morrison, CEO, Caledonia Products

Re: A test of your understanding of basic financial concepts and of the Corporate Tax Code

Please respond to the following questions:

1. What are the differences between the goals of profit maximization and maximization of shareholder wealth? Which goal do you think is more appropriate?
2. What does the risk-return trade-off mean?
3. Why are we interested in cash flows rather than accounting profits in determining the value of an asset?
4. What is an efficient market and what are the implications of efficient markets for us?
5. What is the cause of the agency problem and how do we try to solve it?
6. What do ethics and ethical behavior have to do with finance?
7. Define (a) sole proprietorship, (b) partnership, and (c) corporation.

CASE PROBLEM

ETHICS

LIVING AND DYING WITH ASBESTOS

What happens when you find your most profitable product is dangerous—an ethical dilemma for the financial manager.

Much of what we deal with in financial management centers around the evaluation of projects—when they should be accepted and when they should be terminated. As new information surfaces regarding the future profitability of a project, the firm always has the choice of terminating that project. When this new information raises the question of whether or not it is ethical to produce a profitable project, the decision becomes more difficult. Many times, ethical dilemmas pit profits versus ethics. These decisions become even more difficult when continuing to produce the product is within the law.

Asbestos is a fibrous mineral used for fireproofing, electrical insulation, building materials, brake linings, and chemical filters. If you are exposed long enough to asbestos particles—usually 10 or more years—you can develop a chronic lung inflammation called asbestosis, which makes breathing difficult and infection easy. Also linked to asbestos exposure is mesethelioma, a cancer of the chest lining. This disease sometimes doesn't develop until 40 years after the first exposure. Although the first major scientific conference on the dangers of asbestos was not held until 1964, the asbestos industry knew of the dangers of asbestos 60 years ago.

As early as 1932, the British documented the occupational hazards of asbestos dust inhalation.[a] Indeed, on September 25, 1935, the editors of the trade journal *Asbestos* wrote to Sumner Simpson, president of Raybestos-Manhattan, a leading asbestos company, asking permission to publish an article on the dangers of asbestos. Simpson refused and later praised the magazine for not printing the article. In a letter to Vandivar Brown, secretary of Johns-Manville, another asbestos manufacturer, Simpson observed: "The less said about asbestos the better off we are." Brown agreed, adding that any article on asbestosis should reflect American, not English, data.

In fact, American data were available, and Brown, as one of the editors of the journal, knew it. Working on behalf of Raybestos-Manhattan and Johns-Manville and their insurance carrier, Metropolitan Life Insurance Company, Anthony Lanza had conducted research between 1929 and 1931 on 126 workers with 3 or more years of asbestos exposure. But Brown and others were not pleased with the paper Lanza submitted to them for editorial review. Lanza, said Brown, had failed to portray asbestosis as milder than silicosis, a lung disease caused by long-term inhalation of silica dust and resulting in chronic shortness of breath. Under the then-pending Workmen's Compensation law, silicosis was categorized as a compensable disease. If asbestosis was worse than silicosis or indistinguishable from it, then it too would have to be covered. Apparently Brown didn't want this and thus requested that Lanza depict asbestosis as less serious than silicosis. Lanza complied and also omitted from his published report the fact that more than half the workers examined—67 of 126—were suffering from asbestosis.

Meanwhile, Sumner Simpson was writing F. H. Schulter, president of Thermoid Rubber Company, to suggest that several manufacturers sponsor further asbestos experiments. The sponsors, said Simpson, could exercise oversight prerogatives; they "could determine from time to time after the findings are made whether they wish any publication or not." Added Simpson: "It would be a good idea to distribute the information to the medical fraternity, providing it is of the right type and would not injure our companies." Lest there should be any question about the arbiter of publication, Brown wrote to officials at the laboratory conducting the tests:

> It is our further understanding that the results obtained will be considered the property of those who are advancing the required funds, who will determine whether, to what extent and in what manner they shall be made public. In the event it is deemed desirable that the results be made public, the manuscript of your study will be submitted to us for approval prior to publication.

Industry officials were concerned with more than controlling information flow. They also sought to deny workers early evidence of their asbestosis. Dr. Kenneth Smith, medical director of a Johns-Manville plant in Canada, explained why seven workers he found to have asbestosis should not be informed of their disease:

> It must be remembered that although these men have the X-ray evidence of asbestosis, they are working today and definitely are not disabled from asbestosis. They have not been told of this diagnosis, for it is felt that as long as the man feels well, is happy at home and at work, and his physical condition remains good, nothing should be said. When he becomes disabled and sick, then the diagnosis should be made and the claim submitted *by the Company*. The fibrosis of this disease is irreversible and permanent so that eventually compensation will be paid to each of these men. But as long as the man is not disabled, it is felt that he should not be told of his condition so that he can live and work in peace and the Company can benefit by his many years of experience. Should the man be told of his condition today there is a very definite possibility that he would become mentally and physically ill, simply through the knowledge that he has asbestosis.

When lawsuits filed by asbestos workers who had developed cancer reached the industry in the 1950s, Dr. Smith suggested that the industry retain the Industrial Health Foundation to conduct a cancer study that would, in effect, squelch the asbestos-cancer connection. The asbestos companies refused, claiming that such a study would only bring further unfavorable publicity to the industry, and that there wasn't enough evidence linking asbestos and cancer industry-wide to warrant it.

Shortly before his death in 1977, Dr. Smith was asked whether he had ever recommended to Johns-Manville officials that warning labels be placed on insulation products containing asbestos. He provided the following testimony:

> The reasons why the caution labels were not implemented immediately, it was a business decision as far as I could understand. Here was a recommendation, the corporation is in business to make, to provide jobs for people and make money for stockholders and they had to take into consideration the effects of everything they did, and if the application of a caution label identifying a product as hazardous would cut out sales, there would be serious financial implications. And the powers that be had to make some effort to judge the necessity of the label vs. the consequences of placing the label on the product.

Dr. Smith's testimony and related documents have figured prominently in hundreds of asbestos-related lawsuits, totaling more than $1 billion. In March 1981, a settlement was reached

[a]See Samuel S. Epstein, "The Asbestos 'Pentagon Papers,' " in Mark Green and Robert Massie, Jr., eds., *The Big Business Reader: Essays on Corporate America* (New York: Pilgrim Press, 1980), 154–65. This article is the primary source of the facts and quotations reported here.

in nine separate lawsuits brought by 680 New Jersey asbestos workers at a Raybestos-Manhattan plant. Several asbestos manufacturers, as well as Metropolitan Life Insurance, were named as defendants. Under the terms of the settlement, the workers affected will share in a $9.4 million court-administered compensation fund. Each worker will be paid compensation according to the length of exposure to asbestos and the severity of the disease contracted.

By 1982, an average of 500 new asbestos cases were being filed each month against Manville (as Johns-Manville was now called), and the company was losing more than half the cases that went to trial. In 10 separate cases, juries had also awarded punitive damages, averaging $616,000 a case. By August, 20,000 claims had been filed against the company, and Manville filed for bankruptcy in federal court. This action froze the lawsuits in their place and forced asbestos victims to stand in line with other Manville creditors. After more than 3 years of legal haggling, Manville's reorganization plan was finally approved by the bankruptcy court. The agreement set up a trust fund valued at approximately $2.5 billion to pay Manville's asbestos claimants. To fund the trust, shareholders were required to surrender half the value of their stock, and the company had to give up much of its projected earnings over the next 25 years.[b]

Claims, however, soon overwhelmed the trust, which ran out of money in 1990. With many victims still waiting for payment, federal Judge Jack B. Weinstein ordered the trust to restructure its payments and renegotiate Manville's contributions to the fund. As a result, the most seriously ill victims will now be paid first, but average payments to victims have been lowered significantly, from $145,000 to $43,000. Meanwhile, the trust's stake in Manville has been increased to 80 percent, and Manville has been required to pay $300 million to it in additional dividends.[c]

Questions

1. Should the asbestos companies be held morally responsible in the sense of being capable of making a moral decision about the ill effects of asbestos exposure? Or does it make sense to consider only the principal people involved as morally responsible—for example, Simpson and Brown?
2. Simpson and Brown presumably acted in what they thought were the best profit interests of their companies. Nothing they did was illegal. On what grounds, if any, are their actions open to criticism?
3. Suppose that Simpson and Brown reasoned this way: "While it may be in our firms' short-term interests to suppress data about the ill effects of asbestos exposure, in the long run it may ruin our companies. We could be sued for millions, and the reputation of the entire industry could be destroyed. So we should reveal the true results of the asbestos-exposure research and let the chips fall where they may." Would that be appropriate?
4. If you were a stockholder in Raybestos-Manhattan or Johns-Manville, would you approve of Simpson and Brown's conduct? If not, why not?
5. "Hands of government" proponents would say that it is the responsibility of government, not the asbestos industry, to ensure health and safety with respect to asbestos. In the absence of appropriate government regulations, asbestos manufacturers have no responsibility other than to operate efficiently. Do you agree?
6. Does Dr. Smith's explanation for concealing from workers the nature of their health problems illustrate how adherence to industry and corporate goals can militate against individual moral behavior? Or do you think Dr. Smith did all he was morally obliged to do as an employee of an asbestos firm? What about Lanza's suppression of data in his report?
7. It has been shown that spouses of asbestos workers can develop lung damage and cancer simply by breathing the fibers carried home on work clothes and that people living near asbestos plants experience higher rates of cancer than the general population does. Would it be possible to assign responsibility for these effects to individual members of asbestos companies? Should the companies themselves be held responsible?

[b]See Robert Mokhiber, *Corporate Crime and Violence* (San Francisco: Sierra Club Books, 1988), 285–86; and Arthur Sharplin, "Manville Lives on as Victims Continue to Die," *Business and Society Review* 65 (Spring 1988): 27–28.

[c]"Asbestos Claims to Be Reduced Under New Plan," *The Wall Street Journal* (November 20, 1990): A4; and "MacNeil-Lehrer Newshour," December 18, 1990.

LEARNING OBJECTIVES

After reading this chapter, you should be able to

1. Compute a company's profits as reflected by an income statement.
2. Determine a firm's accounting book value, as presented in a balance sheet.
3. Compute a company's taxes.
4. Measure a company's free cash flows, both from an asset perspective and a financing perspective.
5. Explain the difficulty in comparing financial statements of U.S. firms and foreign companies.

CHAPTER 2

Understanding Financial Statements, Taxes, and Cash Flows

The year was 1985 when Howard Schultz joined a small firm located in Seattle's historic Pike Place Market. The business sold coffee to high-end restaurants and espresso bars.

The company was virtually unknown to the public at that time, but not any more. We all recognize the name today—Starbucks Coffee. You might be interested to know that the name came from Herman Melville's *Moby Dick,* a classic American novel about the 19th century whaling industry.

As director of retail operations and marketing, Schultz was traveling on a business trip to Italy, where he was impressed with the popularity of espresso bars in Milan. He immediately saw the potential for developing a similar coffee bar culture in Seattle.

Schultz returned home to convince the founders of Starbucks to test the coffee bar concept in downtown Seattle. The experiment quickly proved to be successful, leading Schultz to found a new business, Il Giornale. The business offered brewed coffee and espresso beverages made from Starbucks coffee beans.

With the backing of local investors, Il Giornale acquired Starbucks' assets and changed its name to Starbucks Corporation. From that meager beginning, the rest is history. By October 2003, the firm had 7,225 stores in 25 countries. Schultz has since become Chairman of the Board and Chief Global Strategist. Sales for 2003 were expected to exceed $4 billion.

In those early days, Schultz no doubt considered a lot of different factors in evaluating the Starbucks opportunity. After all, he was about to change the way most of us think about coffee and what we are willing to pay for it. Not knowing for certain, we can surmise that he thought a great deal about such issues as the size and growth potential of the market, competition, and the management team.

Schultz would have also considered the economics of the deal, such as projected sales, profits, the amount of capital required, and the potential returns to his investors. Such an analysis would have required him to have a good understanding of income statements, balance sheets, and cash flows—the very topic of this chapter. And now that Starbucks is a large public corporation, investment analysts, along with management, meticulously study the firm' financial statements. So let's begin our own study of financial statements, which will be continued in Chapter 3.

CHAPTER PREVIEW

In this chapter, we view the world of finance primarily as an accountant sees it. To begin, we review the two basic financial statements that are used to understand how a firm is doing financially—the income statement, or what is sometimes called the profit and loss statement, and the balance sheet. We also spend a significant amount of time coming to understand how to measure and interpret a company's cash flows. No skill is more important in our study of finance than being able to calculate a firm's or a project's cash flows. Cash flow is a *very* significant issue for a company and is critical in our understanding of financial management. It will be discussed over and over in the chapters to follow. Thus, it is essential that we begin early to develop a good understanding of cash flows.

BACK TO THE PRINCIPLES

Two principles are especially important in this chapter: ***Principle 3*** *tells us that* ***Cash—Not Profits—Is King.*** *In many respects, cash is more important than profits. Thus, in this chapter, considerable time is devoted to learning how to measure cash flows. Second,* ***Principle 7*** *warns us there may be conflict between management and owners, especially in large firms where managers and owners have different incentives. That is,* ***Managers Won't Work for the Owners Unless It's In Their Best Interest to Do So.*** *Although the management is an agent of the owners, experience suggests that managers do not always act in the best interest of the owners. The incentives for the managers are, at times, different from those of owners. Thus, the firm's common stockholders, as well as other providers of capital (such as bankers), have a need for information that can be used to monitor the managers' actions. Because the owners of large companies do not have access to internal information about the firm's operations, they must rely on public information from any and all sources. One of the main sources of such information is the company's financial statements that are provided by the firm's accountants. Although this information is by no means perfect, it is an important source used by outsiders to assess a company's activities. In this chapter, we learn how to use data from the firm's public financial statements to monitor management's actions.*

Let's begin our study by looking at the basic financial statements that are a primary source of information about a firm's financial performance. Only by understanding the makeup of these statements can we have any hope of learning about business, much less finance.

Objective 1

THE INCOME STATEMENT: MEASURING A COMPANY'S PROFITS

Income statement
The statement of profit or loss for the period, comprised of revenues less expenses for the period.

An **income statement**, or *profit and loss statement*, measures the amount of profits generated by a firm over a given time period. In its most basic form, an income statement can be expressed as follows:

sales − expenses = profits

The income statement answers the question, "How profitable is the business?" In providing this answer, the income statement reports financial information related to five broad areas of business activity:

1. Revenue (sales)—money derived from selling the company's product or service
2. Cost of goods sold—the cost of producing or acquiring the goods or services to be sold
3. Operating expenses—expenses related to (a) marketing and distributing the product or service, and (b) administering the business
4. Financing costs of doing business—the interest paid to the firm's creditors and the dividends paid to preferred stockholders (but not dividends paid to common stockholders)
5. Tax expenses—the amount of taxes owed based on a firm's taxable income

All of these "income statement activities" are illustrated in Table 2-1, where we present the annual income statement for Harley-Davidson, Inc. Looking at the firm's income statement, we see that for 2002:

TABLE 2-1 Harley-Davidson, Inc. Annual Income Statement for the Year Ending December 31, 2002

	2002
Sales	$4,195,197
Cost of goods sold	2,673,129
Gross profit	1,522,068
Selling, general, and administration expenses	465,831
Depreciation	160,119
Total operating expenses	$ 625,950
Operating profit	$ 896,118
Interest expense	17,849
Earnings before taxes	878,269
Provision for income taxes	298,052
Net income	580,217

Operating profit: Also called earnings before interest and taxes, or operating income

$ 896,118: Income from operating activities

17,849: Cost of debt financing

580,217: Income resulting from operating and financing activities

1. Sales or revenues—determined by the amount of product sold times the price per unit—were almost $4.2 billion for the year.
2. The firm's cost of producing or acquiring its product was $2.67 billion.
3. Harley-Davidson spent $466 million in selling and administration expenses, and had approximately $160.1 million in depreciation expense.
4. Given these results, the firm had **operating income**, or **earnings before interest and taxes (EBIT)**, of $896 million.
5. The firm owed $17.8 million in **interest expense**, which is determined by the amount of Harley-Davidson debt and the interest rate paid on the debt.
6. Harley-Davidson owed $298 million in income tax expense, which was approximately 34 percent of the company's **earnings before taxes.**
7. Finally, the **net income** available to Harley-Davidson's owners was equal to $580 million. This income may be distributed to the company's owners or reinvested in the company provided, of course, there is cash available to do so.

Operating income (earnings before interest and taxes)
Profit from sales minus total operating expenses.

Interest expense
Interest paid on a firm's outstanding debt. A firm's interest expense is tax deductible.

Earnings before taxes
Operating income minus interest expense.

Net income
A figure representing the firm's profit or loss for the period. It also represents the earnings available to the firm's common stockholders.

What conclusion can we draw from Harley-Davidson's income statement? Well, for one thing, we learn that for every $1 in sales, Harley-Davidson earned about $.36 in gross profits ($1,522,068 gross profits ÷ $4,195,197 sales), $.21 in operating profits ($896,118 ÷ $4,195,197 sales), and $.138 in net income ($580,217 ÷ $4,195,197).

To determine if these results are good, we must estimate if these profit-to-sales ratios are high enough that shareholder value is being created. We might also gain some insight if we could see how Harley-Davidson's performance compares against that of its competition—more about this in Chapter 3. For the time being, simply remember that the profit-to-sales relationships are important in assessing a firm's performance.

Three additional issues are important in understanding the information contained in an income statement:

1. Operating income (earnings before interest and taxes) is not affected by how the firm is financed, whether with debt or equity. Operating income is the firm's profits from all of its assets, regardless of whether the assets are financed from debt or stock. Understanding this fact is essential when we later want to evaluate management's performance at creating profits from the firm's assets. Just remember that operating income is affected only by management's investment decisions, and not by how the firm is financed.

2. Notice that interest expense is subtracted from income before computing the firm's tax liability, which is not true for dividends paid. In other words, interest is a tax-deductible expense; that is, for every dollar a company spends on interest, its tax expense is reduced proportionately. For example, if a firm's tax rate is 30 percent, $1 paid in interest reduces taxes by $.30, which means that the after-tax cost of a dollar of debt is only $0.70 ($1.00 – $0.30).
3. As we shall see later, the fact that a firm has a positive net income does not necessarily mean it has any cash—possibly a surprising result to us, but one that we will come to understand.

CONCEPT CHECK

1. What does the income statement tell us? Why must we be careful when interpreting the income statement?
2. What is the basic relationship that we see in the income statement?
3. How is operating income different from net income as both relate to the five "business activities" reported in the income statement?

Objective 2

THE BALANCE SHEET: MEASURING A FIRM'S BOOK VALUE

Balance sheet A statement of financial position at a particular date. The form of the statement follows the balance sheet equation: total assets = total liabilities + owners' equity.

Whereas the income statement reports the results from operating the business for a period of time, such as a year, the **balance sheet** provides a snapshot of the firm's financial position at a specific point in time, presenting its asset holdings, liabilities, and owner-supplied capital. In its simplest form, a balance sheet follows this formula:

total assets = outstanding debt + shareholders' equity

Assets represent the resources owned by the firm, whereas the liabilities (debt) and shareholders' equity indicate how those resources are financed.

Figure 2-1 presents the basic components of a balance sheet. On the left side of Figure 2-1, the firm's assets are listed according to their type; on the right side, we see a listing of the different sources of financing a company could use to finance its assets.

TYPES OF ASSETS

As shown in Figure 2-1, a company's assets fall into three categories: (1) current assets, (2) fixed assets, and (3) other assets. Assets on a balance sheet are listed in the order of the length of time necessary to convert them into cash in the ordinary course of business. Current assets, excluding cash itself, are expected to be converted into cash within 12 months, with accounts receivable not taking as long to convert to cash as inventories. Fixed assets, such as equipment, are used over a number of years, and as such will not be converted into cash within the normal operating cycle of business.

Current assets (gross working capital) Current assets are assets that are expected to be converted into cash within a year, consisting primarily of cash, marketable securities, accounts receivable, inventories, and prepaid expenses.

CURRENT ASSETS **Current assets**, or **gross working capital**, as it is sometimes called, comprise those assets that are relatively liquid; that is, those that are expected to be converted into cash within a year. Current assets primarily include cash, marketable securities, accounts receivable, inventories, and prepaid expenses.

FIGURE 2-1 The Balance Sheet: An Overview

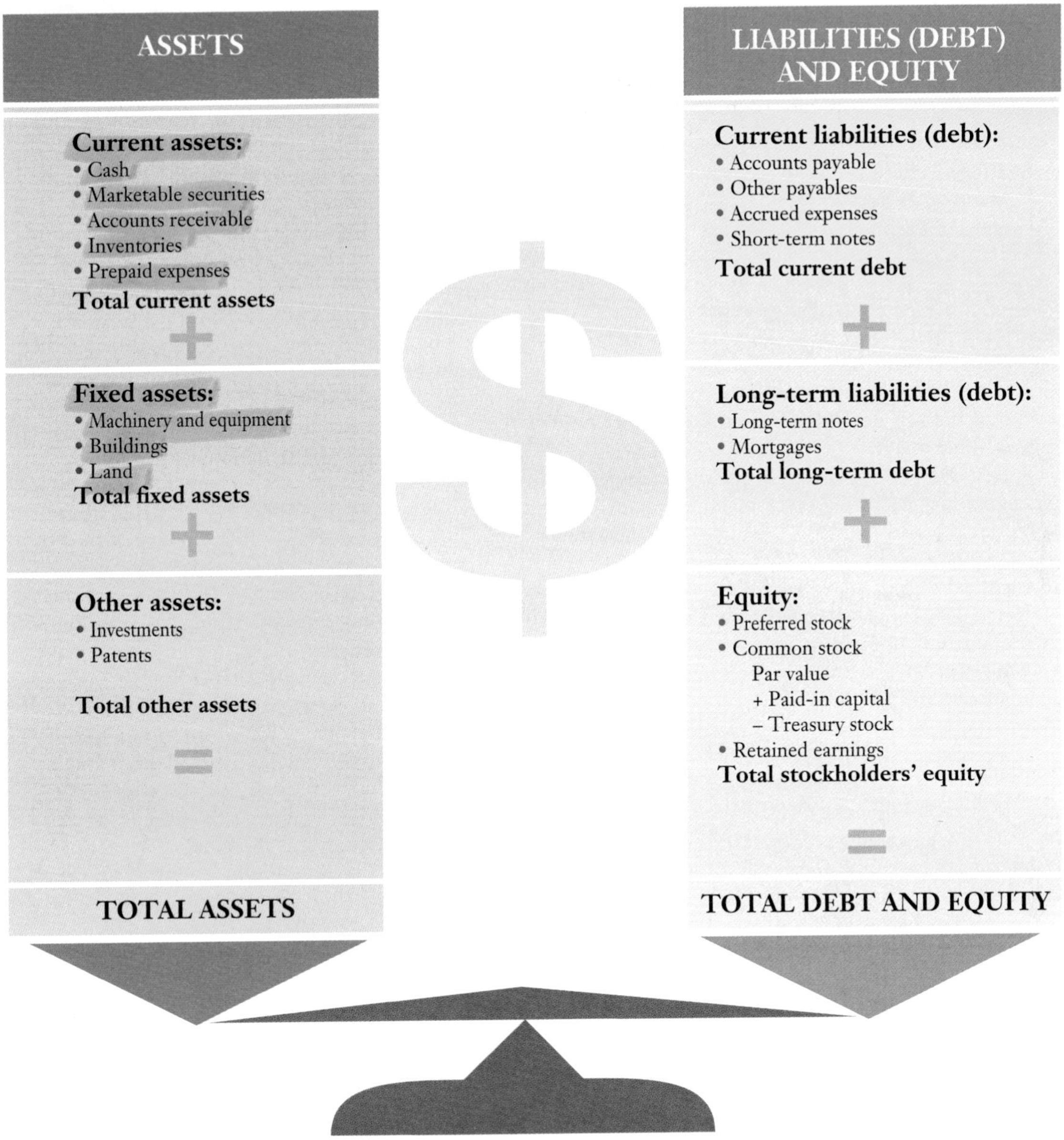

- **Cash.** Every firm must have cash for current business operations. A reservoir of cash is needed because of the unequal flow of funds into (cash receipts) and out of (cash expenditures) the business. The amount of the cash balance is determined not only by the volume of sales, but also by the predictability of cash receipts and cash payments.
- **Accounts receivable.** The firm's **accounts receivable** consists of payments due from its customers who buy on credit.
- **Inventories. Inventory** consists of the raw materials, work-in-progress, and the final products held by a firm for eventual sale.
- **Prepaid expenses.** A company often needs to prepay some of its expenses. For example, insurance premiums may be due before coverage begins, or rent may have to be

Accounts receivable
A promise to receive cash from customers who purchased goods from the firm on credit.

Inventory
Raw materials, work-in-progress, and finished goods held by the firm for eventual sale.

A FOCUS ON HARLEY-DAVIDSON ROAD RULES

THE PATH TO CFO AT HARLEY-DAVIDSON: AN INTERVIEW WITH JIM ZIEMER

For as long as I can remember, I wanted to work at Harley-Davidson. Growing up just three blocks from the plant, I used to watch the test riders who sometimes ate lunch in my neighbor's yard and think "Wouldn't it be great to be paid to ride a motorcycle?"

I rode my first motorcycle, an M-50 Harley, when I was 15 years old. When I was 19, my wish came true; I went to work for the firm as a union employee, operating the elevator used to move parts from floor to floor. They'd punch the sheet metal on the first floor for the tanks and fenders and I'd take it up to the sixth floor where they painted it. I would take tube steel up to the 5th floor where it was bent and welded into frames. Then the bike flowed downward to the first floor for the final assembly. It was really great watching all the components of manufacturing come together into a beautiful motorcycle.

In the meantime, I entered the University of Wisconsin, Milwaukee, to study accounting. Actually, this was a bit of a fluke. When I started college I had no idea of what I wanted to be. I started in the school of engineering, but soon transferred to the school of science, with an interest in physics, and eventually ended up in chemistry. However, my work and studies were abruptly interrupted when I received a letter from Uncle Sam requesting my services in the army. While in the army, I took some accounting and economics courses, and when I got out, I thought, "The quickest way to graduate is to major in accounting." So I returned to Harley-Davidson to work part-time and finish my accounting degree. In my new job, I worked as a timekeeper, which helped me become familiar with all the operations within the plant. It was interesting to watch the gears being cut and the crankcases being machined, and in the process learning all about the inside components of an engine.

Then I got a job in the engineering department. With a limited background in engineering and an interest in accounting, I was put in charge of project management. After graduating, I had a number of jobs, ending up in financial planning, which allowed me to see what happened in the firm as a whole. From there, I worked as the controller in parts and accessories, which meant getting involved in sales and marketing and shipping and receiving.

In 1981, management bought the company from AMF (a conglomerate) through a management buyout, which meant the firm took on a lot of debt. Shortly thereafter, interest rates climbed to 20 percent; it was not a pretty sight. The firm went through a major downsizing that led to laying off about 40 percent of our employees. As a consequence, everybody ended up doing several jobs, and I became director of all the firm's accounting.

In 1986, we decided to take the company public through the initial public offering, which would allow us to get rid of a lot of debt. This was happening when I was working on my MBA, which was a great situation for my master's studies. Finally, in February 1987, I became the vice president and controller at Harley-Davidson. I remember feeling very fortunate; I was 37 years old and the controller of what I thought was a great company. We had a lot of things to prove yet, but we were on our way.

Prepaid expenses Expenses that have been paid in advance. These assets are recorded on the balance sheet and expensed on the income statement as they are used.

Fixed assets Assets comprising equipment, buildings, and land.

Other assets Assets not included in current assets or fixed assets.

Accounting book value The value of an asset as shown on a firm's balance sheet. It represents the historical cost of the asset rather than its current market value or replacement cost.

paid in advance. Thus, **prepaid expenses** are those cash payments recorded on the balance sheet as current assets and then shown as an expense in the income statement as they are used.

FIXED ASSETS **Fixed assets** include machinery and equipment, buildings, and land. Some businesses are more capital-intensive than others; for example, a manufacturer would typically be more capital-intensive than a wholesale operation and, therefore, have more fixed assets.

OTHER ASSETS **Other assets** are all assets that are not current assets or fixed assets, including, for example, intangible assets such as patents, copyrights, and goodwill.

In reporting the dollar amounts of the various types of assets just described, the conventional practice is to report the value of the assets and liabilities on a historical cost basis. Thus, the balance sheet is not intended to represent the current market value of the company, but rather reports the historical transactions recorded at their cost, or what we call a firm's **accounting book value**. Determining a fair value of the business is a different matter.

TYPES OF FINANCING

We now turn to the right side of the balance sheet in Figure 2-1, labeled "Liabilities (Debt) and Equity," which indicates how the firm finances its assets. Financing comes from two main sources: debt (liabilities) and equity. **Debt** is money that has been borrowed and must be repaid at some predetermined date. **Equity**, however, represents the shareholders' investment in the company. See the Finance Matters box, "Financial Statements: Fact or Fiction."

DEBT CAPITAL **Debt capital** is financing provided by a creditor. As shown in Figure 2-1, it is divided into (1) current, or short-term, debt and (2) long-term debt. **Current debt**, or short-term liabilities, includes borrowed money that must be repaid within the next 12 months. Sources of current debt include the following:

- **Accounts payable** represents credit extended by suppliers to a firm when it purchases inventories. The purchasing firm may have 30 or 60 days before paying for inventory that has been purchased. This form of credit extension is also called trade credit.
- **Other payables** include interest payable and income taxes payable that are owed and will come due within the year.
- **Accrued expenses** are short-term liabilities that have been incurred in the firm's operations, but not yet paid. For example, employees perform work that may not be paid for until the following week or month, which are recorded as accrued wages.
- **Short-term notes** represent amounts borrowed from a bank or other lending source that are due and payable within 12 months.

LONG-TERM DEBT **Long-term debt** includes loans from banks or other sources that lend money for longer than 12 months. For example, a firm might borrow money for 5 years to buy equipment, or for as long as 25 to 30 years to purchase real estate, such as a warehouse or an office building.

EQUITY Equity includes the shareholders' investment—both preferred stockholders and common stockholders—in the firm.

- **Preferred stockholders** receive a dividend that is fixed in amount. In the event of liquidation of the firm, these stockholders are paid after the firm's creditors, but before the common stockholders.
- **Common stockholders** are the residual owners of a business. They receive whatever is left over—good or bad—after the creditors and preferred stockholders are paid. The amount of a firm's common equity as reported in the balance sheet is equal to (1) the net amount the company received from selling stock to investors less stock the firm has repurchased from shareholders plus (2) the firm's retained earnings. The amount the firm receives from selling stock is recorded in the common equity section in the accounts of **par value and paid-in capital**. These amounts may be offset by any stock that has been repurchased by the company, which is typically shown as **treasury stock**. **Retained earnings** is the cumulative total of all the net income over the firm's life less the common stock dividends that have been paid over the years. Thus, the common equity capital consists of the following:

common equity = common stock issued (less treasury stock repurchased)
+ cumulative net income over the firm's life
– total dividends paid over the firm's life

which is shown in the balance sheet as:

common equity = common stock (par value + paid-in capital – treasury stock)
+ retained earnings

Debt
Consists of such sources as credit extended by suppliers or a loan from a bank.

Equity
Stockholders' investment in the firm and the cumulative profits retained in the business up to the date of the balance sheet.

Debt capital
Funds provided to the firm by a creditor.

Current debt
Debt due to be paid within 1 year.

Accounts payable
Liability of the firm for goods purchased from suppliers on credit.

Other payables
Interest payable and income taxes payable that are to be paid within 1 year.

Accrued expenses
Expenses that have been incurred but not yet paid in cash.

Short-term notes
Amounts borrowed from a creditor that are due within 1 year.

Long-term debt
Loans from banks or other sources that lend money for longer than 12 months.

Preferred stockholders
Investors who own the firm's preferred stock.

Common stockholders
Investors who own the firm's common stock. Common stockholders are the residual owners of the firm.

Par value and paid-in capital
The amount the firm receives from selling stock to investors.

Treasury stock
The firm's stock that has been issued and reacquired by the firm.

Retained earnings
The cumulative earnings that have been retained and reinvested in the firm over its life (cumulative earnings – cumulative dividends).

FINANCE MATTERS — ETHICS

FINANCIAL STATEMENTS: FACT OR FICTION?

A firm's financial statements are the primary source of information used by investors and creditors for making investment decisions. Firm management is obligated to provide accurate information and motivated to provide financial results that meet the expectations of Wall Street participants. Much of the time both results can be obtained simultaneously. However, there are times where the accurate information will not support the expectations of the investing community. What is management to do?

The requirement for management is to accurately report the firm's financial position. However, in the late 1990s and early 2000s there were instances where the desire to meet Wall Street expectations dominated the obligation to provide accurate information.

Rite Aid executives were charged with overstating the firm's income during the period from May 1997 to May 1999. Correcting this situation required a $1.6 billion restatement of earnings, the largest restatement ever recorded at that time, according to the Securities and Exchange Commission.

In the summer of 2000, Waste Management and their independent auditors, Arthur Andersen, paid $229 million to shareholders to settle charges related to $3.5 billion in accounting irregularities. In November 2002, Waste Management paid an additional $457 million in fines for violating securities laws.

During its 1997 merger with CUC International, Cendant issued false and misleading statements concerning the merger. Additionally, firm officers sold Cendant stock prior to making the accounting problems known to investors. For these actions, the firm paid $2.8 billion.

Energy trading firm Enron used off-the-book partnerships to conceal $1 billion in debt and to inflate the firm's profits. News of these transactions resulted in the firm filing for bankruptcy in December 2002 and criminal charges against former CFO Andy Fastow. Another casualty of the Enron scandal was the accounting firm Arthur Andersen. Andersen was found guilty of obstruction of justice for shredding documents related to the Enron investigation. This felony conviction resulted in the discontinuation of Andersen's auditing business.

Conglomerate Tyco has also seen its share of accounting problems. Former CEO Dennis Kozlowski used millions of dollars in company funds inappropriately and without the consent of the board of directors. As a result of the misuse of company funds, Tyco stock lost 75 percent of its value in 2002.

Telecommunications giant Worldcom saw its fortunes disappear after an internal audit in 2002 revealed the firm had booked operating expenses as capital expenditures in an attempt to report better than actual profits. In July 2002, Worldcom filed Chapter 11 bankruptcy. As of early 2003, approximately $7 billion of accounting discrepancies have been uncovered.

In 2002, Xerox announced plans to restate earnings for the period 1997 to 2001 and to pay a $10 million fine to the SEC for engaging in fraudulent accounting practices. The total amount of improperly recorded revenue for the period could be in excess of $6 billion.

Do these examples indicate that financial statements are not reliable at all? Hardly! These large firms that have been charged with or convicted of misrepresenting their financial result are but a few of the over 7,200 publicly traded firms in the United States. Most firm managers are committed to their obligation to accurately report financial information. Beginning in 2002, the SEC required firm executives to submit a signed document attesting the financial results are accurate. Improper reporting of financial statements can lead to severe consequences for management, including loss of job, fines, and jail time.

Source: *Wall Street Journal*. Eastern Edition (Staff produced copy only) by Saunders-Egodigwe, Long, & Warfield.

THE HARLEY-DAVIDSON, INC. BALANCE SHEET

Balance sheets for Harley-Davidson, Inc. are presented in Table 2-2 for both December 31, 2001 and December 31, 2002, along with the changes in each account during the year. We show the reasons for the change in retained earnings at the bottom of the table. By referring to the two balance sheets, we can see the financial position of the firm both at the beginning and end of 2002. Furthermore, by examining the two balance sheets, along with the income statement for 2002, we will have a more complete picture of the firm's operations. We are then able to see what Harley-Davidson looked like at the beginning of 2002 (balance sheet

TABLE 2-2 Harley-Davidson Inc. Annual Balance Sheet ($000)

	12/31/01	12/31/02	CHANGE
ASSETS			
Cash	$ 635,449	$ 795,728	$160,279
Accounts receivable	775,264	964,465	189,201
Inventories	181,115	218,156	37,041
Other current assets	73,436	88,237	14,801
Total current assets	$1,665,264	$2,066,586	$401,322
Gross plant, property & equipment	$1,705,361	$2,006,256	$300,895
Accumulated depreciation	(813,541)	(973,660)	
Net plant, property, and equipment	$ 891,820	$1,032,596	
Other assets	561,411	762,035	200,624
Total assets	$3,118,495	$3,861,217	$742,722
LIABILITIES AND EQUITY			
LIABILITIES			
Accounts payable	$ 217,051	$ 382,579	$165,528
Accrued expenses	194,683	226,977	32,294
Income taxes payable	65,875	67,886	2,011
Short-term notes	141,191	189,024	47,833
Other interest bearing current liabilities	97,310	123,586	26,276
Total current liabilities	$ 716,110	$ 990,052	$273,942
Long-term debt	646,102	638,250	(7,852)
Total liabilities	$1,362,212	$1,628,302	$266,090
COMMON EQUITY			
Common stock (par value)	$ 3,242	$ 3,254	$ 12
Paid in capital	359,165	386,284	27,119
Retained earnings	1,819,422	2,325,737	506,315
Less treasury stock	(425,546)	(482,360)	(56,814)
Total common equity	$1,756,283	$2,232,915	$476,632
Total liabilities and equity	$3,118,495	$3,861,217	$742,722

HARLEY DAVIDSON INC.

RECONCILIATION OF RETAINED EARNINGS

Retained earnings, December 31, 2001	$1,819,422
2002 net income	580,217
Dividends paid	73,902
Retained earnings, December 31, 2002	$2,325,737

on December 31, 2001), what happened during the year (income statement for 2002), and the final outcome at the end of the year (balance sheet on December 31, 2002).

The firm's investment in assets increased $742.7 million over the year, with most of the growth in cash, accounts receivables, and other assets. The increase in the firm's assets in turn required additional financing. Looking at the debt and equity parts of the balance sheet, we see that management used two primary sources of money to finance the growth:

1. A $506.3 million increase in retained earnings, which is the result of retaining a portion of the firm's net income, rather than paying it out in dividends.
2. Borrowing $273.9 million in additional short-term debt (current liabilities).

We also observe in the common equity section that the firm's net common stock was reduced by $29.7 million. This is due to the increases in common par value

FIGURE 2-2 Harley-Davidson Balance Sheet as of December 31, 2002

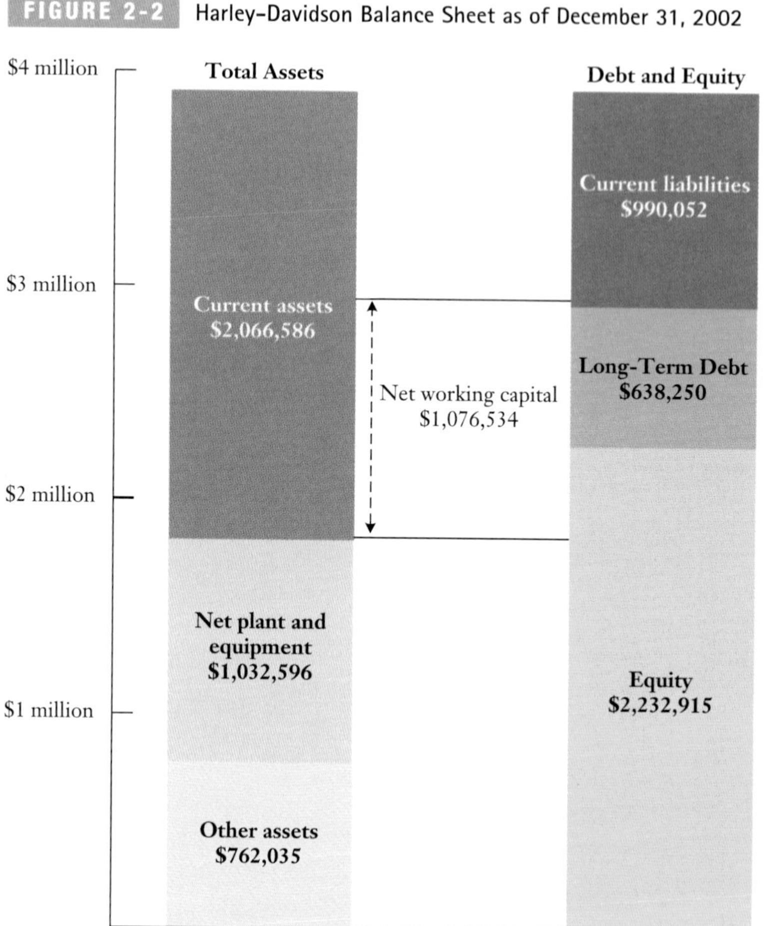

($12 thousand) and paid-in capital ($27.1 million) less the increase in treasury stock of $56.8 million (–$29.7 million = $12 thousand + $27.1 million – $56.8 million).

Note that when we are examining the changes in the balance sheet from one year to the next, as we just did with Harley-Davidson, Inc., we are gaining an understanding of where money came from and how it was used. For Harley-Davidson, we see that the firm invested in additional assets ($742.7 million increase in assets). Where did the money come from? The largest amount came from retaining a part of the firm's profits ($506.3 million). The remainder came from additional short-term borrowing ($273.9 million). Knowing this information is helpful in better understanding Harley-Davidson's finances. In fact, it is such an important matter that we will return to this issue later in the chapter.

To help us visualize Harley-Davidson's financial position, as reflected by its balance sheet, we have graphed the major types of assets and debt and equity in Figure 2-2, as of December 31, 2002. In looking at this graph, we see that for every dollar of assets, there must be a dollar of financing. There can be no exception. If we grow the firm's assets, we had best be prepared to find additional financing. Harley-Davidson has $3,861.2 million in total assets, which represents all of the investments made by creditors and stockholders in the firm. Two other terms related to the balance sheet need mentioning: net working capital and debt/equity mix.

Net working capital
The difference between the firm's current assets and its current liabilities. When the term *working capital* is used, it is frequently intended to mean net working capital.

NET WORKING CAPITAL Earlier we said that the term *current assets* is also called *gross working capital.* We can now define **net working capital** as current assets less current liabilities (current assets – current liabilities). Thus, net working capital compares the amount of current assets (assets that should convert into cash within the next 12 months) to the current liabilities (debt that will be due within 12 months). As shown in Figure 2-2, Harley-Davidson's net working capital is $1,076.5 million ($2,066.6 million current assets – $990.1 million current liabilities). A firm's net working capital is of particular importance to lenders who want to know if a company has adequate liquidity. **Liquidity** is the speed and ease at which an asset can be converted into cash. The more current assets that a firm has relative to its current liabilities, the greater the firm's liquidity. If you loan a company some money, you would want to know that it has adequate liquidity to be able to repay the loan.

Liquidity
The ability of a firm to pay its bills on time, and how quickly a firm converts its liquid assets (accounts receivables and inventories) into cash.

DEBT/EQUITY MIX We can also see that by the end of 2002, Harley-Davidson was financing its assets about 42 percent from debt ($1.63 billion debt ÷ $3.86 billion total assets) and 58 percent from equity ($2.23 billion common equity ÷ $3.86 billion total assets). The debt-equity relationship is an important one to lenders and investors, as we will see on numerous occasions in our studies.

We next want to look briefly at one of the largest expenses a company encounters—taxes.

CONCEPT CHECK

1. Regarding the time frame reported, how is the balance sheet different from the income statement?
2. State the basic balance sheet formula and its meaning.
3. What is the definition of a firm's "accounting book value"?
4. What are the two principal sources of financing? What do these sources consist of?

COMPUTING A COMPANY'S TAXES

Objective 3

Taxes are a critical factor in making many financial decisions. The tax rules can be extremely complex, requiring a lot of specialized expertise to understand them. However, for our purposes, we just need to understand how taxes are computed.

To begin, we should ask, "Who is a taxpayer?" For the most part, there are three basic types of taxable business entities: sole proprietors, partnerships, and corporations. Sole proprietors report their income in their personal tax returns and pay the taxes owed. Partnerships report income from the partnership but do not pay taxes. Each partner reports his or her portion of the income and pays the corresponding taxes. The corporation, as a separate legal entity, reports its income and pays any taxes related to these profits. The owners (stockholders) of the corporation do not report these earnings in their personal tax returns, except when all or a part of the profits are distributed in the form of dividends. Because most firms of any size are corporations, we will restrict our discussion to corporate taxes.

COMPUTING TAXABLE INCOME

The taxable income for a corporation is based on the gross income from all sources less any tax-deductible expenses. *Gross income* equals the firm's dollar sales from its product less the cost of producing or acquiring the product. Tax-deductible expenses include any operating expenses, such as marketing expenses, administrative expenses, and depreciation expense. Also, interest expense paid on the firm's outstanding debt is a tax-deductible expense. However, dividends paid to the firm's stockholders are *not* deductible expenses,

FINANCE MATTERS — ETHICS

WHO CAN WE TRUST IF NOT MANAGEMENT?

On some rare occasions, management provides inaccurate accounting information to investors, even sometimes with the intent to mislead. The management of the third-largest drugstore chain in the United States, Rite Aid, acknowledged that the firm's profits in 1998 and 1999 were not profits at all, but losses—and big ones. The drugstore chain had reportedly overstated its profits by more than $1 billion. Management also reported a net loss of $1.14 billion for the fiscal year ended in February 2000.

The restatement of profits forced the resignation of the founder's son as the CEO and caused the stock price to fall by more than 80 percent.

The Securities and Exchange Commission and the U.S. Attorney's Office were investigating the firm. Management had turned over the results of its own legal and accounting probes to the government agencies. Robert Miller, the firm's new chairman of the board and its Chief Executive Officer, said that Rite Aid would "cooperate fully" with the investigations.

The firm's losses reduced its retained earnings to the point that the outstanding debt was 15 times larger than the amount of equity on the balance sheet. The firm's annual interest expenses were more than the firm's profits. However, Miller predicted that future cash flow, combined with available borrowing power, would be sufficient to service the firm's debt and meet its operating expenses. In a presentation to security analysts, Miller said that the firm's operating problems had been resolved and that "we expect a dramatic improvement in sales" and positive earnings before interest, taxes, depreciation, and amortization next year (2001).

Based on his analysis of the situation, Paul Brown, an accounting professor at New York University, said, "They employed just about every accounting trick out there." For instance, Rite Aid's management had reported expenses as assets and had retroactively increased the useful lives of selected fixed assets, lowering depreciation expense and artificially boosting reported income. Adjustments in a category called "inventory and cost of goods sold" involved some $500 million in misstatement of income, such as recording credits from vendors that had not been earned.

In 2002, a federal grand jury charged the firm's former chief executive and chairman, Martin Grass, with 36 charges, including accounting fraud, fabricating board minutes, lying to the SEC, and tampering with a witness. The government contends Grass inflated Rite Aid's earnings to benefit financially through compensation incentives linked to firm performance. Also charged with accounting fraud were the firm's former chief counsel and CFO. If convicted, the penalties for the former company executives could be millions of dollars in fines and many years in prison.

The lesson learned: Even very large, reputable firms can make some really big mistakes and then try to cover them up by using misleading accounting methods. When this happens, there is a loss of trust that cannot be overcome, typically leading to the firing of management. We can be thankful, however, that we live in a country where these instances are the exception. Even so, it can be very costly to investors when it does happen.

but rather distributions of income. See the Finance Matters box, "Who Can We Trust If Not Management."

When computing depreciation for tax purposes, companies use the *modified accelerated cost recovery system;* however, to avoid unnecessary complexity, we will generally use straight-line depreciation in our study. For instance, if a firm purchases a fixed asset for $12,000 that has a 5-year expected life and a $2,000 anticipated salvage value at the end of that period, straight-line depreciation would be $2,400 per year ($12,000 ÷ 5 years = $2,400). Although there is a $2,000 salvage value, this value is disregarded in computing annual depreciation expense for tax purposes.

To demonstrate how to compute a corporation's taxable income, consider the J&S Corporation, a manufacturer of home accessories. The firm, originally established by Kelly Stites, had sales of $50 million for the year. The cost of producing the accessories totaled $23 million. Operating expenses were $10 million. The corporation has $12.5 million in debt outstanding with an 8 percent interest rate, which has resulted in $1 million in interest expense ($12,500,000 × .08 = $1,000,000). Management paid $1 million in dividends to the

TABLE 2-3 J&S Corporation Taxable Income

Sales		$50,000,000
Cost of goods sold		(23,000,000)
Gross profit		$27,000,000
Operating expenses		
Administrative expenses	$4,000,000	
Depreciation expenses	1,500,000	
Marketing expenses	4,500,000	
Total operating expenses		(10,000,000)
Operating income (earnings before interest and taxes)		$17,000,000
Interest expense		(1,000,000)
Taxable income		$16,000,000

Note: Dividends paid to common stockholders ($1,000,000) are not tax-deductible.

TABLE 2-4 Corporate Tax Rates

RATES	INCOME LEVELS
15%	$0–$50,000
25%	$50,001–$75,000
34%	$75,001–$100,000
39%	$100,001–$335,000
34%	$335,001–$10,000,000
35%	$10,000,001–$15,000,000
38%	$15,000,001–$18,333,333
35%	Over $18,333,333

firm's common stockholders. The taxable income for the J&S Corporation would be $16 million, as shown in Table 2-3.

COMPUTING THE TAXES OWED The taxes to be paid by a corporation on its taxable income are based on the corporate tax rate structure. The specific rates effective for the corporation, as of 2002, are given in Table 2-4. If you wonder about the economic rationale for the rates, don't waste your time. There is none. Politicians, not economists, determine the rates.

Based on the tax rates, J&S Corporation's tax liability would be $5,530,000, as computed in Table 2-5.

The tax rates in Table 2-4 are defined as the **marginal tax rates**, or rates applicable to the next dollar of taxable income. For instance, if a firm has taxable income of $60,000 and is contemplating an investment that would yield $10,000 in additional taxable income, the tax rate to be used in calculating the taxes on this added income is the 25 percent marginal tax rate. However, if the corporation already expects $20 million without the new investment, the extra $10,000 in taxable income would be taxed at 35 percent, the marginal tax rate at the $20 million level of income.

Marginal tax rate
The tax rate that would be applied to the next dollar of taxable income.

For the J&S Corporation, with a taxable income of $16 million, its marginal tax rate is 38 percent; that is, any additional income from new investments will be taxed at a rate of 38 percent—at least until taxable income exceeds $18,333,333. Then the marginal tax rate would decline to 35 percent. Note, however, that while J&S Corporation has a 38 percent *marginal* tax rate, its **average tax rate**—taxes owed relative to the firm's taxable income—is 34.6 percent ($5,530,000 ÷ $16,000,000).

Average tax rate
Taxes owed by the firm divided by the firm's taxable income.

For financial decision making, it is the *marginal tax rate*, rather than the *average tax rate*, that matters because it is the marginal rate that is applied to any additional earnings resulting from a decision. Thus, when making financial decisions involving taxes, *always*

TABLE 2-5 Tax Calculations for J&S Corporation

EARNINGS	×	MARGINAL TAX RATE	=	TAXES
$50,000	×	15%	=	$ 7,500
$75,000–$50,000	×	25%	=	6,250
$100,000–$75,000	×	34%	=	8,500
$335,000–$100,000	×	39%	=	91,650
$10,000,000–$335,000	×	34%	=	3,286,100
$15,000,000–$10,000,000	×	35%	=	1,750,000
$16,000,000–$15,000,000	×	38%	=	380,000
Total tax liability				$5,530,000

use the marginal tax rate in your calculations and *not* the average tax rate. We cannot overemphasize the importance of remembering the preceding statement, which is a specific application of **Principle 4—It's Only What Changes That Counts.** We should always analyze decisions at the margin.

The tax rate structure used in computing the J&S Corporation's taxes assumes that the income occurs in the United States. Given the globalization of the economy, it may well be that some of the income originates in a foreign country. If so, the tax rates, and the method of taxing the firm, frequently vary. International tax rates can vary substantially and the job of the financial manager is to minimize the firm's taxes by reporting as much income as legally allowed in the low tax-rate countries and as little as legally allowed in the high tax-rate countries. Of course, other factors, such as political risk, may discourage efforts to minimize taxes across national borders.

CONCEPT CHECK

1. Distinguish among sole proprietors, partnerships, and corporations in terms of how they are taxed.
2. What is the difference between marginal tax rates and average tax rates?
3. Why do we use marginal tax rates, rather than average tax rates, when making financial decisions?
4. What should be the firm's goal when it comes to international taxes?

Objective 4

MEASURING FREE CASH FLOWS

While an income statement measures a company's profits, profits are not the same as cash flows; profits are calculated on an *accrual* basis rather than a *cash* basis. Accrual-basis accounting records income when it is earned, whether or not the income has been received in cash, and records expenses when they are incurred, even if money has not actually been paid out. For example, sales reported in the income statement include both cash sales and credit sales. Therefore, sales for a given year do not correspond exactly to the actual cash collected from sales. Similarly, a firm must purchase inventory, but some of the purchases are financed by credit rather than by immediate cash payment. Also, under the accrual system, the purchase of equipment that will last for more than 1 year is not shown as an expense in the income statement. Instead, the amount is recorded as an asset and then depreciated over its useful life. An annual depreciation expense (this is not a cash flow) is recorded as a way to match the use of the asset with sales generated from its service. We could give more examples to show why profits differ from cash flows, but the point should be clear: *Profits and cash flows are not the same thing*. Failure to understand and recognize this important fact could cause some real problems.

In measuring cash flows, we could use the conventional accountant's presentation called a *statement of cash flows*. However, we are more interested in considering cash flows from the perspective of the firm's investors, rather than from an accounting view. So, what follows is similar to a conventional cash flow statement presented as part of a company's financial statements, but "not exactly." (For a presentation of an accountant's statement of cash flows, see Appendix 2-A.)

We can think of a firm as a block of assets that produce cash flow, which can be either positive or negative. Once the firm has paid all its operating expenses and made all its investments, the remaining cash flows are free to distribute to the firm's creditors and shareholders—thus, the term **free cash flows**. However, if the free cash flows are negative, the creditors and investors are the ones who make up the shortfall—someone has to do it. Thus, the cash flows that are generated through a firm's assets equal its cash flows paid to—or received from—the company's investors (both creditors and stockholders). They have to be equal; except that if one is positive (negative) the other will be negative (positive). That is,

Free cash flows Amount of cash available from operations after paying for investments in net operating working capital and fixed assets. This cash is available to distribute to the firm's creditors and owners.

+(–) Cash flows from assets = –(+) cash flows from financing

The two calculations simply give us different perspectives about the firm's cash flows. So, let's look at each approach for measuring a company's free cash flows.

Calculating Free Cash Flows: An Asset Perspective

A firm's free cash flows, viewed from an *asset perspective*, are the after-tax cash flows generated from operating the business less the firm's investments in assets; that is:

$$\text{free cash flows} = \text{after-tax operating cash flows} - \text{investment in assets}$$

where the investment in assets may be expressed as follows:

$$\text{investment in assets} = \text{change in net operating working capital} + \text{change in gross fixed assets and other assets}$$

Thus, the procedure for computing a firm's free cash flows on an asset basis involves three steps:

1. Convert the income statement from an accrual basis to a cash basis (compute after-tax cash flows from operations).
2. Calculate the investment in *net* operating working capital.
3. Compute investments made in fixed assets and other assets (investment activities).

For the first step, we compute after-tax cash flows from operations as follows:

Operating income (earnings before interest and taxes)

+	depreciation
=	earnings before interest, taxes, depreciation, and amortization (EBITDA)
–	cash tax payments
=	after-tax cash flows from operations

In the preceding calculation, we determine **earnings before interest, taxes, depreciation, and amortization (EBITDA)** by adding back depreciation to operating income because depreciation is not a cash expense. We then subtract taxes to get the cash flows on an after-tax basis.

Earnings before interest, taxes, depreciation, and amortization (EBITDA) Operating income plus depreciation and amortization expenses.

Let's return to Harley-Davidson, Inc., to illustrate how to compute a firm's after-tax cash flows from operations. Using Harley-Davidson's income statement in Table 2-1, we find that the firm's after-tax cash flow from operations is $760,196,000.

		(in thousands)
After tax cash flows from operations:		
Operating income (See income statement)		$ 896,118
Depreciation (See income statement)		160,119
Earnings before interest, tax, depreciation, and amortization		$1,056,237
Provision for income taxes (see income statement)	$298,052	
Less change in income tax payable (see balance sheets)	2,011	
Cash taxes		$ 296,041
After-tax cash flows from operations		$ 760,196

Note that we made an adjustment in computing the taxes Harley-Davidson actually paid, as opposed to what is shown in the income statement, or what is called cash taxes. The income statement indicated that the *provision for income tax* was $298.05 million. However, look at the balance sheet and notice that *income taxes payable* increased $2.01 million from December 31, 2001 to December 31, 2002. Why would that be? Simply put, management did not pay the full $298.1 million in taxes. Rather they accrued $2.01 million of these taxes instead of paying them. So the cash taxes are computed as follows:

$$\text{Cash taxes} = \text{Provision for income taxes} - \text{change in income taxes payable.}$$
$$= \$298.052 \text{ million} - \$2.011 \text{ million} = \$296.041 \text{ million}$$

For the second step, the increase in net operating working capital is equal to the:

$$\begin{bmatrix} \textit{change in} \\ \text{current assets} \end{bmatrix} - \begin{bmatrix} \text{change in noninterest-bearing} \\ \text{current liabilities} \end{bmatrix}$$

Noninterest-bearing current liabilities Current liabilities other than short-term debt.

Earlier, we said that *net working capital* is equal to current assets minus current, or short-term, debt. However, in computing free cash flows, we only consider the **noninterest-bearing current liabilities** incurred in the normal day-to-day operating activities of buying and selling the firm's goods, such as accounts payable and accrued expenses. Any interest-bearing debt (that is, where you explicitly pay interest for the use of the money) will be included in computing free cash flows from a financing perspective because borrowing money is a financing activity.

For Harley-Davidson, the increase in net operating working capital is found by looking at the firm's balance sheets in Table 2-2 and computing the following:

$$\begin{bmatrix} \textit{change in} \\ \text{current assets} \end{bmatrix} - \begin{bmatrix} \text{change in noninterest-bearing} \\ \text{current liabilities} \end{bmatrix}$$
$$= \$401.322 \text{ million} - \$197.822 \text{ million} = \$203.5 \text{ million}$$

where the noninterest-bearing current liabilities are the firm's accounts payable and accruals.

The final step involves computing the change in *gross* fixed assets (not *net* fixed assets) and any other balance sheet assets that are not already considered. For Harley-Davidson, that includes the change in gross fixed assets and other assets, which equals $501,519,000:

Increase in gross fixed assets	$300,895,000
Increase in other assets	200,624,000
Total increase in long-term assets	$501,519,000

We can now compute Harley-Davidson's free cash flows from an asset perspective as follows:

	(in thousands)
After-tax cash flow operations	$760,196
Less:	
Increase in net operating working capital	(203,500)
Increase in long-term assets	(501,519)
Free cash flows (asset perspective)	$ 55,177

Given the preceding computations, we see that the firm's free cash flows are positive in the amount of $55.2 million. The firm's operations generated $760.2 million; but, the firm used cash to increase its investments in net operating working capital by the amount of $203.5 million and the investment in long-term assets of $501.5 million, leaving $55.2 million over and above what is needed within the business; in other words, these are the *free* cash flows. So, the question should now be: What did Harley-Davidson do with the asset free cash flows? Answer: They gave it to the investors! Let's look at the cash flows going to investors, as indicated by the firm's financial statements.

FREE CASH FLOWS: FINANCING PERSPECTIVE

A firm can either receive money from or distribute money to its investors, or some of both. In general, cash flows between investors and the firm occur in one of four ways. The firm can:

1. Pay interest to creditors.
2. Pay dividends to stockholders.
3. Increase or decrease outstanding debt.
4. Issue or repurchase stock from current investors.

We can illustrate these computations by returning to Harley-Davidson. We want to determine how the $55 plus million was paid to the investors, which we call the **financing cash flows**. When we say *investor*, we include both lenders and the company's shareholders. However, we do *not* include financing provided by accounts payable and accrued expenses, which were recognized earlier as part of the firm's net operating working capital. See the Finance Matters box, "Earnings or Cash: Which is Better?"

Financing cash flows
Financing free cash flows the firm pays to or receives from the investors (lenders and shareholders).

Looking at Harley-Davidson's income statement and the changes in the balance sheets, we see that cash was paid to the firm's investors in the following four ways:

1. Payment of interest to the creditors (income statement)
2. Payment of dividends to the common stockholders (below balance sheet)
3. Reducing the amount of long-term debt outstanding (decrease in long-term debt in the balance sheet)
4. Repurchasing more stock than was issued by the firm (increase in treasury stock less the increase in common stock and paid in capital)

However, the firm received additional financing from its creditors as indicated by the increases in the following interest-bearing current liabilities in the balance sheet:

1. Interest-bearing short-term notes
2. Other interest-bearing current liabilities

EARNINGS OR CASH: WHICH IS BETTER?

In the late 1980s the cable-television industry began measuring its financial health using earnings before interest, taxes, depreciation, and amortization (EBITDA). The industry believed the assets being depreciated were actually holding their value over time, not losing value as the depreciation expense signifies. Therefore, EBITDA was deemed to be an appropriate measure of the financial condition of the firms. This practice of examining a firm's earnings exclusive of depreciation gradually spread beyond the cable-television industry to the point where investors considered EBITDA a proxy for profits or a proxy for cash flow. Critics of this measure insist EBITDA is a proxy for neither of these measures and that it gives a firm too much flexibility in deciding what should be included as an expense to the firm.

Since the financial finagling by Worldcom, EBITDA has come under further scrutiny. Worldcom categorized as much as $7 billion of operating expenses as capital expenditures. Net income reported by Worldcom was overstated since these operating expenses were depreciated over several years rather than being expensed as they occurred. Furthermore, the EBITDA measure excludes any consideration of these expenses since the depreciation cost associated with the inappropriately classified capital expenditures is excluded in this measure.

Chuck Hill, director of research at Thomson Financial/First Call, believes that attention previously given the EBITDA as the focus of earnings reports will diminish, although it will continue to be "a useful tool." Merrill Lynch analyst Jessica Reif Cohen indicated that her firm will use more metrics in evaluating a firm's performance, placing less emphasis on EBITDA.

Media giant Viacom has already begun utilizing a broader range of measures that includes both EBITDA and net income. The firm also includes a measure of free cash flow, calculated as cash flow from operations less capital expenditures. Viacom President Mel Karmazin argues free cash flow is an important measure because it shows "how much cash a company has available to pay down debt, do acquisitions, and buy back stock."

USA Interactive Inc. announced plans to use "cash net income" rather than EBITDA as its preferred measure of profitability. Cash net income is calculated as net income exclusive of expenses such as amortization of intangibles and stock-option expense. A regulatory filing by the firm explains the reason for the change, "USA believes that today's conservative market environment calls for increased focus on the bottom line."

Source: Reprinted by permission of *The Wall Street Journal*, Copyright License number 880501203092.

Let's compute the actual amounts for Harley-Davidson.

	(in thousands)
Interest paid to lenders	$(17,849)
Dividends paid to owners (see balance sheets)	(73,902)
Changes in debt:	
Increase in interest-bearing short-term notes	47,833
Increase in other interest-bearing current liabilities	26,276
Decrease in long-term debt	(7,852)
Net stock repurchase	(29,683)
Free cash flows (financing perspective)	$(55,177)

Thus, the firm paid $17.85 million in interest and $73.9 million in dividends, paid off $7.9 million in long-term debt and repurchased $29.7 million in stock, net of new stock issued ($27,131 increase in par and paid-in capital – $56,814 stock repurchased). However, Harley received money from the firm's short-term creditors in the amount of $74.1 million ($47.8 million + $26.3 million). Add it all up and Harley paid a net amount of $55.2 million to its creditors and shareholders.

It is not a coincidence that Harley-Davidson's cash flows from assets exactly equal its cash flows from financing, except for the signs of the cash flows. They will always equal. The cash flows from the assets, if positive, will be the amount distributed to the investors;

and if the cash flow from the assets is negative, it will be the amount that the investors had to provide to the firm to cover the shortage in asset free cash flows.

Harley-Davidson, Inc.: What Have We Learned?

Based on our review of Harley-Davidson, Inc.'s financial statements, we can now draw some conclusions. To this point, we have learned that:

- For every dollar of sales, Harley-Davidson earns $.36 in gross profits, $.21 in operating income, and $.138 in net income.
- Most of the firm's investments are in current assets and in fixed assets.
- The firm finances its assets using about 42 percent debt and 58 percent equity.
- Harley-Davidson has positive cash flows from assets because the company generated more money from operations than invested.
- The company increased its working capital (current assets), plant and equipment, and other assets.
- In net, $55.12 million were distributed to Harley's investors.

CONCEPT CHECK

1. Why can an income statement not provide a measurement of a firm's cash flows?
2. What is the relationship between a firm's asset and financing free cash flows?
3. When computing a firm's asset free cash flows, why is it necessary to adjust operating income for increases (decreases) in net operating working capital and fixed assets?
4. What impact do positive or negative operating cash flows have on financing cash flows?

Objective 5

FINANCIAL STATEMENTS AND INTERNATIONAL FINANCE

Many countries have different guidelines for firms to use in preparing financial statements. In other words, even if $1 of United States *earnings* is equivalent to 1.10 Euro at the current exchange rate, $1 of earnings in the United States is not the same as 1.10 Euros of earnings in a German firm. The two countries simply have different "Generally Accepted Accounting Principles." In fact, the differences in accounting practices are significant enough that a firm reporting according to German standards could have $100 million in profits, but in the United States, that same company might report a loss. Just imagine what this does for an investor trying to interpret financial statements across different country boundaries.

As a result of this situation, the International Accounting Standards Board (IASB), a private body supported by the worldwide accounting profession, is trying to develop international financial-reporting standards that will minimize the problem. The need for international standards became increasingly urgent as a result of the 1997 Asian crisis, which called attention to the perils of lax accounting in many Asian countries.

In 2002 accounting scandals associated with the downfall of firms such as Enron and Worldcom brought additional attention on the U.S. GAAP standards as compared to the international accounting standards (IAS). Proponents of an international standardized system state GAAP is a rules-based system while IAS is a principles-based system. The principles-based system provides guidelines to firms and auditors to determine if an accounting treatment is true and fair. GAAP, the IAS proponents say, is more prone to accounting creativity—if there is no rule against a procedure, it can be done.

In October 2002, U.S. and European regulators agreed to create a single set of global accounting standards. Differences in the current standards will be identified in 2003 and eliminated by 2005.

Until the international standards are finalized, foreign companies seeking to list their shares in the United States must follow U.S. accounting standards, as developed by the Financial Accounting Standards Board (FASB).

HOW FINANCIAL MANAGERS USE THIS MATERIAL

In this chapter, we have explained the contents of key financial statements—the income statement and the balance sheet. In addition, we have spent considerable time coming to understand cash flows from a finance perspective. Accounting data are the basis for so much that is done in finance. It is used in almost every aspect of financial management, either directly or indirectly. In a firm of any significant size, the data are used both to evaluate historical performance and to project future expectations. Managers are increasingly evaluated and compensated based on their firm's performance, and performance is measured in terms of *financial* performance, usually in terms of profitability. For many executives, up to half of their compensation is tied to performance incentives, frequently to increasing company earnings.

Not only do the financial managers use the data, but financial analysts and lenders rely on the firm's financial information to advise investors and to make loans. Lenders, for example, often require that the firm's earnings before interest, taxes, depreciation, and amortization (EBITDA) cannot fall below a given minimum, usually stated in terms of a ratio of EBITDA to interest and debt principal requirements. Or, they may say that the firm's equity cannot be less than some minimum amount.

Let there be no question, managers throughout an organization rely heavily on financial statements. Failure to understand this information would almost certainly prove fatal to the firm and to the careers of most managers.

SUMMARY

Objective 1

A firm's profits may be viewed as follows:

gross profit = sales – cost of goods sold

earnings before interest and tax (operating profits) = sales – cost of goods sold – operating expenses

net profits (net income) = sales – cost of goods sold – operating expenses – interest expense – taxes

Five activities that drive a company's profits:

1. Revenue derived from selling the company's product or service
2. Cost of producing or acquiring the goods or services to be sold
3. Operating expenses related to (a) marketing and distributing the product or service to the customer and (b) administering the business
4. Financing costs of doing business—namely, the interest paid to the firm's creditors
5. Payment of taxes

Objective 2

The balance sheet presents a company's assets, liabilities, and equity as of a specific date. Total assets must equal debt plus equity. Assets include current assets, fixed assets, and other assets. Debt includes short-term and long-term debt. Equity includes preferred stock, common stock, and retained earnings. All of the numbers in a balance sheet are based on historical costs. As such, they are considered to equal the firm's accounting book value, as opposed to its market value.

Objective 3

For the most part, a company's taxes are determined by multiplying the applicable tax rate times the firm's earnings after all expenses have been paid, including interest expense, but not dividend payments.

Objective 4

Free cash flow is the cash that is distributed to or received from the firm's investors. Free cash flow can be computed from an asset perspective or a financing perspective. In either case, they will be equal; that is:

FREE CASH FLOW FROM		
ASSET PERSPECTIVE		**FINANCING PERSPECTIVE**
Earnings before interest, taxes, depreciation, and amortization (EBITDA) – cash tax payment – additional investments in assets	=	– Interest and dividend payments – decreases in debt and stock or + increases in debt and stock

Objective 5

Foreign firms often follow accounting practices that differ significantly from the Generally Accepted Accounting Principles used by U.S. firms. The reporting differences may provide financial results that are misleading or misinterpreted. Attempts to implement international financial reporting standards have not been embraced by the U.S. accounting profession and the SEC. Therefore, investors viewing financial statements of foreign-based firms must view the data with caution.

KEY TERMS

Accounting book value, 36
Accounts payable, 37
Accounts receivable, 35
Accrued expenses, 37
Average tax rate, 43
Balance sheet, 34
Common stockholders, 37
Current assets (gross working capital), 34
Current debt, 37
Debt, 37
Debt capital, 37
Earnings before interest, taxes, depreciation, and amortization (EBITDA), 45
Earnings before taxes, 33
Equity, 37
Financing cash flows, 47
Fixed assets, 36
Free cash flows, 45
Income statement, 32
Interest expense, 33
Inventory, 35
Liquidity, 41
Long-term debt, 37
Marginal tax rate, 43
Net income, 33
Net working capital, 40
Noninterest-bearing current liabilities, 46
Operating income (earnings before interest and taxes), 33
Other assets, 36
Other payables, 37
Par value and paid-in capital, 37
Preferred stockholders, 37
Prepaid expenses, 36
Retained earnings, 37
Short-term notes, 37
Treasury stock, 37

Go To: www.prenhall.com/keown for downloads and current events associated with this chapter

STUDY QUESTIONS

2-1. A company's financial statements consist of the balance sheet, income statement, and statement of cash flows.

a. Describe the nature of the balance sheet and the income statement.

b. Why have we not used the conventional statement of cash flows in our presentation, computing instead what we call free cash flows?

2-2. What are the differences among gross profits, operating profits, and net income?

2-3. What is the difference between dividends and interest expense?

2-4. Why is it that the common equity section in the balance sheet changes from year to year regardless of whether new shares are bought or sold?

2-5. What is net working capital? How is it different from gross working capital? What is the difference between interest-bearing debt and noninterest-bearing debt?

2-6. Discuss the reasons why one firm could have positive cash flows and be headed for financial trouble, while another firm with negative cash flows could actually be in a good financial position.

2-7. Why is the examination of only the balance sheet and income statement not adequate in evaluating a firm?

2-8. Why do a firm's free cash flows from an asset perspective have to equal its free cash flows from a financing perspective?

SELF-TEST PROBLEMS

ST-1. (*Review of financial statements*) Prepare a balance sheet and income statement for the Wood Corporation, given the following information:

Accumulated depreciation	$38,000
Long-term debt	??
Inventory	5,000
General and administrative expenses	1,000
Interest expense	1,200
Common stock	50,000
Cost of goods sold	6,000
Short-term notes	750
Depreciation expense	600
Sales	13,000
Accounts receivable	10,000
Accounts payable	5,000
Buildings and equipment	120,000
Cash	11,000
Taxes	1,300
Retained earnings	10,250

ST-2. (*Corporate income tax*) Sales for Davies, Inc. during the past year amounted to $4 million. The firm supplies statistical information to engineering companies. Gross profits totaled $1 million, and operating and depreciation expenses were $500,000 and $350,000, respectively. Compute the corporation's tax liability.

ST-3. (*Measuring cash flows*) Given the following information for Neff Industries, compute the firm's free cash flows for the year 2003, first from an asset perspective and then from a financing perspective. What do you learn about the firm from these computations?

Neff Industries Balance Sheet
for December 31, 2002, and December 31, 2003

	2002	2003
Cash	$ 9,000	$ 500
Accounts receivable	12,500	16,000
Inventories	29,000	45,500
Total current assets	$ 50,500	$ 62,000

(continued)

	2002	2003
Land	20,000	26,000
Buildings and equipment	70,000	100,000
Less: allowance for depreciation	(28,000)	(38,000)
Total fixed assets	$ 62,000	$ 88,000
Total assets	$112,500	$150,000
Accounts payable	$ 10,500	$ 22,000
Bank notes	17,000	47,000
Total current liabilities	$ 27,500	$ 69,000
Long-term debt	28,750	22,950
Common stock	31,500	31,500
Retained earnings	24,750	26,550
Total liabilities and equity	$112,500	$150,000

Neff Industries Income Statement
for the Years Ended December 31, 2002, and December 31, 2003

	2002	2003
Sales	$125,000	$160,000
Cost of goods sold	75,000	96,000
Gross profit	$ 50,000	$ 64,000
Operating expense		
Fixed cash operating expense	21,000	21,000
Variable operating expense	12,500	16,000
Depreciation	4,500	10,000
Total operating expense	38,000	47,000
Earnings before interest and taxes	$ 12,000	$ 17,000
Interest	3,000	6,100
Earnings before taxes	$ 9,000	$ 10,900
Taxes	4,500	5,450
Net income	$ 4,500	$ 5,450

STUDY PROBLEMS (SET A)

2-1A. (*Review of financial statements*) Prepare a balance sheet and income statement as of December 31, 2003, for Belmond, Inc., from the following information.

Inventory	$ 6,500
General and administrative expenses	850
Common stock	45,000
Cash	16,550
Operating expenses	1,350
Notes payable	600
Interest expense	900
Depreciation expense	500
Net sales	12,800
Accounts receivable	9,600
Accounts payable	4,800
Long-term debt	55,000
Cost of goods sold	5,750
Buildings and equipment	122,000
Accumulated depreciation	34,000
Taxes	1,440
Retained earnings	?

2-2A. (*Review of financial statements*) Prepare a balance sheet and income statement as of December 31, 2003, for the Sharpe Mfg. Co. from the following information.

Accounts receivable	$120,000
Machinery and equipment	700,000
Accumulated depreciation	236,000
Notes payable	100,000
Net sales	800,000
Inventory	110,000
Accounts payable	90,000
Long-term debt	160,000
Cost of goods sold	500,000
Operating expenses	280,000
Common stock	320,000
Cash	96,000
Retained earnings—prior year	?
Retained earnings—current year	?

2-3A. (*Corporate income tax*) Delaney, Inc. sells minicomputers. During the past year, the company's sales were $4 million. The cost of its merchandise sold came to $2 million, cash operating expenses were $400,000, depreciation expense was $100,000, and the firm paid $150,000 in interest on bank loans. Also, the corporation paid $25,000 in the form of dividends to its own common stockholders. Calculate the corporation's tax liability.

2-4A. (*Corporate income tax*) Potts, Inc. had sales of $6 million during the past year. The cost of goods sold amounted to $3 million. Operating expenses totaled $2.6 million and interest expense was $30,000. Determine the firm's tax liability.

2-5A. (*Measuring cash flows*) Calculate the free cash flows for Pamplin, Inc., for the year ended December 31, 2003, both from an asset and a financing perspective. Interpret your results.

Pamplin, Inc., Balance Sheet at 12/31/02 and 12/31/03

ASSETS	2002	2003
Cash	$ 200	$ 150
Accounts receivable	450	425
Inventory	550	625
Current assets	1,200	1,200
Plant and equipment	2,200	2,600
Less: accumulated depreciation	(1,000)	(1,200)
Net plant and equipment	1,200	1,400
Total assets	$2,400	$2,600

LIABILITIES AND OWNERS' EQUITY	2002	2003
Accounts payable	$ 200	$ 150
Notes payable—current (9%)	0	150
Current liabilities	$ 200	$ 300
Long-term debt	600	600
Owners' equity		
Common stock	$ 300	$ 300
Paid-in capital	600	600
Retained earnings	700	800
Total owners' equity	$1,600	$1,700
Total liabilities and owners' equity	$2,400	$2,600

Pamplin, Inc. Income Statement
for years ending 12/31/02 and 12/31/03 ($ in thousands)

	2002	2003
Sales	$1,200	$1,450
Cost of goods sold	700	850
Gross profit	$ 500	$ 600
Operating expenses	30	40
Depreciation	220	200
Net operating income	$ 250	$ 360
Interest expense	50	60
Net income before taxes	$ 200	$ 300
Taxes (40%)	80	120
Net income	$ 120	$ 180

2-6A. (*Measuring cash flows*) Calculate the free cash flows for T. P. Jarmon Company for the year ended December 31, 2003, both from an asset and a financing perspective. Interpret your results.

T. P. Jarmon Company Balance Sheets
at 12/31/02 and 12/31/03

ASSETS	2002	2003
Cash	$ 15,000	$ 14,000
Marketable securities	6,000	6,200
Accounts receivable	42,000	33,000
Inventory	51,000	84,000
Prepaid rent	1,200	1,100
Total current assets	$115,200	$138,300
Net plant and equipment	286,000	270,000
Total assets	$401,200	$408,300

LIABILITIES AND EQUITY	2002	2003
Accounts payable	$ 48,000	$ 57,000
Notes payable	15,000	13,000
Accruals	6,000	5,000
Total current liabilities	$ 69,000	$ 75,000
Long-term debt	$160,000	$150,000
Common stockholders' equity	$172,200	$183,300
Total liabilities and equity	$401,200	$408,300

T. P. Jarmon Company Income Statement
for the Year Ended 12/31/03

Sales		$600,000
Less: cost of goods sold		460,000
Gross profits		$140,000
Less: expenses		
General and administrative	$30,000	
Interest	10,000	
Depreciation	30,000	
Total operating expenses		$ 70,000
Earnings before taxes		$ 70,000
Less: taxes		27,100
Net income		$ 42,900
Net income		$ 42,900
Less: cash dividends		31,800
To retained earnings		$ 11,100

2-7A. (*Measuring cash flows*) Calculate the free cash flows for Abrams Manufacturing Company for the year ended December 31, 2003, both from an asset and a financing perspective. Interpret your results.

Abrams Manufacturing Balance Sheets
at 12/31/2002 and 12/31/2003

	2002	2003
Cash	$ 89,000	$100,000
Accounts receivable	64,000	70,000
Inventory	112,000	100,000
Prepaid expenses	10,000	10,000
Plant and equipment	238,000	311,000
Accumulated depreciation	(40,000)	(66,000)
Total	$473,000	$525,000
Accounts payable	$ 85,000	$ 90,000
Accrued liabilities	68,000	63,000
Mortgage payable	70,000	0
Preferred stock	0	120,000
Common stock	205,000	205,000
Retained earnings	45,000	47,000
Total liabilities & equity	$473,000	$525,000

Abrams Manufacturing Company Income Statement
for the Year Ended 12/31/03

Sales	$184,000
Cost of sales	60,000
Gross profit	124,000
Selling, general, and administrative expenses	44,000
Depreciation expense	26,000
Operating income	$ 54,000
Interest expense	4,000
Taxes	16,000
Preferred stock dividends	10,000
Net income	$ 24,000

Additional information:
The firm paid $22,000 in common stock dividends during 2003.

2-8A. (*Analyzing free cash flows*) Following you will find our computation of the free cash flows for J. T. Williams. Interpret the information in terms of where cash came from and where it was used.

J.T. WILLIAMS 2003 FREE CASH FLOWS ($ IN THOUSANDS)		
CASH FLOWS FROM AN ASSET PERSPECTIVE		
After-tax cash flows from operations:		
Operating income	$ 156,711	
Depreciation	97,797	
Earnings before interest, tax, depreciation		$254,508
Tax expense	$ 62,333	
Less change in income tax payable	(7,600)	
Less change in deferred taxes	(13,903)	
Cash taxes		40,830
After-tax cash flows from operations		$213,678
Other income (losses)		10,532
		$224,210

(continued)

Change in net operating working capital:		
Change in cash	$ (5,751)	
Change in accounts receivable	(3,326)	
Change in inventories	37,768	
Change in other current assets	20,529	
Change in current assets		$ 49,220
Change in accounts payable	$ 1,662	
Change in accrued expenses	32,283	
Change in noninterest-bearing current debt		33,945
Change in net operating working capital		$ 15,275
Change in fixed assets and other assets:		
Purchase of fixed assets	$257,292	
Change in investments	43,334	
Change in other assets	7,710	
Net cash used for investments		$308,336
Asset free cash flows		$ (99,401)

CASH FLOWS FROM A FINANCING PERSPECTIVE

Interest expense	$ –
Plus increase in long-term debt	7,018
Plus increase in short-term debt	30,577
Less dividends	–
Plus increase in common stock	61,806
Financing free cash flows	$ 99,401

2-9A. (*Analyzing free cash flows*) Following you will find our computation of the free cash flows for Johnson, Inc. Interpret the information in terms of where cash came from and where it was used.

FREE CASH FLOWS FROM AN ASSET PERSPECTIVE ($ IN THOUSANDS)

After-tax cash flows from operations:		
Operating income	$(597,683)	
Depreciation	251,500	
Earnings before interest, tax, depreciation		$ (346,183)
Taxes		–
After-tax cash flows from operations		$ (346,183)
Other income (losses)		(104,388)
		$ (450,571)
Change in net operating working capital:		
Change in cash	$ 332,743	
Change in inventories	191,145	
Change in other current assets	64,036	
Change in current assets		$ 587,924
Change in accounts payable		349,753
Change in net operating working capital		$ 238,171
Change in fixed assets and other assets:		
Purchase of fixed assets	$ 472,768	
Change in investments	1,101,606	
Change in other assets	(154,261)	
Net cash used for investments		$ 1,420,113
Asset free cash flows		$(2,108,855)

FREE CASH FLOWS FROM A FINANCING PERSPECTIVE

Interest expense paid	$(87,966)
Plus increase in long-term debt	1,118,198
Plus increase in short-term debt	13,638
Plus increase in other current liabilities	213,969
Plus increase in common stock	851,016
Financing free cash flows	$2,108,855

WEB WORKS

Go to the Harley-Davidson Website (www.harley-davidson.com) and download the firm's financial statements. Calculate the changes in each asset, debt, and equity balance in the balance sheet from the prior year to the most recent year. Explain the changes that occurred between the two years. (See page 39 for an example). Then compare the operating profit margin (operating income ÷ sales) for the two years. Did they increase or decrease?

INTEGRATIVE PROBLEM

The following financial statements are for Davis & Howard. Assume that you would be meeting with Josh Gray, the firm's controller. Based on the financials and the free cash flow computations, what would you tell Gray about his firm? What questions would you have for him?

Davis & Howard Financials ($ in thousands)

	2002	2003
ASSETS		
Cash	$ 84,527	$ 60,806
Accounts receivable	136,629	194,096
Inventories	107,876	137,448
Prepaid expenses	21,727	32,413
Other current assets	31,287	34,383
Total current assets	$382,046	$459,146
Gross property, plant, and equipment	812,428	874,301
Accumulated depreciation	(420,501)	(469,847)
Net property, plant, and equipment	$391,927	$404,454
Investments	–	2,730
Other assets	19,436	9,555
Total assets	$793,409	$875,885
LIABILITIES		
Short-term debt	$ 15,000	$ 15,000
Notes payable	19,036	18,159
Accounts payable	76,915	117,757
Taxes payable	10,529	11,901
Accrued expenses	101,465	119,685
Total current liabilities	$222,945	$282,502
Long-term debt	128,102	113,307
Other liabilities	125,874	114,166
Total liabilities	$476,921	$509,975
EQUITY		
Common stock	$ 289	$ 289
Paid-in capital	37,776	37,422
Retained earnings	531,695	611,075
Less: treasury stock	253,272	282,876
Total equity	$316,488	$365,910
Total liabilities and equity	$793,409	$875,885

Davis & Howard

RECONCILIATION OF RETAINED EARNINGS ($ IN THOUSANDS)	
Retained earnings, December 31, 2002	$531,695
2003 net income	106,101
Dividends paid	26,912
Other gains	191
Retained earnings, December 31, 2003	$611,075

Davis & Howard Income Statement ($ in thousands)

	2002	2003
Sales	$1,327,610	$1,501,726
Cost of goods sold	1,025,425	1,147,025
Gross profit	$ 302,185	$ 354,701

	2002	2003
Selling, general, and administrative expense	129,986	125,219
Depreciation	47,511	49,346
Operating profit	$ 124,688	$ 180,136
Interest expense	19,352	17,024
Nonoperating income (expense)	7,809	6,659
Income before taxes	$ 113,145	$ 169,771
Provision for income taxes	42,500	63,670
Net income	$ 70,645	$ 106,101

Davis & Howard 2003 Free Cash Flows ($ in thousands)

CASH FLOWS FROM AN ASSET PERSPECTIVE		
After-tax cash flows from operations:		
Operating income	$180,136	
Depreciation	49,346	
Earnings before interest, tax, depreciation		$229,482
Tax expense	$ 63,670	
Less change in income tax payable	(1,372)	
Cash taxes		$ 62,298
After-tax cash flows from operations		$167,184
Other income (losses)		6,850
		$174,034
Change in net operating working capital:		
Change in cash	$ (23,721)	
Change in accounts receivable	57,467	
Change in inventories	29,572	
Change in prepaid expenses	10,686	
Change in other current assets	3,096	
Change in current assets		$ 77,100
Change in accounts payable	$ 40,842	
Change in accrued expenses	18,220	
Change in noninterest-bearing current debt		$ 59,062
Change in net operating working capital		$ 18,038
Change in fixed assets and other assets:		
Purchase of fixed assets	$ 61,873	
Change in investments	2,730	
Change in other assets	(9,881)	
Net cash used for investments		$ 54,722
Asset free cash flows		$101,274
CASH FLOWS FROM A FINANCING PERSPECTIVE		
Interest expense		$ (17,024)
Less decrease in long-term debt		(14,795)
Less decrease in other liabilities		(11,708)
Less decrease in notes payable		(877)
Less dividends		(26,912)
Less decrease in common stock		(29,958)
Financing free cash flows		$(101,274)

STUDY PROBLEMS (SET B)

2-1B. (*Review of financial statements*) Prepare a balance sheet and income statement as of December 31, 2003, for the Warner Company from the following list of items.

Depreciation	$ 66,000
Cash	225,000
Long-term debt	334,000
Sales	573,000
Accounts payable	102,000
General and administrative expenses	79,000
Buildings and equipment	895,000
Notes payable	75,000
Accounts receivable	153,000
Interest expense	4,750
Accrued expenses	7,900
Common stock	289,000
Cost of goods sold	297,000
Inventory	99,300
Taxes	50,500
Accumulated depreciation	263,000
Prepaid expenses	14,500
Taxes payable	53,000
Retained earnings	262,900

2-2B. (*Review of financial statements*) Prepare a balance sheet and income statement as of December 31, 2003, for the Sabine Mfg. Co. from the following list of items. Ignore income taxes and interest expense.

Accounts receivable	$150,000
Machinery and equipment	700,000
Accumulated depreciation	236,000
Notes payable—current	90,000
Net sales	900,000
Inventory	110,000
Accounts payable	90,000
Long-term debt	160,000
Cost of goods sold	550,000
Operating expenses	280,000
Common stock	320,000
Cash	90,000
Retained earnings—prior year	?
Retained earnings—current year	?

2-3B. (*Corporate income tax*) Cook, Inc., sells minicomputers. During the past year, the company's sales were $3.5 million. The cost of its merchandise sold came to $2 million, and cash operating expenses were $500,000; depreciation expense was $100,000, and the firm paid $165,000 in interest on bank loans. Also, the corporation paid $25,000 in dividends to its own common stockholders. Calculate the corporation's tax liability.

2-4B. (*Corporate income tax*) Rose, Inc. had sales of $7 million during the past year. The cost of goods sold amounted to $4 million. Operating expenses totaled $2.6 million and interest expense was $40,000. Determine the firm's tax liability.

2-5B. (*Measuring cash flows*) Calculate the free cash flows for the J. B. Chavez Corporation for the year ended December 31, 2003, both from an asset and a financing perspective. Interpret your results.

J. B. Chavez Corporation, Balance Sheet at 12/31/02 and 12/31/03 ($000)

ASSETS	12/31/02	12/31/03
Cash	$ 225	$ 175
Accounts receivable	450	430
Inventory	575	625
Current assets	$1,250	$1,230
Plant and equipment	$2,200	$2,500
Less: accumulated depreciation	(1,000)	(1,200)
Net plant and equipment	$1,200	$1,300
Total assets	$2,450	$2,530

LIABILITIES AND OWNERS' EQUITY	12/31/02	12/31/03
Accounts payable	$ 250	$ 115
Notes payable—current (9%)	0	115
Current liabilities	$ 250	$ 230
Bonds	$ 600	$ 600
Owners' equity		
Common stock	$ 300	$ 300
Paid-in capital	600	600
Retained earnings	700	800
Total owners' equity	$1,600	$1,700
Total liabilities and owners' equity	$2,450	$2,530

J. B. Chavez Corporation, Income Statement for the years ending 12/31/02 and 12/31/03 ($000)

		2002		2003
Sales		$1,250		$1,450
Cost of goods sold		700		875
Gross profit		$ 550		$ 575
Operating expenses	$ 30		$ 45	
Depreciation	220	250	200	245
Operating income		$ 300		$ 330
Interest expense		50		60
Net income before taxes		$ 250		$ 270
Taxes (40)%		100		108
Net income		$ 150		$ 162

2-6B. (*Measuring cash flows*) Calculate the free cash flows for RPI, Inc., for the year ended December 31, 2003, both from an asset and a financing perspective. Interpret your results.

RPI, Inc., Balance Sheets for 12/31/02 and 12/31/03

ASSETS	2002	2003
Cash	$ 16,000	$ 17,000
Marketable securities	7,000	7,200
Accounts receivable	42,000	38,000
Inventory	50,000	93,000
Prepaid rent	1,200	1,100
Total current assets	$116,200	$156,300
Net plant and equipment	286,000	290,000
Total assets	$402,200	$446,300

LIABILITIES AND STOCKHOLDERS' EQUITY		
	2002	2003
Accounts payable	$ 48,000	$ 55,000
Notes payable	16,000	13,000
Accruals	6,000	5,000
Total current liabilities	$ 70,000	$ 73,000
Long-term debt	$160,000	$150,000
Common stockholders' equity	$172,200	$223,300
Total liabilities and equity	$402,200	$446,300

RPI, Inc., Income Statement for the Year Ended 12/31/03

Sales		$700,000
Less: cost of goods sold		500,000
Gross profits		$200,000
Less: operating and interest expenses		
General and administrative	$50,000	
Interest	10,000	
Depreciation	30,000	
Total expenses		$ 90,000
Profit before taxes		$ 110,000
Less: taxes		27,100
Net income available to common stockholders		$ 82,900
Less: cash dividends		31,800
Change in retained earnings		$ 51,100

2-7B. (*Measuring cash flows*) Calculate the free cash flows for the Cameron Company for the year ended December 31, 2003, both from an asset and a financing perspective. Interpret your results.

Comparative Balance Sheets for December 31, 2002, and December 31, 2003, for the Cameron Company

	2002	2003
Cash	$ 89,000	$ 70,000
Accounts receivable	64,000	70,000
Inventory.	102,000	80,000
Prepaid expenses	10,000	10,000
Total current assets	$265,000	$230,000
Plant and equipment	$238,000	$301,000
Accumulated depreciation	(40,000)	(66,000)
Total assets	$463,000	$465,000
Accounts payable	$ 85,000	$ 80,000
Accrued liabilities	68,000	63,000
Total current liabilities	$153,000	$143,000
Mortgage payable	60,000	0
Preferred stock	0	70,000
Common stock	205,000	205,000
Retained earnings	45,000	47,000
Total debt and equity	$463,000	$465,000

Cameron's 2003 income statement is as follows:

Sales	$204,000
Cost of sales	84,000

Gross profit	$120,000
Selling, general, and administrative expenses	17,000
Depreciation expense	26,000
Operating income	$ 77,000
Interest expense	5,000
Taxes	30,000
Preferred stock dividends	8,000
Net income	$ 34,000

Additional information:
The firm paid $32,000 in common stock dividends during 2003.

2-8B. (*Analyzing free cash flows*) Following you will find our computation of the free cash flows for Hilary's Ice Cream. Interpret the information in terms of where cash came from and where it was used.

Hilary's Free Cash Flows ($ in Thousands)

CASH FLOWS FROM AN ASSET PERSPECTIVE		
After-tax cash flows from operations:		
Operating income	$13,129	
Depreciation	9,202	
Earnings before interest, tax, depreciation		$22,331
Tax expense	$ 1,823	
Less change in income tax payable	1,215	
Less change in deferred taxes	(4,174)	
Cash taxes		$ 4,782
After-tax cash flows from operations		17,549
Other income (losses)		(6,596)
		$10,953
Change in net operating working capital:		
Change in cash	$ (638)	
Change in accounts receivable	7,495	
Change in inventories	847	
Change in other current assets	(2,666)	
Change in current assets		$ 5,038
Change in accounts payable	$ 5,456	
Change in accrued expenses	517	
Change in noninterest-bearing current debt		$ 5,973
Change in net operating working capital		$ (935)
Change in fixed assets and other assets:		
Purchase of fixed assets	$ (757)	
Change in investments	(103)	
Change in other assets	3,060	
Net cash used for investments		$ 2,200
Asset free cash flows		$ 9,688
CASH FLOWS FROM A FINANCING PERSPECTIVE		
Interest expense		$(1,634)
Less decrease in long-term debt		(3,822)
Plus increase in short-term debt		361
Less dividends		–
Less decrease in common stock		(4,593)
Financing free cash flows		$(9,688)

2-9B. (*Analyzing free cash flows*) Following you will find our computation of the free cash flows for **Retail.com**. Interpret the information in terms of where cash came from and where it was used.

Retail.com Cash Flows ($ in Thousands)

CASH FLOWS FROM AN ASSET PERSPECTIVE		
After-tax cash flows from operations:		
Operating income	$(97,324)	
Depreciation	29,312	
Earnings before interest, tax, depreciation		$ (68,012)
Cash taxes		–
After-tax cash flows from operations		(68,012)
Other income (losses)		4,323
		$ (63,689)
Change in net operating working capital:		
Change in cash	$ 76,680	
Change in accounts receivable	3,472	
Change in inventories	2,332	
Change in other current assets	2,478	
Change in current assets		$ 84,962
Change in accounts payable	$ 4,657	
Change in noninterest-bearing current debt		4,657
Change in net operating working capital		$ 80,305
Change in fixed assets and other assets:		
Purchase of fixed assets	$ 31,971	
Change in investments	178,108	
Change in other assets	250	
Net cash used for investments		$ 210,329
Asset free cash flows		$(354,323)
CASH FLOWS FROM A FINANCING PERSPECTIVE		
Interest expense		$ –
Dividends		(23,612)
Less decrease in short-term debt		(137)
Plus increase in other current liabilities		9,609
Plus increase in common stock		368,463
Financing free cash flows		$ 354,323

SELF-TEST SOLUTIONS

ST-1.

INCOME STATEMENT	
Sales	$ 13,000
Cost of goods sold	6,000
Gross profits	$ 7,000
Depreciation expense	600
General and administrative expenses	1,000
Operating expenses	$ 1,600
Operating income	$ 5,400
Interest expense	1,200
Earnings before taxes	$ 4,200
Taxes	1,300
Net income	$ 2,900

BALANCE SHEET	
Cash	$ 11,000
Accounts receivable	10,000
Inventory	5,000
Total current assets	$ 26,000
Buildings and equipment	120,000
Accumulated depreciation	38,000

(continued)

Net buildings and equipment	82,000
Total assets	$108,000
Accounts payable	$ 5,000
Short-term notes	750
Current liabilities	$ 5,750
Long-term debt	$ 42,000
Total debt	$ 47,750
Common stock	50,000
Retained earnings	10,250
Total debt and equity	$108,000

ST-2.

Gross profits	$1,000,000
Operating expenses	500,000
Depreciation	350,000
Taxable income	$ 150,000

EARNINGS	×	MARGINAL TAX RATE	=	TAXES
$50,000	×	0.15	=	$ 7,500
$75,000–$50,000	×	0.25	=	6,250
$100,000–$75,000	×	0.34	=	8,500
$150,000–$100,000	×	0.39	=	19,500
				$41,750

ST-3.

Neff Industries Free Cash Flows
for the Year Ended December 31, 2003

FREE CASH FLOWS: OPERATING PERSPECTIVE	
Operating income	$ 17,000
Plus depreciation expense	10,000
Less tax expense	(5,450)
Less change in income tax payable	0
After-tax cash flows from operations	$ 21,550
Change in net operating working capital	
Change in cash	$ (8,500)
Change in accounts receivable	3,500
Change in inventories	16,500
Change in accounts payable	(11,500)
Change in net operating working capital	$ 0
Change in fixed assets and land	
Purchase of buildings and equipment	$ 30,000
Purchase of land	6,000
Change in fixed assets and land	$ 36,000
Free cash flows (operating perspective)	$ (14,450)

FREE CASH FLOWS: FINANCING PERSPECTIVE	
Increase in short-term notes	$ 30,000
Decrease in long-term notes	(5,800)
Dividends	(3,650)
Interest expense	(6,100)
Free cash flows (financing perspective)	$ 14,450

APPENDIX 2A

Measuring Cash Flows: An Accounting Perspective

In this chapter, we measured cash flows from a finance perspective, or what we called *free cash flows*. However, if you were looking at the financial statements in a firm's annual report, you would see something a bit different from what we presented in this chapter. In addition to the income statement and balance sheet, the firm's accountant would also present a **statement of cash flows**. The purpose of the statement is not to compute *free cash flows*, but rather to measure the change in cash during a period and explain the sources and uses of the cash.

There are two ways that accountants present the cash flow statement: the indirect method and the direct method. We will present the indirect method, since it is generally the preferred format for accountants, and use Harley-Davidson to illustrate the computations. (If you want an explanation and illustration of the direct method, refer to the Web site, **www.prenhall.com/keown**)

STATEMENT OF CASH FLOWS

Three elements are used to determine a firm's cash flows through the indirect method:

1. After-tax cash flows from day-to-day operations
2. Cash flows related to long-term investments, such as plant and equipment
3. Cash flows from financing activities

The statement of cash flows combines the three elements listed above to measure the change in cash for the period.

The data needed to prepare this statement include:

1. **An income statement for the period.** While an income statement does not measure cash flows, its data are necessary for computing cash flows. For example, to measure Harley-Davidson's cash flows for 2002, we need the firm's income statement for the year.
2. **Two balance sheets, one at the beginning of the period and the other at the end of the period.** Again, if we want to compute Harley's cash flows for 2002, we would need the balance sheets for December 31, *2001*, and December 31, *2002*. Graphically, it would appear as follows:

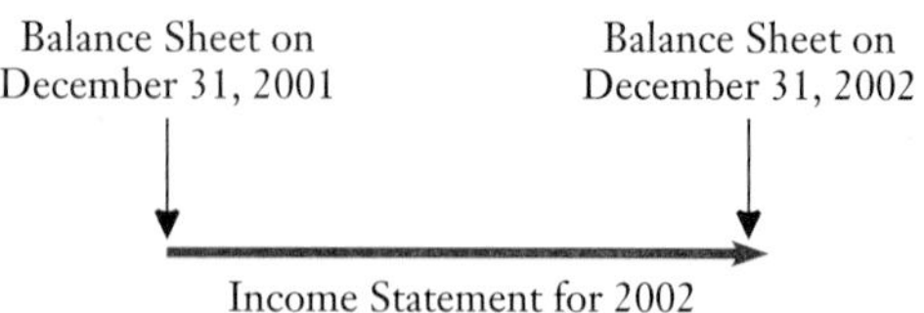

HARLEY-DAVIDSON STATEMENT OF CASH FLOWS

Let's prepare a statement of cash flows for Harley-Davidson for 2002. To do so, we will need to refer back to the company's 2002 income statement (Table 2-1) and the year-ending balance sheets for 2001 and 2002 (Table 2-2).

Cash Flows from Operations

To compute cash from operating activities (the cash flows from day-to-day operations), we begin with net income, and then make adjustments to convert the income statement from an accrual basis to a cash basis. Doing so requires the following computations:

1. Start with the firm's net income.
2. Add back depreciation expense (a non-cash expense).
3. Subtract (add) any increases (decreases) in operating assets. In this context, operating assets are the same as current assets, excluding cash. It is the money invested in accounts receivables, inventories, and other current assets. Thus, if the firm invests more (an increase in the balance sheet) in accounts receivable, it means the firm is extending credit to its customers. In other words, when the firm sells its product or service, it is reported as a sale, which shows up in the income statement. However, since the company has not received the cash, it needed to subtract the change in accounts receivables from net income for the cash that was not collected. The same would be true for inventories and other current assets.
4. Add (subtract) increases (decreases) in short-term operating liabilities. These are the short-term liabilities that are part of the firm's normal operating cycle from the time inventory is acquired, to its sale, and to the time the cash is collected. We can typically identify these liabilities as those that are short term where no interest is paid on the debt, such as accounts payable and accruals.

For Harley-Davidson, the cash flows from operations for 2002 were $699.1 million, computed as follows (in $000):

Net income		$580,217
Depreciation expense		160,119
(Increase) decrease in operating assets (current assets):		
Change in accounts receivables	$(189,201)	
Change in inventories	(37,041)	
Change in other current assets	(14,801)	$(241,043)
Increase (decrease) in short-term operating liabilities (short-term liabilities that do not pay interest):		
Change in income tax payable	$ 2,011	
Change in accounts payables	165,528	
Change in accrued expenses	32,294	199,833
Cash provided by operating activities		$699,126

Cash Flows—Investment Activities

Now that we have calculated the cash flows that were generated from the day-to-day operations at Harley, we will determine the amount of cash used for long-term investments by the firm—the cash flows from investing activities. Relying on Harley's balance sheets, we see that the firm invested $501.5 million in long-term assets—$300.9 million for fixed assets and $200.6 million on other long-term assets, such as patents and intangibles. The computations are as follows (in $000):

Increase in fixed assets	$(300,895)
Increase in other assets	(200,624)
Cash flows from investing activities	$(501,519)

The change in fixed assets, or plant and equipment in the balance sheets, has to be based on *gross* fixed assets rather than *net* fixed assets. After all, *net* fixed assets are affected by *both* the change in gross fixed assets (plant and equipment) *and* depreciation expense for the year. However, the change in gross plant and equipment is totally the result of buying and selling these assets. NEVER take the change in *net* fixed assets, but only the change in *gross* fixed assets. Again: *Never take the change in net fixed assets. It will be wrong.*

Cash Flows—Financing Activities

The last part of cash flows relates to financing activities, including any cash inflows or outflows to or from the firm's investors, both lenders of debt and owners. For 2002, Harley had the following cash flows associated with the firm's financing (in $000):

Dividends paid	$(73,902)
Increase (decrease) in interest-bearing short-term notes	47,833
Increase (decrease) in other interest-bearing current liabilities	26,276
Increase (decrease) in long-term debt	(7,852)
Increase (decrease) in common stock	(29,683)
Cash flows from financing activities	$(37,328)

Thus, Harley had cash inflows from borrowing short-term liabilities of about $74 million ($47.8 million plus $26.3 million). The firm then used cash to pay the common stockholders almost $74 million in dividends, $7.8 million to pay down long-term debt, and $29.7 million to repurchase stock. Also, notice that interest expense is not included as a financing cash flow. Since cash flows from operations begin with net income, as previously calculated, the firm's interest expense has already been deducted as part of cash flows from operations. Finally, note that accounts payables and accruals are not included in financing cash flows. We have already included them in cash flows from operations.

We may now bring all three parts of the cash flows together into a single report, the statement of cash flows, as shown in Table 2A-1.

TABLE 2A-1 Harley-Davidson Cash Flow Statement (Indirect Method)

ADJUSTMENTS TO RECONCILE NET INCOME TO CASH PROVIDED BY OPERATING ACTIVITIES (IN $000)	
Net income	$ 580,217
Depreciation and amortization	160,119
(Increase) decrease in operating assets:	
Change in accounts receivables	(189,201)
Change in inventories	(37,041)
Change in other current assets	(14,801)
Increase (decrease) in operating liabilities:	
Change in income tax payable	2,011
Change in accounts payables	165,528
Change in accrued expenses	32,294
Cash provided by operating activities	$ 699,126
INVESTING ACTIVITIES	
Increase in fixed assets	$(300,895)
Increase in other assets	(200,624)
Cash flows from investing activities	$(501,519)
FINANCING ACTIVITIES	
Dividends paid	$ (73,902)
Increase (decrease) in interest-bearing short-term notes	47,833
Increase (decrease) in other interest-bearing current liabilities	26,276
Increase (decrease) in long-term debt	(7,852)
Increase (decrease) in common stock	(29,683)
Cash flows from financing activities	$ (37,328)
Change in cash	$ 160,279
Beginning cash (Dec. 31, 2001)	635,449
Ending cash (Dec. 31, 2002)	$ 795,728

Thus, Harley's cash flows during 2002 increased $160.3 million, resulting from $699.1 million flowing into the firm from operations, investing $501.5 million in long-term assets, and paying down debt of $37.3 million. As a result, the firm's cash balances on the balance sheet increased from $635.4 million to $795.7 million from December 31, 2001, to December 31, 2002. Now we know where Harley's cash came from and how it was used, which is the purpose of a statement of cash flows.

LEARNING OBJECTIVES

After reading this chapter, you should be able to

1. Calculate a comprehensive set of financial ratios and use them to evaluate the financial health of a company.
2. Apply the DuPont analysis in evaluating a firm's performance.
3. Explain the limitations of ratio analysis.

CHAPTER 3

Evaluating a Firm's Financial Performance

As Harley-Davidson approached its 100th anniversary of operations, Chief Executive Officer Jeffrey Bleustein shared his thoughts about the reasons for the firm's success in its 2001 Annual Report. Bleustein credits the passion and commitment of customers, employees, managers, suppliers, dealers, distributors, and shareholders, whose determination, skill, and efforts have resulted in a successful business. Bleustein went on to report that the firm "achieved its 16th consecutive year of record revenue and earnings." The firm had also reached a level of production output in 2001 that exceeded the 2003 production target! Retail sales increased for the 17th straight year. As Harley-Davidson prepares for the future, Mr. Bleustein said that the firm continues to invest capital to maintain its design superiority and its production capacity. The firm is building new manufacturing facilities, expanding product development sites, and consolidating operations to improve capacity utilization. Clearly 2001 was a successful year for Harley-Davidson in terms of business growth and expansion. In this chapter, we want to examine Harley-Davidson's financial statements to determine if the picture presented by Mr. Bleustein is reflected in the financial performance of the firm. We can do this by examining financial ratios using information from the income statement and balance sheet.

CHAPTER PREVIEW

This chapter is a natural extension of Chapter 2. In this chapter, we restate financial statements in relative terms to gain a more complete understanding about a firm's financial performance. Specifically, we look at key financial relationships in the form of ratios. The specific relationships we consider are:

- The risk that a firm will not have the needed cash to meet debt payments as they come due
- Whether management is generating an attractive rate of return on the capital that has been entrusted to them
- How management chooses to finance the company
- Whether the stockholders are receiving an acceptable rate of return on their investment

BACK TO THE PRINCIPLES

As in Chapter 2, when we talked about financial statements, ***Principle 7*** *continues to be a primary rationale for wanting to evaluate a company's financial performance. As stated in* ***Principle 7, managers won't work for the owners unless it's in their best interest to do so.*** *Thus, the firm's common stockholders have a need for information that can be used to monitor the managers' actions. Interpreting the firm's financial statements through the use of financial ratios is a key source of information that can be used in this monitoring.*

Principle 5 *is also relevant in evaluating a firm's financial performance. This principle tells us that* ***competitive markets make it hard to find exceptionally profitable investments.*** *By* exceptional, *we mean investments that earn rates of return that exceed the opportunity cost of the money invested. Thus, the notion of a rate of return is a primary issue in knowing whether management is creating value. Although far from perfect, certain financial ratios can help us better know if management is finding exceptional investments, or if the investments are in fact just the opposite—exceptionally bad.*

Finally, ***Principle 1*** *is at work in this chapter; that is,* ***The Risk-Return Trade-Off—We won't take on additional risk unless we expect to be compensated with additional return.*** *As we will see, how management chooses to finance the business will affect the company's risk, and, as a result, the stockholders' rate of return on their investment.*

Objective 1

FINANCIAL RATIO ANALYSIS

Financial ratios
Restating the accounting data in relative terms to identify some of the financial strengths and weaknesses of a company.

In Chapter 2, we examined financial statements in absolute dollar terms for the purpose of coming to understand a firm's financial position. We chose to use the financial statements for Harley-Davidson to illustrate the format and content of the statements and to demonstrate an important financial measurement—free cash flows. We next want to restate the accounting data in relative terms, or what we call financial ratios. **Financial ratios** help us identify some of the financial strengths and weaknesses of a company. The ratios give us two ways of making meaningful comparisons of a firm's financial data: (1) We can examine the ratios across time (say, for the last 5 years) to identify any trends; and (2) We can compare the firm's ratios with those of other firms. In short, such a financial analysis will allow us to see if Harley-Davidson is as good as management claims it to be. After all, we need to decide that for ourselves, and not just take the word of Harley-Davidson's management.

Mathematically, a financial ratio is nothing more than a ratio whose numerator and denominator are comprised of financial data. Sounds simple? Well, in concept it is. The objective in using a ratio when analyzing financial information is simply to standardize the information being analyzed so that comparisons can be made between ratios of different firms or possibly the same firm at different points in time. So try to keep this in mind as you read through the discussion of financial ratios. All we are doing is trying to standardize financial data so that we can make comparisons with industry norms or other standards.

In making a comparison of our firm with other companies, we could select a peer group of companies, or we could use industry norms published by firms such as Dun & Bradstreet, Robert Morris Associates, Standard & Poor's, and Prentice Hall. Dun & Bradstreet, for instance, annually publishes a set of 14 key ratios for each of 125 lines of business. Robert Morris Associates, the association of bank loan and credit officers, publishes a set of 16 key ratios for more than 350 lines of business. In both cases, the ratios are classified by industry and by firm size to provide the basis for more meaningful comparisons.

In learning about ratios, we could simply study the different types or categories of ratios, or we could use ratios to answer some important questions about a firm's opera-

TABLE 3-1 Harley-Davidson, Inc., Annual Income Statement ($ in thousands)

	2002
Sales	$4,195,197
Cost of goods sold	2,673,129
Gross profit	$1,522,068
Selling, general, and administration expenses	$ 465,831
Depreciation	160,119
Total operating expenses	625,950
Operating profit	$ 896,118
Interest expense	17,849
Earnings before taxes	$ 878,269
Provision for income taxes	298,052
Net income	$ 580,217

tions. We prefer the latter approach and choose the following four questions as a map in using financial ratios:

1. How liquid is the firm?
2. Is management generating adequate operating profits on the firm's assets?
3. How is the firm financing its assets?
4. Are the owners (stockholders) receiving an adequate return on their investment?

Let's look at each of these questions in turn. In doing so, let's use Harley-Davidson to illustrate the use of ratios in answering these questions. For ease of reference, we again show the Harley-Davidson financial statements in Table 3-1 and Table 3-2.

Question 1: How Liquid Is the Firm?

There are two ways to approach the liquidity question. First, we can look at the firm's assets that are relatively liquid in nature and compare them to the amount of the debt coming due in the near term.[1] Second, we can look at how quickly the firm's liquid assets—namely, accounts receivable and inventories—are being converted into cash.

MEASURING LIQUIDITY: APPROACH 1 The first approach compares cash and the assets that should be converted into cash within the year with the debt (liabilities) that is coming due and payable within the year. The assets here are the *current assets*, and the debt is the *current liabilities* in the balance sheet. Thus we could use the following measure, called the **current ratio**, to estimate a company's relative liquidity:

Current ratio
Current ratio indicates a firm's liquidity, as measured by its liquid assets (current assets) relative to its liquid debt (short-term or current liabilities).

$$\text{current ratio} = \frac{\text{current assets}}{\text{current liabilities}} \tag{3-1}$$

Furthermore, remembering that the three primary current assets include (1) cash, (2) accounts receivable, and (3) inventories, we could make our measure of liquidity more restrictive by *excluding inventories*, the least liquid of the current assets, in the numerator. This revised ratio is called the **acid-test** (or **quick**) **ratio**, and is calculated as follows:

Acid-test (quick) ratio
Acid-test ratio indicates a firm's liquidity, as measured by its liquid assets, excluding inventories, relative to its current liabilities.

$$\text{acid-test ratio} = \frac{\text{current assets} - \text{inventories}}{\text{current liabilities}} \tag{3-2}$$

[1] This approach has long been used in the finance community; however, it really measures solvency, not liquidity. A firm is solvent when its assets exceed its liabilities, which is in essence what we will be measuring by this approach. For an in-depth discussion of this issue, see Chapter 2 of Terry S. Maness and John T. Zietlow, *Short-Term Financial Management* (New York: Dryden Press, 1997).

TABLE 3-2 Harley-Davidson, Inc., Annual Balance Sheet ($000)

	12/31/02
ASSETS	
Cash and equivalents	$ 795,728
Accounts receivable	964,465
Inventories	218,156
Other current assets	88,237
Total current assets	$2,066,586
Gross plant, property, and equipment	$2,006,256
Accumulated depreciation	973,660
Net plant, property, and equipment	$1,032,596
Other assets	762,035
Total assets	$3,861,217
LIABILITIES AND EQUITY	
LIABILITIES	
Accounts payable	$ 382,579
Accrued expenses	226,977
Income taxes payable	67,886
Short-term notes	189,024
Other interest bearing current liabilities	123,586
Total current liabilities	$ 990,052
Long-term debt	638,250
Total liabilities	$1,628,302
COMMON EQUITY	
Common stock (par value)	$ 3,254
Paid in capital	386,284
Retained earnings	2,325,737
Less treasury stock	(482,360)
Total common equity	$2,232,915
Total liabilities and equity	$3,861,217

To demonstrate how to compute the current ratio and acid-test ratio, we will use the 2002 balance sheet for Harley-Davidson (refer to Table 3-2). To have a standard for comparison, we could use industry norms published by Dun and Bradstreet or any of the other sources mentioned earlier. However, we chose instead to calculate the average ratios for a group of similar firms or what could be called a *peer group*. The 2002 results for these first two ratios are as follows:

Harley-Davidson	Peer-Group Average
$\text{current ratio} = \dfrac{\text{current assets}}{\text{current liabilities}} = \dfrac{\$2{,}067\text{M}}{\$990\text{M}} = 2.09 \text{ times}$	1.50 times
$\text{acid-text ratio} = \dfrac{\text{current assets} - \text{inventories}}{\text{current liabilities}} = \dfrac{\$2{,}067 - 218\text{M}}{\$990\text{M}} = 1.87 \text{ times}$	1.06 times

So, in terms of the current ratio and acid-test ratio, Harley-Davidson is more liquid than the average peer-group firm. Harley-Davidson has $2.09 in current assets for every $1 in

A FOCUS ON HARLEY-DAVIDSON
ROAD RULES

WORDS OF ADVICE FROM HARLEY-DAVIDSON COMPANY'S CEO

We asked Jeff Bleustein, Harley-Davidson CEO, what advice he would offer students contemplating a career in business, and this is what he told us:

- ***Understand that not all businesses are the same.*** What works in one environment may not work in another. So, dedicate yourself to your study of fundamentals. In their applications, however, be flexible and open to the differences in company and industry environments that you might encounter.
- ***Be bold and willing to experiment with something different.*** This advice is as meaningful for individuals as it is for companies. Great companies are those that focus on an area, a product, or a set of competencies and then excel at it. If you always follow others you are going to be a mediocre company. Greatness comes from being willing to step out and be uniquely better than the competition.

current liabilities (debt), compared to \$1.50 for comparable firms, and \$1.87 in current assets less inventories per \$1 of current debt, compared to \$1.06 for the peer group. Thus, Harley-Davidson has more liquid assets relative to its short-term debt, an indication that the firm has a greater ability to meet its maturing obligations. See the "A Focus on Harley Davidson" box.

MEASURING LIQUIDITY: APPROACH 2 The second view of liquidity examines the firm's ability to convert accounts receivable and inventory into cash on a timely basis. The conversion of accounts receivable into cash may be measured by computing how long it takes to collect the firm's receivables; that is, how many days of sales are outstanding in the form of accounts receivable? We can answer this question by computing the **average collection period**:

Average collection period
Average collection period indicates how rapidly a firm is collecting its credit, as measured by the average number of days it takes to collect its accounts receivable.

$$\text{average collection period} = \frac{\text{accounts receivable}}{\text{daily credit sales}} \qquad \textbf{(3-3)}$$

If we assume all Harley-Davidson 2002 sales (\$4,195 million in Table 3-1) to be credit sales, as opposed to some cash sales, then the firm's average collection period is 83.9 days, compared to a peer-group norm of 75 days:

	Harley-Davidson	Peer-Group Average
average collection period	$= \dfrac{\text{accounts receivable}}{\text{daily credit sales}}$	
	$= \dfrac{\$964\text{M}}{\$4{,}195\text{M}/365} = \dfrac{964}{11.5} = 83.9$ days	75 days

Thus, Harley-Davidson takes just a little longer to collect its receivables than the average firm in the comparison group—83.9 days compared to 75 days for the peer group.

Accounts receivable turnover ratio
Accounts receivable turnover ratio indicates how rapidly the firm is collecting its credit, as measured by the number of times its accounts receivable are collected or "rolled over" during the year.

We could have reached the same conclusion by measuring how many times accounts receivable are "rolled over" during a year, or the **accounts receivable turnover ratio**. For instance, Harley-Davidson turns its receivables over 4.35 times a year.[2]

[2] We could also measure the accounts receivable turnover by dividing 365 days by the average collection period: $365 \div 83.9 = 4.35$.

Harley-Davidson	Peer-Group Average
$\text{accounts receivable turnover} = \dfrac{\text{credit sales}}{\text{accounts receivable}}$ **(3-4)**	
$= \dfrac{\$4{,}195\text{M}}{\$964\text{M}} = 4.35 \text{ times/year}$	4.87 times/year

Whether we use the average collection period or the accounts receivable turnover ratio, the conclusion is the same. Harley-Davidson is somewhat slower at collecting its receivables than competing firms.[3]

As a general rule, management would want to collect receivables sooner rather than later—that is, reduce collection period and increase turnover ratios. However, it may be that a company's management would intentionally extend longer credit terms as a policy for reasons it deems justifiable. Alternatively, slower collection could mean that management is simply not being as careful at enforcing its collection policies. In other words, it may not be managing receivables effectively.

Inventory turnover ratio Inventory turnover indicates the relative liquidity of inventories, as measured by the number of times a firm's inventories are replaced during the year.

We now want to know the same thing for inventories that we just determined for accounts receivable: How many times are we turning over inventories during the year? In this manner, we gain some insight into the liquidity of inventories. The **inventory turnover ratio** is calculated as follows:

$$\text{inventory turnover} = \frac{\text{cost of goods sold}}{\text{inventory}} \tag{3-5}$$

Note that sales in this ratio is replaced by cost of goods sold. Since the inventory (the denominator) is measured at cost, we want to use a cost-based measure of sales in the numerator. Otherwise, our answer would vary from one firm to the next solely due to differences in how each firm marks up its sales over costs.[4]

Given that Harley-Davidson's cost of goods sold was \$2,673 million (Table 3-1) and its inventory was \$218 million (Table 3-2), the firm's 2002 inventory turnover, along with the peer-group average, is as follows:

Harley-Davidson	Peer-Group Average
$\text{inventory turnover} = \dfrac{\text{cost of goods sold}}{\text{inventory}}$	
$= \dfrac{\$2{,}673\text{M}}{\$218\text{M}} = 12.26 \text{ times/year}$	5.78 times/year

Given the preceding results, we can conclude that Harley-Davidson is clearly excellent in its management of inventory, turning its inventory over 12.26 times per year compared to 5.78 times for the peer group. In other words, Harley-Davidson sells its inventory in 29.77 days on average (365 days ÷ 12.26 times), whereas the average firm takes 63.1 days (365 ÷ 5.78 times).

To conclude, when it comes to Harley-Davidson's liquidity, we see that the firm has high current and acid-test ratios, indicating the firm has sufficient liquid assets to cover liabilities coming due in the next 12 months. However, the firm takes slightly longer to col-

[3] Although it will not be discussed here, we could also evaluate how effectively management is managing accounts receivable by aging the firm's receivables. For example, we could calculate how many of the accounts are 0 to 30 days old, 30 to 60 days old, and over 60 days old.

[4] Whereas our logic may be correct to use cost of goods sold in the numerator, practicality may dictate that we use sales instead. Some suppliers of peer-group norm data use sales in the numerator. Thus, for consistency in our comparisons, we too may need to use sales.

lect its accounts receivable (84 days) than its peer group (75 days). But, Harley-Davidson turns its inventory over twelve times per year, indicating that this asset is very liquid.

In summary, a firm's liquidity—its ability to meet maturing debt obligations (short-term debt) and the ability to convert accounts receivables and inventories into cash on a timely basis—represents an important issue to managers, lenders, and investors. The less liquid the firm, the greater the chance that the firm will be unable to pay creditors when payments are due.

Question 2: Is Management Generating Adequate Operating Profits on the Firm's Assets?

We now begin a different line of thinking that will carry us through all the remaining questions. At this point, we want to know if a firm's profits are sufficient relative to the assets being invested. The question is similar to a question one might ask about the interest being earned on a savings account at the bank. When you invest \$1,000 in a savings account and receive \$40 in interest during the year, you are earning a 4 percent return on your investment (\$40 ÷ \$1,000 = .04 = 4%). With respect to Harley-Davidson, we want to know something similar: the rate of return that management is earning on the firm's assets.

In answering this question, we have several choices as to how we measure profits: gross profits, operating profits, or net income. Gross profits would not be an acceptable choice because it does not include some important information, such as the cost of marketing and distributing the firm's product. Thus we should choose between operating profits and net income. For our purposes, we prefer to use operating profits, because this measure of firm profits is calculated before the costs of the company's financing policies, for example, interest expense, have been deducted. Because financing is explicitly considered in our next question, we want to isolate only the operating aspects of the company's profits at this point. In this way, we are able to compare the profitability of firms with different debt-to-equity mixes. Therefore, to examine the level of operating profits relative to the assets, we would use the **operating income return on investment** (OIROI):

Operating income return on investment
Operating income return on investment indicates the effectiveness of management at generating operating profits on the firm's assets, as measured by operating profits relative to the total assets.

$$\text{operating income return on investment} = \frac{\text{operating income}}{\text{total assets}} \tag{3-6}$$

The operating income return on investment for Harley-Davidson (based on the financial data in Table 3-1 and Table 3-2), and the corresponding peer-group norm, are shown below:

Harley-Davidson	Peer-Group Average
$\text{operating income return on investment} = \frac{\text{operating income}}{\text{total assets}}$	
$= \frac{\$896M}{\$3,861M} = .232 = 23.2\%$	9.8%

Hence we see that Harley-Davidson is earning over twice the return on investment of the average firm in the peer group. Management is generating significantly more income on \$1 of assets than similar firms.[5]

[5] The **return on assets** (ROA) is often used as an indicator of a firm's profitability and is measured as follows: return on assets = net income ÷ total assets.

We choose not to use this ratio because *net income* is influenced both by operating decisions and by how the firm is financed. We want to restrict our attention only to operating activities; financing is considered later in questions 3 and 4. Nevertheless, sometimes the peer-group norm for operating income return on investment is not available. Instead, return on assets is provided. If so, we have no option but to use the return on assets for measuring the firm's profitability.

Return on assets
Return on assets determines the amount of net income produced on a firm's assets by relating net income to total assets.

If we were the managers of Harley-Davidson, we should not be satisfied with merely knowing that we are earning more than a competitive return on the firm's assets. We would also want to know why we are above average. To understand this issue, we may separate the operating income return on investment, OIROI, into two important pieces: the operating profit margin and the total asset turnover. The firm's OIROI is a multiple of these two ratios and may be shown algebraically as follows:

$$\text{OIROI} = \left(\begin{array}{c}\text{operating}\\ \text{profit margin}\end{array}\right) \times \left(\begin{array}{c}\text{total asset}\\ \text{turnover}\end{array}\right) \tag{3-7a}$$

or more completely,

$$\text{OIROI} = \frac{\text{operating income}}{\text{sales}} \times \frac{\text{sales}}{\text{total assets}} \tag{3-7b}$$

Operating profit margin
Operating profit margin indicates management's effectiveness in managing the firm's income statement, as measured by operating profits relative to sales.

OIROI: COMPONENT 1 The first component of the OIROI, the **operating profit margin**, is an extremely important variable in understanding a company's operating profitability. It is important that we know exactly what drives this ratio. In coming to understand the ratio, think about the makeup of the ratio, which may be expressed as follows:

$$\begin{array}{c}\text{operating}\\ \text{profit margin}\end{array} = \frac{\text{operating income}}{\text{sales}}$$

$$= \frac{\begin{array}{c}\text{total}\\ \text{sales}\end{array} - \begin{array}{c}\text{cost of}\\ \text{goods sold}\end{array} - \begin{array}{c}\text{general and}\\ \text{administrative}\\ \text{expenses}\end{array} - \begin{array}{c}\text{marketing}\\ \text{expenses}\end{array}}{\text{sales}} \tag{3-8}$$

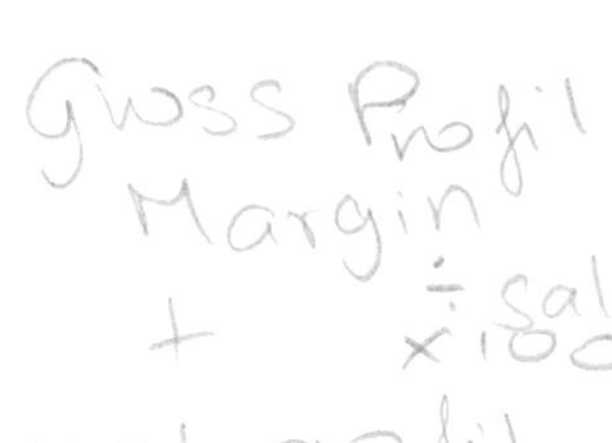

Because total sales equals the number of units sold times the sales price per unit, and the cost of goods sold equals the number of units sold times the cost of goods sold per unit, we may conclude that the driving forces of the operating profit margin are the following:

1. The number of units of product sold[6]
2. The average selling price for each product unit
3. The cost of manufacturing or acquiring the firm's product
4. The ability to control general and administrative expenses
5. The ability to control expenses in marketing and distributing the firm's product

These influences are also apparent simply by looking at the income statement and thinking about what is involved in determining the firm's operating profits or income.[7] For Harley-Davidson and its peer group, the operating profit margins are 21.4 percent and 8.3 percent, respectively, determined as follows:

Harley-Davidson	Peer-Group Average
$\begin{array}{c}\text{operating}\\ \text{profit margin}\end{array} = \dfrac{\text{operating income}}{\text{sales}}$	
$= \dfrac{\$896M}{\$4{,}195M} = .214 = 21.4\%$	8.3%

[6] The number of units affects the operating profit margin only if some of the firm's costs and expenses are fixed. If a company's expenses are all variable in nature, then the ratio would not change as the number of units sold increases or decreases, because the numerator and the denominator would change at the same rate.

Net profit margin
Net profit margin measures the net income of a firm as a percent of sales.

[7] We could have used the **net profit margin**, rather than the operating profit margin, which is measured as follows: net profit margin = net income ÷ sales.

The net profit margin measures the amount of net income per $1 of sales. However, because net income includes both operating expenses and interest expense, this ratio is influenced both by operating activities and financing activities. We prefer to defer the effect of financing decisions until questions 3 and 4, which follow shortly.

Based on these findings, we may conclude that Harley-Davidson is far more than competitive when it comes to keeping costs and expenses in line relative to sales, as is reflected by the operating profit margin. In other words, management is extremely effective in managing the five driving forces of the operating profit margin listed previously. In terms of its high operating profit margin, Harley-Davidson has no equal.

OIROI: COMPONENT 2 As shown in Equation (3-7a), the **total asset turnover** is the second component of the operating income return on investment. The total asset turnover measures the dollar sales per one dollar of assets. The ratio is calculated as follows:

Total asset turnover Total asset turnover indicates management's effectiveness at managing a firm's balance sheet—its assets—as indicated by the amount of sales generated per one dollar of assets.

$$\text{total asset turnover} = \frac{\text{sales}}{\text{total assets}} \tag{3-9}$$

This ratio indicates how efficiently a firm is using its assets in generating sales. For instance, if Company A can generate \$3 in sales with \$1 in assets, compared to \$2 in sales per asset dollar for Company B, we may say that Company A is using its assets more efficiently in generating sales, which is a major determinant in the firm's operating income return on investment.

Returning to Harley-Davidson, the firm's total asset turnover is calculated as follows:

Harley-Davidson	Peer-Group Average
$\text{total asset turnover} = \frac{\text{sales}}{\text{total assets}}$	
$= \frac{\$4{,}195M}{\$3{,}861M} = 1.09 \text{ times}$	1.18 times

Based on the forgoing results, we see that Harley-Davidson generates about \$1.09 in sales per dollar of assets, whereas the competition on average produces \$1.18 from every dollar in assets. That is, Harley-Davidson is using its assets slightly less efficiently than the average firm in its peer group.

While we have concluded that Harley-Davidson utilizes its assets less efficiently than does its peer group, it is also good to see what drives its performance. To determine the factors responsible for Harley-Davidson's performance, we examine the turnover ratios for the primary assets held by the firm—accounts receivables, inventories, and fixed assets. We have already calculated these ratios for accounts receivables and inventories, which are repeated as follows:

	Harley-Davidson	Peer-Group Average
Accounts receivable turnover		
$\frac{\text{credit sales}}{\text{accounts receivable}}$	$= \frac{\$4{,}195M}{\$964M} = 4.35 \text{ times/yr}$	4.87 times/yr
Inventory turnover		
$\frac{\text{cost of goods sold}}{\text{inventory}}$	$= \frac{\$2{,}673M}{\$218M} = 12.26 \text{ times/yr}$	5.78 times/yr

We next calculate a firm's fixed assets turnover ratio as follows:

$$\text{fixed assets turnover} = \frac{\text{sales}}{\text{net fixed assets}} \tag{3-10}$$

	Harley-Davidson	Peer-Group Average
$\frac{\text{sales}}{\text{net fixed assets}} = \frac{\$4{,}195M}{\$1{,}033M}$	= 4.06 times	4.26 times

Given these turnover ratios, we can say that, in general, Harley-Davidson manages its assets efficiently—but some better than others. Management is particularly good at managing the firm's inventories, but somewhat below average in its collection of accounts receivables and at utilizing the firm's fixed assets.

To summarize, a firm's operating income return on investment (OIROI) is a function of two elements, the operating profit margin and the firm's total asset turnover. For Harley-Davidson, the OIROI was determined as follows:

$$\text{OIROI}_{\text{HD}} = 21.4\% \times 1.09 = 23.3\%$$

and for the peer group, this same ratio is

$$\text{OIROI}_{\text{pg}} = 8.3\% \times 1.18 = 9.8\%$$

Based on these findings, we can say with complete confidence that Harley-Davidson is a superstar at managing its income statement, keeping its cost of goods and operating expenses extremely low relative to its sales (as indicated by its high operating profit margin). In terms of managing assets, the firm has much less inventory per dollar of sales than competing firms, which is good. However, the company is not quite as efficient when it comes to managing its accounts receivables and its fixed assets—that is, it has more invested in accounts receivables and fixed assets per dollar of sales than is true for the average firm in the peer group.

Question 3: How Is the Firm Financing Its Assets?

We now turn for the moment to the matter of how the firm is financed. We shall return to the firm's profitability shortly. The basic issue is the use of debt versus equity: Do we finance the assets more by debt or equity? In answering this question, we will use two ratios. Many more could be used. First, we simply ask what percentage of the firm's assets are financed by debt, including *both* short-term and long-term debt, realizing the remaining percentage must be financed by equity. We would compute the **debt ratio** as follows:[8]

Debt ratio
Debt ratio indicates how much debt is used to finance a firm's assets.

$$\text{debt ratio} = \frac{\text{total debt}}{\text{total assets}} \tag{3-11}$$

For Harley-Davidson, debt as a percentage of total assets is 42 percent (taken from Harley-Davidson's balance sheet in Table 3-2) compared to a peer-group norm of 58 percent. The computation is as follows:

	Harley-Davidson	Peer-Group Average
debt ratio $= \frac{\text{total debt}}{\text{total assets}}$		
$= \frac{\$1{,}628M}{\$3{,}861M}$	= .422 = 42.2%	58%

[8] We will often see the relationship stated in terms of debt to equity, or the debt-equity ratio, rather than debt to total assets. We come to the same conclusion with either ratio.

Thus Harley-Davidson uses significantly less debt than the average firm in the peer group.

We should note that companies in general finance about 40 percent of their assets with debt and 60 percent in equity. Firms with more real assets, such as land and buildings (as with Harley-Davidson), are able to finance more of their assets with debt. High-technology firms where the assets are "soft," such as research and development, are less able to acquire debt financing. Thus, the amount of debt a firm uses depends on its proven income record and the availability of assets that can be used as collateral for the loan—and how much risk management is willing to assume.

Our second perspective regarding the firm's financing decisions comes by looking at the income statement. When we borrow money, there is a minimum requirement that the firm pay the interest on the debt. Thus, it is informative to compare the amount of operating income that is available to service the interest with the amount of interest that is to be paid. Stated as a ratio, we compute the number of times we are earning our interest. Thus a **times interest earned** ratio is commonly used when examining the firm's debt position and is computed in the following manner:

Times interest earned
Times interest earned indicates a firm's ability to cover its interest expense, as measured by its earnings before interest and taxes relative to the interest expense.

$$\text{times interest earned} = \frac{\text{operating income}}{\text{interest expense}} \quad \textbf{(3-12)}$$

Based on the income statement for Harley-Davidson (Table 3-1), the firm's times interest earned is 50.2, computed as follows:

Harley-Davidson	Peer-Group Average
$\text{times interest earned} = \frac{\text{operating income}}{\text{interest expense}}$	
$= \frac{\$896.1\text{M}}{\$17.85\text{M}} = 50.2 \text{ times}$	3.93 times

Thus Harley-Davidson is well able to service its interest expense without any difficulty. In fact, the firm's operating income could fall to as little as one-fiftieth (1/50.2) its current level and still have the income to pay the required interest. We should remember, however, that interest is not paid with income but with cash, and that the firm may be required to repay some of the debt principal as well as the interest. Thus, the times interest earned is only a crude measure of the firm's capacity to service its debt. Nevertheless, it does give us a general indication of a company's debt capacity.

Question 4: Are the Owners (Stockholders) Receiving an Adequate Return on Their Investment?

Our one remaining question looks at the accounting return on the common stockholders' investment or **return on common equity**; that is, we want to know if the earnings available to the firm's owners or common equity investors are attractive when compared to the returns of owners of companies in the peer group.

Return on common equity
Return on common equity indicates the accounting rate of return on the stockholders' investment, as measured by net income relative to common equity.

We measure the return to the owners as follows:

$$\text{return on common equity} = \frac{\text{net income}}{\text{common equity including par, paid-in capital, and retained earnings}} \quad \textbf{(3-13)}$$

The return on common equity for Harley-Davidson and the peer group are 26 percent and 12 percent, respectively:

	Harley-Davidson	Peer-Group Average
$\text{return on common equity}$	$= \dfrac{\text{net income}}{\text{common equity}}$	
	$= \dfrac{\$580M}{\$2{,}233M} = .26 = 26\%$	12%

Clearly, the owners of Harley-Davidson are receiving a return on their investment that is very attractive when compared to what owners involved with competing businesses receive. To understand the reasons, we need to draw on what we have already learned, namely that:

1. Harley-Davidson is far more profitable in its operations than its competitors. (Remember, the operating income return on investment, OIROI, was 23.2 percent for Harley-Davidson compared to 9.8 percent for the competition.) Thus, we could expect that Harley-Davidson would have a higher return on common equity.
2. Harley-Davidson uses considerably less debt (more equity) financing than does the average firm in the peer group. As we will see shortly, the more debt a firm uses, the higher its return on equity will be, provided that the firm is earning a return on investment greater than its cost of debt. Thus, given its low debt ratio, Harley-Davidson's higher return for its shareholders has been achieved totally by generating greater profits on the firm's assets, and not through the use of debt financing. Harley-Davidson could further increase its return to the owners by utilizing more debt; however, the more debt a firm uses, the greater the company's financial risk, which translates to more risk to the shareholders as well.

To help us understand the foregoing conclusion about the use of debt and its effect on shareholder return, consider the following example.

Firms A and B are identical in size, both having $1,000 in total assets and both having an operating income return on investment of 14 percent. However, they are different in one respect: Firm A uses no debt, but Firm B finances 60 percent of its investments with debt at an interest cost of 10 percent. For the sake of simplicity, we will assume there are no income taxes. The financial statements for the two companies would be as follows:

	FIRM A	FIRM B
Total assets	$1,000	$1,000
Debt (10% interest rate)	$ 0	$ 600
Equity	1,000	400
Total debt and equity	$1,000	$1,000
Operating income (OIROI = 14%)	$ 140	$ 140
Interest expense (10%)	0	60
Net profit	$ 140	$ 80

Computing the return on common equity for both companies, we see that Firm B has a much more attractive return to its owners, 20 percent compared to Firm A's 14 percent:

$$\text{return on equity} = \frac{\text{net income}}{\text{common equity}}$$

$$\text{Firm A: } \frac{\$140}{\$1{,}000} = .14 = 14\% \qquad \text{Firm B: } \frac{\$80}{\$400} = .20 = 20\%$$

Why the difference? Firm B is earning 14 percent on its investments, but is only having to pay 10 percent for its borrowed money. The difference between the return on the firm's investments and the interest rate, 14 percent less the 10 percent, goes to the owners, thus boosting Firm B's return on equity above that of Firm A. We are seeing the favorable results of debt at work, where we borrow at 10 percent and invest at 14 percent. The result is an increase in the return on equity.

If debt enhances the owners' returns, why would we not use lots of it all the time? We may continue our example to find the answer. Assume now that the economy falls into a deep recession, business declines sharply, and Firms A and B only earn a 6 percent operating income return on investment. Let's recompute the return on common equity now.

	FIRM A	FIRM B
Operating income (OIROI = 6%)	\$60	\$60
Interest expense	0	60
Net profit	\$60	\$ 0
Return on equity:	Firm A: $\frac{\$60}{\$1,000} = .06 = 6\%$	Firm B: $\frac{\$0}{\$400} = .00 = 0\%$

Now the use of debt has a negative influence on the return on equity, with Firm B earning less than Firm A for its owners. This results from the fact that now Firm B earns less than the interest rate of 10 percent; consequently, the equity investors have to make up the difference. Thus, using debt is a two-edged sword; when times are good, debt financing can make them very, very good, but when times are bad, debt financing makes them very, very bad. Thus, financing with debt can potentially enhance the returns of the equity investors, but it also increases the uncertainty or risk for the owners.

Let's review what we have learned about the use of financial ratios in evaluating a company's financial position. We have presented the financial ratios calculated for Harley-Davidson in Table 3-3. The ratios are grouped by the issue being addressed: liquidity, operating profitability, financing, and profits for the owners. As before, we use some ratios for more than one purpose—namely, the turnover ratios for accounts receivable and inventories. These ratios have implications both for the firm's liquidity and its profitability; thus they are listed in both areas. Also, we have included both average collection period and accounts receivable turnover; typically, we would only use one in our analysis, because they are just different ways of expressing the same thing.

Conducting Financial Analysis Over Time

To this point, we have been comparing Harley-Davidson with a peer group as of 2002. As mentioned earlier, we should also be interested in a firm's performance over time. To illustrate this process, Table 3-4 shows the financial ratios for Harley-Davidson for the years 1998 through 2002. Based on the trends, we can draw the following conclusions:

1. The firm's liquidity, as measured by the current and quick ratios, has been relatively stable over time. Although there was a decline in these ratios from 2000 to 2002 the ratios have improved overall during the period. Accounts receivable turnover has also been relatively stable, but has shown slight declines. Inventory turnover improved in 2002 over the previous four years, suggesting that inventory is being managed more efficiently.
2. Operating income return on investment (OIROI) has shown improvement over the five-year period. This improvement was largely the result of a better operating profit margin.

TABLE 3-3 Harley-Davidson's Financial Ratio Analysis

FINANCIAL RATIOS	HARLEY-DAVIDSON	PEER GROUP AVERAGE
1. FIRM LIQUIDITY		
Current ratio $= \frac{\text{current assets}}{\text{current liabilities}}$	$\frac{2{,}067\text{M}}{990\text{M}} = 2.09$ times	1.50 times
Acid-test ratio $= \frac{\text{current assets} - \text{inventories}}{\text{current liabilities}}$	$\frac{2{,}067 - 218\text{M}}{990\text{M}} = 1.87$ times	1.06 times
Average collection period $= \frac{\text{accounts receivable}}{\text{daily credit sales}}$	$\frac{964\text{M}}{4{,}195\text{M}/365} = \frac{964}{11.5} = 83.9$ days	75 days
Accounts receivable turnover $= \frac{\text{credit sales}}{\text{accounts receivable}}$	$\frac{4{,}195\text{M}}{964\text{M}} = 4.35$ times/yr.	4.87 times/yr.
Inventory turnover $= \frac{\text{cost of goods sold}}{\text{inventory}}$	$\frac{2{,}673\text{M}}{218\text{M}} = 12.26$ times/yr.	5.78 times/yr.
2. OPERATING PROFITABILITY		
Operating income return on investment $= \frac{\text{operating income}}{\text{total assets}}$	$\frac{896\text{M}}{3{,}861\text{M}} = 23.2\%$	9.8%
Operating profit margin $= \frac{\text{operating income}}{\text{sales}}$	$\frac{896\text{M}}{4{,}195\text{M}} = 21.4\%$	8.3%
Total asset turnover $= \frac{\text{sales}}{\text{total assets}}$	$\frac{4{,}195\text{M}}{3{,}861\text{M}} = 1.09$ times	1.18 times
Accounts receivable turnover $= \frac{\text{credit sales}}{\text{accounts receivable}}$	$\frac{4{,}195\text{M}}{964\text{M}} = 4.35$ times/yr.	4.87 times/yr.
Inventory turnover $= \frac{\text{cost of goods sold}}{\text{inventory}}$	$\frac{2{,}673\text{M}}{218\text{M}} = 12.25$ times/yr.	5.78 times/yr.
Fixed assets turnover $= \frac{\text{sales}}{\text{net fixed assets}}$	$\frac{4{,}195\text{M}}{1{,}033\text{M}} = 4.06$ times/yr.	4.26 times/yr.
3. FINANCING DECISIONS		
Debt ratio $= \frac{\text{total debt}}{\text{total assets}}$	$\frac{1{,}628\text{M}}{3{,}861\text{M}} = 42.2\%$	58%
Times interest earned $= \frac{\text{operating income}}{\text{interest expense}}$	$\frac{896.1\text{M}}{17.85\text{M}} = 50.2$ times	3.93 times
4. RETURN ON EQUITY		
Return on equity $= \frac{\text{net income}}{\text{common equity}}$	$\frac{580\text{M}}{2{,}233\text{M}} = 26\%$	12%

3. Harley-Davidson reduced its use of debt somewhat over the past five years. During this same time, the times interest earned has shown significant improvement.
4. The firm's return on equity has continued to improve over the five years reaching 26 percent in 2002, with the last year being on the high end of this range. Thus, for these five years, management has been able to consistently provide very attractive returns to the owners.

TABLE 3-4 Harley-Davidson, Inc., Ratio Analysis

	1998	1999	2000	2001	2002
FIRM LIQUIDITY					
Current ratio	1.80	1.83	2.61	2.33	2.09
Acid-test ratio	1.47	1.51	2.22	2.07	1.87
Average collection period	79.87	76.68	75.41	84.49	83.91
Accounts receivable turnover	4.57	4.76	4.84	4.32	4.35
Inventory turnover	8.57	9.26	9.61	11.77	12.26
OPERATING PROFITABILITY					
Operating income return on investment	18.6%	21.0%	22.4%	21.0%	23.2%
Operating profit margin	16.5%	17.2%	17.9%	19.6%	21.4%
Total asset turnover	1.13	1.22	1.25	1.07	1.09
Accounts receivable turnover	4.57	4.76	4.84	4.32	4.35
Inventory turnover	8.57	9.26	9.61	11.77	12.26
Fixed assets turnover	3.45	3.79	4.04	3.75	4.06
FINANCING DECISIONS					
Debt ratio	0.46	0.45	0.42	0.44	0.42
Times interest earned	14.90	15.50	17.97	26.55	50.21
RETURN ON EQUITY					
Return on equity	20.7%	23.0%	24.7%	24.9%	26.0%

From the foregoing trend analysis we are able to see clearly how the firm is performing financially over time, which gives us additional insights not possible from only looking at industry norms.

CONCEPT CHECK

1. How can financial ratios be used to make valuable comparisons?
2. The financial ratios outlined in this chapter have been developed to answer what four important questions?
3. Which number in the income statement should be used to measure profitability relative to total assets, and why? What are the two driving forces behind the operating income return on investment?
4. What is the relationship between the use of debt and the return on common equity for shareholders?

Objective 2

THE DUPONT ANALYSIS: AN INTEGRATIVE APPROACH TO RATIO ANALYSIS

In the previous section, we used ratio analysis to answer four questions thought to be important in understanding a company's financial position. The last three of the four questions dealt with a company's earnings capabilities and the common stockholders' return on the equity capital. In our analysis, we measured the return on equity as follows:

$$\text{return on equity} = \frac{\text{net income}}{\text{common equity}} \qquad \textbf{(3-14)}$$

FIGURE 3-1 DuPont Analysis: Harley-Davidson

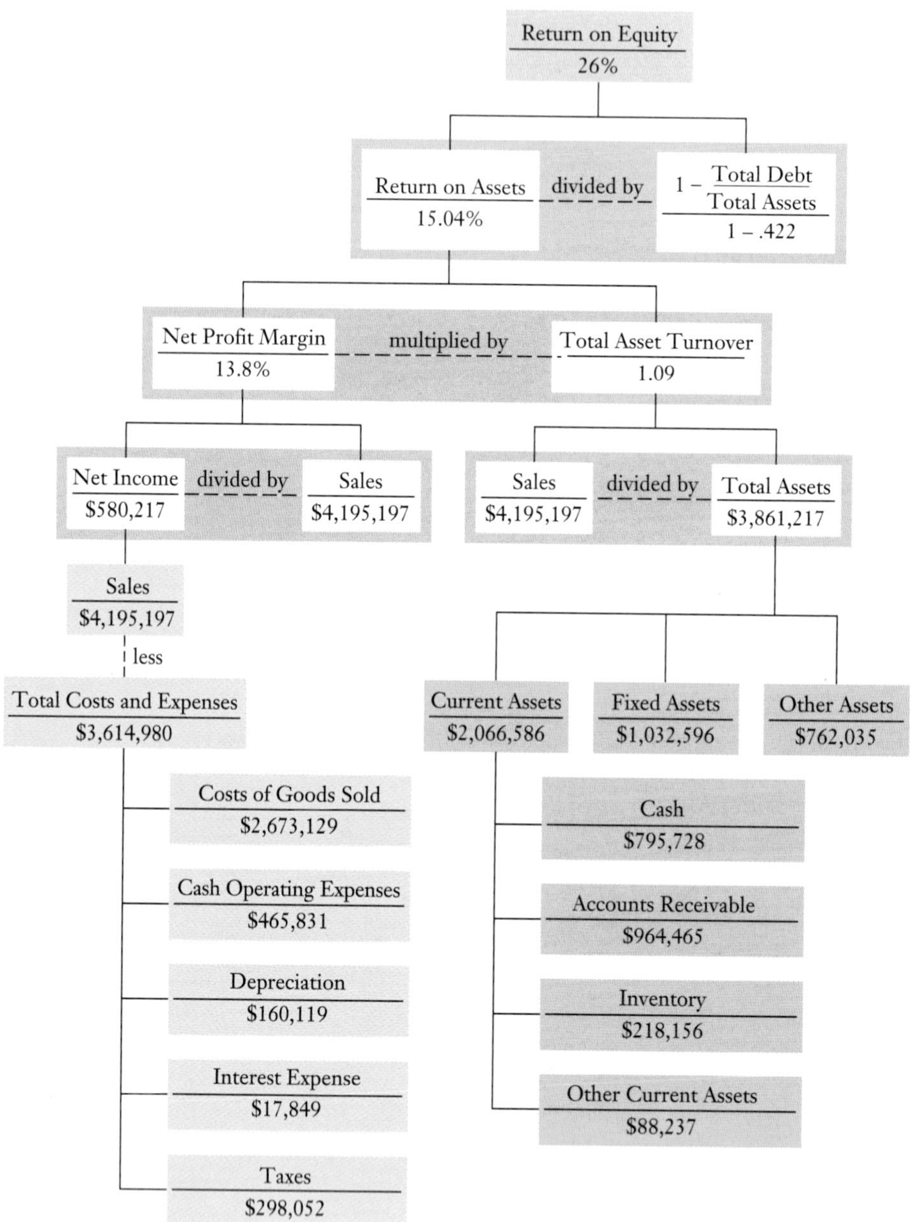

DuPont analysis
The DuPont analysis is an approach to evaluate a firm's profitability and return on equity.

Another approach can be used to evaluate a firm's return on equity. The **DuPont analysis** is a method used to analyze a firm's profitability and return on equity. Figure 3-1 shows graphically the DuPont technique, along with the numbers for Harley-Davidson. Beginning at the top of the figure, we see that the return on equity is calculated as follows:

$$\text{return on equity} = \left(\begin{matrix}\text{return}\\ \text{on assets}\end{matrix}\right) \div \left(1 - \frac{\text{total debt}}{\text{total assets}}\right) \tag{3-15}$$

where the return on assets, or ROA, equals:

$$\text{return on assets} = \frac{\text{net income}}{\text{total assets}} \tag{3-16}$$

Thus we see that the return on equity is a function of (1) the firm's overall profitability (net income relative to the amount invested in assets), and (2) the amount of debt used to finance the assets. Also, the return on assets may be represented as follows:

$$\begin{aligned}\text{return on assets} &= \begin{pmatrix}\text{net profit}\\\text{margin}\end{pmatrix} \times \begin{pmatrix}\text{total asset}\\\text{turnover}\end{pmatrix}\\ &= \left(\frac{\text{net income}}{\text{sales}}\right) \times \left(\frac{\text{sales}}{\text{total assets}}\right)\end{aligned} \tag{3-17}$$

Combining equations (3-15) and (3-17) gives us the basic DuPont equation that shows the firm's return on equity as follows:

$$\begin{aligned}\text{return on equity} &= \begin{pmatrix}\text{net profit}\\\text{margin}\end{pmatrix} \times \begin{pmatrix}\text{total asset}\\\text{turnover}\end{pmatrix} \div \left(1 - \frac{\text{total debt}}{\text{total assets}}\right)\\ &= \left(\frac{\text{net income}}{\text{sales}}\right) \times \left(\frac{\text{sales}}{\text{total assets}}\right) \div \left(1 - \frac{\text{total debt}}{\text{total assets}}\right)\end{aligned} \tag{3-18}$$

Using the DuPont equation and the diagram in Figure 3-1 allows management to see more clearly what drives the return on equity and the interrelationships among the net profit margin, the asset turnover, and the debt ratio. Management is provided with a road map to follow in determining its effectiveness in managing the firm's resources to maximize the return earned on the owners' investment. In addition, the manager or owner can determine why that particular return was earned.

Let's return to Harley-Davidson to demonstrate the use of the DuPont analysis. Taking the information from Harley-Davidson's income statement (Table 3-1) and balance sheet as of December 31, 2002 (Table 3-2), we can calculate the company's return on equity as follows:

$$\begin{aligned}\text{return on equity} &= \left(\frac{\text{net income}}{\text{sales}}\right) \times \left(\frac{\text{sales}}{\text{total assets}}\right) \div \left(1 - \frac{\text{total debt}}{\text{total assets}}\right)\\ &= \frac{580{,}217}{4{,}195{,}197} \times \frac{4{,}195{,}197}{3{,}861{,}217} \div \left(1 - \frac{1{,}628{,}302}{3{,}861{,}217}\right)\\ &= .138 \times 1.086 \div .578\\ &= 26\%\end{aligned}$$

We can also visualize the relationships graphically for Harley-Davidson, as shown in Figure 3-1.

If Harley-Davidson's management wants to improve the company's return on equity, it should carefully examine Figure 3-1 for possible avenues. As we study the figure, we quickly see that improvement in the return on equity can come in one or more of four ways:

1. Increase sales without a disproportionate increase in costs and expenses.
2. Reduce the firm's cost of goods sold or operating expenses shown in the left side of Figure 3-1.

3. Increase the sales relative to the asset base, either by increasing sales or by reducing the amounts invested in company assets. From our earlier examination of Harley-Davidson, we learned that the firm had excessive accounts receivables and fixed assets. Thus management needs to reduce these assets to the lowest point possible, which would in turn result in an increase in the return on assets and then the return on equity.
4. Increase the use of debt relative to equity, but only to the extent that it does not unduly jeopardize the firm's financial position.

The choice between using the four-question approach as described earlier or the DuPont analysis is largely a matter of personal preference. Both approaches are intended to let us see the variables that determine a firm's profitability. There are, however, limitations to either technique because of the inherent limitations in using financial ratios—a topic addressed in the next section.

CONCEPT CHECK

1. In the DuPont analysis, the return on equity is the function of what two factors?
2. What four methods can a firm utilize to improve return on equity?

Objective 3

LIMITATIONS OF RATIO ANALYSIS

We have shown how financial ratios may be used to understand a company's financial position, but anyone who works with these ratios ought to be aware of the limitations involved in their use. The following list includes some of the more important pitfalls that may be encountered in computing and interpreting financial ratios:

1. It is sometimes difficult to identify the industry category to which a firm belongs when the firm engages in multiple lines of business. Thus, we frequently must select our own set of peer firms and construct tailor-made norms. Such was the case with our analysis of Harley-Davidson.
2. Published industry averages are only approximations and provide the user with general guidelines rather than scientifically determined averages of the ratios of all or even a representative sample of the firms within an industry.
3. Accounting practices differ widely among firms and can lead to differences in computed ratios. For example, firms may choose different methods of depreciating their fixed assets.
4. An industry average may not provide a desirable target ratio or norm. At best, an industry average provides a guide to the financial position of the average firm in the industry, which includes all the dogs and the stars. It does not mean it is the ideal or best value for the ratio. Thus, we may choose to compare our firm's ratios with a self-determined peer group or even a single competitor.[9]
5. Many firms experience seasonality in their operations. Thus, balance sheet entries and their corresponding ratios will vary with the time of year when the statements are prepared. For example, a firm may have a fiscal year that ends on June 30, whereas

[9] See Donald F. Cunningham and John T. Rose, "Industry Norms in Financial Statement Analysis: A Comparison of RMA and D&B Benchmark Data," *The Credit and Financial Management Review*, 1995, pp. 42–48, for a comparison of the industry financial ratios provided by Robert Morris Associates with those of Dun and Bradstreet. They find significant differences within the same industry classifications. This finding points out the need to consider carefully the choice of an industry norm. In fact, your analysis may require that you construct your own norm from, say, a list of the four or five firms in a particular industry that might provide the most appropriate standard of comparison for the firm being analyzed.

another company in the same industry may have a December 31 fiscal-year end. To avoid this problem, an average account balance should be used (for several months or quarters during the year) rather than the year-end total. For example, an average of month-end inventory balances might be used to compute a firm's inventory turnover ratio when the firm is subject to a significant seasonality in its sales (and correspondingly in its investment in inventories).

In spite of their limitations, financial ratios provide us with a very useful tool for assessing a firm's financial condition. We should, however, be aware of these potential weaknesses when performing a ratio analysis. In many cases, the real value derived from analyzing financial ratios is that they tell us what questions to ask and what avenues to pursue.

CONCEPT CHECK

1. Why is it difficult to create industry categories, especially among larger companies?
2. What differences in accounting practices create problems in using financial ratios?
3. Why should a firm be careful when making comparisons with industry norms?

HOW FINANCIAL MANAGERS USE THIS MATERIAL

In this chapter, we provided a framework for using the information in evaluating a firm's performance. As stated in Chapter 2, accounting data are the basis for so much that is done in finance. The consequences of certain important management decisions can only be verified by the relationships shown in the financial statements. Such measurements as gross profit margin, operating profit margin, the different asset turnover ratios, debt ratios, and return on investment provide important information about the effectiveness of a management's strategies. For instance, Michael Eisner, the CEO for Disney, received large bonuses based on the company earning a superior return on the common stockholders' investment, as did Al Dunlap when he went to Scott Paper to turn the company around and make it more profitable. Eisner was successful, but Dunlap was not. So, if a manager or a common stockholder wants to know the effectiveness of a firm's strategies, the ultimate test is the rate of return being earned on the company's assets, which is measured, to a large extent, by the accounting data. Without such information, managers cannot make any definite conclusions as to the success of their strategies.

SUMMARY

Financial ratios are the principal tools of financial analysis. Sometimes referred to simply as benchmarks, ratios standardize financial information so that comparisons can be made between firms of varying sizes. *Objective 1*

Two groups find financial ratios useful. The first is comprised of managers who use them to measure and track company performance over time. The focus of their analysis is frequently related to various measures of profitability used to evaluate the performance of the firm from the perspective of the owners. The second group of users of financial ratios includes analysts external to the firm who, for one reason or another, have an interest in the firm's economic well-being. An example of this group would be a loan officer of a commercial bank who wishes to determine the creditworthiness of a loan applicant. Here the focus of the analysis is on the firm's previous use of financial leverage and its ability to pay the interest and principal associated with the loan request.

Financial ratios may be used to answer at least four questions: (1) How liquid is the company? (2) Is management effective at generating operating profits on the firm's assets? (3) How is the firm financed? (4) Are the returns earned by the common stockholders adequate?

Two methods may be used in analyzing financial ratios. The first involves trend analysis for the firm over time; the second involves making ratio comparisons with a selected peer group of similar firms. In our example, a peer group was chosen for analyzing the financial position of Harley-Davidson.

Objective 2

Another approach frequently used to evaluate a firm's profitability and the return on equity is the DuPont analysis. The basic format of the DuPont analysis dissects the return on equity into three drivers, represented as follows:

$$\text{return on equity} = \left(\frac{\text{net income}}{\text{sales}}\right) \times \left(\frac{\text{sales}}{\text{total assets}}\right) \div \left(1 - \frac{\text{total debt}}{\text{total assets}}\right)$$

Objective 3

The following limitations may be encountered in computing and interpreting financial ratios:

1. It is sometimes difficult to identify an appropriate industry category.
2. Published industry averages are only approximations rather than scientifically determined averages.
3. Accounting practices differ widely among firms and can lead to differences in computed ratios.
4. An industry average may not provide a desirable target ratio or norm.
5. Many firms experience seasonality in their operations. Thus, ratios will vary with the time of year when the statements are prepared.

In spite of their limitations, financial ratios provide us with very useful tools for assessing a firm's financial condition.

KEY TERMS

Go To: www.prenhall.com/keown for downloads and current events associated with this chapter

Accounts receivable turnover ratio, 75
Acid-test (quick) ratio, 73
Average collection period, 75
Current ratio, 73
Debt ratio, 80
DuPont analysis, 86
Financial ratios, 72
Inventory turnover ratio, 76
Net profit margin, 78
Operating income return on investment, 77
Operating profit margin, 78
Return on assets, 77
Return on common equity, 81
Times interest earned, 81
Total asset turnover, 79

STUDY QUESTIONS

3-1. Describe the "four-question approach" to using financial ratios.

3-2. Discuss briefly the two perspectives that can be taken in performing ratio analyses.

3-3. Where can we obtain industry norms? What are the limitations of industry average ratios? Discuss briefly.

3-4. What is liquidity, and what is the rationale for its measurement?

3-5. Distinguish between the operating income return on investment and the operating profit margin.

3-6. Why is operating income return on investment a function of operating profit margin and total asset turnover?

3-7. What are the differences among gross profit margin, operating profit margin, and net profit margin?

3-8. Explain what drives a company's return on common equity.

SELF-TEST PROBLEMS

ST-1. (*Ratio analysis and short-term liquidity*) Ray's Tool and Supply Company of Austin, Texas, has been expanding its level of operation for the past two years. The firm's sales have grown rapidly as a result of the expansion in the Austin economy. However, Ray's is a privately held company, and its only source of available funds is a line of credit with the firm's bank. The company needs to expand its inventories to meet the needs of its growing customer base but also wishes to maintain a current ratio of at least 3. If Ray's current assets are $6 million, and its current ratio is now 4, how much can it expand its inventories (financing the expansion with its line of credit) before the target current ratio is violated?

ST-2. Given the following information for Neff Industries, evaluate the firm's performance for the years 2002 and 2003 by using the "four-question approach."

Neff Industries Balance Sheet
for December 31, 2002, and December 31, 2003

	2002	2003
Cash	$ 9,000	$ 500
Accounts receivable	12,500	16,000
Inventories	29,000	45,500
Total current assets	$ 50,500	$ 62,000
Land	20,000	26,000
Buildings and equipment	70,000	100,000
Less: allowance for depreciation	28,000	38,000
Total fixed assets	$ 62,000	$ 88,000
Total assets	$112,500	$150,000
Accounts payable	$ 10,500	$ 22,000
Bank notes	17,000	47,000
Total current liabilities	$ 27,500	$ 69,000
Long-term debt	28,750	22,950
Common stock	31,500	31,500
Retained earnings	24,750	26,550
Total liabilities and equity	$112,500	$150,000

Neff Industries Income Statement
for the Years Ended December 31, 2002, and December 31, 2003

	2002	2003
Sales	$125,000	$160,000
Cost of goods sold	75,000	96,000
Gross profit	$ 50,000	$ 64,000
Operating expenses		
Fixed cash operating expense	21,000	21,000
Variable operating expense	12,500	16,000
Depreciation	4,500	10,000
Total operating expense	$ 38,000	$ 47,000
Earnings before interest and taxes	$ 12,000	$ 17,000
Interest	3,000	6,100
Earnings before taxes	$ 9,000	$ 10,900
Taxes	4,500	5,450
Net income	$ 4,500	$ 5,450

(continued)

INDUSTRY NORMS	
Current ratio	1.80
Acid-test ratio	0.70
Average collection period	37.00
Inventory turnover	2.50
Debt ratio	0.58
Times interest earned	3.80
Gross profit margin	38%
Operating profit margin	10%
Total asset turnover	1.14
Fixed asset turnover	1.40
Operating income return on investment	11.4%
Return on total assets	4.0%
Return on common equity	9.5%

STUDY PROBLEMS (SET A)

3-1A. (*Balance sheet analysis*) Complete the following balance sheet using the following information provided:

Cash		Accounts payable	100,000
Accounts receivable		Long-term debt	
Inventory		Total liabilities	
Current assets		Common equity	
Net fixed assets	1,500,000	Total	$2,100,000
Total	$2,100,000		

Current ratio = 6.0	Total asset turnover = 1.0
Inventory turnover = 8.0	Average collection period = 30 days
Debt ratio = 20%	Gross profit margin = 15%

3-2A. (*Ratio analysis*) The Mitchem Marble Company has a target current ratio of 2.0 but has experienced some difficulties financing its expanding sales in the past few months. The firm has a current ratio of 2.5 with current assets of $2.5 million. If Mitchem expands its receivables and inventories using its short-term line of credit, how much additional short-term funding can it borrow before its current ratio standard is reached?

3-3A. (*Ratio analysis*) The balance sheet and income statement for the J. P. Robard Mfg. Company are as follows:

Balance Sheet ($000)

Cash	$ 500
Accounts receivable	2,000
Inventories	1,000
Current assets	$3,500
Net fixed assets	4,500
Total assets	$8,000
Accounts payable	$1,100
Accrued expenses	600
Short-term notes payable	300
Current liabilities	$2,000
Long-term debt	2,000
Owners' equity	4,000
Total liabilities and owners' equity	$8,000

Income Statement ($000)

Net sales (all credit)	$8,000
Cost of goods sold	(3,300)
Gross profit	$4,700
Operating expenses[a]	(3,000)
Operating income	$1,700
Interest expense	(367)
Earnings before taxes	$1,333
Income taxes (40%)	(533)
Net income	$ 800

[a]Includes depreciation expense of $500 for the year

Calculate the following ratios:

Current ratio	Debt ratio
Times interest earned	Average collection period
Inventory turnover	Fixed asset turnover
Total asset turnover	Gross profit margin
Operating profit margin	Return on equity
Operating income return on investment	

3-4A. (*Analyzing operating income return on investment*) The R. M. Smithers Corporation earned an operating profit margin of 10 percent based on sales of $10 million and total assets of $5 million last year.

a. What was Smithers's total asset turnover ratio?

b. During the coming year, the company president has set a goal of attaining a total asset turnover of 3.5. How much must firm sales rise, other things being the same, for the goal to be achieved? (State your answer in both dollars and percentage increase in sales.)

c. What was Smithers's operating income return on investment last year? Assuming the firm's operating profit margin remains the same, what will the operating income return on investment be next year if the total asset turnover goal is achieved?

3-5A. (*Using financial ratios*) The Brenmar Sales Company had a gross profit margin (gross profits/sales) of 30 percent and sales of $9 million last year. Seventy-five percent of the firm's sales are on credit and the remainder are cash sales. Brenmar's current assets equal $1.5 million, its current liabilities equal $300,000, and it has $100,000 in cash plus marketable securities.

a. If Brenmar's accounts receivable are $562,500, what is its average collection period?

b. If Brenmar reduces its average collection period to 20 days, what will be its new level of accounts receivable?

c. Brenmar's inventory turnover ratio is nine times. What is the level of Brenmar's inventories?

3-6A. (*Ratio analysis*) Using the following financial statements for Pamplin Inc.:

a. Compute the following ratios for both 2002 and 2003.

	INDUSTRY NORM
Current ratio	5.00
Acid-test (quick) ratio	3.00
Inventory turnover	2.20
Average collection period	90.00
Debt ratio	0.33
Times interest earned	7.00
Total asset turnover	0.75
Fixed asset turnover	1.00
Operating profit margin	20%
Return on common equity	9%

b. How liquid is the firm?

c. Is management generating adequate operating profit on the firm's assets?

d. How is the firm financing its assets?

e. Are the common stockholders receiving a good return on their investment?

Pamplin, Inc., Balance Sheet at 12/31/02 and 12/31/03

	2002	2003
ASSETS		
Cash	$ 200	$ 150
Accounts receivable	450	425
Inventory	550	625
Current assets	1,200	1,200
Plant and equipment	2,200	2,600
Less: accumulated depreciation	(1,000)	(1,200)
Net plant and equipment	1,200	1,400
Total assets	$2,400	$2,600
LIABILITIES AND OWNERS' EQUITY		
Accounts payable	$ 200	$ 150
Notes payable—current (9%)	0	150
Current liabilities	$ 200	$ 300
Bonds (8 1/3% interest)	600	600
Owners' equity		
Common stock	$ 300	$ 300
Paid-in capital	600	600
Retained earnings	700	800
Total owners' equity	$1,600	$1,700
Total liabilities and owners' equity	$2,400	$2,600

Pamplin, Inc., Income Statement for Years Ending 12/31/02 and 12/31/03

		2002		2003
Sales (all credit)		$1,200		$1,450
Cost of goods sold		700		850
Gross profit		$ 500		$ 600
Operating expenses	30		40	
Depreciation	220	250	200	240
Operating income		$ 250		$ 360
Interest expense		50		64
Net income before taxes		$ 200		$ 296
Taxes (40%)		80		118
Net income		$ 120		$ 178

3-7A. *(Financial ratios—investment analysis)* The annual sales for Salco, Inc., were $4.5 million last year. The firm's end-of-year balance sheet appeared as follows:

Current assets	$ 500,000	Liabilities	$1,000,000
Net fixed assets	1,500,000	Owners' equity	1,000,000
	$2,000,000		$2,000,000

The firm's income statement for the year was as follows:

Sales	$4,500,000
Less: cost of goods sold	(3,500,000)
Gross profit	$1,000,000
Less: operating expenses	(500,000)
Operating income	$ 500,000
Less: interest expense	(100,000)
Earnings before taxes	$ 400,000
Less: taxes (50%)	(200,000)
Net income	$ 200,000

a. Calculate Salco's total asset turnover, operating profit margin, and operating income return on investment.

b. Salco plans to renovate one of its plants, which will require an added investment in plant and equipment of $1 million. The firm will maintain its present debt ratio of .5 when financing the new investment and expects sales to remain constant, while the operating profit margin will rise to 13 percent. What will be the new operating income return on investment for Salco after the plant renovation?

c. Given that the plant renovation in part (b) occurs and Salco's interest expense rises by $50,000 per year, what will be the return earned on the common stockholders' investment? Compare this rate of return with that earned before the renovation.

3-8A. *(Ratio analysis of loan request)* The T. P. Jarmon Company manufactures and sells a line of exclusive sportswear. The firm's sales were $600,000 for the year just ended, and its total assets exceeded $400,000. The company was started by Mr. Jarmon just 10 years ago and has been profitable every year since its inception. The Chief Financial Officer for the firm, Brent Vehlim, has decided to seek a line of credit from the firm's bank totaling $80,000. In the past, the company has relied on its suppliers to finance a large part of its needs for inventory. However, in recent months, tight money conditions have led the firm's suppliers to offer sizable cash discounts to speed up payments for purchases. Mr. Vehlim wants to use the line of credit to supplant a large portion of the firm's payables during the summer months, which are the firm's peak seasonal sales period.

The firm's two most recent balance sheets were presented to the bank in support of its loan request. In addition, the firm's income statement for the year just ended was provided to support the loan request. These statements are as follows:

T. P. Jarmon Company Balance Sheets for 12/31/02 and 12/31/03

	2002	2003
ASSETS		
Cash	$ 15,000	$ 14,000
Marketable securities	6,000	6,200
Accounts receivable	42,000	33,000
Inventory	51,000	84,000
Prepaid rent	1,200	1,100
Total current assets	$115,200	$138,300
Net plant and equipment	286,000	270,000
Total assets	$401,200	$408,300
LIABILITIES AND EQUITY		
Accounts payable	$ 48,000	$ 57,000
Notes payable	15,000	13,000
Accruals	6,000	5,000
Total current liabilities	$ 69,000	$ 75,000
Long-term debt	$160,000	$150,000
Common stockholders' equity	$172,200	$183,300
Total liabilities and equity	$401,200	$408,300

T. P. Jarmon Company Income Statement for the Year Ended 12/31/03

Sales		$600,000
Less: cost of goods sold		460,000
Gross profits		$140,000
Less: operating and interest expenses		
General and administrative	$30,000	
Interest	10,000	
Depreciation	30,000	
Total		$ 70,000

(continued)

Earnings before taxes	$ 70,000
Less: taxes	27,100
Net income available to common stockholders	$ 42,900
Less: cash dividends	31,800
Change in retained earnings	$ 11,100

Jan Fama, associate credit analyst for the Merchants National Bank of Midland, Michigan, was assigned the task of analyzing Jarmon's loan request.

a. Calculate the financial ratios for 2003 corresponding to the industry norms provided as follows:

	RATIO NORM
Current ratio	1.8
Acid-test ratio	0.9
Debt ratio	0.5
Times interest earned	10.0
Average collection period	20.0
Inventory turnover (based on cost of goods sold)	7.0
Return on common equity	12.0%
Gross profit margin	25.0%
Operating income return on investment	16.8%
Operating profit margin	14.0%
Total asset turnover	1.20
Fixed asset turnover	1.80
Return on assets	6%
Return on equity	12%

b. Which of the ratios reported in the industry norms do you feel should be most crucial in determining whether the bank should extend the line of credit?

c. Use the DuPont analysis to evaluate the firm's financial position.

3-9A. (*Ratio analysis*) HiTech, Inc.'s income statement for 2003 and the balance sheet for December 31, 2003 follow.

Compute the financial ratios for HiTech for 2003 and using the industry norms, evaluate the firm in the following areas:

(1) liquidity
(2) operating profitability
(3) financing policies
(4) return on the shareholders' investment

HiTech Income Statement for Year Ending 2003

	2003
Sales	$29,389,000
Cost of goods sold	9,061,000
Gross profit	$20,328,000
Selling, general, and administrative expense	6,983,000
Depreciation	3,186,000
Operating profit	$10,159,000
Interest expense	41,000
Nonoperating income (expense)	1,110,000
Pretax income	$ 11,228,000
Total income taxes	3,914,000
Net income	$ 7,314,000

HiTech Balance Sheet, For December 31, 2003

	2003
ASSETS	
Cash and equivalents	$11,788,000
Accounts receivable	3,700,000
Inventories	1,478,000
Other current assets	853,000
Total current assets	$17,819,000
Gross plant, property, and equipment	24,360,000
Accumulated depreciation	12,645,000
Net plant, property, and equipment	$11,715,000
Other investments	7,911,000
Intangibles	4,322,000
Other assets	2,082,000
Total assets	$43,849,000
LIABILITIES	
Notes payable	$ 230,000
Accounts payable	1,370,000
Taxes payable	1,695,000
Accrued expenses	3,195,000
Other current liabilities	609,000
Total current liabilities	$ 7,099,000
Long-term debt	955,000
Deferred taxes	3,130,000
Total liabilities	$11,184,000
EQUITY	
Preferred stock	$ 130,000
Common stock	3,334
Capital surplus	7,312,666
Retained earnings	25,219,000
Common equity	$32,535,000
Total equity	32,665,000
Total liabilities and equity	$43,849,000

INDUSTRY NORMS	
FIRM LIQUIDITY	
Current ratio	2.01
Acid-test ratio	1.66
Average collection period	72.64
Accounts receivable turnover	5.02
Inventory turnover	4.42
OPERATING PROFITABILITY	
Operating income return on investment	9%
Operating profit margin	13%
Total asset turnover	0.69
Accounts receivable turnover	5.02
Inventory turnover	4.42
Fixed asset turnover	2.27
FINANCING DECISIONS	
Debt ratio	0.44
Times interest earned	8.87
RETURN ON EQUITY	
Return on equity	12%

INTEGRATIVE PROBLEM

Following are the 1999 to 2003 financial statements for both Blake International and Scott Corp., two head-to-head competitors in the athletic footwear industry.

1. Evaluate the two respective firms in terms of their financial performance over time (1999–2003) as it relates to (1) liquidity, (2) operating profitability, (3) financing assets, and (4) the shareholders' (common equity) return on investment. (A computer spreadsheet is extremely helpful here and will save you some time in doing the assignment.)
2. Compare the two firms' financial performance. How are they different and how are they similar?

Blake International Financial Statements, 1999–2003

INCOME STATEMENTS ($ MILLIONS)

	1999	2000	2001	2002	2003
Sales	$3,481	$3,479	$3,644	$3,225	$2,900
Cost of goods sold	2,083	2,109	2,255	1,997	1,746
Gross profit	$1,398	$1,370	$1,389	$1,228	$1,154
Selling, general, and administrative expense	999	1,065	1,070	1,043	972
Depreciation	35	40	43	45	43
Operating profit	$ 364	$ 265	$ 276	$ 140	$ 139
Interest expense	26	42	64	61	50
Nonoperating income/expense	10	15	5	(8)	1
Special items	(72)	0	(59)	(34)	(62)
Pretax income	$ 276	$ 238	$ 158	$ 37	$ 28
Total income taxes	100	84	12	12	10
Minority interest	11	15	10	1	7
Net income	$ 165	$ 139	$ 136	$ 24	$ 11

BALANCE SHEETS ($ MILLIONS)

	1999	2000	2001	2002	2003
ASSETS					
Cash and equivalents	$ 80	$ 232	$ 210	$ 180	$ 282
Net receivables	507	591	562	518	417
Inventories	635	545	564	535	415
Other current assets	121	95	129	129	129
Total current assets	$1,343	$1,463	$1,465	$1,362	$1,243
Gross plant, property, and equipment	336	357	354	399	422
Accumulated depreciation	144	172	197	226	244
Net plant, property, and equipment	$ 192	$ 185	$ 157	$ 173	$ 178
Other assets	121	138	134	205	143
Total assets	$1,656	$1,786	$1,756	$1,740	$1,564
LIABILITIES					
Long-term debt due in one year	$ 1	$ 53	$ 121	$ 87	$ 185
Notes payable	67	33	41	48	28
Accounts payable	166	196	192	203	154
Taxes payable	53	66	4	82	8
Accrued expenses	145	169	219	192	249
Total current liabilities	$ 432	$ 517	$ 577	$ 612	$ 624
Long-term debt	254	854	639	554	370
Minority interest	31	34	33	33	–
Other liabilities	–	–	–	–	41
Total liabilities	$ 717	$1,405	$1,249	$1,199	$1,035

(continued)

BALANCE SHEETS ($ MILLIONS)	1999	2000	2001	2002	2003
EQUITY					
Preferred stock	$ 44	$ –	$ –	$ 17	$ –
Common stock	1	1	1	1	1
Retained earnings	1,497	998	1,124	1,141	1,146
Less: treasury stock	603	618	618	618	618
Total equity	$ 939	$ 381	$ 507	$ 541	$ 529
Total liabilities and equity	$1,656	$1,786	$1,756	$1,740	$1,564

Scott Corp. Financial Statements, 1999–2003

INCOME STATEMENTS ($ MILLIONS)	1999	2000	2001	2002	2003
Sales	$4,761	$6,471	$9,187	$9,553	$8,777
Cost of goods sold	2,806	3,825	5,365	5,881	5,295
Gross profit	$1,955	$2,646	$3,822	$3,672	$3,482
Selling, general, and administrative expense	1,210	1,589	2,304	2,624	2,427
Depreciation	84	119	158	204	218
Operating profit	$ 661	$ 938	$1,360	$ 844	$ 837
Interest expense	24	40	55	67	51
Nonoperating income/expense	24	1	8	5	(10)
Special items	(11)	–	(18)	(129)	(30)
Pretax income	$ 650	$ 899	$1,295	$ 653	$ 746
Total income taxes	250	346	499	253	295
Preferred dividends	0	0	0	0	0
Net income	$ 400	$ 553	$ 796	$ 400	$ 451

BALANCE SHEETS ($ MILLIONS)	1999	2000	2001	2002	2003
ASSETS					
Cash and equivalents	$ 216	$ 262	$ 445	$ 109	$ 198
Net receivables	1,053	1,346	1,754	1,674	1,556
Inventories	630	931	1,339	1,397	1,199
Prepaid expenses	74	94	157	196	191
Other current assets	73	94	136	157	121
Total current assets	$2,046	$2,727	$3,831	$3,533	$3,265
Gross plant, property, and equipment	891	1,047	1,425	1,820	2,002
Accumulated depreciation	336	404	503	667	736
Net plant, property, and equipment	$ 555	$ 643	$ 922	$1,153	$1,266
Intangibles	496	476	464	435	427
Other assets	46	106	144	276	290
Total assets	$3,143	$3,952	$5,361	$5,397	$5,248
LIABILITIES					
Long-term debt due in one year	$ 32	$ 7	$ 2	$ 2	$ 1
Notes payable	397	445	553	480	419
Accounts payable	298	455	687	585	373
Taxes payable	36	79	54	29	–
Accrued expenses	345	481	571	608	654
Total current liabilities	$1,108	$1,467	$1,867	$1,704	$1,447
Long-term debt	11	10	296	379	386
Deferred taxes	18	2	5	–	–
Other liabilities	41	41	37	53	80
Total liabilities	$1,178	$1,520	$2,205	$2,136	$1,913

(continued)

BALANCE SHEETS ($ MILLIONS)	1999	2000	2001	2002	2003
EQUITY					
Common stock	3	3	3	3	3
Capital surplus	123	155	211	263	334
Retained earnings	1,839	2,274	2,942	2,995	2,998
Total equity	$1,965	$2,432	$3,156	$3,261	$3,335
Total liabilities and equity	$3,143	$3,952	$5,361	$5,397	$5,248

STUDY PROBLEMS (SET B)

3-1B. (*Balance sheet analysis*) Complete the following balance sheet using this information:

Cash		Accounts payable	100,000
Accounts receivable		Long-term debt	
Inventory		Total liabilities	
Current assets		Common equity	
Net fixed assets	1,000,000	Total	$1,300,000
Total	$1,300,000		

Current ratio = 3.0
Inventory turnover = 10.0
Debt ratio = 30%
Total asset turnover = .5
Average collection period = 45 days
Gross profit margin = 30%

3-2B. (*Ratio analysis*) The Allandale Office Supply Company has a target current ratio of 2.0 but has experienced some difficulties financing its expanding sales in the past few months. At present, the firm has a current ratio of 2.75 with current assets of $3 million. If Allandale expands its receivables and inventories using its short-term bank loan (a current liability), how much additional short-term funding can it borrow before its current ratio standard is reached?

3-3B. (*Ratio analysis*) The balance sheet and income statement for the Simsboro Paper Company are as follows:

BALANCE SHEET ($000)		INCOME STATEMENT ($000)	
Cash	$1,000	Net sales (all credit)	$7,500
Accounts receivable	1,500	Cost of goods sold	(3,000)
Inventories	1,000	Gross profit	$4,500
Current assets	$3,500	Operating expenses[a]	(3,000)
Net fixed assets	4,500	Operating income (EPIT)	$1,500
Total assets	$8,000	Interest expense	(367)
Accounts payable	$1,000	Earnings before taxes	$1,133
Accrued expenses	600	Income taxes (40%)	(453)
Short-term notes payable	200	Net income	$ 680
Current liabilities	$1,800		
Long-term debt	2,100		
Owners' equity	4,100		
Total liabilities and owners' equity	$8,000		

[a]Includes depreciation expense of $500 for the year.

Calculate the following ratios:

Current ratio	Debt ratio
Times interest earned	Average collection period
Inventory turnover	Fixed asset turnover
Total asset turnover	Gross profit margin
Operating profit margin	Return on equity
Operating income return on investment	

3-4B. (*Analyzing operating income return on investment*) The R. M. Senchack Corporation earned an operating profit margin of 6 percent based on sales of $11 million and total assets of $6 million last year.

a. What was Senchack's total asset turnover ratio?

b. During the coming year, the company president has set a goal of attaining a total asset turnover of 2.5. How much must firm sales rise, other things being the same, for the total asset goal to be achieved? (State your answer in both dollars and as a percent increase in sales.)

c. What was Senchack's operating income return on investment last year? Assuming the firm's operating profit margin remains the same, what will the operating income return on investment be next year if the total asset turnover goal is achieved?

3-5B. (*Using financial ratios*) Brenda Smith, Inc. had a gross profit margin (gross profits ÷ sales) of 25 percent and sales of $9.75 million last year. Seventy-five percent of the firm's sales are on credit and the remainder are cash sales. Smith's current assets equal $1,550,000, its current liabilities equal $300,000, and it has $150,000 in cash plus marketable securities.

a. If Smith's accounts receivable are $562,500, what is its average collection period?

b. If Smith reduces its average collection period to 20 days, what will be its new level of accounts receivable?

c. Smith's inventory turnover ratio is eight times. What is the level of Smith's inventories?

3-6B. (*Ratio analysis*) Using J. B. Chavez Corporation's financial statements:

a. Compute the following ratios for both 2002 and 2003.

	INDUSTRY NORM
Current ratio	5.00
Acid-test (quick) ratio	3.00
Inventory turnover	2.20
Average collection period	90.00
Debt ratio	0.33
Times interest earned	7.00
Total asset turnover	0.75
Fixed asset turnover	1.00
Operating profit margin	20%
Operating income return on investment	15%
Return on common equity	13.43%

b. How liquid is the firm?

c. Is management generating adequate operating profit on the firm's assets?

d. How is the firm financing its assets?

e. Are the common stockholders receiving a good return on their investment?

J. B. Chavez Corporation, Balance Sheet at 12/31/02 and 12/31/03

ASSETS	12/31/02	12/31/03	LIABILITIES AND OWNERS' EQUITY	12/31/02	12/31/03
Cash	$ 225	$ 175	Accounts payable	$ 250	$ 115
Accounts receivable	450	430	Notes payable—current (9%)	0	115
Inventory	575	625	Current liabilities	$ 250	$ 230
Current assets	$1,250	$1,230	Bonds	$ 600	$ 600
Plant and equipment	$2,200	$2,500	Owners' equity		
Less: accumulated depreciation	(1,000)	(1,200)	Common stock	$ 300	$ 300
Net plant and equipment	$1,200	$1,300	Paid-in capital	600	600
Total assets	$2,450	$2,530	Retained earnings	700	800
			Total owners' equity	$1,600	$1,700
			Total liabilities and owners' equity	$2,450	$2,530

J. B. Chavez Corporation, Income Statement for the Years Ending 12/31/02 and 12/31/03

		2002		2003
Sales		$1,250		$1,450
Cost of goods sold		700		875
Gross profit		$ 550		$ 575
Operating expenses	30		45	
Depreciation	220	250	200	245
Net operating income		$ 300		$ 330
Interest expense		50		60
Net income before taxes		$ 250		$ 270
Taxes (40%)		100		108
Net income		$ 150		$ 162

3-7B. (*Financial ratios—investment analysis*) The annual sales for Mel's, Inc. were $5 million last year. The firm's end-of-year balance sheet appeared as follows:

Current assets	$ 500,000	Liabilities	$1,000,000
Net fixed assets	$1,500,000	Owners' equity	$1,000,000
	$2,000,000		$2,000,000

The firm's income statement for the year was as follows:

Sales	$5,000,000
Less: cost of goods sold	3,000,000
Gross profit	$2,000,000
Less: operating expenses	1,500,000
Operating income	$ 500,000
Less: interest expense	100,000
Earnings before taxes	$ 400,000
Less: taxes (40%)	160,000
Net income	$ 240,000

a. Calculate Mel's total asset turnover, operating profit margin, and operating income return on investment.

b. Mel's plans to renovate one of its plants, which will require an added investment in plant and equipment of $1 million. The firm will maintain its present debt ratio of 0.50 when financing the new investment and expects sales to remain constant, whereas the operating profit margin will rise to 13 percent. What will be the new operating income return on investment for Mel's after the plant renovation?

c. Given that the plant renovation in part (b) occurs and Mel's interest expense rises by $40,000 per year, what will be the return earned on the common stockholders' investment? Compare this rate of return with that earned before the renovation.

3-8B. (*Ratio analysis of loan request*) RPI Inc. is a manufacturer and retailer of high-quality sports clothing and gear. The firm was started several years ago by a group of serious outdoors enthusiasts who felt there was a need for a firm that could provide quality products at reasonable prices. The result was RPI Inc. Since its inception, the firm has been profitable, with sales that last year totaled $700,000 and assets in excess of $400,000. The firm now finds its growing sales outstrip its ability to finance its inventory needs and estimates that it will need to borrow $100,000 in a short-term loan from its bank during the coming year.

The firm's most recent financial statements were provided to its bank as support for the firm's loan request. Joanne Peebie, a loan analyst trainee for the Morristown Bank and Trust, has been assigned the task of analyzing the firm's loan request.

RPI Inc., Balance Sheets for 12/31/02 and 12/31/03

ASSETS	2002	2003	LIABILITIES AND STOCKHOLDERS' EQUITY	2002	2003
Cash	$ 16,000	$ 17,000	Accounts payable	$ 48,000	$ 55,000
Marketable securities	7,000	7,200	Notes payable	16,000	13,000
Accounts receivable	42,000	38,000	Accruals	6,000	5,000
Inventory	50,000	93,000	Total current liabilities	$ 70,000	$ 73,000
Prepaid rent	1,200	1,100	Long-term debt	$160,000	$150,000
Total current assets	$116,200	$156,300	Common stockholders' equity	$172,200	$223,300
Net plant and equipment	286,000	290,000	Total liabilities and equity	$402,200	$446,300
Total assets	$402,200	$446,300			

RPI Inc., Income Statement for the Year Ended 12/31/03

Sales (all credit)		$700,000
Less: cost of goods sold		500,000
Gross profits		$200,000
Less: operating and interest expenses		
General and administrative	$50,000	
Interest	10,000	
Depreciation	30,000	
Total		90,000
Profit before taxes		$ 110,000
Less: taxes		27,100
Net income available to common stockholders		$ 82,900
Less: cash dividends		31,800
Change in retained earnings		$ 51,100

a. Calculate RPI's financial ratios corresponding to these industry norms provided for 2003.

	RATIO NORM		RATIO NORM
Current ratio	1.80	Return on total assets	6.0%
Acid-test ratio	0.90	Gross profit margin	25.0%
Debt ratio	0.50	Operating income return on investment	16.8%
Times interest earned	10.00	Operating profit margin	14.0%
Average collection period	20.00	Total asset turnover	1.20
Inventory turnover (based on cost of goods sold)	7.00	Fixed asset turnover	1.80
		Return on equity	12.0%

b. Which of the ratios reported in these industry norms do you feel should be most crucial in determining whether the bank should extend the loan?

c. Use the DuPont analysis to evaluate the firm's financial position as of December 31, 2003.

3-9B. (*Ratio analysis*) Reynolds Computer's income statement for 2003 and the balance sheet for December 31, 2003 follow.

Compute the financial ratios for Reynolds Computer for 2003, and using your industry norms, evaluate the firm in the following areas:

(1) liquidity
(2) operating profitability
(3) financing policies
(4) return on the shareholders' investment

Reynolds Computer Income Statement for Year Ending 2003

	2003
Sales	$25,265,000
Cost of goods sold	19,891,000
Gross profit	$ 5,374,000
Selling, general, and administrative expense	2,761,000
Depreciation	156,000
Operating profit	$ 2,457,000
Interest expense	34,000
Nonoperating income (expense)	26,000
Pretax income	$ 2,449,000
Total income taxes	785,000
Net income	$ 1,664,000

Reynolds Computer Balance Sheet for December 31, 2003 ($ in thousands)

	2003
ASSETS	
Cash and equivalents	$ 4,132,000
Accounts receivable	2,678,000
Inventories	391,000
Other current assets	480,000
Total current assets	$ 7,681,000
Gross plant, property, and equipment	1,059,000
Accumulated depreciation	294,000
Net plant, property, and equipment	$ 765,000
Other investments	2,721,000
Intangibles	304,000
Other assets	–
Total assets	$11,471,000
LIABILITIES	
Accounts payable	$ 3,538,000
Accrued expenses	337,000
Other current liabilities	1,317,000
Total current liabilities	$ 5,192,000
Long-term debt	508,000
Other liabilities	463,000
Total liabilities	$ 6,163,000
EQUITY	
Common stock	$ 25,750
Capital surplus	3,557,250
Retained earnings	1,725,000
Total equity	$ 5,308,000
Total liabilities and equity	$11,471,000

INDUSTRY NORMS	
FIRM LIQUIDITY	
Current ratio	1.49
Acid-test ratio	1.36
Average collection period	53.38
Accounts receivable turnover	6.84
Inventory turnover	20.87
OPERATING PROFITABILITY	
Operating income return on investment	9%
Operating profit margin	6%
Total asset turnover	1.58
Accounts receivable turnover	6.84

Inventory turnover	20.87
Fixed asset turnover	13.02
FINANCING DECISIONS	
Debt ratio	0.47
Times interest earned	14.79
RETURN ON EQUITY	
Return on equity	13%

SELF-TEST SOLUTIONS

ST-1. Note that Ray's current inventory expansion is as follows:

current ratio = \$6,000,000/current liabilities = 4

Thus, the firm's level of current liabilities is \$1,500,000. If the expansion in inventories is financed entirely with borrowed funds, then the change in inventories is equal to the change in current liabilities, and the firm's current ratio after the expansion can be defined as follows:

$$\text{current ratio} = \frac{\$6{,}000{,}000 + \text{change in inventory}}{\$1{,}500{,}000 + \text{change in inventory}} = 3$$

Note that we set the new current ratio equal to the firm's target of 3. Solving for the change in inventory in the previous equation, we determine that the firm can expand its inventories by \$750,000, finance the expansion with current liabilities, and still maintain its target current ratio.

ST-2. a.

Neff Industries, Ratio Analysis

	INDUSTRY AVERAGES	ACTUAL 2002	ACTUAL 2003
Current ratio	1.80	1.84	0.90
Acid-test ratio	0.70	0.78	0.24
Average collection periods (based on a 365-day year and end-of-year figures)	37.00	36.50	36.50
Inventory turnover	2.50	2.59	2.11
Debt ratio	58%	50%	61.3%
Times interest earned	3.80	4.00	2.79
Gross profit margin	38%	40%	40%
Operating profit margin	10%	9.6%	10.6%
Total asset turnover	1.14	1.11	1.07
Fixed asset turnover	1.40	2.02	1.82
Operating income return on investment	11.4%	10.7%	11.3%
Return on common equity	9.5%	8.0%	9.4%
Return on total assets	4.0%	4.0%	3.6%

b. Neff's liquidity in 2003 is poor, as suggested by the low current ratio and acid-test ratio: also, inventories are turning slowly. In 2003, management is doing a satisfactory job at generating profits on the firm's operating assets, as indicated by the operating income return on investment. Note that the operating income return on investment in 2003 is average, owing to a slightly above-average operating profit margin combined with a slightly below-average asset turnover. The problem with the asset turnover ratio comes from a slow inventory turnover.

Neff has increased its use of debt to the point of using slightly more debt than the average company in the industry. As a result, the firm's coverage of interest has decreased to a point well below the industry norm.

As of 2003, Neff's return on equity is average because the operating income return on investment and the debt ratio are average.

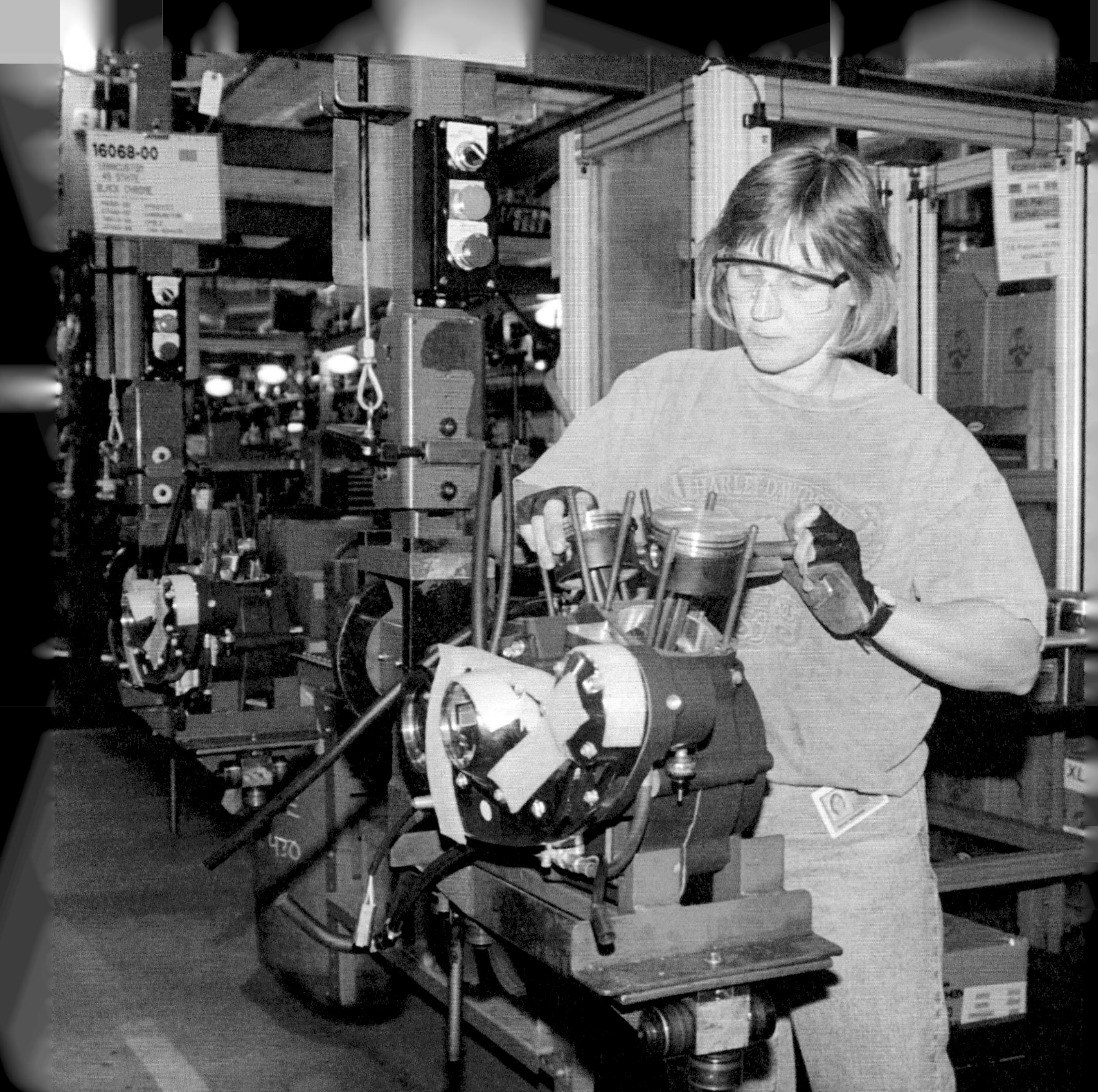

LEARNING OBJECTIVES

After reading this chapter, you should be able to

1. Use the percent of sales method to forecast the financing requirements of a firm.
2. Describe the limitations of the percent of sales forecast method.
3. Calculate a firm's sustainable rate of growth.
4. Prepare a cash budget and use it to evaluate the amount and timing of a firm's financing needs.

CHAPTER 4

Financial Forecasting, Planning, and Budgeting

Forecasting is an integral part of the planning process, yet there are countless examples where our ability to predict the future has been simply awful. During the mid-1980s oil prices were roughly $30 a barrel, and many firms were developing new reserves that would cost well over this amount to produce. Why? Oil prices were projected to continue to rise and many thought the price might eventually reach $50 a barrel by the end of the decade. Then in January 1986, the collapse of the oil producer's cartel, in combination with the benefits of energy conservation efforts, produced a dramatic drop in oil prices to below $10 a barrel.

If forecasting the future is so difficult, and plans are built on forecasts, why do firms engage in planning efforts? The answer, oddly enough, does not lie in the accuracy of the firm's projections, for planning offers its greatest value when the future is the most uncertain. The reason is that planning is the process of thinking about what the future might bring and devising strategies for dealing with the likely outcomes. Planning is thinking in advance, and thinking in advance provides an opportunity to devise contingency plans that can be quickly and easily initiated should the need arise. This increased speed of response to uncertain events means that the firm can reduce the costs of responding to adverse circumstances and quickly respond to take advantage of unexpected opportunities.

Financial managers spend a significant portion of their time planning for their firm's uncertain future. Financial planning entails collecting sales forecasts from marketing personnel and production plans from operations, and then combining them to make projections of the firm's future financing requirements. In this chapter, we will see that the financial plan takes the form of a set of pro forma or planned financial statements and a cash budget. These statements provide a benchmark to which day-to-day actual results can be compared. If actual performance results begin to deviate from the plan, then this provides the financial manager with an early warning signal that her financing plans may be inadequate and appropriate actions can be taken: for example, contacting the firm's banker to request an increase in the firm's prearranged credit line.

CHAPTER PREVIEW

Chapter 4 has two primary objectives: First, we develop an appreciation for the financial manager's role in financial forecasting. Firms go through an annual planning and budgeting exercise in which the financial manager is asked to bring together revenue forecasts from marketing and production plans from operations to develop a forecast of the firm's cash flow. This cash flow forecast then becomes the basis for estimating the firm's financing requirements. Second, we review the pro forma (planned) income statement, the pro forma balance sheet, and the cash budget. These statements constitute the principal elements of the firm's financial forecast and serve as a benchmark against which future performance can be compared.

This chapter emphasizes **Principle 3: Cash—Not Profits—Is King,** and **Principle 7: The Agency Problem—Managers won't work for owners unless it's in their best interest.** Firms pay bills and dividends with cash and investors make mortgage payments using cash, not profits. In addition, financial planning entails the construction of detailed budgets that can be used as an oversight tool for monitoring the activities of the firm's employees.

BACK TO THE PRINCIPLES

Financial decisions are made today in light of our expectations of an uncertain future. Financial forecasting involves making estimates of the future financing requirements of the firm. ***Principle 3: Cash—Not Profits—Is King*** *speaks directly to this problem. Remember that effective financial management requires that consideration be given to cash flow and when it is received or dispersed.*

Objective 1

FINANCIAL FORECASTING

Forecasting in financial management is used to estimate a firm's future financial needs. If the financial manager has not attempted to anticipate his firm's future financing requirements, then a crisis occurs every time the firm's cash inflows fall below its cash outflows. Proper planning means anticipating and preparing for those times in every firm's future when it will need to obtain additional financing and also when the firm will have excess cash. For example, the financing requirements of growth firms frequently outstrip the firm's ability to generate cash. Planning for growth means that the financial manager can anticipate the firm's financing requirements and plan for them well in advance of the need. Advance planning means the financial manager can explore more alternatives and obtain the most favorable set of financing terms available.

The basic steps involved in predicting those financing needs are the following: **Step 1:** Project the firm's sales revenues and expenses over the planning period. **Step 2:** Estimate the levels of investment in current and fixed assets that are necessary to support the projected sales. **Step 3:** Determine the firm's financing needs throughout the planning period.

SALES FORECAST

The key ingredient in the firm's planning process is the *sales forecast.* This projection is generally derived using information from a number of sources. At a minimum, the sales forecast for the coming year would reflect (1) any past trends in sales that are expected to carry through into the new year, and (2) the influence of any events that might materially affect those trends.[1] An example of the latter would be the initiation of a major advertising campaign or a change in the firm's pricing policy.

FORECASTING FINANCIAL VARIABLES

Traditional financial forecasting takes the sales forecast as a given and makes projections of its impact on the firm's various expenses, assets, and liabilities. The amount of financing—as we will see—can vary greatly if sales grow by 1 percent versus 5 percent or 10 percent. The amount of the variation depends on the interplay of the key variables that determine the firm's financing requirements.

PERCENT OF SALES METHOD OF FINANCIAL FORECASTING

Percent of sales method Estimating the level of an expense, asset, or liability for a future period as a percent of the sales forecast.

The most commonly used method for making these projections is the percent of sales method. The **percent of sales method** involves estimating the level of an expense, asset, or liability for a future period as a percent of the sales forecast. The percentage used can

[1] A complete discussion of forecast methodologies is outside the scope of this book. The interested reader will find the following references helpful: F. Gerard Adams, *The Business Forecasting Revolution* (Oxford: Oxford University Press, 1986); C. W. J. Granger, *Forecasting in Business and Economics,* 2d ed. (Boston: Academic Press, 1989); and Paul Newbold and Theodore Bos, *Introductory Business Forecasting* (Cincinnati: Southwestern, 1990).

come from the most recent financial statement as a percent of current sales, from an average computed over several years, from the judgment of the analyst, or from some combination of these sources.

Table 4-1 presents a complete example of the use of the percent of sales method of financial forecasting. In this example, each item in the firm's balance sheet that varies with sales is converted to a percentage of 2003 sales of $10 million. The forecast of the new balance for each item is then calculated by multiplying this percentage times the $12 million in projected sales for the 2004 planning period. This method of forecasting future financing is not as precise or detailed as the method using a cash budget, which is presented later; however, it offers a relatively low-cost and easy-to-use first approximation of the firm's financing needs for a future period.

Note that in the example in Table 4-1, both current and fixed assets are assumed to vary with the level of firm sales. This means that the firm does not have sufficient productive capacity to absorb a projected increase in sales. Thus, if sales were to rise by $1, fixed assets would rise by 40 cents, or 40 percent of the projected increase in sales. Note that if the fixed assets the firm currently owns were sufficient to support the projected level of new sales (such as when the firm has excess capacity), these assets should not be allowed to vary with sales. If this were the case, then fixed assets would not be converted to a percent of sales and would be projected to remain unchanged for the period being forecast.

Also, we note that accounts payable and accrued expenses are the only liabilities allowed to vary with sales. Both of these accounts might reasonably be expected to rise and fall with the level of firm sales; hence the use of the percent of sales forecast.

TABLE 4-1 Using the Percent of Sales Method to Forecast Future Financing Requirements

ASSETS	PRESENT (2003)	PERCENT OF SALES (2003 SALES = $10M)	PROJECTED (BASED ON 2004 SALES = $12M)	
Current assets	$2.0M	$\frac{\$2M}{\$10M} = 20\%$		.2 × $12M = $2.4M
Net fixed assets	$4.0M	$\frac{\$4M}{\$10M} = 40\%$		.4 × $12M = $4.8M
Total	$6.0M			$7.2M
LIABILITIES AND OWNERS' EQUITY				
Accounts payable	$1.0M	$\frac{\$1M}{\$10M} = 10\%$		.10 × $12M = $1.2M
Accrued expenses	1.0M	$\frac{\$1M}{\$10M} = 10\%$		.10 × $12M = $1.2M
Notes payable	.5M	NA[a]	no change	.5M
Long-term debt	$2.0M	NA[a]	no change	2.0M
Total liabilities	$4.5M			$4.9M
Common stock	$ .1M	NA[a]	no change	$ .1M
Paid-in capital	.2M	NA[a]	no change	.2M
Retained earnings	1.2M		$1.2M + [.05 × $12M × (1 − .5)] =	1.5M[b]
Common equity	$1.5M			$1.8M
Total	$6.0M		Total financing provided	$6.7M
			Discretionary financing needed	.5M[c]
			Total	$7.2M

[a]Not applicable. These account balances are assumed not to vary with sales.

[b]Projected retained earnings equals the beginning level ($1.2M) plus projected net income less any dividends paid. In this case, net income is projected to equal 5 percent of sales, and dividends are projected to equal half of net income: .05 × $12M × (1 − .5) = $300,000.

[c]Discretionary financing needed equals projected total assets ($7.2M) less projected total liabilities ($4.9M) less projected common equity ($1.8), or $7.2M × 4.9M − 1.8M = $500,000.

FINANCE MATTERS

ALCOA IMPLEMENTS REAL TIME MANUFACTURING SYSTEM TO REPLACE FORECASTS

In 1998, Alcoa announced it would reduce manufacturing costs by \$1.1 billion by the end of 2000. By mid-2000, the firm had realized savings of \$832 million. The key to its success has been implementation of the Alcoa Business System, an adaptation of Toyota's production methods that focus on managing the business in real time.

Managing in real time requires accurate, real time information in order for the firm to produce material for an actual demand rather than to forecasts. It also means the use of lots of other modern manufacturing techniques like just-in-time inventory control, small-batch production, flexible production lines, quick machine tool changes, and minimal waste of materials. This all sounds great, but how do you make it work? The key to Alcoa's success has been moving production decisions to the workers. A worker who has a problem with equipment or product defect summons a leader who is charged with fixing the problem on the spot. The manufacturing process is a "pull" system in which workers in upstream processes respond to demand requests from workers downstream. Workers often negotiate with coworkers to buy and sell their inputs and outputs with others in the process.

Results of the change in the manufacturing process have increased inventory turns in Brazil to 60 times per year, and in Mississippi, the customer delivery time has been reduced from three weeks to just two days. At its Massena, New York, plant, the speed of production increased fourfold while work-in-process inventories were reduced by 85 percent. Companywide, Alcoa was able to reduce inventories by more than \$250 million while increasing sales to just under \$1 billion.

Furthermore, Alcoa believes it can multiply these savings when suppliers and customers are integrated into the system. Integrating supplier and customer systems requires trust and impeccable reliability from all parties. By focusing on reducing costs and improving responsiveness, Alcoa will continue to revolutionize its manufacturing process and be a leader in the aluminum industry.

Source: Adapted from Thomas A. Stewart, "How Cisco and Alcoa Make Real Time Work," *Fortune*, May 29, 2000.

Spontaneous sources of financing Sources of financing that arise naturally during the course of business. Accounts payable is a primary example.

Discretionary financing Sources of financing that require an explicit decision on the part of the firm's management every time funds are raised.

Because these two categories of current liabilities normally vary directly with the level of sales, they are often referred to as **spontaneous sources of financing**. Chapter 18, which discusses working-capital management, has more to say about these forms of financing. Notes payable, long-term debt, common stock, and paid-in capital are not assumed to vary directly with the level of firm sales. These sources of financing are termed **discretionary financing**, in that the firm's management must make a conscious decision to seek additional financing using any one of them. An example of discretionary financing is a bank note that requires that negotiations be undertaken and an agreement signed setting forth the terms and conditions for the financing. Finally, we note that the level of retained earnings does vary with estimated sales. The predicted change in the level of retained earnings equals the estimated after-tax profits (projected net income) equal to 5 percent of sales, or \$600,000 less the common stock dividends of \$300,000.

Thus using the example from Table 4-1, we estimate that firm sales will increase from \$10 million to \$12 million, which will cause the firm's needs for total assets to rise to \$7.2 million. These assets will then be financed by \$4.9 million in existing liabilities plus spontaneous liabilities; \$1.8 million in owner funds, including \$300,000 in retained earnings from next year's sales; and finally, \$500,000 in discretionary financing, which can be raised by issuing notes payable, selling bonds, offering an issue of stock, or some combination of these sources. By far the most frequently used source of discretionary financing is a bank loan. As we will learn later when we study financial policy, if the need for financing persists, then the firm may later issue bonds or stock to retire the bank loan. See the Finance Matters box, "Alcoa Implements Real Time Manufacturing System to Replace Forecasts."

In summary, we can estimate the firm's needs for discretionary financing, using the percent of sales method of financial forecasting, by following a four-step procedure:

Step 1. Convert each asset and liability account that varies directly with firm sales to a percent of the current year's sales, for example:

$$\frac{\text{current assets}}{\text{sales}} = \frac{\$2M}{\$10M} = .2 \text{ or } 20\%$$

Step 2. Project the level of each asset and liability account in the balance sheet using its percent of sales multiplied by projected sales or by leaving the account balance unchanged where the account does not vary with the level of sales, for example:

projected current assets =

$$\text{projected sales} \times \frac{\text{current assets}}{\text{sales}} = \$12M \times .2 = \$2.4M$$

Step 3. Project the addition to retained earnings available to help finance the firm's operations. This equals projected net income for the period less planned common stock dividends, for example:

projected addition to retained earnings =

$$\text{projected sales} \times \frac{\text{net income}}{\text{sales}} \times \left(1 - \frac{\text{cash dividends}}{\text{net income}}\right)$$

$$= \$12M \times .05 \times [1 - .5] = \$300{,}000$$

Step 4. Project the firm's need for discretionary financing as the projected level of total assets less projected liabilities and owners' equity, for example:

discretionary financing needed=

projected total assets – projected total liabilities – projected owners' equity

$= \$7.2M - \$4.9M - \$1.8M - \$500{,}000$

The Discretionary Financing Needed (DFN) Model

In the preceding discussion, we estimated *DFN* (discretionary financing needed) as the difference in projected total assets and the sum of projected liabilities and owners' equity. We can estimate the projected discretionary financing needs, DFN_{t+1}, directly using the predicted change in sales and corresponding changes in assets, liabilities, and owners' equity as follows:

$$DFN_{t+1} = \begin{matrix}\text{projected}\\ \text{change in}\\ \text{assets}_{t+1}\end{matrix} - \begin{matrix}\text{projected}\\ \text{change in}\\ \text{liabilities}_{t+1}\end{matrix} - \begin{matrix}\text{projected}\\ \text{change in}\\ \text{owners' equity}_{t+1}\end{matrix} \qquad \textbf{(4-1)}$$

To calculate DFN_{t+1} we must estimate each of the components found in equation 4-1. For example, we can project the firm's need for assets using the relationship between assets and sales for the current year multiplied by the projected change in sales for the coming year:

$$\begin{matrix}\text{projected}\\ \text{change in}\\ \text{assets}_{t+1}\end{matrix} = \left[\frac{\text{assets}_t}{\text{sales}_t}\right] \times [\text{sales}_{t+1} - \text{sales}_t]$$

Similarly, the projected change in liabilities can be calculated as the product of the ratio of total firm liabilities to sales for the current year and the projected change in firm sales:

$$\text{projected change in liabilities}_{t+1} = \left[\frac{\text{liabilities}_t}{\text{sales}_t}\right] \times [\text{sales}_{t+1} - \text{sales}_t]$$

We can project the anticipated change in the firm's common equity for the coming year by first estimating net income for the coming year as the product of the net profit margin for the coming year, NPM_{t+1}, and the projected level of firm sales, and then multiplying projected net income by the percent of net income that is retained and not paid out in dividends. Note that b is the percent of firm net income paid in dividends such that $(1 - b)$ is the fraction of net income that is retained. How are we to estimate NPM_{t+1}? One approach that can be used is to simply use the net profit margin for the current period, NPM_t. However, if sales are expected to change, then the firm's net profit margin will probably change as well, so using NPM_t is only a rough approximation.

$$\text{projected change in owner's equity}_{t+1} = [NPM_{t+1} \times \text{sales}_{t+1}] \times (1 - b)$$

Now let's define the terms we have been using with some care:

- *assets*$_t$ = those assets in period t that are expected to change in proportion to the level of sales
- *sales*$_t$ = the level of sales for the period t
- *liabilities*$_t$ = the liabilities in period t that are expected to change in proportion to the level of sales
- NPM_{t+1} = net profit margin projected for period $t + 1$
- b = dividend payout ratio or dividends as a percent of net income; the fraction of the firm's net income that it plans to retain, therefore, is $(1 - b)$

In the preceding example, we assumed that all of the firm's assets, accounts payable, and accrued expenses vary in proportion to sales. Notes payable and long-term debt did not change from the current to projected year. Using the numbers from our example, we estimate DFN_{2001} as follows:

$$\text{projected change in assets}_{2001} = \left[\frac{\$2M + 4M}{10M}\right] \times [\$12M - 10M] = \$1.2M$$

$$\text{projected change in liabilities}_{2001} = \left[\frac{\$1M + 1M}{\$10M}\right] \times [\$12M - 10M] = \$.4M$$

$$\text{projected change in owners' equity}_{2001} = [.05 \times \$12M] \times (1 - .5) = \$.3M$$

$$DFN_{2001} = \$1.2M - .4M - .3M = \$.5M \text{ or } \$500{,}000$$

Analyzing the Effects of Profitability and Dividend Policy on DFN

Using the *DFN* model, we can quickly and easily evaluate the sensitivity of our projected financing requirements to changes in key variables. For example, using the information from the preceding example, we evaluate the effect of net profit margins (*NPM*) equal to

1 percent, 5 percent, and 10 percent in combination with dividend payout ratios of 30 percent, 50 percent, and 70 percent as follows:

Discretionary Financing Needed for Various Net Profit Margins and Dividend Payout Ratios

NET PROFIT MARGIN	DIVIDEND PAYOUT RATIOS (DIVIDENDS ÷ NET INCOME)		
	30%	50%	70%
1%	$716,000	$740,000	$764,000
5%	380,000	500,000	620,000
10%	(40,000)	200,000	440,000

Let's first consider the dividend payout ratio. The higher the dividend payout percentage (b), the lower the retention percentage ($1 - b$). Thus, as we just saw earlier when discussing the *DFN* model, this means that the firm will have less to reinvest and will need more discretionary financing. Consider the row corresponding to a 5 percent net profit margin. If the firm pays out 30 percent of its earnings in dividends (retains 70 percent), then its need for discretionary financing is estimated to be $380,000, whereas a 70 percent dividend payout ratio requires $620,000 in discretionary financing. Later, in Chapter 17, we will learn that firms tend to have dividend policies that are similar to other firms in their industry. For example, firms in high-growth industries pay out a very small fraction of their earnings in dividends. Thus, a firm's discretionary financing needs are in part a function of its growth prospects and industry practice with respect to the payment of dividends.

Discretionary financing needs are also a function of the firm's profitability. The higher the net profit margin is, all things being the same, the lower the firm's need for discretionary financing will be. For example, with a 1 percent net profit margin and 30 percent dividend payout ratio, the firm will require $716,000 in discretionary financing. If the net profit margin were 10 percent with the same payout ratio, the firm would have surplus funds of $40,000. Thus, a firm's discretionary financing needs swing from year to year with the firm's profitability, which is, to a large degree, due to economy-wide and industry influences, and are outside the control of the firm's management. Financial planning is particularly crucial for firms subject to wide variability in their year-to-year profitability.

CONCEPT CHECK

1. If we cannot predict the future perfectly, then why do firms engage in financial forecasting?
2. Why are sales forecasts so important to developing a firm's financial forecast?
3. What is the percent of sales method of financial forecasting?
4. What are some examples of spontaneous and discretionary sources of financing?

Objective 2

LIMITATIONS OF THE PERCENT OF SALES FORECAST METHOD

The percent of sales method of financial forecasting provides reasonable estimates of a firm's financing requirements only where asset requirements and financing sources can be accurately forecast as a constant percent of sales. For example, predicting inventories using the percent of sales method involves the following predictive equation:

$$\text{inventories}_{t+1} = \frac{\text{inventories}_t}{\text{sales}_t} \times \text{sales}_{t+1}$$

FIGURE 4-1 The Relationship Between Inventories and Sales

a. Percent of Sales Forecast

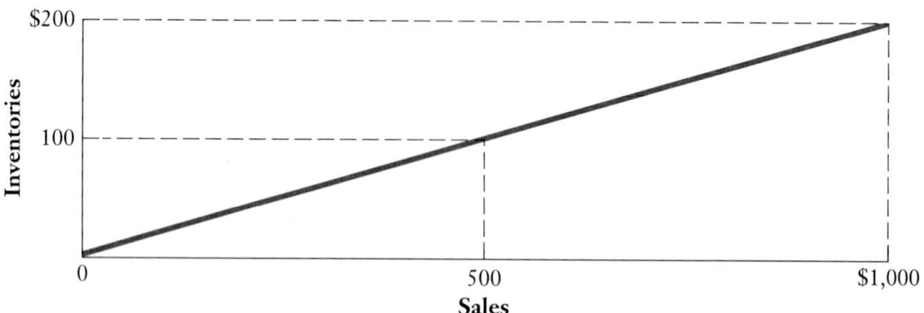

b. Economies of Scale

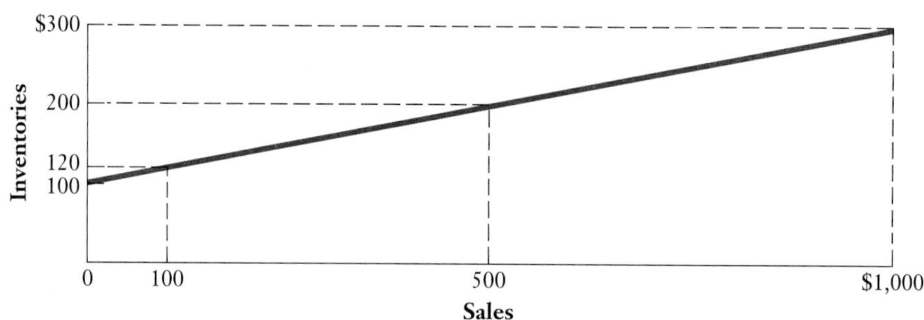

c. Economies of Scale and Lumpy Investments

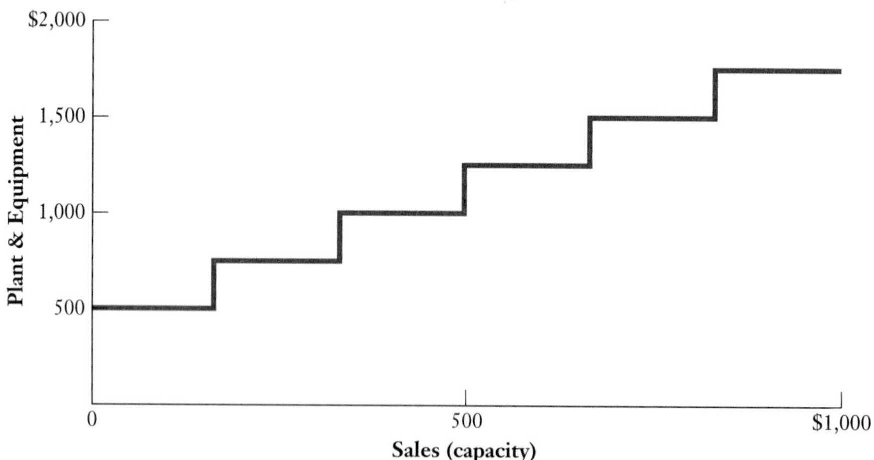

Figure 4-1a depicts this predictive relationship. Note that the percent of sales predictive model is simply a straight line that passes through the origin (that is, has a zero intercept). Thus, the percent of sales model is appropriate where there is no level of inventories that remains constant regardless of the level of firm sales, and inventories rise and fall in direct proportion to changes in the level of sales.

There are some fairly common instances in which this type of relationship fails to describe the relationship between an asset category and sales. Two such examples involve assets for which there are scale economics and assets that must be purchased in discrete quantities ("lumpy assets").

Economies of scale are sometimes realized from investing in certain types of assets such as finished goods inventories. For example, a retail drugstore requires a full range of drug products in order to operate. This inventory can be replenished on a daily basis in response to firm sales. However, a constant level of investment is necessary to open the doors of the enterprise. This means that these assets do not increase in direct proportion to sales. Figure 4-1b reflects one instance in which the firm realizes economies of scale from its investment in inventory. Note that inventories as a percent of sales decline from 120 percent where sales are \$100, to 30 percent where sales equal \$1,000. This reflects the fact that there is a fixed component of inventories (in this case \$100) that the firm must have on hand regardless of the level of sales, plus a variable component (20 percent of sales). In this instance, the predictive equation for inventories is as follows:

$$\text{inventories}_t = a + b \text{ sales}_t$$

In this example, the intercept "a" of the above equation is equal to 100 and the slope "b" equals .20.

Figure 4-1c is an example of *lumpy assets*—that is, assets that must be purchased in large, nondivisible components such as plant and equipment. For example, firms in the semiconductor industry now invest approximately \$2 billion in each new wafer fab (factory) they build. They then spend the next two to three years filling the fab's productive capacity with production. Consequently, when a block of assets is purchased, it creates excess capacity until sales grow to the point where the capacity is fully used. The result is a step function such as the one depicted in Figure 4-1c. Thus, if the firm does not expect sales to exceed the current capacity of its plant and equipment, there would be no projected need for added plant and equipment capacity.

CONCEPT CHECK

1. What, in words, is the fundamental relationship (equation) used in making percent of sales forecasts?
2. Under what circumstances does a firm violate the basic relationship underlying the percent of sales forecast method?

THE SUSTAINABLE RATE OF GROWTH

Objective 3

Growing firms require expenditures for new assets that outstrip the firm's ability to finance those purchases using internally generated profits. This means that the firm must go out and borrow the additional funds or issue new equity. Because selling new shares of stock is a very involved and expensive endeavor, the question arises as to how fast a firm can grow without having to borrow more than the firm's desired debt ratio and without having to sell more stock. This growth rate is referred to as the sustainable

Sustainable rate of growth The maximum rate of growth in sales that the firm can sustain while maintaining its present capital structure (debt and equity mix) and without having to sell new common stock.

rate of growth. Specifically, the **sustainable rate of growth** (g^*) represents the rate at which a firm's sales can grow if it wants to maintain its present financial ratios and does not want to resort to the sale of new equity shares.[2] A simple formula can be derived for g^* where we assume that a firm's assets and liabilities all grow at the same rate as its sales; that is,

$$\text{sustainable rate of growth } (g^*) = ROE(1 - b) \quad \textbf{(4-2)}$$

ROE is the firm's return on equity, which was defined in Chapter 3 as follows:

$$ROE = \frac{\text{net income}}{\text{common equity}}$$

Plowback ratio The percent of a firm's earnings that are reinvested in the firm.

and b is the firm's dividend payout ratio, that is, $\frac{\text{dividends}}{\text{net income}}$. The term $(1 - b)$ is sometimes referred to as the **plowback ratio** because it indicates the fraction of earnings that are reinvested or plowed back into the firm. Thus, $g^* = ROE \times \text{plowback ratio}$. Thus, if a firm pays 40 percent of its earnings out in dividends, it is also reinvesting 60 percent.

Equation (4-2) is deceptively simple. Recall that ROE can also be written as follows:

$$ROE = \left(\frac{\text{net income}}{\text{sales}}\right) \times \left(\frac{\text{sales}}{\text{assets}}\right) \times \left(\frac{\text{assets}}{\text{common equity}}\right)$$

Consequently, a firm's sustainable rate of growth is determined by its ROE (i.e., its anticipated net profit margin, asset turnover, and capital structure), as well as its dividend policy.

EXAMPLE: CALCULATING THE SUSTAINABLE RATE OF GROWTH

Consider the following three firms:

FIRM	NET PROFIT MARGIN	ASSET TURNOVER	LEVERAGE (ASSETS/EQUITY)	PLOWBACK RATIO	g^*
A	15%	1	1.2	50%	9.0%
B	15%	1	1.2	100%	18.0%
C	15%	1	1.5	100%	22.5%

Comparing Firms A and B above, we see that the only difference is that Firm A pays out half its earnings in common dividends (i.e., plows back half its earnings) whereas Firm B retains or plows back all of its earnings. The net result is that Firm B, with its added source of internal equity financing, can grow at twice the rate of Firm A (18 percent compared to only 9 percent). Similarly, comparing Firms B and C, we note that they differ only in that Firm B finances only 83 percent of its assets with equity (i.e., $1 \div 1.2 = .83$) whereas Firm C finances 67 percent ($1 \div 1.5 = .67$) of its assets with equity. The result is that Firm C's sustainable rate of growth is 22.5 percent since it needs \$0.67 per \$1.00 of assets financed from equity versus \$0.83 in equity financing for firm B. This compares to only 18 percent for Firm B.

Before leaving our discussion of the sustainable rate of growth concept, it is important that we stress the underlying assumptions behind equation 4-2. For this equation to accurately depict a firm's sustainable rate of growth, the following assumptions must

[2] For an extensive discussion of this concept, see Robert C. Higgins, "Sustainable Growth with Inflation," *Financial Management* (Autumn 1981): 36–40.

hold: First, the firm's assets must vary as a constant percent of sales (i.e., even fixed assets expand and contract directly with the level of firm sales). Second, the firm's liabilities must all vary directly with firm sales. This means that the firm's management will expand its borrowing (both spontaneous and discretionary) in direct proportion with sales to maintain its present ratio of debt to assets. Finally, the firm pays out a constant proportion of its earnings in common stock dividends regardless of the level of firm sales. Since all three of these assumptions are only rough approximations to the way that firms actually behave, equation 4-2 provides a crude approximation of the firm's actual sustainable rate of growth. However, an estimate of g^* using equation 4-2 can be a very useful first step in the firm's financial planning process.

CONCEPT CHECK

1. What is a firm's sustainable rate of growth?
2. How is a firm's sustainable rate of growth related to the firm's profitability and dividend policy?

FINANCIAL PLANNING AND BUDGETING

Objective 4

As we noted earlier, the primary virtue of the percent of sales method of financial forecasting is its simplicity. To obtain a more precise estimate of the amount and timing of a firm's future financing requirements requires that a cash budget be prepared. The percent of sales method of financial forecasting provides a very useful, low-cost forerunner to the development of the more detailed cash budget, which the firm will ultimately use to estimate its financing needs.

BACK TO THE PRINCIPLES

Elaborate cash budgets are needed so that firms can avoid a cash crisis when anticipated cash inflows fall below cash outflows. This is a direct reflection of ***Principle 3: Cash—Not Profits—Is King.*** *It is cash flow and not accounting profits that pay the firm's bills. In addition, budgets are the critical tool of managerial control.* ***Principle 7: The Agency Problem—Managers won't work for owners unless it's in their best interest*** *speaks to the root source of the problem, and budgets provide one tool for attempting to deal with it. Specifically, budgets provide management with a tool for evaluating performance and consequently maintaining a degree of control over employee actions.*

BUDGET FUNCTIONS

A *budget* is simply a forecast of future events. For example, students preparing for final exams make use of time budgets, which help them allocate their limited preparation time among their courses. Students also must budget their financial resources among competing uses, such as books, tuition, food, rent, clothes, and extracurricular activities.

Budgets perform three basic functions for a firm. First, they indicate the amount and timing of the firm's needs for future financing. Second, they provide the basis for taking corrective action in the event budgeted figures do not match actual or realized figures. Third, budgets provide the basis for performance evaluation. Plans are carried out by people, and budgets provide benchmarks that management can use to evaluate the performance of those responsible for carrying out those plans and, in turn, to control their actions. Thus, budgets are valuable aids in both the planning and controlling aspects of the firm's financial management.

THE CASH BUDGET

Cash budget
A detailed plan of future cash receipts and disbursements.

The **cash budget** represents a detailed plan of future cash flows and is composed of four elements: cash receipts, cash disbursements, net change in cash for the period, and new financing needed.

To demonstrate the construction and use of the cash budget, consider Salco Furniture Company, Inc., a regional distributor of household furniture. Management is in the process of preparing a monthly cash budget for the upcoming period (January through April 2004). Salco's sales are highly seasonal, peaking in the months of February and March. The following information is used to prepare a cash budget:

- Roughly 30 percent of Salco's sales are collected one month after the sale and the balance (70 percent) is collected two months after the sale.
- Salco attempts to pace its purchases with its forecast of future sales. Purchases generally equal 60 percent of sales and are made one month in advance of anticipated sales. Payments are made in the month following the purchase. For example, January sales are estimated at $60,000; thus, December purchases are $36,000 (.60 × $60,000) and are paid in January.
- Wages, salaries, rent, and other cash expenses are recorded in Table 4-2, which gives Salco's cash budget for the four-month period ended in April 2004.
- Additional expenditures are recorded in the cash budget related to the purchase of equipment in the amount of $10,000 in January and the repayment of an $8,000 loan in March.
- In January, Salco will pay $4,000 in interest on its long-term debt. This interest expense corresponds to the period of January through March.
- Interest on the $8,000 short-term note for the period January through March equals $200 and is paid in March.
- A tax payment of $5,200 is made in March.
- Salco currently has a cash balance of $10,000 and maintains a minimum balance of $10,000 to meet any unanticipated shortfall in net cash flow.
- Additional borrowing necessary to maintain that minimum balance is estimated in the final section of Table 4-2. Borrowing takes place at the beginning of the month in which the funds are needed. Interest on borrowed funds equals 12 percent per annum, or 1 percent per month, and is paid in the month following the month in which funds are borrowed. Thus, interest on funds borrowed in February will be paid in March equal to 1 percent of the loan amount outstanding in February.
- The financing needed in Salco's cash budget indicates that the firm's cumulative short-term borrowing will be $3,100 at the end of February and $11,731 in March. In April, the firm will be able to repay all short-term debt incurred in February and March. Note that the cash budget indicates not only the amount of financing needed during the period but also when the funds will be needed.

BUDGET PERIOD

There are no strict rules for determining the length of the budget period. However, as a general rule, it should be long enough to show the effect of management policies, yet short enough so that estimates can be made with reasonable accuracy. Applying this rule of thumb to the Salco example in Table 4-2, it appears that the four-month budget period is too short. The reason is that we cannot tell whether the planned operations of

TABLE 4-2 Salco Furniture Co., Inc., Cash Budget for the Four Months Ended April 30, 2004

WORKSHEET	NOVEMBER	DECEMBER	JANUARY	FEBRUARY	MARCH	APRIL
Sales	$62,000	$50,000	$60,000	$80,000	$85,000	$70,000
Collections:						
First month (30%)		$18,600	$15,000	$18,000	$24,000	$25,500
Second month (70%)		$38,500	$43,400	$35,000	$42,000	$56,000
Total collections		$57,100	$58,400	$53,000	$66,000	$81,500
Purchases (60% of next month's sales)	$30,000	$36,000	$48,000	$51,000	$42,000	$39,000
Payments (one-month lag)		$30,000	$36,000	$48,000	$51,000	$42,000
CASH BUDGET						
Cash receipts						
Collections (see above)		$57,100	$58,400	$53,000	$66,000	$81,500
CASH DISBURSEMENTS						
Purchases		$30,000	$36,000	$48,000	$51,000	$42,000
Wages and salaries			4,000	5,000	6,000	4,000
Rent			3,000	3,000	3,000	3,000
Other expenses			1,000	500	1,200	1,500
Interest expense on existing debt			4,000		200	
Taxes					5,200	
Purchases of equipment			10,000			
Loan repayment					8,000	
Total disbursements			$58,000	$56,500	$74,600	$50,500
Net monthly change			$400	$(3,500)	$(8,600)	$31,000
Plus: beginning cash balance			10,000	10,400	10,000	10,000
Less: interest on short-term borrowing			0	0	31	117
Equals: ending cash balance before short-term borrowing			10,400	6,900	1,369	40,883
Financing needed[a]			0	3,100	8,631	(11,731)[b]
Ending cash balance			10,400	10,000	10,000	29,152
Cumulative borrowing			0	3,100	11,731	0

[a]The amount of financing that is required to raise the firm's ending cash balance up to its $10,000 desired cash balance.

[b]Negative financing needed simply means the firm has excess cash that can be used to retire a part of its short-term borrowing from prior months.

the firm will be successful over the coming fiscal year. That is, for most of the first four-month period, the firm is operating with a cash flow deficit. If this does not reverse in the latter eight months of the year, then a reevaluation of the firm's plans and policies is clearly in order.

Longer-range budgets are also prepared in the form of the capital-expenditure budget. These budgets detail the firm's plans for acquiring plant and equipment over a 5-year, 10-year, or even longer period. Furthermore, firms often develop comprehensive long-range plans extending up to 10 years into the future. These plans are generally not as detailed as the annual cash budget, but they do consider such major components as sales, capital expenditures, new-product development, capital funds acquisition, and employment needs. See the Finance Matters box, "To Bribe or Not to Bribe."

CONCEPT CHECK

1. What is a cash budget and how is it used in financial planning?
2. How long should a firm's budget period be?

FINANCE MATTERS — ETHICS

TO BRIBE OR NOT TO BRIBE

In many parts of the world, bribes and payoffs to public officials are considered the norm in business transactions. This raises a perplexing ethical question. If paying bribes is not considered unethical in a foreign country, should you consider it unethical to make these payments?

This situation provides an example of an ethical issue that gave rise to legislation. The Foreign Corrupt Practices Act of 1977 (as amended in the Omnibus Trade and Competitiveness Act of 1988) established criminal penalties for making payments to foreign officials, political parties, or candidates in order to obtain or retain business. Ethical problems are frequently found in the gray areas just outside the boundaries of current legislation and often lead to the passage of new legislation.

Consider the following question: If you were involved in negotiating an important business deal in a foreign country, and the success or failure of the deal hinged on whether you paid a local government official to help you consummate the deal, would you authorize the payment? Assume that the form of the payment is such that you do not expect to be caught and punished; for example, your company agrees to purchase supplies from a family member of the government official at a price slightly above the competitive price.

HOW FINANCIAL MANAGERS USE THIS MATERIAL

In the introduction, we pointed out examples that illustrate the difficulties involved in making financial forecasts. The difficulty of making a forecast, we learned, often varied directly with the value of the effort. That is, it is precisely where forecasts are most difficult that our attempts and the plans we formulate based upon the forecast are the most valuable.

Every business of any size makes and uses financial forecasts as an integral part of its planning process. The typical firm makes revenue and expense projections for at least one and usually five years. These forecasts are then used to develop pro forma financial statements that can be used to evaluate the financial condition of the firm if the forecast proves to be accurate. In addition, it is common practice to develop one or more contingency plans based on alternative sales and cost outcomes. The alternative scenarios frequently reflect optimistic and pessimistic scenarios.

The forecast methods used in practice can be varied. The firm may actually contract with a consulting firm for long-run forecasts that they feel demand skills not possessed by the finance staff. In the majority of the cases, however, the firm's finance personnel gather information concerning historical revenue and cost relationships and use this as the basis for developing the firm's financial forecast in conjunction with the firm's sales forecast. The sales forecast is frequently constructed by polling the heads of the firm's various operating divisions and then combining the results. In this way, the finance staff relies on the individuals who are directly responsible for the revenues being forecast.

SUMMARY

Objective 1

This chapter develops the role of forecasting within the context of the firm's financial planning activities. Forecasts of the firm's sales revenues and related expenses provide the basis for projecting future financing needs. The most popular method for forecasting financial variables is the percent of sales method.

Objective 2

The percent of sales method presumes that the asset or liability being forecast is a constant percent of sales for all future levels of sales. There are instances where this assumption is not reasonable, and consequently, the percent of sales method does not provide reasonable predictions. One such instance arises where there are economies of scale in the use of the asset being forecast. For example, the firm may need at least $10 million in inventories to open its doors and operate even for sales as low as $100 million per year. If sales double to $200 million, inventories may only increase to $15 million. Thus, inventories do not increase with sales in a constant proportion. A second situation where the percent of sales method fails to work properly is where asset purchases are lumpy. That is, if plant capacity must be purchased in $50 million increments, then plant and equipment will not remain a constant percent of sales.

How serious are these possible problems and should we use the percent of sales method at all? Even in the face of these problems, the percent of sales method predicts reasonably well where predicted sales levels do not differ drastically from the level used to calculate the percent of sales. For example, if the current sales level used in calculating percent of sales for inventories is $40 million, then we can feel more comfortable forecasting the level of inventories corresponding to a new sales level of $42 million than if sales were predicted to rise to $60 million.

Objective 3

A firm's sustainable rate of growth is the maximum rate at which its sales can grow if it is to maintain its present financial ratios and not have to resort to issuing new equity. We calculate the sustainable rate of growth as follows:

$$\text{sustainable rate of growth } (g^*) = ROE\,(1 - b)$$

where ROE is the return earned on common equity and b is the dividend payout ratio (that is, the ratio of dividends to earnings). Consequently, a firm's sustainable rate of growth increases with ROE and decreases with a higher fraction of its earnings paid out in dividends.

Objective 4

The cash budget is the primary tool of financial forecasting and planning. It contains a detailed plan of future cash flow estimates and is comprised of four elements or segments: cash receipts, cash disbursements, net change in cash for the period, and new financing needed. Once prepared, the cash budget also serves as a tool for monitoring and controlling the firm's operations. By comparing actual cash receipts and disbursements to those in the cash budget, the financial manager can gain an appreciation for how well the firm is performing. In addition, deviations from the plan serve as an early warning system to signal the need for external financing in response to either the presence of future investment opportunities or poor business performance.

KEY TERMS

Cash budget, 118

Discretionary financing, 110

Percent of sales method, 108

Plowback ratio, 106

Spontaneous sources of financing, 110

Sustainable rate of growth, 116

Go To: www.prenhall.com/keown for downloads and current events associated with this chapter

STUDY QUESTIONS

4-1. Discuss the shortcomings of the percent of sales method of financial forecasting.

4-2. Explain how a fixed cash budget differs from a variable or flexible cash budget.

4-3. What two basic needs does a flexible (variable) cash budget serve?

4-4. What would be the probable effect on a firm's cash position of the following events?

- **a.** Rapidly rising sales
- **b.** A delay in the payment of accounts payable
- **c.** A more liberal credit policy on sales (to the firm's customers)
- **d.** Holding larger inventories

4-5. How long should the budget period be? Why would a firm not set a rule that all budgets be for a 12-month period?

4-6. A cash budget is usually thought of as a means of planning for future financing needs. Why would a cash budget also be important for a firm that had excess cash on hand?

4-7. Explain why a cash budget would be of particular importance to a firm that experiences seasonal fluctuations in its sales.

SELF-TEST PROBLEMS

ST-1. (*Financial forecasting*) Use the percent of sales method to prepare a pro forma income statement for Calico Sales Co., Inc. Projected sales for next year equal $4 million. Cost of goods sold is expected to be 70 percent of sales, administrative expense equals $500,000, and depreciation expense is $300,000. Interest expense equals $50,000 and income is taxed at a rate of 40 percent. The firm plans to spend $200,000 during the period to renovate its office facility and will retire $150,000 in notes payable. Finally, selling expense equals 5 percent of sales.

ST-2. (*Cash budget*) Stauffer, Inc., has estimated sales and purchase requirements for the last half of the coming year. Past experience indicates that it will collect 20 percent of its sales in the month of the sale, 50 percent of the remainder one month after the sale, and the balance in the second month following the sale. Stauffer prefers to pay for half its purchases in the month of the purchase and the other half the following month. Labor expense for each month is expected to equal 5 percent of that month's sales, with cash payment being made in the month in which the expense is incurred. Depreciation expense is $5,000 per month; miscellaneous cash expenses are $4,000 per month and are paid in the month incurred. General and administrative expenses of $50,000 are recognized and paid monthly. A $60,000 truck is to be purchased in August and is to be depreciated on a straight-line basis over 10 years with no expected salvage value. The company also plans to pay a $9,000 cash dividend to stockholders in July. The company feels that a minimum cash balance of $30,000 should be maintained. Any borrowing will cost 12 percent annually, with interest paid in the month following the month in which the funds are borrowed. Borrowing takes place at the beginning of the month in which the need for funds arises. For example, if during the month of July, the firm should need to borrow $24,000 to maintain its $30,000 desired minimum balance, then $24,000 will be taken out on July 1 with interest owed for the entire month of July. Interest for the month of July would then be paid on August 1. Sales and purchase estimates are shown in the following chart. Prepare a cash budget for the months of July and August (cash on hand June 30 was $30,000, whereas sales for May and June were $100,000 and purchases were $60,000 for each of these months).

MONTH	SALES	PURCHASES
July	$120,000	$50,000
August	150,000	40,000
September	110,000	30,000

STUDY PROBLEMS (SET A)

4-1A. (*Financial forecasting*) Zapatera Enterprises is evaluating its financing requirements for the coming year. The firm has only been in business for one year, but its Chief Financial Officer predicts that the firm's operating expenses, current assets, net fixed assets, and current liabilities will remain at their current proportion of sales.

Last year Zapatera had $12 million in sales with net income of $1.2 million. The firm anticipates that next year's sales will reach $15 million with net income rising to $2 million. Given its present high rate of growth, the firm retains all of its earnings to help defray the cost of new investments.

The firm's balance sheet for the year just ended is as follows:

Zapatera Enterprises, Inc.

BALANCE SHEET	12/31/03	% OF SALES
Current assets	$3,000,000	25%
Net fixed assets	6,000,000	50%
Total	$9,000,000	
LIABILITIES AND OWNERS' EQUITY		
Accounts payable	$3,000,000	25%
Long-term debt	2,000,000	NA[a]
Total liabilities	$5,000,000	
Common stock	1,000,000	NA*
Paid-in capital	1,800,000	NA*
Retained earnings	1,200,000	
Common equity	4,000,000	
Total	$9,000,000	

[a]Not applicable. This figure does not vary directly with sales and is assumed to remain constant for purposes of making next year's forecast of financing requirements.

Estimate Zapatera's total financing requirements (i.e., total assets) for 2004 and its net funding requirements (discretionary financing needed).

4-2A. (*Pro forma accounts receivable balance calculation*) On March 31, 2003, the Sylvia Gift Shop had outstanding accounts receivable of $20,000. Sylvia's sales are roughly evenly split between credit and cash sales, with half the credit sales collected in the month after the sale and the remainder two months after the sale. Historical and projected sales for the gift shop are:

MONTH	SALES	MONTH	SALES
January	$15,000	March	$30,000
February	20,000	April (projected)	40,000

a. Under these circumstances, what should the balance in accounts receivable be at the end of April?

b. How much cash did Sylvia realize during April from sales and collections?

4-3A. (*Financial forecasting*) Sambonoza Enterprises projects its sales next year to be $4 million and expects to earn 5 percent of that amount after taxes. The firm is currently in the process of projecting its financing needs and has made the following assumptions (projections):

(1) Current assets will equal 20 percent of sales, and fixed assets will remain at their current level of $1 million.

(2) Common equity is currently $0.8 million, and the firm pays out half of its after-tax earnings in dividends.

(3) The firm has short-term payables and trade credit that normally equal 10 percent of sales, and it has no long-term debt outstanding.

What are Sambonoza's financing needs for the coming year?

4-4A. (*Financial forecasting—percent of sales*) Tulley Appliances, Inc., projects next year's sales to be $20 million. Current sales are at $15 million based on current assets of $5 million and fixed assets of $5 million. The firm's net profit margin is 5 percent after taxes. Tulley forecasts that current assets will rise in direct proportion to the increase in sales, but fixed assets will increase by only $100,000. Currently, Tulley has $1.5 million in accounts payable (which vary directly with sales), $2 million in long-term debt (due in 10 years), and common equity (including $4 million in retained earnings) totaling $6.5 million. Tulley plans to pay $500,000 in common stock dividends next year.

a. What are Tulley's total financing needs (that is, total assets) for the coming year?

b. Given the firm's projections and dividend payment plans, what are its discretionary financing needs?

c. Based on your projections, and assuming that the $100,000 expansion in fixed assets will occur, what is the largest increase in sales the firm can support without having to resort to the use of discretionary sources of financing?

4-5A. (*Pro forma balance sheet construction*) Use the following industry average ratios to construct a pro forma balance sheet for Carlos Menza, Inc.

Total asset turnover	2 times
Average collection period (assume a 365-day year)	9 days
Fixed asset turnover	5 times
Inventory turnover (based on cost of goods sold)	3 times
Current ratio	2 times
Sales (all on credit)	$4.0 million
Cost of goods sold	75% of sales
Debt ratio	50%

Cash	____	Current liabilities	____
Inventory	____	Long-term debt	____
Accounts receivable	____	Common stock plus	____
Net fixed assets	____	Retained earnings	____
Total	$____	Total	$____

4-6A. (*Cash budget*) The Sharpe Corporation's projected sales for the first eight months of 2004 are as follows:

January	$ 90,000	May	$300,000
February	120,000	June	270,000
March	135,000	July	225,000
April	240,000	August	150,000

Of Sharpe's sales, 10 percent is for cash, another 60 percent is collected in the month following sale, and 30 percent is collected in the second month following sale. November and December sales for 2003 were $220,000 and $175,000, respectively.

Sharpe purchases its raw materials two months in advance of its sales equal to 60 percent of their final sales price. The supplier is paid one month after it makes delivery. For example, purchases for April sales are made in February and payment is made in March.

In addition, Sharpe pays $10,000 per month for rent and $20,000 each month for other expenditures. Tax prepayments of $22,500 are made each quarter, beginning in March.

The company's cash balance at December 31, 2003, was $22,000; a minimum balance of $15,000 must be maintained at all times. Assume that any short-term financing needed to maintain the cash balance is paid off in the month following the month of financing if sufficient funds are available. Interest on short-term loans (12 percent) is paid monthly. Borrowing to meet estimated monthly cash needs takes place at the beginning of the month. Thus, if in the month of April the firm expects to have a need for an additional $60,500, these funds would be borrowed at the beginning of April with interest of $605 ($.12 \times 1/12 \times \$60{,}500$) owed for April and paid at the beginning of May.

a. Prepare a cash budget for Sharpe covering the first seven months of 2004.

b. Sharpe has $200,000 in notes payable due in July that must be repaid or renegotiated for an extension. Will the firm have ample cash to repay the notes?

4-7A. (*Percent of sales forecasting*) Which of the following accounts would most likely vary directly with the level of firm sales? Discuss each briefly.

	YES	NO		YES	NO
Cash	____	____	Notes payable	____	____
Marketable securities	____	____	Plant and equipment	____	____
Accounts payable	____	____	Inventories	____	____

4-8A. (*Financial forecasting—percent of sales*) The balance sheet of the Thompson Trucking Company (TTC) follows:

Thompson Trucking Company Balance Sheet, December 31, 2003 ($ millions)

Current assets	$10	Accounts payable	$ 5
Net fixed assets	15	Notes payable	0
Total	$25	Bonds payable	10
		Common equity	10
		Total	$25

TTC had sales for the year ended 12/31/03 of $50 million. The firm follows a policy of paying all net earnings out to its common stockholders in cash dividends. Thus, TTC generates no funds from its earnings that can be used to expand its operations. (Assume that depreciation expense is just equal to the cost of replacing worn-out assets.)

a. If TTC anticipates sales of $80 million during the coming year, develop a pro forma balance sheet for the firm for 12/31/04. Assume that current assets vary as a percent of sales, net fixed assets remain unchanged, and accounts payable vary as a percent of sales. Use notes payable as a balancing entry.

b. How much "new" financing will TTC need next year?

c. What limitations does the percent of sales forecast method suffer from? Discuss briefly.

4-9A. (*Financial forecasting—discretionary financing needed*) The most recent balance sheet for the Armadillo Dog Biscuit Co. is shown in the following table. The company is about to embark on an advertising campaign, which is expected to raise sales from the current level of $5 million to $7 million by the end of next year. The firm is currently operating at full capacity and will have to increase its investment in both current and fixed assets to support the projected level of new sales. In fact, the firm estimates that both categories of assets will rise in direct proportion to the projected increase in sales.

Armadillo Dog Biscuit Co., Inc. ($ millions)

	PRESENT LEVEL	PERCENT OF SALES	PROJECTED LEVEL
Current assets	$2.0		
Net fixed assets	3.0		
Total	$5.0		
Accounts payable	$0.5		
Accrued expenses	0.5		
Notes payable	–		
Current liabilities	$1.0		
Long-term debt	$2.0		
Common stock	0.5		
Retained earnings	1.5		
Common equity	$2.0		
Total	$5.0		

The firm's net profits were 6 percent of current year's sales but are expected to rise to 7 percent of next year's sales. To help support its anticipated growth in asset needs next year, the firm has suspended plans to pay cash dividends to its stockholders. In past years, a $1.50 per share dividend has been paid annually.

Armadillo's payables and accrued expenses are expected to vary directly with sales. In addition, notes payable will be used to supply the funds that are needed to finance next year's operations and that are not forthcoming from other sources.

a. Fill in the table and project the firm's needs for discretionary financing. Use notes payable as the balancing entry for future discretionary financing needed.

b. Compare Armadillo's current ratio and debt ratio (total liabilities/total assets) before the growth in sales and after. What was the effect of the expanded sales on these two dimensions of Armadillo's financial condition?

c. What difference, if any, would have resulted if Armadillo's sales had risen to $6 million in one year and $7 million only after two years? Discuss only; no calculations are required.

4-10A. (*Forecasting discretionary financing needs*) Fishing Charter, Inc., estimates that it invests 30 cents in assets for each dollar of new sales. However, 5 cents in profits are produced by each dollar of additional sales, of which 1 cent can be reinvested in the firm. If sales rise from their current level of $5 million by $500,000 next year, and the ratio of spontaneous liabilities to sales is .15, what will be the firm's need for discretionary financing? (*Hint:* In this situation you do not know what the firm's existing level of assets is, nor do you know how those assets have been financed. Thus, you must estimate the change in financing needs and match this change with the expected changes in spontaneous liabilities, retained earnings, and other sources of discretionary financing.)

4-11A. (*Preparation of a cash budget*) Harrison Printing has projected its sales for the first eight months of 2004 as follows:

January	$100,000	April	$300,000	July	$200,000
February	120,000	May	275,000	August	180,000
March	150,000	June	200,000		

Harrison collects 20 percent of its sales in the month of the sale, 50 percent in the month following the sale, and the remaining 30 percent two months following the sale. During November and December of 2003 Harrison's sales were $220,000 and $175,000, respectively.

Harrison purchases raw materials two months in advance of its sales equal to 65 percent of its final sales. The supplier is paid one month after delivery. Thus, purchases for April sales are made in February and payment is made in March.

In addition, Harrison pays $10,000 per month for rent and $20,000 each month for other expenditures. Tax prepayments of $22,500 are made each quarter beginning in March. The company's cash balance as of December 31, 2003, was $22,000; a minimum balance of $20,000 must be maintained at all times to satisfy the firm's bank line of credit agreement. Harrison has arranged with its bank for short-term credit at an interest rate of 12 percent per annum (1 percent per month) to be paid monthly. Borrowing to meet estimated monthly cash needs takes place at the end of the month, and interest is not paid until the end of the following month. Consequently, if the firm were to need to borrow $50,000 during the month of April, then it would pay $500 (= .01 × $50,000) in interest during May. Finally, Harrison follows a policy of repaying its outstanding short-term debt in any month in which its cash balance exceeds the minimum desired balance of $20,000.

a. Harrison needs to know what its cash requirements will be for the next six months so that it can renegotiate the terms of its short-term credit agreement with its bank, if necessary. To evaluate this problem, the firm plans to evaluate the impact of a ±20 percent variation in its monthly sales efforts. Prepare a six-month cash budget for Harrison and use it to evaluate the firm's cash needs.

b. Harrison has a $200,000 note due in June. Will the firm have sufficient cash to repay the loan?

4-12A. (*Sustainable rate of growth*) ADP, Inc., is a manufacturer of specialty circuit boards in the personal computer industry. The firm has experienced phenomenal sales growth over its short five-year life. Selected financial statement data are found in the following table:

	2003	2002	2001	2000	1999
Sales	$3,000	$2,200	$1,800	$1,400	$1,200
Net income	150	110	90	70	60
Assets	2,700	1,980	1,620	1,260	1,080
Dividends	60	44	36	28	24
Common equity	812	722	656	602	560
Liabilities	1,888	1,258	964	658	520
Liabilities and equity	2,700	1,980	1,620	1,260	1,080

a. Calculate ADP's sustainable rate of growth for each of the five years of its existence.
b. Compare the actual rates of growth in sales to the firm's sustainable rates calculated in part a. How has ADP been financing its growing asset needs?

4-13A. (*Sustainable rate of growth*) The Carrera Game Company has experienced a 100 percent increase in sales over the last five years. The company president, Jack Carrera, has become increasingly alarmed by the firm's rising debt level even in the face of continued profitability.

	2003	2002	2001	2000	1999
Sales	$60,000	$56,000	$48,000	$36,000	$30,000
Net income	3,000	2,800	2,400	1,800	1,500
Assets	54,000	50,400	43,200	32,400	27,000
Dividends	1,200	1,120	960	720	600
Common equity	21,000	19,200	17,520	16,080	15,000
Liabilities	33,000	31,200	25,680	16,320	12,000
Liabilities and equity	54,000	50,400	43,200	32,400	27,000

a. Calculate the debt to asset ratio, return on common equity, actual rate of growth in firm sales, and retention ratio for each of the five years of data provided.
b. Calculate the sustainable rates of growth for Carrera for each of the last five years. Why has the firm's borrowing increased so dramatically?

4-14A. (*Forecasting inventories*) Findlay Instruments produces a complete line of medical instruments used by plastic surgeons and has experienced rapid growth over the last five years. In an effort to make more accurate predictions of its financing requirements, Findlay is currently attempting to construct a financial planning model based on the percent of sales forecasting method. However, the firm's Chief Financial Analyst (Sarah Macias) is concerned that the projections for inventories will be seriously in error. She recognizes that the firm has begun to accrue substantial economies of scale in its inventory investment and has documented this fact in the following data and calculations:

YEAR	SALES (000)	INVENTORY (000)	% OF SALES
1999	$15,000	1,150	7.67%
2000	18,000	1,180	6.56%
2001	17,500	1,175	6.71%
2002	20,000	1,200	6.00%
2003	25,000	1,250	5.00%
		Average	6.39%

a. Plot Findlay's sales and inventories for the last five years. What is the relationship between these two variables?
b. Estimate firm inventories for 2004, when firm sales are projected to reach $30,000,000. Use the average percent of sales for the last five years, the most recent percent of sales, and your evaluation of the true relationship between the sales and inventories from part a to make three separate predications of inventories.

WEB WORKS

4-1ww. Go to **www.starbucks.com** and use the Investor Relations information to obtain the company's most recent financial statements. Calculate the sustainable rate of growth. How does this compare with the firm's actual rate of growth in revenues over the last three years?

4-2ww. You can find financial information for the Gap at **www.gap.com**. Look in Company Information and determine the company's projected sales. Why are sales forecasts so important to developing a firm's financial forecast?

INTEGRATIVE PROBLEM

Phillips Petroleum is an integrated oil and gas company with headquarters in Bartlesville, Oklahoma, where it was founded in 1917. The company engages in petroleum exploration and production worldwide. In addition, it engages in natural gas gathering and processing, as well as petroleum refining and marketing, primarily in the United States. The company has three operating groups—Exploration and Production, Gas and Gas Liquids, and Downstream Operations, which encompasses Petroleum Products and Chemicals.

Summary Financial Information for Phillips Petroleum Corporation: 1986–1992 (in millions of dollars except for per share figures)

	1986	1987	1988	1989	1990	1991	1992
Sales	10,018.00	10,917.00	11,490.00	12,492.00	13,975.00	13,259.00	12,140.00
Net income	228.00	35.00	650.00	219.00	541.00	98.00	270.00
EPS	0.89	0.06	2.72	0.90	2.18	0.38	1.04
Current assets	2,802.00	2,855.00	3,062.00	2,876.00	3,322.00	2,459.00	2,349.00
Total assets	12,403.00	12,111.00	11,968.00	11,256.00	12,130.00	11,473.00	11,468.00
Current liabilities	2,234.00	2,402.00	2,468.00	2,706.00	2,910.00	2,603.00	2,517.00
Long-term liabilities	8,175.00	7,887.00	7,387.00	6,418.00	6,501.00	6,113.00	5,894.00
Total liabilities	10,409.00	10,289.00	9,855.00	9,124.00	9,411.00	8,716.00	8,411.00
Preferred stock	270.00	205.00	0.00	0.00	0.00	0.00	359.00
Common equity	1,724.00	1,617.00	2,113.00	2,132.00	2,719.00	2,757.00	2,698.00
Dividends per share	2.02	1.73	1.34	0.00	1.03	1.12	1.12

Source: Phillips Annual Reports for the years 1986–1992.

In the mid-1980s, Phillips engaged in a major restructuring following two failed takeover attempts, one led by T. Boone Pickens and the other by Carl Icahn.[a] The restructuring resulted in a $4.5 billion plan to exchange a package of cash and debt securities for roughly half the company's shares and to sell $2 billion worth of assets. Phillips's long-term debt increased from $3.4 billion in late 1984 to a peak of $8.6 billion in April 1985.

During 1992, Phillips was able to strengthen its financial structure dramatically. Its subsidiary, Phillips Gas Company, completed an offering of $345 million of Series A 9.32% Cumulative Preferred Stock. As a result of these actions and prior years' debt reductions, the company lowered its long-term debt to capital ratio over the last five years from 75 to 55 percent. In addition, the firm refinanced over a billion dollars of its debt at reduced rates. A company spokesman said that "Our debt-to-capital ratio is still on the high side, and we'll keep working to bring it down. But the cost of debt is manageable, and we're beyond the point where debt overshadows everything else we do."[b]

Highlights of Phillips's financial condition spanning the years 1986–1992 are found in the preceding table.[c] These data reflect the modern history of the company as a result of its financial restructuring following the downsizing and reorganization of Phillips's operations begun in the mid-1980s.

Phillips's management is currently developing its financial plans for the next five years and wants to develop a forecast of its financing requirements. As a first approximation, they have asked you to develop a model that can be used to make "ballpark" estimates of the firm's financing needs under the proviso that existing relationships found in the firm's financial statements remain the same over the period. Of particular interest is whether or not Phillips will be able to further reduce its reliance on debt financing. You may assume that Phillips's projected sales (in millions) for 1993 through 1997 are as follows: $13,000, $13,500, $14,000, $14,500, and $15,500.

1. Project net income for 1993 to 1997 using the percent of sales method based on an average of this ratio for 1986 to 1992.

[a]This discussion is based on a story in *The New York Times*, January 7, 1986.
[b]From *SEC Online*, 1992.
[c]Extracted from Phillips's Annual Reports for the years represented.

2. Project total assets and current liabilities for the period 1993 to 1997 using the percent of sales method and your sales projections from part 1.
3. Assuming that common equity increases only as a result of the retention of earnings and holding long-term liabilities and preferred stock equal to their 1992 balances, project Phillips's discretionary financing needs for 1993 to 1997. (*Hint:* Assume that total assets and current liabilities vary as a percent of sales as per your answer. In addition, assume that Phillips plans to continue to pay its dividend of $1.12 per share in each of the next five years.)

STUDY PROBLEMS (SET B)

4-1B. (*Financial forecasting*) Hernandez Trucking Company is evaluating its financing requirements for the coming year. The firm has only been in business for three years and the firm's Chief Financial Officer (Eric Stevens) predicts that the firm's operating expenses, current assets, and current liabilities will remain at their current proportion of sales.

Last year, Hernandez had $20 million in sales with net income of $1 million. The firm anticipates that next year's sales will reach $25 million with net income rising to $2 million. Given its present high rate of growth, the firm retains all its earnings to help defray the cost of new investments.

The firm's balance sheet for the year just ended follows:

Hernandez Trucking Company, Inc., Balance Sheet

	12/31/03	% OF SALES
Current assets	$ 4,000,000	20%
Net fixed assets	8,000,000	40%
Total	$12,000,000	
LIABILITIES AND OWNERS' EQUITY		
Accounts payable	$ 3,000,000	15%
Long-term debt	2,000,000	NA[a]
Total liabilities	$ 5,000,000	
Common stock	1,000,000	NA
Paid-in capital	1,800,000	NA
Retained earnings	4,200,000	
Common equity	7,000,000	
Total	$12,000,000	

[a]Not applicable. This figure does not vary directly with sales and is assumed to remain constant for purposes of making next year's forecast of financing requirements.

Estimate Hernandez's total financing requirements for 2004 and its net funding requirements (discretionary financing needed).

4-2B. (*Pro forma accounts receivable balance calculation*) On March 31, 2004, the Floydata Food Distribution Company had outstanding accounts receivable of $52,000. Sales are roughly 40 percent credit and 60 percent cash, with half of the credit sales collected in the month after the sale and the remainder two months after the sale. Historical and projected sales for Floydata Food follow:

MONTH	SALES
January	$100,000
February	100,000
March	80,000
April (projected)	60,000

a. Under these circumstances, what should the balance in accounts receivable be at the end of April?
b. How much cash did Floydata realize during April from sales and collections?

4-3B. (*Financial forecasting*) Simpson, Inc., projects its sales next year to be $5 million and expects to earn 6 percent of that amount after taxes. The firm is currently in the process of projecting its financing needs and has made the following assumptions (projections):

a. Current assets will equal 15 percent of sales and fixed assets will remain at their current level of $1 million.
b. Common equity is presently $0.7 million, and the firm pays out half its after-tax earnings in dividends.
c. The firm has short-term payables and trade credit that normally equal 11 percent of sales and has no long-term debt outstanding.

What are Simpson's financing needs for the coming year?

4-4B. (*Financial forecasting—percent of sales*) Carson Enterprises is in the midst of its annual planning exercise. Bud Carson, the owner, is a mechanical engineer by education and has only modest skills in financial planning. In fact, the firm has operated in the past on a "crisis" basis with little attention paid to the firm's financial affairs until a problem arose. This worked reasonably well for several years, until the firm's growth in sales created a serious cash flow shortage last year. Bud was able to convince the firm's bank to come up with the needed funds, but an outgrowth of the agreement was that the firm would begin to make forecasts of its financing requirements annually. To support its first such effort, Bud has made the following estimates for next year: Sales are currently $18 million with projected sales of $25 million for next year. The firm's current assets equal $7 million, and its fixed assets are $6 million. The best estimate Bud can make is that current assets will equal the current proportion of sales and fixed assets will rise by $100,000. At the present time, the firm has accounts payable of $1.5 million, $2 million in long-term debt, and common equity totaling $9.5 million (including $4 million in retained earnings). Finally, Carson Enterprises plans to continue paying its dividend of $600,000 next year and has a 5 percent profit margin.

a. What are Carson's total financing needs (that is, total assets) for the coming year?
b. Given the firm's projections and dividend payment plans, what are its discretionary financing needs?
c. Based on the projections given and assuming that the $100,000 expansion in fixed assets will occur, what is the largest increase in sales the firm can support without having to resort to the use of discretionary sources of financing?

4-5B. (*Pro forma balance sheet construction*) Use the following industry average ratios to construct a pro forma balance sheet for the V. M. Willet Co.

Total asset turnover	2.5 times
Average collection period (assume a 365-day year)	10 days
Fixed asset turnover	6 times
Inventory turnover (based on cost of goods sold)	4 times
Current ratio	3 times
Sales (all on credit)	$5 million
Cost of goods sold	80% of sales
Debt ratio	60%

Cash	_____	Current liabilities	_____
Accounts receivables	_____	Long-term debt	_____
Inventories	_____	Common stock plus	
Net fixed assets	$_____	retained earnings	$_____
	$_____		$_____

4-6B. (*Cash budget*) The Carmel Corporation's projected sales for the first eight months of 2004 are as follows:

January	$100,000	May	$275,000
February	110,000	June	250,000
March	130,000	July	235,000
April	250,000	August	160,000

Of Carmel's sales, 20 percent is for cash, another 60 percent is collected in the month following sale, and 20 percent is collected in the second month following sale. November and December sales for 2003 were \$220,000 and \$175,000, respectively.

Carmel purchases its raw materials two months in advance of its sales equal to 70 percent of their final sales price. The supplier is paid one month after it makes delivery. For example, purchases for April sales are made in February and payment is made in March.

In addition, Carmel pays \$10,000 per month for rent and \$20,000 each month for other expenditures. Tax prepayments for \$23,000 are made each quarter beginning in March.

The company's cash balance at December 31, 2003, was \$22,000; a minimum balance of \$20,000 must be maintained at all times. Assume that any short-term financing needed to maintain cash balance would be paid off in the month following the month of financing if sufficient funds are available. Interest on short-term loans (12 percent) is paid monthly. Borrowing to meet estimated monthly cash needs takes place at the beginning of the month. Thus, if in the month of April the firm expects to have a need for an additional \$60,500, these funds would be borrowed at the beginning of April with interest of \$605 ($.12 \times 1/12 \times \$60{,}500$) owed for April and paid at the beginning of May.

a. Prepare a cash budget for Carmel covering the first seven months of 2004.
b. Carmel has \$250,000 in notes payable due in July that must be repaid or renegotiated for an extension. Will the firm have ample cash to repay the notes?

4-7B. (*Percent of sales forecasting*) Which of the following accounts would most likely vary directly with the level of firm sales? Discuss each briefly.

	YES	NO		YES	NO
Cash	____	____	Notes payable	____	____
Marketable securities	____	____	Plant and equipment	____	____
Accounts payable	____	____	Inventories	____	____

4-8B. (*Financial forecasting—percent of sales*) The balance sheet of the Chavez Drilling Company (CDC) follows:

Chavez Drilling Company Balance Sheet for January 31, 2003 (\$ millions)

Current assets	\$15	Accounts payable	\$10
Net fixed assets	15	Notes payable	0
Total	\$30	Bonds payable	10
		Common equity	10
		Total	\$30

CDC had sales for the year ended 1/31/03 of \$60 million. The firm follows a policy of paying all net earnings out to its common stockholders in cash dividends. Thus, CDC generates no funds from its earnings that can be used to expand its operations (assume that depreciation expense is just equal to the cost of replacing worn-out assets).

a. If CDC anticipates sales of \$80 million during the coming year, develop a pro forma balance sheet for the firm for 1/31/04. Assume that current assets vary as a percent of sales, net fixed assets remain unchanged, and accounts payable vary as a percent of sales. Use notes payable as a balancing entry.
b. How much "new" financing will CDC need next year?
c. What limitations does the percent of sales forecast method suffer from? Discuss briefly.

4-9B. (*Financial forecasting—discretionary financing needed*) Symbolic Logic Corporation (SLC) is a technological leader in the application of surface mount technology in the manufacture of printed circuit boards used in the personal computer industry. The firm has recently patented an advanced version of its original path-finding technology and expects sales to grow from their present level of \$5 million to \$8 million in the coming year. Since the firm is at present operating at full capacity, it expects to have to increase its investment in both current and fixed assets in proportion to the predicted increase in sales.

The firm's net profits were 7 percent of current year's sales and are expected to be the same next year. To help support its anticipated growth in asset needs next year, the firm has suspended plans to pay cash dividends to its stockholders. In years past, a $1.25 per share dividend has been paid annually.

Symbolic Logic Corporation ($ millions)

	PRESENT LEVEL	PERCENT OF SALES	PROJECTED LEVEL
Current assets	$2.5		
Net fixed assets	3.0		
Total	5.5		
Accounts payable	$1.0		
Accrued expenses	0.5		
Notes payable	–		
Current liabilities	$1.5		
Long-term debt	$2.0		
Common stock	0.5		
Retained earnings	1.5		
Common equity	$2.0		
Total	$5.5		

SLC's payables and accrued expenses are expected to vary directly with sales. In addition, notes payable will be used to supply the funds needed to finance next year's operations and that are not forthcoming from other sources.

a. Fill in the table and project the firm's needs for discretionary financing. Use notes payable as the balancing entry for future discretionary financing needed.

b. Compare SLC's current ratio and debt ratio (total liabilities/total assets) before the growth in sales and after. What was the effect of the expanded sales on these two dimensions of SLC's financial condition?

c. What difference, if any, would have resulted if SLC's sales had risen to $6 million in one year and $8 million only after two years? Discuss only; no calculations are required.

4-10B. (*Forecasting discretionary financing needs*) Royal Charter, Inc., estimates that it invests 40 cents in assets for each dollar of new sales. However, 5 cents in profits are produced by each dollar of additional sales, of which 1 cent can be reinvested in the firm. If sales rise from their present level of $5 million by $500,000 next year, and the ratio of spontaneous liabilities to sales is .15, what will be the firm's need for discretionary financing? (*Hint:* In this situation you do not know what the firm's existing level of assets is, nor do you know how those assets have been financed. Thus, you must estimate the change in financing needs and match this change with the expected changes in spontaneous liabilities, retained earnings, and other sources of discretionary financing. Note that spontaneous liabilities are those liabilities that vary with sales.)

4-11B. (*Preparation of a cash budget*) Halsey Enterprises has projected its sales for the first eight months of 2004 as follows:

January	$120,000	May	$225,000
February	160,000	June	250,000
March	140,000	July	210,000
April	190,000	August	220,000

Halsey collects 30 percent of its sales in the month of the sale, 30 percent in the month following the sale, and the remaining 40 percent two months following the sale. During November and December of 2003, Halsey's sales were $230,000 and $225,000, respectively.

Halsey purchases raw materials two months in advance of its sales equal to 75 percent of its final sales. The supplier is paid in the month after delivery. Thus, purchases for April sales are made in February and payment is made in March.

In addition, Halsey pays $12,000 per month for rent and $20,000 each month for other expenditures. Tax prepayments of $26,500 are made each quarter beginning in March. The company's cash balance as of December 31, 2003, was $28,000; a minimum balance of $25,000 must be maintained at all times to satisfy the firm's bank line of credit agreement. Halsey has arranged with its bank for short-term credit at an interest rate of 12 percent per annum (1 percent per month) to be paid monthly. Borrowing to meet estimated monthly cash needs takes place at the beginning of the month, but interest is not paid until the end of the following month. Consequently, if the firm were to need to borrow $50,000 during the month of April, then it would pay $500 (= .01 × $50,000) in interest during May. Finally, Halsey follows a policy of repaying any outstanding short-term debt in any month in which its cash balance exceeds the minimum desired balance of $25,000.

a. Halsey needs to know what its cash requirements will be for the next six months so that it can renegotiate the terms of its short-term credit agreement with its bank, if necessary. To evaluate this problem the firm plans to assess the impact of a 20 percent variation in its monthly sales efforts. Prepare a six-month cash budget for Halsey and use it to evaluate the firm's cash needs.

b. Halsey has a $200,000 note due in July. Will the firm have sufficient cash to repay the loan?

SELF-TEST SOLUTIONS

ST-1.

Calico Sales Co., Inc., Pro Forma Income Statement

Sales		$4,000,000
Cost of goods sold (70%)		(2,800,000)
Gross profit		1,200,000
Operating expense		
Selling expense (5%)	$ 200,000	
Administrative expense	500,000	
Depreciation expense	300,000	(1,000,000)
Net operating income		200,000
Interest		(50,000)
Earnings before taxes		150,000
Taxes (40%)		(60,000)
Net income		$ 90,000

Although the office renovation expenditure and debt retirement are surely cash outflows, they do not enter the income statement directly. These expenditures affect expenses for the period's income statement only through their effect on depreciation and interest expense. A cash budget would indicate the full cash impact of the renovation and debt retirement expenditures.

ST-2.

	MAY	JUNE	JULY	AUGUST
Sales	$100,000	$100,000	$ 120,000	$ 150,000
Purchases	60,000	60,000	50,000	40,000
Cash receipts:				
Collections from month of sale (20%)	20,000	20,000	24,000	30,000
1 month later (50% of uncollected amount)		40,000	40,000	48,000
2 months later (balance)			40,000	40,000
Total receipts			$ 104,000	$ 118,000
Cash disbursements:				
Payments for purchases—				
From 1 month earlier			$ 30,000	$ 25,000
From current month			25,000	$ 20,000
Total			$ 55,000	$ 45,000
Miscellaneous cash expenses			4,000	4,000
Labor expense (5% of sales)			6,000	7,500
General and administrative expense ($50,000 per month)			50,000	50,000
Truck purchase			0	60,000
Cash dividends			9,000	–
Total disbursements			$ (124,000)	$ (166,500)
Net change in cash			(20,000)	(48,500)
Plus: Beginning cash balance			30,000	30,000
Less: Interest on short-term borrowing (1% of prior month's borrowing)				(200)
Equals: ending cash balance—without borrowing			10,000	(18,700)
Financing needed to reach target cash balance			20,000	48,700
Cumulative borrowing			$ 20,000	$ 68,700

PART 2

Valuation of Financial Assets

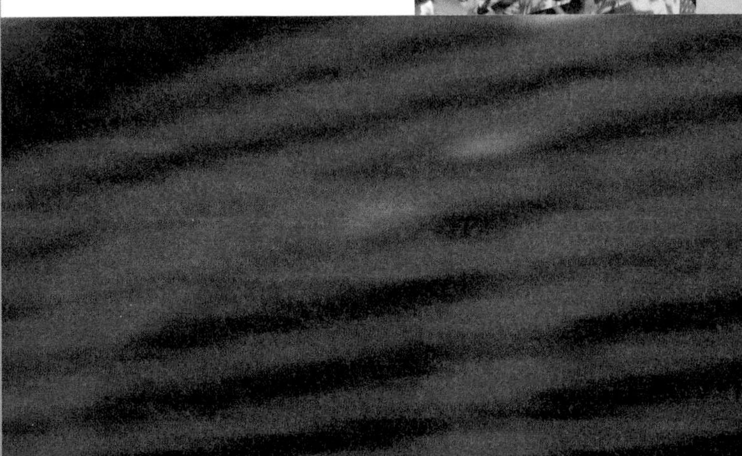

LEARNING OBJECTIVES

After reading this chapter, you should be able to

1. Explain the mechanics of compounding: how money grows over time when it is invested.
2. Determine the future or present value of a sum when there are nonannual compounding periods.
3. Discuss the relationship between compounding (future value) and bringing money back to the present (present value).
4. Define an ordinary annuity and calculate its compound or future value.
5. Differentiate between an ordinary annuity and an annuity due, and determine the future and present value of an annuity due.
6. Deal with complex cash flows.
7. Work with annuities and perpetuities.
8. Calculate the annual percentage yield or effective annual rate of interest and then explain how it differs from the nominal or stated interest rate.

CHAPTER 5

The Time Value of Money

In business and in personal finance, there is probably no single concept with more power or applications than the time value of money. In his landmark book, *A History of Interest Rates*, Homer Sidney noted that if $1,000 were invested for 400 years at 8 percent interest, it would grow to $23 quadrillion—approximately $5 million per person on earth. He was not giving a plan to make the world rich, but effectively pointing out the power of the time value of money.

The time value of money is certainly not a new concept. Benjamin Franklin had a good understanding of how it worked when he bequest $1,000 each to Boston and Philadelphia. With his gift, he left instructions that the cities were to lend the money, charging the going interest rate, to worthy apprentices. Then, after the money had been invested this way for 100 years, they were to use a portion of the investment to build something of benefit to the city and hold some back for the future. In the 213 years that followed, Ben's gift to Boston resulted in the construction of the Franklin Union, helped countless medical students with loans, and still contains over $3 million in the account. Philadelphia, likewise, has reaped significant rewards. Bear in mind that all this came from a combined gift of $2,000 and some serious help from the time value of money.

The power of the time value of money can also be illustrated through a story Andrew Tobias tells in his book *Money Angles*. In the story, a peasant wins a chess tournament sponsored by the king. The king then asks him what he would like as the prize. The peasant answers that, for his village, he would like one piece of grain to be placed on the first square of his chessboard, two pieces on the second square, four on the third, eight on the fourth, and so forth. The king, thinking he was getting off easy, pledged his word of honor that this would be done. Unfortunately for the king, by the time all 64 squares on the chessboard were filled, there were 18.5 million trillion grains of wheat on

CHAPTER PREVIEW

In the next six chapters, we will focus on determining the value of the firm and the value of investment proposals. A key concept that underlies this material is the *time value of money*; that is, a dollar today is worth more than a dollar received a year from now because a dollar today can be invested and earn interest. Intuitively this idea is easy to understand. We are all familiar with the concept of interest. This concept illustrates what economists call an *opportunity cost* of passing up the earning potential of a dollar today. This opportunity cost is the time value of money.

Different investment proposals produce different sets of cash flows over different time periods. How does the manager compare these? We will see that the concept of the time value of money will let us do this. Thus, an understanding of the time value of money is essential to an understanding of financial management, whether basic or advanced. In this chapter, we develop the tools to incorporate **Principle 2: The Time Value of Money—A dollar received today is worth more than a dollar received in the future** into our calculations. In coming chapters, we will use this concept to measure value by bringing the benefits and costs from a project back to the present.

the board—the kernels were compounding at a rate of 100 percent over the 64 squares of the chessboard. Needless to say, no one in the village ever went hungry; in fact, that is so much wheat that if the kernels were one-quarter inch long (the estimate Andrew Tobias provides) they could stretch to the sun and back 391,320 times if laid end to end.

Understanding the techniques of compounding and moving money through time are critical to almost every business decision. It will also help you to understand such varied things as how stocks and bonds are valued, how much you should save for your children's education, and how much your mortgage payments will be.

Objective 1

COMPOUND INTEREST AND FUTURE VALUE

Compound interest Interest that occurs when interest paid on the investment during the first period is added to the principal; then, during the second period, interest is earned on this new sum.

Most of us encounter the concept of compound interest at an early age. Anyone who has ever had a savings account or purchased a government savings bond has received compound interest. **Compound interest** occurs when interest paid on the investment during the first period is added to the principal; then, during the second period, interest is earned on this new sum.

For example, suppose we place \$100 in a savings account that pays 6 percent interest, compounded annually. How will our savings grow? At the end of the first year we have earned 6 percent, or \$6 on our initial deposit of \$100, giving us a total of \$106 in our savings account. The mathematical formula illustrating this relationship is

$$FV_1 = PV(1 + i) \qquad \textbf{(5-1)}$$

where FV_1 = the future value of the investment at the end of one year
i = the annual interest (or discount) rate
PV = the present value, or original amount invested at the beginning of the first year

In our example

$$\begin{aligned} FV_1 &= PV(1 + i) \\ &= \$100\,(1 + .06) \\ &= \$100\,(1.06) \\ &= \$106 \end{aligned}$$

Carrying these calculations one period further, we find that we now earn the 6 percent interest on a principal of \$106, which means we earn \$6.36 in interest during the second year. Why do we earn more interest during the second year than we did during the first? Simply because we now earn interest on the sum of the original principal, or present value, and the interest we earned in the first year. In effect, we are now earning interest on interest—this is the concept of compound interest. Examining the mathematical formula illustrating the earning of interest in the second year, we find

$$FV_2 = FV_1(1 + i) \qquad \textbf{(5-2)}$$

which, for our example, gives

$$\begin{aligned} FV_2 &= \$106\,(1.06) \\ &= \$112.36 \end{aligned}$$

Looking back at equation 5-1 we can see that FV_1, or \$106, is actually equal to $PV(1+i)$, or \$100 (1 + .06). If we substitute these values into equation 5-2, we get

$$FV_2 = PV(1+i)(1+i) = PV(1+i)^2 \quad \textbf{(5-3)}$$

Carrying this forward into the third year, we find that we enter the year with \$112.36 and we earn 6 percent, or \$6.74, in interest, giving us a total of \$119.10 in our savings account. Expressing this mathematically

$$FV_3 = FV_2(1+i) = \$112.36\,(1.06) = \$119.10 \quad \textbf{(5-4)}$$

If we substitute the value in equation 5-3 for FV_2 into equation 5-4, we find

$$FV_3 = PV(1+i)(1+i)(1+i) = PV(1+i)^3 \quad \textbf{(5-5)}$$

By now a pattern is beginning to be evident. We can generalize this formula to illustrate the value of our investment if it is compounded annually at a rate of i for n years to be

$$FV_n = PV(1+i)^n \quad \textbf{(5-6)}$$

→ compounding

where FV_n = the future value of the investment at the end of n years
n = the number of years during which the compounding occurs
i = the annual interest (or discount) rate
PV = the present value or original amount invested at the beginning of the first year

Table 5-1 illustrates how this investment of \$100 would continue to grow for the first 10 years at a compound interest rate of 6 percent. Notice how the amount of interest earned annually increases each year. Again, the reason is that each year interest is received on the sum of the original investment plus any interest earned in the past.

TABLE 5-1 Illustration of Compound Interest Calculations

YEAR	BEGINNING VALUE	INTEREST EARNED	ENDING VALUE
1	\$100.00	\$ 6.00	\$106.00
2	106.00	6.36	112.36
3	112.36	6.74	119.10
4	119.10	7.15	126.25
5	126.25	7.57	133.82
6	133.82	8.03	141.85
7	141.85	8.51	150.36
8	150.36	9.02	159.38
9	159.38	9.57	168.95
10	168.95	10.13	179.08

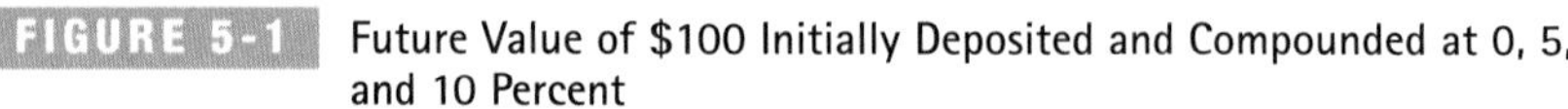

FIGURE 5-1 Future Value of $100 Initially Deposited and Compounded at 0, 5, and 10 Percent

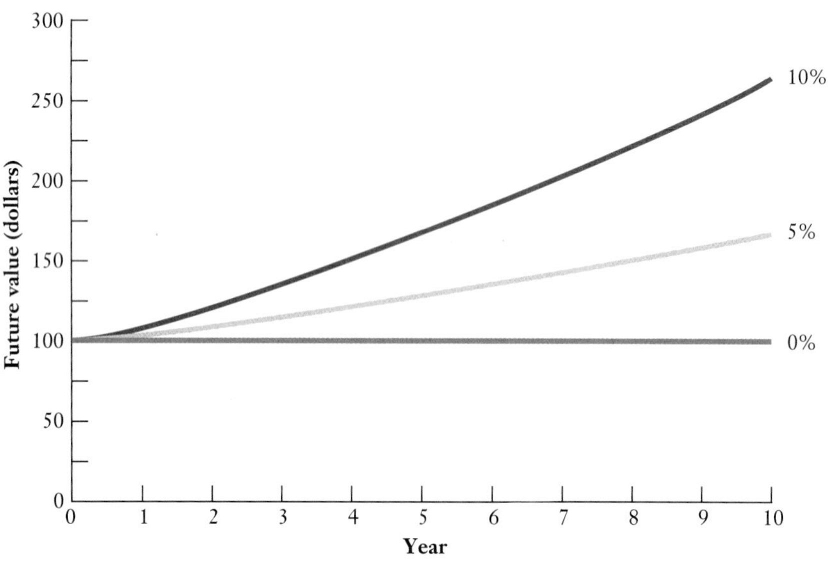

When we examine the relationship between the number of years an initial investment is compounded for and its future value, as shown graphically in Figure 5-1, we see that we can increase the future value of an investment by increasing the number of years we let it compound or by compounding it at a higher interest rate. We can also see this from equation 5-6, because an increase in either i or n while PV is held constant will result in an increase in FV_n.

Keep in mind that future cash flows are assumed to occur at the end of the time period during which they accrue. For example, if a cash flow of $100 occurs in time period 5, it is assumed to occur at the end of time period 5, which is also the beginning of time period 6. In addition, cash flows that occur in time $t = 0$ occur right now; that is, they are already in present dollars.

EXAMPLE: FUTURE VALUE OF A SINGLE FLOW

If we place $1,000 in a savings account paying 5 percent interest compounded annually, how much will our account accrue in 10 years? Substituting $PV = \$1,000$, $i = 5$ percent, and $n = 10$ years into equation 5-6, we get

$$\begin{aligned} FV_n &= PV(1 + i)^n \\ &= \$1,000\,(1 + .05)^{10} \\ &= \$1,000\,(1.62889) \\ &= \$1,628.89 \end{aligned}$$

Thus, at the end of 10 years, we will have $1,628.89 in our savings account.

TABLE 5-2 $FVIF_{i,n}$ or the Compound Sum of $1

n	1%	2%	3%	4%	5%	6%	7%	8%	9%	10%
1	1.010	1.020	1.030	1.040	1.050	1.060	1.070	1.080	1.090	1.100
2	1.020	1.040	1.061	1.082	1.102	1.124	1.145	1.166	1.188	1.210
3	1.030	1.061	1.093	1.125	1.158	1.191	1.225	1.260	1.295	1.331
4	1.041	1.082	1.126	1.170	1.216	1.262	1.311	1.360	1.412	1.464
5	1.051	1.104	1.159	1.217	1.276	1.338	1.403	1.469	1.539	1.611
6	1.062	1.126	1.194	1.265	1.340	1.419	1.501	1.587	1.677	1.772
7	1.072	1.149	1.230	1.316	1.407	1.504	1.606	1.714	1.828	1.949
8	1.083	1.172	1.267	1.369	1.477	1.594	1.718	1.851	1.993	2.144
9	1.094	1.195	1.305	1.423	1.551	1.689	1.838	1.999	2.172	2.358
10	1.105	1.219	1.344	1.480	1.629	1.791	1.967	2.159	2.367	2.594
11	1.116	1.243	1.384	1.539	1.710	1.898	2.105	2.332	2.580	2.853
12	1.127	1.268	1.426	1.601	1.796	2.012	2.252	2.518	2.813	3.138
13	1.138	1.294	1.469	1.665	1.886	2.133	2.410	2.720	3.066	3.452
14	1.149	1.319	1.513	1.732	1.980	2.261	2.579	2.937	3.342	3.797
15	1.161	1.346	1.558	1.801	2.079	2.397	2.759	3.172	3.642	4.177

As the determination of future value can be quite time-consuming when an investment is held for a number of years, the **future-value interest factor** for i and n ($FVIF_{i,n}$), defined as $(1 + i)^n$, has been compiled in the back of the book for various values of i and n. An abbreviated compound interest or future-value interest factor table appears in Table 5-2, with a more comprehensive version of this table appearing in Appendix B at the back of this book. Alternatively, the $FVIF_{i,n}$ values could easily be determined using a calculator. Note that the compounding factors given in these tables represent the value of $1 compounded at rate i at the *end* of the nth period. Thus, to calculate the future value of an initial investment, we need only determine the $FVIF_{i,n}$, using a calculator or the tables in Appendix B, and multiply this times the initial investment. In effect, we can rewrite equation 5-6 as follows:

Future-value interest factor ($FVIF_{i,n}$)
The value $(1 + i)^n$ used as a multiplier to calculate an amount's future value.

$$FV_n = PV(FVIF_{i,n}) \tag{5-6a}$$

EXAMPLE: FUTURE VALUE OF AN ANNUITY

If we invest $500 in a bank where it will earn 8 percent compounded annually, how much will it be worth at the end of seven years? Looking at Table 5-2 in row $n = 7$ and column $i = 8\%$, we find that $FVIF_{8\%,7yrs}$ has a value of 1.714. Substituting this in equation 5-6a, we find

$$\begin{aligned} FV_n &= PV(FVIF_{8\%,7yrs}) \\ &= \$500\,(1.714) \\ &= \$857 \end{aligned}$$

Thus, we will have $857 at the end of seven years.

We will find several uses for equation 5-6: Not only will we find the future value of an investment, but we can also solve for PV, i, or n. When we are given three of the four variables, we can solve for the fourth.

EXAMPLE: SOLVING FOR N

Let's assume that the Chrysler Corporation has guaranteed that the price of a new Jeep will always be $20,000, and you'd like to buy one but currently have only $7,752. How many years will it take for your initial investment of $7,752 to grow to $20,000 if it is invested at 9 percent compounded annually? We can use equation 5-6a to solve for this problem as well. Substituting the known values in equation 5-6a, you find

$$FV_n = PV(FVIF_{i,n})$$
$$\$20{,}000 = \$7{,}752\,(FVIF_{9\%,n\text{yrs}})$$
$$\frac{\$20{,}000}{\$7{,}752} = \frac{\$7{,}752\,(FVIF_{9\%,n\text{yrs}})}{\$7{,}752}$$
$$2.58 = FVIF_{9\%,n\text{yrs}}$$

Thus, you are looking for a value of 2.58 in the $FVIF_{i,n}$ tables, and you know it must be in the 9% column. To finish solving the problem, look down the 9% column for the value closest to 2.58. You find that it occurs in the $n = 11$ row. Thus, it will take 11 years for an initial investment of $7,752 to grow to $20,000 if it is invested at 9 percent compounded annually.

EXAMPLE: SOLVING FOR I

Now let's solve for the compound annual growth rate, and let's go back to that Jeep that always costs $20,000. In 10 years, you'd really like to have $20,000 to buy a new Jeep, but you only have $11,167. At what rate must your $11,167 be compounded annually for it to grow to $20,000 in 10 years? Substituting the known variables into equation 5-6a, you get

$$FV_n = PV(FVIF_{i,n})$$
$$\$20{,}000 = \$11{,}167\,(FVIF_{i,10\text{yrs}})$$
$$\frac{\$20{,}000}{\$11{,}167} = \frac{\$11{,}167\,(FVIF_{i,10\text{yrs}})}{\$11{,}167}$$
$$1.791 = FVIF_{i,10\text{yrs}}$$

You know you are looking in the $n = 10$ row of the $FVIF_{i,n}$ tables for a value of 1.791, and you find this in the $i = 6\%$ column. Thus, if you want your initial investment of $11,167 to grow to $20,000 in 10 years, you must invest it at 6 percent.

Just how powerful is the time value of money? Manhattan Island was purchased by Peter Minuit from the Indians in 1626 for $24 in "knickknacks" and jewelry. If at the end of 1626 the Indians had invested their $24 at 8 percent compounded annually, it would be worth over $103.4 trillion today (by the end of 2004, 378 years later). That's certainly enough to buy back all of Manhattan. In fact, with $103 trillion in the bank, the $90 to

$100 billion you'd have to pay to buy back all of Manhattan would only seem like pocket change. This story illustrates the incredible power of time in compounding. There simply is no substitute for it.

CONCEPT CHECK

1. Principle 2 states that "A Dollar Received Today Is Worth More Than a Dollar Received in the Future." Explain this statement.
2. How does compound interest differ from simple interest?
3. Explain the formula $FV_n = PV(1 + i)^n$

Moving Money Through Time with the Aid of a Financial Calculator

Time value of money calculations can be made simple with the aid of a *financial calculator*. In solving time value of money problems with a financial calculator, you will be given three of four variables and will have to solve for the fourth. Before presenting any solutions using a financial calculator, we will introduce the calculator's five most common keys. (In most time value of money problems, only four of these keys are relevant.) These keys are:

MENU KEY	DESCRIPTION
N	Stores (or calculates) the total number of payments or compounding periods.
I/Y	Stores (or calculates) the interest or discount rate.
PV	Stores (or calculates) the present value of a cash flow or series of cash flows.
FV	Stores (or calculates) the future value, that is, the dollar amount of a final cash flow or the compound value of a single flow or series of cash flows.
PMT	Stores (or calculates) the dollar amount of each annuity payment deposited or received at the end of each year.

When you use a financial calculator, remember that outflows generally have to be entered as negative numbers. In general, each problem will have two cash flows: one an outflow with a negative value, and one an inflow with a positive value. The idea is that you deposit money in the bank at some point in time (an outflow), and at some other point in time you take money out of the bank (an inflow). Also, every calculator operates a bit differently with respect to entering variables. Needless to say, it is a good idea to familiarize yourself with exactly how your calculator functions.

In any problem, you will be given three of four variables. These four variables will always include *N* and *I/Y*; in addition, two out of the final three variables *PV*, *FV*, and *PMT* will also be included. To solve a time value of money problem using a financial calculator, all you need to do is enter the appropriate numbers for three of the four variables, and press the key of the final variable to calculate its value. It is also a good idea to enter zero for any of the five variables not included in the problem in order to clear that variable.

Now let's solve the previous example using a financial calculator. We were trying to find at what rate $100 must be compounded annually for it to grow to $179.10 in 10 years. The solution using a financial calculator would be as follows:

Step 1: Input values of known variables

DATA INPUT	FUNCTION KEY	DESCRIPTION
10	N	Stores $N = 10$ years
−100	PV	Stores $PV = -\$100$
179.10	FV	Stores $FV = \$179.10$
0	PMT	Clears *PMT* to = 0

Step 2: Calculate the value of the unknown variable

FUNCTION KEY	ANSWER	DESCRIPTION
CPT		
I/Y	6.00%	Calculates $I/Y = 6.00\%$

Any of the problems in this chapter can easily be solved using a financial calculator, and the solutions to many examples using a Texas Instrument (TI) BAII Plus financial calculator are provided in the margins. If you are using the TI BAII Plus, make sure that you have selected both the "END MODE" and "one payment per year" ($P/Y = 1$). This sets the payment conditions to a maximum of one payment per period occurring at the end of the period. One final point: You will notice that solutions using the present-value tables versus solutions using a calculator may vary slightly—a result of rounding errors in the tables.

For further explanation of the TI BAII Plus, see Appendix A at the end of the book.

Spreadsheets and the Time Value of Money

Without question, in the real world most calculations involving moving money through time will be carried out with the help of a spreadsheet. While there are several competing spreadsheets, the most popular one is Microsoft Excel. Just as with the keystroke calculations on a financial calculator, a spreadsheet can make easy work of most common financial calculations. Following are some of the most common functions used with Excel when moving money through time:

Calculation	Formula
Present value	= *PV*(rate,number of periods,payment,future value,type)
Future value	= *FV*(rate,number of periods,payment,present value,type)
Payment	= *PMT*(rate,number of periods,present value,future value,type)
Number of periods	= *NPER*(rate,payment,present value,future value,type)
Interest rate	= *RATE*(number of periods,payment,present value,future value,type,guess)

where:

Rate	= *i*, the interest rate or discount rate
Number of periods	= *n*, the number of years or periods
Payment	= *PMT*, the annuity payment deposited or received at the end of each period
Future value	= *FV*, the future value of the investment at the end of *n* periods or years
Present value	= *PV*, the present value of the future sum of money
Type	= when the payment is made (0 if omitted) 0 = at end of period 1 = at beginning of period
Guess	= a starting point when calculating the interest rate; if omitted, the calculations begin with a value of 0.1, or 10%

Just like with a financial calculator, the outflows have to be entered as negative numbers. In general, each problem will have two cash flows—one positive and one negative. The idea is that you deposit money at some point in time (an outflow or negative value) and at some point later in time, you withdraw your money (an inflow or positive value). For example, let's look back at the example on page 141.

Row	A–C	D
1		
2	Spreadsheets and the Time Value of Money	
3		
4	If we invest $500 in a bank where it will earn 8 percent compounded	
5	annually, how much will it be worth at the end of 7 years?	
6		
7	rate (i) =	8%
8	number of periods (n) =	7
9	payment (PMT) =	$0
10	present value (PV) =	$500
11	type (0 = at end of period) =	0
12		
13	Future value =	$856.91
14		
15	Excel formula: =FV(rate,number of periods,payment,present value,type)	
16		
17	Entered value in cell d13: =FV(d7,d8,d9,-d10,d11)	
18	Notice that present value ($500) took on a negative value.	
19		

Sheet1 / Sheet2 / Sheet3

Row	A–C	D
1	Now let's solve for the value of i, just as we did on page 142.	
2		
3	Spreadsheets: Solving for i	
4		
5	In 10 years you'd like to have $20,000 to buy a new Jeep, but you only	
6	have $11,167. At what rate must your $11,167 be compounded	
7	annually for it to grow to $20,000 in 10 years?	
8		
9	number of periods (n) =	10
10	payment (PMT) =	$0
11	present value (PV) =	$11,167
12	future value (FV) =	$20,000
13	type (0 = at end of period) =	0
14	guess =	
15		
16	i =	6.00%
17		
18	Excel formula: =RATE(number of periods,payment,present value,future value,type,guess)	
19		
20	Entered value in cell d16: =RATE(d28,d29,-d30,d31,d32,d33)	
21		
22	Notice that present value ($11,167) took on a negative value.	
23	Also note that if you didn't assign a value to guess, it would begin calculations	
24	with a value of 0.1 or 10%. If it could not come up with a value for i after	
25	20 iterations, you would receive the #NUM! error message. Generally a	
26	guess between 10 and 100 percent will work.	
27		

Sheet1 / Sheet2 / Sheet3

Objective 2

COMPOUND INTEREST WITH NONANNUAL PERIODS

Until now, we have assumed that the compounding period is always annual; however, it need not be, as evidenced by savings and loan associations and commercial banks that compound on a quarterly, and in some cases a daily, basis. Fortunately, this adjustment of the compounding period follows the same format as that used for annual compounding. If we invest our money for five years at 8 percent interest compounded semiannually, we are really investing our money for 10 six-month periods during which we receive 4 percent interest each period. If it is compounded quarterly, we receive 2 percent interest per period for 20 three-month periods. Table 5-3 illustrates the importance of nonannual compounding. For example, if you invested \$100 at 15 percent you would end up with about 5 percent more if it was compounded semiannually instead of annually, and about 10 percent more if the compounding occurred daily. This process can easily be generalized, giving us the following formula for finding the future value of an investment for which interest is compounded in nonannual periods:

$$FV_n = PV\left(1 + \frac{i}{m}\right)^{mn} \qquad \textbf{(5-7)}$$

where FV_n = the future value of the investment at the end of n years
n = the number of years during which the compounding occurs
i = annual interest (or discount) rate
PV = the present value or original amount invested at the beginning of the first year
m = the number of times compounding occurs during the year

CALCULATOR SOLUTION

Data Input	Function Key
20	N
3	I/Y
100	PV
0	PMT

Function Key	Answer
CPT	
FV	–180.61

EXAMPLE: NONANNUAL COMPOUNDING

If we place \$100 in a savings account that yields 12 percent compounded quarterly, what will our investment grow to at the end of five years? Substituting $n = 5$, $m = 4$, $i = 12$ percent, and $PV = \$100$ into equation 5-7, we find

$$\begin{aligned} FV_5 &= \$100\left(1 + \frac{.12}{4}\right)^{4\cdot 5} \\ &= \$100\,(1 + .03)^{20} \\ &= \$100\,(1.806) \\ &= \$180.60 \end{aligned}$$

Thus, we will have \$180.60 at the end of five years. Notice that the calculator solution is slightly different because of rounding errors in the tables, as explained in the previous section, and that it also takes on a negative value.

Obviously, the choice of the interest rate plays a critical role in how much an investment grows, but do small changes in the interest rate have much of an impact on future values? To answer this question, let's look back to Peter Minuit's purchase of Manhattan. If the Indians had invested their \$24 at 10 percent rather than 8 percent compounded annually at the end of 1626, they would have over \$106 quadrillion by the end of 2004 (378 years). That is 106 followed by 15 zeros, or \$106,000,000,000,000,000. Actually, that is enough to buy back not only Manhattan Island, but the entire world and still have plenty left over! Now let's assume a lower interest rate—say, 6 percent. In that case, the

TABLE 5-3 The Value of $100 Compounded at Various Nonannual Periods

FOR 1 YEAR AT *i* PERCENT	*i* = 2%	5%	10%	15%
Compounded annually	$102.00	$105.00	$110.00	$115.00
Compounded semiannually	102.01	105.06	110.25	115.56
Compounded quarterly	102.02	105.09	110.38	115.87
Compounded monthly	102.02	105.12	110.47	116.08
Compounded weekly (52)	102.02	105.12	110.51	116.16
Compounded daily (365)	102.02	105.13	110.52	116.18
FOR 10 YEARS AT *i* PERCENT	***i* = 2%**	**5%**	**10%**	**15%**
Compounded annually	$121.90	$162.89	$259.37	$404.56
Compounded semiannually	122.02	163.86	265.33	424.79
Compounded quarterly	122.08	164.36	268.51	436.04
Compounded monthly	122.12	164.70	270.70	444.02
Compounded weekly (52)	122.14	164.83	271.57	447.20
Compounded daily (365)	122.14	164.87	271.79	448.03

$24 would have only grown to a mere $88.3 billion—less than 1/100th of what it grew to at 8 percent, and only one-millionth of what it would have grown to at 10 percent. With today's real estate prices, you'd have a tough time buying Manhattan, but if you did, you probably couldn't pay your taxes! To say the least, the interest rate is extremely important in investing.

CONCEPT CHECK

1. Why does the future value of a given amount increase when interest is compounded nonannually as opposed to annually?
2. How do you adjust the present and future value formulas when interest is compounded monthly?

PRESENT VALUE

Objective 3

Up until this point, we have been moving money forward in time; that is, we know how much we have to begin with and are trying to determine how much that sum will grow in a certain number of years when compounded at a specific rate. We are now going to look at the reverse question: What is the value in today's dollars of a sum of money to be received in the future? The answer to this question will help us determine the desirability of investment projects in Chapters 9 through 11. In this case, we are moving future money back to the present. We will be determining the **present value** of a lump sum, which in simple terms is the current value of a future payment. What we will be doing is, in fact, nothing other than inverse compounding. The differences in these techniques come about merely from the investor's point of view. In compounding, we talked about the compound interest rate and the initial investment; in determining the present value, we will talk about the discount rate, and the present value of future cash flows. Determination of the discount rate is the subject of Chapter 6, and can be defined as the rate of return available on an investment of equal risk to what is being discounted. Other than that, the technique and the terminology remain the same, and the mathematics are

Present value The current value of a future sum.

simply reversed. In equation 5-6, we attempt to determine the future value of an initial investment. We now want to determine the initial investment or present value. By dividing both sides of equation 5-6 by $(1 + i)^n$, we get

$$PV = FV_n\left[\frac{1}{(1 + i)^n}\right] \tag{5-8}$$

where PV = the present value of the future sum of money
FV_n = the future value of the investment at the end of n years
n = the number of years until the payment will be received
i = the annual discount (or interest) rate

Because the mathematical procedure for determining the present value is exactly the inverse of determining the future value, we also find that the relationships among n, i, and PV are just the opposite of those we observed in future value. The present value of a future sum of money is inversely related to both the number of years until the payment will be received and the discount rate. Graphically, this relationship can be seen in Figure 5-2. Although the present value equation (equation 5-8) will be used extensively in evaluating new investment proposals, it should be stressed that the present value equation is actually the same as the future value or compounding equation (equation 5-6) where it is solved for PV.

CALCULATOR SOLUTION

Data Input	Function Key
10	N
6	I/Y
500	FV
0	PMT
Function Key	**Answer**
CPT	
PV	−279.20

EXAMPLE: PRESENT VALUE OF A FUTURE CASH FLOW

What is the present value of \$500 to be received 10 years from today if our discount rate is 6 percent? Substituting FV_{10} = \$500, n = 10, and i = 6 percent into equation 5-8, we find

$$\begin{aligned} PV &= \$500\left[\frac{1}{(1 + .06)^{10}}\right] \\ &= \$500\left(\frac{1}{1.791}\right) \\ &= \$500\,(.558) \\ &= \$279 \end{aligned}$$

Thus, the present value of the \$500 to be received in 10 years is \$279.

Present-value interest factor ($PVIF_{i,n}$)
The value $[1/(1 + i)^n]$ used as a multiplier to calculate an amount's present value.

To aid in the computation of present values, the **present-value interest factor** for i and n, or $PVIF_{i,n}$, which is equal to $[1/(1 + i)^n]$, has been compiled for various combinations of i and n and appears in Appendix C at the back of this book. An abbreviated version of Appendix C appears in Table 5-4. A close examination shows that the values in Table 5-4 are merely the inverse of those found in Appendix B. This, of course, is as it should be, as the values in Appendix B are $(1 + i)^n$ and those in Appendix C are $[1/(1 + i)^n]$. Now to determine the present value of a sum of money to be received at some future date, we need only determine the value of the appropriate $PVIF_{i,n}$, either by using a calculator or consulting the tables, and multiply it by the future value. In effect, we can use our new notation and rewrite equation 5-8 as follows:

$$PV = FV_n(PVIF_{i,n}) \tag{5-8a}$$

FIGURE 5-2 Present Value of $100 to Be Received at a Future Date and Discounted Back to the Present at 0, 5, and 10 Percent

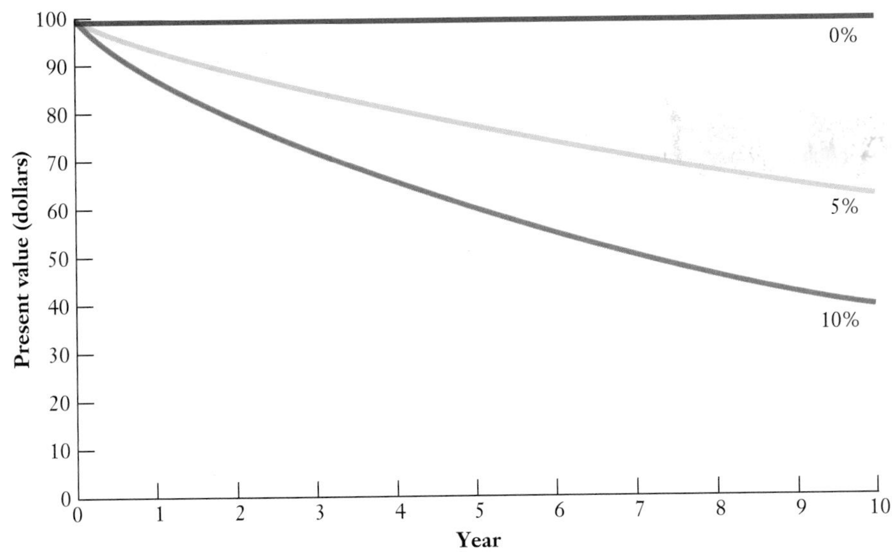

Example: Present Value Calculation

You're on vacation in a rather remote part of Florida and see an advertisement stating that if you take a sales tour of some condominiums, "you will be given $100 just for taking the tour." However, the $100 that you get is in the form of a savings bond that will not pay you the $100 for 10 years. What is the present value of $100 to be received 10 years from today if your discount rate is 6 percent? By looking at the $n = 10$ row and $i = 6\%$ column of Table 5-4, you find the $PVIF_{6\%,10\text{yrs}}$ is .558. Substituting $FV_{10} =$ $100 and $PVIF_{6\%,10\text{yrs}} = .558$ into equation 5-8a, you find

$$PV = \$100\,(PVIF_{6\%,10\text{yrs}})$$
$$= \$100\,(.558)$$
$$= \$55.80$$

Thus, the value in today's dollars of that $100 savings bond is only $55.80.

CALCULATOR SOLUTION

Data Input	Function Key
10	N
6	I/Y
100	FV
0	PMT

Function Key	Answer
CPT	
PV	−55.84

TABLE 5-4 $PVIF_{i,n}$ or the Present Value of $1

n	1%	2%	3%	4%	5%	6%	7%	8%	9%	10%
1	.990	.980	.971	.962	.952	.943	.935	.926	.917	.909
2	.980	.961	.943	.925	.907	.890	.873	.857	.842	.826
3	.971	.942	.915	.889	.864	.840	.816	.794	.772	.751
4	.961	.924	.888	.855	.823	.792	.763	.735	.708	.683
5	.951	.906	.863	.822	.784	.747	.713	.681	.650	.621
6	.942	.888	.837	.790	.746	.705	.666	.630	.596	.564
7	.933	.871	.813	.760	.711	.655	.623	.583	.547	.513
8	.923	.853	.789	.731	.677	.627	.582	.540	.502	.467
9	.914	.837	.766	.703	.645	.592	.544	.500	.460	.424
10	.905	.820	.744	.676	.614	.558	.508	.463	.422	.386
11	.896	.804	.722	.650	.585	.527	.475	.429	.388	.350
12	.887	.789	.701	.625	.557	.497	.444	.397	.356	.319
13	.879	.773	.681	.601	.530	.469	.415	.368	.326	.290
14	.870	.758	.661	.577	.505	.442	.388	.340	.299	.263
15	.861	.743	.642	.555	.481	.417	.362	.315	.275	.239

Dealing with Multiple, Uneven Cash Flows

Again, we only have one present value–future value equation; that is, equations 5-6 and 5-8 are identical. We have introduced them as separate equations to simplify our calculations; in one case, we are determining the value in future dollars and in the other case, the value in today's dollars. In either case, the reason is the same: To compare values on alternative investments and to recognize that the value of a dollar received today is not the same as that of a dollar received at some future date, we must measure the dollar values in dollars of the same time period.

In the chapter opening we discussed Harley-Davidson investing in the costly development of the Buell Lightning Low in 2000 and receiving income on that investment in the year 2003 and beyond. The concept of present value allows us to bring those future cash flows back to the present and view them in terms of today's dollars. Moreover, because all present values are comparable (they are all measured in dollars of the same time period), we can add and subtract the present value of inflows and outflows to determine the present value of an investment. Let's now look at an example of an investment that has two cash flows in different time periods and determine the present value of this investment.

Example: Present Value of a Single Flow and an Annuity

What is the present value of an investment that yields \$500 to be received in five years and \$1,000 to be received in 10 years if the discount rate is 4 percent? Substituting the values of $n = 5$, $i = 4$ percent, and $FV_5 = \$500$; and $n = 10$, $i = 4$ percent, and $FV_{10} =$ \$1,000 into equation 5-8 and adding these values together, we find

$$
\begin{aligned}
PV &= \$500\left[\frac{1}{(1+.04)^5}\right] + \$1{,}000\left[\frac{1}{(1+.04)^{10}}\right] \\
&= \$500\,(PVIF_{4\%,5\text{yrs}}) + \$1{,}000\,(PVIF_{4\%,10\text{yrs}}) \\
&= \$500\,(.822) + \$1{,}000\,(.676) \\
&= \$411 + \$676 \\
&= \$1{,}087
\end{aligned}
$$

Again, present values are comparable because they are measured in the same time period's dollars.

CONCEPT CHECK

1. What is the relationship between the present value equation (5-7) and the future value or compounding equation (5-6)?
2. Why is the present value of a future sum always less than that sum's future value?

Objective 4

ANNUITIES—A LEVEL STREAM

Annuity
A series of equal dollar payments for a specified number of years.

An **annuity** is a series of equal dollar payments for a specified number of years. Because annuities occur frequently in finance—for example, interest payments on bonds are in effect annuities—we will treat them specially. Although compounding and determining the present value of an annuity can be dealt with using the methods we have just described, these processes can be time-consuming, especially for larger annuities. Thus we have modified the formulas to deal directly with annuities.

Although all annuities involve a series of equal dollar payments for a specified number of years, there are two basic types of annuities: an **ordinary annuity** and an **annuity due.** With an ordinary annuity, we assume that the payments occur at the end of each period; with an annuity due, the payments occur at the beginning of each period. Because an annuity due provides the payments earlier (at the beginning of each period instead of the end as with an ordinary annuity), it has a greater present value. After we master ordinary annuities, we will examine annuities due. However, in finance, ordinary annuities are used much more frequently than are annuities due. Thus, in this text, whenever the term "annuity" is used, you should assume that we are referring to an ordinary annuity unless otherwise specified.

Ordinary annuity An annuity in which the payments occur at the end of each period.

Annuity due An annuity in which the payments occur at the beginning of each period.

COMPOUND ANNUITIES

A **compound annuity** involves depositing or investing an equal sum of money at the end of each year for a certain number of years and allowing it to grow. Perhaps we are saving money for education, a new car, or a vacation home. In any case, we want to know how much our savings will have grown by some point in the future.

Compound annuity Depositing an equal sum of money at the end of each year for a certain number of years and allowing it to grow.

Actually, we can find the answer by using equation 5-6, our compounding equation, and compounding each of the individual deposits to its future value. For example, if to provide for a college education we are going to deposit \$500 at the end of each year for the next five years in a bank where it will earn 6 percent interest, how much will we have at the end of five years? Compounding each of these values using equation 5-6, we find that we will have \$2,818.50 at the end of five years.

$$
\begin{aligned}
FV_5 &= \$500\,(1+.06)^4 + \$500\,(1+.06)^3 + \$500\,(1+.06)^2 + \$500\,(1+.06) + \$500 \\
&= \$500\,(1.262) + \$500\,(1.191) + \$500\,(1.124) + \$500\,(1.060) + \$500 \\
&= \$631.00 + \$595.50 + \$562.00 + \$530.00 + \$500.00 \\
&= \$2,818.50
\end{aligned}
$$

CALCULATOR SOLUTION

Data Input	Function Key
5	N
6	I/Y
0	PV
500	PMT

Function Key	Answer
CPT	
FV	–2,818.55

To better understand what's happening, let's look at this problem using a time line. A time line is simply a horizontal line on which the present—time period zero—is at the left-most end. Future time periods are then shown along the line moving from left to right. The dollar amount of the cash flow is shown below the line, with positive values representing cash inflows, and negative values representing cash outflows. We will frequently use time lines to illustrate the timing of an investment's cash flows. In the present example, cash flows of \$500 are received at the end of years one through five and are presented graphically in Table 5-5. From examining the mathematics involved and the graph of the movement of money through time in Table 5-5, we can see that this procedure can be generalized to

$$FV_n = PMT\left[\sum_{t=0}^{n-1}(1+i)^t\right] \tag{5-9}$$

where FV_n = the future value of the annuity at the end of the nth year
PMT = the annuity payment deposited or received at the end of each year
i = the annual interest (or discount) rate
n = the number of years for which the annuity will last

To aid in compounding annuities, the **future-value interest factor for an annuity** for i and n ($FVIFA_{i,n}$), defined as $\left[\sum_{t=0}^{n-1}(1+i)^t\right]$, is provided in Appendix D for various combinations of n and i. An abbreviated version is shown in Table 5-6.

Future-value interest factor for an annuity ($FVIFA_{i,n}$) The value $\left[\sum_{t=0}^{n-1}(1+i)^t\right]$ used as a multiplier to calculate the future value of an annuity.

TABLE 5-5 Illustration of a Five-Year $500 Annuity Compounded at 6 Percent

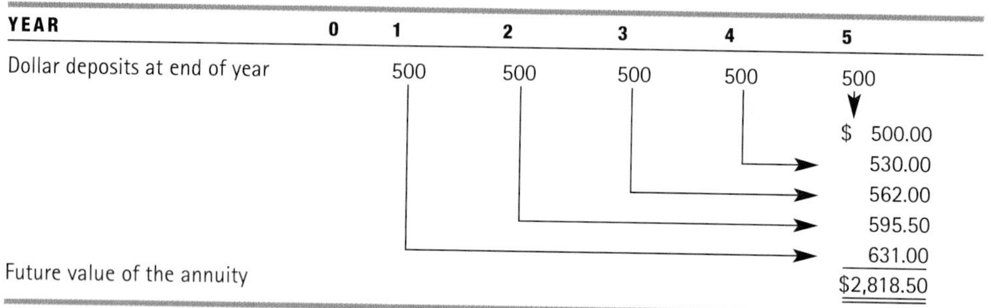

YEAR	0	1	2	3	4	5
Dollar deposits at end of year		500	500	500	500	500
						$ 500.00
						530.00
						562.00
						595.50
						631.00
Future value of the annuity						$2,818.50

Using this new notation, we can rewrite equation 5-9 as follows:

$$FV_n = PMT(FVIFA_{i,n}) \tag{5-9a}$$

The $FVIFA_{i,n}$ can also be calculated as follows:

$$FVIFA_{i,n} = \frac{(1+i)^n - 1}{i} \tag{5-9b}$$

This formula is useful if you don't have a financial calculator or tables.

Reexamining the previous example, in which we determined the value after five years of $500 deposited at the end of each of the next five years in the bank at 6 percent, we would look in the i = 6% column and n = 5 year row and find the value of the $FVIFA_{6\%,5yrs}$ to be 5.637. Substituting this value into equation 5-9a, we get

$$\begin{aligned} FV_5 &= \$500\,(5.637) \\ &= \$2{,}818.50 \end{aligned}$$

This is the same answer we obtained earlier.

Rather than asking how much we will accumulate if we deposit an equal sum in a savings account each year, a more common question is how much we must deposit each year to accumulate a certain amount of savings. This problem frequently occurs with respect to saving for large expenditures and pension funding obligations.

TABLE 5-6 $FVIFA_{i,n}$ or the Sum of an Annuity of $1 for n Years

n	1%	2%	3%	4%	5%	6%	7%	8%	9%	10%
1	1.000	1.000	1.000	1.000	1.000	1.000	1.000	1.000	1.000	1.000
2	2.010	2.020	2.030	2.040	2.050	2.060	2.070	2.080	2.090	2.100
3	3.030	3.060	3.091	3.122	3.152	3.184	3.215	3.246	3.278	3.310
4	4.060	4.122	4.184	4.246	4.310	4.375	4.440	4.506	4.573	4.641
5	5.101	5.204	5.309	5.416	5.526	5.637	5.751	5.867	5.985	6.105
6	6.152	6.308	6.468	6.633	6.802	6.975	7.153	7.336	7.523	7.716
7	7.214	7.434	7.662	7.898	8.142	8.394	8.654	8.923	9.200	9.487
8	8.286	8.583	8.892	9.214	9.549	9.897	10.260	10.637	11.028	11.436
9	9.368	9.755	10.159	10.583	11.027	11.491	11.978	12.488	13.021	13.579
10	10.462	10.950	11.464	12.006	12.578	13.181	13.816	14.487	15.193	15.937
11	11.567	12.169	12.808	13.486	14.207	14.972	15.784	16.645	17.560	18.531
12	12.682	13.412	14.192	15.026	15.917	16.870	17.888	18.977	20.141	21.384
13	13.809	14.680	15.618	16.627	17.713	18.882	20.141	21.495	22.953	24.523
14	14.947	15.974	17.086	18.292	19.598	21.015	22.550	24.215	26.019	27.975
15	16.097	17.293	18.599	20.023	21.578	23.276	25.129	27.152	29.361	31.772

For example, we may know that we need $10,000 for education in eight years; how much must we deposit at the end of each year in the bank at 6 percent interest to have the college money ready? In this case, we know the values of n, i, and FV_n in equation 5-9; what we do not know is the value of *PMT*. Substituting these example values in equation 5-9, we find

$$\$10{,}000 = PMT\left[\sum_{t=0}^{8-1}(1+.06)^t\right]$$

$$\$10{,}000 = PMT(FVIFA_{6\%,8\text{yrs}})$$

$$\$10{,}000 = PMT(9.897)$$

$$\frac{\$10{,}000}{9.897} = PMT$$

$$PMT = \$1{,}010.41$$

Thus, we must deposit $1,010.41 in the bank at the end of each year for eight years at 6 percent interest to accumulate $10,000 at the end of eight years.

CALCULATOR SOLUTION

Data Input	Function Key
8	N
6	I/Y
10,000	FV
0	PV

Function Key	Answer
CPT	
PMT	–1,010.36

EXAMPLE: SOLVING FOR PAYMENT

How much must we deposit in an 8 percent savings account at the end of each year to accumulate $5,000 at the end of 10 years? Substituting the values FV_{10} = $5,000, n = 10, and i = 8 percent into equation 5-9, we find

$$\$5{,}000 = PMT\left[\sum_{t=0}^{10-1}(1+.08)^t\right] = PMT(FVIFA_{8\%,10\text{yrs}})$$

$$\$5{,}000 = PMT(14.487)$$

$$\frac{\$5{,}000}{14.487} = PMT$$

$$PMT = \$345.14$$

Thus, we must deposit $345.14 per year for 10 years at 8 percent to accumulate $5,000.

CALCULATOR SOLUTION

Data Input	Function Key
10	N
8	I/Y
5,000	FV
0	PV

Function Key	Answer
CPT	
PMT	–345.15

PRESENT VALUE OF AN ANNUITY

Pension funds, insurance obligations, and interest received from bonds all involve annuities. To value them, we need to know the present value of each. See the Finance Matters box, "Make a Child (or Yourself) a Millionaire." Although we can find this by using the present-value table in Appendix C, this can be time-consuming, particularly when the annuity lasts for several years. For example, if we wish to know what $500 received at the end of the next five years is worth to us today given the appropriate discount rate of 6 percent, we can simply substitute the appropriate values into equation 5-8, such that

$$PV = \$500\left[\frac{1}{(1+.06)^1}\right] + \$500\left[\frac{1}{(1+.06)^2}\right] + \$500\left[\frac{1}{(1+.06)^3}\right]$$

$$+ \$500\left[\frac{1}{(1+.06)^4}\right] + \$500\left[\frac{1}{(1+.06)^5}\right]$$

$$= \$500\,(.943) + \$500\,(.890) + \$500\,(.840) + \$500\,(.792) + \$500\,(.747)$$

$$= \$2{,}106$$

$PV = \frac{PMT}{r}\left[1 - \frac{1}{(1+r)^t}\right]$ → Present Value of Annuity

FINANCE MATTERS

MAKE A CHILD (OR YOURSELF) A MILLIONAIRE

Thanks a million.

Even if you haven't got a lot of money, you can easily give $1 million or more to your children, grandchildren, or favorite charity. All it takes is a small initial investment and a lot of time.

Suppose your 16-year-old daughter plans to take a summer job, which will pay her at least $2,000. Because she has earned income, she can open an individual retirement account. If you would like to help fund her retirement, Kenneth Klegon, a financial planner in Lansing, Michigan, suggests giving her $2,000 to set up the IRA. He then advises doing the same in each of the next five years, so that your daughter stashes away a total of $12,000.

Result? If the money is invested in stocks, and stocks deliver their historical average annual return of 10 percent, your daughter will have more than $1 million by the time she turns 65.

Using the principles and techniques set out in this chapter, we can easily see how much this IRA investment will accumulate to. We can first take the $2,000 six-year annuity and determine its future value—that is, its value when your daughter is 21 and receives the last payment. This would be done as follows:

$$\begin{aligned} FV &= PMT(FVIFA_{10\%,\,6\text{yrs}}) \\ &= \$2{,}000\,(FVIFA_{10\%,\,6\text{yrs}}) \\ &= \$15{,}431.22 \end{aligned}$$

We could then take this amount that your daughter has when she is 21 and compound it out 44 years to when she is 65, as follows:

$$\begin{aligned} FV &= PV(FVIF_{10\%,\,44\text{yrs}}) \\ &= \$15{,}431.22\,(FVIF_{10\%,\,44\text{yrs}}) \\ &= \$1{,}022{,}535.54 \end{aligned}$$

Thus, your daughter's IRA would have accumulated to $1,022,535.54 by age 65 if it grew at 10 percent compounded annually.

Because of the corrosive effect of inflation, that $1 million will only buy a quarter of what $1 million buys today, presuming the cost of living rises at 3 percent a year.

To determine how much this is worth in today's dollars, if inflation increases at an annual rate of 3 percent over this period, we need only calculate the present value of $1,022,535.54 to be received 49 years from now given a discount rate of 3 percent. This would determine the future value of this IRA measured in dollars with the same spending power as those around when your daughter was 16. This is done as follows:

$$\begin{aligned} PV &= FV(PVIF_{3\%,\,49\text{yrs}}) \\ &= \$1{,}022{,}535.54\,(PVIF_{3\%,\,49\text{yrs}}) \\ &= \$240{,}245.02 \end{aligned}$$

You can change the growth and inflation rates and come up with all kinds of numbers, but one thing holds: There is incredible power in compounding! Nonetheless, your $12,000 gift will go a long way toward paying for your daughter's retirement. The huge gain is possible because of the way stock market compounding works, with money earned each year not only on your initial investment, but also on the gains accumulated from earlier years.

"The beauty of this strategy is that it will grow tax-deferred," Klegon says. "There's no cost. You can set up an IRA with a no-load mutual fund for nothing." Similarly, Mr. Klegon says, once your children enter the workforce full time, you can encourage them to participate in their company's 401(k) plan by reimbursing them for their contributions.

Thus, the present value of this annuity is $2,106.00. From examining the mathematics involved and the graph of the movement of these funds through time in Table 5-7, we see that we are simply summing up the present values of each cash flow. Thus, this procedure can be generalized to

$$PV = PMT\left[\sum_{t=1}^{n} \frac{1}{(1+i)^t}\right] \tag{5-10}$$

where PMT = the annuity payment deposited or received at the end of each year
i = the annual discount (or interest) rate
PV = the present value of the future annuity
n = the number of years for which the annuity will last

TABLE 5-7 Illustration of a 5-Year $500 Annuity Discounted Back to the Present at 6 Percent

YEAR	0	1	2	3	4	5
Dollars received at the end of year		500	500	500	500	500
	$ 471.50 ← (year 1)					
	445.00 ← (year 2)					
	420.00 ← (year 3)					
	396.00 ← (year 4)					
	373.50 ← (year 5)					
Present value of the annuity	$2,106.00					

To simplify the process of determining the present value for an annuity, the **present-value interest factor for an annuity** for i and $n(PVIFA_{i,n})$, defined as $\left[\sum_{t=1}^{n} \frac{1}{(1+i)^t}\right]$, has been compiled for various combinations of i and n in Appendix E, with an abbreviated version provided in Table 5-8.

Present-value interest factor for an annuity ($PVIFA_{i,n}$)

The value $\left[\sum_{t=1}^{n} \frac{1}{(1+i)^t}\right]$ used as a multiplier to calculate the present value of an annuity.

Using this new notation, we can rewrite equation 5-10 as follows:

$$PV = PMT(PVIFA_{i,n}) \tag{5-10a}$$

The $PVIFA_{i,n}$ can also be calculated as follows:

$$PVIFA_{i,n} = \frac{1 - \frac{1}{(1+i)^n}}{i} \tag{5-10b}$$

This formula is useful if you don't have a financial calculator or tables.

Solving the previous example to find the present value of $500 received at the end of each of the next five years discounted back to the present at 6 percent, we look in the $i = 6\%$ column and $n = 5$ year row and find the $PVIFA_{6\%,5\text{yrs}}$ to be 4.212. Substituting the appropriate values into equation 5-10a, we find

$$\begin{aligned} PV &= \$500\,(4.212) \\ &= \$2{,}106 \end{aligned}$$

TABLE 5-8 $PVIFA_{i,n}$ or the Present Value of an Annuity of $1

n	1%	2%	3%	4%	5%	6%	7%	8%	9%	10%
1	0.990	0.980	0.971	0.962	0.952	0.943	0.935	0.926	0.917	0.909
2	1.970	1.942	1.913	1.886	1.859	1.833	1.808	1.783	1.759	1.736
3	2.941	2.884	2.829	2.775	2.723	2.673	2.624	2.577	2.531	2.487
4	3.902	3.808	3.717	3.630	3.546	3.465	3.387	3.312	3.240	3.170
5	4.853	4.713	4.580	4.452	4.329	4.212	4.100	3.993	3.890	3.791
6	5.795	5.601	5.417	5.242	5.076	4.917	4.767	4.623	4.486	4.355
7	6.728	6.472	6.230	6.002	5.786	5.582	5.389	5.206	5.033	4.868
8	7.652	7.326	7.020	6.733	6.463	6.210	5.971	5.747	5.535	5.335
9	8.566	8.162	7.786	7.435	7.108	6.802	6.515	6.247	5.995	5.759
10	9.471	8.983	8.530	8.111	7.722	7.360	7.024	6.710	6.418	6.145
11	10.368	9.787	9.253	8.760	8.306	7.887	7.499	7.139	6.805	6.495
12	11.255	10.575	9.954	9.385	8.863	8.384	7.943	7.536	7.161	6.814
13	12.134	11.348	10.635	9.986	9.394	8.853	8.358	7.904	7.487	7.103
14	13.004	12.106	11.296	10.563	9.899	9.295	8.746	8.244	7.786	7.367
15	13.865	12.849	11.938	11.118	10.380	9.712	9.108	8.560	8.061	7.606

TABLE 5-9 Present Value of a Six-Year Annuity Discounted at 8 Percent

$1 RECEIVED AT THE END OF YEAR	1	2	3	4	5	6
Present value						
.926	←					
.857		←				
.794			←			
.735				←		
.681					←	
.630						←
4.623 Present value of the annuity						

This, of course, is the same answer we calculated when we individually discounted each cash flow to the present. The reason is that we really only have one table: All of the tables are derived from Table 5-2; the Table 5-8 value for an n-year annuity for any discount rate i is merely the sum of the first n values in Table 5-4. We can see this by comparing the value in the present-value-of-an-annuity table (Table 5-8) for $i = 8$ percent and $n = 6$ years, which is 4.623, with the sum of the values in the $i = 8\%$ column and $n = 1, \ldots,$ six rows of the present-value table (Table 5-4), which is equal to 4.623, as shown in Table 5-9.

CALCULATOR SOLUTION

Data Input	Function Key
10	N
5	I/Y
1,000	PMT
0	FV
Function Key	**Answer**
CPT	
PV	−7,721.73

EXAMPLE: PRESENT VALUE OF AN ANNUITY

What is the present value of a 10-year $1,000 annuity discounted back to the present at 5 percent? Substituting $n = 10$ years, $i = 5$ percent, and $PMT = \$1{,}000$ into equation 5-10, we find

$$PV = \$1{,}000\left[\sum_{t=1}^{10}\frac{1}{(1+.05)^t}\right] = \$1{,}000\,(PVIFA_{5\%,10\text{yrs}})$$

Determining the value for the $PVIFA_{5\%,10\text{yrs}}$ from Table 5-8, row $n = 10$, column $i = 5\%$, and substituting it in, we get

$$\begin{aligned} PV &= \$1{,}000\,(7.722) \\ &= \$7{,}722 \end{aligned}$$

Thus, the present value of this annuity is $7,722.

As with our other compounding and present-value tables, given any three of the four unknowns in equation 5-10, we can solve for the fourth. In the case of the present-value-of-an-annuity table, we may be interested in solving for PMT if we know i, n, and PV. The financial interpretation of this action would be: How much can be withdrawn, perhaps as a pension or to make loan payments, from an account that earns i percent compounded annually for each of the next n years if we wish to have nothing left at the end of n years? For an example, if we have $5,000 in an account earning 8 percent interest, how large an annuity can we draw out each year if we want nothing left at the end of five years? In this case, the present value, PV, of the annuity is $5,000, $n = 5$ years, $i = 8$ percent, and PMT is unknown. Substituting this into equation 5-10, we find

CALCULATOR SOLUTION

Data Input	Function Key
5	N
8	I/Y
5,000	PV
0	FV
Function Key	**Answer**
CPT	
PMT	−1,252.28

$$\begin{aligned} \$5{,}000 &= PMT(3.993) \\ \$1{,}252.19 &= PMT \end{aligned}$$

Thus, this account will fall to zero at the end of five years if we withdraw \$1,252.19 at the end of each year.

> **CONCEPT CHECK**
> 1. How could you determine the future value of a three-year annuity using the formula for the future value of a single cash flow?
> 2. What is the $PVIFA_{10\%,3yrs}$? Now add up the values for the $PVIF_{10\%,nyrs}$ for $n = 1, 2,$ and 3. What is this value? Why do these values have the relationship they do?

ANNUITIES DUE

Objective 5

Because annuities due are really just ordinary annuities in which all the annuity payments have been shifted forward by one year, compounding them and determining their present value is actually quite simple. Remember, with an annuity due, each annuity payment occurs at the beginning of each period rather than at the end of the period. Let's first look at how this affects our compounding calculations.

Because an annuity due merely shifts the payments from the end of the year to the beginning of the year, we now compound the cash flows for one additional year. Therefore, the compound sum of an annuity due is simply

$$FV_n(\text{annuity due}) = PMT(FVIFA_{i,n})(1 + i)$$

For example, earlier we calculated the value of a five-year ordinary annuity of \$500 invested in the bank at 6 percent to be \$2,818.50. If we now assume this to be a five-year annuity due, its future value increases from \$2,818.50 to \$2,987.61.

$$\begin{aligned} FV_5 &= \$500\,(FVIFA_{6\%,5yrs})(1 + .06) \\ &= \$500\,(5.637)(1.06) \\ &= \$2{,}987.61 \end{aligned}$$

Likewise, with the present value of an annuity due, we simply receive each cash flow one year earlier—that is, we receive it at the beginning of each year rather than at the end of each year. Thus, since each cash flow is received one year earlier, it is discounted back for one less period. To determine the present value of an annuity due, we merely need to find the present value of an ordinary annuity and multiply that by $(1 + i)$, which in effect cancels out one year's discounting.

$$PV(\text{annuity due}) = PMT(PVIFA_{i,n})(1 + i)$$

Reexamining the earlier example where we calculated the present value of a five-year ordinary annuity of \$500 given an appropriate discount rate of 6 percent, we now find that if it is an annuity due rather than an ordinary annuity, the present value increases from \$2,106 to \$2,232.36.

$$\begin{aligned} PV &= \$500\,(PVIFA_{6\%,5yrs})(1 + .06) \\ &= \$500\,(4.212)(1.06) \\ &= \$2{,}232.36 \end{aligned}$$

The result of all this is that both the future and present values of an annuity due are larger than that of an ordinary annuity because in each case all payments are received earlier. Thus, when *compounding* an annuity due, it compounds for one additional year;

whereas when *discounting* an annuity due, the cash flows are discounted for one less year. Although annuities due are used with some frequency in accounting, their usage is quite limited in finance. Therefore, in the remainder of this text, whenever the term *annuity* is used, you should assume that we are referring to an ordinary annuity.

EXAMPLE: PRESENT VALUE OF AN ANNUITY DUE

The Virginia State Lottery runs like most other state lotteries: You must select six out of 44 numbers correctly in order to win the jackpot. If you come close, there are some significantly lesser prizes—we will ignore them for now. For each million dollars in the lottery jackpot, you receive $50,000 per year for 20 years, and your chance of winning is 1 in 7.1 million. One of the recent advertisements for the Virginia State Lottery went as follows: "Okay, you got two kinds of people. You've got the kind who play Lotto all the time and the kind who play Lotto some of the time. You know, like only on a Saturday when they stop in at the store on the corner for some peanut butter cups and diet soda and the jackpot happens to be really big. I mean, my friend Ned? He's like, 'Hey, it's only 2 million dollars this week.' Well, hellloooo, anybody home? I mean, I don't know about you, but I wouldn't mind having a measly 2 mill coming *my* way. . . ."

What is the present value of these payments? The answer to this question depends upon what assumption you make as to the time value of money—in this case, let's assume that your required rate of return on an investment with this level of risk is 10 percent. Keep in mind that the Lotto is an annuity due—that is, on a $2 million lottery you would get $100,000 immediately and $100,000 at the end of each of the next 19 years. Thus, the present value of this 20-year annuity due discounted back to present at 10 percent becomes:

$$
\begin{aligned}
PV_{\text{annuity due}} &= PMT(PVIFA_{i\%,n\text{yrs}})(1+i) \\
&= \$100{,}000\ (PVIFA_{10\%,20\text{yrs}})(1+.10) \\
&= \$100{,}000\ (8.514)(1.10) \\
&= \$851{,}400\ (1.10) \\
&= \$936{,}540
\end{aligned}
$$

Thus, the present value of the $2 million Lotto jackpot is less than $1 million if 10 percent is the appropriate discount rate. Moreover, because the chance of winning is only 1 in 7.1 million, the expected value of each dollar "invested" in the lottery is only (1/7.1 million) × ($936,540) = 13.19 cents. That is, for every dollar you spend on the lottery, you should expect to get (*on average*) about 13 cents back—not a particularly good deal. Although this ignores the minor payments for coming close, it also ignores taxes. In this case, it looks like "my friend Ned" is doing the right thing by staying clear of the lottery. Obviously, the main value of the lottery is entertainment. Unfortunately, without an understanding of the time value of money, it can sound like a good investment.

CONCEPT CHECK

1. How does an annuity due differ from an ordinary annuity?
2. Why are both the future and present values greater for an annuity due than for an ordinary annuity?

AMORTIZED LOANS

The procedure of solving for *PMT* is also used to determine what payments are associated with paying off a loan in equal installments over time. Loans that are paid off this way, in equal periodic payments, are called **amortized loans**. For example, suppose you want to buy a used car. To do this, you borrow $6,000 to be repaid in four equal payments at the end of each of the next four years, and the interest rate that is paid to the lender is 15 percent on the outstanding portion of the loan. To determine what the annual payment associated with the repayment of this debt will be, we simply use equation 5-10 and solve for the value of *PMT*, the annual annuity. Again, we know three of the four values in that equation, *PV*, *i*, and *n*. *PV*, the present value of the future annuity, is $6,000; *i*, the annual interest rate, is 15 percent; and *n*, the number of years for which the annuity will last, is four years. *PMT*, the annuity payment received (by the lender and paid by you) at the end of each year, is unknown. Substituting these values into equation 5-10, we find

Amortized loan
A loan paid off in equal installments.

CALCULATOR SOLUTION

Data Input	Function Key
4	N
15	I/Y
6,000	PV
0	FV

Function Key	Answer
CPT	
PMT	−2,101.59

$$\$6{,}000 = PMT\left[\sum_{t=1}^{4} \frac{1}{(1+.15)^t}\right]$$

$$\$6{,}000 = PMT(PVIFA_{15\%,4yrs})$$

$$\$6{,}000 = PMT(2.855)$$

$$\$2{,}101.58 = PMT$$

To repay the principal and interest on the outstanding loan in four years, the annual payments would be $2,101.58. The breakdown of interest and principal payments is given in the **loan amortization schedule** in Table 5-10, with very minor rounding errors. As you can see, the interest payment declines each year as the loan outstanding declines, and more of the principal is repaid each year.

Loan amortization schedule
A breakdown of loan payments into interest and principal payments.

CONCEPT CHECK

1. What is an amortized loan?

	A–J
1	Now let's look at a loan amortization problem where the payments occur
2	monthly using a spreadsheet.
3	
4	Spreadsheets: the Loan Amortization Problem
5	
6	To buy a new house you take out a 25 year mortgage for $100,000.
7	What will your monthly interest rate payments be if the interest rate
8	on your mortgage is 8 percent?
9	
10	Two things to keep in mind when you're working this problem: first, you'll
11	have to convert the annual rate of 8 percent into a monthly rate by dividing it
12	by 12, and second, you'll have to convert the number of periods into months
13	by multiplying 25 times 12 for a total of 300 months.
14	
15	Excel formula: =PMT(rate,number of periods,present value,future value,type)
16	
17	rate (I) = 8%/12
18	number of periods (n) = 300
19	present value (PV) = $100,000
20	future value (FV) = $0
21	type (0 = at end of period) = 0
22	
23	Entered values in cell d25: =PMT((8/12)%,d18,d19,d20,d21)
24	
25	monthly mortgage payment = ($771.82)
26	
27	Notice that monthly payments take on a negative value because you
28	pay them.
29	

Sheet1 / Sheet2 / Sheet3

TABLE 5-10 Loan Amortization Schedule Involving a $6,000 Loan at 15 Percent to Be Repaid in Four Years

YEAR	ANNUITY	INTEREST PORTION OF THE ANNUITY[a]	REPAYMENT OF THE PRINCIPAL PORTION OF THE ANNUITY[b]	OUTSTANDING LOAN BALANCE AFTER THE ANNUITY PAYMENT
1	$2,101.58	$900.00	$1,201.58	$4,798.42
2	2,101.58	719.76	1,381.82	3,416.60
3	2,101.58	512.49	1,589.09	1,827.51
4	2,101.58	274.07	1,827.51	

[a]The interest portion of the annuity is calculated by multiplying the outstanding loan balance at the beginning of the year by the interest rate of 15 percent. Thus, for year 1 it was $6,000.00 × .15 = $900.00, for year 2 it was $4,798.42 × .15 = $719.76, and so on.

[b]Repayment of the principal portion of the annuity was calculated by subtracting the interest portion of the annuity (column 2) from the annuity (column 1).

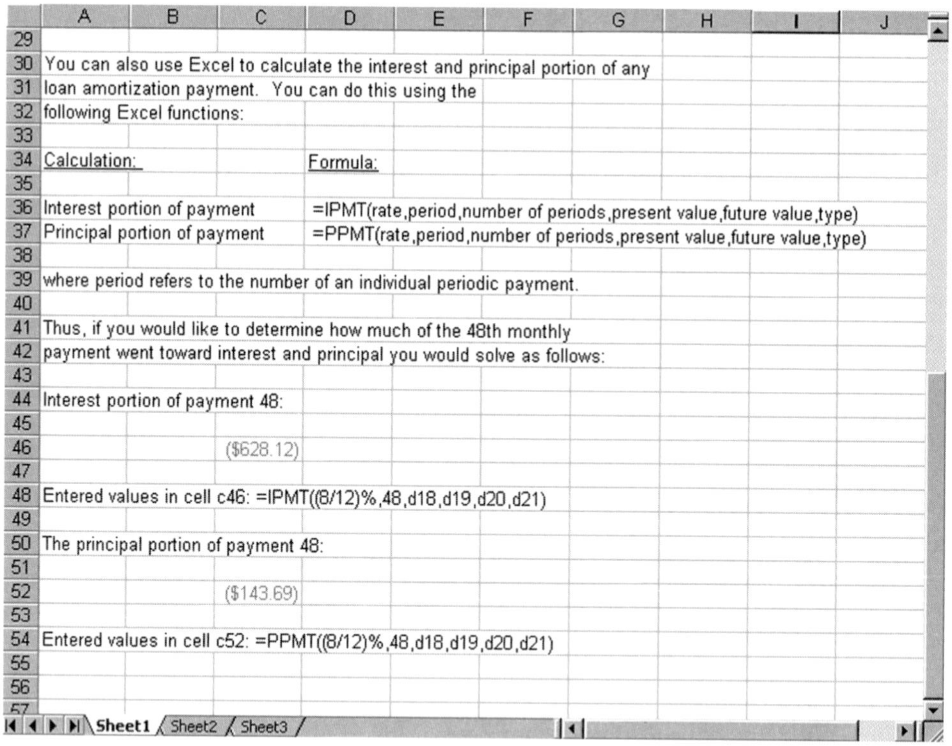

You can also use Excel to calculate the interest and principal portion of any loan amortization payment. You can do this using the following Excel functions:

Calculation:	Formula:
Interest portion of payment	=IPMT(rate,period,number of periods,present value,future value,type)
Principal portion of payment	=PPMT(rate,period,number of periods,present value,future value,type)

where period refers to the number of an individual periodic payment.

Thus, if you would like to determine how much of the 48th monthly payment went toward interest and principal you would solve as follows:

Interest portion of payment 48:

($628.12)

Entered values in cell c46: =IPMT((8/12)%,48,d18,d19,d20,d21)

The principal portion of payment 48:

($143.69)

Entered values in cell c52: =PPMT((8/12)%,48,d18,d19,d20,d21)

Sheet1 Sheet2 Sheet3

Objective 6

PRESENT VALUE OF COMPLEX STREAM

Although some projects will involve a single cash flow and some annuities, many projects will involve uneven cash flows over several years. Chapter 9, which examines investments in fixed assets, presents this situation repeatedly. There we will be comparing not only the present value of cash flows between projects, but also the cash inflows and outflows within a particular project, trying to determine that project's present value. However, this will not be difficult because the present value of any cash flow is measured in today's dol-

TABLE 5-11 Illustration of an Example of Present Value of an Uneven Stream Involving One Annuity Discounted to Present at 6 Percent

YEAR	0	1	2	3	4	5	6	7	8	9	10
Dollars received at end of year		500	200	–400	500	500	500	500	500	500	500
	$ 471.50 ← (year 1)										
	178.00 ← (year 2)										
	–336.00 ← (year 3)										
				$2,791 ← (years 4–10)							
	$2,344.44 ← ($2,791)										
Total present value	$2,657.94										

lars and thus can be compared, through addition for inflows and subtraction for outflows, to the present value of any other cash flow also measured in today's dollars.

YEAR	CASH FLOW	YEAR	CASH FLOW
1	$500	6	$500
2	200	7	500
3	–400	8	500
4	500	9	500
5	500	10	500

For example, if we wished to find the present value of the cash flows provided above given a 6 percent discount rate, we would merely discount the flows back to the present and total them by adding in the positive flows and subtracting the negative ones. However, this problem also contains the annuity of $500 that runs from years 4 through 10. To accommodate this, we can first discount the annuity back to the beginning of period 4 (or end of period 3) by multiplying it by the value of $PVIFA_{6\%,7yrs}$ and get its present value at that point in time. We then multiply this value times the $PVIF_{6\%,3yrs}$ in order to bring this single cash flow (which is the present value of the seven-year annuity) back to the present. In effect, we discount twice—first back to the end of period 3, then back to the present. This is shown graphically in Table 5-11 and numerically in Table 5-12. Thus, the present value of this uneven stream of cash flows is $2,657.94.

TABLE 5-12 Determination of the Present Value of an Uneven Stream Involving One Annuity Discounted to Present at 6 Percent

1. Present value of $500 received at the end of 1 year = $500(.943) =	$ 471.50
2. Present value of $200 received at the end of 2 years = $200(.890) =	178.00
3. Present value of a $400 outflow at the end of 3 years = –$400(.840) =	–336.00
4. (a) Value at the end of year 3 of a $500 annuity, years 4 through 10 = $500(5.582) = $2,791	
(b) Present value of $2,791 received at the end of year 3 = $2,791(.840) =	$2,344.44
5. Total present value =	$2,657.94

EXAMPLE: PRESENT VALUE OF MULTIPLE CASH FLOWS

What is the present value of an investment involving \$200 received at the end of years 1 through 5, a \$300 cash outflow at the end of year 6, and \$500 received at the end of years 7 through 10, given a 5 percent discount rate? Here we have two annuities, one that can be discounted directly back to the present by multiplying it by the value of the $PVIFA_{5\%,5yrs}$ and one that must be discounted twice to bring it back to the present. This second annuity, which is a four-year annuity, must first be discounted back to the beginning of period 7 (or end of period 6) by multiplying it by the value of the $PVIFA_{5\%,4yrs}$. Then the present value of this annuity at the end of period 6 (which can be viewed as a single cash flow) must be discounted back to the present by multiplying it by the value of the $PVIF_{5\%,6yrs}$. To arrive at the total present value of this investment, we subtract the present value of the \$300 cash outflow at the end of year 6 from the sum of the present value of the two annuities. Table 5-13 shows this graphically; Table 5-14 gives the calculations. Thus, the present value of this series of cash flows is \$1,964.66.

Remember, once the cash flows from an investment have been brought back to present they can be combined by adding and subtracting to determine the project's total present value.

TABLE 5-13 Illustration of an Example of Present Value of an Uneven Stream Involving Two Annuities Discounted to Present at 5 Percent

YEAR	0	1	2	3	4	5	6	7	8	9	10
Dollars received at end of year		200	200	200	200	200	−300	500	500	500	500
	\$ 865.80										
	−223.80										
							\$1,773				
	1,322.66										
Total present value	\$1,964.66										

TABLE 5-14 Determination of Present Value of an Example with Uneven Stream Involving Two Annuities Discounted to Present at 5 Percent

1. Present value of first annuity, years 1 through 5 = \$200(4.329) =	\$ 865.80
2. Present value of \$300 cash outflow = −\$300(.746) =	−223.80
3. (a) Value at end of year 6 of second annuity, years 7 through 10 = \$500(3.546) = \$1,773	
(b) Present value of \$1,773 received at the end of year 6 = \$1,773(.746) =	1,322.66
4. Total present value =	\$1,964.66

CONCEPT CHECK

1. If you wanted to calculate the present value of an investment that produced cash flows of \$100 received at the end of year 1 and \$700 at the end of year 2, how would you do it?

PERPETUITIES AND INFINITE ANNUITIES

Objective 7

A **perpetuity** is an annuity that continues forever; that is, every year from its establishment, this investment pays the same dollar amount. An example of a perpetuity is preferred stock that yields a constant dollar dividend infinitely. Determining the present value of a perpetuity is delightfully simple; we merely need to divide the constant flow by the discount rate.[1] For example, the present value of a $100 perpetuity discounted back to the present at 5 percent is $100/.05 = $2,000. Thus, the equation representing the present value of a perpetuity is

Perpetuity
An annuity that continues forever.

$$PV = \frac{PP}{i} \tag{5-11}$$

→ Perpetuity

where PV = the present value of the perpetuity
PP = the constant dollar amount provided by the perpetuity
i = the annual interest (or discount) rate

EXAMPLE: PRESENT VALUE OF A PERPETUITY

What is the present value of a $500 perpetuity discounted back to the present at 8 percent? Substituting PP = $500 and i = .08 into equation (5-11), we find

$$PV = \frac{\$500}{.08} = \$6{,}250$$

Thus, the present value of this perpetuity is $6,250.

CONCEPT CHECK

1. What is a perpetuity?
2. When *i*, the annual interest (or discount) rate, increases, what happens to the present value of a perpetuity? Why?

MAKING INTEREST RATES COMPARABLE

Objective 8

In order to make intelligent decisions about where to invest or borrow money, it is important that we make the stated interest rates comparable. Unfortunately, some rates are quoted as compounded annually, whereas others are quoted as compounded quarterly or compounded daily. But we already know that it is not fair to compare interest rates with different compounding periods to each other. Thus, the only way interest rates can logically be compared is to convert them to some common compounding period and then compare them. That is what is done with the *annual percentage yield.* In order to understand the process of making different interest rates comparable, it is first necessary to define the **nominal** or **quoted interest rate**.

Nominal or quoted interest rate
The stated rate of interest on the contract.

The nominal or quoted rate is the rate of interest stated on the contract. For example, if you shop around for loans and are quoted 8 percent compounded annually and 7.85 percent

[1] See Chapter 8 for a mathematical derivation.

compounded quarterly, then 8 percent and 7.85 percent would both be nominal rates. Unfortunately, because on one the interest is compounded annually, but on the other interest is compounded quarterly, they are not comparable. In fact, it is never appropriate to compare nominal rates *unless* they include the same number of compounding periods per year. To make them comparable, we must calculate their equivalent rate at some common compounding period. We do this by calculating the **annual percentage yield (APY)** or **effective annual rate (EAR)**. This is the annual compound rate that produces the same return as the nominal or quoted rate.

Annual percentage yield (APY) or effective annual rate (EAR)
The annual compound rate that produces the same return as the nominal or quoted rate.

Let's assume that you are considering borrowing money from a bank at 12 percent compounded monthly. To convert this to an *APY*, we must determine the annual rate that would produce the same return as the nominal rate. In the case of a 12 percent loan compounded monthly, by looking in the *FVIF* table in the back of the book, we see that the future value of $1 in one year at 12 percent compounded monthly (that is, compounded at 1 percent per month for 12 one-month periods) is $1.1268 ($FVIF_{1\%,12\text{periods}} = 1.1268$). This tells us that 12.68 percent is the *APY*, because if we compound $1 at the nominal rate of 12 percent compounded monthly, we would have $1.1268 after one year.

Generalizing on this process, we can calculate the *APY* using the following equation:

$$APY \text{ or } EAR = (1 + \text{quoted rate}/m)^m - 1 \quad \textbf{(5-12)}$$

where *APY* or *EAR* is the annual percentage yield and m is the number of compounding periods within a year. Given the wide variety of compounding periods used by businesses and banks, it is important to know how to make these rates comparable so that logical decisions can be made.

Objective 9

THE MULTINATIONAL FIRM: THE TIME VALUE OF MONEY

From **Principle 1: The Risk-Return Tradeoff—We won't take on additional risk unless we expect to be compensated with additional return,** we found that investors demand a return for delaying consumption, as well as an additional return for taking on added risk. The discount rate that we use to move money through time should reflect this return for delaying consumption; and it should reflect anticipated inflation. In the United States, anticipated inflation is quite low, although it does tend to fluctuate over time. Elsewhere in the world, however, the inflation rate is difficult to predict because it can be dramatically high and undergo huge fluctuations.

Let's look at Argentina, keeping in mind that similar examples abound in Central and South America and Eastern Europe. At the beginning of 1992, Argentina introduced the fifth currency in 22 years, the new peso. The austral, the currency that was replaced, was introduced in June 1985 and was initially equal in value to $1.25 U.S. currency. Five and a half years later, it took 100,000 australs to equal $1. Inflation had reached the point where the stack of money needed to buy a candy bar was bigger and weighed more than the candy bar itself, and many workers received their weeks' wages in grocery bags. Needless to say, if we were to move australs through time, we would have to use an extremely high interest or discount rate. Unfortunately, in countries suffering from hyperinflation, inflation rates tend to fluctuate dramatically, and this makes estimating the expected inflation rate even more difficult. For example, in 1989 the inflation rate in Argentina was 4,924 percent; in 1990 it dropped to 1,344 percent; in 1991 it was only 84 percent; in 1992, only 18 percent; and in 1997 it had fallen to 0.3 percent. However, as inflation in Argentina dropped, inflation in Brazil heated up, going from 426 percent in 1991 to 1,094 percent in 1995, and finally coming under control in 1999 and 2000. But while inflation in one area of the world is finally controlled, it pops up in another area—for example, in mid-2000 inflation in Turkey was over 60 percent. Finally, at the extreme, in 1993 in Serbia the inflation rate reached 360,000,000,000,000,000 percent.

The bottom line on all this is that because of the dramatic fluctuations in inflation that can take place in the international setting, choosing the appropriate discount rate of moving money through time is an extremely difficult process.

CONCEPT CHECK

1. How does the international setting complicate the choice of the appropriate interest rate to use when discounting cash flows back to the present?

HOW FINANCIAL MANAGERS USE THIS MATERIAL

Almost all business decisions involve cash flow occurring in different time periods. It is the techniques and tools introduced in this chapter that allow you to compare these cash flows and, therefore, make the appropriate decision. Perhaps you'll work for Marriott and you'll be deciding whether to build a hotel resort or some new time-share units on the beachfront land Marriott owns on Hilton Head Island. That's a decision that involves spending the money right now to build the complex and then, sometime in the future, either selling the time-share units or receiving rent from tourists at the new hotel resort. It's an understanding of the time value of money that allows you to compare these cash flows that occur in different time periods. In fact, any time you're evaluating a new product, the time value of money comes into play. In short, there isn't another tool in business that is more essential to making good decisions.

As you will see later, the time value of money also plays a central role in determining the price that a share of common stock sells for. That is to say, it was an understanding of the time value of money that allowed the folks at Friendly Ice Cream to determine that Friendly's common stock should be offered to the public at $18 per share when it was first sold. Those same people use the time value of money to determine how much they should save for their children's college education and for retirement, and whether they should refinance their home mortgage. Truly, the concept of the time value of money is one that not only affects all corporate finance decisions, but also affects all personal finance decisions.

SUMMARY

To make decisions, financial managers must compare the costs and benefits of alternatives that do not occur during the same time period. Whether to make profitable investments or to take advantage of favorable interest rates, financial decision making requires an understanding of the time value of money. Managers who use the time value of money in all of their financial calculations assure themselves of more logical decisions. The time value process first makes all dollar values comparable; because money has a time value, it moves all dollar flows either back to the present or out to a common future date. All time value formulas presented in this chapter actually stem from the single compounding formula $FV_n = PV(1 + i)^n$. The formulas are used to deal simply with common financial situations, for example, discounting single flows, compounding annuities, and discounting annuities. Table 5-15 provides a summary of these calculations.

TABLE 5-15 Summary of Time Value of Money Equations[a]

	CALCULATION	EQUATION
Objective 1	Future value of a single payment	$FV_n = PV(1+i)^n$ or $PV(FVIF_{i,n})$
Objective 2	Future value of a single payment with nonannual compounding	$FV_n = PV\left(1+\frac{i}{m}\right)^{mn}$
Objective 3	Present value of a single payment	$PV = FV_n\left[\frac{1}{(1+i)^n}\right]$ or $FV_n(PVIF_{i,n})$
Objective 4	Future value of an annuity	$FV_n = PMT\left[\sum_{t=0}^{n-1}(1+i)^t\right]$ or $PMT(FVIFA_{i,n})$
Objective 5	Present value of an annuity	$PV = PMT\left[\sum_{t=1}^{n}\frac{1}{(1+i)^t}\right]$ or $PMT(PVIFA_{i,n})$
	Present value of a perpetuity	$PV = \frac{PP}{i}$
Objective 6	Annual percentage yield (APY)	$APY = \left(1+\frac{\text{quoted rate}}{m}\right)^m - 1$

Notation: FV_n = the future value of the investment at the end of n years
n = the number of years until payment will be received or during which compounding occurs
i = the annual interest or discount rate
PV = the present value of the future sum of money
m = the number of times compounding occurs during the year
PMT = the annuity payment deposited or received at the end of each year
PP = the constant dollar amount provided by the perpetuity

[a]Related tables appear in Appendices B through E at the end of the book.

KEY TERMS

Go To: www.prenhall.com/keown for downloads and current events associated with this chapter

Amortized loan, 159
Annual percentage yield (APY) or effective annual rate (EAR), 164
Annuity, 150
Annuity due, 151
Compound annuity, 151
Compound interest, 138
Future-value interest factor ($FVIF_{i,n}$), 141
Future-value interest factor for an annuity ($FVIFA_{i,n}$), 151
Loan amortization schedule, 159
Nominal or quoted interest rate, 163
Ordinary annuity, 151
Perpetuity, 163
Present value, 147
Present-value interest factor ($PVIF_{i,n}$), 148
Present-value interest factor for an annuity ($PVIFA_{i,n}$), 155

STUDY QUESTIONS

5-1. What is the time value of money? Why is it so important?

5-2. The processes of discounting and compounding are related. Explain this relationship.

5-3. How would an increase in the interest rate (i) or a decrease in the holding period (n) affect the future value (FV_n) of a sum of money? Explain why.

5-4. Suppose you were considering depositing your savings in one of three banks, all of which pay 5 percent interest; bank A compounds annually, bank B compounds semiannually, and bank C compounds daily. Which bank would you choose? Why?

5-5. What is the relationship between the $PVIF_{i,n}$ (Table 5-4) and the $PVIFA_{i,n}$ (Table 5-8)? What is the $PVIFA_{10\%,10yrs}$? Add up the values of the $PVIF_{10\%,n}$ for $n = 1, \ldots, 10$. What is this value? Why do these values have the relationship they do?

5-6. What is an annuity? Give some examples of annuities. Distinguish between an annuity and a perpetuity.

SELF-TEST PROBLEMS

ST-1. You place \$25,000 in a savings account paying annual compound interest of 8 percent for three years and then move it into a savings account that pays 10 percent interest compounded annually. How much will your money have grown at the end of six years?

ST-2. You purchase a boat for \$35,000 and pay \$5,000 down and agree to pay the rest over the next 10 years in 10 equal annual payments that include principal payments plus 13 percent of compound interest on the unpaid balance. What will be the amount of each payment?

ST-3. For an investment to grow eightfold in nine years, at what rate would it have to grow?

STUDY PROBLEMS (SET A)

5-1A. (*Compound interest*) To what amount will the following investments accumulate?

a. \$5,000 invested for 10 years at 10 percent compounded annually
b. \$8,000 invested for 7 years at 8 percent compounded annually
c. \$775 invested for 12 years at 12 percent compounded annually
d. \$21,000 invested for 5 years at 5 percent compounded annually

5-2A. (*Compound value solving for* n) How many years will the following take?

a. \$500 to grow to \$1,039.50 if invested at 5 percent compounded annually
b. \$35 to grow to \$53.87 if invested at 9 percent compounded annually
c. \$100 to grow to \$298.60 if invested at 20 percent compounded annually
d. \$53 to grow to \$78.76 if invested at 2 percent compounded annually

5-3A. (*Compound value solving for* i) At what annual rate would the following have to be invested?

a. \$500 to grow to \$1,948.00 in 12 years
b. \$300 to grow to \$422.10 in 7 years
c. \$50 to grow to \$280.20 in 20 years
d. \$200 to grow to \$497.60 in 5 years

5-4A. (*Present value*) What is the present value of the following future amounts?

a. \$800 to be received 10 years from now discounted back to the present at 10 percent
b. \$300 to be received 5 years from now discounted back to the present at 5 percent
c. \$1,000 to be received 8 years from now discounted back to the present at 3 percent
d. \$1,000 to be received 8 years from now discounted back to the present at 20 percent

5-5A. (*Compound annuity*) What is the accumulated sum of each of the following streams of payments?

a. \$500 a year for 10 years compounded annually at 5 percent
b. \$100 a year for 5 years compounded annually at 10 percent
c. \$35 a year for 7 years compounded annually at 7 percent
d. \$25 a year for 3 years compounded annually at 2 percent

5-6A. (*Present value of an annuity*) What is the present value of the following annuities?

a. \$2,500 a year for 10 years discounted back to the present at 7 percent
b. \$70 a year for 3 years discounted back to the present at 3 percent
c. \$280 a year for 7 years discounted back to the present at 6 percent
d. \$500 a year for 10 years discounted back to the present at 10 percent

5-7A. (*Compound value*) Brian Mosallam, who recently sold his Porsche, placed $10,000 in a savings account paying annual compound interest of 6 percent.

a. Calculate the amount of money that will have accrued if he leaves the money in the bank for 1, 5, and 15 years.
b. If he moves his money into an account that pays 8 percent or one that pays 10 percent, rework part (a) using these new interest rates.
c. What conclusions can you draw about the relationship between interest rates, time, and future sums from the calculations you have done above?

5-8A. (*Compound interest with nonannual periods*) Calculate the amount of money that will be in each of the following accounts at the end of the given deposit period:

ACCOUNT	AMOUNT DEPOSITED	ANNUAL INTEREST RATE	COMPOUNDING PERIOD (COMPOUNDED EVERY __ MONTHS)	DEPOSIT PERIOD (YEARS)
Theodore Logan III	$ 1,000	10%	12	10
Vernell Coles	95,000	12	1	1
Thomas Elliott	8,000	12	2	2
Wayne Robinson	120,000	8	3	2
Eugene Chung	30,000	10	6	4
Kelly Cravens	15,000	12	4	3

5-9A. (*Compound interest with nonannual periods*)

a. Calculate the future sum of $5,000, given that it will be held in the bank five years at an annual interest rate of 6 percent.
b. Recalculate part (a) using a compounding period that is (1) semiannual and (2) bimonthly.
c. Recalculate parts (a) and (b) for a 12 percent annual interest rate.
d. Recalculate part (a) using a time horizon of 12 years (annual interest rate is still 6 percent).
e. With respect to the effect of changes in the stated interest rate and holding periods on future sums in parts (c) and (d), what conclusions do you draw when you compare these figures with the answers found in parts (a) and (b)?

5-10A. (*Solving for* i *in annuities*) Nicki Johnson, a sophomore mechanical engineering student, receives a call from an insurance agent who believes that Nicki is an older woman ready to retire from teaching. He talks to her about several annuities that she could buy that would guarantee her an annual fixed income. The annuities are as follows:

ANNUITY	INITIAL PAYMENT INTO ANNUITY (AT $t = 0$)	AMOUNT OF MONEY RECEIVED PER YEAR	DURATION OF ANNUITY (YEARS)
A	$50,000	$8,500	12
B	60,000	7,000	25
C	70,000	8,000	20

If Nicki could earn 11 percent on her money by placing it in a savings account, should she place it instead in any of the annuities? Which ones, if any? Why?

5-11A. (*Future value*) Sales of a new finance book were 15,000 copies this year and were expected to increase by 20 percent per year. What are expected sales during each of the next three years? Graph this sales trend and explain.

5-12A. (*Future value*) Reggie Jackson, formerly of the New York Yankees, hit 41 home runs in 1980. If his home-run output grew at a rate of 10 percent per year, what would it have been over the following five years?

5-13A. (*Loan amortization*) Mr. Bill S. Preston, Esq., purchased a new house for $80,000. He paid $20,000 down and agreed to pay the rest over the next 25 years in 25 equal annual payments that include principal payments plus 9 percent compound interest on the unpaid balance. What will these equal payments be?

5-14A. (*Solving for* PMT *in an annuity*) To pay for your child's education, you wish to have accumulated $15,000 at the end of 15 years. To do this, you plan to deposit an equal amount into the bank at the end of each year. If the bank is willing to pay 6 percent compounded annually, how much must you deposit each year to obtain your goal?

5-15A. (*Solving for* i *in compound interest*) If you were offered $1,079.50 10 years from now in return for an investment of $500 currently, what annual rate of interest would you earn if you took the offer?

5-16A. (*Future value of an annuity*) In 10 years, you plan to retire and buy a house in Oviedo, Florida. The house you are looking at currently costs $100,000 and is expected to increase in value each year at a rate of 5 percent. Assuming you can earn 10 percent annually on your investments, how much must you invest at the end of each of the next 10 years to be able to buy your dream home when you retire?

5-17A. (*Compound value*) The Aggarwal Corporation needs to save $10 million to retire a $10 million mortgage that matures in 10 years. To retire this mortgage, the company plans to put a fixed amount into an account at the end of each year for 10 years. The Aggarwal Corporation expects to earn 9 percent annually on the money in this account. What equal annual contribution must it make to this account to accumulate the $10 million by the end of 10 years?

5-18A. (*Compound interest with nonannual periods*) After examining the various personal loan rates available to you, you find that you can borrow funds from a finance company at 12 percent compounded monthly or from a bank at 13 percent compounded annually. Which alternative is the most attractive?

5-19A. (*Present value of an uneven stream of payments*) You are given three investment alternatives to analyze. The cash flows from these three investments are as follows:

Investment

END OF YEAR	A	B	C
1	$10,000		$10,000
2	10,000		
3	10,000		
4	10,000		
5	10,000	$10,000	
6		10,000	50,000
7		10,000	
8		10,000	
9		10,000	
10		10,000	10,000

Assuming a 20 percent discount rate, find the present value of each investment.

5-20A. (*Present value*) The Kumar Corporation plans to issue bonds that pay no interest but can be converted into $1,000 at maturity, seven years from their purchase. To price these bonds competitively with other bonds of equal risk, it is determined that they should yield 10 percent, compounded annually. At what price should the Kumar Corporation sell these bonds?

5-21A. (*Perpetuities*) What is the present value of the following?

a. A $300 perpetuity discounted back to the present at 8 percent
b. A $1,000 perpetuity discounted back to the present at 12 percent
c. A $100 perpetuity discounted back to the present at 9 percent
d. A $95 perpetuity discounted back to the present at 5 percent

5-22A. (*Present value of an annuity due*) What is the present value of a 10-year annuity due of $1,000 annually given a 10 percent discount rate?

5-23A. (*Solving for* n *with nonannual periods*) About how many years would it take for your investment to grow fourfold if it were invested at 16 percent compounded semiannually?

5-24A. (*Present value of an uneven stream of payments*) You are given three investment alternatives to analyze. The cash flows from these three investments are as follows:

Investment

END OF YEAR	A	B	C
1	$2,000	$2,000	$5,000
2	3,000	2,000	5,000
3	4,000	2,000	−5,000
4	−5,000	2,000	−5,000
5	5,000	5,000	15,000

What is the present value of each of these three investments if 10 percent is the appropriate discount rate?

5-25A. (*Complex present value*) How much do you have to deposit today so that beginning 11 years from now you can withdraw $10,000 a year for the next five years (periods 11 through 15) plus an *additional* amount of $20,000 in the last year (period 15)? Assume an interest rate of 6 percent.

5-26A. (*Loan amortization*) On December 31, Beth Klemkosky bought a yacht for $50,000, paying $10,000 down and agreeing to pay the balance in 10 equal annual installments that include both the principal and 10 percent interest on the declining balance. How big would the annual payments be?

5-27A. (*Solving for* i *in an annuity*) You lend a friend $30,000, which your friend will repay in five equal annual payments of $10,000, with the first payment to be received one year from now. What rate of return does your loan receive?

5-28A. (*Solving for* i *in compound interest*) You lend a friend $10,000, for which your friend will repay you $27,027 at the end of five years. What interest rate are you charging your "friend"?

5-29A. (*Loan amortization*) A firm borrows $25,000 from the bank at 12 percent compounded annually to purchase some new machinery. This loan is to be repaid in equal annual installments at the end of each year over the next five years. How much will each annual payment be?

5-30A. (*Present-value comparison*) You are offered $1,000 today, $10,000 in 12 years, or $25,000 in 25 years. Assuming that you can earn 11 percent on your money, which should you choose?

5-31A. (*Compound annuity*) You plan to buy some property in Florida five years from today. To do this, you estimate that you will need $20,000 at that time for the purchase. You would like to accumulate these funds by making equal annual deposits in your savings account, which pays 12 percent annually. If you make your first deposit at the end of this year, and you would like your account to reach $20,000 when the final deposit is made, what will be the amount of your deposits?

5-32A. (*Complex present value*) You would like to have $50,000 in 15 years. To accumulate this amount, you plan to deposit each year an equal sum in the bank, which will earn 7 percent interest compounded annually. Your first payment will be made at the end of the year.

a. How much must you deposit annually to accumulate this amount?

b. If you decide to make a large lump-sum deposit today instead of the annual deposits, how large should this lump-sum deposit be? (Assume you can earn 7 percent on this deposit.)

c. At the end of five years, you will receive $10,000 and deposit this in the bank toward your goal of $50,000 at the end of 15 years. In addition to this deposit, how much must you deposit in equal annual deposits to reach your goal? (Again, assume you can earn 7 percent on this deposit.)

5-33A. (*Comprehensive present value*) You are trying to plan for retirement in 10 years and currently you have $100,000 in a savings account and $300,000 in stocks. In addition, you plan to add to your savings by depositing $10,000 per year in your *savings account* at the end of each of the next five years and then $20,000 per year at the end of each year for the final five years until retirement.

a. Assuming your savings account returns 7 percent compounded annually and your investment in stocks will return 12 percent compounded annually, how much will you have at the end of 10 years? (Ignore taxes.)

b. If you expect to live for 20 years after you retire, and at retirement you deposit all of your savings in a bank account paying 10 percent, how much can you withdraw each year after retirement (20 equal withdrawals beginning one year after you retire) to end up with a zero balance at death?

5-34A. (*Loan amortization*) On December 31, Son-Nan Chen borrowed $100,000, agreeing to repay this sum in 20 equal annual installments that include both the principal and 15 percent interest on the declining balance. How large will the annual payments be?

5-35A. (*Loan amortization*) To buy a new house you must borrow $150,000. To do this, you take out a $150,000, 30-year, 10 percent mortgage. Your mortgage payments, which are made at the end of each year (one payment each year), include both principal and 10 percent interest on the declining balance. How large will your annual payments be?

5-36A. (*Present value*) The state lottery's million-dollar payout provides for $1 million to be paid over 19 years in $50,000 amounts. The first $50,000 payment is made immediately and the 19 remaining $50,000 payments occur at the end of each of the next 19 years. If 10 percent is the appropriate discount rate, what is the present value of this stream of cash flows? If 20 percent is the appropriate discount rate, what is the present value of the cash flows?

5-37A. (*Compounding an annuity due*) Find the future value at the end of year 10 of an annuity due of $1,000 per year for 10 years compounded annually at 10 percent. What would be the future value of this annuity if it were compounded annually at 15 percent?

5-38A. (*Present value of an annuity due*) Determine the present value of an annuity due of $1,000 per year for 10 years discounted back to the present at an annual rate of 10 percent. What would be the present value of this annuity due if it were discounted at an annual rate of 15 percent?

5-39A. (*Present value of a future annuity*) Determine the present value of an ordinary annuity of $1,000 per year for 10 years with the first cash flow from the annuity coming at the end of year 8 (that is, no payments at the end of years 1 through 7 and annual payments at the end of years 8 through 17) given a 10 percent discount rate.

5-40A. (*Solving for* i *in compound interest—financial calculator needed*) In September 1963, the first issue of the comic book *X-MEN* was issued. The original price for the issue was 12 cents. By September 2000, 38 years later, the value of this comic book had risen to $6,500. What annual rate of interest would you have earned if you had bought the comic in 1963 and sold it in 2000?

5-41A. (*Comprehensive present value*) You have just inherited a large sum of money, and you are trying to determine how much you should save for retirement and how much you can spend now. For retirement, you will deposit today (January 1, 2004) a lump sum in a bank account paying 10 percent compounded annually. You don't plan on touching this deposit until you retire in five years (January 1, 2009), and you plan on living for 20 additional years and then to drop dead on December 31, 2028. During your retirement, you would like to receive income of $50,000 per year to be received the first day of each year, with the first payment on January 1, 2009, and the last payment on January 1, 2028. Complicating this objective is your desire to have one final three-year fling during which time you'd like to track down all the original members of *Leave It to Beaver* and *The Brady Bunch* and get their autographs. To finance this, you want to receive $250,000 on January 1, 2024, and *nothing* on January 1, 2025 and January 1, 2026, because you will be on the road. In addition, after you pass on (January 1, 2029), you would like to have a total of $100,000 to leave to your children.

- **a.** How much must you deposit in the bank at 10 percent on January 1, 2004, to achieve your goal? (Use a time line to answer this question.)
- **b.** What kinds of problems are associated with this analysis and its assumptions?

5-42A. (*Spreadsheet problem*) If you invest $900 in a bank where it will earn 8 percent compounded annually, how much will it be worth at the end of seven years? Use a spreadsheet to do your calculations.

5-43A. (*Spreadsheet problem*) In 20 years you would like to have $250,000 to buy a vacation home, but you have only $30,000. At what rate must your $30,000 be compounded annually for it to grow to $250,000 in 20 years? Use a spreadsheet to calculate your answer.

5-44A. (*Spreadsheet problem*) You take out a 25-year mortgage for $300,000 to buy a new house. What will your monthly interest rate payments be if the interest rate on your mortgage is 8 percent? Use a spreadsheet to calculate your answer. Now, calculate the portion of the 48th monthly payment that goes toward interest and principal.

5-45A. (*Future and present value using a calculator*) Bill Gates' billions! Over the past few years Microsoft founder Bill Gates' net worth has fluctuated between $30 and $130 billion. In early 2003 it was about $33 billion—after he reduced his stake in Microsoft from 21 percent to around 14 percent by moving billions into his charitable foundation. Let's see what Bill Gates can do with his money in the following problems.

- **a.** I'll take Manhattan? Manhattan's native tribe sold Manhattan Island to Peter Minuit for $24 in 1626. Now, 378 years later in 2004, Bill Gates wants to buy the island from the "current natives." How much would Bill have to pay for Manhattan if the "current natives" want a 6 percent annual return on the original $24 purchase price?

b. Microsoft Seattle? Bill Gates decides to pass on Manhattan and instead plans to buy the city of Seattle, Washington, for $200 billion in 10 years. How much would Mr. Gates have to invest today at 10 percent compounded annually in order to purchase Seattle in 10 years?

c. Now assume Bill Gates only wants to invest half his net worth today, $50 billion, in order to buy Seattle for $200 billion in 10 years. What annual rate of return would he have to earn in order to complete his purchase in 10 years?

d. Margaritaville? Instead of buying and running large cities, Bill Gates is considering quitting the rigors of the business world and retiring to work on his golf game. To fund his retirement, Bill Gates would invest his $100 billion fortune in safe investments with an expected annual rate of return of 7 percent. Also, Mr. Gates wants to make 40 equal annual withdrawals from this retirement fund beginning a year from today. How much can Mr. Gates' annual withdrawal be in this case?

5-46A. (*Compounding using a calculator*) Bart Simpson, age 10, wants to be able to buy a really cool new car when he turns 16. His really cool car costs $15,000 today, and its cost is expected to increase 3 percent annually. Bart wants to make one deposit today (he can sell his mint-condition original Nuclear Boy comic book) into an account paying 7.5 percent annually in order to buy his car in six years. How much will Bart's car cost, and how much does Bart have to save today in order to buy this car at age 16?

5-47A. (*Compounding using a calculator*) Lisa Simpson wants to have $1,000,000 in 45 years by making equal annual end-of-the-year deposits into a tax-deferred account paying 8.75 percent annually. What must be Lisa's annual deposit?

5-48A. (*Compounding using a calculator*) Springfield mogul Montgomery Burns, age 80, wants to retire at age 100 in order to steal candy from babies full time. Once Mr. Burns retires, he wants to withdraw $1 billion at the beginning of each year for 10 years from a special off-shore account that will pay 20 percent annually. In order to fund his retirement, Mr. Burns will make 20 equal end-of-the-year deposits in this same special account that will pay 20 percent annually. How much money will Mr. Burns need at age 100, and how large of an annual deposit must be made to fund this retirement fund amount?

5-49A. (*Compounding using a calculator and annuities due*) Imagine Homer Simpson actually invested the $100,000 he earned providing Mr. Burns entertainment five years ago at 7.5 percent annual interest and starts investing an additional $1,500 a year today and at the beginning of each year for 20 years at the same 7.5 percent annual rate. How much money will Homer have 20 years from today?

5-50A. (*Nonannual compounding using a calculator*) Prof. Finance is thinking about trading cars. He estimates he will still have to borrow $25,000 to pay for his new car. How large will Prof. Finance's monthly car loan payment be if he can get a five-year (60 equal monthly payments) car loan from the VTech Credit Union at 6.2 percent APR?

5-51A. (*Nonannual compounding using a calculator*) Bowflex's television ads say you can get a fitness machine that sells for $999 for $33 a month for 36 months. What is the APR for this Bowflex loan?

5-52A. (*Nonannual compounding using a calculator*) Ford's current incentives include 4.9 percent APR financing for 60 months or $1,000 cash back on a Mustang. Let's assume Suzie Student wants to buy the premium Mustang convertible, which costs $25,000, and she has no down payment other than the cash back from Ford. If she chooses the $1,000 cash back, Suzie can borrow from the VTech Credit Union at 6.9 percent APR for 60 months (Suzie's credit isn't as good as that of Prof. Finance). What will Suzie Student's monthly payment be under each option? Which option should she choose?

5-53A. (*Nonannual compounding using a calculator*) Ronnie Rental plans to invest $1,000 at the end of each quarter for four years into an account that pays 6.4 percent APR compounded quarterly. He will use this money as a down payment on a new home at the end of the four years. How large will his down payment be four years from today?

5-54A. (*Calculating an APY*) Your Grandma asks for your help in choosing a CD. CD #1 pays 4.95 percent APR compounded daily. CD #2 pays 5.0 percent APR compounded monthly. What is the annual percentage yield (the APY or EAR) of each CD, and which CD do you recommend to your Grandma?

5-55A. (*Nonannual compounding using a calculator*) Dennis Rodman has a $5,000 debt balance on his Visa card that charges 12.9 percent APR compounded monthly. Dennis' current minimum monthly payment is 3 percent of his debt balance, which is $150. How many months (round up) will it take Dennis Rodman to pay off his credit card if he pays the current minimum payment of $150 at the end of each month?

5-56A. (*Nonannual compounding using a calculator*) Should we have bet the kids' college fund at the dog track? In the early 2000s investors suffered substantial declines of mutual funds used in tax-sheltered college savings plans (called 529 plans) around the country. One specific case discussed in the article was a college professor (let's call him Prof. ME) with two young children who, two years ago, had deposited $160,000 hoping to have $420,000 available 12 years later when the first child started college. However, the account's balance is now only $140,000. Let's figure out what is needed to get Prof. ME's college savings plan back on track.

a. What was the original annual rate of return needed to reach Prof. ME's goal when he started the fund two years ago?

b. Now with only $140,000 in the fund and 10 years remaining until his first child starts college, what annual rate of return would the fund have to earn to reach Prof. ME's $420,000 goal if he adds nothing to the account?

c. Shocked by his experience of the past two years, Prof. ME feels the college fund has invested too much in stocks and wants a low risk fund in order to ensure he has the necessary $420,000 in 10 years and is willing to make end-of-the-month deposits to the fund as well. He finds he can get a fund that promises to pay a guaranteed return of 6 percent compounded monthly. Prof. ME decides to transfer the $140,000 to this new fund and make the necessary monthly deposits. How large of a monthly deposit must Prof. ME make into this new fund?

d. Now, Prof. ME gets sticker shock from the necessary monthly deposit he has to make into the guaranteed fund in the last question, and decides to invest the $140,000 today and $500 at the end of each month for the next 10 years into a fund consisting of 50 percent stock and 50 percent bonds and hope for the best. What APR would the fund have to earn in order to reach Prof. ME's $420,000 goal?

WEB WORKS

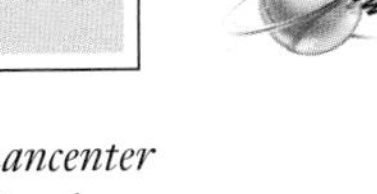

5-1WW. How fast will my money grow? Use the *financial calculator provided by Financenter* (**partners.financenter.com/financenter/calculate/us-eng/savings14.fcs**) to determine how long it will take $50,000 to grow to $90,000 if it earns 10 percent. Again using the *financial calculator provided by Financenter* (**partners.financenter.com/financenter/calculate/us-eng/savings14.fcs**), if you start with $50,000 and invest an additional $250 per month every month, how long will it take to grow to $90,000 if it earns 10 percent?

5-2WW. How much money will you need to start with if you make no additional investments? You want to have $90,000 in six years and your investment will grow at 10 percent. Use the *financial calculator provided by Financenter* (**partners.financenter.com/financenter/calculate/us-eng/savings14.fcs**) to determine how much money you will need to start with.

5-3WW. Financial calculators. Compare some of the different financial calculators that are available on the Internet. Look at both the *Financial Visions calculators* (**www.fvisions.com/consumercalculators/modules.htm**) and the *USA Today's Internet calculators* (**www.usatoday.com/money/calculator.htm**)—consumer loan, tuition, new car, mortgage, retirement, and 401(k) calculators. Also check out *Kiplinger Online calculators* (**www.kiplinger.com/tools/index.html**) which include saving and investing, mutual funds, bonds, stocks, home, auto, credit cards, and budgeting online calculators. Finally look at *Mortgage and Financial Calculators by Hugh Chou* (**www.interest.com/hugh/calc/**). Which financial calculators do you find to be the most useful? Why?

5-4WW. Understanding annuities. Home mortgage payments are an annuity, as are any loans where the payments remain constant. In effect, if you can understand annuities, you'll understand how mortgages and other loans are calculated. What would your monthly loan payments be if you bought a new 60-inch television for $3,400? You put $300 down, and plan to finance the loan over 36 months at 12 percent interest. In addition, when you bought the new television, you received $100 for the trade-in of your old set. Use an *online financial calculator* (**www.calcbuilder.com/cgi-bin/calcs/AUT5.cgi/Kiplinger**) to determine your answer.

5-5WW. College Savings Planning. Try out *Great Western Bank's College Savings Planner* (**www.greatwesternbank.com/College.html**). Enter data in every field except for the monthly savings. Let the interest rate vary and see the effect on how much you must save. What did you learn from this? How does the interest level you can earn affect how much you must save?

INTEGRATIVE PROBLEM

For your job as the business reporter for a local newspaper, you are given the task of putting together a series of articles that explains the power of the time value of money to your readers. Your editor would like you to address several specific questions in addition to demonstrating for the readership the use of the time value of money techniques by applying them to several problems. What would be your response to the following memorandum from your editor?

TO: Business Reporter

FROM: Perry White, Editor, *Daily Planet*

RE: Upcoming Series on the Importance and Power of the Time Value of Money

In your upcoming series on the time value of money, I would like to make sure you cover several specific points. In addition, before you begin this assignment, I want to make sure we are all reading from the same script, because accuracy has always been the cornerstone of the *Daily Planet*. In this regard, I'd like responses to the following questions before we proceed:

1. What is the relationship between discounting and compounding?
2. What is the relationship between the $PVIF_{i,n}$ and $PVIFA_{i,n}$?
3. a. What will $5,000 invested for 10 years at 8 percent compounded annually grow to?
   b. How many years will it take $400 to grow to $1,671, if it is invested at 10 percent compounded annually?
   c. At what rate would $1,000 have to be invested to grow to $4,046 in 10 years?
4. Calculate the future sum of $1,000, given that it will be held in the bank for five years and earn 10 percent compounded semiannually.
5. What is an annuity due? How does this differ from an ordinary annuity?
6. What is the present value of an ordinary annuity of $1,000 per year for seven years discounted back to the present at 10 percent? What would be the present value if it were an annuity due?
7. What is the future value of an ordinary annuity of $1,000 per year for seven years compounded at 10 percent? What would be the future value if it were an annuity due?
8. You have just borrowed $100,000, and you agree to pay it back over the next 25 years in 25 equal end-of-year annual payments that include the principal payments plus 10 percent compound interest on the unpaid balance. What will be the size of these payments?
9. What is the present value of a $1,000 perpetuity discounted back to the present at 8 percent?
10. What is the present value of a $1,000 annuity for 10 years with the first payment occurring at the end of year 10 (that is, ten $1,000 payments occurring at the end of year 10 through year 19) given an appropriate discount rate of 10 percent?
11. Given a 10 percent discount rate, what is the present value of a perpetuity of $1,000 per year if the first payment does not begin until the end of year 10?
12. What is the annual percentage yield (*APY*) on an 8 percent bank loan compounded quarterly?

STUDY PROBLEMS (SET B)

5-1B. (*Compound interest*) To what amount will the following investments accumulate?

a. $4,000 invested for 11 years at 9 percent compounded annually
b. $8,000 invested for 10 years at 8 percent compounded annually

c. \$800 invested for 12 years at 12 percent compounded annually
d. \$21,000 invested for 6 years at 5 percent compounded annually

5-2B. (*Compound value solving for* n) How many years will the following take?

a. \$550 to grow to \$1,043.90 if invested at 6 percent compounded annually
b. \$40 to grow to \$88.44 if invested at 12 percent compounded annually
c. \$110 to grow to \$614.79 if invested at 24 percent compounded annually
d. \$60 to grow to \$78.30 if invested at 3 percent compounded annually

5-3B. (*Compound value solving for* i) At what annual rate would the following have to be invested?

a. \$550 to grow to \$1,898.60 in 13 years
b. \$275 to grow to \$406.18 in 8 years
c. \$60 to grow to \$279.66 in 20 years
d. \$180 to grow to \$486.00 in 6 years

5-4B. (*Present value*) What is the present value of the following future amounts?

a. \$800 to be received 10 years from now discounted back to the present at 10 percent
b. \$400 to be received 6 years from now discounted back to the present at 6 percent
c. \$1,000 to be received 8 years from now discounted back to the present at 5 percent
d. \$900 to be received 9 years from now discounted back to the present at 20 percent

5-5B. (*Compound annuity*) What is the accumulated sum of each of the following streams of payments?

a. \$500 a year for 10 years compounded annually at 6 percent
b. \$150 a year for 5 years compounded annually at 11 percent
c. \$35 a year for 8 years compounded annually at 7 percent
d. \$25 a year for 3 years compounded annually at 2 percent

5-6B. (*Present value of an annuity*) What is the present value of the following annuities?

a. \$3,000 a year for 10 years discounted back to the present at 8 percent
b. \$50 a year for 3 years discounted back to the present at 3 percent
c. \$280 a year for 8 years discounted back to the present at 7 percent
d. \$600 a year for 10 years discounted back to the present at 10 percent

5-7B. (*Compound value*) Trish Nealon, who recently sold her Porsche, placed \$20,000 in a savings account paying annual compound interest of 7 percent.

a. Calculate the amount of money that will have accrued if she leaves the money in the bank for 1, 5, and 15 years.
b. If she moves her money into an account that pays 9 percent or one that pays 11 percent, rework part (a) using these new interest rates.
c. What conclusions can you draw about the relationship among interest rates, time, and future sums from the calculations you have done?

5-8B. (*Compound interest with nonannual periods*) Calculate the amount of money that will be in each of the following accounts at the end of the given deposit period:

ACCOUNT	AMOUNT DEPOSITED	ANNUAL INTEREST RATE	COMPOUNDING PERIOD (COMPOUNDED EVERY __ MONTHS)	DEPOSIT PERIOD (YEARS)
Korey Stringer	\$ 2,000	12%	2	2
Erica Moss	50,000	12	1	1
Ty Howard	7,000	18	2	2
Rob Kelly	130,000	12	3	2
Mary Christopher	20,000	14	6	4
Juan Diaz	15,000	15	4	3

5-9B. (*Compound interest with nonannual periods*)

a. Calculate the future sum of \$6,000, given that it will be held in the bank five years at an annual interest rate of 6 percent.
b. Recalculate part (a) using a compounding period that is (1) semiannual and (2) bimonthly.

c. Recalculate parts (a) and (b) for a 12 percent annual interest rate.
d. Recalculate part (a) using a time horizon of 12 years (annual interest rate is still 6 percent).
e. With respect to the effect of changes in the stated interest rate and holding periods on future sums in parts (c) and (d), what conclusions do you draw when you compare these figures with the answers found in parts (a) and (b)?

5-10B. (*Solving for* i *in annuities*) Ellen Denis, a sophomore mechanical engineering student, receives a call from an insurance agent, who believes that Ellen is an older woman ready to retire from teaching. He talks to her about several annuities that she could buy that would guarantee her an annual fixed income. The annuities are as follows:

ANNUITY	INITIAL PAYMENT INTO ANNUITY (AT $t = 0$)	AMOUNT OF MONEY RECEIVED PER YEAR	DURATION OF ANNUITY (YEARS)
A	$50,000	$8,500	12
B	60,000	7,000	25
C	70,000	8,000	20

If Ellen could earn 12 percent on her money by placing it in a savings account, should she place it instead in any of the annuities? Which ones, if any? Why?

5-11B. (*Future value*) Sales of a new marketing book were 10,000 copies this year and were expected to increase by 15 percent per year. What are expected sales during each of the next three years? Graph this sales trend and explain.

5-12B. (*Future value*) Reggie Jackson, formerly of the New York Yankees, hit 41 home runs in 1980. If his home-run output grew at a rate of 12 percent per year, what would it have been over the following five years?

5-13B. (*Loan amortization*) Stefani Moore purchased a new house for $150,000. She paid $30,000 down and agreed to pay the rest over the next 25 years in 25 equal annual payments that include principal payments plus 10 percent compound interest on the unpaid balance. What will these equal payments be?

5-14B. (*Solving for* PMT *in an annuity*) To pay for your child's education, you wish to have accumulated $25,000 at the end of 15 years. To do this, you plan to deposit an equal amount into the bank at the end of each year. If the bank is willing to pay 7 percent compounded annually, how much must you deposit each year to obtain your goal?

5-15B. (*Solving for* i *in compound interest*) If you were offered $2,376.50 10 years from now in return for an investment of $700 currently, what annual rate of interest would you earn if you took the offer?

5-16B. (*Future value of an annuity*) In 10 years, you plan to retire and buy a house in Marco Island, Florida. The house you are looking at currently costs $125,000 and is expected to increase in value each year at a rate of 5 percent. Assuming you can earn 10 percent annually on your investments, how much must you invest at the end of each of the next 10 years to be able to buy your dream home when you retire?

5-17B. (*Compound value*) The Knutson Corporation needs to save $15 million to retire a $15 million mortgage that matures in 10 years. To retire this mortgage, the company plans to put a fixed amount into an account at the end of each year for 10 years. The Knutson Corporation expects to earn 10 percent annually on the money in this account. What equal annual contribution must it make to this account to accumulate the $15 million by the end of 10 years?

5-18B. (*Compound interest with nonannual periods*) After examining the various personal loan rates available to you, you find that you can borrow funds from a finance company at 24 percent compounded monthly or from a bank at 26 percent compounded annually. Which alternative is the most attractive?

5-19B. (*Present value of an uneven stream of payments*) You are given three investment alternatives to analyze. The cash flows from these three investments are as follows:

Investment

END OF YEAR	A	B	C
1	$15,000		$20,000
2	15,000		
3	15,000		
4	15,000		
5	15,000	$15,000	
6		15,000	60,000
7		15,000	
8		15,000	
9		15,000	
10		15,000	20,000

Assuming a 20 percent discount rate, find the present value of each investment.

5-20B. (*Present value*) The Shin Corporation is planning on issuing bonds that pay no interest but can be converted into $1,000 at maturity, eight years from their purchase. To price these bonds competitively with other bonds of equal risk, it is determined that they should yield 9 percent, compounded annually. At what price should the Shin Corporation sell these bonds?

5-21B. (*Perpetuities*) What is the present value of the following?

a. A $400 perpetuity discounted back to the present at 9 percent
b. A $1,500 perpetuity discounted back to the present at 13 percent
c. A $150 perpetuity discounted back to the present at 10 percent
d. A $100 perpetuity discounted back to the present at 6 percent

5-22B. (*Present value of an annuity due*) What is the present value of a five-year annuity due of $1,000 annually given a 10 percent discount rate?

5-23B. (*Solving for* n *with nonannual periods*) About how many years would it take for your investment to grow sevenfold if it were invested at 10 percent compounded semiannually?

5-24B. (*Present value of an uneven stream of payments*) You are given three investment alternatives to analyze. The cash flows from these three investments are as follows:

Investment

END OF YEAR	A	B	C
1	$5,000	$1,000	$10,000
2	5,000	3,000	10,000
3	5,000	5,000	10,000
4	−15,000	10,000	10,000
5	15,000	−10,000	−40,000

What is the present value of each of these three investments if 10 percent is the appropriate discount rate?

5-25B. (*Complex present value*) How much do you have to deposit today so that beginning 11 years from now you can withdraw $10,000 a year for the next five years (periods 11 through 15), plus an *additional* amount of $15,000 in the last year (period 15)? Assume an interest rate of 7 percent.

5-26B. (*Loan amortization*) On December 31, Loren Billingsley bought a yacht for $60,000, paying $15,000 down and agreeing to pay the balance in 10 equal annual installments that include both the principal and 9 percent interest on the declining balance. How big will the annual payments be?

5-27B. (*Solving for* i *in an annuity*) You lend a friend $45,000, which your friend will repay in five equal annual payments of $9,000 with the first payment to be received one year from now. What rate of return does your loan receive?

5-28B. (*Solving for* i *in compound interest*) You lend a friend $15,000, for which your friend will repay you $37,313 at the end of five years. What interest rate are you charging your "friend"?

5-29B. (*Loan amortization*) A firm borrows $30,000 from the bank at 13 percent compounded annually to purchase some new machinery. This loan is to be repaid in equal annual installments at the end of each year over the next four years. How much will each annual payment be?

5-30B. (*Present value comparison*) You are offered $1,000 today, $10,000 in 12 years, or $25,000 in 25 years. Assuming that you can earn 11 percent on your money, which should you choose?

5-31B. (*Compound annuity*) You plan to buy some property in Florida five years from today. To do this, you estimate that you will need $30,000 at that time for the purchase. You would like to accumulate these funds by making equal annual deposits in your savings account, which pays 10 percent annually. If you make your first deposit at the end of this year and you would like your account to reach $30,000 when the final deposit is made, what will be the amount of your deposits?

5-32B. (*Complex present value*) You would like to have $75,000 in 15 years. To accumulate this amount, you plan to deposit each year an equal sum in the bank, which will earn 8 percent interest compounded annually. Your first payment will be made at the end of the year.

a. How much must you deposit annually to accumulate this amount?
b. If you decide to make a large lump-sum deposit today instead of the annual deposits, how large should this lump-sum deposit be? (Assume you can earn 8 percent on this deposit.)
c. At the end of five years, you will receive $20,000 and deposit this in the bank toward your goal of $75,000 at the end of 15 years. In addition to this deposit, how much must you deposit in equal annual deposits to reach your goal? (Again, assume you can earn 8 percent on this deposit.)

5-33B. (*Comprehensive present value*) You are trying to plan for retirement in 10 years and currently you have $150,000 in a savings account and $250,000 in stocks. In addition, you plan to add to your savings by depositing $8,000 per year in your *savings account* at the end of each of the next five years and then $10,000 per year at the end of each year for the final five years until retirement.

a. Assuming your savings account returns 8 percent compounded annually and your investment in stocks will return 12 percent compounded annually, how much will you have at the end of 10 years? (Ignore taxes.)
b. If you expect to live 20 years after you retire, and at retirement you deposit all of your savings in a bank account paying 11 percent, how much can you withdraw each year after retirement (20 equal withdrawals beginning one year after you retire) to end up with a zero-balance at death?

5-34B. (*Loan amortization*) On December 31, Eugene Chung borrowed $200,000, agreeing to repay this sum in 20 equal annual installments that include both the principal and 10 percent interest on the declining balance. How large will the annual payments be?

5-35B. (*Loan amortization*) To buy a new house, you must borrow $250,000. To do this, you take out a $250,000, 30-year, 9 percent mortgage. Your mortgage payments, which are made at the end of each year (one payment each year), include both principal and 9 percent interest on the declining balance. How large will your annual payments be?

5-36B. (*Present value*) The state lottery's million-dollar payout provides for $1 million to be paid over 24 years in $40,000 amounts. The first $40,000 payment is made immediately with the 24 remaining $40,000 payments occurring at the end of each of the next 24 years. If 10 percent is the appropriate discount rate, what is the present value of this stream of cash flows? If 20 percent is the appropriate discount rate, what is the present value of the cash flows?

5-37B. (*Compounding an annuity due*) Find the future value at the end of year 5 of an annuity due of $1,000 per year for five years compounded annually at 5 percent. What would be the future value of this annuity if it were compounded annually at 8 percent?

5-38B. (*Present value of an annuity*) Determine the present value of an annuity due of $1,000 per year for 15 years discounted back to the present at an annual rate of 12 percent. What would be the present value of this annuity due if it were discounted at an annual rate of 15 percent?

5-39B. (*Present value of a future annuity*) Determine the present value of an ordinary annuity of $1,000 per year for 10 years with the first cash flow from the annuity coming at the end of year 8 (that is, no payments at the end of years 1 through 7 and annual payments at the end of years 8 through 17) given a 15 percent discount rate.

5-40B. (*Solving for* i *in compound interest—financial calculator needed*) In March 1963, issue number 39 of *Tales of Suspense* was issued. The original price for that issue was 12 cents. By March of 2001, 38 years later, the value of this comic book had risen to $3,500. What annual rate of interest would you have earned if you had bought the comic in 1963 and sold it in 2001?

5-41B. (*Comprehensive present value*) You have just inherited a large sum of money and you are trying to determine how much you should save for retirement and how much you can spend now. For retirement you will deposit today (January 1, 2005) a lump sum in a bank account paying 10 percent compounded annually. You don't plan on touching this deposit until you retire in five years (January 1, 2010), and you plan on living for 20 additional years and then drop dead on December 31, 2029. During your retirement, you would like to receive income of $60,000 per year to be received the first day of each year, with the first payment on January 1, 2010, and the last payment on January 1, 2029. Complicating this objective is your desire to have one final three-year fling, during which time you'd like to track down all the original members of *The Mr. Ed Show* and *The Monkees* and get their autographs. To finance this, you want to receive $300,000 on January 1, 2025, and *nothing* on January 1, 2026, and January 1, 2027, as you will be on the road. In addition, after you pass on (January 1, 2030), you would like to have a total of $100,000 to leave to your children.

a. How much must you deposit in the bank at 10 percent on January 1, 2005, in order to achieve your goal? (Use a time line in order to answer this question.)

b. What kinds of problems are associated with this analysis and its assumptions?

SELF-TEST SOLUTIONS

ST-1. This is a compound interest problem in which you must first find the future value of $25,000 growing at 8 percent compounded annually for three years and then allow that future value to grow for an additional three years at 10 percent. First, the value of the $25,000 after three years growing at 8 percent is

$$FV_3 = PV(1 + i)^n$$
$$FV_3 = \$25{,}000\,(1 + .08)^3$$
$$FV_3 = \$25{,}000\,(1.260)$$
$$FV_3 = \$31{,}500$$

Thus, after three years, you have $31,500. Now this amount is allowed to grow for three years at 10 percent. Plugging this into equation 5-6, with $PV = \$31{,}500$, $i = 10$ percent, $n = 3$ years, we solve for FV_3:

$$FV_3 = \$31{,}500(1 + .10)^3$$
$$FV_3 = \$31{,}500(1.331)$$
$$FV_3 = \$41{,}926.50$$

Thus, after six years, the $25,000 will have grown to $41,926.50.

ST-2. This loan amortization problem is actually just a present-value-of-an-annuity problem in which we know the values of i, n, and PV, and are solving for PMT. In this case, the value of i is 13 percent, n is 10 years, and PV is $30,000. Substituting these values into equation 5-10, we find

$$\$30{,}000 = PMT\left[\sum_{t=1}^{10} \frac{1}{(1 + .13)^t}\right]$$

$$\$30{,}000 = PMT(5.426)$$
$$\$5{,}528.93 = PMT$$

ST-3. This is a simple compound interest problem in which FV_9 is eight times larger than PV. Here again, three of the four variables are known: $n = 9$ years, $FV_9 = 8$, and $PV = 1$, and we are solving for i. Substituting these values into equation 5-6, we find

$$FV_9 = PV(1 + i)^n$$
$$FV_9 = PV(FVIF_{i,n})$$
$$8 = 1\,(FVIF_{i,\text{9yrs}})$$
$$8.00 = FVIF_{i,\text{9yrs}}$$

Thus, we are looking for an $FVIF_{i,\text{9yrs}}$ with a value of 8 in Appendix B, which occurs in the nine-year row. If we look in the nine-year row for a value of 8.00, we find it in the 26 percent column (8.004). Thus, the answer is 26 percent.

LEARNING OBJECTIVES

After reading this chapter, you should be able to

1. Describe the relationship between the average returns that investors have earned and riskiness of these returns.
2. Explain the effects of inflation on rates of return.
3. Describe *term structure of interest rates.*
4. Define and measure the expected rate of return of an individual investment.
5. Define and measure the riskiness of an individual investment.
6. Explain how diversifying investments affects the riskiness and expected rate of return of a portfolio or combination of assets.
7. Measure the market risk of an individual asset.
8. Calculate the market risk of a portfolio of investments.
9. Explain the relationship between an investor's required rate of return on an investment and the riskiness of the investment.

CHAPTER 6

Risk and Rates of Return

One of the most important concepts in all of finance deals with risk and return, and our first principle addresses this topic. As an illustration of risk and return, consider what was happening to the stock price of many of the high-tech stocks during 2000.

From January 1, 2000, through March 10, 2000, the Nasdaq Composite Index, dominated by such firms as Microsoft, Oracle, and Intel, increased 25 percent in value—not bad for a mere two months. Many of us probably wished that we had been so "smart" as to buy a group of these high-tech stocks. But by January 2003, the Nasdaq was down 74 percent from its March 2000, high. Imagine how you would feel if you had jumped on the bandwagon in 2000. However, these highly volatile price changes were part of the 1999–2002 landscape if you bought and sold high-tech stocks. In other words, these stocks may produce high rates of return to their owners, but they are risky investments, as signified by their high volatility. As the owner of high-tech stocks during this time, you may have eaten well on the good days, but you certainly didn't sleep very well some nights. Welcome to the world where high rates of return go hand in hand with high risk.

CHAPTER PREVIEW

The need to recognize risk in financial decisions has already been emphasized in earlier chapters. In Chapter 1, we introduced **Principle 1: The Risk-Return Trade-Off—We won't take an additional risk unless we expect to be compensated with additional returns.** In the previous chapter, we observed the importance of the discount rate in comparing financial assets and investment proposals. But we assumed the interest rate to be a given. Now we want to examine where the appropriate rate comes from. We will see that risk is a prime factor in setting the appropriate rate.

There is an intuitive aspect to thinking about risk. Let's approach this by looking at an industry, a firm, and an individual investment proposal. For instance, think intuitively about different industries, such as soft drinks, computers, and biotechs. Which one would we expect to be the most stable? The obvious answer is soft drinks. We can reasonably anticipate this industry to keep chugging along. The computer industry, however, is more volatile. What happens if Intel introduces a faster chip? Will people buy it in large numbers? And the biotech industry is more volatile still—will a cure for AIDS be found? If so, we can imagine that there would be a big payoff, but a lot of money could be spent along the way.

Now consider individual companies involved in seeking an AIDS cure. There are large companies, such as GlaxoSmithKline and Pfizer, and small startups. Do we have any basis for thinking the larger companies have a better chance than the smaller ones? Does size imply financial commitment or superior resources?

Now think about a particular company, such as Pfizer. Finding an AIDS cure could give it a huge boost in profits. But Pfizer has many different products. An AIDS cure may not be as important to Pfizer's future as it would be for a one-product startup company.

In all of these cases, we have an intuitive sense of differences in prospects. We will now turn to how this intuitive sense flows into the returns one can expect to receive from a particular investment

(continued)

proposal. We will see the relationship between risk and average returns of different investments. We will show how we can quantify this concept of risk, and how this determines the interest rate we used in discounting to compare projects. The concept of risk is a crucial one for the financial manager. This chapter will show where it comes from and how it can be used to compare financial assets.

Three principles will serve as the foundation for this chapter. Keeping them in mind throughout will be helpful in your study. These axioms are **Principle 1: The Risk-Return Trade-Off—We won't take on additional risk unless we expect to be compensated with additional returns; Principle 3: Cash—Not Profits—Is King; Principle 9: All Risk Is Not Equal—Some risk can be diversified away, and some cannot.**

Watch for these principles and let them be the thread that connects the ideas presented in this chapter. Let's now begin our study by looking at what we mean by the expected rate of return and how it can be measured.

Objective 1

RATES OF RETURN IN THE FINANCIAL MARKETS

In the financial markets where stocks and bonds are sold, net users of money, such as companies that make investments, have to compete with one another for capital. To obtain financing for projects that will benefit a firm's stockholders, a company must offer investors a rate of return that is *competitive* with the next best investment alternative available to the investor. This rate of return on the next best investment alternative to the saver is known as the investor's **opportunity cost of funds**.

Opportunity cost of funds
The next best rate of return available to the investor for a given level of risk.

As managers, we need to understand the investor's opportunity cost of investing; that is, what could an investor earn by investing in another company of similar risk? Only by answering this question can a financial manager begin to understand whether the shareholders are receiving a fair return on their investments. Also, from an investor's perspective, there is a need to know the historical experience of other investors in the capital markets; otherwise, there is no basis for knowing what can be reasonably expected in terms of rates of returns.

THE RELATIONSHIP BETWEEN RISK AND RATES OF RETURN

History can tell us a great deal about the returns that investors earn in the financial markets. A primary source for an historical perspective comes from Ibbotson and Sinquefield's *Stocks, Bonds, Bills, and Inflation*, which examines the realized rates of return for a wide variety of securities spanning the period from 1926 through 2002. Their data are comprehensive and extremely useful both to investors and financial managers in their respective needs for understanding rates of returns in the capital markets. In their results, they summarize, among other things, the annual returns for different portfolios of securities, five of them being:[1]

1. Common stocks of small firms
2. Common stocks of large companies
3. Long-term corporate bonds
4. Long-term U.S. government bonds
5. U.S. Treasury bills

[1] Roger G. Ibbotson and Rex A. Sinquefield, *Stocks, Bonds, Bills, and Inflation: Historical Return* (1926–1999) (Chicago, IL: Ibbotson Associates, 2003).

TABLE 6-1 Annual Rates of Return 1926–2002

SECURITIES	NOMINAL AVERAGE ANNUAL RETURNS	STANDARD DEVIATION OF RETURNS	REAL AVERAGE ANNUAL RETURNS[a]	RISK PREMIUM[b]
Small-company Stocks	16.9%	33.2%	13.8%	13.1%
Large-company Stocks	12.2	20.5	9.1	8.4
Long-term Corporate Bonds	6.2	8.7	3.1	2.4
Long-term Government Bonds	5.8	9.4	2.7	2.0
U.S. Treasury Bills	3.8	3.2	0.7	0.0

[a]Real return equals the nominal return less the average inflation rate from 1926 through 2002 of 3.1 percent.

[b]Risk premium equals the nominal return less the average risk-free rate (Treasury bills) of 3.8 percent.

Source: R. G. Ibbotson and R. A. Sinquefield, *Stocks, Bonds, Bills, and Inflation: Historical Returns* (Chicago, IL: Ibbotson Associates, 2003): 31. © Ibbotson Associates.

Before comparing the actual rates of returns and their variability (risk), we should first think about what to expect. First, we would intuitively expect a Treasury bill to be the least risky of the five portfolios. Because a Treasury bill has a short-term maturity date, the price is less volatile (less risky) than the price of a long-term government security.[2] In turn, because there is a chance of default on a corporate bond, which is essentially nonexistent for government securities, a long-term government bond is less risky than a long-term corporate bond. Finally, common stock of large companies is more risky than a corporate bond, with small-company stocks being more risky than the portfolio of large-firm stocks.

By smaller firm, we do not mean the "mom-and-pop" store down on the corner, but rather the smallest companies listed on the New York Stock Exchange (the bottom 20 percent, to be exact). It is believed that these smaller companies are more risky than the really large firms. Why might that be? First, smaller businesses experience greater risk in their operations—they are more sensitive to business downturns, and some operate in niche markets that can quickly appear and then quickly disappear. Second, they rely more heavily on debt financing than do larger firms. These differences create more variability in their profits and cash flows, which translates into greater risk.

With the foregoing in mind, we should expect different rates of return to the holders of these varied securities. If the market rewards an investor for assuming risk, the average annual rates of return should increase as risk increases.

A comparison of the annual rates of return for the five portfolios listed previously for the years 1926 to 2002 is provided in Table 6-1. Four attributes of these returns are included: (1) the *nominal* average annual rate of return; (2) the standard deviation of the returns, which measures the volatility or riskiness of the portfolios; (3) the *real* average annual rate of return, which is the nominal return less the inflation rate; and (4) the risk premium, which represents the additional return received beyond the risk-free rate (Treasury bill rate) for assuming risk.

Looking first at the two columns of average annual returns and standard deviations, we gain an overview of the risk-return relationships that have existed over the 76 years ending in 2002. For the most part, there has been a positive relationship between risk and

[2] For an explanation of the greater volatility for long-term bonds relative to short-term bonds, see Chapter 7.

return, with Treasury bills being the least risky and common stocks of small companies being the most risky.

The return information in Table 6-1 demonstrates that common stock has been the investor's primary inflation hedge (returns are greater than the inflation rate) in the long run—the average inflation rate has been 3.1 percent—and offered the highest risk premium. However, it is equally apparent that the common stockholder is exposed to sizable risk, as demonstrated by a 20.5 percent standard deviation for large-company stocks and a 33.2 percent standard deviation for small-company stocks. In fact, in the 1926 to 2002 time frame, large-company common shareholders received negative returns in 22 of the 76 years, compared with only 1 in 76 for Treasury bills.

Objective 2

THE EFFECTS OF INFLATION ON RATES OF RETURN AND THE FISHER EFFECT

Real rate of interest The nominal rate of interest less the expected rate of inflation over the maturity of the fixed-income security. This represents the expected increase in actual purchasing power to the investor.

When a rate of interest is quoted, it is generally the nominal, or observed rate. The **real rate of interest**, in contrast, represents the rate of increase in actual purchasing power, after adjusting for inflation. For example, if you have \$100 today and lend it to someone for a year at a nominal rate of interest of 11.3 percent, you will get back \$111.30 in one year. But if during the year prices of goods and services rise by 5 percent, it will take \$105 at year end to purchase the same goods and services that \$100 purchased at the beginning of the year. What was your increase in purchasing power over the year? The quick and dirty answer is found by subtracting the inflation rate from the nominal rate, 11.3 – 5 = 6.3 percent, but this is not exactly correct. To be more precise, let the nominal rate of interest be represented by k_{rf}, the anticipated rate of inflation by *IRP*, and the real rate of interest by k^*. Using these notations, we can express the relationship among the nominal interest rate, the rate of inflation, and the real rate of interest as follows:

$$1 + k_{rf} = (1 + k^*)\,(1 + IRP) \qquad \textbf{(6-1)}$$

or

$$k_{rf} = k^* + IRP + (k^* \times IRP)$$

Consequently, the nominal rate of interest (k_{rf}) is equal to the sum of the real rate of interest (k^*), the inflation rate (*IRP*), and the product of the real rate and the inflation rate. This relationship among nominal rates, real rates, and the rate of inflation has come to be called the *Fisher effect.*[3] It means that the observed nominal rate of interest includes both the real rate and an *inflation premium*, as noted in the previous section.

Substituting into equation 6-1 using a nominal rate of 11.3 percent and an inflation rate of 5 percent, we can calculate the real rate of interest, k^*, as follows:

$$\begin{aligned} k_{rf} &= k^* + IRP + (k^* \times IRP) \\ .113 &= k^* + .05 + .05k^* \\ k^* &= .06 = 6\% \end{aligned}$$

Thus, at the new higher prices, your purchasing power will have increased by only 6 percent, although you have \$11.30 more than you had at the start of the year. To see why, let's assume that at the outset of the year one unit of the market basket of

[3] This relationship was analyzed many years ago by Irving Fisher. For those who want to explore "Fisher's theory of interest" in more detail, a fine overview is contained in Peter N. Ireland, "Long-Term Interest Rates and Inflation: A Fisherian Approach," *Federal Reserve Bank of Richmond, Economic Quarterly* 82 (Winter 1996), pp. 22–26.

goods and services costs $1, so you could purchase 100 units with your $100. At the end of the year you have $11.30 more, but each unit now costs $1.05 (remember the 5 percent rate of inflation). How many units can you buy at the end of the year? The answer is $111.30 ÷ $1.05 = 106, which represents a 6 percent increase in real purchasing power.[4]

THE TERM STRUCTURE OF INTEREST RATES

Objective 3

The relationship between a debt security's rate of return and the length of time until the debt matures is known as the **term structure of interest rates** or the **yield to maturity**. For the relationship to be meaningful to us, all the factors other than maturity, meaning factors such as the chance of the bond defaulting, must be held constant.

Term structure of interest rates (yield to maturity) Relationship between a debt security's rate of return and the length of time until the debt matures.

Thus, the term structure reflects observed rates or yields on similar securities, except for the length of time until maturity, at a particular moment in time.

Figure 6-1 shows an example of the term structure of interest rates. The curve is upward sloping, indicating that longer terms to maturity command higher returns, or yields. In this hypothetical term structure, the rate of interest on a five-year note or bond is 11.5 percent, whereas the comparable rate on a 20-year bond is 13 percent.

As we might expect, the term structure of interest rates changes over time, depending on the environment. The particular term structure observed today may be quite different from the term structure a month ago and different still from the term structure one month from now. A perfect example of the changing term structure, or yield curve, was witnessed during the period around the September 11, 2001, attack on the World Trade Center and the Pentagon. Figure 6-2 shows the yield curve one day before the attack and again just two weeks later. The change is noticeable, particularly for short-term interest rates. Investors quickly developed fears about the prospect of increased inflation caused by the crisis and consequently increased their required rates of return.

Although the upward-sloping term-structure curves in Figures 6-1 and 6-2 are the ones most commonly observed, yield curves can assume several shapes. Sometimes the term structure is downward sloping; at other times it rises and then falls (hump-backed);

[4] Recall our discussion of the time value of money in Chapter 5.

FIGURE 6-1 The Term Structure of Interest Rates

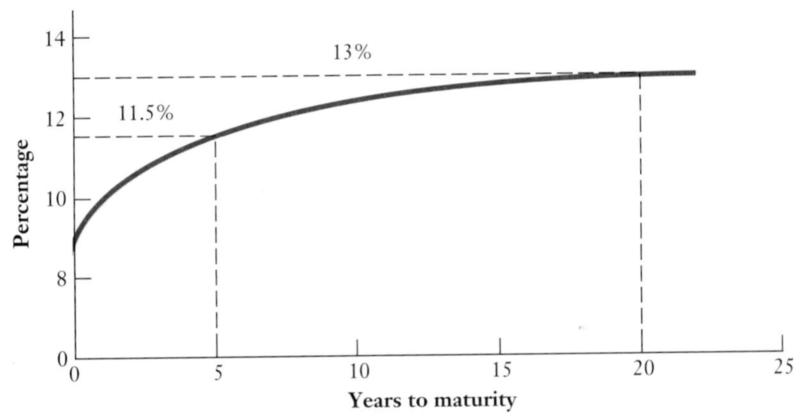

FIGURE 6-2 Changes in the Term Structure of Interest Rates for Government Securities around the period of the September 11th, 2001, attack on the United States

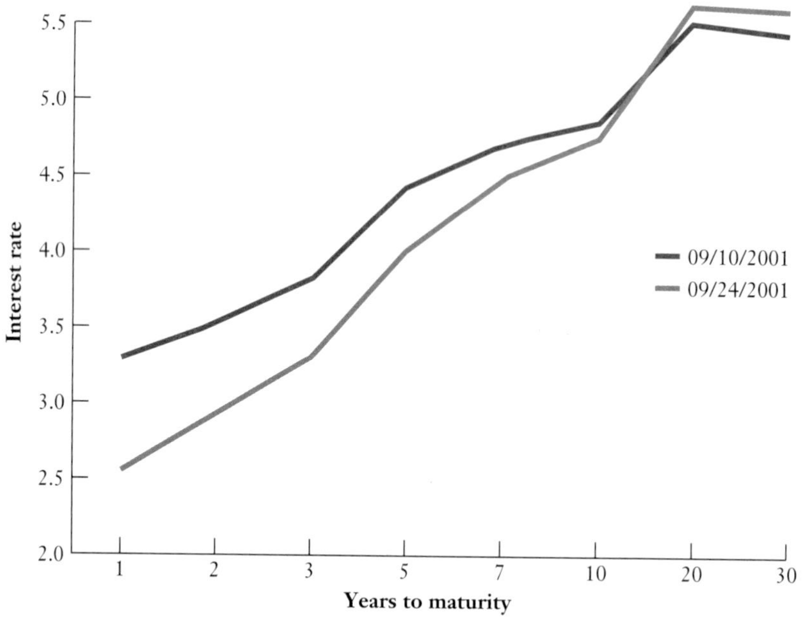

and at still other times it may be relatively flat. Figure 6-3 shows some yield curves at different points in time.

Now that we have looked at actual rates of returns earned by investors, let's next examine specifically how risk and return are measured, both for individual assets and a portfolio of assets. In so doing, we will gain a better understanding of the underlying concepts relating to risk and returns.

FIGURE 6-3 Historical Term Structures of Interest Rates for Government Securities

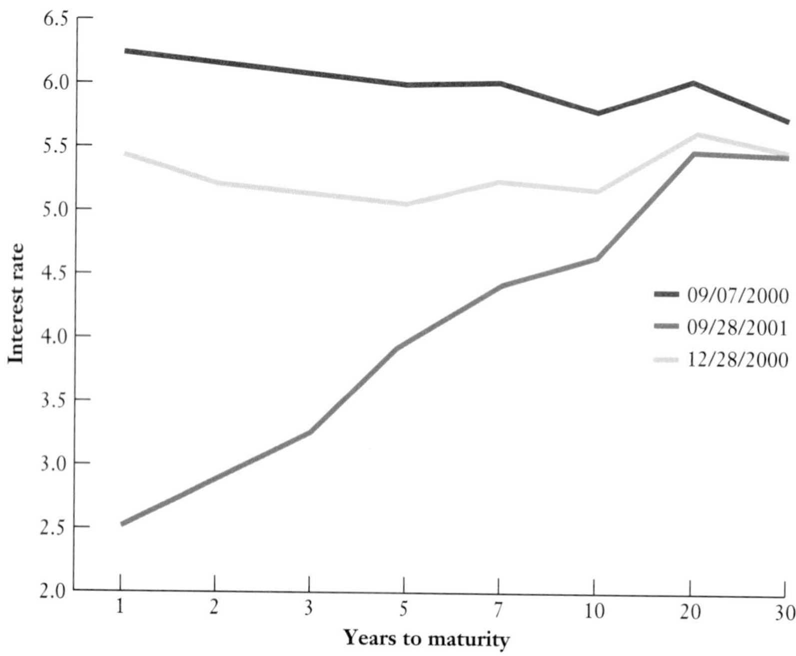

EXPECTED RETURN

Objective 4

The *expected return* from an investment, either by an individual investor or a company, is determined by the different possible outcomes that could occur from making the investment. The expected benefits or returns that an investment generates come in the form of cash flows. *Cash flows*, not accounting profits, should be used to measure returns. This principle holds true regardless of the type of security, whether it is a debt instrument, preferred stock, common stock, or any mixture of these (such as convertible bonds).

In an uncertain world, an accurate measurement of expected future cash flows is not easy for an investor to ascertain. The uncertainty of making an investment is apparent any time you buy stock and watch the price of the stock fluctuate. At the firm level, uncertainty comes to play in almost any decision made, but particularly when investing in new product lines or entering a new geographical market. At the extreme, how would Motorola predict its cash flows in a country where the government is prone to imposing regulations restricting foreign expansion? With a lot of *uncertainty*, we can say without hesitation (that is, with certainty).

While we can talk about uncertainty in general terms, it helps to crystallize our thoughts by an illustration: Assume you are considering an investment costing $10,000, where the future cash flows from owning the security depend on the state of the economy, as estimated in Table 6-2.

In any given year, the investment could produce any one of three possible cash flows depending on the particular state of the economy. With this information, how should we select the cash flow estimate that means the most for measuring the investment's expected rate of return? One approach is to calculate an *expected* cash flow. The expected cash flow is simply the weighted average of the *possible* cash flow outcomes such that the weights are the probabilities of the occurrence of the various states of the economy. Let X_i designate the *i*th possible cash flow, n reflects the number of possible states of the economy, and $P(X_i)$ indicates the probability that the *i*th cash flow or state of economy will occur. The expected cash flow, $\overline{X}$, can then be calculated as follows:

$$\overline{X} = X_1P(X_1) + X_2P(X_2) + \cdots + X_nP(X_n) \qquad \textbf{(6-2)}$$

or

$$\overline{X} = \sum_{i=1}^{n} X_iP(X_i)$$

For the present illustration,

$$\overline{X} = (.2)(\$1{,}000) + (.3)(\$1{,}200) + (.5)(\$1{,}400) = \$1{,}260$$

In addition to computing an expected dollar return from an investment, we can also calculate an **expected rate of return** earned on the $10,000 investment. As the last

Expected rate of return The weighted average of all possible returns where the returns are weighted by the probability that each will occur.

TABLE 6-2 Measuring the Expected Return

STATE OF THE ECONOMY	PROBABILITY OF THE STATE[a]	CASH FLOWS FROM THE INVESTMENT	PERCENTAGE RETURN (CASH FLOW ÷ INVESTMENT COST)
Economic recession	20%	$1,000	10% (= $1,000 ÷ $10,000)
Moderate economic growth	30%	1,200	12% (= $1,200 ÷ $10,000)
Strong economic growth	50%	1,400	14% (= $1,400 ÷ $10,000)

[a]The probabilities assigned to the three possible economic conditions have to be determined subjectively, which requires management to have a thorough understanding of both the investment cash flows and the general economy.

column in Table 6-2 shows, the \$1,400 cash inflow, assuming strong economic growth, represents a 14 percent return (\$1,400 ÷ \$10,000). Similarly, the \$1,200 and \$1,000 cash flows result in 12 percent and 10 percent returns, respectively. Using these percentage returns in place of the dollar amounts, the expected rate of return, $\bar{k}$, may be expressed as follows:

$$\bar{k} = k_1P(k_1) + k_2P(k_2) + \cdots + k_nP(k_n) \quad \textbf{(6-3)}$$

$$\bar{k} = \sum_{i=1}^{n} k_iP(k_i)$$

where k_i = the ith possible rate of return
$P(k_i)$ = the probability of the ith possible rate of return

In our example:

$$\bar{k} = (.2)(10\%) + (.3)(12\%) + (.5)(14\%) = 12.6\%$$

Now let's consider the other side of the investment coin: risk.

BACK TO THE PRINCIPLES

In the forgoing example, we were interested in cash flows—not earnings—in computing the investment's rate of return. This is not an unimportant distinction, as noted in ***Principle 3: Cash—Not Profits—Is King.*** *Since we spend cash to make an investment, we want to receive cash in return. Thus, cash is what matters.*

CONCEPT CHECK

1. When we speak of "benefits" from investing in an asset, what do we mean?
2. Why is it difficult to measure future cash flows?
3. Define "expected rate of return."

Objective 5

RISK

Because we live in a world of uncertainty, how we perceive risk and integrate it into our decisions is vitally important in almost all dimensions of our life; certainly, risk must be considered in financial decision making. The Greek poet and statesman Solon, writing in the sixth century B.C., stated:

> There is risk in everything that one does, and no one knows where he will make his landfall when his enterprise is at its beginning. One man, trying to act effectively, fails to foresee something and falls into great and grim ruination, but to another man, one who is acting ineffectively, a god gives good fortune in everything and escape from his folly.[5]

Although Solon would have given more of the credit to Zeus than we might for the outcomes of our ventures, his insight reminds us that life has always been uncertain; thus

[5] Translated by Arthur W. H. Adkins from the Greek text of Solon's poem "Prosperity, Justice and the Hazards of Life," in M. L. West, ed., *lambi et Elegi Gracci ante Alexandrum canttati*, vol. 2 (Oxford: Clarendon Press, 1972).

FINANCE MATTERS — ETHICS

WHIM OF THE GODS?

What is it that distinguishes the thousands of years of history from what we think of as modern times? The answer goes way beyond the progress of science, technology, capitalism, and democracy.

The distant past was studded with brilliant scientists, mathematicians, inventors, technologists, and political philosophers. Hundreds of years before the birth of Christ, the skies had been mapped, the great library of Alexandria built, and Euclid's geometry taught. Demand for technological innovation in warfare was as insatiable then as it is today. Coal, oil, iron, and copper have been at the service of human beings for millennia, and travel and communication mark the very beginnings of recorded civilization.

The revolutionary idea that defines the boundary between modern times and the past is the mastery of risk: the notion that the future is more than a whim of the gods and that men and women are not passive before nature. Until human beings discovered a way across that boundary, the future was a mirror of the past or the murky domain of oracles and soothsayers who held a monopoly over knowledge of anticipated events.

Peter Bernstein in *Against the Gods, the Remarkable Story of Risk*, John Wiley & Sons (October 1996).

we need to acknowledge and compensate as best we can for the risks we encounter. See the Finance Matters box, "Whim of the Gods?"

Without intending to be trite, risk means different things to different people, depending on the context and on how they feel about taking chances. For the student, risk is the possibility of failing an exam, or the chance of not making his or her best grades. For the coal miner or the oil field worker, risk is the chance of an explosion in the mine or at the well site. For the retired person, risk means perhaps not being able to live comfortably on a fixed income. For the entrepreneur, risk is the chance that a new venture will fail. In a financial context, we want to understand risk so that we can assess the level of risk inherent in an investment.

To gain a basic understanding of investment risk, we might ask: "What is risk and how is it measured?" To begin, we will answer this question when we are only making a single investment, and then for a portfolio, or group of investments.

RISK AND A SINGLE INVESTMENT

To help us grasp the fundamental meaning of risk, consider two possible investments:

1. The first investment is a U.S. Treasury bill, which is a government security that matures in 90 days and promises to pay an annual return of 6 percent. If we purchase and hold this security for 90 days, we are virtually assured of receiving no more and no less than 6 percent. For all practical purposes, the risk of loss is nonexistent.
2. The second investment involves the purchase of the stock of a local publishing company. Looking at the past returns of the firm's stock, we have made the following estimate of the annual returns from the investment:

CHANCE (PROBABILITY) OF OCCURRENCE	RATE OF RETURN ON INVESTMENT
1 chance in 10 (10%)	−10%
2 chances in 10 (20%)	5%
4 chances in 10 (40%)	15%
2 chances in 10 (20%)	25%
1 chance in 10 (10%)	40%

Investing in the publishing company could conceivably provide a return as high as 40 percent if all goes well, or we could lose 10 percent if everything goes against the firm. However, in future years, both good and bad, we could expect a 15 percent return on average computed as follows:[6]

$$\bar{k} = (.10)(-10\%) + (.20)(5\%) + (.40)(15\%) + (.20)(25\%) + (.10)(40\%) = 15\%$$

Comparing the Treasury bill investment with the publishing company investment, we see that the Treasury bill offers an expected 6 percent rate of return, whereas the publishing company has an expected rate of return of 15 percent. However, our investment in the publishing firm is clearly more "risky"—that is, there is greater uncertainty about the final outcome. Stated somewhat differently, there is a greater variation or dispersion of possible returns, which in turn implies greater **risk**.[7] Figure 6-4 shows these differences graphically in the form of discrete probability distributions.

Risk
The prospect of an unfavorable outcome. This concept has been measured operationally as the standard deviation or beta, which will be explained later.

Although the return from investing in the publishing firm is clearly less certain than for Treasury bills, quantitative measures of risk are useful when the difference between two investments is not so evident. Just as we used the time value of money in Chapter 5 to compare cash flow streams of different investments, we need a way to compare the riskiness of different projects. Furthermore, the problem is similar for a financial manager who must consider different investments. At times the choice is obvious, but at others it is not—so the manager needs a way to be more precise in analyzing a project's level of risk. The standard deviation (σ) is such a measure. The **standard deviation** is simply the square root of the average squared deviation of each possible return from the expected return; that is

Standard deviation
A measure of the spread or dispersion about the mean of a probability distribution. We calculate it by squaring the difference between each outcome and its expected value, weighting each squared difference by its associated probability, summing over all possible outcomes, and taking the square root of this sum.

$$\sigma = \sqrt{\sum_{i=1}^{n} (k_i - \bar{k})^2 P(k_i)} \tag{6-4}$$

where n = the number of possible outcomes or different rates of return on the investment
k_i = the value of the ith possible rate of return
$\bar{k}$ = the expected rate of return
$P(k_i)$ = the chance or probability that the ith outcome or return will occur

For the publishing company, the standard deviation would be 12.85 percent, determined as follows:

$$\sigma = \begin{bmatrix} (-10\% - 15\%)^2(.10) + (5\% - 15\%)^2(.20) \\ + (15\% - 15\%)^2(.40) + (25\% - 15\%)^2(.20) \\ + (40\% - 15\%)^2(.10) \end{bmatrix}^{\frac{1}{2}}$$

$$= \sqrt{165\%} = 12.85\%$$

Although the standard deviation of returns provides us with a quantitative measure of an asset's riskiness, how should we interpret the result? What does it mean? Is the

[6] We assume that the particular outcome or return earned in one year does *not* affect the return earned in the subsequent year. Technically speaking, the distribution of returns in any year is assumed to be independent of the outcome in any prior year.

[7] How can we possibly view variations above the expected return as risk? Should we not be concerned only with the negative deviations? Some would agree and view risk as only the negative variability in returns from a predetermined minimum acceptable rate of return. However, as long as the distribution of returns is symmetrical, the same conclusions will be reached.

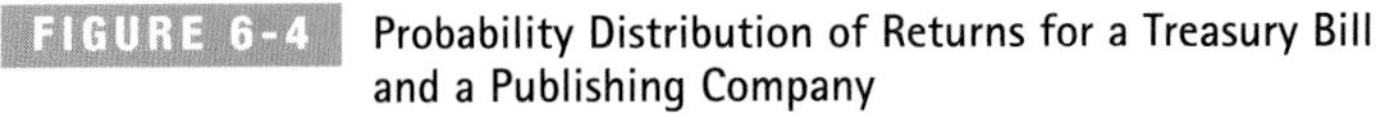

FIGURE 6-4 Probability Distribution of Returns for a Treasury Bill and a Publishing Company

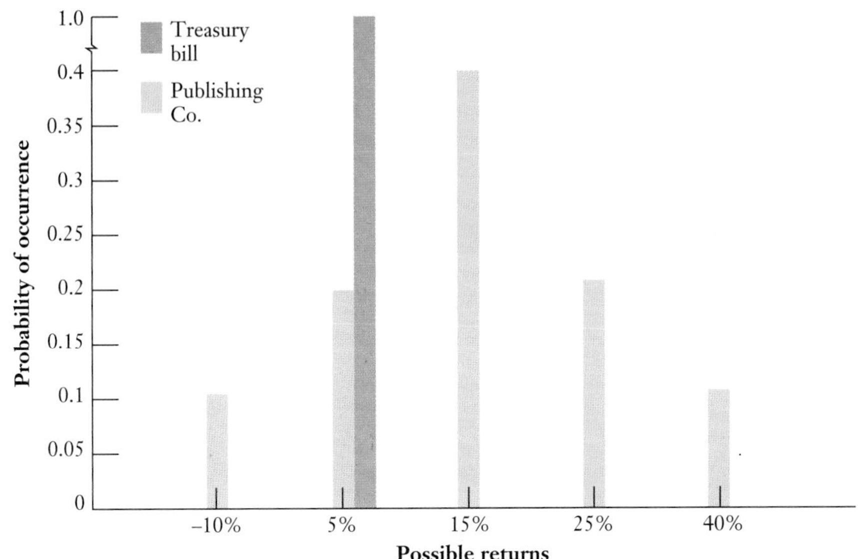

12.85 percent standard deviation for the publishing company investment good or bad? First, we should remember that statisticians tell us that two-thirds of the time, an event will fall within plus or minus one standard deviation of the expected value (assuming the distri-bution is normal; that is, shaped like a bell). Thus, given a 15 percent expected return and a standard deviation of 12.85 percent for the publishing company investment, we may reasonably anticipate that the actual returns will fall between 2.15 percent and 27.85 percent (15% ± 12.85%) two-thirds of the time—not much certainty with this investment.

A second way to interpret the standard deviation as a measure of risk is to compare the investment in the publishing firm against other investments. The attractiveness of a security with respect to its return and risk cannot be determined in isolation. Only by examining other available alternatives can we reach a conclusion about a particular investment's risk. For example, if another investment—say, an investment in a firm that owns a local radio station—has the same expected return as the publishing company, 15 percent, but with a standard deviation of 7 percent, we would consider the risk associated with the publishing firm, 12.85 percent, to be excessive. In the technical jargon of modern portfolio theory, the radio company investment is said to "dominate" the publishing firm investment. In commonsense terms, this means that the radio company investment has the same expected return as the publishing company investment but is less risky.

What if we compare the investment in the publishing company with one in a quick oil-change franchise, an investment in which the expected rate of return is an attractive 24 percent, but in which the standard deviation is estimated at 18 percent? Now what should we do? Clearly, the oil-change franchise has a higher expected rate of return, but it also has a larger standard deviation. In this example, we see that the real challenge in selecting the better investment comes when one investment has a higher expected rate of return but also exhibits greater risk. *Here the final choice is determined by our attitude toward risk, and there is no single right answer.* You might select the publishing company, whereas I might choose the oil-change investment, and neither of us would be wrong. We would simply be expressing our tastes and preferences about risk and return.

CONCEPT CHECK

1. Define "risk."
2. How does the standard deviation help us to measure the riskiness of an investment?
3. Does greater risk imply a bad investment?

Objective 

RISK AND DIVERSIFICATION

In the preceding discussion, we defined risk as the variability of anticipated returns as measured by the standard deviation. However, more can be said about risk, especially as to its nature, when either an individual or a firm holds more than one asset. Let's consider for the moment how risk is affected if we diversify our investment by holding a variety of securities.

To begin, assume that the date is January 17, 2003. When you awake this morning, you follow your daily routine, which includes reading *The Wall Street Journal.* You always begin by scanning "What's News—Business and Finance," with an eye for anything related to the stocks you own—and there they are. Two of your stocks made the front page, the first being Sun Microsystems. The firm reported a record loss for the quarter due to losses in investment-related expenses. The firm also reported that operating profits increased slightly. The result: their stock fell 4 percent on the announcements. That hurts! The only consolation is the article on Bank One, another one of your investments reported that its net income increased 56 percent in the fourth quarter as a result of business growth in its consumer division. In response, the company's stock increased 1.3 percent—not as much as your loss in Sun Microsystems, but it helps. You also notice that these events occurred on a day that the overall market on the New York Stock Exchange decreased by 0.29 percent.

Clearly, what we have described about Sun Microsystems and Bank One were events unique to these two companies, and as we would expect, the investors reacted accordingly; that is, the value of the stock changed in light of the new information. Although we might have wished we had owned only Bank One stock at the time, most of us would prefer to avoid such uncertainties; that is, we are risk averse. Instead, we would like to reduce the risk associated with our investment portfolio without having to accept a lower expected return. Good news: It is possible by diversifying our portfolio!

If we diversify our investments across different securities rather than invest in only one stock, the variability in the returns of our portfolio should decline. The reduction in risk will occur if the stock returns within our portfolio do not move precisely together over time—that is, if they are not perfectly correlated. Figure 6-5 shows graphically what we can expect to happen to the variability of returns as we add additional stocks to the portfolio. The reduction occurs because some of the volatility in returns of a stock are unique to that security. The unique return variability of a single stock tends to be countered by the unique variability of another security. However, we should not expect to eliminate all risk from our portfolio. In practice, it would be rather difficult to cancel all the variations in returns of a portfolio, because stock prices have some tendency to move together; that is, a rising stock market tends to boost *most* (not all) stocks. Furthermore, investing in Intel, Microsoft, and Dell Computer would provide little reduction in the variability of returns. These firms are concentrated in the same industry, and as a result, their stocks tend to move together. In contrast, investing in Coca-Cola, ExxonMobil, and Citibank would have a greater effect on the variability of returns. To be even more effective at reducing the variabil-

FIGURE 6-5 Variability of Returns Compared with Size of Portfolio

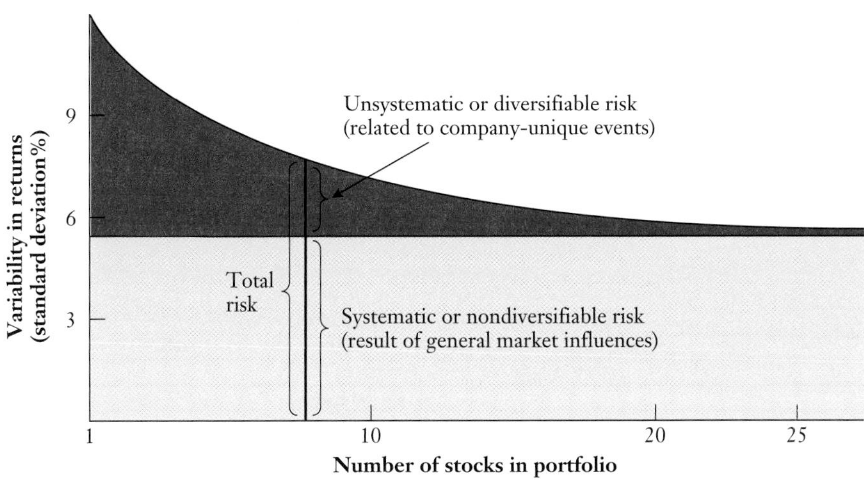

ity of returns, we could invest in various large and small firms in different industries, as well as foreign companies. But even then, you will not be able to remove all the risk (variation in returns). Thus, we can divide the total risk (total variability) of our portfolio into two types of risk: (1) **firm-specific** or **company-unique risk** and (2) **market-related risk**. Company-unique risk might also be called **diversifiable risk**, because it can be diversified away. Market risk is **nondiversifiable risk**; it cannot be eliminated, no matter how much we diversify. These two types of risk are shown graphically in Figure 6-5.

Firm-specific risk or company-unique risk (diversifiable risk or unsystematic risk)
The portion of the variation in investment returns that can be eliminated through investor diversification. This diversifiable risk is the result of factors that are unique to the particular firm.

Market-related risk (nondiversifiable risk or systematic risk)
The portion of variations in investment returns that cannot be eliminated through investor diversification. This variation results from factors that affect all stocks.

Total risk declines until we have approximately 20 securities, and then the decline becomes very slight. The remaining risk, which would typically be about 40 percent of the total risk, is the portfolio's market risk. At this point, our portfolio is highly correlated with all securities in the marketplace. Events that affect our portfolio now are not so much unique events but changes in the general economy or major political events. Examples include changes in general interest rates, changes in tax legislation that affects companies, or increasing public concern about the effect of business practices on the environment.

Because we can remove the company-unique, or unsystematic, risk there is no reason to believe that the market will reward us with additional returns for assuming risk that could be avoided by simply diversifying. Our new measure of risk should therefore measure how responsive a stock or portfolio is to changes in a *market portfolio*, such as the New York Stock Exchange or the S&P 500 Index.[8] This relationship could be determined by plotting past returns—say, on a monthly basis—of a particular stock or a portfolio of stocks against the returns of the *market portfolio* for the same period. The market portfolio is one that only has systematic (nondiversifiable) risk. We frequently use the stocks making up the S&P 500 Index (500 largest U.S. companies) as a surrogate for the overall market portfolio.

[8] The New York Stock Exchange Index is an index that reflects the performance of all stocks listed on the New York Stock Exchange. The Standard & Poor's (S&P) 500 Index is similarly an index that measures the combined performance of the companies that constitute the largest 500 companies in the United States, as designated by Standard & Poor's.

BACK TO THE PRINCIPLES

We have just explained ***Principle 9: All Risk Is Not Equal—Some risk can be diversified away, and some cannot.*** *As we diversify our portfolio, we reduce the effects of company-unique risk, but some risk—nondiversifiable or market risk—still remains, no matter how much we diversify.*

RISK AND DIVERSIFICATION ILLUSTRATED[9]

To see an actual case of the effects of diversification on rates of return, we can draw on a study by Ibbotson Associates. To demonstrate the effect of diversification on risk and rates of return, compare three portfolios (A, B, and C) consisting of the following investments:

	INVESTMENT MIX IN PORTFOLIO		
TYPES OF SECURITIES	**A**	**B**	**C**
Short-term government securities (Treasury bills)	0%	63%	34%
Long-term government bonds	100%	12%	14%
Large-company stocks	0%	25%	52%
	100%	100%	100%

Figure 6-6 shows the average returns and standard deviations of the three portfolios. The results show that an investor can use diversification to improve the risk-return characteristics of a portfolio. Specifically, we see that:

1. Portfolio A, which consists entirely of long-term government bonds, had an average annual return of 5.5 percent with a standard deviation of 11.3 percent.[10]
2. In Portfolio B, we have diversified across all three security types, with the majority of the funds (63 percent) now invested in Treasury bills and a lesser amount (25 percent) in stocks. The effects are readily apparent. The average returns of the two portfolios, A and B, are identical, but the risk associated with Portfolio B is almost half that of Portfolio A—standard deviation of 6.1 percent for Portfolio B compared to 11.3 percent for Portfolio A. Notice that risk has been reduced in Portfolio B even though stocks, a far more risky security, have been included in the portfolio. How could this be? Simple: Stocks behave differently than both government bonds and Treasury bills, with the effect being a less risky (lower standard deviation) portfolio.
3. Portfolio B demonstrates how an investor can reduce risk while keeping returns constant, and Portfolio C, with its increased investment in stocks (52 percent), shows how an investor can increase average returns while keeping risk constant. This portfolio has a risk level identical to that of long-term government bonds alone (Portfolio A), but achieves a higher average return of 8 percent, compared to 5.5 percent for the government bond portfolio.

The conclusion to be drawn from this example is clear: The market rewards diversification. By diversifying our investments, we can indeed lower risk without sacrificing expected return, or we can increase expected return without having to assume more risk.

The preceding example gives us real-world evidence as to the merits of diversification; however, a clarification is in order. Note that the diversification in the preceding

[9] This presentation is based on material developed by Ibbotson Associates. Copyright 1994.

[10] In this example, Ibbotson Associates use 1970–1993 data to compute the standard deviation for the long-term government bonds; all other computations use the total 1926–1993 time frame.

FIGURE 6-6 The Effect of Diversification on Average Returns and Risk

Portfolio		Average Annual Return	Risk (Standard Deviation)
A	100% Long-term government bonds	5.5%	11.3%
B	25% Large company stocks 12% Long-term government bonds 63% Treasury bills	5.5%	6.1%
C	52% Large company stocks 14% Long-term government bonds 34% Treasury bills	8.0%	11.3%

Large company stocks   Long-term government bonds   Treasury bills

NOTE: Adapted from Ibbotson Associates, Copyright 1994, Chicago, Illinois.

example is across different asset types—Treasury bills versus long-term government bonds versus common stocks. Diversifying among different kinds of assets—such as stocks, bonds, and real estate—is called **asset allocation**, as compared to diversification within the different asset classes—such as investing only in PepsiCo, National Semiconductor, and American Airlines. The benefit we receive from diversifying is far greater through effective asset allocation than through merely selecting individual securities (e.g., stocks) to include within an asset category. For instance, Brinson, Singer, and Beebower studied quarterly data from 82 large U.S. pension funds over the period 1977 to 1987.[11] They found that the asset allocation decision accounted for over 91 percent of the differences among the returns of pension funds. Deciding what specific securities to hold accounted for only 4.6 percent of the variation in the different pension returns.[12]

Asset allocation
Identifying and selecting the asset classes appropriate for a specific investment portfolio and determining the proportions of these assets within the given portfolio.

CONCEPT CHECK

1. Give specific examples of systematic and unsystematic risk. How many different securities must be owned to essentially diversify away unsystematic risk?
2. What method is used to measure a firm's market risk?
3. What is a measure of a market portfolio? Is the risk of this portfolio systematic, unsystematic, or a combination of both?

[11] Gary P. Brinson, Brian D. Singer, and Gilbert L. Beebower, "Determinants of Portfolio Performance," *Financial Analysts Journal* (May–June 1991).

[12] It is also interesting to know that Brinson, Singer, and Beebower found that timing investments explained a meager 1.8 percent of the variation in pension fund returns. That is, none of the investors of these pension funds were any better than their peers at timing market movements when making investments.

Objective 7

MEASURING MARKET RISK

To help clarify the idea of systematic risk, let's examine the relationship between the common stock returns of Harley-Davidson, Inc., and the returns of the S&P 500 Index. The monthly returns for Harley-Davidson and for the S&P 500 Index for the 24 months ending May 2002 are presented in Table 6-3 and in Figure 6-7. These monthly returns, or holding-period returns, as they are often called, are calculated as follows:[13]

$$k_t = \frac{P_t}{P_{t-1}} - 1 \tag{6-5}$$

where k_t = the holding-period return in month t for a particular firm such as Harley-Davidson or for a market portfolio such as the S&P 500 Index

P_t = a firm's stock price such as Harley-Davidson (or the S&P 500 Index) at the end of month t

For instance, the holding-period return for Harley-Davidson and the S&P 500 Index for April 2001 is computed as follows:

$$\text{Harley-Davidson return} = \frac{\text{stock price at the end of April 2001}}{\text{stock price at the end of March 2001}} - 1$$

$$= \frac{\$46.09}{\$37.95} - 1 = .2145 = 21.45\%$$

$$\text{S\&P 500 index return} = \frac{\text{index value at the end of April 2001}}{\text{index value at the end of March 2001}} - 1$$

$$= \frac{\$1{,}249.46}{\$1{,}160.33} - 1 = 0.768 = 7.68\%$$

At the bottom of Table 6-3, we have also computed the average of the returns for the 24 months, both for Harley-Davidson and for the S&P 500, and the standard deviation for these returns. Because we are using historical return data, we assume each observation has an equal probability of occurrence. Thus, the average return, $\bar{k}$, is found by summing the returns and dividing by the number of months; that is,

$$\text{average return} = \frac{\sum_{t=1}^{n} \text{return in month } t}{\text{number of months}} = \frac{\sum_{t=1}^{n} (k_t)}{n} \tag{6-6}$$

and the standard deviation is computed as:

$$\text{standard deviation} = \sqrt{\frac{\sum_{t=1}^{n} (\text{return in month } t - \text{average return})^2}{\text{number of months} - 1}} \tag{6-7}$$

$$= \sqrt{\frac{\sum_{t=1}^{n} (k_t - \bar{k})^2}{n-1}}$$

[13] For simplicity's sake, we are ignoring the dividend that the investor receives from the stock as part of the total return. In other words, letting D_t equal the dividend received by the investor in month t, the holding period return would more accurately be measured as: $k_t = \frac{P_t + D_t}{P_{t-1}} - 1$

TABLE 6-3 Monthly Holding-Period Returns, Harley-Davidson and the S&P 500 Index, May 2000–May 2002

	HARLEY-DAVIDSON		S&P 500 INDEX	
MONTH AND YEAR	**PRICE**	**RETURN**	**PRICE**	**RETURN**
2000				
May	$37.25	–	$1,420.60	–
June	38.50	3.36%	1,454.60	2.39%
July	44.88	16.56%	1,430.83	−1.63%
August	49.81	11.00%	1,517.68	6.07%
September	47.88	−3.89%	1,436.51	−5.35%
October	48.19	0.65%	1,429.40	−0.49%
November	45.44	−5.71%	1,314.95	−8.01%
December	39.75	−12.52%	1,320.28	0.41%
2001				
January	$45.39	14.19%	$1,366.01	3.46%
February	43.35	−4.49%	1,239.94	−9.23%
March	37.95	−12.46%	1,160.33	−6.42%
April	46.09	21.45%	1,249.46	7.68%
May	46.97	1.91%	1,255.82	0.51%
June	47.08	0.23%	1,224.42	−2.50%
July	51.61	9.62%	1,211.23	−1.08%
August	48.59	−5.85%	1,133.58	−6.41%
September	40.50	−16.65%	1,040.94	−8.17%
October	45.26	11.75%	1,059.78	1.81%
November	52.58	16.17%	1,139.45	7.52%
December	54.31	3.29%	1,148.08	0.76%
2002				
January	$57.00	4.95%	$1,130.20	−1.56%
February	51.26	−10.07%	1,106.73	−2.08%
March	55.13	7.55%	1,147.39	3.67%
April	52.99	−3.88%	1,076.92	−6.14%
May	52.58	−0.77%	1,067.14	−0.91%
Average monthly return		1.93%		−1.07%
Standard deviation		10.16%		4.86%

In looking at Table 6-3 and Figure 6-7, we notice the following things about Harley-Davidson's holding-period returns over the two years ending in May 2002:

1. Harley-Davidson's stockholders have had higher average monthly returns than the average stock in the S&P 500 Index, 1.93 percent compared to −1.07 percent. That's the good news.
2. The bad news is Harley-Davidson's greater volatility of returns—in other words, greater risk—as evidenced by Harley-Davidson's higher standard deviation. As shown at the bottom of Table 6-3, the standard deviation of the returns is 10.16 percent for Harley-Davidson versus 4.86 percent for the S&P 500 Index. Harley-Davidson's more volatile returns are also evident in Figure 6-7, where we see Harley-Davidson's returns frequently being higher and lower than the corresponding S&P 500 returns.
3. We should also notice the tendency of Harley-Davidson's stock price to increase (decrease) when the value of the S&P 500 Index increases (decreases). In 18 of the

FIGURE 6-7 Monthly Holding-Period Returns: Harley-Davidson and the S&P 500 Index, June 2000 through May 2002

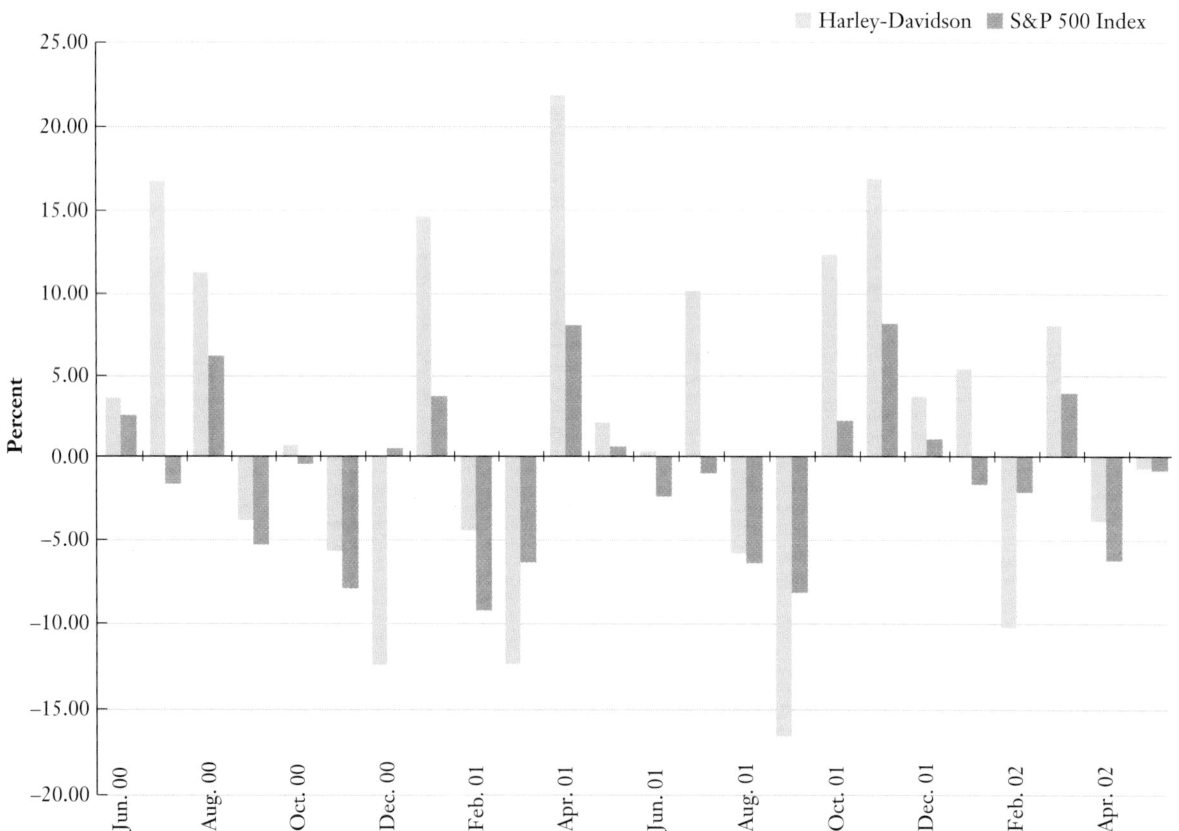

24 months, Harley-Davidson's returns were positive (negative) when the S&P 500 Index returns were positive (negative). That is, there is a positive, although not perfect, relationship between Harley-Davidson's stock returns and the S&P 500 Index returns.

With respect to our third observation, that there is a relationship between the stock returns for Harley-Davidson and the S&P 500 Index, it is helpful to see this relationship by graphing Harley-Davidson's returns against the S&P 500 Index returns. We provide such a graph in Figure 6-8. In the figure, we have plotted Harley-Davidson's returns on the vertical axis and the returns for the S&P 500 Index on the horizontal axis. Each of the 24 dots in the figure represents the returns for Harley-Davidson and the S&P 500 Index for a particular month. For instance, the returns for March 2002 for Harley-Davidson and the S&P 500 Index were 7.55 percent and 3.67 percent, respectively, which are noted in the figure.

Characteristic line The line of "best fit" through a series of returns for a firm's stock relative to the market returns. The slope of the line, frequently called beta, represents the average movement of the firm's stock returns in response to a movement in the market's returns.

In addition to the dots in the graph, we have drawn a line of "best fit," which we call the **characteristic line**. The slope of the characteristic line measures the average relationship between a stock's returns and those of the S&P 500 Index; or stated differently, the slope of the line indicates the average movement in a stock's price to a movement in the S&P 500 Index price. For Harley-Davidson, the slope of the line is 1.6, which simply

FIGURE 6-8 Monthly Holding-Period Returns: Harley-Davidson and the S&P 500 Index

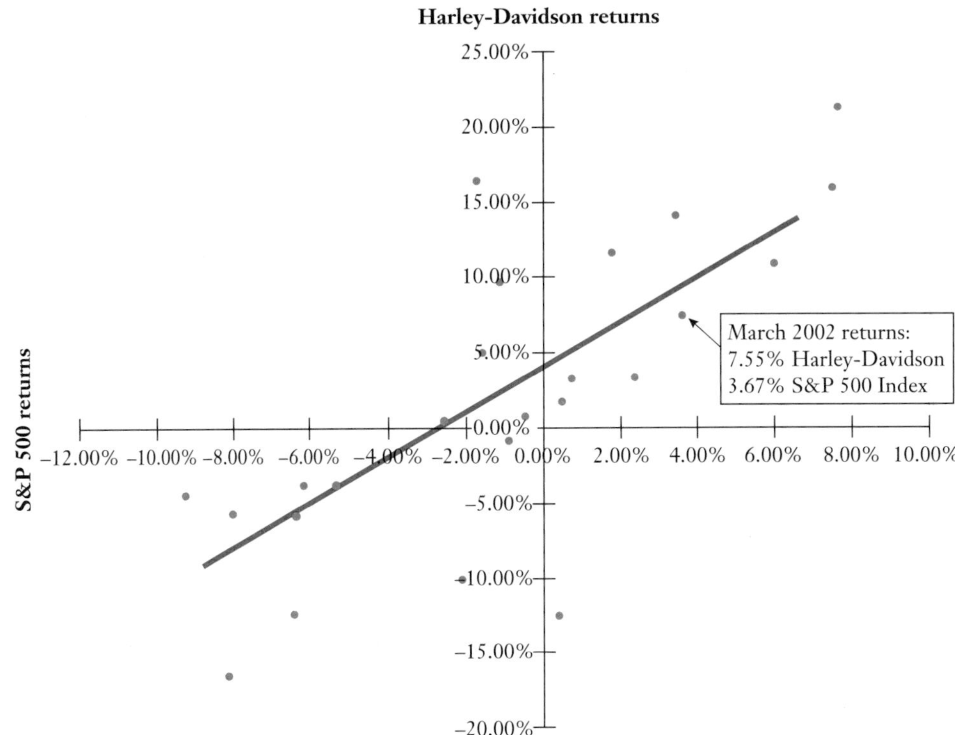

equals the rise of the line relative to the run of the line.[14] A slope of 1.6 as for Harley-Davidson, means that as the market return (S&P 500 Index returns) increases or decreases 1 percentage point, the return for Harley-Davidson on average increases or decreases 1.6 percentage points.

We can also think of the 1.6 slope of the characteristic line as indicating that Harley-Davidson's returns are 1.6 times as volatile on average as those of the overall market (S&P 500 Index). This slope has come to be called **beta** in investor jargon, and measures the average relationship between a stock's returns and the market's returns. It is a term you will see almost anytime you read an article written by a financial analyst about the riskiness of a stock.

Beta
A measure of the relationship between an investment's returns and the market's returns. This is a measure of the investment's nondiversifiable risk.

Looking once again at Figure 6-8, we see that the dots (returns) are scattered all about the characteristic line—most of the returns do not fit neatly on the characteristic line. That is, the average relationship may be 1.6, but the variation in Harley-Davidson's returns is only partly explained by the stock's average relationship with the S&P 500 Index. There are other driving forces unique to Harley-Davidson that also affect the firm's stock returns. (Earlier, we called this company-unique risk.) If we were, however, to diversify our holdings and own, say, 20 stocks with betas of 1.6, we could essentially eliminate the variation about the characteristic line. That is, we would remove almost all the volatility in returns, except for what is caused by the general market, which is

[14] Linear regression analysis is the statistical technique used to determine the slope of the line of best fit.

FIGURE 6-9 Holding-Period Returns: Hypothetical 20-Stock Portfolio and the S&P 500 Index

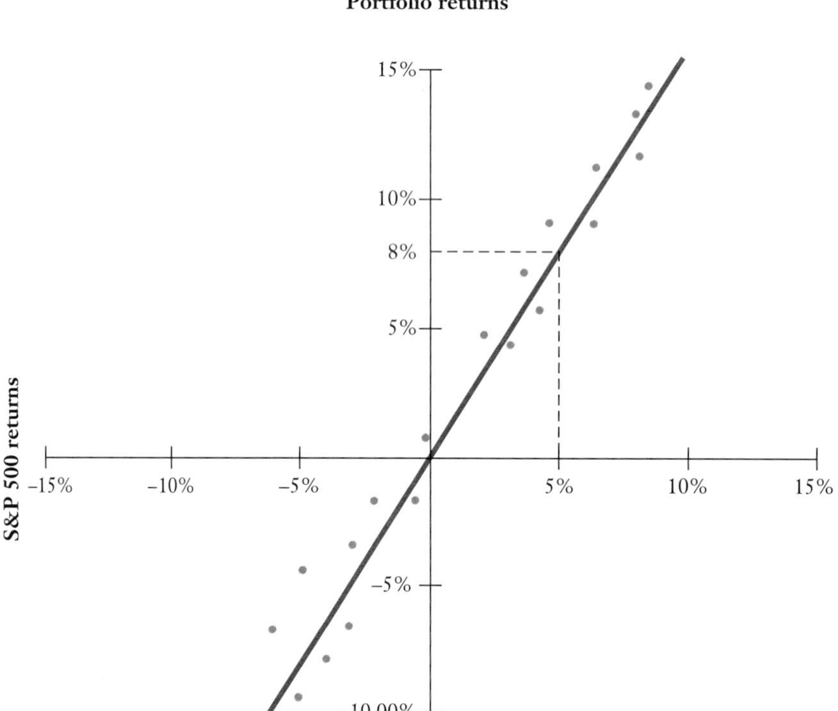

represented by the slope of the line in Figure 6-8. If we plotted the returns of our 20-stock portfolio against the S&P 500 Index, the points in our new graph would fit nicely along a straight line with a slope of 1.6, which means that the beta of the portfolio is also 1.6. The new graph would look something like the one shown in Figure 6-9. In other words, by diversifying our portfolio, we can essentially eliminate the variations about the characteristic line, leaving only the variation in returns for a company that comes from variations in the general market returns.

So beta—the slope of the characteristic line—is a measure of a firm's market risk or systematic risk, which is the risk that remains for a company even after we have diversified our portfolio. It is this risk—and only this risk—that matters for any investors who have broadly diversified portfolios.

We have said that beta is a measure of a stock's systematic risk, but how should we interpret a specific beta? For instance, when is a beta considered low and when is it considered high? In general, a stock with a beta of 0 has no systematic risk; a stock with a beta of 1 has systematic or market risk equal to the "typical" stock in the marketplace; and a stock with a beta exceeding 1 has more market risk than the typical stock. Most stocks, however, have betas between 0.60 and 1.60.

We should also realize that calculating beta is no exact science. The final estimate of a firm's beta is heavily dependent on one's methodology. For instance, it matters whether you use 24 months in your measurement or 60 months, as most professional investment companies do. Take our computation of Harley-Davidson's beta. We said Harley-

Davidson's beta was 1.6 but Standard & Poor's and Value Line, two well-known investment services, have estimated Harley-Davidson's beta to be 1.40 and 1.20, significantly different results from what is found. This disparity comes in part as a result of using different data and different time periods. The difference in results can be observed by comparing Standard & Poor's and Value Line's beta estimates for a number of firms as follows:

	S&P	VALUE LINE
Starbucks	1.11	0.90
McDonald's	0.71	0.90
Briggs & Stratton	0.76	1.00
ExxonMobil	0.40	0.80
Fossil	1.54	1.10
Dell	2.07	1.25

Thus, although close in many instances, even the professionals may not agree in their measurement of a given firm's beta.

In conclusion, remember that the slope of the characteristic line is called beta and it is a measure of a stock's systematic or market risk. The slope of the characteristic line indicates the average response of a stock's returns to the change in the market as a whole. How an investor and a financial manager use beta will be explained in the section that follows. We will see it again in Chapter 12 when we explain how a firm computes its cost of capital.

To this point, we have talked about measuring an individual stock's beta. We will now consider how to measure the beta for a portfolio of stocks.

CONCEPT CHECK

1. Explain the meaning of a stock's holding-period return.
2. After reviewing Figure 6-8, explain the difference between the plotted dots and the firm's characteristic line. What must be done to eliminate the variations?

MEASURING A PORTFOLIO'S BETA

Objective 8

From Figure 6-8, we see that the stock price of Harley-Davidson moves 1.6 percent on average for a 1 percent change in the market. However, we also see a lot of fluctuation around this characteristic line. If we were to diversify our holdings and own 20 stocks with betas of about 1.6, like that of Harley-Davidson, we could essentially eliminate the variation around the line; that is, we would remove almost all the volatility in returns, except for what is caused by the general market, represented by the slope of the line. If we plotted the returns of our 20-stock portfolio against the S&P 500 Index, the points in our new graph would fit nicely along a straight line with a slope of 1.6. The new graph would look something like the one that was shown in Figure 6-9.

What if we were to diversify our portfolio, as we have just suggested, but instead of acquiring stocks with the same beta as Harley-Davidson (1.6), we buy eight stocks with betas of 1 and 12 stocks with betas of 1.5. What is the beta of our portfolio? As it works out, the **portfolio beta** is merely the average of the individual stock betas. Actually, the portfolio beta is a weighted average of the individual securities' betas, the weights being

Portfolio beta The relationship between a portfolio's returns and the market's different returns. It is a measure of the portfolio's nondiversifiable risk.

FIGURE 6-10 Holding-Period Returns: High- and Low-Beta Portfolios and the S&P 500 Index

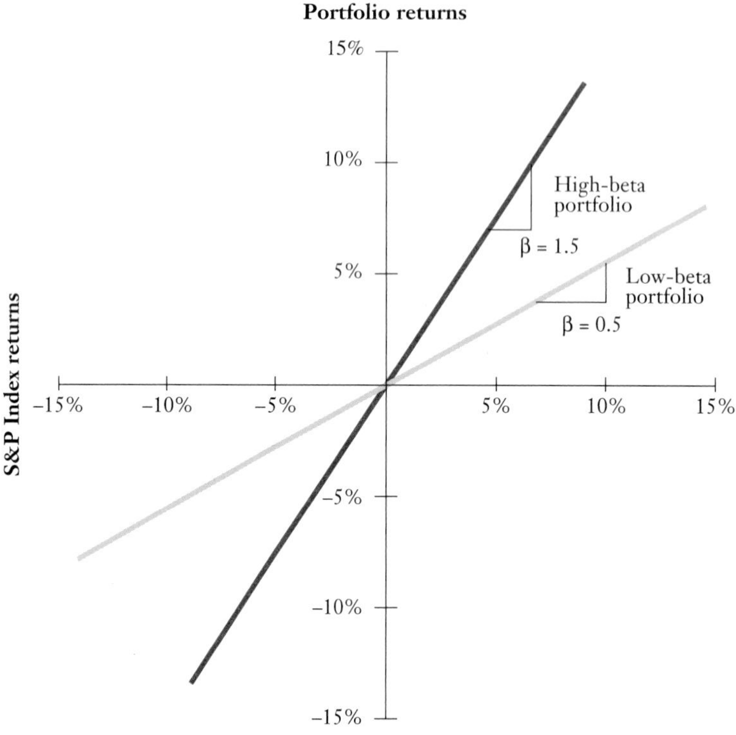

equal to the proportion of the portfolio invested in each security. Thus, the beta (β) of a portfolio consisting of *n* stocks is equal to:

$$\beta_{\text{portfolio}} = \sum_{j=1}^{n} (\text{percentage invested in stock}\, j) \times (\beta \text{ of stock}\, j) \tag{6-8}$$

So, assuming we bought equal amounts of each stock in our new 20-stock portfolio, the beta would simply be 1.3, calculated as follows:

$$\begin{aligned}\beta_{\text{portfolio}} &= \left(\frac{8}{20} \times 1.0\right) + \left(\frac{12}{20} \times 1.50\right)\\ &= 1.3\end{aligned}$$

Thus, whenever the general market increases or decreases 1 percent, our new portfolio's returns would on average change 1.3 percent, which says that our new portfolio has more systematic or market risk than has the market as a whole.

We can conclude that the beta of a portfolio is determined by the betas of the individual stocks. If we have a portfolio consisting of stocks with low betas, then our portfolio will have a low beta. The reverse is true as well. Figure 6-10 presents these situations graphically.

Although portfolio betas tend to be stable, individual betas are not necessarily stable and not always particularly meaningful. A classic example of how individual stock betas can be misleading comes from Burton G. Malkiel's book *A Random Walk Down Wall Street.*[15] Malkiel describes how Meade Johnson (following its takeover by Bristol-Myers) had a negative beta in the 1960s. Apparently, Meade Johnson introduced a product called "Metrecal," a dietary supplement that Meade Johnson sold to consumers, who drank this instead of eating their normal lunches. In any case, the public loved it, and Meade Johnson's stock shot up in price just as the market sank into a deep slump. As the market rebounded in 1963 and 1964, the Metrecal fad died and Meade Johnson dropped in price, again moving in an opposite direction from the market. Later in the 1960s, just as the market began to drop, Meade Johnson reintroduced the exact same product, this time called "Nutrament," telling consumers to buy it and drink it in addition to their normal lunch to put on weight. Once again, Meade Johnson's stock price went up as the market went down. The result of all this was that Meade Johnson had a negative beta. Needless to say, it would be unfortunate if capital-budgeting decisions were made using Meade Johnson's beta as the yardstick by which they were measured. The point here is that betas for individual stocks are not always reliable. In fact, typically only about 30 percent of the variation in returns of a stock can be statistically related (correlated) to the market portfolio, and sometimes as low as 5 percent.

In summary, beta is the underlying basis often used for measuring a security's or a portfolio's risk. It also proves useful to a financial manager when attempting to specify what the relationship should be between an investor's required rate of return and the stock's or portfolio's risk—market risk, that is. In other words, a financial manager can use beta to estimate an *appropriate* required rate of return for the firm's stockholders. The use of beta in this regard is the topic of the following section and will be seen again in later chapters.

CONCEPT CHECK

1. How is the beta of a portfolio determined?
2. Explain what a portfolio beta of 1.5 means.

THE INVESTOR'S REQUIRED RATE OF RETURN

Objective 9

In this section, we examine the concept of the investor's required rate of return, especially as it relates to the riskiness of the asset, and then we see how the required rate of return is measured.

BACK TO THE PRINCIPLES

The point should be increasingly clear: In the words of ***Principle 9: All Risk Is Not Equal—Some risk can be diversified away, and some cannot.*** *As we diversify our portfolio, we reduce the effects of company-unique risk, but some risk—called by different names such as nondiversifiable, systematic, or market risk—still remains no matter how much we diversify. It is therefore the market risk that we must be concerned about. Beta is a measure of this risk and is represented by the slope of the characteristic line. The slope of the characteristic line indicates the average response of a stock's returns to the change in the market as a whole.*

[15] Burton Malkiel, *A Random Walk Down Wall Street*, 4th ed. (New York: W.W. Norton, 1996).

THE REQUIRED RATE OF RETURN CONCEPT

..e of return ..tract an investor ..se or hold a security. ..lso the discount rate that ..quates the present value of the cash flows with the value of the security.

The **investor's required rate of return** can be defined as the minimum rate of return necessary to attract an investor to purchase or hold a security. This definition considers the investor's opportunity cost of making an investment; that is, if an investment is made, the investor must forgo the return available from the next best investment. This forgone return is the opportunity cost of funds and consequently is the investor's required rate of return. In other words, we invest with the intention of achieving a rate sufficient to warrant making the investment. The investment will be made only if the purchase price is low enough relative to expected future cash flows to provide a rate of return greater than or equal to our required rate of return. To help us better understand the nature of an investor's required rate of return, we can separate the return into its basic components: the *risk-free rate of return* plus a *risk premium*. Expressed as an equation:

$$k = k_{rf} + k_{rp} \tag{6-9}$$

where k = the investor's required rate of return
k_{rf} = the risk-free return
k_{rp} = the risk premium

Risk-free or riskless rate of return The rate of return on risk-free investments. The interest rate on short-term U.S. government securities is commonly used to measure this rate.

Risk premium The additional rate of return we expect to earn above the risk-free rate for assuming risk.

As noted earlier in the chapter, the **risk-free rate of return**, k_{rf}, rewards us for deferring consumption, and not for assuming risk; that is, the risk-free return reflects the basic fact that we invest today so that we can consume more later. By itself, the risk-free rate should be used only as the required rate of return, or discount rate, for *riskless* investments. Typically, our measure for the risk-free rate is the rate of return on a U.S. government security.

The **risk premium**, k_{rp}, is the additional return we expect to receive for assuming risk.[16] As the level of risk increases, we will demand additional expected returns. Even though we may or may not actually receive this incremental return, we must have reason to expect it; otherwise, why expose ourselves to the chance of losing all or part of our money?

EXAMPLE: COMPUTING THE REQUIRED RATE OF RETURN

To demonstrate the required rate of return concept, let us take IBM, which has bonds that mature in 2009. Based on the market price of these bonds on January 16, 2003, we can determine that investors were expecting a 5.1-percent return. The 90-day Treasury bill rate at that time was about 1.8 percent, which means that IBM bondholders were requiring a risk premium of 3.3 percent. Stated as an equation, we have

$$\begin{aligned} \text{required rate}\,(k) &= \text{risk-free rate}\,(k_{rf}) + \text{risk premium}\,(k_{rp}) \\ &= 1.8\% + 3.3\% \\ &= 5.1\% \end{aligned}$$

MEASURING THE REQUIRED RATE OF RETURN

We have seen that (1) systematic risk is the only relevant risk—the rest can be diversified away, and (2) the required rate of return, k, equals the risk-free rate, k_{rf}, plus a risk premium, k_{rp}. We can now put these elements together to estimate required rates

[16] The risk premium here can be thought of as a composite of a "default risk premium" (reflected in the difference in a corporate bond's rate of return and the rate on a government bond with a similar maturity date) and "term structure" premium (reflected in the difference in the 90-day Treasury bill rate and the long-term government bond rate).

of return. Looking at equation 6-9, the really tough task is how to estimate the risk premium.

The finance profession has had difficulty in developing a practical approach to measure the investor's required rates of return; however, financial managers often use a method called the **capital asset pricing model (CAPM)**. The capital asset pricing model is an equation that equates the expected rate of return on a stock to the risk-free rate plus a risk premium for the stock's systematic risk. Although not without its critics, the CAPM provides an intuitive approach for thinking about the return that an investor should require on an investment, given the asset's systematic or market risk.

Capital asset pricing model (CAPM)
An equation stating that the expected rate of return on an investment is a function of (1) the risk-free rate, (2) the investment's systematic risk, and (3) the expected risk premium for the market portfolio of all risky securities.

Equation 6-9, as previously shown, provides the natural starting point for measuring the investor's required rate of return and sets us up to use the CAPM. Rearranging this equation to solve for the risk premium (k_{rp}), we have

$$k_{rp} = k - k_{rf} \tag{6-10}$$

which simply says that the risk premium for a security, k_{rp}, equals the security's expected return, k, less the risk-free rate existing in the market, k_{rf}. For example, if the expected return for a security is 15 percent and the risk-free rate is 5 percent, the risk premium is 10 percent. Also, if the expected return for the market, k_m, is 13 percent, and the risk-free rate, k_{rf}, is 5 percent, the risk premium, k_{rp}, for the general market would be 8 percent. This 8 percent risk premium would apply to any security having systematic (nondiversifiable) risk equivalent to the general market, or a beta of 1.

In the same market, a security with a beta of 2 should provide a risk premium of 16 percent, or twice the 8 percent risk premium existing for the market as a whole. Hence, in general, the appropriate required rate of return for the jth security, k_j, should be determined by

$$k_j = k_{rf} + \beta_j(k_m - k_{rf}) \tag{6-11}$$

Equation 6-11 is the CAPM. This equation designates the risk-return trade-off existing in the market, where risk is defined in terms of beta. Figure 6-11 graphs the CAPM

FIGURE 6-11 Security Market Line

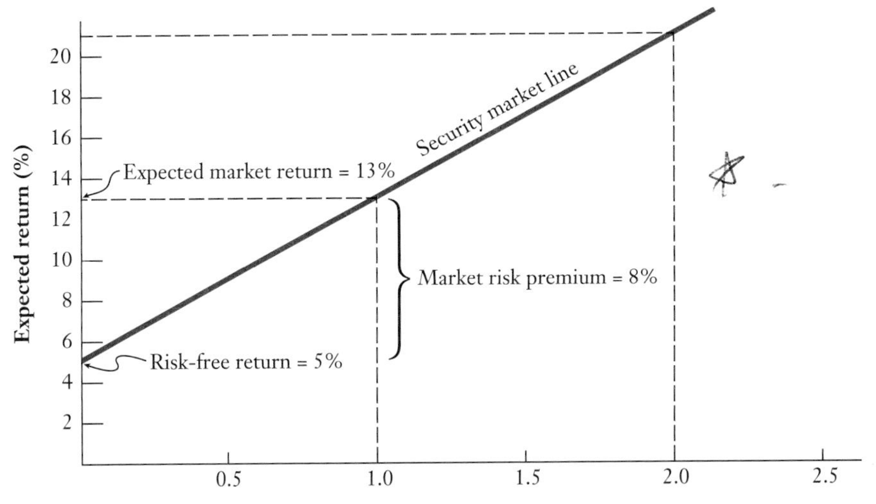

security market line The return line that reflects the attitudes of investors regarding the minimal acceptable return for a given level of systematic risk.

as the **security market line.**[17] As presented in this figure, securities with betas equal to 0, 1, and 2 should have required rates of return as follows:

$$\text{If } \beta_j = 0: k_j = 5\% + 0(13\% - 5\%) = 5\%$$
$$\text{If } \beta_j = 1: k_j = 5\% + 1(13\% - 5\%) = 13\%$$
$$\text{If } \beta_j = 2: k_j = 5\% + 2(13\% - 5\%) = 21\%$$

where the risk-free rate, k_{rf}, is 5 percent and the expected market return, k_m, is 13 percent.[18]

EXAMPLE: MEASURING A STOCK'S RETURN

To illustrate the use of beta in estimating a fair rate of return for a given stock, consider General Electric. Standard and Poor's estimates GE's beta to be 1.05. As we saw earlier in the chapter the risk premium for large-company stocks (return on large-company stocks less a risk-free rate) has been about 8.8 percent over the last seven decades. The risk-free rate of return (U.S. Treasury bill) in early 2003 was about 1.8 percent. Thus, an investor should expect an 11.04 percent rate of return from investing in GE, computed as follows:

$$k_{GE} = k_{rf} + \beta_{GE}(k_m - k_{rf})$$
$$= 1.8\% + 1.05\ (8.8)$$
$$= 1.8\% + 9.24\% = 11.04$$

The previous explanations rely on the capital asset pricing model (CAPM)—and beta—as our standard bearer for estimating a stock's market risk and the rate of return that we should expect for a given beta.

BACK TO THE PRINCIPLES

*The conclusion of the matter is that **Principle 1** is alive and well. It tells us, **We won't take on additional risk unless we expect to be compensated with additional return.** That is, there is a risk-return trade-off in the market.*

[17] Two key assumptions are made in using the security market line. First, we assume that the marketplace where securities are bought and sold is highly efficient. Market efficiency indicates that the price of an asset responds quickly to new information, thereby suggesting that the price of a security reflects all available information. As a result, the current price of a security is considered to represent the best estimate of its future price. Second, the model assumes that a perfect market exists. A perfect market is one in which information is readily available to all investors at a nominal cost. Also, securities are assumed to be infinitely divisible, with any transaction costs incurred in purchasing or selling a security being negligible. Furthermore, investors are assumed to be single-period wealth maximizers who agree on the meaning and the significance of the available information. Finally, within the perfect market, all investors are *price takers*, which simply means that a single investor's actions cannot affect the price of a security. These assumptions are obviously not descriptive of reality. However, from the perspective of positive economics, the mark of a good theory is the accuracy of its predictions, not the validity of the simplifying assumptions that underlie its development.

[18] For a more in-depth explanation of the CAPM, see B. Rosenberg, "The Capital Asset Pricing Model and the Market Model," *Journal of Portfolio Management* (Winter 1981): 5–16.

CONCEPT CHECK

1. How does opportunity cost affect an investor's required rate of return?
2. What are the two components of the investor's required rate of return?
3. How does beta fit into factoring the risk premium in the CAPM equation?
4. Assuming the market is efficient, what is the relationship between a stock's price and the security market line?

HOW FINANCIAL MANAGERS USE THIS MATERIAL

We have now completed our study of risk, and most importantly, how rates of return for investments are explicitly tied to risk. The greater the risk, the greater the required rate of return needed to attract investors. This concept, although presented at this point mostly from an investor's perspective, holds equally well for a financial manager considering an investment to develop a new product line. Thus, this chapter will serve as the basis for much that we do in later chapters when it comes to evaluating investment decisions. However, because any investment decision made by a firm should be linked to the goal of enhancing shareholder value, we will next study the concepts and procedures for valuing bonds and stocks. See the Finance Matters box, "Does Beta Always Work?"

FINANCE MATTERS **ETHICS**

DOES BETA ALWAYS WORK?

At the start of 1998, Apple Computer was in deep trouble. As a result, its stock price fluctuated wildly—far more than that of other computer firms, such as IBM. However, based on the capital asset pricing model (CAPM) and its measure of beta, the required return of Apple's investors would have been only 8 percent at the time, compared to 12 percent for IBM's stockholders. Equally interesting, when Apple's situation improved in the spring of that year, and its share price became less volatile, Apple's investors—at least according to the CAPM—would have required a rate of return of 11 percent—a 3-percentage-point increase from the earlier required rate of return. That is not what intuition would suggest should have happened.

So what should we think? Just when Apple's future was most in doubt and its shares most volatile, its beta was only 0.47, suggesting that Apple's stock was only half as volatile as the overall stock market. In reality, beta is meaningless here. The truth is that Apple was in such a dire condition that its stock price simply decoupled itself from the stock market. So as IBM and its peer-stock prices moved up and down with the rest of the market, Apple shares reacted solely to news about the company, without regard for the market's movements. Beta thus created the false impression that Apple shares were more stable than the stock market.

The lesson here is that beta may at times be misleading when used with individual companies. Instead, its use is far more reliable when applied to a portfolio of companies. A firm that was interested in acquiring Apple Computer in 1998, for instance, would, most likely, not have been planning to buy other computer companies in the same circumstances. If an interested acquirer used beta in computing the required rate of return for the acquisition, it would without a doubt have overvalued Apple.

So does that mean that CAPM is worthless? No, not as long as company-unique risk is not the main driving force in a company's stock price movements, or if investors are able to diversify away specific company risk. Then they would bid up the price of such shares until they reflect only market risk. For example, a mutual fund that specializes in "distress stocks" might purchase a number of Apple Computer-type companies, each with its own problems, but for different reasons. For such investors, beta works pretty well. Thus, the moral of the story is: Don't use beta without some common sense and good judgment.

SUMMARY

We have referred to the discount rate as the interest rate or the opportunity cost of funds. At that point, we considered a number of important factors that influence interest rates, including the price of time, expected or anticipated inflation, the risk premium related to maturity (liquidity), and variability of future returns.

In this chapter, we looked at the relationship between risk and rates of returns.

Objective 1

Ibbotson Associates has provided us with annual rates of return earned on different types of security investments as far back as 1926. They summarize, among other things, the annual returns for five portfolios of securities made up of (1) common stocks of small firms, (2) common stocks of large companies, (3) long-term corporate bonds, (4) long-term U.S. government bonds, and (5) U.S. Treasury bills. A comparison of the annual rates of return for these respective portfolios for the years 1926 to 2001 shows there to be a positive relationship between risk and return, with Treasury bills being least risky and common stocks of small firms being most risky.

Objective 2

The rate of inflation has an effect on the nominal rate of return that an investor receives on an investment. That is, part of the return on an investment is to keep an investor from losing purchasing power from holding an investment.

Objective 3

The term structure of interest rates (also called the yield to maturity) compares the rates of return of similar securities to their respective times to maturity. For instance, if long-term government bonds offer a higher rate of return than do U.S. Treasury bills, then the yield curve is upward sloping. But if the Treasury bill is paying a higher rate of interest than its long-term counterparts are, then the yield curve is downward sloping.

Objective 4

In a world of uncertainty, we cannot make forecasts with certainty. Thus, we must speak in terms of *expected* events. The expected return on an investment may therefore be stated as the arithmetic mean or average of all possible outcomes where those outcomes are weighted by the probability that each will occur.

Objective 5

Risk, for our purposes, is the prospect of an unfavorable outcome and may be measured by the standard deviation.

Objective 6

We have made an important distinction between nondiversifiable risk and diversifiable risk. We concluded that the only relevant risk given the opportunity to diversify our portfolio is a security's nondiversifiable risk, which we called by two other names: systematic risk and market risk.

Objective 7

A security's market risk is represented by beta, the slope of the characteristic line. Beta measures the average responsiveness of a security's returns to the movement of the general market, such as the S&P 500. If beta is 1, the security's returns move 1-to-1 with the market returns; if beta is 1.5, the security's returns move up and down 1.5 percent for every 1 percent change in the market's returns.

Objective 8

A portfolio's beta is simply a weighted average of the individual stock's betas, where the weights are the percentage of funds invested in each stock. The portfolio beta measures the average responsiveness of the portfolio's returns to the movement of the general market, such as the S&P 500.

Objective 9

The capital asset pricing model (CAPM), even with its weaknesses, provides an intuitive framework for understanding the risk-return relationship. The CAPM suggests that investors determine an appropriate required rate of return, depending upon the amount of systematic risk inherent in a security. This minimum acceptable rate of return is equal to the risk-free rate plus a return premium for assuming risk.

KEY TERMS

Asset allocation, 195
Beta, 199
Capital asset pricing model (CAPM), 205
Characteristic line, 198
Expected rate of return, 187
Firm-specific risk or company-unique risk (diversifiable risk or unsystematic risk), 193
Investor's required rate of return, 204
Market-related risk (nondiversifiable risk or systematic risk), 193
Opportunity cost of funds, 182
Portfolio beta, 201
Real rate of interest, 184
Risk, 190
Risk-free or riskless rate of return, 204
Risk premium, 204
Security market line, 206
Standard deviation, 190
Term structure of interest rates (yield to maturity), 185

Go To: www.prenhall.com/keown for downloads and current events associated with this chapter

STUDY QUESTIONS

6-1. Over the past seven decades, we have had the opportunity to observe the rates of return and variability of these returns for different types of securities. Summarize these observations.

6-2. Explain the effect of inflation on rates of return.

6-3. Explain the concept "term structure of interest rates."

6-4. **a.** What is meant by the investor's required rate of return?

b. How do we measure the riskiness of an asset?

c. How should the proposed measurement of risk be interpreted?

6-5. What is (a) unsystematic risk (company-unique or diversifiable risk) and (b) systematic risk (market or nondiversifiable risk)?

6-6. What is the meaning of beta? How is it used to calculate k, the investor's required rate of return?

6-7. Define the security market line. What does it represent?

6-8. How do we measure the beta for a portfolio?

6-9. If we were to graph the returns of a stock against the returns of the S&P 500 Index, and the points did not follow a very ordered pattern, what could we say about that stock? If the stock's returns tracked the S&P 500 returns very closely, then what could we say?

SELF-TEST PROBLEMS

ST-1. *(Expected return and risk)* Universal Corporation is planning to invest in a security that has several possible rates of return. Given the following probability distribution of the returns, what is the expected rate of return on the investment? Also, compute the standard deviation of the returns. What do the resulting numbers represent?

PROBABILITY	RETURN
.10	−10%
.20	5%
.30	10%
.40	25%

ST-2. *(Capital asset pricing model)* Using the CAPM, estimate the appropriate required rate of return for the following three stocks, given that the risk-free rate is 5 percent, and the expected return for the market is 17 percent.

STOCK	BETA
A	.75
B	.90
C	1.40

ST-3. *(Expected return and risk)* Given the following holding-period returns, calculate the average returns and the standard deviations for the Kaifu Corporation and for the market.

MONTH	KAIFU CORP.	MARKET
1	4%	2%
2	6	3
3	0	1
4	2	−1

ST-4. *(Holding-period returns)* From the following price data, compute the holding-period returns.

TIME	STOCK PRICE
1	$10
2	13
3	11
4	15

ST-5.

a. *(Security market line)* Determine the expected return and beta for the following portfolio:

STOCK	PERCENTAGE OF PORTFOLIO	BETA	EXPECTED RETURN
1	40%	1.00	12%
2	25	0.75	11
3	35	1.30	15

b. Given the preceding information, draw the security market line and show where the securities fit on the graph. Assume that the risk-free rate is 8 percent and that the expected return on the market portfolio is 12 percent. How would you interpret these findings?

STUDY PROBLEMS (SET A)

6-1A. *(Inflation and interest rates)* What would you expect the nominal rate of interest to be if the real rate is 4.5 percent and the expected inflation rate is 7.3 percent?

6-2A. *(Inflation and interest rates)* Assume the expected inflation rate is 3.8 percent. If the current real rate of interest is 6.4 percent, what should the nominal rate of interest be?

6-3A. *(Expected rate of return and risk)* Pritchard Press, Inc., is evaluating a security. One-year Treasury bills are currently paying 3.1 percent. Calculate the following investment's expected return and its standard deviation. Should Pritchard invest in this security?

PROBABILITY	RETURN
.15	−1%
.30	2%
.40	3%
.15	8%

6-4A. (*Expected rate of return and risk*) Syntex, Inc., is considering an investment in one of two common stocks. Given the information that follows, which investment is better, based on risk (as measured by the standard deviation) and return?

COMMON STOCK A		COMMON STOCK B	
PROBABILITY	RETURN	PROBABILITY	RETURN
.30	11%	.20	−5%
.40	15%	.30	6%
.30	19%	.30	14%
		.20	22%

6-5A. (*Expected rate of return and risk*) Friedman Manufacturing, Inc., has prepared the following information regarding two investments under consideration. Which investment should be accepted?

COMMON STOCK A		COMMON STOCK B	
PROBABILITY	RETURN	PROBABILITY	RETURN
.20	−2%	.10	4%
.50	18%	.30	6%
.30	27%	.40	10%
		.20	15%

6-6A. (*Required rate of return using CAPM*)

a. Compute a fair rate of return for Intel common stock, which has a 1.2 beta. The risk-free rate is 6 percent and the market portfolio (New York Stock Exchange stocks) has an expected return of 16 percent.

b. Why is the rate you computed a fair rate?

6-7A. (*Estimating beta*) From the following graph relating the holding-period returns for Aram, Inc., to the S&P 500 Index, estimate the firm's beta.

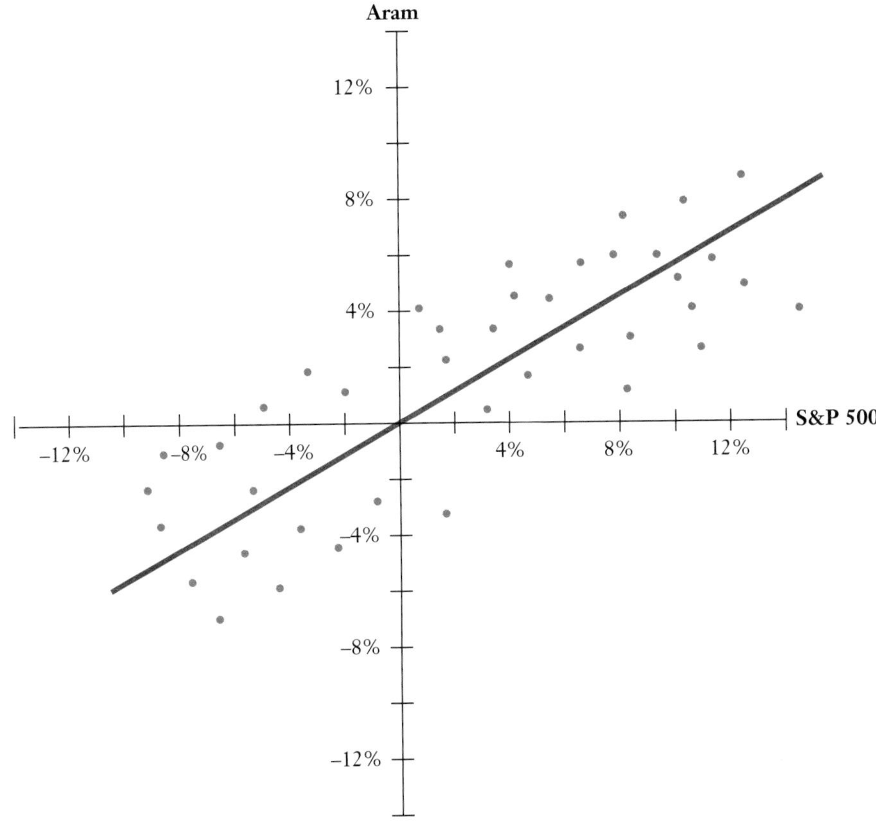

6-8A. (*Capital asset pricing model*) Johnson Manufacturing, Inc., is considering several investments. The rate on Treasury bills is currently 6.75 percent, and the expected return for the market is 12 percent. What should be the required rates of return for each investment (using the CAPM)?

SECURITY	BETA
A	1.50
B	.82
C	.60
D	1.15

6-9A. (*Capital asset pricing model*) CSB, Inc. has a beta of .765. If the expected market return is 11.5 percent and the risk-free rate is 7.5 percent, what is the appropriate required rate of return of CSB (using the CAPM)?

6-10A. (*Capital asset pricing model*) The expected return for the general market is 12.8 percent, and the risk premium in the market is 4.3 percent. Tasaco, LBM, and Exxos have betas of .864, .693, and .575, respectively. What are the appropriate required rates of return for the three securities?

6-11A. (*Computing holding-period returns*) From the following price data, compute the holding-period returns for Asman and Salinas.

TIME	ASMAN	SALINAS
1	$10	$30
2	12	28
3	11	32
4	13	35

How would you interpret the meaning of a holding-period return?

6-12A. (*Measuring risk and rates of return*)

a. Given the following holding-period returns, compute the average returns and the standard deviations for the Zemin Corporation and for the market.

MONTH	ZEMIN CORP.	MARKET
1	6%	4%
2	3	2
3	1	−1
4	−3	−2
5	5	2
6	0	2

b. If Zemin's beta is 1.54 and the risk-free rate is 8 percent, what would be an appropriate required return for an investor owning Zemin? (*Note:* Because the preceding returns are based on monthly data, you will need to annualize the returns to make them comparable with the risk-free rate. For simplicity, you can convert from monthly to yearly returns by multiplying the average monthly returns by 12.)

c. How does Zemin's historical average return compare with the return you believe to be a fair return, given the firm's systematic risk?

6-13A. (*Portfolio beta and security market line*) You own a portfolio consisting of the following stocks:

STOCK	PERCENTAGE OF PORTFOLIO	BETA	EXPECTED RETURN
1	20%	1.00	16%
2	30%	0.85	14%
3	15%	1.20	20%
4	25%	0.60	12%
5	10%	1.60	24%

The risk-free rate is 7 percent. Also, the expected return on the market portfolio is 15.5 percent.

a. Calculate the expected return of your portfolio. (*Hint:* The expected return of a portfolio equals the weighted average of the individual stock's expected return, where the weights are the percentage invested in each stock.)

b. Calculate the portfolio beta.

c. Given the information preceding, plot the security market line on paper. Plot the stocks from your portfolio on your graph.

d. From your plot in part (c), which stocks *appear* to be your winners and which ones appear to be losers?

e. Why should you consider your conclusion in part (d) to be less than certain?

6-14A. (*Expected return, standard deviation, and capital asset pricing model*) Following you will find the end-of-month prices, both for the Market Index and for Mathews, Inc. common stock.

a. Using the following data, calculate the holding-period returns for each month from August 2002 to July 2003.

		PRICES	
	MONTH AND YEAR	MARKET	MATHEWS CORP.
2002	July	$1,328.72	$34.50
	August	1,320.41	41.09
	September	1,282.71	37.16
	October	1,362.93	38.72
	November	1,388.91	38.34
	December	1,469.25	41.16
2003	January	1,394.46	49.47
	February	1,366.42	56.50
	March	1,498.58	65.97
	April	1,452.43	63.41
	May	1,420.60	62.34
	June	1,454.60	66.84
	July	1,430.83	66.75

b. Calculate the average monthly return and the standard deviation of these returns both for the Market and Mathews.

c. Develop a graph that shows the relationship between the Mathews stock returns and the Market Index. (Show the Mathews returns on the vertical axis and the Market Index returns on the horizontal, as done in Figure 6-8.)

d. From your graph, describe the nature of the relationship between Mathews stock returns and the returns for the Market Index.

6-15A. (*Expected rate of return and risk*) Jones Corporation has collected information on the following three investments. Which investment is the most favorable based on the information presented?

STOCK 1		STOCK 2		STOCK 3	
PROBABILITY	RETURN	PROBABILITY	RETURN	PROBABILITY	RETURN
0.15	2%	0.25	–3%	0.1	–5%
0.4	7%	0.5	20%	0.4	10%
0.3	10%	0.25	25%	0.3	15%
0.15	15%			0.2	30%

6-16A. (*Capital asset pricing model*) Anita, Inc. is considering the following investments. The current rate on Treasury bills is 5.5 percent, and the expected return for the market is 11 percent. Using the CAPM, what rates of return should Anita require for each individual security?

STOCK	BETA
H	0.75
T	1.4
P	0.95
W	1.25

6-17A. (*Computing holding-period returns*) From the following price data, compute the holding-period returns for Williams and Davis.

TIME	WILLIAMS	DAVIS
1	33	19
2	27	15
3	35	14
4	39	23

6-18A. (*Required rate of return using CAPM*) Whitney common stock has a beta of 1.2. The expected rate of return for the market is 9 percent and the risk-free rate is 5 percent.

- **a.** Compute a fair rate of return based on this information.
- **b.** What would be a fair rate if the beta were .85?
- **c.** What would be the effect on the fair rate if the expected return for the market improved to 12 percent?

WEB WORKS

Using an internet search engine, conduct a search for "risk and return." What do you find?

INTEGRATIVE PROBLEM

Note: Although not absolutely necessary, you are advised to use a computer spreadsheet to work the following problems.

1. Use the price data on page 215 for the Market Index, Reynolds Computer, and Andrews to calculate the holding-period returns for the 24 months ending May 2003.
2. Calculate the average monthly holding-period return and the standard deviation of these returns for the Market Index, Reynolds Computer, and Andrews.
3. Plot (a) the holding-period returns for Reynolds Computer against the Market Index, and (b) the Andrews holding-period returns against the Market Index. (Use Figure 6-8 as the format for the graph.)
4. From your graphs in question 3, describe the nature of the relationship between the Reynolds Computer stock returns and the returns for the Market Index. Make the same comparison for Andrews.
5. Assume that you have decided to invest one-half of your money in Reynolds Computer and the remaining amount in Andrews. Calculate the monthly holding-period returns for your two-stock portfolio. (*Hint:* The monthly return for the portfolio is the average of the two stocks' monthly returns.)
6. Plot the returns of your two-stock portfolio against the Market Index as you did for the individual stocks in question 3. How does this graph compare to the graphs for the individual stocks? Explain the difference.
7. The returns on an *annualized* basis that were realized from holding long-term government bonds for the 24 months ending May 2003 appear on page 215. Calculate the average *monthly* holding-period return and the standard deviation of these returns. (*Hint:* You will need to convert the annual returns to monthly returns by dividing each return by 12 months.)
8. Now assume that you have decided to invest equal amounts of money in Reynolds Computer, Andrews, and the long-term government securities. Calculate the monthly returns for your three-asset portfolio. What are the average return and standard deviation?
9. Make a comparison of the average returns and the standard deviations for the individual assets and the two portfolios that we designed. What conclusions can be reached by your comparisons?
10. The betas for Reynolds Computer and Andrews are 1.96 and 1.49, respectively. Compare the meaning of these betas relative to the preceding standard deviations calculated.
11. The Treasury bill rate at the end of May 2003 was approximately 6 percent. Given the betas for Reynolds Computer and Andrews and using the preceding data for the Market Index as a measure for the market portfolio expected return, estimate an appropriate required rate of return given the level of systematic risk for each stock.

	MONTH	END OF MONTH PRICES MARKET	REYNOLDS	ANDREWS
2001	May	$1,090.82	$20.60	$24.00
	June	1,133.84	23.20	26.72
	July	1,120.67	27.15	20.94
	August	957.28	25.00	15.78
	September	1,017.01	32.88	18.09
	October	1,098.67	32.75	21.69
	November	1,163.63	30.41	23.06
	December	1,229.23	36.59	28.06
2002	January	1,279.64	50.00	26.03
	February	1,238.33	40.06	26.44
	March	1,286.37	40.88	28.06
	April	1,335.18	41.19	36.94
	May	1,301.84	34.44	36.88
	June	1,372.71	37.00	37.56
	July	1,328.72	40.88	23.25
	August	1,320.41	48.81	22.88
	September	1,282.71	41.81	24.78
	October	1,362.93	40.13	27.19
	November	1,388.91	43.00	26.56
	December	1,469.25	51.00	24.25
2003	January	1,394.46	38.44	32.00
	February	1,366.42	40.81	35.13
	March	1,498.58	53.94	44.81
	April	1,452.43	50.13	30.23
	May	1,420.60	43.13	34.00

LONG-TERM GOVERNMENT BONDS

	MONTH	ANNUALIZED RATE OF RETURN		MONTH	ANNUALIZED RATE OF RETURN
2001	June	5.70%	2002	June	6.04%
	July	5.68		July	5.98
	August	5.54		August	6.07
	September	5.20		September	6.07
	October	5.01		October	6.26
	November	5.25		November	6.15
	December	5.06		December	6.35
2002	January	5.16	2003	January	6.63
	February	5.37		February	6.23
	March	5.58		March	6.05
	April	5.55		April	5.85
	May	5.81		May	6.15

STUDY PROBLEMS (SET B)

6-1B. *(Inflation and interest rates)* Assume the expected inflation rate is 5 percent. If the current real rate of interest is 7 percent, what should the nominal rate of interest be?

6-2B. *(Inflation and interest rates)* What would you expect the nominal rate of interest to be if the real rate is 5 percent and the expected inflation rate is 3 percent?

6-3B. *(Expected rate of return and risk)* B. J. Gautney Enterprises is evaluating a security. One-year Treasury bills are currently paying 2.9 percent. Calculate the following investment's expected return and its standard deviation. Should Gautney invest in this security?

PROBABILITY	RETURN
.15	–3%
.30	2%
.40	4%
.15	6%

6-4B. (*Expected rate of return and risk*) Kelly B. Stites, Inc., is considering an investment in one of two common stocks. Given the information that follows, which investment is better, based on risk (as measured by the standard deviation) and return?

SECURITY A		SECURITY B	
PROBABILITY	**RETURN**	**PROBABILITY**	**RETURN**
.20	−2%	.10	5%
.50	19%	.30	7%
.30	25%	.40	12%
		.20	14%

6-5B. (*Expected rate of return and risk*) Clevenger Manufacturing, Inc., has prepared the following information regarding two investments under consideration. Which investment should be accepted?

COMMON STOCK A		COMMON STOCK B	
PROBABILITY	**RETURN**	**PROBABILITY**	**RETURN**
.20	10%	.15	6%
.60	13%	.30	8%
.20	20%	.40	15%
		.15	19%

6-6B. (*Required rate of return using CAPM*)

a. Compute a *fair* rate of return for Compaq common stock, which has a 1.5 beta. The risk-free rate is 8 percent and the market portfolio (New York Stock Exchange stocks) has an expected return of 16 percent.

b. Why is the rate you computed a fair rate?

6-7B. (*Estimating beta*) From the following graph relating the holding-period returns for Bram, Inc., to the S&P 500 Index, estimate the firm's beta.

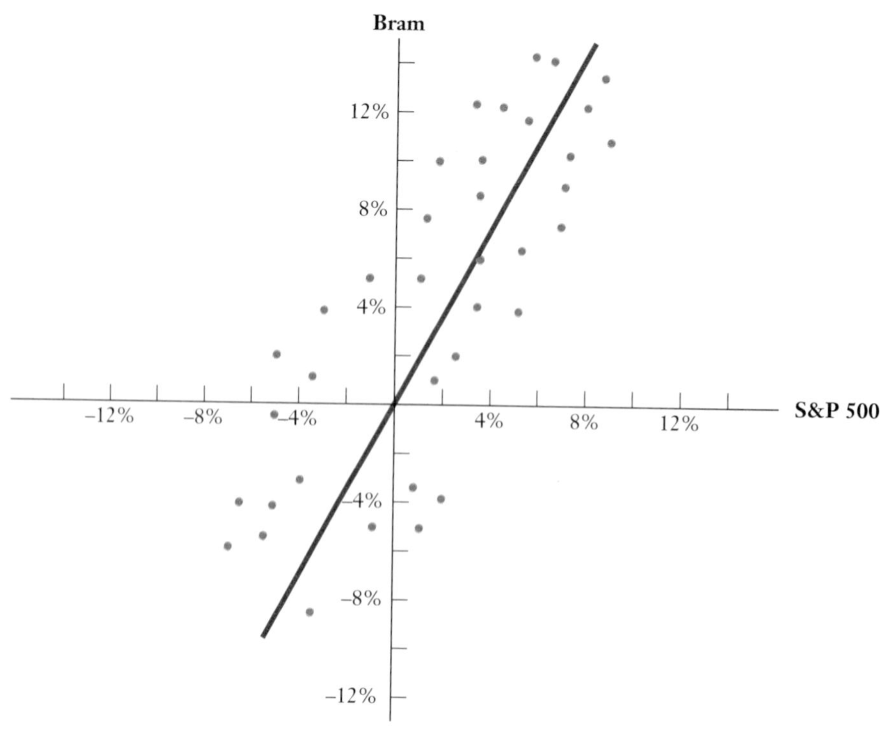

6-8B. (*Capital asset pricing model*) Bobbi Manufacturing, Inc., is considering several investments. The rate on Treasury bills is currently 6.75 percent, and the expected return for the market is 12 percent. What should be the required rates of return for each investment (using the CAPM)?

SECURITY	BETA
A	1.40
B	.75
C	.80
D	1.20

6-9B. (*Capital asset pricing model*) Breckenridge, Inc., has a beta of .85. If the expected market return is 10.5 percent and the risk-free rate is 7.5 percent, what is the appropriate required return of Breckenridge (using the CAPM)?

6-10B. (*Capital asset pricing model*) The expected return for the general market is 12.8 percent, and the risk premium in the market is 4.3 percent. Dupree, Yofota, and MacGrill have betas of .82, .57, and .68, respectively. What are the appropriate required rates of return for the three securities?

6-11B. (*Computing holding-period returns*) From the following price data, compute the holding-period returns for O'Toole and Baltimore.

TIME	O'TOOLE	BALTIMORE
1	$22	$45
2	24	50
3	20	48
4	25	52

How would you interpret the meaning of a holding-period return?

6-12B. (*Measuring risk and rates of return*)

a. Given the following holding-period returns, compute the average returns and the standard deviations for the Sugita Corporation and for the market.

MONTH	SUGITA CORP.	MARKET
1	1.8%	1.5%
2	−0.5	1.0
3	2.0	0.0
4	−2.0	−2.0
5	5.0	4.0
6	5.0	3.0

b. If Sugita's beta is 1.18 and the risk-free rate is 8 percent, what would be an appropriate required return for an investor owning Sugita? (*Note:* Because the preceding returns are based on monthly data, you will need to annualize the returns to make them comparable with the risk-free rate. For simplicity, you can convert from monthly to yearly returns by multiplying the average monthly returns by 12.)

c. How does Sugita's historical average return compare with the return you believe to be a fair return, given the firm's systematic risk?

6-13B. (*Portfolio beta and security market line*) You own a portfolio consisting of the following stocks:

STOCK	PERCENTAGE OF PORTFOLIO	BETA	EXPECTED RETURN
1	10%	1.00	12%
2	25	0.75	11
3	15	1.30	15
4	30	0.60	9
5	20	1.20	14

The risk-free rate is 8 percent. Also, the expected return on the market portfolio is 11.6 percent.

a. Calculate the expected return of your portfolio. (*Hint:* The expected return of a portfolio equals the weighted average of the individual stock's expected return, where the weights are the percentage invested in each stock.)

b. Calculate the portfolio beta.

c. Given the preceding information, plot the security market line on paper. Plot the stocks from your portfolio on your graph.

d. From your plot in part (c), which stocks *appear* to be your winners and which ones *appear* to be losers?

e. Why should you consider your conclusion in part (d) to be less than certain?

6-14B. (*Expected return, standard deviation, and capital asset pricing model*) Following you will find the end-of-month prices, both for the Market Index and for Hilary's common stock.

a. Using the following data, calculate the holding-period returns for each month from August 2002 to July 2003.

		PRICES	
	MONTH	MARKET	HILARY'S
2002	July	$1,328.72	$21.00
	August	1,320.41	19.50
	September	1,282.71	17.19
	October	1,362.93	16.88
	November	1,388.91	18.06
	December	1,469.25	24.88
2003	January	1,394.46	22.75
	February	1,366.42	26.25
	March	1,498.58	33.56
	April	1,452.43	43.31
	May	1,420.60	43.50
	June	1,454.60	43.50
	July	1,430.83	43.63

b. Calculate the average monthly return and the standard deviation of these returns both for the Market and Hilary's.

c. Develop a graph that shows the relationship between the Hilary's stock returns and the Market Index. (Show the Hilary's returns on the vertical axis and the Market Index returns on the horizontal as done in Figure 6-8.)

d. From your graph, describe the nature of the relationship between Hilary's stock returns and the returns for the Market Index.

6-15B. (*Expected rate of return and risk*) Moody, Inc., has collected information on the following three investments. Which investment is the most favorable based on the information presented?

STOCK A		STOCK B		STOCK C	
PROBABILITY	RETURN	PROBABILITY	RETURN	PROBABILITY	RETURN
.1	−4%	.13	4%	.2	−2%
.3	2%	.4	10%	.25	5%
.4	13%	.27	19%	.45	14%
.2	17%	.2	23%	.1	25%

6-16B. (*Capital asset pricing model*) Grace Corporation is considering the following investments. The current rate on Treasury bills is 5.5 percent, and the expected return for the market is 11 percent. Using the CAPM, what rates of return should Grace require for each individual security?

STOCK	BETA
K	1.12
G	1.3
B	0.75
U	1.02

6-17B. (*Computing holding-period returns*) From the following price data, compute the holding-period returns for Watkins and Fisher.

TIME	WATKINS	FISHER
1	40	27
2	45	31
3	43	35
4	49	36

6-18B. (*Required rate of return using CAPM*) Hilary's common stock has a beta of 0.95. The expected rate of return for the market is 7 percent and the risk-free rate is 4 percent.

a. Compute a fair rate of return based on this information.
b. What would be a fair rate if the beta were 1.25?
c. What would be the effect on the fair rate if the expected return for the market improved to 10 percent?

SELF-TEST SOLUTIONS

ST-1.

(A) PROBABILITY $P(k_i)$	(B) RETURN (k_i)	EXPECTED RETURN $(\bar{k})$ (A) × (B)	WEIGHTED DEVIATION $(k_i - \bar{k})^2 P(k_i)$
.10	−10%	−1%	52.9%
.20	5%	1%	12.8%
.30	10%	3%	2.7%
.40	25%	10%	57.6%
		$\bar{k}$ = 13%	σ^2 = 126.0%
			σ = 11.22%

From our studies in statistics, we know that if the distribution of returns were normal, then Universal could expect a return of 13 percent with a 67 percent possibility that this return would vary up or down by 11.22 percent between 1.78 percent (13% – 11.22%) and 24.22 percent (13% + 11.22%). However, it is apparent from the probabilities that the distribution is not normal.

ST-2.

Stock A	5% + .75(17% – 5%) = 14%
Stock B	5% + .90(17% – 5%) = 15.8%
Stock C	5% + 1.40(17% – 5%) = 21.8%

ST-3.

Kaifu

Average return:

$$\frac{4\% + 6\% + 0\% + 2\%}{4} = 3\%$$

Standard deviation:

$$\sqrt{\frac{(4\% - 3\%)^2 + (6\% - 3\%)^2 + (0\% - 3\%)^2 + (2\% - 3\%)^2}{4 - 1}} = 2.58$$

Market

Average return:

$$\frac{2\% + 3\% + 1\% - 1\%}{4} = 1.25$$

Standard deviation:

$$\sqrt{\frac{(2\% - 1.25\%)^2 + (3\% - 1.25\%)^2 + (1\% - 1.25\%)^2 + (-1\% - 1.25\%)^2}{4 - 1}} = 1.71\%$$

ST-4.

TIME	STOCK PRICE	HOLDING-PERIOD RETURN
1	$10	
2	13	($13 ÷ $10) – 1 = 30.0%
3	11	($11 ÷ $13) – 1 = –15.4%
4	15	($15 ÷ $11) – 1 = 36.4%

ST-5. **a.** Portfolio expected return:

$$(.4 \times 12\%) + (.25 \times 11\%) + (.35 \times 15\%) = 12.8\%$$

Portfolio beta:

$$(.4 \times 1) + (.25 \times .75) + (.35 \times 1.3) = 1.04$$

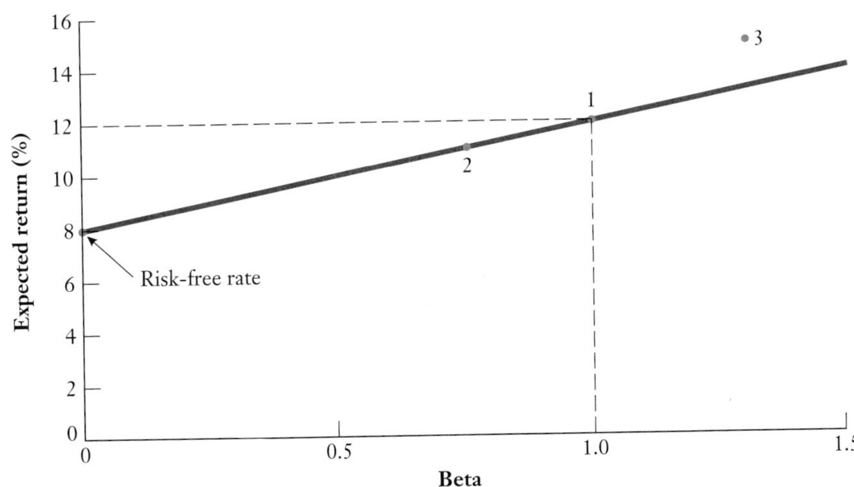

b. Stocks 1 and 2 seem to be right in line with the security market line, which suggests that they are earning a fair return, given their systematic risk. Stock 3, however, is earning more than a fair return (above the security market line). We might be tempted to conclude that security 3 is undervalued. However, we may be seeing an illusion; it is possible to misspecify the security market line by using bad estimates in our data.

LEARNING OBJECTIVES

After reading this chapter, you should be able to

1. Distinguish between different kinds of bonds.
2. Explain the more popular features of bonds.
3. Define the term *value* as used for several different purposes.
4. Explain the factors that determine value.
5. Describe the basic process for valuing assets.
6. Estimate the value of a bond.
7. Compute a bondholder's expected rate of return.
8. Explain five important relationships that exist in bond valuation.

CHAPTER 7

Valuation and Characteristics of Bonds

Practically all companies use debt to finance their firms, and many of those companies issue bonds, just one form of debt. Bonds provide investors a fixed income each year in the form of interest. Just as you can open a savings account at a bank and earn interest on your savings, so can you buy a bond that pays interest and then repays your principal on a designated date when the bond matures. Many of these bonds are traded in the public capital markets. Three examples of companies that have issued bonds to investors include the telecommunications firm, AT&T; the power company, Illinois Power; and the funeral service provider, Service Corporation. Each of these bonds pays $67.50 in interest each year on a bond that will repay the investor $1,000 when it matures. However, while these bonds are similar in terms of their interest payment, investors do not value them the same. In mid-2002, they were selling for the following amounts:

AT&T	$1,037.50
Illinois Power	$ 995.00
Service Corp.	$ 905.00

Why would there be differences in the values of these bonds? Why would AT&T's bonds be worth more than Illinois Power's bonds? And why would the Service Corp. bonds sell for this low price? They all pay the same amount of interest. Why would investors pay $1,037.50 for a bond that promises $67.50 in interest, when they could buy Service Corp. bonds for only $905.00? Or a more general question, "What determines a bond's value?" Read on and you will find the answer to this puzzle.

CHAPTER PREVIEW

Knowing the fair value or price of an asset is no easy matter. The *Maxims* of the French writer La Rochefoucauld, written over three centuries ago, still speak to us: "The greatest of all gifts is the power to estimate things at their true worth." Understanding how to value financial securities is essential if managers are to meet the objective of maximizing the value of the firm. If they are to maximize the investors' value, they must know what drives the value of an asset. Specifically, they need to understand how bonds and stocks are valued in the marketplace; otherwise, they cannot act in the best interest of the firm's investors.

A bond is one form of a company's long-term debt. In this chapter, we begin by identifying the different kinds of bonds. We next look at the features or characteristics of most bonds. We then examine the concepts of and procedures for valuing an asset and apply these ideas to valuing bonds, one form of a company's long-term debt. We now begin our study by considering the different kinds of bonds.

Objective 1

Bond
A type of debt or a long-term promissory note, issued by the borrower, promising to pay its holder a predetermined and fixed amount of interest each year.

TYPES OF BONDS

A **bond** is a type of debt or long-term promissory note, issued by the borrower, promising to pay its holder a predetermined and fixed amount of interest per year. However, there is a wide variety of such creatures. Just to mention a few, we have:

- Debentures
- Subordinated debentures
- Mortgage bonds
- Eurobonds
- Zero and very low coupon bonds
- Junk bonds

The following sections briefly explain each of these types of bonds.

DEBENTURES

Debenture
Any unsecured long-term debt.

The term **debenture** applies to any unsecured long-term debt. Because these bonds are unsecured, the earning ability of the issuing corporation is of great concern to the bondholder. They are also viewed as being riskier than secured bonds and as a result must provide investors with a higher yield than secured bonds provide. Often, the issuing firm attempts to provide some protection to the holder of the bond by prohibiting the firm from issuing more secured long-term debt that would further tie up the firm's assets and leave the bondholders less protected. To the issuing firm, the major advantage of debentures is that no property has to be secured by them. This allows the firm to issue debt and still preserve some future borrowing power.

SUBORDINATED DEBENTURES

Subordinated debenture
A debenture that is subordinated to other debentures in being paid in the case of insolvency.

Many firms have more than one issue of debentures outstanding. In this case a hierarchy may be specified, in which some debentures are given subordinated standing in case of insolvency. The claims of the **subordinated debentures** are honored only after the claims of secured debt and unsubordinated debentures have been satisfied.

MORTGAGE BONDS

Mortgage bond
A bond secured by a lien on real property

A **mortgage bond** is a bond secured by a lien on real property. Typically, the value of the real property is greater than that of the mortgage bonds issued. This provides the mortgage bondholders with a margin of safety in the event the market value of the secured property declines. In the case of foreclosure, the trustees have the power to sell the secured property and use the proceeds to pay the bondholders. In the event that the proceeds from this sale do not cover the bonds, the bondholders become general creditors, similar to debenture bondholders, for the unpaid portion of the debt.

EUROBONDS

Eurobonds
Bonds issued in a country different from the one in whose currency the bond is denominated—for instance, a bond issued in Europe or in Asia by an American company that pays interest and principal to the lender in U.S. dollars.

Eurobonds are not so much a different type of security. They are simply securities, in this case bonds, issued in a country different from the one in whose currency the bond is denominated. For example, a bond that is issued in Europe or in Asia by an American company and that pays interest and principal to the lender in U.S. dollars would be considered a Eurobond. Thus, even if the bond is not issued in Europe, it merely needs to be sold in a country different from the one in whose currency it is denominated to be considered a Eurobond. The Eurobond market actually has its roots in the 1950s and 1960s as the U.S. dollar became increasingly popular because of its role as the primary international reserve. In recent years, as the U.S. dollar has gained a reputation for being one of the most stable currencies, demand for Eurobonds has increased. The primary attractions of Eurobonds to borrowers, aside from favorable rates, are the relative lack of regulation (Eurobonds are not registered with the Securities and Exchange Commission [SEC]), less rigorous disclosure requirements than those of the SEC, and the speed with which they can be issued. Interestingly, not only are Eurobonds not registered with the SEC, but they may not be offered to U.S. citizens and residents during their initial distribution.

Zero and Very Low Coupon Bonds

Zero and very low coupon bonds allow the issuing firm to issue bonds at a substantial discount from their $1,000 face value with a zero or very low coupon rate. The investor receives a large part (or all with zero coupon bonds) of the return from the appreciation of the bond. For example, in 1998, 21st Century Telecom Group, Inc., a telecommunications firm, issued $43 million of debt maturing in 2008 with a zero coupon rate. These bonds were sold at a 57 percent discount from their par value; that is, investors only paid $430 for a bond with a $1,000 par value. Investors who purchased these bonds for $430 and hold them until they mature in 2008 will receive an 8.8 percent yield to maturity, with all of this yield coming from appreciation of the bond. However, 21st Century Telecom Group, Inc., will have no cash outflows until these bonds mature; at that time it will have to pay back $100 million even though it only received $43 million when the bonds were first issued.

Zero and very low coupon bonds
Bonds issued at a substantial discount from their $1,000 face value that pay no or little interest.

As with any form of financing, there are both advantages and disadvantages of issuing zero or very low coupon bonds. As already mentioned, the disadvantage is when the bonds mature, 21st Century Telecom Group will face an extremely large cash outflow, much greater than the cash inflow it experienced when the bonds were first issued. The advantages of zero and low coupon bonds are, first, that annual cash outflows associated with interest payments do not occur with zero coupon bonds and are at a relatively low level with low coupon bonds. Second, because there is relatively strong investor demand for this type of debt, prices tend to be bid up and yields tend to be bid down. That is to say, 21st Century Telecom Group was able to issue zero coupon bonds at about half a percent less than it would have been if they had been traditional coupon bonds. Finally, 21st Century Telecom Group is able to deduct the annual amortization of the discount from taxable income, which will provide a positive annual cash flow to 21st Century Telecom Group.

Junk Bonds (High-Yield Bonds)

Junk bonds are high-risk debt with ratings of BB or below by Moody's and Standard & Poor's. The lower the rating, the higher the chance of default; the lowest class is CC for Standard & Poor's and Ca for Moody's. Originally, the term was used to describe bonds issued by "fallen angels"; that is, firms with sound financial histories that were facing severe financial problems and suffering from poor credit ratings.

Junk or high-yield bonds
Bonds rated BB or below.

Junk bonds are also called **high-yield bonds** for the high interest rates they pay the investor, typically having an interest rate of between 3 and 5 percent more than AAA grade long-term debt.

Before the mid-1970s, smaller firms simply did not have access to the capital markets because of the reluctance of investors to accept speculative grade bonds. However, by the late 1980s, junk bonds became the way to finance hostile takeovers—buying a firm without the management's approval. For example, the purchase of RJR Nabisco for some $20 billion by the investment group KKR was largely accomplished by junk bond financing. However, the eventual bankruptcy of Drexel Burnham Lambert, the investment bank most responsible for developing a large junk bond market, the jailing of the "king of junk bonds" Michael Milken, and increasing interest rates brought an end to the extensive use of junk bonds for financing corporate takeovers. (Michael Milken, a partner at Drexel Burnham Lambert, used to have an annual conference in Beverly Hills, California, nicknamed "The Predator's Ball," for attracting takeover investors and corporate raiders who needed junk bond financing to accomplish their takeovers.)

When corporate takeovers subsided from their highs, most people thought the junk bond was forever dead. By 1990, the junk bond market was virtually nonexistent. Then, in 1992, with investors looking for higher interest rates and a rebounding economy, the junk bond market was revitalized. The following year, new junk bond issues reached a record \$62 billion. Also, by 1995, less than 20 percent of the proceeds from junk bonds were being used to finance mergers and acquisitions, compared to 60 percent in the 1980s. In addition, in 1995, more than 800 companies had issued junk bonds, up from several hundred in the 1980s. Then in early 1998, the junk bond market suffered a sudden, jarring setback that led to the market for these bonds essentially dying. By year-end 1998, the capital market had returned to relatively moderate levels, in part because the Federal Reserve lowered interest rates. The borrowers in the 1990s came from a variety of industries, including manufacturing, media, retailing, consumer products, financial services, and housing. Also, credit quality improved. Only 17 percent of new issues in 1995 fell into the lower ratings of creditworthiness, compared with 66 percent in 1988.

BACK TO THE PRINCIPLES

Some have thought junk bonds were fundamentally different from other securities, but they are not. They are bonds with a great amount of risk, and therefore promise high expected returns. Thus, ***Principle 1: The Risk-Return Trade-off—We won't take on additional risk unless we expect to be compensated with additional return.***

In 2001, new issues of junk bonds totaled more than \$87.6 billion, double the \$38.8 billion issued in 2000. Junk bond issues represented around 10 percent of all corporate bonds issued in 2001, compared to 5.8 percent of the total in 2000. In 2002 the new issues of junk bonds fell to \$58.1 billion; however, this represented 9.8 percent of all corporate bonds issued that year. Contrary to the conventional wisdom of the early 1990s, the junk bond market is alive and well. See the Finance Matters box, "Junk Bonds: A Very Risky Business."

CONCEPT CHECK

1. What is the difference in the nature and associated risk among debentures, subordinated debentures, and mortgage bonds? How would investors respond to the varying types of risk?
2. How does an investor receive a return from a zero or very low coupon bond? Why would a company be able to deduct amortized interest over the life of the bond even though there are no cash outflows associated with interest?
3. Why do junk bonds typically have a higher interest rate than other types of bonds? Why has this market been revitalized?

FINANCE MATTERS — ETHICS

JUNK BONDS: A VERY RISKY BUSINESS

Investors in high-yield bonds in the late 1990s have discovered how risky these securities can be. Fitch Ratings reports that 40 percent of all junk bonds issued during the period 1997 through 1999 have defaulted as of the end of June 2002. Most of the defaults have occurred in the telecommunications and media sectors. Junk bonds issued in 1998 have had the highest share of defaulted bonds in 2000, 2001, and 2002. March 1998 turned out to be the worst month to invest in junk bonds. Thirteen bond issues in that month had defaulted by June 2002.

Mariarosa Verde, senior director of credit-market research at Fitch, reports that start-up telecommunications companies issued high-yield bonds to raise large amounts of debt capital. The telecom companies raised more than $100 billion of debt capital. Their ability to borrow at this significant level led to overcapacity in the industry, which resulted in the collapse of pricing power for the firms. Default rates on debt by these firms began to increase.

Ed Mally, managing director of high-yield research at CIBC World Capital Markets, notes that in good times, default rates on high-yield bonds are around 2 percent, while in bad times the default rate rises to about 12 percent. Default rates are determined by comparing the amount of debt defaulted in a particular period to the total amount of debt outstanding, regardless of when it was issued. Thus, the 40 percent default rate during this narrow interval from 1998 to 2002 highlights a particularly grim time for high-yield investors and illustrates there is great risk associated with investing in high-yield bonds.

Now that you have an understanding of the kinds of bonds firms might issue, let's look at some of the characteristics and terminology of bonds.

TERMINOLOGY AND CHARACTERISTICS OF BONDS

Objective 2

Now that we have learned about the types of bonds, we need to look at the specific characteristics and terminology used in describing bonds. Only then will we be prepared to learn how to value a bond.

When a firm or nonprofit institution needs financing, one source is bonds. As already noted, this type of financing instrument is simply a long-term promissory note, issued by the borrower, promising to pay its holder a predetermined and fixed amount of interest each year. Some of the more important terms and characteristics that you might hear about bonds are as follows:

- Claims on assets and income
- Par value
- Coupon interest rate
- Maturity
- Indenture
- Current yield
- Bond ratings

Let's consider each in turn.

CLAIMS ON ASSETS AND INCOME

In the case of insolvency, claims of debt in general, including bonds, are honored before those of both common stock and preferred stock. However, different types of debt may also have a hierarchy among themselves as to the order of their claim on assets.

Bonds also have a claim on income that comes ahead of common and preferred stock. In general, if interest on bonds is not paid, the bond trustees can classify the firm as insolvent and force it into bankruptcy. Thus, the bondholder's claim on income is more likely to be honored than that of common and preferred stockholders, whose dividends are paid at the discretion of the firm's management.

PAR VALUE

Par value of a bond
The bond's face value that is returned to the bondholder at maturity, usually $1,000.

The **par value of a bond** is its face value that is returned to the bondholder at maturity. In general, corporate bonds are issued in denominations of $1,000, although there are some exceptions to this rule. Also, when bond prices are quoted, either by financial managers or in the financial press, prices are generally expressed as a percentage of the bond's par value. For example, a Lucent bond was recently quoted in the *Wall Street Journal* as selling for 77.88. That does not mean you can buy the bond for $77.88. It means that this bond is selling for 77.88 percent of its par value of $1,000. Hence, the market price of this bond is actually $778.80. At maturity in 2006, the bondholder will receive the $1,000.

COUPON INTEREST RATE

Coupon interest rate
A bond's coupon interest rate indicates what percentage of the par value of the bond will be paid out annually in the form of interest.

The **coupon interest rate** on a bond indicates the percentage of the par value of the bond that will be paid out annually in the form of interest. Thus, regardless of what happens to the price of a bond with an 8 percent coupon interest rate and a $1,000 par value, it will pay out $80 annually in interest until maturity (.08 × $1,000 = $80).

MATURITY

Maturity
The length of time until the bond issuer returns the par value to the bondholder and terminates the bond.

The **maturity** of a bond indicates the length of time until the bond issuer returns the par value to the bondholder and terminates or redeems the bond.

INDENTURE

Indenture
The legal agreement or contract between the firm issuing the bonds and the bond trustee who represents the bondholders.

An **indenture** is the legal agreement between the firm issuing the bonds and the bond trustee who represents the bondholders. The indenture provides the specific terms of the loan agreement, including a description of the bonds, the rights of the bondholders, the rights of the issuing firm, and the responsibilities of the trustee. This legal document may run 100 pages or more in length, with the majority of it devoted to defining protective provisions for the bondholder. The bond trustee, usually a banking institution or trust company, is then assigned the task of overseeing the relationship between the bondholder and the issuing firm, protecting the bondholder, and seeing that the terms of the indenture are carried out.

Typically, the restrictive provisions included in the indenture attempt to protect the bondholders' financial position relative to that of other outstanding securities. Common provisions involve (1) prohibiting the sale of accounts receivable, (2) limiting common stock dividends, (3) restricting the purchase or sale of fixed assets, and (4) setting limits on additional borrowing. Not allowing the sale of accounts receivable is specified because such sales would benefit the firm's short-run liquidity position at the expense of its future liquidity position. Common stock dividends may not be allowed if the firm's liquidity falls below a specified level, or the maximum dividend payout may be limited to some fraction, say 50 percent or 60 percent of earnings under any circumstance. Fixed-asset restrictions generally require lender permission before the liquidation of any fixed asset or prohibit the use of any existing fixed asset as collateral on new loans. Constraints on additional borrowing usually involve limiting the amount and type of additional long-term debt that can be issued. All of these restrictions have one thing in common: They attempt to prohibit actions that would improve the status of other securities at the expense of bonds and to protect the status of bonds from being weakened by any managerial action.

CURRENT YIELD

The **current yield** on a bond refers to the ratio of the annual interest payment to the bond's current market price. If, for example, we have a bond with an 8 percent coupon interest rate, a par value of $1,000, and a market price of $700, it would have a current yield of

Current yield The ratio of the annual interest payment to the bond's market price.

$$\text{current yield} = \frac{\text{annual interest payment}}{\text{market price of the bond}} \tag{7-1}$$

$$= \frac{0.08 \times \$1000}{\$700} = \frac{\$80}{\$700} = 0.114 = 11.4\%$$

BOND RATINGS

John Moody first began to rate bonds in 1909. Since that time three rating agencies—Moody's, Standard & Poor's, and Fitch Investor Services—have provided ratings on corporate bonds. These ratings involve a judgment about the future risk potential of the bond. (See the Finance Matters box, "Fitch Affirms Belo Corporation's 'BBB-' Rating Outlook Changed to Stable.") Although they deal with expectations, several historical factors seem to play a significant role in their determination. Bond ratings are favorably affected by (1) a greater reliance on equity as opposed to debt in financing the firm, (2) profitable operations, (3) a low variability in past earnings, (4) large firm size, and (5) little use of subordinated debt. In turn, the rating a bond receives affects the rate of return demanded on the bond by the investors. The poorer the bond rating, the higher the rate of return demanded in the capital markets. Table 7-1 provides an example and description of these ratings. Thus, bond ratings are extremely important for the financial manager. They provide an indicator of default risk that in turn affects the rate of return that must be paid on borrowed funds.

FINANCE MATTERS — ETHICS

BOND RATING: FITCH AFFIRMS BELO CORPORATION'S "BBB-" RATING OUTLOOK CHANGED TO STABLE

The following news announcement was released regarding Fitch Ratings changing its rating outlook on Belo Corporation's senior unsecured debt. The following is an excerpt from the announcement.

> Fitch Ratings has affirmed Belo Corp. (Belo) 'BBB-' senior unsecured debt and changed the Rating Outlook to Stable from Negative . . .
>
> Credit protection measures have been reestablished at levels consistent with the current 'BBB-' rating and the combination of improved business trends and the company's focus on additional credit strengthening provides for a Stable Rating Outlook.
>
> Improved advertising trends at both television and newspaper operations and lower operating costs combined with the company's program to strengthening the balance sheet have produced meaningful improvements in leverage in 2002. Lower operating costs reflect internal cost reduction initiatives as well as benefits from lower newsprint prices in newspaper operations. Reductions in capital expenditures and the cessation of share repurchases in 2001 have allowed the company to reduce debt balances to $1.44 billion at year-end 2002 from $1.70 billion at year-end 2001. The ratio of cash flow to debt has improved accordingly to 3.4 times (×) in 2002 from 4.9× in 2001.
>
> The company remains focused on further improvements to the balance sheet in 2003. Fitch notes, however, that while current business trends are favorable, earnings comparisons in 2003 will be made more difficult by higher newsprint prices in the newspaper operations, the absence of political advertising in the television operations, and increases in company-wide employee benefits costs. The effect on advertising revenues of a foreign military conflict adds to the uncertainties. Nevertheless, Belo typically generates solid free cash flow after capital expenditures and dividends and the company should be able to effect additional reductions in debt given the continuing hiatus on share repurchases.

Source: "Fitch Affirms Belo Corp.'s 'BBB-' Rating; Outlook Changed to Stable," Fitch Rating, February 26, 2003.

TABLE 7-1 Standard & Poor's Corporate Bond Ratings

AAA	An obligation rated 'AAA' has the highest rating assigned by Standard & Poor's. The obligor's capacity to meet its financial commitment on the obligation is extremely strong.
AA	An obligation rated 'AA' differs from the highest-rated obligations only to a small degree. The obligor's capacity to meet its financial commitment on the obligation is very strong.
A	An obligation rated 'A' is somewhat more susceptible to the adverse effects of changes in circumstances and economic conditions than obligations in higher-rated categories. However, the obligor's capacity to meet its financial commitment on the obligation is still strong.
BBB	An obligation rated 'BBB' exhibits adequate protection parameters. However, adverse economic conditions or changing circumstances are more likely to lead to a weakened capacity of the obligor to meet its financial commitment on the obligation.
BB, B, CCC, CC, and C	Obligations rated 'BB', 'B', 'CCC', 'CC', and 'C' are regarded as having significant speculative characteristics. 'BB' indicates the least degree of speculation and 'C' the highest. While such obligations will likely have some quality and protective characteristics, these may be outweighed by large uncertainties or major exposures to adverse conditions.
BB	An obligation rated 'BB' is less vulnerable to nonpayment than other speculative issues. However, it faces major ongoing uncertainties or exposure to adverse business, financial, or economic conditions which could lead to the obligor's inadequate capacity to meet its financial commitment on the obligation.
B	An obligation rated 'B' is more vulnerable to nonpayment than obligations rated 'BB', but the obligor currently has the capacity to meet its financial commitment on the obligation. Adverse business, financial, or economic conditions will likely impair the obligor's capacity or willingness to meet its financial commitment on the obligation.
CCC	An obligation rated 'CCC' is currently vulnerable to nonpayment, and is dependent upon favorable business, financial, and economic conditions for the obligor to meet its financial commitment on the obligation. In the event of adverse business, financial, or economic conditions, the obligor is not likely to have the capacity to meet its financial commitment on the obligation.
CC	An obligation rated 'CC' is currently highly vulnerable to nonpayment.
C	A subordinated debt or preferred stock obligation rated 'C' is currently highly vulnerable to nonpayment. The 'C' rating may be used to cover a situation where a bankruptcy petition has been filed or similar action taken, but payments on this obligation are being continued. A 'C' also will be assigned to a preferred stock issue in arrears on dividends or sinking fund payments, but that is currently paying.
D	An obligation rated 'D' is in payment default. The 'D' rating category is used when payments on an obligation are not made on the date due even if the applicable grace period has not expired, unless Standard & Poor's believes that such payments will be made during the grace period. The 'D' rating also will be used upon the filing of a bankruptcy petition or the taking of a similar action if payments on an obligation are jeopardized.

Plus (+) or Minus (–): The ratings from 'AA' to 'CCC' may be modified by the addition of a plus (+) or minus (–) sign to show relative standing within the major rating categories.

Source: *Standard & Poor's Fixed Income Investor,* Vol. 8 (1980). Reprinted with permission of Standard & Poor's, a division of The McGraw-Hill Companies, Inc.

BACK TO THE PRINCIPLES

When we say that a lower bond rating means a higher interest rate charged by the investors (bondholders), we are observing an application of ***Principle 1: The Risk-Return Trade-Off—We won't take on additional risk unless we expect to be compensated with additional return.***

We are now ready to think about bond valuation. But, to begin, we must first clarify precisely what we mean by value. Next, we need to understand the basic concepts of valuation and the process for valuing an asset. Then we may apply these concepts to valuing a bond—and in Chapter 8 to valuing stocks.

CONCEPT CHECK

1. What are some of the important features of a bond? Which features determine the cash flows associated with a bond?
2. What restrictions are typically included in an indenture in order to protect the bondholder?
3. How does the bond rating affect an investor's required rate of return? What actions could a firm take to receive a more favorable rating?

DEFINITIONS OF VALUE

Objective 3

The term *value* is often used in different contexts, depending on its application. Examples of different uses of this term include the following:

Book value is the value of an asset as shown on a firm's balance sheet. It represents the historical cost of the asset rather than its current worth. For instance, the book value of a company's preferred stock is the amount the investors originally paid for the stock and therefore the amount the firm received when the stock was issued.

Book value
The value of an asset as shown on a firm's balance sheet. It represents the historical cost of the asset rather than its current market value or replacement cost.

Liquidation value is the dollar sum that could be realized if an asset were sold individually and not as part of a going concern. For example, if a firm's operations were discontinued and its assets were divided up and sold, the sales price would represent the asset's liquidation value.

Liquidation value
The amount that could be realized if an asset were sold individually and not as a part of a going concern.

The **market value** of an asset is the observed value for the asset in the marketplace. This value is determined by supply and demand forces working together in the marketplace, where buyers and sellers negotiate a mutually acceptable price for the asset. For instance, the market price for Ford Motor Company common stock on November 5, 2002, was $8.90. This price was reached by a large number of buyers and sellers working through the New York Stock Exchange. In theory, a market price exists for all assets. However, many assets have no readily observable market price because trading seldom occurs. For instance, the market price for the common stock of Blanks Engraving, a Dallas-based, family-owned firm, would be more difficult to establish than the market value of J. C. Penney's common stock.

Market value
The observed value for the asset in the marketplace.

The **intrinsic** or **economic value** of an asset—also called the fair value—is the present value of the asset's expected future cash flows. This value is the amount an investor should be willing to pay, given the amount, timing, and riskiness of future cash flows. Once the investor has estimated the intrinsic value of a security, this value could be compared with its market value when available. If the intrinsic value is greater than the market value, then the security is undervalued in the eyes of the investor. Should the market value exceed the investor's intrinsic value, then the security is overvalued.

Intrinsic or economic value
The present value of the asset's expected future cash flows. This value is the amount the investor considers to be a fair value, given the amount, timing, and riskiness of future cash flows.

We hasten to add that if the securities market is working efficiently, the market value and the intrinsic value of a security will be equal. Whenever a security's intrinsic value differs from its current market price, the competition among investors seeking opportunities to make a profit will quickly drive the market price back to its intrinsic value. Thus, we may define an **efficient market** as one in which the values of all securities at any instant fully reflect all available public information, which results in the market value and the intrinsic value being the same. If the markets are efficient, it is extremely difficult for an investor to make extra profits from an ability to predict prices.

Efficient market
A market in which the values of securities at any instant in time fully reflect all available information, which results in the market value and the intrinsic value being the same.

BACK TO THE PRINCIPLES

*The fact that investors have difficulty identifying securities that are undervalued relates to **Principle 6: Efficient Capital Markets—The markets are quick and the prices are right.** In an efficient market, the price reflects all available public information about the security, and therefore, it is priced fairly.*

The idea of efficient markets has recently been challenged by proponents of behavioral finance, an emerging area of research. Behavioral finance theory suggests that market investors are irrational, past stock prices can be used to predict future stock price changes, and analysis of stock price trends and financial reports can be used to enhance returns to the investor. While behavioral finance supporters and efficient market proponents have differing beliefs about investor and market behavior, they both conclude that investors cannot consistently beat the market.

Efficient market theory is based on the belief that stock price movements are responses by investors as they incorporate all publicly available information into their investment decisions. This does not mean that all market participants are rational, but that irrational investors are irrational in different ways that tend to cancel out each other. Behavioral finance supporters say that investors are not always rational and often make judgment errors that are both systematic and predictable. Behavioral research has shown that investment errors come from overconfidence—investors are not sufficiently diversified, they trade too frequently, and they rely too heavily on the recent past to forecast future stock performance.

The stock market bubble of the late 1990s provides evidence to support the behavioral finance theory. High price-earnings ratios, Internet companies with soaring stock prices but negative earnings, and a perception that the past performance of the market would continue into the future are indications that market investors had succumbed to fads and mass hysteria. The efficient market proponents explain the stock market bubble as a risky, but not foolish, response by investors to the information available.

Behaviorists conclude that although stock market investors are often irrational, the markets do perform well and that an individual investor trying to outguess the behavior of the market participants will usually fail. Efficient market proponents believe that for the market to be efficient, there must be rational investors who believe there are market inefficiencies that can be exploited to generate excess returns.

Both the behaviorists and the efficient market supporters agree that investors can be successful by considering factors which are under their control. Specifically, investors should be properly diversified, they should minimize transaction costs by maintaining a "buy and hold" strategy, and they should invest in index funds.[1]

CONCEPT CHECK

1. Explain the difference between the four different values of a bond. Why should the market value equal the intrinsic value?
2. How does risk play a role in the three basic factors of asset valuation?

Objective 4

DETERMINANTS OF VALUE

For our purposes, the value of an asset is its intrinsic value or the present value of its expected future cash flows, where these cash flows are discounted back to the present using the investor's required rate of return. This statement is true for valuing all assets and serves as the basis of almost all that we do in finance. Thus, value is affected by three elements:

1. The amount and timing of the asset's expected cash flows
2. The riskiness of these cash flows
3. The investor's required rate of return for undertaking the investment

The first two factors are characteristics of the asset; the third one, the required rate of return, is the minimum rate of return necessary to attract an investor to purchase or hold a security, which is determined by the rates of return available on similar investments, or

[1] "Is the Market Rational?" Justin Fox, *Fortune*, December 3, 2002.

what is called the **opportunity cost of funds**. This rate must be high enough to compensate the investor for the risk perceived in the asset's future cash flows. (The required rate of return was explained in Chapter 6.)

Opportunity cost of funds The next best rate of return available to the investor for a given level of risk.

BACK TO THE PRINCIPLES

Our discussions should remind us of three of our principles that help us understand finance:

Principle 1: The Risk-Return Trade-off—We won't take on additional risk unless we expect to be compensated with additional return.

Principle 2: The Time Value of Money—A dollar received today is worth more than a dollar received in the future.

Principle 3: Cash—Not Profits—Is King.

Determining the economic worth or value of an asset always relies on these three principles. Without them, we would have no basis for explaining value. With them, we can know that the amount and timing of cash, not earnings, drive value. Also, we must be rewarded for taking risk; otherwise, we will not invest.

Figure 7-1 depicts the basic factors involved in valuation. As the figure shows, finding the value of an asset involves the following steps:

1. Assessing the asset's characteristics, which include the amount and timing of the expected cash flows and the riskiness of these cash flows
2. Determining the investor's required rate of return, which embodies the investor's attitude about assuming risk and perception of the riskiness of the asset
3. Discounting the expected cash flows back to the present, using the investor's required rate of return as the discount rate

FIGURE 7-1 Basic Factors Determining an Asset's Value

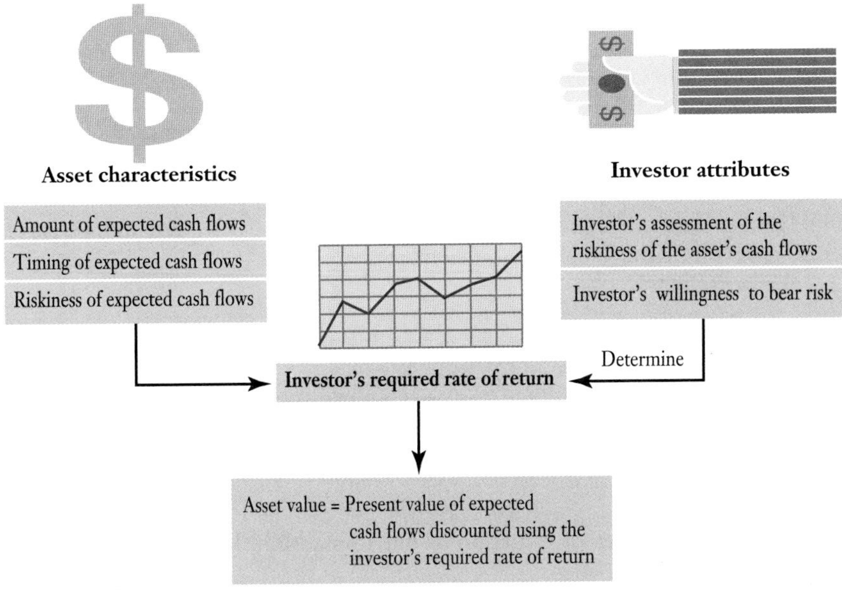

Thus, intrinsic value is a function of the cash flows yet to be received, the riskiness of these cash flows, and the investor's required rate of return.

CONCEPT CHECK

1. What are the three important elements of asset valuation?

Objective 5

VALUATION: THE BASIC PROCESS

The valuation process can be described as follows: It is assigning value to an asset by calculating the present value of its expected future cash flows using the investor's required rate of return as the discount rate. The investor's required rate of return, k, is determined by the level of the risk-free rate of interest and the risk premium that the investor feels is necessary to compensate for the risks assumed in owning the asset. Therefore, a basic asset valuation model can be defined mathematically as follows:

$$V = \frac{C_1}{(1+k)^1} + \frac{C_2}{(1+k)^2} + \cdots + \frac{C_n}{(1+k)^n} \tag{7-2}$$

or

$$V = \sum_{t=1}^{n} \frac{C_t}{(1+k)^t}$$

where C_t = cash flow to be received at time t
V = the intrinsic value or present value of an asset producing expected future cash flows, C_t, in years 1 through n
k = the investor's required rate of return

Using equation 7-2, there are three basic steps in the valuation process:

Step 1. Estimate C_t in equation 7-2, which is the amount and timing of the future cash flows the asset is expected to provide.
Step 2. Determine k, the investor's required rate of return.
Step 3. Calculate the intrinsic value, V, as the present value of expected future cash flows discounted at the investor's required rate of return.

Equation 7-2, which measures the present value of future cash flows, is the basis of the valuation process. It is the most important equation in this chapter, because all the remaining equations in this chapter and in Chapter 8 are merely reformulations of this one equation. If we understand equation 7-2, all the valuation work we do, and a host of other topics as well, will be much clearer in our minds.

CONCEPT CHECK

1. What two factors determine an investor's required rate of return?
2. How does the required rate of return affect an asset's value?

With the forgoing principles of valuation as our foundation, let's now look at how bonds are valued.

FIGURE 7-2 Data Requirements for Bond Valuation

(A) Cash Flow Information	Periodic interest payments For example, $65 per year Principal amount or par value For example, $1,000
(B) Time to Maturity	For example, 12 years
(C) Investor's Required Rate of Return	For example, 8 percent

BOND VALUATION

Objective 6

The value of a bond is the present value both of future interest to be received and the par or maturity value of the bond. It's that simple.

The process for valuing a bond, as depicted in Figure 7-2, requires knowing three essential elements: (1) the amount and timing of the cash flows to be received by the investor, (2) the time to maturity of the loan, and (3) the investor's required rate of return. The amount of cash flows is dictated by the periodic interest to be received and by the par value to be paid at maturity. Given these elements, we can compute the value of the bond, or the present value. See the Finance Matters box, "Reading a Bond Quote in *The Wall Street Journal*" on page 237.

EXAMPLE: VALUING A BOND

Consider a bond issued by AT&T with a maturity date of 2022 and a stated coupon rate of 8.5 percent.[a] On January 1, 2003, with 20 years left to maturity, investors owning the bonds are requiring a 7.5 percent rate of return. We can calculate the value of the bonds to these investors using the following three-step valuation procedure:

Step 1. Estimate the amount and timing of the expected future cash flows. Two types of cash flows are received by the bondholder:

a. Annual interest payments equal to the coupon rate of interest times the face value of the bond. In this example, the bond's coupon interest rate is 8.5 percent; thus the annual interest payment is $\$85 = .085 \times \$1{,}000$. These interest payments will be received by the bondholder in each of the 20 years before the bond matures (2003 through 2022 = 20 years).

b. The face value of the bond of $1,000 to be received in 2022. To summarize, the cash flows received by the bondholder are as follows:

YEAR	1	2	3	4	...	19	20
	$85	$85	$85	$85	...	$85	85 1,000 $1,085

[a]AT&T pays interest to its bondholders on a semiannual basis on January 15 and July 15. However, for the moment, assume the interest is to be received annually. The effect of semiannual payments is examined later.

(continued)

Step 2. Determine the investor's required rate of return by evaluating the riskiness of the bond's future cash flows. A 7.5 percent required rate of return for the bondholders is given. In Chapter 6, we learned how this rate is determined. For now, simply realize that the investor's required rate of return is equal to a rate earned on a risk-free security plus a risk premium for assuming risk.

Step 3. Calculate the intrinsic value of the bond as the present value of the expected future interest and principal payments discounted at the investor's required rate of return.

The present value of AT&T bonds is as follows:

$$\text{bond value} = V_b = \frac{\$\text{ interest in year 1}}{(1 + \text{required rate of return})^1} + \frac{\$\text{ interest in year 2}}{(1 + \text{required rate of return})^2} + \cdots + \frac{\$\text{ interest in year 20}}{(1 + \text{required rate of return})^{20}} + \frac{\$\text{ par value of bond}}{(1 + \text{required rate of return})^{20}} \quad \textbf{(7-3a)}$$

or, summing over the interest payments,

$$V_b = \underbrace{\sum_{t=1}^{20} \frac{\$\text{ interest in year } t}{(1 + \text{required rate of return})^t}}_{\text{present value of interest}} + \underbrace{\frac{\$\text{ par value of bond}}{(1 + \text{required rate of return})^{20}}}_{\text{present value of par value}}$$

The forgoing equation is a restatement in a slightly different form of equation 7-2. Recall that equation 7-2 states that the value of an asset is the present value of future cash flows to be received by the investor.

Using I_t to represent the interest payment in year t, M to represent the bond's maturity (or par) value, and k_b to equal the bondholder's required rate of return, we may express the value of a bond maturing in year n as follows:

$$V_b = \sum_{t=1}^{n} \frac{\$I_t}{(1 + k_b)^t} + \frac{\$M}{(1 + k_b)^n} \quad \textbf{(7-3b)}$$

Finding the value of the AT&T bonds may be represented graphically as follows:

YEAR	0	1	2	3	4	5	6	...	20
Dollars received at end of year		$85	$85	$85	$85	$85	$85	...	$85 $1,000 $1,085
Present value	$1,102 ←								

CALCULATOR SOLUTION

Data Input	Function Key
20	N
7.5	I/Y
85	PMT
1000	FV

Function Key	Answer
CPT PV	–1,102

Using the TI BAII Plus, we find the value of the bond to be $1,102, as calculated in the margin.[b] Thus, if investors consider 7.5 percent to be an appropriate required rate of return in view of the risk level associated with AT&T bonds, paying a price of $1,102 would satisfy their return requirement.

[b]As noted in Chapter 5, we are using the TI BAII Plus. You may want to return to the Chapter 5 section "Moving Money through Time with the Aid of a Financial Calculator" or Appendix A to see a more complete explanation of using the TI BAII Plus.

FINANCE MATTERS — ETHIC

READING A BOND QUOTE IN *THE WALL STREET JOURNAL*

Following is a section of *The Wall Street Journal* that gives the quotes for November 5, 2002, for some of the corporate bonds traded on the New York Stock Exchange on that date.

U.S. Exchange Bonds

BONDS	CUR. YLD.	VOL.	CLOSE	NET CHG.
Lucent 6½28	16.6	104	39.13	+0.13
Malan 9½04	cv	103	95.13	+0.13
NrurU 5.95s03	6.0	10	100	−0.16
NETelTel 4⅝05	4.6	6	101.13	+0.88
NYTel 6⅛10	6.0	10	101.75	−0.50
NYTel 7s25	7.0	105	100	+2.25
Noram 6s12	cv	42	66.50	+1.50
Nortel 4¼08	cv	10	48	+10.00
OldRep 7s07	6.7	15	104.50	+0.38
ParkerD 5½04	cv	15	89.25	−0.25
PhilPt 7.92s23	7.6	21	104.75	+0.13
PSEG 8 03	8.7	100	102.13	−0.38

The bonds shown in the list as "Lucent 6½28" were issued by Lucent Technologies. They pay a 6½ percent coupon interest rate (indicated by the "6½"), or $65 interest paid annually (actually $32.50 paid semiannually) on a par value of $1,000, and they mature in 2028 (28 is the last two digits of the year the bonds mature). The closing price of the bonds on November 5, 2002, was 39.13, which is stated as a percentage of the bond's $1,000 par value; thus, the bond's closing price on November 5, 2002, was $391.30 = .3913 × 1000. The current yield on the bond is 16.6 percent, calculated as the annual interest divided by the closing price, or $65/$391.30 = 16.6 percent. During the day, 104 bonds were traded on the exchange, as reflected by the "VOL." heading.[a] Finally, the net change ("NET CHG.") in the price of the bond from the previous day's close was an increase of .13 percent.

[a] There may have been more than 104 bonds changing hands on November 5, 2002. Many bond trades are negotiated directly between institutional investors or through bankers and are not listed in *The Wall Street Journal.*

We can also solve for the value of AT&T's bonds using a spreadsheet. The solution using Excel appears as follows:

	A	B	C	D
1	Required rate of return	Rate	0.075	
2	Years left to maturity	Nper	20	
3	Annual interest payment	Pmt	85	
4	Future value	FV	1,000	
5	Present value	PV	($1,102)	
6			↑	
7				
8				
9	Equation: = PV (Rate, Nper, Pmt, FV) = PV (C1, C2, C3, C4)			

SEMIANNUAL INTEREST PAYMENTS

In the preceding AT&T illustration, the interest payments were assumed to be paid annually. However, companies typically pay interest to bondholders semiannually. For example, consider Time Warner's bonds maturing in 11 years that pay \$91.25 per year, but the interest is dispersed semiannually (\$45.625 each January 15 and July 15).

Several steps are involved in adapting equation 7-3b for semiannual interest payments.[2] First, thinking in terms of *periods* instead of years, a bond with a life of n years paying interest semiannually has a life of $2n$ periods. In other words, a five-year bond ($n = 5$) that remits its interest on a semiannual basis actually makes 10 payments. Yet although the number of periods has doubled, the *dollar* amount of interest being sent to the investors for each period and the bondholders' required rate of return are half of the equivalent annual figures. I_t becomes $I_t/2$ and k_b is changed to $k_b/2$; thus, for semiannual compounding, equation 7-3b becomes

$$V_b = \sum_{t=1}^{2n} \frac{\$I_t/2}{\left(1+\frac{k_b}{2}\right)^t} + \frac{\$M}{\left(1+\frac{k_b}{2}\right)^{2n}} \quad \text{(7-4)}$$

CALCULATOR SOLUTION

Data Input	Function Key
$2n \rightarrow 2 \times 11 = 22$	N
7.2% ÷ 2 = 3.6	I/Y
\$91.25 ÷ 2 = 45.625	PMT
1000	FV
Function Key	**Answer**
CPT PV	−1,145

Assuming the Time Warner bondholders' annual required rate of return is 7.2 percent, we can use the TI BAII Plus calculator, as shown in the margin, to find the bond value, but now assuming semiannual interest payments. Thus, the value of a bond paying \$45.625 in semiannual interest for 11 years, where the investor has a 7.2 percent required rate of return, would be \$1,145.

This solution using a spreadsheet would look as follows:

	A	B	C	D
1	Required rate of return	Rate	0.036	
2	Periods left to maturity	Nper	22	
3	Semiannual interest payment	Pmt	45.625	
4	Future value	FV	1,000	
5	Present value	PV	(\$1,145)	
6			↑	
7				
8				
9	Equation: = PV (Rate, Nper, Pmt, FV) = PV (C1, C2, C3, C4)			

CONCEPT CHECK

1. What does it mean if your required rate of return for investing in a bond is different from the expected rate of return implied by its current market price? As an investor, what would you do if this were true?
2. How do semiannual payments affect the asset valuation equation?

Objective 7

THE BONDHOLDER'S EXPECTED RATE OF RETURN (YIELD TO MATURITY)

Theoretically, each investor could have a different required rate of return for a particular security. However, the financial manager is only interested in the required rate of return

[2] The logic for calculating the value of a bond that pays interest semiannually is similar to the material presented in Chapter 5 where compound interest with nonannual periods was discussed.

that is implied by the market prices of the firm's securities. In other words, the consensus of a firm's investors about the expected rate of return is reflected in the current market price of the stock.

To measure the bondholder's **expected rate of return,** $\bar{k}_b$, we would find the discount rate that equates the present value of the future cash flows (interest and maturity value) with the current market price of the bond.[3] The expected rate of return for a bond is also the rate of return the investor will earn if the bond is held to maturity, or the **yield to maturity**. Thus, when referring to bonds, the terms *expected rate of return* and *yield to maturity* are often used interchangeably.

Expected rate of return
The discount rate that equates the present value of the future cash flows (interest and maturity value) with the current market price of the bond. It is the rate of return an investor will earn if a bond is held to maturity.

Yield to maturity
The same as the expected rate of return.

To illustrate this concept, consider the Brister Corporation's bonds, which are selling for $1,100. The bonds carry a coupon interest rate of 9 percent and mature in 10 years. (Remember, the coupon rate determines the interest payment—coupon rate × par value.)

In determining the expected rate of return ($\bar{k}_b$) implicit in the current market price, we need to find the rate that discounts the anticipated cash flows back to a present value of $1,100, the current market price (P_0) for the bond.

Finding the expected rate of return for a bond using the present value tables is done by trial and error. We have to keep trying new rates until we find the discount rate that results in the present value of the future interest and maturity value of the bond just equaling the current market value of the bond. If the expected rate is somewhere between rates in the present value tables, we then must interpolate between the rates.

For our example, if we try 7 percent, the bond's present value is $1,140.16. Because the present value of $1,140.16 is greater than the market price of $1,100, we should next try a higher rate. Increasing the discount rate, say, to 8 percent gives a present value of $1,066.90. (These computations are shown in the following chart.) Now the present value is less than the market price; thus, we know that the investor's expected rate of return is between 7 percent and 8 percent.

YEARS	CASH FLOW	7% PRESENT VALUE FACTORS	PRESENT VALUE	8% PRESENT VALUE FACTORS	PRESENT VALUE
1–10	$90 per year	7.024	$ 632.16	6.710	$ 603.90
10	$1,000 in year 10	0.508	508.00	0.463	$ 463.00
		Present value at 7%	$1,140.16	Present value at 8%	$1,066.90

CALCULATOR SOLUTION

Data Input	Function Key
10	N
1100	PV
90	+/– PMT
1000	+/– FV

Function Key	Answer
CPT I/Y	7.54

The actual expected return for the Brister Corporation bondholders is 7.54 percent, which may be found by using the TI BAII Plus calculator as presented in the margin, or by using a computer spreadsheet as follows:

	A	B	C	D
1	Years left to maturity	Nper	10	
2	Annual interest payment	Pmt	90	
3	Present value	PV	–1,100	
4	Future value	FV	1,000	
5	Required rate of return	Rate	7.54%	
6			▲	
7				
8				
9				
10	Equation: = RATE (Nper, Pmt, –PV, FV) = RATE (C1, C2, C3, C4)			

[3] When we speak of computing an expected rate of return, we are not describing the situation very accurately. Expected rates of return are ex ante (before the fact) and are based on "expected and unobservable future cash flows" and, therefore, can only be "estimated."

Given our understanding of bond valuation and a bondholder's expected rate of return, let's discover what else a financial manager needs to know to understand why bond prices and interest rates perform as they do.

Objective 8

BOND VALUATION: FIVE IMPORTANT RELATIONSHIPS

We have now learned to find the value of a bond (V_b), given (1) the amount of interest payments, (2) the maturity or par value, (3) the length of time to maturity, and (4) the investor's required rate of return. We also know how to compute the expected rate of return, $\bar{k}_b$, which also happens to be the *current interest rate* on the bond, given (1) the current market value, (2) the amount of interest payments, (3) the maturity value, and (4) the length of time to maturity. We now have the basics. However, a financial manager needs to know more in order to understand how the firm's bonds will react to changing conditions. So let's go further in our understanding of bond valuation by studying several important relationships.

FIRST RELATIONSHIP

The value of a bond is inversely related to changes in the investor's present required rate of return (the current interest rate). In other words, as interest rates increase (decrease), the value of the bond decreases (increases).

To illustrate, assume that an investor's required rate of return for a given bond is 12 percent. The bond has a par value of $1,000 and annual interest payments of $120, indicating a 12 percent coupon interest rate ($120 ÷ $1,000 = 12%). Assuming a five-year maturity date, the bond would be worth $1,000, computed as follows by using equation 7-3a:

CALCULATOR SOLUTION

Data Input	Function Key
5	N
12	I/Y
120	+/– PMT
1000	+/– FV
Function Key	**Answer**
CPT PV	$1000.00

$$V_b = \frac{I_1}{(1+k_b)^1} + \cdots + \frac{I_n}{(1+k_b)^n} + \frac{M}{(1+k_b)^n}$$

$$= \sum_{t=1}^{n} \frac{I_t}{(1+k_b)^t} + \frac{M}{(1+k_b)^n}$$

$$= \sum_{t=1}^{5} \frac{\$120}{(1+.12)^t} + \frac{\$1,000}{(1+.12)^5} = \$1,000$$

Using present value tables, as explained in Chapter 5, we have:

CALCULATOR SOLUTION

Data Input	Function Key
5	N
15	I/Y
120	+/– PMT
1000	+/– FV
Function Key	**Answer**
CPT PV	$899.24

$$V_b = \$120\,(PVIFA_{12\%,5\text{yrs}}) + \$1,000\,(PVIF_{12\%,5\text{yrs}})$$
$$V_b = \$120\,(3.605) + \$1,000\,(.567)$$
$$= \$432.60 + \$567.00$$
$$= \$999.60 \cong \$1,000.00$$

If, however, the investor's required rate of return increases from 12 percent to 15 percent, the value of the bond would decrease to $899.24, computed as follows:

$$V_b = \$120\,(PVIFA_{15\%,5\text{yrs}}) + \$1,000\,(PVIF_{15\%,5\text{yrs}})$$
$$V_b = \$120\,(3.352) + \$1,000\,(.497)$$
$$= \$402.24 + \$497.00$$
$$= \$899.24$$

CALCULATOR SOLUTION

Data Input	Function Key
5	N
9	I/Y
120	+/– PMT
1000	+/– FV
Function Key	**Answer**
CPT PV	$1,116.80

In contrast, if the investor's required rate of return decreases to 9 percent, the bond would increase in value to $1,116.80:

$$V_b = \$120\,(PVIFA_{9\%,5\text{yrs}}) + \$1,000\,(PVIF_{9\%,5\text{yrs}})$$
$$V_b = \$120\,(3.890) + \$1,000\,(.650)$$
$$= \$466.80 + \$650.00$$
$$= \$1,116.80$$

FIGURE 7-3 Value and Required Rates for a Five-Year Bond at 12 Percent Coupon Rate

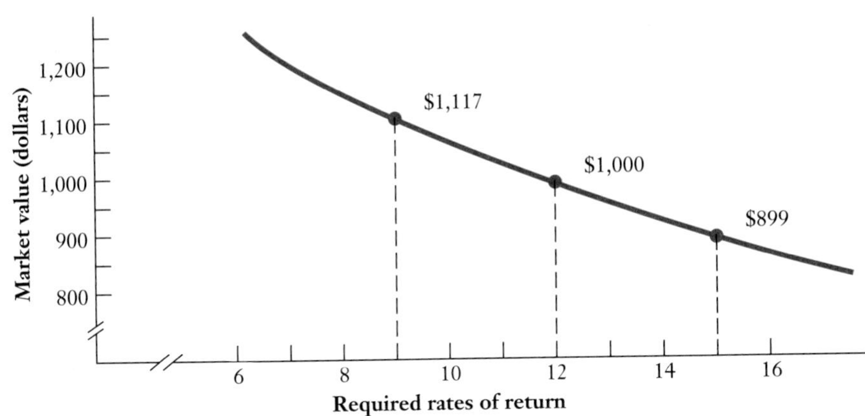

This inverse relationship between the investor's required rate of return and the value of a bond is presented in Figure 7-3. Clearly, as an investor demands a higher rate of return, the value of the bond decreases. Because the interest payments and par value are fixed, the higher rate of return the investor desires can be achieved only by paying less for the bond. Conversely, a lower required rate of return yields a higher market value for the bond.

Changes in bond prices represent an element of uncertainty for the bond investor as well as the financial manager. If the current interest rate (required rate of return) changes, the price of the bond also fluctuates. An increase in interest rates causes the bondholder to incur a loss in market value. Because future interest rates and the resulting bond value cannot be predicted with certainty, a bond investor is exposed to the risk of changing values as interest rates vary. This risk has come to be known as **interest-rate risk.**

Interest-rate risk
The variability in a bond's value (risk) caused by changing interest rates.

SECOND RELATIONSHIP

The market value of a bond will be less than the par value if the investor's required rate is above the coupon interest rate; but it will be valued above par value if the investor's required rate of return is below the coupon interest rate.

Using the previous example, we observed that:

1. The bond has a *market* value of $1,000, equal to the par or maturity value, when the investor's required rate of return equals the 12 percent coupon interest rate. In other words, if

required rate	=	*coupon rate,*	then	*market value*	=	*par value*
12%	=	12%	then	$1,000	=	$1,000

2. When the required rate is 15 percent, which exceeds the 12 percent coupon rate, the market value falls below par value to $899.24; that is, if

required rate	>	*coupon rate,*	then	*market value*	<	*par value*
15%	>	12%	then	$899.24	<	$1,000

In this case, the bond sells at a discount below par value; thus, it is called a **discount bond.**

Discount bond
A bond that is selling below its par value.

TABLE 7-2 Values Relative to Maturity Dates

	MARKET VALUE IF MATURITY IS		
REQUIRED RATE	5 YEARS	2 YEARS	CHANGE IN VALUE
9%	$1,116.80	$1,053.08	−$63.72
12	1,000.00	1,000.00	.00
15	899.24	951.12	51.88

3. When the required rate is 9 percent, or less than the 12 percent coupon rate, the market value, $1,116.80, exceeds the bond's par value. In this instance, if

required rate	<	*coupon rate,*	then	*market value*	>	*par value*
9%	<	12%	then	$1,116.80	>	$1,000

The bond is now selling at a premium above par value; thus, it is a **premium bond.**

Premium bond A bond that is selling above its par value.

THIRD RELATIONSHIP

As the maturity date approaches, the market value of a bond approaches its par value.

Continuing to draw from our example, the bond has five years remaining until the maturity date. The bond sells at a discount below par value ($899.24) when the required rate is 15 percent; it sells at a premium above par value ($1,116.80) when the required rate is only 9 percent.

In addition to knowing value today, an investor would also be interested in knowing how these values would change over time, assuming no change in the current interest rates. For example, how will these values change when only two years remain until maturity rather than five years? Table 7-2 shows (1) the values with five years remaining to maturity, (2) the values as recomputed with only two years left until the bonds mature, and (3) the changes in values between the five-year bonds and the two-year bonds. The following conclusions can be drawn from these results:

1. The premium bond sells for less as maturity approaches. The price decreases from $1,116.80 to $1,053.08 over the three years.
2. The discount bond sells for more as maturity approaches. The price increases from $899.24 to $951.12 over the three years.

The change in prices over the entire life of the bond is shown in Figure 7-4. The graph clearly demonstrates that the value of a bond, either a premium or a discount bond, approaches par value as the maturity date becomes closer in time.

FOURTH RELATIONSHIP

Long-term bonds have greater interest rate risk than do short-term bonds.

As already noted, a change in current interest rates (required rate of return) causes a change in the market value of a bond. However, the impact on value is greater for long-term bonds than it is for short-term bonds.

In Figure 7-3, we observed the effect of interest rate changes on a five-year bond paying a 12 percent coupon interest rate. What if the bond did not mature until 10 years from today instead of five years? Would the changes in market value be the same? Absolutely not. The changes in value would be more significant for the 10-year bond. For example, if we vary the current interest rates (the bondholder's required rate of return) from 9 percent to 12 percent and then to 15 percent, as we did earlier with the five-year bond, the values for both the five-year and the 10-year bonds would be as follows:

FIGURE 7-4 Value of a 12 percent Coupon Bond During the Life of the Bond

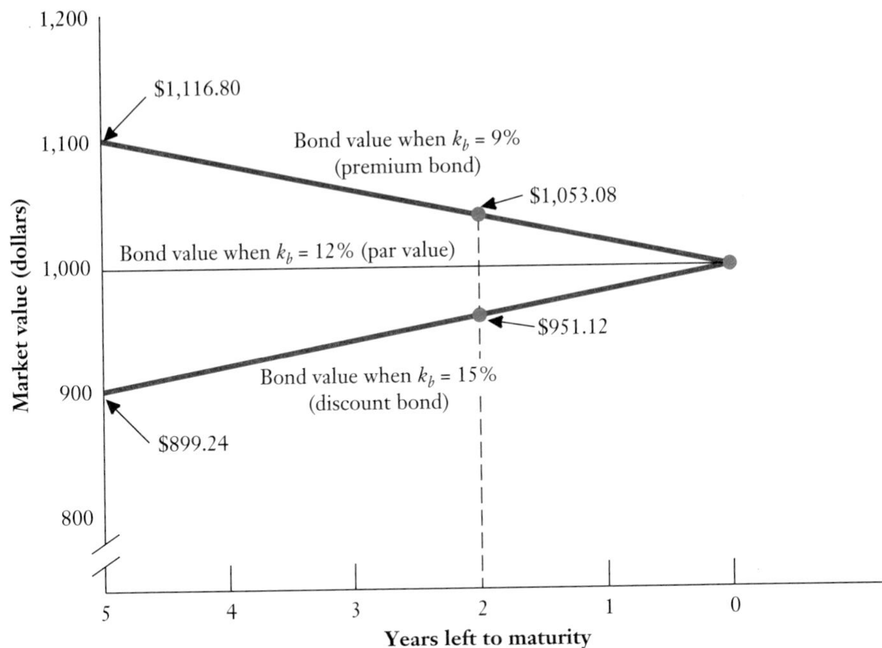

	MARKET VALUE FOR A 12% COUPON RATE BOND MATURING IN	
REQUIRED RATE	5 YEARS	10 YEARS
9%	$1,116.80	$1,192.16
12	1,000.00	1,000.00
15	899.24	849.28

Using these values and the required rates, we can graph the changes in values for the two bonds relative to different interest rates. These comparisons are provided in Figure 7-5. The figure clearly illustrates that the price of the long-term bond (say, 10 years) is more responsive or sensitive to interest rate changes than the price of a short-term bond (say, five years).

The reason long-term bond prices fluctuate more than short-term bond prices in response to interest rate changes is simple. Assume an investor bought a 10-year bond yielding a 12 percent interest rate. If the current interest rate for bonds of similar risk increased to 15 percent, the investor would be locked into the lower rate for 10 years. If, however, a shorter-term bond had been purchased—say, one maturing in two years—the investor would have to accept the lower return for only two years and not the full 10 years. At the end of year 2, the investor would receive the maturity value of $1,000 and could buy a bond offering the higher 15 percent rate for the remaining eight years. Thus, interest rate risk is determined, at least in part, by the length of time an investor is required to commit to an investment. However, the holder of a long-term bond may take some comfort from the fact that long-term interest rates are usually not as volatile as

FIGURE 7-5 Market Values of a 5-Year and a 10-Year Bond at Different Required Rates

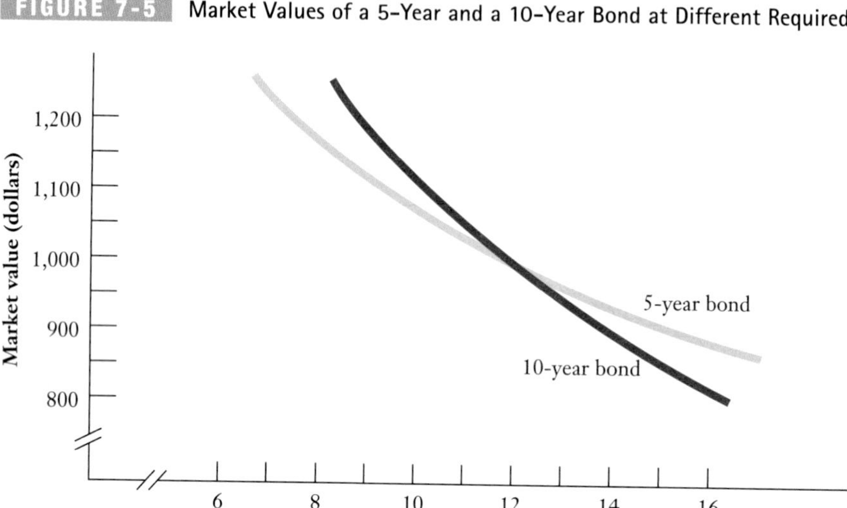

short-term rates. If the short-term rate changed 1 percentage point, for example, it would not be unusual for the long-term rate to change only 0.3 percentage points.

FIFTH RELATIONSHIP

The sensitivity of a bond's value to changing interest rates depends not only on the length of time to maturity, but also on the pattern of cash flows provided by the bond.

It is not at all unusual for two bonds with the same maturity to react differently to a change in interest rates. Consider two bonds, A and B, both with 10-year maturities. Although the bonds are similar in terms of maturity date and the contractual interest rate, the structure of the interest payments is different for each bond. Bond A pays $100 interest annually, with the $1,000 principal being repaid at the end of the tenth year. Bond B is a zero-coupon bond; it pays no interest until the bond matures. At that time, the bondholder receives $1,593.70 in interest plus $1,000 in principal. The value of both bonds, assuming a market interest rate (required rate of return) of 10 percent, is $1,000. However, if interest rates fell to 6 percent, bond A's market value would be $1,294, compared with $1,447 for bond B. Why the difference? Both bonds have the same maturity, and each promises the same 10 percent rate of return. The answer lies in the differences in their cash flow patterns. Bond B's cash flows are received in the more distant future on average than are the cash flows for bond A. Because a change in interest rates always has a greater impact on the present value of later cash flows than on earlier cash flows (due to the effects of compounding), bonds with cash flows coming later, on average, will be more sensitive to interest rate changes than will bonds with earlier cash flows. This phenomenon was recognized in 1938 by Macaulay, who devised the concept of duration.

Duration
A measure of how responsive a bond's price is to changing interest rates. Also, it is a weighted average time to maturity in which the weight attached to each year is the present value of the cash flow for that year.

The **duration** of a bond is simply a measure of the responsiveness of its price to a change in interest rates. The greater the relative percentage change in a bond price in response to a given percentage change in the interest rate, the longer the duration. In computing duration, we consider not only the maturity or term over which cash flows are received but also the time pattern of interim cash flows. Specifically, duration is a weighted average time to maturity in which the weight attached to each year is the present value of the cash flow for that year. A measurement of duration may be represented as follows:

$$\text{duration} = \frac{\sum_{t=1}^{n} \frac{tC_t}{(1 + k_b)^t}}{P_0} \tag{7-5}$$

where t = the year the cash flow is to be received
n = the number of years to maturity
C_t = the cash flow to be received in year t
k_b = the bondholder's required rate of return
P_0 = the bond's present value

For our two bonds, A and B, duration would be calculated as follows:

$$\text{duration bond A} = \left\{ \frac{(1)\frac{\$100}{(1.1)^1} + (2)\frac{\$100}{(1.1)^2} + (3)\frac{\$100}{(1.1)^3} + \cdots + (9)\frac{\$100}{(1.1)^9} + (10)\frac{\$1{,}100}{(1.1)^{10}}}{\$1{,}000} \right\} = 6.759$$

$$\text{duration bond B} = \left\{ \frac{(1)\frac{0}{(1.1)^1} + (2)\frac{0}{(1.1)^2} + (3)\frac{0}{(1.1)^3} + \cdots + (9)\frac{0}{(1.1)^9} + (10)\frac{\$2{,}593.70}{(1.1)^{10}}}{\$1{,}000} \right\} = 10$$

Thus, although both bonds have the same maturity, 10 years, the zero coupon bond (bond B) is more sensitive to interest rate changes, as suggested by its higher duration, which in this instance equals its maturity. The lesson learned: in assessing a bond's sensitivity to changing interest rates, the bond's duration is the more appropriate measure, not the term to maturity.

CONCEPT CHECK

1. Explain the relationship between bond value and investor's required rate of return.
2. As interest rates increase, why does the price of a long-term bond decrease more than the price of a short-term bond?
3. Why does a bond sell at a premium when the coupon rate is higher than the required rate of return, and vice versa?
4. As the maturity date of a bond approaches, what happens to the price of a discount bond? Is the result the same if the bond is a premium bond?
5. What bond characteristics influence the duration measurement? Why is duration the more appropriate measure of a bond's sensitivity to interest rates than term to maturity?

HOW FINANCIAL MANAGERS USE THIS MATERIAL

To be effective as a financial manager, we must have a good understanding of the capital markets, where a company's bonds and stocks are issued and are bought and sold. The forgoing presentation has provided us the foundation to that understanding. Much of what has been said has been from an investor's perspective, but it is crucial that the financial manager see the "territory" from that perspective as well. Otherwise, the manager is likely to be blindsided by the markets. Also, many firms not only issue bonds, but also buy and sell bonds of other companies as well as the federal and state governments. The financial manager then becomes an investor in his or her own right.

SUMMARY

Valuation is an important issue if we are to manage the company effectively. An understanding of the concepts and how to compute the value of a security underlie much of what we do in finance and in making correct decisions for the firm as a whole. Only if we know what matters to our investors can we maximize the firm's value.

Objective 1 There are a variety of types of bonds, including:

- Debentures
- Subordinated debentures
- Mortgage bonds
- Eurobonds
- Zero and very low coupon bonds
- Junk bonds

Objective 2 Some of the more popular terms and characteristics that you might hear about bonds include the following:

- Claims on assets and income
- Par value
- Coupon interest rate
- Maturity
- Indenture
- Current yield
- Bond ratings

Objective 3 Value is defined differently depending on the context. But for us, value is the present value of future cash flows expected to be received from an investment discounted at the investor's required rate of return.

Objective 4 Three basic factors determine an asset's value: (1) the amount and timing of future cash flows, (2) the riskiness of the cash flows, and (3) the investor's attitude about the risk.

Objective 5 The valuation process can be described as follows: It is assigning value to an asset by calculating the present value of its expected future cash flows using the investor's required rate of return as the discount rate. The investor's required rate of return, k, equals the risk-free rate of interest plus a risk premium to compensate the investor for assuming risk.

Objective 6 The value of a bond is the present value both of future interest to be received and the par or maturity value of the bond.

Objective 7 To measure the bondholder's expected rate of return, we find the discount rate that equates the present value of the future cash flows (interest and maturity value) with the current market price of the bond. The expected rate of return for a bond is also the rate of return the investor will earn if the bond is held to maturity, or the yield to maturity.

Objective 8

Five key relationships exist in bond valuation:

1. A decrease in interest rates (required rates of return) will cause the value of a bond to increase; an interest rate increase will cause a decrease in value. The change in value caused by changing interest rates is called interest rate risk.
2. If the bondholder's required rate of return (current interest rate):
   a. Equals the coupon interest rate, the bond will sell at par, or maturity value.
   b. Exceeds the bond's coupon rate, the bond will sell below par value, or at a *discount*.
   c. Is less than the bond's coupon rate, the bond will sell above par value, or at a *premium*.
3. As a bond approaches maturity, the market price of the bond approaches the par value.
4. A bondholder owning a long-term bond is exposed to greater interest rate risk than one owning a short-term bond.
5. The sensitivity of a bond's value to interest rate changes is not only affected by the time to maturity, but also by the time pattern of interim cash flows, or its *duration*.

KEY TERMS

Bond, 224
Book value, 231
Coupon interest rate, 228
Current yield, 229
Debenture, 224
Discount bond, 241
Duration, 244
Efficient market, 231
Eurobonds, 224
Expected rate of return, 239
Indenture, 228
Interest-rate risk, 241
Intrinsic or economic value, 231
Junk or high-yield bonds, 225
Liquidation value, 231
Market value, 231
Maturity, 228
Mortgage bond, 224
Opportunity cost of funds, 233
Par value of a bond, 228
Premium bond, 242
Subordinated debenture, 224
Yield to maturity, 239
Zero and very low coupon bonds, 225

Go To: www.prenhall.com/keown for downloads and current events associated with this chapter

STUDY QUESTIONS

7-1. What are the basic differences among book value, liquidation value, market value, and intrinsic value?

7-2. What is a general definition of the intrinsic value of a security?

7-3. Explain the three factors that determine the intrinsic or economic value of an asset.

7-4. Explain the relationship between an investor's required rate of return and the value of a security.

7-5. **a.** How does a bond's par value differ from its market value?

b. Explain the differences among a bond's coupon interest rate, the current yield, and a bondholder's required rate of return.

7-6. Describe the bondholder's claim on the firm's assets and income.

7-7. What factors determine a bond's rating? Why is the rating important to the firm's manager?

7-8. Distinguish between debentures and mortgage bonds.

7-9. Define (a) Eurobonds, (b) zero coupon bonds, and (c) junk bonds.

7-10. Define the bondholder's expected rate of return.

7-11. How does the market value of a bond differ from its par value when the coupon interest rate does not equal the bondholder's required rate of return?

7-12. Differentiate between a premium bond and discount bond. What happens to the premium or discount for a given bond over time?

7-13. Why is the value of a long-term bond more sensitive to a change in interest rates than that of a short-term bond?

7-14. Explain duration.

SELF-TEST PROBLEMS

ST-1. (*Bond valuation*) Trico bonds have a coupon rate of 8 percent, a par value of $1,000, and will mature in 20 years. If you require a return of 7 percent, what price would you be willing to pay for the bond? What happens if you pay *more* for the bond? What happens if you pay *less* for the bond?

ST-2. (*Bond valuation*) Sunn Co.'s bonds, maturing in 7 years, pay 8 percent on a $1,000 face value. However, interest is paid semiannually. If your required rate of return is 10 percent, what is the value of the bond? How would your answer change if the interest were paid annually?

ST-3. (*Bondholder's expected rate of return*) Sharp Co. bonds are selling in the market for $1,045. These 15-year bonds pay 7 percent interest annually on a $1,000 par value. If they are purchased at the market price, what is the expected rate of return?

ST-4. (*Duration*) Calculate the value and the duration for the following bonds:

BOND	YEARS TO MATURITY	ANNUAL INTEREST	MATURITY VALUE
Argile	10	$80	$1,000
Terathon	15	65	1,000

The required rate of return is 8 percent.

STUDY PROBLEMS (SET A)

7-1A. (*Bond valuation*) Calculate the value of a bond that matures in 12 years and has a $1,000 face value. The coupon interest rate is 8 percent and the investor's required rate of return is 12 percent.

7-2A. (*Bond valuation*) Enterprise, Inc., bonds have a 9 percent coupon rate. The interest is paid semiannually and the bonds mature in eight years. Their par value is $1,000. If your required rate of return is 8 percent, what is the value of the bond? What is its value if the interest is paid annually?

7-3A. (*Bondholder's expected rate of return*) The market price is $900 for a 10-year bond ($1,000 par value) that pays 8 percent interest (4 percent semiannually). What is the bond's expected rate of return?

7-4A. (*Bondholder's expected rate of return*) Fitzgerald's 20-year bonds pay 9 percent interest annually on a $1,000 par value. If bonds sell at $945, what is the bond's expected rate of return?

7-5A. (*Bondholder's expected rate of return*) XYZ International's bonds mature in 12 years and pay 7 percent interest annually. If you purchase the bonds for $1,150, what is your expected rate of return?

7-6A. (*Bond valuation*) Waco Industries 15-year, $1,000 par value bonds pay 8 percent interest annually. The market price of the bonds is $1,085, and your required rate of return is 10 percent.

a. Compute the bond's expected rate of return.
b. Determine the value of the bond to you, given your required rate of return.
c. Should you purchase the bond?

7-7A. (*Bond valuation*) You own a bond that pays $100 in annual interest, with a $1,000 par value. It matures in 15 years. Your required rate of return is 12 percent.

a. Calculate the value of the bond.
b. How does the value change if your required rate of return (*i*) increases to 15 percent or (*ii*) decreases to 8 percent?
c. Explain the implications of your answers in part (b) as they relate to interest rate risk, premium bonds, and discount bonds.
d. Assume that the bond matures in five years instead of 15 years. Recompute your answers in part (b).
e. Explain the implications of your answers in part (d) as they relate to interest rate risk, premium bonds, and discount bonds.

7-8A. (*Bondholder's expected return*) Abner Corporation's bonds mature in 15 years and pay 9 percent interest annually. If you purchase the bonds for $1,250, what is your expected rate of return?

7-9A. (*Bond valuation*) Telink Corporation bonds pay $110 in annual interest, with a $1,000 par value. The bonds mature in 20 years. Your required rate of return is 9 percent.

a. Calculate the value of the bond.
b. How does the value change if (*i*) your required rate of return (*k*) increases to 12 percent or (*ii*) decreases to 6 percent?
c. Interpret your findings in parts (a) and (b).

7-10A. (*Duration*) Calculate the value and the duration for the following bonds:

BOND	YEARS TO MATURITY	ANNUAL INTEREST	MATURITY VALUE
P	5	$100	$1,000
Q	5	70	1,000
R	10	120	1,000
S	10	80	1,000
T	15	65	1,000

Your required rate of return is 8 percent.

7-11A. (*Bond valuation*) Vail Inc.'s seven-year $1,000 par bonds pay 9 percent interest. Your required rate of return is 7 percent. The current market price for the bond is $1,100.

a. Determine the expected rate of return.
b. What is the value of the bonds to you given your required rate of return?
c. Should you purchase the bond at the current market price?

7-12A. (*Bondholder's expected return*) Jennifer Corporation's $1,000 bonds pay 5 percent interest annually and have 12 years until maturity. You can purchase the bond for $915.

a. What return do you expect to earn on this bond?
b. Should you purchase the bond if your required rate of return is 9 percent?

7-13A. (*Duration*) Determine the value and duration for the following bonds given a required return of 7 percent.

BOND	YEARS TO MATURITY	ANNUAL INTEREST	MATURITY VALUE
I	7	130	$1,000
II	6	90	1,000
III	12	110	1,000
IV	5	125	1,000
V	10	80	1,000

7-14A. (*Bond valuation*) Stanley, Inc. issues 15-year $1,000 bonds that pay $85 annually. The market price for the bonds is $960. Your required rate of return is 9 percent.

a. What is the value of the bond to you?
b. What happens to the value if your required rate of return (*i*) increases to 11 percent or (*ii*) decreases to 7 percent?
c. Under which of the circumstances in part (b) should you purchase the bond?

WEB WORKS

Find a bond indenture or at least a sample bond indenture online and list at least three rights of the bondholders and three rights of the issuing firm.

INTEGRATIVE PROBLEM

Following you will find data on $1,000 par value bonds issued by Young Corporation, Thomas Resorts, and Entertainment, Inc. at the end of 2003. Assume you are thinking about buying these bonds as of January 2004. Answer the following questions for each of these bonds:

1. Calculate the values of the bonds if your required rates of return are as follows: Young Corp., 6 percent; Thomas Resorts, 9 percent; and Entertainment, Inc., 8 percent:

	YOUNG CORP.	THOMAS RESORTS	ENTERTAINMENT, INC.
Coupon interest rates	7.8%	7.5%	7.975%
Years to maturity	10	17	4

2. In December 2003, the bonds were selling for the following amounts:

Young Corp.	$1,030
Thomas Resorts	$ 973
Entertainment, Inc.	$1,035

What were the expected rates of return for each bond?

3. How would the values of the bonds change if (*i*) your required rate of return (*k*) increases 3 percentage points or (*ii*) your required rate of return (*k*) decreases 3 percentage points?
4. Explain the implications of your answers in questions 2 and 3 as they relate to interest rate risk, premium bonds, and discount bonds.
5. Compute the duration for each of the bonds. Interpret your results.
6. What are some of the things you can conclude from these computations?
7. Should you buy the bonds? Explain.

STUDY PROBLEMS (SET B)

7-1B. (*Bond valuation*) Calculate the value of a bond that matures in 10 years and has a $1,000 face value. The coupon interest rate is 9 percent and the investor's required rate of return is 15 percent.

7-2B. (*Bond valuation*) Pybus, Inc., bonds have a 10 percent coupon rate. The interest is paid semiannually and the bonds mature in 11 years. Their par value is $1,000. If your required rate of return is 9 percent, what is the value of the bond? What is it if the interest is paid annually?

7-3B. (*Bondholder's expected return*) A bond's market price is $950. It has a $1,000 par value, will mature in eight years, and pays 9 percent interest (4.5 percent semiannually). What is your expected rate of return?

7-4B. (*Bondholder's expected rate of return*) Doisneau 20-year bonds pay 10 percent interest annually on a $1,000 par value. If you buy the bonds at $975, what is your expected rate of return?

7-5B. (*Bondholder's expected return*) Hoyden Co.'s bonds mature in 15 years and pay 8 percent interest annually. If you purchase the bonds for $1,175, what is your expected rate of return?

7-6B. (*Bond valuation*) Fingen 14-year, $1,000 par value bonds pay 9 percent interest annually. The market price of the bonds is $1,100 and your required rate of return is 10 percent.

a. Compute the bond's expected rate of return.
b. Determine the value of the bond to you, given your required rate of return.
c. Should you purchase the bond?

7-7B. (*Bond valuation*) Arizona Public Utilities issued a bond that pays $80 in interest, with a $1,000 par value. It matures in 20 years. Your required rate of return is 7 percent.

a. Calculate the value of the bond.
b. How does the value change if your required rate of return (*i*) increases to 10 percent or (*ii*) decreases to 6 percent?
c. Explain the implications of your answers in part (b) as they relate to interest rate risk, premium bonds, and discount bonds.
d. Assume that the bond matures in 10 years instead of 20 years. Recompute your answers in part (b).
e. Explain the implications of your answers in part (d) as they relate to interest rate risk, premium bonds, and discount bonds.

7-8B. (*Bondholder's expected return*) Zebner Corporation's bonds mature in 14 years and pay 7 percent interest annually. If you purchase the bonds for $1,110, what is your expected rate of return?

7-9B. (*Bond valuation*) Visador Corporation bonds pay $70 in annual interest, with a $1,000 par value. The bonds mature in 17 years. Your required rate of return is 8.5 percent.

a. Calculate the value of the bond.
b. How does the value change if your required rate of return (*k*) (*i*) increases to 11 percent or (*ii*) decreases to 6 percent?
c. Interpret your finding in parts (a) and (b).

7-10B. (*Duration*) Calculate the value and the duration for the following bonds:

BOND	YEARS TO MATURITY	ANNUAL INTEREST	MATURITY VALUE
A	5	$90	$1,000
B	5	60	1,000
C	10	120	1,000
D	15	90	1,000
E	15	75	1,000

Your required rate of return is 7 percent.

7-11B. (*Bond valuation*) Carl Corporation four-year $1,000 par bonds pay 12 percent interest. Your required rate of return is 9 percent. The current market price for the bond is $1,350.

a. Determine the expected rate of return.
b. What is the value of the bonds to you given your required rate of return?
c. Should you purchase the bond at the current market price?

7-12B. (*Bondholder's expected return*) Blake Company's $1,000 bonds pay 8 percent interest annually and have 25 years until maturity. You can purchase the bond for $915.

a. What return do you expect to earn on this bond?
b. Should you purchase the bond if your required rate of return is 11 percent?

7-13B. (*Duration*) Determine the value and duration for the following bonds given a required return of 10 percent.

BOND	YEARS TO MATURITY	ANNUAL INTEREST	MATURITY VALUE
J	4	$95	$1,000
P	12	115	1,000
Y	16	80	1,000
Q	20	70	1,000
Z	15	130	1,000

7-14B. (*Bond valuation*) International, Inc., issues 20-year $1,000 bonds that pay $120 annually. The market price for the bonds is $1,250. Your required rate of return is 8 percent.

- **a.** What is the value of the bond to you?
- **b.** What happens to the value if your required rate of return (*i*) increases to 13 percent or (*ii*) decreases to 6 percent?
- **c.** Under which of the circumstances in part (b) should you purchase the bond?

SELF-TEST SOLUTIONS

ST-1.

$$\text{Value } (V_b) = \sum_{t=1}^{20} \frac{\$80}{(1.07)^t} + \frac{\$1{,}000}{(1.07)^{20}}$$

Thus,

present value of interest:	$80 (10.594) =	$ 847.52
present value of par value:	$1,000 (0.258) =	258.00
	Value (V_b) =	$1,105.52

If you pay more for the bond, your required rate of return will not be satisfied. In other words, by paying an amount for the bond that exceeds $1,105.52, the expected rate of return for the bond is less than the required rate of return. If you have the opportunity to pay less for the bond, the expected rate of return exceeds the 7 percent required rate of return.

ST-2. If interest is paid semiannually:

$$\text{Value } (V_b) = \sum_{t=1}^{14} \frac{\$40}{(1+0.05)^t} + \frac{\$1{,}000}{(1+0.05)^{14}}$$

Thus,

$$\$40\,(9.899) = \$395.96$$
$$\$1{,}000\,(0.505) = 505.00$$
$$\text{Value } (V_b) = \$900.96$$

If interest is paid annually:

$$\text{Value } (V_b) = \sum_{t=1}^{7} \frac{\$80}{(1.10)^t} + \frac{\$1{,}000}{(1.10)^7}$$
$$V_b = \$80\,(4.868) + \$1{,}000\,(0.513)$$
$$V_b = \$902.44$$

ST-3.

$$\$1{,}045 = \sum_{t=1}^{15} \frac{\$70}{(1+\bar{k}_b)^t} + \frac{\$1{,}000}{(1+\bar{k}_b)^{15}}$$

At 6%: $70 (9.712) + $1, 000 (0.417) = $1,096.84

At 7%: Value must equal $1,000.

Interpolation:

Expected rate of return: $\bar{k}_b = 6\% + \frac{\$51.84}{\$96.84}(1\%) = 6.54\%$

CALCULATOR SOLUTION

Data Input	Function Key
15	N
70	+/– PMT
1,000	+/– FV
1,045	PV
Function Key	**Answer**
CPT I/Y	6.52

ST-4.

	BOND			
	ARGILE $1,000 (VALUE)		TERATHON $872 (VALUE)	
YEAR	C_t	$(t)(PV(C_t))$	C_t	$(t)(PV(C_t))$
1	$ 80	$ 74	$ 65	$ 60
2	80	137	65	111
3	80	191	65	155
4	80	235	65	191
5	80	272	65	221
6	80	302	65	246
7	80	327	65	265
8	80	346	65	281
9	80	360	65	293
10	1,080	5,002	65	301
11			65	307
12			65	310
13			65	311
14			65	310
15			1,065	5,036
Sum of $(t)(PV(C_t))$		$7,246		$8,398
Duration		7.25		9.63

LEARNING OBJECTIVES

After reading this chapter, you should be able to

1. Identify the basic characteristics and features of preferred stock.
2. Value preferred stock.
3. Identify the basic characteristics and features of common stock.
4. Value common stock.
5. Calculate a stock's expected rate of return.

CHAPTER 8

Stock Valuation

If you had invested $100 in Harley-Davidson, Inc., common stock at the time its stock began trading publicly on July 8, 1986, and reinvested all dividends, the value of your investment on December 31, 2001, would have been approximately $16,630. Compared to the average share price for the firms included in the Standard & Poor's 500, that is excellent performance, as shown in the graph on the following page. In this chapter, we look closely at common stock and what determines the value investors think a stock is worth.

CHAPTER PREVIEW

In Chapter 7, we developed a general concept about valuation, where economic value was defined as the present value of the expected future cash flows generated by the asset. We then applied that concept to valuing bonds.

We now give our attention to valuing stocks, both preferred stock and common stock. As already noted at the outset of our study of finance and on several occasions since, the financial manager's objective should be to maximize the value of the firm's common stock. Thus, we need to understand what determines stock value.

As we have done in all other chapters, it is important to begin by identifying the principles that are important in understanding the topic to be studied—in this case, the basic considerations in issuing and valuing stock. These principles are as follows: **Principle 1: The Risk-Return Trade-Off—We won't take on additional risk unless we expect to be compensated with additional return; Principle 2: The Time Value of Money—A dollar received today is worth more than a dollar received in the future; Principle 3: Cash—Not Profits—Is King; Principle 7: The Agency Problem—Managers won't work for the owners unless it's in their best interest.**

The first three principles relate to our definition of value—present value of cash flows. The last principle, Principle 7, indicates that the value of a firm's stock is in part dictated by the willingness of management to work in the best interest of the owners, which for most large companies are not the same group.

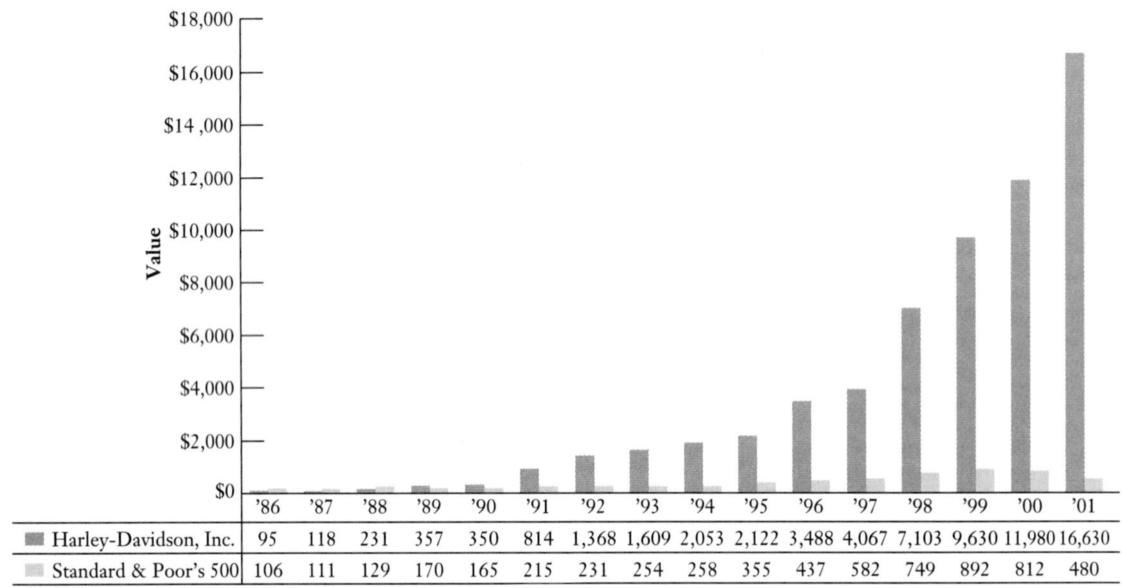

	'86	'87	'88	'89	'90	'91	'92	'93	'94	'95	'96	'97	'98	'99	'00	'01
Harley-Davidson, Inc.	95	118	231	357	350	814	1,368	1,609	2,053	2,122	3,488	4,067	7,103	9,630	11,980	16,630
Standard & Poor's 500	106	111	129	170	165	215	231	254	258	355	437	582	749	892	812	480

If you had invested $100 in Harley-Davidson, Inc. common stock during their IPO on July 8, 1986, and had reinvested all dividends the value of your investment on December 31, 2001, would have been approximately $16,630.

Objective 1

FEATURES AND TYPES OF PREFERRED STOCK

Preferred stock
A hybrid security with characteristics of both common stock and bonds. It is similar to common stock because it has no fixed maturity date, the nonpayment of dividends does not bring on bankruptcy, and dividends are not deductible for tax purposes. Preferred stock is similar to bonds in that dividends are limited in amount.

Preferred stock is often referred to as a hybrid security because it has many characteristics of both common stock and bonds. Preferred stock is similar to common stock in that it has no fixed maturity date, the nonpayment of dividends does not bring on bankruptcy, and dividends are not deductible for tax purposes. However, preferred stock is similar to bonds in that dividends are fixed in amount.

The size of the preferred stock dividend is generally fixed either as a dollar amount or as a percentage of a stock's par value. For example, American Express has issued $1.75 preferred stock, whereas Citigroup has some 6.231 percent preferred stock outstanding. The par value on the Citigroup preferred stock is $250; hence, each share pays 6.231% × $250, or $15.58 in dividends annually. Because these dividends are fixed, preferred stockholders do not share in the residual earnings of the firm but are limited to their stated annual dividend.

In examining preferred stock, we will first discuss several features common to almost all preferred stock. Next we will investigate features less frequently included and take a brief look at methods of retiring preferred stock. We will then learn how to value preferred stock.

Although each issue of preferred stock is unique, a number of characteristics are common to almost all issues. Some of these more frequent traits include:

- multiple classes of preferred stock
- preferred stock's claim on assets and income
- cumulative dividends
- protective provisions
- convertibility

Other features that are less common include:

- adjustable rates
- participation
- payment-in-kind (PIK)

In addition, there are provisions frequently used to retire an issue of preferred stock, including the ability of the firm to call its preferred stock or to use a sinking-fund provision to repurchase preferred shares. All of these features are presented in the discussion that follows.

Multiple Classes

If a company desires, it can issue more than one series or class of preferred stock, and each class can have different characteristics. In fact, it is quite common for firms that issue preferred stock to issue more than one series. For example, Public Storage has 16 different issues of preferred stock outstanding. These issues can be further differentiated in that some are convertible into common stock and others are not, and they have varying priority status regarding assets in the event of bankruptcy.

Claim on Assets and Income

Preferred stock has priority over common stock with regard to claims on assets in the case of bankruptcy. If a firm is liquidated, the preferred stock claim is honored after that of bonds and before that of common stock. Multiple issues of preferred stock may be given an order of priority. Preferred stock also has a claim on income prior to common stock. That is, the firm must pay its preferred stock dividends before it pays common stock dividends. Thus, in terms of risk, preferred stock is safer than common stock because it has a prior claim on assets and income. However, it is riskier than long-term debt because its claims on assets and income come after those of bonds.

Cumulative Feature

Most preferred stocks carry a cumulative feature. **Cumulative preferred stock** requires all past unpaid preferred stock dividends to be paid before any common stock dividends are declared. This feature provides some degree of protection for the preferred shareholder. Without a cumulative feature, management might be tempted not to pay preferred dividends when common stock dividends were passed. Because preferred stock does not have the dividend enforcement power of interest from bonds, the cumulative feature is necessary to protect the rights of preferred stockholders.

Cumulative preferred stock Requires all past unpaid preferred stock dividends to be paid before any common stock dividends are declared.

Protective Provisions

In addition to the cumulative feature, protective provisions are common to preferred stock. These **protective provisions** generally allow for voting rights in the event of nonpayment of dividends, or they restrict the payment of common stock dividends if sinking-fund payments are not met or if the firm is in financial difficulty. In effect, the protective features included with preferred stock are similar to the restrictive provisions included with long-term debt.

Protective provisions Provisions for preferred stock that are included in the terms of the issue to protect the investor's interest.

To examine typical protective provisions, consider Tenneco Corporation and Reynolds Metals preferred stocks. The Tenneco preferred stock has a protective provision that provides preferred stockholders with voting rights whenever six quarterly dividends are in arrears. At that point, the preferred shareholders are given the power to elect a majority of the board of directors. The Reynolds Metals preferred stock includes a protective provision that precludes the payment of common stock dividends during any period in which the preferred stock sinking fund is in default. Both provisions, which yield protection beyond that provided by the cumulative provision and thereby reduce shareholder risk, are desirable. Given these protective provisions for the investor, they reduce the cost of preferred stock to the issuing firm.

Convertibility

Convertible preferred stock
Convertible preferred stock allows the preferred stockholder to convert the preferred stock into a predetermined number of shares of common stock, if he or she so chooses.

Much of the preferred stock that is issued today is **convertible** at the discretion of the holder into a predetermined number of shares of common stock. In fact, today about one-third of all preferred stock issued has a convertibility feature. The convertibility feature is, of course, desirable to the investor and thus reduces the cost of the preferred stock to the issuer.

Adjustable Rate Preferred Stock

Adjustable rate preferred stock
Preferred stock intended to provide investors with some protection against wide swings in the stock value that occur when interest rates move up and down. The dividend rate changes along with prevailing interest rates.

Adjustable rate preferred stock was developed to provide investors with some protection against wide swings in principal that occur when interest rates move up and down. With this kind of preferred stock, quarterly dividends fluctuate with interest rates under a formula that ties the dividend payment at either a premium or discount to the highest of (1) the three-month Treasury bill rate, (2) the 10-year Treasury bond rate, or (3) the 20-year Treasury bond rate. For instance, BankAmerica has adjustable rate preferred stock, where the dividend rate is adjusted every three months to 2 percentage points below the highest of the interest rates on three U.S. Treasury securities, but no lower than 6.5 percent and no greater than 14.5 percent.

Although adjustable rate preferred stock allows dividend rates to be tied to the rates on Treasury securities, it also provides a maximum and a minimum level to which they can climb or fall, called the *dividend rate band.* The purpose of allowing the dividend rate on this preferred stock to fluctuate is, of course, to minimize the fluctuation in the value of the preferred stock. In times of high and fluctuating interest rates, this is a very appealing feature indeed.

Auction rate preferred stock
Variable rate preferred stock in which the dividend rate is set by an auction process.

Another type of adjustable rate preferred stock is **auction rate preferred stock**. With this stock, the dividend rate is set every 49 days by an auction process. At each auction, buyers and sellers place bids for shares, specifying the yield they are willing to accept for the next seven-week period. The yield is then set at the lowest level necessary to match buyers and sellers. As a result, the yield offered on auction rate preferred stock accurately reflects current interest rates, while keeping the market price of these securities at par.

Participation

Participating preferred stock
Allows the preferred stockholder to participate in earnings beyond the payment of the stated dividend.

Although *participating* features are infrequent in preferred stock, their inclusion can greatly affect its desirability to investors and cost to the issuing firm. The **participation feature** allows the preferred stockholder to participate in earnings beyond the payment of the stated dividend. This is usually done in accordance with some set formula. For example, Borden Series A preferred stock currently provides for a dividend of *no less than* 60 cents per share, to be determined by the board of directors.[1] Preferred stock of this sort actually resembles common stock as much as it does normal preferred stock. Although a participating feature is certainly desirable from the point of view of the investor, it is infrequently included in preferred stock.

PIK Preferred

PIK preferred stock
Investors receive no dividends initially; they merely get more preferred stock, which in turn pays dividends in even more preferred stock.

One byproduct of the acquisition boom of the late 1980s was the creation of payment-in-kind (PIK) preferred stock. With **PIK preferred**, investors receive no dividends initially; they merely get more preferred stock, which in turn pays dividends in even more preferred stock. Eventually (usually after five or six years if all goes well for the issuing company), cash dividends should replace the preferred stock dividends. Needless to say, the

[1] During the early 1990s, Borden ran into financial problems. By fall of 1994, the firm was being restructured financially and later acquired, which altered some of the agreements with investors. As a result, the Borden Series A preferred shareholders did not participate in earnings in the ensuing years.

issuing firm has to offer hefty dividends, generally ranging from 12 percent to 18 percent, to entice investors to purchase PIK preferred.

Retirement Features

Although preferred stock does not have a set maturity associated with it, issuing firms generally provide for some method of retirement. If preferred stock could not be retired, issuing firms could not take advantage of falling interest rates. In other words, if interest rates decline, a financial manager would want to retire (pay off) the preferred stock that is currently outstanding and issue new debt or preferred stock at the lower rate. Without the retirement feature, the manager would be unable to do so.

Most preferred stock has some type of **call provision** associated with it. A call provision allows a company to repurchase its preferred stock (or bonds) from holders at stated prices over a given time period. In fact, the Securities and Exchange Commission discourages the issuance of preferred stock without some call provision. The SEC has taken this stance on the grounds that if a method of retirement is not provided, the issuing firm will not be able to retire its preferred stock if interest rates fall.

Call provision
Lets the company buy its preferred stock back from the investor, usually at a premium price above the stock's par value.

The call feature on preferred stock usually involves an initial premium above the par value or issuing price of the preferred of approximately 10 percent. Then over time, the call premium generally falls. By setting the initial call price above the initial issue price and allowing it to decline slowly over time, the firm protects the investor from an early call that carries no premium. A call provision also allows the financial manager to plan the retirement of its preferred stock at predetermined prices.

A **sinking fund** provision requires the firm periodically to set aside an amount of money for the retirement of its preferred stock. This money is then used to purchase the preferred stock in the open market or through the use of the call provision, whichever method is cheaper. Although preferred stock does not have a maturity date associated with it, the use of a call provision in addition to a sinking fund can effectively create a maturity date. For example, a Quaker Oats issue of preferred stock has an annual sinking fund, operating between the years 1981 and 2005, which requires the annual elimination of a minimum of 20,000 shares and a maximum of 40,000 shares. The minimum payments are designed so that the entire issue will be retired by the year 2005. If any sinking fund payments are made above the minimum amount, the issue will be retired prior to 2005. Thus, the size of the outstanding issue decreases each year after 1981.

Sinking fund
A fund that requires the firm periodically to set aside an amount of money for the retirement of its preferred stock. This money is then used to purchase the preferred stock in the open market or through the use of the call provision, whichever method is cheaper.

VALUING PREFERRED STOCK

Objective 2

As already explained, the owner of preferred stock generally receives a *constant income* from the investment in each period. However, the return from preferred stock comes in the form of *dividends* rather than *interest*. In addition, whereas bonds generally have a specific maturity date, most preferred stocks are perpetuities (nonmaturing). In this instance, finding the value (present value) of preferred stock, V_{ps}, with a level cash flow stream continuing indefinitely, may best be explained by an example.

Example: Valuing Preferred Stock

Consider Con Edison's preferred stock issue. In the same way that we valued bonds in Chapter 7, we will use a three-step valuation procedure to value preferred stocks.

Step 1: Estimate the amount and timing of the receipt of the future cash flows the preferred stock is expected to provide. Con Edison's preferred stock pays an annual dividend of $5.00. The shares do not have a maturity date; that is, they go to perpetuity.

(continued)

Step 2: Evaluate the riskiness of the preferred stock's future dividends and determine the investor's required rate of return. For Con Edison, assume that the investor's required rate of return is 6.02 percent.[a]

Step 3: Calculate the economic or intrinsic value of the share of preferred stock, which is the present value of the expected dividends discounted at the investor's required rate of return. The valuation model for a share of preferred stock (V_{ps}) is therefore defined as follows:

$$V_{ps} = \frac{\text{dividend in year 1}}{(1 + \text{required rate of return})^1} + \frac{\text{dividend in year 2}}{(1 + \text{required rate of return})^2} + \cdots + \frac{\text{dividend in infinity}}{(1 + \text{required rate of return})^\infty}$$

$$= \frac{D_1}{(1 + k_{ps})^1} + \frac{D_2}{(1 + k_{ps})^2} + \cdots + \frac{D_\infty}{(1 + k_{ps})^\infty}$$

$$V_{ps} = \sum_{t=1}^{\infty} \frac{D_t}{(1 + k_{ps})^t} \quad \textbf{(8-1)}$$

Because the dividends for preferred stock represent a perpetuity—they continue indefinitely—equation 8-1 can be reduced to the following relationship:[b]

$$V_{ps} = \frac{\text{annual dividend}}{\text{required rate of return}} = \frac{D}{k_{ps}} \quad \textbf{(8-2)}$$

Equation 8-2 represents the present value of a perpetuity (an infinite stream of constant cash flows). We can determine the value of the Con Edison preferred stock, using equation 8-2, as follows:

$$V_{ps} = \frac{D}{k_{ps}} = \frac{\$5.00}{.0602} = \$83.06$$

[a]How do we know the investor's required rate of return is 6.02 percent? Return to Chapter 6 for an explanation of how we ascertain an investor's required rate of return.

[b]To verify this result, consider the following equation:

(i) $$V_{ps} = \frac{D_1}{(1 + k_{ps})^1} + \frac{D_2}{(1 + k_{ps})^2} + \cdots + \frac{D_n}{(1 + k_{ps})^n}$$

If we multiply both sides of this equation by $(1 + k_{ps})$, we have

(ii) $$V_{ps}(1 + k_{ps}) = D_1 + \frac{D_2}{(1 + k_{ps})^1} + \cdots + \frac{D_n}{(1 + k_{ps})^{n-1}}$$

Subtracting (i) from (ii) yields

$$V_{ps}(1 + k_{ps} - 1) = D_1 + \frac{D_n}{(1 + k_{ps})^n}$$

As n approaches infinity, $D_n/(1 + k_{ps})^n$ approaches zero. Consequently,

$$V_{ps}k_{ps} = D_1 \text{ and } V_{ps} = \frac{D_1}{k_{ps}}$$

Because $D_1 = D_2 = \cdots = D_n$, we need not designate the year. Therefore,

(iii) $$V_{ps} = \frac{D}{k_{ps}}$$

In summary, the value of a preferred stock is the present value of all future dividends. But because most preferred stocks are nonmaturing—the dividends continue to infinity—we therefore have to come up with another way for finding value as represented by equation 8-2.

BACK TO THE PRINCIPLES

Valuing preferred stock relies on three of our principles presented in Chapter 1, namely:

- ***Principle 1: The Risk-Return Trade-Off—We won't take on additional risk unless we expect to be compensated with additional return.***
- ***Principle 2: The Time Value of Money—A dollar received today is worth more than a dollar received in the future.***
- ***Principle 3: Cash—Not Profits—Is King.***

As we have already observed with bonds, determining the economic worth or value of an asset always relies on these three principles. Without them, we would have no basis for explaining value. With them, we can know that the amount and timing of cash, not earnings, drives value. Also, we must be rewarded for taking risk; otherwise, we will not invest.

CONCEPT CHECK

1. What features of preferred stock are different from bonds?
2. What provisions are available to protect a preferred stockholder?
3. What cash flows associated with preferred stock are included in the valuation model (equation 8-1)? Why is the valuation model simplified in equation 8-2?

See the "Focus on Harley-Davidson: Road Rules" box.

CHARACTERISTICS OF COMMON STOCK

Objective 3

Common stock
Common stock shares represent the ownership in a corporation.

Common stock represents ownership in the corporation. Bondholders can be viewed as creditors, whereas the common stockholders are the true owners of the firm. Common stock does not have a maturity date, but exists as long as the firm does. Nor does common stock have an upper limit on its dividend payments. Dividend payments must be declared by the firm's board of directors before they are issued. In the event of bankruptcy, the common stockholders—as owners of the corporation—cannot exercise claims on assets until the firm's creditors, including the bondholders and preferred shareholders, have been satisfied.

In examining common stock, we will look first at several of its features or characteristics. Then we will focus on valuing common stock.

CLAIM ON INCOME

As the owners of the corporation, the common shareholders have the right to the residual income after bondholders and preferred stockholders have been paid. This income may be paid directly to the shareholders in the form of dividends or retained and reinvested by the firm. Although it is obvious the shareholder benefits immediately from the distribution of income in the form of dividends, the reinvestment of earnings also benefits the shareholder.

A FOCUS ON HARLEY-DAVIDSON ROAD RULES

A CONVERSATION WITH PAT DAVIDSON, DIRECTOR OF INVESTOR RELATIONS AT HARLEY-DAVIDSON

1. **Could you tell us about your background and how you came to be Director of Investor Relations at Harley-Davidson?**
   Let me begin by stating that I am not a member of the founding Davidson family and yes, I do own and ride a Harley. I came to Harley-Davidson in 1992 after graduating from the MBA program at the Kellogg School at Northwestern University. Before that I had worked for Motorola in Austin, Texas for three years as a product engineer. After I arrived at Harley-Davidson I worked in a number of jobs, gaining a broad exposure to the firm, its business, and its culture. In 1999, I was appointed to the job of Director of Investor Relations.

2. **Just what is Investor Relations?**
   When compared to most other business functions like marketing, accounting, finance, or human resources, the Investor Relations function is a relatively new one in many businesses. However, the importance of Investor Relations has increased dramatically in recent years with the rise of the common stock ownership and the growing importance of institutional investors, including mutual fund managers.

   The primary function of Investor Relations is to serve as the interface between the company and the Wall Street investor community. However, the company's IRO (Investor Relations Officer) has many other responsibilities. For example, the IRO is responsible for helping to develop and communicate the company's key messages to the investing public concerning the firm's strategic direction and its prospects for future performance. This includes company statements regarding its strategy, budgets, and forecasts as well as developments that are under consideration. At Harley-Davidson, this is done primarily with the CFO and our Communications group, but also includes interaction with other members of our Functional Leadership Group and our CEO.

   The Investor Relations Officer is responsible for a company's disclosure record, so the IRO is always involved when information regarding the company is disclosed to the investment community. It is important that companies do not improperly or inadvertently disclose information that is material. This requires a policing effort to make certain that the company is acting responsibly and within the law.

   The Investor Relations Office is also a key conduit for information about company performance and strategy back to management from the street. Thus, Investor Relations can often present an external view of the company, which can be helpful in gauging investor sentiment.

3. **How does the Investor Relations Officer communicate with "the street"?**
   We use three principal methods to communicate with investors and security analysts:

   - Broker-sponsored investor conferences where the CEO or CFO presents the Harley-Davidson story
   - One-on-one meetings between the company and an institutional investor
   - Company-sponsored meetings

   Whenever we disclose material information, we take steps to do it publicly and obey all relevant securities regulations. Before moving on to your next question, let me also point out that Harley-Davidson has an active individual investor program run by Michelle Updike. Through this program we receive a large number of information requests from a variety of sources. For example, students often contact us and we are happy to help, provided they have performed some initial background work trying to understand Harley-Davidson.

4. **Would you recommend that students target a career in Investor Relations?**
   Like most things in life, the answer is "it depends." Investor Relations can be a great career for people with a hunger for knowledge and the curiosity for understanding how things work. An effective IRO must possess superior knowledge about the company and its industry. This requires that the IRO work with the company's marketing research team to develop a better understanding of the company's competitors and the strategic threat they pose.

   In total, the Investor Relations position requires a person who is very familiar with the company and its industry. This requires an understanding of the big picture, as well as enough detailed knowledge to be able to provide information valued by investors. An Investor Relations Officer gets too much credit when the stock price goes up and too much blame when the stock price goes down, but it sure makes for an interesting job.

5. **To give us a better understanding of your job, please trace through the events in a typical day.**

   - Stop by Jim Ziemer's (CFO) office to chat with him and Jim Brostowitz (Treasurer) on the upcoming week.

- Talk with analyst in Boston regarding next week's one-on-one meeting with our CEO and CFO.
- Discuss upcoming conference particulars with analyst in Milwaukee.
- Meet with Vice President of Dealer Service and Director of Business Planning to review recent activity in the heavyweight motorcycle market.
- Review internal income statements and cash-flow models with Michelle Updike (Assistant IR officer).
- Review the Investor Relations portion of Harley-Davidson.com to determine if any changes or updating are required.
- Set up a plant tour for portfolio managers from Denver who are visiting next week and need to be on a plane by 4:30 P.M. And, of course, there is a significant portion of my time spent on the phone and on the computer responding to e-mail.

Plowing earnings back into the firm should result in an increase in the value of the firm, in its earning power, and in its future dividends. This action in turn results in an increase in the value of the stock. In effect, residual income is distributed directly to shareholders in the form of dividends or indirectly in the form of capital gains (a rising stock price) on their common stock.

The right to residual income has both advantages and disadvantages for the common stockholder. The advantage is that the potential return is limitless. Once the claims of the more senior securities (bonds and preferred stock) have been satisfied, the remaining income flows to the common stockholders in the form of dividends or capital gains. The disadvantage: If the bond and preferred stock claims on income totally absorb earnings, common shareholders receive nothing. In years when earnings fall, it is the common shareholder who suffers first.

Claim on Assets

Just as common stock has a residual claim on income, it also has a residual claim on assets in the case of liquidation. Only after the claims of debt holders and preferred stockholders have been satisfied do the claims of common shareholders receive attention. Unfortunately, when bankruptcy does occur, the claims of the common shareholders generally go unsatisfied. This residual claim on assets adds to the risk of common stock. Thus, although common stock has historically provided a higher return than other securities, averaging 12 percent annually since the late 1920s, it also has more risks associated with it.

Voting Rights

The common shareholders elect the board of directors and are in general the only security holders given a vote. Early in the twentieth century, it was not uncommon for a firm to issue two classes of common stock that were identical, except that only one carried voting rights. For example, both the Parker Pen Co. and the Great Atlantic and Pacific Tea Co. (A&P) had two such classes of common stock. This practice was virtually eliminated by (1) the Public Utility Holding Company Act of 1935, which gave the Securities and Exchange Commission the power to require that newly issued common stock carry voting rights; (2) the New York Stock Exchange's refusal to list common stock without voting privileges; and (3) investor demand for the inclusion of voting rights. However, with the merger boom of the 1980s, dual classes of common stock with different voting rights again emerged, this time as a defensive tactic used to prevent takeovers. See the Finance Matters box, "Buffett on the Stock Market."

FINANCE MATTERS

BUFFETT ON THE STOCK MARKET

In 1999, when Warren Buffett discussed his expectations for the stock market, he could not have known for certain the stock market would be headed for three consecutive down years. Buffett explained why he believed the stock market could not sustain the level of growth experienced over the prior 17 years. Two of Buffett's "doubtful conditions" were, in fact, realized: interest rates did fall and the level of corporate profits relative to GDP remained at the 6 percent level. His third condition concerns firm selection for investment. As we now know, much of the stock market bubble was due to investment in Internet firms that were unable to achieve financial performance commensurate with the stock price. As a result, the bull market of the 1990s gave way to a bear market in the early years of the 2000s. Now here is what Buffett had to say in 1999.

During the 17-year period from 1981 to 1998, bond investors realized an annual return of more than 13 percent while stock investors earned a return of 19 percent. But should investors expect these investments to continue to provide such phenomenal returns? No, according to Warren Buffett, chairman of Berkshire Hathaway. While Buffett usually avoids speaking of market projections, in 1999 he addressed the reasons he believed stock and bond returns were likely to be well below the returns of the prior 17-year period.

One reason that returns are likely to fall is that stocks are overvalued. In 1998 profits for the Fortune 500 companies were $334,335,000,000 and market value on March 15, 1999, was $9,907,233,000,000. This implies that investors are paying $30 for each $1 in profits. This overvaluation has been a factor in the extraordinary returns of the past and is not likely to continue into the future. While markets sometimes behave in ways not linked to value, eventually value does become important. Investors cannot get out of a firm more than what the business earns.

In July 1999 Paine Webber and Gallup Organization surveyed investors and found that those with less than five years experience expected stock returns to be 22.6 percent over the next 10 years. More experienced investors believed a return of 12.9 percent was more reasonable. Mr. Buffett believes that both estimates are too high. He says that in order for an investor to realize such high returns three doubtful conditions must occur.

First, interest rates must fall. The return an investor realizes from his or her investment is tied to the risk-free rate earned from government securities. When interest rates fall, security prices increase. Therefore, for investors to earn a significantly higher return on their investments, the government must lower the rate on government securities well below the 6 percent level in 1999.

Second, corporate profits in relation to GDP would have to rise. Since 1990, after-tax corporate profits as a percent of GDP have been around 6 percent. Buffett expects this rate to remain within the range of 4 percent to 6.5 percent as a result of competition among firms. If GDP is expected to grow at 5 percent per year and corporate profits remain at 6 percent of GDP, firm values will not grow at the 12.9 percent—or 22.6 percent—rate investors expect. After all, a firm's value cannot grow faster than its earnings do.

Finally, Buffett says that the key to earning significant profits from investments is not in selecting the industry but rather in selecting the company that has the competitive advantage and can provide persistent growth for the investors. Historically, industries that have impacted the economy, such as automobiles and aviation, have seen more companies fail than succeed. Identifying the companies that are sustainable over the long term is difficult at best.

While investors may not see double-digit returns long term, the securities market still provides an opportunity to increase wealth and to enjoy a progressively higher standard of living.,

Source: "Buffett on the Stock Market," Warren Buffett, *Fortune*, November 22, 1999.

Proxy
A proxy gives a designated party the temporary power of attorney to vote for the signee at the corporation's annual meeting.

Proxy fights
When rival groups compete for proxy votes in order to control the decisions made in a stockholder meeting.

Common shareholders not only have the right to elect the board of directors, but they also must approve any change in the corporate charter. A typical charter change might involve the authorization to issue new stock or perhaps a merger proposal.

Voting for directors and charter changes occur at the corporation's annual meeting. Whereas shareholders may vote in person, the majority generally vote by proxy. A **proxy** gives a designated party the temporary power of attorney to vote for the signee at the corporation's annual meeting. The firm's management generally solicits proxy votes and, if the shareholders are satisfied with its performance, has little problem securing them. However, in times of financial distress or when management takeovers are being attempted, **proxy fights**—battles between rival groups for proxy votes—occur.

Although each share of stock carries the same number of votes, the voting procedure is not always the same from company to company. The two procedures commonly used are majority and cumulative voting. Under **majority voting**, each share of stock allows the shareholder one vote, and each position on the board of directors is voted on separately. Because each member of the board of directors is elected by a simple majority, a majority of shares has the power to elect the entire board of directors.

With **cumulative voting**, each share of stock allows the shareholder a number of votes equal to the number of directors being elected. The shareholder can then cast all of his or her votes for a single candidate or split them among the various candidates. The advantage of a cumulative voting procedure is that it gives minority shareholders the power to elect a director. See the Finance Matters box, "Reading a Stock Quote in *The Wall Street Journal*."

Majority voting
Each share of stock allows the shareholder one vote, and each position on the board of directors is voted on separately. As a result, a majority of shares has the power to elect the entire board of directors.

Cumulative voting
Each share of stock allows the shareholder a number of votes equal to the number of directors being elected. The shareholder can then cast all of his or her votes for a single candidate or split them among the various candidates.

FINANCE MATTERS

READING A STOCK QUOTE IN *The Wall Street Journal*

Following is a section of *The Wall Street Journal* that gives the quotes for some of the stocks traded on the New York Stock Exchange on August 8, 2002.

52 WEEKS HI	LO	STOCK	SYM	DIV	YLD %	PE	VOL 100S	HI	LO	CLOSE		NET CHG
57.25	32.00	HarleyDav	HDI	0.16	0.30	29	13,477	46.59	44.38	46.45	+	0.86
62.15	28.94	HarmanInt	HAR	0.10	0.20	28	3,498	42.20	39.88	41.88	+	1.46
51.35	22.00	HarrahEntri	HET		. . .	19	18,076	48.25	46.75	48.19	+	1.88
38.70	26.42	Harris	HRS	0.20	0.60	27	4,527	33.82	31.85	33.36	+	1.16
44.48	25.85	Harsco	HSC	1.00	3.30	16	1,451	30.03	28.73	30.03	+	0.99
22.68	13.63	HarteHanks	HHS	.10f	0.50	22	2,552	19.85	18.86	19.71	+	0.65

These stocks include Harley-Davidson and others that are listed in *The Wall Street Journal* on a daily basis. To help us understand how to read the quotes, consider Harley-Davidson:

- The 52-week *Hi* column shows that Harley-Davidson stock reached a high of 57.25 during the past year.
- The 52-week *Lo* column shows that Harley-Davidson stock sold for a low of 32.00 during the past year.
- The *Stock* (HarleyDav) and *Sym* (HDI) columns give an abbreviated version of the corporation's name and the ticker symbol, respectively.
- *Div*, the dividend column, gives the amount of dividend that Harley-Davidson paid its common stockholders in the last year, 16 cents per share.
- *Yld%* (.3%) is the stock's dividend yield—the amount of the dividend divided by the day's closing price (0.16 ÷ 46.45).
- *PE* (29) gives the current market price (46.45) divided by the firm's earnings per share.
- The amount of Harley-Davidson stock traded on August 8, 2002, is represented in the *Vol 100s* column. On this day 1,347,700 shares were traded.
- Harley-Davidson stock traded at a high price of 46.59 (*Hi*) and a low price of 44.38 (*Lo*) during the day.
- The previous day's closing price is subtracted from the closing price (*Close*) of 46.45 on August 8, 2002, for a net change (*Net Chg*) of 0.86.

BACK TO THE PRINCIPLES

In theory, the shareholders pick the corporate board of directors, generally through proxy voting, and the board of directors in turn picks the management. Unfortunately, in reality the system frequently works the other way around. Shareholders are offered a slate of nominees selected by management from which to choose. The end result is that management effectively selects the directors, who then may have more allegiance to the managers than to the shareholders. This in turn sets up the potential for agency problems in which a divergence of interests between managers and shareholders is allowed to exist, with the board of directors not monitoring the managers on behalf of the shareholders as they should. The result: ***Principle 7: The Agency Problem—Managers won't work for the owners unless it's in their best interest.*** *A former president for Archer-Daniels-Midland is one example among many of the agency problem. At one time, he would place his own family members and personal friends on the firm's board, paying them at rates twice the norm.*

Preemptive rights
The right of a common shareholder to maintain a proportionate share of ownership in the firm. When new shares are issued, common shareholders have the first right of refusal.

Rights
Certificates issued to shareholders giving them an option to purchase a stated number of new shares of stock at a specified price during a 2- to 10-week period.

PREEMPTIVE RIGHTS

The **preemptive right** entitles the common shareholder to maintain a proportionate share of ownership in the firm. When new shares are issued, common shareholders have the first right of refusal. If a shareholder owns 25 percent of the corporation's stock, then he or she is entitled to purchase 25 percent of the new shares. Certificates issued to the shareholders giving them an option to purchase a stated number of new shares of stock at a specified price typically during a 2- to 10-week period are called **rights**. These rights can be exercised (generally at a price set by management below the common stock's current market price), can be allowed to expire, or can be sold in the open market.

FINANCE MATTERS — ETHICS

ETHICS: KEEPING PERSPECTIVE

Ethical and moral lapses in the business and financial community, academia, politics, and religion fill the daily press. But the rash of insider-trading cases on Wall Street against recent graduates of top business and law schools seems particularly disturbing because the cream of the crop, with six-figure incomes and brilliant careers ahead, is being convicted.

Most appear to have been very bright, highly motivated overachievers, driven by peer rivalries to win a game in which the score had a dollar sign in front of it. Although there have been a few big fish, most sold their futures for $20,000 to $50,000 of illicit profits. They missed the point—that life is a marathon, not a sprint.

In fact, most business school graduates become competent executives, managing people and resources for the benefit of society. The rewards—the titles and money—are merely byproducts of doing a good job.

To illustrate the point, consider the owner of a small company who had the opportunity to acquire a contract with a large Fortune 500 company to produce a product for the large firm. Verbal agreement was reached on the deal, but when the owner met with the president of the large company to sign the contract, the price of the product to be produced by the small firm was $0.25 per unit higher than originally agreed upon—in the small company owner's favor. When questioned, the president of the large firm informed the small firm owner she was to deposit the difference in a personal account and then periodically send the money to the president's personal bank account. Because the small firm owner was not directly profiting from the president's clearly unethical behavior, should she have accepted the terms? It would have increased her firm's profits—but only by a legitimate amount. How about the president of the large company? Why would he be willing to act unethically for what would have meant $40,000 or $50,000 to him?

LIMITED LIABILITY

Although the common shareholders are the actual owners of the corporation, their liability in the case of bankruptcy is limited to the amount of their investment. The advantage is that investors who might not otherwise invest their funds in the firm become willing to do so. See the Finance Matters box, "Ethics: Keeping Perspective."

VALUING COMMON STOCK

Objective 4

Like both bonds and preferred stock, a common stock's value is equal to the present value of all future cash flows expected to be received by the stockholder. However, in contrast to bonds, common stock does not promise its owners interest income or a maturity payment at some specified time in the future. Nor does common stock entitle the holder to a predetermined constant dividend, as does preferred stock. For common stock, the dividend is based on (1) the profitability of the firm, and (2) on management's decision to pay dividends or to retain the profits to grow the firm.

Thus, dividends will vary with a firm's profitability and its stage of growth. In a company's early years, little if any dividends are typically paid. The funds are needed to finance the firm's growth—to capture the opportunity that was identified by the founders. As a company's growth slows—additional investment opportunities become less attractive—and the business becomes more profitable, the financial manager will then begin paying dividends to the common stockholders. As the firm eventually reaches maturity and growth is no longer a priority, the financial manager should increase the dividends even more. In short, a firm's stage of growth has direct implications on the dividends to be paid and on the value of the stock.

THE GROWTH FACTOR IN VALUING COMMON STOCK

What is meant by the term *growth* when used in the context of valuing common stock? A company can grow in a variety of ways. It can become larger by borrowing money to invest in new projects. Likewise, it can issue new stock for expansion. Management could also acquire another company to merge with the existing firm, which would increase the firm's assets. In all of these cases, the firm is growing through the use of new financing, by issuing debt or common stock. Although management could accurately say that the firm has grown, the original stockholders may or may not participate in this growth. Growth is realized through the infusion of new capital. The firm's assets have clearly increased, but unless the original investors increase their investment in the firm, they will own a smaller portion of the expanded business.

Another means of growing is internal growth, which comes from management retaining some or all of the firm's profits for reinvestment in the firm, in turn resulting in the growth of future earnings and hopefully the value of the existing common stock. Although not a direct investment in the company—the shareholders did not send the firm any additional money—the retention of profits is a form of investment by the current common stockholders. The money made from existing product lines could be distributed to the shareholders, but instead is retained as a source of financing future growth. In this way, the current stockholders participate in the growth of the company. It is this internal growth (no financing was acquired from new external sources) that matters in valuing the shares of the present common stockholders.[2]

[2] We are not arguing that the existing common stockholders never benefit from the use of external financing; however, such benefit is more evasive when dealing with competitive capital markets.

Example: Understanding Internal Growth

To illustrate the nature of internal growth, assume that the return on equity for PepsiCo is 16 percent.[a] If PepsiCo's management decides to pay all the profits out in dividends to its stockholders, the firm will experience no growth internally. It might become larger by borrowing more money or issuing new stock, but internal growth will come only through the retention of profits. If, however, PepsiCo retains all the profits, the stockholders' investment in the firm would grow by the amount of profits retained, or by 16 percent. If, however, management kept only 50 percent of the profits for reinvestment, the common shareholders' investment would increase only by half of the 16 percent return on equity, or by 8 percent. Generalizing this relationship, we have

$$g = ROE \times r; \tag{8-3}$$

where g = the growth rate of future earnings and the growth in the common stockholders' investment in the firm

ROE = the return on equity (net income/common book value)

r = the company's percentage of profits retained, called the profit-retention rate.[b]

Therefore, if only 25 percent of the profits were retained by PepsiCo, we would expect the common stockholders' investment in the firm and the value of the stock price to increase or grow by only 4 percent; that is,

$$g = 16\% \times 0.25 = 4\%$$

[a]The return on equity is the percentage return on the common shareholders' investment in the company and is computed as follows:

$$\text{return on equity} = \frac{\text{net income}}{(\text{par value} + \text{paid in capital} + \text{retained earnings})}$$

[b]The retention rate is also equal to (1 – the percentage of profits paid out in dividends). The percentage of profits paid out in dividends is often called the dividend-payout ratio.

In summary, common stockholders frequently rely on an increase in the stock price as a source of return. If the company is retaining a portion of its earnings for reinvestment, future profits and dividends should grow. This growth should be reflected in an increased market price of the common stock in future periods, provided that the return on the funds reinvested exceeds the investor's required rate of return. Therefore, both types of return (dividends and price appreciation) are necessary in the development of a valuation model for common stock.

To explain this process, let us begin by examining how an investor—and financial manager—might value a common stock that is to be held for only one year.

Common Stock Valuation—Single Holding Period

For an investor holding a common stock for only one year, the value of the stock should equal the present value of both the expected dividend to be received in one year, D_1, and the anticipated market price of the share at year end, P_1. If k_{cs} represents a common stockholder's required rate of return, the value of the security, V_{cs}, would be

$$V_{cs} = \begin{bmatrix}\text{present value of dividend}\\ \text{received in 1 year } (D_1)\end{bmatrix} + \begin{bmatrix}\text{present value of market price}\\ \text{received in 1 year } (P_1)\end{bmatrix}$$

$$= \frac{D_1}{(1 + k_{cs})} + \frac{P_1}{(1 + k_{cs})}$$

EXAMPLE: SINGLE-PERIOD STOCK VALUATION

Suppose an investor is contemplating the purchase of RMI common stock at the beginning of this year. The dividend at year end is expected to be \$1.64, and the market price by the end of the year is projected to be \$22. If the investor's required rate of return is 18 percent, the value of the security would be

$$V_{cs} = \frac{\$1.64}{(1 + .18)} + \frac{\$22}{(1 + .18)}$$

$$= \$1.39 + \$18.64$$

$$= \$20.03$$

Once again we see that valuation is a three-step process. First, we estimate the expected future cash flows from common stock ownership (a \$1.64 dividend and a \$22 end-of-year expected share price). Second, we estimate the investor's required rate of return by assessing the riskiness of the expected cash flows (assumed to be 18 percent). Finally, we discount the expected dividend and end-of-year share price back to the present at the investor's required rate of return.

COMMON STOCK VALUATION—MULTIPLE HOLDING PERIODS

Because common stock has no maturity date and is frequently held for many years, a multiple-holding-period valuation model is needed. This model is an equation used to value stock that has no maturity date, but continues in perpetuity (or as long as the firm exists). The general common stock valuation model can be defined as follows:

$$V_{cs} = \frac{D_1}{(1 + k_{cs})^1} + \frac{D_2}{(1 + k_{cs})^2} + \cdots + \frac{D_n}{(1 + k_{cs})^n} + \cdots + \frac{D_\infty}{(1 + k_{cs})^\infty} \quad \textbf{(8-4)}$$

Equation 8-4 indicates that we are discounting the dividend at the end of the first year, D_1, back one year; the dividend in the second year, D_2, back two years; the dividend in the *n*th year back *n* years; and the dividend in infinity back an infinite number of years. The required rate of return is k_{cs}. In using equation 8-4, note that the value of the stock is established at the beginning of the year, say January 1, 2004. The most recent past dividend D_0 would have been paid the previous day, December 31, 2003. Thus, if we purchased the stock on January 1, the first dividend would be received in 12 months, on December 31, 2004, which is represented by D_1.

Fortunately, equation 8-4 can be reduced to a much more manageable form if dividends grow each year at a constant rate, g. The constant-growth common stock valuation equation may be represented as follows:[3]

$$\text{common stock value} = \frac{\text{dividend in year 1}}{\text{required rate of return} - \text{growth rate}} \tag{8-7}$$

$$V_{cs} = \frac{D_1}{k_{cs} - g}$$

Consequently, the intrinsic value (present value) of a share of common stock whose dividends grow at a constant annual rate in perpetuity can be calculated using equation 8-5. Although the interpretation of this equation may not be intuitively obvious, simply remember that it solves for the present value of the future dividend stream growing at a rate, g, to infinity, assuming that k_{cs} is greater than g.

Example: Valuing Common Stock

Consider the valuation of a share of common stock that paid a \$2 dividend at the end of last year and is expected to pay a cash dividend every year from now to infinity. Each year the dividends are expected to grow at a rate of 10 percent. Based on an assessment of the riskiness of the common stock, the investor's required rate of return is 15 percent. Using this information, we would compute the value of the common stock as follows:

1. Because the \$2 dividend was paid last year (actually yesterday), we must compute the next dividend to be received, that is, D_1, where

$$\begin{aligned} D_1 &= D_0\,(1 + g) \\ &= \$2\,(1 + .10) \\ &= \$2.20 \end{aligned}$$

[3] Where common stock dividends grow at a constant rate of g every year, we can express the dividend in any year in terms of the dividend paid at the end of the previous year, D_0. For example, the expected dividend one year hence is simply $D_0(1 + g)$. Likewise, the dividend at the end of t years is $D_0(1 + g)^t$. Using this notation, the common stock valuation equation in equation 8-4 can be written as follows:

$$V_{cs} = \frac{D_0(1 + g)^1}{(1 + k_{cs})^1} + \frac{D_0(1 + g)^2}{(1 + k_{cs})^2} + \cdots + \frac{D_0(1 + g)^n}{(1 + k_{cs})^n} + \cdots + \frac{D_0(1 + g)^\infty}{(1 + k_{cs})^\infty} \tag{8-5}$$

If both sides of equation 8-5 are multiplied by $(1 + k_{cs})/(1 + g)$ and then equation 8-4 is subtracted from the product, the result is

$$\frac{V_{cs}(1 + k_{cs})}{(1 + g)} - V_{cs} = D_0 - \frac{D_0(1 + g)^\infty}{(1 + k_{cs})^\infty} \tag{8-6}$$

If $k_{cs} > g$, which normally should hold, $[D_0(1 + g^\infty)/(1 + k_{cs})^\infty]$ approaches zero. As a result,

$$\frac{V_{cs}(1 + k_{cs})}{(1 + g)} - V_{cs} = D_0$$

$$V_{cs}\left(\frac{1 + k_{cs}}{1 + g}\right) - V_{cs}\left(\frac{1 + g}{1 + g}\right) = D_0$$

$$V_{cs}\left[\frac{(1 + k_{cs}) - (1 + g)}{1 + g}\right] = D_0$$

$$V_{cs}(k_{cs} - g) = D_0(1 + g)$$

$$V_{cs} = \frac{D_1}{k_{cs} - g} \tag{8-7}$$

2. Now, using equation 8-7

$$V_{cs} = \frac{D_1}{k_{cs} - g}$$

$$= \frac{\$2.20}{.15 - .10}$$

$$= \$44$$

We have argued that the value of a common stock is equal to the present value of all future dividends, which is without question a fundamental premise of finance. In practice, however, managers, along with many security analysts, often talk about the relationship between stock value and earnings, rather than dividends. We would encourage you to be very cautious in using earnings to value a stock. Even though it may be a popular practice, the evidence available suggests that investors look to the cash flows generated by the firm, not the earnings, for value. A firm's value truly is the present value of the cash flows it produces. (We look at this issue in Appendix 8A.)

We now turn to our last issue in stock valuation, that of the stockholder's expected returns, a matter of key importance to the financial manager.

BACK TO THE PRINCIPLES

Valuing common stock is no different from valuing preferred stock; the pattern of the cash flows changes, but nothing else. Thus, the valuation of common stock relies on the same three principles that were used in valuing preferred stock:

- ***Principle 1: The Risk-Return Trade-Off—We won't take on additional risk unless we expect to be compensated with additional return.***
- ***Principle 2: The Time Value of Money—A dollar received today is worth more than a dollar received in the future.***
- ***Principle 3: Cash—Not Profits—Is King.***

CONCEPT CHECK

1. What features of common stock indicate ownership in the corporation versus preferred stock or bonds?
2. What are the two ways that a shareholder benefits from ownership?
3. How does internal growth versus the infusion of new capital affect the original shareholders?
4. If a corporation decides to retain its earnings, when would the value of the market price actually decrease?
5. What is the three-step process for common stock valuation? Explain the difference in the equations for a single holding period and multiple holding periods.

A FOCUS ON HARLEY-DAVIDSON
ROAD RULES

THE VALUE OF THE HARLEY-DAVIDSON BRAND

Take the following test: If you want to buy a book, what company or store name comes to mind? Chances are it's one of the big book retailers like Barnes & Noble or perhaps Amazon.com. The fact that you are aware of these companies when book purchases come to mind is very valuable to the respective firms. Thus, owning a brand name can be a tremendous source of value. Furthermore, the brand is a source of valuable assets to the firm that doesn't appear on a traditional balance sheet. These assets are sometimes referred to as market-based assets and include customer loyalty, name awareness, and perceived quality. In addition, owning a brand can be a source of new and valuable opportunities for the firm. For example, Harley-Davidson is the leading producer of heavyweight motorcycles in the world. Virtually since its inception, the company sold functional riding gear, including riding jackets dating back to 1906. However, in 1989 the company introduced an expanded line of clothing called "Harley-Davidson MotorClothes" that carry the Harley-Davidson brand and are sold in motorcycle dealerships and specialty Harley-Davidson clothing shops around the world. A large part of this decision was predicated on the brand image that the company enjoyed based on its motorcycle product line. To date, the venture has proven very successful, producing over $130 million in revenues during 1999.

Protecting the Brand

Something so valuable as the company brand must be cherished and carefully managed and protected. At Harley-Davidson, for example, the "Bar & Shield" company emblem doesn't go on just anything. In fact, one of the company's corporate strategic objectives is to "Strengthen the Harley-Davidson brand." In producing a Harley-Davidson product, whether branded or licensed, the company looks for authentic products that are consistent with, and relevant to, the Harley-Davidson brand image.

Brand Management and the Creation of Shareholder Value

Expenditures made on advertising that are directed at enhancing customer awareness of the firm and its products are really investments in the firm's brand. However, the accounting profession doesn't see it this way. That is, generally accepted accounting principles (GAAP) call for the expensing of all advertising expenditures in the period in which they are made such that no asset is ever recorded on the firm's balance sheet to reflect the value that these expenditures might have created by enhancing the value of the firm's brand.

But what exactly is the value of a firm's brand and how should we think about its determinants? Conceptually, it is quite easy to imagine that a firm's brand has value when it leads customers to think of the firm's products and services when a need arises. However, coming to understand how much value the brand has is a really tough problem. Perhaps the best way to begin is to review briefly the sources of value from any productive asset. These include the amount, timing, and riskiness of future cash-flow expectations. Thus, the firm's brand has value insofar as it can increase future cash-flow expectations, shorten the time until customers make their purchases (thus shortening the time to receipt of future cash flows), and reduce the risk of future cash flows by increasing the loyalty of customers and the likelihood that they will purchase the firm's product.

Want to Know More about the Interface between Marketing and Finance?

The following references address the marketing-finance interface and provide valuable grounding for financial specialists and marketers. In fact, these papers received the prize for best practical and theoretical article from the *Journal of Marketing*, the premier journal of marketers.

Rajendra K. Srivastava, Tasadduz A. Shervani, and Liam Fahey, 1998. Market-based assets and shareholder value: A framework for analysis. *Journal of Marketing* 62 (January), 2–18.

Rajendra K. Srivastava, Tasadduz A. Shervani, and Liam Fahey, 1999. Marketing, business processes, and shareholder value: An organizationally embedded view of marketing activities and the discipline of marketing. *Journal of Marketing* 63 (Special Issue), 168–179.

Objective 5

STOCKHOLDER'S EXPECTED RATE OF RETURN

As stated in Chapter 7, the expected rate of return on a bond is the return the bondholder expects to receive on the investment by paying the existing market price for the security. This rate of return is of interest to the financial manager because it tells the manager about the investor's expectations, which in turn affects the firm's cost of financing new projects. The same can be said for the financial manager needing to know the expected rate of return of the firm's stockholders, which is the topic of this next section.

The Preferred Stockholder's Expected Rate of Return

In computing the preferred stockholder's expected rate of return, we use the valuation equation for preferred stock. Earlier, equation 8-2 specified the value of a preferred stock (V_{ps}) as

$$V_{ps} = \frac{\text{annual dividend}}{\text{required rate of return}} = \frac{D}{k_{ps}}$$

Solving equation 8-2 for the preferred stockholder's required rate of return (k_{ps}), we have:

$$k_{ps} = \frac{\text{annual dividend}}{\text{intrinsic value}} = \frac{D}{V_{ps}} \quad \textbf{(8-8)}$$

That is, the preferred stockholder's *required* rate of return simply equals the stock's annual dividend divided by the intrinsic value. We may also restate equation 8-8 to solve for a preferred stock's *expected* rate of return, $\bar{k}_{ps}$ as follows:[4]

$$\bar{k}_{ps} = \frac{\text{annual dividend}}{\text{market price}} = \frac{D}{P_0} \quad \textbf{(8-9)}$$

Note that we have merely substituted the current market price, P_0, for the intrinsic value, V_{ps}. The expected rate of return $\bar{k}_{ps}$ therefore, equals the annual dividend relative to the price the stock is presently selling for, P_0. Thus, the expected rate of return, $\bar{k}_{ps}$ is the rate of return the investor can expect to earn from the investment if bought at the current market price. For example, if the present market price of preferred stock is \$83.06 and it pays a \$5.00 annual dividend, the expected rate of return implicit in the present market price is

$$\bar{k}_{ps} = \frac{D}{P_0} = \frac{\$5.00}{\$83.06} = 6.02\%$$

Therefore, investors at the margin (who pay \$83.06 per share for a preferred security that is paying \$5.00 in annual dividends) are expecting a 6.02 percent rate of return.

The Common Stockholder's Expected Rate of Return

The valuation equation for common stock was defined earlier in equation 8-4 as

$$\text{value} = \frac{\text{dividend in year 1}}{(1 + \text{required rate of return})^1} + \frac{\text{dividend in year 2}}{(1 + \text{required rate of return})^2} + \cdots + \frac{\text{dividend in year infinity}}{(1 + \text{required rate of return})^\infty}$$

$$V_{cs} = \frac{D_1}{(1 + k_{cs})^1} + \frac{D_2}{(1 + k_{cs})^2} + \cdots + \frac{D_\infty}{(1 + k_{cs})^\infty}$$

$$V_{cs} = \sum_{t=1}^{\infty} \frac{D_t}{(1 + k_{cs})^t}$$

[4] We will use $\bar{k}$ to represent a security's expected rate of return versus k for the investor's required rate of return.

Owing to the difficulty of discounting to infinity, we made the key assumption that the dividends, D_t, increase at a constant annual compound growth rate of g. If this assumption is valid, equation 8-4 was shown to be equivalent to

$$\text{value} = \frac{\text{dividend in year 1}}{\text{required rate of return} - \text{growth rate}}$$

$$V_{cs} = \frac{D_1}{k_{cs} - g}$$

Thus, V_{cs} represents the maximum value that an investor having a required rate of return of k_{cs} would pay for a security having an anticipated dividend in year 1 of D_1 that is expected to grow in future years at rate g. Solving for k_{cs}, we can compute the common stockholder's required rate of return as follows:[5]

$$k_{cs} = \underbrace{\left(\frac{D_1}{V_{cs}}\right)}_{\text{dividend yield}} + \underbrace{g}_{\text{annual growth rate}} \tag{8-10}$$

From this equation, the common stockholder's required rate of return is equal to the dividend yield plus a growth factor. Although the growth rate, g, applies to the growth in the company's dividends, given our assumptions the stock's value may also be expected to increase at the same rate. For this reason, g represents the annual percentage growth in the stock value. In other words, the investor's required rate of return is satisfied by receiving dividends and capital gains, as reflected by the expected percentage growth rate in the stock price.

As was done for preferred stock earlier, we may revise equation 8-10 to measure a common stock's *expected* rate of return, $\bar{k}_{cs}$. Replacing the intrinsic value, V_{cs}, in equation 8-10 with the stock's current market price, P_0, we may express the stock's expected rate of return as follows:

$$\bar{k}_{cs} = \frac{\text{dividend in year 1}}{\text{market price}} + \text{growth rate} = \frac{D_1}{P_0} + g \tag{8-11}$$

Example: Computing Expected Rate of Return

As an example of computing the expected rate of return for a common stock where dividends are anticipated to grow at a constant rate to infinity, assume that a firm's common stock has a current market price of \$44. If the expected dividend at the conclusion of this year is \$2.20 and dividends and earnings are growing at a 10 percent annual rate (last year's dividend was \$2), the expected rate of return implicit in the \$44 stock price is as follows:

$$\bar{k}_{cs} = \frac{\$2.20}{\$44} + 10\% = 15\%$$

[5] At times, the expected dividend at year end (D_1) is not given. Instead, we might only know the most recent dividend (paid yesterday), that is, D_0. If so, we must restate the equation as follows:

$$V_{cs} = \frac{D_1}{(k_{cs} - g)} = \frac{D_0(1 + g)}{(k_{cs} - g)}$$

As a final note, we should understand that the *expected* rate of return implied by a given market price equals the *required* rate of return for investors at the margin. For these investors, the expected rate of return is just equal to their required rate of return, and therefore they are willing to pay the current market price for the security. These investors' required rate of return is of particular significance to the financial manager, because it represents the cost of new financing to the firm.

CONCEPT CHECK

1. In computing the required rate of return, why should the growth factor be added to the dividend yield?
2. How does an efficient market affect the required and expected rates of return?

HOW FINANCIAL MANAGERS USE THIS MATERIAL

In this chapter, we have looked at the nature and process for valuing both preferred stock and common stock—sources of equity capital for a business. Although we have taken an investor perspective in much of what we have said, we are ultimately interested in the implications of valuation for a financial manager. But a financial manager must first and foremost view valuation from the investor's vantage point. What matters to the investor should matter to the financial manager. Otherwise, a financial manager cannot be effective in enhancing firm value—the criterion for evaluating much that the financial manager does. This relationship will become increasingly clear as we move into future chapters dealing with making capital investments and financing these expenditures.

SUMMARY

Objective 1

Valuation is an important process in financial management. An understanding of valuation, both the concepts and procedures, supports the financial officer's objective of maximizing the value of the firm.

Preferred stock has no fixed maturity date and the dividends are fixed in amount. Following are some of the more frequent characteristics of preferred stock:

- There are multiple classes of preferred stock.
- Preferred stock has a priority of claim on assets and income over common stock.
- Any dividends, if not paid as promised, must be paid before any common stock dividends may be paid. That is, they are cumulative.
- Protective provisions are included in the contract for the preferred shareholder in order to reduce the investor's risk.
- Many preferred stocks are convertible into common stock shares.

For a few preferred stocks:

- The dividend rate may be adjustable as interest rates change.
- The preferred stockholder may be allowed to participate in the firm's earnings in certain situations.
- The preferred stockholder may receive dividends in the form of more shares—payment-in-kind (PIK).

In addition, there are provisions frequently used to retire an issue of preferred stock, such as the ability for the firm to call its preferred stock or to use a sinking fund provision.

Objective 2

Value is the present value of future cash flows discounted at the investor's required rate of return. Although the valuation of any security entails the same basic principles, the procedures used in each situation vary. For example, we learned in Chapter 7 that valuing a bond involves calculating the present value of future interest to be received plus the present value of the principal returned to the investor at the maturity of the bond.

For securities with cash flows that are constant in each year but with no specified maturity, such as preferred stock, the present value equals the dollar amount of the annual dividend divided by the investor's required rate of return; that is,

$$\text{preferred stock value} = \frac{\text{dividend}}{\text{required rate of return}}$$

Objective 3

Bondholders and preferred stockholders can be viewed as creditors, whereas the common stockholders are the owners of the firm. Common stock does not have a maturity date, but exists as long as the firm does. Nor does common stock have an upper limit on its dividend payments. Dividend payments must be declared by the firm's board of directors before they are issued. In the event of bankruptcy, the common stockholders, as owners of the corporation, cannot exercise claims on assets until the firm's creditors, including the bondholders and preferred shareholders, have been satisfied. However, common stockholders' liability is limited to the amount of their investment.

The common shareholders are in general the only security holders given a vote. Common shareholders have the right to elect the board of directors and to approve any change in the corporate charter. Although each share of stock carries the same number of votes, the voting procedure is not always the same from company to company.

The preemptive right entitles the common shareholder to maintain a proportionate share of ownership in the firm.

Objective 4

For common stock where the future dividends are expected to increase at a constant growth rate, value may be given by the following equation:

$$\text{common stock value} = \frac{\text{dividend in year 1}}{\text{required rate of return} - \text{growth rate}}$$

Growth here relates to *internal* growth only, where management retains part of the firm's profits to be reinvested and thereby grow the firm—as opposed to growth through issuing new stock or acquiring another firm.

Growth in and of itself does not mean that we are creating value for the stockholders. Only if we are reinvesting at a rate of return that is greater than the investors' required rate of return will growth result in increased value to the firm. In fact, if we are investing at rates less than the required rate of return for our investors, the value of the firm will actually decline.

Objective 5

The expected rate of return on a security is the required rate of return of investors who are willing to pay the present market price for the security, but no more. This rate of return is important to the financial manager because it equals the required rate of return of the firm's investors.

The expected rate of return for preferred stock is computed as follows:

$$\text{expected return preferred stock} = \frac{\text{annual dividend}}{\text{stock market price}}$$

The expected rate of return for common stock is calculated as follows:

$$\text{expected return common stock} = \frac{\text{dividend in year 1}}{\text{stock market price}} + \text{dividend growth rate}$$

Go To:
www.prenhall.com/keown
for downloads and current events associated with this chapter

KEY TERMS

Adjustable rate preferred stock, 258

Auction rate preferred stock, 258

Call provision, 259

Common stock, 261

Convertible preferred stock, 258

Cumulative preferred stock, 257

Cumulative voting, 265

Majority voting, 265

Participating preferred stock, 258
PIK preferred stock, 258
Preemptive rights, 266
Preferred stock, 256
Protective provisions, 257
Proxy, 264
Proxy fights, 264
Rights, 266
Sinking fund, 259

STUDY QUESTIONS

8-1. Why is preferred stock referred to as a hybrid security? It is often said to combine the worst features of common stock and bonds. What is meant by this statement?

8-2. Because preferred stock dividends in arrears must be paid before common stock dividends, should they be considered a liability and appear on the right side of the balance sheet?

8-3. Why would a preferred stockholder want the stock to have a cumulative dividend feature and other protective provisions?

8-4. Distinguish between fixed rate preferred stock and adjustable rate preferred stock. What is the rationale for a firm issuing adjustable rate preferred stock?

8-5. What is PIK preferred stock?

8-6. Why is preferred stock frequently convertible? Why would it be callable?

8-7. Compare valuing preferred stock and common stock.

8-8. Define the investor's *expected* rate of return.

8-9. State how the investor's required rate of return is computed.

8-10. The common stockholders receive two types of return from their investment. What are they?

SELF-TEST PROBLEMS

ST-1. (*Preferred stock valuation*) What is the value of a preferred stock where the dividend rate is 16 percent on a $100 par value? The appropriate discount rate for a stock of this risk level is 12 percent.

ST-2. (*Preferred stockholder expected return*) You own 250 shares of Dalton Resources' preferred stock, which currently sells for $38.50 per share and pays annual dividends of $3.25 per share.

a. What is your expected return?
b. If you require an 8 percent return, given the current price, should you sell or buy more stock?

ST-3. (*Preferred stock valuation*) The preferred stock of Armlo pays a $2.75 dividend. What is the value of the stock if your required return is 9 percent?

ST-4. (*Common stock valuation*) Crosby Corporation's common stock paid $1.32 in dividends last year and is expected to grow indefinitely at an annual 7 percent rate. What is the value of the stock if you require an 11 percent return?

ST-5. (*Common stockholder expected return*) Blackburn & Smith's common stock currently sells for $23 per share. The company's executives anticipate a constant growth rate of 10.5 percent and an end-of-year dividend of $2.50.

a. What is your expected rate of return?
b. If you require a 17 percent return, should you purchase the stock?

STUDY PROBLEMS (SET A)

8-1A. (*Preferred stock valuation*) Calculate the value of a preferred stock that pays a dividend of $6 per share and your required rate of return is 12 percent.

8-2A. (*Measuring growth*) If Pepperdine, Inc.'s return on equity is 16 percent and the management plans to retain 60 percent of earnings for investment purposes, what will be the firm's growth rate?

8-3A. (*Preferred stock valuation*) What is the value of a preferred stock where the dividend rate is 14 percent on a $100 par value? The appropriate discount rate for a stock of this risk level is 12 percent.

8-4A. (*Preferred stockholder expected return*) Solitron's preferred stock is selling for $42.16 and pays $1.95 in dividends. What is your expected rate of return if you purchase the security at the market price?

8-5A. (*Preferred stockholder expected return*) You own 200 shares of Somner Resources' preferred stock, which currently sells for $40 per share and pays annual dividends of $3.40 per share.

a. What is your expected return?
b. If you require an 8 percent return, given the current price, should you sell or buy more stock?

8-6A. (*Common stock valuation*) You intend to purchase Marigo common stock at $50 per share, hold it one year, and sell after a dividend of $6 is paid. How much will the stock price have to appreciate for you to satisfy your required rate of return of 15 percent?

8-7A. (*Common stockholder expected return*) Made-It's common stock currently sells for $22.50 per share. The company's executives anticipate a constant growth rate of 10 percent and an end-of-year dividend of $2.

a. What is your expected rate of return if you buy the stock for $22.50?
b. If you require a 17 percent return, should you purchase the stock?

8-8A. (*Common stock valuation*) Header Motor, Inc., paid a $3.50 dividend last year. At a constant growth rate of 5 percent, what is the value of the common stock if the investors require a 20 percent rate of return?

8-9A. (*Measuring growth*) Given that a firm's return on equity is 18 percent and management plans to retain 40 percent of earnings for investment purposes, what will be the firm's growth rate?

8-10A. (*Common stockholder expected return*) The common stock of Zaldi Co. is selling for $32.84. The stock recently paid dividends of $2.94 per share and has a projected constant growth rate of 9.5 percent. If you purchase the stock at the market price, what is your expected rate of return?

8-11A. (*Common stock valuation*) Honeywag common stock is expected to pay $1.85 in dividends next year, and the market price is projected to be $42.50 by year end. If the investor's required rate of return is 11 percent, what is the current value of the stock?

8-12A. (*Common stockholder expected return*) The market price for Hobart common stock is $43. The price at the end of one year is expected to be $48, and dividends for next year should be $2.84. What is the expected rate of return?

8-13A. (*Preferred stock valuation*) Pioneer's preferred stock is selling for $33 in the market and pays a $3.60 annual dividend.

a. What is the expected rate of return on the stock?
b. If an investor's required rate of return is 10 percent, what is the value of the stock for that investor?
c. Should the investor acquire the stock?

8-14A. (*Common stock valuation*) The common stock of NCP paid $1.32 in dividends last year. Dividends are expected to grow at an 8 percent annual rate for an indefinite number of years.

a. If NCP's current market price is $23.50, what is the stock's expected rate of return?
b. If your required rate of return is 10.5 percent, what is the value of the stock for you?
c. Should you make the investment?

8-15A. (*Common stockholder expected return*) In October 2003, Michael, Inc. was expecting to pay an annual dividend of $1.12 in 2004. The firm's stock was selling for $49. The stock's beta is 1.10.

a. What is Michael, Inc.'s dividend yield?
b. Based on the Ibbotson Associates data presented in Chapter 6 (Table 6-1, p. 183), compute the expected rate of return for this stock. (Use the CAPM approach described in Chapter 6.)
c. What growth rate would you have to use in the multiple-period valuation model to get the same expected return as in part (b)?

8-16A. (*Common stockholder expected return*) Access the Internet to gather the following information for Johnson & Johnson.

- **a.** The earnings per share and dividends per share for the past five years.
- **b.** The common stock price.

Assuming that the annual growth rate in earnings per share for the past four years is a reasonable estimate of the growth in share price for the indefinite future, which it may not be, estimate the expected rate of return for the stock.

8-17A. (*Preferred stock valuation*) Kendra Corporation's preferred shares are trading for $25 in the market and pay a $4.50 annual dividend. Assume that you, the investor, have a required rate of return of 14 percent.

- **a.** What is the expected rate of return on the stock?
- **b.** What is the stock's value to you, the investor?
- **c.** Should you purchase the stock?

8-18A. (*Common stock valuation*) Wayne, Inc.'s outstanding common stock is currently selling in the market for $33. Dividends of $2.30 per share were paid last year, and the company expects annual growth of 5 percent.

- **a.** What is the value of the stock to you, given a 15 percent required rate of return?
- **b.** Determine the expected rate of return for the stock.
- **c.** Should you purchase this stock?

8-19A. (*Measuring growth*) XYZ's return on equity is 17 percent and management has plans to retain 30 percent of earnings for investment in the company.

- **a.** What will be the company's growth rate?
- **b.** How would the growth rate change if management (*i*) increased retained earnings to 40 percent or (*ii*) decreased retention to 25 percent?

8-20A. (*Common stockholder expected return*) Carpenter Corporation's common stock is selling for $29.50 and recently paid dividends of $1.75 per share. The company has an expected growth rate of 4 percent.

- **a.** What is the stock's expected rate of return?
- **b.** Should you make the investment if your required rate of return is 14 percent?

WEB WORKS

Find the web page of a company that interests you. Look for a link that takes you to investor information, about the firm. Examine the types of information that the firm provides to its stockholders.

INTEGRATIVE PROBLEM

You are considering three investments. The first is a bond that is selling in the market at $1,200. The bond has a $1,000 par value, pays interest at 14 percent, and is scheduled to mature in 12 years. For bonds of this risk class, you believe that a 12 percent rate of return should be required. The second investment that you are analyzing is a preferred stock ($100 par value) that sells for $80 and pays an annual dividend of $12. Your required rate of return for this stock is 14 percent. The last investment is a common stock ($25 par value) that recently paid a $3 dividend. The firm's earnings per share have increased from $4 to $8 in 10 years, which also reflects the expected growth in dividends per share for the indefinite future. The stock is selling for $25, and you think a reasonable required rate of return for the stock is 20 percent.

1. Calculate the value of each security based on your required rate of return.
2. Which investment(s) should you accept? Why?

3. If your required rates of return changed to 14 percent for the bond, 16 percent for the preferred stock, and 18 percent for the common stock, how would your answers to parts 1 and 2 change?
4. Assuming again that your required rate of return for the common stock is 20 percent, but the anticipated constant growth rate changes to 12 percent, how would your answers to questions 1 and 2 change?

STUDY PROBLEMS (SET B)

8-1B. (*Preferred stock valuation*) Calculate the value of a preferred stock that pays a dividend of $7 per share when your required rate of return is 10 percent.

8-2B. (*Measuring growth*) If the Stanford Corporation's return on equity is 24 percent and management plans to retain 70 percent of earnings for investment purposes, what will be the firm's growth rate?

8-3B. (*Preferred stock valuation*) What is the value of a preferred stock where the dividend rate is 16 percent on a $100 par value? The appropriate discount rate for a stock of this risk level is 12 percent.

8-4B. (*Preferred stockholder expected return*) Shewmaker's preferred stock is selling for $55.16 and pays $2.35 in dividends. What is your expected rate of return if you purchase the security at the market price?

8-5B. (*Preferred stockholder expected return*) You own 250 shares of McCormick Resources' preferred stock, which currently sells for $38.50 per share and pays annual dividends of $3.25 per share.

a. What is your expected return?
b. If you require an 8 percent return, given the current price, should you sell or buy more stock?

8-6B. (*Common stock valuation*) You intend to purchase Bama, Inc., common stock at $52.75 per share, hold it one year, and sell after a dividend of $6.50 is paid. How much will the stock price have to appreciate if your required rate of return is 16 percent?

8-7B. (*Common stockholder expected return*) Blackburn & Smith's common stock currently sells for $23 per share. The company's executives anticipate a constant growth rate of 10.5 percent and an end-of-year dividend of $2.50.

a. What is your expected rate of return?
b. If you require a 17 percent return, should you purchase the stock?

8-8B. (*Common stock valuation*) Gilliland Motor, Inc., paid a $3.75 dividend last year. At a growth rate of 6 percent, what is the value of the common stock if the investors require a 20 percent rate of return?

8-9B. (*Measuring growth*) Given that a firm's return on equity is 24 percent and management plans to retain 60 percent of earnings for investment purposes, what will be the firm's growth rate?

8-10B. (*Common stockholder expected return*) The common stock of Bouncy-Bob Moore Co. is selling for $33.84. The stock recently paid dividends of $3 per share and has a projected growth rate of 8.5 percent. If you purchase the stock at the market price, what is your expected rate of return?

8-11B. (*Common stock valuation*) Honeybee common stock is expected to pay $1.85 in dividends next year, and the market price is projected to be $40 by year end. If the investor's required rate of return is 12 percent, what is the current value of the stock?

8-12B. (*Common stock valuation*) The market price for M. Simpson & Co.'s common stock is $44. The price at the end of one year is expected to be $47, and dividends for next year should be $2. What is the expected rate of return?

8-13B. (*Preferred stock valuation*) Green's preferred stock is selling for $35 in the market and pays a $4 annual dividend.

a. What is the expected rate of return on the stock?
b. If an investor's required rate of return is 10 percent, what is the value of the stock for that investor?
c. Should the investor acquire the stock?

8-14B. (*Common stock valuation*) The common stock of KPD paid $1 in dividends last year. Dividends are expected to grow at an 8 percent annual rate for an indefinite number of years.

a. If KPD's current market price is $25, what is the stock's expected rate of return?
b. If your required rate of return is 11 percent, what is the value of the stock for you?
c. Should you make the investment?

8-15B. (*Common stockholder expected return*) In October 2003, Dorothy Corp. was expecting to pay an annual dividend of $1.20 in 2004. The firm's stock was selling for $54. The stock's beta is 0.90.

a. What is Dorothy Corp.'s dividend yield?
b. Based on the Ibbotson Associates data presented in Chapter 6 (Table 6-1, p. 183), compute the expected rate of return for this stock. (Use the CAPM approach described in Chapter 6.)
c. What growth rate would you have to use in the multiple-period valuation model to get the same expected return as in part (b)?

8-16B. (*Expected rate of return*) Access the Internet to gather the following information for First Union Corporation.

a. The earnings per share and dividends per share for the past five years.
b. The common stock price.

Assuming that the annual growth rate in earnings per share for the past four years is a reasonable estimate of the growth in share price for the indefinite future, which it may not be, estimate the expected rate of return for the stock.

8-17B. (*Preferred stock valuation*) Melissa Corporation's preferred shares are trading for $19.50 in the market and pay a $2.25 annual dividend. Assume that you, the investor, have a required rate of return of 10 percent.

a. What is the expected rate of return on the stock?
b. What is the stock's value to you, the investor?
c. Should you purchase the stock?

8-18B. (*Common stock valuation*) Adam, Inc.'s outstanding common stock is currently selling in the market for $26. Dividends of $1.95 per share were paid last year, and the company expects annual growth of 5 percent.

a. What is the value of the stock to you, given a 12 percent required rate of return?
b. Determine the expected rate of return for the stock.
c. Should you purchase this stock?

8-19B. (*Measuring growth*) Thomas, Inc.'s return on equity is 13 percent and management has plans to retain 20 percent of earnings for investment in the company.

a. What will be the company's growth rate?
b. How would the growth rate change if management (*i*) increased retained earnings to 35 percent or (*ii*) decreased retention to 13 percent?

8-20B. (*Common stockholder expected return*) Arthur Corporation's common stock is selling for $33.75 and recently paid dividends of $3.15 per share. The company has an expected growth rate of 7 percent.

a. What is the stock's expected rate of return?
b. Should you make the investment if your required rate of return is 11 percent?

SELF-TEST SOLUTIONS

ST-1.

$$\text{value } (V_{ps}) = \frac{.16 \times \$100}{.12} = \frac{\$16}{.12} = \$133.33$$

ST-2.

a. $$\text{expected return} = \frac{\text{dividend}}{\text{market price}} = \frac{\$3.25}{\$38.50} = 0.0844 = 8.44\%$$

b. Given your 8 percent required rate of return, the stock is worth \$40.62 to you:

$$\text{value} = \frac{\text{dividend}}{\text{required rate of return}} = \frac{\$3.25}{0.08} = \$40.62$$

Because the expected rate of return (8.44%) is greater than your required rate of return (8%) or because the current market price (\$38.50) is less than \$40.62, the stock is undervalued and you should buy.

ST-3.

$$\text{value } (V_{ps}) = \frac{\text{dividend}}{\text{required rate of return}} = \frac{\$2.75}{0.09} = \$30.56$$

ST-4.

$$\text{value } (V_{cs}) = \left(\frac{\text{last year dividend } (1 + \text{growth rate})}{\text{required rate of return} - \text{growth rate}}\right) = \frac{\$1.32\ (1.07)}{0.11 - 0.07} = \$35.31$$

ST-5.

a. $$\text{expected rate of return } (\bar{k}_{cs}) = \frac{\text{dividend in year 1}}{\text{market price}} + \text{growth rate}$$

$$\bar{k}_{cs} = \frac{\$2.50}{\$23.00} + 0.105 = .2137$$

$$\bar{k}_{cs} = 21.37\%$$

b. The value of the stock for you would be \$38.46. Thus, the expected rate of return exceeds your required rate of return, which means that the value of the security to you is greater than the current market price. Thus, you should buy the stock.

$$V_{cs} = \frac{\$2.50}{.17 - .105} = \$38.46$$

APPENDIX 8A

The Relationship between Value and Earnings

In understanding the relationship between a firm's earnings and the market price of its stock, it is helpful to look first at the relationship for a nongrowth firm and then expand our view to include the growth firm.

THE RELATIONSHIP BETWEEN EARNINGS AND VALUE FOR THE NONGROWTH COMPANY

When we speak of a nongrowth firm, we mean one that retains no profits for the purpose of reinvestment. The only investments made are for the purpose of maintaining status quo—that is, investing the amount of the depreciation taken on fixed assets so that the firm does not lose its current earnings capacity. The result is both constant earnings and a constant dividend stream to the common stockholder, because the firm is paying all earnings out in the form of dividends (dividend in year *t* equals earnings in year *t*). This type of common stock is essentially no different from a preferred stock. Recalling our earlier discussion about valuing a preferred stock, we may value the nongrowth common stock similarly, expressing our valuation in one of two ways:

$$\text{value of a nongrowth common stock } (V_{ng}) = \frac{\text{earnings per share}_1}{\text{required rate of return}} \quad \textbf{(8A-1)}$$

$$= \frac{\text{dividend per share}_1}{\text{required rate of return}} \quad \textbf{(8A-2)}$$

or

$$V_{ng} = \frac{EPS_1}{k_{cs}} = \frac{D_1}{k_{cs}}$$

EXAMPLE: VALUING NO-GROWTH STOCK

The Reeves Corporation expects its earnings per share this year to be $12, which is to be paid out in total to the investors in the form of dividends. If the investors have a required rate of return of 14 percent, the value of the stock would be $85.71:

$$V_{ng} = \frac{\$12}{.14} = \$85.71$$

In this instance, the relationship between value and earnings per share is direct and unmistakable. If earnings per share increases (decreases) 10 percent, then the value of the share should increase (decrease) 10 percent; that is, the ratio of price to earnings will be a constant, as will the ratio of earnings to price. A departure from the constant relationship would occur only if the investors change their required rate of return, owing to a change in their perception about such things as risk or anticipated inflation. Thus, there is good reason to perceive a relationship between next year's earnings and share price for the nongrowth company.

THE RELATIONSHIP BETWEEN EARNINGS AND VALUE FOR THE GROWTH FIRM

Turning our attention now to the growth firm, one that does reinvest its profits back into the business, we will recall that our valuation model depended on dividends and earnings increasing at a constant growth rate. Returning to equation 8-5, we valued a common stock where dividends were expected to increase at a constant growth rate as follows:

$$\text{value} = \frac{\text{dividend}_1}{\text{required rate of return} - \text{growth rate}}$$

or

$$V_{cs} = \frac{D_1}{k_{cs} - g}$$

Although equation 8-7 is certainly the conventional way of expressing value of the growth stock, it is not the only means. We could also describe the value of a stock as the present value of the dividend stream provided from the firm's existing assets plus the present value of any future growth resulting from the reinvestment of future earnings. We could represent this concept notationally as follows:

$$V_{cs} = \frac{EPS_1}{k_{cs}} + NVDG \tag{8A-3}$$

where EPS_1/k_{cs} = the present value of the cash flow stream provided by the existing assets
$NVDG$ = the net value of any dividend growth resulting from the reinvestment of future earnings

The first term, EPS_1/k_{cs}, is immediately understandable given our earlier rationale about nongrowth stocks. The second term, the net value of future dividend growth ($NVDG$), needs some clarification.

To begin our explanation of $NVDG$, let r equal the fraction of a firm's earnings that are retained in the business, which implies that the dividend in year 1 (D_1) would equal $(1 - r) \times EPS_1$. Next assume that any earnings that are reinvested yield a rate of ROE (return on equity). Thus, from the earnings generated in year 1, we would be investing the percentage of earnings retained, r; times the firm's earnings per share, EPS_1, or $r \times EPS_1$. In return, we should expect to receive a cash flow in all future years equal to the expected return on our investment, ROE, times the amount of our investment, or $r \times EPS_1 \times ROE$. Because cash inflows represent an annuity continuing in perpetuity, the present value from reinvesting a part of the firm's earnings in year 1 (PV_1) would be equal to the present value of the new cash flows less the cost of the investment:

$$PV_1 = \underbrace{\left(\frac{r \times EPS_1 \times ROE}{k_{cs}}\right)}_{\substack{\text{present value}\\\text{of increased}\\\text{cash flows}}} - \underbrace{(r \times EPS)}_{\substack{\text{amount of cash}\\\text{retained and}\\\text{reinvested}}} \tag{8A-4}$$

If we continued to reinvest a fixed percentage of earnings each year and earned ROE on these investments, there would also be a net present value in all the following years; that is, we would have a $PV_2, PV_3, PV_4 \ldots PV_\infty$. Also, because r and ROE are both constant, the series of PVs will increase at a constant growth rate of $r \times ROE$. We may therefore use the *constant-growth valuation model* to value $NVDG$ as follows:

$$NVDG = \frac{PV_1}{k_{cs} - g} \qquad \textbf{(8A-5)}$$

Thus, we may now establish the value of a common stock as the sum of (1) a present value of a constant stream of earnings generated from the firm's assets already in place and (2) the present value of an increasing dividend stream coming from the retention of profits; that is,

$$V_{cs} = \frac{EPS_1}{k_{cs}} + \frac{PV_1}{k_{cs} - g} \qquad \textbf{(8A-6)}$$

EXAMPLE: COMPARING TWO VALUATION METHODS

The Upp Corporation should earn \$8 per share this year, of which 40 percent will be retained within the firm for reinvestment and 60 percent paid in the form of dividends to the stockholders. Management expects to earn an 18 percent return on any funds retained. Let us use both the constant-growth dividend model and the *NVDG* model to compute Upp's stock value, assuming the investors have a 12 percent required rate of return.

CONSTANT-GROWTH DIVIDEND MODEL

Because we are assuming that the Upp's *ROE* will be constant and that management faithfully intends to retain 40 percent of earnings each year to be used for new investments, the dividend stream flowing to the investor should increase by 7.2 percent each year, which we know by solving for $r \times ROE$, or (.4)(18%). The dividend for this year will be \$4.80, which is the dividend-payout ratio of $(1 - r)$ times the expected earnings per share of \$8 (.60 × \$8 = \$4.80). Given a 12 percent required rate of return for the investors, the value of the security may be shown to be \$100.

$$\begin{aligned} V_{cs} &= \frac{D_1}{k_{cs} - g} \\ &= \frac{\$4.80}{.12 - .072} \\ &= \$100 \end{aligned}$$

NVDG MODEL

Restructuring the problem to compute separately the present value of the no-growth stream and the present value of future growth opportunities, we may again determine the value of the stock to be \$100. Solving first for value assuming a no-growth scenario,

$$\begin{aligned} V_{ng} &= \frac{EPS_1}{k_{cs}} \\ &= \frac{\$8}{.12} \\ &= \$66.67 \end{aligned} \qquad \textbf{(8A-7)}$$

We next estimate the value of the future growth opportunities coming from reinvesting corporate profits each year, which is

$$NVDG = \frac{PV_1}{k_{cs} - g} \qquad \textbf{(8A-8)}$$

(continued)

Knowing k_{cs} to be 12 percent and the growth rate to be 7.2 percent, we lack knowing only PV_1, which can easily be determined using equation 8A-4:

$$PV_1 = \left(\frac{r \times EPS_1 \times ROE}{k_{cs}}\right) - r \times EPS_1$$

$$= \left(\frac{(.4)(\$8)(.18)}{.12}\right) - (.4)(\$8)$$

$$= \$4.80 - \$3.20$$

$$= \$1.60$$

The *NVDG* may now be computed:

$$NVDG = \frac{\$1.60}{.12 - .072}$$

$$= \$33.33$$

Thus, the value of the combined streams is \$100:

$$V_{cs} = \$66.67 + \$33.33 = \$100$$

From the preceding example, we see that the value of the growth opportunities represents a significant portion of the total value, 33 percent to be exact. Furthermore, in looking at the *NVDG* model, we observe that value is influenced by the following: (1) the size of the firm's beginning earnings per share, (2) the percentage of profits retained, and (3) the spread between the return generated on new investments and the investor's required rate of return. The first factor relates to firm size; the second to management's decision about the firm's earnings retention rate. Although the first two factors are not unimportant, the last one is the key to wealth creation by management. *Simply because management retains profits does not mean that wealth is created for the stockholders.* Wealth comes only if the return on equity from the investments, *ROE*, is greater than the investor's required rate of return, k_{cs}. Thus, we should expect the market to assign value not only to the reported earnings per share for the current year but also to the anticipated growth opportunities that have a marginal rate of return that exceed the required rate of return of the firm's investors.

STUDY PROBLEMS (SET A)

8A-1. *(Valuation of common stock—*NVDG *model)* The Burgon Co. management expects the firm's earnings per share to be \$5 this forthcoming year. The firm's policy is to pay out 35 percent of its earnings in the form of dividends. In looking at the investment opportunities available to the firm, the return on equity should be 20 percent for the foreseeable future. Use the *NVDG* model to find the value of the company's stock. The stockholder's required rate of return is 16 percent. Verify your results with the constant-growth dividend model.

8A-2. *(Valuation of common stock—*NVDG *model)* You want to know the impact of retaining earnings on the value of your firm's stock. Given the following information, calculate the value of the stock under the different scenarios described in part d.

a. Earnings per share on existing assets should be about \$7 this forthcoming year.
b. The stockholder's required rate of return is 18 percent.
c. The expected return on equity may be as low as 16 percent or as high as 24 percent, with an expected return of 18 percent.
d. You are considering three earnings-retention policies on a long-term basis: (1) retain no earnings, instead distributing all earnings to stockholders in the form of dividends; (2) retain 30 percent of earnings; or (3) retain 60 percent of earnings.

PART 3

Investment in Long-Term Assets

CHAPTER 9
CAPITAL-BUDGETING DECISION CRITERIA

CHAPTER 10
CASH FLOWS AND OTHER TOPICS IN CAPITAL BUDGETING

CHAPTER 11
CAPITAL BUDGETING AND RISK ANALYSIS

CHAPTER 12
COST OF CAPITAL

CHAPTER 13
MANAGING FOR SHAREHOLDER VALUE

LEARNING OBJECTIVES

After reading this chapter, you should be able to

1. Discuss the difficulty of finding profitable projects in competitive markets.
2. Determine whether a new project should be accepted using the payback period.
3. Determine whether a new project should be accepted using the net present value.
4. Determine whether a new project should be accepted using the profitability index.
5. Determine whether a new project should be accepted using the internal rate of return.
6. Explain the importance of ethical considerations in capital-budgeting decisions.
7. Discuss the trends in the use of different capital-budgeting criteria.

CHAPTER 9

Capital-Budgeting Decision Criteria

In 2003, Universal Studios broke ground on its newest theme park. What made this event so noteworthy was not just the cost of between $1 and $2 billion, but the location: Shanghai, China. Universal's first venture into China will take almost four years to complete and is going to be a big undertaking. In fact, this new park is expected to be larger than Universal's theme park in Osaka, Japan, which drew over 110 million visitors in its first year. This is all part of a high-stakes competition between Disney and Universal to capture the Asian tourist dollar. While they both have theme parks in Japan, the competition has now moved into China, with Disney currently involved in the construction of a park in Hong Kong.

Universal picked Shanghai because, in addition to being China's financial center with a high standard of living, it is also one of China's most popular tourist destinations, annually drawing 2 million foreign visitors. This park will also give Universal a foothold in mainland China from which to expand.

To say the least, the stakes involved with a $1 to $2 billion investment are so large that the outcome of this decision will have a major effect on Universal's future. Was this a good or a bad decision? Only time will tell. The question is how Universal went about making this decision to spend well over $1 billion. They did it using the decision criteria we will examine in this chapter.

This chapter is actually the first of two chapters dealing with the process of decision making with respect to investment in fixed assets—that is, should a proposed project be accepted or rejected? We will refer to this process as capital budgeting. In this chapter, we will look at methods used to evaluate new projects. When deciding whether to accept a new project, we will focus on free cash flows that represent the benefits generated from accepting a capital budgeting proposal. In the following chapter, we will examine what a free cash flow is and how we measure it. Then in Chapter 11 we will look at how risk enters into this process.

CHAPTER PREVIEW

Capital budgeting is the process by which the firm renews and reinvents itself—adapting old projects to the times and finding new ones. It involves comparing cash inflows that may spread out over many years with cash outflows that generally occur close to the present. As a result, much of this chapter relies heavily on **Principle 2: The Time Value of Money—A dollar received today is worth more than a dollar received in the future.** We will begin this chapter with a look at finding profitable projects. As you will see, **Principle 5: The Curse of Competitive Markets—Why it's hard to find exceptionally profitable projects** helps explain this. Next we will look at the purpose and importance of capital budgeting. We will then consider four commonly used criteria for determining acceptability of investment proposals. Keep in mind during all this that what we are actually doing is developing a framework for decision making.

Objective 1

FINDING PROFITABLE PROJECTS

Without question, it is easier to *evaluate* profitable projects than it is to *find* them. In competitive markets, generating ideas for profitable projects is extremely difficult. The competition is brisk for new profitable projects, and once they have been uncovered competitors generally rush in, pushing down prices and profits. For this reason, a firm must have a systematic strategy for generating **capital-budgeting** projects. Without this flow of new projects and ideas, the firm cannot grow or even survive for long, being forced to live off the profits from existing projects with limited lives. So where do these ideas come from for new products, for ways to improve existing products, or for ways to make existing products more profitable? The answer is from inside the firm—from everywhere inside the firm. See the Finance Matters box, "Dinnertime Blues: The Green and Bear It Approach to Finding New Projects."

Capital budgeting
The decision-making process with respect to investment in fixed assets.

BACK TO THE PRINCIPLES

The fact that profitable projects are difficult to find relates directly to ***Principle 5: The Curse of Competitive Markets—Why it's hard to find exceptionally profitable projects.*** *When we introduced that principle we stated that successful investments involve the reduction of competition by creating barriers to entry either through product differentiation or cost advantages. The key to locating profitable projects is to understand how and where they exist.*

Typically, a firm has a research and development department that searches for ways to improve existing products or find new products. These ideas may come from within the R&D department or be based on referral ideas from executives, sales personnel, anyone in the firm, or even from customers. For example, at Ford Motor Company prior to the 1980s, ideas for product improvement had typically been generated in Ford's research and development department. Unfortunately, this strategy was not enough to keep Ford from losing much of its market share to the Japanese. In an attempt to cut costs and improve product quality, Ford moved from strict reliance on an R&D department to seeking the input of employees at all levels for new ideas. Bonuses are now provided to workers for their cost-cutting suggestions, and assembly line personnel who can see the production process from a hands-on point of view are now brought into the hunt for new projects. The effect on Ford has been positive and significant. Although not all suggested projects prove to be profitable, many new ideas generated from within the firm turn out to be good ones.

Keep in mind that new capital-budgeting projects don't necessarily mean coming up with a new product; it may be taking an existing product and applying it to a new market. That's certainly been the direction that McDonald's has taken in recent years. Today, McDonald's operates in over 118 countries with more than 30,000 restaurants. One of the biggest is a 700-seat McDonald's in Moscow. Was this an expensive venture? It certainly was; in fact, the food plant that McDonald's built to supply burgers, buns, fries, and everything else sold there cost over $60 million. In addition to the costs, it differs from opening an outlet in the United States in a number of ways. First, in order to keep the quality of what McDonald's sells identical to what is served at any McDonald's anywhere in the world, McDonald's spent six years in putting together a supply chain that would provide the necessary raw materials at the quality level McDonald's demanded. On top of that, there are risks associated with the Russian economy and its currency that are well beyond the scope of what is experienced in the United States. However, since it opened, it has proven to be enormously successful. It all goes to show that not all capital-

FINANCE MATTERS

DINNERTIME BLUES: THE GREEN AND BEAR IT APPROACH TO FINDING NEW PROJECTS

How do you expand the market for a product like ketchup? It seems like there's only so much ketchup a person will use and the goal might just be to take market share away from your competitors. That's not an answer that Heinz was satisfied with, and so, in the fall of 2000, Heinz introduced green ketchup. How and why did they come up with the idea for such a thing?

The answer is simple, capital budgeting. While capital budgeting is decision making with respect to investment in long-term assets, it also involves coming up with those ideas. In the food industry one of the recent trends has been toward "eatertainment"—that is, making kids' food more fun to eat. Market research has shown that kids just like to be entertained when they eat. That's the reason behind the success of Dannon Sprinkl'ins Color Creations, a vanilla yogurt packaged with a different colored sprinkle under each cup lid. Stir in the sprinkle and the yogurt changes colors—the green crystals turn the yogurt blue and the red turns it yellow. It is also the reason behind the success of Quaker Oats Sea Adventures, which advertises, "A blue sea with sharks, treasures, and divers magically appears as you stir!" It even hit the computer industry with the introduction of the iMac.

To say the least, the people at Heinz were excited when their marketing found that grade school children in test groups from coast to coast said they wanted their ketchup in colors. According to Kelly Stitt, the brand manager for Heinz, "Kids live a world of color. Everything is bright, bold color." The bottom line is that kids wanted ketchup in green, and also in blue. For Heinz, it was one step at a time—they initially just went with the green, but they did it in a plastic bottle that squirts a thin stream so kids can draw with it.

What techniques did Heinz use to make their decision to go forward with this project? They used the same capital budgeting techniques we introduced in this chapter. Many times good capital budgeting projects are not just a great idea for a new project, but are also the result of good marketing research. In effect, although our capital budgeting techniques can do a good job of evaluating projects, a good project has it roots in good product development—knowing consumer wants and delivering them. That means coming up with sales forecasts that are accurate—that anticipate moves by competitors—because although our capital budgeting criteria are good at evaluating proposals, the results are only as good as what is input into the models.

How did this all work out? The answer is pretty well. Green ketchup is gone, being replaced with purple, pink, orange, and teal, but the Heinz EZ Squirt brand ketchup—the colored variety—is a success, and has helped Heinz increase its total market share from around 45 percent to 58 percent in just a few years.

It has even spilled over into other markets, with new products being introduced that are simply color variations of older products. For example, in March of 2001, Frito-Lay introduced Cheetos, Mystery Colorz, adding color to the snack aisle. The product looks and tastes like traditional Cheetos, but turns either blue or green upon being eaten, painting the snacker's tongue. Similarly Ore-Ida, a subsidiary of Heinz, introduced Kool Blue, a blue version of the traditional fry. It even took matters further with Cocoa Crisper, a chocolate-flavored French fry.

Source: Based on Paul Lukas, "The Color of Money and Ketchup," *Fortune* (August 14, 2000): 38; Constance L. Hays, "Go Play With Your Food, Dear," *The New York Times* (July 16, 2000): 2; Lisa Gutierrez, "In Living Color It's Fast Becoming a Mix-and-Match World, from Food to Appliances," *The Kansas City Star* (July 18, 2000): E1; Damian Whitworth, "Green Ketchup Is Latest Heinz Variety," *The Times of London* (July 11, 2000): 4m; Kristen Hays, "Heinz Looks to New Green Ketchup for a Pot of Gold," *Chicago Sun-Times* (July 10, 2000): 4; Gabrielle Glaser, "Dinner Time Blues, Novelty Foods Aimed at Kids Have Made the Jump from Snacktime," *The Oregonian* (April 27, 2003): L9; Sherri Day, "Tonight's Menu: Special Effects. Foodmakers Entice Kids with Color," *The New York Times* (March 13, 2003): 1; and Sarah Mulholland, "Over the Rainbow; Retailers Wonder if Odd-Colored Foods will Retain their Popularity and Profitability in the Long Run," *Supermarket News* (August 19, 2002): 33.

budgeting projects have to be new products, they can also be existing products in new markets.

Another way an existing product can be applied to a new market is illustrated by Kimberly-Clark, the manufacturers of Huggies disposable diapers. They took their existing product line, made it more waterproof, and began marketing it as disposable swim pants call Little Swimmers. Sara Lee Hosiery boosted its market by expanding its offerings to appeal to more customers and more customer needs; for example, it introduced Sheer Energy pantyhose for support, Just My Size pantyhose aimed at larger sizes, and recently introduced Silken Mist pantyhose aimed at African-American women in shades better suited for darker skin tones.

These are big investments and go a long way toward determining the future of the company, but they don't always work as planned. Just look at Burger King's development of its new french fries. It looked like a slam dunk great idea. They took an uncooked french fry and coated it with a layer of starch that made it crunchier and kept it hot longer. Spending over $70 million on the new fries, they even gave away 15 million orders on a "Free Fryday." Unfortunately, they didn't go down with consumers and Burger King was left to eat the loss. Given the size of the investment we're talking about, you can see why capital budgeting is so important.

We will consider four commonly used criteria for determining acceptability of investment proposals. The first is the payback period and it is the least sophisticated, in that it does not incorporate the time value of money into its calculations; the remaining three do take it into account. For the time being, the problem of incorporating risk into the capital-budgeting decision is ignored. This issue will be examined in Chapter 11. In addition, we will assume that the appropriate discount rate, required rate of return, or cost of capital is given. The determination of this rate is the topic of Chapter 12.

CONCEPT CHECK

1. Why is it so difficult to find an exceptionally profitable project?
2. Why is the search for new, profitable projects so important?

Objective 2

PAYBACK PERIOD

Payback period
A capital-budgeting criterion defined as the number of years required to recover the initial cash investment.

The **payback period** is the number of years needed to recover the initial cash outlay of the capital budgeting project. As this criterion measures how quickly the project will return its original investment, it deals with free cash flows, which measure the true timing of the benefits, rather than accounting profits. Unfortunately, it also ignores the time value of money and does not discount these free cash flows back to the present. The accept-reject criterion centers on whether the project's payback period is less than or equal to the firm's maximum desired payback period. For example, if a firm's maximum desired payback period is three years and an investment proposal requires an initial cash outlay of $10,000 and yields the following set of annual free cash flows, what is its payback period? Should the project be accepted?

	AFTER-TAX FREE CASH FLOW
Year 1	$ 2,000
Year 2	4,000
Year 3	3,000
Year 4	3,000
Year 5	10,000

In this case, after three years the firm will have recaptured $9,000 on an initial investment of $10,000, leaving $1,000 of the initial investment still to be recouped. During the fourth year, a total of $3,000 will be returned from this investment. Assuming cash will flow into the firm at a constant rate over the year, it will take one-third of the year ($1,000/$3,000) to recapture the remaining $1,000. Thus, the payback period on this project is 3⅓ years, which is more than the desired payback period. Using the payback period criterion, the firm would reject this project without even considering the $10,000 cash flow in year 5.

TABLE 9-1 Payback Period Example

PROJECTS	A	B
Initial cash outlay	–$10,000	–$10,000
Annual free cash flows:		
Year 1	$ 6,000	$ 5,000
Year 2	4,000	5,000
Year 3	3,000	0
Year 4	2,000	0
Year 5	1,000	0

Although the payback period is used frequently, it does have some rather obvious drawbacks, which can best be demonstrated through the use of an example. Consider two investment projects, A and B, which involve an initial cash outlay of $10,000 each and produce the annual free cash flows shown in Table 9-1. Both projects have a payback period of two years; therefore, in terms of the payback period criterion, both are equally acceptable. However, if we had our choice, it is clear we would select A over B, for at least two reasons. First, regardless of what happens after the payback period, project A returns our initial investment to us earlier within the payback period. Thus, because there is a time value of money, the cash flows occurring within the payback period should not be weighted equally, as they are. In addition, all cash flows that occur after the payback period are ignored. This violates the principle that investors desire more in the way of benefits rather than less—a principle that is difficult to deny, especially when we are talking about money.

To deal with the criticism that the payback period ignores the time value of money, some firms use the **discounted payback period** approach. The discounted payback period method is similar to the traditional payback period except that it uses discounted free cash flows rather than actual undiscounted free cash flows in calculating the payback period. The discounted payback period is defined as the number of years needed to recover the initial cash outlay from the *discounted free cash flows.* The accept-reject criterion then becomes whether the project's discounted payback period is less than or equal to the firm's maximum desired discounted payback period. Using the assumption that the required rate of return on projects A and B illustrated in Table 9-1 is 17 percent, the discounted cash flows from these projects are given in Table 9-2. On project A, after three years, only $74 of the initial outlay remain to be recaptured, whereas year 4 brings in a discounted free cash flow of $1,068. Thus, if the $1,068 comes in a constant rate over the year, it will take 7/100s of the year ($74/$1,068) to recapture the remaining $74. The discounted payback period for project A is 3.07 years, calculated as follows:

Discounted payback period A variation of the payback period decision criterion defined as the number of years required to recover the initial cash outlay from the discounted net cash flows.

$$\text{discounted payback period}_A = 3.0 + \$74/\$1{,}068 = 3.07 \text{ years}$$

If project A's discounted payback period was less than the firm's maximum desired discounted payback period, then project A would be accepted. Project B, however, does not have a discounted payback period because it never fully recovers the project's initial cash outlay, and thus should be rejected. The major problem with the discounted payback period comes in setting the firm's maximum desired discounted payback period. This is an arbitrary decision that affects which projects are accepted and which ones are rejected. Thus, although the discounted payback period is superior to the traditional payback period, in that it accounts for the time value of money in its calculations, its use is limited by the arbitrariness of the process used to select the maximum desired payback period. Moreover, as we will soon see, the net present value criterion is theoretically superior and no more difficult to calculate.

Although these deficiencies limit the value of the payback period and discounted payback period as tools for investment evaluation, these methods do have several positive

TABLE 9-2 Discounted Payback Period Example Using a 17 Percent Required Rate of Return

PROJECT A

YEAR	UNDISCOUNTED FREE CASH FLOWS	$PVIF^*_{17\%,n}$	DISCOUNTED FREE CASH FLOWS	CUMULATIVE DISCOUNTED FREE CASH FLOWS
0	–$10,000	1.0	–$10,000	–$10,000
1	6,000	.855	5,130	– 4,870
2	4,000	.731	2,924	– 1,946
3	3,000	.624	1,872	– 74
4	2,000	.534	1,068	994
5	1,000	.456	456	1,450

PROJECT B

YEAR	UNDISCOUNTED FREE CASH FLOWS	$PVIF_{17\%,n}$	DISCOUNTED FREE CASH FLOWS	CUMULATIVE DISCOUNTED FREE CASH FLOWS
0	–$10,000	1.0	–$10,000	–$10,000
1	5,000	.855	4,275	– 5,725
2	5,000	.731	3,655	– 2,070
3	0	.624	0	– 2,070
4	0	.534	0	– 2,070
5	0	.456	0	– 2,070

*These are present value factors from Appendix C in the back of the book. If you're using a financial calculator, simply discount each cash flow individually back to the present.

features. First, they deal with free cash flows, as opposed to accounting profits, and therefore focus on the true timing of the project's benefits and costs, even though the traditional payback period does not adjust the cash flows for the time value of money. Second, they are easy to visualize, quickly understood, and easy to calculate. Finally, although the payback period and discounted payback period methods have serious deficiencies, they are often used as rough screening devices to eliminate projects whose returns do not materialize until later years. These methods emphasize the earliest returns, which in all likelihood are less uncertain, and provide for the liquidity needs of the firm. Although their advantages are certainly significant, their disadvantages severely limit their value as discriminating capital-budgeting criteria.

BACK TO THE PRINCIPLES

The final three capital-budgeting criteria all incorporate ***Principle 2: The Time Value of Money—A dollar received today is worth more than a dollar received in the future*** *in their calculations. If we are at all to make rational business decisions we must recognize that money has a time value. In examining the following capital-budgeting techniques, you will notice that this principle is the driving force behind each of them.*

CONCEPT CHECK

1. What are some of the shortcomings of the payback period?
2. Why do you think the payback period is used as frequently as it is?
3. What is the major problem with the discounted payback period?

NET PRESENT VALUE

Objectiv

The **net present value (*NPV*)** of an investment proposal is equal to the present value of its free cash flows less the investment's initial outlay. The net present value can be expressed as follows:

Net present value (N... A capital-budgeting decision criterion defined as the present value of the free cash flows after tax less the project's initial outlay.

$$NPV = \sum_{t=1}^{n} \frac{FCF_t}{(1+k)^t} - IO \tag{9-1}$$

where FCF_t = the annual free cash flow in time period t (this can take on either positive or negative values)
k = the appropriate discount rate; that is, the required rate of return or cost of capital[1]
IO = the initial cash outlay
n = the project's expected life

The project's net present value gives a measurement of the *net value* of an investment proposal in terms of today's dollars. Because all cash flows are discounted back to the present, comparing the difference between the present value of the annual free cash flows and the investment outlay is appropriate. The difference between the present value of the annual free cash flows and the initial outlay determines the net value of accepting the investment proposal in terms of today's dollars. Whenever the project's *NPV* is greater than or equal to zero, we will accept the project; whenever the *NPV* is negative, we will reject the project. Note that if the project's net present value is zero, then it returns the required rate of return and should be accepted. This accept-reject criterion can be stated as:

$NPV \geq 0.0$: Accept
$NPV < 0.0$: Reject

The following example illustrates the use of the net present value capital-budgeting criterion.

EXAMPLE: CALCULATING THE NPV WITH UNEVEN CASH FLOWS

Ski-Doo is considering new machinery that would reduce manufacturing costs associated with its Mach Z snowmobile, for which the after-tax cash flows are shown in Table 9-3. If the firm has a 12 percent required rate of return, the present value of the free cash flows is $47,678, as calculated in Table 9-4. Subtracting the $40,000 initial outlay leaves a net present value of $7,678. Because this value is greater than zero, the net present value criterion indicates that the project should be accepted.

TABLE 9-3 *NPV* Illustration of investment in New Machinery

	FREE CASH FLOW		FREE CASH FLOW
Initial outlay	–$40,000	Year 3	13,000
Year 1	15,000	Year 4	12,000
Year 2	14,000	Year 5	11,000

(continued)

[1] The required rate of return or cost of capital is the rate of return necessary to justify raising funds to finance the project or, alternatively, the rate of return necessary to maintain the firm's current market price per share. These terms will be defined in greater detail in Chapter 12.

TABLE 9-4 Calculation for *NPV* Illustration of Investment in New Machinery

	FREE CASH FLOW	PRESENT VALUE* FACTOR AT 12 PERCENT	PRESENT VALUE
Year 1	$15,000	.893	$13,395
Year 2	14,000	.797	11,158
Year 3	13,000	.712	9,256
Year 4	12,000	.636	7,632
Year 5	11,000	.567	6,237
Present value of free cash flows			$47,678
Initial outlay			–40,000
Net present value			$7,678

*These are present value factors from the back of the book. If you're using a financial calculator, simply discount each cash flow individually back to the present.

Note in the Ski-Doo example that the worth of the net present value calculation is a function of the accuracy of cash-flow predictions.

The *NPV* criterion is the capital-budgeting decision tool we will find most favorable. First of all, it deals with free cash flows rather than accounting profits. Also, it is sensitive to the true timing of the benefits resulting from the project. Moreover, recognizing that, the time value of money allows comparison of the benefits and costs in a logical manner. Finally, because projects are accepted only if a positive net present value is associated with them, the acceptance of a project using this criterion will increase the value of the firm, which is consistent with the goal of maximizing the shareholders' wealth.

EXAMPLE: CALCULATING THE NPV WITH EVEN CASH FLOWS

A firm is considering the purchase of a new computer system, which will cost $30,000 initially, to aid in credit billing and inventory management. The free cash flows resulting from this project are provided in Table 9-5. The required rate of return demanded by the firm is 10 percent. To determine the system's net present value, the three-year $15,000 cash flow annuity is first discounted back to the present at 10 percent. From Appendix E in the back of this book, we find that $PVIFA_{10\%,3yrs}$ is 2.487. Thus, the pres-ent value of this $15,000 annuity is $37,305 ($15,000 × 2.487).

TABLE 9-5 *NPV* Example Problem of Computer System

	FREE CASH FLOW		FREE CASH FLOW
Initial outlay	–$30,000	Year 2	15,000
Year 1	15,000	Year 3	15,000

Seeing that the cash inflows have been discounted back to the present, they can now be compared with the initial outlay, because both of the flows are now stated in terms of today's dollars. Subtracting the initial outlay ($30,000) from the present value of the free cash flows ($37,305), we find that the system's net present value is $7,305. Because the *NPV* on this project is positive, the project should be accepted.

The disadvantage of the *NPV* method stems from the need for detailed, long-term forecasts of free cash flows accruing from the project's acceptance. Despite this drawback, the net present value is the theoretically correct criterion in that it measures the impact of a project's acceptance on the value of the firm's equity. The following example provides an additional illustration of its application.

Spreadsheets and the Net Present Value

While we can calculate the *NPV* by hand, it is more common that it will be done with the help of a spreadsheet. Just as with the keystroke calculations on a financial calculator, a spreadsheet can make easy work of the *NPV* calculations. The only real glitch here is that Excel, along with most other spreadsheets, only calculates the present value of the future cash flows and ignores the initial outlay in its *NPV* calculations. Sound strange? Well, it is. It is essentially just a carry-forward of an error in one of the first spreadsheets. That means that the actual *NPV* is the Excel calculated *NPV*, minus the initial outlay:

actual *NPV* = Excel calculated *NPV* – initial outlay

This can be input into a spreadsheet cell as: =*NPV*(rate, inflow 1, inflow 2, . . . inflow 29) – initial outlay.

Spreadsheets and Net Present Value

Looking back at the Ski-Doo example in Table 9.4, we can use a spreadsheet to calculate the Net Present Value. However, we must keep in mind that the NPV formula in Excel only calculates the present value of the future cash flows, and ignores the initial outlay. Thus, you have to be sure to subtract out the initial outlay in order to get the correct number.

Back to the example in Table 9.4, given a 12 percent discount rate and the following after-tax cash flows, the Net Present Value could be calculated as follows:

rate (i) = 12%

Year	Cash Flow
Initial Outlay	($40,000)
1	$15,000
2	$14,000
3	$13,000
4	$12,000
5	$11,000

NPV = $7,674.63

Excel formula: =NPV(rate,inflow 1, inflow2, ... ,inflow 29)

Again, from the Excel NPV calculation we must then subtract out the initial outlay in order to calculate the actual NPV.

Entered value in cell c26: =NPV(D16,D20:D24)-40000

Sheet1 Sheet2 Sheet3

CONCEPT CHECK

1. Provide an intuitive definition of the net present value of a project.
2. Suppose a project has a net present value of $10 million. What does that mean?

Objective 4

PROFITABILITY INDEX (BENEFIT/COST RATIO)

Profitability index (*PI*) (or Benefit/Cost Ratio) A capital-budgeting decision criterion defined as the ratio of the present value of the future free cash flows to the initial outlay.

The **profitability index (*PI*)**, or **benefit/cost ratio**, is the ratio of the present value of the future free cash flows to the initial outlay. Although the net present value investment criterion gives a measure of the absolute dollar desirability of a project, the profitability index provides a relative measure of an investment proposal's desirability—that is, the ratio of the present value of its future benefits to its initial cost. The profitability index can be expressed as follows:

$$PI = \frac{\sum_{t=1}^{n} \frac{FCF_t}{(1+k)^t}}{IO} \tag{9-2}$$

where FCF_t = the annual free cash flow in time period t (this can take on either positive or negative values)

k = the appropriate discount rate; that is, the required rate of return or cost of capital

IO = the initial cash outlay

n = the project's expected life

The decision criterion is this: Accept the project if the *PI* is greater than or equal to 1.00, and reject the project if the *PI* is less than 1.00.

$PI \geq 1.0$: Accept

$PI < 1.0$: Reject

Looking closely at this criterion, we see that it yields the same accept-reject decision as the net present value criterion. Whenever the present value of the project's net cash flows is greater than its initial cash outlay, the project's net present value will be positive, signaling a decision to accept. When this is true, the project's profitability index will also be greater than 1, as the present value of the free cash flows (the *PI*'s numerator) is greater than its initial outlay (the *PI*'s denominator). Thus, these two decision criteria will always yield the same accept-reject decision, although they will not necessarily rank acceptable projects in the same order. This problem of conflicting ranking will be dealt with at a later point.

Because the net present value and profitability index criteria are essentially the same, they have the same advantages over the other criteria examined. Both employ cash flows, recognize the timing of the cash flows, and are consistent with the goal of maximization of shareholders' wealth. The major disadvantage of this criterion, similar to the net present value criterion, is that it requires detailed free cash flow forecasts over the entire life of the project.

EXAMPLE: CALCULATING THE PROFITABILITY INDEX

A firm with a 10 percent required rate of return is considering investing in a new machine with an expected life of six years. The after-tax cash flows resulting from this investment are given in Table 9-6. Discounting the project's future free cash flows back to the present yields a present value of \$53,667; dividing this value by the initial outlay of \$50,000 gives a profitability index of 1.0733, as shown in Table 9-7. This tells us that the present value of the future benefits accruing from this project is 1.0733 times the level of the initial outlay. Because the profitability index is greater than 1.0, the project should be accepted.

TABLE 9-6 *PI* Illustration of Investment in New Machinery

	FREE CASH FLOW		FREE CASH FLOW
Initial outlay	–$50,000	Year 4	$12,000
Year 1	15,000	Year 5	14,000
Year 2	8,000	Year 6	16,000
Year 3	10,000		

TABLE 9-7 Calculation for *PI* Illustration of Investment in New Machinery

	FREE CASH FLOW	PRESENT VALUE* FACTOR AT 10 PERCENT	PRESENT VALUE
Initial outlay	–$50,000	1.000	–$50,000
Year 1	15,000	0.909	13,635
Year 2	8,000	0.826	6,608
Year 3	10,000	0.751	7,510
Year 4	12,000	0.683	8,196
Year 5	14,000	0.621	8,694
Year 6	16,000	0.564	9,024

$$PI = \frac{\sum_{t=1}^{n} \frac{FCF_t}{(1+k)^t}}{IO}$$

$$= \frac{\$13,635 + \$6,608 + \$7,510 + \$8,196 + \$8,694 + \$9,024}{\$50,000}$$

$$= \frac{\$53,667}{\$50,000}$$

$$= 1.0733$$

*These are present value factors from Appendix C in the back of the book. If you're using a financial calculator, simply discount each cash flow individually back to the present.

CONCEPT CHECK

1. Provide an intuitive definition of the profitability index of a project.
2. Suppose a project has a profitability index of 0.94. What does that mean?
3. Why do the net present value and profitability index always give the same accept or reject decision for any project?

INTERNAL RATE OF RETURN

Objective 5

The **internal rate of return (*IRR*)** attempts to answer this question: What rate of return does this project earn? For computational purposes, the internal rate of return is defined as the discount rate that equates the present value of the project's future net cash flows with the project's initial cash outlay. Mathematically, the internal rate of return is defined as the value of *IRR* in the following equation:

$$IO = \sum_{t=1}^{n} \frac{FCF_t}{(1+IRR)^t} \quad \text{(9-3)}$$

Internal rate of return (*IRR*) A capital-budgeting decision criterion that reflects the rate of return a project earns. Mathematically, it is the discount rate that equates the present value of the inflows with the present value of the outflows.

where FCF_t = the annual free cash flow in time period t
(this can take on either positive or negative values)
IO = the initial cash outlay
n = the project's expected life
IRR = the project's internal rate of return

In effect, the *IRR* is analogous to the concept of the yield to maturity for bonds, which was examined in Chapter 7. In other words, a project's internal rate of return is simply the rate of return that the project earns.

The decision criterion is this: Accept the project if the internal rate of return is greater than or equal to the required rate of return. We reject the project if its internal rate of return is less than this required rate of return. This accept-reject criterion can be stated as:

$IRR >$ required rate of return: Accept
$IRR <$ required rate of return: Reject

If the internal rate of return on a project is equal to the shareholders' required rate of return, then the project should be accepted, because the firm is earning the rate that its shareholders require. However, the acceptance of a project with an internal rate of return below the investors' required rate of return will decrease the firm's stock price.

If the *NPV* is positive, then the *IRR* must be greater than the required rate of return, *k*. Thus, all the discounted cash flow criteria are consistent and will give similar accept-reject decisions. In addition, because the internal rate of return is another discounted cash flow criterion, it exhibits the same general advantages and disadvantages as both the net present value and profitability index, but has an additional disadvantage of being tedious to calculate if a financial calculator is not available.

An additional disadvantage of the *IRR* relative to the *NPV* deals with the implied reinvestment rate assumptions made by these two methods. The *NPV* method implicitly assumes that cash flows received over the life of the project are reinvested back in projects that earn the required rate of return. That is, if we have a mining project with a 10-year expected life that produces a $100,000 cash flow at the end of the second year, the *NPV* technique assumes that this $100,000 is reinvested over the period years 3 through 10 at the required rate of return. The use of the *IRR*, however, implies that cash flows over the life of the project can be reinvested at the *IRR*. Thus, if the mining project we just looked at has a 40 percent *IRR*, the use of the *IRR* implies that the $100,000 cash flow that is received at the end of year 2 could be reinvested at 40 percent over the remaining life of the project. In effect, *the* NPV *method implicitly assumes that cash flows over the life of the project can be reinvested at the project's required rate of return, whereas the use of the* IRR *method implies that these cash flows could be reinvested at the* IRR. The better assumption is the one made by the *NPV*, that cash flows could be reinvested at the required rate of return, because these cash flows will either be (1) returned in the form of dividends to shareholders who demand the required rate of return on their investment, or (2) reinvested in a new investment project. If these cash flows are invested in a new project, then they are simply substituting for external funding on which the required rate of return is demanded. Thus, the opportunity cost of these funds is the required rate of return. The bottom line to all this is that the *NPV* method makes the best reinvestment rate assumption and, as such, is superior to the *IRR* method. Why should we care which method is used if both methods give similar accept-reject decisions? The answer, as we will see in the next chapter, is that although they may give the same accept-reject decision, they may rank projects differently in terms of desirability.

Computing the *IRR* with a Financial Calculator

With today's calculators, the determination of an internal rate of return is merely a matter of a few keystrokes as illustrated in Appendix A. In Chapter 5, whenever we were solving time value of money problems for i, we were really solving for the internal rate of return. For instance, in Chapter 5, when we solved for the rate that \$100 must be compounded annually for it to grow to \$179.10 in 10 years, we were actually solving for that problem's internal rate of return. Thus, with financial calculators we need only input the initial outlay, the cash flows, and their timing, and then press the function key ***I/Y*** or the ***IRR*** button to calculate the internal rate of return. On some calculators, it is necessary to press the compute key, ***CPT***, before pressing the function key to be calculated.

Computing the *IRR* for Even Cash Flows Using the Time Value Tables

In this section, we are going to put our spreadsheets and calculators aside and obtain a better understanding of the *IRR* by examining the mathematical process of calculating internal rates of return.

The calculation of a project's internal rate of return can either be very simple or relatively complicated. As an example of a straightforward solution, assume that a firm with a required rate of return of 10 percent is considering a project that involves an initial outlay of \$45,555. If the investment is taken, the free cash flows are expected to be \$15,000 per annum over the project's four-year life. In this case, the internal rate of return is equal to *IRR* in the following equation:

$$\$45{,}555 = \frac{\$15{,}000}{(1 + IRR)^1} + \frac{\$15{,}000}{(1 + IRR)^2} + \frac{\$15{,}000}{(1 + IRR)^3} + \frac{\$15{,}000}{(1 + IRR)^4}$$

From our discussion of the present value of an annuity in Chapter 5, we know that this equation can be reduced to

$$\$45{,}555 = \$15{,}000 \left[\sum_{t=1}^{4} \frac{1}{(1 + IRR)^t} \right]$$

Appendix E gives values for the $PVIFA_{i,n}$ for various combinations of i and n, which further reduces this equation to

$$\$45{,}555 = \$15{,}000\ (PVIFA_{i,4\text{yrs}})$$

Dividing both sides by \$15,000, this becomes

$$3.037 = PVIFA_{i,4\text{yrs}}$$

Hence we are looking for a $PVIFA_{i,4\text{yrs}}$ of 3.037 in the four-year row of Appendix E. This value occurs when i equals 12 percent, which means that 12 percent is the internal rate of return for the investment. Therefore, because 12 percent is greater than the 10 percent required return, the project should be accepted.

Computing the *IRR* for Uneven Cash Flows Using the Time Value Tables

Unfortunately, although solving for the *IRR* is quite easy when using a financial calculator or spreadsheet, it can be solved directly in the tables only when the future after-tax net cash flows are in the form of an annuity or a single payment. With a calculator, the process is simple: One need only key in the initial cash outlay, the cash flows, and their timing, and press the ***IRR*** button. When a financial calculator is not available and these flows are in the form of an uneven series of flows, a trial-and-error approach is necessary. To do this, we first determine the present value of the future free cash flows using an arbitrary discount rate. If the present value of the future free cash flows at this discount rate is larger than the initial outlay, the rate is increased; if it is smaller than the initial outlay, the discount rate is lowered and the process begins again. This search routine is continued until the present value of the future free cash flows is equal to the initial outlay. The interest rate that creates this situation is the internal rate of return. This is the same basic process that a financial calculator uses to calculate an *IRR*.

To illustrate the procedure, consider an investment proposal that requires an initial outlay of $3,817 and returns $1,000 at the end of year 1, $2,000 at the end of year 2, and $3,000 at the end of year 3. In this case, the internal rate of return must be determined using trial and error. This process is presented in Table 9-8, in which an arbitrarily selected discount rate of 15 percent was chosen to begin the process.

TABLE 9-8 Computing *IRR* for Uneven Free Cash Flows Without a Financial Calculator

Initial outlay	−$3,817	$FCF_{year\ 2}$	2,000
$FCF_{year\ 1}$	1,000	$FCF_{year\ 3}$	3,000

Solution:

Step 1: Pick an arbitrary discount rate and use it to determine the present value of the free cash flows.

Step 2: Compare the present value of the free cash flows with the initial outlay; if they are equal, you have determined the *IRR*.

Step 3: If the present value of the free cash flows is larger than (less than) the initial outlay, raise (lower) the discount rate.

Step 4: Determine the present value of the free cash flows and repeat step 2.

1. TRY *i* = 15 PERCENT:

	FREE CASH FLOWS	PRESENT VALUE FACTOR AT 15 PERCENT	PRESENT VALUE
Year 1	$1,000	.870	$ 870
Year 2	2,000	.756	1,512
Year 3	3,000	.658	1,974
Present value of inflows			$4,356
Initial outlay			−$3,817

2. TRY *i* = 20 PERCENT:

	FREE CASH FLOWS	PRESENT VALUE FACTOR AT 20 PERCENT	PRESENT VALUE
Year 1	$1,000	.833	$ 833
Year 2	2,000	.694	1,388
Year 3	3,000	.579	1,737
Present value of inflows			$3,958
Initial outlay			−$3,817

3. TRY *i* = 22 PERCENT:

	FREE CASH FLOWS	PRESENT VALUE FACTOR AT 22 PERCENT	PRESENT VALUE
Year 1	$1,000	.820	$ 820
Year 2	2,000	.672	1,344
Year 3	3,000	.551	1,653
Present value of inflows			$3,817
Initial outlay			−$3,817

Obviously, 15 percent isn't the *IRR* for this project, because the present value of the free cash flows discounted back to present at 15 percent ($4,356) doesn't equal the initial outlay ($3,817). How do we make the present value of the future free cash flows smaller? We raise the discount rate. Thus, we tried 20 percent next. Again, 20 percent isn't the *IRR* for this project because the present value of the free cash flows discounted back to present at 20 percent ($3,958) doesn't equal the initial outlay ($3,817)—although it's closer than it was at 15 percent. Once more, we need to make the present value of the future free cash flows smaller so we try a higher discount rate—22 percent. At 22 percent, we have found the project's internal rate of return, because the present value of the future free cash flows equals the initial outlay. The project's internal rate of return is then compared with the firm's required rate of return, and if the *IRR* is the larger, the project is accepted.

EXAMPLE: CALCULATING THE IRR

A firm with a required rate of return of 10 percent is considering three investment proposals. Given the information in Table 9-9, management plans to calculate the internal rate of return for each project and determine which projects should be accepted.

TABLE 9-9 Evaluating Three Investment Proposal Examples Using the IRR

	A	B	C
Initial outlay	–$10,000	–$10,000	–$10,000
FCF year 1	3,362	0	1,000
FCF year 2	3,362	0	3,000
FCF year 3	3,362	0	6,000
FCF year 4	3,362	13,605	7,000

Because project A is an annuity, we can easily calculate its internal rate of return by determining the $PVIFA_{i,4yrs}$ necessary to equate the present value of the future free cash flows with the initial outlay. This computation is done as follows:

$$IO = \sum_{t=1}^{n} \frac{FCF_t}{(1 + IRR)^t}$$

$$\$10{,}000 = \sum_{t=1}^{4} \frac{\$3{,}362}{(1 + IRR)^t}$$

$$\$10{,}000 = \$3{,}362\,(PVIFA_{i,4yrs})$$

$$2.974 = (PVIFA_{i,4yrs})$$

We are looking for a $PVIFA_{i,4yrs}$ of 2.974, in the four-year row of Appendix E, which occurs in the $i = 13$ percent column. Thus, 13 percent is the internal rate of return. Because this rate is greater than the firm's required rate of return of 10 percent, the project should be accepted.

Project B involves a single future free cash flow of $13,605, resulting from an initial outlay of $10,000; thus, its internal rate of return can be determined directly from the present-value table in Appendix C, as follows:

$$IO = \frac{FCF_t}{(1 + IRR)^t}$$

(continued)

$$\$10{,}000 = \frac{\$13{,}605}{(1 + IRR)^4}$$

$$\$10{,}000 = \$13{,}605\,(PVIF_{i,4\text{yrs}})$$

$$.735 = (PVIF_{i,4\text{yrs}})$$

This tells us that we should look for a $PVIF_{i,4\text{yrs}}$ of .735 in the four-year row of Appendix C, which occurs in the $i = 8$ percent column. We may therefore conclude that 8 percent is the internal rate of return. Because this rate is less than the firm's required rate of return of 10 percent, project B should be rejected.

The uneven nature of the future free cash flows associated with project C necessitates the use of the trial-and-error method. The internal rate of return for project C is equal to the value of *IRR* in the following equation:

$$\$10{,}000 = \frac{\$1{,}000}{(1 + IRR)^1} + \frac{\$3{,}000}{(1 + IRR)^2} + \frac{\$6{,}000}{(1 + IRR)^3} + \frac{\$7{,}000}{(1 + IRR)^4}$$

Arbitrarily selecting a discount rate of 15 percent and substituting it for *IRR* reduces the value of the right side of the equation to \$11,090, as shown in Table 9-10. Therefore, because the present value of the future free cash flows is larger than the initial outlay, we must raise the discount rate to find the project's internal rate of return. Substituting 20 percent for the discount rate, the right side of the equation now becomes \$9,763. As this is less than the initial outlay of \$10,000, we must now decrease the discount rate. In other words, we know that the internal rate of return for this project is between 15 and 20 percent. Because the present value of the future flows discounted back to present at 20 percent was only \$237 too low, a discount rate of 19 percent is selected. As shown in Table 9-10, a discount rate of 19 percent reduces the present value of the future inflows down to \$10,009, which is approximately the same as the initial outlay. Consequently, project C's internal rate of return is approximately 19 percent.[a] Because the internal rate of return is greater than the firm's required rate of return of 10 percent, this investment should be accepted.

[a]If desired, the actual rate can be more precisely approximated through interpolation as follows:

DISCOUNT RATE	PRESENT VALUE		
19%	\$10,009	difference \$9	difference \$246
IRR	10,000		
20%	9,763		

Thus $IRR = 19\% + (\$9/\$246) \cdot 1\% = 19.04\%$

TABLE 9-10 Computing *IRR* for Project C

TRY *i* = 15 PERCENT:

	FREE CASH FLOWS	PRESENT VALUE FACTOR AT 15 PERCENT	PRESENT VALUE
Year 1	\$1,000	.870	\$ 870
Year 2	3,000	.756	2,268
Year 3	6,000	.658	3,948
Year 4	7,000	.572	4,004
Present value of free cash flows			\$11,090
Initial outlay			–\$10,000

(continued)

TRY i = 20 PERCENT:

	FREE CASH FLOWS	PRESENT VALUE FACTOR AT 20 PERCENT	PRESENT VALUE
Year 1	$1,000	.833	$ 833
Year 2	3,000	.694	2,082
Year 3	6,000	.579	3,474
Year 4	7,000	.482	3,374
Present value of free cash flows			$ 9,763
Initial outlay			–$10,000

TRY i = 19 PERCENT:

	FREE CASH FLOWS	PRESENT VALUE FACTOR AT 19 PERCENT	PRESENT VALUE
Year 1	$1,000	.840	$ 840
Year 2	3,000	.706	2,118
Year 3	6,000	.593	3,558
Year 4	7,000	.499	3,493
Present value of free cash flows			$10,009
Initial outlay			–$10,000

SPREADSHEETS AND THE INTERNAL RATE OF RETURN

Calculating the *IRR* using a spreadsheet is extremely simple. Once the cash flows have been entered on the spreadsheet, all you need to do is input the Excel *IRR* formula into a spreadsheet cell and let the spreadsheet do the calculations for you. Of course, at least one of the cash flows must be positive and at least one must be negative. The *IRR* formula to be input into a spreadsheet cell is: ***=IRR*(values)**, where values is simply the range of cells where the cash flows are stored.

	A	B	C	D	E	F	G
1							
2		**Spreadsheets and the IRR**					
3							
4	The three investment proposals just examined have the following						
5	cash flows:						
6							
7	Year	Project A	Project B	Project C			
8	Initial Outlay	($10,000)	($10,000)	($10,000)			
9	1	3,362	0	1,000			
10	2	3,362	0	3,000			
11	3	3,362	0	6,000			
12	4	3,362	13,605	7,000			
13							
14	IRR=	13.001%	8.000%	19.040%			
15							
16	Excel Formula: =IRR(values)						
17							
18	where:						
19	values =	the range of cells where the cash flows are stored.					
20		Note: There must be at least one positive and one					
21		negative cash flow.					
22							
23	Entered value in cell B14:=IRR(B8:B12)						
24	Entered value in cell C14:=IRR(C8:C12)						
25	Entered value in cell D14:=IRR(D8:D12)						
26							
27							

Sheet1 / Sheet2 / Sheet3

VIEWING THE *NPV–IRR* RELATIONSHIP: THE NET PRESENT VALUE PROFILE

Net present value profile A graph showing how a project's net present value changes as the discount rate changes.

Perhaps the easiest way to understand the relationship between the internal rate of return and the net present value is to view it graphically through the use of a **net present value profile**. A net present value profile is simply a graph showing how a project's net present value changes as the discount rate changes. To graph a project's net present value profile, you simply need to determine the project's net present value first using a zero percent discount rate, then slowly increase the discount rate until a representative curve has been plotted. How does the *IRR* enter into the net present value profile? The *IRR* is the discount rate at which the net present value is zero.

Let's look at an example of a project that involves an initial outlay of $105,517 with free cash flows expected to be $30,000 per year over the project's five-year life. Calculating the *NPV* of this project at several different discount rates results in the following:

DISCOUNT RATE	PROJECT'S *NPV*
0%	$44,483
5%	$24,367
10%	$ 8,207
13%	$ 0
15%	–$ 4,952
20%	–$15,799
25%	–$24,839

Plotting these values, we get the net present value profile in Figure 9-1.

Where is the *IRR* in this figure? Recall that the *IRR* is the discount rate that equates the present value of the inflows with the present value of the outflows; thus, the *IRR* is the point where the *NPV* is equal to zero. In this case, 13 percent.

From the net present value profile, you can easily see how a project's net present value varies inversely with the discount rate—as the discount rate is raised, the net present value

FIGURE 9-1 Net Present Value Profile

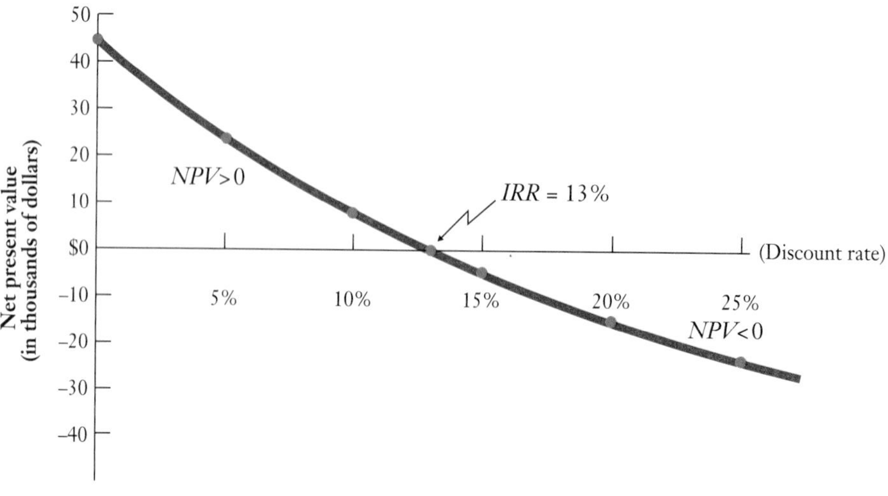

drops. From looking at a project's net present value profile, you can also see how sensitive the project is to your selection of the discount rate. The more sensitive the *NPV* is to the discount rate, the more important it is that you use the correct one in your calculations.

COMPLICATIONS WITH *IRR*: MULTIPLE RATES OF RETURN

Although any project can have only one *NPV* and one *PI*, a single project under certain circumstances can have more than one *IRR*. The reason for this can be traced to the calculations involved in determining the *IRR*. Equation 9-3 states that the *IRR* is the discount rate that equates the present value of the project's future free cash flows with the project's initial outlay:

$$IO = \sum_{t=1}^{n} \frac{FCF_t}{(1 + IRR)^t}$$

However, because equation 9-3 is a polynomial of a degree n, it has n solutions. Now if the initial outlay (IO) is the only negative cash flow and all the annual free cash flows (FCF_t) are positive, then all but one of these n solutions is either a negative or an imaginary number, and there is no problem. But problems occur when there are sign reversals in the cash flow stream; in fact, there can be as many solutions as there are sign reversals. A normal pattern with a negative initial outlay and positive annual free cash flows after that (−, +, +, . . . , +) has only one sign reversal, hence only one positive *IRR*. However, a pattern with more than one sign reversal can have more than one *IRR*.[2]

	FREE CASH FLOW
Initial outlay	−$ 1,600
Year 1	+$10,000
Year 2	−$10,000

In the preceding pattern of free cash flows, there are two sign reversals, from −$1,600 to +$10,000 and then from +$10,000 to −$10,000, so there can be as many as two positive *IRR*s that will make the present value of the future cash flows equal to the initial outlay. In fact, two internal rates of return solve this problem, 25 and 400 percent. Graphically, what we are solving for is the discount rate that makes the project's *NPV* equal to zero; as Figure 9-2 illustrates, this occurs twice.

Which solution is correct? The answer is that neither solution is valid. Although each fits the definition of *IRR*, neither provides any insight into the true project returns. In summary, when there is more than one sign reversal in the cash flow stream, the possibility of multiple *IRR*s exists, and the normal interpretation of the *IRR* loses its meaning. In this case, try the *NPV* criterion instead. See the "Focus on Harley-Davidson: Road Rules" box.

Modified internal rate of return (*MIRR*)
A variation of the *IRR* capital-budgeting decision criterion defined as the discount rate that equates the present value of the project's annual cash outlays with the present value of the project's terminal value, where the terminal value is defined as the sum of the future value of the project's free cash flows compounded to the project's termination at the project's required rate of return.

MODIFIED INTERNAL RATE OF RETURN

The primary drawback of the internal rate of return relative to the net present value method is the reinvestment rate assumption made by the internal rate of return. Recently, a new technique, the **modified internal rate of return (*MIRR*)**, has gained popularity as an alternative to the *IRR* method because it allows the decision maker to directly specify the

[2] This example is taken from James H. Lorie and Leonard J. Savage, "Three Problems in Rationing Capital," *Journal of Business* 28 (October 1955): 229–39.

FIGURE 9-2 Multiple *IRR*s

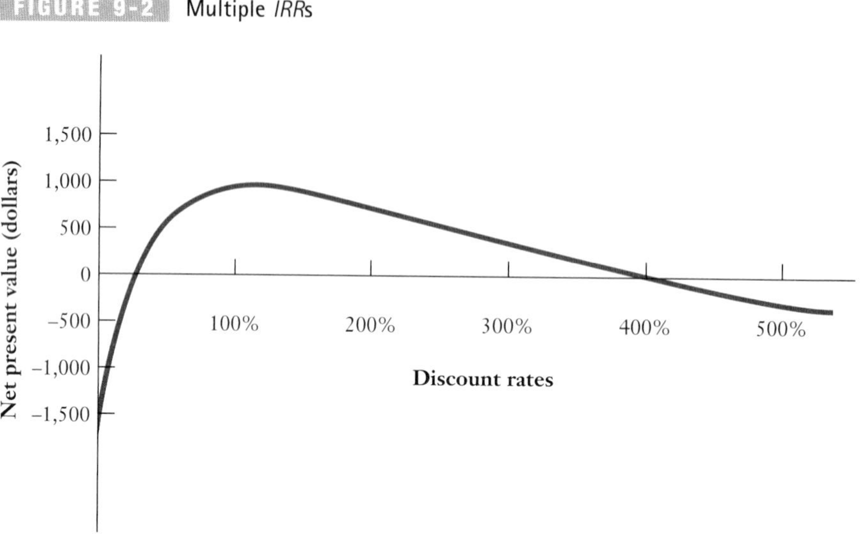

appropriate reinvestment rate. As a result, the *MIRR* provides the decision maker with the intuitive appeal of the *IRR* coupled with an improved reinvestment rate assumption.

The driving force behind the *MIRR* is the assumption that all free cash flows over the life of the project are reinvested at the required rate of return until the termination of the project. Thus, to calculate the *MIRR*, we take all the annual free cash *in*flows,

A FOCUS ON HARLEY-DAVIDSON

ROAD RULES

DECISION MAKING AT HARLEY-DAVIDSON—AN INTERVIEW WITH DAVE COTTELEER

Dave Cotteleer took his first finance class at Northern Illinois University, and in that class was introduced to discounted cash-flow decision techniques like net present value and the internal rate of return. Little did he know then that he would actually be using what he learned in that undergraduate finance course years later in his job as Manager for Planning and Control for Materials Management at Harley-Davidson, where he oversees major initiatives in materials management. As Dave says "It is vitally important to understand these techniques when making a multi-million dollar expenditure. To boil a decision down to its value today is critical."

As Manager for Planning and Control, the job of deciding whether or not to buy purchasing software for Harley fell into his lap. In the past, Harley had used different packages to handle purchasing in different parts of the firm. The software package that Harley was considering was extremely comprehensive in nature, overseeing purchasing for all areas of Harley business. It would result in common systems across the company that would reduce support and maintenance costs in addition to reducing the amount of integration needed.

How did Dave go about making this decision? His first task was to identify all the benefits to Harley from the system being considered. That meant asking the purchasing people to identify any and all benefits and the timing of those benefits. For example, if this purchasing software allowed for inventory to be reduced by 30 percent, what was the timing of that 30 percent reduction? Once the benefits and their timing were identified, they were quantified. Finally, the costs of the purchase and installation of the software and the timing of those costs had to be identified, since all costs weren't expected to occur at the same time. Once this was done, these cash flows were discounted back to the present and the final decision was made. What is the key to making good decisions? A strong understanding of basic finance and capital budgeting. As Dave Cotteleer says, "Finance is in everything—in marketing, purchasing, management, production and accounting. You've got to understand it if you're to be successful."

$ACIF_t$s, and find their future value at the end of the project's life, compounded at the required rate of return. We will call this the project's *terminal value*, or *TV*. We then calculate the present value of the project's free cash *outflows*. We do this by discounting all free cash *outflows*, $ACOF_t$, back to the present at the required rate of return. If the initial outlay is the only free cash *outflow*, then the initial outlay is the present value of the free cash *outflows*. The *MIRR* is the discount rate that equates the present value of the free cash *outflows* with the present value of the project's *terminal value*.[3] Mathematically, the modified internal rate of return is defined as the value of *MIRR* in the following equation:

$$PV_{outflows} = PV_{inflows}$$

$$\sum_{t=0}^{n} \frac{ACOF_t}{(1+k)^t} = \frac{\sum_{t=0}^{n} ACIF_t(1+k)^{n-t}}{(1+MIRR)^n} \tag{9-4}$$

$$PV_{outflows} = \frac{TV}{(1+MIRR)^n}$$

where $ACOF_t$ = the annual free cash *outflow* in time period t
$ACIF_t$ = the annual free *inflow* in time period t
TV = the terminal value of the *ACIF*s compounded at the required rate of return to the end of the project
n = the project's expected life
$MIRR$ = the project's modified internal rate of return
k = the appropriate discount rate; that is, the required rate of return or cost of capital

EXAMPLE: CALCULATING THE MIRR

Let's look at an example of a project with a three-year life and a required rate of return of 10 percent assuming the following cash flows are associated with it:

	FREE CASH FLOWS		FREE CASH FLOWS
Initial outlay	−$6,000	Year 2	$3,000
Year 1	2,000	Year 3	4,000

The calculation of the *MIRR* can be viewed as a three-step process, which is also shown graphically in Figure 9-3.

Step 1. Determine the present value of the project's free cash *outflows*. In this case, the only *outflow* is the initial outlay of $6,000, which is already at the present, thus it becomes the present value of the cash *outflows*.

(continued)

[3] You will notice that we differentiate between annual cash *inflows* and annual cash *outflows*, compounding all the *inflows* to the end of the project and bringing all the *outflows* back to the present as part of the present value of the costs. Although there are alternative definitions of the *MIRR*, this is the most widely accepted definition. For an excellent discussion of the *MIRR*, see William R. McDaniel, Daniel E. McCarty, and Kenneth A. Jessell, "Discounted Cash Flow with Explicit Reinvestment Rates: Tutorial and Extension," *The Financial Review* (August 1988): 369–85.

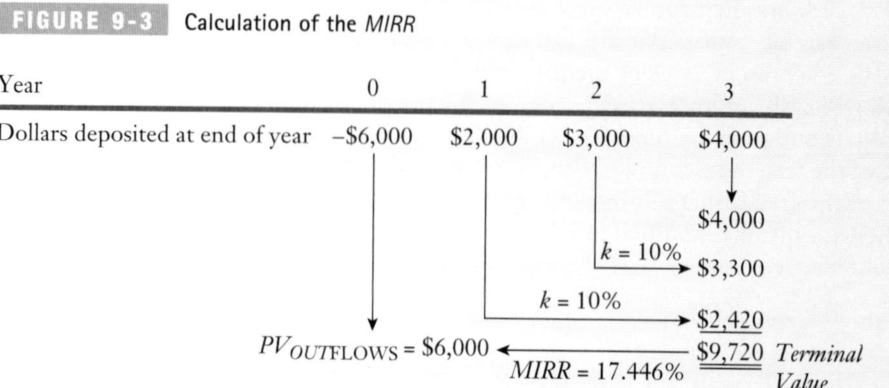

FIGURE 9-3 Calculation of the *MIRR*

Step 2. Determine the terminal value of the project's free cash *in*flows. To do this, we merely use the project's required rate of return to calculate the future value of the project's three cash *in*flows at the termination of the project. In this case, the *terminal value* becomes $9,720.

Step 3. Determine the discount rate that equates the present value of the *terminal value* and the present value of the project's cash *out*flows. Thus the *MIRR* is calculated to be 17.446 percent.

For our example, the calculations are as follows:

$$\$6{,}000 = \frac{\sum_{t=1}^{3} ACIF_t(1+k)^{n-t}}{(1+MIRR)^n}$$

$$\$6{,}000 = \frac{\$2{,}000\,(1+.10)^2 + \$3{,}000\,(1+.10)^1 + \$4{,}000\,(1+.10)^0}{(1+MIRR)^3}$$

$$\$6{,}000 = \frac{\$2{,}420 + \$3{,}300 + \$4{,}000}{(1+MIRR)^3}$$

$$\$6{,}000 = \frac{\$9{,}720}{(1+MIRR)^3}$$

$$MIRR = 17.446\%$$

Thus, the *MIRR* for this project (17.446 percent) is less than its *IRR*, which comes out to 20.614 percent. In this case, it only makes sense that the *IRR* should be greater than the *MIRR*, because the *IRR* allows intermediate cash *in*flows to grow at the *IRR* rather than the required rate of return.

In terms of decision rules, if the project's *MIRR* is greater than or equal to the project's required rate of return, then the project should be accepted; if not, it should be rejected:

MIRR ≥ required rate of return: Accept
MIRR < required rate of return: Reject

Because of the frequent use of the *IRR* in the real world as a decision-making tool and its limiting reinvestment rate assumption, the *MIRR* has become increasingly popular as an alternative decision-making tool.

SPREADSHEETS AND THE MODIFIED INTERNAL RATE OF RETURN

As with other financial calculations using a spreadsheet, calculating the *MIRR* is extremely simple. The only difference between this calculation and that of the traditional *MIRR* is that with a spreadsheet you also have the option of specifying both a *financing rate* and a *reinvestment rate*. The financing rate refers to the rate at which you borrow the money needed for the investment, while the reinvestment rate is the rate at which you reinvest the cash flows. Generally, it is assumed that these two values are one and the same. Thus, we enter in the value of *k*, the appropriate discount rate, for both of these values. Once the cash flows have been entered on the spreadsheet, all you need to do is input the Excel *MIRR* formula into a spreadsheet cell and let the spreadsheet do the calculations for you. Of course, as with the *IRR* calculation, at least one of the cash flows must be positive and at least one must be negative. The *MIRR* formula to be input into a spreadsheet cell is: **=*MIRR*(values,finance rate,reinvestment rate)**, where values is simply the range of cells where the cash flows are stored, and *k* is entered for both the finance rate and the reinvestment rate.

Expt opp loss - expected opportunity loss (EOL) is the cost of not picking the best solution.

Using a Spreadsheet to Calculate the MIRR

Looking back on the previous example, we can also calculate the MIRR using a spreadsheet. However, with a spreadsheet you also have the option of specifying both a financing rate and a reinvestment rate. The *financing rate* would be the rate you borrow the money you need for the investment, while the *reinvestment rate* is the rate at which you reinvest the cash flows. In our calculations we assume these values to be identical. Thus we will put *k*, the appropriate discount rate in for both of these values. Going back to the previous example:

Year	Cash Flow
Initial Outlay	($6,000)
1	2,000
2	3,000
3	4,000

MIRR = 17.446%

Excel formula: =MIRR(values, finance rate, reinvestment rate)

Entered value in cell C20: =MIRR(C15:C18,10%,10%)

where:

values = the range of cells where the cash flows are stored. Note: There must be at least one positive and one negative cash flow.

finance rate = the rate at which you borrow the money needed for the investment. Generally assumed to be *k*.

reinvestment rate = the reinvestment rate. Generally assumed to be *k*.

CONCEPT CHECK

1. Provide an intuitive definition of an internal rate of return for a project.
2. What does a net present value profile tell you and how is it constructed?
3. What is the difference between the *IRR* and the *MIRR*?
4. Why do the net present value and profitability index always give the same accept or reject decision for any project?

Objective 6

ETHICS IN CAPITAL BUDGETING

Although it may not seem obvious, ethics has a role in capital budgeting. Any actions that violate ethical standards can cause a loss of trust, which can, in turn, have a negative and long-lasting effect on the firm. The Finance Matters box "Bad Apple for Baby" outlines one such violation. In this case, it deals with ethical lapses at Beech-Nut and demonstrates the consequences of those actions. No doubt the decisions of the Beech-Nut executives were meant to create wealth, but in fact, they cost Beech-Nut tremendously.

FINANCE MATTERS — ETHICS

BAD APPLE FOR BABY

When we introduced **Principle 10: Ethical Behavior Is Doing the Right Thing, and Ethical Dilemmas Are Everywhere in Finance** in Chapter 1, we noted that acting in an ethical manner is not only morally correct, but that it is congruent with our goal of maximization of shareholder wealth. In this case, we can directly relate unethical behavior to a loss of shareholder wealth.

It's a widely held, but hard-to-prove belief that a company gains because it is perceived as more socially responsive than its competitors. Over the years, the three major manufacturers of baby food—Gerber Products, Beech-Nut Nutrition, and H. J. Heinz—had, with almost equal success, gone out of their way to build an image of respectability.

Theirs is an almost perfect zero-sum business. They know, at any given time, how many babies are being born. They all pay roughly the same price for their commodities, and their manufacturing and distribution costs are almost identical. So how does one company gain a market share edge over another, especially in a stagnant or declining market?

The answer for Beech-Nut was to sell a cheaper, adulterated product. Beginning in 1977, the company began buying a chemical concoction, made up mostly of sugar and water, and labeling it as apple juice. Sales of that product brought Beech-Nut an estimated $60 million between 1977 and 1982, while reducing material costs about $250,000 annually.

When various investigators tried to do something about it, the company stonewalled. Among other things, they shipped the bogus juice out of a plant in New York to Puerto Rico, to put it beyond the jurisdiction of federal investigators, and they even offered the juice as a give-away to reduce their stocks after they were finally forced to discontinue selling it.

In the end, the company pleaded guilty to 215 counts of introducing adulterated food into commerce and violating the Federal Food, Drug, and Cosmetic Act. The FDA fined Beech-Nut $2 million.

In addition, Beech-Nut's president, Neils Hoyvald, and its vice president of operations, John Lavery, were found guilty of similar charges. Each were sentenced to a year and one day in jail and a $100,000 fine.

Why did they do it? The Fort Washington, Pa.-based company will not comment. But perhaps some portion of motive can be inferred from a report Hoyvald wrote to Nestle, the company which had acquired Beech-Nut in the midst of his cover-up. "It is our feeling that we can report safely now that the apple juice recall has been completed. If the recall had been effectuated in early June [when the FDA had first ordered it], over 700,000 cases in inventory would have been affected; due to our many delays, we were only faced with having to destroy 20,000 cases."

One thing is clear: Two executives of a company with an excellent reputation breached a trust and did their company harm.

The most damaging event a business can suffer is a loss of the public's confidence in its ethical standards. In the financial world, we have seen this happen with the insider trading scandal at Drexel Burnham Lambert that brought down the firm and at Bridgestone/Firestone when it kept silent about problems with ATX and Wilderness tires, used mainly on Ford Explorers. At Beech-Nut, the loss in consumer confidence that accompanied this scandal resulted in a drop of Beech-Nut's share of the overall baby food market from 19.1 percent to 15.8 percent. Thus, although this violation of ethics resulted in a short-run gain for Beech-Nut, much more was lost in the long run for many years to come.

Source: Stephen Kindel, "Bad Apple for Baby," *Financial World* (June 27, 1989): 48. Reprinted by permission.

BACK TO THE PRINCIPLES

*Ethics and ethical considerations continually crop up when capital-budgeting decisions are being made. This brings us back to the fundamental **Principle 10: Ethical Behavior Is Doing the Right Thing, and Ethical Dilemmas Are Everywhere in Finance.** As "Bad Apple for Baby" points out, the most damaging event a business can experience is a loss of the public's confidence in its ethical standards. In making capital-budgeting decisions we must be aware of this, and that ethical behavior is doing the right thing and it is the right thing to do.*

A GLANCE AT ACTUAL CAPITAL-BUDGETING PRACTICES

Objective 7

During the past 50 years, the popularity of each of the capital-budgeting methods has shifted rather dramatically. In the 1950s and 1960s, the payback period method dominated capital budgeting; but through the 1970s and 1980s, the internal rate of return and the net present value techniques slowly gained in popularity until they are today used by virtually all major corporations in decision making. Table 9-11 provides the results of a survey of the 100 largest Fortune 500 firms, showing the popularity of the internal rate of return and net present value methods.

Interestingly, although most firms use the *NPV* and *IRR* as their primary techniques, most firms also use the payback period as a secondary decision method for capital budgeting. In a sense, they are using the payback period to control for risk. The logic behind this is that the payback period dramatically emphasizes early cash flows, which are presumably more certain—that is, have less risk—than cash flows occurring later in a project's life. Managers believe its use will lead to projects with more certain cash flows.

A reliance on the payback period came out even more dramatically in a study of the capital-budgeting practices of 12 large manufacturing firms.[4] This study also showed that, although the discounted cash flow methods are used at most firms, the simple payback criterion was the measure relied on primarily in one-third of the firms examined. The use of the payback period seemed to be even more common for smaller projects, with firms severely simplifying the discounted cash flow analysis or relying primarily on the payback period. Thus, although discounted cash flow decision techniques have become more widely accepted, their use depends to an extent on the size of the project.

[4] Marc Ross, "Capital Budgeting Practices of Twelve Large Manufacturers," *Financial Management* 15 (Winter 1986): 15–22.

TABLE 9-11 1992 Survey of Capital-Budgeting Practices of the 100 Largest Fortune 500 Industrial Firms

	PERCENT OF FIRMS		
INVESTMENT EVALUATION METHODS USED	A PRIMARY METHOD	A SECONDARY METHOD	TOTAL USING THIS METHOD
Internal rate of return	88%	11%	99%
Net present value	63%	22%	85%
Payback period	24%	59%	83%
Profitability index	15%	18%	33%

Source: "Capital Budgeting in 1992: A Survey," Harold Bierman, Jr., *Financial Management* (Autumn 1993). Reprinted by permission of Harold J. Bierman, Jr. and the Financial Management Association, International, University of South Florida, College of Business Administration #3331, Tampa, FL 33620, (813)974-2084.

CONCEPT CHECK

1. What capital-budgeting criteria seem to be used most frequently in the real world? Why do you think this is so?

The Multinational Firm: Capital Budgeting

Without question, the key to success in capital budgeting is to identify good projects, and for many companies, these good projects are found overseas. Just look at the success that Coca-Cola has had in the international markets, with over 80 percent of its beverage profit coming from foreign markets and earning more in Japan than in the United States. This success abroad also holds true for Exxon, which earns over half its profits from abroad and is involved in gas and oil exploration projects in West Africa, the Caspian Sea, Russia, the Gulf of Mexico, and South America.

But how do you enter those markets initially? One approach that has been used successfully is through international joint ventures or strategic alliances. Under these arrangements, two or more corporations merge their skills and resources on a specific project, trading things like technology and access to marketing channels. For example, GM and Suzuki Motors recently announced a strategic alliance that will provide Suzuki with access to Europe, North America, South America, and Africa, where GM has a strong presence, and provide GM with access to the Asia Pacific region, where Suzuki is well-established. As John F. Smith, Jr., the GM Chairman and CEO, said at the announcement of this joint venture, "Each company has specific competencies and market strengths, which can be better leveraged to the mutual benefit of both parties through this agreement."

An example of a successful market penetration using joint ventures is that of the U.S. oil giant Armco, which formed a joint venture with Mitsubishi to sell Armco's lightweight plastics in Japan. Similarly, Georgia Pacific and Canfor Japan Corporation recently announced a joint venture in which Georgia Pacific will gain access to Canfor's marketing expertise in Japan to sell pulp and paper products there. H. J. Heinz Co. announced a joint venture with an Indonesian firm to gain access to its Indonesian marketing channels. Joint ventures also provide a way to get around trade barriers. For example, India and Mexico require joint ventures for entry into their markets. As a result, U.S. firms like Apple Computer and Hewlett-Packard have been forced to enter into Mexican joint ventures in order to be allowed to ship their products into Mexico.

What is the alternative to not looking abroad for projects? It is losing out on potential revenues. Keep in mind that firms like Xerox, Hewlett-Packard, Dow Chemical, IBM, and Gillette all earn more than 50 percent of their profits from sales abroad. International boundaries no longer apply in finance.

CONCEPT CHECK

1. What methods do corporations use to enter the international markets?

HOW FINANCIAL MANAGERS USE THIS MATERIAL

Without taking on new projects, a company simply wouldn't continue to exist. For example, Smith-Corona's inability to come up with a product to replace the typewriters that it produced resulted in that company going under in 1996. Finding new profitable projects and correctly evaluating them are central to the firm's continued existence—and that's what capital budgeting is all about. It may be your decision to buy a Burger King franchise and open a Burger King restaurant. Or you may decide to help in Burger King's introduction of the Big King, a new burger that looks an awful lot like the Big Mac, or new fries that are crispier. Whatever your decision, when you're making an investment in fixed assets, it's a capital-budgeting decision. It may also involve taking a product that didn't work and trying to redesign it in such a way that it does. That's what 3Com Corporation did with the Palm Pilot electronic datebook and scheduler, which succeeded with small size and simplicity where Apple's Newton and Motorola's Envoy failed.

Much of what is done within a business involves the capital-budgeting process. Many times it's referred to as strategic planning, but it generally involves capital-budgeting decisions. You may be involved in market research dealing with a proposed new product, on its marketing plan, or in analyzing its costs—these are all part of the capital-budgeting process. Once all this information has been gathered, it is analyzed using the techniques and tools that we have presented in this chapter. Actually, almost any decision can be analyzed using the framework we presented here. That's because the net present value method "values" the project under consideration. That is, it looks at the present value of its benefits relative to the present value of its costs, and if the present value of the benefits outweighs the costs, the project is accepted. That's a pretty good decision rule, and it can be applied to any decision a business faces.

SUMMARY

Before a profitable project can be adopted, it must be identified or found. Unfortunately, coming up with ideas for new products, for ways to improve existing products, or for ways to make existing products more profitable is extremely difficult. In general, the best source of ideas for these new, potentially profitable products is found within the firm.

Objective 1

The process of capital budgeting involves decision making with respect to investment in fixed assets. We examine five commonly used criteria for determining the acceptance or rejection of capital-budgeting proposals. The first method, the payback period, does not incorporate the time value of money into its calculations, although a variation of it, the discounted payback period, does. The discounted methods, net present value, profitability index, internal rate of return, and MIRR do account for the time value of money. These methods are summarized in Table 9-12.

TABLE 9-12 Capital-Budgeting Criteria

Objective 2

1. A. Payback period = number of years required to recapture the initial investment

   Accept if payback ≤ maximum acceptable payback period
   Reject if payback > maximum acceptable payback period

   Advantages:
   - Uses free cash flows
   - Is easy to calculate and understand
   - May be used as rough screening device

   Disadvantages:
   - Ignores the time value of money
   - Ignores free cash flows occurring after the payback period
   - Selection of the maximum acceptable payback period is arbitrary

(continued)

TABLE 9-12 Continued

B. Discounted payback period = the number of years needed to recover the initial cash outlay from the *discounted free cash flows*

Accept if discounted payback ≤ maximum acceptable discounted payback period
Reject if discounted payback > maximum acceptable discounted payback period

Advantages:
- Uses free cash flows
- Is easy to calculate and understand
- Considers time value of money

Disadvantages:
- Ignores free cash flows occurring after the discounted payback period
- Selection of the maximum acceptable discounted payback period is arbitrary

Objective 3

2. Net present value = present value of the annual free cash flows less the investment's initial outlay

$$NPV = \sum_{t=1}^{n} \frac{FCF_t}{(1+k)^t} - IO$$

where FCF_t = the annual free cash flow in time period t (this can take on either positive or negative values)
k = the appropriate discount rate; that is, the required rate of return or the cost of capital
IO = the initial cash outlay
n = the project's expected life

Accept if $NPV \geq 0.0$
Reject if $NPV < 0.0$

Advantages:
- Uses free cash flows
- Recognizes the time value of money
- Is consistent with the firm's goal of shareholder wealth maximization

Disadvantages:
- Requires detailed long-term forecasts of a project's free cash flows
- Sensitivity to the choice of the discount rate

Objective 4

3. Profitability index = the ratio of the present value of the future free cash flows to the initial outlay

$$PI = \frac{\sum_{t=1}^{n} \frac{FCF_t}{(1+k)^t}}{IO}$$

Accept if $PI \geq 1.0$
Reject if $PI < 1.0$

Advantages:
- Uses free cash flows
- Recognizes the time value of money
- Is consistent with the firm's goal of shareholder wealth maximization

Disadvantages:
- Requires detailed long-term forecasts of a project's free cash flows

Objective 5

4. Internal rate of return = the discount rate that equates the present value of the project's future free cash flows with the project's initial outlay

$$IO = \sum_{t=1}^{n} \frac{FCF_t}{(1+IRR)^t}$$

where IRR = the project's internal rate of return

Accept if $IRR \geq$ the required rate of return
Reject if $IRR <$ the required rate of return

(continued)

TABLE 9-12 Continued

Advantages:
- Uses free cash flows
- Recognizes the time value of money
- Is in general consistent with the firm's goal of shareholder wealth maximization

Disadvantages:
- Requires detailed long-term forecasts of a project's free cash flows
- Possibility of multiple *IRR*s
- Assumes cash flows over the life of the project are reinvested at the *IRR*

5. Modified internal rate of return = the discount rate that equates the present value of the project's cash *out*flows with the present value of the project's *terminal value*

$$\sum_{t=0}^{n} \frac{ACOF_t}{(1+k)^t} = \frac{\sum_{t=0}^{n} ACIF_t(1+k)^{n-t}}{(1+MIRR)^n}$$

$$PV_{\text{outflows}} = \frac{TV}{(1+MIRR)^n}$$

where $ACOF_t$ = the annual free cash *out*flow in time period t
$ACIF_t$ = the annual free cash *in*flow in time period t
TV = the terminal value of *ACIF*s compounded at the required rate of return to the end of the project

Accept if $MIRR \geq$ the required rate of return
Reject if $MIRR <$ the required rate of return

Advantages:
- Uses free cash flows
- Recognizes the time value of money
- In general, is consistent with the goal of maximization of shareholder wealth

Disadvantages:
- Requires detailed long-term forecasts of a project's free cash flows

Objective 6

Ethics and ethical decisions crop up in capital budgeting. Just as with all other areas of finance, violating ethical considerations results in a loss of public confidence, which can have a significant negative effect on shareholder wealth.

Objective 7

Over the past 40 years, the discounted capital-budgeting decision criteria have continued to gain in popularity and today dominate in the decision-making process.

KEY TERMS

Capital budgeting, 290

Discounted payback period, 293

Internal rate of return (*IRR*), 299

Modified internal rate of return (*MIRR*), 307

Net present value (*NPV*), 295

Net present value profile, 306

Payback period, 292

Profitability index (*PI*) (or benefit/cost ratio), 298

Go To:
www.prenhall.com/keown
for downloads and current events associated with this chapter

STUDY QUESTIONS

9-1. Why is the capital-budgeting decision so important? Why are capital-budgeting errors so costly?

9-2. What are the criticisms of the use of the payback period as a capital-budgeting technique? What are its advantages? Why is it so frequently used?

9-3. In some countries, expropriation of foreign investments is a common practice. If you were considering an investment in one of those countries, would the use of the payback period criterion seem more reasonable than it otherwise might? Why?

9-4. Briefly compare and contrast the *NPV*, *PI*, and *IRR* criteria. What are the advantages and disadvantages of using each of these methods?

9-5. What is the advantage of using the *MIRR* as opposed to the *IRR* decision criteria?

SELF-TEST PROBLEMS

ST-1. You are considering a project that will require an initial outlay of $54,200. This project has an expected life of five years and will generate after-tax cash flows to the company as a whole of $20,608 at the end of each year over its five-year life. In addition to the $20,608 free cash flow from operations during the fifth and final year, there will be an additional cash inflow of $13,200 at the end of the fifth year associated with the salvage value of a machine, making the cash flow in year 5 equal to $33,808. Thus, the free cash flows associated with this project look like this:

YEAR	FREE CASH FLOW	YEAR	FREE CASH FLOW
0	−$54,200	3	$20,608
1	20,608	4	20,608
2	20,608	5	33,808

Given a required rate of return of 15 percent, calculate the following:

- **a.** Payback period
- **b.** Net present value
- **c.** Profitability index
- **d.** Internal rate of return

Should this project be accepted?

STUDY PROBLEMS (SET A)

9-1A. (IRR *calculation*) Determine the internal rate of return on the following projects:

- **a.** An initial outlay of $10,000 resulting in a single free cash flow of $17,182 after 8 years
- **b.** An initial outlay of $10,000 resulting in a single free cash flow of $48,077 after 10 years
- **c.** An initial outlay of $10,000 resulting in a single free cash flow of $114,943 after 20 years
- **d.** An initial outlay of $10,000 resulting in a single free cash flow of $13,680 after 3 years

9-2A. (IRR *calculation*) Determine the internal rate of return on the following projects:

- **a.** An initial outlay of $10,000 resulting in a free cash flow of $1,993 at the end of each year for the next 10 years
- **b.** An initial outlay of $10,000 resulting in a free cash flow of $2,054 at the end of each year for the next 20 years
- **c.** An initial outlay of $10,000 resulting in a free cash flow of $1,193 at the end of each year for the next 12 years
- **d.** An initial outlay of $10,000 resulting in a free cash flow of $2,843 at the end of each year for the next 5 years

9-3A. (IRR *calculation*) Determine the internal rate of return to the nearest percent on the following projects:

- **a.** An initial outlay of $10,000 resulting in a free cash flow of $2,000 at the end of year 1, $5,000 at the end of year 2, and $8,000 at the end of year 3
- **b.** An initial outlay of $10,000 resulting in a free cash flow of $8,000 at the end of year 1, $5,000 at the end of year 2, and $2,000 at the end of year 3
- **c.** An initial outlay of $10,000 resulting in a free cash flow of $2,000 at the end of years 1 through 5 and $5,000 at the end of year 6

9-4A. (NPV, PI, *and* IRR *calculations*) Fijisawa, Inc., is considering a major expansion of its product line and has estimated the following free cash flows associated with such an expansion. The initial outlay associated with the expansion would be $1,950,000, and the project would generate free cash flows of $450,000 per year for six years. The appropriate required rate of return is 9 percent.

- **a.** Calculate the net present value.
- **b.** Calculate the profitability index.
- **c.** Calculate the internal rate of return.
- **d.** Should this project be accepted?

9-5A. (*Payback period, net present value, profitability index, and internal rate of return calculations*) You are considering a project with an initial cash outlay of $80,000 and expected free cash flows of $20,000 at the end of each year for six years. The required rate of return for this project is 10 percent.

- **a.** What are the project's payback and discounted payback periods?
- **b.** What is the project's *NPV?*
- **c.** What is the project's *PI?*
- **d.** What is the project's *IRR?*

9-6A. (*Net present value, profitability index, and internal rate of return calculations*) You are considering two independent projects, project A and project B. The initial cash outlay associated with project A is $50,000 and the initial cash outlay associated with project B is $70,000. The required rate of return on both projects is 12 percent. The expected annual free cash flows from each project are as follows:

YEAR	PROJECT A	PROJECT B
0	–$50,000	–$70,000
1	12,000	13,000
2	12,000	13,000
3	12,000	13,000
4	12,000	13,000
5	12,000	13,000
6	12,000	13,000

Calculate the *NPV, PI,* and *IRR* for each project and indicate if the project should be accepted.

9-7A. (*Payback period calculations*) You are considering three independent projects, project A, project B, and project C. The required rate of return is 10 percent on each. Given the following free cash flow information, calculate the payback period and discounted payback period for each.

YEAR	PROJECT A	PROJECT B	PROJECT C
0	–$1,000	–$10,000	–$5,000
1	600	5,000	1,000
2	300	3,000	1,000
3	200	3,000	2,000
4	100	3,000	2,000
5	500	3,000	2,000

If you require a three-year payback for both the traditional and discounted payback period methods before an investment can be accepted, which projects would be accepted under each criterion?

9-8A. (NPV *with varying rates of return*) Dowling Sportswear is considering building a new factory to produce aluminum baseball bats. This project would require an initial cash outlay of $5,000,000 and will generate annual free cash inflows of $1 million per year for eight years. Calculate the project's *NPV* given:

a. A required rate of return of 9 percent
b. A required rate of return of 11 percent
c. A required rate of return of 13 percent
d. A required rate of return of 15 percent

9-9A. (*Internal rate of return calculations*) Given the following free cash flows, determine the internal rate of return for the three independent projects A, B, and C.

	PROJECT A	PROJECT B	PROJECT C
Initial Investment:	–$50,000	–$100,000	–$450,000
Cash Inflows:			
Year 1	$10,000	$ 25,000	$200,000
Year 2	15,000	25,000	200,000
Year 3	20,000	25,000	200,000
Year 4	25,000	25,000	–
Year 5	30,000	25,000	–

9-10A. (NPV *with varying required rates of return*) Big Steve's, makers of swizzle sticks, is considering the purchase of a new plastic stamping machine. This investment requires an initial outlay of $100,000 and will generate free cash inflows of $18,000 per year for 10 years. For each of the listed required rates of return, determine the project's net present value.

a. The required rate of return is 10 percent.
b. The required rate of return is 15 percent.
c. Would the project be accepted under part (a) or (b)?
d. What is this project's internal rate of return?

9-11A. (MIRR *calculation*) Emily's Soccer Mania is considering building a new plant. This project would require an initial cash outlay of $10 million and will generate annual free cash inflows of $3 million per year for 10 years.

Calculate the project's *MIRR*, given:

a. A required rate of return of 10 percent
b. A required rate of return of 12 percent
c. A required rate of return of 14 percent

WEB WORKS

In 2000, after a major investment and three years of development, Harley-Davidson introduced the Buell Blast. This fun-to-ride, sporty motorcycle was low-cost, lightweight, and aimed directly at 18- to 34-year-old Generation X-ers in the hopes of bringing a new generation of customers into motorcycling. That's because Harley was facing a problem—its customer base was rapidly aging. In fact, over the past 10 years the average age of a Harley rider has risen from 38 to 46. In addition, Harley wanted to add more women to its customer base, and it accomplished this through its Buell motorcycle division. These smaller, sportier, less expensive motorcycles are more appropriate for less experienced motorcyclists. It is Harley's hope that once these new customers find the fun in motorcycling, they will eventually graduate to Harleys.

Take a look at the Harley-Davidson Web site (**www.harley-davidson.com**). What type of customer do you think the Harley-Davidson motorcycles appeal to? Now find the Buell Motorcycle Company Web site (**www.buell.com/en_us**). What type of customer do these motorcycles appeal to? What do you think of Harley's strategy?

INTEGRATIVE PROBLEM

Your first assignment in your new position as assistant financial analyst at Caledonia Products is to evaluate two new capital-budgeting proposals. Because this is your first assignment, you have been asked not only to provide a recommendation, but also to respond to a number of questions aimed at judging your understanding of the capital-budgeting process. This is a standard procedure for all new financial analysts at Caledonia and will serve to determine whether you are moved directly into the capital-budgeting analysis department or are provided with remedial training. The memorandum you received outlining your assignment follows:

TO: The New Financial Analysts

FROM: Mr. V. Morrison, CEO, Caledonia Products

RE: Capital-Budgeting Analysis

Provide an evaluation of two proposed projects, both with five-year expected lives and identical initial outlays of $110,000. Both of these projects involve additions to Caledonia's highly successful Avalon product line, and as a result, the required rate of return on both projects has been established at 12 percent. The expected free cash flows from each project are as follows:

	PROJECT A	PROJECT B
Initial Outlay	–$110,000	–$110,000
Year 1	20,000	40,000
Year 2	30,000	40,000
Year 3	40,000	40,000
Year 4	50,000	40,000
Year 5	70,000	40,000

In evaluating these projects, please respond to the following questions:

1. Why is the capital-budgeting process so important?
2. Why is it difficult to find exceptionally profitable projects?
3. What is the payback period on each project? If Caledonia imposes a three-year maximum acceptable payback period, which of these projects should be accepted?
4. What are the criticisms of the payback period?
5. What is the discounted payback period for each of these projects? If Caledonia requires a three-year maximum acceptable discounted payback period on new projects, which of these projects should be accepted?
6. What are the drawbacks or deficiencies of the discounted payback period? Do you feel either the payback or discounted payback period should be used to determine whether or not these projects should be accepted? Why or why not?
7. Determine the net present value for each of these projects. Should they be accepted?
8. Describe the logic behind the net present value.
9. Determine the profitability index for each of these projects. Should they be accepted?
10. Would you expect the net present value and profitability index methods to give consistent accept-reject decisions? Why or why not?
11. What would happen to the net present value and profitability index for each project if the required rate of return increased? If the required rate of return decreased?
12. Determine the internal rate of return for each project. Should they be accepted?
13. How does a change in the required rate of return affect the project's internal rate of return?
14. What reinvestment rate assumptions are implicitly made by the net present value and internal rate of return methods? Which one is better?
15. Determine the modified internal rate of return for each project. Should they be accepted? Do you feel it is a better evaluation technique than is the internal rate of return? Why or why not?

STUDY PROBLEMS (SET B)

9-1B. (IRR *calculation*) Determine the internal rate of return on the following projects:

a. An initial outlay of $10,000 resulting in a single cash flow of $19,926 after 8 years
b. An initial outlay of $10,000 resulting in a single cash flow of $20,122 after 12 years
c. An initial outlay of $10,000 resulting in a single cash flow of $121,000 after 22 years
d. An initial outlay of $10,000 resulting in a single cash flow of $19,254 after 5 years

9-2B. (IRR *calculation*) Determine the internal rate of return on the following projects:

a. An initial outlay of $10,000 resulting in a cash flow of $2,146 at the end of each year for the next 10 years

b. An initial outlay of $10,000 resulting in a cash flow of $1,960 at the end of each year for the next 20 years

c. An initial outlay of $10,000 resulting in a cash flow of $1,396 at the end of each year for the next 12 years

d. An initial outlay of $10,000 resulting in a cash flow of $3,197 at the end of each year for the next 5 years

9-3B. (IRR *calculation*) Determine the internal rate of return to the nearest percent on the following projects:

a. An initial outlay of $10,000 resulting in a cash flow of $3,000 at the end of year 1, $5,000 at the end of year 2, and $7,500 at the end of year 3

b. An initial outlay of $12,000 resulting in a cash flow of $9,000 at the end of year 1, $6,000 at the end of year 2, and $2,000 at the end of year 3

c. An initial outlay of $8,000 resulting in a cash flow of $2,000 at the end of years 1 through 5 and $5,000 at the end of year 6

9-4B. (NPV, PI, *and* IRR *calculations*) Gecewich, Inc., is considering a major expansion of its product line and has estimated the following cash flows associated with such an expansion. The initial outlay associated with the expansion would be $2,500,000 and the project would generate incremental free cash flows of $750,000 per year for six years. The appropriate required rate of return is 11 percent.

a. Calculate the net present value.

b. Calculate the profitability index.

c. Calculate the internal rate of return.

d. Should this project be accepted?

9-5B. (*Payback period, net present value, profitability index, and internal rate of return calculations*) You are considering a project with an initial cash outlay of $160,000 and expected free cash flows of $40,000 at the end of each year for six years. The required rate of return for this project is 10 percent.

a. What is the project's payback period?

b. What is the project's *NPV?*

c. What is the project's *PI?*

d. What is the project's *IRR?*

9-6B. (*Net present value, profitability index, and internal rate of return calculations*) You are considering two independent projects, project A and project B. The initial cash outlay associated with project A is $45,000, whereas the initial cash outlay associated with project B is $70,000. The required rate of return on both projects is 12 percent. The expected annual free cash inflows from each project are as follows:

YEAR	PROJECT A	PROJECT B	YEAR	PROJECT A	PROJECT B
0	–$45,000	–$70,000	4	$12,000	$14,000
1	12,000	14,000	5	12,000	14,000
2	12,000	14,000	6	12,000	14,000
3	12,000	14,000			

Calculate the *NPV, PI,* and *IRR* for each project and indicate if the project should be accepted.

9-7B. (*Payback period calculations*) You are considering three independent projects, project A, project B, and project C. Given the following free cash flow information, calculate the payback period for each.

YEAR	PROJECT A	PROJECT B	PROJECT C
0	–900	–$9,000	–$7,000
1	600	5,000	2,000
2	300	3,000	2,000
3	200	3,000	2,000
4	100	3,000	2,000
5	500	3,000	2,000

If you require a three-year payback period before an investment can be accepted, which projects would be accepted?

9-8B. (NPV *with varying required rates of return*) Mo-Lee's Sportswear is considering building a new factory to produce soccer equipment. This project would require an initial cash outlay of $10,000,000 and will generate annual free cash inflows of $2,500,000 per year for eight years. Calculate the project's *NPV* given:

- **a.** A required rate of return of 9 percent
- **b.** A required rate of return of 11 percent
- **c.** A required rate of return of 13 percent
- **d.** A required rate of return of 15 percent

9-9B. (*Internal rate of return calculations*) Given the following cash flows, determine the internal rate of return for projects A, B, and C.

YEAR	PROJECT A	PROJECT B	PROJECT C
Initial Investment:	–$75,000	–$95,000	–$395,000
Cash Inflows:			
Year 1	$10,000	$25,000	$150,000
Year 2	10,000	25,000	150,000
Year 3	30,000	25,000	150,000
Year 4	25,000	25,000	–
Year 5	30,000	25,000	–

9-10B. (NPV *with varying required rates of return*) Bert's, makers of gourmet corn dogs, is considering the purchase of a new corn dog "molding" machine. This investment requires an initial outlay of $150,000 and will generate free cash inflows of $25,000 per year for 10 years. For each of the listed required rates of return, determine the project's net present value.

- **a.** The required rate of return is 9 percent.
- **b.** The required rate of return is 15 percent.
- **c.** Would the project be accepted under part (a) or (b)?
- **d.** What is this project's internal rate of return?

9-11B. (MIRR *calculation*) Artie's Soccer Stuff is considering building a new plant. This plant would require an initial cash outlay of $8 million and will generate annual free cash inflows of $2 million per year for eight years. Calculate the project's *MIRR* given:

- **a.** A required rate of return of 10 percent
- **b.** A required rate of return of 12 percent
- **c.** A required rate of return of 14 percent

CASE PROBLEM

ETHICS

FORD'S PINTO

Ethics Case: The Value of Life

There was a time when the "made in Japan" label brought a predictable smirk of superiority to the face of most Americans. The quality of most Japanese products usually was as low as their price. In fact, few imports could match their domestic counterparts, the proud products of "Yankee know-how." But by the late 1960s, an invasion of foreign-made goods chiseled a few worry lines into the countenance of American industry. And in Detroit, worry was fast fading to panic as the Japanese, not to mention the Germans, began to gobble up more and more of the subcompact auto market.

Never one to take a back seat to the competition, Ford Motor Company decided to meet the threat from abroad head-on. In 1968, Ford executives decided to produce the Pinto. Known inside the company as "Lee's car," after Ford president Lee Iacocca, the Pinto was to weigh no more than 2,000 pounds and cost no more than $2,000.

Eager to have its subcompact ready for the 1971 model year, Ford decided to compress the normal drafting-board-to-showroom time of about three-and-a-half years into two. The compressed schedule meant that any design changes typically made before production-line tooling would have to be made during it.

Before producing the Pinto, Ford crash-tested 11 of them, in part to learn if they met the National Highway Traffic Safety Administration (NHTSA) proposed safety standard that all autos be able to withstand a fixed-barrier impact of 20 miles per hour without fuel loss. Eight standard-design Pintos failed the tests. The three cars that passed the test all had some kind of gas-tank modification. One had a plastic baffle between the front of the tank and the differential housing; the second had a piece of steel between the tank and the rear bumper; and the third had a rubber-lined gas tank.

Ford officials faced a tough decision. Should they go ahead with the standard design, thereby meeting the production time table but possibly jeopardizing consumer safety? Or should they delay production of the Pinto by redesigning the gas tank to make it safer and thus concede another year of subcompact dominance to foreign companies?

To determine whether to proceed with the original design of the Pinto fuel tank, Ford decided to use a capital-budgeting approach, examining the expected costs and the social benefits of making the change. Would the social benefits of a new tank design outweigh design costs, or would they not?

To find the answer, Ford had to assign specific values to the variables involved. For some factors in the equation, this posed no problem. The costs of design improvement, for example, could be estimated at $11 per vehicle. But what about human life? Could a dollar-and-cents figure be assigned to a human being?

NHTSA thought it could. It had estimated that society loses $200,725 every time a person is killed in an auto accident. It broke down the costs as follows:

FUTURE PRODUCTIVITY LOSSES	
Direct	$ 132,000
Indirect	41,300
MEDICAL COSTS	
Hospital	700
Other	425
Property damage	1,500
Insurance administration	4,700
Legal and court expenses	3,000
Employer losses	1,000
Victim's pain and suffering	10,000
Funeral	900
Assets (lost consumption)	5,000
Miscellaneous accident costs	200
Total per fatality	$200,725[a]

[a]Ralph Drayton, "One Manufacturer's Approach to Automobile Safety Standards," *CTLA News 8* (February 1968): 11.

Ford used NHTSA and other statistical studies in its cost-benefit analysis, which yielded the following estimates:

BENEFITS	
Savings:	180 burn deaths, 180 serious burn injuries, 2,100 burned vehicles
Unit cost:	$200,000 per death, $67,000 per injury, $700 per vehicle
Total benefit:	(180 × $200,000) + (180 × $67,000) + (2,100 × $700) = $49.5 million

COSTS	
Sales:	11 million cars, 1.5 million light trucks
Unit cost:	$11 per car, $11 per truck
Total cost:	12.5 million × $11 = $137.5 million[a]

[a]Mark Dowie, "Pinto Madness," *Mother Jones* (September–October 1977): 20. See also Russell Mokhiber, *Corporate Crime and Violence* (San Francisco: Sierra Club Books, 1988): 373–82, and Francis T. Cullen, William J. Maakestad, and Gary Cavender, *Corporate Crime Under Attack: The Ford Pinto Case and Beyond* (Cincinnati: Anderson Publishing, 1987).

Because the costs of the safety improvement outweighed its benefits, Ford decided to push ahead with the original design.

Here is what happened after Ford made this decision:

> Between 700 and 2,500 persons died in accidents involving Pinto fires between 1971 and 1978. According to sworn testimony of Ford engineer Harley Copp, 95 percent of them would have survived if Ford had located the fuel tank over the axle (as it had done on its Capri automobiles).
>
> NHTSA's standard was adopted in 1977. The Pinto then acquired a rupture-proof fuel tank. The following year Ford was obliged to recall all 1971–1976 Pintos for fuel-tank modifications.
>
> Between 1971 and 1978, approximately fifty lawsuits were brought against Ford in connection with rear-end accidents in the Pinto. In the Richard Grimshaw case, in addition to awarding over $3 million in compensatory damages to the victims of a Pinto crash, the jury awarded a landmark $125 million in punitive damages against Ford. The judge reduced punitive damages to $3.5 million.
>
> On August 10, 1978, eighteen-year-old Judy Ulrich, her sixteen-year-old sister Lynn, and their eighteen-year-old cousin Donna, in their 1973 Ford Pinto, were struck from the rear by a van near Elkhart, Indiana. The gas tank of the Pinto exploded on impact. In the fire that resulted, the three teenagers were burned to death. Ford was charged with criminal homicide. The judge presiding over the twenty-week trial advised jurors that Ford should be convicted if it had clearly disregarded the harm that might result from its actions and that disregard represented a substantial deviation from acceptable standards of conduct. On March 13, 1980, the jury found Ford not guilty of criminal homicide.

For its part, Ford has always denied that the Pinto is unsafe compared with other cars of its type and era. The company also points out that in every model year the Pinto met or surpassed the government's own standards. But what the company doesn't say is that successful lobbying by it and its industry associates was responsible for delaying for nine years the adoption of NHTSA's 20 miles-per-hour crash standard. And Ford critics claim that there were more than forty European and Japanese models in the Pinto price and weight range with a safer gas-tank position. "Ford made an extremely irresponsible decision," concludes auto safety expert Byron Bloch, "when they placed such a weak tank in such a ridiculous location in such a soft rear end."

Questions

1. Do you think Ford approached this question properly?
2. What responsibilities to its customers do you think Ford had? Were their actions ethically appropriate?

3. Would it have made a moral or ethical difference if the \$11 savings had been passed on to Ford's customers? Could a rational customer have chosen to save \$11 and risk the more dangerous gas tank? Would that have been similar to making air bags optional? What if Ford had told potential customers about its decision?
4. Should Ford have been found guilty of criminal homicide in the Ulrich case?
5. If you, as a financial manager at Ford, found out about what had been done, what would you do?

Source: Reprinted by permission from William Shaw and Vincent Barry, "Ford's Pinto," *Moral Issues in Business*, 6th ed. (New York: Wadsworth, 1995), 84–86. © by Wadsworth, Inc.

SELF-TEST SOLUTIONS

ST-1.

a. $$\text{Payback period} = \frac{\$54{,}000}{\$20{,}608} = 2.620 \text{ years}$$

b. $$\begin{aligned} NPV &= \sum_{t=1}^{n} \frac{FCF_t}{(1+k)^t} \\ &= \sum_{t=1}^{4} \frac{\$20{,}608}{(1+.15)^t} + \frac{\$33{,}808}{(1+.15)^5} - \$54{,}200 \\ &= \$20{,}608\,(2.855) + \$33{,}808\,(.497) - \$54{,}200 \\ &= \$58{,}836 + \$16{,}803 - \$54{,}200 \\ &= \$21{,}439 \end{aligned}$$

c. $$\begin{aligned} PI &= \frac{\sum_{t=1}^{n} \frac{FCF_t}{(1+k)^t}}{IO} \\ &= \frac{\$75{,}639}{\$54{,}200} \\ &= 1.396 \end{aligned}$$

d. $$IO = \sum_{t=1}^{n} \frac{FCF_t}{(1+IRR)^t}$$

$$\$54{,}200 = \$20{,}608\,(PVIFA_{IRR\%,4\text{yrs}}) + \$33{,}808\,(PVIF_{IRR\%,5\text{yrs}})$$

Try 29 percent:

$$\begin{aligned} \$54{,}200 &= \$20{,}608\,(2.203) + \$33{,}808\,(.280) \\ &= \$45{,}399 + \$9{,}466 \\ &= \$54{,}865 \end{aligned}$$

Try 30 percent:

$$\begin{aligned} \$54{,}200 &= \$20{,}608\,(2.166) + \$33{,}808\,(.269) \\ &= \$44{,}637 + \$9{,}094 \\ &= \$53{,}731 \end{aligned}$$

Thus, the *IRR* is just below 30 percent. The project should be accepted because the *NPV* is positive, the *PI* is greater than 1.0, and the *IRR* is greater than the required rate of return of 15 percent.

LEARNING OBJECTIVES

After reading this chapter, you should be able to

1. Identify the guidelines by which we measure cash flows.
2. Explain how a project's benefits and costs—that is, its incremental after-tax cash flows—are calculated.
3. Explain how the capital-budgeting decision process changes when a limit is placed on the dollar size of the capital budget, or there are mutually exclusive projects.

CHAPTER 10

Cash Flows and Other Topics in Capital Budgeting

A major capital-budgeting decision led Harley-Davidson to introduce the Buell Blast in 2000 and the Lightning Low XB95 in 2003. This multi-million dollar investment by Harley in smaller, lighter motorcycles designed for the new or novices rider who is not yet ready for the traditionally heavier Harley-Davidson bike was targeted directly at younger and female riders. Although this capital-budgeting decision may, on the surface, seem like a relatively simple decision, the forecasting of the expected cash flows associated with the Buell Blast were, in fact, quite complicated.

To begin with, Harley-Davidson had two goals in mind when it introduced the Buell Blast. First, it was trying to expand into a new market made up of Generation X-ers. Second, it wanted to expand the market for existing products by introducing more people to motorcycling. That is, the Buell Blast was meant to not only produce its own sales, but eventually result in increased sales in Harley's heavier cruiser and touring bikes as the Blast customers move up to these larger bikes. The Lightning Low was also aimed at bringing in new riders, specifically female riders.

While the motorcycle industry has enjoyed tremendous growth over the past 12 years with over 7 million riders out there now, representing an increase of 30 percent in just 12 years, the demographics of the motorcycle rider has changed considerably. In particular, the median age of a rider has risen 8 years over the past 12 years. This aging of the motorcycle-riding population played a major role in the decision to go forward with the Blast, and from early returns, it looks like it was, in fact, an excellent decision.

How exactly do you measure the cash flows that come from the introduction of a new product line? What do you do about cash flows that the new product brings to other product lines? In the previous chapter, we looked at decision criteria, assuming the cash flows were known. In this chapter, we will see how difficult and complex it is estimating those cash flows. We will also gain an understanding of what a relevant cash flow is. We will evaluate projects relative to their base case—that is, what will happen to the company as a whole if the project is not carried out. In the case of Harley's Buell Blast and Lightning Low, we will also look at the sales that these new products brought down the line to Harley's cruising and touring bikes. Did the introduction of the Buell Blast and Lightning Low result in eventual sales to Harley's other lines? What is the future level of cash flows to Harley-Davidson as a whole versus the level without the introduction of the Buell Blast and Lightning Low? Questions such as these lead us to an understanding of what are and what are not relevant cash flows. As you will see in the future, these questions are generally answered by those in marketing and management, but regardless of your area of concentration, they are important questions to understand.

CHAPTER PREVIEW

This chapter continues our discussion of decision rules for deciding whether to invest in new projects. First we will examine what is a relevant cash flow and how to calculate the relevant cash flow. This will be followed by a discussion of the problems created when the number of projects that can be accepted or the total budget is limited. This chapter will rely on **Principle 3: Cash—Not Profits—Is King, Principle 4: Incremental Cash Flows—It's only what changes that counts,** and **Principle 5: The Curse of Competitive Markets.** Be on the lookout for these important concepts.

Objective 1

GUIDELINES FOR CAPITAL BUDGETING

To evaluate investment proposals, we must first set guidelines by which we measure the value of each proposal. In effect, we will be deciding what is and what isn't a relevant cash flow.

USE FREE CASH FLOWS RATHER THAN ACCOUNTING PROFITS

We will use free cash flows, not accounting profits, as our measurement tool. The firm receives and is able to reinvest free cash flows, whereas accounting profits are shown when they are earned rather than when the money is actually in hand. Unfortunately, a firm's accounting profits and cash flows may not be timed to occur together. For example, capital expenses, such as vehicles and plant and equipment, are depreciated over several years, with their annual depreciation subtracted from profit. Free cash flows correctly reflect the timing of benefits and costs—that is, when the money is received, when it can be reinvested, and when it must be paid out.

BACK TO THE PRINCIPLES

If we are to make intelligent capital-budgeting decisions, we must accurately measure the timing of the benefits and costs, that is, when we receive money and when it leaves our hands. ***Principle 3: Cash—Not Profits—Is King*** *speaks directly to this. Remember, it is cash inflows that can be reinvested and cash outflows that involve paying out money.*

THINK INCREMENTALLY

Unfortunately, calculating cash flows from a project may not be enough. Decision makers must ask: What new cash flows will the company as a whole receive if the company takes on a given project? What if the company does not take on the project? Interestingly, we may find that not all cash flows a firm expects from an investment proposal are incremental in nature. In measuring cash flows, however, the trick is to *think* incrementally. In doing so, we will see that only *incremental after-tax cash flows* matter. As such, our guiding rule in deciding if a cash flow is incremental will be to look at the company with, versus without, the new product. These incremental after-tax cash flows to the company as a whole are many times referred to as *free cash flows.* As you will see in the upcoming sections, this may be easier said than done.

BACK TO THE PRINCIPLES

In order to measure the true effects of our decisions, we will analyze the benefits and costs of projects on an incremental basis, which relates directly to ***Principle 4: Incremental Cash Flows—It's only what changes that counts.*** *In effect, we will ask ourselves what the cash flows will be if the project is taken on versus what they will be if the project is not taken on.*

BEWARE OF CASH FLOWS DIVERTED FROM EXISTING PRODUCTS

Assume for a moment that we are managers of a firm considering a new product line that might compete with one of our existing products and possibly reduce its sales. In determining the cash flows associated with the proposed project, we should consider only the incremental sales brought to the company as a whole. New-product sales achieved at the cost of losing sales of other products in our line are not considered a benefit of adopting the new product. For example, when General Foods Post Cereal Division introduced its Dino Pebbles, the product competed directly with the company's Fruity Pebbles. (In fact, the two were actually the same product, with an addition to the former of dinosaur-shaped marshmallows.) Post meant to target the market niche held by Kellogg's Marshmallow Krispies, but there was no question that sales recorded by Dino Pebbles bit into—literally cannibalized—Post's existing product line.

Remember that we are only interested in the sales dollars to the firm if this project is accepted, as opposed to what the sales dollars would be if the project is rejected. Just moving sales from one product line to a new product line does not bring anything new into the company, but if sales are captured from our competitors or if sales that would have been lost to new competing products are retained, then these are relevant incremental cash flows. In each case, these are the incremental cash flows to the firm—looking at the firm as a whole with the new product versus without the new product.

Look for Incidental or Synergistic Effects

Although in some cases a new project may take sales away from a firm's current projects, in other cases a new effort may actually bring new sales to the existing line. For example, in 2000 GM's Pontiac division introduced the Aztek, an in-your-face looking sport-ute. The idea was not only to sell lots of Azteks, but also to help lure back young customers to Pontiac's other car lines. From 1994 until the introduction of the Aztek, the average age of Pontiac buyers had risen from 40 to 42. Thus, the hope was that Aztek would bring younger customers into showrooms, who would in turn either buy an Aztek, or lock onto another one of Pontiac's products. Thus, in evaluating the Aztek, if managers were to look only at the revenue from new Aztek sales, they would miss the incremental cash flow to Pontiac as a whole that results from new customers who would not have otherwise purchased a Pontiac automobile, but did so only after being lured into a Pontiac showroom to see an Aztek. This is called a *synergistic effect*. The cash flow comes from any Pontiac sale that would not have occurred if a customer had not visited a Pontiac showroom to see an Aztek.

This is very similar to what Harley-Davidson did with the Buell Blast and Lightning Low. This youth-oriented sports bike is not only intended to generate sales on its own, but also to serve as a feeder for Harley-Davidson's cruising and touring bikes, as Blast riders grow older and trade up. Thus, the incremental sales from the Buell Blast and Lightning Low can only be measured by looking at all cash flows that accrue to Harley-Davidson as a whole from its introduction. The bottom line: Any cash flow to any part of the company that may result from the decision at hand must be considered when making that decision.

Work in Working-Capital Requirements

Many times, a new project will involve additional investment in working capital. This may take the form of new inventory to stock a sales outlet, additional investment in accounts receivable resulting from additional credit sales, or increased investment in cash to operate additional cash registers, and more. For most projects, some of the funds to support the new level of working capital will come from money owed to suppliers (accounts receivable). Still, the firm will generally have to provide some funds to working capital. Working-capital requirements are considered a cash flow even though they do not leave the company. How can investment in inventory be considered a cash outflow when the goods are still in the store? Because the firm does not have access to the inventory's cash value, the firm cannot use the money for other investments. Generally, working-capital requirements are tied up over the life of the project. When the project terminates, there is usually an offsetting cash inflow as the working capital is recovered. (Although this offset is not perfect because of the time value of money.)

Consider Incremental Expenses

Just as cash inflows from a new project are measured on an incremental basis, expenses should also be measured on an incremental basis. For example, if introducing a new product line necessitates training the sales staff, the after-tax cash flow associated with the training program must be considered a cash outflow and charged against the project. If accepting a new project dictates that a production facility be reengineered, the after-tax cash flows associated with that capital investment should be charged against the project. Again, any incremental after-tax cash flow affecting the company as a whole is a relevant cash flow whether it is flowing in or flowing out.

For example, Harley-Davidson offered buyers of the Buell Blast a "Riders Edge" schooling program to help them learn how to drive a motorcycle safely and minimize any fear of the unknown. The idea here is, of course, to make it easier for nonriders or novices to enter biking. This is also an incremental expense, one that would not have happened if the Buell Blast had not been introduced. As such it is a relevant cash flow. The bottom line is to look at the company's cash flows as a whole with this project versus without this project. The decision is then based on the difference in those cash flows.

Remember That Sunk Costs Are Not Incremental Cash Flows

Only cash flows that are affected by the decision made at the moment are relevant in capital budgeting. The manager asks two questions: (1) Will this cash flow occur if the project is accepted? (2) Will this cash flow occur if the project is rejected? *Yes* to the first question and *no* to the second equals an incremental cash flow. For example, let's assume you are considering introducing a new taste treat called "Puddin' in a Shoe." You would like to do some test marketing before production. If you are considering the decision to test market and have not yet done so, the costs associated with the test marketing are relevant cash flows. Conversely, if you have already test marketed, the cash flows involved in test marketing are no longer relevant in project evaluation. It's a matter of timing. Regardless of what you might decide about future production, the cash flows allocated to marketing have already occurred. Cash flows that have already taken place are often referred to as "sunk costs" because they have been sunk into the project and cannot be undone. As a rule, any cash flows that are not affected by the accept-reject decision should not be included in capital-budgeting analysis.

Account for Opportunity Costs

Now we will focus on the cash flows that are lost because a given project consumes scarce resources that would have produced cash flows if that project had been rejected. This is the opportunity cost of doing business. For example, a product may use valuable floor space in a production facility. Although the cash flow is not obvious, the real question remains: What else could be done with this space? The space could have been rented out, or another product could have been stored there. The key point is that opportunity-cost cash flows should reflect net cash flows that would have been received if the project under consideration were rejected. Again, we are analyzing the cash flows to the company as a whole, with or without the project.

Decide If Overhead Costs Are Truly Incremental Cash Flows

Although we certainly want to include any incremental cash flows resulting in changes from overhead expenses such as utilities and salaries, we also want to make sure that

FINANCE MATTERS

UNIVERSAL STUDIOS

In 1999, a major capital-budgeting decision led Universal Studios to build its Islands of Adventure theme park. The purpose of this $2.6 billion investment by Universal was to take direct aim at the first crack of the tourist's dollar in Orlando. Although this capital-budgeting decision may, on the surface, seem like a relatively simple decision, forecasting the expected cash flows associated with this theme park was, in fact, quite complicated.

To begin with, Universal was introducing a product that competes directly with itself. The original Universal Studios features rides like "Back to the Future" and "Jaws." Are there enough tourist dollars to support both theme parks, or will the new Islands of Adventure park simply cannibalize ticket sales to the older Universal Studios? In addition, what happens when Disney counters with a new park of its own? We will evaluate projects relative to their base case—that is, what will happen if the project is not carried out? In the case of Universal's Islands of Adventure, we could ask what would happen to attendance at the original Universal Studios if the new park was not opened, versus what the attendance would be with the new park. Will tourist traffic through the Islands of Adventure lead to additional sales of the brands and businesses visibly promoted and available in the new park that fall under Universal's and Seagrams's corporate umbrella?

From Universal's point of view, the objective may be threefold: to increase its share of the tourist market; to keep from losing market share as the tourists look for the latest in technological rides and entertainment; and to promote Universal's, and its parent company Seagrams', other brands and products. However, for companies in very competitive markets, the evolution and introduction of new products may serve more to preserve market share than to expand it. Certainly, that's the case in the computer market, where Dell, Compaq, and IBM introduce upgraded models that continually render current models obsolete. The bottom line here is that, with respect to estimating cash flows, things are many times more complicated than they first appear. As such, we have to dig deep to understand how a firm's free cash flows are affected by the decision at hand.

How did all this turn out? . . . It must have turned out reasonably well because Universal followed up this investment by dropping another $100 million on new rides based on Universal franchises: the Mummy, Shrek, and Jimmy Neutron. Then in October of 2003, Universal's theme parks changed ownership as NBC signed a deal to merge with Universal with the new media conglomerate called NBC Universal which will control NBC, more than a dozen local television stations, several cable networks, and five theme parks and will be owned by NBC's parent company, General Electric.

these are truly incremental cash flows. Many times, overhead expenses—heat, light, rent—would occur whether a given project were accepted or rejected. There is often not a single specific project to which these expenses can be allocated. Thus, the question is not whether the project benefits from overhead items, but whether the overhead costs are incremental cash flows associated with the project—and relevant to capital budgeting.

IGNORE INTEREST PAYMENTS AND FINANCING FLOWS

In evaluating new projects and determining cash flows, we must separate the investment decision from the financing decision. Interest payments and other financing cash flows that might result from raising funds to finance a project should not be considered incremental cash flows. If accepting a project means we have to raise new funds by issuing bonds, the interest charges associated with raising funds are not a relevant cash outflow. When we discount the incremental cash flows back to the present at the required rate of return, we are implicitly accounting for the cost of raising funds to finance the new project. In essence, the required rate of return reflects the cost of the funds needed to support the project. Managers first determine the desirability of the project and then determine how best to finance it. See the Finance Matters box, "Universal Studios."

CONCEPT CHECK

1. What is an incremental cash flow? What is a sunk cost? What are opportunity costs?
2. If Ford introduces a new auto line, might some of the cash flows from that new car line be diverted from existing product lines? How should you deal with this?

Objective 2

AN OVERVIEW OF THE CALCULATIONS OF A PROJECT'S FREE CASH FLOWS

In measuring cash flows, we will be interested only in the *incremental*, or differential, *after-tax cash flows* that can be attributed to the proposal being evaluated. That is, we will focus our attention on the difference in the firm's after-tax cash flows *with* versus *without* the project—the project's free cash flows. The worth of our decision depends on the accuracy of our cash flow estimates. For this reason, we first examined the question of what cash flows are relevant. Now we will see that, in general, a project's free cash flows will fall into one of three categories: (1) the initial outlay, (2) the annual free cash flows, and (3) the terminal cash flow. Once we have taken a look at these categories, we will take on the task of measuring these free cash flows.

INITIAL OUTLAY

Initial outlay
The immediate cash outflow necessary to purchase the asset and put it in operating order.

The **initial outlay** involves the immediate cash outflow necessary to purchase the asset and put it in operating order. This amount includes the cost of installing the asset (the asset's purchase price plus any expenses associated with shipping or installation) and any nonexpense cash outlays, such as increased working-capital requirements. If we are considering a new sales outlet, there might be additional cash flows associated with net investment in working capital in the form of increased inventory and cash necessary to operate the sales outlet. Although these cash flows are not included in the cost of the asset or even expensed on the books, they must be included in our analysis. The after-tax cost of expense items incurred as a result of new investment must also be included as cash outflows—for example, any training expenses or special engineering expenses that would not have been incurred otherwise.

Finally, if the investment decision is a replacement decision, the cash inflow associated with the selling price of the old asset, in addition to any tax effects resulting from its sale, must be included.

Determining the initial outlay is a complex matter. Table 10-1 summarizes some of the more common calculations involved in determining the initial outlay. This list is by no means exhaustive, but it should give you a framework for thinking about the initial outlay. At this point, we should realize that the incremental nature of the cash flow is of great

TABLE 10-1 Summary of Typical Initial Outlay Incremental After-Tax Cash Flows

1. Installed cost of asset
2. Additional nonexpense outlays incurred (for example, working-capital investments)
3. Additional expenses on an after-tax basis (for example, training expenses)
4. In a replacement decision, the *after-tax* cash flow associated with the sale of the old machine

importance. In many cases, if the project is not accepted, then status quo for the firm will simply not continue. In calculating incremental cash flows, we must be realistic in estimating what the cash flows to the company would be if the new project is not accepted.

TAX EFFECTS—SALE OF OLD MACHINE Potentially, one of the most confusing initial outlay calculations is for a replacement project involving the incremental tax payment associated with the sale of an old machine. There are three possible tax situations dealing with the sale of an old asset:

1. The old asset is sold for a price above the depreciated value. Here the difference between the old machine's selling price and its depreciated value is considered a taxable gain and taxed at the marginal corporate tax rate. If, for example, the old machine was originally purchased for $15,000, had a book value of $10,000, and was sold for $17,000, assuming the firm's marginal corporate tax rate is 34 percent, the taxes due from the gain would be ($17,000 – $10,000) × (.34), or $2,380.
2. The old asset is sold for its depreciated value. In this case, no taxes result, as there is neither a gain nor a loss in the asset's sale.
3. The old asset is sold for less than its depreciated value. In this case, the difference between the depreciated book value and the salvage value of the asset is a taxable loss and may be used to offset capital gains and thus results in tax savings. For example, if the depreciated book value of the asset is $10,000 and it is sold for $7,000 we have a $3,000 loss. Assuming the firm's marginal corporate tax rate is 34 percent, the cash inflow from tax savings is ($10,000 – $7,000) × (.34), or $1,020.

Annual Free Cash Flows

Annual free cash flows come from operating cash flows, changes in working capital, and any capital spending that might take place. In our calculations we'll begin with our pro forma statements and work from there. From there we will have to make adjustments for interest, depreciation, and working capital, along with any capital expenditures that might occur.

ACCOUNTING FOR INTEREST Any increase in interest payments incurred as a result of issuing bonds to finance the project will *not* be included, as the costs of funds needed to support the project are implicitly accounted for by discounting the project back to the present using the required rate of return.

ACCOUNTING FOR DEPRECIATION AND TAXES Finally, an adjustment for the incremental change in taxes should be included that reflect the fact that while depreciation is considered an expense from an accounting perspective, it does not involve any cash flows.

Depreciation plays an important role in the calculation of cash flows. Although it is not a cash flow item, it lowers profits, which in turn lowers taxes. For students developing a foundation in corporate finance, it is the concept of depreciation, not the calculation of it, that is important. The reason the calculation of depreciation is deemphasized is that it is extremely complicated, and its calculation changes every few years as Congress enacts new tax laws. Through all this, bear in mind that although depreciation is not a cash flow item, it does affect cash flows by lowering the level of profits on which taxes are calculated.

DEPRECIATION CALCULATION The Revenue Reconciliation Act of 1993 largely left intact the modified version of the Accelerated Cost Recovery System introduced in the Tax Reform Act of 1986. Although this was examined earlier, a review is appropriate here. This modified version of the old accelerated cost recovery system (ACRS) is used for most tangible depreciable property placed in service beginning in 1987. Under this method, the life of the asset is determined according to the asset's class life, which is assigned by the IRS; for example, most computer equipment has a five-year asset life. It also allows for only a half-year's deduction in the first year and a half-year's deduction in the year after the recovery period. The asset is then depreciated using the 200 percent declining balance method or an optional straight-line method.

For our purposes, depreciation is calculated using a simplified straight-line method. This simplified process ignores the half-year convention that allows only a half-year's deduction in the year the project is placed in service and a half-year's deduction in the first year after the recovery period. By ignoring the half-year convention and assuming a zero salvage value, we are able to calculate annual depreciation by taking the project's initial depreciable value and dividing by its depreciable life as follows:

$$\text{annual depreciation using the simplified straight-line method} = \frac{\text{initial depreciable value}}{\text{depreciable life}}$$

The initial depreciable value is equal to the cost of the asset plus any expenses necessary to get the new asset into operating order.

This is not how depreciation would actually be calculated. The reason we have simplified the calculation is to allow you to focus directly on what should and should not be included in the cash flow calculations. Moreover, because the tax laws change rather frequently, we are more interested in recognizing the tax implications of depreciation than in understanding the specific depreciation provisions of the current tax laws.

Our concern with depreciation is to highlight its importance in generating cash flow estimates and to indicate that the financial manager must be aware of the current tax provisions when evaluating capital-budgeting proposals.

WORKING CAPITAL While depreciation is an expense, but not a cash-flow item, working capital is a cash-flow item, but not an expense. In fact, very few projects do not require some increased investment in working capital. It is only natural for inventory levels to increase as a firm begins production of a new product. Likewise, much of the sales of the new product may be on credit, resulting in an increase in accounts receivable. Offsetting some of this may be a corresponding increase in accounts payable, as the firm buys raw materials on credit.

The increased working capital minus any additional short-term liabilities that were generated is the change in net working capital. Thus, we need only look at the difference between the beginning and ending levels of investment in working capital less any additional short-term liabilities to calculate the change in net working capital. Complicating all of this are two things: the current portion of long-term debt and cash. Because the current portion of long-term debt is already counted as part of the financing for the project, including it as part of working capital would double-count it.

Cash is more complicated. The only change in the level of cash held that should be considered to be a cash flow is cash that is required for the operation of the business and does not earn interest. For example, an increase in teller cash associated with opening a new sales outlet would be a relevant cash-flow item. However, if as a result of the operation of the new project the firm increases its level of idle cash, this would not be considered a cash-flow item. The firm can earn interest on this idle cash, so it would be inappropriate to consider it a cash-outflow item.

Terminal Cash Flow

The calculation of the terminal cash flow is a bit unique in that it generally includes the salvage value of the project plus or minus any taxable gains or losses associated with its sale.

TABLE 10-2 Summary of Typical Terminal Cash Flows on After-Tax Basis

1. The after-tax salvage value of the project
2. Cash outlays associated with the project's termination
3. Recapture of nonexpense outlays that occurred at the project's initiation (for example, working capital investments)

Under the current tax laws, in most cases there will be tax payments associated with the salvage value at termination. This is because the current laws allow all projects to be depreciated to zero, and if a project has a book value of zero at termination and a positive salvage value, then that salvage value will be taxed. The tax effects associated with the salvage value of the project at termination are determined exactly like the tax effects on the sale of the old machine associated with the initial outlay. The salvage value proceeds are compared with the depreciated value, in this case zero, to determine the tax.

In addition to the salvage value, there may be a cash outlay associated with the project termination. For example, at the close of a strip-mining operation, the mine must be refilled in an ecologically acceptable manner. Finally, any working capital outlay required at the initiation of the project—for example, increased inventory needed for the operation of a new plant—will be recaptured at the termination of the project. In effect, the increased inventory required by the project can be liquidated when the project expires. Table 10-2 provides a general list of some of the factors that might affect a project's terminal cash flow.

Cash Flows: Why Accounting Income Doesn't Measure Up

Why not use profits after tax as our measure of these cash flows? The answer is that we can, but first we've got to correct four problems:

- **Depreciation (and any other non-cash flow charges).** When accountants calculate a firm's net income, one of the expenses they subtract out is depreciation. However, depreciation is a non-cash flow expense. If you think about it, depreciation comes about because you bought a fixed asset (for example, you built a plant) in an earlier period, and now, through depreciation, you're expensing it over time—but depreciation does not actually involve a cash flow. That means net income understates cash flows by this amount. Therefore, we'll want to compensate for this by adding depreciation back in to our measure of accounting income when calculating cash flows.
- **Interest expenses.** There's no question that if you take on a new project, you'll have to pay for it somehow—either through internal cash flow or selling new stocks or bonds. In other words, there's a cost to that money. We will recognize that when we discount future cash flows back to the present at the required rate of return. Remember, the project's required rate of return is the rate of return that you must earn to justify taking on the project. It recognizes the risk of the project and the fact that there is an opportunity cost of money. If we discount the future cash flows back to the present and also subtract out interest expenses, then we'd be double counting for the cost of money—accounting for the cost of money once when we subtracted out interest expenses and once when we discounted the cash flows back to the present. Therefore, we want to make sure interest expenses *aren't subtracted out.* That means we'll want to ignore interest and make sure that financing flows are not included.

- **Changes in net working capital.** Many projects require an increased investment in working capital. For example, some of the new sales may be credit sales resulting in an increased investment in accounts receivable. Also, in order to produce and sell the product, the firm may have to increase its investment in inventory. However, some of this increased working capital investment may be financed by an increase in accounts payable. Since all these potential changes are changes in assets and liabilities, they don't affect accounting income. The bottom line here is that if this project brings with it a positive change in net working capital, then it means money is going to be tied up in increased working capital, and this would be a cash outflow. That means we'll have to make sure we account for any changes in net working capital that might occur.
- **Changes in capital spending.** From an accounting perspective, the cash flow associated with the purchase of a fixed asset is not an expense. That means that when Marriott spends $50 million building a new hotel resort there is a significant cash outflow, but there is no accompanying expense. Instead, the $50 million cash outflow creates an annual depreciation expense over the life of the hotel. We'll want to make sure we include any changes in capital spending in our cash flow calculations.

Now let's put this all together and measure the project's free cash flows.

Measuring the Cash Flows

Cash flow calculations can be broken down into three basic parts: cash flows from operations, cash flows associated with working capital requirements, and capital spending cash flows. Let's begin our discussion by looking at three different, but equivalent, methods for measuring cash flows from operations, then move on and discuss measuring cash flows from working capital requirements and capital spending.

PROJECT'S CHANGE IN OPERATING CASH FLOWS There are a number of different ways that are used to calculate operating cash flows, all getting at the same thing—the after-tax differential cash flows that the project's operations bring in. We'll begin by looking at the pro forma approach because it is the one used most frequently, with its inputs taken directly from pro forma statements.

OCF Calculation: The Pro Forma Approach An easy way to calculate operating cash flows is to take the information provided on the project's pro forma income statement where interest payments are ignored and simply convert the accounting information into cash-flow information. To do this we take advantage of the fact that the difference between the change in sales and the change in costs should be equal to the change in EBIT plus depreciation.

Under this method, the calculation of a project's operating cash flow involves three steps. First, we determine the company's *Earnings Before Interest and Taxes (EBIT)* with and without this project. Second, we subtract out the change in taxes. Keep in mind that in calculating the change in taxes, we will ignore any interest expenses. Third, we adjust this value for the fact that depreciation, a non-cash flow item, has been subtracted out in the calculation of EBIT. We do this by adding back depreciation. Thus, operating cash flows are calculated as follows:

operating cash flows = change in earnings before interest and taxes
− change in taxes
+ change in depreciation

Now let's take a look at three alternative methods for calculating the change in operating cash flows. The reason we've presented alternative methods for calculating operating cash flows is because they are all used and talked about in the real world; hence, you should be familiar with them. In addition, you'll notice that they all give you the same result. That's because they all do the same thing—they just do it in different ways.

Alternative OCF Calculation 1: Add Back Approach Since financing flows (for example, interest payments) are not included in our pro forma income statement, we can go directly to the bottom line of our income statement and adjust for the fact that depreciation, a non-cash flow item, has been subtracted out in the calculations:

$$\text{operating cash flows} = \text{net income} + \text{depreciation}$$

This method for determining operating cash flows is commonly used. That's because it is so simple—and if financing flows are ignored, it is also correct.

Alternative OCF Calculation 2: Definitional Approach Since we are trying to measure the change in operating cash flows, we can simply calculate the change in revenues minus cash expenses minus taxes:

$$\begin{aligned}\text{operating cash flows} = {} & \text{change in revenues} \\ & - \text{change in cash expenses} \\ & - \text{change in taxes}\end{aligned}$$

All we've done here is to take the definition of operating cash flows and put it into practice.

Alternative OCF Calculation 3: Depreciation Tax Shield Approach Under the depreciation tax shield approach we begin by ignoring depreciation and calculating net profits after tax as revenues less cash expenses. We then adjust for the fact that incremental depreciation will reduce taxes—referred to as the depreciation tax shield, which is calculated as depreciation times tax rate:

$$\begin{aligned}\text{operating cash flows} = {} & (\text{revenues} - \text{cash expenses}) \times (1 - \text{tax rate}) \\ & + (\text{change in depreciation} \times \text{tax rate})\end{aligned}$$

EXAMPLE: CALCULATING OPERATING CASH FLOWS

Let's look at an example to show the equivalency of the three methods. Assume that a new project will annually generate revenues of $1,000,000 and cash expenses including both fixed and variable costs of $500,000, while increasing depreciation by $150,000 per year. In addition, let's assume that the firm's marginal tax rate is 34 percent. Given this, the firm's change in net profit after tax can be calculated as:

revenue	$1,000,000
– cash expenses	500,000
– depreciation	150,000
= EBIT	$ 350,000
– taxes (34%)	119,000
= net income	$ 231,000

As you can see, regardless of which method you use to calculate operating cash flows, you get the same answer:

OCF Calculation: Pro Forma Approach

$$\begin{aligned}\text{operating cash flows} = {} & \text{change in earnings before interest and taxes} \\ & - \text{change in taxes} + \text{change in depreciation} \\ = {} & \$350{,}000 - \$119{,}000 + \$150{,}000 = \$381{,}000\end{aligned}$$

(continued)

Alternative OCF Calculation 1: Add Back Approach

$$\begin{aligned}\text{operating cash flows} &= \text{net income} + \text{depreciation}\\ &= \$231{,}000 + \$150{,}000 = \$381{,}000\end{aligned}$$

Alternative OCF Calculation 2: Definitional Approach

$$\begin{aligned}\text{operating cash flows} &= \text{change in revenues} - \text{change in cash expenses}\\ &\quad - \text{change in taxes}\\ &= \$1{,}000{,}000 - \$500{,}000 - 119{,}000 = \$381{,}000\end{aligned}$$

Alternative OCF Calculation 3: Depreciation Tax Shield Approach

$$\begin{aligned}\text{operating cash flows} &= (\text{revenues} - \text{cash expenses}) \times (1 - \text{tax rate})\\ &\quad + (\text{change in depreciation} \times \text{tax rate})\\ &= (\$1{,}000{,}000 - \$500{,}000) \times (1 - .34)\\ &\quad + (\$150{,}000 \times .34) = \$381{,}000\end{aligned}$$

You'll notice that interest payments are nowhere to be found. That's because we ignore them when we're calculating operating cash flows. You'll also notice that we end up with the same answer regardless of how we work the problem.

CASH FLOWS FROM THE CHANGE IN NET WORKING CAPITAL As we mentioned earlier in this chapter, many times a new project will involve additional investment in working capital—perhaps new inventory to stock a new sales outlet or simply additional investment in accounts receivable. There also may be some spontaneous short-term financing—for example, increases in accounts payable—that result from the new project. Thus, the change in net working capital is the additional investment in working capital minus any additional short-term liabilities that were generated.

CASH FLOWS FROM THE CHANGE IN CAPITAL SPENDING While there is generally a large cash outflow associated with a project's initial outlay, there may also be additional capital spending requirements over the life of the project. For example, you may know ahead of time that the plant will need some minor retooling in the second year of the project in order to keep the project abreast of new technological changes that are expected to take place. In effect, we will look at the company with and without the new project, and any changes in capital spending that occur are relevant.

PUTTING IT TOGETHER: CALCULATING A PROJECT'S FREE CASH FLOWS Thus, a project's free cash flows are:

$$\begin{aligned}\text{project's free cash flows} &= \text{project's change in operating cash flows}\\ &\quad - \text{change in net working capital}\\ &\quad - \text{change in capital spending}\end{aligned}$$

The question now becomes: Which method should we use for estimating the change in operating cash flows? The answer is that it doesn't matter, but the most commonly used method is method 1, the pro forma approach. Generally, that's how the information is presented by those in marketing and accounting who work on the sales forecasts for new products. Thus, we can rewrite the formula for a project's free cash flows given above, inserting the pro forma approach for calculating a project's change in operating cash flows, and we get:

project's free cash flows = change in earnings before interest and taxes
– change in taxes
+ change in depreciation
– change in net working capital
– change in capital spending

To estimate the changes in EBIT, taxes, depreciation, net working capital, and capital spending, we start with estimates of how many units we expect to sell, what the costs—both fixed and variable—will be, what the selling price will be, and what the required capital investment will be. From there we can put together a pro forma statement that should provide us with the data we need to estimate the project's free cash flows. However, you must keep in mind that our capital budgeting decision will only be as good as our estimates of the costs and future demand. In fact, most capital budgeting decisions that turn out to be bad decisions are not bad decisions because the decision maker used a bad decision rule, but because the estimates of future demand and costs were inaccurate. Let's look at an example.

EXAMPLE: CALCULATING A PROJECT'S FREE CASH FLOWS

You are considering expanding your product line, which currently consists of Lee's Press On Nails, to take advantage of the fitness craze. The new product you are considering introducing is called "Press On Abs." You feel you can sell 100,000 of these per year for four years (after which time this project is expected to shut down as forecasters predict healthy looks will no longer be in vogue, being replaced with the couch potato look). The Press On Abs would sell for $6.00 each with variable costs of $3.00 for each one produced, while annual fixed costs associated with production would be $90,000. In addition, there would be a $200,000 initial expenditure associated with the purchase of new production equipment. It is assumed that this initial expenditure will be depreciated using the simplified straight-line method down to zero over four years. This project will also require a one-time initial investment of $30,000 in net working capital associated with inventory. Finally, assume that the firm's marginal tax rate is 34 percent.

Initial Outlay Let's begin by estimating the initial outlay. In this example, the initial outlay will be the $200,000 initial expenditure plus the investment of $30,000 in net working capital, for a total of $230,000.

Annual Free Cash Flows Next, Table 10-3 calculates the annual change in earnings before interest and taxes. This calculation begins with the change in sales (Δ Sales) and subtracts the change in fixed and variable costs, in addition to the change in depreciation to calculate the change in earnings before interest and taxes or EBIT. Annual depreciation was calculated using the simplified straight-line method, which is simply the depreciable value of the asset ($200,000) divided by the asset's expected life, which is four years. Taxes are then calculated assuming a 34 percent marginal tax rate. Once we have calculated EBIT and taxes, we don't need to go any further, since these are the only two values from the pro forma income statement that we need. In addition, in this example there is not any annual increase in working capital associated with the project under consideration. Also notice that we have ignored any interest payments and financing flows that might have occurred. As mentioned earlier, when we discount the free cash flows back to the present at the required rate of return, we are implicitly accounting for the cost of the funds needed to support the project.

(continued)

TABLE 10-3 Calculation of the Annual Change in Earnings Before Interest and Taxes for the Press On Abs Project

Δ sales (100,000 units at $6.00/unit)	$600,000
Less: Δ variable costs (variable cost $3.00/unit)	300,000
Less: Δ fixed costs	90,000
Equals:	$210,000
Less: Δ depreciation ($200,000/4 years)	50,000
Equals: Δ EBIT	$160,000
Less: Δ taxes (taxed at 34%)	54,400
Equals: Δ net income	$105,600

The project's annual *change in operating cash flow* is calculated using all four methods in Table 10-4. The project's annual *free cash flow* is simply the *change in operating cash flow* less any *change in net working capital* and less any *change in capital spending*. In this example there are no changes in net working capital and capital spending over the life of the project. This is not the case for all projects that you will consider. For example, on a project where sales increased annually, it is likely that working capital will also increase each year to support a larger inventory and a higher level of accounts receivable. Similarly, on some projects the capital expenditures may be spread out over several years. The point here is that what we are trying to do is look at the firm with this

TABLE 10-4 Annual Change in Operating Cash Flow, Press On Abs Project

OCF CALCULATION: PRO FORMA APPROACH	
Δ Earnings before interest and taxes (EBIT)	$160,000
Minus: Δ taxes	−54,400
Plus: Δ depreciation	+50,000
Equals: Δ operating cash flow	$155,600
ALTERNATIVE CALCULATION 1: ADD BACK APPROACH	
Δ net income	$105,600
Plus: Δ depreciation	+50,000
Equals: Δ operating cash flow	$155,600
ALTERNATIVE CALCULATION 2: DEFINITIONAL APPROACH	
Δ revenues (100,000 units at $6.00/unit)	$600,000
Minus: Δ cash expenses (Δ variable and Δ fixed costs)	−390,000
Minus: Δ taxes	−54,400
Equals: Δ operating cash flow	$155,600
ALTERNATIVE CALCULATION 3: DEPRECIATION TAX SHIELD APPROACH	
Δ revenues (100,000 units at $6.00/unit)	$600,000
Minus: Δ cash expenses (Δ variable and Δ fixed costs)	−390,000
Equals:	$210,000
Times: one minus the tax rate (1 − .34)	$138,600
Plus: Δ depreciation times the tax rate ($50,000 × .34)	17,000
Equals: Δ operating cash flow	$155,600

TABLE 10-5 Terminal Free Cash Flow, Press On Abs Project

Δ earnings before interest and taxes (EBIT)	$160,000
Minus: Δ taxes	−54,400
Plus: Δ depreciation	+50,000
Minus: change in net working capital	−(30,000)
Equals: Δ free cash flow	$185,600

FIGURE 10-1 Free Cash Flow Diagram for Press On Abs

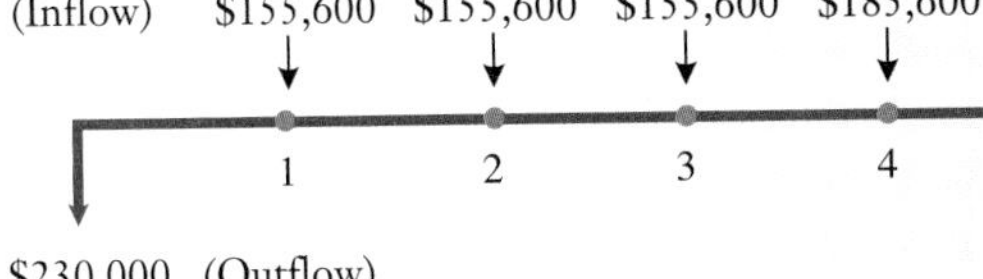

project and without this project and measure the change in cash flows other than any interest payments and financing flows that might have occurred.

Terminal Cash Flow For this project, the terminal cash flow is quite simple. The only unusual cash flow at the project's termination is the recapture of the net working capital associated with the project. In effect, the investment in inventory of $30,000 is liquidated when the project is shut down in four years. Keep in mind that in calculating free cash flow we subtract out the change in net working capital, but since the change in net working capital is negative (we are reducing our investment in inventory), we are subtracting a negative number, which has the effect of adding it back in. Thus, working capital was a negative cash flow when the project began and we invested in inventory, and at termination it became a positive offsetting cash flow when the inventory was liquidated. The calculation of the terminal free cash flow using method 1, the pro forma approach is illustrated in Table 10-5.

If we were to construct a free cash flow diagram from this example (Figure 10-1), it would have an initial outlay of $230,000, the free cash flows during years 1 through 3 would be $155,600, and the free cash flow in the terminal year would be $185,600. Free cash flow diagrams similar to Figure 10-1 will be used through the remainder of this chapter with arrows above the time line indicating cash inflows and arrows below the time line denoting outflows.

A Comprehensive Example: Calculating Free Cash Flows

Now let's put what we know about capital budgeting together and look at a capital-budgeting decision for a firm in the 34 percent marginal tax bracket with a 15 percent required rate of return or cost of capital. The project we are considering involves the introduction of a new electric scooter line by Raymobile. Our first task is that of estimating cash flows. This project is expected to last five years and then, because this is somewhat

TABLE 10-6 Raymobile Scooter Line Capital-Budgeting Example

Cost of new plant and equipment: $9,700,000
Shipping and installation costs: $ 300,000

Unit Sales:

Year	Units Sold
1	50,000
2	100,000
3	100,000
4	70,000
5	50,000

Sales price per unit: $150/unit in years 1–4, $130/unit in year 5

Variable cost per unit: $80/unit

Annual fixed costs: $500,000

Working capital requirements: There will be an initial working capital requirement of $100,000 just to get production started. Then, for each year, the *total* investment in net working capital will be equal to 10 percent of the dollar value of sales for that year. Thus, the investment in working capital will increase during years 1 through 3, then decrease in year 4. Finally, all working capital is liquidated at the termination of the project at the end of year 5.

The depreciation method: We use the simplified straight-line method over five years. It is assumed that the plant and equipment will have no salvage value after five years. Thus, annual depreciation is $2,000,000/year for five years.

of a fad project, to be terminated. Thus, our first task becomes that of estimating the initial outlay, the annual free cash flows, and the terminal free cash flow. Given the information in Table 10-6, we want to determine the free cash flows associated with the project. Once we had that, we could easily calculate the project's net present value, the profitability index, and the internal rate of return, and apply the appropriate decision criteria.

SECTION I, TABLE 10-7: CALCULATING CHANGE IN EBIT, TAXES, AND DEPRECIATION To determine the differential annual free cash flows, we first need to determine the annual change in operating cash flow. To do this we will take the change in EBIT, subtract out the change in taxes, and then add in the change in depreciation. This is shown in Section I of Table 10-7 on page 343. We first determine what the change in sales revenue will be by multiplying the units sold times the sale price. From the change in sales revenue we subtract out variable costs, which were given as dollars per unit sold. Then, the change in fixed costs is subtracted out, and the result is earnings before depreciation, interest, and taxes (EBDIT). Subtracting the change in depreciation from EBDIT then leaves us with the change in earnings before interest and taxes (EBIT). From the change in EBIT we can then calculate the change in taxes, which are assumed to be 34 percent of EBIT.

SECTION II, TABLE 10-7: CALCULATING OPERATING CASH FLOW Using the calculations provided in Section I of Table 10-7, we then calculate the operating cash flow in Section II of Table 10-7. As you recall, the operating cash flow is simply EBIT minus taxes, plus depreciation.

SECTION III, TABLE 10-7: CALCULATING CHANGE IN NET WORKING CAPITAL To calculate the free cash flow from this project, we subtract the change in net working capital and the change in capital spending from operating cash flow. Thus, the first step becomes determining the change in net working capital, which is shown in Section III of Table 10-7. The change in net working capital generally includes both increases in inventory and increases in accounts receivable that naturally occur as sales

TABLE 10-7 Calculation of Free Cash Flow for Raymobile Scooters

YEAR	0	1	2	3	4	5
Section I. Calculate the change in EBIT, taxes, and depreciation (this becomes an input in the calculation of operating cash flow in Section II)						
Units sold		50,000	100,000	100,000	70,000	50,000
Sale price		$150	$150	$150	$150	$130
Sales revenue		7,500,000	15,000,000	15,000,000	10,500,000	6,500,000
Less: variable costs		4,000,000	8,000,000	8,000,000	5,600,000	4,000,000
Less: fixed costs		500,000	500,000	500,000	500,000	500,000
Equals: EBDIT		3,000,000	6,500,000	6,500,000	4,400,000	2,000,000
Less: depreciation		2,000,000	2,000,000	2,000,000	2,000,000	2,000,000
Equals: EBIT		1,000,000	4,500,000	4,500,000	2,400,000	0
Taxes (@34%)		340,000	1,530,000	1,530,000	816,000	0
Section II. Calculate operating cash flow (this becomes an input in the calculation of free cash flow in Section IV)						
Operating Cash Flow:						
EBIT		$1,000,000	$4,500,000	$4,500,000	$2,400,000	0
Minus: taxes		340,000	1,530,000	1,530,000	816,000	0
Plus: depreciation		2,000,000	2,000,000	2,000,000	2,000,000	2,000,000
Equals: operating cash flows		2,660,000	4,970,000	4,970,000	3,584,000	2,000,000
Section III. Calculate the net working capital (this becomes an input in the calculation of free cash flows in Section IV)						
Change in Net Working Capital:						
Revenue		$7,500,000	$15,000,000	$15,000,000	$10,500,000	$6,500,000
Initial working capital requirement	100,000					
Net working capital needs		750,000	1,500,000	1,500,000	1,050,000	650,000
Liquidation of working capital						650,000
Change in working capital	100,000	650,000	750,000	0	(450,000)	(1,050,000)
Section IV. Calculate free cash flow (using information calculated in Sections II and III, in addition to the change in capital spending)						
Free Cash Flow:						
Operating cash flow		$2,660,000	$4,970,000	$4,970,000	$3,584,000	$2,000,000
Minus: change in net working capital	100,000	650,000	750,000	0	(450,000)	(1,050,000)
Minus: change in capital spending	10,000,000	0	0	0	0	0
Free cash flow	(10,100,000)	2,010,000	4,220,000	4,970,000	4,034,000	3,050,000

increase from the introduction of the new product line. Some of the increase in accounts receivable may be offset by increases in accounts payable, but, in general, most new projects involve some type of increase in net working capital. In this example, there is an initial working capital requirement of $100,000. In addition, for each year the total investment in net working capital will be equal to 10 percent of sales for each year. Thus, the investment in working capital for year 1 is $750,000 (because sales are estimated to be $7,500,000). Working capital will already be at $100,000, so the change in net working capital will be $650,000. Net working capital will continue to increase during years 1 through 3, then decrease in year 4. Finally, all working capital is liquidated at the termination of the project at the end of year 5.

SECTION IV, TABLE 10-7: CALCULATING FREE CASH FLOW With the operating cash flow and the change in net working capital already calculated, the calculation of the project's free cash flow becomes easy. All that is missing is the change in capital spending, which in this example will simply be the $9,700,000 for plant and equipment plus the $300,000 for shipping and installation. Thus, change in capital spending

FIGURE 10-2 Free Cash-Flow Diagram for the Raymobile Scooter Line

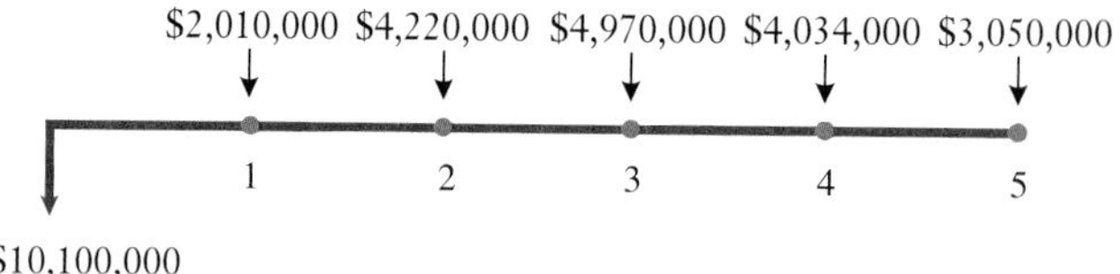

becomes $10,000,000. We then need to merely take operating cash flow and subtract from it both the change in net working capital and the change in capital spending. This is done in Section IV of Table 10-7. A free cash-flow diagram for this project is provided in Figure 10-2.

CASH FLOW DIAGRAM Using the information provided in Section IV of Table 10-7 and Figure 10-2, we easily calculate the *NPV, PI,* and *IRR* for this project.

CONCEPT CHECK

1. In general, a project's cash flows will fall into one of three categories. What are these categories?
2. What is a free cash flow? How do we calculate it?
3. What is depreciation? Where does it come from?
4. Although depreciation is not a cash flow item, it plays an important role in the calculation of cash flows. How does depreciation affect a project's cash flows?

BACK TO THE PRINCIPLES

In this chapter, it is easy to get caught up in the calculations and forget that before the calculations can be made, someone has to come up with the idea for the project. In some of the example problems, you may see projects that appear to be extremely profitable. Unfortunately, as we learned in ***Principle 5: The Curse of Competitive Markets—Why it's hard to find exceptionally profitable projects,*** *it is unusual to find projects with dramatically high returns because of the very competitive nature of business. Thus, keep in mind that capital budgeting not only involves the estimation and evaluation of the project's cash flows, but it also includes the process of coming up with the idea for the project in the first place.*

Objective 3

COMPLICATIONS IN CAPITAL BUDGETING: CAPITAL RATIONING AND MUTUALLY EXCLUSIVE PROJECTS

Capital rationing
The placing of a limit by the firm on the dollar size of the capital budget.

The use of our capital-budgeting decision rules implies that the size of the capital budget is determined by the availability of acceptable investment proposals. However, a firm may place a limit on the dollar size of the capital budget. This situation is called **capital rationing**. As we will see, an examination of capital rationing

FIGURE 10-3 Projects Ranked by *IRR*

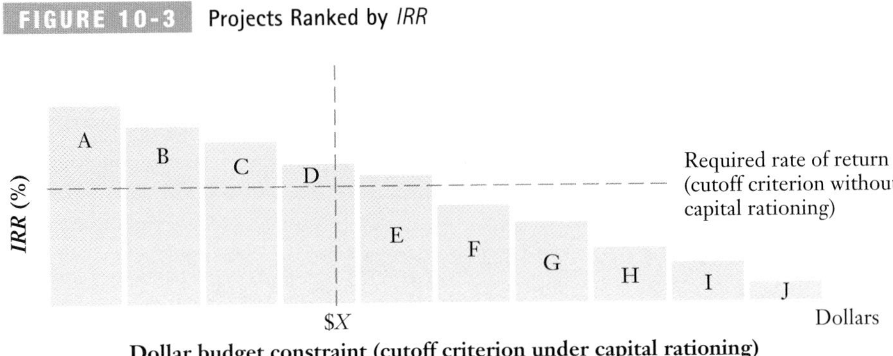

will not only enable us to deal with complexities of the real world but will also serve to demonstrate the superiority of the *NPV* method over the *IRR* method for capital budgeting.

Using the internal rate of return as the firm's decision rule, a firm accepts all projects with an internal rate of return greater than the firm's required rate of return. This rule is illustrated in Figure 10-3, where projects A through E would be chosen. However, when capital rationing is imposed, the dollar size of the total investment is limited by the budget constraint. In Figure 10-3, the budget constraint of $*X* precludes the acceptance of an attractive investment, project E. This situation obviously contradicts prior decision rules. Moreover, the solution of choosing the projects with the highest internal rate of return is complicated by the fact that some projects may be indivisible; for example, it is meaningless to recommend that half of project D be acquired.

Rationale for Capital Rationing

We will first ask why capital rationing exists and whether or not it is rational. In general, three principal reasons are given for imposing a capital-rationing constraint. First, management may think market conditions are temporarily adverse. In the period surrounding the stock market crash of 1987, this reason was frequently given. At that time, interest rates were high, and stock prices were depressed, which made the cost of funding projects high. Second, there may be a shortage of qualified managers to direct new projects; this can happen when projects are of a highly technical nature. Third, there may be intangible considerations. For example, management may simply fear debt, wishing to avoid interest payments at any cost. Or perhaps issuance of common stock may be limited to maintain a stable dividend policy.

Despite strong evidence that capital rationing exists in practice, the question remains as to its effect on the firm. In brief, the effect is negative, and to what degree depends on the severity of the rationing. If the rationing is minor and short-lived, the firm's share price will not suffer to any great extent. In this case, capital rationing can probably be excused, although it should be noted that any capital rationing that rejects projects with positive net present values is contrary to the firm's goal of maximization of shareholders' wealth. If the capital rationing is a result of the firm's decision to dramatically limit the number of new projects or to limit total investment to internally generated funds, then this policy will eventually have a significantly negative effect on the firm's share price. For example, a lower share price will eventually result from lost competitive advantage if, owing to a decision to arbitrarily limit its capital budget, a firm fails to upgrade its products and manufacturing process.

TABLE 10-8 Capital-Rationing Example of Five Indivisible Projects

PROJECT	INITIAL OUTLAY	PROFITABILITY INDEX	NET PRESENT VALUE
A	$200,000	2.4	$280,000
B	200,000	2.3	260,000
C	800,000	1.7	560,000
D	300,000	1.3	90,000
E	300,000	1.2	60,000

Capital Rationing and Project Selection

If the firm decides to impose a capital constraint on investment projects, the appropriate decision criterion is to select the set of projects with the highest net present value subject to the capital constraint. In effect, you are selecting the projects that increase shareholder wealth the most, because the net present value is the amount of wealth that is created when a project is accepted. This guideline may preclude merely taking the highest-ranked projects in terms of the profitability index or the internal rate of return. If the projects shown in Figure 10-3 are divisible, the last project accepted may be only partially accepted. Although partial acceptances may be possible in some cases, the indivisibility of most capital investments prevents it. If a project is a sales outlet or a truck, it may be meaningless to purchase half a sales outlet or half a truck.

To illustrate this procedure, consider a firm with a budget constraint of $1 million and five indivisible projects available to it, as given in Table 10-8. If the highest-ranked projects were taken, projects A and B would be taken first. At that point, there would not be enough funds available to take project C; hence, projects D and E would be taken. However, a higher total net present value is provided by the combination of projects A and C. Thus, projects A and C should be selected from the set of projects available. This illustrates our guideline: to select the set of projects that maximize the firm's net present value.

Project Ranking

In the past, we have proposed that all projects with a positive net present value, a profitability index greater than 1.0, or an internal rate of return greater than the required rate of return be accepted, assuming there is no capital rationing. However, this acceptance is not always possible. In some cases, when two projects are judged acceptable by the discounted cash flow criteria, it may be necessary to select only one of them, as they are mutually exclusive.

Mutually exclusive projects
A set of projects that perform essentially the same task, so that acceptance of one will necessarily mean rejection of the others.

Mutually exclusive projects occur when a set of investment proposals perform essentially the same task; acceptance of one will necessarily mean rejection of the others. For example, a company considering the installation of a computer system may evaluate three or four systems, all of which may have positive net present values; however, the acceptance of one system will automatically mean rejection of the others. In general, to deal with mutually exclusive projects, we will simply rank them by means of the discounted cash flow criteria and select the project with the highest ranking. On occasion, however, problems of conflicting ranking may arise. As we will see, in general the net present value method is the preferred decision-making tool because it leads to the selection of the project that increases shareholder wealth the most.

Problems in Project Ranking

There are three general types of ranking problems: the size disparity problem, the time disparity problem, and the unequal lives problem. Each involves the possibility of conflict in the ranks yielded by the various discounted cash flow capital-budgeting decision criteria. As noted previously, when one discounted cash flow criterion gives an accept signal, they will all give an accept signal, but they will not necessarily rank all projects in the same order. In most cases, this disparity is not critical; however, for mutually exclusive projects, the ranking order is important.

SIZE DISPARITY The *size disparity problem* occurs when mutually exclusive projects of unequal size are examined. This problem is most easily clarified with an example.

EXAMPLE: THE SIZE DISPARITY RANKING PROBLEM

Suppose a firm is considering two mutually exclusive projects, A and B, both with required rates of return of 10 percent. Project A involves a $200 initial outlay and cash inflow of $300 at the end of one year, whereas project B involves an initial outlay of $1,500 and a cash inflow of $1,900 at the end of one year. The net present value, profitability index, and internal rate of return for these projects are given in Figure 10-4.

In this case, if the net present value criterion is used, project B should be accepted, whereas if the profitability index or the internal rate of return criterion is used, project A should be chosen. The question now becomes: Which project is better? The answer depends on whether capital rationing exists. Without capital rationing, project B is better because it provides the largest increase in shareholders' wealth; that is, it has a larger net present value. If there is a capital constraint, the problem then focuses on what can be done with the additional $1,300 that is freed if project A is chosen (costing $200, as opposed to $1,500). If the firm can earn more on project A plus the proj-ect financed with the additional $1,300 ($1,500 – $200) freed up if project A as opposed to project B is chosen, then project A and the marginal project should be accepted. In effect, we are attempting to select the set of projects that maximize the firm's *NPV.* Thus, if the marginal project has a net present value greater than $154.40 ($227.10 – $72.70), selecting it plus project A with a net present value of $72.70 will provide a net present value greater than $227.10, the net present value for project B.

FIGURE 10-4 Size Disparity Ranking Problem

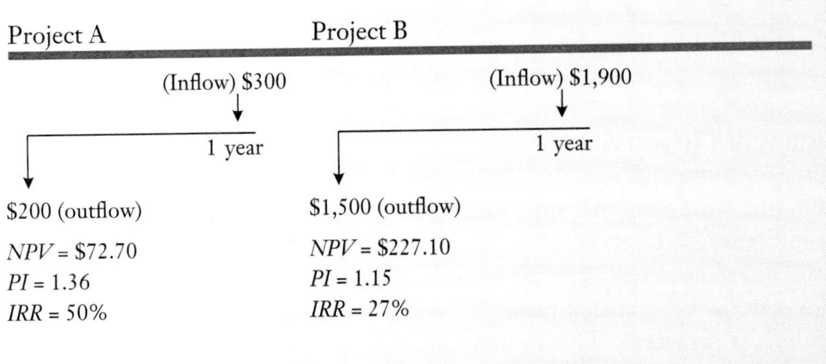

In summary, whenever the size disparity problem results in conflicting rankings between mutually exclusive projects, the project with the largest net present value will be selected, provided there is no capital rationing. When capital rationing exists, the firm should select the set of projects with the largest net present value.

FIGURE 10-5 Time Disparity Ranking Problem

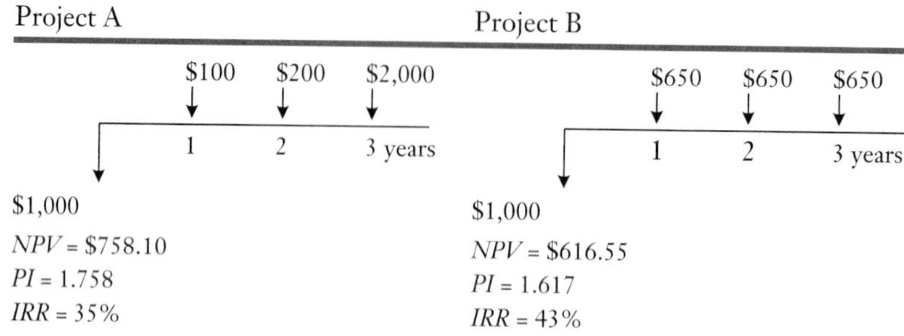

TIME DISPARITY The *time disparity problem* and the conflicting rankings that accompany it result from the differing reinvestment assumptions made by the net present value and internal rate of return decision criteria. The *NPV* criterion assumes that cash flows over the life of the project can be reinvested at the required rate of return or cost of capital, whereas the *IRR* criterion implicitly assumes that the cash flows over the life of the project can be reinvested at the internal rate of return. Again, this problem may be illustrated through the use of an example.

Suppose a firm with a required rate of return or cost of capital of 10 percent and with no capital constraint is considering the two mutually exclusive projects illustrated in Figure 10-5. The net present value and profitability index indicate that project A is the better of the two, whereas the internal rate of return indicates that project B is the better. Project B receives its cash flows earlier than project A, and the different assumptions made as to how these flows can be reinvested result in the difference in rankings. Which criterion should be followed depends on which reinvestment assumption is used. The net present value criterion is preferred in this case because it makes the most acceptable assumption for the wealth-maximizing firm. It is certainly the most conservative assumption that can be made, because the required rate of return is the lowest possible reinvestment rate. Moreover, as we have already noted, the net present value method maximizes the value of the firm and the shareholders' wealth. An alternate solution, as discussed in Chapter 9, is to use the *MIRR* method.

UNEQUAL LIVES The final ranking problem to be examined centers on the question of whether it is appropriate to compare mutually exclusive projects with different life spans.

Suppose a firm with a 10 percent required rate of return is faced with the problem of replacing an aging machine and is considering two replacement machines, one with a three-year life and one with a six-year life. The relevant cash flow information for these projects is given in Figure 10-6.

Examining the discounted cash flow criteria, we find that the net present value and profitability index criteria indicate that project B is the better project, whereas the internal rate of return favors project A. This ranking inconsistency is caused by the different life spans of the projects being compared. In this case, the decision is a difficult one because the projects are not comparable.

The problem of incomparability of projects with different lives arises because future profitable investment proposals may be rejected without being included in the analysis. This can easily be seen in a replacement problem such as the present example, in which two mutually exclusive machines with different lives are being considered. In this case, a

FIGURE 10-6 Unequal Lives Ranking Problem

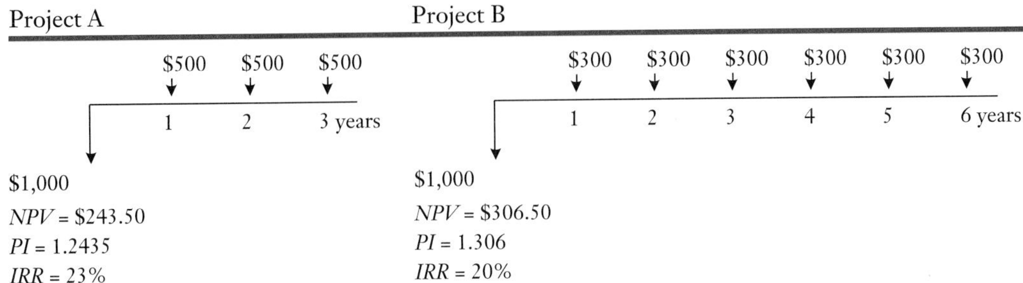

comparison of the net present values alone on each of these projects would be misleading. If the project with the shorter life were taken, at its termination the firm could replace the machine and receive additional benefits, whereas acceptance of the project with the longer life would exclude this possibility, a possibility that is not included in the analysis. The key question thus becomes: Does today's investment decision include all future profitable investment proposals in its analysis? If not, the projects are not comparable. In this case, if project B is taken, then the project that could have been taken after three years when project A terminates is automatically rejected without being included in the analysis. Thus, acceptance of project B not only forces rejection of project A, but also forces rejection of any replacement machine that might have been considered for years 4 through 6 without including this replacement machine in the analysis.

There are several methods to deal with this situation. The first option is to assume that the cash inflows from the shorter-lived investment will be reinvested at the required rate of return until the termination of the longer-lived asset. Although this approach is the simplest, merely calculating the net present value, it actually ignores the problem at hand—that of allowing for participation in another replacement opportunity with a positive net present value. The proper solution thus becomes the projection of reinvestment opportunities into the future—that is, making assumptions about possible future investment opportunities. Unfortunately, whereas the first method is too simplistic to be of any value, the second is extremely difficult, requiring extensive cash flow forecasts. The final technique for confronting the problem is to assume that reinvestment opportunities in the future will be similar to the current ones. The two most common ways of doing this are by creating a replacement chain to equalize life spans or calculating the project's equivalent annual annuity (EAA). Using a replacement chain, the present example would call for the creation of a two-chain cycle for project A; that is, we assume that project A can be replaced with a similar investment at the end of three years. Thus, project A would be viewed as two A projects occurring back to back, as illustrated in Figure 10-7. The net present value on this replacement chain is $426.50, which can be compared with project B's net present value. Therefore, project A should be accepted because the net present value of its replacement chain is greater than the net present value of project B.

One problem with replacement chains is that, depending on the life of each project, it can be quite difficult to come up with equivalent lives. For example, if the two projects had 7- and 13-year lives, because the lowest common denominator is 7 × 13 = 91, a 91-year replacement chain would be needed to establish equivalent lives. In this case, it is easier to determine the project's **equivalent annual annuity (*EAA*)**. A project's *EAA* is simply an annuity cash flow that yields the same present value as the project's *NPV*. To calculate a project's *EAA*, we need only calculate a project's *NPV* and then divide that

Equivalent annual annuity (*EAA*) An annual cash flow that yields the same present value as the project's *NPV*. It is calculated by dividing the project's *NPV* by the appropriate $PVIFA_{i,n}$.

FIGURE 10-7 Replacement Chain Illustration: Two Project A's Back to Back

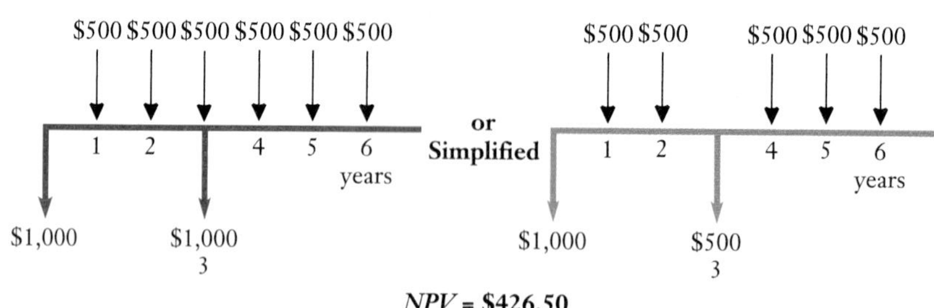

number by the $PVIFA_{i,n}$ to determine the dollar value of an n-year annuity that would produce the same *NPV* as the project. This can be done in two steps as follows:

Step 1. *Calculate the project's NPV.* In Figure 10-6 we determined that project A had an *NPV* of $243.50, whereas project B had an *NPV* of $306.50.

Step 2. *Calculate the EAA.* The *EAA* is determined by dividing each project's *NPV* by the $PVIFA_{i,n}$ where i is the required rate of return and n is the project's life. This determines the level of an annuity cash flow that would produce the same *NPV* as the project. For project A the $PVIFA_{10\%,3yrs}$ is equal to 2.487, whereas the $PVIFA_{10\%,6yrs}$ for project B is equal to 4.355. By dividing each project's *NPV* by the appropriate $PVIFA_{i,n}$ we determine the *EAA* for each project:

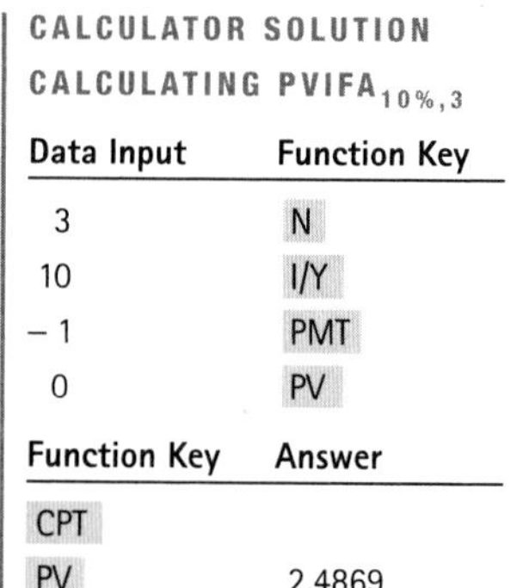

CALCULATOR SOLUTION
CALCULATING PVIFA$_{10\%,3}$

Data Input	Function Key
3	N
10	I/Y
– 1	PMT
0	PV

Function Key	Answer
CPT	
PV	2.4869

$$
\begin{aligned}
EAA_A &= NPV/PVIFA_{i,n} \\
&= \$243.50/2.487 \\
&= \$97.91 \\
EAA_B &= \$306.50/4.355 \\
&= \$70.38
\end{aligned}
$$

How do we interpret the *EAA*? For a project with an n-year life, it tells us what the dollar value is of an n-year annual annuity that would provide the same *NPV* as the project. Thus, for project A, it means that a three-year annuity of $97.91 given a discount rate of 10 percent would produce a net present value the same as project A's net present value, which is $243.50. We can now compare the equivalent annual annuities directly to determine which project is better. We can do this because we now have found the level of annual annuity that produces an *NPV* equivalent to the project's *NPV.* Thus, because they are both annual annuities, they are comparable. An easy way to see this is to use the *EAAs* to create infinite-life replacement chains. To do this, we need only calculate the present value of an infinite stream or perpetuity of equivalent annual annuities. This is done by using the present value of an infinite annuity formula—that is, simply dividing the equivalent annual annuity by the appropriate discount rate. In this case we find:

$$
\begin{aligned}
NPV_{\infty,A} &= \$97.91/.10 \\
&= \$979.10 \\
NPV_{\infty,B} &= \$70.38/.10 \\
&= \$703.80
\end{aligned}
$$

Here we have calculated the present value of an infinite-life replacement chain. Because the *EAA* method provides the same results as the infinite-life replacement chain, it really doesn't matter which method you prefer to use.

CONCEPT CHECK

1. What is capital rationing and why does it occur?
2. What are mutually exclusive projects? Give an example.

Options in Capital Budgeting

The use of our discounted cash-flow decision criteria like the *NPV* method provides an excellent framework within which to evaluate projects. However, what happens if the project being analyzed has the potential to be modified after some future uncertainty has been resolved? For example, if a project that had an expected life of 10 years turns out to be better than anticipated, it may be expanded or continued past 10 years, perhaps going for 20 years. However, if its cash flows do not meet expectations, it may not last a full 10 years—it might be scaled back, abandoned, or sold. In addition, it might be delayed for a year or two. This flexibility is something that the *NPV* and our other decision criteria had a difficult time dealing with. In fact, the *NPV* may actually understate the value of the project because the future opportunities associated with the possibility of modifying the project may have a positive value. It is this value of flexibility that we will be examining using options.

Three of the most common option types that can add value to a capital-budgeting project are (1) the option to delay a project until the future cash flows are more favorable—this option is common when the firm has exclusive rights, perhaps a patent, to a product or technology; (2) the option to expand a project, perhaps in size or even to new products that would not have otherwise been feasible; and (3) the option to abandon a project if the future cash flows fall short of expectations.

THE OPTION TO DELAY A PROJECT There is no question that the estimated cash flows associated with a project can change over time. In fact, as a result of changing expected cash flows, a project that currently has a negative net present value may have a positive net present value in the future. Let's look at the example of an eco-car—a car with a hybrid gasoline engine and an electric motor. Perhaps you've developed a high-voltage nickel-metal hydride battery that you plan on using, coupled with a gasoline engine, to power an automobile. However, as you examine the costs of introducing an eco-car capable of producing 70 miles per gallon, you realize that it is still relatively expensive to manufacture the nickel-metal hydride battery and the market for such a car would be quite small. Thus, this project seems to have a negative net present value. Does that mean that the rights to the high-voltage nickel-metal hydride battery have no value? No, they have value because you may be able to improve on this technology in the future and make the battery more efficient and less expensive, and they also have value because oil prices may rise, which would lead to a bigger market for fuel-efficient cars. In effect, the ability to delay this project with the hope that technological and market conditions will change, making this project profitable, lends value to this project.

Another example of the option to delay a project until the future cash flows are more favorable involves a firm that owns the oil rights to some oil-rich land and is considering an oil-drilling project. After all of the costs and the expected oil output are considered, this project may have a negative net present value. Does that mean the firm should give away its oil rights or that those oil rights have no value? Certainly not; there is a chance that in the future oil prices could rise to the point that this negative net present value project could become a positive net present value project. It is this ability to delay development that provides value. Thus, the value in this seemingly negative *NPV* project is provided by the option to delay the project until the future cash flows are more favorable.

THE OPTION TO EXPAND A PROJECT Just as we saw with the option to delay a project, the estimated cash flows associated with a project can change over time, making it valuable to expand a project. Again, this flexibility to adjust production to demand has value. For example, a firm may build a production plant with excess capacity so that if the product has more than anticipated demand, it can simply increase production. Alternatively, taking on this project may provide the firm with a foothold in a new industry and lead to other products that would not have otherwise been feasible. This reasoning has led many firms to expand into e-businesses, hoping to gain know-how and expertise that will lead to other profitable projects down the line. It also provides some of the rationale for research and development expenditures in which the future project is not well defined.

Let's go back to our example of the eco-car and examine the option to expand that project. One of the reasons that most of the major automobile firms are introducing eco-cars is that they feel that if gas prices surge beyond the $2 per gallon price, these hybrids may be the future of the industry, and the only way to gain the know-how and expertise to produce an eco-car is to do it. If the cost of technology declines and the demands increase—perhaps pushed on by increases in gas prices—then they will be ready to expand into full-fledged production. This point becomes clear when you look at the Honda Insight, which is a two-passenger, three-cylinder car with a gas engine and electric motor. It provides 65 miles per gallon, and Honda expects to sell between 7,000 and 8,000 a year. On every Insight that Honda sells, analysts estimate that Honda loses about $8,000. A Honda spokesman says that Honda expects to break even "in a couple of years." Still, this project makes sense because only through it can Honda gain the technological and production expertise to produce an eco-car profitably. Moreover, the technology Honda develops with the Insight may have profitable applications for other cars or in other areas. In effect, it is the option of expanding production in the future that brings value to this project.

THE OPTION TO ABANDON A PROJECT The option to abandon a project as the estimated cash flows associated with a project can change over time also has value. Again, it is this flexibility to adjust to new information that provides the value. For example, a project's sales in the first year or two may not live up to expectations, with the project being barely profitable. The firm may then decide to liquidate the project and sell the plant and all of the equipment, and that liquidated value may be more than the value of keeping the project going.

Again, let's go back to our example of the eco-car and, this time, examine the option to abandon that project. If after a few years the cost of gas falls dramatically while the cost of technology remains high, the eco-car may not become profitable. At that point Honda may decide to abandon the project and sell the technology, including all the patent rights it has developed. In effect, the original project, the eco-car, may not be of value, but the technology that has been developed may be. In effect, the value of abandoning the project and selling the technology may be more than the value of keeping the project running. Again, it is the value of flexibility associated with the possibility of modifying the project in the future—in this case abandoning the project—that can produce positive value.

OPTIONS IN CAPITAL BUDGETING: THE BOTTOM LINE Because of the potential to be modified in the future after some future uncertainty has been resolved, we may find that a project with a negative net present value based upon its expected free cash flows is a "good" project and should be accepted—this demonstrates the value of options. In addition, we may find that a project with a positive net present value may be of more value if its acceptance is delayed. Options also explain the logic that drives firms to take on negative net present value projects that allow them to enter new markets. The option to abandon a project explains why firms hire employees on a temporary basis rather than permanently, why they may lease rather than buy equipment, and why they may enter into contracts with suppliers on an annual basis rather than long term.

CONCEPT CHECK

1. Give an example of an option to delay a project. Why might this be of value?
2. Give an example of an option to expand a project. Why might this be of value?
3. Give an example of an option to abandon a project. Why might this be of value?

THE MULTINATIONAL FIRM: INTERNATIONAL COMPLICATIONS IN CALCULATING EXPECTED FREE CASH FLOWS

The process of measuring the incremental after-tax cash flows to the company as a whole gets a bit more complicated when we are dealing with competition from abroad. One area in which this is certainly true is in calculating the right base case; that is, what the firm's free cash flows would be if the project is not taken on. In determining what free cash flows will be in the future, we must always be aware of potential competition from abroad. We need only look to the auto industry to see that competition from abroad can be serious. During the 1970s, who would have thought that firms like Toyota, Honda, and Nissan could enter the U.S. markets and actually challenge the likes of Ford and GM? The end result of this is that the opening of the markets to international competition has not only led to increased opportunities, but it has also led to increased difficulties in estimating expected free cash flows.

There are also other intangible benefits from investing in countries like Germany and Japan, where cutting-edge technology is making its way into the marketplace. Here, investment abroad provides a chance to observe the introduction of new innovations on a first-hand basis. This allows firms like IBM, GE, and 3Com to react more quickly to any technological advances and product innovations that might come out of Germany or Japan.

Finally, international markets can be viewed as an option to expand if a product is well received at home. For example, McDonald's was much more of a hit at home than anyone ever expected 30 years ago. Once it conquered the United States, it moved abroad. There is much uncertainty every time McDonald's opens a new store in another country; it is unlikely that any new store will be without problems stemming from cultural differences. What McDonald's learns in the first store opened in a new country is then used in modifying any new stores that it opens in that country. In effect, opening that first store in a new country provides the option to expand, and that option to expand and the value of the flexibility to adjust to the future make opening that first store in a new country a good project.

HOW FINANCIAL MANAGERS USE THIS MATERIAL

Not only is the financial manager responsible for finding and then properly evaluating new projects, but the financial manager must be certain that the numbers going into the analysis are correct. Let's look at what the financial managers at Burger King faced when they decided to introduce the Big King, a new burger that looks an awful lot like the Big

Mac. The first task they face is to estimate what the sales from this new product will be—a task that is easier said than done. Not only will sales be dependent upon how good the product is, or in this case, how good the product tastes, but they will also be dependent upon how good a job the marketing department does in selling the public on this new product. But just looking at sales is not enough. To properly perform the analysis on this product, Burger King needs to know what portion of sales will simply be sales diverted from Whoppers, and what portion of sales will be new to Burger King as a whole. In other words, when it introduces the Big King, how much of the sales are from new customers—those "Big Mac attack" eaters?

This is truly an area where finance and marketing meet. Much of the job of the financial manager is to make sure that the numbers are correct. That is, have the marketing people considered any synergistic effects? If new customers are drawn into Burger King, are they likely to buy a drink and some fries—two very high markup sales? Will they bring in their families or friends when they make their Big King purchase? How about the increased inventory associated with carrying the Big King line? If it all sounds pretty complex, that's because it *is* complex. But more important, it is a decision that has a dramatic effect on the future direction of the firm, and it is an ongoing decision. That is, once the product is introduced and you see how the public reacts, you will continuously reevaluate the product to determine if it should be abandoned or expanded.

Look at the "New Coke." Cola-Cola spent an enormous amount of money test marketing and promoting that product, only to find the public didn't really like it after all. Once it realized that, the next capital-budgeting decision it made was, given the new sales estimates, to abandon the product. In effect, capital budgeting involves reinventing the company, and in order to make a good decision, you've got to have good information going into your capital-budgeting decision model. An awful lot of time and many jobs—maybe your job—revolve around making these decisions.

SUMMARY

Objective 1

In this chapter, we examined the measurement of free cash flows associated with a firm's investment proposals that are used to evaluate those proposals. Relying on **Principle 3: Cash—Not Profits—Is King,** and **Principle 4: Incremental Cash Flows—It's only what changes that counts,** we focused only on free cash flows—that is, the incremental or different after-tax cash flows attributed to the investment proposal. Care was taken to be wary of cash flows diverted from existing products, look for incidental or synergistic effects, consider working-capital requirements, consider incremental expenses, ignore sunk costs, account for opportunity costs, examine overhead costs carefully, and ignore interest payments and financing flows.

Objective 2

In general, a project's free cash flows fall into one of three categories: (1) the initial outlay, (2) the annual free cash flows, and (3) the terminal cash flow.

To measure a project's benefits, we use the project's free cash flows. These free cash flows include:

project's free cash flows = project's change in operating cash flows
− change in net working capital
− change in capital spending

We can rewrite this, inserting our calculation for project's change in operating cash flows:

project's free cash flows = change in earnings before interest and taxes
− change in taxes
+ change in depreciation
− change in net working capital
− change in capital spending

Objective 3

We also examined capital rationing and the problems it can create by imposing a limit on the dollar size of the capital budget. Although capital rationing does not, in general, lead to the goal of maximization of shareholders' wealth, it does exist in practice. We discussed problems associated with the evaluation of mutually exclusive projects. Mutually exclusive projects occur when we have a set of investment proposals that perform essentially the same task. In general, to deal with mutually exclusive projects, we rank them by means of the discounted cash flow criteria and select the project with the highest ranking. Conflicting rankings may arise because of the size disparity problem, the time disparity problem, and unequal lives. The problem of incomparability of projects with different lives is not simply a result of the different lives; rather, it arises because future profitable investment proposals may be rejected without being included in the analysis. Replacement chains and equivalent annual annuities are possible solutions to this problem.

How do we deal with a project that has the potential to be modified after some future uncertainty has been resolved? This flexibility to be modified is something that the *NPV* and our other decision criteria had a difficult time dealing with. It is this value of flexibility that we examined using options. Three of the most common types of options that can add value to a capital budgeting project are (1) the option to delay a project until the future cash flows are more favorable—this option is common when the firm has exclusive rights, perhaps a patent, to a product or technology; (2) the option to expand a project, perhaps in size or even to new products that would not have otherwise been feasible; and (3) the option to abandon a project if the future cash flows fall short of expectations.

KEY TERMS

Capital rationing, 344

Equivalent annual annuity (*EAA*), 349

Initial outlay, 332

Mutually exclusive projects, 346

Go To: **www.prenhall.com/keown** for downloads and current events associated with this chapter

STUDY QUESTIONS

10-1. Why do we focus on cash flows rather than accounting profits in making our capital-budgeting decisions? Why are we interested only in incremental cash flows rather than total cash flows?

10-2. If depreciation is not a cash flow item, why does it affect the level of cash flows from a project in any way?

10-3. If a project requires additional investment in working capital, how should this be treated in calculating cash flows?

10-4. How do sunk costs affect the determination of cash flows associated with an investment proposal?

10-5. What are mutually exclusive projects? Why might the existence of mutually exclusive projects cause problems in the implementation of the discounted cash flow capital-budgeting decision criteria?

10-6. What are common reasons for capital rationing? Is capital rationing rational?

10-7. How should managers compare two mutually exclusive projects of unequal size? Would your approach change if capital rationing existed?

10-8. What causes the time disparity ranking problem? What reinvestment rate assumptions are associated with the net present value and internal rate of return capital-budgeting criteria?

10-9. When might two mutually exclusive projects having unequal lives be incomparable? How should managers deal with this problem?

SELF-TEST PROBLEMS

ST-1. The Easterwood Corporation, a firm in the 34 percent marginal tax bracket with a 15 percent required rate of return or cost of capital, is considering a new project. This project involves the introduction of a new product. This project is expected to last five years and then, because this is somewhat of a fad project, to be terminated. Given the following information, determine the free cash flows associated with the project, the project's net present value, the profitability index, and the internal rate of return. Apply the appropriate decision criteria.

Cost of new plant and equipment: $20,900,000

Shipping and installation costs: $ 300,000

Unit sales:

Year	Units Sold
1	100,000
2	130,000
3	160,000
4	100,000
5	60,000

Sales price per unit: $500/unit in years 1–4, $380/unit in year 5

Variable cost per unit: $260/unit

Annual fixed costs: $300,000

Working-capital requirements: There will be an initial working-capital requirement of $500,000 just to get production started. For each year, the total investment in net working capital will be equal to 10 percent of the dollar value of sales for that year. Thus, the investment in working capital will increase during years 1 through 3, then decrease in year 4. Finally, all working capital is liquidated at the termination of the project at the end of year 5.

The depreciation method: Use the simplified straight-line method over five years. It is assumed that the plant and equipment will have no salvage value after five years.

ST-2. The J. Serrano Corporation is considering signing a one-year contract with one of two computer-based marketing firms. Although one is more expensive, it offers a more extensive program and thus will provide higher after-tax net cash flows. Assume these two options are mutually exclusive and that the required rate of return is 12 percent. Given the following after-tax net cash flows:

YEAR	OPTION A	OPTION B
0	–$50,000	–$100,000
1	70,000	130,000

a. Calculate the net present value.
b. Calculate the profitability index.
c. Calculate the internal rate of return.
d. If there is no capital-rationing constraint, which project should be selected? If there is a capital-rationing constraint, how should the decision be made?

STUDY PROBLEMS (SET A)

10-1A. (*Capital gains tax*) The J. Harris Corporation is considering selling one of its old assembly machines. The machine, purchased for $30,000 five years ago, had an expected life of 10 years and an expected salvage value of zero. Assume Harris uses simplified straight-line depreciation, creating depreciation of $3,000 per year, and could sell this old machine for $35,000. Also assume a 34 percent marginal tax rate.

a. What would be the taxes associated with this sale?
b. If the old machine were sold for $25,000, what would be the taxes associated with this sale?
c. If the old machine were sold for $15,000, what would be the taxes associated with this sale?
d. If the old machine were sold for $12,000, what would be the taxes associated with this sale?

10-2A. (*Relevant cash flows*) Captins' Cereal is considering introducing a variation of its current breakfast cereal, Crunch Stuff. This new cereal will be similar to the old with the exception that it will contain sugarcoated marshmallows shaped in the form of stars. The new cereal will be called Crunch Stuff n' Stars. It is estimated that the sales for the new cereal will be $25 million; however, 20 percent of those sales will be former Crunch Stuff customers who have switched to Crunch Stuff n' Stars who would not have switched if the new product had not been introduced. What is the relevant sales level to consider when deciding whether or not to introduce Crunch Stuff n' Stars?

10-3A. (*Calculating free cash flows*) Racin' Scooters is introducing a new product and has an expected change in EBIT of $475,000. Racin' Scooters has a 34 percent marginal tax rate. This project will also produce $100,000 of depreciation per year. In addition, this project will also cause the following changes:

	WITHOUT THE PROJECT	WITH THE PROJECT
Accounts receivable	$45,000	$63,000
Inventory	65,000	80,000
Accounts payable	70,000	94,000

What is the project's free cash flow?

10-4A. (*Calculating free cash flows*) Visible Fences is introducing a new product and has an expected change in EBIT of $900,000. Visible Fences has a 34 percent marginal tax rate. This project will also produce $300,000 of depreciation per year. In addition, this project will also cause the following changes:

	WITHOUT THE PROJECT	WITH THE PROJECT
Accounts receivable	$55,000	$63,000
Inventory	55,000	70,000
Accounts payable	90,000	106,000

What is the project's free cash flow?

10-5A. (*Calculating operating cash flows*) Assume that a new project will annually generate revenues of $2,000,000 and cash expenses, including both fixed and variable costs, of $800,000, while increasing depreciation by $200,000 per year. In addition, let's assume that the firm's marginal tax rate is 34 percent. Calculate the operating cash flows using the pro forma and 3 alternatives.

10-6A. (*Calculating operating cash flows*) Assume that a new project will annually generate revenues of $3,000,000 and cash expenses, including both fixed and variable costs, of $900,000, while increasing depreciation by $400,000 per year. In addition, let's assume that the firm's marginal tax rate is 34 percent. Calculate the operating cash flows using all three methods.

10-7A. (*Calculating free cash flows*) You are considering expanding your product line that currently consists of skateboards to include gas-powered skateboards, and you feel you can sell 10,000 of these per year for 10 years (after which time this project is expected to shut down with solar-powered skateboards taking over). The gas skateboards would sell for $100 each with variable costs of $40 for each one produced, while annual fixed costs associated with production would be $160,000. In addition, there would be a $1,000,000 initial expenditure associated with the purchase of new production equipment. It is assumed that this initial expenditure will be depreciated using the simplified straight-line method down to zero over 10 years. This project will also require a one-time initial investment of $50,000 in net working capital associated with inventory and that working capital investment will be recovered when the project is shut down. Finally, assume that the firm's marginal tax rate is 34 percent.

a. What is the initial outlay associated with this project?
b. What are the annual free cash flows associated with this project for years 1 through 9?

c. What is the terminal cash flow in year 10 (that is, what is the free cash flow in year 10 plus any additional cash flows associated with termination of the project)?
d. What is the project's *NPV* given a 10 percent required rate of return?

10-8A. (*Calculating free cash flows*) You are considering new elliptical trainers and you feel you can sell 5,000 of these per year for five years (after which time this project is expected to shut down when it is learned that being fit is unhealthy). The elliptical trainers would sell for $1,000 each with variable costs of $500 for each one produced, while annual fixed costs associated with production would be $1,000,000. In addition, there would be a $5,000,000 initial expenditure associated with the purchase of new production equipment. It is assumed that this initial expenditure will be depreciated using the simplified straight-line method down to zero over five years. This project will also require a one-time initial investment of $1,000,000 in net working capital associated with inventory and that working capital investment will be recovered when the project is shut down. Finally, assume that the firm's marginal tax rate is 34 percent.
a. What is the initial outlay associated with this project?
b. What are the annual free cash flows associated with this project for years 1 through 9?
c. What is the terminal cash flow in year 10 (that is, what is the free cash flow in year 10 plus any additional cash flows associated with termination of the project)?
d. What is the project's *NPV* given a 10 percent required rate of return?

10-9A. (*New project analysis*) The Chung Chemical Corporation is considering the purchase of a chemical analysis machine. Although the machine being considered will result in an increase in earnings before interest and taxes of $35,000 per year, it has a purchase price of $100,000, and it would cost an additional $5,000 after tax to properly install this machine. In addition, to properly operate this machine, inventory must be increased by $5,000. This machine has an expected life of 10 years, after which it will have no salvage value. Also, assume simplified straight-line depreciation and that this machine is being depreciated down to zero, a 34 percent marginal tax rate, and a required rate of return of 15 percent.
a. What is the initial outlay associated with this project?
b. What are the annual after-tax cash flows associated with this project for years 1 through 9?
c. What is the terminal cash flow in year 10 (what is the annual after-tax cash flow in year 10 plus any additional cash flows associated with termination of the project)?
d. Should this machine be purchased?

10-10A. (*New project analysis*) Raymobile Motors is considering the purchase of a new production machine for $500,000. The purchase of this machine will result in an increase in earnings before interest and taxes of $150,000 per year. To operate this machine properly, workers would have to go through a brief training session that would cost $25,000 after tax. In addition, it would cost $5,000 after tax to install this machine properly. Also, because this machine is extremely efficient, its purchase would necessitate an increase in inventory of $30,000. This machine has an expected life of 10 years, after which it will have no salvage value. Assume simplified straight-line depreciation and that this machine is being depreciated down to zero, a 34 percent marginal tax rate, and a required rate of return of 15 percent.
a. What is the initial outlay associated with this project?
b. What are the annual after-tax cash flows associated with this project for years 1 through 9?
c. What is the terminal cash flow in year 10 (what is the annual after-tax cash flow in year 10 plus any additional cash flows associated with termination of the project)?
d. Should this machine be purchased?

10-11A. (*New project analysis*) Garcia's Truckin' Inc. is considering the purchase of a new production machine for $200,000. The purchase of this machine will result in an increase in earnings before interest and taxes of $50,000 per year. To operate this machine properly, workers would have to go through a brief training session that would cost $5,000 after tax. In addition, it would cost $5,000 after tax to install this machine properly. Also, because this machine is extremely efficient, its purchase would necessitate an increase in inventory of $20,000. This machine has an expected life of 10 years, after which it will have no salvage value. Finally, to purchase the new machine, it appears that the firm would have to borrow $100,000 at 8 percent interest from its local bank, resulting in additional interest payments of $8,000 per year. Assume simplified straight-line depreciation and that this machine is being depreciated down to zero, a 34 percent marginal tax rate, and a required rate of return of 10 percent.

a. What is the initial outlay associated with this project?
b. What are the annual after-tax cash flows associated with this project for years 1 through 9?
c. What is the terminal cash flow in year 10 (what is the annual after-tax cash flow in year 10 plus any additional cash flows associated with termination of the project)?
d. Should this machine be purchased?

10-12A. (*Comprehensive problem*) Traid Winds Corporation, a firm in the 34 percent marginal tax bracket with a 15 percent required rate of return or cost of capital, is considering a new project. This project involves the introduction of a new product. This project is expected to last five years and then, because this is somewhat of a fad project, to be terminated. Given the following information, determine the free cash flows associated with the project, the project's net present value, the profitability index, and the internal rate of return. Apply the appropriate decision criteria.

Cost of new plant and equipment:		$14,800,000
Shipping and installation costs:		$ 200,000
Unit sales:	Year	Units Sold
	1	70,000
	2	120,000
	3	120,000
	4	80,000
	5	70,000

Sales price per unit: $300/unit in years 1–4, $250/unit in year 5

Variable cost per unit: $140/unit

Annual fixed costs: $700,000

Working-capital requirements: There will be an initial working-capital requirement of $200,000 just to get production started. For each year, the total investment in net working capital will be equal to 10 percent of the dollar value of sales for that year. Thus, the investment in working capital will increase during years 1 through 3, then decrease in year 4. Finally, all working capital is liquidated at the termination of the project at the end of year 5.

The depreciation method: Use the simplified straight-line method over five years. It is assumed that the plant and equipment will have no salvage value after five years.

10-13A. (*Comprehensive problem*) The Shome Corporation, a firm in the 34 percent marginal tax bracket with a 15 percent required rate of return or cost of capital, is considering a new project. This project involves the introduction of a new product. This project is expected to last five years and then, because this is somewhat of a fad project, to be terminated. Given the following information, determine the free cash flows associated with the project, the project's net present value, the profitability index, and the internal rate of return. Apply the appropriate decision criteria.

Cost of new plant and equipment:		$6,900,000
Shipping and installation costs:		$ 100,000
Unit sales:	Year	Units Sold
	1	80,000
	2	100,000
	3	120,000
	4	70,000
	5	70,000

Sales price per unit: $250/unit in years 1–4, $200/unit in year 5

Variable cost per unit: $130/unit

Annual fixed costs: $300,000

Working-capital requirements: There will be an initial working-capital requirement of $100,000 just to get production started. For each year, the total investment in net working capital will be equal to 10 percent of the dollar value of sales for that year. Thus, the investment in working capital will increase during years 1 through 3, then decrease in year 4. Finally, all working capital is liquidated at the termination of the project at the end of year 5.

The depreciation method: Use the simplified straight-line method over five years. It is assumed that the plant and equipment will have no salvage value after five years.

10-14A. (*Size disparity ranking problem*) The D. Dorner Farms Corporation is considering purchasing one of two fertilizer-herbicides for the upcoming year. The more expensive of the two is better and will produce a higher yield. Assume these projects are mutually exclusive and that the required rate of return is 10 percent. Given the following after-tax net cash flows:

YEAR	PROJECT A	PROJECT B
0	–\$500	–\$5,000
1	700	6,000

a. Calculate the net present value.
b. Calculate the profitability index.
c. Calculate the internal rate of return.
d. If there is no capital-rationing constraint, which project should be selected? If there is a capital-rationing constraint, how should the decision be made?

10-15A. (*Time disparity ranking problem*) The State Spartan Corporation is considering two mutually exclusive projects. The cash flows associated with those projects are as follows:

YEAR	PROJECT A	PROJECT B
0	–\$50,000	–\$50,000
1	15,625	0
2	15,625	0
3	15,625	0
4	15,625	0
5	15,625	\$100,000

The required rate of return on these projects is 10 percent.

a. What is each project's payback period?
b. What is each project's net present value?
c. What is each project's internal rate of return?
d. What has caused the ranking conflict?
e. Which project should be accepted? Why?

10-16A. (*Unequal lives ranking problem*) The B. T. Knight Corporation is considering two mutually exclusive pieces of machinery that perform the same task. The two alternatives available provide the following set of after-tax net cash flows:

YEAR	EQUIPMENT A	EQUIPMENT B
0	–\$20,000	–\$20,000
1	12,590	6,625
2	12,590	6,625
3	12,590	6,625
4		6,625
5		6,625
6		6,625
7		6,625
8		6,625
9		6,625

Equipment A has an expected life of three years, whereas equipment B has an expected life of nine years. Assume a required rate of return of 15 percent.

a. Calculate each project's payback period.
b. Calculate each project's net present value.
c. Calculate each project's internal rate of return.
d. Are these projects comparable?
e. Compare these projects using replacement chains and *EAA*. Which project should be selected? Support your recommendation.

10-17A. (*EAAs*) The Andrzejewski Corporation is considering two mutually exclusive projects, one with a three-year life and one with a seven-year life. The after-tax cash flows from the two projects are as follows:

YEAR	PROJECT A	PROJECT B
0	−$50,000	−$50,000
1	20,000	36,000
2	20,000	36,000
3	20,000	36,000
4	20,000	
5	20,000	
6	20,000	
7	20,000	

a. Assuming a 10 percent required rate of return on both projects, calculate each project's *EAA*. Which project should be selected?

b. Calculate the present value of an infinite-life replacement chain for each project.

10-18A. (*Capital rationing*) Cowboy Hat Company of Stillwater, Oklahoma, is considering seven capital investment proposals, for which the funds available are limited to a maximum of $12 million. The projects are independent and have the following costs and profitability indexes associated with them:

PROJECT	COST	PROFITABILITY INDEX
A	$4,000,000	1.18
B	3,000,000	1.08
C	5,000,000	1.33
D	6,000,000	1.31
E	4,000,000	1.19
F	6,000,000	1.20
G	4,000,000	1.18

a. Under strict capital rationing, which projects should be selected?

b. What problems are there with capital rationing?

WEB WORKS

If you're an automaker, you've got to be ready for the next generation of cars. While they may be extremely efficient gas-powered vehicles, they could also be a hybrid—gas and electricity powered or even propelled by electricity generated by a hydrogen-oxygen chemical reaction. Given all the uncertainty associated with the future direction of automobiles and how they will be powered, it only makes sense to explore all avenues and make sure you're not left behind. That is, if you want to be a leader in this market and if it does in fact develop, you'll have an early presence in it, developing and refining your potential product line. That's the whole idea behind an option to expand a product line.

In the fuel-efficient automobile market, the Toyota Prius and the Honda Insight have taken the initial lead, with Ford's Prodigy, GM's Precipt, and now Daimler's ESX3 entering the competition. This is not an inexpensive effort; in fact, it has been estimated that the Toyota Prius, which employs an expensive electric-alone drive for much of its duty cycle, produces a loss per vehicle sold of approximately $10,000. Thinking about the discussion in this chapter dealing with the option to expand a product, why do you think they are willing to take on this type of loss-producing project? Does this make sense to you?

Now take a look at some of the different products being developed in this area. Which ones do you think have the highest chance of success? For example, Honda's new FCX car (**hondacorporate.com/?onload=fcx**) works on fuel cells. Check out how they work at **www.howstuffworks.com/fuel-cell.htm**.

Also, take a look at what Toyota is doing at **www.toyota.com** and also look at what Ford is doing (**www.ford.com/en/innovation/engineFuelTechnology/default.htm**). In addition, check out GM's new efforts (**www.gmev.com/**).

Has your opinion on whether or not these are appropriate projects to take on changed at all?

INTEGRATIVE PROBLEM

It's been two months since you took a position as an assistant financial analyst at Caledonia Products. Although your boss has been pleased with your work, he is still a bit hesitant about unleashing you without supervision. Your next assignment involves both the calculation of the cash flows associated with a new investment under consideration and the evaluation of several mutually exclusive projects. Given your lack of tenure at Caledonia, you have been asked not only to provide a recommendation, but also to respond to a number of questions aimed at judging your understanding of the capital-budgeting process. The memorandum you received outlining your assignment follows:

TO: The Assistant Financial Analyst

FROM: Mr. V. Morrison, CEO, Caledonia Products

RE: Cash Flow Analysis and Capital Rationing

We are considering the introduction of a new product. Currently we are in the 34 percent marginal tax bracket with a 15 percent required rate of return or cost of capital. This project is expected to last five years and then, because this is somewhat of a fad project, to be terminated. The following information describes the new project:

Cost of new plant and equipment: $7,900,000

Shipping and installation costs: $ 100,000

Unit sales:

Year	Units Sold
1	70,000
2	120,000
3	140,000
4	80,000
5	60,000

Sales price per unit: $300/unit in years 1–4, $260/unit in year 5

Variable cost per unit: $180/unit

Annual fixed costs: $200,000

Working-capital requirements: There will be an initial working-capital requirement of $100,000 just to get production started. For each year, the total investment in net working capital will be equal to 10 percent of the dollar value of sales for that year. Thus, the investment in working capital will increase during years 1 through 3, then decrease in year 4. Finally, all working capital is liquidated at the termination of the project at the end of year 5.

The depreciation method: Use the simplified straight-line method over five years. It is assumed that the plant and equipment will have no salvage value after five years.

1. Should Caledonia focus on cash flows or accounting profits in making our capital-budgeting decisions? Should we be interested in incremental cash flows, incremental profits, total free cash flows, or total profits?
2. How does depreciation affect free cash flows?
3. How do sunk costs affect the determination of cash flows?
4. What is the project's initial outlay?

5. What are the differential cash flows over the project's life?
6. What is the terminal cash flow?
7. Draw a cash flow diagram for this project.
8. What is its net present value?
9. What is its internal rate of return?
10. Should the project be accepted? Why or why not?

You have also been asked for your views on three unrelated sets of projects. Each set of projects involves two mutually exclusive projects. These projects follow:

11. Caledonia is considering two investments with one-year lives. The more expensive of the two is the better and will produce more savings. Assume these projects are mutually exclusive and that the required rate of return is 10 percent. Given the following after-tax net cash flows:

YEAR	PROJECT A	PROJECT B
0	–$195,000	–$1,200,000
1	240,000	1,650,000

a. Calculate the net present value.
b. Calculate the profitability index.
c. Calculate the internal rate of return.
d. If there is no capital-rationing constraint, which project should be selected? If there is a capital-rationing constraint, how should the decision be made?

12. Caledonia is considering two additional mutually exclusive projects. The cash flows associated with these projects are as follows:

YEAR	PROJECT A	PROJECT B
0	–$100,000	–$100,000
1	32,000	0
2	32,000	0
3	32,000	0
4	32,000	0
5	32,000	$200,000

The required rate of return on these projects is 11 percent.

a. What is each project's payback period?
b. What is each project's net present value?
c. What is each project's internal rate of return?
d. What has caused the ranking conflict?
e. Which project should be accepted? Why?

13. The final two mutually exclusive projects that Caledonia is considering involve mutually exclusive pieces of machinery that perform the same task. The two alternatives available provide the following set of after-tax net cash flows:

YEAR	EQUIPMENT A	EQUIPMENT B
0	–$100,000	–$100,000
1	65,000	32,500
2	65,000	32,500
3	65,000	32,500
4		32,500
5		32,500
6		32,500
7		32,500
8		32,500
9		32,500

Equipment A has an expected life of three years, whereas equipment B has an expected life of nine years. Assume a required rate of return of 14 percent.

- **a.** Calculate each project's payback period.
- **b.** Calculate each project's net present value.
- **c.** Calculate each project's internal rate of return.
- **d.** Are these projects comparable?
- **e.** Compare these projects using replacement chains and *EAAs*. Which project should be selected? Support your recommendation.

STUDY PROBLEMS (SET B)

10-1B. (*Capital gains tax*) The R. T. Kleinman Corporation is considering selling one of its old assembly machines. The machine, purchased for $40,000 five years ago, had an expected life of 10 years and an expected salvage value of zero. Assume Kleinman uses simplified straight-line depreciation, creating depreciation of $4,000 per year, and could sell this old machine for $45,000. Also assume a 34 percent marginal tax rate.

- **a.** What would be the taxes associated with this sale?
- **b.** If the old machine were sold for $40,000, what would be the taxes associated with this sale?
- **c.** If the old machine were sold for $20,000, what would be the taxes associated with this sale?
- **d.** If the old machine were sold for $17,000, what would be the taxes associated with this sale?

10-2B. (*Relevant cash flows*) Fruity Stones is considering introducing a variation of its current breakfast cereal, Jolt 'n Stones. This new cereal will be similar to the old with the exception that it will contain more sugar in the form of small pebbles. The new cereal will be called Stones 'n Stuff. It is estimated that the sales for the new cereal will be $100 million; however, 40 percent of those sales will be from former Fruity Stones customers who have switched to Stones 'n Stuff who would not have switched if the new product had not been introduced. What is the relevant sales level to consider when deciding whether or not to introduce Stones 'n Stuff?

10-3B. (*Calculating free cash flows*) Tetious Dimensions is introducing a new product and has an expected change in EBIT of $775,000. Tetious Dimensions has a 34 percent marginal tax rate. This project will also produce $200,000 of depreciation per year. In addition, this project will also cause the following changes:

	WITHOUT THE PROJECT	WITH THE PROJECT
Accounts receivable	$55,000	$89,000
Inventory	100,000	180,000
Accounts payable	70,000	120,000

What is the project's free cash flow?

10-4B. (*Calculating free cash flows*) Duncan Motors is introducing a new product and has an expected change in EBIT of $300,000. Duncan Motors has a 34 percent marginal tax rate. This project will also produce $50,000 of depreciation per year. In addition, this project will also cause the following changes:

	WITHOUT THE PROJECT	WITH THE PROJECT
Accounts receivable	$33,000	$23,000
Inventory	25,000	40,000
Accounts payable	50,000	86,000

What is the project's free cash flow?

10-5B. (*New project analysis*) The Guo Chemical Corporation is considering the purchase of a chemical analysis machine. The purchase of this machine will result in an increase in earnings before interest and taxes of $70,000 per year. The machine has a purchase price of $250,000, and it would cost an additional $10,000 after tax to install this machine properly. In addition, to operate this machine properly, inventory must be increased by $15,000. This machine has an expected life of 10 years, after which it will have no salvage value. Also, assume simplified straight-line depreciation and that this machine is being depreciated down to zero, a 34 percent marginal tax rate, and a required rate of return of 15 percent.

a. What is the initial outlay associated with this project?
b. What are the annual after-tax cash flows associated with this project for years 1 through 9?
c. What is the terminal cash flow in year 10 (what is the annual after-tax cash flow in year 10 plus any additional cash flow associated with termination of the project)?
d. Should this machine be purchased?

10-6B. (*New project analysis*) El Gato's Motors is considering the purchase of a new production machine for $1 million. The purchase of this machine will result in an increase in earnings before interest and taxes of $400,000 per year. To operate this machine properly, workers would have to go through a brief training session that would cost $100,000 after tax. In addition, it would cost $50,000 after tax to install this machine properly. Also, because this machine is extremely efficient, its purchase would necessitate an increase in inventory of $150,000. This machine has an expected life of 10 years, after which it will have no salvage value. Assume simplified straight-line depreciation and that this machine is being depreciated down to zero, a 34 percent marginal tax rate, and a required rate of return of 12 percent.

a. What is the initial outlay associated with this project?
b. What are the annual after-tax cash flows associated with this project for years 1 through 9?
c. What is the terminal cash flow in year 10 (what is the annual after-tax cash flow in year 10 plus any additional cash flows associated with termination of the project)?
d. Should this machine be purchased?

10-7B. (*New project analysis*) Weir's Truckin' Inc. is considering the purchase of a new production machine for $100,000. The purchase of this new machine will result in an increase in earnings before interest and taxes of $25,000 per year. To operate this machine properly, workers would have to go through a brief training session that would cost $5,000 after tax. In addition, it would cost $5,000 after-tax to install this machine properly. Also, because this machine is extremely efficient, its purchase would necessitate an increase in inventory of $25,000. This machine has an expected life of 10 years, after which it will have no salvage value. Finally, to purchase the new machine, it appears that the firm would have to borrow $80,000 at 10 percent interest from its local bank, resulting in additional interest payments of $8,000 per year. Assume simplified straight-line depreciation and that this machine is being depreciated down to zero, a 34 percent marginal tax rate, and a required rate of return of 12 percent.

a. What is the initial outlay associated with this project?
b. What are the annual after-tax cash flows associated with this project for years 1 through 9?
c. What is the terminal cash flow in year 10 (what is the annual after-tax cash flow in year 10 plus any additional cash flows associated with termination of the project)?
d. Should this machine be purchased?

10-8B. (*Comprehensive problem*) The Dophical Corporation, a firm in the 34 percent marginal tax bracket with a 15 percent required rate of return or cost of capital, is considering a new project. This project involves the introduction of a new product. This project is expected to last five years and then, because this is somewhat of a fad product, to be terminated. Given the following information, determine the free cash flows associated with the project, the project's net present value, the profitability index, and the internal rate of return. Apply the appropriate decision criteria.

Cost of new plant and equipment: $198,000,000
Shipping and installation costs: $ 2,000,000
Unit sales:

Year	Units Sold
1	1,000,000
2	1,800,000
3	1,800,000
4	1,200,000
5	700,000

Sales price per unit: $800/unit in years 1–4, $600/unit in year 5

Variable cost per unit: $400/unit

Annual fixed costs: $10,000,000

Working-capital requirements: There will be an initial working-capital requirement of $2,000,000 just to get production started. For each year, the total investment in net working capital will equal 10 percent of the dollar value of sales for that year. Thus, the investment in working capital will increase during years 1 through 3, then decrease in year 4. Finally, all working capital is liquidated at the termination of the project at the end of year 5.

The depreciation method: Use the simplified straight-line method over five years. It is assumed that the plant and equipment will have no salvage value after five years.

10-9B. (*Comprehensive problem*) The Kumar Corporation, a firm in the 34 percent marginal tax bracket with a 15 percent required rate of return or cost of capital, is considering a new project. This project involves the introduction of a new product. This project is expected to last five years and then, because this is somewhat of a fad product, to be terminated. Given the following information, determine the free cash flows associated with the project, the project's net present value, the profitability index, and the internal rate of return. Apply the appropriate decision criteria.

Cost of new plant and equipment: $9,900,000
Shipping and installation costs: $ 100,000
Unit sales:

Year	Units Sold
1	70,000
2	100,000
3	140,000
4	70,000
5	60,000

Sales price per unit: $280/unit in years 1–4, $180/unit in year 5

Variable cost per unit: $140/unit

Annual fixed costs: $300,000

Working-capital requirements: There will be an initial working-capital requirement of $100,000 just to get production started. For each year, the total investment in net working capital will equal 10 percent of the dollar value of sales for that year. Thus, the investment in working capital will increase during years 1 through 3, then decrease in year 4. Finally, all working capital is liquidated at the termination of the project at the end of year 5.

The depreciation method: Use the simplified straight-line method over five years. It is assumed that the plant and equipment will have no salvage value after five years.

10-10B. (*Size disparity ranking problem*) The Unk's Farms Corporation is considering purchasing one of two fertilizer-herbicides for the upcoming year. The more expensive of the two is the better and will produce a higher yield. Assume these projects are mutually exclusive and that the required rate of return is 10 percent. Given the following after-tax net cash flows:

YEAR	PROJECT A	PROJECT B
0	–$650	–$4,000
1	800	5,500

a. Calculate the net present value.
b. Calculate the profitability index.
c. Calculate the internal rate of return.
d. If there is no capital-rationing constraint, which project should be selected? If there is a capital-rationing constraint, how should the decision be made?

10-11B. (*Time disparity ranking problem*) The Z. Bello Corporation is considering two mutually exclusive projects. The cash flows associated with those projects are as follows:

YEAR	PROJECT A	PROJECT B
0	–$50,000	–$50,000
1	16,000	0
2	16,000	0
3	16,000	0
4	16,000	0
5	16,000	$100,000

The required rate of return on these projects is 11 percent.

a. What is each project's payback period?
b. What is each project's net present value?
c. What is each project's internal rate of return?
d. What has caused the ranking conflict?
e. Which project should be accepted? Why?

10-12B. (*Unequal lives ranking problem*) The Battling Bishops Corporation is considering two mutually exclusive pieces of machinery that perform the same task. The two alternatives available provide the following set of after-tax net cash flows:

YEAR	EQUIPMENT A	EQUIPMENT B
0	–$20,000	–$20,000
1	13,000	6,500
2	13,000	6,500
3	13,000	6,500
4		6,500
5		6,500
6		6,500
7		6,500
8		6,500
9		6,500

Equipment A has an expected life of three years, whereas equipment B has an expected life of nine years. Assume a required rate of return of 14 percent.

a. Calculate each project's payback period.
b. Calculate each project's net present value.
c. Calculate each project's internal rate of return.
d. Are these projects comparable?
e. Compare these projects using replacement chains and *EAAs*. Which project should be selected? Support your recommendation.

10-13B. (*EAAs*) The Anduski Corporation is considering two mutually exclusive projects, one with a five-year life and one with a seven-year life. The after-tax cash flows from the two projects are as follows:

YEAR	PROJECT A	PROJECT B
0	–$40,000	–$40,000
1	20,000	25,000
2	20,000	25,000

(continued)

YEAR	PROJECT A	PROJECT B
3	20,000	25,000
4	20,000	25,000
5	20,000	25,000
6	20,000	
7	20,000	

a. Assuming a 10 percent required rate of return on both projects, calculate each project's *EAA*. Which project should be selected?

b. Calculate the present value of an infinite-life replacement chain for each project.

10-14B. (*Capital rationing*) The Taco Toast Company is considering seven capital investment projects, for which the funds available are limited to a maximum of $12 million. The projects are independent and have the following costs and profitability indexes associated with them:

a. Under strict capital rationing, which projects should be selected?

b. What problems are associated with imposing capital rationing?

PROJECT	COST	PROFITABILITY INDEX
A	$4,000,000	1.18
B	3,000,000	1.08
C	5,000,000	1.33
D	6,000,000	1.31
E	4,000,000	1.19
F	6,000,000	1.20
G	4,000,000	1.18

SELF-TEST SOLUTIONS

ST-1. Step 1: First calculate the initial outlay.

YEAR	0	1	2	3	4	5
Section I. Calculate the change in EBIT, Taxes, and Depreciation (this becomes an input in the calculation of operating cash flow in Section II)						
Units sold		100,000	130,000	160,000	100,000	60,000
Sale price		$500	$500	$500	$500	$380
Sales revenue		$50,000,000	$65,000,000	$80,000,000	$50,000,000	$22,800,000
Less: variable costs		26,000,000	33,800,000	41,600,000	26,000,000	15,600,000
Less: fixed costs		$ 300,000	$ 300,000	$ 300,000	$ 300,000	$ 300,000
Equals: EBDIT		$23,700,000	$30,900,000	$38,100,000	$23,700,000	$ 6,900,000
Less: depreciation		$ 4,240,000	$ 4,240,000	$ 4,240,000	$ 4,240,000	$ 4,240,000
Equals: EBIT		$19,460,000	$26,660,000	$33,860,000	$19,460,000	$ 2,660,000
Taxes (@34%)		$ 6,616,400	$ 9,064,400	$ 11,512,400	$ 6,616,400	$ 904,400
Section II. Calculate Operating Cash Flow (this becomes an input in the calculation of free cash flow in Section IV)						
Operating Cash Flow:						
EBIT		$19,460,000	$26,660,000	$33,860,000	$19,460,000	$ 2,660,000
Minus: taxes		$ 6,616,400	$ 9,064,400	$ 11,512,400	$ 6,616,400	$ 904,400
Plus: depreciation		$ 4,240,000	$ 4,240,000	$ 4,240,000	$ 4,240,000	$ 4,240,000
Equals: operating cash flow		$17,083,600	$21,835,600	$26,587,600	$17,083,600	$ 5,995,600

YEAR	0	1	2	3	4	5
Section III. Calculate the Net Working Capital (this becomes an input in the calculation of free cash flows in Section IV)						
Change in Net Working Capital:						
Revenue:		$ 50,000,000	$ 65,000,000	$ 80,000,000	$ 50,000,000	$ 22,800,000
Initial working-capital requirement	$ 500,000					
Net working-capital needs		$ 5,000,000	$ 6,500,000	$ 8,000,000	$ 5,000,000	$ 2,280,000
Liquidation of working capital						$ 2,280,000
Change in working capital	$ 500,000	$ 4,500,000	$ 1,500,000	$ 1,500,000	($ 3,000,000)	($ 5,000,000)
Section IV. Calculate Free Cash Flow (using information calculated in Sections II and III, in addition to change in capital spending)						
Free Cash Flow:						
Operating cash flow		$ 17,083,600	$ 21,835,600	$ 26,587,600	$ 17,083,600	$ 5,995,600
Minus: change in net working capital	$ 500,000	$ 4,500,000	$ 1,500,000	$ 1,500,000	($ 3,000,000)	($ 5,000,000)
Minus: change in capital spending	$ 21,200,000	0	0	0	0	0
Free cash flow	($ 21,700,000)	$12,583,600	$20,335,600	$25,087,600	$20,083,600	$10,995,600
NPV	$38,064,020					

Step 2: Calculate the differential cash flows over the project's life.

Thus, the cash flow in the final year will be equal to the annual net cash flow in that year of $20,608 plus the terminal cash flow of $13,200 for a total of $33,808.

ST-2.

a.

$$NPV_A = \$70{,}000\left[\frac{1}{(1+.12)^1}\right] - \$50{,}000$$
$$= \$62{,}500 - \$50{,}000$$
$$= 12{,}500$$

$$NPV_B = \$130{,}000\left[\frac{1}{(1+.12)^1}\right] - \$100{,}000$$
$$= 116{,}071 = \$100{,}000$$
$$= 160{,}071$$

b.

$$PI_A = \frac{\$62{,}500}{\$50{,}000}$$
$$= 1.250$$
$$PI_B = \frac{\$116{,}071}{\$100{,}000}$$
$$= 1.1607$$

c.

$$\$50{,}000 = \$70{,}000\,(PVIF_{i,1\text{yr}})$$
$$.7143 = PVIF_{i,1\text{yr}}$$

Looking for a value of $PVIF_{i,1\text{yr}}$ in Appendix C, a value of .714 is found in the 40 percent column. Thus, the *IRR* is 40 percent.

$$\$100{,}000 = \$130{,}000(PVIF_{i,1\text{yr}})$$
$$.7692 = PVIF_{i,1\text{yr}}$$

Looking for a value of $PVIF_{i,1\text{yr}}$ in Appendix C, a value of .769 is found in the 30 percent column. Thus, the *IRR* is 30 percent.

d. If there is no capital rationing, project B should be accepted because it has a larger net present value. If there is a capital constraint, the problem focuses on what can be done with the additional $50,000 (the additional money that could be invested if project A, with an initial outlay of $50,000, were selected over project B, with an initial outlay of $100,000). In the capital constraint case, if Serrano can earn more on project A plus the marginal project financed with the additional $50,000 than it can on project B, then project A and the marginal project should be accepted.

LEARNING OBJECTIVES

After reading this chapter, you should be able to

1. Explain what the appropriate measure of risk is for capital-budgeting purposes.
2. Determine the acceptability of a new project using both the certainty equivalent and risk-adjusted discount rate methods of adjusting for risk.
3. Explain the use of simulation and probability trees for imitating the performance of a project under evaluation.

CHAPTER 11

Capital Budgeting and Risk Analysis

In the previous two chapters, we assumed that all projects had the same level of risk. In this chapter, we will discard that assumption and incorporate risk into the capital-budgeting decision. As international competition increases and technology changes at an ever-quickening pace, risk and uncertainty play an increasingly important role in business decisions. In this chapter, we will examine problems in measuring risk and approaches for dealing with it as it affects business decisions.

We will look at risks faced in decisions like the one made by Harley-Davidson to develop and introduce the Harley-Davidson Buell Blast model, a lightweight, one-cylinder motorcycle, and the Lightning Low XB9S, two motorcycles designed specifically for first-time riders, both male and female—a group not targeted by Harley-Davidson in over 30 years. How would the public react to a lightweight bike from Harley? Harley-Davidson hopes that the Blast and Lightning Low will get more young people and women on an easy-to-handle, fun bike and give them the new excitement of motorcycling. Will it accomplish this task? Because the Blast is easier to ride and light as a feather while the Lightning Low is shorter compared with the heavier cruising and touring "Harley Hogs," will it take away from Harley's big-bike image? The bottom line is that before Harley-Davidson introduced the Buell Blast and Lightning Low, it didn't know how the public would react to them. That is, the expected future free cash flows from these projects were far from certain. How should Harley evaluate projects with uncertain returns that stretch well into the future? Certainly, it shouldn't treat all projects in the same way, but how should Harley ensure that the decisions it makes correctly reflect a project's uncertainty? Complicating Harley's task is the question of what is the appropriate measure of risk for a new project. How well a firm does in answering these questions and evaluating capital-budgeting projects will determine its future. These are "strategic" decisions that are made by all of the firm's employees—those in management, accounting, information technology, and marketing—working together.

Principle 1: The Risk-Return Trade-Off states that investors demand a higher return for taking on additional risk; in this chapter, we modify our capital-budgeting decision criterion to allow for different levels of risk for different projects. In so doing we will try to understand how a company like Harley-Davidson, or any other firm, deals with the risk and uncertainty that surrounds its capital-budgeting decisions.

CHAPTER PREVIEW

This chapter completes our discussion of decision rules for when to invest in new projects. In Chapter 9, we introduced the different capital-budgeting decision criteria, and in Chapter 10, we looked at measuring a project's relevant cash flows. Through all of this discussion of capital-budgeting techniques, we implicitly assumed that the level of risk associated with each investment was the same. In this chapter, we lift that assumption. We begin with a discussion of what measure of risk is relevant in capital-budgeting decisions. We then look at various ways of incorporating risk into the capital-budgeting decision and how to measure that risk.

To do this, we will be relying heavily on **Principle 1: The Risk-Return Trade-Off—We won't take on additional risk unless we expect to be compensated with additional return** and **Principle 9: All Risk Is Not Equal—Some risk can be diversified away, and some cannot.**

Objective 1

RISK AND THE INVESTMENT DECISION

Up to this point, we have ignored risk in capital budgeting; that is, we have discounted expected cash flows back to the present and ignored any uncertainty that there might be surrounding that estimate. In reality, the future cash flows associated with the introduction of a new sales outlet or a new product are estimates of what is *expected* to happen in the future, not necessarily what *will* happen in the future. For example, when Coca-Cola decided to replace Classic Coke with its "New Coke," you can bet that the expected cash flows it based its decision on were nothing like the cash flows it realized. As a result, it didn't take Coca-Cola long to reintroduce Classic Coke. In effect, the cash flows we have discounted back to the present have been our best estimate of the expected future cash flows. A cash-flow diagram based on the possible outcomes of an investment proposal rather than the expected values of these outcomes appears in Figure 11-1.

In this section, we will assume that under conditions of risk we do not know beforehand what cash flows will actually result from a new project. However, we do have expectations concerning the possible outcomes and are able to assign probabilities to these outcomes. Stated another way, although we do not know the cash flows resulting from the acceptance of a new project, we can formulate the probability distributions from which the flows will be drawn.

As we learned in Chapter 6, risk occurs when there is some question as to the future outcome of an event. We will now proceed with an examination of the logic behind this definition. Again, risk is defined as the potential variability in future cash flows.

The fact that variability reflects risk can easily be shown with a coin toss. Consider the possibility of flipping a coin—heads you win, tails you lose—for 25 cents with your finance professor. Most likely, you would be willing to take on this game because the utility gained from winning 25 cents is about equal to the utility lost if you lose 25 cents. Conversely, if the flip is for $1,000, you may be willing to play only if you are offered more than $1,000 if you win—say, you win $1,500 if it turns out heads and lose $1,000 if it turns out tails. In each case, the probability of winning and losing is the same; that is, there is an equal chance that the coin will land heads or tails. In each case, however, the width of the dispersion changes, which is why the second coin toss is more risky and why you may not take the chance unless the payoffs are altered. The key here is the fact that only the dispersion changes; the probability of winning or losing is the same in each case. Thus, the potential variability in future returns reflects the risk.

The final question to be addressed is whether or not individuals are in fact risk averse. Although we do see people gambling when the odds of winning are against them, it

FIGURE 11-1 Cash-Flow Diagram Based on Possible Outcomes

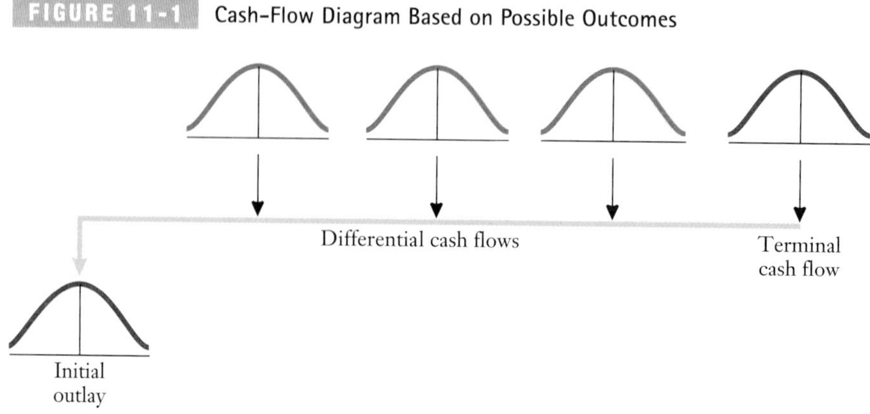

should be stressed that monetary return is not the only possible return they may receive. A nonmonetary, psychic reward accrues to some gamblers, allowing them to fantasize that they will break the bank, never have to work again, and retire to some island. Actually, the heart of the question is how wealth is measured. Although gamblers appear to be acting as risk seekers, they actually attach an additional nonmonetary return to gambling; the risk is in effect its own reward. When this is considered, their actions seem totally rational. It should also be noted that although gamblers appear to be pursuing risk on one hand, on the other hand in other endeavors they are also eliminating some risk by purchasing insurance and diversifying their investments.

In the remainder of this chapter, we assume that although future cash flows are not known with certainty, the probability distribution from which they come can be estimated. Also, as illustrated in Chapter 6, because the dispersion of possible outcomes reflects risk, we are prepared to use a measure of dispersion or variability later in the chapter when we quantify risk.

In the pages that follow, there are only two basic issues that we address: (1) What is risk in terms of capital-budgeting decisions, and how should it be measured? (2) How should risk be incorporated into capital-budgeting analysis?

What Measure of Risk Is Relevant in Capital Budgeting?

Before we begin our discussion of how to adjust for risk, it is important to determine just what type of risk we are to adjust for. In capital budgeting, a project's risk can be looked at on three levels. First, there is the **project standing alone risk**, which is a project's risk ignoring the fact that much of this risk will be diversified away as the project is combined with the firm's other projects and assets.

Project standing alone risk
The risk of a project standing alone is measured by the variability of the asset's expected returns. That is, it is the risk of a project ignoring the fact that it is only one of many projects within the firm, and the firm's stock is but one of many stocks within a stockholder's portfolio.

Second, we have the **project's contribution-to-firm risk**, which is the amount of risk that the project contributes to the firm as a whole; this measure considers the fact that some of the project's risk will be diversified away as the project is combined with the firm's other projects and assets, but *ignores* the effects of diversification of the firm's shareholders. Finally, there is **systematic risk**, which is the risk of the project from the viewpoint of a well-diversified shareholder; this measure considers the fact that some of a project's risk will be diversified away as the project is combined with the firm's other projects, and, in addition, some of the remaining risk will be diversified away by shareholders as they combine this stock with other stocks in their portfolios. This is shown graphically in Figure 11-2.

Project's contribution-to-firm risk
The amount of risk that a project contributes to the firm as a whole. That is, it is a project's risk considering the effects of diversification among different projects within the firm, but ignoring the effects of shareholder diversification within the portfolio.

Systematic risk
The risk of a project measured from the point of view of a well-diversified shareholder. That is, it is a project's risk taking into account the fact that this project is only one of many projects within the firm, and the firm's stock is but one of many stocks within a stockholder's portfolio.

Should we be interested in the project standing alone risk? The answer is *no*. Perhaps the easiest way to understand why not is to look at an example. Let's take the case of research and development projects at Johnson & Johnson. Each year, Johnson & Johnson takes on hundreds of new R&D projects, knowing that they only have about a 10 percent probability of being successful. If they are successful, the profits can be enormous; if they fail, the investment is lost. If the company has only one project, and it is an R&D project, the company would have a 90 percent chance of failure. Thus, if we look at these R&D projects individually and measure their project standing alone risk, we would have to judge them to be enormously risky. However, if we consider the effect of the diversification that comes about from taking on several hundred independent R&D projects a year, all with a 10 percent chance of success, we can see that each R&D project does not add much in the way of risk to Johnson & Johnson. In short, because much of a project's risk is diversified away within the firm, project standing alone risk is an inappropriate measure of the level of risk of a capital-budgeting project.

Should we be interested in the project's contribution-to-firm risk? Once again, the answer is *no*, provided investors are well diversified, and there is no chance of bankruptcy. From our earlier discussion of risk in Chapter 6, we saw that, as shareholders, if

FIGURE 11-2 Looking at Three Measures of a Project's Risk

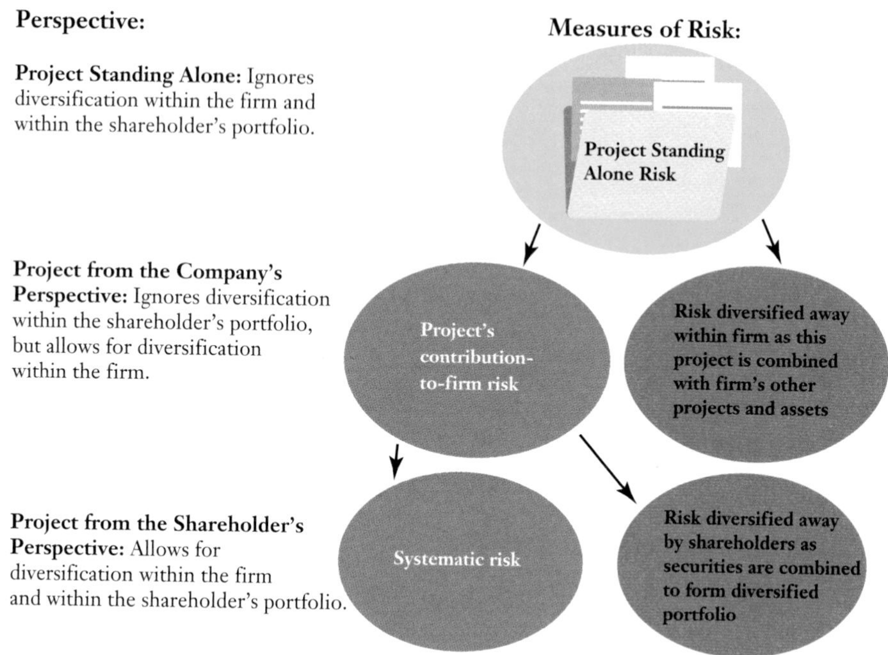

we combined our stocks with other stocks to form a diversified portfolio, much of the risk of our security would be diversified away. Thus, all that affects the shareholders is the systematic risk of the project and, as such, it is all that is theoretically relevant for capital budgeting.

CONCEPT CHECK

1. In capital budgeting, a project's risk can be looked at on three levels. What are they and what are the measures of risk?
2. Is a project's stand alone risk the appropriate level of risk for capital budgeting? Why or why not?
3. What is systematic risk?
4. What type of risk affects all shareholders and is theoretically the correct measure for capital budgeting?

BACK TO THE PRINCIPLES

Our discussion of capital budgeting and risk is based on ***Principle 9: All Risk Is Not Equal—Some risk can be diversified away, and some cannot.*** *That principle describes how difficult it is to measure a project's risk as a result of diversification. This is because diversification takes place both within the firm, where the new project is just one of many projects, and in the shareholder's portfolio, where the company's stock is just one of many stocks he or she holds.*

Measuring Risk for Capital-Budgeting Purposes and a Dose of Reality—Is Systematic Risk All There Is?

According to the capital asset pricing model (CAPM), systematic risk is the only relevant risk for capital-budgeting purposes; however, reality complicates this somewhat. In many instances, a firm will have undiversified shareholders, including owners of small corporations. Because they are not diversified, for those shareholders the relevant measure of risk is the project's contribution-to-firm risk.

The possibility of bankruptcy also affects our view of what measure of risk is relevant. Because the project's contribution-to-firm risk can affect the possibility of bankruptcy, this may be an appropriate measure of risk in the real world, where there is a cost associated with bankruptcy. First, if a firm fails, its assets, in general, cannot be sold for their true economic value. Moreover, the amount of money actually available for distribution to stockholders is further reduced by liquidation and legal fees that must be paid. Finally, the opportunity cost associated with the delays related to the legal process further reduces the funds available to the shareholder. Therefore, because there are costs associated with bankruptcy, reduction of the chance of bankruptcy has a very real value associated with it.

Indirect costs of bankruptcy also affect other areas of the firm, including production, sales, and the quality and efficiency of management. For example, firms with a higher probability of bankruptcy may have a more difficult time recruiting and retaining quality managers because jobs with that firm are viewed as being less secure. Suppliers also may be less willing to sell on credit. Finally, customers may lose confidence and fear that the firm may not be around to honor the warranty or to supply spare parts for the product in the future. As a result, as the probability of bankruptcy increases, the eventual bankruptcy may become self-fulfilling as potential customers and suppliers flee. The end result is that the project's contribution-to-firm risk is also a relevant risk measure for capital budgeting.

Finally, problems in measuring a project's systematic risk make its implementation extremely difficult. As we will see later on in this chapter, it is much easier talking about a project's systematic risk than it is measuring it.

Given all this, what do we use? The answer is that we will give consideration to both measures. We know in theory systematic risk is correct. We also know that bankruptcy costs and undiversified shareholders violate the assumptions of the theory, which brings us back to the concept of a project's contribution-to-firm risk. Still, the concept of systematic risk holds value for capital-budgeting decisions, because that is the risk for which shareholders are compensated. As such, we will concern ourselves with both the project's contribution-to-firm risk and the project's systematic risk, and not try to make any specific allocation of importance between the two for capital-budgeting purposes.

BACK TO THE PRINCIPLES

All the methods used to compensate for risk in capital budgeting find their roots in fundamental ***Principle 1: The Risk-Return Trade-Off.*** *In fact, the risk-adjusted discount method, to be described later, puts this concept directly into play.*

Objective 2

METHODS FOR INCORPORATING RISK INTO CAPITAL BUDGETING

In the past two chapters, we ignored any risk differences between projects. This assumption is simple but not valid; different investment projects do in fact contain different levels of risk. We will now look at two methods for incorporating risk into the analysis. The first method, the *certainty equivalent approach*, attempts to incorporate the manager's utility function into the analysis. The second method, the *risk-adjusted discount rate*, is based on the notion that investors require higher rates of return on more risky projects.

CERTAINTY EQUIVALENT APPROACH

Certainty equivalent approach
A method for incorporating risk into the capital-budgeting decision in which the decision maker substitutes a set of equivalent riskless cash flows for the expected cash flows and then discounts these cash flows back to the present.

Certainty equivalent
The amount of cash a person would require with certainty to make him or her indifferent between this certain sum and a particular risky or uncertain sum.

The **certainty equivalent approach** involves a direct attempt to allow the decision maker to incorporate his or her utility function into the analysis. The financial manager is allowed to substitute the certain dollar amount that he or she feels is equivalent to the expected but risky cash flow offered by the investment for that risky cash flow in the capital-budgeting analysis. In effect, a set of riskless cash flows is substituted for the original risky cash flows, between both of which the financial manager is indifferent. The key here is that the financial manager is indifferent between picking from the risky distribution and the certain cash flow.

To illustrate the concept of a **certainty equivalent**, let us look at a simple coin toss. Assume you can play the game only once and if it comes out heads, you win $10,000, and if it comes out tails, you win nothing. Obviously, you have a 50 percent chance of winning $10,000 and a 50 percent chance of winning nothing, with an expected value of $5,000. Thus, $5,000 is your uncertain expected value outcome. The certainty equivalent then becomes the amount you would demand to make you indifferent with regard to playing and not playing the game. If you are indifferent with respect to receiving $3,000 for certain and not playing the game, then $3,000 is the certainty equivalent. However, someone else may not have as much fear of risk as you do and as a result, will have a different certainty equivalent.

To simplify future calculations and problems, let us define the certainty equivalent coefficient (α_t) that represents the ratio of the certain outcome to the risky or expected outcome, between which the financial manager is indifferent. In equation form, α_t can be represented as follows:

$$\alpha_t = \frac{\text{certain cash flow}_t}{\text{risky or expected cash flow}_t} \tag{11-1}$$

Thus, the alphas (α_t) can vary between 0, in the case of extreme risk, and 1, in the case of certainty. To obtain the value of the equivalent certain cash flow, we need only multiply the risky cash flow in years t times the α_t. When this is done, we are indifferent with respect to this certain cash flow and the risky cash flow. In the preceding example of the simple coin toss, the certain cash flow was $3,000, whereas the risky cash flow was $5,000, the expected value of the coin toss; thus, the certainty equivalent coefficient is $3,000/$5,000 = 0.6. In summary, by multiplying the certainty equivalent coefficient (α_t) times the expected but risky cash flow, we can determine an equivalent certain cash flow.

Once this risk is taken out of the project's cash flows, those cash flows are discounted back to the present at the risk-free rate of interest, and the project's net present value or profitability index is determined. If the internal rate of return is calculated, it is then compared with the risk-free rate of interest rather than the firm's required rate of return in determining whether or not it should be accepted or rejected. The certainty equivalent method can be summarized as follows:

$$NPV = \sum_{t=1}^{n} \frac{\alpha_t FCF_t}{(1 + k_{rf})^t} - IO \qquad \textbf{(11-2)}$$

where α_t = the certainty equivalent coefficient in period t
FCF_t = the annual expected free cash flow in period t
IO = the initial cash outlay
n = the project's expected life
k_{rf} = the risk-free interest rate

The certainty equivalent approach can be summarized as follows:

Step 1: Risk is removed from the cash flows by substituting equivalent certain cash flows for the risky cash flows. If the certainty equivalent coefficient (α_t) is given, this is done by multiplying each risky cash flow by the appropriate α_t value.

Step 2: These riskless cash flows are then discounted back to the present at the riskless rate of interest.

Step 3: The normal capital-budgeting criteria are then applied, except in the case of the internal rate of return criterion, where the project's internal rate of return is compared with the risk-free rate of interest rather than the firm's required rate of return.

EXAMPLE: CERTAINTY EQUIVALENTS

A firm with a 10 percent required rate of return is considering building new research facilities with an expected life of five years. The initial outlay associated with this project involves a certain cash outflow of $120,000. The expected cash inflows and certainty equivalent coefficients, α_t, are as follows:

YEAR	EXPECTED CASH FLOW	CERTAINTY EQUIVALENT COEFFICIENT AT α_t
1	$10,000	0.95
2	20,000	0.90
3	40,000	0.85
4	80,000	0.75
5	80,000	0.65

The risk-free rate of interest is 6 percent. What is the project's net present value?

To determine the net present value of this project using the certainty equivalent approach, we must first remove the risk from the future cash flows. We do so by multiplying each expected cash flow by the corresponding certainty equivalent coefficient, α_t, as shown below:

EXPECTED CASH FLOW	CERTAINTY EQUIVALENT COEFFICIENT α_t	α_t (EXPECTED CASH FLOW) = EQUIVALENT RISKLESS CASH FLOW
$10,000	0.95	$ 9,500
20,000	0.90	18,000
40,000	0.85	34,000
80,000	0.75	60,000
80,000	0.65	52,000

(continued)

The equivalent riskless cash flows are then discounted back to the present at the riskless interest rate, not the firm's required rate of return. The required rate of return would be used if this project had the same level of risk as a typical project for this firm. However, these equivalent cash flows have no risk at all; hence, the appropriate discount rate is the riskless rate of interest. The equivalent riskless cash flows can be discounted back to the present at the riskless rate of interest, 6 percent, as follows:

YEAR	EQUIVALENT RISKLESS CASH FLOW	PRESENT VALUE FACTOR AT 6 PERCENT	PRESENT VALUE
1	$ 9,500	0.943	$ 8,958.50
2	18,000	0.890	16,020.00
3	34,000	0.840	28,560.00
4	60,000	0.792	47,520.00
5	52,000	0.747	38,844.00

NPV = −$120,000 + $8,958.50 + $16,020 + $28,560 + $47,520 + $38,844 = $19,902.50

Applying the normal capital-budgeting decision criteria, we find that the project should be accepted, as its net present value is greater than zero.

The real problem with the certainty equivalent risk adjustment technique is that it is so arbitrary. That is, two excellent managers might look at the same project and come up with different certainty equivalent values. Which one is right? The answer is that they are both right, they just have different levels of risk aversion. Because it is so slippery, the certainty equivalent method is not used very often.

Risk-Adjusted Discount Rates

The use of risk-adjusted discount rates is based on the concept that investors demand higher returns for more risky projects. This is the basic axiom behind **Principle 1: The Risk-Return Trade-Off** and the CAPM.

The required rate of return on any investment should include compensation for delaying consumption equal to the risk-free rate of return, plus compensation for any risk taken on. If the risk associated with the investment is greater than the risk involved in a typical endeavor, the discount rate is adjusted upward to compensate for this added risk. Once the firm determines the appropriate required rate of return for a project with a given level of risk, cash flows are discounted back to the present at the **risk-adjusted discount rate**. Then the normal capital-budgeting criteria are applied, except in the case of the internal rate of return. For the *IRR*, the hurdle rate with which the project's internal rate of return is compared now becomes the risk-adjusted discount rate. Expressed mathematically, the net present value using the risk-adjusted discount rate becomes

Risk-adjusted discount rate
A method for incorporating the project's level of risk into the capital-budgeting process, in which the discount rate is adjusted upward to compensate for higher than normal risk or downward to adjust for lower than normal risk.

$$NPV = \sum_{t=1}^{n} \frac{FCF_t}{(1 + k^*)^t} - IO \qquad \textbf{(11-3)}$$

where FCF_t = the annual expected free cash flow in time period t
IO = the initial cash outlay
k^* = the risk-adjusted discount rate
n = the project's expected life

The logic behind the risk-adjusted discount rate stems from the idea that if the level of risk in a project is different from that in the firm's typical project, then management must incorporate the shareholders' probable reaction to this new endeavor into the decision-making process. If the project has more risk than a typical project, then a higher required rate of return should apply. Otherwise, a project may appear to have a positive net present value, but if you had used the appropriate, higher required rate of return, the project may actually have a negative net present value. Thus, marginal projects may lower the firm's share price—that is, reduce shareholders' wealth. This will occur as the market raises its required rate of return on the firm to reflect the addition of a more risky project, whereas the incremental cash flows resulting from the acceptance of the new project are not large enough to offset this change fully. By the same logic, if the project has less than normal risk, a reduction in the required rate of return is appropriate. Thus, the risk-adjusted discount method attempts to apply more stringent standards—that is, require a higher rate of return—to projects that will increase the firm's risk level.

EXAMPLE: RISK ADJUSTED DISCOUNT RATE

A toy manufacturer is considering the introduction of a line of fishing equipment with an expected life of five years. In the past, this firm has been quite conservative in its investment in new products, sticking primarily to standard toys. In this context, the introduction of a line of fishing equipment is considered an abnormally risky project. Management thinks that the normal required rate of return for the firm of 10 percent is not sufficient. Instead, the minimally acceptable rate of return on this project should be 15 percent. The initial outlay would be $110,000, and the expected free cash flows from this project are as given below:

YEAR	EXPECTED CASH FLOW
1	$30,000
2	30,000
3	30,000
4	30,000
5	30,000

Discounting this annuity back to the present at 15 percent yields a present value of the future cash flows of $100,560. Because the initial outlay on this project is $110,000, the net present value becomes –$9,440, and the project should be rejected. If the normal required rate of return of 10 percent had been used as the discount rate, the project would have been accepted with a net present value of $3,730.

In practice, when the risk-adjusted discount rate is used, projects are generally grouped according to purpose, or risk class; then the discount rate preassigned to that purpose or risk class is used. For example, a firm with an overall required rate of return of 12 percent might use the following rate-of-return categorization:

PROJECT	REQUIRED RATE OF RETURN
Replacement decision	12%
Modification or expansion of existing product line	15
Project unrelated to current operations	18
Research and development operations	25

FINANCE MATTERS

RISK HAPPENS: THE FUTURE DOESN'T STAND STILL

In high-tech areas a frequent problem is that while we can forecast the future, that forecast constantly changes as technology changes. The telecommunications sector shows how quickly things can change. Look, for example, to Conxus Communications. In the mid-1990s they came up with a great idea to take advantage of the wireless telecommunications technology of the time. They developed a product called Pocketalk—a wireless answering machine that you carry in your pocket, kind of like a high-tech pager—with the ability to deliver voice messages. To develop the product they turned to Motorola for help, and after three years they were ready to launch Pocketalk. The problem was that during the three years needed to develop the product and technological infrastructure to make it work, cell phones hit the market. The bottom line was that Pocketalk was a failure. What went wrong? Conxus didn't continue to monitor the market, and while Pocketalk was initially aimed at a strong market, that market was a moving target. By the time Pocketalk was ready to sell, its market had disappeared.

The purpose of this categorization of projects is to make their evaluation easier, but it also introduces a sense of the arbitrary into the calculations that makes the evaluation less meaningful. The trade-offs involved in the preceding classification are obvious; time and effort are minimized, but only at the cost of precision. See the Finance Matters box, "Risk Happens: The Future Doesn't Stand Still."

Certainty Equivalent versus Risk-Adjusted Discount Rate Methods

The primary difference between the certainty equivalent approach and the risk-adjusted discount rate approach involves the point at which the adjustment for risk is incorporated into the calculations. The certainty equivalent penalizes or adjusts downward the value of the expected annual free cash flows, FCF_t, which results in a lower net present value for a risky project. The risk-adjusted discount rate, conversely, leaves the cash flows at their expected value and adjusts the required rate of return, k, upward to compensate for added risk. In either case, the project's net present value is being adjusted downward to compensate for additional risk. The computational differences are illustrated in Table 11-1.

TABLE 11-1 Computational Steps in Certainty Equivalent and Risk-Adjusted Discount Rate Methods

CERTAINTY EQUIVALENT	RISK-ADJUSTED DISCOUNT RATE
STEP 1: Adjust the free cash flows, FCF_t, downward for risk by multiplying them by the corresponding certainty equivalent coefficient, α_t.	STEP 1: Adjust the discount rate upward for risk, or down in the case of less than normal risk.
STEP 2: Discount the certainty equivalent riskless cash flows back to the present using the risk-free rate of interest.	STEP 2: Discount the expected free cash flows back to the present using the risk-adjusted discount rate.
STEP 3: Apply the normal decision criteria, except in the case of the internal rate of return, where the risk-free rate of interest replaces the required rate of return as the hurdle rate.	STEP 3: Apply the normal decision criteria except in the case of the internal rate of return, where the risk-adjusted discount rate replaces the required rate of return as the hurdle rate.

In addition to the difference in point of adjustment for risk, the risk-adjusted discount rate makes the implicit assumption that risk becomes greater as we move further out in time. Although this is not necessarily a good or bad assumption, we should be aware of it and understand it. Let's look at an example in which the risk-adjusted discount rate is used and then determine what certainty equivalent coefficients, α_t, would be necessary to arrive at the same solution.

EXAMPLE: COMPARING THE CERTAINTY EQUIVALENT AND RISK ADJUSTED DISCOUNT RATE METHODS

Assume that a firm with a required rate of return of 10 percent is considering introducing a new product. This product has an initial outlay of $800,000, an expected life of 10 years, and free cash flows of $100,000 each year during its life. Because of the increased risk associated with this project, management is requiring a 15 percent rate of return. Let us also assume that the risk-free rate of return is 6 percent.

If the firm chose to use the certainty equivalent method, the certainty equivalent cash flows would be discounted back to the present at 6 percent, the risk-free rate of interest. The present value of the $100,000 cash flow occurring at the end of the first year discounted back to the present at 15 percent is $87,000. The present value of this $100,000 flow discounted back to the present at the risk-free rate of 6 percent is $94,300. Thus, if the certainty equivalent approach were used, a certainty equivalent coefficient, α_1, of .9226 ($87,000 ÷ $94,300 = 0.9226) would be necessary to produce a present value of $87,000. In other words, the same results can be obtained in the first year by using the risk-adjusted discount rate and adjusting the discount rate up to 15 percent or by using the certainty equivalent approach and adjusting the expected cash flows by a certainty equivalent coefficient of 0.9226.

Under the risk-adjusted discount rate, the present value of the $100,000 cash flow occurring at the end of the second year becomes $75,600. To produce an identical present value under the certainty equivalent approach, a certainty equivalent coefficient of 0.8494 would be needed. Following this through for the life of the project yields the certainty equivalent coefficients given in Table 11-2.

TABLE 11-2 Certainty Equivalent Coefficients Yielding Same Results as Risk-Adjusted Discount Rate of 15 Percent in Illustrative Example

YEAR	1	2	3	4	5	6	7	8	9	10
α_t:	0.9226	0.8494	0.7833	0.7222	0.6653	0.6128	0.5654	0.5215	0.4797	0.4427

What does this analysis suggest? It indicates that if the risk-adjusted discount rate method is used, we are adjusting downward the value of future cash flows that occur further in the future more severely than earlier cash flows.

In summary, the use of the risk-adjusted discount rate assumes that risk increases over time and that cash flows occurring further in the future should be more severely penalized. If performed properly, either of these methods can do a good job of adjusting for risk. However, by far the most popular method of risk adjustment is the risk-adjusted discount rate. The reason for the popularity of the risk-adjusted discount rate over the certainty equivalent approach is purely and simply its ease of implementation.

Risk-Adjusted Discount Rate and Measurement of a Project's Systematic Risk

When we initially talked about systematic risk or a beta, we were talking about measuring it for the entire firm. As you recall, although we could estimate a firm's beta using historical data, we did not have complete confidence in our results. As we will see, estimating the appropriate level of systematic risk for a single project is even more fraught with difficulties. To truly understand what it is that we are trying to do and the difficulties that we will encounter, let us step back a bit and examine systematic risk and the risk adjustment for a project.

What we are trying to do is to use the CAPM to determine the level of risk and the appropriate risk-return trade-offs for a particular project. We will then take the expected return on this project and compare it to the risk-return trade-offs suggested by the CAPM to determine whether or not the project should be accepted. If the project appears to be a typical one for the firm, using the CAPM to determine the appropriate risk-return trade-offs and then judging the project against them may be a warranted approach. But if the project is not a typical project, what do we do? Historical data generally do not exist for a new project. In fact, for some capital investments, for example, a truck or a new building, historical data would not have much meaning. What we need to do is make the best out of a bad situation. We either (1) fake it—that is, use historical accounting data, if available, to substitute for historical price data in estimating systematic risk; or (2) we attempt to find a substitute firm in the same industry as the capital-budgeting project and use the substitute firm's estimated systematic risk as a proxy for the project's systematic risk.

BETA ESTIMATION USING ACCOUNTING DATA When we are dealing with a project that is identical to the firm's other projects, we need only estimate the level of systematic risk for the firm and use that estimate as a proxy for the project's risk. Unfortunately, when projects are not typical of the firm, this approach does not work. For example, when R. J. Reynolds introduces a new food through one of its food products divisions, this new product most likely carries with it a different level of systematic risk than is typical for Reynolds as a whole.

To get a better approximation of the systematic risk level on this project, we could estimate the level of systematic risk for the food division and use that as a proxy for the project's systematic risk. Unfortunately, historical stock price data are available only for the company as a whole and, as you recall, historical stock return data are generally used to estimate a firm's beta. Thus, we are forced to use *accounting return data* rather than historical stock return data for the division to estimate the division's systematic risk. To estimate a project's beta using accounting data we need only run a time series regression of the division's return on assets (net income/total assets) on the market index (the S&P 500). The regression coefficient from this equation would be the project's accounting beta and would serve as an approximation for the project's true beta or measure of systematic risk. Alternatively, a multiple regression model based on accounting data could be developed to explain betas. The results of this model could then be applied to firms that are not publicly traded to estimate their betas.

How good is the accounting beta technique? It certainly is not as good as a direct calculation of the beta. In fact, the correlation between the accounting beta and the beta calculated on historical stock return data is only about 0.6; however, better luck has been experienced with multiple regression models used to predict betas. Unfortunately, in many cases, there may not be any realistic alternative to the calculation of the accounting beta. Owing to the importance of adjusting for a project's risk, the accounting beta method is much preferred to doing nothing.

THE PURE PLAY METHOD FOR ESTIMATING A PROJECT'S BETA Whereas the accounting beta method attempts to directly estimate a project's or division's beta, the **pure play method** attempts to identify publicly traded firms that are engaged solely in the same business as the project or division. Once the proxy or pure play firm is identified, its systematic risk is determined and then used as a proxy for the project's or division's level of systematic risk. What we are doing is looking for a publicly traded firm on the outside that looks like our project, and using that firm's required rate of return to judge our project. In doing so, we are presuming that the systematic risk of the proxy firm is identical to that of the project.

Pure play method
A method of estimating a project's beta that attempts to identify a publicly traded firm that is engaged solely in the same business as the project, and uses that beta as a proxy for the project's beta.

In using the pure play method, it should be noted that a firm's capital structure (that is, the way it raises money in the capital markets) is reflected in its beta. When the capital structure of the proxy firm is different from that of the project's firm, some adjustment must be made for this difference. Although not a perfect approach, it does provide some insights as to the level of systematic risk a project might have. It also provides a good framework from which to view risk.

CONCEPT CHECK

1. What is the most commonly used method for incorporating risk into the capital-budgeting decision? How is this technique related to Principle 1?
2. Describe two methods for estimating a project's systematic risk.

Objective 3

OTHER APPROACHES TO EVALUATING RISK IN CAPITAL BUDGETING

SIMULATION

Another method for evaluating risk in the investment decision is through the use of **simulation**. The certainty equivalent and risk-adjusted discount rate approaches provided us with a single value for the risk-adjusted net present value, whereas a simulation approach gives us a probability distribution for the investment's net present value or internal rate of return. Simulation imitates the performance of the project under evaluation. This is done by randomly selecting observations from each of the distributions that affect the outcome of the project, combining those observations to determine the final output of the project, and continuing with this process until a representative record of the project's probable outcome is assembled. Today this process is much simpler due to the fact that spreadsheets like Excel have add-in programs that allow for simulations. In effect, what was once a major effort is now a simple task with spreadsheets.

Simulation
The process of imitating the performance of an investment project under evaluation using a computer. This is done by randomly selecting observations from each of the distributions that affect the outcome of the project, combining those observations to determine the final output of the project, and continuing with this process until a representative record of the project's probable outcome is assembled.

The easiest way to develop an understanding of the computer simulation process is to follow through an example simulation for an investment project evaluation. Suppose Merck is considering a new drug for the treatment of Alzheimer's disease. The simulation process is portrayed in Figure 11-3. First, the probability distributions are determined for all the factors that affect the project's returns; in this case, let us assume these include the market size, selling price, fixed costs, market growth rate, investment required, residual value of investment, share of market (which results in physical sales volume), operating costs, and useful life of facilities.

Then the computer randomly selects one observation from each of the probability distributions, according to its chance of actually occurring in the future. These nine observations are combined, and a net present value or internal rate of return figure is calculated. This process is repeated as many times as desired, until a representative distribution of

FIGURE 11-3 Capital-Budgeting Simulation for Proposed New Alzheimer's Drug

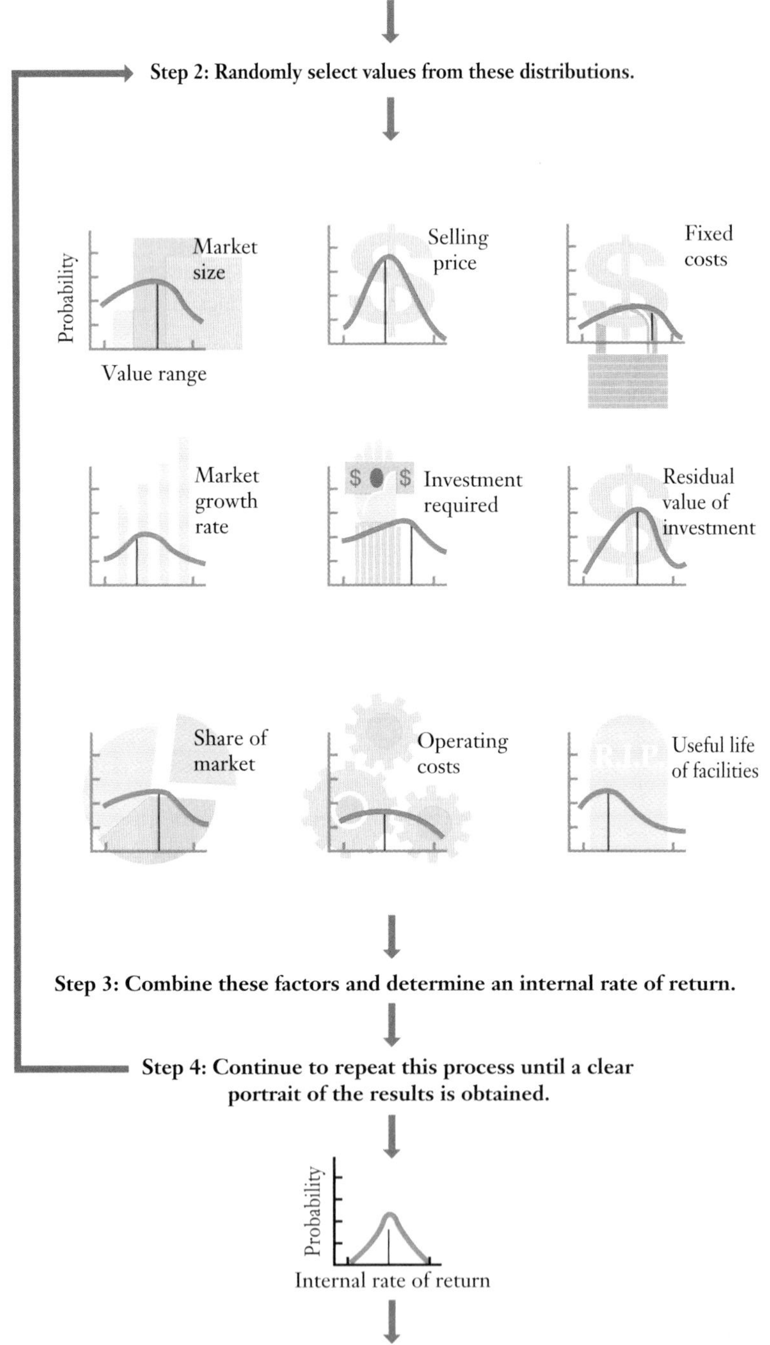

FIGURE 11-4 Output from Simulation of a Proposed New Drug for the Treatment of Alzheimer's Disease

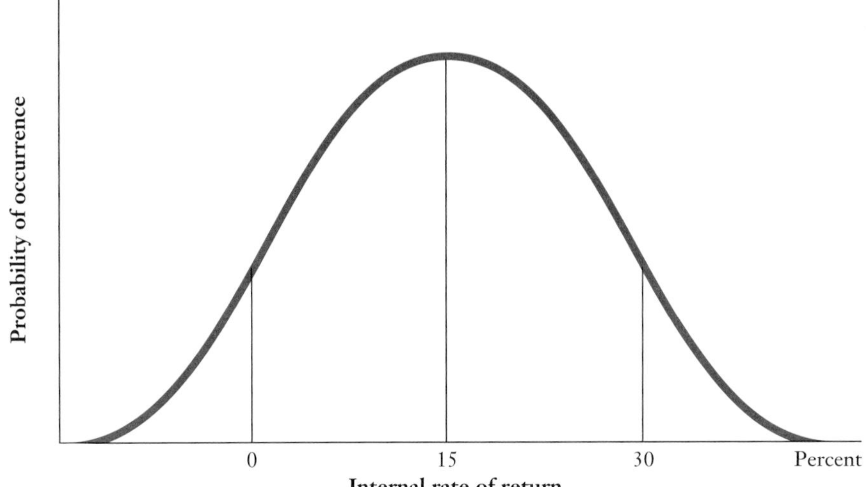

possible future outcomes is assembled. Thus, the inputs to a simulation include all the principal factors affecting the project's profitability, and the simulation output is a probability distribution of net present values or internal rates of return for the project. The decision maker bases the decision on the full range of possible outcomes. The project is accepted if the decision maker feels that enough of the distribution lies above the normal cutoff criteria ($NPV \geq 0$, $IRR \geq$ required rate of return).

Suppose that the output from the simulation of Merck's Alzheimer's disease drug project is as given in Figure 11-4. This output provides the decision maker with the probability of different outcomes occurring in addition to the range of possible outcomes. Sometimes called **scenario analysis**, this examination identifies the range of possible outcomes under the worst, best, and most likely case. Merck's management will examine the distribution to determine the project's level of risk and then make the appropriate adjustment.

Scenario analysis
Simulation analysis that focuses on an examination of the range of possible outcomes.

You'll notice that although the simulation approach helps us to determine the amount of total risk that a project has, it does not differentiate between systematic and unsystematic risk. Because systematic risk cannot be diversified away for free, the simulation approach does not provide a complete method of risk assessment. However, it does provide important insights as to the total risk level of a given investment project. Now we will look briefly at how the simulation approach can be used to perform sensitivity analysis.

SENSITIVITY ANALYSIS THROUGH THE SIMULATION APPROACH

Sensitivity analysis involves determining how the distribution of possible net present values or internal rates of returns for a particular project is affected by a change in one particular input variable. This is done by changing the value of one input variable while holding all other input variables constant. The distribution of possible net present values or internal rates of return that is generated is then compared with the distribution of possible returns generated before the change was made to determine the effect of the change. For this reason, sensitivity analysis is commonly called "*What if?*" analysis.

Sensitivity analysis
The process of determining how the distribution of possible returns for a particular project is affected by a change in one particular input variable.

For example, in analyzing the proposal for a new drug for the treatment of Alzheimer's disease, Merck's management may wish to determine the effect of a more pessimistic forecast of the anticipated market growth rate. After the more pessimistic forecast replaces the original forecast in the model, the simulation is rerun. The two outputs are then compared to determine how sensitive the results are to the revised estimate of the market growth rate.

By modifying assumptions made about the values and ranges of the input factors and rerunning the simulation, management can determine how sensitive the outcome of the project is to these changes. If the output appears to be highly sensitive to one or two of the input factors, the financial managers may then wish to spend additional time refining those input estimates to make sure they are accurate.

Fortunately, as with most other things, there is help on the Web. In fact, in the Cash Flow Business Owner's Toolkit Web site (**www.toolkit.cch.com/tools/cfsens_m.asp**) there is a Sensitivity Analysis Worksheet that you can download for free. This worksheet is an Excel 5.0 template you can use to see what happens if your sales are 5 percent more or less than the forecast.

PROBABILITY TREES

Probability tree
A schematic representation of a problem in which all possible outcomes are graphically displayed.

A **probability tree** is a graphic exposition of the sequence of possible outcomes; it presents the decision maker with a schematic representation of the problem in which all possible outcomes are pictured. Moreover, the computations and results of the computations are shown directly on the tree, so that the information can be easily understood.

To illustrate the use of a probability tree, suppose a firm is considering an investment proposal that requires an initial outlay of $1 million and will yield cash flows for the next two years. During the first year, let us assume there are three possible outcomes, as shown in Table 11-3. Graphically, each of these three possible alternatives is represented on the probability tree shown in Figure 11-5 as one of the three possible branches.

TABLE 11-3 Possible Outcomes in Year 1

	PROBABILITY		
	.5	.3	.2
	Outcome 1	Outcome 2	Outcome 3
Cash flow	$600,000	$700,000	$800,000

FIGURE 11-5 First Stage of a Probability-Tree Diagram

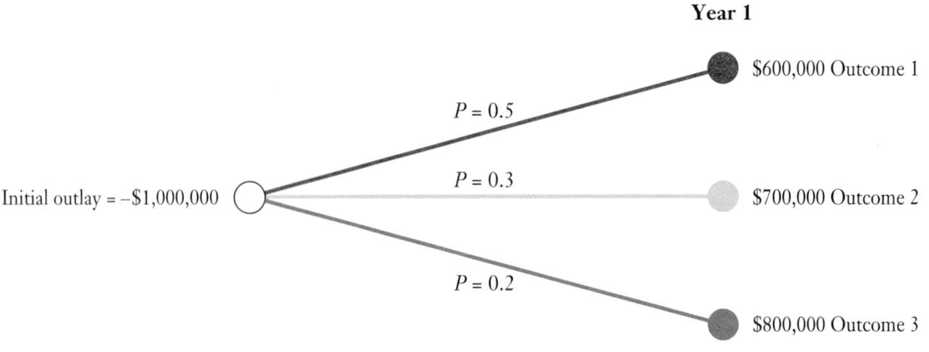

TABLE 11-4 Conditional Outcomes and Probabilities for Year 2

	IF OUTCOME 1		IF OUTCOME 2		IF OUTCOME 3	
Year 1	ACF_1 = $600,000 Then		ACF_1 = $700,000 Then		ACF_1 = $800,000 Then	
Year 2	ACF_2	Probability	ACF_2	Probability	ACF_2	Probability
	$300,000	.2	$300,000	.2	$400,000	.2
	600,000	.8	500,000	.3	600,000	.7
			700,000	.5	800,000	.1

The second step in the probability tree is to continue drawing branches in a similar manner so that each of the possible outcomes during the second year is represented by a new branch. For example, if outcome 1 occurs in year 1, then there would be a 20 percent chance of a $300,000 cash flow and an 80 percent chance of a $600,000 cash flow in year 2, as shown in Table 11-4. Two branches would be sent out from the outcome 1 node, reflecting these two possible outcomes. The cash flows that occur if outcome 1 takes place and the probabilities associated with them are called *conditional outcomes* and *conditional probabilities* because they can occur only if outcome 1 occurs during the first year. Finally, to determine the probability of the sequence of a $600,000 flow in year 1 and a $300,000 outcome in year 2, the probability of the $600,000 flow (.5) is multiplied by the conditional probability of the second flow (.2), telling us that this sequence has a 10 percent chance of occurring; this is called its **joint probability**. Letting the values in Table 11-4 represent the conditional outcomes and their respective conditional probabilities, we can complete the probability tree, as shown in Figure 11-6.

Joint probability
The probability of two different sequential outcomes occurring.

The financial manager, by examining the probability tree, is provided with the expected internal rate of return for the investment, the range of possible outcomes, and a listing of each possible outcome with the probability associated with it. In this case, the expected internal rate of return is 14.74 percent, and there is a 10 percent chance of incurring the worst possible outcome with an internal rate of return of −7.55 percent. There is a 2 percent probability of achieving the most favorable outcome, an internal rate of return of 37.98 percent.

Decision making with probability trees does not mean simply the acceptance of any project with an internal rate of return greater than the firm's required rate of return, because the project's required rate of return has not yet been adjusted for risk. As a result, the financial decision maker must examine the entire distribution of possible internal rates of return. Then, based on that examination, he or she must decide, given her or his aversion to risk, if enough of this distribution is above the appropriate (risk-adjusted) required rate of return to warrant acceptance of the project. Thus, the probability tree allows the manager to quickly visualize the possible future events, their probabilities, and their outcomes. In addition, the calculation of the expected internal rate of return and enumeration of the distribution should aid the financial manager in determining the risk level of the project. However, just as with the simulation approach, probability trees do not differentiate between systematic and unsystematic risk.

Other Sources of Risk: Time Dependence of Cash Flows

Up to this point, in all approaches other than the probability tree, we have assumed that the cash flow in one period is independent of the cash flow in the previous period. Although this assumption is appealing because it is simple, in many cases it is also invalid.

FIGURE 11-6 Probability Tree

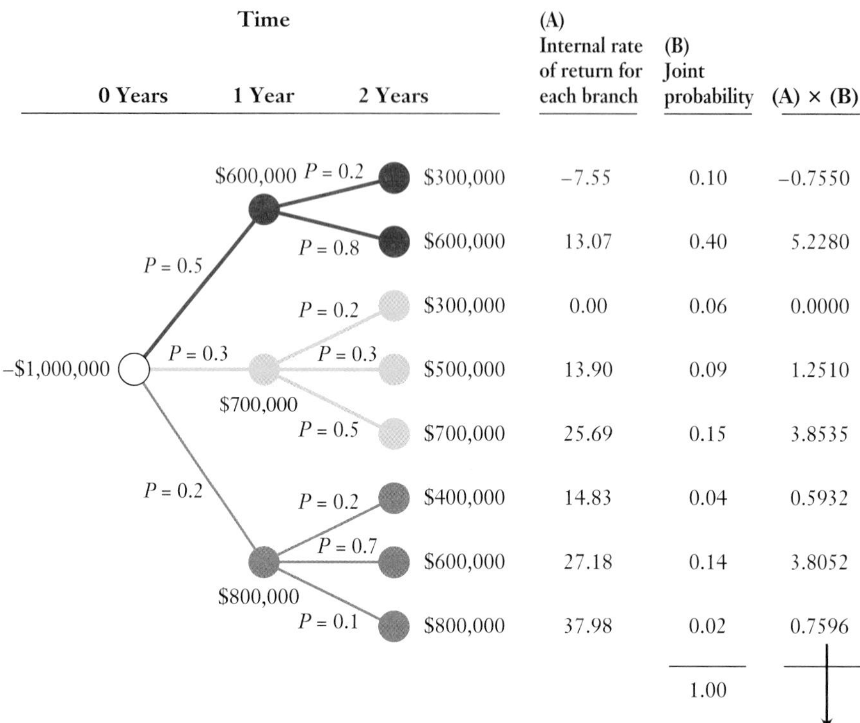

For example, if a new product is introduced and the initial public reaction is poor, resulting in low initial cash flows, then cash flows in future periods are likely to be low. An extreme example of this is Coca-Cola's experience with the "New Coke." Poor consumer acceptance and sales in the first year were followed by even poorer results in the second year. If the New Coke had been received favorably during its first year, it quite likely would have done well in the second year. The end effect of time dependence of cash flows is to increase the risk of the project over time. That is, because large cash flows in the first period lead to large cash flows in the second period, and low cash flows in the first period lead to low cash flows in the second period, the probability distribution of possible net present values tends to be wider than if the cash flows were not dependent over time. The greater the degree of correlation between flows over time, the greater will be the dispersion of the probability distribution. See the Finance Matters box, "Financial Engineering at Merck."

CONCEPT CHECK

1. Explain how simulations work.
2. What is scenario analysis? What is sensitivity analysis? When would you perform sensitivity analysis?

FINANCE MATTERS

FINANCIAL ENGINEERING AT MERCK

The risks that pharmaceutical firms face in product development are great. It costs $359 million and takes 10 years to bring a new drug to market. Then, once the drug has reached the market, 70 percent of the new drugs introduced do not cover their costs. Rather than simply using an estimate of the project's expected net present value, Merck relies on a simulation approach. It examines the returns on proposed new drugs over a 20-year period, allowing for any and all complexities that it can foresee. The excerpt that follows illustrates this.

Last year Merck & Co., Inc., invested well over $2 billion in R&D and capital expenditures combined. The company spent much of the money on risky, long-term projects that are notoriously difficult to evaluate. Indeed, the critics of modern finance would argue that such projects should not be subjected to rigorous financial analysis, because such analysis fails to reflect the strategic value of long-term investments. Yet at Merck, it is those projects with the longest time horizon that receive the most intense and financially sophisticated analyses. In fact, Merck's financial function is active and influential with a highly quantitative, analytical orientation. The company is seldom, if ever, criticized for being shortsighted.

Why doesn't all this analysis choke off long-term investing, as critics of modern finance theory say it should? In part because Merck is a leader in building financial models of scientific and commercial processes and in using those models to improve business decisions. Rather than relying on static, single-point forecasts, Merck's models use probability distributions for numerous variables and come up with a range of possible outcomes that both stimulate discussion and facilitate decision making.

For example, Merck's Research Planning Model, now 10 years old, and its Revenue Hedging Model, now four years old, integrate economics, finance, statistics, and computer science to produce disciplined, quantitative analyses of specific elements of Merck's business. These models do not make decisions. Instead, they provide Merck executives with cogent information both about risks and returns and about financial performance for specific projects and activities.

One of the key aspects of the simulation approach used by Merck is the ability to perform sensitivity analysis by changing the value of specific variables and seeing how the results are affected. In this way, Merck can determine where to spend more time in forecasting and where they should spend time and money trying to improve efficiency.

Source: Reprinted by permission of *Harvard Business Review*. From "Scientific Management at Merck: An Interview with CFO Judy Lewent" by Nancy A. Nichols (Jan.–Feb. 1994).

THE MULTINATIONAL FIRM: CAPITAL BUDGETING AND RISK

Along with all the benefits from going multinational come the risks. One of the major risks involves currency fluctuations. For example, in 1998, Boeing introduced the Boeing Business Jet, a new versatile business jet that combines fuel efficiency for short flights with globe-spanning range. Boeing produces these planes in the United States, paying workers and suppliers in U.S. dollars. Boeing then exports them all over the world in many different currencies. What happens if the value of the foreign currency falls in the time between placement of the order and receipt of the payment? Can this happen? The answer is that it can happen. In fact, on April 1, 1998, the value of the Yugoslav dinar fell by 43 percent against the U.S. dollar. That means if Boeing had sold a Business Jet to a customer in Yugoslavia for Yugoslav dinars, Boeing would have received the same number of dinars stated in the contract, but they would have been worth 43 percent less. Risks from economic and currency problems abroad can be devastating. For example, the Asian and Latin American economic crisis of 1998 resulted in GM's Latin America/Africa/Mid-East division showing a loss of $161 million in the fourth quarter of 1998 compared with income of $192 million in the fourth quarter of 1997. Also, GM's Asia/Pacific's losses totaled $116 million in the fourth quarter of 1998, compared with a loss of $27 million in the prior-year period. Currency risks also came into play in 2000, but this time from a place that might at first appear safe—Europe. In fact, between January 1, 1999, and the end of 2000, the value of the currency of the European Union, the Euro, fell by about 28 percent. This dramatic drop in the Euro had a major impact on the bottom-line profits of almost every company that did business in Europe. For example, Harley-Davidson, which posted record profits in the third quarter of 2000, pointed out the "negative effects of European currencies" on its profits. McDonald's, however, reported that the Euro's fall would slash its full-year earnings by about 5 percent, while Goodyear's third quarter profits dropped by 30 percent as a result of the Euro. The bottom line here is that when a firm's capital budgeting goes across its border, it adds some new risks to the decision.

HOW FINANCIAL MANAGERS USE THIS MATERIAL

If financial managers could see into the future, the material in this chapter would be unnecessary. Unfortunately, they can't—in fact, no one can. What that means for capital-budgeting decision making is that you're never really sure how the market will react to your new project. Moreover, not all projects have the same level of risk and, as a result, you have to look at each project individually and make some adjustment for risk. On top of all that, we have the problem of measuring risk.

What does all this mean for you as a financial manager? It means that you not only must understand how risk is measured and the fact that all risk is not the same (in effect, **Principle 9**), but you must also make an adjustment for risk within the capital-budgeting process.

Looking back at Burger King and its introduction of the Big King burger aimed at competing with the McDonald's Big Mac, after all the test marketing, there is still a good deal of uncertainty as to how the public will react to this product. Remember, when McDonald's introduced the Arch Deluxe several years ago? That was McDonald's attempt to bring older customers back into McDonald's by providing a more sophisticated burger. They went through extensive test marketing and thought they had a winner, but it didn't sell that way. To determine how much risk and uncertainty there is with a new product, the financial manager must rely heavily on those making the sales forecast. Once they provide the estimate of risk, it is the financial manager's job to react to this and incorporate it into the capital-budgeting process, looking at the best and worst case scenarios and trying to determine just how risky the project is. That may be your job.

SUMMARY

Objective 1

In this chapter, we examine the problem of incorporating risk into the capital-budgeting decision. First we explore just what type of risk to adjust for: project standing alone risk, the project's contribution-to-firm risk, or the project's systematic risk. In theory, systematic risk is the appropriate risk measure, but bankruptcy costs and the issue of undiversified shareholders also give weight to considering a project's contribution-to-firm risk as the appropriate risk measure. Both measures of risk have merit, and we avoid making any specific allocation of importance between the two in capital budgeting.

Objective 2

Two commonly used methods for incorporating risk into capital budgeting are (1) the certainty equivalent method and (2) risk-adjusted discount rates. The certainty equivalent approach involves a direct attempt to incorporate the decision maker's utility function into the analysis. Under this method, cash flows are adjusted downward by multiplying them by certainty equivalent coefficients, α_t's, which transform the risky cash flows into equivalent certain cash flows in terms of desirability. A project's net present value using the certainty equivalent method for adjusting for risk becomes

$$NPV = \sum_{t=1}^{n} \frac{\alpha_t FCF_t}{(1 + k_{rf})^t} - IO \quad \textbf{(11-2)}$$

The risk-adjusted discount rate involves an upward adjustment of the discount rate to compensate for risk. This method is based on the concept that investors demand higher returns for riskier projects.

Objective 3

The simulation and probability tree methods are used to provide information as to the location and shape of the distribution of possible outcomes. Decisions could be based directly on these methods, or they could be used to determine input into either certainty equivalent or risk-adjusted discount method approaches.

KEY TERMS

Certainty equivalent, 376

Certainty equivalent approach, 376

Joint probability, 387

Probability tree, 386

Project's contribution-to-firm risk, 373

Project standing alone risk, 373

Pure play method, 383

Risk-adjusted discount rate, 378

Scenario analysis, 385

Sensitivity analysis, 385

Simulation, 383

Systematic risk, 373

Go To: **www.prenhall.com/keown** for downloads and current events associated with this chapter

STUDY QUESTIONS

11-1. In Chapter 9, we examined the payback period capital-budgeting decision criterion. Often this capital-budgeting criterion is used as a risk-screening device. Explain the rationale behind its use.

11-2. The use of the risk-adjusted discount rate assumes that risk increases over time. Justify this assumption.

11-3. What are the similarities and differences between the risk-adjusted discount rate and the certainty equivalent methods for incorporating risk into the capital-budgeting decision?

11-4. What is the value of using the probability tree method for evaluating capital-budgeting projects?

11-5. Explain how simulation works. What is the value in using a simulation approach?

11-6. What does time dependence of cash flows mean? Why might cash flows be time dependent? Give some examples.

SELF-TEST PROBLEMS

ST-1. G. Norohna and Co. is considering two mutually exclusive projects. The expected values for each project's cash flows are as follows:

YEAR	PROJECT A	PROJECT B
0	–$300,000	–$300,000
1	100,000	200,000
2	200,000	200,000
3	200,000	200,000
4	300,000	300,000
5	300,000	400,000

The company has decided to evaluate these projects using the certainty equivalent method. The certainty equivalent coefficients for each project's cash flows are as follows:

YEAR	PROJECT A	PROJECT B
0	1.00	1.00
1	.95	.90
2	.90	.80
3	.85	.70
4	.80	.60
5	.75	.50

Given that this company's normal required rate of return is 15 percent and the after-tax risk-free rate is 8 percent, which project should be selected?

STUDY PROBLEMS (SET A)

11-1A. (*Risk-adjusted* NPV) The Hokie Corporation is considering two mutually exclusive projects. Both require an initial outlay of $10,000 and will operate for five years. The probability distributions associated with each project for years 1 through 5 are given as follows:

Probability Distribution for Cash Flow Years 1–5 (the same cash flow each year)

PROJECT A		PROJECT B	
PROBABILITY	CASH FLOW	PROBABILITY	CASH FLOW
.15	$4,000	.15	$ 2,000
.70	5,000	.70	6,000
.15	6,000	.15	10,000

Because project B is the riskier of the two projects, the management of Hokie Corporation has decided to apply a required rate of return of 15 percent to its evaluation but only a 12 percent required rate of return to project A.

a. Determine the expected value of each project's annual cash flows.
b. Determine each project's risk-adjusted net present value.
c. What other factors might be considered in deciding between these two projects?

11-2A. (*Risk-adjusted* NPV) The Goblu Corporation is evaluating two mutually exclusive projects, both of which require an initial outlay of $100,000. Each project has an expected life of five years. The probability distributions associated with the annual cash flows from each project are as follows:

Probability Distribution for Cash Flow Years 1–5 (the same cash flow each year)

PROJECT A		PROJECT B	
PROBABILITY	CASH FLOW	PROBABILITY	CASH FLOW
.10	$35,000	.10	$10,000
.40	40,000	.20	30,000
.40	45,000	.40	45,000
.10	50,000	.20	60,000
		.10	80,000

The normal required rate of return for Goblu is 10 percent, but because these projects are riskier than most, it is requiring a higher-than-normal rate of return on them. Project A requires a 12 percent rate of return and project B requires a 13 percent rate of return.

a. Determine the expected value for each project's cash flows.

b. Determine each project's risk-adjusted net present value.

c. What other factors might be considered in deciding between these projects?

11-3A. *(Certainty equivalents)* The V. Coles Corp. is considering two mutually exclusive projects. The expected values for each project's cash flows are as follows:

YEAR	PROJECT A	PROJECT B
0	–$1,000,000	–$1,000,000
1	500,000	500,000
2	700,000	600,000
3	600,000	700,000
4	500,000	800,000

Management has decided to evaluate these projects using the certainty equivalent method. The certainty equivalent coefficients for each project's cash flows are as follows:

YEAR	PROJECT A	PROJECT B
0	1.00	1.00
1	.95	.90
2	.90	.70
3	.80	.60
4	.70	.50

Given that this company's normal required rate of return is 15 percent and the after-tax risk-free rate is 5 percent, which project should be selected?

11-4A. *(Certainty equivalents)* Neustal, Inc., has decided to use the certainty equivalent method in determining whether or not a new investment should be made. The expected cash flows associated with this investment and the estimated certainty equivalent coefficients are as follows:

YEAR	EXPECTED VALUES FOR CASH FLOWS	CERTAINTY EQUIVALENT COEFFICIENTS
0	–$90,000	1.00
1	25,000	0.95
2	30,000	0.90
3	30,000	0.83
4	25,000	0.75
5	20,000	0.65

Given that Neustal's normal required rate of return is 18 percent and that the after-tax risk-free rate is 7 percent, should this project be accepted?

11-5A. *(Risk-adjusted discount rates and risk classes)* The G. Wolfe Corporation is examining two capital-budgeting projects with five-year lives. The first, project A, is a replacement project; the second, project B, is a project unrelated to current operations. The G. Wolfe Corporation uses the risk-adjusted discount rate method and groups projects according to purpose and then uses a required rate of return or discount rate that has been preassigned to that purpose or risk class. The expected cash flows for these projects are as follows:

	PROJECT A	PROJECT B
Initial Investment:	$250,000	$400,000
Cash Inflows:		
Year 1	$ 30,000	$135,000
Year 2	40,000	135,000
Year 3	50,000	135,000
Year 4	90,000	135,000
Year 5	130,000	135,000

The purpose or risk classes and preassigned required rates of return are as follows:

PURPOSE	REQUIRED RATE OF RETURN
Replacement decision	12%
Modification or expansion of existing product line	15
Project unrelated to current operations	18
Research and development operations	20

Determine the project's risk-adjusted net present value.

11-6A. (*Certainty equivalents*) Nacho Nachtmann Company uses the certainty equivalent approach when it evaluates risky investments. The company presently has two mutually exclusive investment proposals with an expected life of four years each to choose from with money it received from the sale of part of its toy division to another company. The expected net cash flows are as follows:

YEAR	PROJECT A	PROJECT B
0	−$50,000	−$50,000
1	15,000	20,000
2	15,000	25,000
3	15,000	25,000
4	45,000	30,000

The certainty equivalent coefficients for the net cash flows are as follows:

YEAR	PROJECT A	PROJECT B
0	1.00	1.00
1	.95	.90
2	.85	.85
3	.80	.80
4	.70	.75

Which of the two investment proposals should be chosen, given that the after-tax risk-free rate of return is 6 percent?

11-7A. (*Probability trees*) The M. Solt Corporation is evaluating an investment proposal with an expected life of two years. This project will require an initial outlay of $1,200,000. The resultant possible cash flows are as follows:

Possible Outcomes in Year 1

	PROBABILITY		
	.6	.3	.1
	Outcome 1	Outcome 2	Outcome 3
Cash flow =	$700,000	$850,000	$1,000,000

Conditional Outcomes and Probabilities for Year 2

If ACF_1 = $700,000		If ACF_1 = $850,000		If ACF_1 = $1,000,000	
ACF_2	Probability	ACF_2	Probability	ACF_2	Probability
$ 300,000	.3	$ 400,000	.2	$ 600,000	.1
700,000	.6	700,000	.5	900,000	.5
1,100,000	.1	1,000,000	.2	1,100,000	.4
		1,300,000	.1		

a. Construct a probability tree representing the possible outcomes.
b. Determine the joint probability of each possible sequence of events taking place.
c. What is the expected *IRR* of this project?
d. What is the range of possible *IRR*s for this project?

11-8A. (*Probability trees*) Sega, Inc. is considering expanding its operations into computer-based lacrosse games. Sega feels that there is a three-year life associated with this project, and it will initially involve an investment of $100,000. It also believes there is a 60 percent chance of success and a cash flow of $100,000 in year 1 and a 40 percent chance of failure and a $10,000 cash flow in year 1. If the project fails in year 1, there is a 60 percent chance that it will produce cash flows of only $10,000 in years 2 and 3. There is also a 40 percent chance that it will *really* fail and Sega will earn nothing in year 2 and get out of this line of business, with the project terminating and no cash flow occurring in year 3. If, conversely, this project succeeds in the first year, then cash flows in the second year are expected to be $200,000, $175,000, or $150,000 with probabilities of .30, .50, and .20, respectively. Finally, if the project succeeds in the third and final year of operation, the cash flows are expected to be either $30,000 more or $20,000 less than they were in year 2, with an equal chance of occurrence.

a. Construct a probability tree representing the possible outcomes.
b. Determine the joint probability of each possible sequence of events.
c. What is the expected *IRR*?
d. What is the range of possible *IRR*s for this project?

WEB WORKS

You've decided to use the pure play method for estimating a project's beta. Let's assume that your new product is in the pharmaceutical industry. That means the first thing you'll have to do is calculate the beta on a drug company—let's pick Pfizer for this—that most closely matches your new product. To do this let's use the *MoneyCentral* site, which is a research site for the Microsoft network. If you have the company's ticker symbol, which is a unique one-to four-place alphabetical "nickname" for a company—for Pfizer the ticker symbol is pfe—you can go to a company report (**moneycentral.msn.com/investor/research/profile.asp?**) which provides a one-page overview of the company, including its beta.

You can also find the beta on Yahoo! Finance:

1. From the Yahoo home page (**www.yahoo.com**), choose "Yahoo! Finance" (first link under "Info").
2. Enter the ticker symbol in the first box; choose "Basic" from the second box; click on "Get".
3. Click on "Profile" in the "More Info" box.
4. Go to the table at the bottom of the page. Beta will be the fourth item in the first column.

Just as with MoneyCentral, in order to get the information for a given firm, you need to know its ticker symbol. The *MoneyCentral* site is a place to find the ticker symbol if you don't know it.

1. Let's look up four companies using both MoneyCentral and Yahoo! Finance:
   - Pfizer (pfe)
   - Amazon.com (amzn)
   - Aetna (aet)
   - Intel (intc)

What do you think the betas would be for these companies? Remember that the beta of the market is 1.0, less risky companies would be less than 1, and more risky ones would be more than 1.

Were you close? Are the betas on both sites the same? Why might there be differences in the betas?

INTEGRATIVE PROBLEM

It's been four months since you took a position as an assistant financial analyst at Caledonia Products. During that time, you've had a promotion and now are working as a special assistant for capital budgeting to the CEO. Your latest assignment involves the analysis of several risky projects. Because this is your first assignment dealing with risk analysis, you have been asked not only to provide a recommendation on the projects in question, but also to respond to a number of questions aimed at judging your understanding of risk analysis and capital budgeting. The memorandum you received outlining your assignment follows:

TO: The Special Assistant for Capital Budgeting

FROM: Mr. V. Morrison, CEO, Caledonia Products

RE: Capital Budgeting and Risk Analysis

Provide a written response to the following questions:

1. In capital budgeting, risk can be measured from three perspectives. What are those three measures of a project's risk?
2. According to the CAPM, which measurement of a project's risk is relevant? What complications does reality introduce into the CAPM view of risk and what does that mean for our view of the relevant measure of a project's risk?
3. What are the similarities and differences between the risk-adjusted discount rate and certainty equivalent methods for incorporating risk into the capital-budgeting decision?
4. Why might we use the probability tree technique for evaluating capital-budgeting projects?
5. Explain how simulation works. What is the value of using a simulation approach?
6. What is sensitivity analysis and what is its purpose?
7. What does time dependence of cash flows mean? Why might cash flows be time dependent? Give some examples.
8. Caledonia Products is using the certainty equivalent approach to evaluate two mutually exclusive investment proposals with an expected life of four years. The expected net cash flows are as follows:

YEAR	PROJECT A	PROJECT B
0	–$150,000	–$200,000
1	40,000	50,000
2	40,000	60,000
3	40,000	60,000
4	100,000	50,000

The certainty equivalent coefficients for the net cash flows are as follows:

YEAR	PROJECT A	PROJECT B
0	1.00	1.00
1	.90	.95
2	.85	.85
3	.80	.80
4	.70	.75

Which of the two investment proposals should be chosen, given that the after-tax risk-free rate of return is 7 percent?

9. Caledonia is considering an additional investment project with an expected life of two years and would like some insights on the level of risk this project has using the probability tree method. The initial outlay on this project would be $600,000, and the resultant possible cash flows are as follows:

Possible Outcomes in Year 1

	PROBABILITY		
	.4	.4	.2
	Outcome 1	Outcome 2	Outcome 3
Cash flow =	$300,000	$350,000	$450,000

Conditional Outcomes and Probabilities for Year 2

If ACF_1 = $300,000		If ACF_1 = $350,000		If ACF_1 = $450,000	
ACF_2	Probability	ACF_2	Probability	ACF_2	Probability
$ 200,000	.3	$ 250,000	.2	$ 300,000	.2
300,000	.7	450,000	.5	500,000	.5
		650,000	.3	700,000	.2
				1,000,000	.1

a. Construct a probability tree representing the possible outcomes.
b. Determine the joint probability of each possible sequence of events taking place.
c. What is the expected *IRR* of this project?
d. What is the range of possible *IRR*s for this project?

STUDY PROBLEMS (SET B)

11-1B. (*Risk-adjusted* NPV) The Cake-O-Las Corporation is considering two mutually exclusive projects. Each of these projects requires an initial outlay of $10,000 and will operate for five years. The probability distributions associated with each project for years 1 through 5 are given as follows:

Probability Distribution for Cash Flow Years 1–5 (the same cash flow each year)

PROJECT A		PROJECT B	
PROBABILITY	CASH FLOW	PROBABILITY	CASH FLOW
.20	$5,000	.20	$ 3,000
.60	6,000	.60	7,000
.20	7,000	.20	11,000

Because project B is the riskier of the two projects, the management of Cake-O-Las Corporation has decided to apply a required rate of return of 18 percent to its evaluation but only a 13 percent required rate of return to project A.

a. Determine the expected value of each project's annual cash flows.
b. Determine each project's risk-adjusted net present value.
c. What other factors might be considered in deciding between these two projects?

11-2B. (*Risk-adjusted* NPV) The Dorf Corporation is evaluating two mutually exclusive projects, both of which require an initial outlay of $125,000. Each project has an expected life of five years. The probability distributions associated with the annual cash flows from each project are as follows:

Probability Distribution for Cash Flow Years 1–5 (the same cash flow each year)

PROJECT A		PROJECT B	
PROBABILITY	CASH FLOW	PROBABILITY	CASH FLOW
.10	$40,000	.10	$20,000
.40	45,000	.20	40,000
.40	50,000	.40	55,000
.10	55,000	.20	70,000
		.10	90,000

The normal required rate of return for Dorf is 10 percent, but because these projects are riskier than most, Dorf is requiring a higher-than-normal rate of return on them. On project A, it is requiring an 11 percent rate of return, and on project B, a 13 percent rate of return.

a. Determine the expected value for each project's cash flows.
b. Determine each project's risk-adjusted net present value.
c. What other factors might be considered in deciding between these projects?

11-3B. (*Certainty equivalents*) The Temco Corp. is considering two mutually exclusive projects. The expected values for each project's cash flows are as follows:

YEAR	PROJECT A	PROJECT B
0	−$100,000	−$100,000
1	600,000	600,000
2	750,000	650,000
3	600,000	700,000
4	550,000	750,000

Temco has decided to evaluate these projects using the certainty equivalent method. The certainty equivalent coefficients for each project's cash flows are as follows:

YEAR	PROJECT A	PROJECT B
0	1.00	1.00
1	.90	.95
2	.90	.75
3	.75	.60
4	.65	.60

Given that this company's normal required rate of return is 15 percent and the after-tax risk-free rate is 5 percent, which project should be selected?

11-4B. (*Certainty equivalents*) Perumperal, Inc., has decided to use the certainty equivalent method in determining whether or not a new investment should be made. The expected cash flows associated with this investment and the estimated certainty equivalent coefficients are as follows:

YEAR	EXPECTED CASH FLOW	CERTAINTY EQUIVALENT COEFFICIENT AT
0	−$100,000	1.00
1	30,000	.95
2	25,000	.90
3	30,000	.83
4	20,000	.75
5	25,000	.65

Given that Perumperal's normal required rate of return is 18 percent and that the after-tax risk-free rate is 8 percent, should this project be accepted?

11-5B. (*Risk-adjusted discount rates and risk classes*) The Kick 'n' MacDonald Corporation is examining two capital-budgeting projects with five-year lives. The first, project A, is a replacement project; the second, project B, is a project unrelated to current operations. The Kick 'n' MacDonald Corporation uses the risk-adjusted discount rate method and groups projects according to purpose and then uses a required rate of return or discount rate that has been preassigned to that purpose or risk class. The expected cash flows for these projects are as follows:

	PROJECT A	PROJECT B
Initial Investment:	$300,000	$450,000
Cash Inflows:		
Year 1	$ 30,000	$130,000
Year 2	40,000	130,000
Year 3	50,000	130,000
Year 4	80,000	130,000
Year 5	120,000	130,000

The purpose-risk classes and preassigned required rates of return are as follows:

PURPOSE	REQUIRED RATE OF RETURN
Replacement decision	13%
Modification or expansion of existing product line	16
Project unrelated to current operations	18
Research and development operations	20

Determine the project's risk-adjusted net present value.

11-6B. (*Certainty equivalents*) The M. Jose Company uses the certainty equivalent approach when it evaluates risky investments. The company presently has two mutually exclusive investment proposals, with an expected life of four years each, to choose from with money it received from the sale of part of its toy division to another company. The expected net cash flows are as follows:

YEAR	PROJECT A	PROJECT B
0	–$75,000	–$75,000
1	20,000	25,000
2	20,000	30,000
3	15,000	30,000
4	50,000	25,000

The certainty equivalent coefficients for the net cash flows are as follows:

YEAR	PROJECT A	PROJECT B
0	1.00	1.00
1	.95	.95
2	.85	.85
3	.80	.80
4	.70	.75

Which of the two investment proposals should be chosen, given that the after-tax risk-free rate of return is 7 percent?

11-7B. (*Probability trees*) The Buckeye Corporation is evaluating an investment proposal with an expected life of two years. This project will require an initial outlay of $1,300,000. The resultant possible cash flows are as follows:

Possible Outcomes in Year 1

	PROBABILITY		
	.6	.3	.1
	Outcome 1	Outcome 2	Outcome 3
Cash flow =	$750,000	$900,000	$1,500,000

Conditional Outcomes and Probabilities for Year 2

If ACF_1 = $750,000		If ACF_1 = $900,000		If ACF_1 = $1,500,000	
ACF_2	Probability	ACF_2	Probability	ACF_2	Probability
$ 300,000	.10	$ 400,000	.2	$ 600,000	.3
700,000	.50	700,000	.5	900,000	.6
1,100,000	.40	900,000	.2	1,100,000	.1
		1,300,000	.1		

a. Construct a probability tree representing the possible outcomes.
b. Determine the joint probability of each possible sequence of events taking place.
c. What is the expected *IRR* of this project?
d. What is the range of possible *IRR*s for this project?

11-8B. (*Probability trees*) Mac's Buffaloes, Inc., is considering expanding its operations into computer-based basketball games. Mac's Buffaloes feels that there is a three-year life associated with this project, and it will initially involve an investment of $120,000. It also feels there is a 70 percent chance of success and a cash flow of $100,000 in year 1 and a 30 percent chance of "failure" and a $10,000 cash flow in year 1. If the project "fails" in year 1, there is a 60 percent chance that it will produce cash flows of only $10,000 in years 2 and 3. There is also a 40 percent chance that it will really fail and Mac's Buffaloes will earn nothing in year 2 and get out of this line of business, with the project terminating and no cash flow occurring in year 3. If, however, this project succeeds in the first year, then cash flows in the second year are expected to be $225,000, $180,000, or $140,000 with probabilities of .30, .50, and .20, respectively. Finally, if the project succeeds in the third and final year of operation, the cash flows are expected to be either $30,000 more or $20,000 less than they were in year 2, with an equal chance of occurrence.

a. Construct a probability tree representing the possible outcomes.
b. Determine the joint probability of each possible sequence of events.
c. What is the expected *IRR?*
d. What is the range of possible *IRR*s for this project?

CASE PROBLEM

ETHICS

MADE IN THE U.S.A.: DUMPED IN BRAZIL, AFRICA . . .

Ethics in Dealing with Uncertainty in Capital Budgeting, or What Happens When a Project Is No Longer Sellable

In an uncertain world, capital budgeting attempts to determine what the future of a new product will bring and how then to act on that forecast. We never know for certain what the future will bring, but we do arrive at some idea of what the distribution of possible outcomes looks like. Unfortunately, when there is uncertainty, the outcome is not always a good one. For example, what happens if the government rules that our product is not safe? The answer is that we must abandon the product. The question then becomes what to do with the inventory we currently have on hand. We certainly want to deal with it in a way that is in the best interests of our shareholders. We also want to obey the law and act ethically. As with most ethical questions, there isn't necessarily a right or wrong answer.

When it comes to the safety of young children, fire is a parent's nightmare. Just the thought of their young ones trapped in their cribs and beds by a raging nocturnal blaze is enough to make most mothers and fathers take every precaution to ensure their children's safety. Little wonder that when fire-retardant children's pajamas hit the market in the mid-1970s, they proved an overnight success. Within a few short years, more than 200 million pairs were sold, and the sales of millions more were all but guaranteed. For their manufacturers, the future could not have been brighter. Then, like a bolt from the blue, came word that the pajamas were killers.

In June 1977, the U.S. Consumer Product Safety Commission (CPSC) banned the sale of these pajamas and ordered the recall of millions of pairs. Reason: The pajamas contained the flame-retardant chemical Tris (2,3-dibromoprophyl), which had been found to cause kidney cancer in children.

Whereas just months earlier the 100 medium- and small-garment manufacturers of the Tris-impregnated pajamas couldn't fill orders fast enough, suddenly they were worrying about how to get rid of the millions of pairs now sitting in warehouses. Because of its toxicity, the sleepwear couldn't even be thrown away, let alone be sold. Indeed, the CPSC left no doubt about how the pajamas were to be disposed of—buried or burned or used as industrial wiping cloths. All meant millions of dollars in losses for manufacturers.

The companies affected—mostly small, family-run operations employing fewer than 100 workers—immediately attempted to shift blame to the mills that made the cloth. When that attempt failed, they tried to get the big department stores that sold the pajamas and the chemical companies that produced Tris to share the financial losses. Again, no sale. Finally, in desperation, the companies lobbied in Washington for a bill making the federal government partially responsible for the losses. It was the government, they argued, that originally had required the companies to add Tris to pajamas and then had prohibited their sale. Congress was sympathetic; it passed a bill granting companies relief. But President Carter vetoed it.

While the small firms were waging their political battle in the halls of Congress, ads began appearing in the classified pages of *Women's Wear Daily*. "Tris-Tris-Tris. . . . We will buy any fabric containing Tris," read one. Another said, "Tris—we will purchase any large quantities of garments containing Tris."[a] The ads had been placed by exporters, who began buying up the pajamas, usually at 10 to 30 percent of the normal wholesale price. Their intent was clear: to dump[b] the carcinogenic pajamas on overseas markets.[c]

Tris is not the only example of dumping. In 1972, 400 Iraqis died and 5,000 were hospitalized after eating wheat and barley treated with a U.S.-banned organic mercury fungicide. Winstrol, a synthetic male hormone that had been found to stunt the growth of American children, was made available in Brazil as an appetite stimulant for children. Depo-Provera, an injectable contraceptive known to cause malignant tumors in animals, was shipped overseas to 70 countries where it was used in U.S.-sponsored population control programs. And 450,000 baby pacifiers, of the type known to have caused choking deaths, were exported for sale overseas.

Manufacturers that dump products abroad clearly are motivated by profit or at least by the hope of avoiding financial losses resulting from having to withdraw a product from the market. For government and health agencies that cooperate in the exporting of dangerous products, the motives are more complex.

For example, as early as 1971, the dangers of the Dalkon Shield intrauterine device were well documented.[d] Among the adverse reactions were pelvic inflammation, blood poisoning, pregnancies resulting in spontaneous abortions, tubal pregnancies, and uterine perforations. A number of deaths were even attributed to the device. Faced with losing its domestic market, A. H. Robins Co., manufacturer of the Dalkon Shield, worked out a deal with the Office of Population within the U.S. Agency for International Development (AID), whereby AID bought thousands of the devices at a reduced price for use in population-control programs in 42 countries.

Why do governmental and population-control agencies approve for sale and use overseas birth control devices proved dangerous in the United States? They say their motives are humanitarian. Because the rate of dying in childbirth is high in Third World countries, almost any birth control device is preferable to none. Third World scientists and government officials frequently support this argument. They insist that denying their countries access to the contraceptives of their choice is tantamount to violating their countries' national sovereignty.

Apparently this argument has found a sympathetic ear in Washington, for it turns up in the "notification" system that regulates the export of banned or dangerous products overseas. Based on the principles of national sovereignty, self-determination, and free trade, the notification system requires that foreign governments be notified whenever a product is banned, deregulated, suspended, or canceled by an American regulatory agency. The State Department, which implements the system, has a policy statement on the subject that reads in part: "No country should establish itself as the arbiter of others' health and safety standards. Individual governments are generally in the best position to establish standards of public health and safety."

Critics of the system claim that notifying foreign health officials is virtually useless. For one thing, other governments

[a]Mark Hosenball, "Karl Marx and the Pajama Game," *Mother Jones* (November 1979): 47.

[b]"Dumping" is a term apparently coined by *Mother Jones* magazine to refer to the practice of exporting to overseas countries products that have been banned or declared hazardous in the United States.

[c]Unless otherwise noted, the facts and quotations reported in this case are based on Mark Dowie, "The Corporate Crime of the Century," *Mother Jones* (November 1971) and Russell Mokhiber, *Corporate Crime and Violence* (San Francisco: Sierra Club Books, 1988): 181–95. See also Jane Kay, "Global Dumping of U.S. Toxics Is Big Business," *San Francisco Examiner* (September 23, 1990): A2.

[d]See Mark Dowie and Tracy Johnston, "A Case of Corporate Malpractice," *Mother Jones* (November 1976).

rarely can establish health standards or even control imports into their countries. Indeed, most of the Third World countries where banned or dangerous products are dumped lack regulatory agencies, adequate testing facilities, and well-staffed customs departments.

Then there's the problem of getting the word out about hazardous products. In theory, when a government agency such as the Environmental Protection Agency or the Food and Drug Administration (FDA) finds a product hazardous, it is supposed to inform the State Department, which is to notify local health officials. But agencies often fail to inform the State Department of the product they have banned or found harmful. And when it is notified, its communiqués typically go no further than the U.S. embassies abroad. One embassy official even told the General Accounting Office that he "did not routinely forward notification of chemicals not registered in the host country because it may adversely affect U.S. exporting." When foreign officials are notified by U.S. embassies, they sometimes find the communiqués vague or ambiguous or too technical to understand.

In an effort to remedy these problems, at the end of his term in office, President Jimmy Carter issued an executive order that (1) improved export notice procedures; (2) called for publishing an annual summary of substances banned or severely restricted for domestic use in the United States; (3) directed the State Department and other federal agencies to participate in the development of international hazards alert systems; and (4) established procedures for placing formal export licensing controls on a limited number of extremely hazardous substances. In one of his first acts as president, however, Ronald Reagan rescinded the order. Later in his administration, the law that formerly prohibited U.S. pharmaceutical companies from exporting drugs that are banned or not registered in this country was weakened to allow the export to 21 countries of drugs not yet approved for use in the United States.

But even if communication procedures were improved or the export of dangerous products forbidden, there are ways that companies can circumvent these threats to their profits—for example, by simply changing the name of the product or by exporting the individual ingredients of a product to a plant in a foreign country. Once there, the ingredients can be reassembled and the product dumped.[e] Upjohn, for example, through its Belgian subsidiary, continues to produce Depo-Provera, which the FDA has consistently refused to approve for use in this country. And the prohibition on the export of dangerous drugs is not that hard to sidestep. "Unless the package bursts open on the dock," one drug company executive observes, "you have no chance of being caught."

Unfortunately for us, in the case of pesticides, the effects of overseas dumping are now coming home. The Environmental Protection Agency bans from the United States all crop uses of DDT and Dieldrin, which kill fish, cause tumors in animals, and build up in the fatty tissue of humans. It also bans heptachlor, chlordane, leptophos, endrin, and many other pesticides, including 2,4,5-T (which contains the deadly poison dioxin, the active ingredient in Agent Orange, the notorious defoliant used in Vietnam) because they are dangerous to human beings. No law, however, prohibits the sale of DDT and these other U.S.-banned pesticides overseas, where—thanks to corporate dumping—they are routinely used in agriculture. The FDA now estimates, through spot checks, that 10 percent of our imported food is contaminated with illegal residues of banned pesticides. And the FDA's most commonly used testing procedure does not even check for 70 percent of the pesticides known to cause cancer.

[e]Mark Dowie, "A Dumper's Guide to Tricks of the Trade," *Mother Jones* (November 1979): 25.

Questions

1. Was the dumping in this case ethical? Those involved in the dumping might have argued that the people receiving the pajamas would not have otherwise had access to such clothing and were notified of the health and safety hazards. Does this affect your feelings about the case? What do you think about the exportation of the Dalkon Shield? Can it be justified because the rate of dying during childbirth in Third World countries is extremely high, and, as such, any effective birth control device is better than none?
2. What obligations did the financial managers have to their shareholders to do whatever is possible to avoid major financial losses associated with these products?
3. Is it still immoral or unethical to dump goods when doing so does not violate any U.S. laws? How about when those receiving the goods know the dangers? Why do you think dumpers dump? Do you think they believe what they are doing is ethically acceptable?

Source: Adapted by permission from William Shaw and Vincent Barry, "Made in the U.S.A.: Dumped in Brazil, Africa . . .", *Moral Issues in Business*, 6th ed. (New York: Wadsworth, 1995): 28–31.

SELF-TEST SOLUTIONS

ST-1. Project A:

YEAR	(A) EXPECTED CASH FLOW	(B) α_t	(A × B) (EXPECTED CASH FLOW) × (α_t)	PRESENT VALUE FACTOR AT 8%	PRESENT VALUE
0	−$300,000	1.00	−$300,000	1.000	−$300,000
1	100,000	.95	95,000	0.926	87,970
2	200,000	.90	180,000	0.857	154,260
3	200,000	.85	170,000	0.794	134,980
4	300,000	.80	240,000	0.735	176,400
5	300,000	.75	225,000	0.681	153,225
					NPV_A = $406,835

Project B:

YEAR	(A) EXPECTED CASH FLOW	(B) α_t	(A × B) (EXPECTED CASH FLOW) × (α_t)	PRESENT VALUE FACTOR AT 8%	PRESENT VALUE
0	−$300,000	1.00	−$300,000	1.000	−$300,000
1	200,000	.90	180,000	0.926	166,680
2	200,000	.80	160,000	0.857	137,120
3	200,000	.70	140,000	0.794	111,160
4	300,000	.60	180,000	0.735	132,300
5	400,000	.50	200,000	0.681	136,460
					NPV_B = $383,720

Thus, project A should be selected, because it has the higher *NPV*.

LEARNING OBJECTIVES

After reading this chapter, you should be able to

1. Describe the concepts underlying the firm's cost of capital (technically, its weighted average cost of capital) and the purpose for its calculation.
2. Calculate the after-tax cost of debt, preferred stock, and common equity.
3. Calculate a firm's weighted average cost of capital.
4. Describe the procedure used by PepsiCo to estimate the cost of capital for a multiple division firm.
5. Use the cost of capital to evaluate new investment opportunities.

CHAPTER 12

Cost of Capital

The Home Depot and Briggs & Stratton operate in very different industries; but they do have certain things in common. Both firms are faced with the need to assess two types of financial performance. In one instance, it is the anticipated performance of what seems like a never-ending stream of new capital investment opportunities related to rapid growth, and in the other, it is the operating performance of the firm as a whole. Consider the following scenarios:

- In the face of tremendous growth, the Home Depot's capital expenditures expanded from $864.2 million in 1994 to more than $2,749 million in 2003. As the firm analyzes its growing appetite for capital, it is essential that it undertake only those investments that are wealth enhancing to the firm's shareholders. How should the firm choose among its investment opportunities?
- Briggs & Stratton, however, tries to reward its employees with bonuses that reflect value created during the year. To properly assess the bonuses, the firm must first know what is expected of it by the firm's investors. That is, what minimum rate of return must the firm earn if it is to be assured of creating value for the firm's shareholders?

Home Depot needs a benchmark return that can be used to evaluate new project proposals. Similarly, Briggs & Stratton needs a benchmark return to use in evaluating whether the firm's ongoing operations are creating additional shareholder value.

In both of these instances, the firm needs an estimate of its cost of capital. We discussed the use of the cost of capital in the context of a firm's investment decisions in Chapters 9 through 11 and we return to a discussion of the use of the cost of capital in evaluating a firm's operating performance in Chapter 13.

CHAPTER PREVIEW

Having studied the linkage between risk and rates of return for securities (Chapter 6) and the valuation of bonds and stocks (Chapters 7 and 8), we are prepared to consider the firm's cost of capital. A firm's cost of capital serves as the linkage between its financing and investment decisions. The cost of capital becomes the hurdle rate that must be achieved by an investment before it will increase shareholder wealth. The term *cost of capital* is frequently used interchangeably with the firm's *required rate of return*, the *hurdle rate for new investments*, the *discount rate for evaluating a new investment*, and the firm's *opportunity cost of funds*. Regardless of the term used, the basic concept is the same. The cost of capital is the rate that must be earned on an investment project if the project is to increase the value of the common stockholder's investment.

The cost of capital is also the appropriate basis for evaluating the periodic performance of a division or even an entire firm. In this case, the cost of capital becomes the key determinant of the capital cost associated with a firm's investments.

In this chapter, we will discuss the fundamental determinants of a firm's cost of capital as well as the rationale for its calculation and use. This will entail estimating the cost of debt capital, preferred stock, and common stock. Chapter 16 takes up consideration of the impact of the firm's financing mix on the cost of capital.

This chapter emphasizes principles 1, 2, 3, 6, 8, and 9: **Principle 1: The Risk-Return Trade-Off—We won't take on additional risk unless we expect to be compensated with additional return; Principle 2: The Time Value of Money—A dollar received today is worth more than a dollar received in the future; Principle 3: Cash—Not Profits—Is King; Principle 6: Efficient Capital Markets—The markets are quick and the prices are right; Principle 8: Taxes Bias Business Decisions; Principle 9: All Risk Is Not Equal—Some risk can be diversified away, and some cannot.**

Objective 1

THE COST OF CAPITAL: KEY DEFINITIONS AND CONCEPTS

INVESTOR OPPORTUNITY COSTS, REQUIRED RATES OF RETURN, AND THE COST OF CAPITAL

Investor's required rate of return The minimum rate of return necessary to attract an investor to purchase or hold a security.

In Chapter 9, we referred to the discount rate used in calculating *NPV* simply as the appropriate discount rate. In this chapter, we define what we mean by this term. Specifically, the appropriate discount rate primarily reflects the **investor's required rate of return**. In Chapter 6, we defined the investor's required rate of return for a security as the *minimum rate of return necessary to attract an investor to purchase or hold a security*. This rate of return considers the investor's opportunity cost of making an investment; that is, if an investment is made, the investor must forgo the return available on the next-best investment. This forgone return then is the opportunity cost of undertaking the investment and, consequently, is the investor's required rate of return.

Is the investor's required rate of return the same thing as the cost of capital? Not exactly. Two basic considerations drive a wedge between the investor's required rate of return and the cost of capital to the firm. First, there are taxes. When a firm borrows money to finance the purchase of an asset, the interest expense is deductible for federal income tax calculations. Consider a firm that borrows at 9 percent and then deducts its interest expense from its revenues before paying taxes at a rate of 34 percent. For each dollar of interest it pays, the firm reduces its taxes by 34 cents. Consequently, the actual cost of borrowing to the firm is only 5.94 percent. We calculate the after-tax cost of debt in this case as follows: $.09 - (.34 \times .09) = .09(1 - .34) = 0.0594 = 5.94\%$. The second thing that causes the firm's cost of capital to differ from the investor's required rate of return is any transaction costs incurred when a firm raises funds by issuing a particular type of security, sometimes called **flotation costs**. For example, if a firm sells new shares of common stock for \$25 per share but incurs transaction costs of \$5 per share, then the cost of capital for the new common equity is increased. Assume that the investor's required rate of return is 15 percent for each \$25 share, then $.15 \times \$25 = \$3.75$ must be earned each year to satisfy the investor's required return. However, the firm has only \$20 to invest, so the cost of capital (k) is calculated as the rate of return that must be earned on the \$20 net proceeds, which will produce a dollar return of \$3.75; that is,

Flotation costs The underwriter's spread and issuing costs associated with the issuance and marketing of new securities.

$$\$20k = \$25 \times .15 = \$3.75$$

$$k = \frac{\$3.75}{\$20.00} = .1875 \text{ or } 18.75\%$$

We will have more to say about both of these considerations as we discuss the costs of the individual sources of capital to the firm.

FINANCIAL POLICY AND THE COST OF CAPITAL

Financial policy The firm's policies regarding the sources of financing and the particular mix in which they will be used.

Weighted average cost of capital The average of the after-tax costs of each of the sources of capital used by a firm to finance a project. The weights reflect the proportion of the total financing raised from each source.

A firm's **financial policy**—that is, the policies regarding the sources of finances it plans to use and the particular mix (proportions) in which they will be used—governs its use of debt and equity financing. The particular mixture of debt and equity that the firm utilizes can impact the firm's cost of capital. However, in this chapter, we will assume that the firm maintains a fixed financial policy that is defined by the firm's debt-to-equity ratio. Determination of the target mix of debt and equity financing is the subject of Chapter 16.

The firm's overall cost of capital will reflect the combined costs of all the sources of financing used by the firm. We refer to this overall cost of capital as the firm's **weighted average cost of capital**. The weighted average cost of capital is the weighted average of the after-tax costs of each of the sources of capital used by a firm to finance a project where the weights reflect the proportion of total financing raised from each source.

Consequently, the weighted average cost of capital is the rate of return that the firm must earn on its investments so that it can compensate both its creditors and stockholders with their individual required rates of return. Let's now turn to a discussion of how the costs of debt and equity can be estimated.

CONCEPT CHECK

1. Define the concept of an investor's required rate of return.
2. How is the investor's required rate of return related to the firm's cost of capital?
3. Define a firm's financial policy.
4. What is meant by the phrase "a firm's weighted average cost of capital"?

Objective 2

DETERMINING INDIVIDUAL COSTS OF CAPITAL

In order to attract new investors, companies have created a wide variety of financing instruments or securities. In this chapter, we will stick to three basic types: debt, preferred stock, and common stock. In calculating the respective cost of financing from each of these financing instruments, we estimate the investor's required rate of return properly adjusted for any transaction or flotation costs associated with each funding source. In addition, because we will be discounting after-tax cash flows, we should adjust our cost of capital for any influence of corporate taxes. In summary, the cost of a particular source of capital is equal to the investor's required rate of return after adjusting for the effects of both flotation costs and corporate taxes.

THE COST OF DEBT

The investor's required rate of return on debt is simply the return that creditors demand when they lend to the firm. In Chapter 7 we estimated this required rate of return by solving the following bond valuation equation:

$$P_d = \sum_{t=1}^{n} \frac{\text{interest paid in period } t\ (I_t)}{(1 + \text{bondholder's required rate of return } (k_d))^t} + \frac{\text{maturity value of the debt } (\$M)}{(1 + \text{bondholder's required rate of return } (k_d))^n} \quad \textbf{(12-1)}$$

where P_d is the market price of the debt security and n is the number of periods to maturity. Should the firm incur flotation costs such as brokerage commissions and legal and accounting fees in issuing the debt, then the cost of debt capital, k_d, is found as follows:

$$\begin{array}{c}\text{net proceeds}\\ \text{per bond } (NP_d)\end{array} = \sum_{t=1}^{n} \frac{\$I_t}{(1 + \$k_d)^t} + \frac{\$M}{(1 + k_d)^n} \quad \textbf{(12-2)}$$

The adjustment for flotation costs simply involves replacing the market price of the bond with the net proceeds per bond (NP_d) received by the firm after paying these costs. The result of this adjustment is that the discount rate that solves equation 12-2 is now the firm's cost of debt financing before adjusting for the effect of corporate taxes—that is, the before-tax cost of debt (k_d). The final adjustment we make is to account for the fact that interest is tax deductible. Thus, the after-tax cost of debt capital is simply $k_d(1 - T_c)$, where T_c is the corporate tax rate.

As we learned in Chapter 6, the interest payments on bonds are generally the same for each period. Under these conditions, equation 12-2 can be restated using the interest factors in the present value tables in Appendices B and C as follows:

$$NP_d = \$I_t(PVIFAk_{d,n}) + \$M(PVIFk_{d,n}) \quad \textbf{(12-2a)}$$

BACK TO THE PRINCIPLES

When we calculate the bondholder's required rate of return, we are discounting the interest and principal payments to the bondholder back to the present using a discount rate that makes this present value equal the current price of the firm's bonds. In essence, we are valuing the bond, which relies on two basic principles of finance: ***Principle 1: The Risk-Return Trade-Off—We won't take on additional risk unless we expect to be compensated with additional return,*** *and* ***Principle 2: The Time Value of Money—A dollar received today is worth more than a dollar received in the future.***

In addition, the calculation of the bondholder's required rate of return relies on the observed market price of the firm's bonds to be an accurate reflection of their worth. Buyers and sellers only stop trading when they are convinced that the price properly reflects all available information. ***Principle 6: Efficient Capital Markets—The markets are quick and the prices are right.*** *What we mean here, very simply, is that investors are ever vigilant and quickly act on information that affects the riskiness and, consequently, the price of a firm's bonds and other securities.*

CALCULATOR SOLUTION

Data Input	Function Key
30	N
978.31	+/– PV
77.50	PMT
1,000	FV
Function Key	**Answer**
CPT I/Y	7.94%

EXAMPLE: THE COST OF DEBT CAPITAL

TRW, Inc., plans to offer a new bond issue but first wants to estimate the cost of new debt capital. The firm's investment banker estimates that a 30-year bond with a $1,000 face value and 7.75 percent coupon paid annually (7.75% × $1,000 = 77.50) could be sold to investors for $990.81. Equation 12-1 can be used to solve for the investor's required rate of return, as illustrated in Chapter 6. In this case, TRW's creditors require a 7.83 percent rate of return. The cost of capital to the firm is higher than 7.83 percent, however, because the firm will have to pay flotation costs of $12.50 per bond when it issues the security. The flotation costs reduce the net proceeds to TRW to $978.31 = $990.81 – $12.50. Substituting into equation 12-2, we estimate the before-tax cost of capital for the bond issue is 7.94 percent. Once again, we can solve equation 12-2 using a financial calculator, as illustrated in the margin.

One final adjustment is necessary to obtain an estimate of the firm's after-tax cost of debt capital. Assuming that TRW is in the 34 percent corporate income tax bracket, we estimate the after-tax cost of debt capital as follows:

$$\text{after-tax cost of debt} = k_d(1 - T_c)$$

$$\text{after-tax cost of debt} = 7.94\%(1 - .34) = 5.24\%$$

BACK TO THE PRINCIPLES

The tax deductibility of interest expense makes debt financing less costly to the firm. This is an example of ***Principle 8: Taxes Bias Business Decisions.*** *The tax deductibility of interest, other things remaining constant, serves to encourage firms to use more debt in their capital structure than they might otherwise use.*

THE COST OF PREFERRED STOCK

Determining the cost of preferred stock is very straightforward because of the simple nature of the cash flows paid to the holders of preferred shares. You will recall from Chapter 7 that the value of a preferred stock is simply

$$\text{price of preferred stock}(P_{ps}) = \frac{\text{preferred stock dividend}}{\text{required rate of return for preferred stockholder}} \quad \textbf{(12-3)}$$

where P_{ps} is the current market price of the preferred shares. Solving for the preferred stockholder's required rate of return, we get the following:

$$\text{required rate of return for preferred stockholder} = \frac{\text{preferred stock dividend}}{\text{price of preferred stock}} \quad \textbf{(12-4)}$$

Once again, where flotation costs are incurred when new preferred shares are sold, the investor's required rate of return is less than the cost of preferred capital to the firm. To calculate the cost of preferred stock, we must adjust the required rate of return to reflect these flotation costs. We replace the price of a preferred share in equation 12-4 with the net proceeds per share from the sale of new preferred shares (NP_{ps}). The resulting formula can be used to calculate the cost of preferred stock to the firm.

$$\text{cost of preferred stock}(k_{ps}) = \frac{\text{preferred stock dividend}}{\text{net proceeds per preferred share}} \quad \textbf{(12-5)}$$

What about corporate taxes? In the case of preferred stock, no tax adjustment must be made because preferred dividends are not tax deductible to the firm.

EXAMPLE: THE COST OF PREFERRED STOCK

On March 26, 2003, Ford Motor Company had an issue of preferred stock trading on the NYSE that had a closing price of \$23.45 and paid an annual dividend of \$2.25 per share. Assume that if the firm were to sell an issue of preferred stock with the same characteristics as its outstanding issue, it would incur flotation costs of \$2.00 per share and the shares would sell for their March 26, 2003, closing price. What is Ford's cost of preferred stock?

Substituting into equation 12-5, we get the following cost of preferred stock for Ford:

$$k_{ps} = \frac{\$2.25}{(\$23.45 - \$2.00)} = .1049 \text{ or } 10.49\%$$

Note that there is no adjustment for taxes, as preferred dividends are not tax deductible—that is, preferred dividends are paid after corporate taxes, unlike bond interest, which is paid with before-tax dollars.

THE COST OF COMMON EQUITY

Common equity is unique in two respects. First, the cost of common equity is more difficult to estimate than the cost of debt or preferred stock because the common stockholder's required rate of return is not observable. This results from the fact that common stockholders are the residual owners of the firm, which means that their return is equal to what is left of the firm's earnings after paying the firm's bondholders their contractually set interest and principal payments and the preferred stockholders their promised dividends. Second, common equity can be obtained from either the retention of firm earnings or through the sale of new shares. The cost associated with each of these sources is different because the firm does not incur any flotation costs when it retains earnings but does when it sells new common shares.

We discuss two methods for estimating the common stockholder's required rate of return, which is the foundation for our estimate of the firm's cost of equity capital. These methods are based on the dividend growth model and the capital asset pricing model, which were both discussed earlier in Chapter 8 when we discussed stock valuation.

THE DIVIDEND GROWTH MODEL

Recall from Chapter 8 that the value of a firm's common stock is equal to the present value of all future dividends. Where dividends are expected to grow at a rate g forever and this rate g is less than the investor's required rate of return, k_{cs}, then the value of a share of common stock, P_{cs}, can be written as:

$$P_{cs} = \frac{D_1}{k_{cs} - g} \tag{12-6}$$

where D_1 is the dividend expected to be received by the firm's common shareholders one year hence. The expected dividend is simply equal to the current dividend multiplied by 1 plus the annual rate of growth in dividends (i.e., $D_1 = D_0(1 + g)$). The investor's required rate of return then is found by solving equation 12-6 for k_{cs}.

$$k_{cs} = \frac{D_1}{P_{cs}} + g \tag{12-7}$$

Note that k_{cs} is the investor's required rate of return for investing in the firm's stock. It also serves as our estimate of the cost of equity capital, where new equity capital is obtained by retaining a part of the firm's current period earnings. Recall that common equity financing can come from one of two sources: the retention of earnings (i.e., earnings not paid out in dividends to the common stockholders) or from the sale of new common shares. When the firm retains earnings, it doesn't incur any flotation costs, thus the investor's required rate of return is the same as the firm's cost of new equity capital in this instance.

If the firm issues new shares to raise equity capital, then it incurs flotation costs. Once again we adjust the investor's required rate of return for flotation costs by substituting the net proceeds per share, NP_{cs}, for the stock price, P_{cs}, in equation 12-7 to estimate the cost of new common stock, k_{ncs}.

$$k_{ncs} = \frac{D_1}{NP_{cs}} + g \tag{12-8}$$

EXAMPLE: ESTIMATING THE COST OF COMMON STOCK USING THE DIVIDEND GROWTH MODEL

On July 1, 2002, the common stock of Wal-Mart closed at $54.40 per share. In 2001 Wal-Mart paid a dividend of $0.28. If dividends are expected to grow at a rate of 14.6 percent per year into the foreseeable future, then the expected dividend for 2002 is 25 cents. What is the investor's required rate of return (i.e., the cost of retained earnings) for Wal-Mart?

$$k_{cs} = \frac{D_1}{P_{cs}} + g = \frac{\$0.28(1.146)}{\$54.40} + .146 = .1518 \text{ or } 15.18\%$$

Should Wal-Mart decide to issue new common stock, it will incur a flotation cost. If these costs are approximately 6 percent of the share price or \$3.00 per share, what is the resulting cost of new common equity capital?

$$k_{ncs} = \frac{D_1}{NP_{cs}} + g = \frac{\$.28(1.146)}{\$54.40 - \$3.00} + .146 = .1522 \text{ or } 15.22\%$$

Thus, when Wal-Mart retains earnings, we estimate its cost of equity to be 15.18 percent compared to 15.22 percent if the firm issues new equity.

BACK TO THE PRINCIPLES

The dividend growth model for common stock valuation relies on three of the fundamental principles of finance. First, stock value is equal to the present value of expected future dividends. This reflects ***Principle 2: The Time Value of Money—A dollar received today is worth more than a dollar received in the future.*** *Furthermore, dividends represent actual cash receipts to stockholders and are incorporated into the valuation model in a manner that reflects the timing of their receipt. This attribute of the dividend growth model reflects* ***Principle 3: Cash—Not Profits—Is King.*** *Finally, the rate used to discount the expected future dividends back to the present reflects the riskiness of the dividends. The higher the riskiness of the dividend payments, the higher the investor's required rate of return. This reflects* ***Principle 1: The Risk-Return Trade-Off—We won't take on additional risk unless we expect to be compensated with additional return.***

ISSUES IN IMPLEMENTING THE DIVIDEND GROWTH MODEL

The principal advantage of the dividend growth model is its simplicity. To estimate an investor's required rate of return, the analyst needs only to observe the current dividend and stock price and to estimate the rate of growth in future dividends. The primary drawback relates to the applicability or appropriateness of the valuation model. That is, the dividend growth model is based on the fundamental assumption that dividends are expected to grow at a constant rate g forever. To avoid this assumption, analysts frequently utilize more complex valuation models in which dividends are expected to grow for, say, five years at one rate and then grow at a lower rate from year 6 forward. We will not consider these more complex models here.

Even if the constant growth rate assumption is acceptable, we must arrive at an estimate of that growth rate. We could estimate the rate of growth in historical dividends ourselves or go to published sources of growth rate expectations. Investment advisory services such as Value Line provide their own analysts' estimates of earnings growth rates (generally spanning up to five years), and the Institutional Brokers' Estimate System (I/B/E/S) collects and publishes earnings per share forecasts made by over 1,000 analysts for a broad list of stocks. These estimates are helpful but still require the careful judgment of the analyst in their use, because they relate to earnings (not dividends) and only extend five years into the future (not forever, as required by the dividend growth model). Nonetheless, these estimates provide a useful guide to making your initial dividend growth rate estimate.

The Capital Asset Pricing Model

Capital asset pricing model (CAPM)
A statement of the relationship between expected returns and risk in which risk is captured by the systematic risk (beta) for the risky asset. The expected return is equal to the sum of the risk-free rate of interest and a risk premium equal to the product of beta and the market risk premium.

Recall from Chapter 6 that the **capital asset pricing model (CAPM)** provides a basis for determining the investor's expected or required rate of return from investing in common stock. The model depends on three things:

1. the risk-free rate, k_{rf},
2. the systematic risk of the common stock's returns relative to the market as a whole or the stock's beta coefficient, β; and
3. the market risk premium, which is equal to the difference in the expected rate of return for the market as a whole—that is, the expected rate of return for the "average security" minus the risk-free rate, or in symbols, $k_m - k_{rf}$.

Using the CAPM, the investor's required rate of return can be written as follows:

$$k_c = k_{rf} + \beta(k_m - k_{rf}) \qquad \textbf{(12-9)}$$

See the Finance Matters box, "IPOs: Should a Firm Go Public?"

Example: Estimating the Cost of Common Stock Using the CAPM

Wal-Mart's common stock has a beta coefficient of .987. Furthermore, on July 6, 2002, the risk-free rate was 5.52 percent, and the expected rate of return on the market portfolio of all risky assets was approximately 14 percent. Using the CAPM from equation 12-9, we can estimate Wal-Mart's cost of capital as follows:

$$\begin{aligned} k_c &= k_{rf} + \beta(k_m - k_{rf}) \\ &= 0.0552 + 0.987\ (0.14 - 0.0552) = .1389 \text{ or } 13.89\% \end{aligned}$$

Note that the required rate of return we have estimated is the cost of internal common equity because no transaction costs are considered.

Issues in Implementing the CAPM

The CAPM approach has two primary advantages. First, the model is simple and easy to understand and implement. The model variables are readily available from public sources with the possible exception of beta coefficients for small and/or nonpublicly traded firms. Second, because the model does not rely on dividends or any assumption about the growth rate in dividends, it can be applied to companies that do not currently pay dividends or are not expected to experience a constant rate of growth in dividends.

Using the CAPM requires that we obtain estimates of each of the three model variables—k_{rf}, β, and $k_m - k_{rf}$. Let's consider each in turn. First, the analyst has a wide range of U.S. government securities upon which to base an estimate of the risk-free rate. Treasury securities with maturities from 30 days to 20 years are readily available, but the CAPM offers no guidance as to the appropriate choice. In fact, the model itself assumes that there is but one risk-free rate, and it corresponds to a one-period return (the length of the period is not specified, however). Consequently, we are left to our own judgment as to which maturity we should use to represent the risk-free rate. For applications of the cost of capital involving long-term capital expenditure decisions, it seems reasonable to select a risk-free rate of comparable maturity. So, if we are calculating the cost of capital to be used as the basis for evaluating investments that will provide returns over the next 20 years, it

FINANCE MATTERS

IPOs: SHOULD A FIRM GO PUBLIC?

When a privately owned company decides to distribute its shares to the general public, it goes through a process known as an initial public offering or IPO. There are a number of advantages to having a firm's shares traded in the public equity market. These include the following:

- New capital is raised. When the firm sells its shares to the public, it acquires new capital that can be invested in the firm.
- The firm's owners gain liquidity of their share holdings. Publicly traded shares are more easily bought and sold so that the owners can more easily liquidate all or a part of their interest in the firm.
- The firm gains future access to the public capital market. Once a firm has raised capital in the public markets, it is easier to go back a second and third time.
- Being a publicly traded firm may benefit the firm's business. Public firms tend to enjoy a higher profile than their privately held counterparts. This may make it easier to make sales and attract vendors to supply goods and services to the firm.

However, all is not rosy as a publicly held firm. There are a number of potential disadvantages including the following:

- Reporting requirements can be onerous. Publicly held firms are required to file periodic reports with the Securities and Exchange Commission (SEC). This is not only onerous in terms of the time and effort required, but some business owners feel they must reveal information to their competitors that could be potentially damaging.
- Private equity investors now must share any new wealth with the new public investors. Now that the firm is a publicly held company, the new shareholders share on an equal footing with the company founders in the good (and bad) fortune of the firm.
- The private investors lose a degree of control of the organization. Outsiders gain voting control over the firm to the extent that they own its shares.
- An IPO is expensive. A typical firm may spend 15 to 25 percent of the money raised on expenses directly connected to the IPO. This cost is increased further if we consider the cost of lost management time and disruption of business associated with the IPO process.
- Exit of company owners is usually limited. The company founders may want to sell their shares through the IPO, but this is not allowed for an extended period of time. Therefore, the IPO is not usually a good mechanism for cashing out the company founders.
- Everyone involved faces legal liability. The IPO participants are jointly and severally liable for each others' actions. This means that they can be sued for any omissions from the IPO prospectus should the public market valuation fall below the IPO offering price.

A careful weighing of the financial consequences of each of these advantages and disadvantages can provide a company's owners (and management) with some basis for answering the question of whether they want to become a public corporation.

Source: Professor Ivo Welch's Web site at http://welch.som.yale.edu provides a wealth of information concerning IPOs.

seems appropriate to use a risk-free rate corresponding to a U.S. Treasury bond of comparable maturity.

Second, estimates of security beta coefficients are available from a wide variety of investment advisory services, including Merrill Lynch and Value Line, among others. Alternatively, we could collect historical stock market returns for the company of interest as well as a general market index (such as the Standard and Poor's 500 Index) and estimate the stock's beta as the slope of the relationship between the two return series—as we did in Chapter 6. However, because beta estimates are widely available for a large majority of publicly traded firms, analysts frequently rely on published sources for betas.

Finally, estimation of the market risk premium can be accomplished by looking at the history of stock returns and the premium earned over (under) the risk-free rate of interest. In Chapter 6, we reported a summary of the historical returns earned on risk-free securities and common stocks in Table 6-1. We saw that on average over the last 76 years, common stocks have earned a premium of roughly 6.4 percent over long-term government bonds. Thus, for our purposes, we will utilize this estimate of the market risk premium ($k_m - k_{rf}$) when estimating the investor's required rate of return on equity using the CAPM.

BACK TO THE PRINCIPLES

The capital asset pricing model, or CAPM, is a formal representation of ***Principle 1: The Risk-Return Trade-Off—We won't take on additional risk unless we expect to be compensated with additional return.*** *By "formal" we mean that the specific method of calculating the additional returns needed to compensate for additional risk is specified in the form of an equation—the CAPM. The CAPM's recognition of systematic or nondiversifiable risk as the source of risk that is rewarded in the capital market is a reflection of* ***Principle 9: All Risk Is Not Equal—Some risk can be diversified away, and some cannot.***

CONCEPT CHECK

1. How do you estimate a firm's cost of new debt financing?
2. What are two alternative approaches to estimating a firm's cost of equity financing?
3. What are flotation costs and how do they impact a firm's cost of capital when it issues new bonds or equity?

Objective 3

THE WEIGHTED AVERAGE COST OF CAPITAL

Capital structure The mix of long-term sources of funds used by the firm.

Now that we have calculated the individual costs of capital for each of the sources of financing the firm might use, we turn to the combination of these capital costs into a single weighted average cost of capital. To estimate the weighted average cost of capital, we need to know the cost of each of the sources of capital used and the capital structure mix. We use the term **capital structure** to refer to the proportions of each source of financing used by the firm. Although a firm's capital structure can be quite complex, we will focus our examples on the three basic sources of capital: bonds, preferred stock, and common equity.

In words, we calculate the weighted average cost of capital for a firm that uses only debt and common equity using the following equation:

$$\begin{matrix}\textit{weighted}\\ \textit{average cost}\\ \textit{of capital}\end{matrix} = \left[\begin{matrix}\textit{after-tax}\\ \textit{cost of}\\ \textit{debt}\end{matrix} \times \begin{matrix}\textit{proportion}\\ \textit{of debt}\\ \textit{financing}\end{matrix}\right] + \left[\begin{matrix}\textit{cost of}\\ \textit{equity}\end{matrix} \times \begin{matrix}\textit{proportion}\\ \textit{of equity}\\ \textit{financing}\end{matrix}\right]$$

For example, if a firm borrows money at 6 percent after taxes, pays 10 percent for equity, and raises its capital in equal proportions from debt and equity, its weighted average cost of capital is 8 percent, that is,

$$\begin{matrix}\textit{weighted}\\ \textit{average cost}\\ \textit{of capital}\end{matrix} = [.06 \times .5] + [.10 \times .5] = .08 \text{ or } 8\%$$

In practice, the calculation of the cost of capital is generally more complex than this example. For one thing, firms often have multiple debt issues with different required rates of return, and they also use preferred equity as well as common equity financing. Furthermore, when new common equity capital is raised, it is sometimes the result of retaining and reinvesting the firm's current period earnings and, at other times, it involves a new stock offering. In the case of retained earnings, the firm does not incur the costs associated with selling new common stock. This means that equity from retained earnings is less costly than a new stock offering. In the examples that follow, we will address each of these complications.

Capital Structure Weights

A critical element in the analysis of new investments is an estimate of the cost of capital—the discount rate—to be used to calculate the *NPV* for the project. We calculate a cost of capital so we can evaluate the firm's investment opportunities. Remember that the cost of capital should reflect the riskiness of the project being evaluated, so that a firm may calculate multiple costs of capital where it makes investments in multiple divisions or business units having different risk characteristics. Thus, for the calculated cost of capital to be meaningful, it must correspond directly to the riskiness of the particular project being analyzed. That is, in theory the cost of capital should reflect the particular way in which the funds are raised (the capital structure used) and the systematic risk characteristics of the project. Consequently, the correct way to calculate capital structure weights is to use the actual dollar amounts of the various sources of capital actually used by the firm.[1]

In practice, the mixture of financing sources used by a firm will vary from year to year. For this reason, many firms find it expedient to use **target capital structure proportions** in calculating the firm's weighted average cost of capital. For example, a firm might use its target mix of 40 percent debt and 60 percent equity to calculate its weighted average cost of capital even though, in that particular year, it raised the majority of its financing requirements by borrowing. Similarly, it would continue to use the target proportions in the subsequent year when it might raise the majority of its financing needs by reinvesting earnings or through a new stock offering.

Target capital structure proportions
The mix of financing sources that the firm plans to maintain through time.

Calculating the Weighted Average Cost of Capital

The weighted average cost of capital, k_{wacc}, is simply a weighted average of all the capital costs incurred by the firm. Table 12-1 illustrates the procedure used to estimate k_{wacc} for a firm that has debt, preferred stock, and common equity in its target capital structure

[1] There are instances when we will want to calculate the cost of capital for the firm as a whole. In this case, the appropriate weights to use are based upon the market value of the various capital sources used by the firm. Market values rather than book values properly reflect the sources of financing used by a firm at any particular point in time. However, where a firm is privately owned, it is not possible to get market values of its securities, and book values are often used.

TABLE 12-1 Calculating the Weighted Average Cost of Capital

PANEL A: COMMON EQUITY RAISED BY RETAINING EARNINGS

SOURCE OF CAPITAL	CAPITAL STRUCTURE WEIGHTS ×	COST OF CAPTIAL =	PRODUCT
Bonds	w_d	$k_d(1 - T_c)$	$w_d \times k_d(1 - T_c)$
Preferred stock	w_{ps}	k_{ps}	$w_{ps} \times k_{ps}$
Common equity			
Retained earnings	w_{cs}	k_{cs}	$w_{cs} \times k_{cs}$
Sum =	100%		k_{wacc}

PANEL B: COMMON EQUITY RAISED BY SELLING NEW COMMON STOCK

SOURCE OF CAPITAL	CAPITAL STRUCTURE WEIGHTS ×	COST OF CAPTIAL =	PRODUCT
Bonds	w_d	$k_d(1 - T_c)$	$w_d \times k_d(1 - T_c)$
Preferred stock	w_{ps}	k_{ps}	$w_{ps} \times k_{ps}$
Common equity			
New stock offering	w_{ncs}	k_{ncs}	$w_{ncs} \times k_{ncs}$
Sum =	100%		k_{wacc}

mix. Note that in Panel A, the firm is able to finance all its target capital structure requirements for common equity through the retention of firm earnings, and in Panel B, it utilizes a new equity offering. For example, if the firm targets 75 percent equity financing and has current earnings of \$750,000, then it can raise up to \$750,000/.75 = \$1,000,000 in new financing before it has to sell new equity. For \$1,000,000 or less in capital spending, the firm's weighted average cost of capital would be calculated using the cost of equity from retained earnings (following Panel A of Table 12-1). For more than \$1,000,000 in new capital, the cost of capital would rise to reflect the impact of the higher cost of using new common stock (following Panel B of Table 12-1).

EXAMPLE: ESTIMATING THE WEIGHTED AVERAGE COST OF CAPITAL

Ash, Inc.'s capital structure and estimated capital costs are found in Table 12-2. Note that the sum of the capital structure weights must sum to 100 percent if we have properly accounted for all sources of financing and in the correct amounts. For example, Ash plans to invest a total of \$3 million in common equity into the \$5 million investment. Because Ash has earnings equal to the \$3,000,000 it needs in new equity financing, the entire amount of new equity will be raised by retaining earnings.

We calculate the weighted average cost of capital following the procedure described in Panel A of Table 12-1 and using the information found in Table 12-2. The resulting calculations are found in Panel A of Table 12-3, in which Ash, Inc.'s weighted average cost of capital for up to \$5,000,000 in new financing is found to be 12.7 percent.

If Ash needs more than \$5,000,000, then it will not have any retained earnings to provide the additional equity capital. Thus, to maintain its desired 60 percent equity financing proportion, Ash will now have to issue new equity that costs 18 percent. Panel B of Table 12-3 contains the calculation of Ash's weighted average cost of capital for more than \$5,000,000. The resulting cost is 13.9 percent.

In practice, many firms calculate only one cost of capital using a cost of equity capital that ignores the transaction costs associated with raising new equity capital. In essence, they would use the capital cost calculated for Ash in Panel A of Table 12-3 regardless of the level of new financing for the year. Although this is technically incorrect, it is understandable given the difficulties involved in estimating equity capital costs.[a]

[a]For a discussion of the imprecise nature of equity capital cost estimates, see Eugene F. Fama and Kenneth R. French, 1997, "Industry Cost of Equity," *Journal of Financial Economics 43*, 153–93.

TABLE 12-2 Calculating Structure and Capital Costs for Ash, Inc.

SOURCE OF CAPITAL	AMOUNT OF FUNDS RAISED (\$)	PERCENTAGE OF TOTAL	AFTER-TAX COST OF CAPITAL
Bonds	\$1,750,000	35%	7%
Preferred stock	250,000	5%	13%
Common equity			
Retained earnings	3,000,000	60%	16%
	\$5,000,000	100%	

TABLE 12-3 Weighted Average Cost of Capital for Ash, Inc.

PANEL A: COST OF CAPITAL FOR $0 TO $5,000,000 IN NEW CAPITAL			
SOURCE OF CAPITAL	CAPITAL STRUCTURE WEIGHTS	AFTER-TAX COST OF CAPITAL	PRODUCT
Bonds	35%	7%	2.45%
Preferred stock	5%	13%	0.65%
Common equity			
Retained earnings	60%	16%	9.60%
	100%	k_{wacc}	= 12.70%

PANEL B: COST OF CAPITAL FOR MORE THAN $5,000,000			
SOURCE OF CAPITAL	CAPITAL STRUCTURE WEIGHTS	AFTER-TAX COST OF CAPITAL	PRODUCT
Bonds	35%	7%	2.45%
Preferred stock	5%	13%	0.65%
Common equity			
Common stock	60%	18%	10.80%
	100%	k_{wacc}	= 13.90%

COST OF CAPITAL IN PRACTICE: BRIGGS & STRATTON

Briggs & Stratton is the world's largest producer of air-cooled gasoline engines. For many years, the firm also was the world's largest producer of locks for automobiles and trucks. However, on February 27, 1995, the automobile lock business was spun off to the stockholders, leaving Briggs & Stratton in a single business (producing air-cooled gasoline engines for outdoor power equipment).

Each year Briggs & Stratton engages in the exercise of estimating its cost of capital. The process entails a calculation very similar to that used by the hypothetical Ash, Inc. The differences, as we shall see, relate to simplifications, not additional complexities. The example calculations we present here are based upon estimates made on March 27, 2003.

COST OF EQUITY

Briggs & Stratton uses the CAPM to estimate its cost of equity capital as follows:

$$k_c = k_{rf} + \beta(k_m - k_{rf}) \quad \textbf{(12-9)}$$

$$k_c = .0538 + .80(.06) = .1018 \text{ or } 10.18\%$$

The risk-free rate (k_{rf}) is estimated using 30-year government bond interest rates from March 27, 2003. The firm's beta coefficient (β) is taken from MSN moneycentral.com. Finally, the market risk premium ($k_m - k_{rf}$) is estimated as the historical average difference in the return to equities and long-term government bonds.

Note that Briggs & Stratton does not make any adjustment for the influence of transaction costs nor does it bother with the nuance of estimating the fraction of its target equity component that could come from retained earnings.

HOW DO MANAGERS RESOLVE ETHICAL DECISIONS?

What makes a managerial choice an ethical one? Brief et al.[a] (1991) suggest that if the decision entails reflection on the moral significance of the choice, then the choice is an ethical one. How do managers resolve ethical dilemmas? There is some evidence suggesting that two factors come to bear on ethical choices: values and accountability.

We will consider two social value systems that are present in Western society, which are particularly relevant to the study of finance. These are the Smithian and Humanitarian value systems. The Smithian system is derived from the writings of the 19th-century moral philosopher and political economist Adam Smith. This value system is reflected in the current-day teachings of economists such as Milton Friedman[b] (1962). Briefly, this system holds that when individuals pursue their own self-interest in the marketplace, they contribute to the good of society. At the firm level, this system provides the basis for the market system and is used as the basis for corporate self-interest. In contrast, the Humanitarian system is based on the fundamental premise of the equality of individuals in society. This system seeks to protect individuals from the harshness of the market system and to promote equality of opportunity.

Personal value systems are not the only influence on managerial decisions that have ethical implications. Managers are influenced by their perception of the value systems of the individuals to whom they are held accountable. That is, ethical choices made by managers are influenced by the values they believe are held by the person to whom they are accountable.[c] Arendt (1951, 1977) provides evidence that suggests that the effects of accountability may be more profound than those of the individual manager's values. Consequently, the potentially overpowering effects of hierarchical accountability may lead individual managers not to construe the moral significance attached to the choices they make. They may see no choice but to comply with the higher authority. Brief et al. (1991) provide empirical evidence bearing on the question of the relative importance of personal values versus accountability in the choices made by individuals. Using a set of experiments involving 135 M.B.A. students, they concluded that personal values may not be related to how an individual chooses to resolve ethical dilemmas when the choices (values) of the higher authority are known explicitly.

Note that we have not addressed the normative issue: How should ethical dilemmas be resolved? Instead, we have addressed the question, How do managers actually deal with ethical choices? The principal finding of the studies we have reviewed is that the *perceived values of one's superiors* have a profound impact on the way in which a subordinate resolves ethical dilemmas. So choose your superior carefully.

Sources: [a]A. Brief, J. M. Dukerich, and L. I. Doran, "Resolving Ethical Dilemmas in Management: Experimental Investigations of Values, Accountability and Choice," *Journal of Applied Social Psychology* 21 (1991): 380–96; [b]M. Friedman, *Capitalism and Freedom* (Chicago: University of Chicago Press, 1962); [c]H. Arendt, *The Origins of Totalitarianism* (New York: Harcourt Brace, 1951); H. Arendt, *Eichmann in Jerusalem* (New York: Penguin Books, 1977).

COST OF DEBT

We estimate the cost of debt for Briggs & Stratton using the 6 percent yield on bonds of comparable credit rating to Briggs & Stratton. A tax rate of 38 percent is then used to calculate the after-tax cost of debt financing as follows:

$$k_d\,(1 - \text{tax rate}) = .06\,(1 - .38) = .0372 \text{ or } 3.72\%$$

WEIGHTED AVERAGE COST OF CAPITAL FOR 2003

The weighted average cost of capital is calculated using a formula very similar to the one laid out in equation 12-2. The only difference—as we see following—is the lumping of all equity financing into one component with no special consideration being given to the cost of retained earnings versus the sale of new equity, that is,

$$k_{wacc} = K_d\,(1 - T_c)\,w_d + k_c w_{cs} \quad \textbf{(12-10)}$$

where k_d and k_c are the costs of debt and equity, T_c is the corporate tax rate, and w_d and w_{cs} are the weights attached to debt and equity, respectively.

TABLE 12-4 Weighted Average Cost of Capital for Briggs & Stratton, 2003

SOURCE OF CAPITAL	PERCENT OF CAPITAL		COST OF CAPITAL		WEIGHTED COST OF CAPITAL
Debt	30.5%	×	3.72%	=	1.1%
Equity	69.5%	×	10.18%	=	7.1%
	100.0%				8.2%

The capital structure weights are based on market values on March 27, 2003. The weighted average cost of capital for 2003 is calculated in Table 12-4.

CONCEPT CHECK

1. What does the term "capital structure" mean and how is it used in evaluating a firm's weighted average cost of capital?
2. What is the source of capital structure weights that a firm should use when calculating its weighted average cost of capital?

CALCULATING DIVISIONAL COSTS OF CAPITAL: PEPSICO, INC.

Objective 4

If a firm operates in multiple industries where each has its own particular risk characteristics, should it use different capital costs for each division? **Principle 1** suggests that the financial manager should recognize these risk differences in estimating the cost of capital to use in each division. This is exactly what PepsiCo did prior to February 1997, when it operated in three basic industries.

PepsiCo went to great lengths to estimate the cost of capital for each of its three major operating divisions (restaurants, snack foods, and beverages).[2] We will briefly summarize the basic elements of the calculations involved in these estimates, including the cost of debt financing, the cost of common equity, the target capital structure weights, and the weighted average cost of capital.

Table 12-5 contains the estimates of the after-tax cost of debt for each of PepsiCo's three divisions. Table 12-6 contains the estimates of the cost of equity capital using the CAPM. We will not explain the intricacies of their method for estimating divisional betas, except to say that they make use of beta estimates for a number of competitor firms from each of the operating divisions, which involves making appropriate adjustments for differences in the use of financial leverage across the competitor firms used in the analysis.[3]

The weighted average cost of capital for each of the divisions is estimated in Table 12-7 using the capital costs estimated in Tables 12-5 and 12-6 and using PepsiCo's target capital structure weights for each operating division. Note that the weighted average costs of capital for all three divisions fall within a very narrow range, between 10.08 percent and 10.29 percent.

[2] PepsiCo spun off its restaurants division in February 1997. However, the example used here was based on the pre-spinoff company.

[3] This method of using betas from comparable firms is sometimes referred to as the pure play method, because the analyst seeks independent beta estimates for firms engaged in only one business (i.e., restaurants or beverages). The betas for these pure play companies are then used to estimate the beta for a business or division.

TABLE 12-5 Estimating PepsiCo's Cost of Debt

	PRETAX COST OF DEBT	×	(1 − TAX RATE)	AFTER-TAX COST OF DEBT
Restaurants	8.93%	×	.62	5.54%
Snack foods	8.43%	×	.62	5.23%
Beverages	8.51%	×	.62	5.28%

TABLE 12-6 Cost of Equity Capital for PepsiCo's Operating Divisions

	RISK-FREE RATE	+	BETA	EXPECTED MARKET RETURN	−	RISK-FREE RATE	=	COST OF EQUITY
Restaurants	7.28%	+	1.17	(11.48%	−	7.28%)	=	12.20%
Snack foods	7.28%	+	1.02	(11.48%	−	7.28%)	=	11.56%
Beverages	7.28%	+	1.07	(11.48%	−	7.28%)	=	11.77%

TABLE 12-7 PepsiCo's Weighted Average Cost of Captial for Each of Its Operating Divisions

	COST OF EQUITY TIMES THE TARGET EQUITY RATIO	+	COST OF DEBT TIMES THE TARGET DEBT RATIO	=	WEIGHTED AVERAGE COST OF CAPITAL
Restaurants	(12.20%)(0.70)	+	(5.54%)(0.30)	=	10.20%
Snack foods	(11.56%)(0.80)	+	(5.23%)(0.20)	=	10.29%
Beverages	(11.77%)(0.74)	+	(5.28%)(0.26)	=	10.08%

CONCEPT CHECK

1. Why do firms calculate individual costs of capital for their operating divisions?
2. How should divisional costs of capital be used in evaluating a firm's new investment opportunities?

Objective 5

USING A FIRM'S COST OF CAPITAL TO EVALUATE NEW CAPITAL INVESTMENTS

Now that we have learned the principles used to estimate a firm's cost of capital, it is tempting to use this capital cost to evaluate all the firm's investment opportunities. This can produce some very expensive mistakes. *Recall that the cost of capital depends primarily on the use of the funds, not their source.* Consequently, the appropriate cost of capital for individual investment opportunities should, in theory and practice, reflect the individual risk characteristics of the investment. With this principle in mind, we reason that the firm's weighted average cost of capital is the appropriate discount rate for estimating a project's *NPV* only when the project has similar risk characteristics to the firm. This would be true, for example, when the investment involves expanding an existing facility but would not be true when the investment involves entering into a completely new business with different risk characteristics.

What does it mean to say that a firm and an investment opportunity have similar risk characteristics? We can think of an investment's risk characteristics as coming from two sources: business risk and financial risk. By **business risk** we mean the potential variability in the firm's expected earnings before interest and taxes (EBIT). In Chapter 6, we learned that investors should not be worried about total variability but should only be concerned about systematic variability. **Financial risk** refers to the added variability in earnings available to a firm's shareholders and the added chance of insolvency caused by the use of securities bearing a fixed rate of return in the firm's financial structure. For example, in Chapter 3, we learned that firms that use higher levels of financial leverage also experience higher volatility in earnings available to the common stockholders. This higher volatility leads investors to require higher rates of return, which means a higher cost of capital for the project.

Business risk
The potential variability in a firm's earnings before interest and taxes resulting from the nature of the firm's business endeavors.

Financial risk
The added variability in earnings available to a firm's shareholders and the additional risk of insolvency caused by the use of financing sources that require a fixed return.

In summary, the firm's weighted average cost of capital is the appropriate discount rate for evaluating the *NPV* of investments whose business and financial risks are similar to those of the firm as a whole. See Table 12-8 on page 422 for a summary of the formulas involved in estimating the weighted average cost of capital. If either of these sources of project risk is different from the risks of the firm, then the analyst must alter the estimate of the cost of capital to reflect these differences. If financial risk is different, then this calls for the use of different financial mix ratios when calculating the weighted average cost of capital, as well as estimates of individual capital costs that properly reflect these financial risks. If operating-risk characteristics differ, then once again capital costs must be adjusted to reflect this difference. In our discussion of PepsiCo, we saw that it estimates three different weighted average costs of capital to reflect what it feels are meaningful differences in the operating and financial risk characteristics of its three operating divisions. This practice reflects PepsiCo's adherence to the principle that the cost of capital is primarily a function of the use of the capital (i.e., the riskiness of the different operating divisions). See the Finance Matters box, "Why Do Interest Rates Differ Between Countries?"

BACK TO THE PRINCIPLES

The firm's weighted average cost of capital provides the appropriate discount rate for evaluating new projects only where the projects offer the same riskiness as the firm as a whole. This limitation of the usefulness of the firm's weighted average cost of capital is a direct extension of ***Principle 1: The Risk-Return Trade-Off—We won't take on additional risk unless we expect to be compensated with additional return.*** *If project risk differs from that of the firm, then the firm's cost of capital (which reflects the risk of the firm's investment portfolio) is no longer the appropriate cost of capital for the project. For this reason, firms that invest in multiple divisions or business units that have different risk characteristics should calculate a different cost of capital for each division. In theory, each individual investment opportunity has its own unique risk attri-butes and correspondingly should have a unique cost of capital. However, given the impreciseness with which we estimate the cost of capital, we generally calculate the cost of capital for each operating division of the firm, not each project.*

CONCEPT CHECK

1. What determines a firm's business risk?
2. What is meant by a firm's financial risk?

TABLE 12-8 Summary of Cost of Capital Formulas

1. The After-Tax Cost of Debt, $k_d(1 - T_c)$
   a. Calculate the before-tax cost of debt, k_d, as follows:

$$NP_d = \sum_{t=1}^{n} \frac{\$I_t}{(1 + k_d)^t} + \frac{\$M}{(1 + k_d)^n} \qquad (12\text{-}2)$$

   where NP_d is the net proceeds received by the firm from the sale of each bond; $\$I_t$ is the dollar amount of interest paid to the investor in period t for each bond; $\$M$ is the maturity value of each bond paid in period n; k_d is the before-tax cost of debt to the firm; and n is the number of periods to maturity.

   b. Calculate the after-tax cost of debt as follows:

   after-tax cost of debt $= k_d(1 - T_c)$

   where T_c is the corporate tax rate.

2. The Cost of Preferred Stock, k_{ps}

$$k_{ps} = \frac{\text{preferred stock dividend}}{NP_{ps}} \qquad (12\text{-}5)$$

   where NP_{ps} is the net proceeds per share of new preferred stock sold after flotation costs.

3. The Cost of Common Equity
   a. Method 1: dividend growth mode

   Calculate the cost of internal common equity (retained earnings), k_c, as follows:

$$k_{cs} = \frac{D_1}{P_{cs}} + g \qquad (12\text{-}7)$$

   where D_1 is the expected dividend for the next year, P_{cs} is the current price of the firm's common stock, and g is the rate of growth in dividends per year.

   Calculate the cost of external common equity (new stock offering), k_{ncs}, as follows:

$$k_{ncs} = \frac{D_1}{NP_{cs}} + g \qquad (12\text{-}8)$$

   where NP_{cs} is the net proceeds to the firm after flotation costs per share of stock sold.

   b. Method 2: capital asset pricing model, k_c

$$k_c = k_{rf} + \beta(k_m - k_{rf}) \qquad (12\text{-}9)$$

   where the risk-free rate is k_{rf}; the systematic risk of the common stock's returns relative to the market as a whole or the stock's beta coefficient is β; and the market risk premium, which is equal to the difference in the expected rate of return for the market as a whole (i.e., the expected rate of return for the "average security" minus the risk-free rate), is $k_m - k_{rf}$.

4. The Weighted Average Cost of Capital

$$k_{wacc} = w_d \times k_d(1 - T_c) + w_{ps} \times k_{ps} + w_{cs} \times k_{cs} + w_{ncs} \times k_{ncs}$$

   where the w_i terms represent the market value weights associated with the firm's use of each of its sources of financing. Note that we are simply calculating a weighted average of the costs of each of the firm's sources of capital where the weights reflect the firm's relative use of each source.

FINANCE MATTERS

WHY DO INTEREST RATES DIFFER BETWEEN COUNTRIES?

If borrowers and lenders can freely obtain money in one country and invest it in another, why are interest rates not the same the world over? Stated somewhat differently, if capital markets are fully integrated and money flows to the highest rate of interest, it would seem that the forces of competition would make interest rates the same for a given risk borrower.

Let's consider a hypothetical example to see how this might work. Assume that a U.S. borrower can borrow 1,000 yen in Japan for a 5 percent interest paying back 1,050 yen in one year. Alternatively, the U.S. firm can borrow an equivalent amount in the United States and pay 15.5 percent interest. Why the big difference? Is capital 10.5 percent cheaper in Japan, and if so, why don't U.S. firms simply switch to the Japanese capital market for their funds? The answer, as we will now illustrate, lies in the differences in the anticipated rates of inflation for Japan versus the United States.

Although it was not obvious in the preceding example, we assumed a zero rate of inflation for the Japanese economy and a 10 percent rate of inflation for the U.S. economy. With a zero anticipated rate of inflation, the nominal rate of interest in Japan is equal to the real rate of 5 percent. Under these assumptions, the nominal rate in the United States can be calculated using the Fisher model as follows:[a]

U.S. nominal = (1 + real rate, U.S.)
rate of interest (1 + inflation rate, U.S.) − 1
= (1 + .05)(1 + .10) − 1 = .155 or 15.5%

To understand the reason for the different interest rates in Japan and the United States, we must extend the Fisher model to its international counterpart.

The International Fisher Effect

In an international context, we must recognize that there can be different rates of inflation among the different countries of the world. For example, the Fisher model for the nominal rate in the home or domestic country ($r_{n,h}$) is a function of the real interest rate in the home country ($r_{r,h}$) and the anticipated rate of inflation in the home country (i_h). For the domestic economy, the Fisher relationship can be described as follows:

$$r_{n,h} = (1 + r_{r,h})(1 + i_h) - 1 = r_{r,h} + (i_h)(r_{r,h}) + i_h \quad \textbf{(1a)}$$

[a]The Fisher model or Fisher effect was introduced earlier in Chapter 2.

Using "*f*" as a subscript to denote a foreign country, we can define a similar relationship for any foreign country (Japan in our previous example):

$$r_{n,f} = (1 + r_{r,f})(1 + i_f) - 1 = r_{r,f} + (i_f)(r_{r,f}) + i_f \quad \textbf{(1b)}$$

The international version of the Fisher model prescribes that real returns will be equalized across countries through arbitrage, that is,

$$r_{r,h} = r_{r,f}$$

Solving for the real rates of interest in equations 1a and 1b and equating the results produces the international version of the Fisher model, that is,

$$r_{n,h} - (i_h)(r_{r,h}) - i_h = r_{n,f} - (i_f)(r_{r,f}) - i_f \quad \textbf{(2)}$$

For simplicity analysts frequently ignore the intermediate product terms on both sides of equation 3 such that equation 2 reduces to the following:

$$r_{n,h} - i_h = r_{n,f} - i_f$$

Rearranging terms, we get the following relationship between nominal interest rates in the domestic and foreign country and the differences in anticipated inflation in the two countries:

$$r_{n,h} - r_{n,f} = i_h - i_f \quad \textbf{(3)}$$

Thus, differences in observed nominal rates of interest should equal differences in the expected rates of inflation between the two countries. This means that when we compare the interest rates for similar loans in two countries and they are not the same, we should immediately suspect that the expected rates of inflation for the two economies differ by an amount roughly equal to the interest rate differential!

Interest Rates and Currency Exchange Rates: Interest Rate Parity

Economists have formalized the relationship between interest rates of different countries in the interest rate parity theorem. This theorem is as follows:

$$\frac{(1 + r_{n,h})}{(1 + r_{n,f})} = \frac{E_1}{E_0} \quad \textbf{(4)}$$

(continued)

WHY DO INTEREST RATES DIFFER BETWEEN COUNTRIES? *(continued)*

where $r_{n,b}$ is the domestic one-period rate of interest, $r_{n,f}$ is the corresponding rate of interest in a foreign country, and the E_j are exchange rates corresponding to the current period (i.e., the spot rate, E_0) and one-period hence (i.e., the one-period forward rate, E_1).

To illustrate, let's consider the previous example where the domestic one-period interest rate ($r_{n,b}$) is 15.5 percent, the Japanese rate of interest ($r_{n,f}$) is 5 percent, the spot exchange ratio (E_0) is \$1 to 1 yen, and the forward exchange rate (E_1) is \$1.10 to 1 yen. Substituting into equation 1 produces the following result:

$$\frac{(1 + .155)}{(1 + .05)} = \frac{1.1}{1} = 1.10$$

The key thing to note here is that nominal interest rates are tied to exchange rates, and as we learned earlier, differences in nominal rates of interest are tied to expected rates of inflation.

Why would we expect the interest rate parity relationship to hold? The answer lies in the greed of investors who stand ready to engage in arbitrage (trading) to enforce this relationship (within the bounds of transaction costs). Formally, we rely on the fundamental dictum of an efficient market (the law of one price). Very simply, the exchange-adjusted prices of identical loans must be within transaction costs of equality or the opportunity exists for traders to buy the low-cost loan and sell the higher priced loan for a profit.

Source: W. Carl Kester and Timothy A. Luehrman, "What Makes You Think U.S. Capital Is So Expensive?" *Journal of Applied Corporate Finance* (Summer 1992): 29–41.

HOW FINANCIAL MANAGERS USE THIS MATERIAL

The opportunity cost of capital is critically important for every firm, and most publicly traded firms estimate it at least annually and some revise their estimate quarterly. The cost of capital is not an abstract concept but a very important factor of corporate business decision making. Most firms rely on the weighted average cost of capital (calculated using current investor required rates of return and target financing proportions or weights).

Our discussion was kept purposely basic because this reflects the way in which the cost of capital is actually calculated. Specifically, firms that have two or more operating divisions will usually estimate a cost of capital for each division. However, when using the cost of capital for evaluating operating results and determining incentive compensation, even multi-division firms sometimes use a single weighted average cost of capital. This is sometimes done to simplify the basis for determining bonuses, and in other instances, it is done in an effort to remove the cost of capital as an element of discussion in determining compensation. The key fact here is that firms do calculate their cost of capital, they use it to make investment decisions and to determine incentive compensation, and they "try to keep it simple."

SUMMARY

Objective 1

Consider the following investment opportunity. The investment requires that the firm invest \$75 million to renovate a production facility that will provide after-tax savings to the firm of \$25 million per year over the next five years. In Chapter 9, we learned that the proper way to evaluate whether or not to undertake the investment involves calculating its net present value (*NPV*). To calculate *NPV*, we must estimate both project cash flows and an appropriate discount rate. In this chapter, we have learned that the proper discount rate is a weighted average of the after-tax costs of all the firm's sources of financing. In addition, we have learned that the cost of capital for any source of financing is estimated by first calculating the investor's required rate of return, then making appropriate adjustments for flotation costs and corporate taxes (where appropriate). If the weighted average cost of capital is 12 percent, then the *NPV* of the plant renovation is \$15,120 and the investment should be made. The reason is that the project is expected to increase the wealth of the firm's shareholders by \$15,120. Very simply, the project is expected to return a present value amount of \$15,120 more than the firm's sources of capital require, and since the common stockholders get any residual value left after returning the promised return to each of the other sources of capital, they receive the *NPV*.

Objective 2

To calculate the after-tax cost of debt capital, we must first calculate the before-tax cost of capital using the following formula:

$$NP_d = \sum_{t=1}^{n} \frac{\$I_t}{(1+k_d)^t} + \frac{\$M}{(1+k_d)^n} \quad \textbf{(12-2)}$$

where NP_d = the net proceeds received by the firm from the sale of each bond

$\$I_t$ = the dollar amount of interest paid to the investor in period t for each bond

$\$M$ = the maturity value of each bond paid in period n

k_d = the before-tax cost of debt to the firm

n = the number of periods to maturity

Next, we adjust for the effects of corporate taxes because the bond interest is deducted from the firm's taxable income.

after-tax cost of debt = $k_d(1 - \text{corporate tax rate})$

The cost of preferred stock is relatively easy to calculate. We calculate the dividend yield on the preferred issue using net proceeds from the sale of each new share as follows:

$$\text{cost of preferred stock} = \frac{\text{preferred stock dividend}}{\text{net proceeds per preferred share}} \quad \textbf{(12-5)}$$

Note that no adjustment is made for corporate taxes because preferred stock dividends, unlike bond interest, are paid with after-tax earnings.

Common equity can be obtained by the firm in one of two ways. First, the firm can retain a portion of its net income after paying common dividends. The retention of earnings constitutes a means of raising common-equity financing internally—that is, no capital market issuance of securities is involved. Second, the firm can also raise equity capital through the sale of a new issue of common stock.

We discussed two methods for estimating the cost of common equity. The first involved using the dividend growth model:

$$k_{cs} = \frac{D_1}{P_{cs}} + g \quad \textbf{(12-7)}$$

where g is the rate at which dividends are expected to grow forever, k_{cs} is the investor's required rate of return, and P_{cs} is the current price of a share of common stock. When a new issue of common shares is issued, the firm incurs flotation costs. These costs reduce the amount of funds the firm receives per share. Consequently, the cost of external common equity using the dividend growth model requires that we substitute the new proceeds per share, NP_{cs}, for share price:

$$k_{ncs} = \frac{D_1}{NP_{cs}} + g \quad \textbf{(12-8)}$$

The second method for estimating the cost of common equity involves the use of the capital asset pricing model (CAPM), which we first discussed in Chapter 6. There we learned that the

CAPM provides a basis for evaluating investor's required rates of return on common equity, k_c, using three variables:

1. the risk-free rate, k_{rf};
2. the systematic risk of the common stock's returns relative to the market as a whole or the stock's beta coefficient, β; and
3. the market risk premium which is equal to the difference in the expected rate of return for the market as a whole—that is, the expected rate of return for the "average security" minus the risk-free rate, $k_m - k_{rf}$.

The CAPM is written as follows:

$$k_c = k_{rf} + \beta(k_m - k_{rf}) \quad \textbf{(12-9)}$$

We found that all of the variables on the right side of equation (12-9) could be obtained from public sources for larger, publicly traded firms. However, for non-publicly traded firms, the CAPM is more difficult to apply in the estimation of investor-required rates of return.

Objective 3

The firm's weighted average cost of capital, k_{wacc}, can be defined as follows:

$$k_{wacc} = w_d \times k_d(1 - T_c) + w_{ps} \times k_{ps} + w_{cs} \times k_{cs} + w_{ncs} \times k_{ncs}$$

where the w terms represent the market value weights associated with the firm's use of each of its sources of financing. Note that we are simply calculating a weighted average of the costs of each of the firm's sources of capital where the weights reflect the firm's relative use of each source.

The weights used to calculate k_{wacc} should theoretically reflect the market values of each capital source as a fraction of the total market value of all capital sources (i.e., the market value of the firm). However, the analyst frequently finds the use of market value weights is impractical, either because the firm's securities are not publicly traded or because all capital sources are not used in proportion to their makeup of the firm's target capital structure in every financing episode. In these instances, we found that the weights should be the firm's long-term target financial mix.

Objective 4

Objective 5

The firm's weighted average cost of capital will reflect the operating or business risk of the firm's present set of investments and the financial risks attendant upon the way in which those assets are financed. Therefore, this cost of capital estimate is useful only for evaluating new investment opportunities that have similar business and financial risks. Remember that the primary determinant of the cost of capital for a particular investment is the risk of the investment itself, not the source of the capital. Multidivision firms such as PepsiCo resolve this problem by calculating a different cost of capital for each of their major operating divisions.

KEY TERMS

Go To: www.prenhall.com/keown for downloads and current events associated with this chapter

STUDY QUESTIONS

12-1. Define the term *cost of capital.*

12-2. Why do we calculate a firm's weighted average cost of capital?

12-3. In computing the cost of capital, which sources of capital do we consider?

12-4. How does a firm's tax rate affect its cost of capital? What is the effect of the flotation costs associated with a new security issue?

12-5. **a.** Distinguish between internal common equity and new common stock.
b. Why is a cost associated with internal common equity?
c. Describe the two approaches that could be used in computing the cost of common equity.

12-6. What might we expect to see in practice in the relative costs of different sources of capital?

SELF-TEST PROBLEMS

ST-1. (*Individual costs of capital*) Compute the cost for the following sources of financing:

a. A $1,000 par value bond with a market price of $970 and a coupon interest rate of 10 percent. Flotation costs for a new issue would be approximately 5 percent. The bonds mature in 10 years and the corporate tax rate is 34 percent.
b. A preferred stock selling for $100 with an annual dividend payment of $8. If the company sells a new issue, the flotation cost will be $9 per share. The company's marginal tax rate is 30 percent.
c. Internally generated common stock totaling $4.8 million. The price of the common stock is $75 per share, and the dividend per share was $9.80 last year. The dividend is not expected to change in the future.
d. New common stock where the most recent dividend was $2.80. The company's dividends per share should continue to increase at an 8 percent growth rate into the indefinite future. The market price of the stock is currently $53; however, flotation costs of $6 per share are expected if the new stock is issued.

ST-2. (*Weighted average cost of capital*) The capital structure for the Carion Corporation is provided below. The company plans to maintain its debt structure in the future. If the firm has a 5.5 percent after-tax cost of debt, a 13.5 percent cost of preferred stock, and an 18 percent cost of common stock, what is the firm's weighted average cost of capital?

CAPITAL STRUCTURE ($000)	
Bonds	$1,083
Preferred stock	268
Common stock	3,681
	$5,032

STUDY PROBLEMS (SET A)

12-1A. (*Individual or component costs of capital*) Compute the cost for the following:

a. A bond that has a $1,000 par value (face value) and a contract or coupon interest rate of 11 percent. A new issue would have a flotation cost of 5 percent of the $1,125 market value. The bonds mature in 10 years. The firm's average tax rate is 30 percent and its marginal tax rate is 34 percent.
b. A new common stock issue that paid a $1.80 dividend last year. The par value of the stock is $15, and earnings per share have grown at a rate of 7 percent per year. This growth rate is expected to continue into the foreseeable future. The company maintains a constant dividend-earnings ratio of 30 percent. The price of this stock is now $27.50, but 5 percent flotation costs are anticipated.
c. Internal common equity where the current market price of the common stock is $43. The expected dividend this coming year should be $3.50, increasing thereafter at a 7 percent annual growth rate. The corporation's tax rate is 34 percent.
d. A preferred stock paying a 9 percent dividend on a $150 par value. If a new issue is offered, flotation costs will be 12 percent of the current price of $175.

e. A bond selling to yield 12 percent after flotation costs, but prior to adjusting for the marginal corporate tax rate of 34 percent. In other words, 12 percent is the rate that equates the net proceeds from the bond with the present value of the future cash flows (principal and interest).

12-2A. (*Individual or component costs of capital*) Compute the cost for the following:

a. A bond selling to yield 8 percent after flotation costs, but prior to adjusting for the marginal corporate tax rate of 34 percent. In other words, 8 percent is the rate that equates the net proceeds from the bond with the present value of the future cash flows (principal and interest).

b. A new common stock issue that paid a $1.05 dividend last year. The par value of the stock is $2, and the earnings per share have grown at a rate of 5 percent per year. This growth rate is expected to continue into the foreseeable future. The company maintains a constant dividend-earnings ratio of 40 percent. The price of this stock is now $25, but 9 percent flotation costs are anticipated.

c. A bond that has a $1,000 par value and a contract or coupon interest rate of 12 percent. A new issue would net the company 90 percent of the $1,150 market value. The bonds mature in 20 years, the firm's average tax rate is 30 percent, and its marginal tax rate is 34 percent.

d. A preferred stock paying a 7 percent dividend on a $100 par value. If a new issue is offered, the company can expect to net $85 per share.

e. Internal common equity where the current market price of the common stock is $38. The expected dividend this forthcoming year should be $3, increasing thereafter at a 4 percent annual growth rate. The corporation's tax rate is 34 percent.

12-3A. (*Cost of equity*) Salte Corporation is issuing new common stock at a market price of $27. Dividends last year were $1.45 and are expected to grow at an annual rate of 6 percent forever. Flotation costs will be 6 percent of market price. What is Salte's cost of equity?

12-4A. (*Cost of debt*) Belton is issuing a $1,000 par value bond that pays 7 percent annual interest and matures in 15 years. Investors are willing to pay $958 for the bond. Flotation costs will be 11 percent of market value. The company is in an 18 percent tax bracket. What will be the firm's after-tax cost of debt on the bond?

12-5A. (*Cost of preferred stock*) The preferred stock of Walter Industries sells for $36 and pays $2.50 in dividends. The net price of the security after issuance costs is $32.50. What is the cost of capital for the preferred stock?

12-6A. (*Cost of debt*) The Zephyr Corporation is contemplating a new investment to be financed 33 percent from debt. The firm could sell new $1,000 par value bonds at a net price of $945. The coupon interest rate is 12 percent, and the bonds would mature in 15 years. If the company is in a 34 percent tax bracket, what is the after-tax cost of capital to Zephyr for bonds?

12-7A. (*Cost of preferred stock*) Your firm is planning to issue preferred stock. The stock sells for $115; however, if new stock is issued, the company would receive only $98. The par value of the stock is $100 and the dividend rate is 14 percent. What is the cost of capital for the stock to your firm?

12-8A. (*Cost of internal equity*) Pathos Co.'s common stock is currently selling for $21.50. Dividends paid last year were $.70. Flotation costs on issuing stock will be 10 percent of market price. The dividends and earnings per share are projected to have an annual growth rate of 15 percent. What is the cost of internal common equity for Pathos?

12-9A. (*Cost of equity*) The common stock for the Bestsold Corporation sells for $58. If a new issue is sold, the flotation costs are estimated to be 8 percent. The company pays 50 percent of its earnings in dividends, and a $4 dividend was recently paid. Earnings per share five years ago were $5. Earnings are expected to continue to grow at the same annual rate in the future as during the past five years. The firm's marginal tax rate is 34 percent. Calculate the cost of (a) internal common and (b) external common.

12-10A. (*Cost of debt*) Sincere Stationery Corporation needs to raise $500,000 to improve its manufacturing plant. It has decided to issue a $1,000 par value bond with a 14 percent annual coupon rate and a 10-year maturity. The investors require a 9 percent rate of return.

a. Compute the market value of the bonds.
b. What will the net price be if flotation costs are 10.5 percent of the market price?
c. How many bonds will the firm have to issue to receive the needed funds?
d. What is the firm's after-tax cost of debt if its average tax rate is 25 percent and its marginal tax rate is 34 percent?

12-11A. (*Cost of debt*)

a. Rework problem 12-10A assuming a 10 percent coupon rate. What effect does changing the coupon rate have on the firm's after-tax cost of capital?
b. Why is there a change?

12-12A. (*Weighted average cost of capital*) The target capital structure for QM Industries is 40 percent common stock, 10 percent preferred stock, and 50 percent debt. If the cost of equity for the firm is 18 percent, the cost of preferred stock is 10 percent, the before-tax cost of debt is 8 percent, and the firm's tax rate is 35 percent, what is QM's weighted average cost of capital?

12-13A. (*Weighted average cost of capital*) Crypton Electronics has a capital structure consisting of 40 percent common stock and 60 percent debt. A debt issue of $1,000 par value 6 percent bonds, maturing in 15 years and paying annual interest, will sell for $975. Flotation costs for the bonds will be $15 per bond. Common stock of the firm is currently selling for $30 per share. The firm expects to pay a $2.25 dividend next year. Dividends have grown at the rate of 5 percent per year and are expected to continue to do so for the foreseeable future. Flotation costs for the stock issue are 5 percent of the market price. What is Crypton's cost of capital where the firm's tax rate is 30 percent?

12-14A. (*Weighted average cost of capital*) As a member of the Finance Department of Ranch Manufacturing, your supervisor has asked you to compute the appropriate discount rate of use when evaluating the purchase of new packaging equipment for the plant. You have determined the market value of the firm's capital structure as follows:

SOURCE OF CAPITAL	MARKET VALUES
Bonds	$4,000,000
Preferred stock	$2,000,000
Common stock	$6,000,000

To finance the purchase, Ranch Manufacturing will sell 10-year bonds paying 7 percent per year at the market price of $1,050. Flotation costs for issuing the bonds are 4 percent of the market price. Preferred stock paying a $2.00 dividend can be sold for $25; the cost of issuing these shares is $3 per share. Common stock for Ranch Manufacturing is currently selling for $55 per share. The firm paid a $3 dividend last year and expects dividends to continue growing at a rate of 10 percent per year. Flotation costs for issuing new common stock will be $5 per share and the firm's tax rate is 30 percent. What discount rate should you use to evaluate the equipment purchase?

INTEGRATIVE PROBLEM

The capital structure for Nealon, Inc., follows:

Nealon, Inc., Balance Sheet

TYPE OF FINANCING	PERCENTAGE OF FUTURE FINANCING
Bonds (8%, $1,000 par, 16-year maturity)	38%
Preferred stock (5,000 shares outstanding, $50 par, $1.50 dividend)	15%
Common stock	47%
Total	100%

Flotation costs are (a) 15 percent of market value for a new bond issue, (b) \$1.21 per share for common stock, and (c) \$2.01 per share for preferred stock. The dividends for common stock were \$2.50 last year and are projected to have an annual growth rate of 6 percent. The firm is in a 34 percent tax bracket. What is the weighted average cost of capital if the firm finances are in the following proportions?

Market prices are \$1,035 for bonds, \$19 for preferred stock, and \$35 for common stock. There will be sufficient internal common equity funding (i.e., retained earnings) available such that the firm does not plan to issue new common stocks.

WEB WORKS

12-1WW. You can find the latest IPOs at **www.hoovers.com**. Use the IPO Central to find the latest IPO pricing and filings. Go to the IPO Scorecard and find the total number and value of IPOs for the most recent quarter.

12-2WW. The Federal Reserve Bank monitors interest rates on a wide variety of financial instruments.

a. Go to **www.federalreserve.gov/releases/h15/update/** and find the most recent rates for U.S. Treasury Bills with four-week, three-month, and six-month maturities.

b. The term structure of interest rates contains the rates of interest on U.S. Treasury securities. Use the above site to determine the most recent rates for one- to thirty-year U.S. securities. Graph the term structure and comment on the relationship between rates and term to maturity.

12-3WW. Go to **www.yahoo.com** and look up financial information for Dell Computers. How does the expected growth rate in Dell earnings for the next five years compare to its industry sector and the S&P 500? Can Dell's earnings grow indefinitely at these rates? Why or why not?

STUDY PROBLEMS (SET B)

12-1B. (*Individual or component costs of capital*) Compute the cost for the following:

a. A bond that has a \$1,000 par value (face value) and a contract or coupon interest rate of 12 percent. A new issue would have a flotation cost of 6 percent of the \$1,125 market value. The bonds mature in 10 years. The firm's average tax rate is 30 percent and its marginal tax rate is 34 percent.

b. A new common stock issue that paid a \$1.75 dividend last year. The par value of the stock is \$15, and earnings per share have grown at a rate of 8 percent per year. This growth rate is expected to continue into the foreseeable future. The company maintains a constant dividend/earnings ratio of 30 percent. The price of this stock is now \$28, but 5 percent flotation costs are anticipated.

c. Internal common equity in which the current market price of the common stock is \$43.50. The expected dividend this coming year should be \$3.25, increasing thereafter at a 7 percent annual growth rate. The corporation's tax rate is 34 percent.

d. A preferred stock paying a 10 percent dividend on a \$125 par value. If a new issue is offered, flotation costs will be 12 percent of the current price of \$150.

e. A bond selling to yield 13 percent after flotation costs, but prior to adjusting for the marginal corporate tax rate of 34 percent. In other words, 13 percent is the rate that equates the net proceeds from the bond with the present value of the future cash flows (principal and interest).

12-2B. (*Individual or component costs of capital*) Compute the cost of the following:

a. A bond selling to yield 9 percent after flotation costs, but prior to adjusting for the marginal corporate tax rate of 34 percent. In other words, 9 percent is the rate that equates the net proceeds from the bond with the present value of the future flows (principal and interest).

b. A new common stock issue that paid a $1.25 dividend last year. The par value of the stock is $2, and the earnings per share have grown at a rate of 6 percent per year. This growth rate is expected to continue into the foreseeable future. The company maintains a constant dividend/earnings ratio of 40 percent. The price of this stock is now $30, but 9 percent flotation costs are anticipated.

c. A bond that has a $1,000 par value (face value) and a contract or coupon interest rate of 13 percent. A new issue would net the company 90 percent of the $1,125 market value. The bonds mature in 20 years, the firm's average tax rate is 30 percent, and its marginal tax rate is 34 percent.

d. A preferred stock paying a 7 percent dividend on a $125 par value. If a new issue is offered, the company can expect to net $90 per share.

e. Internal common equity where the current market price of the common stock is $38. The expected dividend this coming year should be $4, increasing thereafter at a 5 percent annual growth rate. This corporation's tax rate is 34 percent.

12-3B. (*Cost of equity*) Falon Corporation is issuing new common stock at a market price of $28. Dividends last year were $1.30 and are expected to grow at an annual rate of 7 percent forever. Flotation costs will be 6 percent of market price. What is Falon's cost of equity?

12-4B. (*Cost of debt*) Temple is issuing a $1,000 par value bond that pays 8 percent annual interest and matures in 15 years. Investors are willing to pay $950 for the bond. Flotation costs will be 11 percent of market value. The company is in a 19 percent tax bracket. What will be the firm's after-tax cost of debt on the bond?

12-5B. (*Cost of preferred stock*) The preferred stock of Gator Industries sells for $35 and pays $2.75 in dividends. The net price of the security after issuance costs is $32.50. What is the cost of capital for the preferred stock?

12-6B. (*Cost of debt*) The Walgren Corporation is contemplating a new investment to be financed 33 percent from debt. The firm could sell new $1,000 par value bonds at a net price of $950. The coupon interest rate is 13 percent, and the bonds would mature in 15 years. If the company is in a 34 percent tax bracket, what is the after-tax cost of capital to Walgren for bonds?

12-7B. (*Cost of preferred stock*) Your firm is planning to issue preferred stock. The stock sells for $120; however, if new stock is issued, the company would receive only $97. The par value of the stock is $100, and the dividend rate is 13 percent. What is the cost of capital for the stock to your firm?

12-8B. (*Cost of internal equity*) The common stock for Oxford, Inc., is currently selling for $22.50. Dividends last year were $.80. Flotation costs on issuing stock will be 10 percent of market price. The dividends and earnings per share are projected to have an annual growth rate of 16 percent. What is the cost of internal common equity for Oxford?

12-9B. (*Cost of equity*) The common stock for the Hetterbrand Corporation sells for $60. If a new issue is sold, the flotation cost is estimated to be 9 percent. The company pays 50 percent of its earnings in dividends, and a $4.50 dividend was recently paid. Earnings per share five years ago were $5. Earnings are expected to continue to grow at the same annual rate in the future as during the past five years. The firms' marginal tax rate is 35 percent. Calculate the cost of (a) internal common and (b) external common stock.

12-10B. (*Cost of debt*) Gillian Stationery Corporation needs to raise $600,000 to improve its manufacturing plant. It has decided to issue a $1,000 par value bond with a 15 percent annual coupon rate and a 10-year maturity. If the investors require a 10 percent rate of return:

a. Compute the market value of the bonds.

b. What will the net price be if flotation costs are 11.5 percent of the market price?

c. How many bonds will the firm have to issue to receive the needed funds?

d. What is the firm's after-tax cost of debt if its average tax rate is 25 percent and its marginal tax rate is 34 percent?

12-11B. (*Cost of debt*)

a. Rework problem 12-10B assuming a 10 percent coupon rate. What effect does changing the coupon rate have on the firm's after-tax cost of capital?

b. Why is there a change?

12-12B. (*Weighted cost of capital*) The capital structure for the Bias Corporation follows. The company plans to maintain its debt structure in the future. If the firm has a 6 percent after-tax cost of debt, a 13.5 percent cost of preferred stock, and a 19 percent cost of common stock, what is the firm's weighted cost of capital?

CAPITAL STRUCTURE ($000)	
Bonds	$1,100
Preferred stock	250
Common stock	3,700
	$5,050

12-13B. The target capital structure for Jowers Manufacturing is 50 percent common stock, 15 percent preferred stock, and 35 percent debt. If the cost of equity for the firm is 20 percent, the cost of preferred stock is 12 percent, and the before-tax cost of debt is 10 percent, what is Jower's cost of capital? The firm's marginal tax rate is 34 percent.

12-14B. Bane Industries has a capital structure consisting of 60 percent common stock and 40 percent debt. A debt issue of $1,000 par value, 8 percent bonds, maturing in 20 years and paying semiannually, will sell for $1,100. Flotation costs for the bonds will be $20 per bond. Common stock of the firm is currently selling for $80 per share. The firm expects to pay a $2 dividend next year. Dividends have grown at the rate of 8 percent per year and are expected to continue to do so for the foreseeable future. Flotation costs for the stock issue are 10 percent of the market price. What is Bane's cost of capital? The firm's marginal tax rate is 34 percent.

12-15B. As a consultant to GBH Skiwear, you have been asked to compute the appropriate discount rate to use to evaluate the purchase of a new warehouse facility. You have determined the market value of the firm's capital structure as follows:

SOURCE OF CAPITAL	MARKET VALUE
Bonds	$500,000
Preferred stock	$100,000
Common stock	$400,000

To finance the purchase, GBH will sell 20-year bonds, paying 8 percent per year, at the market price of $950. Flotation costs for issuing the bonds are 6 percent of the market price. Preferred stock paying a $2.50 dividend can be sold for $35; the cost of issuing these shares is $5 per share. Common stock for GBH is currently selling for $50 per share. The firm paid a $2 dividend last year and expects dividends to continue growing at a rate of 8 percent per year. Flotation costs for issuing new common stock will be 10 percent of the market price. The firm's marginal tax rate is 34 percent. What discount rate should you use to evaluate the warehouse project? What discount rate should you use to evaluate the equipment purchase?

SELF-TEST SOLUTIONS

The following notations are used in this group of problems:

where k_d = the before-tax cost of debt
k_{ps} = the cost of preferred stock
k_{cs} = the cost of internal common stock
k_{ncs} = the cost of new common stock
t = the marginal tax rate
D_t = the dollar dividend per share, where D_0 is the most recently paid dividend and D_1 is the forthcoming dividend
P_0 = the value (present value) of a security
NP_0 = the value of a security less any flotation costs incurred in issuing the security

ST-1.

a. $$\$921.50 = \sum_{t=1}^{n} \frac{\$100}{(1 + k_d)^t} + \frac{\$1,000}{(1 + k_d)^{10}}$$

RATE	VALUE		
11%	\$940.90	\$19.40	\$53.90
k_d%	\$921.50		
12%	\$887.00		

$$k_d = 0.11 + \left(\frac{\$19.40}{\$53.90}\right) 0.01 = .1136 = 11.36\%$$

$$k_d(1 - t) = 11.36\%(1 - 0.34) = 7.50\%$$

b. $$k_{ps} = \frac{D}{NP_0}$$

$$k_{ps} = \frac{\$8}{\$100 - \$9} = .0879 = 8.79\%$$

c. $$k_{cs} = \frac{D_1}{P_0} + g$$

$$k_{cs} = \frac{\$9.80}{\$75} + 0\% = .1307 = 13.07\%$$

d. $$k_{ncs} = \frac{D_1}{NP_0} + g$$

$$k_{ncs} = \frac{\$2.80\ (1 + 0.08)}{\$53 - \$6} + 0.08 = .1443 = 14.43\%$$

ST-2.

Carion Corporation—Weighted Cost of Capital

	CAPITAL STRUCTURE	WEIGHTS	INDIVIDUAL COSTS	WEIGHTED COSTS
Bonds	\$1,083	0.2152	5.5%	1.18%
Preferred stock	268	0.0533	13.5%	0.72%
Common stock	3,681	0.7315	18.0%	13.17%
	\$5,032	1.0000		15.07%

LEARNING OBJECTIVES

After reading this chapter, you should be able to

1. Use Market Value Added to identify the value created for shareholders by a publicly held firm.
2. Estimate the value of the firm, which we will refer to as its enterprise value, using the discounted free cash-flow model.
3. Identify the value drivers that can be managed to create shareholder value.
4. Define, compute, and interpret a firm's return on invested capital, and Economic Value Added (EVA)®.[1]
5. Discuss the structure of typical managerial compensation packages and the issues that arise in designing them.

[1] EVA® is a registered trademark of the Stern Stewart and Company.

CHAPTER 13

Managing for Shareholder Value

We are a nation of stockholders. More than 41 percent of American families own shares of common stock in either their personal portfolio, their retirement portfolio, or both.[2] Furthermore, these equity holdings constitute about 40 percent of their total financial assets, and this fraction has been growing. The reason for investing in the common shares of a firm are obvious, as Danny DeVito, playing the role of "Larry the Liquidator" in the movie *Other People's Money,* stated when addressing the annual shareholders meeting of the New England Wire and Cable Company: "Lest we forget, the reason you became a stockholder in the first place was to make money." In the movie, Larry the Liquidator was unhappy with the past performance of the New England Wire and Cable Company and he saw the opportunity to "make a buck or two" by buying the firm and restructuring it.

CHAPTER PREVIEW

We have spent a lot of time addressing the problems that firms encounter when making investment decisions designed to maximize shareholder wealth. In Chapters 9 through 11, we discussed the use of net present value and other tools of discounted cash-flow analysis to analyze project cash flows and compare them to the investments required. Furthermore, in Chapter 12, we addressed the problem of assessing the proper required rate of return for a firm's investments. What happens once the investment is made and the firm has bought and put into operation the new assets that were the object of the capital expenditure analysis? How can we be sure that these assets will be managed and operated so as to maximize shareholder value? This chapter answers these questions. Specifically, we address the fundamental problem of managing a firm's operations to create as much shareholder value as possible.

We introduce the subject of managing for shareholder value by introducing the free cash-flow model of firm value. This model is widely used to develop an understanding of the value of the business. We then identify the basic determinants of firm value in this model and then provide the value drivers that managers can focus upon.

Firm performance is evaluated periodically in an effort to determine whether the firm's management is on track to create shareholder value. As a consequence, we need measures of quarterly and annual performance that can be used to assess that performance and pay for success or penalize failure. Firms have used a wide variety of performance measures including firm earnings, earnings growth, and return on investment, to name a few. Recently, however, economic value added has been widely recommended as an improvement on traditional accounting-based performance measures.

This chapter emphasizes **Principle 1: The Risk-Return Trade-off—We won't take on additional risk unless we expect to be compensated with additional return; Principle 2: The Time Value of Money—A dollar received today is worth more than a dollar received in the future; Principle 3: Cash—Not Profits—Is King; and Principle 7: The Agency Problem—Managers won't work for owners unless it's in their best interest.** We are particularly attentive to Principle 7 as it describes the agency problem that arises between managers and stockholders. In fact, there would be no need for the use of periodic performance measures and reward (compensation) systems based upon them if it were not for this basic problem.

[2] Based on the Survey of Consumer Finances and reported by Kennickell, Starr-McCluer, and Sunden, "Family Finances in the U.S.: Recent Evidence from the Survey of Consumer Finances," *Federal Reserve Bulletin,* January 1997, 1–28.

In real life, the Harley-Davidson Company offers a shareholder experience that has been totally different from the fictional New England Wire and Cable Company. Harley's CEO and President, Jeffrey Bleustein, describes the firm's stockholder performance in the following quote from his letter to the shareholders contained in the company's 1999 annual report:

> Dear Fellow Shareholder: It is my privilege to share with you in this Annual Report the results of Harley-Davidson's fourteenth consecutive record year of financial performance. Our consistent growth has had a clear benefit to investors—a shareholder who purchased $10,000 of Harley-Davidson stock when we first went public in 1986 would be a millionaire today—for many, a dream came true. (Harley-Davidson Annual Report, 1999)

You would not expect to find Larry the Liquidator making an appearance at the Harley-Davidson shareholders meeting unless it was to lead a cheer!

Harley's shares had increased in value from 65 cents to $50.43 from 1986 to July 1, 2002. This resulted in an average compound rate of return of 29 percent per year! Thus, Harley's management has been very successful in managing the firm to create shareholder value. How did this happen? In our discussions of capital budgeting and the cost of capital (Chapters 9–12), we learned that managers create shareholder value by identifying and undertaking investments that earn returns greater than the firm's cost of raising money (i.e., the firm's weighted average cost of capital). Let's put this notion to the test by reviewing Harley's performance during 2001. In that year, the firm earned an annual rate of return of 17.69 percent on its investments while its cost of capital was only 11.62 percent.[3] Clearly, shareholder value was created.

The issue we address in this chapter then boils down to addressing the problems associated with making sure that the firm maintains a return on its investments that meets or exceeds its cost of capital. We present economic value added, or *EVA*®, as a performance measure that is designed to accomplish this goal.

Throughout the text we have promoted the notion that a firm's management should make decisions that lead to increased shareholder value. To investors, this is not a controversial statement. After all, the common shareholders do "own" the firm. In fact, it is not uncommon to see corporate mission statements that endorse shareholder value maximization as the firm's primary goal. For example, the Disney 1999 annual report states "Disney's overriding objective is to create shareholder value by continuing to be the world's premier entertainment company from a creative, strategic, and financial standpoint." Unfortunately, the incentives of a firm's management are not always aligned with those of the firm's stockholders. As a consequence, many (perhaps even most) large corporations are not run on a day-to-day basis so as to maximize shareholder wealth.[4] In fact, many proceed to destroy shareholder value year after year.

In this chapter we use the free cash-flow valuation model that serves as the basis for estimating project value in an analysis of new capital expenditure proposals to estimate the value of the business enterprise. We then link this valuation to value drivers that can be used by managers for setting performance goals that can be tied directly to firm value. Next we look at *EVA*® as a measure of firm or business unit performance. This performance measure has become very popular among firms that have focused their efforts on the creation of shareholder value. Finally, we discuss the fundamental issues arising in establishing an incentive compensation program that encourages employees to engage in activities that create shareholder value. Here we learn that compensation based on performance measures that are linked directly to the creation of shareholder value is critical. In fact, if compensation is not tied to performance measures, the value creation process is ultimately doomed to failure. The old adage that what gets measured and rewarded gets done is the guiding principle behind managing the firm to create value for its shareholders.

[3] Reported in Shawn Tully, MVA Performance Ranking: United States, *Fortune*, 1999.

[4] In their book on value-based management, McTaggart, Kontes, and Mankins go so far as to assert that "the great majority of large corporations throughout the world are not managed with the objective of maximizing wealth or shareholder value," *Managing for Shareholder Returns: The Value Imperative* (New York: Free Press, 1994), p. 41.

Objective 1

WHO ARE THE TOP CREATORS OF SHAREHOLDER VALUE?

Table 13-1 contains a list of the five top and bottom wealth creators for 2001 among the 1,000 largest U.S. corporations. The ranking is based on **market value added (*MVA*)**, which was devised by Stern Stewart and Company to measure how much wealth a firm has created at a particular moment in time.[5] *MVA* is computed as follows:

Market value added (*MVA*) The difference in the market value of the firm and the capital that has been invested in it.

$$\text{market value added} = \text{firm value} - \text{invested capital} \quad \textbf{(13-1)}$$

By *firm value*, we mean the market values of the firm's outstanding debt and equity securities. Invested capital is a bit more problematic. Conceptually, a firm's **invested capital** is the sum of all the funds that have been invested in it. Although this sum is related to the firm's total assets, it is not quite the same thing.[6] But for right now, let's just think of invested capital as total assets.

Invested capital Total amount of funds invested in a firm.

[5] Although we do not report it here, a similar ranking called the Shareholder Scoreboard is prepared by L.E.K. Consulting LLC and published in the *Wall Street Journal*. This ranking, however, uses the total return to shareholders over 1-, 3-, 5-, and 10-year holding periods to assess wealth creation/destruction. Total return includes price appreciation or depreciation, and any reinvestment from cash dividends, rights and warrant offerings, and cash equivalents, such as stock received in spinoffs. Returns are also adjusted for stock splits, stock dividends, and recapitalizations. (See *Wall Street Journal* Interactive edition, February 24, 2000.)

[6] Accounting conventions used in constructing the firm's balance sheet distort the reporting of the firm's invested capital, so that we have to make some adjustments to the firm's total assets from its balance sheet. Stern Stewart has identified over 160 such adjustments; however, we will mention only one important one here to provide a flavor for the types of adjustments that are required. The example we use is the adjustment made for research and development (R&D) expenditures. Generally accepted accounting principles (GAAP) call for the expensing of 100 percent of the firm's R&D expenditures in the year in which the expenditure is made. This practice fails to recognize the future value that the firm's management anticipates receiving from these expenditures. As a consequence, expenditures for R&D, unlike expenditures made for new plant and equipment, are not reflected in the total assets of the company. This treatment of R&D has the effect of understating the total investment that has been made in the firm. Stern Stewart adds R&D back to the firm's total assets and amortizes it over several future years. The net effect of this adjustment is to inflate book value to be more clearly reflective of the total investment that has been made in the firm.

TABLE 13-1 America's Top and Bottom Creators of Shareholder Value for 2001 ($ Millions)

COMPANY NAME	MARKET VALUE ADDED (MVA)	INVESTED CAPITAL	RETURN ON INVESTED CAPITAL	COST OF CAPITAL (WACC)
TOP FIVE WEALTH CREATORS FOR 2001				
General Electric Co.	339,200	82,111	20.0%	9.4%
Microsoft Corp.	325,872	26,343	21.5%	13.7%
Wal-Mart Stores	221,166	65,677	12.4%	8.9%
Intel Corp.	169,980	41,397	9.0%	16.2%
Citigroup, Inc.	155,695	104,210	14.7%	12.0%
BOTTOM FIVE WEALTH CREATORS FOR 2001				
AOL Time Warner Inc.	(23,382)	201,885	6.0%	9.6%
Qwest Communication Intl. Inc.	(24,238)	78,435	1.8%	9.3%
AT&T Corp.	(28,356)	167,129	0.8%	9.6%
Lucent Technologies Inc.	(37,112)	73,356	−10.3%	12.3%
JDS Uniphase Corp.	(37,577)	48,348	−52.4%	14.3%

Source: Stern Stewart and Company, 2002

Let's take a look at the firms listed in Table 13-1 whose performance places them at the top and bottom of the list of wealth creators. The names of the firms at the top of the list are probably very familiar to you. For example, investors have invested roughly $82 billion in the assets of top-ranked GE. The market value of this investment at the end of 2001 was over $520 billion. On the other end of the spectrum we see JDS Uniphase, whose investors have entrusted over $48 billion to the firm's management, which is worth almost $38 billion less than their investment at the end of 2001. Table 13-1 also provides information concerning the rates of return earned on each firm's invested capital as well as the market's assessment of the firm's cost of capital. These last two pieces of information highlight the fundamental paradigm of creating shareholder value—that is, firms that earn higher rates of return than their capital costs create shareholder wealth, while those that fail this simple test destroy it.

How is it that some firms can create so much value for their shareholders while others destroy it?[7] Value creation, very simply, results from the marriage of opportunity and execution. Opportunities must be recognized and, in some cases, created, and this is the stuff of which business strategy is made. However, opportunity is not enough. Firms have to have employees who are ready, willing, and able to take advantage of business opportunities. It is on this side of the value creation equation that we focus our attention. Specifically, managing for shareholder value requires that we resolve two separate issues: First, we must identify a set of performance measures that are both linked to value creation and are under the control of the firm's management. Second, we must design a system of incentives that encourages employees to base their decisions on these performance metrics in their day-to-day decisions. In essence, we must develop a performance measurement and reward system that encourages managers to think and act like business owners. Let's consider how this might be accomplished.

CONCEPT CHECK

1. What is Market Value Added and how is it calculated?
2. What is the fundamental paradigm for creating shareholder value?

Objective 2

BUSINESS VALUATION—THE KEY TO CREATING SHAREHOLDER VALUE

To understand how shareholder value is created we must first understand how firms are valued in the capital markets. There are two competing valuation paradigms that have been used to explain the value of a firm's common stock in the capital market: the accounting model and the discounted cash flow model. Figure 13-1 captures the essential elements of both.

THE ACCOUNTING MODEL

Although both the accounting and discounted cash flow models *can be* consistent in theory, they are not generally used in a consistent manner and they can lead manage-

[7] Although the 1990s produced the longest bull market for common stock in recorded history, many firms have struggled and even lost value for their shareholders. The manufacturing sector was particularly hard hit with only one in eight manufacturers outperforming the S&P 500 since 1988 and one-third experiencing a decline in the value of their shares (Wise and Baumgartner, 1999).

FIGURE 13-1 Competing Models of Equity Valuation

	Accounting (earnings) Model	Discounted Cash Flow Model
Equity value	(price-earnings ratio) × (earnings per share)	Present value of future cash flows
Value drivers	Determinants of accounting earnings and the price-earnings ratio	Determinants of firm future cash flows and the opportunity cost of capital

ment to act in very different ways as it tries to manage for shareholder value. If management uses the accounting model to think about the value of its equity, then it will focus on reported earnings in conjunction with the market's valuation of those earnings as reflected in the price-earnings ratio. For example, if the price-earnings ratio is 20, then a $1 increase in earnings per share will create $20 in additional equity value per share. Similarly, a $1 loss in earnings per share will lead to a drop of $20 in share value. To see what's wrong with this theory of equity valuation, consider the following scenario. In 2001, Intel Corporation spent $3.796 billion on research and development (R&D) designed to identify the products that would become the source of future revenues for the company. This total represents 55 cents per share after taxes. On July 1, 2002, the firm's price-earnings multiple was 67.46, reflecting earnings per share of $0.26 and a share price of $17.54. Ask yourself the following question: "Do you believe that Intel's stock price would have been $37.10 higher (i.e., 55 cents in R&D per share times 67.46), or $54.64, if Intel had not spent anything on R&D? Of course not! Intel's expenditures for R&D are its life's blood in creating new products that drive its future profitability. Without its R&D, the firm's stream of new products would evaporate, as would its future cash flows. This simple example serves to caution against managing for shareholder value by managing the firm's reported accounting earnings.

We learned in our discussion of capital budgeting that the discounted cash-flow valuation model incorporates investor expectations of future cash flows into the indefinite future as well as the opportunity cost of funds when estimating value. In this model, the R&D investment used in the previous example would lead to a reduction in cash flow during the period in which the expenditure is being made, but would correspondingly increase future cash flows when the anticipated rewards of the investment are being reaped. Hence, the appropriate model for our use in managing the firm for shareholder value is one that focuses on the cash-flow consequences of the firm's decisions for the future, not just the current period, because this is how investors view their investments.

Free Cash-Flow Valuation Model

The **free cash-flow model** for valuing a firm provides a method for analyzing value as the present value of the firm's projected free cash flows for all future years (1 through infinity). Pragmatically, of course, we cannot forecast free cash flows for an infinite future, so we generally project them for a finite number of years called the *planning period*,

Free cash-flow model Method of valuing a firm by calculating the present value of all future free cash flows.

Terminal value
The estimated value of the firm at the end of the planning period or the present value of the firm's free cash flows to be received after the end of the planning period.

and then capture the value of all subsequent free cash flows using the concept of a **terminal value.**[8]

To illustrate the use of the free cash-flow valuation model, let's consider a model based on a four-year planning period; that is, we project free cash flows for a firm over a period of four years into the future. For years 5 and beyond we capture the value of the estimated free cash flows in the terminal value of the firm at the end of year 4. The value of the firm under this circumstance is reflected in the following model:

$$\text{firm value} = \frac{\text{free cash flow}_1}{(1 + k_{wacc})^1} + \frac{\text{free cash flow}_2}{(1 + k_{wacc})^2} + \frac{\text{free cash flow}_3}{(1 + k_{wacc})^3} + \frac{\text{free cash flow}_4}{(1 + k_{wacc})^4} + \frac{\text{terminal value}_4}{(1 + k_{wacc})^4} \quad \textbf{(13-2)}$$

To estimate the value of the firm, we discount future free cash flows for years 1 through 4, as well as the terminal value, back to the present using the firm's weighted average cost of capital (k_{wacc}). Let's now consider how the terminal value component of the model captures the firm's free cash flows for years 5 and beyond.

There are many ways to estimate the terminal value at the end of year 4 depending upon the pattern of future free cash flows the firm is expected to generate. For simplicity, we will assume that the firm's free cash flows for years 5 through infinity are all equal to the free cash flow for year 4. In other words, free cash flows for years 5, 6, and so forth do not grow after year 4. Technically, this means that terminal value at the end of year 3 is equal to the present value of a level perpetuity. We learned in Chapter 5 that the present value of a level perpetuity is calculated as follows:

$$\text{terminal value}_4 = \frac{\text{free cash flow}_5}{k_{wacc}} \quad \textbf{(13-3)}$$

Recall that free cash flow_5 is equal to free cash flow_4.

BACK TO THE PRINCIPLES

When we calculate the value of the firm using the free cash-flow model, we are using the same basic model we used earlier to estimate the value of a capital investment proposal. The three basic determinants of value are the same. We rely on two fundamental principles of finance when we utilize the free cash flow model to value a firm: ***Principle 1: The Risk-Return Trade-Off,*** *because we discount the expected firm free cash flows using the firm's risk adjusted weighted average cost of capital, and* ***Principle 3: Cash—Not Profits—Is King,*** *as we estimate the firm's free cash flow and not the firm's profits as the basis for valuation.*

[8] Free cash flow provides the basis for valuing the firm as an entity and is calculated as follows:

CALCULATION OF FREE CASH FLOW		EXPLANATION
Net operating income (NOI)		Estimated as revenues less cost of goods sold and operating expenses
Less:	taxes	Taxes estimated on the level of NOI
Equals:	net operating income after tax	NOPAT
Plus:	depreciation expense	Add back noncash depreciation
Less:	new investments made during the period	
	additional net working capital	Increases in current assets less accounts payable and other noninterest-bearing liabilities
	capital expenditures (CAPEX)	New investments made in plant and equipment during the period
Equals:	free cash flow	Cash available to pay dividends, interest, and principal.

EXAMPLE OF FREE CASH-FLOW VALUATION

Table 13-2 contains projections for Kramerica, Inc., spanning the next four years of the firm's operations. Specifically, the table includes pro forma income statements (Panel A), current and pro forma balance sheets (Panel B), and free cash-flow estimates (Panel C). Note that the calculation of free cash flow follows the procedure laid out earlier in

TABLE 13-2 Income Statements, Balance Sheets, and Free Cash-Flow Estimates for Kramerica, Inc.

PANEL A. PRO FORMA INCOME STATEMENTS

	YEARS			
	1	2	3	4
Sales	$56,000.00	$62,720.00	$70,246.40	$70,246.40
Cost of goods sold	(22,400.00)	(25,088.00)	(28,098.56)	(28,098.56)
Gross profit	$33,600.00	$37,632.00	$42,147.84	$42,147.84
Operating expenses (excluding depreciation)	(16,800.00)	(18,816.00)	(21,073.92)	(21,073.92)
Depreciation expense	(4,000.00)	(4,240.00)	(4,508.80)	(4,809.86)
Operating income (earnings before interest and taxes)	$12,800.00	$14,576.00	$16,565.12	$16,264.06
Less: interest expense	(1,000.00)	(1,400.00)	(1,568.00)	(1,756.16)
Earnings before taxes	$11,800.00	$13,176.00	$14,997.12	$14,507.90
Less: taxes	(3,540.00)	(3,952.80)	(4,499.14)	(4,352.37)
Net income	$ 8,260.00	$ 9,223.20	$10,497.98	$10,155.53

PANEL B. CURRENT AND PRO FORMA BALANCE SHEETS

	CURRENT PERIOD	PRO FORMA BALANCE SHEETS				
	0	1	2	3	4	5
Current assets	$ 7,500.00	$ 8,400.00	$ 9,408.00	$10,536.96	$10,536.96	$10,536.96
Property, plant, and equipment	20,000.00	22,400.00	25,088.00	28,098.56	28,098.56	28,098.56
Total	$27,500.00	$30,800.00	$34,496.00	$38,635.52	$38,635.52	$38,635.52
Accruals and payables	$ 2,500.00	$ 2,800.00	$ 3,136.00	$ 3,512.32	$ 3,512.32	$ 3,512.32
Long-term debt	10,000.00	14,000.00	15,680.00	17,561.60	17,561.60	17,561.60
Equity	15,000.00	14,000.00	15,680.00	17,561.60	17,561.60	17,561.60
Total	$27,500.00	$30,800.00	$34,496.00	$38,635.52	$38,635.52	$38,635.52
Invested capital[a]	$25,000.00	$28,000.00	$31,360.00	$35,123.20	$35,123.20	$35,123.20

PANEL C. ESTIMATION OF FREE CASH FLOW

	1	2	3	4 AND BEYOND
Sales	$56,000.00	$62,720.00	$70,246.40	$70,246.40
Operating income (earnings before interest and taxes)	12,800.00	14,576.00	16,565.12	16,264.06
Less: cash tax payments	(3,840.00)	(4,372.80)	(4,969.54)	(4,879.22)
Net operating profits after taxes (NOPAT)	$ 8,960.00	$10,203.20	$11,595.58	$11,384.84
Plus: depreciation expense	4,000.00	4,240.00	4,508.80	4,809.86
Less investments:				
In net working capital	$ (600.00)	$ (672.00)	$ (752.64)	$ –
In new capital (CAPEX)	(6,400.00)	(6,928.00)	(7,519.36)	(4,809.86)
Total net investment for the period	$ (7,000.00)	$ (7,600.00)	$ (8,272.00)	$ (4,809.86)
Free cash flow[b]	$ 5,960.00	$ 6,843.20	$ 7,832.38	$11,384.84

[a]Invested capital is the total amount of funds invested in the assets of the firm that is financed by interest-bearing liabilities such as notes payable and bonds plus equity invested by the firm's preferred and common shareholders. In this example, invested capital = total assets – accruals & payables.

[b]Free cash flow = NOPAT + depreciation expense – total net investment for the period.

Chapter 2 and used in our earlier discussions of capital budgeting. Let's consider the underlying basis for the projections:

- **Estimated revenues.** Kramerica's sales are predicted to grow at a rate of 12 percent per year over the first three years before leveling off in year 4. For example, revenue for year 1 is predicted to be $56,000 = $50,000 (1 + .12).
- **Estimated gross profits.** Gross profits are projected to equal 60 percent of firm sales such that in year 1, gross profit = .60 × $56,000 = $33,600.
- **Estimated operating expenses.** We estimate operating expenses before depreciation to be 30 percent of revenues. Depreciation expense for the year is based on the level of property, plant, and equipment for the previous year. This total grows over the years as the firm acquires more depreciable assets.
- **Investment in net working capital.** Each year the firm must invest in additional current assets to support its growth in sales. However, at least a part of this investment is financed by noninterest-bearing liabilities such as accounts payable and accrued expenses. Thus, each year Kramerica will have to invest an amount in net working capital equal to the difference in the new current assets it needs to support the firm's growing sales and the corresponding change in noninterest-bearing current liabilities. We refer to this total as the firm's investment in net working capital for the period.[9] Kramerica is assumed to invest 15 percent of each additional dollar in firm sales in current assets. However, 5 percent of this amount is spontaneously financed by accruals and payables. Thus, for each dollar in sales, Kramerica needs to raise 10 cents in new capital. For example, firm sales are expected to increase by $6,000 over the first year from $50,000 to $56,000. Thus, the anticipated need for new investment in net working capital for the first year of the planning period will be 10 percent of $6,000, or $600.
- **Capital expenditures (CAPEX).** New expenditures for property, plant, and equipment are included in Panel C of Table 13-2. To simplify our analysis, we follow common practice and assume that accounting depreciation expense on the firm's investment in plant and equipment at the beginning of each year is just equal to the cost of replacing plant and equipment that wears out during the year. This assumption is obvious when we look at the *CAPEX* for year 4, which is equal to depreciation expense for the year. The reason for this, you will recall, is that sales stop growing after year 3, and the only *CAPEX* the firm incurs is to replace worn-out assets. In addition, during the first three years when sales are growing at 12 percent per year, we estimate that Kramerica will have to invest an amount equal to 40 percent of the year-to-year increase in sales. Thus, in year 1 when sales rise by $6,000 over year 0, we estimate that the firm will have to spend $2,400 = .40 × $6,000 on new property, plant, and equipment in addition to the cost of replacing worn-out fixed assets in an amount equal to year 1's depreciation expense of $4,000. The net result is *CAPEX* equal to $6,400 in year 1.

Substituting Kramerica's weighted average cost of capital of 15 percent and the year 5 (same as year 4) free cash flow of $11,384.84 into equation 13-3, we estimate Kramerica's terminal value at the end of year 4 (i.e., the present value of the firm's free cash flows for years 5 through infinity) to be $75,898.97:

[9] Traditionally, net working capital is defined to be the difference in current assets and current liabilities. However, for purposes of valuing the firm, we are interested only in the financing provided by noninterest-bearing current liabilities (e.g., accounts payable and deferred expenses). Thus, when a firm's sales increase and it needs additional current assets (such as accounts receivable and inventories) to support the added sales, this need is partially offset by noninterest-bearing current liabilities. Thus, the net new investment a firm must make to finance current assets as its sales grow is represented by the difference between the added current assets and additional noninterest-bearing current liabilities.

$$\text{terminal value}_4 = \frac{\textit{free cash flows}_5}{K_{wacc}} = \frac{\$11{,}384.84}{.15} = \$75{,}898.97$$

Finally, substituting our estimate of the terminal value into equation 13-2 along with the free cash flows for years 1 through 4 from Table 13-2, we estimate the firm's enterprise value to be $65,412:

$$\begin{matrix}\text{firm}\\\text{value}\end{matrix} = \left[\frac{\$5{,}960.00}{(1+.15)^1} + \frac{\$6{,}843.20}{(1+.15)^2} + \frac{\$7{,}832.38}{(1+.15)^3} + \frac{\$11{,}384.84}{(1+.15)^4} + \frac{\$75{,}898.97}{(1+.15)^4}\right]$$

$$\begin{matrix}\text{firm}\\\text{value}\end{matrix} = \$22{,}016 + 43{,}396 = \$65{,}411.77$$

We estimate the value of the firm's equity by subtracting the value of Kramerica's interest-bearing liabilities from firm value.[10] In our example, we assume that Kramerica has interest-bearing liabilities of $10,000, such that the equity value is $55,411.77. To value Kramerica's equity we make use of the following relationship:[11]

$$\begin{matrix}\text{firm}\\\text{value}\end{matrix} = \begin{matrix}\text{debt}\\\text{value}\end{matrix} + \begin{matrix}\text{equity}\\\text{value}\end{matrix} \qquad \textbf{(13-4)}$$

Recall that this is simply the balance sheet equation for the firm, with one significant difference. In this case we are using market, as opposed to book, values. Solving for equity value:

$$\text{equity value} = \$65{,}411.77 - \$10{,}000 = \$55{,}411.77$$

Kramerica, Inc., has a total of 2,000 shares of outstanding stock. Thus, we calculate the value per share of the firm's equity to be $27.71:

$$\begin{matrix}\text{share}\\\text{value}\end{matrix} = \frac{\text{equity value}}{\text{number of shares}} = \frac{\$55{,}411.77}{2{,}000} = \$27.71$$

CONCEPT CHECK

1. What is the free cash-flow valuation model?
2. What does the terminal value in the free cash-flow valuation model represent?

VALUE DRIVERS

Objective **3**

Let's now consider how we can use our free cash-flow valuation model to manage the firm for shareholder value. Stated differently, what are the "knobs and controls" that managers can tweak to increase firm value? We will refer to these knobs and controls as *value drivers* and can identify them by reviewing the assumptions that underlie the free

[10] Technically, we have estimated the value of the firm's invested capital to be $65,412. To get the value of the entire firm we have to add back to this total the firm's accruals and payables of $2,500, or $65,412 + 2,500 = $67,912.

[11] See footnote 9 for an explanation as to why we only deduct long-term interest-bearing debt rather than total liabilities.

cash-flow estimates for Kramerica, Inc., that were presented in Table 13-2. Consider the following list of model assumptions—parameter values used in Table 13-2—and classification as either value driver or historical value:

Model Assumptions and Forecast Variables

	VALUE	VALUE DRIVER OR HISTORICAL VALUE
SALES GROWTH FOR YEARS 1–3	**12%**	**VALUE DRIVER**
Gross profit margin	60%	Value driver
Operating expenses (before depreciation)	30%	Value driver
Net working capital-to-sales ratio	10%	Value driver
Property, plant, and equipment-to-sales ratio	40%	Value driver
Beginning sales	$50,000	Historical value
Cash tax rate	30%	Historical value
Total liabilities	$10,000	Historical value
Cost of capital	15.0%	Value driver
Number of shares	2,000	Historical value

Note that four of the items represent historical values (sales, total liabilities, the corporate tax rate, and the number of common shares outstanding) for the previous year. These four items provide the base values for our analysis and are not decision variables over which management has any control.[12] The remaining five items represent **value drivers**.

Value drivers
Variables that affect firm value and can be controlled or influenced by the firm's management.

The value drivers represent the variables that are in some degree under the control or influence of the firm's management and that are connected in some meaningful way to the determinants of firm value. For example, management may be able to initiate a new compensation program for the firm's sales force that would increase the projected rate of growth in firm sales. It might institute cost-control procedures that would lead to an increase in the gross profit margin or a decrease in the ratio of operating expenses to sales. Or it might engage in a repurchase of the firm's shares financed by borrowing (a leveraged recapitalization) that could lead to a reduction in the firm's cost of capital. Thus, the value drivers meet all the requirements we set forth previously. The firm's management can influence them and each is linked to the determination of the value of the firm and, consequently, equity value.

Table 13-3 contains a list of potential strategies that the firm's management might consider in an effort to manage each of the value drivers that we have identified here. While these strategies have the potential for impacting firm value in a beneficial way, it is not certain that they will. For example, the firm might spend $40 million on a new advertising campaign that only leads to improvements in firm cash flow valued at $35 million, in which case $5 million in value would be destroyed. Thus, each of these strategies must be analyzed by management and decisions made based upon the anticipated merits of the specific proposal.

CONCEPT CHECK

1. What are value drivers? Give some examples.
2. How can management use value drivers to improve firm performance?

[12] The tax rate paid by the firm is, to some degree, a manageable variable because the tax code is a very complex structure that provides some decision flexibility on the part of the firm's tax specialists. However, we will eschew further consideration of tax management issues here—they should be left to the tax specialists, although the issues raised are real and consequential in their value impact on the firm.

TABLE 13-3 Value Drivers and Managing for Shareholder Value

VALUE DRIVERS	VALUE-ENHANCING STRATEGIES
Sales growth for years 1–3	• Implement a new promotional campaign to promote exciting or new products • Form a distributional alliance to enter a new market • Invest in R&D to create new products • Acquire a competitor firm
Operating profit margin	• Initiate cost-control programs to reduce operating and administrative expenses • Invest in a promotional campaign aimed at improving the brand image of your products or services in an effort to support premium pricing policies
Net working capital-to-sales ratio	• Initiate inventory control policies designed to reduce the time that inventory is held before sale • Implement a program of credit analysis and control designed to either decrease the time customers take to pay for their purchases or to incorporate penalties for late payment • Negotiate more lenient credit terms from the firm's suppliers
Property, plant, and equipment-to-sales ratio	• Consider outsourcing of production to strategic partners who might be more efficient in their operations in an effort to reduce the firm's need for plant and equipment • Implement stringent controls over the acquisition of new plant and equipment to assure that all purchases are economically viable • Improve maintenance of existing plant and equipment to improve up time, which reduces the need for additional plant and equipment
Cost of capital	• Review the firm's financial policies to assure that financing is being obtained from the lowest-cost sources • Approach large institutional investors in an effort to develop direct sources of financing for the firm's new capital needs, thus bypassing the significant costs associated with using the public capital markets

ECONOMIC VALUE ADDED (*EVA*)®

Objective 4

Earlier we used Market Value Added (*MVA*) to measure the total wealth created by a firm at a particular point in time. As such, *MVA* is a reflection of investor expectations regarding the total value they expect the firm to create in the future less the total capital invested in the firm. Stated like this, we can see a direct analogy between *MVA* and net present value (*NPV*) for the firm as a whole. However, the manager must evaluate the performance of the firm over specific intervals of time—say, one year. For this purpose, we calculate the firm's **economic value added**, or ***EVA***®. *EVA* for year t is defined as follows:

Economic value added The difference in a firm's net operating profit after taxes (NOPAT) and the capital charge for the period (i.e., the product of the firm's cost of capital and its invested capital at the beginning of the period).

$$EVA_t = \begin{bmatrix} \text{net operating} \\ \text{profit after} \\ \text{tax } (NOPAT)_t \end{bmatrix} - \begin{bmatrix} \text{weighted average} \\ \text{cost of} \\ \text{capital } (k_{wacc}) \end{bmatrix} \times \begin{bmatrix} \text{invested} \\ \text{capital}_{t-1} \end{bmatrix} \quad \text{(13-5)}$$

Note that *EVA* is related to accounting profits (i.e., *NOPAT* = net operating income ([1 – tax rate]) but differs in that it incorporates a charge for the capital invested in the firm. This **capital charge** is equal to the product of the firm's invested capital at the beginning of the period and the firm's weighted average cost of capital and is deducted from the period's net operating profit after tax (*NOPAT*) to estimate *EVA*. The result is a measure of the contribution of the firm's operations for the period to the value of the firm.

Capital charge The firm's invested capital at the beginning of the period multiplied by the firm's weighted average cost of capital. This value is deducted from the firm's net operating profit after taxes (*NOPAT*) to estimate *EVA*.

The relationship between the future *EVA*s and *MVA* is an important one, the reason being that managing for shareholder value entails increasing *MVA*. However, we manage a firm's *EVA*, which is related to *MVA* in the following way: *MVA* is the present value of

TABLE 13-4 Calculation of Economic Value Added (*EVA*) for Kramerica, Inc.

PANEL A. METHOD I FOR CALCULATING *EVA*®

	YEARS				
	0	1	2	3	4 AND BEYOND
Sales		\$56,000.00	\$62,720.00	\$70,246.40	\$70,246.40
Operating income		\$12,800.00	\$14,576.00	\$16,565.12	16,264.06
Less cash tax payments		(3,840.00)	(4,372.80)	(4,969.54)	(4,879.22)
Net operating profits after taxes (*NOPAT*)		\$ 8,960.00	\$10,203.20	\$11,595.58	\$11,384.84
Less capital charge = invested capital × K_{wacc}		(3,750.00)	(4,200.00)	(4,704.00)	(5,268.48)
Economic value added		\$ 5,210.00	\$ 6,003.20	\$ 6,891.58	\$ 6,116.36

PANEL B. METHOD II FOR CALCULATING *EVA*®

	0	1	2	3	4 AND BEYOND
Return on invested capital (*ROIC*) = $NOPAT_{(t)} \div IC_{(t-1)}$		35.84%	36.44%	36.98%	32.41%
Cost of capita! (K_{wacc})		15%	15%	15%	15%
Invested capital (Table 13-2)	\$25,000.00	\$28,000.00	\$31,360.00	\$35,123.20	\$35,123.20
Economic value added		\$ 5,210.00	\$ 6,003.20	\$ 6,891.58	\$ 6,116.36

$EVA(1) = (.3584 - .15) \times \$25{,}000 = \$5{,}210$

all future *EVA*s over the life of the firm. Thus, managing the firm in ways that increase *EVA* will generally lead to a higher *MVA*.[13]

EXAMPLE CALCULATION OF *EVA*

Let's take a look at the *EVA*s anticipated by Kramerica, Inc., based on the projections of future performance discussed earlier regarding free cash-flow valuation. Table 13-4 contains estimates of Kramerica's *EVA* for years 1–4. In Panel A we see that *EVA* is positive for every year, indicating that value is being created in each period. For example, in year 1 Kramerica's *EVA* is \$5,210, reflecting the fact that during this year Kramerica expects to earn \$8,960 in after-tax operating income (*NOPAT*), which exceeds capital costs of \$3,750 (i.e., .15 × \$25,000) by \$5,210. Kramerica's capital cost for year 1 is computed as the product of the firm's weighted average cost of capital of 15 percent and its invested capital of \$25,000. Earlier, when we introduced the notion of a firm's invested capital, we indicated that it was related to the firm's total assets, but because of the way that accountants prepare the firm's balance sheet, this was not exactly the case. For example, Stern Stewart recommends a number of adjustments to the firm's reported accounting numbers for the express purpose of converting both *NOPAT* and capital from an accounting book value to economic book value.[14] In the Kramerica example used here, none of these adjustments is required.

[13] This is a simplistic interpretation of the use of *EVA* that sometimes does not hold. For example, there are situations in which very large capital investments lead to a decrease in *EVA* in the near term that is more than offset by future increases in *EVA*. Thus, simply maximizing *EVA* is not always the same thing as maximizing *MVA*. Discussion of the limitations of *EVA* as an indicator of value creation is beyond the scope of this text. The interested reader is referred to Martin and Petty (2001) for a detailed treatment of these and other related issues.

[14] While Stern Stewart mentions some 162 adjustments, only 10 to 15 adjustments are more typically made. These adjustments are made for three reasons: (1) To convert from accrual to cash accounting (eliminating many of the reserves that the accountants have created in the financial statements; e.g., reserves for bad debt or LIFO reserves). (2) To capitalize market-building expenditures that have been expensed in the past (converting from a liquidating perspective to a going-concern perspective; e.g., capitalizing expensed R&D). (3) To remove cumulative unusual losses or gains after taxes (converting from successful-efforts to full-cost accounting).

Panel B of Table 13-4 contains an alternative definition of *EVA* that is completely equivalent to the definition found in equation 13-5. The alternative definition is:

$$EVA_t = \left(\begin{matrix}\text{return on invested}\\ \text{capital }(ROIC)_t\end{matrix} - \begin{matrix}\text{weighted average}\\ \text{cost of capital}(K_{wacc})\end{matrix}\right) \times \begin{matrix}\text{invested}\\ \text{capital }(IC)_{t-1}\end{matrix} \quad \textbf{(13-6)}$$

In this alternative format, we can see that a firm creates value only when it earns a rate of **return on invested capital** (i.e., $NOPAT_t$/invested capital_{t-1}) that exceeds the firm's cost of capital. If this difference is positive, then *EVA* is positive. Going back to Table 13-1, we can see that all five of the top wealth creators earned rates of return on their invested capital that far exceeded their cost of capital during 2001. Similarly, the bottom five wealth creators all failed to earn a rate of return on their invested capital that was as high as their cost of capital, and the return earned was actually negative in two cases.

Return on invested capital The ratio of net operating income after tax for the period divided by the firm's invested capital at the end of the previous period.

CONCEPT CHECK

1. Define economic value added and explain how to interpret it.
2. How is market value added related to economic value added?

HOW DO THEY DO IT?

Back in Table 13-1 we identified the top and bottom five wealth creators among America's 1,000 largest corporations. Let's see how they faired in managing the value drivers we identified using our free cash-flow valuation model and EVA analysis. Table 13-5 contains selected value drivers for each of these firms. We include only two value drivers in this example (fixed asset turnover and net profit margin), and in both cases it is clear that the top performers simply do better than their industry peers. For example, the average net profit margin for the top performers versus their industry peers is 11.8 percent compared to only 4 percent. However, when we look at the bottom five performers the comparison is reversed, with the bottom performers averaging a

TABLE 13-5 Value Drivers for the Top and Bottom Five Wealth Creators for 2002

	FIXED ASSET TURNOVER		NET PROFIT MARGIN			
TOP FIVE PERFORMERS	**FIRM**	**INDUSTRY**	**FIRM**	**INDUSTRY**	**RETURN ON INVESTED CAPITAL**	**COST OF CAPITAL**
General Electric Co.	3.1	3.0	11.2%	6.7%	20.0%	9.4%
Microsoft Corp.	12.4	8.9	27.0%	15.5%	21.5%	13.7%
Wal-Mart Stores	5.0	4.9	3.1%	2.9%	12.4%	8.9%
Intel Corp.	1.6	1.6	4.9%	−13.5%	9.0%	16.2%
Citigroup, Inc.	NA	NA	12.8%	8.6%	14.7%	12.0%
Average	5.5	4.6	11.8%	4.0%	15.5%	12.0%
BOTTOM FIVE PERFORMERS						
AOL Time Warner Inc.	3.7	2.6	−12.9%	−5.9%	6.0%	9.6%
Qwest Communication Intl. Inc.	0.7	1.0	−20.1%	−0.2%	1.8%	9.3%
AT&T Corp.	1.1	1.0	−13.0%	0.2%	0.8%	9.6%
Lucent Technologies Inc.	3.9	3.1	−96.0%	−47.5%	−10.3%	12.3%
JDS Uniphase Corp.	1.3	3.1	NA	−47.5%	−52.4%	14.3%
Average	2.1	2.2	−35.5%	−20.2%	−10.8%	11.0%

FINANCE MATTERS — ETHICS

EVA SUCCESS STORY—MANITOWOC CO.

Manitowoc is a manufacturer of construction cranes, ice machines, and Great Lakes shipping vessels that a decade ago was suffering from the effects of the construction recession of the mid-1980s. However, since 1995 Manitowoc's share price has increased fivefold. The booming economy of the 1990s certainly helped produce this result but that's not all. Manitowoc got religion—*EVA* religion, that is. Here's their inspiring story of shareholder value creation.

In 1986 and 1987 Manitowoc did not receive a single order for a new crane. Not to worry, the firm had a $100 million cash reserve that allowed the firm to ride out the recession until 1990, when the board promoted a newly hired Chief Operating Officer to replace the retiring CEO. The new CEO inherited a firm with a debt-free balance sheet so when tough times came, no creditors showed up at the door demanding control over the firm to repay their claims. In addition, the firm had storerooms crammed full of dusty parts dating back to the 1940s. To make matters even worse, Manitowoc's customers used the firm like a bank by taking two months to pay their bills.

In 1991 the firm's CFO heard a talk about *EVA*® and the CEO adopted the concept. The results were striking. Headquarters staff was cut from 127 to 30, Manitowoc's two crane factories were consolidated into one plant, and inventories were reduced from $84 million to $34 million over a period of two years. In addition, the firm started charging interest on late payments. These changes have shown up in dramatically improved firm performance. For example, the crane division's operating margin (net operating income before depreciation, interest, and taxes, as a percent of sales) is 16 percent compared to rival Terex's 11.5 percent.

Source: Abstracted from Michelle Conlin, "Manitowoc Co. Used to Be a Rust Belt Bum—Until Management Got Evangelical About Not Wasting Capital," *Forbes* (April 19, 1999).

–35.5 percent net profit margin compared to –20.2 percent for the industry. Finally, when we analyze the return on invested capital for the top performers, we find that four of the five firms earned rates of return that exceeded their costs of capital, whereas none of the bottom tier performers earned a return as high as their cost of capital. The message is clear. Manage your value drivers to beat the competition and you will create shareholder value. See the Finance Matters box, "EVA Success Story—Manitowoc Co."

BACK TO THE PRINCIPLES

The basic problem we attempt to address in paying for performance relates to ***Principle 7: The Agency Problem.*** *Specifically, individual managers will seek to follow their own self-interests whenever self-interest and shareholder interests come into conflict unless they are paid to do otherwise. Consequently, the theory behind paying for performance relies on developing methods for paying employees to make decisions that favor shareholder interests as well as their own.*

Objective 5

PAYING FOR PERFORMANCE

Financial economists beginning with Berle and Means (1932) have recognized the fundamental problems that arise where ownership and control of the modern corporation are separated. Where a firm's owners (stockholders) are different than its management, an agency problem arises. In essence, managers control the firm and can at times make decisions that benefit themselves at the expense of the firm's stockholders. The proponents of *EVA* propose that where the contributions of individuals and groups toward the creation of shareholder value are measured using *EVA* and rewards are structured accordingly, shareholder and manager interests will be aligned. In essence, they argue that such a reward system pays employees to behave like owners. The benefits of getting employees to act like owners is summed up in the following quote from Robert Kidder, CEO of Duracell:[15]

> When managers become owners, they begin to think a lot harder about taking money out of mature businesses and investing in growth areas. And I think that happens as a fairly natural consequence of greater ownership. It's certainly not happening because all of a sudden we put in new controls at headquarters. In fact, today we have fewer controls than we had as part of Kraft. What's different is that the proposals for change are coming from the bottom up rather than from the top down.

See the Best Practices box, "How Are Executives Paid?"

Basic Components of a Firm's Compensation Policy

Before we delve into the intricacies of linking pay to performance, let's first step back and review the basic elements of a firm's compensation program. Managerial compensation plans generally provide for three types of compensation, as depicted in Figure 13-2.

- **Base pay** is the fixed salary component of compensation.
- The **bonus payment** is generally a quarterly, semi-annual, or annual cash payment that is dependent upon firm performance compared to targets set at the beginning of the period. *EVA* provides one such performance measure that can be used in this regard.
- **Long-term compensation** consists of stock options and grants that are also made periodically to employees.[16] This type of compensation is the most direct method available to the firm to align the interests of the firm's employees with those of its shareholders.

Note that both bonus and long-term compensation are "at-risk" in that both depend upon performance of the individual and the firm. We often use the term **incentive**, or **performance-based compensation**, to describe this at-risk component of managerial compensation.

Designing a Compensation Program

A firm's compensation program can be very complex. In this section we lay out the fundamental issues that every firm's program must address in terms of four issues:

1. How much should be paid for a particular job?
2. What portion of the total compensation package should be in base salary and what part should be incentive based?

Base pay
Fixed amount of compensation paid to an employee.

Bonus payment
Compensation paid to an employee that is dependent upon the firm's performance compared to predetermined targets.

Long-term compensation
Compensation paid to the employee as an incentive to align the employee's actions to the firm's goal of maximizing shareholder wealth. The most common form of long-term compensation is stock options.

Incentive (performance-based) compensation
Compensation such as bonus and long-term compensation that is designed to motivate the employee to align employee actions with shareholder wealth creation.

[15] This quote was taken from the Stern Steward Roundtables, *Discussing the Revolution in Corporate Finance*, edited by Donald H. Chew, Jr. (Malden, MA: Blackwell Business, 1998).

[16] We discuss options in Chapter 21, where we review the tools of risk management. At this point it is sufficient to understand that a stock option provides the holder with the right to buy (a call option) shares of the firm's stock at a specified price (the exercise or strike price).

FIGURE 13-2 Components of the Typical Managerial Compensation Package

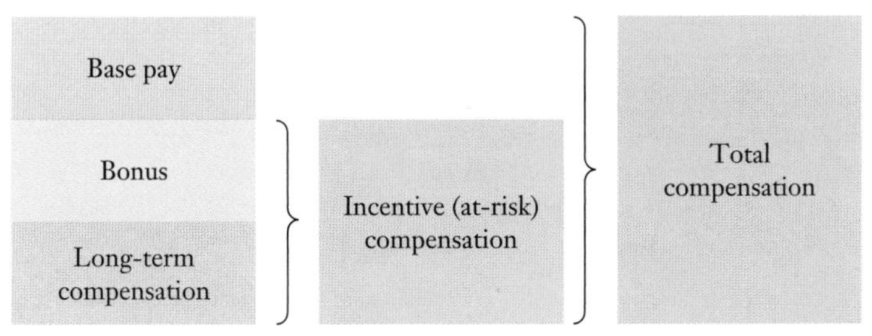

BEST PRACTICES

HOW ARE EXECUTIVES PAID?

Although the specifics of executive pay can vary dramatically from firm to firm, we can discuss them in terms of four basic components: (*i*) a base salary, (*ii*) short-term incentives in the form of an annual bonus, (*iii*) long-term incentives (generally in the form of stock grants or options and multi-year accounting-based performance plans), and (*iv*) the ubiquitous catch-all category "other." For example, consider the description of General Electric's executive compensation policies excerpted below:

> **General Electric Corporation—**
> **Compensation Policies for Executive Officers (2001)**
> The company's basic compensation program for executive officers currently consists of the following elements: annual payments of salary and bonuses; annual grants of stock options; and periodic grants of restricted stock units (RSUs) and other contingent long-term financial performance awards. (General Electric Corporation Proxy Statement for 2001 dated March 8, 2002)

There are a number of additional components of a firm's CEO pay or perks that have become increasingly more controversial in recent years. These include things such as personal use of the corporate jet, golden handshakes, golden parachutes, company loans, re-pricing of stock options, special bonuses, retirement and insurance plans, and even fresh-cut flowers. However, the bulk of executive compensation comes from items (*i*)–(*iii*) as we illustrate in Figure 13-3.

Salary

Figure 13-3 summarizes executive compensation for firms in mining and manufacturing firms in the S&P 500 for the period of 1994–2000. Note that base salary is an important, but declining (in percentage terms), component of executive compensation. CEO salaries declined from just over 30 percent in 1994 to less than 20 percent in 2000. This decrease in importance of salary was not a result of a decrease in the average salary paid but to the dramatic increase in total compensation from other forms of pay. Similar observations apply to the other industry groups and even to smaller publicly held firms.

FIGURE 13-3

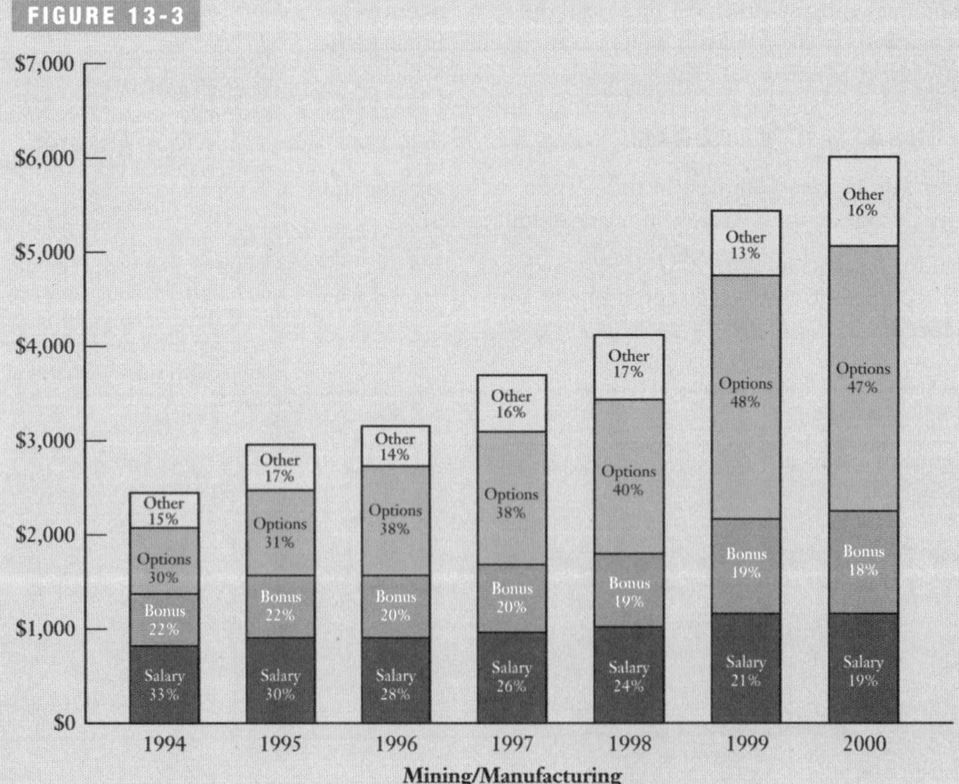

Source: Execucom database.

Short-term incentive compensation (annual bonuses)
Companies generally pay an annual bonus based on the firm's performance during the last fiscal year, hence short-term incentive compensation. Short-term incentive plans have three basic attributes: (1) one or more performance metrics, (2) a target level of performance, and (3) a structural relationship between pay and performance. Most firms use some form of accounting profit as one of their metrics. However, non-financial performance measures related to "individual performance" including subjective assessments of goal achievement and objective comparisons against prescribed goals are also used.

Figure 13-3 indicates that the dollar size of short-term bonuses increased over the 1994–2000 period. However, the relative importance of the short-term bonus (like salary) has declined.

Long-term incentive compensation
Long-term incentive plans reward executives for long-term performance, typically three to five years of performance. The form of payment for long-term compensation may be in cash, stock options, or restricted shares of company stock. Restrictions are frequently used with respect to equity-based compensation. The restriction may be related to employee longevity or firm performance.

The compensation pattern we see in Figure 13-3 demonstrates very clearly that the growing component of executive compensation has been options. We have more to say about best practices in the use of stock options in a subsequent "best practices" box. Basically, using stock options with a fixed exercise price can create some serious problems and may actually encourage managers to undertake bad projects.

3. How should incentive pay be linked to performance?
4. Finally, what portion of the incentive pay should be paid as a cash bonus and what portion should be in long-term (equity) compensation?

The design of a compensation program that supports the creation of shareholder value must arrive at satisfactory answers to all four of these questions. We will touch on each issue briefly; however, from the perspective of creating shareholder value, our primary focus is on issue number 3.

ISSUE 1: HOW MUCH TO PAY? How much to pay for a particular job is dictated by market forces outside the firm's control. That is, the total value of the entire compensation package for a given employee must meet a market test. The firm will only be able to hire good employees if it offers a competitive level of total compensation.[17] This means that companies must be ever vigilant in comparing their pay scales with their competitors in the labor market. The size of the total compensation package may determine where you go to work, but the mix of base pay and performance-based pay will determine how hard you will work. Thus, the key to creating shareholder value lies in linking the incentive portion of the compensation package to the value drivers identified earlier in the chapter.

ISSUE 2: BASE PAY VERSUS AT-RISK OR INCENTIVE COMPENSATION
What fraction of the total compensation package should be tied to performance or placed at-risk? There are no hard-and-fast rules for determining the mix of variable (at-risk) versus fixed compensation. However, in practice, the firm's highest-ranking employees generally have a larger fraction of their total compensation "at-risk" and the fraction declines with the employee's rank in the firm. For example, in 1999, Johnson & Johnson Medical (annual report) used the following scheme to define its target percent of base pay for its incentive pool:

Base Salary	Target % of Base Pay
$64,000–88,999	10%
89,000–112,999	15%
113,000–156,999	20%

[17] For example, the Dana Corporation's 1999 proxy statement indicates that the firm ". . . compares Dana's compensation practices to those of a group of comparable companies. The comparison group . . . currently consists of 22 companies . . ." (p. 11).

BEST PRACTICES

EMPLOYEE COMPENSATION POLICIES

The board of directors, through the compensation committee, is responsible for determining the firm's compensation policies and overseeing their implementation. In practice, the role of the board is more involved in the oversight of management-determined plans as opposed to originating compensation plans of its own. Nevertheless, there are some basic principles of compensation program design that are considered to be leading edge in terms of best pay practices. The principal elements of best practice include the following elements:

1. Linking pay to performance.
2. Utilizing performance measures that are both linked to the firm's goal of creating shareholder wealth and that are under the influence of the employee being evaluated (i.e., in the employee's "line of sight").
3. Making sure that the level of overall compensation is competitive such that employee retention is not an issue.

Figure 13-4 illustrates how the appropriate compensation policy (performance metric and performance targets) vary with the position of the employee in the firm. For example, for the CEO and top executives it is appropriate to tie compensation to market-based performance metrics since these executives have broad responsibility for the firm's operations and rightfully should be accountable to stockholders for the performance of the firm's shares. However, as we move down into the organization to operating executives and frontline managers, the appropriate performance metrics relate to the things that are under their control. For operating unit executives who have both revenue and expense control responsibilities it is appropriate to measure operating profit at the business unit level, whereas lower level managers' performance should be measured based on the specific value drivers (revenue or cost or units) for which they are accountable.

To this point we have focused on "pay for performance" as the factor motivation underlying the design of a compensation policy (points 1 and 2 above). However, there is one additional factor that must be considered. This is point 3, retention. Fundamentally, retention issues are addressed in terms of the overall level of compensation. Standard practice entails the use of compensation surveys that identify the overall level of compensation paid for specific jobs. These surveys are the primary tool used by compensation consultants and for obvious reasons are kept proprietary. Suffice it to say that there exist compensation surveys that contain the distribution of pay for a wide variety of industries and specific jobs, and this information is used to determine levels of pay. For example, a firm might try to maintain pay levels at the 50th percentile for their employees.

FIGURE 13-4

Employee Position in Firm	Performance Measure	Performance Target
CEO & Corporate Executives	Stockmarket returns (prices)	Exceed peer or market expectations
Operating unit executives	Operating unit performance	Exceeds performance target(s)
Frontline managers and employees	Value drivers	Exceed performance targets

In 1999, however, Motel 6 set its incentive pay based on employee responsibilities and title. A manager had 10 percent of base salary subject to incentive compensation while a vice president had 25 percent subject to incentive compensation (annual report for 1999). For most firms, basing the fraction of an employee's compensation that is at-risk on either salary level or responsibilities simply mirrors the responsibilities of the firm's top managers and their ability to control firm performance. See the Best Practices box, "Employee Compensation Policies."

ISSUE 3: LINKING PAY TO PERFORMANCE The procedure used to link the level of incentive compensation to performance is the same regardless of the particular performance measure that is chosen, so let's begin by looking at an unbounded incentive compensation payout formula.[18]

$$\text{incentive pay} = \begin{pmatrix}\text{base}\\\text{pay}\end{pmatrix}\begin{pmatrix}\text{fraction}\\\text{of pay}\\\text{at-risk}\end{pmatrix}\left(\frac{\text{actual performance}}{\text{target performance}}\right) \quad \textbf{(13-7)}$$

Note that in equation 13-7 incentive pay is unbounded. That is, there are no limits specified as to the maximum or minimum levels of incentive pay that can be earned. Incentive pay is a function of the portion of the employee's compensation that is at-risk or subject to firm performance (the product of base pay and fraction of pay at-risk) and the firm's actual performance for the period relative to a target level of performance. Note that we have not yet specified the measure of firm performance. Historically, it should be noted that performance has been measured in terms of profits or revenue growth. For example, see the description of the Harley-Davidson Short-Term Incentive Program found in the "Focus on Harley-Davidson" discussion later in this chapter. Alternatively, some firms base performance on a return on investment measure. For example, in 1996, John Deere used return on assets as its primary performance metric.

To illustrate this basic model of incentive pay found in equation 13-7, consider the case of an employee whose base pay is $40,000 and who has a target bonus equal to 25 percent of his base pay or expected incentive compensation (i.e., dependent on firm performance) equal to $10,000. The employee's expected total compensation *if* the firm meets its performance target will equal $50,000, which is the sum of the $40,000 base pay plus the $10,000 incentive compensation. Substituting into equation 13-7 to calculate the incentive compensation, we get:

$$\text{incentive pay} = \$40{,}000 \times .25 \times 1.0 = \$10{,}000$$

If we assume that the ratio of actual to target performance is 1.1, then his incentive or at-risk pay for the year is $11,000 (i.e., $40,000 × .25 × 1.1 = $11,000) and total compensation for the period will equal $51,000. The basic system would differ across employees only in terms of the level of employee base pay and the percent of that base pay that is at-risk or subject to incentive compensation.

Figure 13-5 illustrates how incentive compensation varies with firm performance. This example represents an **unbounded incentive compensation plan** because it varies directly with actual performance in relation to target performance with no floor (minimum) or cap (maximum).[19] Employees are "incentivized" to improve firm performance regardless of the level of firm performance in such a system.

Unbounded incentive compensation plan
An incentive program that has no minimum or maximum performance targets that limit the payment of incentive pay.

Most firms, however, do not use an unbounded incentive pay program. Instead they use a system that provides for a minimum, or threshold, level of performance (in relation to the target level) before the incentive plan kicks in, and a maximum level of performance (again in relation to the target) above which no incentive pay is rewarded. We refer to these plans as **bounded incentive pay programs**. The minimum and maximum performance levels are sometimes referred to as "golfing points" because of the adverse incentives that they have on employee work effort (i.e., they go play golf rather than work harder).

Bounded incentive pay programs
Incentive pay programs that place upper and lower limits on the levels of firm performance for which incentive compensation will be awarded to employees.

[18] The discussion that follows is very basic. In most firms incentive pay is based on multiple performance metrics. For example, executives may receive 75 percent of their incentive pay based on financial results and 25 percent based on personal objectives. In other cases incentive pay might be based on individual performance, financial performance, and strategic performance.

[19] Implicit in our discussion is the assumption that the performance metric is bounded from below at zero.

FIGURE 13-5 Pure (Unbounded) Incentive Pay-for-Performance System

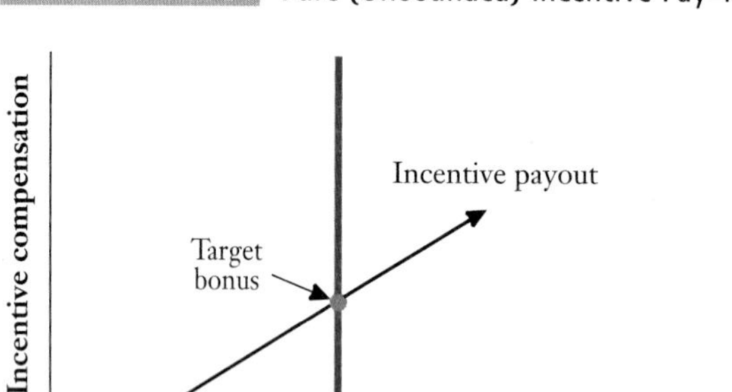

Figure 13-6 contains an example of an 80/120 plan for which the minimum or threshold level of performance at which incentive compensation will be paid is 80 percent of the target level of performance. The maximum performance for which incentive pay will be awarded is 120 percent of the target performance. Incentive compensation is only paid for performance levels that fall within the 80/120 range. Consequently, there is a wide range of performance for which no incentive pay is awarded (i.e., performance above 120 percent or below 80 percent of the target level). As a result of the boundaries, this type of program encourages employees to work to meet their performance targets only within the range of performance for which the payout varies with performance.

This type of bounded incentive payment plan also has some unfortunate effects on employee incentives to improve firm performance. Specifically, consider the effects on employee incentives under an 80/120 bonus plan that uses firm earnings to measure performance. Under this plan, managers have an incentive to select accounting procedures

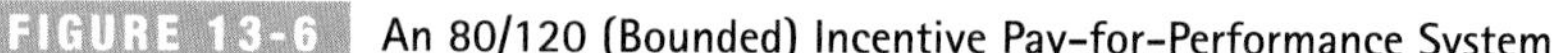

FIGURE 13-6 An 80/120 (Bounded) Incentive Pay-for-Performance System

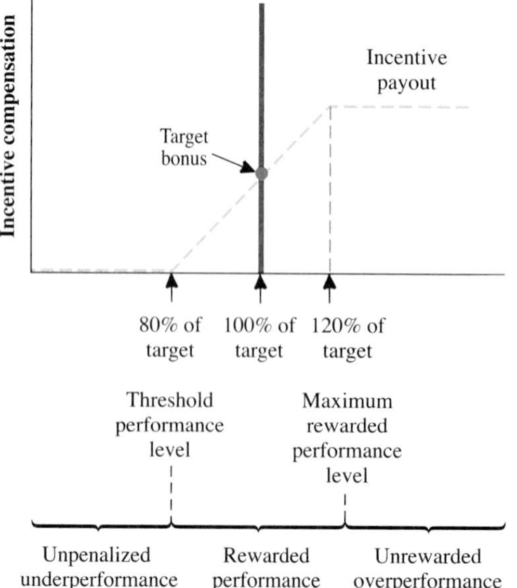

and accruals to increase the present value of their bonus. For example, as it becomes obvious that the firm's performance for the evaluation period (usually one quarter or one year) will fall below the 80 percent threshold, employees have no direct pay-for-performance incentive to work harder in order to raise firm performance during the remainder of the performance evaluation period. In fact, they have an incentive to reduce current period performance even further in the hopes that it will lower the performance target for the coming period. In addition, reducing current period performance may allow management to shift some or all of the unrewarded performance from the current to the subsequent evaluation period when it hopes to be rewarded for it.

A similar perversity arises at the upper end of the performance spectrum when management sees that the firm may exceed the upper bound on the incentive compensation program. For example, if it looks like the firm's performance is going to surpass the maximum payout level, then the employees once again lose the incentive to improve performance. This occurs for two reasons. First of all, they are not paid for performance above the maximum, and second, they may be able to postpone some of the current period's business until the coming period when they can count it toward incentive pay for that period. See the Best Practices box, "Executive Stock Options."

ISSUE 4: PAYING WITH A CASH BONUS VERSUS EQUITY The amount of incentive pay is determined by firm performance and the particulars of the payout function (i.e., whether it is bounded or not). However, the form of the compensation is also an important component of a firm's compensation program. Specifically, the firm can pay in cash, stock, or some mixture of the two. If the firm chooses stock, then the employees are rewarded for current performance and are also provided with a long-term incentive to improve performance.

The importance of stock options is reflected in the fact that they currently account for more than half of total CEO compensation in the largest U.S. companies and about 30 percent of senior operating managers' pay. Furthermore, options and stock grants now constitute almost half of the board of directors' pay. Obviously, equity-based compensation is an important and valuable tool in a firm's compensation package. Baker, Jensen, and Murphy (1988) summarize the case for equity-based compensation as follows:

> Compensation practitioners argue that fundamental changes in the "corporate culture" occur when employees are made partial owners of the firm. The effects of these plans include "rooting for the home team" and a growing awareness of and interest in the corporate bottom line. We do not understand how these effects translate into increased productivity, nor do we have a well-developed economic theory of the creation and effects of corporate culture.

This is a very brief overview of the use of equity-based pay as an important component of a firm's overall compensation program. There are a number of important issues that arise in determining just who should receive equity-based pay within the organization and how that pay should be structured. However, discussion of these issues is beyond the scope of this book. The interested reader will find the discussion by Rappaport (1999) very helpful in coming to understand these issues.

CONCEPT CHECK

1. Define each of the following components of a firm's compensation plan: base pay, bonus, long-term compensation, incentive-based compensation, and at-risk compensation.
2. Describe a bounded and an unbounded incentive pay program. What are the behavioral implications of the bounded program?

BEST PRACTICES

EXECUTIVE STOCK OPTIONS

Executive stock options are call options that give the recipient the right to purchase a share of company stock at a pre-specified "exercise" price on or before a pre-specified date. The exercise price is almost always set equal to the market price of the firm's shares on the day the option is awarded, and the option term is typically 5 to 10 years. Furthermore, executive stock options are generally restricted such that the executive cannot exercise or sell the options until they vest, and vesting typically occurs over time. For example, an option grant made today may vest over four years, with 25 percent of the award being exercisable in the year of the grant, and an additional 25 percent vesting each year for the next three years. If the executive should leave the firm before the vesting is complete, then the options are generally forfeited (although in some cases, such as a change in control of the firm, vesting may be accelerated).

Stock option grants now dominate the pay of top executives in the United States. Their popularity rose dramatically during the 1980s and 1990s, but their use has not been free of controversy. The problems we discuss arise out of the fact that the incentive effects of owning stock options are not the same as owning equity. For example, executive stock options offer the executive an opportunity to participate in the wealth effects of a growing stock price but do not expose the executive to the analogous effects of a faltering stock price. This can provide an incentive for executives to undertake very risky (volatile) investments since this maximizes the value of the stock options. Furthermore, if an executive has the power to manipulate firm earnings temporarily so as to produce a temporary uptick in the price of the firm's shares, then he may be tempted to do so in order to cash out his options. Finally, stock options, like stock grants, suffer from the "free rider" problem. That is, everyone who receives shares or options receives the same benefit from a rising stock price, even though their actions may not have contributed to the increased value of the shares. For example, in a bull market all companies' stock prices will increase even though the relative performance of a particular firm may not have changed at all.

One way to address the free rider problem is to "index" the exercise price for the stock options to an industry or general market index. To illustrate, consider the situation where stock options are granted with an exercise price equal to the current market price of the shares ($50). Now assume that by the time the options vest a year later the general market index has risen by 10 percent such that the firm's shares are trading at $55. The executives that received the option grant will realize a windfall of $5 per share on their options even though the increase in value was not due to their efforts at all. With an indexed option the exercise price could be indexed to the general market such that the exercise price is increased to $55. With a properly constructed indexed exercise price it is possible to reward only truly exceptional performance rather than free riders.

If indexed executive stock options offer the potential to resolve the free rider problem, why don't we see them much in compensation practice? The answer that is generally given is that the accounting rules for expensing options make it disadvantageous to issue indexed options. Basically, the accounting rules for reporting executive compensation as an expense of the period require that the value of stock options be recorded *only* where the exercise price differs from the current market price. Thus, to set a "variable" or "indexed" exercise price would automatically require that the firm issuing the stock options expense them in the period in which they are offered. This is of consequence where investors naively use reported earnings as a signal of firm value without digging further into the firm's compensation practices and accounting for the effects of executive stock options.

HOW FINANCIAL MANAGERS USE THIS MATERIAL

Capital-budgeting procedures are designed to help managers make new investments that promise returns that are higher than the firm's cost of capital. However, promising and delivering these returns are not always the same thing. Forecast project benefits and costs are not always realized, and it is up to the firm's management to oversee operations so as to achieve the greatest value possible from its investments. However, when firms are managed by non-owner employees, the problem of properly motivating employees to make shareholder wealth-maximizing decisions arises. This is where managing for shareholder value comes into prominence. Firms must measure and reward periodic performance of the firm in a way that encourages good decisions. This is a difficult task, but recent developments in the use of economic value added have helped a number of firms

A FOCUS ON HARLEY-DAVIDSON

ROAD RULES

THE ANNUAL BONUS PROGRAM FOR HARLEY-DAVIDSON EMPLOYEES

The employees at Harley-Davidson participate in an annual bonus program called STIP, for Short-Term Incentive Plan.[a] The STIP program is a variable compensation program that rewards financial performance and continuous improvement of defined measures. The program was designed to provide eligible employees with cash rewards when company performance improves. Furthermore, the program is continually reviewed and may be amended annually. For our purposes, we review the basic elements of the system in place for 2000 to illustrate the fundamental characteristics of the program.

How Is the STIP Payout Determined?

The cash payout for 2000 is determined by company-wide performance based on both financial and quality measures. The specific payout reflects how the company performs against the 2000 STIP measures.

For 2000, the financial performance measure for the STIP plan is based on earnings growth rate (EGR), which is calculated by comparing 2000 earnings before interest and taxes (EBIT) to 1999 EBIT. The amount of the payout is then based on the company's actual EGR for the year. The higher the EGR is, the higher the bonus payout.

The second performance measure in the STIP program for 2000 is based on quality and, for 2000, is comprised of two quality measures. The first quality performance standard relates to the number of warranty claims received within 30 days following registration, per hundred motorcycles produced from January through September 2000. The second quality measure relates to the establishment of a companywide, five-year Quality Plan. With this standard a bonus is awarded for completing the plan.

Summing Up

The STIP program at Harley-Davidson constitutes the firm's annual bonus program and is but one form of compensation paid to employees. They also receive pay that is subject to merit raises and some employees participate in a stock option program. Note also that the STIP payout is based on overall company performance and not the performance of the individual or group in which the individual participates. Another interesting feature of the program is that it is "uncapped." That is, the maximum bonus depends on firm performance and is not limited or capped at any particular percentage of target bonus pay. Finally, the program is very flexible in that the performance measures can be changed from year to year depending upon the perceived needs of the firm. For 2000 the performance measures reflect both financial performance (operating earnings) and quality.

[a]The description given here is a simplification of the actual program but captures the essence of the program for 2000.

in this regard. In addition, most publicly held firms choose to make owners out of their employees by granting them shares of stock or giving them the option to buy shares.

Shareholder value maximization represents a melding of multiple business disciplines by focusing on the measurement and rewarding of performance that creates shareholder value. Traditionally, the periodic measurement of firm performance has been discussed in managerial accounting classes while compensation programs were discussed in human relations management courses. Stock options are discussed in finance courses and the overall design of business strategy falls within the realm of strategic management. Shareholder value management represents an attempt to bring all of these topics together in the context of managing the firm for value creation.

SUMMARY

Using performance measures that are directly linked to firm value as the basis for compensating managers has been found to be a very powerful tool for focusing behavior on the goal of shareholder wealth maximization. However, as simple as the idea might sound, its implementation can be fraught with difficulties. In this chapter, we laid out a framework for analyzing both the choice of a performance measure and a discussion of the issues that must be addressed when linking performance to pay.

Objective 1

Which firms create shareholder value and which ones destroy it? This sounds like a very difficult question but, in fact, it is pretty easy to address. Recalling our discussion of project net present value, we determined that a new investment was expected to create value for the firm's shareholders if the anticipated value of its cash flows (i.e., the present value of expected future cash flows) was greater than the amount of money required to undertake the investment. Well, it may surprise you to learn that there is an analogous measure for the firm as a whole and it is called market value added, or *MVA*. However, when we measure *MVA* for a publicly held firm (i.e., a firm whose shares of stock are traded in the public capital market) we don't have to do the discounting of future cash flows to estimate the market value of the firm. So, we can assess the market's assessment of whether a firm is creating value for its shareholders directly using *MVA*, which is calculated as the difference in the market value of the firm (i.e., the sum of the market values of all the firm's securities—debt and equity) less the total capital invested in the firm.

Objective 2

Throughout this text we have argued that the underlying basis for understanding the determinants of firm value lie in the discounted cash-flow model. The model was described as follows:

$$\text{firm value} = \frac{\text{free cash flow}_1}{(1 + k_{wacc})^1} + \frac{\text{free cash flow}_2}{(1 + k_{wacc})^2} + \frac{\text{free cash flow}_3}{(1 + k_{wacc})^3} + \frac{\text{terminal value}_3}{(1 + k_{wacc})^3} \quad \textbf{(13-2)}$$

With this model of firm value in mind, we then considered the underlying drivers of free cash flow. We referred to these as value drivers.

Objective 3

We identified a key set of value drivers in the free cash-flow valuation model including operating profit margins and asset intensity (i.e., the efficiency with which the firm uses its assets to generate sales). These drivers, in turn, have their determinants in the actions taken by the firm's management. For example, instituting a just-in-time inventory control program can lead to reductions in inventories and, consequently, an increase in the efficiency with which assets are utilized. Other things remaining the same, this could lead to a reduction in expenses and an increase in firm value.

Objective 4

Economic value added represents a measure of performance that can be used to capture the success or failure of the firm (or a business unit) to create shareholder value over a specific interval of time such as one year. *EVA* is defined in either of two equivalent ways:

$$EVA_t = \begin{bmatrix}\text{net operating} \\ \text{profit after} \\ \text{tax } (NOPAT)_t\end{bmatrix} - \begin{bmatrix}\text{weighted average} \\ \text{cost of} \\ \text{capital } (k_{wacc})\end{bmatrix} \times \begin{matrix}\text{invested} \\ \text{capital}_{t-1}\end{matrix} \quad \textbf{(13-5)}$$

We observed that although *EVA* is related to accounting profits, it differs in that it incorporates a charge for the capital invested in the firm equal to the product of the firm's invested capital at the beginning of the period and the firm's weighted average cost of capital. The result is a measure of the contribution of the firm's operations for the period to the value of the firm. If *EVA* is positive, then value was created in the period, and if it is negative, value was destroyed.[20] An alternative definition of *EVA* focuses on the rates of return earned on capital compared to the cost of capital:

$$EVA_t = \left(\begin{matrix}\text{return on invested} \\ \text{capital } (ROIC)_t\end{matrix} - \begin{matrix}\text{weighted average} \\ \text{cost of capital } (K_{wacc})\end{matrix}\right) \times \begin{matrix}\text{invested} \\ \text{capital } (IC)_{t-1}\end{matrix} \quad \textbf{(13-6)}$$

Either formulation provides the same estimate of *EVA*, which can then be used as a measure of the performance of the firm for a specific period of time. A growing number of firms are now using *EVA* and similar performance measures as the basis for determining incentive or at-risk compensation for their employees.

Objective 5

Managerial compensation programs typically are comprised of three basic components: base pay, bonus, and long-term compensation. Base pay is the salary component that does not vary with the performance of the firm. The bonus and long-term compensation components are based on

[20] This is a simplistic interpretation of *EVA* that sometimes does not hold. Discussion of the limitations of *EVA* as an indicator of value creation is beyond the scope of this text. The interested reader is referred to Martin and Petty (2001) for a detailed treatment of these and other related issues.

the performance of the firm compared to a target set prior to the start of the period. Because these latter components of compensation vary with firm performance, they are considered to be *at-risk*.

There are four fundamental issues that every managerial compensation program must address:

- **How much should be paid for a particular job?** We found that this issue is generally addressed by deferring to the labor market and the going rate of pay for the job.
- **What portion of the total compensation package should be in base salary and what part should be incentive based?** Although no strict guidelines were given, we do know that, in general, the higher the position in the firm's managerial hierarchy, the greater the proportion of pay that is based on firm performance.
- **How should incentive pay be linked to performance?** Typically, firms pay out incentive compensation to their employees over a limited range of performance. For example, if performance exceeds 80 percent of the target performance level set by upper management but is less than 120 percent of the target, incentive compensation will be paid. However, should firm performance drop below 80 percent of the target level, no incentive pay will be awarded for the period. Should performance exceed 120 percent of the target, no incentive pay is awarded for performance in excess of the 120 percent cap. These upper and lower bounds on incentive pay are often referred to by those affected as *golfing points* because the employees have no financial incentive to work hard once it becomes obvious that one of these boundaries will be violated.
- **What portion of the incentive pay should be paid as a cash bonus and what portion should be in long-term (equity) compensation?** Equity in the company is growing in popularity as a medium of payment for incentive-based compensation. Giving employees shares of stock has the double effect of both compensating them for superior performance in the current period and also giving them an added incentive to perform well in the future.

KEY TERMS

Base pay, 449

Bonus payment, 449

Bounded incentive pay programs, 453

Capital charge, 445

Economic value added, 445

Free cash-flow model, 439

Incentive (performance-based compensation), 449

Invested capital, 437

Long-term compensation, 449

Market value added (MVA), 437

Return on invested capital, 447

Terminal value, 440

Unbounded incentive compensation plan, 453

Value drivers, 444

Go To: **www.prenhall.com/keown** for downloads and current events associated with this chapter

STUDY QUESTIONS

13-1. What is the accounting model of equity valuation and what are its limitations?

13-2. What is the free cash-flow valuation model?

13-3. List and describe four value drivers. How can a firm's management take explicit steps to manage these value drivers?

13-4. What is economic value added, how is it calculated, and how is it related to market value added?

13-5. List and discuss the fundamental components of a firm's compensation program.

13-6. List and discuss the four basic issues that must be addressed in designing a firm's compensation program.

SELF-TEST PROBLEMS

ST-1. The earnings per share of Creamco, Inc., for the current year are $2 per share and the firm has 4 million shares outstanding. The dairy products industry in which Creamco competes consists of a relatively small number of producers and the common stock of those that are publicly traded generally trade at price multiples of about 18 times earnings.

a. Based on the information provided, what price would you expect Creamco's shares to sell for?

b. Creamco has an opportunity to construct a new dairy processing plant in nearby Weatherford, Texas. The new plant will offer state-of-the-art facilities and allow the firm to reduce its waste by 15 percent. However, if plant construction begins next year, it will interrupt the firm's operations such that earnings per share may drop by as much as 10 cents for the year. What effect, if any, would you anticipate that the decision to undertake the new investment will have on Creamco's stock price?

ST-2. Zaap.com, Inc. is a privately held B2B startup that offers inventory management services to clients. Client firms are generally small- to medium-sized manufacturing firms that cannot afford sophisticated inventory control practices. Zaap.com provides its services via the Internet by connecting the manufacturers directly to their suppliers and managing the ordering and payment interface. Zaap.com plans to sell its shares to the general public within the next 18 months and wants to get some idea what the firm's stock will be worth. An investment banker located in Dallas who specializes in assisting high-tech startups to go public has evaluated the company's future prospects and made the following estimates of future free cash flows:

	YEARS			
	1	2	3	4
Sales	$100,000.00	$115,000.00	$132,250.00	$132,250.00
Operating income (earnings before interest and taxes)	16,000.00	18,400.00	21,160.00	21,160.00
Less cash tax payments	(4,800.00)	(5,520.00)	(6,348.00)	(6,348.00)
Net operating profits after taxes (*NOPAT*)	$ 11,200.00	$ 12,880.00	$ 14,812.00	$ 14,812.00
Less investments:				
Investment in net working capital	(1,695.65)	(1,950.00)	(2,242.50)	–
Capital expenditures (*CAPEX*)	(2,347.83)	(2,700.00)	(3,105.00)	–
Total investments	$ (4,043.48)	$ (4,650.00)	$ (5,347.50)	$ –
Free cash flow	$ 7,156.52	$ 8,230.00	$ 9,464.50	$ 14,812.00

Furthermore, the firm's investment banker had done a study of the firm's cost of capital and estimated the weighted average cost of capital to be approximately 12 percent.

a. What is the value of Zaap.com based on these estimates?

b. Given that Zaap.com's invested capital in year 0 is $31,304.35, what is the firm's market value added?

c. If Zaap.com has 2,000 shares of common stock outstanding and liabilities valued at $4,000, what is the value per share of its stock?

ST-3. The management of Zaap.com (from ST-2) wishes to estimate *EVA* for each of the next four years of the firm's operations. An evaluation of the firm's invested capital reveals the following values beginning with the current period (year 0):

	YEARS				
	0	1	2	3	4
Current assets	$15,652.17	$17,347.83	$19,297.83	$21,540.33	$21,540.33
Property, plant, and equipment	15,652.17	18,000.00	20,700.00	23,805.00	23,805.00
Invested capital	31,304.34	35,347.83	39,997.83	45,345.33	45,345.33

a. Calculate Zaap.com's *EVA*s for years 1 through 4. What do these values tell you about the value being created by Zaap.com?

b. What is Zaap.com's return on invested capital (*ROIC*) for each of the years 1 through 4? Relate the firm's *ROIC* to your *EVA* estimates.

STUDY PROBLEMS (SET A)

13-1A. (*Accounting model valuation*) Dynegy Corporation's earnings for 2001 were $1.90 per share and its closing stock price for the year was $25.50. Analysts' estimates of 2002 earnings per share are about $1.06. Use the accounting valuation model to estimate Dynegy's stock price.

13-2A. (*Free cash flow model valuation*) The Bergman Corporation sold its shares to the general public in 2003. The firm's estimated free cash flows for the next four years are as follows:

	YEARS			
	1	2	3	4
Sales	$30,000.00	$33,000.00	$36,300.00	$36,300.00
Operating income	4,800.00	5,280.00	5,808.00	5,808.00
Less cash tax payments	(1,440.00)	(1,584.00)	(1,742.40)	(1,742.40)
Net operating profits after taxes (*NOPAT*)	$ 3,360.00	$ 3,696.00	$ 4,065.60	$ 4,065.60
Less investments:				
Investment in net working capital	(354.55)	(390.00)	(429.00)	–
Capital expenditures (*CAPEX*)	(490.91)	(540.00)	(594.00)	–
Total investments	$ (845.46)	$ (930.00)	$ (1,023.00)	$ –
Free cash flow	$ 2,514.54	$ 2,766.00	$ 3,042.60	$ 4,065.60

Bergman estimated that its free cash flows would form a level perpetuity beginning in year 4. Furthermore, the firm's investment banker conducted a study of the firm's cost of capital and estimated the weighted average cost of capital to be approximately 12 percent.

a. What is the value of Bergman using the free cash-flow valuation model?

b. Given that Bergman's invested capital in year 0 is $9,818.18, what is the market value added for Bergman?

c. If Bergman has 2,000 shares of common stock outstanding and liabilities valued at $4,000, what is the value per share of its stock?

13-3A. (*Calculating economic value added*) The management of the Bergman Corporation (from problem 13-2A) wishes to estimate *EVA* for each of the next three years of the firm's operations. An evaluation of the firm's invested capital reveals the following values beginning with the current period (year 0):

	YEARS				
	0	1	2	3	4
Current assets	$4,909.09	$ 5,263.64	$ 5,653.64	$ 6,082.64	$ 6,082.64
Property, plant, and equipment	4,909.09	5,400.00	5,940.00	6,534.00	6,534.00
Invested capital	$9,818.18	$10,663.64	$11,593.64	$12,616.64	$12,616.64

a. Calculate Bergman's *EVA*s for years 1 through 4. What do these values tell you about the value being created by Bergman?

b. What is Bergman's return on invested capital (*ROIC*) for each of the years 1 through 4? Relate the firm's *ROIC* to your *EVA* estimates.

c. Bergman's *EVA*s for years 4 and beyond form a level perpetuity equal to the *EVA* for year 3. Calculate the present value of the firm's *EVA*s for years 1 through infinity. How does this present value compare to the market value added for the firm (see part *b* of problem 13-2A)? You can assume that the free cash-flow value of Bergman from problem 13-2a is $30,730.95.

13-4A. (*Incentive compensation*) The management of Seligman Manufacturing has decided to tie employee compensation to *EVA* performance of the firm. The firm's CFO, Virginia Whitten, is to make a presentation to the CEO and board of directors illustrating how the program will work under both an unbounded and a bounded plan for awarding incentive compensation. To illustrate the two plans, Virginia has chosen to use the compensation for a typical plant manager. Under the proposed compensation plan, a plant manager would receive a base pay level of $100,000 plus incentive pay equal to 20 percent of this base pay if the firm hits its *EVA* performance targets exactly.

a. Calculate the plant manager's incentive pay and total compensation for actual *EVA* performance of $15,000,000; $20,000,000; and $30,000,000 if the target level of *EVA* performance is set at $20,000,000.

b. Now estimate the plant manager's incentive pay and total compensation for the same three levels of *EVA* performance and target *EVA* but with a bounded incentive pay system that has a floor equal to 80 percent of the target performance level and a cap at 120 percent. What are the incentive effects for the plant manager of placing the floor and cap on target performance when determining the incentive pay?

WEB WORKS

13-1WW. You can learn more about *EVA* at **www.sternstewart.com.** What are Stern-Stewart's four Ms? Why do you think that these factors are important to maximizing shareholder value? Identify three companies that use *EVA*. Notice that companies outside of the United States also use *EVA*.

13-2WW. Go to a company's Web site that uses *EVA* (identified in the previous exercise). Does the company report its *EVA* in its financial statements?

INTEGRATIVE PROBLEM

Jason Jeffries was still a bit stunned as he pressed the lever on the water cooler just outside his boss's office. Just minutes before, Jason had left the office of Sarah Burchette, a partner at PerformancePlus and Jason's immediate supervisor. During their brief visit, Sarah had informed him that the firm wanted to broaden its practice to include new-economy Internet firms. To get the ball rolling for the firm's new target market, she asked Jason to work up a performance analysis for RealNetworks Inc. and present it to the company's partners in two weeks. This meant that Jason would have to come to grips with just how much value RealNetworks was creating and how it was doing it. Jason was thrilled with the opportunity to lead the effort but very concerned that he would not have enough time to come up with anything meaningful. After all, rationalizing the market valuations of Internet firms was not easy even to the most savvy investors.

After graduating with an MBA from a well-known university in the southwestern United States, Jason had joined the staff of a regional consulting firm, PerformancePlus, where he entered the firm's practice as an associate with a specialty in finance. PerformancePlus specializes in the design of compensation programs that provide greater employee incentives to create shareholder value. The principal tool used in its performance appraisal practice is economic value added, or *EVA*®, which was developed by Stern Stewart and Company.

RealNetworks Inc. is a Washington corporation that provides software products for "streaming" audio, video, text, animation, and other media content over the Internet. Its products include RealAudio and RealVideo. The leadership of the firm, and many industry watchers, believe that streaming media technology is essential to the evolution of the World Wide Web as a mass communications medium because it allows the Internet to compete more effectively with traditional media.[21]

[21] Based on RealNetworks's 10K filing for the period ended December 31, 1998.

The historical performance of RealNetworks is similar to that of many other new economy Internet firms. The company has experienced very rapid sales growth but has yet to produce a profit (see Panel A of Exhibit 1). In fact, the firm has experienced increasing losses in every year; in 1998, the firm lost over $20 million. In spite of these continued and growing losses, RealNetworks's stock price closed just under $9 per share in 1998, giving the firm a market capitalization of $1,204,467.

Exhibit 1. Selected Financial Statements—RealNetworks, Inc.

PANEL A. GAAP ACCOUNTING EARNINGS

	(US $ THOUSANDS)		
	1996	**1997**	**1998**
Revenue	$14,012	$ 32,720	$ 64,839
Cost of sales	(2,185)	(6,465)	(12,390)
Gross profit	$11,827	$ 26,255	$ 52,449
General and administration	(3,491)	(6,024)	(9,841)
Selling, marketing, and advertising	(7,540)	(20,124)	(32,451)
Research and development	(4,812)	(13,268)	(29,401)
Goodwill amortization	–	–	(1,596)
Net operating profit	$ (4,016)	$(13,161)	$(20,840)

PANEL B. GAAP BALANCE SHEETS

	(U.S. $ THOUSANDS)			
	DEC-95	**DEC-96**	**DEC-97**	**DEC-98**
ASSETS				
Cash and equivalents	$ 6,116	$19,595	$ 92,028	$ 89,777
Net receivables	717	3,381	15,779	4,941
Inventories	3	61	167	–
Other current assets	143	491	1,885	3,212
Total current assets	$ 6,979	$23,528	$109,859	$ 97,930
Gross plant, property, and equipment	692	3,462	7,896	12,355
Accumulated depreciation	98	783	2,753	6,082
Net plant, property, and equipment	$ 594	$ 2,679	$ 5,143	$ 6,273
Investments at equity	–	–	816	–
Intangibles	–	–	–	9,048
Other assets	1	261	886	14,808
TOTAL ASSETS	$7,574	$26,468	$116,704	$128,059
LIABILITIES				
Accounts payable	$ 185	$ 2,405	$ 2,136	$ 3,563
Accrued expenses	200	1,318	3,653	10,418
Other current liabilities	646	2,912	16,550	23,742
Total current liabilities	1,031	6,635	22,339	37,723
Long-term debt	–	–	963	987
Other liabilities	–	–	15,500	5,833
EQUITY				
Preferred stock—redeemable	$ 7,654	$23,153	–	–
Preferred stock—nonredeemable	14	14	–	–
Total preferred stock	$ 7,668	$23,167	–	–
Common stock	–	1	31	34
Capital surplus	921	2,543	95,557	117,546
Retained earnings	(2,046)	(5,878)	(17,686)	(34,064)
Common equity	$(1,125)	$ (3,334)	$ 77,902	$ 83,516
TOTAL EQUITY	$ 6,543	$19,833	$ 77,902	$ 83,516
TOTAL LIABILITIES AND EQUITY	7,574	26,468	116,704	128,059
COMMON SHARES OUTSTANDING	148	2,140	123,464	134,296

a. Evaluate RealNetworks' profitability over the 1996–1998 period.
b. What do you think is the appropriate number for RealNetworks' invested capital at the end of 1998? Note that both marketing and R&D expenditures are expensed fully against revenues in the year in which the expenditures are made. Do you think that this distorts total assets as an indication of the firm's invested capital? Explain.
c. Explain how you would go about evaluating the *EVA* for 1996–1998. What problems do you see in carrying out the analysis?

STUDY PROBLEMS (SET B)

13-1B. (*Accounting model valuation*) The Harley-Davidson Corporation's earnings for 2001 were $1.45 per share and its closing stock price for the year was $54.31. Analyst estimates of 2002 earnings per share are about $1.72. Use the accounting valuation model to estimate Harley-Davidson's stock price.

13-2B. (*Free cash-flow model valuation*) The Hackberg Corporation sold its shares to the general public in 2003. The firm's estimated free cash flows for the next four years are as follows:

	YEARS			
	1	2	3	4
Sales	$34,500.00	$37,950.00	$41,745.00	$41,745.00
Operating income	5,865.00	6,451.50	7,096.65	7,096.65
Less cash tax payments	(1,642.20)	(1,806.42)	(1,987.06)	(1,987.06)
Net operating profits after taxes (*NOPAT*)	$ 4,222.80	$ 4,645.08	$ 5,109.59	$ 5,109.59
Less investments:				
Investment in net working capital	(407.73)	(448.50)	(493.35)	–
Capital expenditures (*CAPEX*)	(564.55)	(621.00)	(683.10)	–
Total investments	$ (972.28)	$ (1,069.50)	$ (1,176.45)	–
Free cash flow	$ 3,250.52	$ 3,575.58	$ 3,933.14	$ 5,109.59

Hackberg estimated that its free cash flow would form a level perpetuity beginning in year 4. Furthermore, the firm's investment banker did a study of the firm's cost of capital and estimated the weighted average cost of capital to be approximately 15 percent.

a. What is the value of Hackberg?
b. Given that Hackberg's invested capital in year 0 is $11,290.91, what is the market value added for Hackberg?
c. If Hackberg has 4,000 shares of common stock outstanding and liabilities valued at $6,000, what is the value per share of its stock?

13-3B. (*Calculating economic value added*) The management of the Hackberg Corporation (from problem 13-2B) wishes to estimate *EVA* for each of the next four years of the firm's operations. An evaluation of the firm's invested capital reveals the following values beginning with the current period (year 0):

	YEARS				
	0	1	2	3	4
Current assets	$ 5,645.45	$ 6,053.18	$ 6,501.68	$ 6,995.03	$ 6,995.03
Property, plant, and equipment	5,645.45	6,210.00	$ 6,831.00	7,514.10	7,514.10
Invested capital	$11,290.90	$12,263.18	$13,332.68	$14,509.13	$14,509.13

a. Calculate Hackberg's *EVAs* for years 1 through 4. What do these values tell you about the value being created by Hackberg?
b. What is Hackberg's return on invested capital (*ROIC*) for each of the years 1 through 4? Relate the firm's *ROIC* to your *EVA* estimates.

c. Hackberg's *EVA*s for years 4 and beyond form a level perpetuity equal to the *EVA* for year 3. Calculate the present value of the firm's *EVA*s for years 1 through infinity. How does this present value compare to the market value added for the firm (see part *b* of problem 13-2B)? You can assume that the free cash-flow value of Hackberg from problem 13-2B is $30,513.88.

13-4B. (*Incentive compensation*) The management of Shook Manufacturing has decided to tie employee compensation to *EVA* performance of the firm. The firm's CFO, Mark Shephard, is to make a presentation to the CEO and board of directors illustrating how the program will work under both an unbounded and a bounded plan for awarding incentive compensation. To illustrate the two plans, Mark has chosen to use the compensation for a typical division manager. Under the proposed compensation plan, a division manager would receive a base pay level of $150,000 plus incentive pay equal to 30 percent of this base pay if the firm hits its *EVA* performance targets exactly.

a. Calculate the division manager's incentive pay and total compensation for actual *EVA* performance of $20,000,000; $30,000,000; and $40,000,000 if the target level of *EVA* performance is set at $30,000,000.

b. Now estimate the division manager's incentive pay and total compensation for the same three levels of *EVA* performance and target *EVA* but with a bounded incentive pay system that has a floor equal to 80 percent of the target performance level and a cap at 120 percent. What are the incentive effects for the division manager of placing the floor and cap on target performance when determining the incentive pay?

SELF-TEST SOLUTIONS

ST-1. **a.** $$\text{price-earnings multiple} = \frac{\text{stock price}}{\text{earnings per share}}$$

$$18 = \frac{\text{stock price}}{\$2.00}$$

$$\text{stock price} = 18 \times \$2.00 = \$36.00$$

b. Although the new processing plant will reduce earnings per share by 10 cents, this project should not have a negative impact on the stock price. It is reasonable to think the stock price may increase as a result of the new facility and the reduction in waste.

ST-2. **a.** $$\text{terminal value} = \frac{\$14,812}{.12} = 123,433.33$$

$$\text{value of the firm} = PV \text{ of free cash flows} = \frac{\$7,156.52}{(1.12)^1} + \frac{\$8,230.00}{(1.12)^2} + \frac{\$9,464.50}{(1.12)^3} + \frac{\$123,433.33}{(1.12)^3}$$

$$= \$107,544.71$$

b. $$\begin{aligned} MVA &= \text{firm value} - \text{invested capital} \\ &= \$107,544.71 - \$31,304.05 \\ &= \$76,240.66 \end{aligned}$$

c. $$\begin{aligned} \text{firm value} &= \text{debt value} + \text{equity value} \\ \$107,544.71 &= \$4,000 + \text{equity value} \\ \text{equity value} &= \$103,544.71 \end{aligned}$$

$$\text{value per share of stock} = \frac{\text{equity value}}{\text{shares outstanding}}$$

$$= \frac{\$103,544.71}{2,000} = \$51.77$$

ST-3. **a.** $EVA_t = NOPAT_t - (k_{wacc} \times IC_{t-1})$

$k_{wacc} = 12\%$

	YEAR 1	YEAR 2	YEAR 3	YEAR 4
$NOPAT_t$	$11,200	$12,880	$14,812	$14,812
IC_{t-1}	31,304.35	35,347.83	39,997.83	45,345.33
EVA_t	7,443.48	8,638.61	10,012.26	9,370.56

EVA is positive for each of the four years under review, indicating that Zapp.com is creating value for its shareholders.

b. $ROIC_t = \dfrac{NOPAT_t}{IC_{t-1}}$

	YEAR 1	YEAR 2	YEAR 3	YEAR 4
$NOPAT_t$	$11,200	$12,880	$14,812	$14,812
IC_{t-1}	31,304.35	35,347.83	39,997.83	45,345.33
$ROIC_t$	35.8%	36.4%	37.0%	32.7%

As we would expect, the firm's *ROIC* is greater than its cost of capital and, thus, the firm is creating value for its shareholders. When *ROIC* is greater than the firm's cost of capital, we would see positive *EVA*s, which we did in part *a* of this problem.

SUGGESTED READINGS

Berle, Adolph, and Gardner Means. 1932. *The modern corporation and private property* (New York: Macmillan).

Copeland, Tom, Tim Koller, and Jack Murrin. 1994. *Valuation: Measuring and managing the value of companies*, 2nd edition (New York: John Wiley & Sons, Inc.).

Martin, John D., and J. William Petty. 2001. *Value-based management: The corporate response to the shareholder revolution* (Boston: Harvard Business School Press).

McTaggart, James M., Peter W. Kontes, and Michael C. Mankins. 1994. *The value imperative: Managing for superior shareholder returns* (New York: The Free Press).

Rappaport, Alfred. 1986. *Creating shareholder value: The new standard for business performance* (New York: The Free Press).

Rappaport, Alfred. 1999. New thinking on how to link executive pay with performance. *Harvard Business Review*, March/April: 91–101.

Stewart, G. Bennett III. 1991. *The quest for value* (New York: Harper Business).

PART 4

Capital Structure and Dividend Policy

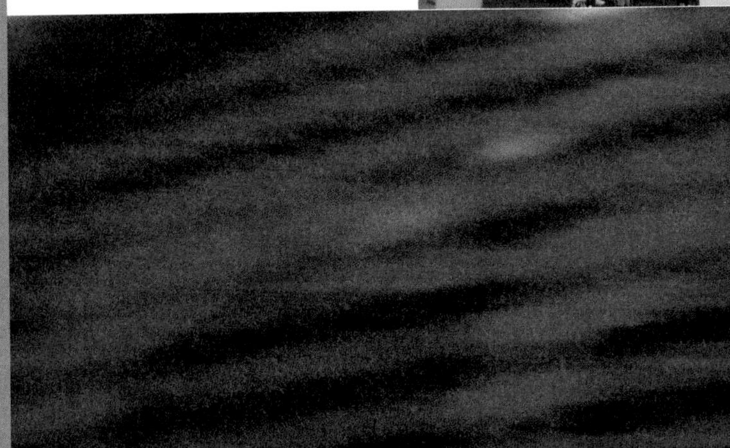

LEARNING OBJECTIVES

After reading this chapter, you should be able to

1. Understand the historical relationship between internally generated corporate sources of funds and externally generated sources of funds.
2. Understand the financing mix that tends to be used by firms raising long-term financial capital.
3. Explain why financial markets exist in a developed economy.
4. Explain the financing process by which savings are supplied and raised by major sectors in the economy.
5. Describe the key components of the U.S. financial market system.
6. Understand the role of the investment banking business in the context of raising corporate capital.
7. Distinguish between privately placed securities and publicly offered securities.
8. Be acquainted with the concepts of securities flotation costs and securities markets regulations.

CHAPTER 14

Raising Capital in the Financial Markets

From February 4, 1994, through November 6, 2002, the Federal Reserve System (Fed), the nation's central bank, voted to change the "target" federal funds rate on 32 different occasions. Fourteen of these interest rate changes were in the upward direction. Eighteen decisions, therefore, moved short-term interest rates downward, indicating a loosening of monetary policy. Eleven consecutive times, in fact, during calendar year 2001 Federal Reserve policy makers chose to reduce the target federal funds rate. Such a pervasive stance occurs during periods of slowing aggregate economic activity, which we will shortly review. The federal funds rate is a short-term market rate of interest, influenced by the Fed, that serves as a sensitive indicator of the direction of future changes in interest rates.

We will review here five different interest rate cycles that have confronted major corporate officers, like those at Harley-Davidson or the Walt Disney Company. This will emphasize how alert and flexible top-level executives must be in planning their firms' cash availability and cash distributions within an always uncertain global economic environment. The discussion also stresses that interest rate changes induce changes in the cost of capital to firms, and thereby, affects their capital budgeting decisions. The funds-management process, as you will shortly see, is continual. An overview of the five distinct cycles is displayed below.

Recent Interest Rate Cycles

PHASE AND TIME PERIOD	MAIN CONCERN OR RISK	POLICY ACTION
1. Early 1994	Inflation	Raise interest rates
2. Early 1997	Inflation	Raise interest rates
3. Fall 1998	International pressures	Lower interest rates
4. Summer 1999	Tight labor markets, strong aggregate, real growth, and inflation	Raise interest rates
5. Early 2001	Contracting manufacturing output, slower business capital spending, equity market sell-off, and formal recession	Lower interest rates

CHAPTER PREVIEW

This chapter focuses on the market environment in which long-term financial capital is raised. Long-term funds are raised in the capital market. By the term *capital market*, we mean all institutions and procedures that facilitate transactions in long-term financial instruments (such as common stocks and bonds).

The sums involved in tapping the capital markets can be vast. For example, new corporate securities offered to the investing marketplace for cash during 2001 totaled $1.54 trillion. To be able to distribute and absorb security offerings of such enormous size, an economy must have a well-developed financial market system. To use that system effectively, the financial manager must possess a basic understanding of its structure. This chapter will help you gain that understanding.

As you work through this chapter, be on the lookout for direct applications of several of our principles that form the basics of business financial management. Specifically, your attention will be directed to: **Principle 1: The Risk-Return Trade-Off—We won't take on additional risk unless we expect to be compensated with additional return; Principle 6: Efficient Capital Markets—The markets are quick and the prices are right;** and **Principle 10: Ethical Behavior Is Doing the Right Thing, and Ethical Dilemmas Are Everywhere in Finance.**

In early 1994, the central bank feared that inflationary pressures were building up in the U.S. economy and decided to take action, via raising nominal short-term interest rates, to stem those pressures by slowing down aggregate economic growth. The Fed remained committed to a course of higher interest rates throughout 1994 and the first half of 1995; then, on July 6, 1995, these monetary policy makers reversed course and began a series of three interest rate decreases. For over a year, from January 31, 1996, to March 25, 1997, the Fed stayed on the sidelines and let the nation's financial markets direct the course of interest rates.

But, during the first quarter of 1997, the Fed again became concerned that increased inflationary pressures were building up within the U.S. economic system. For example, the national economy was growing at a faster inflation-adjusted rate in the 1997 first quarter than was experienced in the first quarter of 1987—the year of the major equity market crash which later occurred during October of that year. As a result, the Fed chose to raise the target federal funds rate on March 25, 1997. The March 1997 interest rate increase directed by the Fed was followed by almost a year and a half of the central bank returning to the sidelines and observing the important relationship between the rate of inflation and real economic growth.

Then, during the Fall months of 1998, unfavorable international pressures from Brazil and Russia, among others, caused the commercial lending system to pull in the reins. This put financing strains on corporate America. Fearing a widening international economic slowdown, the Fed engineered a quick sequence of three more interest rate decreases that ended on November 17, 1998, aimed at stabilizing both the credit and equity markets. By the way, this maneuvering by the central bank in 1998 did, in fact, work.

Once again, commencing on June 30, 1999, the Fed became concerned about the relationship among (1) tight labor markets; (2) strong aggregate real economic growth, usually monitored by rates of change in real gross domestic product (GDP); and (3) the rate of observed inflation as well as inflationary expectations. During this phase of the business cycle, the Fed chose to increase short-term interest rates on six different occasions over the period ended May 16, 2000.

Realize that at this stage of the business cycle the U.S. economy was in uncharted territory, as the remarkable economic expansion that began in March 1991 *entered* its tenth year at the close of the 2000 first quarter. Such good performance within the aggregate domestic economy stood out, as it marked the longest, uninterrupted period of expansion in the United States, dating back to 1854 when reliable records began to be maintained. Thus, the Fed continued its vigilant monitoring stance by putting upward pressure on short-term interest rates in the hopes of meeting its twin objectives of supporting (1) maximum sustainable employment and (2) price stability. The "good times" began to be stressed during the summer of 2000. A wide-ranging series of events that included (1) a contracting manufacturing sector, (2) slower business investment in plant and equipment, (3) an equity market sell-off that made the term "dot-com" a less-than-desirable word, and (4) a build-up of business inventories notably suggested that the United States was poised to enter the tenth recession since the end of World War II.

So, on January 3, 2001, the Fed began a concerted drive that lasted across all of that year to stimulate the domestic economy by driving interest rates lower and reducing the cost of capital funds to businesses. In the midst of these record 11 interest-rate cuts, the United States officially slipped into recession in March of 2001. Thus, the record-setting U.S. commercial expansion ended at a duration of 120 months, outpacing the 106-month expansion from February 1961 into December 1969.

The implications for business financial officers and other corporate decision makers are important. The 32 monetary policy actions and resultant interest rate changes discussed here are displayed in the accompanying table.

From a financial management viewpoint, the 14 overt actions by the Fed to raise rates caused the *opportunity cost of funds* to rise. This means that firms like Harley-Davidson and the Walt Disney Company, for example, endured increases in their respective cost of capital funds.

This, in turn, made it more difficult for real capital projects to be financed and be included in those firms' capital budgets.

Changes in the Target Federal Funds Rate and Commercial Bank Prime Lending Rate
February 1994–December 2002

DATE	OLD TARGET RATE %	NEW TARGET RATE %	PRIME LENDING RATE %
		1994	
February 4	3.00	3.25	6.00 (no change)
March 22	3.25	3.50	6.25
April 18	3.50	3.75	6.75
May 17	3.75	4.25	7.25
August 16	4.25	4.75	7.75
November 19	4.75	5.50	8.50
		1995	
February 1	5.50	6.00	9.00
July 6	6.00	5.75	8.75
December 19	5.75	5.50	8.50
		1996	
January 31	5.50	5.25	8.25
		1997	
March 25	5.25	5.50	8.50
		1998	
September 29	5.50	5.25	8.25
October 15	5.25	5.00	8.00
November 17	5.00	4.75	7.75
		1999	
June 30	4.75	5.00	8.00
August 24	5.00	5.25	8.25
November 16	5.25	5.50	8.50
		2000	
February 2	5.50	5.75	8.75
March 21	5.75	6.00	9.00
May 16	6.00	6.50	9.50
		2001	
January 3	6.50	6.00	9.00
January 31	6.00	5.50	8.50
March 20	5.50	5.00	8.00
April 18	5.00	4.50	7.50
May 15	4.50	4.00	7.00
June 27	4.00	3.75	6.75
August 21	3.75	3.50	6.50

(continued)

DATE	OLD TARGET RATE %	NEW TARGET RATE %	PRIME LENDING RATE %
		2001	
September 17	3.50	3.00	6.00
October 2	3.00	2.50	5.50
November 6	2.50	2.00	5.00
December 11	2.00	1.75	4.75
		2002	
November 6	1.75	1.25	4.25

Do you need current interest rate data? Just go to **www.federalreserve.gov/** and you will be at the Federal Reserve Board's Web site. Once you get there, click on "Research and Data" then examine the H.15 report called "Selected Interest Rates." This provides you with a long-term perspective on interest rate levels in the United States for a wide variety of instruments.

The 18 decisions to lower the target federal funds rate had the exact opposite effect (i.e., the given firm's cost of capital funds decreased). In this latter case, the company can take on more capital projects.

Also note in the far right column of the table that the commercial bank prime lending rate typically changes in the same direction and at about the same time that a shift in the federal funds rate occurs. The prime lending rate is the interest rate that banks charge their *most* creditworthy customers. Thus, the transmission of the central bank's policy move to the explicit cost of funds that the firm faces in the financial markets happens quickly. The commercial banking industry helps it along.

As you read this chapter you will learn about (1) the importance of financial markets to a developed economy and (2) how funds are raised in the financial markets. This will help you, as an emerging business executive specializing in accounting, finance, marketing, or strategy, understand the basics of acquiring financial capital in the funds marketplace.

Objective 1

THE FINANCIAL MANAGER, INTERNAL AND EXTERNAL FUNDS, AND FLEXIBILITY

At times, internally generated funds will not be sufficient to finance all of the firm's proposed expenditures. In these situations, the corporation may find it necessary to attract large amounts of financial capital externally or otherwise forgo projects that are forecast to be profitable.[1] Year in and year out, business firms in the nonfinancial corporate sector of the U.S. economy rely heavily on the nation's financial market system to raise cash.

Table 14-1 displays the relative internal and external sources of funds for such corporations over the 1981 to 2000 period. Notice that the percentage of external funds raised in any given year can vary substantially from that of other years. In 1982, for example, the nonfinancial business sector raised 25.4 percent of its funds in the financial markets. This was substantially less than the 39.4 percent raised externally only one year earlier, during 1981. After that, the same type of significant adjustment made by financial managers is evident. During 1988, we see that nonfinancial firms raised 36.3 percent of new funds in the external markets. By the end of 1991, this proportion dropped drastically to 9.7 percent.

Such adjustments illustrate an important point: Financial executives are perpetually on their toes regarding market conditions and the state of the overall economy. Changes in market conditions influence the precise way corporate funds will be raised.

[1] By *externally generated,* we mean that the funds are obtained by means other than through retentions or depreciation. Funds from these latter two sources are commonly called *internally generated funds.*

TABLE 14-1 Nonfinancial Corporate Business Sources of Funds: 1981–2000

YEAR	TOTAL SOURCES ($ BILLIONS)	PERCENT INTERNAL FUNDS	PERCENT EXTERNAL FUNDS
2000	1,166.9	68.1	31.9
1999	1,200.1	62.5	37.5
1998	899.8	79.4	20.6
1997	967.6	75.6	24.4
1996	812.0	83.4	16.6
1995	878.4	70.7	29.3
1994	733.7	77.3	22.7
1993	593.1	81.6	18.4
1992	560.5	78.2	21.8
1991	471.7	90.3	9.7
1990	535.5	76.9	23.1
1989	567.9	70.4	29.6
1988	634.2	63.7	36.3
1987	564.7	66.6	33.4
1986	538.8	62.5	37.5
1985	493.8	71.3	28.7
1984	511.4	65.8	34.2
1983	444.6	65.7	34.3
1982	331.7	74.6	25.4
1981	394.4	60.6	39.4
Mean	–	72.3	27.7

Sources: *Economic Report of the President,* February 1995, p. 384; *Federal Reserve Bulletin,* June 2000, Table 1.57; and *Flow of Funds Accounts of the U.S.,* First Quarter 2000, Table F. 102, and Third Quarter 2001, Table F. 102.

High relative interest rates, for instance, will deter use of debt instruments by the financial manager.

The financial market system must be both organized and resilient. Periods of economic recession test the financial markets and those firms that continually use the markets. Economic contractions are especially challenging to financial decision makers because all recessions are unique. This forces financing policies to become unique.

During the 1981 to 1982 recession, which lasted 16 months, interest rates remained high by historic standards during the worst phases of the downturn. This occurred because policy makers at the Fed decided to wring a high rate of inflation out of the economy by means of a tight monetary policy. Simultaneously, stock prices were depressed. These business conditions induced firms to forgo raising funds via external means. During 1982, 74.6 percent of corporate funds were generated internally (see Table 14-1). The same general pattern followed after the 1990 to 1991 recession ended in the first quarter of 1991. During 1991, businesses paid down their short-term borrowing and relied on internally generated sources for 90.3 percent of their net financing needs.

Corporate profitability also plays a role in the determination of the internal-external financing choice. In March 2000, the U.S. economy began the tenth year of economic expansion that ended during March 2001. The good economy translated into good corporate profits. Other things held equal, greater profits reduce the need for external financing. For example, in 1998 the reliance of firms on external finance dropped to 20.6 percent of their total funds sources. Whereas, when profits were more strained over the 1981 to 1984 period, financial managers relied more heavily on the market system for an average of 33 percent of their total funds needed.

The collective behavior of companies that results in firms retaining internally generated cash rather than paying it to stockholders as dividends or to creditors (bondholders)

FIGURE 14-1 Non-Financial Corporate Business Sources of Funds 1981–2000

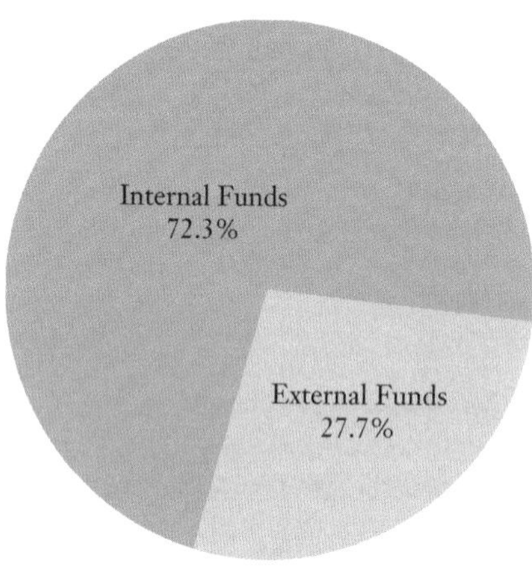

1981–2000

as interest is referred to by financial economists and analysts as the *internal capital market*.[2] This is because the firm allocates the cash flows to new projects. However, if the cash payments were made directly to stockholders and creditors, the funds would ultimately be allocated to new projects through the external capital markets.

As Figure 14-1 shows, the internal capital market accounted for 72.3 percent of non-financial corporations' sources of funds over the 1981–2000 period. Changing economic conditions will cause this relationship to shift persistently because financial executives will continually adjust to the new information that encompasses the business cycle, interest rates, and stock prices.

The point here is an important one for the executive: As economic activity and policy shape the environment of the financial markets, financial managers must understand the meaning of the economic ups and downs and remain flexible in their decision-making processes. Remaining excessively rigid leads to financing mistakes. Those mistakes will generate costs that are ultimately borne by the firm's stockholders.

CONCEPT CHECK

1. What distinguishes the internal capital market from the external capital market?
2. What important factor(s) might affect a firm's internal-external financing choice?

Objective 2

THE MIX OF CORPORATE SECURITIES SOLD IN THE CAPITAL MARKET

When corporations decide to raise cash in the capital market, what type of financing vehicle is most favored? Many individual investors think that common stock is the answer to this question. This is understandable, given the coverage of the level of common stock

[2] A lengthier discussion on the relationship of the internal capital market to the external capital market is found in M. Berlin, "Jack of All Trades? Product Diversification in Nonfinancial Firms," *Business Review*, Federal Reserve Bank of Philadelphia (May–June 1999), pp. 19, 23.

TABLE 14-2 Corporate Securities Offered for Cash—Nonfinancial Corporations, Three-Year Cash Weighted Average, 1999–2001

TOTAL VOLUME ($ MILLIONS)	PERCENT EQUITIES	PERCENT BONDS AND NOTES
$1,326,850	23.1	76.9

Source: *Federal Reserve Bulletin*, Table 1.46, February 2003, A29.

prices by the popular news media. All of the major television networks, for instance, quote the closing price of the Dow Jones Industrial Average on their nightly news broadcasts. Common stock, though, is not the financing method relied on most heavily by corporations. The answer to this question is *corporate bonds. The corporate debt markets clearly dominate the corporate equity markets when new funds are being raised.* This is a long-term relationship—it occurs year after year. Table 14-2 highlights this fact for the recent time period of 1999 to 2001.

In Table 14-2, we see the annual average volume (in millions of dollars) of corporate securities sold for cash over the 1999 to 2001 period. The percentage breakdown between equities (both common and preferred stocks) and bonds and notes (corporate debt) is also displayed. Notice that debt-type instruments represented a full 76.9 percent of the annual average dollar amount offered to investors by nonfinancial corporations over this three-year time frame. Equities, therefore, represented the other 23.1 percent. We learned from our discussions of the cost of capital and planning the firm's financing mix that the U.S. tax system inherently favors debt as a means of raising capital. Quite simply, interest expense is deductible from other income when computing the firm's federal tax liability, whereas the dividends paid on both preferred and common stock are not.

Financial executives responsible for raising corporate cash know this. When they have a choice between marketing new bonds and marketing new preferred stock, the outcome is usually in favor of bonds. The after-tax cost of capital on the debt is less than that incurred on preferred stock. Likewise, if the firm has unused debt capacity and the general level of equity prices is depressed, financial executives favor the issuance of debt securities over the issuance of new common stock.

CONCEPT CHECK

1. Why might firms prefer to issue new debt securities rather than new common stock?
2. How does the U.S. tax system affect a firm's financing choices?

WHY FINANCIAL MARKETS EXIST

Objective 3

Financial markets are institutions and procedures that facilitate transactions in all types of financial claims. The purchase of your home, the common stock you may own, and your life insurance policy all took place in some type of financial market. Why do financial markets exist? What would the economy lose if our complex system of financial markets were not developed? We will address these questions here.

Financial markets Those institutions and procedures that facilitate transactions in all types of financial claims (securities).

Some *economic units*, such as households, firms, or governments, spend more during a given period than they earn. Other economic units spend less on current consumption than they earn. For example, business firms in the aggregate usually spend more during a specific period than they earn. Households in the aggregate spend less on current consumption than they earn. As a result, some mechanism is needed to facilitate the transfer of savings from those economic units with a surplus to those with a deficit. That is precisely the function of financial markets. Financial markets exist in order to allocate the supply of savings in the economy to the demanders of those savings. The central characteristic of a financial market is that it acts as the vehicle through which the forces of demand and supply for a specific type of financial claim (such as a corporate bond) are brought together.

BACK TO THE PRINCIPLES

In this chapter, we cover material that introduces the financial manager to the process involved in raising funds in the nation's capital markets and also rely on the logic that lies behind the determination of interest rates and required rates of return in those capital markets.

We will see that the United States has a highly developed, complex, and competitive system of financial markets that allows for the quick transfer of savings from those economic units with a surplus of savings to those economic units with a savings deficit. Such a system of highly developed financial markets allows great ideas (such as the personal computer) to be financed and increases the overall wealth of the economy. Consider your wealth, for example, compared to that of the average family in Russia. Russia lacks a complex system of financial markets to facilitate transactions in financial claims (securities). As a result, real capital formation there has suffered.

Thus, we return now to ***Principle 6: Efficient Capital Markets—The markets are quick and the prices are right.*** *Financial managers like our system of capital markets because they trust it. This trust stems from the fact that the markets are "efficient." Managers trust prices in the securities markets because those prices quickly and accurately reflect all available information about the value of the underlying securities. This means that expected risks and expected cash flows matter more to market participants than do simpler things such as accounting changes and the sequence of past price changes in a specific security. With security prices and returns (such as interest rates) competitively determined, more financial managers (rather than fewer) participate in the markets and help ensure the basic concept of efficiency.*

Now, why would the economy suffer without a developed financial market system? The answer is that the wealth of the economy would be less without the financial markets. The rate of capital formation would not be as high if financial markets did not exist. This means that the net additions during a specific period to the stocks of (1) dwellings, (2) productive plant and equipment, (3) inventory, and (4) consumer durables would occur at lower rates. Figure 14-2 helps clarify the rationale behind this assertion. The abbreviated balance sheets in the figure refer to firms or any other type of economic units that operate in the private as opposed to governmental sectors of the economy. This means that such units cannot issue money to finance their own activities.

Real assets Tangible assets such as houses, equipment, and inventories.

Financial assets Claims for future payment by one economic unit on another.

At stage 1 in Figure 14-2, only real assets exist in the hypothetical economy. **Real assets** are tangible assets, such as houses, equipment, and inventories. They are distinguished from **financial assets**, which represent claims for future payment on other economic units. Common and preferred stocks, bonds, bills, and notes all are types of financial assets. If only real assets exist, then savings for a given economic unit, such as a firm, must be accumulated in the form of real assets. If the firm has a great idea for a new product, that new product can be developed, produced, and distributed only out of company savings (retained earnings). Furthermore, all investment in the new product must occur simultaneously as the savings are generated. If you have the idea, and we have the savings, there is no mechanism to transfer our savings to you. This is not a good situation.

FIGURE 14-2 Development of a Financial Market System

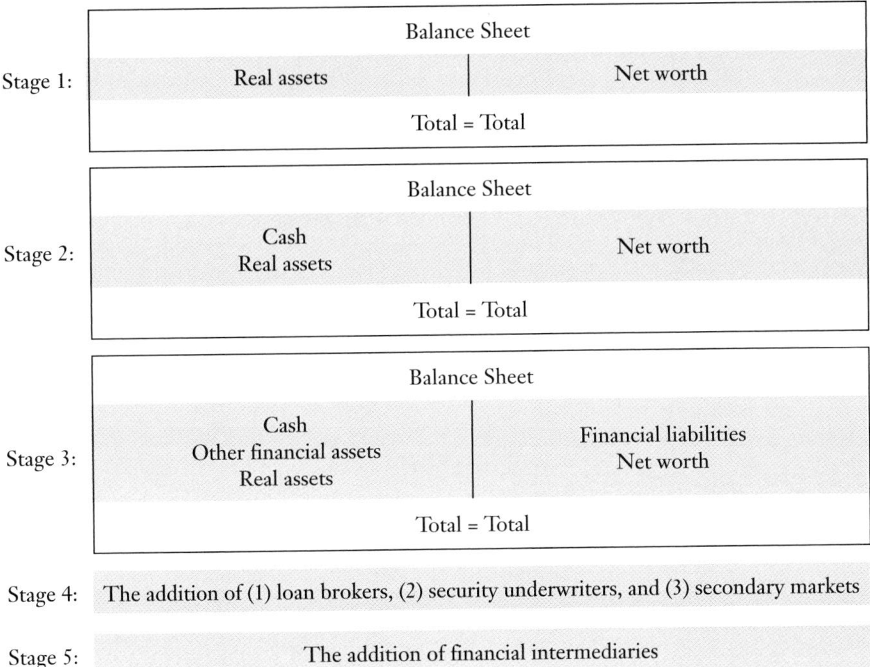

At stage 2, paper money (cash) comes into existence in the economy. Here, at least, you can *store* your own savings in the form of money.

Thus, you can finance your great idea by drawing down your cash balances. This is an improvement over stage 1, but there is still no effective mechanism to transfer our savings to you. You see, we will not just hand you our dollar bills. We will want a receipt.

The concept of a receipt that represents the transfer of savings from one economic unit to another is a monumental advancement. The economic unit with excess savings can lend the savings to an economic unit that needs them. To the lending unit, these receipts are identified as "other financial assets" in stage 3 of Figure 14-2. To the borrowing unit, the issuance of financial claims (receipts) shows up as "financial liabilities" on the stage 3 balance sheet. The economic unit with surplus savings will earn a rate of return on those funds. The borrowing unit will pay that rate of return, but it has been able to finance its great idea.

In stage 4, the financial market system moves further toward full development. Loan brokers come into existence. These brokers help locate pockets of excess savings and channel such savings to economic units needing the funds. Some economic units will actually purchase the financial claims of borrowing units and sell them at a higher price to other investors; this process is called **underwriting**. Underwriting is discussed in more detail later in this chapter. In addition, **secondary markets** develop. Secondary markets simply represent trading existing financial claims. If you buy your brother's General Motors common stock, you have made a secondary market transaction. Secondary markets reduce the risk of investing in financial claims. Should you need cash, you can liquidate your claims in the secondary market. This induces savers to invest in securities.

Underwriting
The purchase and subsequent resale of a new security issue. The risk of selling the new issue at a profitable price is assumed (underwritten) by an investment banker.

Secondary markets
Transactions in currently outstanding securities.

The progression toward a developed and complex system of financial markets ends with stage 5. Here, financial intermediaries come into existence. You can think of financial intermediaries as the major financial institutions with which you are used to dealing.

These include commercial banks, savings and loan associations, credit unions, life insurance companies, and mutual funds. Financial intermediaries share a common characteristic: They offer their own financial claims, called **indirect securities**, to economic units with excess savings. The proceeds from selling their indirect securities are then used to purchase the financial claims of other economic units. These latter claims can be called **direct securities**. Thus, a mutual fund might sell mutual fund shares (its indirect security) and purchase the common stocks (direct securities) of some major corporations. A life insurance company sells life insurance policies and purchases huge quantities of corporate bonds. Financial intermediaries thereby involve many small savers in the process of capital formation. This means there are more "good things" for everybody to buy.

Indirect securities The unique financial claims issued by financial intermediaries. Mutual fund shares are an example.

Direct securities The pure financial claims issued by economic units to savers. These can later be transformed into indirect securities.

A developed financial market system provides for a greater level of wealth in the economy. In the absence of financial markets, savings are not transferred to the economic units most in need of those funds. It is difficult, after all, for a household to build its own automobile. The financial market system makes it *easier* for the economy to build automobiles and all the other goods that economic units like to accumulate.

CONCEPT CHECK

1. What are financial markets?
2. Why will an economy suffer without a developed financial market system?
3. What distinguishes a real asset from a financial asset?
4. Can you distinguish between direct securities and indirect securities?

Objective 4

FINANCING OF BUSINESS: THE MOVEMENT OF FUNDS THROUGH THE ECONOMY

We now understand the crucial role that financial markets play in a capitalist economy. At this point, we will take a brief look at how funds flow across some selected sectors of the U.S. economy. In addition, we will focus a little more closely on the process of financial intermediation that was introduced in the preceding section. Some actual data are used to sharpen our knowledge of the financing process. We will see that financial institutions play a major role in bridging the gap between savers and borrowers in the economy. Nonfinancial corporations, we already know, are significant borrowers of financial capital.

THE FINANCING PROCESS

Table 14-3 shows how funds were supplied and raised by the major sectors of the U.S. economy over the five-year period from 1995 through 1999. The dollar amounts (in billions) are annual averages over those five years. We will specifically make comments on three of the five sectors identified in the table.

Households' net increase in financial liabilities exceeded their net increase in financial assets to the extent of $50.3 billion, as shown in the right-hand column of the table. In the jargon of economics, the household sector was a *savings-deficit* sector over this period.

This financing behavior was unusual because the household sector over long periods of time is typically a major *savings-surplus* sector. This means the household sector normally is a key net supplier of funds to the financial markets. Actually, and for example, over the six-year period of 1991 through 1996, the household sector supplied an

TABLE 14-3 Sector View of Flow of Funds in U.S. Financial Markets for 1995–1999

SECTOR	[1] FUNDS RAISED $ BILLIONS	[2] FUNDS SUPPLIED $ BILLIONS	[2] – [1] NET FUNDS SUPPLIED $ BILLIONS
Households[a]	447.4	397.1	–50.3
Nonfinancial corporate business	447.5	383.8	–63.7
U.S. government	73.9	62.9	–11.0
State and local governments	56.4	48.4	–8.0
Foreign	320.2	561.7	241.5

(Billions of Dollars, 5-Year Averages)

[a]Includes personal trusts and nonprofit organizations.

Source: *Flow of Funds Accounts, First Quarter 2000,* Flow of Funds Section, Statistical Release Z.1 (Washington, DC: Board of Governors of the Federal Reserve System, June 9, 2000).

annual average of $170.0 billion to the markets. Since 1991, the household sector has been a savings-surplus sector for all years except the recent three covering the period 1997 through 1999. So why were those three years any different? We can see and understand the difference merely by looking at data from 1999. Because of prevailing low interest rates in the U.S. credit markets, households took on a huge $411.0 billion in mortgages to finance home purchases. The result made the household sector a net user of financial capital in that year, and similar financing behavior was followed in the previous two years.

Notice that over the subject five years, as detailed in Table 14-3, the nonfinancial business sector was likewise a savings-deficit sector to the net extent of $63.7 billion on average for each year. This means nonfinancial firms, such as General Motors, raised $63.7 billion more in the financial markets than they supplied to the markets. While the nonfinancial business sector often is a savings-deficit sector, it can at times be a savings-surplus sector depending on aggregate economic conditions. The most important of those conditions is the level of corporate profitability.

Table 14-3 further highlights how important foreign financial investment is to the activity of the U.S. economy. On average, the foreign sector supplied a net $241.5 billion to the domestic capital markets for each year of the 1995 through 1999 period. Thus, it was a crucial *savings-surplus* sector. Back in 1982, the foreign sector raised—rather than supplied—$29.9 billion in the U.S. financial markets! This illustrates the dynamic nature of financial management and why financial-management practitioners have to be in tune with current business conditions. Actual capital-budgeting decisions, like those explored in earlier chapters, are made in the corporate board room—not within the rather sterile confines of an end-of-chapter problem.

We have seen here that the financial market system must exist to facilitate the orderly and efficient flow of savings from the surplus sectors to the deficit sectors of the economy. Over long periods, the nonfinancial business sector is typically dependent on the household sector to finance its investment needs. In addition, foreign financing plays an important role in the U.S. economy.

MOVEMENT OF SAVINGS

Figure 14-3 provides a useful way to summarize our discussion of (1) why financial markets exist and (2) the movement of funds through the economy. It also serves as an introduction to the role of the investment banker—a subject discussed in detail later in this chapter.

FIGURE 14-3 Three Ways to Transfer Financial Capital in the Economy

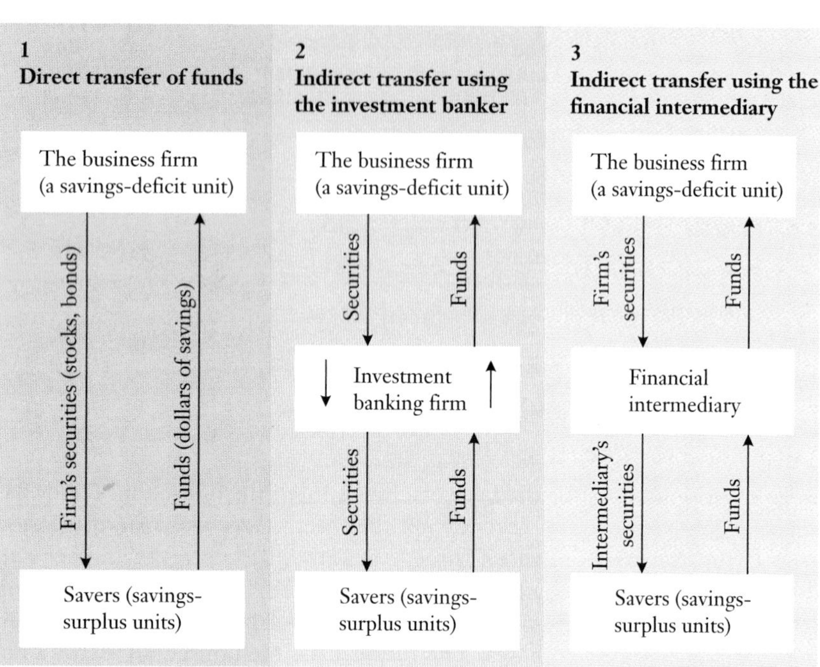

We see that savings are ultimately transferred to the business firm in need of cash in three ways:

1. **The direct transfer of funds.** Here the firm seeking cash sells its securities directly to savers (investors) who are willing to purchase them in hopes of earning a reasonable rate of return. New business formation is a good example of this process at work. The new business may go directly to a saver or group of savers called *venture capitalists.* The venture capitalists will lend funds to the firm or take an equity position in the firm if they feel the product or service the new firm hopes to market will be successful.
2. **Indirect transfer using the investment banker.** In a common arrangement under this system, the managing investment banking house will form a syndicate of several investment bankers. The syndicate will buy the entire issue of securities from the firm that is in need of financial capital. The syndicate will then sell the securities at a higher price to the investing public (the savers) than it paid for them. Merrill Lynch Capital Markets and Goldman Sachs are examples of investment banking firms. They tend to be called "houses" by those who work in the financial community. Notice that under this second method of transferring savings, the securities being issued just pass through the investment banking firm. They are not transformed into a different type of security.
3. **Indirect transfer using the financial intermediary.** This is the type of system life insurance companies and pension funds operate within. The financial intermediary collects the savings of individuals and issues its own (indirect) securities in exchange for these savings. The intermediary then uses the funds collected from the individual savers to acquire the business firm's (direct) securities, such as stocks and bonds.

We all benefit from the three transfer mechanisms displayed in Figure 14-3. Capital formation and economic wealth are greater than they would be in the absence of this financial market system.

CONCEPT CHECK

1. What is the difference between a savings-surplus sector and a savings-deficit sector? Give an example of each.
2. Why cannot all sectors be savings-deficit sectors?

COMPONENTS OF THE U.S. FINANCIAL MARKET SYSTEM

Objective 5

Numerous approaches exist for classifying the securities markets. At times, the array can be confusing. An examination of four sets of dichotomous terms can help provide a basic understanding of the structure of the U.S. financial markets.

PUBLIC OFFERINGS AND PRIVATE PLACEMENTS

When a corporation decides to raise external capital, those funds can be obtained by making a public offering or a private placement. In a **public offering**, both individual and institutional investors have the opportunity to purchase the securities. The securities are usually made available to the public at large by a managing investment banking firm and its underwriting (risk-taking) syndicate. The firm does not meet the ultimate purchasers of the securities in the public offering. The public market is an impersonal market.

Public offering
A security offering where all investors have the opportunity to acquire a portion of the financial claims being sold.

In a **private placement**, also called a **direct placement**, the securities are offered and sold to a limited number of investors. The firm will usually hammer out, on a face-to-face basis with the prospective buyers, the details of the offering. In this setting, the investment banking firm may act as a finder by bringing together potential lenders and borrowers. The private placement market is a more personal market than its public counterpart. We will now relate the private placement market to the need by firms for venture capital.

Private placement (direct placement)
A security offering limited to a small number of potential investors.

THE PRIVATE PLACEMENT MARKET AND VENTURE CAPITAL Private placements can be separated logically into two forms: (1) the organized private equity market and (2) the organized private debt market. Both of these markets are actively participated in by venture capitalists. Because issuing public equity or debt is not workable for new, small, or even most medium-sized firms, these younger business units seek out the financial capital of firms that specialize in rather risky company investments—the so-called venture capitalists.

The unseasoned firm finds that its need for financial capital is not appealing to the broader public markets owing to: (1) small absolute size, (2) a very limited or no historical track record of operating results, and (3) obscure growth prospects.[3] Thus, the venture capitalist who is willing to accept such risks jumps into these more cloudy markets in hopes of a greater return (reward). This economic logic should remind you of **Principle 1: The Risk-Return Trade-Off—We won't take on additional risk unless we expect to be compensated with additional return.**

On the equity investment side, the venture capitalist firm will frequently acquire a meaningful dollar stake in the start-up firm. In exchange for this risk-taking, the venture capital firm will occupy a seat or seats on the young firm's board of directors and will take an active part in monitoring management activities, strategies, and

[3] A useful discussion on financing challenges to younger firms is provided by Stephen Prowse, "Equity Capital and Entrepreneurs," in *Equity for Rural America: From Wall Street to Main Street*, Federal Reserve Bank of Kansas City, August 1999, pp. 10–26.

TABLE 14-4 Why Major Companies Participate in the Organized Private Equity Market

QUESTION

If you have made equity investments in other companies during the previous year, what were your objectives?

RESPONSES	PERCENT
1. Capital appreciation	34.2
2. Strategic alliance	76.3
3. An alternative/precursor to outright acquisition	15.8
4. To outsource research and development	21.1
5. To boost exposure to the Internet/technology	23.7
6. To acquire a minority stake as part of a separate acquisition or as consideration in another deal	10.5

capital-budgeting decisions. Other private equity investors with less financial capital committed to the venture will be given "observational rights" (as distinct from voting rights) at regular meetings of the board. This tendency reminds you of **Principle 7: The Agency Problem—Managers won't work for owners unless it's in their best interest.**

The private equity market is not the sole province of pure venture capital firms. Numerous established and well-known companies such as Microsoft, Intel, and Xerox have for years taken "minority investment positions" in emerging corporations or have created their own separate venture capital subsidiaries. The subsidiary approach has two major benefits to the seasoned company: (1) An incentive is created for human capital to remain with the firm, and (2) great ideas are retained as intellectual capital rather than departing as the basis for a start-up operation.

The other side of the subsidiary approach is for the seasoned company to acquire a minority equity interest in an emerging firm. This choice allows the established corporation to use the private equity market and gain access to new technology by investing directly in start-up organizations rather than taking the risks associated with internal research and development.

Along these lines, a survey of 1,600 Chief Financial Officers published in August 2000 reported that a whopping 76.3 percent of the responding CFOs said that the main objective of taking an equity position in another firm was to create some form of a strategic alliance.[4] Other reasons for participating in the private equity market through minority investments are displayed in Table 14-4.

So we see that investment in young firms does not just come from venture capital companies; numerous established corporations use the private equity market to help fund start-up firms.

In recent years, the dollar volume of financing activity in the private equity market has benefited enormously from the rapid growth of the venture capital industry. We know that the U.S. economy emerged from the ninth recession since the end of World War II during March 1991. Table 14-5 displays the peaks and troughs of the last 10 U.S. business cycles. That roughly dates the beginning of the hot growth pattern of pure (dedicated) U.S. venture capital firms.[5]

[4] CFO Forum, "The New R&D: Corporations Are Making More Minority Investments in Strategic Partners," *Institutional Investor*, August 2000, p. 34.

[5] Additional information and data on venture capital are available from the National Venture Capital Association and Venture Economics. Their Internet sites are *www.nvca.org* and *www.ventureeconomics.com*, respectively.

TABLE 14-5 Post-World War II U.S. Business Cycle Contractions

START OF RECESSION (PEAKS)	END (TROUGHS)	LENGTH (MONTHS)
November 1948	October 1949	11
July 1953	May 1954	10
August 1957	April 1958	8
April 1960	February 1961	10
December 1969	November 1970	11
November 1973	March 1975	16
January 1980	July 1980	6
July 1981	November 1982	16
July 1990	March 1991	8
March 2001	Not yet dated	–

Source: National Bureau of Economic Research. See www.nber.org.cycles.html. Reprinted by permission of The National Bureau of Economic Research.

Notice in Figure 14-4 that U.S.-based venture capital companies had $250.0 billion of financial capital under management at the end of 2001. Also observe that, back in 1992, the amount under management was a significantly lesser $29.4 billion. Uninterrupted domestic economic growth provides a stable environment for venture capital activities, whether it be on the investment side by the venture capital fund, or on the operations side by the start-up firm with the great idea that needs financing.

But, when domestic growth slows, *additional* investments by venture capital firms also abate. A glance at Figure 14-5 in conjunction with Table 14-5 bears this out. As Table 14-5 shows, the tenth post-World War II recession began in March 2001. As recently as June 18, 2003, the end of this downturn had not been "dated" by the National Bureau of Economic Research (NBER). The NBER has an official group known as the "Business Cycle Dating Committee" that puts the fine points on the

FIGURE 14-4 Venture Capital Under Management

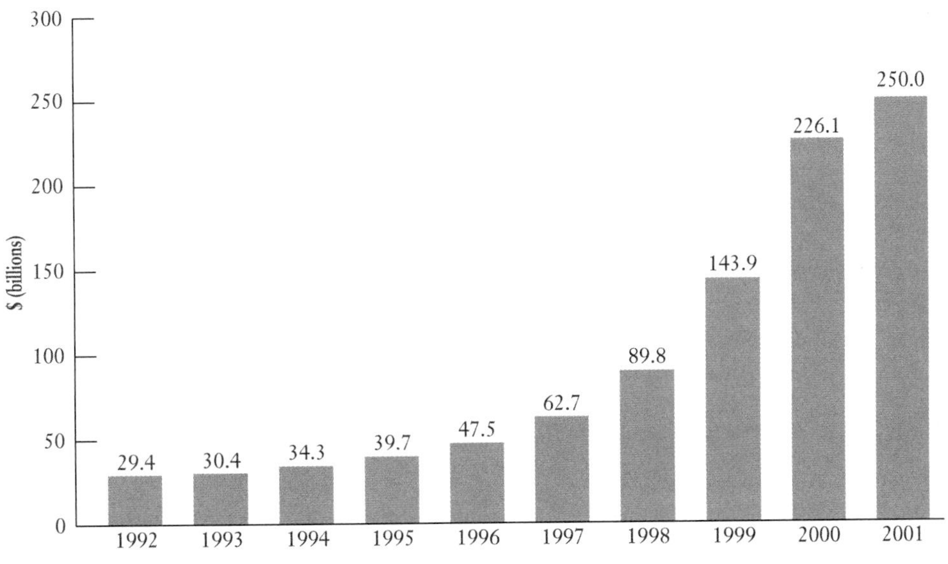

Source: *National Venture Capital Association, 2002 Yearbook*, p.17.

FIGURE 14-5 Changes in Financial Capital under Management from Previous Year ($ Billions)

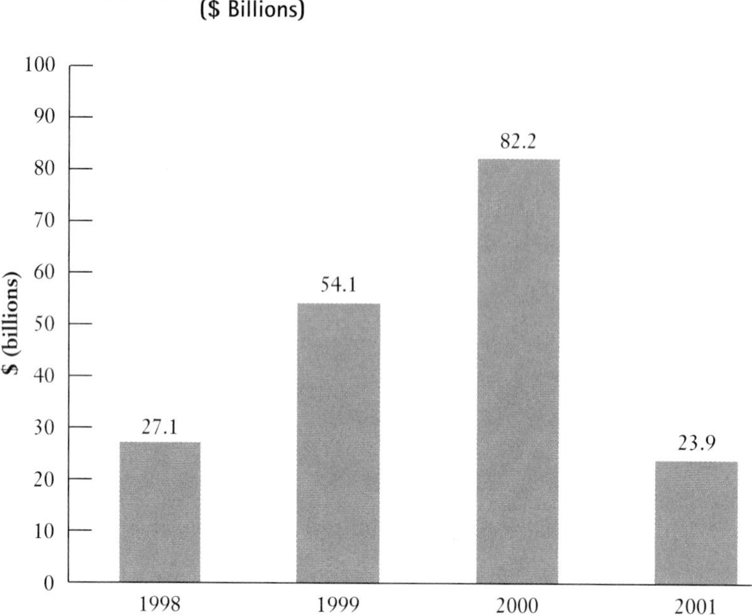

Source: Raw data from *National Venture Capital Association 2002 Yearbook*, p. 17. Calculations by author.

peaks and troughs of the U.S. business cycle.[6] There is a group with which you want to go to Friday evening "happy hour."

We see from Figure 14-5 that the propensity of venture capital firms to commit new funds to projects (such as firms in their portfolios) slowed drastically in 2001—the year the last recession officially began. Specifically, only $23.9 billion of additional financial capital was committed to management in 2001 versus a much more robust $82.2 billion in the previous year of 2000. The financial executive in the venture capital industry is directly impacted by the stage of the U.S. business cycle. The private equity market will rebound as the U.S. economy rebounds.[7] See the An Entrepreneur's Perspective box, "Financing the Deal: The Venture Capitalist's Approach."

Primary Markets and Secondary Markets

Primary markets Transactions in securities offered for the first time to potential investors.

Primary markets are those in which securities are offered for the *first* time to potential investors. A new issue of common stock by AT&T is a primary market transaction. This type of transaction increases the total stock of financial assets outstanding in the economy.

As mentioned in our discussion of the development of the financial market system, *secondary markets* represent transactions in currently outstanding securities. If the first buyer of the AT&T stock subsequently sells it, he or she does so in the secondary market. All transactions after the initial purchase take place in the secondary market. The sales do *not* affect the total stock of financial assets that exist in the economy. Both the money market and the capital market, described next, have primary and secondary sides.

[6] On June 18, 2003, concerning the recession that commenced in March 2001, the NBER said: "According to the most recent data, the U.S. economy continues to experience growth in income and output but employment continues to decline. Because of the divergent behavior of various indicators, the NBER's Business Cycle Dating Committee believes that additional time is needed before interpreting the movements of the economy over the past two years." See www.nber.org/cycles/recessions.pdf.

[7] A short and useful volume published by the American Enterprise Institute provides a quick introduction to venture capital funds and the private equity market. See C. Beltz, ed. *Financing Entrepreneurs* (Washington, D.C.: AEI Press, 1994).

AN ENTREPRENEUR'S PERSPECTIVE

FINANCING THE DEAL: THE VENTURE CAPITALIST'S APPROACH

High-potential ventures typically grow at rates that cannot be financed by the entrepreneur alone. At some point, outside money must be brought in to help finance the firm. At that time, the entrepreneur enters the "private equity markets" for money, which for early stage capital may come from formal venture capital or business angels.

If a prospective investor comes to believe a venture is a good opportunity, then the negotiation process begins. The primary concern becomes how the two parties—the investor and the entrepreneur—will share the future cash flows, *if they occur*, and how they will share the risk of the venture. Each party, of course, wants to receive more of the cash (i.e., have a larger percentage ownership of the firm) and to assume less of the risk. A good deal is one where both parties feel good about how the cash and risk are to be shared—a win-win deal.

The investor's ownership share in a firm and the eventual cash flows that hopefully will be received are driven by an investor's required rate of return. The investor's required rate of return is affected by several factors: (1) the attractiveness or quality of the investment, (2) how the financing is structured, and (3) the stage of the investment. If an investment is particularly attractive, an investor is willing to accept a lower ownership percentage in the company for a given amount of investment. Secondly, we can structure the financing in ways that either increase or decrease the investor's risk exposure—and in turn affect the required rate of return. Finally, the stage of the investment drives the investor's required rate of return.

The investor's target internal rates of return (*IRRs*) for high-risk, high-potential ventures can be quite high. For instance, to invest in a start-up firm, investors might use a 75 percent target rate of return, or for a first stage firm, the target might be a 50 percent rate of return. However, investors know that it is totally unlikely that the investor will receive such high returns from all the investments, as some of the investments will be total losers. Thus, some of the other investments must produce really high returns in order to provide 25 to 30 percent rates of returns on the overall portfolio.

Valuing and Structuring the Deal: An Illustration

To illustrate the process of valuing and structuring a deal, consider an example of a firm, Bear, Inc., that you started last year. At that time, you invested $1 million. Wanting to take the firm to the next level, you have approached a venture capitalist about making an additional $2 million investment in the company.

The investor believes the opportunity is a good one and wants to own common equity in the company; thus, the question becomes what percentage of the stock will you own and how much will the investor own?

Given that Bear, Inc., is seeking first-stage financing, we expect the investor to have a required rate of return (discount rate) of 50 percent. For this rate of return and assuming that the investment will be for five years, the investor would need to receive $15,187,500 when exiting the investment, computed as follows on a spreadsheet:

Investor's required rate of return	50%
Number of years (periods)	5
Annual dividends (payments)	0
Investment amount (present value)	$(2,000,000)
Solve for the investor's future value needed to earn a 50% rate of return	$15,187,500

Payments are zero because the investor will not receive any annual dividends.

What is the likelihood that the investor will receive the $15.2 million in five years? Well, it depends on the value of the firm as a whole at the end of the five years. If the firm has significant value, then the investor will receive a portion of that value. If it does not, then there will be little or no value to "harvest."

Let's assume that if all goes as planned—which it never does—the company's total stockholder value will be $35 million in five years. The venture capitalist needs to receive $15,187,500 at that time in order to earn a 50 percent rate of return. Thus, the venture capitalist would need to own 43.39 percent of the firm's stock, computed as follows:

$$\text{venture capitalist's ownership percentage} = \frac{\text{venture capitalist's equity value}}{\text{firm's equity value}}$$

$$= \frac{\$15{,}187{,}500}{\$35{,}000{,}000} = 43.39\%$$

Consequently, as the founder, you would own the remaining 56.61 percent of the common stock (56.61% = 100% – 43.39%), which would entitle you to $19,812,500, the portion of the $35 million that remains after the venture capitalist is paid.

As the owner, you might think that the venture capitalist is being greedy to expect to take 43 percent of *your* company. Who does he think he is? So you "shop the deal" with other venture capitalists, and behold, you find out that they are "greedy" as well. You might try to "bootstrap" the financing by borrowing against your house or whatever it takes to get some of the needed money and then figure out ways to get by on less. But before you do, at least know what rate of return you will earn if the opportunity performs as projected. You invested $1 million one year ago, which means that you will have invested for six years by the time the venture capitalist will have

(continued)

FINANCING THE DEAL: THE VENTURE CAPITALIST'S APPROACH (CONTINUED)

invested for five years. Given that you expect to receive $19,812,500 in value five years from now (six years since you made the investment), your rate of return would be 64 percent, calculated as follows:

Number of years (periods)	6
Annual interest/dividends (payments)	–
Your original investment (present value)	$(1,000,000)
Total future firm value	$35,000,000
Venture capitalist's future equity value	15,187,500
Your future equity value	$19,812,500
Your rate of return	64%
(Note: to 3 decimals this IRR = 64.496%)	

This return is not bad, but you still may think that you should receive an even better return; after all, this was your idea and you have shed a lot of blood, sweat, and tears. However, you realize that you cannot capture the opportunity without the additional capital. Thus, you need to see if the financing can be structured in a way that the investor will accept a lower rate of return, which usually occurs by the owner assuming more of the risk. This is when the real negotiations begin.

Money Market and Capital Market

Money market All institutions and procedures that facilitate transactions in short-term credit instruments.

Capital market All institutions and procedures that facilitate transactions in long-term financial instruments.

The key distinguishing feature between the money and capital markets is the maturity period of the securities traded in them. The **money market** refers to all institutions and procedures that provide for transactions in short-term debt instruments generally issued by borrowers with very high credit ratings. By financial convention, *short-term* means maturity periods of one year or less. Notice that equity instruments, either common or preferred, are not traded in the money market. The major instruments issued and traded are U.S. Treasury bills, various federal agency securities, bankers' acceptances, negotiable certificates of deposit, and commercial paper. Keep in mind that the money market is an intangible market. You do not walk into a building on Wall Street that has the words "Money Market" etched in stone over its arches. Rather, the money market is primarily a telephone and computer market.

The **capital market** refers to all institutions and procedures that provide for transactions in long-term financial instruments. *Long-term* here means having maturity periods that extend beyond one year. In the broad sense, this encompasses term loans and financial leases, corporate equities, and bonds. The funds that comprise the firm's capital structure are raised in the capital market. Important elements of the capital market are the organized security exchanges and the over-the-counter markets.

Organized Security Exchanges and Over-the-Counter Markets

Organized security exchanges Formal organizations involved in the trading of securities. They are tangible entities that conduct auction markets in listing securities.

Over-the-counter markets All security markets except the organized exchanges.

Organized security exchanges are tangible entities; they physically occupy space (such as a building or part of a building), and financial instruments are traded on their premises. The **over-the-counter markets** include all security markets *except* the organized exchanges. The money market, then, is an over-the-counter market. Because both markets are important to financial officers concerned with raising *long-term capital*, some additional discussion is warranted.

Organized Security Exchanges

For practical purposes there are seven major security exchanges in the United States. These are the (1) New York Stock Exchange, (2) American Stock Exchange, (3) Chicago Stock Exchange, (4) Pacific Stock Exchange, (5) Philadelphia Stock Exchange, (6) Boston

Stock Exchange, and (7) Cincinnati Stock Exchange. The New York Stock Exchange (NYSE) and the American Stock Exchange (AMEX) are called *national* exchanges, whereas the others are loosely described as *regionals*. All of these seven active exchanges are registered with the Securities and Exchange Commission (SEC). Firms whose securities are traded on the registered exchanges must comply with reporting requirements of both the specific exchange and the SEC.

An example of the prominent stature of the NYSE is provided by the sheer number of companies that have stocks listed on this exchange. In 2001, the NYSE handled such listings from 2,798 firms—up from 1,885 some 10 years earlier. This represented a 48.4 percent absolute increase in the number of firms listed over this period. Even though the NASDAQ, soon to be discussed, has surpassed the NYSE in trading volume, the NYSE remains the preeminent exchange in the United States. The collapse in market value of numerous high-tech and "dot.com" firms during the years of 2000 to 2001 just reinforced the importance of the NYSE to the general credibility of the U.S. financial market system. The total market value of shares listed on the NYSE in 2001 amounted to $11.71 trillion, up from $3.71 trillion in 1991.[8] As a point of comparison, the nominal value of gross domestic product for the United States as of the 2001 fourth quarter was $10.22 trillion.[9]

The business of an exchange, including securities transactions, is conducted by its *members*. Members are said to occupy "seats." There are 1,366 seats on the NYSE, a number that has remained constant since 1953. Major brokerage firms own seats on the exchanges. An officer of the firm is designated to be the member of the exchange, and this membership permits the brokerage house to use the facilities of the exchange to effect trades. During 2002, the prices of seats that were exchanged for cash ranged from a low of $2.0 million to a high of $2.55 million.[10] The high price in 1999 of $2.65 million was an all-time high.

STOCK EXCHANGE BENEFITS Both corporations and investors enjoy several benefits provided by the existence of organized security exchanges. These include

1. **Providing a continuous market.** This may be the most important function of an organized security exchange. A continuous market provides a series of continuous security prices. Price changes from trade to trade tend to be smaller than they would be in the absence of organized markets. The reasons are that there is a relatively large sales volume in each security, trading orders are executed quickly, and the range between the price asked for a security and the offered price tends to be narrow. The result is that price volatility is reduced.
2. **Establishing and publicizing fair security prices.** An organized exchange permits security prices to be set by competitive forces. They are not set by negotiations off the floor of the exchange, where one party might have a bargaining advantage. The bidding process flows from the supply and demand underlying each security. This means the specific price of a security is determined in the manner of an auction. In addition, the security prices determined at each exchange are widely publicized.
3. **Helping business raise new capital.** Because a continuous secondary market exists where prices are competitively determined, it is easier for firms to float new security offerings successfully. This continuous pricing mechanism also facilitates the determination of the offering price of a new issue. This means that comparative values are easily observed.

[8] New York Stock Exchange, *Fact Book for the year 2001* (New York, April 2002), p. 105.

[9] U.S. Department of Commerce, Bureau of Economic Analysis, January 30, 2002, *Gross Domestic Product: Fourth Quarter 2001* (Advance), Table 3.

[10] New York Stock Exchange, *2002 Fact Book* Online (New York, 2003), www.nysedata.com/factbook.

TABLE 14-6 A Sample of NYSE Listing Requirements for Domestic (U.S.) Companies

PROFITABILITY (EARNINGS)
Earnings before taxes (EBT) for the most recent year must be at least $2.5 million. For the two years preceding that, EBT must be at least $2.0 million.
MARKET VALUE
The market value of publicly held stock must be at least $100.0 million. For initial public offerings (IPOs), the value must be at least $60.0 million.
PUBLIC OWNERSHIP (DISTRIBUTION CRITERIA)
There must be at least 1.1 million publicly held common shares. There must be at least 2,000 holders of 100 shares or more.

Source: New York Stock Exchange, *2002 Fact Book* Online (New York, 2003), www.nysedata.com/factbook.

LISTING REQUIREMENTS To receive the benefits provided by an organized exchange, the firm must seek to have its securities listed on the exchange. An application for listing must be filed and a fee paid. The requirements for listing vary from exchange to exchange; those of the NYSE are the most stringent. The general criteria for listing fall into these categories: (1) profitability, (2) size, (3) market value, and (4) public ownership. To give you the flavor of an actual set of listing requirements, a selected sample of those set forth by the NYSE are displayed in Table 14-6.

Over-the-Counter Markets

Many publicly held firms do not meet the listing requirements of major stock exchanges. Others may want to avoid the reporting requirements and fees required to maintain a listing. As an alternative, their securities may trade in the over-the-counter markets. On the basis of sheer numbers (not dollar volume), more stocks are traded over-the-counter than on organized exchanges. As far as secondary trading in corporate bonds is concerned, the over-the-counter markets are where the action is. In a typical year, more than 90 percent of corporate bond business takes place over-the-counter.

Most over-the-counter transactions are done through a loose network of security traders who are known as broker-dealers and brokers. Brokers do not purchase securities for their own account, whereas dealers do. Broker-dealers stand ready to buy and sell specific securities at selected prices. They are said to "make a market" in those securities. Their profit is the spread or difference between the price they will pay for a security (bid price) and the price at which they will sell the security (asked price).

A fine source of up-to-the-minute price quotes for securities listed or traded on the NASDAQ, AMEX, or NYSE is provided at the Nasdaq Stock Market's Web site. Go to **www.nasdaq.com**. Price and volume data for certain indices like that of the NASDAQ and the Dow Jones Industrial Average are continuously displayed.

PRICE QUOTES AND THE NASDAQ The availability of prices is not as continuous in the over-the-counter market as it is on an organized exchange. Since February 8, 1971, however, when a computerized network called NASDAQ came into existence, the availability of prices in this market has improved substantially. NASDAQ stands for National Association of Security Dealers Automated Quotation System. It is a telecommunications system that provides a national information link among the brokers and dealers operating in the over-the-counter markets. Subscribing traders have a terminal that allows them to obtain representative bids and ask prices for thousands of securities traded over-the-counter. NASDAQ is a quotation system, not a transactions system. The final trade is still consummated by direct negotiation between traders.

The NASDAQ system has become an increasingly important element of the U.S. financial market system in recent years. It provides a nationwide communications element that was lacking in the over-the-counter side of the securities markets.

The Nasdaq Stock Market, Inc., describes itself as a "screen-based, floorless market." It now is actually home to the securities of more companies than the NYSE; in 2002 some 3,600 public companies had securities traded by means of the NASDAQ system. It has become highly popular as the trading mechanism of choice of several fast-growth sectors in the United States, including the high-technology sector. The common stock of computer chip maker Intel Corporation, for example, is traded via the NASDAQ as is that of Dell and Starbucks.[11]

NASDAQ price quotes for many stocks are published daily in *The Wall Street Journal*. This same financial newspaper also publishes prices on hundreds of other stocks traded over-the-counter. Local papers supply prices on stocks of regional interest.

CONCEPT CHECK

1. What are the differences between (a) public offerings and private placements, (b) primary markets and secondary markets, (c) the money market and the capital market, and (d) tangible-organized security exchanges and over-the-counter markets?
2. What benefits are derived from the existence of stock exchanges?
3. Briefly describe what is meant by the "NASDAQ system."

THE INVESTMENT BANKER

Objective 6

We touched briefly on the investment banking industry and the investment banker earlier in this chapter when we described various methods for transferring financial capital (see Figure 14-3). The investment banker is to be distinguished from the commercial banker in that the former's organization is not a permanent depository for funds. For the moment, it is important for you to learn about the role of the investment banker in the funding of commercial activity because of the importance of this institution within the financial market system.

Most corporations do not frequently raise long-term capital. The activities of working-capital management go on daily, but attracting long-term capital is, by comparison, episodic. The sums involved can be huge, so these situations are considered of great importance to financial managers. Because most managers are unfamiliar with the subtleties of raising long-term funds, they enlist the help of an expert. That expert is an investment banker.

DEFINITION

The **investment banker** is a financial specialist involved as an intermediary in the merchandising of securities. He or she acts as a "middle person" by facilitating the flow of savings from those economic units that want to invest to those units that want to raise funds. We use the term *investment banker* to refer both to a given individual and to the organization for which such a person works, variously known as an *investment banking firm* or an *investment banking house*. Although these firms are called investment bankers, they perform no depository or lending functions. The activities of commercial banking and investment banking as we know them today were separated by the Banking Act of 1933 (also known as the Glass-Steagall Act of 1933). Then, after considerable political debate, the Financial Modernization Act was passed by the U.S. Congress on November 12, 1999. This recent legislation is also referred to as the Gramm-Leach-Bliley Act of 1999, in honor of its congressional sponsors. The act actually repealed significant portions of the Depression-era

Investment banker A financial specialist who underwrites and distributes new securities and advises corporate clients about raising external financial capital.

[11] See www.nasdaq.com/investorrelations/ar2002/pdf/NDQ_AR_2002_complete.pdf.

Glass-Steagall Act and is aimed at increasing competitiveness among modern financial services companies. Through the creation of operating subsidiaries, the act provides for business combinations among banks, underwriters of financial securities (investment bankers), insurance firms, and securities brokers. Here we focus on investment banking and its important middleman role. That is most easily understood in terms of the basic functions of investment banking.

Functions

The investment banker performs three basic functions: (1) underwriting, (2) distributing, and (3) advising.

UNDERWRITING The term *underwriting* is borrowed from the field of insurance. It means "assuming a risk." The investment banker assumes the risk of selling a security issue at a satisfactory price. A satisfactory price is one that will generate a profit for the investment banking house.

Syndicate
A group of investment bankers who contractually assist in the buying of a new security issue.

The procedure goes like this. The managing investment banker and its syndicate will buy the security issue from the corporation in need of funds. The **syndicate** is a group of other investment bankers who are invited to help buy and resell the issue. The managing house is the investment banking firm that originated the business because its corporate client decided to raise external funds. On a specific day, the firm that is raising capital is presented with a check (cash) in exchange for the securities being issued. At this point, the investment banking syndicate owns the securities. The corporation has its cash and can proceed to use it. The firm is now immune from the possibility that the security markets might turn sour. If the price of the newly issued security falls below that paid to the firm by the syndicate, the syndicate will suffer a loss. The syndicate, of course, hopes that the opposite situation will result. Its objective is to sell the new issue to the investing public at a price per security greater than its cost.

DISTRIBUTING Once the syndicate owns the new securities, it must get them into the hands of the ultimate investors. This is the distribution or selling function of investment banking. The investment banker may have branch offices across the United States, or it may have an informal arrangement with several security dealers who regularly buy a portion of each new offering for final sale. It is not unusual to have 300 to 400 dealers involved in the selling effort. The syndicate can properly be viewed as the security wholesaler, and the dealer organization can be viewed as the security retailer.

ADVISING The investment banker is an expert in the issuance and marketing of securities. A sound investment banking house will be aware of prevailing market conditions and can relate those conditions to the particular type of security that should be sold at a given time. Business conditions may be pointing to a future increase in interest rates. The investment banker might advise the firm to issue its bonds in a timely fashion to avoid the higher yields that are forthcoming. The banker can analyze the firm's capital structure and make recommendations as to what general source of capital should be issued. In many instances, the firm will invite its investment banker to sit on the board of directors. This permits the banker to observe corporate activity and make recommendations on a regular basis.

Distribution Methods

Several methods are available to the corporation for placing new security offerings in the hands of final investors. The investment banker's role is different in each of these. Sometimes, in fact, it is possible to bypass the investment banker. These methods are described in this section. Private placements, because of their importance, are treated separately later in the chapter.

NEGOTIATED PURCHASE In a negotiated underwriting, the firm that needs funds makes contact with an investment banker, and deliberations concerning the new issue begin. If all goes well, a *method* is negotiated for determining the price the investment banker and the syndicate will pay for the securities. For example, the agreement might state that the syndicate will pay $2 less than the closing price of the firm's common stock on the day before the offering date of a new stock issue. The negotiated purchase is the most prevalent method of securities distribution in the private sector. It is generally thought to be the most profitable technique as far as investment bankers are concerned.

COMPETITIVE BID PURCHASE The method by which the underwriting group is determined distinguishes the competitive bid purchase from the negotiated purchase. In a competitive underwriting, several underwriting groups bid for the right to purchase the new issue from the corporation that is raising funds. The firm does not directly select the investment banker. The investment banker that underwrites and distributes the issue is chosen by an auction process. The syndicate willing to pay the greatest dollar amount per new security will win the competitive bid.

Most competitive bid purchases are confined to three situations, compelled by legal regulations: (1) railroad issues, (2) public utility issues, and (3) state and municipal bond issues. The argument in favor of competitive bids is that any undue influence of the investment banker over the firm is mitigated and the price received by the firm for each security should be higher. Thus, we would intuitively suspect that the cost of capital in a competitive bid situation would be less than in a negotiated purchase situation. Evidence on this question, however, is mixed. One problem with the competitive bid purchase as far as the fundraising firm is concerned is that the benefits gained from the advisory function of the investment banker are lost. It may be necessary to use an investment banker for advisory purposes and then by law exclude that same banker from the competitive bid process.

COMMISSION OR BEST-EFFORTS BASIS Here, the investment banker acts as an agent rather than as a principal in the distribution process. The securities are *not* underwritten. The investment banker attempts to sell the issue in return for a fixed commission on each security actually sold. Unsold securities are returned to the corporation. This arrangement is typically used for more speculative issues. The issuing firm may be smaller or less established than the investment banker would like. Because the underwriting risk is not passed on to the investment banker, this distribution method is less costly to the issuer than a negotiated or competitive bid purchase. However, the investment banker only has to give it his or her "best effort." A successful sale is not guaranteed.

PRIVILEGED SUBSCRIPTION Occasionally, the firm may feel that a distinct market already exists for its new securities. When a new issue is marketed to a definite and select group of investors, it is called a **privileged subscription**. Three target markets are typically involved: (1) current stockholders, (2) employees, or (3) customers. Of these, distributions directed at current stockholders are the most prevalent. Such offerings are called *rights offerings*. In a privileged subscription, the investment banker may act only as a selling agent. It is also possible that the issuing firm and the investment banker might sign a *standby agreement*, which would obligate the investment banker to underwrite the securities that are not accepted by the privileged in·estors.

Privileged subscription
The process of marketing a new security issue to a select group of investors.

DIRECT SALE In a **direct sale**, the issuing firm sells the securities directly to the investing public without involving an investment banker. Even among established corporate giants, this procedure is relatively rare. A variation of the direct sale, though, was used more frequently in the 1970s than in previous decades. This involves the private placement of a new issue by the fundraising corporation *without* use of an investment banker as an intermediary. Texaco, Mobil Oil (prior to its merger with Exxon), and

Direct sale
The sale of securities by the corporation to the investing public without the services of an investment banking firm.

TABLE 14-7 Leading U.S. Investment Bankers, 2002
Global Stocks and Bonds

FIRM	PROCEEDS (BILLIONS OF DOLLARS)	PERCENT OF MARKET
Citigroup/Salomon Smith Barney	$414.9	10.6%
Merrill Lynch	316.8	8.1
Credit Suisse First Boston	309.4	7.9
Morgan Stanley	286.4	7.3
J.P. Morgan Chase	286.1	7.3
Lehman Brothers	269.6	6.9
UBS Warburg	248.2	6.4
Goldman Sachs	232.5	6.0
Deutsche Bank AG	231.6	5.9
Banc of America Securities	164.6	4.2

Source: *Wall Street Journal*. Eastern Edition (Staff produced copy only). Copyright © 2003 by Dow Jones & Company, Inc. Reproduced with permission of Dow Jones & Company, Inc. in the format Textbook via Copyright Clearance Center.

International Harvester (now Navistar) are examples of large firms that have followed this procedure.

INDUSTRY LEADERS All industries have their leaders, and investment banking is no exception. We have discussed investment bankers at some length in this chapter. Table 14-7 gives us some idea who the major players are within the investment banking industry. It lists the top 10 houses in 2002 based on the dollar volume of security issues that were managed. Notice in the table that the U.S. investment banking industry is a highly concentrated one. The top five bankers with regard to underwriting volume during 2002 accounted for a full 41.2 percent of the total market. This degree of concentration is pervasive over time.

BEST PRACTICES

SELECTION CRITERIA FOR AN INVESTMENT BANKER

Dr. David R. Klock is CEO and Chairman of the Board of Directors of CompBenefits Corporation, headquartered in Atlanta, Georgia. Dr. Klock holds a Ph.D. in Finance from the University of Illinois and is a nationally known insurance economist. The firm, CompBenefits, is a privately held national leader in providing a wide range of dental and vision insurance products. The firm's annual revenues are in the vicinity of $285 million annually. The firm continually works with venture capitalists who provide equity capital and access to debt capital in the nation's financial market system. Dr. Klock authored the checklist below that deals with selecting an investment banker within the context of seeking what are called "strategic buyers" by venture capital firms. Dr. Klock is highly familiar with the field, having spent time at the investment banking firm of Goldman Sachs earlier in his career.

I. Competency

- Technical skills/resources of total team
- People skills/resources of total team
- Knowledge of the firm
- Knowledge of key potential buyers and their needs/ability to pay

II. Connections

- Recent firm history of working with potential buyers
- Individual banker's recent history of working with key potential buyers
- Reputation of investment banking firm with potential buyers
- Intangibles

III. Conviction on Enterprise Value of the Firm

- Valuation range and strength of valuation methods/matrix
- Ability to strongly tell firm's story and to be heard/understood by key individuals at potential buyers
- Level of commitment to this transaction within the banking firm

CONCEPT CHECK

1. What is the main difference between an investment banker and a commercial banker?
2. What are the three major functions that an investment banker performs?
3. What are the five key methods by which securities are distributed to final investors?

MORE ON PRIVATE PLACEMENTS: THE DEBT SIDE

Objective 7

Earlier in this chapter we discussed the private placement market and its important relationship to the market for venture capital. There we emphasized the private equity side of private placements. Here we take a closer look at the debt side of the private placement market and how it is used by more seasoned corporations as distinct from "start-ups." Thus, when we talk of private placements in this section, we are focusing on debt contracts. This debt side of the private placement market is always a significant portion of the total private market.

Private placements are an alternative to the sale of securities to the public or to a restricted group of investors through a privileged subscription. Any type of security can be privately placed (directly placed). The major investors in private placements are large financial institutions. Based on the volume of securities purchased, the three most important investor groups are (1) life insurance companies, (2) state and local retirement funds, and (3) private pension funds.

In arranging a private placement, the firm may (1) avoid the use of an investment banker and work directly with the investing institutions or (2) engage the services of an investment banker. If the firm does not use an investment banker, of course, it does not have to pay a fee. Conversely, investment bankers can provide valuable advice in the private placement process. They are usually in contact with several major institutional investors; thus, they will know if a firm is in a position to invest in its proposed offering, and they can help the firm evaluate the terms of the new issue.

Private placements have advantages and disadvantages compared with public offerings. The financial manager must carefully evaluate both sides of the question. The advantages associated with private placements are these:

1. **Speed.** The firm usually obtains funds more quickly through a private placement than a public offering. The major reason is that registration of the issue with the SEC is not required.
2. **Reduced flotation costs.** These savings result because the lengthy registration statement for the SEC does not have to be prepared, and the investment banking underwriting and distribution costs do not have to be absorbed.
3. **Financing flexibility.** In a private placement, the firm deals on a face-to-face basis with a small number of investors. This means that the terms of the issue can be tailored to meet the specific needs of the company. For example, all of the funds need not be taken by the firm at once. In exchange for a commitment fee, the firm can "draw down" against the established amount of credit with the investors. This provides some insurance against capital market uncertainties, and the firm does not have to borrow the funds if the need does not arise. There is also the possibility of renegotiation. The terms of the debt issue can be altered. The term to maturity, the interest rate, or any restrictive covenants can be discussed among the affected parties.

The following disadvantages of private placements must be evaluated:

1. **Interest costs.** It is generally conceded that interest costs on private placements exceed those of public issues. Whether this disadvantage is enough to offset the reduced flotation costs associated with a private placement is a determination the financial manager must make. There is some evidence that on smaller issues—say, $500,000 as opposed to $30 million—the private placement alternative would be preferable.
2. **Restrictive covenants.** Dividend policy, working-capital levels, and the raising of additional debt capital may all be affected by provisions in the private-placement debt contract. That is not to say that such restrictions are always absent in public debt contracts. Rather, the financial officer must be alert to the tendency for these covenants to be especially burdensome in private contracts.
3. **The possibility of future SEC registration.** If the lender (investor) should decide to sell the issue to a public buyer before maturity, the issue must be registered with the SEC. Some lenders, then, require that the issuing firm agree to a future registration at their option.

CONCEPT CHECK

1. Within the financial markets, what do we mean by "private placements"?
2. What are the possible advantages and disadvantages of private placements?

Objective 8

FLOTATION COSTS

Flotation costs
The underwriter's spread and issuing costs associated with the issuance and marketing of new securities.

The firm raising long-term capital incurs two types of **flotation costs**: (1) the underwriter's spread and (2) issuing costs. Of these two costs, the underwriter's spread is the larger. The *underwriter's spread* is simply the difference between the gross and net proceeds from a given security issue expressed as a percent of the gross proceeds. The *issue costs* include (1) printing and engraving, (2) legal fees, (3) accounting fees, (4) trustee fees, and (5) several other miscellaneous components. The two most significant issue costs are printing and engraving and legal fees.

Data published by the SEC have consistently revealed two relationships about flotation costs. First, the costs associated with issuing common stock are notably greater than the costs associated with preferred stock offerings. In turn, preferred stock costs exceed those of bonds. Second, flotation costs (expressed as a percent of gross proceeds) decrease as the size of the security issue increases.

In the first instance, the stated relationship reflects the fact that issue costs are sensitive to the risks involved in successfully distributing a security issue. Common stock is riskier to own than corporate bonds. Underwriting risk is, therefore, greater with common stock than with bonds. Thus, flotation costs just mirror these risk relationships. In the second case, a portion of the issue costs is fixed. Legal fees and accounting costs are good examples. So, as the size of the security issue rises, the fixed component is spread over a larger gross proceeds base. As a consequence, average flotation costs vary inversely with the size of the issue.

CONCEPT CHECK

1. What are the two major categories of flotation costs?
2. Are flotation costs greater for a new bond issue or a new common stock issue?

REGULATION

Since late 1986, there has been a renewal of public interest in the regulation of the country's financial markets. The key event was a massive insider trading scandal that made the name Ivan F. Boesky one of almost universal recognition—but unfortunately, in a negative sense. This was followed by the October 19, 1987, crash of the equity markets. In early 1990, the investing community (both institutional and individual) became increasingly concerned over a weakening in the so-called "junk bond market." Then several financial failures and breakdowns in corporate governance and democracy made firms such as Enron, WorldCom, Global Crossing, Adelphia, Tyco, Arthur Andersen, and HealthSouth household names in a negative context over the very recent 2001 to 2003 time frame. The accompanying notoriety associated with these firms and their key management personnel led Congress to pass the Sarbanes-Oxley Act of 2002. This recent act is reviewed later in this section. The upshot of all of this enhanced awareness is a new appreciation of the crucial role that regulation plays in the financial system.

Following the severe economic downturn of 1929 to 1932, Congressional action was taken to provide for federal regulation of the securities markets. State statutes (blue sky laws) also govern the securities markets where applicable, but the federal regulations are clearly more pressing and important. The major federal regulations are reviewed here.

PRIMARY MARKET REGULATIONS

The new issues market is governed by the Securities Act of 1933. The intent of the act is important. It aims to provide potential investors with accurate, truthful disclosure about the firm and the new securities being offered to the public. This does *not* prevent firms from issuing highly speculative securities. The SEC says nothing whatsoever about the possible investment worth of a given offering. It is up to the investor to separate the junk from the jewels. The SEC does have the legal power and responsibility to enforce the 1933 act.

Full public disclosure is achieved by the requirement that the issuing firm file a registration statement with the SEC containing requisite information. The statement details particulars about the firm and the new security being issued. During a minimum 20-day waiting period, the SEC examines the submitted document. In numerous instances, the 20-day wait has been extended by several weeks. The SEC can ask for additional information that was omitted in order to clarify the original document. The SEC can also order that the offering be stopped.

During the registration process, a preliminary prospectus (the "red herring") may be distributed to potential investors. When the registration is approved, the final prospectus must be made available to the prospective investors. The prospectus is actually a condensed version of the full registration statement. If, at a later date, the information in the registration statement and the prospectus is found to be lacking, purchasers of the new issue who incurred a loss can sue for damages. Officers of the issuing firm and others who took part in the registration and marketing of the issue may suffer both civil and criminal penalties.

Generally, the SEC defines public issues as those that are sold to more than 25 investors. Some public issues need not be registered. These include

1. Relatively small issues, where the firm sells less than \$1.5 million of new securities per year. Such issues of less than \$1.5 million are not entirely regulation-free. They are monitored through what is usually called the *small-issues exemption.* These small issues, then, fall under the auspices of Regulation A, which is just a very short offering statement compared to the full-blown registration statement. The latter is very onerous; it often ends up in the 50–100 page range.

2. Issues that are sold entirely intrastate.
3. Issues that are basically short-term instruments. This translates into maturity periods of 270 days or less.
4. Issues that are already regulated or controlled by some other federal agency. Examples here are the Federal Power Commission (public utilities) and the Interstate Commerce Commission (railroads).

Secondary Market Regulations

Secondary trading is regulated by the Securities Exchange Act of 1934. This act created the SEC to enforce securities laws. The Federal Trade Commission enforced the 1933 act for one year. The major aspects of the 1934 act can be best presented in outline form:

1. Major security exchanges must register with the SEC. This regulates the exchanges and places reporting requirements on the firms whose securities are listed on them.
2. Insider trading is regulated. Insiders can be officers, directors, employees, relatives, major investors, or anyone having information about the operation of the firm that is not public knowledge. If an investor purchases the security of the firm in which the investor is an insider, he or she must hold it for at least six months before disposing of it. Otherwise, profits made from trading the stock within a period of less than six months must be returned to the firm. Furthermore, insiders must file with the SEC a monthly statement of holdings and transactions in the stock of their corporation.[12]
3. Manipulative trading of securities by investors to affect stock prices is prohibited.
4. The SEC is given control over proxy procedures.
5. The Board of Governors of the Federal Reserve System is given responsibility for setting margin requirements. This affects the flow of credit into the securities markets. Buying securities on margin simply means using credit to acquire a portion of the subject financial instruments.

Securities Acts Amendments of 1975

The Securities Acts Amendments of 1975 touched on three important issues. First, Congress mandated the creation of a national market system (NMS). Only broad goals for this national exchange were identified by Congress. Implementation details were left to the SEC and, to a much lesser extent, the securities industry in general. Congress was really expressing its desire for (1) widespread application of auction market trading principles, (2) a high degree of competition across markets, and (3) the use of modern electronic communication systems to link the fragmented markets in the country into a true NMS. The NMS is still a goal toward which the SEC and the securities industry are moving. Agreement as to its final form and an implementation date have not occurred.

A second major alteration in the habits of the securities industry also took place in 1975. This was the elimination of fixed commissions (fixed brokerage rates) on public transactions in securities. This was closely tied to the desire for an NMS in that fixed brokerage fees provided no incentive for competition among brokers. A third consideration of the 1975 amendments focused on such financial institutions as commercial

[12] On November 14, 1986, the SEC announced that Ivan F. Boesky had admitted to illegal insider trading after an intensive investigation. Boesky at the time was a very well-known Wall Street investor, speculator, and arbitrageur. Boesky was an owner or part owner in several companies, including an arbitrage fund named Ivan F. Boesky & Co. L. P. Boesky agreed to pay the U.S. government $50 million, which represented a return of illegal profits, and another $50 million in civil penalties; to withdraw permanently from the securities industry; and to plead guilty to criminal charges. The far-reaching investigation continued into 1987 and implicated several other prominent investment figures.

banks and insurance firms. These financial institutions were prohibited from acquiring membership on stock exchanges in order to reduce or save commissions on their own trades.

Shelf Registration

On March 16, 1982, the SEC began a new procedure for registering new issues of securities. Formally it is called SEC Rule 415; informally, the process is known as a **shelf registration**, or a **shelf offering**. The essence of the process is rather simple. Rather than go through the lengthy, full registration process each time the firm plans an offering of securities, it can get a blanket order approved by the SEC. A master registration statement that covers the financing plans of the firm over the coming two years is filed with the SEC. On approval, the firm can market some or all of the securities over this two-year period. The securities are sold in a piecemeal fashion, or "off the shelf." Prior to each specific offering, a short statement about the issue is filed with the SEC.

Shelf registration (shelf offering) A procedure for issuing new securities where the firm obtains a master registration statement approved by the SEC.

Corporations raising funds approve of this new procedure. The tedious, full registration process is avoided with each offering pulled off the shelf. This should result in a saving of fees paid to investment bankers. Moreover, an issue can more quickly be brought to the market. Also, if market conditions change, an issue can easily be redesigned to fit the specific conditions of the moment.

As is always the case, there is another side to the story. Recall that the reason for the registration process in the first place is to give investors useful information about the firm and the securities being offered. Under the shelf registration procedure, some of the information about the issuing firm becomes old as the two-year horizon unfolds. Some investment bankers feel they do not have the proper amount of time to study the firm when a shelf offering takes place.

Sarbanes-Oxley Act of 2002

As previously mentioned, several disappointing lapses in corporate behavior became public knowledge after the year 2000. Numerous unflattering instances of poor judgment occurred involving the major fundamental building blocks of Western capitalism. These included the (1) public accounting industry, (2) legal industry, (3) investment banking industry, (4) security analysts' industry, and (5) subject firms themselves, even involving their elected boards of directors. Both individual investors and some institutional investors lost hugely significant amounts of invested capital as a result of this monumental breakdown in corporate morality.

One glaring example involved the board of the energy-sector company, Enron Corporation. Enron failed financially in December 2001. Prior to that formal failure (bankruptcy) the firm's board of directors overtly voted on two occasions to temporarily suspend its own "code of ethics" to permit its CFO to engage in risky personal financial ventures that involved the financial structure and cash flow streams of Enron. This should remind you of our **Principle 10: Ethical behavior is doing the right thing, and ethical dilemmas are everywhere in finance.**

In a research paper that focused on accounting practices at energy firms, Richard Bassett and Mark Storrie summarized the problems at Enron as follows:[13]

> In brief, Enron's senior management and others engaged in a systematic attempt to use various accounting and reporting techniques to mislead investors.

[13] Richard Bassett and Mark Storrie, "Accounting at Energy Firms After Enron: Is the Cure Worse Than the Disease?" *Policy Analysis:* Cato Project on Corporate Governance, Audit and Tax Reform, No. 469, February 12, 2003, p. 2.

TABLE 14-8 Sarbanes–Oxley Act of 2002

Key Elements

TITLE	AREA OF EMPHASIS
I	Public Company Accounting Oversight Board
II	Auditor Independence
III	Corporate Responsibility
IV	Enhanced Financial Disclosures
V	Analyst Conflicts of Interest
VI	Commission Resources and Authority
VII	Studies and Reports
VIII	Corporate and Criminal Fraud Accountability
IX	White-Collar Crime Penalty Enhancements
X	Corporate Tax Returns
XI	Corporate Fraud and Accountability

Source: U.S. Congress, *H.R. 3763.* Passed by the 107th Congress of the United States on July 25, 2002; signed by President Bush on July 30, 2002.

Under intense public scrutiny resulting from a large series of corporate indiscretions like those previously noted, Congress passed in July 2002 the Public Company Accounting Reform and Investor Protection Act, commonly known as the Sarbanes-Oxley Act of 2002. The act contains 11 "titles" which are displayed in Table 14-8.[14] Those 11 titles provide the flavor of the act which tightened significantly the latitudes given to corporate advisors (like accountants, lawyers, company officers, and boards of directors) who have access to or influence company decisions.

In effect, such advisors are now held strictly accountable in law for any instances of misconduct. The act very simply and directly identified its purpose as being "To protect investors by improving the accuracy and reliability of corporate disclosures made pursuant to the securities laws, and for other purposes." In a speech given in March 2003, SEC Commissioner Paul S. Atkins directly recognized the relationship of the act to corporate valuations. He said:[15]

> Fundamentally, Sarbanes-Oxley acknowledges the importance of stockholder value. Without equity investors and their confidence, our economic growth and continued technological innovations would be slowed. Sarbanes-Oxley strengthens the role of directors as representatives of stockholders and reinforces the role of management as stewards of the stockholders' interest.

As evidenced by being the initial title of the act, a critical part of this law was the creation of the Public Company Accounting Oversight Board. This board's purpose is to regulate the accounting industry relative to public companies that they audit. Table 14-9 highlights the composition of the board's membership and its duties. As recently as June 30, 2003, the oversight board itself published a set of ethics rules to police its own set of activities.[16] This ethics code was sent to the SEC for approval as it was intended to "insulate itself from perceptions or accusations of conflicts of interest."

[14] The full Sarbanes-Oxley Act can be viewed at the Library of Congress Web site at http://thomas.loc.gov.

[15] Paul S. Atkins, "The Sarbanes-Oxley Act of 2002: Goals, Content, and Status of Implementation," Speech by the SEC Commissioner, March 25, 2003, p. 2 of 6. See www.sec.gov/news/speech/spch032503psa.htm.

[16] See www.money.cnn.com/2003/06/30/news/companies/accounting_ethics.reut/index.htm.

TABLE 14-9 Public Company Accounting Oversight Board

I. THE BOARD: ESTABLISHMENT OF AN INDEPENDENT OVERSIGHT BOARD FOR AUDITORS

The board consists of five financially literate members, appointed for five-year terms. Two of the members must be or have been certified public accountants, and the remaining members must not be nor have ever been CPAs. Members cannot share in the profits or receive payments from a public accounting firm (other than fixed continuing payments such as retirement benefits). Members are appointed by the SEC, after consultation with the chairman of the Federal Reserve Board and the Secretary of the Treasury. Members can be removed from the board by the SEC for good cause.

II. BOARD DUTIES:

1. Register public accounting firms.
2. Establish or adopt, by rule, auditing, quality control, ethics independence, and other standards relating to the preparation of audit reports for issuers.
3. Conduct inspections of audit firms.
4. Conduct investigations and disciplinary proceedings, and impose appropriate sanctions.
5. Conduct such other duties or functions as necessary and appropriate.
6. Enforce compliance with the act, the rules of the board, professional standards, and the securities laws relating to the preparation and issuance of audit reports and the obligations and liabilities of accountants with respect thereto.
7. Set the budget and manage the operations of the board and its staff.

Source: *Sarbanes-Oxley Act of 2002.*

CONCEPT CHECK

1. What are the main elements of the Securities Act of 1933 and the Securities Exchange Act of 1934?
2. What is meant by "insider trading"?
3. What is a "shelf registration"?
4. What is the purpose of the Sarbanes-Oxley Act of 2002?

THE MULTINATIONAL FIRM: EFFICIENT FINANCIAL MARKETS AND INTERCOUNTRY RISK

We have discussed and demonstrated in this chapter that the United States has a highly developed, complex, and competitive system of financial markets that allows for the quick transfer of savings from those economic units with a surplus of savings to those economic units with a savings deficit. Such a system of robust and credible financial markets allows great ideas (like the personal computer) to be financed and increases the overall wealth of the given economy. Real capital formation—for example, a Ford Motor Company manufacturing plant in Livonia, Michigan—is enhanced by the financial market mechanism.

One major reason why underdeveloped countries are indeed underdeveloped is that they lack a financial market system that has the confidence of those who must use it—like the multinational firm. The multinational firm with cash to invest in foreign markets will weigh heavily the integrity of both the financial system and the political system of the prospective foreign country.

A lack of integrity on either the financial side or the political stability side will retard direct investment in the lesser-developed nation. Consider the Walt Disney Company headquartered in Burbank, California. Disney common stock trades on the NYSE (ticker symbol DIS), while the firm has significant overseas real investments in projects known as the Disneyland Paris Resort and Tokyo Disneyland. Disney has confidence in the French financial markets, and those of western Europe and Japan. As an example, that confidence led Disney executives to launch three new projects in Japan during 1998—a new theme park and two new hotels.[17]

However, Disney did not launch any new projects in Thailand because the basic currency in Thailand, called the "baht," lost a full 98 percent of its value against the U.S. dollar over the short period from June 1997 to February 1998. Profits generated in Thailand and measured by the baht would have bought significantly fewer U.S. dollars after the devaluation. This type of situation is typically referred to as *exchange rate risk*. Currencies, too, trade within financial markets and those risks are closely studied by wise multinational firms.

CONCEPT CHECK

1. Identify one major reason why underdeveloped countries remain underdeveloped.
2. Give an example of "foreign exchange risk."

HOW FINANCIAL MANAGERS USE THIS MATERIAL

Corporate financial executives are constantly balancing the internal demand for funds against the costs of raising external financial capital. In order to finance favorable projects, the financial executive at times will have to choose between issuing new debt, preferred stock, or common stock. Further, the executive will decide whether to raise the external capital via a public offering or private placement of the new securities to a limited number of potential investors. Most of these activities will involve the counsel of an investment banking firm and an awareness of securities markets regulations.

We know that when financial executives decide to raise cash in the capital market, the issuance of corporate debt clearly dominates other forms of financing instruments. This preference rests on economic logic: Interest expense is deductible from other taxable income when computing the firm's tax liability; dividends paid on either preferred stock or common stock are not. This puts **Principle 8: Taxes Bias Business Decisions** into action. Stated alternatively, firms would rather suffer a lower tax bill as opposed to a higher tax bill. Wouldn't you? As a result of this knowledge, U.S. corporate executives raised 75.3 percent of their external cash from bonds and notes (debt capital) during the 1996 to 1999 period.

Financial executives are fully aware of **Principle 8,** but also the need to create wealth for their common stock investors. The use of fixed-income financing (leverage) has to be wisely done—not overdone, or it will ultimately raise overall capital costs and the risk of bankruptcy. The Walt Disney Company displays this perspective in the following statement: "Disney shareholders benefit from the prudent leverage in the company's capital structure represented by total borrowings of $11.1 billion at year end. Attractive borrowing rates help to reduce the company's overall cost of capital, thereby creating value for shareholders. Disney still has substantial financial flexibility to borrow, should sound business opportunities present themselves."[18]

[17] The Walt Disney Company, *Annual Report*, 1998, pp. 24–25, 57.

[18] The Walt Disney Company, *Annual Report* (1997), 17.

SUMMARY

This chapter centers on the market environment in which corporations raise long-term funds, including the structure of the U.S. financial markets, the institution of investment banking, and the various methods for distributing securities.

When corporations go to the capital market for cash, the most favored financing method is debt. The corporate debt markets clearly dominate the equity markets when new funds are raised. The U.S. tax system inherently favors debt capital as a fundraising method. In an average year over the 1981 to 1996 period, bonds and notes made up 75.6 percent of external cash that was raised, and 75.3 percent over the more recent 1996 to 1999 period. **Objective 1** **Objective 2**

The function of financial markets is to allocate savings efficiently in the economy to the ultimate demander (user) of the savings. In a financial market, the forces of supply and demand for a specific financial instrument are brought together. The wealth of an economy would not be as great as it is without a fully developed financial market system. **Objective 3**

Most years, households are a net supplier of funds to the financial markets. The nonfinancial business sector is most always a net borrower of funds. Both life insurance companies and private pension funds are important buyers of corporate securities. Savings are ultimately transferred to the business firm seeking cash by means of (1) the direct transfer, (2) the indirect transfer using the investment banker, or (3) the indirect transfer using the financial intermediary. **Objective 4**

Corporations can raise funds through public offerings or private placements. The public market is impersonal in that the security issuer does not meet the ultimate investors in the financial instruments. In a private placement, the securities are sold directly to a limited number of institutional investors. **Objective 5**

The primary market is the market for new issues. The secondary market represents transactions in currently outstanding securities. Both the money and capital markets have primary and secondary sides. The *money market* refers to transactions in short-term debt instruments. The *capital market*, in contrast, refers to transactions in long-term financial instruments. Trading in the money and capital markets can occur in either the organized security exchanges or the over-the-counter market. The money market is exclusively an over-the-counter market.

The investment banker is a financial specialist involved as an intermediary in the merchandising of securities. He or she performs the functions of (1) underwriting, (2) distributing, and (3) advising. Major methods for the public distribution of securities include (1) the negotiated purchase, (2) the competitive bid purchase, (3) the commission or best-efforts basis, (4) privileged subscriptions, and (5) direct sales. The direct sale bypasses the use of an investment banker. The negotiated purchase is the most profitable distribution method to the investment banker. It also provides the greatest amount of investment banking services to the corporate client. **Objective 6**

Privately placed debt provides an important market outlet for corporate bonds. Major investors in this market are (1) life insurance firms, (2) state and local retirement funds, and (3) private pension funds. Several advantages and disadvantages are associated with private placements. The financial officer must weigh these attributes and decide if a private placement is preferable to a public offering. **Objective 7**

Flotation costs consist of the underwriter's spread and issuing costs. The flotation costs of common stock exceed those of preferred stock, which, in turn, exceed those of debt. Moreover, flotation costs as a percent of gross proceeds are inversely related to the size of the security issue. **Objective 8**

The new issues market is regulated at the federal level by the Securities Act of 1933. It provides for the registration of new issues with the SEC. Secondary market trading is regulated by the Securities Exchange Act of 1934. The Securities Acts Amendments of 1975 placed on the SEC the responsibility for devising a national market system. This concept is still being studied. The shelf registration procedure (SEC Rule 415) was initiated in March 1982. Under this regulation and with the proper filing of documents, firms that are selling new issues do not have to go through the old, lengthy registration process each time the firm plans an offering of securities.

On July 30, 2002, President Bush signed into law the Public Company Accounting Reform and Investor Protection Act, commonly known as the Sarbanes-Oxley Act of 2002. Its intended purpose as stated in the act is "To protect investors by improving the accuracy and reliability of corporate disclosures made pursuant to the securities laws, and for other purposes."

KEY TERMS

Go To: **www.prenhall.com/keown** for downloads and current events associated with this chapter

Capital market, 486
Direct sale, 491
Direct securities, 478
Financial assets, 476
Financial markets, 475
Flotation costs, 494
Indirect securities, 478
Investment banker, 489
Money market, 486
Organized security exchanges, 486
Over-the-counter markets, 486
Primary markets, 484
Private placement (direct placement), 481
Privileged subscription, 491
Public offering, 481
Real assets, 476
Secondary markets, 477
Shelf registration (shelf offering), 497
Syndicate, 490
Underwriting, 477

STUDY QUESTIONS

14-1. What are financial markets? What function do they perform? How would an economy be worse off without them?

14-2. Define in a technical sense what we mean by *financial intermediary*. Give an example of your definition.

14-3. Distinguish between the money and capital markets.

14-4. What major benefits do corporations and investors enjoy because of the existence of organized security exchanges?

14-5. What are the general categories examined by an organized exchange in determining whether an applicant firm's securities can be listed on it?

(Specific numbers are not needed here, but rather areas of investigation.)

14-6. Why do you think most secondary market trading in bonds takes place over-the-counter?

14-7. What is an investment banker, and what major functions does he or she perform?

14-8. What is the major difference between a negotiated purchase and a competitive bid purchase?

14-9. Why is an investment banking syndicate formed?

14-10. Why might a large corporation want to raise long-term capital through a private placement rather than a public offering?

14-11. As a recent business school graduate, you work directly for the corporate treasurer. Your corporation is going to issue a new security plan and is concerned with the probable flotation costs. What tendencies about flotation costs can you relate to the treasurer?

14-12. When corporations raise funds, what type of financing vehicle (instrument or instruments) is most favored?

14-13. What is the major (most significant) savings-surplus sector in the U.S. economy?

14-14. Identify three distinct ways that savings are ultimately transferred to business firms in need of cash.

WEB WORKS

14-1WW. Table 14-5 in the text identified all of the U.S. business cycle contractions that have occurred since the end of World War II. The tenth of these recessions began in March 2001 according to the National Bureau of Economic Research (NBER). Visit the NBER's Web site at **www.NBER.ORG** and determine when this research group suggested that the last recession officially ended.

14-2WW. Negative real interest rates occur when the rate of inflation exceeds the rate of interest on fixed-income financing instruments like corporate bonds, government bonds, and U.S. Treasury bills. Negative real rates of interest generally are associated with slow periods of economic growth. During such periods corporations usually prefer to raise external cash via new debt issues rather than equity issues. Two Web sites can give you insights into whether current real rates of interest are negative or positive. Visit **www.federalreserve.gov** to check on the H.15 Selected Interest Rates report to assess nominal interest rates. Then check on **www.stats.bls.gov** to assess several different inflation indices. Estimate the level of the real rate of interest on the 10-year Treasury note (and any other maturity period that excites you), using more than one inflation index. *Hint:* The consumer price index and producer price index for finished goods are two commonly used indicators looked at by security and financial analysts.

14-3WW. Visit **www.nvca.org** and assess whether or not the private equity markets have recovered their momentum since the general business contraction that commenced during 2001. This is the Web site of the National Venture Capital Association. Would you characterize the state of the private equity markets as either "hot" or "tepid"?

LEARNING OBJECTIVES

After reading this chapter, you should be able to

1. Understand the difference between business risk and financial risk.
2. Use the technique of break-even analysis in a variety of analytical settings.
3. Distinguish among the financial concepts of operating leverage, financial leverage, and combined leverage.
4. Calculate the firm's degree of operating leverage, financial leverage, and combined leverage.
5. Explain why a firm with a high business risk exposure might logically choose to employ a low degree of financial leverage in its financial structure.
6. Understand how business risk and global sales impact the multinational firm.

CHAPTER 15

Analysis and Impact of Leverage

The 2001 annual report of Harley-Davidson, Inc., in a discussion on financial performance, points out that for 2001, the firm's net income increased by 25.9 percent compared with the year 2000. Harley also noted that its sales revenue jumped by a smaller, but pleasant 15.7 percent. Note that Harley's increase in reported net income was 1.650 times the percentage increment in sales. Such disparate relationships between earnings increments and sales increments are commonly reported by numerous firms. Some other actual examples follow here.

In 1996, the Coca-Cola Company posted only a moderate sales increase of 2.9 percent over the level of reported sales for 1995. This firm's change in net income, however, rose by a pleasant 16.9 percent over the same one-year period. Thus, the relative change in net income was 5.83 times the relative fluctuation in sales (i.e., 16.9 percent/2.9 percent). Such disparity in the relationship between sales fluctuations and net income fluctuations is not peculiar to Coca-Cola.

Consider that in 1993, Phillips Petroleum saw its sales rise by only 3.2 percent, yet its net income rose by a whopping 35 percent. Further, Archer Daniels Midland experienced a sales rise of 6.3 percent and a 12.7 percent increase in net income.

We know that sales fluctuations are not always in the positive direction. Over the 1992 to 1993 time frame, Chevron Corporation, the large integrated oil company,

CHAPTER PREVIEW

Our work in earlier chapters allowed us to develop an understanding of how financial assets are valued in the marketplace. Drawing on the tenets of valuation theory, we presented various approaches to measuring the cost of funds to the business organization. This chapter presents concepts that relate to the valuation process and the cost of capital; it also discusses the crucial problem of planning the firm's financing mix.

The cost of capital provides a direct link between the formulation of the firm's asset structure and its financial structure. This is illustrated in Figure 15-1. Recall that the cost of capital is a basic input to the time-adjusted capital-budgeting models. It therefore affects the capital-budgeting, or asset-selection, process. The cost of capital is affected, in turn, by the composition of the right side of the firm's balance sheet—that is, its financial structure.

This chapter examines tools that can be useful aids to the financial manager in determining the firm's proper financial structure. First, we review the technique of break-even analysis. This provides the foundation for the relationships to be highlighted in the remainder of the chapter. We then examine the concept of operating leverage, some consequences of the firm's use of financial leverage, and the impact on the firm's earnings stream when operating and financial leverage are combined in various patterns.

As you work through this chapter, you will be reminded of several of the principles that form the basics of business financial management and decision making. These will be emphasized: **Principle 1: The Risk-Return Trade-Off—We won't take on additional risk unless we expect to be compensated with additional return; Principle 3: Cash—Not Profits—Is King;** and **Principle 6: Efficient Capital Markets—The markets are quick and the prices are right.** Our immediate tasks are to distinguish two types of risk that confront the firm and to clarify some key terminology that will be used throughout this and the subsequent chapter.

FIGURE 15-1 Cost of Capital as a Link between Firm's Asset Structure and Financial Structure

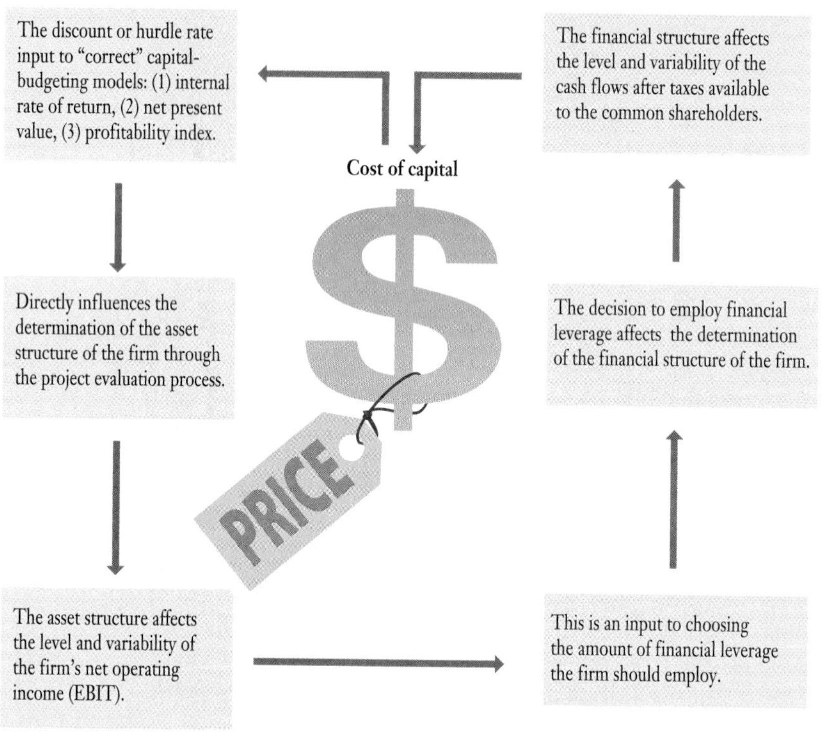

The discount or hurdle rate input to "correct" capital-budgeting models: (1) internal rate of return, (2) net present value, (3) profitability index.

Directly influences the determination of the asset structure of the firm through the project evaluation process.

The asset structure affects the level and variability of the firm's net operating income (EBIT).

This is an input to choosing the amount of financial leverage the firm should employ.

The decision to employ financial leverage affects the determination of the financial structure of the firm.

The financial structure affects the level and variability of the cash flows after taxes available to the common shareholders.

Cost of capital

PRICE

The annual report of Harley-Davidson, Inc., is easily accessed at **www.reportgallery.com**. This excellent site promotes itself as having links to over 2,200 annual reports and those of most "Fortune 500" companies. You can verify the financial performance numbers for Harley that were presented early in the chapter's opening. Just find their 2001 annual report and inspect pages 37 and 41.

endured a 3.6 percent contraction in sales revenues; yet its net income contracted by a larger and more painful 19.4 percent.

What is it about the nature of businesses that causes changes in sales revenues to translate into larger variations in net income and finally the earnings available to the common shareholders? It would actually be a good planning tool for managers to be able to decompose such fluctuations into those policies that are associated with the operating side of the business, as distinct from those policies associated with the financing side of the business. Such knowledge could be put to effective use when the firm builds its strategic plan. This chapter will show you how to do just that.

Objective 1

BUSINESS AND FINANCIAL RISK

In this chapter, we become more precise in assessing the causes of variability in the firm's expected revenue streams. It is useful to think of business risk as induced by the firm's investment decisions. That is, the composition of the firm's assets determines its exposure to business risk. In this way, business risk is a direct function of what appears on the left side of the company's balance sheet. Financial risk is properly attributed to the manner in which the firm's managers have decided to arrange the right side of the company's balance sheet. The choice to use more financial leverage means that the firm will experience greater exposure to financial risk. The tools developed here will help you quantify the firm's business and financial risk. A solid understanding of these tools will make you a better financial manager.

FIGURE 15-2 Subjective Probability Distribution of Next Year's EBIT

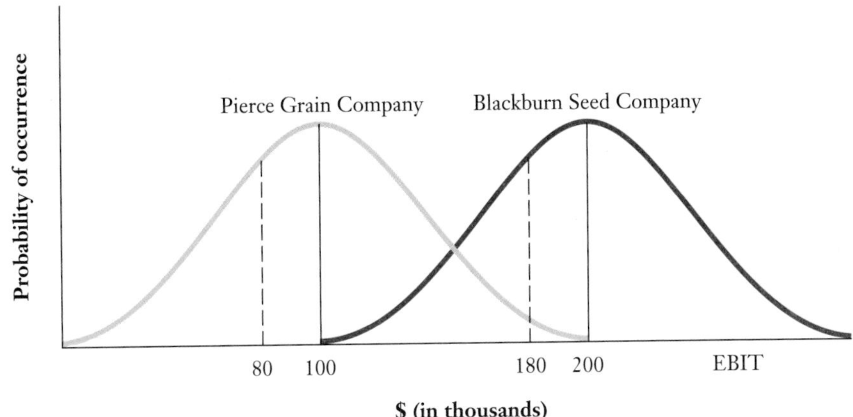

In studying capital-budgeting techniques, we referred to **risk** as the likely variability associated with expected revenue or income streams. As our attention is now focused on the firm's financing decision rather than its investment decision, it is useful to separate the income stream variations attributable to (1) the company's exposure to business risk and (2) its decision to incur financial risk.

Risk
The likely variability associated with expected revenue or income streams.

Business risk refers to the relative dispersion (variability) in the firm's expected earnings before interest and taxes (EBIT).[1] Figure 15-2 shows a subjectively estimated probability distribution of next year's EBIT for the Pierce Grain Company and the same type of projection for Pierce's larger competitor, the Blackburn Seed Company. The expected value of EBIT for Pierce is $100,000, with an associated standard deviation of $20,000. If next year's EBIT for Pierce fell one standard deviation short of the expected $100,000, the actual EBIT would equal $80,000. Blackburn's expected EBIT is $200,000, and the size of the associated standard deviation is $20,000. The standard deviation for the expected level of EBIT is the same for both firms. We would say that Pierce's degree of business risk exceeds Blackburn's because of its larger coefficient of variation of expected EBIT as follows:

Business risk
The relative dispersion in the firm's expected earnings before interest and taxes.

$$\text{Pierce's coefficient of variation of expected EBIT} = \frac{\$12{,}000}{\$100{,}000} = .20$$

$$\text{Blackburn's coefficient of variation of expected EBIT} = \frac{\$20{,}000}{\$200{,}000} = .10$$

The relative dispersion in the firm's EBIT stream, measured here by its expected coefficient of variation, is the *residual* effect of several causal influences. Dispersion in operating income does not *cause* business risk; rather, this dispersion, which we call business risk, is the *result* of several influences. Some of these are listed in Table 15-1, along with an example of each particular attribute. Notice that the company's cost structure, product demand characteristics, and intra-industry competitive position all affect its business risk exposure. Such business risk is a direct result of the firm's investment decision. It

[1] If what the accountants call "other income" and "other expenses" are equal to zero, then EBIT is equal to net operating income. These terms will be used interchangeably.

TABLE 15-1 Concept of Business Risk

BUSINESS RISK ATTRIBUTE	EXAMPLE[a]
1. Sensitivity of the firm's product demand to general economic conditions	If GDP declines, does the firm's sales level decline by a greater percentage?
2. Degree of competition	Is the firm's market share small in comparison with other firms that produce and distribute the same product(s)?
3. Product diversification	Is a large proportion of the firm's sales revenue derived from a single major product or product line?
4. Operating leverage	Does the firm utilize a high level of operating leverage resulting in a high level of fixed costs?
5. Growth prospects	Are the firm's product markets expanding and (or) changing, making income estimates and prospects highly volatile?
6. Size	Does the firm suffer a competitive disadvantage due to lack of size in assets, sales, or profits that translates into (among other things) difficulty in tapping the capital market for funds?

[a]Affirmative responses indicate greater business risk exposure.

is the firm's asset structure, after all, that gives rise to both the level and variability of its operating profits.

Financial risk
The additional variability in earnings available to the firm's common stockholders, and the additional chance of insolvency borne by the common stockholder caused by the use of financial leverage.

Financial leverage
Financing a portion of the firm's assets with securities bearing a fixed or limited rate of return.

Financial risk, conversely, is a direct result of the firm's financing decision. In the context of selecting a proper financing mix, this risk applies to (1) the additional variability in earnings available to the firm's common shareholders; and (2) the additional chance of insolvency borne by the common shareholder caused by the use of financial leverage.[2] **Financial leverage** means financing a portion of the firm's assets with securities bearing a fixed (limited) rate of return in hopes of increasing the ultimate return to the common stockholders. The decision to use debt or preferred stock in the financial structure of the corporation means that those who own the common shares of the firm are exposed to financial risk. Any given level of variability in EBIT will be *magnified* by the firm's use of financial leverage, and such additional variability will be embodied in the variability of earnings available to the common stockholder and earnings per share. If these magnifications are negative, the common stockholder has a higher chance of insolvency than would have existed had the use of fixed-charge securities (debt and preferred stock) been avoided.

Operating leverage
The incurrence of fixed operating costs in the firm's income stream.

The closely related concepts of business and financial risk are crucial to the problem of financial structure design. This follows from the impact of these types of risk on the variability of the earnings stream flowing to the company's shareholders. In the rest of this chapter, we study techniques that permit a precise assessment of the earnings stream variability caused by (1) operating leverage and (2) financial leverage. We have already defined financial leverage. Table 15-1 shows that the business risk of the enterprise is influenced by the use of what is called *operating leverage*. **Operating leverage** refers to the incurrence of fixed operating costs in the firm's income stream. To understand the nature and importance of operating leverage, we need to draw upon the basics of cost-volume-profit analysis, or *break-even analysis*.

[2] Note that the concept of financial risk used here differs from that used in our examination of cash and marketable securities management in Chapter 19.

CONCEPT CHECK

1. Explain the concept of "business risk" within the context of financial structure management.
2. Explain the concept of "financial risk" within the context of financial structure management.
3. Distinguish between "financial leverage" and "operating leverage."

BREAK-EVEN ANALYSIS

Objective 2

The break-even analysis concepts presented in this section are often covered in many of your other classes, such as basic accounting principles and managerial economics. This just shows you how important and accepted this tool is within the realm of business decision making. The "Objective and Uses" section identifies five typical uses of the break-even model. You can probably add an application or two of your own. Hotels and motels, for instance, know exactly what their break-even occupancy rate is. This break-even occupancy rate gives them an operating target. This operating target, in turn, often becomes a crucial input to the hotel's advertising strategy. You may not want to become a financial manager—but you do want to understand how to compute break-even points.

The technique of break-even analysis is familiar to legions of businesspeople. It is usefully applied in a wide array of business settings, including both small and large organizations. This tool is widely accepted by the business community for two reasons: It is based on straightforward assumptions, and companies have found that the information gained from the break-even model is beneficial in decision-making situations.

OBJECTIVE AND USES

The objective of *break-even analysis* is to determine the *break-even quantity of output* by studying the relationships among the firm's cost structure, volume of output, and profit. Alternatively, the firm ascertains the break-even level of sales dollars that corresponds to the break-even quantity of output. We will develop the fundamental relationships by concentrating on units of output, and then extend the procedure to permit direct calculation of the break-even sales level.

What is meant by the break-even quantity of output? It is that quantity of output, denominated in units, that results in an EBIT level equal to zero. Use of the break-even model, therefore, enables the financial officer (1) to determine the quantity of output that must be sold to cover all operating costs, as distinct from financial costs, and (2) to calculate the EBIT that will be achieved at various output levels.

The many actual and potential applications of the break-even approach include the following:

1. **Capital expenditure analysis.** As a complementary technique to discounted cash flow evaluation models, the break-even model locates in a rough way the sales volume needed to make a project economically beneficial to the firm. It should not be used to replace the time-adjusted evaluation techniques.
2. **Pricing policy.** The sales price of a new product can be set to achieve a target EBIT level. Furthermore, should market penetration be a prime objective, a price could be set that would cover slightly more than the variable costs of production and provide

only a partial contribution to the recovery of fixed costs. The negative EBIT at several possible sales prices can then be studied.

3. **Labor contract negotiations.** The effect of increased variable costs resulting from higher wages on the break-even quantity of output can be analyzed.
4. **Cost structure.** The choice of reducing variable costs at the expense of incurring higher fixed costs can be evaluated. Management might decide to become more capital-intensive by performing tasks in the production process through use of equipment rather than labor. Application of the break-even model can indicate what the effects of this trade-off will be on the break-even point for the given product.
5. **Financing decisions.** Analysis of the firm's cost structure will reveal the proportion that fixed operating costs bear to sales. If this proportion is high, the firm might reasonably decide not to add any fixed financing costs on top of the high fixed operating costs.

Essential Elements of the Break-Even Model

To implement the break-even model, we must separate the production costs of the company into two mutually exclusive categories: fixed costs and variable costs. You will recall from your study of basic economics that in the long run, all costs are variable. Break-even analysis, therefore, is a short-run concept.

Assumed Behavior of Costs

Fixed costs (indirect costs) Costs that do not vary in total dollar amount as sales volume or quantity of output changes.

FIXED COSTS **Fixed costs**, also referred to as **indirect costs**, do not vary in total amount as sales volume or the quantity of output changes over some *relevant* range of output. Total fixed costs are independent of the quantity of product produced and equal some constant dollar amount. As production volume increases, fixed cost per unit of product falls, as fixed costs are spread over larger and larger quantities of output. Figure 15-3 graphs the behavior of total fixed costs with respect to the company's relevant range of output. This total is shown to be unaffected by the quantity of product that is manufactured and sold. Over some other relevant output range, the amount of total fixed costs might be higher or lower for the same company.

In a manufacturing setting, some specific examples of fixed costs are:

1. Administrative salaries
2. Depreciation
3. Insurance

FIGURE 15-3 Fixed-Cost Behavior over Relevant Range of Output

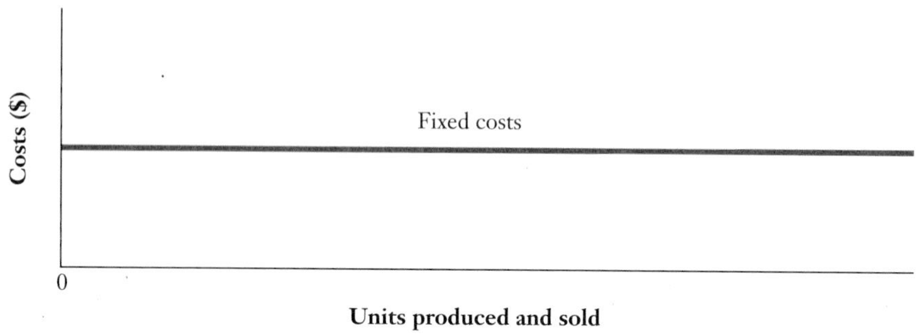

4. Lump sums spent on intermittent advertising programs
5. Property taxes
6. Rent

VARIABLE COSTS **Variable costs** are sometimes referred to as **direct costs.** Variable costs are fixed per unit of output but vary in total as output changes. Total variable costs are computed by taking the variable cost per unit and multiplying it by the quantity produced and sold. The break-even model assumes proportionality between total variable costs and sales. Thus, if sales rise by 10 percent, it is assumed that variable costs will rise by 10 percent. Figure 15-4 graphs the behavior of total variable costs with respect to the company's relevant range of output. Total variable costs are seen to depend on the quantity of product that is manufactured and sold. Notice that if zero units of the product are manufactured, then variable costs are zero, but fixed costs are greater than zero. This implies that some contribution to the coverage of fixed costs occurs as long as the selling price per unit exceeds the variable cost per unit. This helps explain why some firms will operate a plant even when sales are temporarily depressed—that is, to provide some increment of revenue toward the coverage of fixed costs.

Variable costs (direct costs) Costs that are fixed per unit of output but vary in total as output changes.

For a manufacturing operation, some examples of variable costs include:

1. Direct labor
2. Direct materials
3. Energy costs (fuel, electricity, natural gas) associated with the production area
4. Freight costs for products leaving the plant
5. Packaging
6. Sales commissions

MORE ON BEHAVIOR OF COSTS No one believes that all costs behave as neatly as we have illustrated the fixed and variable costs in Figures 15-3 and 15-4. Nor does any law or accounting principle dictate that a certain element of the firm's total costs always be classified as fixed or variable. This will depend on each firm's specific circumstances. In one firm, energy costs may be predominantly fixed, whereas in another they may vary with output.[3]

[3] In a greenhouse operation, where plants are grown (manufactured) under strictly controlled temperatures, heat costs will tend to be fixed whether the building is full or only half full of seedlings. In a metal stamping operation, where levers are being produced, there is no need to heat the plant to as high a temperature when the machines are stopped and the workers are not there. In this latter case, the heat costs will tend to be variable.

FIGURE 15-4 Variable-Cost Behavior over Relevant Range of Output

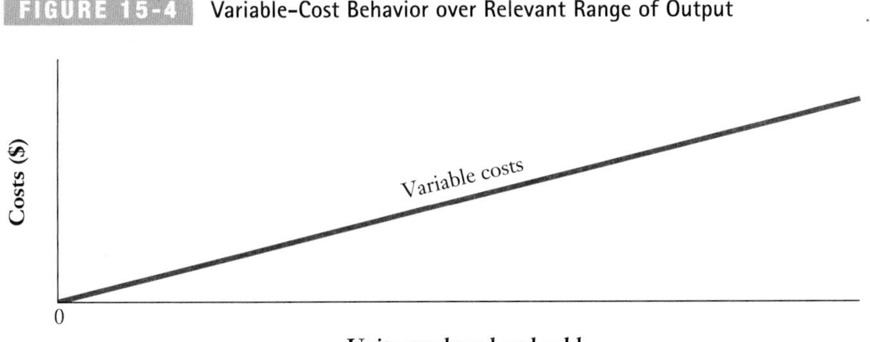

FIGURE 15-5 Semivariable Cost Behavior over Relevant Range of Output

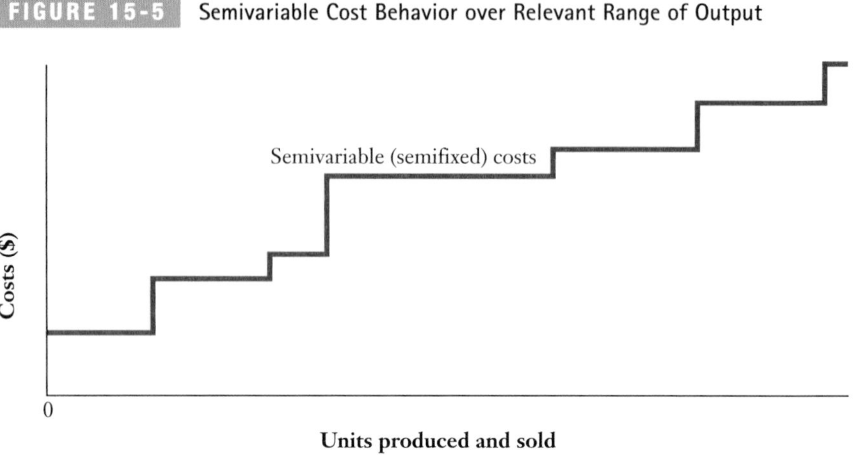

Semivariable costs (semifixed costs) Costs that exhibit the joint characteristics of both fixed and variable costs over different ranges of output.

Furthermore, some costs may be fixed for a while, then rise sharply to a higher level as a higher output is reached, remain fixed, and then rise again with further increases in production. Such costs may be termed either **semivariable** or **semifixed**.

The label is your choice, because both are used in industrial practice. An example might be the salaries paid production supervisors. Should output be cut back by 15 percent for a short period, the management of the organization is not likely to lay off 15 percent of the supervisors. Similarly, commissions paid to salespeople often follow a stepwise pattern over wide ranges of success. This sort of cost behavior is shown in Figure 15-5.

To implement the break-even model and deal with such a complex cost structure, the financial manager must (1) identify the most relevant output range for planning purposes, and then (2) approximate the cost effect of semivariable items over this range by segregating a portion of them to fixed costs and a portion to variable costs. In the actual business setting this procedure is not fun. It is not unusual for the analyst who deals with the figures to spend considerably more time allocating costs to fixed and variable categories than in carrying out the actual break-even calculations.

Total Revenue and Volume of Output

Total revenue Total sales dollars.

Volume of output The firm's level of operations expressed either in sales dollars or as units of output.

Besides fixed and variable costs, the essential elements of the break-even model include total revenue from sales and volume of output. **Total revenue** means sales dollars and is equal to the selling price per unit multiplied by the quantity sold. The **volume of output** refers to the firm's level of operations and may be indicated either as a unit quantity or as sales dollars.

Finding the Break-Even Point

Finding the break-even point in terms of units of production can be accomplished in several ways. All approaches require the essential elements of the break-even model just described. The break-even model is a simple adaptation of the firm's income statement expressed in the following analytical format:

$$\text{sales} - (\text{total variable cost} + \text{total fixed cost}) = \text{profit} \quad \textbf{(15-1)}$$

On a units of production basis, it is necessary to introduce (1) the price at which each unit is sold and (2) the variable cost per unit of output. Because the profit item studied in break-even analysis is EBIT, we will use that acronym instead of the word "profit." In terms of units, the income statement shown in equation (15-1) becomes the break-even model by setting EBIT equal to zero:

(sales price per unit) (units sold) – [(variable cost per unit) (units sold)
+ (total fixed cost)] = EBIT = $0 **(15-2)**

Our task now becomes finding the number of units that must be produced and sold in order to satisfy equation (15-2)—that is, to arrive at an EBIT = $0. This can be done by (1) trial-and-error analysis, (2) contribution-margin analysis, or (3) algebraic analysis. Each approach will be illustrated using the same set of circumstances.

PROBLEM SITUATION

Even though the Pierce Grain Company manufactures several different products, it has observed over a lengthy period that its product mix is rather constant. This allows management to conduct its financial planning by use of a "normal" sales price per unit and "normal" variable cost per unit. The "normal" sales price and variable cost per unit are calculated from the constant product mix. It is like assuming that the product mix is one big product. The selling price is $10 and the variable cost is $6. Total fixed costs for the firm are $100,000 per year. What is the break-even point in units produced and sold for the company during the coming year?

TRIAL-AND-ERROR ANALYSIS The most cumbersome approach to determining the firm's break-even point is to employ the trial-and-error technique illustrated in Table 15-2. The process simply involves the arbitrary selection of an output level and the calculation of a corresponding EBIT amount. When the level of output is found that results in an EBIT = $0, the break-even point has been located. Notice that Table 15-2 is just equation 15-2 in worksheet form. For the Pierce Grain Company, total operating costs will be covered when 25,000 units are manufactured and sold. This tells us that if sales equal $250,000, the firm's EBIT will equal $0.

TABLE 15-2 Pierce Grain Company Sales, Cost, and Profit Schedule

(1) UNITS SOLD	(2) UNIT SALES PRICE	(3) = (1) × (2) SALES	(4) UNIT VARIABLE COST	(5) = (1) × (4) TOTAL VARIABLE COST	(6) TOTAL FIXED COST	(7) = (5) + (6) TOTAL COST	(8) = (3) – (7) EBIT	
1. 10,000	$10	$100,000	$6	$ 60,000	$100,000	$160,000	$–60,000	1.
2. 15,000	10	150,000	6	90,000	100,000	190,000	–40,000	2.
3. 20,000	10	200,000	6	120,000	100,000	220,000	–20,000	3.
4. 25,000	10	250,000	6	150,000	100,000	250,000	0	4.
5. 30,000	10	300,000	6	180,000	100,000	280,000	20,000	5.
6. 35,000	10	350,000	6	210,000	100,000	310,000	40,000	6.

INPUT DATA	OUTPUT DATA
Unit sales price = $10	Break-even point in units = 25,000 units produced and sold
Unit variable cost = $ 6	Break-even point in sales = $250,000
Total fixed cost = $100,000	

Contribution margin Unit sales price minus unit variable cost.

CONTRIBUTION-MARGIN ANALYSIS Unlike trial and error, use of the contribution-margin technique permits direct computation of the break-even quantity of output. The **contribution margin** is the difference between the unit selling price and unit variable costs, as follows:

Unit sales price
– Unit variable cost
= Unit contribution margin

The use of the word "contribution" in the present context means contribution to the coverage of fixed operating costs. For the Pierce Grain Company, the unit contribution margin is:

Unit sales price	$10
Unit variable cost	– 6
Unit contribution margin	$ 4

If the annual fixed costs of $100,000 are divided by the unit contribution margin of $4, we find the break-even quantity of output for Pierce Grain is 25,000 units. With much less effort, we have arrived at the identical result found by trial and error. Figure 15-6 portrays the contribution-margin technique for finding the break-even point.

ALGEBRAIC ANALYSIS To explain the algebraic method for finding the break-even output level, we need to adopt some notation. Let:

Q = the number of units sold
Q_B = the break-even level of Q
P = the unit sales price
F = total fixed costs anticipated over the planning period
V = the unit variable cost

Equation 15-2, the break-even model, is repeated as equation 15-2a with the model symbols used in place of words. The break-even model is then solved for Q, the number

FIGURE 15-6 Contribution-Margin Approach to Break-Even Analysis

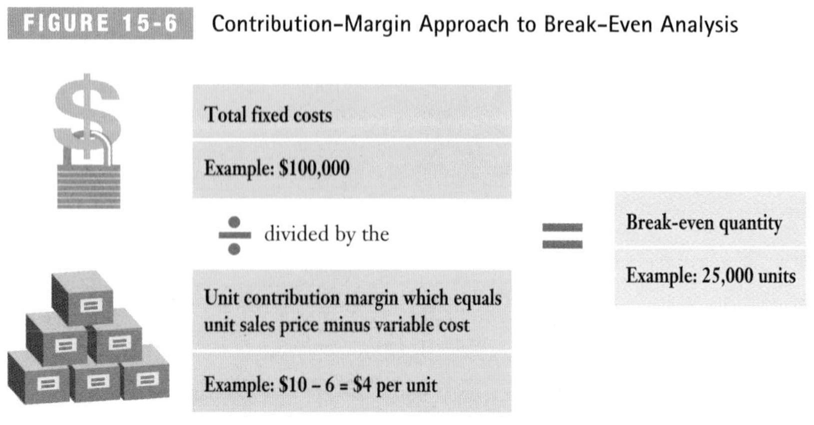

of units that must be sold in order that EBIT will equal \$0. We label the break-even point quantity Q_B.

$$(P \cdot Q) - [(V \cdot Q) + (F)] = \text{EBIT} = \$0 \tag{15-2a}$$
$$(P \cdot Q) - (V \cdot Q) - F = \$0$$
$$Q(P - V) = F$$

$$Q_B = \frac{F}{P - V} \tag{15-3}$$

Observe that equation 15-3 says: divide total fixed operating costs, F, by the unit contribution margin, $P - V$, and the break-even level of output, Q_B, will be obtained. The contribution-margin analysis is nothing more than equation 15-3 in different garb.

Application of equation 15-3 permits direct calculation of Pierce Grain's break-even point, as follows:

$$Q_B = \frac{F}{P - V} = \frac{\$100{,}000}{\$10 - \$6} = 25{,}000 \text{ units}$$

Break-Even Point in Sales Dollars

In dealing with the multiproduct firm, it is convenient to compute the break-even point in terms of sales dollars rather than units of output. Sales, in effect, become a common denominator associated with a particular product mix. Furthermore, an outside analyst may not have access to internal unit cost data. He or she may, however, be able to obtain annual reports for the firm. If the analyst can separate the firm's total costs as identified from its annual reports into their fixed and variable components, he or she can calculate a general break-even point in sales dollars.

We will illustrate the procedure using the Pierce Grain Company's cost structure contained in Table 15-2. Suppose that the information on line 5 of Table 15-2 is arranged in the format shown in Table 15-3. We will refer to this type of financial statement as an **analytical income statement**. This distinguishes it from audited income statements published, for example, in the annual reports of public corporations. If we are aware of the simple mathematical relationships on which cost-volume-profit analysis is based, we can use Table 15-3 to find the break-even point in sales dollars for the Pierce Grain Company.

Analytical income statement
A financial statement used by internal analysts that differs in composition from audited or published financial statements.

First, let us explore the logic of the process. Recall from equation 15-1 that

sales – (total variable cost + total fixed cost) = EBIT

If we let total sales = S, total variable cost = VC, and total fixed cost = F, the preceding relationship becomes

$$S - (VC + F) = \text{EBIT}$$

TABLE 15-3 Pierce Grain Company Analytical Income Statement

Sales	\$300,000
Less: total variable costs	180,000
Revenue before fixed costs	\$120,000
Less: total fixed costs	100,000
EBIT	\$ 20,000

Because variable cost per unit of output and selling price per unit are *assumed* constant over the relevant output range in break-even analysis, the ratio of total sales to total variable cost, *VC/S*, is a constant for any level of sales. This permits us to rewrite the previous expression as:

$$S - \left[\left(\frac{VC}{S}\right)S\right] - F = \text{EBIT}$$

and

$$S\left(1 - \frac{VC}{S}\right) - F = \text{EBIT}$$

At the break-even point, however, EBIT = 0, and the corresponding break-even level of sales can be represented as S^*. At the break-even level of sales, we have

$$S^*\left(1 - \frac{VC}{S}\right) - F = 0$$

or

$$S^*\left(1 - \frac{VC}{S}\right) = F$$

Therefore,

$$S^* = \frac{F}{1 - \frac{VC}{S}} \qquad \textbf{(15-4)}$$

The application of equation 15-4 to Pierce Grain's analytical income statement in Table 15-3 permits the break-even sales level for the firm to be directly computed, as follows:

$$S^* = \frac{\$100{,}000}{1 - \frac{\$180{,}000}{\$300{,}000}}$$

$$= \frac{\$100{,}000}{1 - .60} = \$250{,}000$$

Notice that this is indeed the same break-even sales level for Pierce Grain that is indicated on line 4 of Table 15-2.

Graphic Representation, Analysis of Input Changes, and Cash Break-Even Point

In making a presentation to management, it is often effective to display the firm's cost-volume-profit relationships in the form of a chart. Even those individuals who truly enjoy analyzing financial problems find figures and equations dry material at times. Furthermore, by quickly scanning the basic break-even chart, the manager can approximate the EBIT amount that will prevail at different sales levels.

Such a chart has been prepared for the Pierce Grain Company. Figure 15-7 has been constructed for this firm using the input data contained in Table 15-2. Total fixed costs of $100,000 are added to the total variable costs associated with each production level to form the total costs line. When 25,000 units of product are manufactured and sold, the

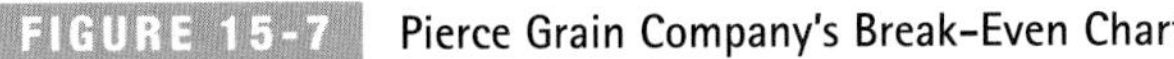
FIGURE 15-7 Pierce Grain Company's Break-Even Chart

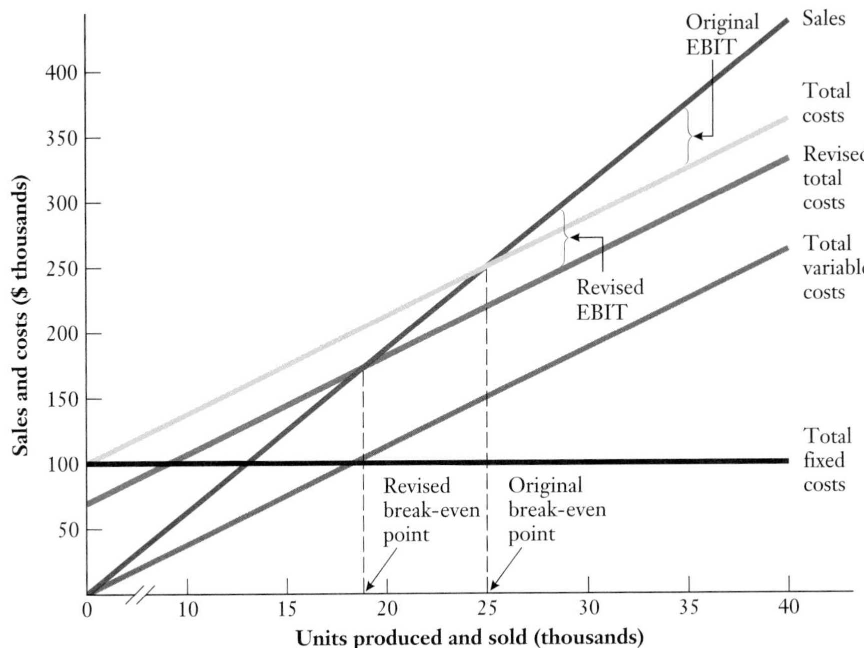

sales line and total costs line intersect. This means, of course, the EBIT that would exist at that volume of output is zero. Beyond 25,000 units of output, notice that sales revenues exceed the total costs line. This causes a positive EBIT. This positive EBIT, or profits, is labeled "original EBIT" in Figure 15-7.

The unencumbered nature of the break-even model makes it possible to quickly incorporate changes in the requisite input data and generate the revised output. Suppose a favorable combination of events causes Pierce Grain's fixed costs to decrease by \$25,000. This would put total fixed costs for the planning period at a level of \$75,000 rather than the \$100,000 originally forecast. Total costs, being the sum of fixed and variable costs, would be lower by \$25,000 at all output levels. The revised total costs line in Figure 15-7 reflects Pierce Grain's reduction in fixed costs. Under these revised conditions, the new break-even point in units would be as follows:

$$Q_B = \frac{\$75{,}000}{\$10 - \$6} = 18{,}750 \text{ units}$$

The revised break-even point of 18,750 units is identified in Figure 15-7, along with the revised EBIT amounts that would prevail at differing output and sales levels. The chart clearly indicates that at any specific production and sales level, the revised EBIT would exceed the original EBIT. This must be the case, as the revised total costs line lies below the original total costs line over the entire relevant output range. The effect on the break-even point caused by other changes in (1) the cost structure or (2) the pricing policy can be analyzed in a similar fashion.

Cash break-even analysis A variation from traditional break-even analysis that removes (deducts) noncash expenses from the cost items.

The data in Figure 15-7 can be used to demonstrate another version of basic cost-volume-profit analysis. This can be called **cash break-even analysis**. If the company's fixed- or variable-cost estimates allow for any noncash expenses, then the resultant break-even point is higher on an accounting profit basis than on a cash basis. This means the firm's production and sales levels do not have to be as great to cover the cash costs of manufacturing the product.

What are these noncash expenses? The largest and most significant is depreciation expense. Another category is prepaid expenses. Insurance policies are at times paid to cover a three-year cycle. Thus, the time period for which the break-even analysis is being performed might *not* involve an actual cash outlay for insurance coverage.

For purposes of illustration, assume that noncash expenses for Pierce Grain amount to $25,000 over the planning period and that all of these costs are fixed. We can compare the revised total costs line in Figure 15-7, which implicitly assumes a lower fixed *cash* cost line, with the sales revenue line to find the cash break-even point. Provided Pierce Grain can produce and sell 18,750 units over the planning horizon, revenues from sales will be equal to cash operating costs.

BACK TO THE PRINCIPLES

The preceding discussion on cash break-even analysis reinforces the importance of ***Principle 3: Cash—Not Profits—Is King.*** *By use of this modified version of regular break-even analysis, we are reminded that only cash can be reinvested into the firm's operations, as distinct from retained earnings. Cash is used to pay operating expenses, acquire real capital, and distribute earnings in the form of cash dividends. Another way of understanding* ***Principle 3*** *is as follows: Accounting profits are an opinion—cash is reality. Financial asset values are based on the firm's ability to generate cash flows. You cannot be misled over long time periods by cash-flow generation. Note that this emphasis on reality also relates to our discussion of value-based management techniques (economic value added and market value added).*

Limitations of Break-Even Analysis

Earlier we identified some of the applications of break-even analysis. This technique is a useful tool in many settings. It must be emphasized, however, that break-even analysis provides a *beneficial guide* to managerial action, not the final answer. The use of cost-volume-profit analysis has limitations, which should be kept in mind. These include the following:

1. The cost-volume-profit relationship is assumed to be linear. This is realistic only over narrow ranges of output.
2. The total revenue curve (sales curve) is presumed to increase linearly with the volume of output. This implies any quantity can be sold over the relevant output range at that *single* price. To be more realistic, it is necessary in many situations to compute *several* sales curves and corresponding break-even points at differing prices.
3. A constant production and sales mix is assumed. Should the company decide to produce more of one product and less of another, a new break-even point would have to be found. Only if the variable cost-to-sales ratios were identical for products involved would the new calculation be unnecessary.
4. The break-even chart and the break-even computation are static forms of analysis. Any alteration in the firm's cost or price structure dictates that a new break-even point be calculated. Break-even analysis is more helpful, therefore, in stable industries than in dynamic ones. See the Finance Matters box, "General Motors: Pricing Strategy in a Slow Aggregate Economy."

FINANCE MATTERS

GENERAL MOTORS: PRICING STRATEGY IN A SLOW AGGREGATE ECONOMY

In the previous chapter we pointed out that the U.S. economy slipped into a formal recession during the initial quarter of 2001. As late as the summer of 2003 the economic recovery in the United States was muted at best. In fact, the highest grade corporate bonds (those rated Aaa by Moody's) were yielding only 5.06 percent during the week of June 27, 2003, compared to a 22-year average (1981–2002) of 9.08 percent. Short-term interest rates were considerably lower. The target federal funds rate, for example, was set by Federal Reserve policy makers at a mere 1.00 percent. This put the commercial bank prime lending rate at 4.00 percent. The combination of (a) the slow overall economy and (b) extraordinarily low borrowing rates gave automobile manufacturers ample incentives to vigorously compete for sales via their pricing strategies.

The discussion just ended on break-even analysis demonstrated how firms and their financial analysts can use the contribution margin metric to help formulate their pricing plans. Next, in an excerpt from a General Motors press release of July 2003, we see how that giant firm uses the break-even concept. Notice also the reference to GM's limited flexibility relative to managing fixed costs. This will directly relate to our subsequent discussion on "operating leverage."

> Over the past year and a half, GM has driven the U.S. auto industry into a price war of historic proportions as it battled the effects of a slowing economy. Last month GM's average per-vehicle incentive hit $3,934, a 51 percent increase over June 2002 and the highest average among large automakers.

With limited room to cut fixed costs, GM executives have defended their strategy as the best way to maximize profits and keep its factories running. GM's inventories were about 21 percent above normal at the end of June.

Source: Reuters at www.money.com/2003/07/08/pf/autos/gm_incentives.reut/index.htm.

CONCEPT CHECK

1. Distinguish among "fixed costs," "variable costs," and "semivariable costs."
2. Define the term "contribution margin."
3. When is it useful or necessary to compute the break-even point in terms of sales dollars rather than units of output?

OPERATING LEVERAGE

Objective 3

If *fixed* operating costs are present in the firm's cost structure, so is *operating leverage.* Fixed operating costs do not include interest charges incurred from the firm's use of debt financing. Those costs will be incorporated into the analysis when financial leverage is discussed.

So operating leverage arises from the firm's use of fixed operating costs. But what is operating leverage? Operating leverage is the responsiveness of the firm's EBIT to fluctuations in sales. By continuing to draw on our data for the Pierce Grain Company, we can illustrate the concept of operating leverage. Table 15-4 contains data for a study of a possible fluctuation in the firm's sales level. It is assumed that Pierce Grain is currently operating at an annual sales level of $300,000. This is referred to in the tabulation as the base sales level at t (time period zero). The question is: How will Pierce Grain's EBIT level respond to a positive 20 percent change in sales? A sales volume of $360,000, referred to as the forecast sales level at $t + 1$, reflects the 20 percent sales rise anticipated over the planning period. Assume that the planning period is one year.

Operating leverage relationships are derived within the mathematical assumptions of cost-volume-profit analysis. In the present example, this means that Pierce Grain's

TABLE 15-4 Concept of Operating Leverage: Increase in Pierce Grain Company Sales

ITEM	BASE SALES LEVEL, t	FORECAST SALES LEVEL, $t + 1$
Sales	$300,000	$360,000
Less: total variable costs	180,000	216,000
Revenue before fixed costs	$120,000	$144,000
Less: total fixed costs	100,000	100,000
EBIT	$ 20,000	$ 44,000

variable cost-to-sales ratio of .6 will continue to hold during time period $t + 1$, and the fixed costs will hold steady at $100,000.

Given the forecasted sales level for Pierce Grain and its cost structure, we can measure the responsiveness of EBIT to the upswing in volume. Notice in Table 15-4 that EBIT is expected to be $44,000 at the end of the planning period. The percentage change in EBIT from t to $t + 1$ can be measured as follows:

$$\text{percentage change in EBIT} = \frac{\$44{,}000_{t+1} - \$20{,}000_t}{\$20{,}000_t} = \frac{\$24{,}000}{\$20{,}000} = 120\%$$

We know that the projected fluctuation in sales amounts to 20 percent of the base period, t, sales level. This is verified:

$$\text{percentage change in sales} = \frac{\$360{,}000_{t+1} - \$300{,}000_t}{\$300{,}000_t} = \frac{\$60{,}000}{\$300{,}000} = 20\%$$

By relating the percentage fluctuation in EBIT to the percentage fluctuation in sales, we can calculate a specific measure of operating leverage. Thus, we have:

$$\frac{\text{degree of operating leverage}}{\text{from the base sales level}_{(s)}} = DOL_s = \frac{\text{percentage change in EBIT}}{\text{percentage change in sales}} \tag{15-5}$$

Applying equation 15-5 to our Pierce Grain data gives:

$$DOL_{\$300{,}000} = \frac{120\%}{20\%} = 6 \text{ times}$$

Unless we understand what the specific measure of operating leverage tells us, the fact that we may know it is equal to six times is nothing more than sterile information. For Pierce Grain, the inference is that for *any* percentage fluctuation in sales from the base level, the percentage fluctuation in EBIT will be six times as great. If Pierce Grain expected only a 5 percent rise in sales over the coming period, a 30 percent rise in EBIT would be anticipated as follows:

$$(\text{percentage change in sales}) \times (DOL_s) = \text{percentage change in EBIT}$$
$$(5\%) \times (6) = 30\%$$

We will now return to the postulated 20 percent change in sales. What if the direction of the fluctuation is expected to be negative rather than positive? What is in store for

TABLE 15-5 Concept of Operating Leverage: Decrease in Pierce Grain Company Sales

ITEM	BASE SALES LEVEL, t	FORECAST SALES LEVEL, $t+1$
Sales	$300,000	$240,000
Less: total variable costs	180,000	144,000
Revenue before fixed costs	$120,000	$ 96,000
Less: total fixed costs	100,000	100,000
EBIT	$ 20,000	$ –4,000

Pierce Grain? Unfortunately for Pierce Grain (but fortunately for the analytical process), we will see that the operating leverage measure holds in the negative direction as well. This situation is displayed in Table 15-5.

At the $240,000 sales level, which represents the 20 percent decrease from the base period, Pierce Grain's EBIT is expected to be –$4,000. How sensitive is EBIT to this sales change? The magnitude of the EBIT fluctuation is calculated as:[4]

$$\text{percentage change in EBIT} = \frac{-\$4{,}000_{t+1} - \$20{,}000_t}{\$20{,}000_t} = \frac{-\$24{,}000}{\$20{,}000} = -120\%$$

Making use of our knowledge that the sales change was equal to –20 percent permits us to compute the specific measure of operating leverage as:

$$DOL_{\$300{,}000} = \frac{-120\%}{-20\%} = 6 \text{ times}$$

What we have seen, then, is that the degree of operating leverage measure works in the positive or the negative direction. A negative change in production volume and sales can be magnified severalfold when the effect on EBIT is calculated.

To this point, our calculations of the degree of operating leverage have required two analytical income statements: one for the base period and a second for the subsequent period that incorporates the possible sales alteration. This cumbersome process can be simplified. If unit cost data are available to the financial manager, the relationship can be expressed directly in the following manner:

$$DOL_s = \frac{Q(P-V)}{Q(P-V)-F} \tag{15-6}$$

Observe in equation 15-6 that the variables were all previously defined in our algebraic analysis of the break-even model. Recall that Pierce sells its product at $10 per unit, the unit variable cost is $6, and total fixed costs over the planning horizon are $100,000. Still assuming that Pierce is operating at a $300,000 sales volume, which means output (Q) is 30,000 units, we can find the degree of operating leverage by application of equation 15-6:

$$DOL_{\$300{,}000} = \frac{30{,}000\ (\$10 - \$6)}{30{,}000\ (\$10 - \$6) - \$100{,}000} = \frac{\$120{,}000}{\$20{,}000} = 6 \text{ times}$$

[4] Some students have conceptual difficulty in computing these percentage changes when negative amounts are involved. Notice by inspection in Table 15-5 that the *difference* between an EBIT amount of +$20,000 at t and –$4,000 at $t+1$ is –$24,000.

Whereas equation 15-6 requires us to know unit cost data to carry out the computations, the next formulation we examine does not. If we have an analytical income statement for the base period, then equation 15-6 can be employed to find the firm's degree of operating leverage:

$$DOL_s = \frac{\text{revenue before fixed costs}}{\text{EBIT}} = \frac{S - VC}{S - VC - F} \tag{15-7}$$

Use of equation 15-7 in conjunction with the base period data for Pierce Grain shown in either Table 15-4 or 15-5 gives:

$$DOL_{\$300,000} = \frac{\$120,000}{\$20,000} = 6 \text{ times}$$

The three versions of the operating leverage measure all produce the same result. Data availability will sometimes dictate which formulation can be applied. The crucial consideration, though, is that you grasp what the measurement tells you. For Pierce Grain, a 1 percent change in sales will produce a 6 percent change in EBIT.

Before we complete our discussion of operating leverage and move on to the subject of financial leverage, ask yourself, "Which type of leverage is more under the control of management?" You will probably (and correctly) come to the conclusion that the firm's managers have less control over its operating cost structure and almost complete control over its financial structure. What the firm actually produces, for example, will determine to a significant degree the division between fixed and variable costs. There is more room for substitution among the various sources of financial capital than there is among the labor and real capital inputs that enable the firm to meet its production requirements. Thus, you can anticipate more arguments over the choice to use a given degree of financial leverage than the corresponding choice over operating leverage use.

IMPLICATIONS

As the firm's scale of operations moves in a favorable manner above the break-even point, the degree of operating leverage at each subsequent (higher) sales base will decline. In short, the greater the sales level, the lower the degree of operating leverage. This is demonstrated in Table 15-6 for the Pierce Grain Company. At the break-even sales level for Pierce Grain, the degree of operating leverage is *undefined*, because the denominator in any of the computational formulas is zero. Notice that beyond the break-even point of 25,000 units, the degree of operating leverage declines. It will decline at a decreasing rate

TABLE 15-6 Pierce Grain Company Degree of Operating Leverage Relative to Different Sales Bases

UNITS PRODUCED AND SOLD	SALES DOLLARS	DOL_s
25,000	$ 250,000	Undefined
30,000	300,000	6.00
35,000	350,000	3.50
40,000	400,000	2.67
45,000	450,000	2.25
50,000	500,000	2.00
75,000	750,000	1.50
100,000	1,000,000	1.33

FIGURE 15-8 Pierce Grain Company Degree of Operating Leverage Relative to Different Sales Bases

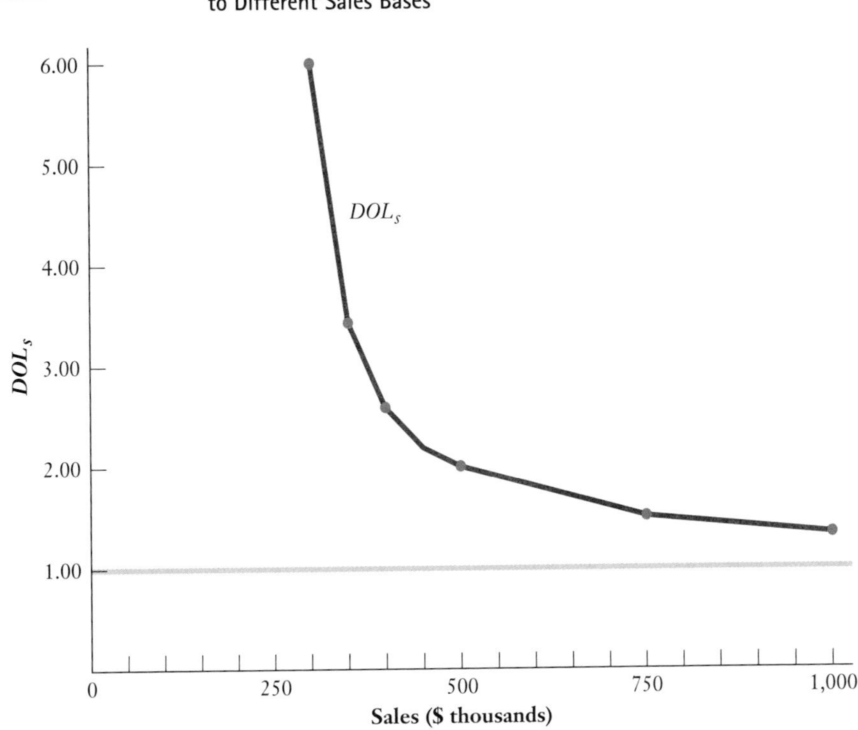

and asymptotically approach a value of 1.00. As long as some fixed operating costs are present in the firm's cost structure, however, operating leverage exists, and the degree of operating leverage (DOL_s) will exceed 1.00. Operating leverage is present, then, whenever the firm faces the following situation:

$$\frac{\text{percentage change in EBIT}}{\text{percentage change in sales}} > 1.00$$

The data in Table 15-6 are presented in graphic form in Figure 15-8.

CONCEPT CHECK

1. If a firm's degree of operating leverage happens to be six times, what precisely does that mean?
2. What does the degree of operating leverage concept suggest when a negative shock in production volume and sales occurs?
3. When is operating leverage present in the firm's cost structure? What condition is necessary for operating leverage not to be present in the firm's cost structure?

The greater the firm's degree of operating leverage, the more its profits will vary with a given percentage change in sales. Thus, operating leverage is definitely an attribute of the business risk that confronts the company. From Table 15-6 and Figure 15-8, we have seen that the degree of operating leverage falls as sales increase past the firm's break-even point. The sheer size and operating profitability of the firm, therefore, affect and can lessen its business-risk exposure.

The manager considering an alteration in the firm's cost structure will benefit from an understanding of the operating leverage concept. It might be possible to replace part of the labor force with capital equipment (machinery). A possible result is an increase in fixed costs associated with the new machinery and a reduction in variable costs attributable to a lower labor bill. This conceivably could raise the firm's degree of operating leverage at a specific sales base. If the prospects for future sales increases are high, then increasing the degree of operating leverage might be a prudent decision. The opposite conclusion will be reached if sales prospects are unattractive.

FINANCIAL LEVERAGE

Objective 4

We have defined *financial leverage* as the practice of financing a portion of the firm's assets with securities bearing a fixed rate of return in hope of increasing the ultimate return to the common shareholders. In the present discussion, we focus on the responsiveness of the company's earnings per share to changes in its EBIT. For the time being, then, the return to the common stockholder being concentrated upon is earnings per share. We are *not* saying that earnings per share is the appropriate criterion for all financing decisions. In fact, the weakness of such a contention will be examined in the next chapter. Rather, the use of financial leverage produces a certain type of *effect*. This effect can be illustrated clearly by concentrating on an earnings-per-share criterion.

Let us assume that the Pierce Grain Company is in the process of getting started as a going concern. The firm's potential owners have calculated that $200,000 is needed to purchase the necessary assets to conduct the business. Three possible financing plans have been identified for raising the $200,000; they are presented in Table 15-7. In plan A, no financial risk is assumed: The entire $200,000 is raised by selling 2,000 common shares, each with a $100 par value. In plan B, a moderate amount of financial risk is assumed: 25 percent of the assets are financed with a debt issue that carries an 8 percent annual interest rate. Plan C would use the most financial leverage: 40 percent of the assets would be financed with a debt issue costing 8 percent.[5]

[5] In actual practice, moving from a 25 to a 40 percent debt ratio would probably result in a higher interest rate on the additional bonds. That effect is ignored here to let us concentrate on the ramifications of using different proportions of debt in the financial structure.

TABLE 15-7 Pierce Grain Company Possible Financial Structures

PLAN A: 0% DEBT			
		Total debt	$ 0
		Common equity	200,000[a]
Total assets	$200,000	Total liabilities and equity	$200,000
PLAN B: 25% DEBT AT 8% INTEREST RATE			
		Total debt	$ 50,000
		Common equity	150,000[b]
Total assets	$200,000	Total liabilities and equity	$200,000
PLAN C: 40% DEBT AT 8% INTEREST RATE			
		Total debt	$ 80,000
		Common equity	120,000[c]
Total assets	$200,000	Total liabilities and equity	$200,000

[a]2,000 common shares outstanding; [b]1,500 common shares outstanding; [c]1,200 common shares outstanding

TABLE 15-8 Pierce Grain Company Analysis of Financial Leverage at Different EBIT Levels

(1) EBIT	(2) INTEREST	(3) = (1) − (2) EBT	(4) = (3) × .5 TAXES	(5) = (3) − (4) NET INCOME TO COMMON	(6) EARNINGS PER SHARE	
PLAN A: 0% DEBT; $200,000 COMMON EQUITY, 2,000 SHARES						
$ 0	$ 0	$ 0	$ 0	$ 0	$ 0	
20,000	0	20,000	10,000	10,000	5.00	100%
40,000	0	40,000	20,000	20,000	10.00	
60,000	0	60,000	30,000	30,000	15.00	
80,000	0	80,000	40,000	40,000	20.00	
PLAN B: 25% DEBT; 8% INTEREST RATE; $150,000 COMMON EQUITY, 1,500 SHARES						
$ 0	$4,000	$(4,000)	$(2,000)[a]	$(2,000)	$(1.33)	
20,000	4,000	16,000	8,000	8,000	5.33	125%
40,000	4,000	36,000	18,000	18,000	12.00	
60,000	4,000	56,000	28,000	28,000	18.67	
80,000	4,000	76,000	38,000	38,000	25.33	
PLAN C: 40% DEBT; 8% INTEREST RATE; $120,000 COMMON EQUITY, 1,200 SHARES						
$ 0	$6,400	$(6,400)	$(3,200)[a]	$(3,200)	$(2.67)	
20,000	6,400	13,600	6,800	6,800	5.67	147%
40,000	6,400	33,600	16,800	16,800	14.00	
60,000	6,400	53,600	26,800	26,800	22.33	
80,000	6,400	73,600	36,800	36,800	30.67	

[a]The negative tax bill recognizes the credit arising from the carryback and carryforward provision of the tax code.

Table 15-8 presents the impact of financial leverage on earnings per share associated with each fundraising alternative. If EBIT should increase from $20,000 to $40,000, then earnings per share would rise by 100 percent under plan A. The same positive fluctuation in EBIT would occasion an earnings per share rise of 125 percent under plan B, and 147 percent under plan C. In plans B and C, the 100 percent increase in EBIT (from $20,000 to $40,000) is magnified to a greater than 100 percent increase in earnings per share. The firm is employing financial leverage, and exposing its owners to financial risk, when the following situation exists:

$$\frac{\text{percentage change in earnings per share}}{\text{percentage change in EBIT}} > 1.00$$

By following the same general procedures that allowed us to analyze the firm's use of operating leverage, we can lay out a precise measure of financial leverage. Such a measure deals with the sensitivity of earnings per share to EBIT fluctuations. The relationship can be expressed as:

$$\text{degree of financial leverage } (DFL) \text{ from base EBIT level} = DFL_{EBIT} = \frac{\text{percentage change in earnings per share}}{\text{percentage change in EBIT}} \quad \textbf{(15-8)}$$

Use of equation 15-8 with each of the financing choices outlined for Pierce Grain is shown subsequently. The base EBIT level is $20,000 in each case.

$$\text{Plan A: } DFL_{\$20,000} = \frac{100\%}{100\%} = 1.00 \text{ time}$$

$$\text{Plan B: } DFL_{\$20,000} = \frac{125\%}{100\%} = 1.25 \text{ times}$$

$$\text{Plan C: } DFL_{\$20,000} = \frac{147\%}{100\%} = 1.47 \text{ times}$$

FINANCE MATTERS

IBM: INTERNATIONAL INFLUENCES ON REVENUE GROWTH

In 1996, IBM posted an increase in sales of some 5.6 percent. But the company's change in net income was a much greater 30.0 percent. This is exactly the type of magnification effect that we are studying within this chapter. The management discussion from IBM's 1996 *Annual Report* highlights several concepts explored in this and other chapters of the text.

IBM's management identifies the building blocks of its strategic plan. The emphasis on sales growth remains intact. Notice the closing reference to cash-flow generation—this should remind you of **Principle 3: Cash—Not Profits—Is King.** Companies do, in fact, think about the important concepts that we discuss in this text.

IBM's financial performance in 1996 reflects continued progress toward its strategic goals of revenue growth, an expanded portfolio of industry-specific customer solutions (especially through network computing), and an increasingly competitive cost and expense structure.

The company reported record revenue of nearly $76 billion, 30 percent net earnings growth over 1995, and ended the year with over $8 billion in cash. The company also continued to align itself for strategic growth by investing almost $20 billion in critical high-growth and advanced technology businesses, research and development, acquisitions, and repurchases of its common shares.

The company's results were also affected adversely by the continued weakness of the European economy and the continued strengthening of the U.S. dollar. Without the currency effect, year-to-year revenue growth would have been 9 percent compared with the reported growth of 6 percent.

Although excellent progress was made in 1996, the company must continue to implement strategic actions to further improve its competitiveness. These actions include an ongoing focus on revenue growth and stable net income margins, while at the same time maintaining a strong balance sheet and cash flows for long-term growth.

Source: IBM *Annual Report* (1996): 44.

Like operating leverage, the *degree of financial leverage* concept performs in the negative direction as well as the positive. Should EBIT fall by 10 percent, the Pierce Grain Company would suffer a 12.5 percent decline in earnings per share under plan B. If plan C were chosen to raise the necessary financial capital, the decline in earnings would be 14.7 percent. Observe that the greater the *DFL*, the greater the fluctuations (positive or negative) in earnings per share. The common stockholder is required to endure greater variations in returns when the firm's management chooses to use more financial leverage rather than less. The *DFL* measure allows the variation to be quantified. See the Finance Matters box, "IBM: International Influences on Revenue Growth."

Rather than taking the time to compute percentage changes in EBIT and earnings per share, the *DFL* can be found directly, as follows:

$$DFL_{EBIT} = \frac{EBIT}{EBIT - I} \qquad \textbf{(15-9)}$$

In equation 15-9, the variable, *I*, represents the total interest expense incurred on *all* the firm's contractual debt obligations. If six bonds are outstanding, *I* is the sum of the interest expense on all six bonds. If the firm has preferred stock in its financial structure, the dividend on such issues must be inflated to a before-tax basis and included in the computation of *I*.[6] In this latter instance, *I* is in reality the sum of all fixed financing costs.

[6] Suppose (1) preferred dividends of $4,000 are paid annually by the firm and (2) it faces a 40 percent marginal tax rate. How much must the firm earn *before* taxes to make the $4,000 payment out of after-tax earnings? Because preferred dividends are not tax deductible to the paying company, we have $4,000/(1 – .40) = $6,666.67. The Tax Reform Act of 1986 provided for the taxation of corporate incomes at a maximum rate of 34 percent for tax years beginning after June 30, 1987. This maximum rate applies to taxable incomes over $75,000. Under this new tax provision, the firm would need to earn only $6,060.61 before taxes to make the $4,000 preferred dividend payment. That is, $4,000/(1 – .34) = $6,060.61. Note that from a financial policy viewpoint, the 1986 tax act reduced *somewhat* the tax shield advantages of corporate debt financing and simultaneously reduced the tax bias against preferred stock and common stock financing.

Equation 15-9 has been applied to each of Pierce Grain's financing plans (Table 15-8) at a base EBIT level of \$20,000. The results are as follows:

$$\text{Plan A: } DFL_{\$20{,}000} = \frac{\$20{,}000}{\$20{,}000 - 0} = 1.00 \text{ time}$$

$$\text{Plan B: } DFL_{\$20{,}000} = \frac{\$20{,}000}{\$20{,}000 - \$4{,}000} = 1.25 \text{ times}$$

$$\text{Plan C: } DFL_{\$20{,}000} = \frac{\$20{,}000}{\$20{,}000 - \$6{,}400} = 1.47 \text{ times}$$

As you probably suspected, the measures of financial leverage shown previously are identical to those obtained by use of equation 15-8. This will always be the case.

BACK TO THE PRINCIPLES

The effect on the earnings stream available to the firm's common stockholders from combining operating and financial leverage in large degrees is dramatic. When the use of both leverage types is indeed heavy, a large sales increase will result in a very large rise in earnings per share. Be aware, though, that the very same thing happens in the opposite direction should the sales change be negative! Piling heavy financial leverage use on a high degree of operating leverage, then, is a very risky way to do business.

Thus, the firm will not "fool the markets" by combining high degrees of operating and financial leverage. Recall ***Principle 6: Efficient Capital Markets—The markets are quick and the prices are right.*** *We stated in Chapter 1 that efficient markets deal with the speed with which information is impounded into security prices. Should the firm become overlevered in the eyes of the markets—say, stemming from an overly large issue of new debt securities—then the company's stock price will quickly be adjusted downward. The capital markets fully understand the double-edged sword of leverage use. Things go well when revenues rise; things do not go well when revenues fall. And, leverage use, either operating or financial, magnifies the original fluctuations in the revenues. Be aware.*

CONCEPT CHECK

1. If a firm's degree of financial leverage happens to be 1.25 times, what precisely does that mean?
2. What does the degree of financial leverage concept suggest when a negative shock in earnings before interest and taxes (EBIT) occurs?
3. From the viewpoint of the company's shareholders, explain the difference between enduring a degree of financial leverage of five times versus two times.

COMBINATION OF OPERATING AND FINANCIAL LEVERAGE

Objective 5

Changes in sales revenues cause greater changes in EBIT. Additionally, changes in EBIT translate into larger variations in both earnings per share (EPS) and total earnings available to the common shareholders (EAC), if the firm chooses to use financial leverage. It

Calculating the degree of combined leverage from some base sales level is not difficult. All that is needed is "top line" data (i.e., sales, also called revenues, in many annual reports) and bottom line data (i.e., earnings per share) for consecutive time periods. Give it a try by using the Walt Disney Company as the subject firm. Disney maintains a good Web site at **www.disney.com/investors**. At that site financial documents can be ordered online. Alternatively, you can find the latest Disney annual report at **www.hoovers.com**. The latter site provides links through the SEC for numerous annual reports called 10-K filings. Brief company overviews (fact sheets) are provided on the Hoover's site without going to the SEC site.

should be no surprise, then, to find out that combining operating and financial leverage causes further large variations in earnings per share. This entire process is visually displayed in Figure 15-9.

Because the risk associated with possible earnings per share is affected by the use of combined or total leverage, it is useful to quantify the effect. For an illustration, we refer once more to the Pierce Grain Company. The cost structure identified for Pierce Grain in our discussion of break-even analysis still holds. Furthermore, assume that plan B, which carried a 25 percent debt ratio, was chosen to finance the company's assets. Turn your attention to Table 15-9.

In Table 15-9, an increase in output for Pierce Grain from 30,000 to 36,000 units is analyzed. This increase represents a 20 percent rise in sales revenues. From our earlier discussion of operating leverage and the data in Table 15-9, we can see that this 20 percent increase in sales is magnified into a 120 percent rise in EBIT. From this base sales level of $300,000 the degree of operating leverage is six times.

The 120 percent rise in EBIT induces a change in earnings per share and earnings available to the common shareholders of 150 percent. The degree of financial leverage is therefore 1.25 times.

The upshot of the analysis is that the 20 percent rise in sales has been magnified to 150 percent, as reflected by the percentage change in earnings per share. The formal measure of combined leverage can be expressed as follows:

$$\begin{pmatrix}\text{degree of combined}\\ \text{leverage from the}\\ \text{base sales level}\end{pmatrix} = DCL_s = \left(\frac{\begin{matrix}\text{percentage change in}\\ \text{earnings per share}\end{matrix}}{\text{percentage change in sales}}\right) \tag{15-10}$$

This equation was used in the bottom portion of Table 15-9 to determine that the degree of combined leverage from the base sales level of $300,000 is 7.50 times. Pierce Grain's use of both operating and financial leverage will cause any percentage change in sales (from the specific base level) to be magnified by a factor of 7.50 when the effect on earnings per share is computed. A 1 percent change in sales, for example, will result in a 7.50 percent change in earnings per share.

Notice that the degree of combined leverage is actually the *product* (not the simple sum) of the two independent leverage measures. Thus, we have:

$$(DOL_s) - (DFL_{EBIT}) = DCL_s \tag{15-11}$$

or

$$(6) \times (1.25) = 7.50 \text{ times}$$

FIGURE 15-9 Leverage and Earnings Fluctuations

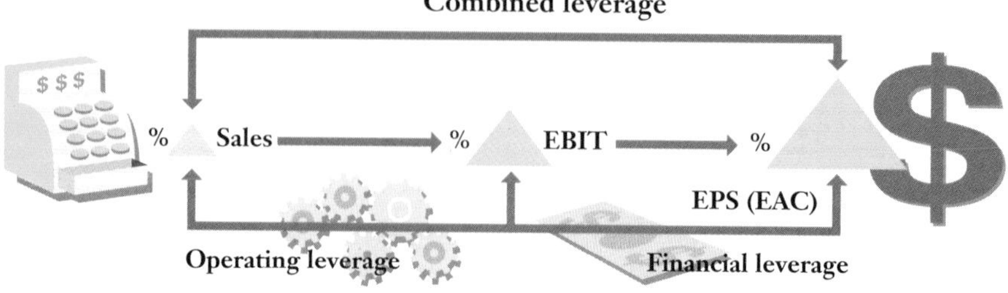

TABLE 15-9 Pierce Grain Company Combined Leverage Analysis

ITEM	BASE SALES LEVEL, t	FORECAST SALES LEVEL, $t+1$	SELECTED PERCENTAGE CHANGES
Sales	$300,000	$360,000	+20
Less: total variable costs	180,000	216,000	
Revenue before fixed costs	$120,000	$144,000	
Less: total fixed costs	100,000	100,000	
EBIT	$ 20,000	$ 44,000	+120
Less: interest expense	4,000	4,000	
Earnings before taxes (EBT)	$ 16,000	$ 40,000	
Less: taxes at 50%	8,000	20,000	
Net income	$ 8,000	$ 20,000	+150
Less: preferred dividends	0	0	
Earnings available to common (EAC)	$ 8,000	$ 20,000	+150
Number of common shares	1,500	1,500	
Earnings per share (EPS)	$ 5.33	$ 13.33	+150

$$\text{Degree of operating leverage} = DOL_{\$300{,}000} = \frac{120\%}{20\%} = 6 \text{ times}$$

$$\text{Degree of financial leverage} = DFL_{\$20{,}000} = \frac{150\%}{120\%} = 1.25 \text{ times}$$

$$\text{Degree of combined leverage} = DCL_{\$300{,}000} = \frac{150\%}{20\%} = 7.50 \text{ times}$$

It is possible to ascertain the degree of combined leverage in a direct fashion, without determining any percentage fluctuations or the separate leverage values. We need only substitute the appropriate values into equation 15-12:[7]

$$DCL_s = \frac{Q(P-V)}{Q(P-V)-F-I} \tag{15-12}$$

The variable definitions in equation 15-12 are the same ones that have been employed throughout this chapter. Use of equation 15-12 with the information in Table 15-9 gives:

$$\begin{aligned} DCL_{\$300,000} &= \frac{\$30{,}000\ (\$10-\$6)}{\$30{,}000\ (\$10-\$6)-\$100{,}000-\$4{,}000} \\ &= \frac{\$120{,}000}{\$16{,}000} \\ &= 7.5 \text{ times} \end{aligned}$$

See the Finance Matters box, "The Coca-Cola Company Financial Policies."

IMPLICATIONS

The total risk exposure the firm assumes can be managed by combining operating and financial leverage in different degrees. Knowledge of the various leverage measures aids the financial officer in determining the proper level of overall risk that should be

[7] As was the case with the degree of financial leverage metric, the variable, I, in the combined leverage measure must include the before-tax equivalent of any preferred dividend payments when preferred stock is in the financial structure.

FINANCE MATTERS

THE COCA-COLA COMPANY FINANCIAL POLICIES

The fact that financial leverage effects can be measured provides management the opportunity to shape corporate policy formally around the decision to use or avoid the use of leverage-inducing financial instruments. The Coca-Cola Company has very specific policies on the use of financial leverage. The learning objectives of this chapter, then, comprise more than mere academic, intellectual exercises. The material is, in fact, the stuff of boardroom-level discussion.

We stated in Chapter 1 that the goal of the firm is to maximize shareholder wealth, and this means maximizing the price of the firm's existing common stock. The Coca-Cola Company has accepted this approach to management as its "primary objective." To accomplish the objective, the company has developed a strategy that centers on investment in its core business—the high-return soft drink business. Notice that Coca-Cola also speaks clearly about "optimizing" its cost of capital through properly designed financial policies. This is a good time to review the cost of capital linkage identified in Figure 15-1 and ponder its meaning.

Determining an appropriate (optimal) financing mix is a crucial activity of financial management. Companies use different approaches to seek an optimal range of financial leverage use. The Coca-Cola Company searches for a "prudent" level of debt use that is affected by (1) its projected cash flows, (2) interest coverage ratios, and (3) ratio of long-term debt to total capitalization. Further, the company is highly concerned about the bond ratings that it receives from major rating agencies.

Management's primary objective is to maximize share-owner value over time. To accomplish this objective, the Coca-Cola Company and subsidiaries (the Company) have developed a comprehensive business strategy that emphasizes maximizing long-term cash flows. This strategy focuses on continuing aggressive investment in the high-return soft drink business, increasing returns on existing investments and optimizing the cost of capital through appropriate financial policies. The success of this strategy is evidenced by the growth in the Company's cash flows and earnings, its increased returns on total capital and equity, and the total return to its share owners over time.

Management seeks investments that strategically enhance existing operations and offer cash returns that exceed the Company's long-term after-tax weighted average cost of capital, estimated by management to be approximately 11 percent as of January 1, 1994. The Company's soft drink business generates inherent high returns on capital, providing an attractive area for continued investment.

Maximizing share-owner value necessitates optimizing the Company's cost of capital through appropriate financial policies.

The Company maintains debt levels considered prudent based on the Company's cash flows, interest coverage, and the percentage of debt to the Company's total capital. The Company's overall cost of capital is lowered by the use of debt financing, resulting in increased return to share owners.

The Company's capital structure and financial policies have resulted in long-term credit ratings of "AA" from Standard & Poor's and "Aa3" from Moody's, as well as the highest credit ratings available for its commercial paper programs. The Company's strong financial position and cash flows allow for opportunistic access to financing in financial markets around the world.

Source: The Coca-Cola Company, *Annual Report* (1993): 44–46.

accepted. If a high degree of business risk is inherent to the specific line of commercial activity, then a low posture regarding financial risk would minimize *additional* earnings fluctuations stemming from sales changes. Conversely, the firm that by its very nature incurs a low level of fixed operating costs might choose to use a high degree of financial leverage in the hope of increasing earnings per share and the rate of return on the common equity investment.

CONCEPT CHECK

1. Explain the degree of combined leverage concept.
2. When would the degree of operating leverage and the degree of combined leverage be equal?

BACK TO THE PRINCIPLES

Our analysis of business risk, financial risk, and the three measurements of leverage use all relate directly to ***Principle 1: The Risk-Return Trade-Off—We won't take on additional risk unless we expect to be compensated with additional return.*** *Should the firm decide to "pile on" heavy financial leverage use on top of a high degree of business risk exposure, then we would expect the firm's overall cost of capital to rise and its stock price to fall. This underscores the critical nature of designing the firm's financing mix to both the financial manager and the stockholders. This central area of financial decision making is explored further in the next chapter on "Planning the Firm's Financing Mix."*

THE MULTINATIONAL FIRM: BUSINESS RISK AND GLOBAL SALES

Objective 6

Early in this chapter we defined business risk as the relative dispersion (variability) in the firm's expected earnings before interest and taxes (EBIT). When we discussed operating leverage and the degree of operating leverage concept, we learned that changes or shocks to the firm's overall sales level will cause a greater percentage change in EBIT if fixed operating costs are present in the firm's cost structure. Thus, any event that induces a fluctuation in measured sales will impact a firm's business risk and its resulting EBIT.

Business risk is multidimensional and international. It is directly affected by several factors, including (1) the sensitivity of the firm's product demand to general economic conditions, (2) the degree of competition to which the firm is exposed, (3) product diversification, (4) growth prospects, and (5) global sales volume and production output. The latter factor is especially important to the multinational firm, and such firms are aware of it. Some seek to take advantage of it in an aggressive manner.

Consider the Coca-Cola Company. In his statement to shareholders published in 1998, Mr. M. Douglas Ivester, the Chairman of Coke's Board of Directors and its Chief Executive Officer, commented on the firm's commercial strategy in both China and Russia.[8] He said: "In China, the world's largest market, our volume soared another 30 percent in 1997. But the average resident of China still drinks just six of our products a year—certainly a business in its infancy." Notice that while Coke's presence in China increases its total business risk exposure, this exposure is viewed by Mr. Ivester as a commercial opportunity for the firm. See the Finance Matters box, "The Relationship Among Sales, Cash Flow, and Leverage."

Next, in his discussion of the Russian market, Mr. Ivester offered: "In Russia, where we took the lead over our largest competitor in 1996, we widened that lead to 3-to-1 in 1997; we opened four more plants there on October 1, bringing our system's Russian investment to $650 million and pointing to strong future growth." Here we see that Coke is both cultivating the Russian consumer and simultaneously investing in plant and equipment there. Thus, Coke's broad commercial strategy, which impacts business risk, also encompasses the capital-budgeting decision discussed earlier in this text.

CONCEPT CHECK

1. Identify several factors that directly affect a firm's business risk.
2. How might a firm's commercial strategy be influenced by its presence in foreign markets?

[8] The Coca-Cola Company, *Annual Report*, 1997: 5–6.

FINANCE MATTERS

THE RELATIONSHIP AMONG SALES, CASH FLOW, AND LEVERAGE

We spent considerable time in earlier chapters studying capital-budgeting techniques and discussed the search by firms for projects with positive net present values. The spending by firms on real capital projects is an important topic not only for the specific firms involved, but also for the aggregate economy. This is because high levels of real capital spending over time are associated with high levels of societal wealth. Societies that do not invest tend to be poor. So, it follows that national economic policymaking is concerned with what variables do affect the spending by companies on projects.

Mr. Kopcke and Mr. Howrey of the Federal Reserve Bank of Boston studied the investment spending of 396 domestic manufacturing corporations and found some interesting relationships among the variables that seem to influence the size of firms' capital budgets.

The authors of this study have put forth a reasonable conclusion concerning the relationship between capital spending and the firm's choice to use or avoid financial leverage. They suggest that *both* capital budgets and financial leverage use depend on expected profits. This is close to asserting that the specific firm's capacity to generate future cash flows is a major determinant of its financing mix. This should remind you of **Principle 3: Cash—Not Profits—Is King.** In the present context, the firm's ability to service its debt contracts depends on its ability to generate future cash flows.

Also, we see that these researchers suggest that general business conditions (that is, strong or weak) affect not only the size of the firm's capital budget, but also management's decision to use financial leverage in the financing of that capital budget. Such a logical combination of (1) the state of business conditions and (2) the expectation of future profits (cash flows) means that the underlying nature of the business in which the firm operates should be the most important factor affecting its ultimate financing mix. That is, *business risk* and commercial strategy directly affect the specific firm's decision to use financial leverage.

Perhaps it is not surprising that leverage, liquidity, and other variables should influence capital spending so little once the general business climate (represented by sales or cash flow) has been taken into account. The choice of leverage, like capital spending, depends on the prospect for profit. A good business climate can foster both investment and debt financing. In these cases, higher leverage does not deter investment; instead, it may appear to facilitate investment.

At other times, companies may increase their leverage while they reduce their capital spending, if the return on existing capital is great compared to that foreseen on new investments. In these cases, higher leverage may appear to deter investment. In any of these cases, appearances can be deceiving, because investment and leverage jointly depend on business conditions, and this dependency entails no consistent relationship between indebtedness and investment.

For the making of economic policy, the evidence suggests that the familiar macroeconomic incentives for investment would be no less effective today than they have been in the past. In particular, the volume of investment spending would appear to respond to monetary and fiscal policies in the customary way. Profits and cash flow might increase as a result of either rising sales or a tax cut.

Source: R. W. Kopcke with M. M. Howrey, "A Panel Study of Investment: Sales, Cash Flow, the Cost of Capital, and Leverage," *New England Economic Review* (January/February 1994): 23.

HOW FINANCIAL MANAGERS USE THIS MATERIAL

The Introduction to this chapter pointed out how fluctuations of specific magnitudes in sales at Harley-Davidson, Coca-Cola, Phillips Petroleum, Archer Daniels Midland, and Chevron actually became even *larger* relative changes in net income and earnings available to the respective firm's common stockholders. The material presented in the chapter allows financial managers to explain this phenomenon to various constituencies such as other managers, shareholders, and financial analysts who follow their firm's stock performance.

Based on the logic, models, and inherent assumptions within the models, managers can more precisely *estimate* the interaction that stems from combining operating leverage with financial leverage. The risks that shareholders are asked to assume because of management choices involving cost structure and financial structure are clarified.

Using some of the same theory and logic, managers develop a distinct linkage among the firm's forecasted sales revenues, cost structure, pricing decisions, and advertising programs. The break-even model, although conceptually simple, is operationally powerful. Its understandability is its strength.

In the hotel industry, managers use the break-even model to determine the property's break-even occupancy rate. This becomes an input to the hotel's pricing policy. To achieve a desired total break-even sales revenue might require a change in the rate charged per room night. In this instance, the hotel's competition has to be assessed and an advertising program put in place that on a forecast basis will permit the break-even occupancy rate to be achieved.

Because firms are in business to generate a profit (and not just "break-even"), the break-even analysis will then extend into a format for achieving minimum target profit levels. So, the break-even model is an essential part of the manager's strategy formulation toolkit.

SUMMARY

Objective 1

In this chapter, we begin to study the process of arriving at an appropriate financial structure for the firm. We examine tools that can assist the financial manager in this task. We are mainly concerned with assessing the variability in the firm's residual earnings stream (either earnings per share or earnings available to the common shareholders) induced by the use of operating and financial leverage. This assessment builds on the tenets of break-even analysis.

Objective 2

Break-even analysis permits the financial manager to determine the quantity of output or the level of sales that will result in an EBIT level of zero. This means the firm has neither a profit nor a loss before any tax considerations. The effect of price changes, cost structure changes, or volume changes on profits (EBIT) can be studied. To make the technique operational, it is necessary that the firm's costs be classified as fixed or variable. Not all costs fit neatly into one of these two categories. Over short planning horizons, though, the preponderance of costs can be assigned to either the fixed or variable classification. Once the cost structure has been identified, the break-even point can be found by use of (1) trial-and-error analysis, (2) contribution-margin analysis, or (3) algebraic analysis.

Objective 3

Operating leverage is the responsiveness of the firm's EBIT to changes in sales revenues. It arises from the firm's use of fixed operating costs. When fixed operating costs are present in the company's cost structure, changes in sales are magnified into even greater changes in EBIT. The firm's degree of operating leverage from a base sales level is the percentage change in EBIT divided by the percentage change in sales. All types of leverage are two-edged swords. When sales decrease by some percentage, the negative impact upon EBIT will be even larger.

Objective 4

A firm employs financial leverage when it finances a portion of its assets with securities bearing a fixed rate of return. The presence of debt and/or preferred stock in the company's financial structure means that it is using financial leverage. When financial leverage is used, changes in EBIT translate into larger changes in earnings per share. The concept of the degree of financial leverage dwells on the sensitivity of earnings per share to changes in EBIT. The *DFL* from a base EBIT level is defined as the percentage change in earnings per share divided by the percentage change in EBIT. All other things equal, the more fixed-charge securities the firm employs in its financial structure, the greater its degree of financial leverage. Clearly, EBIT can rise or fall. If it falls, and financial leverage is used, the firm's shareholders endure negative changes in earnings per share that are larger than the relative decline in EBIT. Again, leverage is a two-edged sword.

Objective 5

Firms use operating and financial leverage in various degrees. The joint use of operating and financial leverage can be measured by computing the degree of combined leverage, defined as the percentage change in earnings per share divided by the percentage change in sales. This measure allows the financial manager to ascertain the effect on total leverage caused by adding financial leverage on top of operating leverage. Effects can be dramatic, because the degree of combined leverage is the product of the degrees of operating and financial leverage. Table 15-10 summarizes the salient concepts and calculation formats discussed in this chapter.

Objective 6

Business risk is both multidimensional and international. It is directly affected by several factors, including (1) the sensitivity of the firm's product demand to general economic conditions,

TABLE 15-10 Summary of Leverage Concepts and Calculations

TECHNIQUE	DESCRIPTION OR CONCEPT	CALCULATION	TEXT REFERENCE
BREAK-EVEN ANALYSIS			
1. Break-even point quantity	Total fixed costs divided by the unit contribution margin	$Q_B = \frac{F}{P - V}$	(15-3)
2. Break-even sales level	Total fixed costs divided by 1 minus the ratio of total variable costs to the associated level of sales	$S^* = \frac{F}{1 - \frac{VC}{S}}$	(15-4)
OPERATING LEVERAGE			
3. Degree of operating leverage	Percentage change in EBIT divided by the percentage change in sales; or revenue before fixed costs divided by revenue after fixed costs, EBIT	$DOL_s = \frac{Q(P - V)}{Q(P - V) - F}$	(15-6)
FINANCIAL LEVERAGE			
4. Degree of financial leverage	Percentage change in earnings per share divided by the percentage change in EBIT; or EBIT divided by EBT.[a]	$DFL_{EBIT} = \frac{EBIT}{EBIT - I}$	(15-9)
COMBINED LEVERAGE			
5. Degree of combined leverage	Percentage change in earnings per share divided by the percentage change in sales; or revenue before fixed costs divided by EBT.[a]	$DCL_s = \frac{Q(P - V)}{Q(P - V) - F - I}$	(15-12)

[a]The use of EBT here presumes no preferred dividend payments. In the presence of preferred dividend payments, replace EBT with earnings available to common stock (EAC).

(2) the degree of competition to which the firm is exposed, (3) product diversification, (4) growth prospects, and (5) global sales. On the latter factor, we explored how the Coca-Cola Company related the firm's commercial strategy to include sales prospects in the huge markets of both China and Russia.

KEY TERMS

Go To: www.prenhall.com/keown for downloads and current events associated with this chapter

Analytical income statement, 515
Business risk, 507
Cash break-even analysis, 517
Contribution margin, 514
Financial leverage, 508
Financial risk, 508
Fixed costs (indirect costs), 510
Operating leverage, 508
Risk, 507
Semivariable costs (semifixed costs), 512
Total revenue, 512
Variable costs (direct costs), 511
Volume of output, 512

STUDY QUESTIONS

15-1. Distinguish between business risk and financial risk. What gives rise to, or causes, each type of risk?

15-2. Define the term *financial leverage*. Does the firm use financial leverage if preferred stock is present in the capital structure?

15-3. Define the term *operating leverage.* What type of effect occurs when the firm uses operating leverage?

15-4. What is the difference between the (ordinary) break-even point and the cash break-even point? Which will be the greater?

15-5. A manager in your firm decides to employ break-even analysis. Of what shortcomings should this manager be aware?

15-6. What is meant by total risk exposure? How may a firm move to reduce its total risk exposure?

15-7. If a firm has a degree of combined leverage of three times, what does a negative sales fluctuation of 15 percent portend for the earnings available to the firm's common stock investors?

15-8. Break-even analysis assumes linear revenue and cost functions. In reality, these linear functions over large output and sales levels are highly improbable. Why?

SELF-TEST PROBLEMS

ST-1. *(Break-even point)* You are a hard-working analyst in the office of financial operations for a manufacturing firm that produces a single product. You have developed the following cost structure information for this company. All of it pertains to an output level of 10 million units. Using this information, find the break-even point in units of output for the firm.

Return on operating assets	= 30%
Operating asset turnover	= 6 times
Operating assets	= $20 million
Degree of operating leverage	= 4.5 times

ST-2. *(Leverage analysis)* You have developed the following analytical income statement for your corporation. It represents the most recent year's operations, which ended yesterday. Your supervisor in the financial studies office has just handed you a memorandum that asked for written responses to the following questions:

a. At this level of output, what is the degree of operating leverage?
b. What is the degree of financial leverage?
c. What is the degree of combined leverage?
d. What is the firm's break-even point in sales dollars?
e. If sales should increase by 30 percent, by what percent would earnings before taxes (and net income) increase?

Sales	$20,000,000
Variable costs	12,000,000
Revenue before fixed costs	$ 8,000,000
Fixed costs	5,000,000
EBIT	$ 3,000,000
Interest expense	1,000,000
Earnings before taxes	$ 2,000,000
Taxes (0.50)	1,000,000
Net income	$ 1,000,000

f. Prepare an analytical income statement that verifies the calculations from part (e).

ST-3. *(Fixed costs and the break-even point)* Bonaventure Manufacturing expects to earn $210,000 next year after taxes. Sales will be $4 million. The firm's single plant is located on the outskirts of Olean, New York. The firm manufactures a combined bookshelf and desk unit used extensively in college dormitories. These units sell for $200 each and have a variable cost per unit of $150. Bonaventure experiences a 30 percent tax rate.

a. What are the firm's fixed costs expected to be next year?
b. Calculate the firm's break-even point in both units and dollars.

STUDY PROBLEMS (SET A)

15-1A. (*Sales mix and break-even point*) CheeMortal music store sells four kinds of musical instruments—pianos, violins, cellos, and flutes. The current sales mix for the store and the contribution margin ratio (unit contribution margin divided by unit sales price) for these product lines are as follows:

PRODUCT LINE	PERCENT OF TOTAL SALES	CONTRIBUTION MARGIN RATIO
Piano	24.5%	32%
Violin	15.0%	40%
Cello	39.5%	38%
Flute	21.0%	51%

Total sales for the next year are forecast to be $250,000. Total fixed costs will be $50,000.

a. Prepare a table showing (1) sales, (2) total variable costs, and (3) the total contribution margin associated with each product line.

b. What is the aggregate contribution margin ratio indicative of the sales mix? (Round off to two decimals.)

c. At this sales mix, what is the break-even point in dollars?

15-2A. (*Break-even point*) Napa Valley Winery (NVW) is a boutique winery that produces a high-quality, nonalcoholic red wine from organically grown cabernet sauvignon grapes. It sells each bottle for $30. NVW's chief financial officer, Jackie Cheng, has estimated variable costs to be 70 percent of sales. If NVW's fixed costs are $360,000, how many bottles of its wine must NVW sell to break even?

15-3A. (*Operating leverage*) In light of a sales agreement that Napa Valley Winery (see description in Problem 15-2A) just signed with a national chain of health food restaurants, NVW's CFO Jackie Cheng is estimating that NVW's sales in the next year will be 50,000 bottles at $30 per bottle. If variable costs are expected to be 70 percent of sales, what is NVW's expected degree of operating leverage?

15-4A. (*Break-even point and operating leverage*) Some financial data for each of three firms are as follows:

	JAKE'S LAWN CHAIRS	SARASOTA SKY LIGHTS	JEFFERSON WHOLESALE
Average selling price per unit	$ 32.00	$ 875.00	$ 97.77
Average variable cost per unit	$ 17.38	$ 400.00	$ 87.00
Units sold	18,770	2,800	11,000
Fixed costs	$120,350	$850,000	$89,500

a. What is the profit for each company at the indicated sales volume?

b. What is the break-even point in units for each company?

c. What is the degree of operating leverage for each company at the indicated sales volume?

d. If sales were to decline, which firm would suffer the largest relative decline in profitability?

15-5A. (*Leverage analysis*) You have developed the following analytical income statement for your corporation. It represents the most recent year's operations, which ended yesterday.

Sales	$45,750,000
Variable costs	22,800,000
Revenue before fixed costs	$22,950,000
Fixed costs	9,200,000
EBIT	$13,750,000
Interest expense	1,350,000
Earnings before taxes	$12,400,000
Taxes (.50)	6,200,000
Net income	$ 6,200,000

Your supervisor in the controller's office has just handed you a memorandum asking for written responses to the following questions:

a. At this level of output, what is the degree of operating leverage?
b. What is the degree of financial leverage?
c. What is the degree of combined leverage?
d. What is the firm's break-even point in sales dollars?
e. If sales should increase by 25 percent, by what percent would earnings before taxes (and net income) increase?

15-6A. *(Break-even point and operating leverage)* Footwear, Inc., manufactures a complete line of men's and women's dress shoes for independent merchants. The average selling price of its finished product is $85 per pair. The variable cost for this same pair of shoes is $58. Footwear, Inc., incurs fixed costs of $170,000 per year.

a. What is the break-even point in pairs of shoes for the company?
b. What is the dollar sales volume the firm must achieve to reach the break-even point?
c. What would be the firm's profit or loss at the following units of production sold: 7,000 pairs of shoes? 9,000 pairs of shoes? 15,000 pairs of shoes?
d. Find the degree of operating leverage for the production and sales levels given in part (c).

15-7A. *(Break-even point and operating leverage)* Zeylog Corporation manufactures a line of computer memory expansion boards used in microcomputers. The average selling price of its finished product is $180 per unit. The variable cost for these same units is $110. Zeylog incurs fixed costs of $630,000 per year.

a. What is the break-even point in units for the company?
b. What is the dollar sales volume the firm must achieve to reach the break-even point?
c. What would be the firm's profit or loss at the following units of production sold: 12,000 units? 15,000 units? 20,000 units?
d. Find the degree of operating leverage for the production and sales levels given in part (c) above.

15-8A. *(Break-even point and operating leverage)* Some financial data for each of three firms are as follows:

	BLACKSBURG FURNITURE	LEXINGTON CABINETS	WILLIAMSBURG COLONIALS
Average selling price per unit	$ 15.00	$ 400.00	$ 40.00
Average variable cost per unit	$ 12.35	$ 220.00	$ 14.50
Units sold	75,000	4,000	13,000
Fixed costs	$35,000	$100,000	$70,000

a. What is the profit for each company at the indicated sales volume?
b. What is the break-even point in units for each company?
c. What is the degree of operating leverage for each company at the indicated sales volume?
d. If sales were to decline, which firm would suffer the largest relative decline in profitability?

15-9A. *(Fixed costs and the break-even point)* A & B Beverages expects to earn $50,000 next year after taxes. Sales will be $375,000. The store is located near the shopping district surrounding Blowing Rock University. Its average product sells for $27 a unit. The variable cost per unit is $14.85. The store experiences a 40 percent tax rate.

a. What are the store's fixed costs expected to be next year?
b. Calculate the store's break-even point in both units and dollars.

15-10A. *(Break-even point and profit margin)* Mary Clark, a recent graduate of Clarion South University, is planning to open a new wholesaling operation. Her target operating profit margin is 26 percent. Her unit contribution margin will be 50 percent of sales. Average annual sales are forecast to be $3,250,000.

a. How large can fixed costs be for the wholesaling operation and still allow the 26 percent operating profit margin to be achieved?
b. What is the break-even point in dollars for the firm?

15-11A. (*Leverage analysis*) You have developed the following analytical income statement for your corporation. It represents the most recent year's operations, which ended yesterday. Your supervisor in the controller's office has just handed you a memorandum asking for written responses to the following questions:

a. At this level of output, what is the degree of operating leverage?
b. What is the degree of financial leverage?

Sales	$30,000,000
Variable costs	13,500,000
Revenue before fixed costs	$16,500,000
Fixed costs	8,000,000
EBIT	$ 8,500,000
Interest expense	1,000,000
Earnings before taxes	$ 7,500,000
Taxes (.50)	3,750,000
Net income	$ 3,750,000

c. What is the degree of combined leverage?
d. What is the firm's break-even point in sales dollars?
e. If sales should increase by 25 percent, by what percent would earnings before taxes (and net income) increase?

15-12A. (*Break-even point*) You are a hard-working analyst in the office of financial operations for a manufacturing firm that produces a single product. You have developed the following cost structure information for this company. All of it pertains to an output level of 10 million units. Using this information, find the break-even point in units of output for the firm.

Return on operating assets	= 25%
Operating asset turnover	= 5 times
Operating assets	= $20 million
Degree of operating leverage	= 4 times

15-13A. (*Break-even point and operating leverage*) Allison Radios manufactures a complete line of radio and communication equipment for law enforcement agencies. The average selling price of its finished product is $180 per unit. The variable cost for these same units is $126. Allison Radios incurs fixed costs of $540,000 per year.

a. What is the break-even point in units for the company?
b. What is the dollar sales volume the firm must achieve in order to reach the break-even point?
c. What would be the firm's profit or loss at the following units of production sold: 12,000 units? 15,000 units? 20,000 units?
d. Find the degree of operating leverage for the production and sales levels given in part (c).

15-14A. (*Break-even point and operating leverage*) Some financial data for each of three firms are as follows:

	OVIEDO SEEDS	GAINESVILLE SOD	ATHENS PEACHES
Average selling price per unit	$ 14.00	$ 200.00	$ 25.00
Average variable cost per unit	$ 11.20	$ 130.00	$ 17.50
Units sold	100,000	10,000	48,000
Fixed costs	$25,000	$100,000	$35,000

a. What is the profit for each company at the indicated sales volume?
b. What is the break-even point in units for each company?
c. What is the degree of operating leverage for each company at the indicated sales volume?
d. If sales were to *decline*, which firm would suffer the largest relative decline in profitability?

15-15A. (*Fixed costs and the break-even point*) Dot's Quik-Stop Party Store expects to earn \$40,000 next year after taxes. Sales will be \$400,000. The store is located near the fraternity-row district of Cambridge Springs State University and sells only kegs of beer for \$20 a keg. The variable cost per keg is \$8. The store experiences a 40 percent tax rate.

- **a.** What are the Party Store's fixed costs expected to be next year?
- **b.** Calculate the firm's break-even point in both units and dollars.

15-16A. (*Fixed costs and the break-even point*) Albert's Cooling Equipment hopes to earn \$80,000 next year after taxes. Sales will be \$2 million. The firm's single plant is located on the edge of Slippery Rock, Pennsylvania, and manufactures only small refrigerators. These are used in many of the dormitories found on college campuses. Refrigerators sell for \$80 per unit and have a variable cost of \$56. Albert's experiences a 40 percent tax rate.

- **a.** What are the firm's fixed costs expected to be next year?
- **b.** Calculate the firm's break-even point both in units and dollars.

15-17A. (*Break-even point and selling price*) Gerry's Tool and Die Company will produce 200,000 units next year. All of this production will be sold as finished goods. Fixed costs will total \$300,000. Variable costs for this firm are relatively predictable at 75 percent of sales.

- **a.** If Gerry's Tool and Die wants to achieve an earnings before interest and taxes level of \$240,000 next year, at what price per unit must it sell its product?
- **b.** Based on your answer to part (a), set up an analytical income statement that will verify your solution.

15-18A. (*Break-even point and selling price*) Parks Castings, Inc., will manufacture and sell 200,000 units next year. Fixed costs will total \$300,000, and variable costs will be 60 percent of sales.

- **a.** The firm wants to achieve an earnings before interest and taxes level of \$250,000. What selling price per unit is necessary to achieve this result?
- **b.** Set up an analytical income statement to verify your solution to part (a).

15-19A. (*Break-even point and profit margin*) A recent business graduate of Midwestern State University is planning to open a new wholesaling operation. His target operating profit margin is 28 percent. His unit contribution margin will be 50 percent of sales. Average annual sales are forecast to be \$3,750,000.

- **a.** How large can fixed costs be for the wholesaling operation and still allow the 28 percent operating profit margin to be achieved?
- **b.** What is the break-even point in dollars for the firm?

15-20A. (*Operating leverage*) Rocky Mount Metals Company manufactures an assortment of woodburning stoves. The average selling price for the various units is \$500. The associated variable cost is \$350 per unit. Fixed costs for the firm average \$180,000 annually.

- **a.** What is the break-even point in units for the company?
- **b.** What is the dollar sales volume the firm must achieve to reach the break-even point?
- **c.** What is the degree of operating leverage for a production and sales level of 5,000 units for the firm? (Calculate to three decimal places.)
- **d.** What will be the projected effect upon earnings before interest and taxes if the firm's sales level should increase by 20 percent from the volume noted in part (c)?

15-21A. (*Break-even point and operating leverage*) The Portland Recreation Company manufactures a full line of lawn furniture. The average selling price of a finished unit is \$25. The associated variable cost is \$15 per unit. Fixed costs for Portland average \$50,000 per year.

- **a.** What is the break-even point in units for the company?
- **b.** What is the dollar sales volume the firm must achieve to reach the break-even point?
- **c.** What would be the company's profit or loss at the following units of production sold: 4,000 units? 6,000 units? 8,000 units?
- **d.** Find the degree of operating leverage for the production and sales levels given in part (c).
- **e.** What is the effect on the degree of operating leverage as sales rise above the break-even point?

15-22A. (*Fixed costs*) Detroit Heat Treating projects that next year its fixed costs will total \$120,000. Its only product sells for \$12 per unit, of which \$7 is a variable cost. The management of Detroit is considering the purchase of a new machine that will lower the variable cost per unit to \$5. The new machine, however, will add to fixed costs through an increase in depreciation expense. How large can the *addition to* fixed costs be to keep the firm's break-even point in units produced and sold unchanged?

15-23A. (*Operating leverage*) The management of Detroit Heat Treating did not purchase the new piece of equipment (see problem 15-22A). Using the existing cost structure, calculate the degree of operating leverage at 30,000 units of output. Comment on the meaning of your answer.

15-24A. (*Leverage analysis*) An analytical income statement for Detroit Heat Treating is shown below. It is based on an output (sales) level of 40,000 units. You may refer to the original cost structure data in problem (15-22A).

Sales	\$480,000
Variable costs	280,000
Revenue before fixed costs	\$200,000
Fixed costs	120,000
EBIT	\$ 80,000
Interest expense	30,000
Earnings before taxes	\$ 50,000
Taxes	25,000
Net income	\$ 25,000

a. Calculate the degree of operating leverage at this output level.
b. Calculate the degree of financial leverage at this level of EBIT.
c. Determine the combined leverage effect at this output level.

15-25A. (*Break-even point*) You are employed as a financial analyst for a single-product manufacturing firm. Your supervisor has made the following cost structure information available to you, all of which pertains to an output level of 1,600,000 units.

Return on operating assets	= 15%
Operating asset turnover	= 5 times
Operating assets	= \$3 million
Degree of operating leverage	= 8 times

Your task is to find the break-even point in units of output for the firm.

15-26A. (*Fixed costs*) Des Moines Printing Services is forecasting fixed costs next year of \$300,000. The firm's single product sells for \$20 per unit and incurs a variable cost per unit of \$14. The firm may acquire some new binding equipment that would lower variable cost per unit to \$12. The new equipment, however, would add to fixed costs through the price of an annual maintenance agreement on the new equipment. How large can this increase in fixed costs be and still keep the firm's present break-even point in units produced and sold unchanged?

15-27A. (*Leverage analysis*) Your firm's cost analysis supervisor supplies you with the following analytical income statement and requests answers to the four questions listed following the statement.

Sales	\$12,000,000
Variable costs	9,000,000
Revenue before fixed costs	\$ 3,000,000
Fixed costs	2,000,000
EBIT	\$ 1,000,000
Interest expense	200,000
Earnings before taxes	\$ 800,000
Taxes	400,000
Net income	\$ 400,000

a. At this level of output, what is the degree of operating leverage?
b. What is the degree of financial leverage?
c. What is the degree of combined leverage?
d. What is the firm's break-even point in sales dollars?

15-28A. (*Leverage analysis*) You are supplied with the following analytical income statement for your firm. It reflects last year's operations.

Sales	$16,000,000
Variable costs	8,000,000
Revenue before fixed costs	$ 8,000,000
Fixed costs	4,000,000
EBIT	$ 4,000,000
Interest expense	1,500,000
Earnings before taxes	$ 2,500,000
Taxes	1,250,000
Net income	$ 1,250,000

a. At this level of output, what is the degree of operating leverage?
b. What is the degree of financial leverage?
c. What is the degree of combined leverage?
d. If sales should increase by 20 percent, by what percent would earnings before taxes (and net income) increase?
e. What is your firm's break-even point in sales dollars?

15-29A. (*Sales mix and break-even point*) Toledo Components produces four lines of auto accessories for the major Detroit automobile manufacturers. The lines are known by the code letters A, B, C, and D. The current sales mix for Toledo and the contribution margin ratio (unit contribution margin divided by unit sales price) for these product lines are as follows:

PRODUCT LINE	PERCENT OF TOTAL SALES	CONTRIBUTION MARGIN RATIO
A	33⅓%	40%
B	41⅔	32
C	16⅔	20
D	8⅓	60

Total sales for next year are forecast to be $120,000. Total fixed costs will be $29,400.

a. Prepare a table showing (1) sales, (2) total variable costs, and (3) the total contribution margin associated with each product line.
b. What is the aggregate contribution margin ratio indicative of this sales mix?
c. At this sales mix, what is the break-even point in dollars?

15-30A. (*Sales mix and break-even point*) Because of production constraints, Toledo Components (see problem 15-29A) may have to adhere to a different sales mix for next year. The alternative plan is outlined as follows:

PRODUCT LINE	PERCENT OF TOTAL SALES
A	25%
B	36⅔
C	33⅓
D	5

a. Assuming all other facts in problem 15-29A remain the same, what effect will this different sales mix have on Toledo's break-even point in dollars?
b. Which sales mix will Toledo's management prefer?

WEB WORKS

15-1WW. Reading the "Finance Matters" box dealing with General Motors' pricing strategy found at the end of the break-even analysis discussion in this chapter will provide a useful background for this exercise. Pricing strategies and adjustments are more likely to occur when interest rates are low than when these rates are high. This is because the firm can borrow at lower rates in the financial marketplace, which offsets the total cost of any pricing incentives offered to potential customers.

The Web site **www.bankrate.com/ust/ratehm.asp** provides a listing of current major interest rates that are important to both corporate executives and investors. Here you can find: (a) various lending rates such as the prime lending rate and federal funds target rate, (b) rates on U.S. Treasury securities of differing maturities, and (c) other selected interest rates, such as on long-term corporate bonds.

Go to this site and inspect the current level of the prime interest rate and compare it to that rate one year earlier. Has the prime rate increased or decreased from a year ago? Given this information, and assuming you work for a major automobile manufacturer, would you recommend to your financial executive superior that the firm consider increasing or decreasing any pricing incentives aimed at your firm's customers?

15-2WW. The Coca-Cola company consistently publishes an outstanding and useful annual report, found at **www.coca-cola.com** or accessed through **www.reportgallery.com**. Coca-Cola is one of the few firms that we are aware of which actually includes a "glossary" in its annual report. For 2002 it is on the inside back cover. Many of the entries in their glossary are of a financial nature. Check out (a) dividend payout ratio, (b) economic profit, (c) operating margin, and (d) return on common equitiy. Then see how their listings stack up against those noted in the glossary to this text. You will notice that the resulting definitions are very close in each case.

Hint: These concepts drive the decision-making processes of financial executives. Thus, you want to make such concepts a part of your everyday vocabulary.

INTEGRATIVE PROBLEM

Imagine that you were hired recently as a financial analyst for a relatively new, highly leveraged ski manufacturer located in the foothills of Colorado's Rocky Mountains. Your firm manufactures only one product, a state-of-the-art snow ski. The company has been operating up to this point without much quantitative knowledge of the business and financial risks it faces.

Ski season just ended, however, so the president of the company has started to focus more on the financial aspects of managing the business. He has set up a meeting for next week with the CFO, Maria Sanchez, to discuss matters such as the business and financial risks faced by the company. Accordingly, Maria has asked you to prepare an analysis to assist her in her discussions with the president.

As a first step in your work, you compiled the following information regarding the cost structure of the company.

Output level	50,000 units
Operating assets	\$2,000,000
Operating asset turnover	7 times
Return on operating assets	35%
Degree of operating leverage	5 times
Interest expense	\$400,000
Tax rate	35%

As the next step, you need to *determine the break-even point in units of output* for the company. One of your strong points has been that you always prepare supporting workpapers, which show how you arrive at your conclusions. You know Maria would like to see such workpapers for this analysis to facilitate her review of your work.

Thereafter you will have the information you require to *prepare an analytical income statement* for the company. You are sure that Maria would like to see this statement; in addition, you know that you need it to be able to answer the following questions. You also know Maria expects you to prepare, in a format that is presentable to the president, answers to the questions to serve as a basis for her discussions with the president.

1. What is the degree of financial leverage?
2. What is the degree of combined leverage?
3. What is the firm's break-even point in sales dollars?
4. If sales should increase by 30 percent (as the president expects), by what percent would EBT (earnings before taxes) and net income increase?
5. Prepare another analytical income statement, this time to verify the calculations from question (4).

STUDY PROBLEMS (SET B)

15-1B. (*Break-even point*) Roberto Martinez is the chief financial analyst at New Wave Pharmaceuticals (NWP), a company that produces a vitamin claimed to prevent the common cold. Roberto has been asked to determine the company's break-even point in units. He obtained the following information from the company's financial statements for the year just ended. In addition, he found out from NWP's production manager that the company produced 40 million units in that year. What will Roberto determine the break-even point to be?

Sales	$20,000,000
Variable costs	16,000,000
Revenue before fixed costs	$ 4,000,000
Fixed costs	2,400,000
EBIT	$ 1,600,000

15-2B. (*Leverage analysis*) New Wave Pharmaceuticals (see description and data in Problem 15-1B) is concerned that recent unfavorable publicity about the questionable medicinal benefits of other vitamins will temporarily hurt NWP's sales even though such assertions do not apply to NWP's vitamin. Accordingly, Roberto has been asked to determine the company's level of risk based on the financial information for the year just ended. In addition to the data described in Problem 15-1B, Roberto learned from the company's financial statements that the company incurred $800,000 of interest expense in the year just ended. What will Roberto determine the (a) degree of operating leverage, (b) degree of financial leverage, and (c) degree of combined leverage to be?

15-3B. (*Break-even point and operating leverage*) Avitar Corporation manufactures a line of computer memory expansion boards used in microcomputers. The average selling price of its finished product is $175 per unit. The variable cost for these same units is $115. Avitar incurs fixed costs of $650,000 per year.

a. What is the break-even point in units for the company?

b. What is the dollar sales volume the firm must achieve to reach the break-even point?

c. What would be the firm's profit or loss at the following units of production sold: 10,000 units? 16,000 units? 20,000 units?

d. Find the degree of operating leverage for the production and sales levels given in part (c).

15-4B. (*Break-even point and operating leverage*) Some financial data for each of three firms are as follows:

	DURHAM FURNITURE	RALEIGH CABINETS	CHARLOTTE COLONIALS
Average selling price per unit	$ 20.00	$ 435.00	$ 35.00
Average variable cost per unit	$ 13.75	$ 240.00	$ 15.75
Units sold	80,000	4,500	15,000
Fixed costs	$40,000	$150,000	$60,000

a. What is the profit for each company at the indicated sales volume?
b. What is the break-even point in units for each company?
c. What is the degree of operating leverage for each company at the indicated sales volume?
d. If sales were to decline, which firm would suffer the largest relative decline in profitability?

15-5B. (*Fixed costs and the break-even point*) Cypress Books expects to earn $55,000 next year after taxes. Sales will be $400,008. The store is located near the shopping district surrounding Sheffield University. Its average product sells for $28 a unit. The variable cost per unit is $18. The store experiences a 45 percent tax rate.

a. What are the store's fixed costs expected to be next year?
b. Calculate the store's break-even point in both units and dollars.

15-6B. (*Break-even point and profit margin*) A recent graduate of Neeley University is planning to open a new wholesaling operation. Her target operating profit margin is 28 percent. Her unit contribution margin will be 45 percent of sales. Average annual sales are forecast to be $3,750,000.

a. How large can fixed costs be for the wholesaling operation and still allow the 28 percent operating profit margin to be achieved?
b. What is the break-even point in dollars for the firm?

15-7B. (*Leverage analysis*) You have developed the following analytical income statement for your corporation. It represents the most recent year's operations, which ended yesterday.

Sales	$40,000,000
Variable costs	16,000,000
Revenue before fixed costs	$24,000,000
Fixed costs	10,000,000
EBIT	$14,000,000
Interest expense	1,150,000
Earnings before taxes	$12,850,000
Taxes	3,750,000
Net income	$ 9,100,000

Your supervisor in the controller's office has just handed you a memorandum asking for written responses to the following questions:

a. At this level of output, what is the degree of operating leverage?
b. What is the degree of financial leverage?
c. What is the degree of combined leverage?
d. What is the firm's break-even point in sales dollars?
e. If sales should increase by 20 percent, by what percent would earnings before taxes (and net income) increase?

15-8B. (*Break-even point*) You are a hard-working analyst in the office of financial operations for a manufacturing firm that produces a single product. You have developed the following cost structure information for this company. All of it pertains to an output level of 7 million units. Using this information, find the break-even point in units of output for the firm.

Return on operating assets	= 25%
Operating asset turnover	= 5 times
Operating assets	= $18 million
Degree of operating leverage	= 6 times

15-9B. (*Break-even point and operating leverage*) Matthew Electronics manufactures a complete line of radio and communication equipment for law enforcement agencies. The average selling price of its finished product is $175 per unit. The variable costs for these same units is $140. Matthew's incurs fixed costs of $550,000 per year.

a. What is the break-even point in units for the company?
b. What is the dollar sales volume the firm must achieve to reach the break-even point?

c. What would be the firm's profit or loss at the following units of production sold: 12,000 units? 15,000 units? 20,000 units?

d. Find the degree of operating leverage for the production and sales levels given in part (c).

15-10B. (*Break-even point and operating leverage*) Some financial data for each of three firms are as follows:

	FARM CITY SEEDS	EMPIRE SOD	GOLDEN PEACHES
Average selling price per unit	$ 15.00	$ 190.00	$ 28.00
Average variable cost per unit	$ 11.75	$ 145.00	$ 19.00
Units sold	120,000	9,000	50,000
Fixed costs	$30,000	$110,000	$33,000

a. What is the profit for each company at the indicated sales volume?

b. What is the break-even point in units for each company?

c. What is the degree of operating leverage for each company at the indicated sales volume?

d. If sales were to *decline*, which firm would suffer the largest relative decline in profitability?

15-11B. (*Fixed costs and the break-even point*) Keller's Keg expects to earn $38,000 next year after taxes. Sales will be $420,002. The store is located near the fraternity-row district of Blue Springs State University and sells only kegs of beer for $17 a keg. The variable cost per keg is $9. The store experiences a 35 percent tax rate.

a. What are Keller's Keg's fixed costs expected to be next year?

b. Calculate the firm's break-even point both in units and in dollars.

15-12B. (*Fixed costs and the break-even point*) Mini-Kool hopes to earn $70,000 next year after taxes. Sales will be $2,500,050. The firm's single plant manufactures only small refrigerators. These are used in many recreational campers. The refrigerators sell for $75 per unit and have a variable cost of $58. Mini-Kool experiences a 45 percent tax rate.

a. What are the firm's fixed costs expected to be next year?

b. Calculate the firm's break-even point both in units and dollars.

15-13B. (*Break-even point and selling price*) Heritage Chain Company will produce 175,000 units next year. All of this production will be sold as finished goods. Fixed costs will total $335,000. Variable costs for this firm are relatively predictable at 80 percent of sales.

a. If Heritage Chain wants to achieve an earnings before interest and taxes level of $270,000 next year, at what price per unit must it sell its product?

b. Based on your answer to part (a), set up an analytical income statement that will verify your solution.

15-14B. (*Break-even point and selling price*) Thomas Appliances will manufacture and sell 190,000 units next year. Fixed costs will total $300,000, and variable costs will be 75 percent of sales.

a. The firm wants to achieve an earnings before interest and taxes level of $250,000. What selling price per unit is necessary to achieve this result?

b. Set up an analytical income statement to verify your solution to part (a).

15-15B. (*Break-even point and profit margin*) A recent business graduate of Dewey University is planning to open a new wholesaling operation. His target operating profit margin is 25 percent. His unit contribution margin will be 60 percent of sales. Average annual sales are forecast to be $4,250,000.

a. How large can fixed costs be for the wholesaling operation and still allow the 25 percent operating profit margin to be achieved?

b. What is the break-even point in dollars for the firm?

15-16B. (*Operating leverage*) The B. H. Williams Company manufactures an assortment of woodburning stoves. The average selling price for the various units is $475. The associated variable cost is $350 per unit. Fixed costs for the firm average $200,000 annually.

a. What is the break-even point in units for the company?

b. What is the dollar sales volume the firm must achieve to reach the break-even point?

c. What is the degree of operating leverage for a production and sales level of 6,000 units for the firm? (Calculate to three decimal places.)

d. What will be the projected effect on earnings before interest and taxes if the firm's sales level should increase by 13 percent from the volume noted in part (c) above?

15-17B. (*Break-even point and operating leverage*) The Palm Patio Company manufactures a full line of lawn furniture. The average selling price of a finished unit is $28. The associated variable cost is $17 per unit. Fixed costs for Palm Patio average $55,000 per year.

a. What is the break-even point in units for the company?

b. What is the dollar sales volume the firm must achieve to reach the break-even point?

c. What would be the company's profit or loss at the following units of production sold: 4,000 units? 6,000 units? 8,000 units?

d. Find the degree of operating leverage for the production and sales levels given in part (c).

e. What is the effect on the degree of operating leverage as sales rise above the break-even point?

15-18B. (*Fixed costs*) Tropical Sun projects that next year its fixed costs will total $135,000. Its only product sells for $13 per unit, of which $6 is a variable cost. The management of Tropical is considering the purchase of a new machine that will lower the variable cost per unit to $5. The new machine, however, will add to fixed costs through an increase in depreciation expense. How large can the *addition* to fixed costs be to keep the firm's break-even point in units produced and sold unchanged?

15-19B. (*Operating leverage*) The management of Tropical Sun did not purchase the new piece of equipment (see problem 15-18B). Using the existing cost structure, calculate the degree of operating leverage at 40,000 units of output. Comment on the meaning of your answer.

15-20B. (*Leverage analysis*) An analytical income statement for Tropical Sun follows. It is based on an output (sales) level of 50,000 units. You may refer to the original cost structure data in problem (15-18B).

Sales	$650,000
Variable costs	300,000
Revenue before fixed costs	$350,000
Fixed costs	135,000
EBIT	$215,000
Interest expense	60,000
Earnings before taxes	$155,000
Taxes	70,000
Net income	$ 85,000

a. Calculate the degree of operating leverage at this output level.

b. Calculate the degree of financial leverage at this level of EBIT.

c. Determine the combined leverage effect at this output level.

15-21B. (*Break-even point*) You are employed as a financial analyst for a single-product manufacturing firm. Your supervisor has made the following cost structure information available to you, all of which pertains to an output level of 1,700,000 units.

Return on operating assets	= 16 percent
Operating asset turnover	= 6 times
Operating assets	= $3.25 million
Degree of operating leverage	= 9 times

Your task is to find the break-even point in units of output for the firm.

15-22B. (*Fixed costs*) Sausalito Silkscreen is forecasting fixed costs next year of $375,000. The firm's single product sells for $25 per unit and incurs a variable cost per unit of $13. The firm may acquire some new binding equipment that would lower variable cost per unit to $11. The new equipment, however, would add to fixed costs through the price of an annual maintenance agreement on the new equipment. How large can this increase in fixed costs be and still keep the firm's present break-even point in units produced and sold unchanged?

15-23B. (*Leverage analysis*) Your firm's cost analysis supervisor supplies you with the following analytical income statement and requests answers to the four questions listed following the statement.

Sales	$13,750,000
Variable costs	9,500,000
Revenue before fixed costs	$ 4,250,000
Fixed costs	3,000,000
EBIT	$ 1,250,000
Interest expense	250,000
Earnings before taxes	$ 1,000,000
Taxes	430,000
Net income	$ 570,000

a. At this level of output, what is the degree of operating leverage?
b. What is the degree of financial leverage?
c. What is the degree of combined leverage?
d. What is the firm's break-even point in sales dollars?

15-24B. (*Leverage analysis*) You are supplied with the following analytical income statement for your firm. It reflects last year's operations.

Sales	$18,000,000
Variable costs	7,000,000
Revenue before fixed costs	$11,000,000
Fixed costs	6,000,000
EBIT	$ 5,000,000
Interest expense	1,750,000
Earnings before taxes	$ 3,250,000
Taxes	1,250,000
Net income	$ 2,000,000

a. At this level of output, what is the degree of operating leverage?
b. What is the degree of financial leverage?
c. What is the degree of combined leverage?
d. If sales should increase by 15 percent, by what percent would earnings before taxes (and net income) increase?
e. What is your firm's break-even point in sales dollars?

15-25B. (*Sales mix and the break-even point*) Wayne Automotive produces four lines of auto accessories for the major Detroit automobile manufacturers. The lines are known by the code letters A, B, C, and D. The current sales mix for Wayne and the contribution margin ratio (unit contribution margin divided by unit sales price) for these product lines are as follows:

PRODUCT LINE	PERCENT OF TOTAL SALES	CONTRIBUTION MARGIN RATIO
A	$25\frac{2}{3}$%	40%
B	$41\frac{1}{3}$	32
C	$19\frac{2}{3}$	20
D	$13\frac{1}{3}$	60

Total sales for next year are forecast to be $150,000. Total fixed costs will be $35,000.

a. Prepare a table showing (1) sales, (2) total variable costs, and (3) the total contribution margin associated with each product line.
b. What is the aggregate contribution margin ratio indicative of this sales mix?
c. At this sales mix, what is the break-even point in dollars?

15-26B. (*Sales mix and the break-even point*) Because of production constraints, Wayne Automotive (see problem 15-25B) may have to adhere to a different sales mix for next year. The alternative plan is outlined as follows:

PRODUCT LINE	PERCENT OF TOTAL SALES
A	33⅓%
B	41⅔
C	16⅔
D	8⅓

a. Assuming all other facts in problem 15-25B remain the same, what effect will this different sales mix have on Wayne's break-even point in dollars?
b. Which sales mix will Wayne's management prefer?

SELF-TEST SOLUTIONS

ST-1. *Step 1: Compute the operating profit margin:*

(margin) × (turnover) = return on operating assets
(M) × (6) = 0.30
M = 0.30/6 = 0.05

Step 2. Compute the sales level associated with the given output level:

$$\frac{\text{sales}}{\$20{,}000{,}000} = 6$$

$$\text{sales} = \$120{,}000{,}000$$

Step 3. Compute EBIT:

(.05)($120,000,000) = $6,000,000 = EBIT

Step 4. Compute revenue before fixed costs. Because the degree of operating leverage is 4.5 times, revenue before fixed costs (RBF) is 4.5 times EBIT, as follows:

RBF = (4.5)($6,000,000) = $27,000,000

Step 5. Compute total variable costs:

$$\begin{aligned}(\text{sales}) - (\text{total variable costs}) &= \$27{,}000{,}000\\ \$120{,}000{,}000 - (\text{total variable costs}) &= \$27{,}000{,}000\\ \text{total variable costs} &= \$93{,}000{,}000\end{aligned}$$

Step 6. Compute total fixed costs:

$$\begin{aligned}\text{RBF} - \text{fixed costs} &= \text{EBIT}\\ \$27{,}000{,}000 - \text{fixed costs} &= \$6{,}000{,}000\\ \text{Fixed costs} &= \$21{,}000{,}000\end{aligned}$$

Step 7. Find the selling price per unit (P), *and the variable cost per unit* (V):

$$P = \frac{\text{sales}}{\text{output in units}} = \frac{\$120{,}000{,}000}{10{,}000{,}000} = \$12.00$$

$$V = \frac{\text{total variable costs}}{\text{output in units}} = \frac{\$93{,}000{,}000}{10{,}000{,}000} = \$9.30$$

Step 8. Compute the break-even point:

$$Q_B = \frac{F}{P - V} = \frac{\$21{,}000{,}000}{\$12.00 - \$9.30}$$

$$= \frac{\$21{,}000{,}000}{\$2.70} = 7{,}777{,}778 \text{ units}$$

The firm will break even when it produces and sells 7,777,778 units.

ST-2. **a.** $\dfrac{\text{Revenue before fixed costs}}{\text{EBIT}} = \dfrac{\$8{,}000{,}000}{\$3{,}000{,}000} = \underline{\underline{2.67 \text{ times}}}$

b. $\dfrac{\text{EBIT}}{\text{EBIT} - I} = \dfrac{\$3{,}000{,}000}{\$2{,}000{,}000} = \underline{\underline{1.50 \text{ times}}}$

c. $DCI_{20,000,000} = (2.67)(1.50) = \underline{\underline{4.00 \text{ times}}}$

d. $S^* = \dfrac{F}{1 - \dfrac{VC}{S}} = \dfrac{\$5{,}000{,}000}{1 - \dfrac{\$12M}{\$20M}} = \dfrac{\$5{,}000{,}000}{1 - 0.60} = \dfrac{\$5{,}000{,}000}{0.40} = \underline{\underline{\$12{,}500{,}000}}$

e. (30%)(4.00) = 120%

f.

Sales	$26,000,000
Variable costs	15,600,000
Revenue before fixed costs	$10,400,000
Fixed costs	5,000,000
EBIT	$ 5,400,000
Interest expense	1,000,000
Earnings before taxes	$ 4,400,000
Taxes (0.50)	2,200,000
Net income	$ 2,200,000

We know that sales have increased by 30 percent to $26 million from the base sales level of $20 million.

Let us focus now on the change in earnings before taxes. We can compute that change as follows:

$$\frac{\$4{,}400{,}000 - \$2{,}000{,}000}{\$2{,}000{,}000} = \frac{\$2{,}400{,}000}{\$2{,}000{,}000} = 120\%$$

Because the tax rate was held constant, the percentage change in net income will also equal 120 percent. The fluctuations implied by the degree of combined leverage measure are therefore accurately reflected in this analytical income statement.

ST-3. **a.**

$$\begin{aligned}
\{(P \cdot Q) - [V \cdot Q + (F)]\}(1 - T) &= \$210{,}000 \\
[(\$4{,}000{,}000) - (\$3{,}000{,}000) - F](.7) &= \$210{,}000 \\
(\$1{,}000{,}000 - F)(.7) &= \$210{,}000 \\
\$700{,}000 - .7F &= \$210{,}000 \\
.7F &= \$490{,}000 \\
F &= \underline{\underline{\$700{,}000}}
\end{aligned}$$

Fixed costs next year, then, are expected to be $700,000.

b.

$$Q_B = \frac{F}{P - V} = \frac{\$700{,}000}{\$50} = \underline{\underline{14{,}000 \text{ units}}}$$

$$S^* = \frac{F}{1 - \dfrac{VC}{S}} = \frac{\$700{,}000}{1 - .75} = \frac{\$700{,}000}{.25} = \underline{\underline{\$2{,}800{,}000}}$$

The firm will break even (EBIT = 0) when it sells 14,000 units. With a selling price of $200 per unit, the break-even sales level is $2,800,000.

LEARNING OBJECTIVES

After reading this chapter, you should be able to

1. Understand the concept of an optimal capital structure.
2. Explain the main underpinnings of capital structure theory.
3. Distinguish between the independence hypothesis and dependence hypothesis as these concepts relate to capital structure theory; identify the Nobel Prize winners in economics who are the leading proponents of the independence hypothesis.
4. Understand and be able to graph the moderate position on capital structure importance.
5. Incorporate the concepts of agency costs and free cash flow into a discussion on capital structure management.
6. Use the basic tools of capital structure management.
7. Understand the relationship between exposure to foreign currency risk and financial risk.
8. Understand corporate financing policies in practice.

CHAPTER 16

Planning the Firm's Financing Mix

The United States was recession-free from April 1991 until March 2001 when the tenth post-World War II recession officially commenced. This was the longest expansion, 120 months, in the history of credible business-cycle recordkeeping in the United States, dating back to 1853. It took until July 17, 2003, for the National Bureau of Economic Research to announce that a "trough in business activity occurred in the U.S. economy in November 2001." A trough means a recession has ended. Note that this announcement happened a full 21 months after the recession was said to have ended. Business cycle "dating" is an art subject to considerable debate among financial economists and executives. Even though this recession was officially over, the nation's labor markets continued to languish into July of 2003, marked by very slow growth in payroll jobs. This post-recession adjustment period was a challenging one for many American businesses that had loaded their balance sheets with debt over the "good times" of the 120-month expansion.

Financial executives had to delicately manage cash flows to service existing debt contracts or face bankruptcy. These same executives had to give considerable thought as to how to finance the next (incremental) capital project.

Along these lines, Harley-Davidson, Inc., has taken a rather moderate approach to financial risk in the management of its funds sources. For reporting year 2001, Harley ranked 466th among the *Fortune* 500 largest domestic corporations with sales revenues of $3.36 billion. Even though the overall economy was slow, Harley improved to a ranking of 392 for 2002 within this same set of 500 companies. For 2001, Harley generated $698.2 million in earnings before interest and taxes (i.e., EBIT) and incurred interest expense of $24.8 million. This put its times interest earned ratio at 28.2 times (i.e.,

CHAPTER PREVIEW

In this chapter, we direct our attention to the determination of an appropriate financing mix for the firm. Think of the right side of the firm's balance sheet as a big pie. That pie can be sliced into different-sized pieces. One piece might be labeled *long-term debt*, another labeled *preferred equity*, and yet another, *common equity*. We want to mix the pieces together in an optimal fashion that will make the pie as large as possible.

That task is the focal point of this chapter, and it is one that all chief financial officers confront. In some instances, just changing the labels on the slices of the pie might not change its size—but in other cases, it might. That is the challenge of financial structure management. The total value of the firm is represented by the ultimate size of the pie. More value (pie) is better than less value (pie). Keep this in mind while you work through the chapter.

As you study this chapter on financial structure theory, decision making, and policy, you will be made aware of a full five of the ten principles, first noted and explained in Chapter 1, that underlie the basics of business financial management. Specifically, your attention will be directed to: **Principle 1: The Risk-Return Trade-Off—We won't take on additional risk unless we expect to be compensated with additional return; Principle 3: Cash—Not Profits—Is King; Principle 6: Efficient Capital Markets—The markets are quick and prices are right; Principle 7: The Agency Problem—Managers won't work for the owners unless it's in their best interest;** and **Principle 8: Taxes Bias Business Decisions.**

$698.2/$24.8) for 2001. So in an adverse economic year, Harley's EBIT could slip to about one-twenty-eighth of its 2001 amount and the firm would still be able to pay its contractual debt obligations. This is a very safe interest coverage ratio. Should you not already be familiar with it, the times interest earned ratio is defined in Table 16-7 in this chapter.

Similarly, another company that pays explicit attention to managing its financing mix is the Georgia-Pacific Corporation. This firm is one of the world's leaders in the manufacturing and distribution of building products, pulp, and paper. The firm employs about 47,500 individuals and ranked exactly 100 among the *Fortune* 500 largest domestic corporations at the end of 1996. Georgia-Pacific posted sales revenues of $13 billion for 1996 and possessed $12.8 billion in assets.

Georgia-Pacific's 1996 Annual Report contained a separate section on "Financial Strategy." On that subject, the management of the firm said: "Georgia-Pacific's objective is to provide superior returns to our shareholders. To achieve this goal, our financial strategy must complement our operating strategy. We must maintain a capital structure that minimizes our cost of capital while providing flexibility in financing our capital (expenditure) requirements."

As you learn the material in this chapter, you will be able to make positive contributions to company financing strategies such as those put forth previously by Harley and the Georgia-Pacific Corporation. In dealing with the firm's financing mix, you can help the firm avoid making serious financial errors, the consequences of which usually last for several years.

Objective 1

KEY TERMS AND GETTING STARTED

Financial structure
The mix of all funds sources that appear on the right side of the balance sheet.

Capital structure
The mix of long-term sources of funds used by the firm. Basically, this concept omits short-term liabilities.

Financial structure design
The management activity of seeking the proper mix of all financing components in order to minimize the cost of raising a given amount of funds.

We now direct our attention to the determination of an appropriate financing mix for the firm. First, we must distinguish between financial structure and capital structure. **Financial structure** is the mix of all items that appear on the right side of the company's balance sheet. **Capital structure** is the mix of the *long-term* sources of funds used by the firm. The relationship between financial and capital structure can be expressed in equation form:

$$\text{(financial structure)} - \text{(current liabilities)} = \text{capital structure} \quad \textbf{(16-1)}$$

Prudent **financial structure design** requires answers to the following two questions:

1. What should be the maturity composition of the firm's sources of funds; in other words, how should a firm best divide its total fund sources between short- and long-term components?
2. In what proportions relative to the total should the various forms of permanent financing be utilized?

The major influence on the maturity structure of the financing plan is the nature of the assets owned by the firm. A company heavily committed to real capital investment, represented primarily by fixed assets on its balance sheet, *should* finance those assets with permanent (long-term) types of financial capital. Furthermore, the permanent portion of the firm's investment in current assets should likewise be financed with permanent capital. Alternatively, assets held on a temporary basis are to be financed with temporary sources. The present discussion assumes that the bulk of the company's current liabilities are comprised of temporary capital.

This hedging concept is discussed in Chapter 18. Accordingly, our focus in this chapter is an answer to the second of the two questions noted previously—this process is usually called *capital structure management.*

The *objective* of capital structure management is to mix the permanent sources of funds used by the firm in a manner that will maximize the company's common stock

TABLE 16-1 Balance Sheet

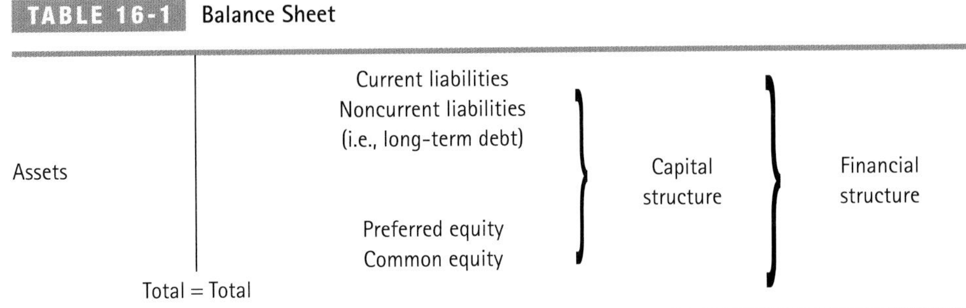

Assets	Liabilities and equity		
Assets	Current liabilities		Financial structure
	Noncurrent liabilities (i.e., long-term debt)	Capital structure	
	Preferred equity		
	Common equity		
Total = Total			

price. Alternatively, this objective may be viewed as a search for the funds mix that will minimize the firm's composite cost of capital. We can call this proper mix of funds sources the **optimal capital structure**.

Optimal capital structure The unique capital structure that minimizes the firm's composite cost of long-term capital.

Table 16-1 looks at equation 16-1 in terms of a simplified balance sheet format. It helps us visualize the overriding problem of capital structure management. The sources of funds that give rise to financing fixed costs (long-term debt and preferred equity) must be combined with common equity in the proportions most suitable to the investing marketplace. If that mix can be found, then, holding all other factors constant, the firm's common stock price will be maximized.

Whereas equation 16-1 quite accurately indicates that the corporate capital structure may be viewed as an absolute dollar *amount*, the *real* capital structure problem is one of balancing the array of funds sources in a proper manner. Our use of the term *capital structure* emphasizes this latter problem of relative magnitude, or proportions.

The rest of this chapter will cover three main areas. First, we discuss the theory of capital structure to provide a perspective. Second, we examine the basic tools of capital structure management. We conclude with a real-world look at actual capital structure management.

CONCEPT CHECK

1. What is the objective of capital structure management?
2. What is the main attribute of a firm's optimal capital structure?

A GLANCE AT CAPITAL STRUCTURE THEORY

Objective 2

It pays to understand the essential components of capital structure theory. The assumption of excessive financial risk can put the firm into bankruptcy proceedings. Some argue that the decision to use little financial leverage results in an undervaluation of the firm's shares in the marketplace. The effective financial manager must know how to find the area of optimum financial leverage use—this will enhance share value, all other considerations held constant. Thus, grasping the theory will make you better able to formulate a sound financial structure policy.

An enduring controversy within financial theory concerns the effect of financial leverage on the overall cost of capital to the enterprise. The heart of the argument may be stated in the form of a question: Can the firm affect its overall cost of funds, either favorably or unfavorably, by varying the mixture of financing sources used?

This controversy has taken many elegant forms in the finance literature. Most of these presentations appeal more to academics than to financial management practitioners. To emphasize the ingredients of capital structure theory that have practical applications for business financial management, we will pursue an intuitive, or nonmathematical, approach to reach a better understanding of the underpinnings of this *cost of capital–capital structure argument.*

THE IMPORTANCE OF CAPITAL STRUCTURE

It makes economic sense for the firm to strive to minimize the cost of using financial capital. Both capital costs and other costs, such as manufacturing costs, share a common characteristic in that they potentially reduce the size of the cash dividend that could be paid to common stockholders.

We saw in Chapter 8 that the ultimate value of a share of common stock depends in part on the returns investors expect to receive from holding the stock. Cash dividends comprise all (in the case of an infinite holding period) or part (in the case of a holding period less than infinity) of these expected returns. Now hold constant all factors that could affect share price except capital costs. If these capital costs could be kept at a minimum, the dividend stream flowing to the common stockholders would be maximized. This, in turn, would maximize the firm's common stock price.

If the firm's cost of capital can be affected by its capital structure, then capital structure management is clearly an important subset of business financial management.

ANALYTICAL SETTING

The essentials of the capital structure controversy are best highlighted within a framework that economists would call a "partial equilibrium analysis." In a partial equilibrium analysis, changes that *do* occur in several factors and have an impact on a certain key item are ignored to study the effect of changes in a main factor on that same item of interest. Here, two items are simultaneously of interest: (1) K_0, the firm's composite cost of capital, and (2) P_0, the market price of the firm's common stock. The firm's use of financial leverage is the main factor that is allowed to vary in the analysis. This means that important financial decisions, such as investing policy and dividend policy, are held constant throughout the discussion. We are concerned with the effect of changes in the financing mix on share price and capital costs.

Our analysis will be facilitated if we adopt a *simplified* version of the basic dividend valuation model presented in Chapter 8 in our study of valuation principles, and in Chapter 12 in our assessment of the cost of capital. That model is shown as equation 16-2:

$$P_0 = \sum_{t=1}^{\infty} \frac{D_t}{(1 + K_c)^t} \tag{16-2}$$

where P_0 = the current price of the firm's common stock
D_t = the cash dividend per share expected by investors during period t
K_c = the cost of common equity capital

We can strip away some complications by making the following assumptions concerning the valuation process implicit in equation 16-2:

1. Cash dividends paid will not change over the infinite holding period. Thus $D_1 = D_2 = D_3 = \cdots = D_\infty$. There is no expected growth by investors in the dividend stream.
2. The firm retains none of its current earnings. This means that *all* of each period's per-share earnings are paid to stockholders in the form of cash dividends. The firm's dividend payout ratio is 100 percent. Cash dividends per share in equation 16-2, then, also equal earnings per share for the same period.

Under these assumptions, the cash dividend flowing to investors can be viewed as a level payment over an infinite holding period. The payment stream is perpetual, and according to the mathematics of perpetuities, equation 16-2 reduces to equation 16-3, where E_t represents earnings per share during period t.

$$P_0 = \frac{D_t}{K_c} = \frac{E_t}{K_c} \tag{16-3}$$

In addition to the suppositions just noted, the analytical setting for the discussion of capital structure theory includes the following assumptions:

1. Corporate income is not subject to any taxation. The major implication of removing this assumption is discussed later.
2. Capital structures consist of only stocks and bonds. Furthermore, the degree of financial leverage used by the firm is altered by the issuance of common stock with the proceeds used to retire existing debt, or the issuance of debt with the proceeds used to repurchase stock. This permits leverage use to vary but maintains constancy of the total book value of the firm's capital structure.
3. The expected values of all investors' forecasts of the future levels of net operating income (EBIT) for each firm are identical. Say that you forecast the average level of EBIT to be achieved by General Motors over a very long period ($n \rightarrow \infty$). Your forecast will be the same as our forecast, and both will be equal to the forecasts of all other investors interested in General Motors common stock. In addition, we do not expect General Motors' EBIT to grow over time. Each year's forecast is the same as any other year's. This is consistent with our assumption underlying equation 16-3, where the firm's dividend stream is not expected to grow.
4. Securities are traded in perfect or efficient financial markets. This means that transaction costs and legal restrictions do not impede any investors' incentives to execute portfolio changes that they expect will increase their wealth. Information is freely available. Moreover, corporations and individuals that are equal credit risks can borrow funds at the same rates of interest.

This completes our description of the analytical setting. We now discuss three differing views on the relationship between use of financial leverage and common stock value.

The discussion and illustrations of the two extreme positions on the importance of capital structure that follow are meant to highlight the critical differences between differing viewpoints. This is not to say that the markets really behave in strict accordance with either position—they don't. The point is to identify polar positions on how things might work. Then by relaxing various restrictive assumptions, a more useful theory of how financing decisions are actually made becomes possible. That results in the third, or moderate, view.

Objective 2

EXTREME POSITION 1: INDEPENDENCE HYPOTHESIS (NOI THEORY)[1]

The crux of this position is that the firm's composite cost of capital, K_0, and common stock price, P_0, are both *independent* of the degree to which the company chooses to use financial leverage. In other words, no matter how modest or excessive the firm's use of

[1] The net operating income and net income capitalization methods, which are referred to here as "extreme positions 1 and 2," were first presented in comprehensible form by Durand. See David Durand, "Costs of Debt and Equity Funds for Business: Trends and Problems of Measurement," *Conference on Research in Business Finance* (New York: National Bureau of Economic Research, 1952), reprinted in Ezra Solomon, ed., *The Management of Corporate Capital* (New York: Free Press), 91–116. The leading proponents of the independence hypothesis in its various forms are Professors Modigliani and Miller. See Franco Modigliani and Merton H. Miller, "The Cost of Capital, Corporation Finance and Theory of Investment," *American Economic Review* 48 (June 1958): 261–97; Franco Modigliani and Merton H. Miller, "Corporate Income Taxes and the Cost of Captial: A Correction," *American Economic Review* 53 (June 1963): 433–43; and Merton H. Miller, "Debt and Taxes," *Journal of Finance* 32 (May 1977): 261–75.

debt financing, its common stock price will not be affected. Let us illustrate the mechanics of this point of view.

Suppose that Rix Camper Manufacturing Company has the following financial characteristics:

Shares of common stock outstanding = 2,000,000 shares
Common stock price, P_0 = \$10 per share
Expected level of net operating income (EBIT) = \$2,000,000
Dividend payout ratio = 100 percent

Currently, the firm uses no financial leverage; its capital structure consists entirely of common equity. Earnings per share and dividends per share equal \$1 each. When the capital structure is all common equity, the cost of common equity, K_c, and the weighted cost of capital, K_0 are equal. If equation 16-3 is restated in terms of the cost of common equity, we have for Rix Camper:

$$K_c = \frac{D_t}{P_0} = \frac{\$1}{\$10} = 10\%$$

Now, the management of Rix Camper decides to use some debt capital in its financing mix. The firm sells \$8 million worth of long-term debt at an interest rate of 6 percent. With no taxation of corporate income, this 6 percent interest rate is the cost of debt capital, K_d. The firm uses the proceeds from the sale of the bonds to repurchase 40 percent of its outstanding common shares. After the capital-structure change has been accomplished, Rix Camper Manufacturing Company has the financial characteristics displayed in Table 16-2.

Based on the preceding data, we notice that the recapitalization (capital structure change) of Rix Camper will result in a dividend paid to owners that is 26.7 percent higher than it was when the firm used no debt in its capital structure. Will this higher dividend result in a lower composite cost of capital to Rix and a higher common stock price? According to the principles of the independence hypothesis, the answer is "No."

The independence hypothesis suggests that the total market value of the firm's outstanding securities is *unaffected* by the manner in which the right side of the balance sheet is arranged. That is, the sum of the market value of outstanding debt plus the sum of the market value of outstanding common equity will always be the *same* regardless of how

TABLE 16-2 Rix Camper Manufacturing Company Financial Data Reflecting the Capital Structure Adjustment

CAPITAL STRUCTURE INFORMATION	
Shares of common stock outstanding = 1,200,000	
Bonds at 6 percent = \$8,000,000	
EARNINGS INFORMATION	
Expected level of net operating income (EBIT)	\$2,000,000
Less: Interest expense	480,000
Earnings available to common stockholders	\$1,520,000
Earnings per share (E_t)	1.267
Dividends per share (D_t)	1.267
Percentage change in both earnings per share and dividends per share relative to the unlevered capital structure	26.7 percent

much or little debt is actually used by the company. If capital structure has no impact on the total market value of the company, then that value is arrived at by the marketplace's capitalizing (discounting) the firm's expected net operating income stream. Therefore the independence hypothesis rests on what is called the **net operating income (NOI) approach to valuation**.

Net operating income (NOI) approach to valuation
The concept from financial theory that suggests the firm's capital structure has no impact on its market valuation.

The format is a very simple one, and the market value of the firm's common stock turns out to be a residual of the valuation process. Recall that before Rix Camper's recapitalization, the total market value of the firm was \$20 million (2 million common shares times \$10 per share). The firm's cost of common equity, K_c, and its weighted cost of capital, K_0, were each equal to 10 percent. The composite discount rate, K_0, is used to arrive at the market value of the firm's securities. After the recapitalization, we have for Rix Camper:

Expected level of net operating income	\$ 2,000,000
capitalized at K_0 = 10 percent	
= Market value of debt and equity	\$20,000,000
− Market value of the new debt	8,000,000
= Market value of the common stock	\$12,000,000

With this valuation format, what is the market price of each share of common stock? Because we know that 1.2 million shares of stock are outstanding after the capital-structure change, the market price per share is \$10 (\$12 million/1.2 million). This is exactly the market value per share, P_0, that existed *before* the change.

Now, if the firm is using some debt that has an *explicit cost* of 6 percent, K_d, and the weighted (composite) cost of capital, K_0, is 10 percent, it stands to reason that the cost of common equity, K_c, has risen above its previous level of 10 percent. What will the cost of common equity be in this situation? As we did previously, we can take equation 16-3 and restate it in terms of K_c, the cost of common equity. After the recapitalization, the cost of common equity for Rix Camper is shown to *rise* to 12.67 percent:

$$K_c = \frac{D_t}{P_0} = \frac{\$1.267}{\$10} = 12.67\%$$

The cost of common equity for Rix Camper is 26.7 percent higher than it was before the capital structure shift. Notice in Table 16-2 that this is *exactly* equal to the percentage increase in earnings and dividends per share that accompanies the same capital structure adjustment. This highlights a fundamental relationship that is an integral part of the independence hypothesis. It concerns the perceived behavior in the firm's cost of common equity as expected dividends (earnings) increase relative to a financing mix change:

percentage change in K_c = percentage change in D_t

In this framework, the use of a greater degree of financial leverage may result in greater earnings and dividends, but the firm's cost of common equity will rise at precisely the same rate as the earnings and dividends do. Thus, the inevitable trade-off between the higher expected return in dividends and earnings (D_t and E_t) and increased risk that accompanies the use of debt financing manifests itself in a linear relationship between the cost of common equity (K_c) and financial leverage use. This view of the relationship between the firm's cost of funds and its financing mix is shown graphically in Figure 16-1. Figure 16-2 relates the firm's stock price to its financing mix under the same set of assumptions.

In Figure 16-1, the firm's overall cost of capital, K_0, is shown to be unaffected by an increased use of financial leverage. If more debt is used in the capital structure, the cost of

FIGURE 16-1 Capital Cost and Financial Leverage: No Taxes—Independence Hypothesis (NOI Theory)

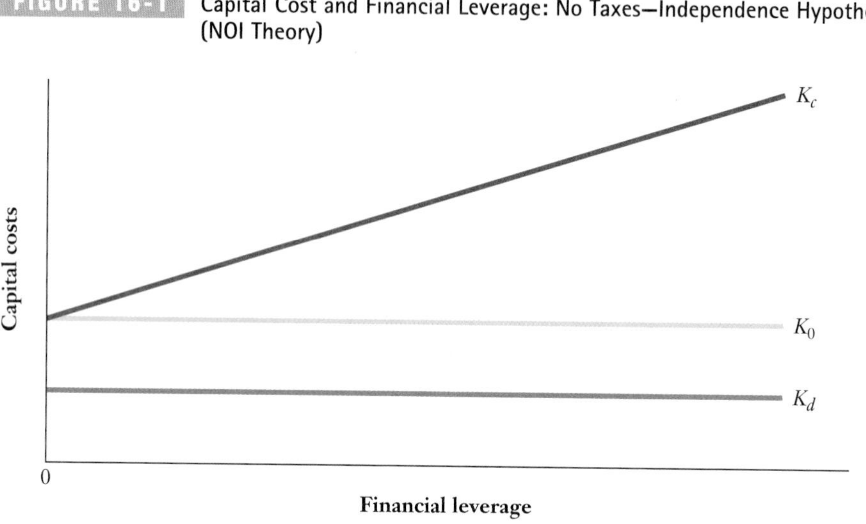

common equity will rise at the same rate additional earnings are generated. This will keep the composite cost of capital to the corporation unchanged. Figure 16-2 shows that because the cost of capital will not change with the leverage use, neither will the firm's stock price.

Explicit cost of capital The cost of capital for any funds source considered in isolation from other funds sources.

Implicit cost of debt The change in the cost of common equity caused by the choice to use additional debt.

Debt financing, then, has two costs—its **explicit cost of capital**, K_d, calculated according to the formats outlined in Chapter 12, and an implicit cost. The **implicit cost of debt** is the change in the cost of common equity brought on by using financial leverage (additional debt). The real cost of debt is the sum of these explicit and implicit costs. In general, the real cost of *any* source of capital is its explicit cost, plus the change that it induces in the cost of any other source of funds.

Followers of the independence hypothesis argue that the use of financial leverage brings a change in the cost of common equity large enough to offset the benefits of higher dividends to investors. Debt financing is not as cheap as it first appears to be. This will keep the composite cost of funds constant. The implication for management is that one capital structure is as good as any other; financial officers should not waste time searching for an optimal capital structure. One capital structure, after all, is as beneficial as any other, because all result in the same weighted cost of capital.

FIGURE 16-2 Stock Price and Financial Leverage: No Taxes—Independence Hypothesis (NOI Theory)

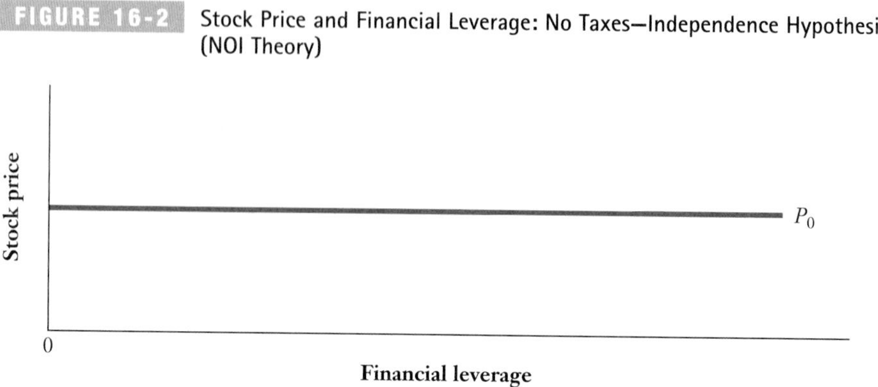

BACK TO THE PRINCIPLES

The suggestion from capital-structure theory that one capital structure is just as good as any other within a perfect ("pure") market framework relies directly on ***Principle 1: The Risk-Return Trade-Off—We won't take on additional risk unless we expect to be compensated with additional return.*** *This means that using more debt in the capital structure will not be ignored by investors in the financial markets. These rational investors will require a higher return on common stock investments in the firm that uses more leverage (rather than less), to compensate for the increased uncertainty stemming from the addition of the debt securities in the capital structure.*

EXTREME POSITION 2: DEPENDENCE HYPOTHESIS (NI THEORY)

Objective 3

The dependence hypothesis is at the opposite pole from the independence hypothesis. It suggests that both the weighted cost of capital, K_0, and common stock price, P_0, *are* affected by the firm's use of financial leverage. No matter how modest or excessive the firm's use of debt financing, both its cost of debt capital, K_d, and cost of equity capital, K_c, will not be affected by capital structure management. Because the cost of debt is less than the cost of equity, greater financial leverage will lower the firm's composite cost of capital indefinitely. Greater use of debt financing will thereby have a favorable effect on the company's common stock price. By returning to the Rix Camper situation, we can illustrate this point of view.

The same capital structure shift is being evaluated. That is, management will market \$8 million of new debt at a 6 percent interest rate and use the proceeds to purchase its own common shares. Under this approach, the market is assumed to capitalize (discount) the expected earnings available to the common stockholders to arrive at the aggregate market value of the common stock. The market value of the firm's common equity is *not* a residual of the valuation process. After the recapitalization, the firm's cost of common equity, K_c, will still be equal to 10 percent. Thus, a 10 percent cost of common equity is applied in the following format:

Expected level of net operating income	\$ 2,000,000
– Interest expense	480,000
= Earnings available to common stockholders capitalized at	\$ 1,520,000
K_c = 10 percent	
= Market value of the common stock	\$15,200,000
+ Market value of the new debt	8,000,000
= Market value of debt and equity	\$23,200,000

When we assume that the firm's capital structure consists only of debt and common equity, earnings available to the common stockholders is synonymous with net income. In the valuation process outlined previously, it is net income that is actually capitalized to arrive at the market value of the common equity. Because of this, the dependence hypothesis is also called the **net income (NI) approach to valuation.**

Net income (NI) approach to valuation
The concept from financial theory that suggests the firm's capital structure has a direct impact upon and can increase its market valuation.

Notice that the total market value of the firm's securities has risen to \$23.2 million from the \$20 million level that existed before the firm moved from the unlevered to the levered capital structure. The per-share value of the common stock is also shown to rise under this valuation format. With 1.2 million shares of stock outstanding, the market price per share is \$12.67 (\$15.2 million/1.2 million).

This increase in the stock price to \$12.67 represents a 26.7 percent rise over the previous level of \$10 per share. This is exactly equal to the percentage change in earnings per

FIGURE 16-3 Capital Costs and Financial Leverage: No Taxes—Dependence Hypothesis (NI Theory)

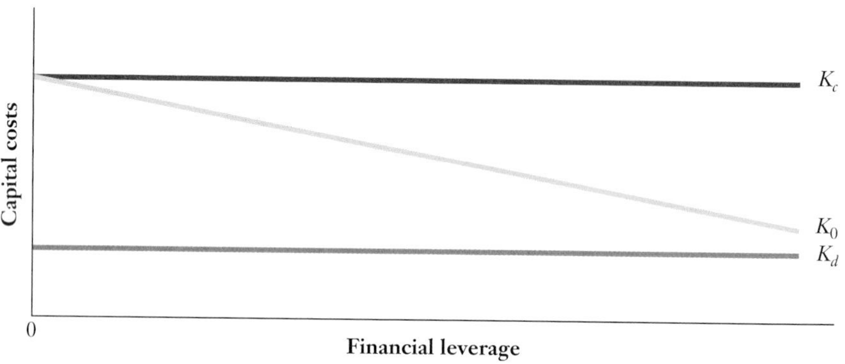

share and dividends per share calculated in Table 16-1. This permits us to characterize the dependence hypothesis in a very succinct fashion:

percentage change in $K_c = 0$ percent < percentage change in D_t
(over all degrees of leverage)

percentage change in P_0 = percentage change in D_t

The dependence hypothesis suggests that the *explicit and implicit* costs of debt are one and the same. The use of more debt does *not* change the firm's cost of common equity. Using more debt, which is explicitly cheaper than common equity, will lower the firm's composite cost of capital, K_0. If you take the market value of Rix Camper's common stock according to the net income theory of \$15.2 million and express it as a percent of the total market value of the firm's securities, you get a market value weight of .655 (\$15.2 million/ \$23.2 million). In a similar fashion, the market value weight of Rix Camper's debt is found to be .345 (\$8 million/\$23.2 million). After the capital structure adjustment, the firm's weighted cost of capital becomes:

$$K_0 = (.345)(6.00\%) + (.655)(10.00\%) = 8.62\%$$

So, changing the financing mix from all equity to a structure including both debt and equity lowered the composite cost of capital from 10 percent to 8.62 percent. The ingredients of the dependence hypothesis are illustrated in Figures 16-3 and 16-4.

FIGURE 16-4 Stock Price and Financial Leverage: No Taxes—Dependence Hypothesis (NI Theory)

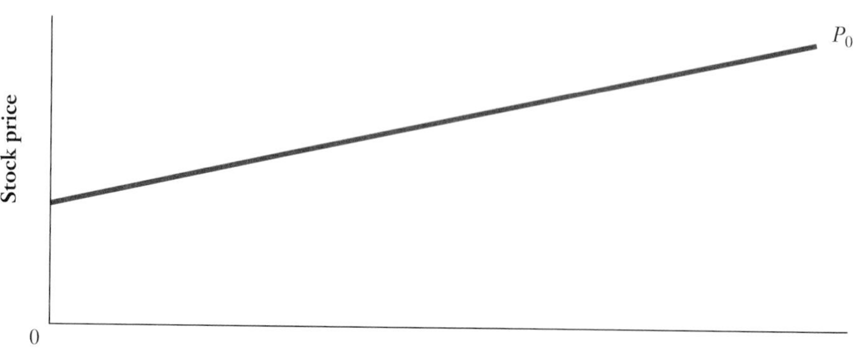

The implication for management from Figures 16-3 and 16-4 is that the firm's cost of capital, K_0, will decline as the debt-to-equity ratio increases. This also implies that the company's common stock price will rise with increased leverage use. Because the cost of capital decreases continuously with leverage, the firm should use as much leverage as is possible. Next we will move toward reality in the analytical setting of our capital structure discussion. This is accomplished by relaxing some of the major assumptions that surrounded the independence and dependence hypotheses.

Moderate Position: Corporate Income Is Taxed and Firms May Fail

In general, an analysis of extreme positions may be useful in that you are forced to sharpen your thinking not only about the poles, but also the situations that span the poles. In microeconomics, the study of perfect competition and monopoly provides a better understanding of the business activity that occurs in the wide area between these two model markets. In a similar fashion, the study of the independence and dependence hypotheses of the importance of capital structure helps us formulate a more informed view of the possible situations between those polar positions.

We turn now to a description of the cost of capital–capital structure relationship that has rather wide appeal to both business practitioners and academics. This moderate view (1) admits to the fact that interest expense is tax deductible, and (2) acknowledges that the probability of the firm's suffering bankruptcy costs is directly related to the company's use of financial leverage.

TAX DEDUCTIBILITY OF INTEREST EXPENSE This portion of the analysis recognizes that corporate income is subject to taxation. Furthermore, we assume that interest expense is tax deductible for purposes of computing the firm's tax bill. In this environment, the use of debt financing should result in a higher total market value for the firm's outstanding securities. We will see why subsequently.

We continue with our Rix Camper Manufacturing Company example. First, consider the total cash payments made to all security holders (holders of common stock plus holders of bonds). In the no-tax case, the sum of cash dividends paid to common shareholders plus interest expense amounted to $2 million both (1) when financing was all by common equity, and (2) after the proposed capital structure adjustment to a levered situation was accomplished. The *sum* of the cash flows that Rix Camper could pay to its contributors of debt and equity capital was not affected by its financing mix.

When corporate income is taxed by the government, however, the sum of the cash flows made to *all* contributors of financial capital *is* affected by the firm's financing mix. Table 16-3 illustrates this point.

TABLE 16-3 Rix Camper Manufacturing Company Cash Flows to All Investors—The Case of Taxes

	UNLEVERED CAPITAL STRUCTURE	LEVERED CAPITAL STRUCTURE
Expected level of net operating income	$2,000,000	$2,000,000
Less: interest expense	0	480,000
Earnings before taxes	$2,000,000	$1,520,000
Less: taxes at 50%	1,000,000	760,000
Earnings available to common stockholders	$1,000,000	$ 760,000
Expected payments to all security holders	$1,000,000	$1,240,000

Tax shield
The element from the federal tax code that permits interest costs to be deductible when computing the firm's tax bill. The dollar difference (the shield) flows to the firm's security holders.

If Rix Camper makes the capital structure adjustment identified in the preceding sections of this chapter, the total payments to equity and debtholders will be $240,000 *greater* than under the all-common-equity capitalization. Where does this $240,000 come from? The government's take, through taxes collected, is lower by that amount. This difference, which flows to the Rix Camper security holders, is called the **tax shield** on interest. In general, it may be calculated by equation 16-4, where r_d is the interest rate paid on the debt, M is the principal amount of the debt, and t is the firm's marginal tax rate:

$$\text{tax shield} = r_d(M)(t) \tag{16-4}$$

The moderate position on the importance of capital structure presumes that the tax shield must have value in the marketplace. Accordingly, this tax benefit will increase the total market value of the firm's outstanding securities relative to the all-equity capitalization. Financial leverage does affect firm value. Because the cost of capital is just the other side of the valuation coin, financial leverage also affects the firm's composite cost of capital. Can the firm increase firm value indefinitely and lower its cost of capital continuously by using more and more financial leverage? Common sense would tell us "No!" So would most financial managers and academicians. The acknowledgment of bankruptcy costs provides one possible rationale.

BACK TO THE PRINCIPLES

*The preceding section on the "Tax Deductibility of Interest Expense" is a compelling example of **Principle 8: Taxes Bias Business Decisions.** We have just seen that corporations have an important incentive provided by the tax code to finance projects with debt securities rather than new issues of common stock. The interest expense on the debt issue will be tax deductible. The common stock dividends will not be tax deductible. So firms can indeed increase their total after-tax cash flows available to all investors in their securities by using financial leverage. This element of the U.S. tax code should also remind you of **Principle 3: Cash—Not Profits—Is King.***

THE LIKELIHOOD OF FIRM FAILURE The probability that the firm will be unable to meet the financial obligations identified in its debt contracts increases as more debt is employed. The highest costs would be incurred if the firm actually went into bankruptcy proceedings. Here, assets would be liquidated. If we admit that these assets might sell for something less than their perceived market values, equity investors and debtholders could both suffer losses. Other problems accompany bankruptcy proceedings. Lawyers and accountants have to be hired and paid. Managers must spend time preparing lengthy reports for those involved in the legal action.

Milder forms of financial distress also have their costs. As their firm's financial condition weakens, creditors may take action to restrict normal business activity. Suppliers may not deliver materials on credit. Profitable capital investments may have to be forgone, and dividend payments may even be interrupted. At some point, the expected cost of default will be large enough to outweigh the tax shield advantage of debt financing.[2] The firm will turn to other sources of financing, mainly common equity. At this point, the real cost of debt is thought to be higher than the real cost of common equity.

[2] Even this argument that the trade-off between costs and the tax shield benefit of debt financing can lead to an optimal structure has its detractors. See Robert A. Haugen and Lemma W. Senbet, "The Insignificance of Bankruptcy Costs to the Theory of Optimal Capital Structure," *Journal of Finance* 33 (May 1978): 383–93.

MODERATE VIEW: SAUCER-SHAPED COST OF CAPITAL CURVE

Objective 4

This moderate view of the relationship between financing mix and the firm's cost of capital is depicted in Figure 16-5. The result is a saucer-shaped (or U-shaped) average cost of capital curve, K_0. The firm's average cost of equity, K_0, is seen to rise over all positive degrees of financial leverage use. For a while, the firm can borrow funds at a relatively low cost of debt, K_d. Even though the cost of equity is rising, it does not rise at a fast enough rate to offset the use of the less expensive debt financing. Thus, between points 0 and *A* on the financial-leverage axis, the average cost of capital declines and stock price rises.

Eventually, the threat of financial distress causes the cost of debt to rise. In Figure 16-5, this increase in the cost of debt shows up in the average cost of debt curve, K_d, at point *A*. Between points *A* and *B*, mixing debt and equity funds produces an average cost of capital that is (relatively) flat. The firm's **optimal range of financial leverage** lies between points *A* and *B*. All capital structures between these two points are optimal because they produce the lowest composite cost of capital. As we said in the introduction to this chapter, finding this optimal range of financing mixes is the objective of capital structure management.

Optimal range of financial leverage
The range of various financial structure combinations that generate the lowest composite cost of capital for the firm.

Point *B* signifies the firm's debt capacity. **Debt capacity** is the maximum proportion of debt the firm can include in its capital structure and still maintain its lowest composite cost of capital. Beyond point *B*, additional fixed-charge capital can be attracted only at very costly interest rates. At the same time, this excessive use of financial leverage would cause the firm's cost of equity to rise at a faster rate than previously. The composite cost of capital would then rise quite rapidly, and the firm's stock price would decline.

Debt capacity
The maximum proportion of debt that the firm can include in its capital structure and still maintain its lowest composite cost of capital.

This version of the moderate view as it relates to the firm's stock price is characterized subsequently. The notation is the same as that found in our discussion of the independence and dependence hypotheses.

1. Between points 0 and *A*: 0 < percentage change in P_0 < percentage change in D_t
2. Between points *A* and *B*: percentage change in $P_0 = 0$
3. Beyond point *B*: percentage change in $P_0 < 0$

FIGURE 16-5 Capital Costs and Financial Leverage: The Moderate View, Considering Taxes and Financial Distress

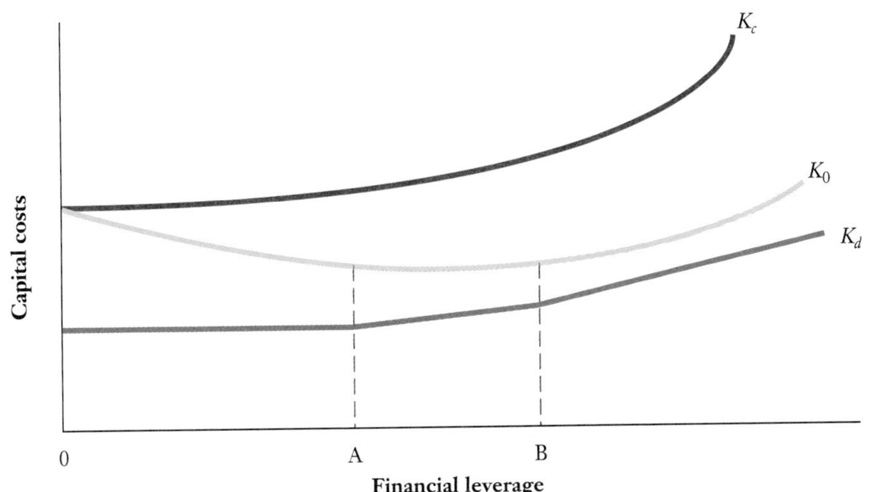

Firm Value, Agency Costs, Static Trade-Off Theory, and the Pecking Order Theory

Given the same task or assignment, it is quite likely that you will do it better for yourself than for someone else. If you are paid well enough, you might do the job about as effectively for that other person. Once you receive compensation, your work will be evaluated by someone. This process of evaluation is called "monitoring" within most discussions on agency costs.

This describes the heart of what is called the "agency problem." As American businesses have grown in size, the owners and managers have become (for the most part) separate groups of individuals. An inherent conflict exists, therefore, between managers and shareholders for whom managers act as agents in carrying out their objectives (for example, corporate goals). The following discussion relates the agency problem to the financial decision-making process of the firm.

In Chapter 1 of this text, we mentioned the *agency problem.* Recall that the agency problem gives rise to *agency costs,* which tend to occur in business organizations because ownership and management control are often separate. Thus the firm's managers can be properly thought of as agents for the firm's stockholders.[3] To ensure that agent-managers act in the stockholders' best interests requires that they have (1) proper incentives to do so and (2) that their decisions are monitored. The incentives usually take the form of executive compensation plans and perquisites. The perquisites might be a bloated support staff, country club memberships, luxurious corporate planes, or other amenities of a similar nature. Monitoring requires that certain costs be borne by the stockholders, such as (1) bonding the managers, (2) auditing financial statements, (3) structuring the organization in unique ways that limit useful managerial decisions, and (4) reviewing the costs and benefits of management perquisites. This list is indicative, not exhaustive. The main point is that monitoring costs are ultimately covered by the owners of the company—its common stockholders.

Capital structure management also gives rise to agency costs. Agency problems stem from conflicts of interest, and capital-structure management encompasses a natural conflict between stockholders and bondholders. Acting in the stockholders' best interests might cause management to invest in extremely risky projects. Existing investors in the firm's bonds could logically take a dim view of such an investment policy. A change in the risk structure of the firm's assets would change the business risk exposure of the firm. This could lead to a downward revision of the bond rating the firm currently enjoys. A lowered bond rating in turn would lower the current market value of the firm's bonds. Clearly, bondholders would be unhappy with this result.

To reduce this conflict of interest, the creditors (bond investors) and stockholders may agree to include several protective covenants in the bond contract. These bond covenants were discussed in more detail in Chapter 7, but essentially they may be thought of as restrictions on managerial decision making. Typical covenants restrict payment of cash dividends on common stock, limit the acquisition or sale of assets, or limit further debt financing. To make sure that the protective covenants are complied with by manage-

[3] Economists have studied the problems associated with control of the corporation for decades. An early, classic work on this topic was A. A. Berle, Jr., and G. C. Means, *The Modern Corporation and Private Property* (New York: Macmillan, 1932). The recent emphasis in corporate finance and financial economics stems from the important contribution of Michael C. Jensen and William H. Meckling, "Theory of the Firm: Managerial Behavior, Agency Costs and Ownership Structure," *Journal of Financial Economics* 3 (October 1976): 306–60. Professors Jensen and Smith have analyzed the bondholder-stockholder conflict in a very clear style. See Michael C. Jensen and Clifford W. Smith, Jr., "Stockholder, Manager, and Creditor Interests: Applications of Agency Theory," in Edward I. Altman and Marti G. Subrahmanyam, eds., *Recent Advances in Corporate Finance* (Homewood, IL: Richard D. Irwin, 1985): 93–131.

FIGURE 16-6 Agency Costs of Debt: Trade-Offs

No Protective Bond Covenants	Many Protective Bond Covenants
High interest rates	Low interest rates
Low monitoring costs	High monitoring costs
No lost operating efficiencies	Many lost operating efficiencies

ment means that monitoring costs are incurred. Like all monitoring costs, they are borne by common stockholders. Further, like many costs, they involve the analysis of an important trade-off.

Figure 16-6 displays some of the trade-offs involved with the use of protective bond covenants. Note (in the left panel of Figure 16-6) that the firm might be able to sell bonds that carry no protective covenants only by incurring very high interest rates. With no protective covenants, there are no associated monitoring costs. Also, there are no lost operating efficiencies, such as being able to move quickly to acquire a particular company in the acquisitions market. Conversely, the willingness to submit to several covenants could reduce the explicit cost of the debt contract, but would involve incurring significant monitoring costs and losing some operating efficiencies (which also translates into higher costs). When the debt issue is first sold, then, a trade-off will be arrived at between incurring monitoring costs, losing operating efficiencies, and enjoying a lower explicit interest cost.

Next we have to consider the presence of monitoring costs at low levels of leverage and at higher levels of leverage. When the firm operates at a low debt-to-equity ratio, there is little need for creditors to insist on a long list of bond covenants. The financial risk is just not there to require that type of activity. The firm will likewise benefit from low explicit interest rates when leverage is low. When the debt-to-equity ratio is high, however, it is logical for creditors to demand a great deal of monitoring. This increase in agency costs will raise the implicit cost (the true total cost) of debt financing. It seems logical, then, to suggest that monitoring costs will rise as the firm's use of financial leverage increases. Just as the likelihood of firm failure (financial distress) raises a company's overall cost of capital (K_0), so do agency costs. On the other side of the coin, this means that total firm value (the total market value of the firm's securities) will be *lower* owing to the presence of agency costs of debt. Taken together, the presence of agency costs and the costs associated with financial distress argue in favor of the concept of an *optimal* capital structure for the individual firm.

This general approach to understanding or explaining capital-structure decision making has come to be known in the finance literature as the "static trade-off theory." The label follows the essential form of the implied model wherein the present value (benefits) of tax shields that stem from increased leverage use are "traded-off" against both the rising costs of the likelihood of financial distress and the rising agency costs associated with increased debt usage.[4]

[4] Portions of the static trade-off model were contained in the original Modigliani and Miller 1958 article noted in footnote 1 in this chapter. It drew much increased attention, however, after the publication of Stewart C. Myers' presidential address to the American Finance Association. See Stewart C. Myers, "The Capital Structure Puzzle," *Journal of Finance* 39 (July 1984): 575–92. As might be expected, not all of the attention is complimentary concerning the usefulness of the static trade-off model.

FIGURE 16-7 Firm Value Considering Taxes, Agency Costs, and Financial Distress Costs

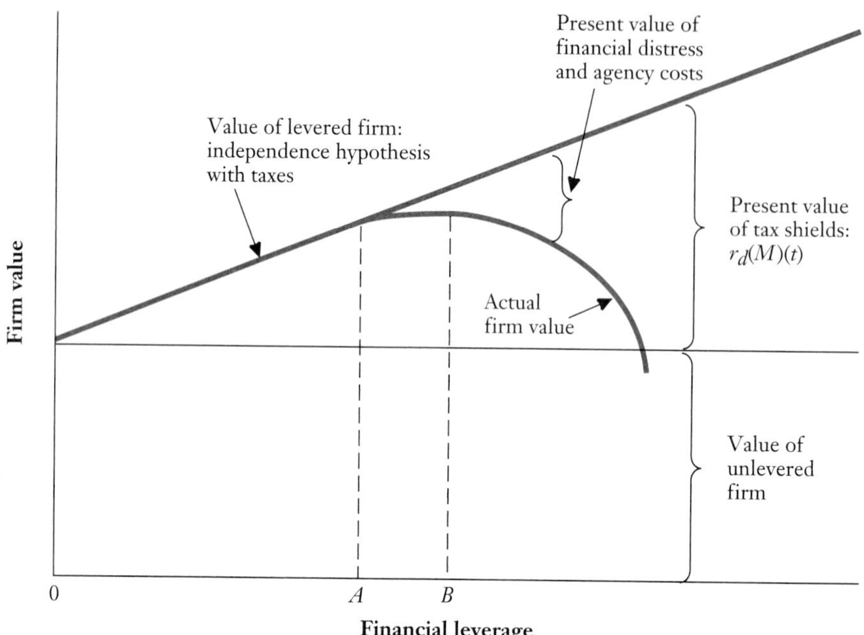

This discussion can be summarized by introducing equation 16-5 for the value of the levered firm. It represents the static trade-off model.

$$\begin{aligned}\text{market value of levered firm} &= \text{market value of unlevered firm} + \text{present value of tax shields} \\ &\quad - \left(\text{present value of financial distress costs} + \text{present value of agency costs}\right)\end{aligned} \tag{16-5}$$

The relationship expressed in equation 16-5 is presented graphically in Figure 16-7. There we see that the tax shield effect is dominant until point *A* is reached. After point *A*, the rising costs of the likelihood of firm failure (financial distress) and agency costs cause the market value of the levered firm to decline. The objective for the financial manager here is to find point *B* by using all of his or her analytical skill; this must also include a good dose of seasoned judgment. At point *B*, the actual market value of the levered firm is maximized, and its composite cost of capital (K_0) is at a minimum. The implementation problem is that the precise costs of financial distress and monitoring can only be estimated by subjective means; a definite mathematical solution is not available. Thus, planning the firm's financing mix always requires good decision making and management judgment.

An alternative view aimed at predicting how managers will finance their firm's capital budgets is now known in the financial-economics literature as the "pecking order theory." The germ of this approach is found in the works of Gordon Donaldson. Specifically, see his two volumes: *Corporate Debt Capacity* (Cambridge, MA: Division of Research, Harvard University, 1961) and *Strategy for Financial Mobility* (Cambridge, MA: Division of Research, Harvard University, 1969).

Myers then expanded on Donaldson's insights in the "Capital Structure Puzzle," noted below, and in several other places, including "Still Searching for Optimal Capital

Structure," which appeared in R. W. Kopcke and E. S. Rosengren, eds., *Are the Distinctions between Debt and Equity Disappearing?* (Boston: Federal Reserve Bank of Boston, 1989), pages 80–95.

In this latter article, Myers succinctly summarized the pecking order theory of capital structure with these four points (see pages 84–85):

1. Firms adapt dividend policy to investment opportunities. Note that this assumption is close to the concept of the *residual dividend theory* discussed in Chapter 17.
2. Firms prefer to finance investment opportunities with internally generated funds first; then external financial capital will be sought.
3. When external financing is needed, the firm will first choose to issue debt securities; issuing equity-type securities will be done last.
4. As more external financing is required to fund projects with positive net present values, the financing pecking order will be followed. This means a preference toward more risky debt, then to convertibles, preferred equity, and common equity as the last preference.

The upshot of this pecking order theory is that *no* precisely defined target leverage ratio really exists. This is because observed leverage ratios (that is, total debt to total assets) merely reflect the cumulative external financing needs of the firm over time.

Agency Costs, Free Cash Flow, and Capital Structure

Objective 5

In 1986, Professor Michael C. Jensen further extended the concept of agency costs into the area of capital structure management. The contribution revolves around a concept that Jensen labels "free cash flow." Professor Jensen defines free cash flow as follows:[5]

> Free cash flow is cash flow in excess of that required to fund all projects that have positive net present values when discounted at the relevant cost of capital.

Jensen then puts forth that substantial free cash flow can lead to misbehavior by managers and poor decisions that are *not* in the best interests of the firm's common stockholders. In other words, managers have an incentive to hold on to the free cash flow and have "fun" with it, rather than "disgorging" it, say, in the form of higher cash dividend payments.

But all is not lost. This leads to what Jensen calls his "control hypothesis" for debt creation. By levering up, the firm's shareholders will enjoy increased control over their management team. For example, if the firm issues new debt and uses the proceeds to retire outstanding common stock, then management is obligated to pay out cash to service the debt—this simultaneously reduces the amount of free cash flow available to management with which to have fun.

We can also refer to this motive for financial leverage use as the "threat hypothesis." Management works under the threat of financial failure—therefore, according to the "free cash flow theory of capital structure," it works more efficiently. This is supposed to reduce the agency costs of free cash flow which will in turn be recognized by the marketplace in the form of greater returns on the common stock.

Note that the *free cash flow theory of capital structure* does not give a theoretical solution to the question of just how much financial leverage is enough. Nor does it suggest how much leverage is too much leverage. It is a way of thinking about why shareholders and their boards of directors might use more debt to control management behavior and decisions. The basic decision tools of capital structure management still have to be utilized. They will be presented later in this chapter.

[5] Michael Jensen, "Agency Costs of Free Cash Flow, Corporate Finance, and Takeovers," *American Economic Review* 76 (May 1986): 323–29.

BACK TO THE PRINCIPLES

The discussions on agency costs, free cash flow, and the control hypothesis for debt creation return us to ***Principle 7: The Agency Problem—Managers won't work for the owners unless it's in their best interest.*** *The control hypothesis put forth by Jensen suggests that managers will work harder for shareholder interests when they have to "sweat it out" to meet contractual interest payments on debt securities. But we also learned that managers and bond investors can have a conflict that leads to agency costs associated with using debt capital. Thus, the theoretical benefits that flow from minimizing the agency costs of free cash flow by using more debt will cease when the rising agency costs of debt exactly offset those benefits. You can see how very difficult it is, then, for financial managers to precisely identify their true optimal capital structure.*

MANAGERIAL IMPLICATIONS

Where does our examination of capital structure theory leave us? The upshot is that the determination of the firm's financing mix is centrally important to the financial manager. The firm's stockholders are affected by capital structure decisions.

At the very least, and before bankruptcy costs and agency costs become detrimental, the tax shield effect will cause the shares of a levered firm to sell at a higher price than they would if the company had avoided debt financing. Owing to both the risk of failure and agency costs that accompany the excessive use of leverage, the financial manager must exercise caution in the use of fixed-charge capital. This problem of searching for the optimal range of use of financial leverage is our next task.[6]

CONCEPT CHECK

1. What is the enduring controversy within the subject of capital structure theory?
2. Can you name the two financial economists, both of whom have won the Nobel Prize in economics, who back in 1958 challenged the importance of capital structure management?
3. Can you explain the independence hypothesis as it relates to capital structure management?
4. Can you explain the moderate view of the relationship between a firm's financing mix and its average cost of capital?
5. How do agency costs and free cash flow relate to capital structure management?

Objective 6

BASIC TOOLS OF CAPITAL STRUCTURE MANAGEMENT

You have now developed a workable knowledge of capital structure theory. This makes you better equipped to search for your firm's optimal capital structure. Several tools are available to help you in this search process and simultaneously help you make prudent financing choices. These tools are decision oriented. They assist us in answering this question: "The next time we need $20 million, should we issue common stock or sell long-term bonds?"

[6] The relationship between capital structure and enterprise valuation by the marketplace continues to stimulate considerable research output. The complexity of the topic is reviewed in Stewart C. Myers, "The Capital Structure Puzzle," *Journal of Finance* 39 (July 1984): 575–92. Ten useful papers are contained in Benjamin M. Friedman, ed., *Corporate Capital Structures in the United States* (Chicago: National Bureau of Economic Research and the University of Chicago Press, 1985).

TABLE 16-4 Pierce Grain Company Possible Capital Structures

PLAN A: 0% DEBT			
		Total debt	$ 0
		Common equity	200,000[a]
Total assets	$200,000	Total liabilities and equity	$200,000
PLAN B: 25% DEBT AT 8% INTEREST RATE			
		Total debt	$ 50,000
		Common equity	150,000[b]
Total assets	$200,000	Total liabilities and equity	$200,000
PLAN C: 40% DEBT AT 8% INTEREST RATE			
		Total debt	$ 80,000
		Common equity	120,000[c]
Total assets	$200,000	Total liabilities and equity	$200,000

[a]2,000 common shares outstanding; [b]1,500 common shares outstanding; [c]1,200 common shares outstanding

Recall from Chapter 15 that the use of financial leverage has two effects on the earnings stream flowing to the firm's common stockholders. For clarity of exposition, Tables 15-7 and 15-8 are repeated here as Tables 16-4 and 16-5. Three possible financing mixes for the Pierce Grain Company are contained in Table 16-4, and an analysis of the corresponding financial leverage effects is displayed in Table 16-5.

TABLE 16-5 Pierce Grain Company Analysis of Financial Leverage at Different EBIT Levels

(1) EBIT	(2) INTEREST	(3) = (1) − (2) EBT	(4) = (3) × .5 TAXES	(5) = (3) − (4) NET INCOME TO COMMON	(6) EARNINGS PER SHARE	
PLAN A: 0% DEBT; $200,000 COMMON EQUITY, 2,000 SHARES						
$ 0	$ 0	$ 0	$ 0	$ 0	$ 0	
20,000	0	20,000	10,000	10,000	5.00	} 100%
40,000	0	40,000	20,000	20,000	10.00	
60,000	0	60,000	30,000	30,000	15.00	
80,000	0	80,000	40,000	40,000	20.00	
PLAN B: 25% DEBT; 8% INTEREST RATE; $150,000 COMMON EQUITY, 1,500 SHARES						
$ 0	$4,000[a]	$ (4,000)	$ (2,000)[a]	$ (2,000)	$ (1.33)	
20,000	4,000	16,000	8,000	8,000	5.33	} 125%
40,000	4,000	36,000	18,000	18,000	12.00	
60,000	4,000	56,000	28,000	28,000	18.67	
80,000	4,000	76,000	38,000	38,000	25.33	
PLAN C: 40% DEBT; 8% INTEREST RATE; $120,000 COMMON EQUITY, 1,200 SHARES						
$ 0	$6,400	$ (6,400)	$ (3,200)[a]	$ (3,200)	$ (2.67)	
20,000	6,400	13,600	6,800	6,800	5.67	} 147%
40,000	6,400	33,600	16,800	16,800	14.00	
60,000	6,400	53,600	26,800	26,800	22.33	
80,000	6,400	73,600	36,800	36,800	30.67	

[a]The negative tax bill recognizes the credit arising from the carryback and carryforward provision of the tax code.

The *first financial leverage effect* is the added variability in the earnings-per-share stream that accompanies the use of fixed-charge securities in the company's capital structure. By means of the degree-of-financial-leverage measure (DFL_{EBIT}) we explained how this variability can be quantified. The firm that uses more financial leverage (rather than less) will experience larger relative changes in its earnings per share (rather than smaller) following EBIT fluctuations. Assume that Pierce Grain elected financing plan C rather than plan A. Plan C is highly levered and plan A is unlevered. A 100 percent increase in EBIT from $20,000 to $40,000 would cause earnings per share to rise by 147 percent under plan C, but only 100 percent under plan A. Unfortunately, the effect would operate in the negative direction as well. A given change in EBIT is *magnified* by the use of financial leverage. This magnification is reflected in the variability of the firm's earnings per share. See the Finance Matters box, "Ben Bernanke on the Free Cash Theory of Capital Structure and the Buildup in Corporate Debt."

FINANCE MATTERS

BEN BERNANKE ON THE FREE CASH THEORY OF CAPITAL STRUCTURE AND THE BUILDUP IN CORPORATE DEBT

Business journalists and academic researchers alike generated several explanations for the seemingly heavy use of debt financing by corporations that persisted over most of the 1980s. Not all analysts accepted Jensen's control hypothesis for debt creation. Professor Bernanke had his doubts. He reviews Jensen's free cash flow theory and comments on the 1980s buildup in corporate leverage. The "incentive-based approach" is Bernanke's term for the free cash flow theory of capital structure.

The idea is that the financial structure of firms influences the incentives of "insiders" (managers, directors, and large shareholders with some operational interest in the business) and that, in particular, high levels of debt may increase the willingness of insiders to work hard and make profit-maximizing decisions. This incentive-based approach makes a valuable contribution to our understanding of a firm's capital structure. But while this theory might explain why firms like to use debt in general, does it explain why the use of debt has increased so much in recent years?

Michael Jensen, a founder and leading proponent of the incentive-based approach to capital structure, argues that it can. Jensen focuses on a recent worsening of what he calls the "free cash flow" problem. Free cash flow is defined as the portion of a corporation's cash flow that it is unable to invest profitably within the firm. Companies in industries that are profitable but no longer have much potential for expansion—the U.S. oil industry, for example—have a lot of free cash flow.

Why is free cash flow a problem? Jensen argues that managers are often tempted to use free cash flow to expand the size of the company, even if the expansion is not profitable. This is because managers feel that their power and job satisfaction are enhanced by a growing company; so given that most managers' compensation is at best weakly tied to the firm's profitability, Jensen argues that managers will find it personally worthwhile to expand even into money-losing operations. In principle, the board of directors and shareholders should be able to block these unprofitable investments; however, in practice, the fact that the management typically has far more information about potential investments than do outside directors and shareholders makes it difficult to second-guess the managers' recommendations.

How More Leverage Can Help

The company manager with lots of free cash flow may attempt to use that cash to increase his power and perquisites, at the expense of the shareholders. Jensen argues that the solution to the free cash-flow problem is more leverage. For example, suppose that management uses the free cash flow of the company, plus the proceeds of new debt issues, to repurchase stock from the outside shareholders—that is, to do a management buyout. This helps solve the free cash flow problem in several ways. The personal returns of the managers are now much more closely tied to the profits of the firm, which gives them incentives to be more efficient. Second, the releveraging process removes the existing free cash from the firm, so that any future investment projects will have to be financed externally; thus, future projects will have to meet the market test of being acceptable to outside bankers or bond purchasers. Finally, the high interest payments implied by releveraging impose a permanent discipline on the managers; in order to meet these payments, they will have to ruthlessly cut money-losing operations, avoid questionable investments, and take other efficiency-promoting actions.

According to Jensen, a substantial increase in free cash flow problems—resulting from deregulation, the maturing of some large industries, and other factors—is a major source of the recent debt expansion. Jensen also points to a number of institutional factors that have promoted increased leverage. These include relaxed restrictions on mergers, which have lowered the barriers to corporate takeovers created by the antitrust laws and increased financial sophistication, such as the greatly expanded operations of takeover specialists like Drexel Burnham Lambert Inc. and the development of the market for "junk bonds." Jensen's diagnosis is not controversial: it's quite plausible that these factors, plus changing norms about what constitutes an "acceptable" level of debt, explain at least part of the trend toward increased corporate debt. One important piece of evidence in favor of this explanation is that net equity issues have been substantially negative since 1983. This suggests that much of the proceeds of the new debt issues is being used to repurchase outstanding shares. This is what we would expect if corporations are attempting to releverage their existing assets, rather than using debt to expand their asset holdings. However, the implied conclusion—that the debt buildup is beneficial overall to the economy—is considerably more controversial.

Criticisms of the Incentive-Based Rationale for Increased Debt

Jensen and other advocates of the incentive-based approach to capital structure have made a cogent theoretical case for the beneficial effects of debt finance, and many architects of large-scale restructurings have given improved incentives and the promise of greater efficiency as a large part of the rationale for increased leverage. The idea that leverage is beneficial has certainly been embraced by the stock market: even unsubstantiated rumors of a potential leveraged buyout (LBO) have been sufficient to send the stock price of the targeted company soaring, often by 40 percent or more. At a minimum, this indicates that stock market participants *believe* that higher leverage increases profitability. Proponents of restructuring interpret this as evidence that debt is good for the economy.

There are, however, criticisms of this conclusion. First, the fact that the stock market's expectations of company profitability rise when there is a buyout is not proof that profits will rise in actuality. It is still too soon to judge whether the increased leverage of the 1980s will lead to a sustained increase in profitability. One might think of looking to historical data for an answer to this question. But buyouts in the 1960s and 1970s were somewhat different in character from more recent restructurings, and, in any case, the profitability evidence on the earlier episodes is mixed.

Even if the higher profits expected by the stock market do materialize, there is contention over where they are likely to come from. The incentive-based theory of capital structure says they will come from improved efficiency. But some opponents have argued that the higher profits will primarily reflect transfers to the shareholders from other claimants on the corporation—its employees, customers, suppliers, bondholders, and the government. Customers may be hurt if takeovers are associated with increased monopolization of markets. Bondholders have been big losers in some buyouts, as higher leverage has increased bankruptcy risk and thus reduced the value of outstanding bonds. The government may have lost tax revenue, as companies, by increasing leverage, have increased their interest deductions (although there are offsetting effects here, such as the taxes paid by bought-out shareholders on their capital gains). The perception that much of the profits associated with releveraging and buyouts comes from "squeezing" existing beneficiaries of the corporation explains much of the recent political agitation to limit these activities.

The debt buildup can also be criticized from the perspective of incentive-based theories themselves. Two points are worth noting: first, the principal problem that higher leverage is supposed to address is the relatively weak connection between firms' profits and managers' personal returns, which reduces managers' incentives to take profit-maximizing actions. But if this is truly the problem, it could be addressed more directly—without subjecting the company to serious bankruptcy risk—simply by changing managerial compensation schemes to include more profit-based incentives.

The Downside of Debt Financing

Increased debt is not the optimal solution to all incentive problems. For example, it has been shown, as a theoretical proposition, that managers of debt-financed firms have an incentive to choose riskier projects over safe ones; this is because firms with fixed-debt obligations enjoy all of the upside potential of high-risk projects but share the downside losses with the debt holders, who are not fully repaid if bad investment outcomes cause the firm to fail.

That high leverage does not always promote efficiency can be seen when highly leveraged firms suffer losses and find themselves in financial distress. When financial problems hit, the need to meet interest payments may force management to take a very short-run perspective, leading them to cut back production and employment, cancel even potentially profitable expansion projects, and sell assets at fire-sale prices. Because the risk of bankruptcy is so great, firms in financial distress cannot make long-term agreements; they lose customers and suppliers who are afraid they cannot count on an ongoing relationship, and they must pay wage premiums to hire workers.

These efficiency losses, plus the direct costs of bankruptcy (such as legal fees), are the potential downside of high leverage.

Source: Ben Bernanke, "Is There Too Much Corporate Debt?" *Business Review*, Federal Reserve Bank of Philadelphia (September–October 1989): 5–8.

The *second financial leverage effect* concerns the level of earnings per share at a given EBIT under a given capital structure. Refer to Table 16-5. At the EBIT level of $20,000, earnings per share would be $5, $5.33, and $5.67 under financing arrangements A, B, and C, respectively. Above a critical level of EBIT, the firm's earnings per share will be higher if greater degrees of financial leverage are employed. Conversely, below some critical level of EBIT, earnings per share will suffer at greater degrees of financial leverage. Whereas the first financial-leverage effect is quantified by the degree-of-financial-leverage measure (DFL_{EBIT}), the second is quantified by what is generally referred to as EBIT–EPS analysis. EPS refers, of course, to earnings per share. The rationale underlying this sort of analysis is simple. Earnings is one of the key variables that influences the market value of the firm's common stock. The effect of a financing decision on EPS, then, should be understood because the decision will probably affect the value of the stockholders' investment.

EBIT–EPS Analysis

Example: Analyzing Financing Choices

Assume that plan B in Table 16-5 is the existing capital structure for Pierce Grain Company. Furthermore, the asset structure of the firm is such that EBIT is expected to be $20,000 per year for a very long time. A capital investment is available to Pierce Grain that will cost $50,000. Acquisition of this asset is expected to raise the projected EBIT level to $30,000, permanently. The firm can raise the needed cash by (1) selling 500 shares of common stock at $100 each or (2) selling new bonds that will net the firm $50,000 and carry an interest rate of 8.5 percent. These capital structures and corresponding EPS amounts are summarized in Table 16-6.

TABLE 16-6 Pierce Grain Company Analysis of Financing Choices

PART A: CAPITAL STRUCTURES	EXISTING CAPITAL STRUCTURE		WITH NEW COMMON STOCK FINANCING		WITH NEW DEBT FINANCING
Long-term debt at 8%	$ 50,000	Long-term debt at 8%	$ 50,000	Long-term debt at 8%	$ 50,000
Common stock	150,000	Common stock	200,000	Long-term debt at 8.5%	50,000
				Common stock	150,000
Total liabilities and equity	$200,000	Total liabilities and equity	$250,000	Total liabilities and equity	$250,000
Common shares outstanding	1,500	Common shares outstanding	2,000	Common shares outstanding	1,500

PART B: PROJECTED EPS LEVELS	EXISTING CAPITAL STRUCTURE	WITH NEW COMMON STOCK FINANCING	WITH NEW DEBT FINANCING
EBIT	$ 20,000	$ 30,000	$ 30,000
Less: interest expense	4,000	4,000	8,250
Earnings before taxes (EBT)	$ 16,000	$ 26,000	$ 21,750
Less: taxes at 50%	8,000	13,000	10,875
Net income	$ 8,000	$ 13,000	$ 10,875
Less: preferred dividends	0	0	0
Earnings available to common	$ 8,000	$ 13,000	$ 10,875
EPS	$ 5.33	$ 6.50	$ 7.25

At the projected EBIT level of $30,000, the EPS for the common stock and debt alternatives are $6.50 and $7.25, respectively. Both are considerably above the $5.33 that would occur if the new project were rejected and the additional financial capital were not raised. Based on a criterion of selecting the financing plan that will provide the highest EPS, the bond alternative is favored. But what if the basic business risk to which the firm is exposed causes the EBIT level to vary over a considerable range? Can we be sure that the bond alternative will *always* have the higher EPS associated with it? The answer, of course, is "No." When the EBIT level is subject to uncertainty, a graphic analysis of the proposed financing plans can provide useful information to the financial manager.

GRAPHIC ANALYSIS The EBIT–EPS analysis chart allows the decision maker to visualize the impact of different financing plans on EPS over a range of EBIT levels. The relationship between EPS and EBIT is linear. Therefore, to construct the chart we only need two points for each alternative. Part B of Table 16-6 already provides us with one of these points. The answer to the following question for each choice gives us the second point: At what EBIT level will the EPS for the plan be exactly zero? If the EBIT level just covers the plan's financing costs (on a before-tax basis), then EPS will be zero. For the stock plan, an EPS of zero is associated with an EBIT of $4,000. The $4,000 is the interest expense incurred under the existing capital structure. If the bond plan is elected, the interest costs will be the present $4,000 plus $4,250 per year arising from the new debt issue. An EBIT of $8,250, then, is necessary to provide a zero EPS with the bond plan.

The EBIT–EPS analysis chart representing the financing choices available to the Pierce Grain Company is shown as Figure 16-8. EBIT is charted on the horizontal axis and EPS on the vertical axis. The intercepts on the horizontal axis represent the before-tax equivalent financing charges related to each plan. The straight lines for each plan tell us the EPS amounts that will occur at different EBIT amounts.

FIGURE 16-8 EBIT–EPS Analysis Chart

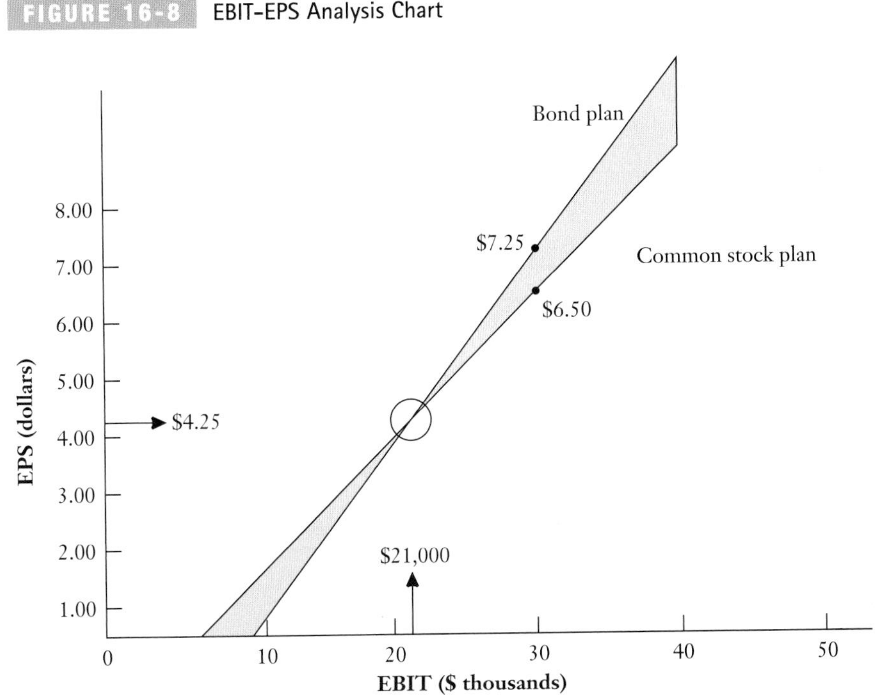

Notice that the bond-plan line has a *steeper slope* than the stock-plan line. This ensures that the lines for each financing choice will *intersect*. Above the intersection point, EPS for the plan with greater leverage will exceed that for the plan with lesser leverage. The intersection point, encircled in Figure 16-8, occurs at an EBIT level of $21,000 and produces EPS of $4.25 for each plan. When EBIT is $30,000, notice that the bond plan produces EPS of $7.25 and the stock plan, $6.50. Below the intersection point, EPS with the stock plan will *exceed* that with the more highly levered bond plan. The steeper slope of the bond-plan line indicates that with greater leverage, EPS is more sensitive to EBIT changes. This same concept was discussed in Chapter 15 when we derived the degree of financial leverage measure.

EBIT–EPS indifference point
The level of earnings before interest and taxes (EBIT) that will equate earnings per share (EPS) between two different financing plans.

COMPUTING INDIFFERENCE POINTS The point of intersection in Figure 16-8 is called the **EBIT–EPS indifference point**. It identifies the EBIT level at which the EPS will be the same regardless of the financing plan chosen by the financial manager. This indifference point, sometimes called the break-even point, has major implications for financial planning. At EBIT amounts in excess of the EBIT indifference level, the more heavily levered financing plan will generate a higher EPS. At EBIT amounts below the EBIT indifference level, the financing plan involving less leverage will generate a higher EPS. It is important, then, to know the EBIT indifference level.

We can find it graphically, as in Figure 16-8. At times it may be more efficient, though, to calculate the indifference point directly. This can be done by using the following equation:

$$\underset{\textit{EPS: Stock Plan}}{\frac{(EBIT - I)(1 - t) - P}{S_s}} = \underset{\textit{EPS: Bond Plan}}{\frac{(EBIT - I)(1 - t) - P}{S_b}} \tag{16-6}$$

where S_s and S_b are the number of common shares outstanding under the stock and bond plans, respectively, I is interest expense, t is the firm's income tax rate, and P is preferred dividends paid. In the present case, P is zero because there is no preferred stock outstanding. If preferred stock is associated with one of the financing alternatives, keep in mind that the preferred dividends, P, are not tax deductible. Equation 16-6 *does* take this fact into consideration.

For the present example, we calculate the indifference level of EBIT as:

$$\frac{(EBIT - \$4{,}000)(1 - 0.5) - 0}{2{,}000} = \frac{(EBIT - \$8{,}250)(1 - 0.5) - 0}{1{,}500}$$

When the expression is solved for EBIT, we obtain $21,000. If EBIT turns out to be $21,000, then EPS will be $4.25 under both plans.

UNCOMMITTED EARNINGS PER SHARE AND INDIFFERENCE POINTS The calculations that permitted us to solve for Pierce Grain's EBIT–EPS indifference point made no explicit allowance for the repayment of the bond principal. This procedure is not that unrealistic. It only presumes the debt will be perpetually outstanding. This means that when the current bond issue matures, a new bond issue will be floated. The proceeds from the newer issue would be used to pay off the maturity value of the older issue.

Sinking fund
A cash reserve used for the orderly and early retirement of the principal amount of a bond issue. Payments into the fund are known as sinking fund payments.

Many bond contracts, however, require that **sinking fund payments** be made to a bond trustee. A **sinking fund** is a real cash reserve that is used to provide for the orderly and early retirement of the principal amount of the bond issue. Most often the sinking fund payment is a mandatory fixed amount and is required by a clause in the bond indenture. Sinking fund payments can represent a sizable cash drain on the firm's liquid resources. Moreover, sinking fund payments are a return of borrowed principal, so they are *not* tax deductible to the firm.

Because of the potentially serious nature of the cash drain caused by sinking fund requirements, the financial manager might be concerned with the uncommitted earnings per share (UEPS) related to each financing plan. The calculation of UEPS recognizes that sinking fund commitments have been honored. UEPS can be used, then, for discretionary spending—such as the payment of cash dividends to common stockholders or investment in capital facilities.

If we let *SF* be the sinking fund payment required in a given year, the EBIT–UEPS indifference point can be calculated as:

$$\overset{\text{UEPS: Stock Plan}}{\frac{(EBIT - I)(1 - t) - P - SF}{S_s}} = \overset{\text{UEPS: Bond Plan}}{\frac{(EBIT - I)(1 - t) - P - SF}{S_b}} \quad \textbf{(16-7)}$$

If several bond issues are already outstanding, then *I* in equations 16-6 and 16-7 for the stock plan consists of the sum of their related interest payments. For the bond plan, *I* would be the sum of existing plus new interest charges. In equation 16-7 the same logic applies to the sinking fund variable, *SF.* The indifference level of EBIT based on UEPS will always exceed that based on EPS.

A WORD OF CAUTION Above the EBIT–EPS indifference point, a more heavily levered financial plan promises to deliver a larger EPS. Strict application of the criterion of selecting the financing plan that produces the highest EPS might have the firm issuing debt most of the time it raised external capital. Our discussion of capital structure theory taught us the dangers of that sort of action.

The primary weakness of EBIT–EPS analysis is that it disregards the implicit costs of debt financing. The effect of the specific financing decision on the firm's cost of common equity capital is totally ignored. Investors should be concerned with both the *level and variability* of the firm's expected earnings stream. EBIT–EPS analysis considers only the level of the earnings stream and ignores the variability (riskiness) inherent in it. Thus, this type of analysis must be used in conjunction with other basic tools in reaching the objective of capital structure management.

BACK TO THE PRINCIPLES

The companion techniques of EBIT–EPS analysis and uncommitted earnings per share analysis are well-known within the corporate financial planning groups of corporations. It is useful to emphasize that these tools of capital structure management are best utilized if we relate them to both ***Principle 3: Cash—Not Profits—Is King,*** *and* ***Principle 6: Efficient Capital Markets—The markets are quick and the prices are right.***

Thus, the cash flows, as opposed to accounting profits, that are available to the firm after a financing choice is made will drive market prices. Recall from Chapter 1 that we said efficient markets *will not be fooled by accounting changes that merely manipulate reported earnings. In the context of using these tools, then, the proper way to think of earnings per share and uncommitted earnings per share is on a cash basis rather than on an accounting accrual basis. The firm services its debt contracts not out of accounting earnings, but out of cash flows.*

Comparative Leverage Ratios

In Chapter 3, we explored the overall usefulness of financial ratio analysis. Leverage ratios are one of the categories of financial ratios identified in that chapter. We emphasize here that the computation of leverage ratios is one of the basic tools of capital structure management.

Two types of leverage ratios must be computed when a financing decision faces the firm. We call these *balance sheet leverage ratios* and *coverage ratios*. The firm's balance sheet supplies inputs for computing the balance sheet leverage ratios. In various forms, these balance sheet metrics compare the firm's use of funds supplied by creditors with those supplied by owners.

Inputs to the coverage ratios *generally* come from the firm's income statement. At times, the external analyst may have to consult balance sheet information to construct some of these needed estimates. On a privately placed debt issue, for example, some fraction of the current portion of the firm's long-term debt might have to be used as an estimate of that issue's sinking fund. Coverage ratios provide estimates of the firm's ability to service its financing contracts. High coverage ratios, compared with a standard, imply unused debt capacity. See the Finance Matters box, "The Walt Disney Company on Capital Costs and Capital Structure."

FINANCE MATTERS

THE WALT DISNEY COMPANY ON CAPITAL COSTS AND CAPITAL STRUCTURE

At the end of fiscal year 1998, the Walt Disney Company had a total market capitalization of $65 billion; this placed it among the 40 largest corporations in the United States, while its sales revenues of $23 billion placed it 53rd on the 1999 *Fortune* 500 list. This multinational giant with 117,000 employees provides several real examples of the capital structure concepts presented in this chapter.

In the discussion that follows from Disney management, notice how the firm (1) relates capital costs to shareholder value, (2) believes in the "prudent degree of leverage" concept, (3) is concerned with its interest coverage ratio—measured as earnings before net interest, taxes, depreciation, and amortization or EBITDA divided by net interest expense, and (4) strives to maintain a minimum desired or target bond rating. Within the accompanying graph you will see that Disney's coverage ratio for fiscal year 1998 of EBITDA to net interest expense is 8.1 times (i.e., $5,019 million/$622 million).

Disney's solid balance sheet allows the company to borrow at attractive rates, helping to reduce the overall cost of capital and thereby creating value for shareholders. As of year end, Disney maintained total borrowings of approximately $12 billion and a debt-to-total-capital ratio of 38 percent. The company believes that this level of debt represents a prudent degree of leverage, which provides for substantial financial flexibility to borrow should business opportunities present themselves. As measured by the ratio of earnings before net interest, taxes, depreciation, and amortization (EBITDA) to net interest expense, the company covered its interest costs by a factor of more than eight times for the year ended September 30.

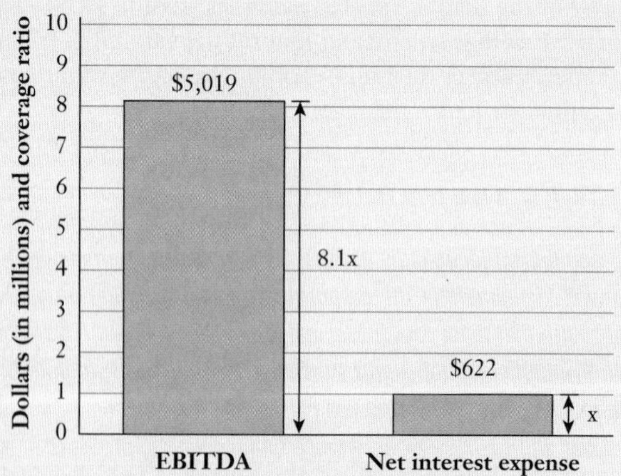

The company monitors its cash flow, interest coverage, and its debt-to-total-capital ratio with the long-term goal of maintaining a strong single-A or better credit rating.

Source: The Walt Disney Company, *1998 Annual Report*, 12.

TABLE 16-7 Comparative Leverage Ratios: Worksheet for Analyzing Financing Plans

RATIOS	COMPUTATION METHOD	EXISTING RATIO	RATIO WITH NEW COMMON STOCK FINANCING	RATIO WITH NEW DEBT FINANCING
BALANCE SHEET LEVERAGE RATIOS				
1. Debt ratio	$\frac{\text{total liabilities}}{\text{total assets}}$	___%	___%	___%
2. Long-term debt to total capitalization	$\frac{\text{long-term debt}}{\text{long-term debt} + \text{net worth}}$	___%	___%	___%
3. Total liabilities to net worth	$\frac{\text{total liabilities}}{\text{net worth}}$	___%	___%	___%
4. Common equity ratio	$\frac{\text{common equity}}{\text{total assets}}$	___%	___%	___%
COVERAGE RATIOS				
1. Times interest earned	$\frac{\text{EBIT}}{\text{annual interest expense}}$	___ times	___ times	___ times
2. Times burden covered	$\frac{\text{EBIT}}{\text{interest} + \frac{\text{sinkingfund}}{1-t}}$	___ times	___ times	___ times
3. Cash flow overall coverage	$\frac{\text{EBIT} + \text{lease expense} + \text{depreciation}}{\text{interest} + \text{lease expense} + \frac{\text{preferred dividends}}{1-t} + \frac{\text{principal payments}}{1-t}}$	___ times	___ times	___ times

A WORKSHEET Table 16-7 is a sample worksheet used to analyze financing choices. The objective of the analysis is to determine the effect each financing plan will have on key financial ratios. The financial officer can compare the existing level of each ratio with its projected level, taking into consideration the contractual commitments of each alternative.

In reality, we know that EBIT might be expected to vary over a considerable range of outcomes. For this reason the coverage ratios should be calculated several times, each at a different level of EBIT. If this is accomplished over all possible values of EBIT, a probability distribution for each coverage ratio can be constructed. This provides the financial manager with much more information than simply calculating the coverage ratios based on the expected value of EBIT.

An efficient way to find various financial leverage ratios is to go to **www.quicken.com/investments**. Once there, type in the stock market ticker symbol of the firm you are analyzing (e.g., for Disney it would be DIS). Once the stock quote comes up, click on "Fundamentals." Under the heading of "Financial Strength," you will find several leverage ratios. You can then repeat the process for several firms in the same industry and quite quickly have your own set of comparative leverage ratios.

INDUSTRY NORMS The comparative leverage ratios calculated according to the format laid out in Table 16-7, or in a similar format, have additional utility to the decision maker if they can be compared with some standard. Generally, corporate financial analysts, investment bankers, commercial bank loan officers, and bond-rating agencies rely on industry classes from which to compute "normal" ratios. Although industry groupings may actually contain firms whose basic business risk exposure differs widely, the practice is entrenched in American business behavior.[7] At the very least, then, the financial officer must be interested in *industry standards* because almost everybody else is.

[7] An approach to grouping firms based on several component measures of business risk, as opposed to ordinary industry classes, is reported in John D. Martin, David F. Scott, Jr., and Robert F. Vandell, "Equivalent Risk Classes: A Multidimensional Examination," *Journal of Financial and Quantitative Analysis* 14 (March 1979): 101–18.

FINANCE MATTERS

GEORGIA-PACIFIC ON CAPITAL STRUCTURE

The introduction to this chapter referred to the Georgia-Pacific Corporation's financial strategies and management of its capital structure. The following discussion further illustrates the care that this firm's key officers place on managing its financing mix and also alerts you to the subject of the next section.

Georgia-Pacific tries to balance the mix of debt and equity in a way that will benefit our shareholders, by keeping our weighted average cost of capital low, while retaining the flexibility needed to finance attractive internal projects or acquisitions. Risk factors that contribute to the volatility of our cash flows include economic cycles, changes in industry capacity, environmental regulations, and litigation.

On a market-value basis, our debt-to-capital ratio was 47 percent (year-end 1996). By employing this capital structure, we believe that our weighted average cost of capital is nearly optimized—at approximately 10 percent. Although reducing debt significantly would somewhat reduce the marginal cost of debt, significant debt reduction would likely increase our weighted average cost of capital by raising the proportion of higher-cost equity.

Considering Georgia-Pacific's ability to generate strong cash flow—even at the bottom of the cycle—we believe the current debt structure is quite manageable. In fact, combining the lowest full-year cash flows from building products and pulp and paper operations over recent business cycles would still provide enough cash to pay taxes, cover interest on $5.5 billion of debt, pay dividends, and fund several hundred million dollars of reinvestment needed to maintain our facilities in competitive condition.

Source: *Georgia-Pacific 1996 Annual Report*, 15.

Several published studies indicate that capital structure ratios vary in a significant manner among industry classes.[8] For example, random samplings of the common equity ratios of large retail firms seem to differ statistically from those of major steel producers. The major steel producers use financial leverage to a lesser degree than do the large retail organizations. On the whole, firms operating in the *same* industry tend to exhibit capital structure ratios that cluster around a central value, which we call a norm. Business risk will vary from industry to industry. As a consequence, the capital structure norms will vary from industry to industry.

This is not to say that all companies in the industry will maintain leverage ratios "close" to the norm. For instance, firms that are very profitable may display *high* coverage ratios and *high* balance sheet leverage ratios. The moderately profitable firm, though, might find such a posture unduly risky. Here the usefulness of industry normal leverage ratios is clear. If the firm chooses to deviate in a material manner from the accepted values for the key ratios, it must have a sound reason. See the Finance Matters box, "Georgia-Pacific on Capital Structure."

Companywide Cash Flows: What Is the Worst that Could Happen?

In Chapter 3, we noted that liquidity ratios are designed to measure the ability of the firm to pay its bills on time. Financing charges are just another type of bill that eventually comes due for payment. Interest charges, preferred dividends, lease charges, and principal payments all must be paid on time, or the company risks being caught in bankruptcy proceedings. To a lesser extent, dispensing with financing charges on an other than timely

[8] See, for example, Eli Schwartz and J. Richard Aronson, "Some Surrogate Evidence in Support of the Concept of Optimal Financial Structure," *Journal of Finance* 22 (March 1967): 10–18; David F. Scott, Jr., "Evidence on the Importance of Financial Structure," *Financial Management* 1 (Summer 1972): 45–50; and David F. Scott, Jr., and John D. Martin, "Industry Influence on Financial Structure," *Financial Management* 4 (Spring 1975): 67–73.

basis can result in severely restricted business operations. We have just seen that coverage ratios provide a measure of the safety of one general class of payment—financing charges. Coverage ratios, then, and liquidity ratios are very close in concept.

A more comprehensive method is available for studying the impact of capital structure decisions on corporate cash flows. The method is simple but nonetheless very valuable. It involves the preparation of a series of cash budgets under (1) different economic conditions and (2) different capital structures. The net cash flows under these different situations can be examined to determine if the financing requirements expose the firm to a degree of default risk too high to bear.

In work that has been highly acclaimed, Donaldson has suggested that the firm's debt-carrying capacity (defined in the broad sense here to include preferred dividend payments and lease payments) ought to depend on the net cash flows the firm could expect to receive during a recessionary period.[9] In other words, *target capital structure proportions* could be set by planning for the "worst that could happen." An example will be of help.

Suppose that a recession is expected to last for one year.[10] Moreover, the end of the year represents the bottoming-out, or worst portion of the recession. Equation 16-8 defines the cash balance, CB_r, the firm could expect to have at the end of the recession period.[11]

$$CB_r = C_0 + (C_s + OR) - (P_a + RM + \ldots + E_n) - FC \quad \textbf{(16-8)}$$

where C_0 = the cash balance at the beginning of the recession
C_s = collection from sales
OR = other cash receipts
P_a = payroll expenditures
RM = raw material payments
E_n = the last of a long series of expenditures over which management has little control (nondiscretionary expenditures)
FC = fixed financial charges associated with a specific capital structure

If we let the net of total cash receipts and nondiscretionary expenditures be represented by NCF_r, then equation 16-8 can be simplified to:

$$CB_r = C_0 + NCF_r - FC \quad \textbf{(16-9)}$$

The inputs to equation 16-9 come from a detailed cash budget. The variable representing financing costs, FC, can be changed in accordance with several alternative financing plans to ascertain if the net cash balance during the recession, CB_r, might fall below zero.

Suppose that some firm typically maintains $500,000 in cash and marketable securities. This amount would be on hand at the start of the recession period. During the economic decline, the firm projects that its net cash flows from operations, NCF_r, will be $2 million. If the firm currently finances its assets with an unlevered capital structure, its cash balance at the worst point of the recession would be:

$$CB_r = \$500{,}000 + \$2{,}000{,}000 - \$0 = \$2{,}500{,}000$$

This procedure allows us to study many different situations.[12] Assume that the same firm is considering a shift in its capitalization such that annual interest and sinking fund

[9] Refer to Gordon Donaldson, "New Framework for Corporate Debt Policy," *Harvard Business Review* 40 (March–April 1962): 117–31; Gordon Donaldson, *Corporate Debt Capacity* (Boston: Division of Research, Graduate School of Business Administration, Harvard University, 1961), chap. 7; and Gordon Donaldson, "Strategy for Financial Emergencies," *Harvard Business Review* 47 (November–December 1969): 67–79.

[10] The analysis can readily be extended to cover a recessionary period of several years. All that is necessary is to calculate the cash budgets over a similar period.

[11] For the most part, the present notation follows that of Donaldson.

[12] It is not difficult to improve the usefulness of this sort of analysis by applying the technique of simulation to the generation of the various cash budgets. This facilitates the construction of probability distributions of net cash flows under differing circumstances.

payments will be $2,300,000. If a recession occurred, the firm's cash balance at the end of the adverse economic period would be:

$$CB_r = \$500{,}000 + \$2{,}000{,}000 - \$2{,}300{,}000 = \$200{,}000$$

The firm ordinarily maintains a liquid asset balance of $500,000. Thus, the effect of the proposed capital structure on the firm's cash balance during adverse circumstances might seem too risky for management to accept. When the chance of being out of cash is too high for management to bear, the use of financial leverage has been pushed beyond a reasonable level. According to this tool, the appropriate level of financial leverage is reached when the chance of being out of cash is exactly equal to that which management will assume.

CONCEPT CHECK

1. Explain the meaning of the EBIT–EPS indifference point.
2. How are various leverage ratios and industry norms used in capital structure management?

Objective 7

THE MULTINATIONAL FIRM: BEWARE OF CURRENCY RISK

When the euro was introduced as a new currency by the 11 countries comprising the European Union on January 1, 1999, it took .8455 euros to buy $1 in foreign exchange markets. By November 15, 2000, it took a greater 1.1663 euros to acquire that same U.S. dollar. That amounted to a relative increase of 37.94 percent as measured in euros to buy that dollar ([1.1663/.8455] – 1). The euro depreciated in value against the dollar; the dollar appreciated against the euro. Such variations in the value of foreign currencies can at times cause big headaches for U.S. financial executives.

The financial-economic reason underlying the headache is straightforward. The U.S. multinational firm, for financial reporting purposes, must convert earnings denominated in foreign currencies into dollars. So, firms with large volumes of sales in non-U.S. markets are exposed to a large degree of currency risk. You can understand, then, that firms with an already high exposure to currency value changes might reasonably choose to avoid incurring high levels of financial risk. The currency risk challenge occurs quite often.

Consider that on September 14, 2000, the common stock price of Colgate-Palmolive declined by 16 percent after security analysts warned of likely lower reported earnings due to a high level of European sales exposure and euro conversion risk. On that same day, McDonalds' common stock fell by 5 percent for the same reason—a decline in the relative value of the euro. And, a few weeks earlier, Harley-Davidson reported on July 12, 2000, that its gross profit margin declined due partially to "weakening European currencies." Managing currency risk, then, is a daily activity for the finance function of the multinational firm. Note that Chapter 22 on International Finance includes a more detailed discussion of currency risk and management.

CONCEPT CHECK

1. Why can a stronger value of the U.S. dollar relative to a foreign currency like the euro pose a problem for financial executives of multinational firms?
2. Why might firms that derive a large proportion of their total sales from overseas markets choose not to utilize large degrees of financial leverage?

HOW FINANCIAL MANAGERS USE THIS MATERIAL

Objective 8

Our study of capital structure management has included examples of actual practice from several corporations including Georgia-Pacific, Texas Instruments, Medtronic, and General Mills. More emphasis and examples dealing with how financial managers use the main concepts from this chapter are presented in this section.

We have discussed (1) the concept of an optimal capital structure, (2) the search for an appropriate range of financial leverage, and (3) the fundamental tools of capital structure management. Now we will examine some opinions and practices of financial executives that support our emphasis on the importance of capital structure management. See the Finance Matters box, "Corporate Policies on Using Financial Leverage."

The Conference Board has surveyed 170 senior financial officers with respect to their capital structure practices.[13] Of these 170 executives, 102, or 60 percent, stated that they *do* believe there is an optimum capital structure for the corporation. Sixty-five percent of the responding practitioners worked for firms with annual sales in excess of $200 million. One executive who subscribed to the optimal capital structure concept stated:

> In my opinion, there is an optimum capital structure for companies. However, this optimum capital structure will vary by individual companies, industries, and then is subject to changing economies, by money markets, earnings trends, and prospects . . . the circumstances and the lenders will determine an optimum at different points in time.[14]

This survey and others consistently point out that (1) financial officers set target debt ratios for their companies, and (2) the values for those ratios are influenced by a conscious evaluation of the basic business risk to which the firm is exposed.

The Coca-Cola Company maintains an extensive and useful Internet site, where you can read about the firm's financial strategies in its latest annual report. Within that site the company provides an extensive "Investor Center," available at www.coca-cola.com. Once you access this site you can click on the firm's most-recent annual report. On page 50 of the 2002 Annual Report, for example, you will find the section on "Financial Strategies." Now you can review Coke's debt policy, bond ratings, and various measures of financial leverage use (e.g., the interest coverage ratio). Many of the concepts discussed in this chapter are touched upon by Coke's management's elaboration on "Debt Financing." Further, if you return to the main page of the Investor Center, you can read about Coke's "Code of Business Conduct." The latter will remind you of our **Principle 10.**

TARGET DEBT RATIOS

Selected comments from financial executives point to the widespread use of target debt ratios. A vice-president and treasurer of the American Telephone and Telegraph Company (AT&T) described his firm's debt ratio policy in terms of a range:

> All of the foregoing considerations led us to conclude, and reaffirm for a period of many years, that the proper range of our debt was 30 percent to 40 percent of total capital. Reasonable success in meeting financial needs under the diverse market and economic conditions that we have faced attests to the appropriateness of this conclusion.[15]

In a similar fashion, the president of Fibreboard Corporation identified his firm's target debt ratio and noted how it is related to the uncertain nature of the company's business:

> Our objective is a 30 percent ratio of debt to capitalization. We need that kind of flexibility to operate in the cyclical business we are in.[16]

In the Conference Board survey mentioned earlier, 84 of the 102 financial officers who subscribed to the optimal capital structure concept stated that their firm *has* a target debt ratio.[17] The most frequently mentioned influence on the level of the target debt ratio was ability to meet financing charges. Other factors identified as affecting the target

[13] Francis J. Walsh, Jr., *Planning Corporate Capital Structures* (New York: The Conference Board, 1972).

[14] Walsh, *Planning Corporate Capital Structures*, 14.

[15] John J. Scanlon, "Bell System Financial Policies," *Financial Management* 1 (Summer 1972): 16–26.

[16] *Business Week* (December 6, 1976): 30.

[17] Walsh, *Planning Corporate Capital Structures*, 17.

FINANCE MATTERS

CORPORATE POLICIES ON USING FINANCIAL LEVERAGE

Managements continually face the challenge of determining how much financial leverage is enough. The statements that follow from Texas Instruments, General Mills, and Medtronic, Inc., deal with this difficult financial policy question.

Texas Instruments

TI's financial condition continued to strengthen in 1993. The company made further progress toward management's goal of reducing TI's debt-to-total capital ratio and generated positive cash flow net of additions to property, plant, and equipment.

TI's debt-to-total-capital ratio was .28 at the end of the year, down .01 from the third quarter and down .05 from year-end 1992. TI's goal is to reduce this ratio to about .25.

General Mills

Our major financial targets for top-decile performance include: Meeting or exceeding a 20 percent after-tax return on invested capital and 38 percent return on equity. Our ROC and ROE, before unusual items, have averaged 21 percent and 43 percent, respectively, during the past three years.

Maintaining a balance sheet with a strong A bond rating is important. Financial ratios, including a cash flow to debt ratio of 53 percent and a fixed charge coverage of 7.8 times, continued strong in 1993. The purchase of 6.3 million shares for our treasury, which both increased debt and reduced stockholders' equity, increased our debt-to-capital ratio to 63 percent.

Medtronic

The company's capital structure consists of equity and interest-bearing debt. The company utilizes long-term debt minimally. Interest-bearing debt as a percent of total capital was 10.9 percent at April 30, 1993, compared with 10.1 percent and 12.6 percent at April 30, 1992 and 1991, respectively. These ratios are well within the company's financial objective of maintaining a debt-to-total-capital ratio not exceeding 30 percent.

Source: *Texas Instruments, 1993 Annual Report,* 36; *General Mills, 1993 Annual Report,* 19; and *Medtronic, 1993 Annual Report,* 36.

were (1) maintaining a desired bond rating, (2) providing an adequate borrowing reserve, and (3) exploiting the advantages of financial leverage.

WHO SETS TARGET DEBT RATIOS?

From the preceding discussion, we know that firms *do* use target debt ratios in arriving at financing decisions. But who sets or influences these target ratios? This and other questions concerning corporate financing policy were investigated in one study published in 1982.[18] This survey of the 1,000 largest industrial firms in the United States (as ranked by total sales dollars) involved responses from 212 financial executives.

In one portion of this study, the participants were asked to rank several possible influences on their target leverage (debt) ratios. Table 16-8 displays the percentage of responses ranked either number one or number two in importance. Ranks past the second are omitted in that they were not very significant. Notice that the most important influence is the firm's own management group and staff of analysts. This item accounted for 85 percent of the responses ranked number one. Of the responses ranked number two in importance, investment bankers dominated the outcomes and accounted for 39 percent of such replies. The role of investment bankers in the country's capital market system is explored in some detail in Chapter 14. Also notice that comparisons with ratios of industry competitors and commercial bankers have some impact on the determination of leverage targets.

[18] David F. Scott, Jr., and Dana J. Johnson, "Financing Policies and Practices in Large Corporations," *Financial Management* 11 (Summer 1982): 51–59.

TABLE 16-8 Setting Target Financial Structure Ratios

	RANK	
TYPE OF INFLUENCE	**1**	**2**
Internal management and staff analysts	85%	7%
Investment bankers	3	39
Commercial bankers	0	9
Trade creditors	1	0
Security analysts	1	4
Comparative industry ratios	3	23
Other	7	18
Total	100%	100%

Source: "Financing Policies and Practices in Large Corporations," David F. Scott and Dana J. Johnson, *Financial Management* 11, Summer 1982. Reprinted by permission of the Financial Management Association, International, University of South Florida, College of Business Administration #3331, Tampa, FL 33620, (813) 974-2084.

Debt Capacity

Previously in this chapter, we noted that the firm's debt capacity is the maximum proportion of debt that it can include in its capital structure and still maintain its lowest composite cost of capital. But how do financial executives make the concept of debt capacity operational? Table 16-9 is derived from the same 1982 survey, involving 212 executives, mentioned previously. These executives defined debt capacity in a wide variety of ways. The most popular approach was as a target percentage of total capitalization. Twenty-seven percent of the respondents thought of debt capacity in this manner. Forty-three percent of the participating executives remarked that debt capacity is defined in terms of some balance-sheet-based financial ratio (see the first three items in Table 16-9). Maintaining a specific bond rating was also indicated to be a popular approach to implementing the debt capacity concept.

We learned that one method used by financial executives to implement the debt-capacity concept is to maintain a specific bond rating. This means the firm will issue new debt only as long as the desired (target) bond rating is not impaired. Now, suppose your firm wishes to maintain a bond rating of Aaa in the Moody's system of ratings. We want to know what the likely before-tax cost of debt of a bond rated Aaa is today. Such information is available at www.federalreserve.gov. At this site you can retrieve the H.15 (for daily data) report called "Selected Interest Rates." Toward the bottom of this report you will find the current yields on Aaa- and Baa-rated corporate bonds.

Business Risk

The single most important factor that should affect the firm's financing mix is the underlying nature of the business in which it operates. In Chapter 15, we defined business risk as the relative dispersion in the firm's expected stream of EBIT. If the nature of the firm's

TABLE 16-9 Definitions of Debt Capacity in Practice

STANDARD OR METHOD	**1,000 LARGEST CORPORATIONS (PERCENT USING)**
Target percent of total capitalization (long-term debt to total capitalization)	27%
Long-term debt to net worth ratio (or its inverse)	14
Long-term debt to total assets	2
Interest (or fixed charge) coverage ratio	6
Maintain bond ratings	14
Restrictive debt covenants	4
Most adverse cash flow	4
Industry standard	3
Other	10
No response	16
Total	100%

Source: "Financing Policies and Practices in Large Corporations," David F. Scott and Dana J. Johnson, *Financial Management* 11, Summer 1982. Reprinted by permission of the Financial Management Association, International, University of South Florida, College of Business Administration #3331, Tampa, FL 33620, (813) 974-2084.

business is such that the variability inherent in its EBIT stream is high, then it would be unwise to impose a high degree of financial risk on top of this already uncertain earnings stream.

Corporate executives are likely to point this out in discussions of capital structure management. A financial officer in a large steel firm related:

> The nature of the industry, the marketplace, and the firm tend to establish debt limits that any prudent management would prefer not to exceed. Our industry is capital intensive and our markets tend to be cyclical. . . . The capability to service debt while operating in the environment described dictates a conservative financial structure.[19]

Notice how that executive was concerned with both his firm's business risk exposure and its cash flow capability for meeting any financing costs. The AT&T financial officer referred to earlier also has commented on the relationship between business and financial risk:

> In determining how much debt a firm can safely carry, it is necessary to consider the basic risks inherent in that business. This varies considerably among industries and is related essentially to the nature and demand for an industry's product, the operating characteristics of the industry, and its ability to earn an adequate return in an unknown future.[20]

Also, refer back to the introduction to this chapter. Recall that the management of Georgia-Pacific said:

> Georgia-Pacific's objective is to provide superior returns to our shareholders. To achieve this goal, our financial strategy must complement our operating strategy.[21]

It appears clear that the firm's capital structure cannot be properly designed without a thorough understanding of its commercial strategy.

Financial Managers and Theory

Earlier in this chapter, we discussed a moderate view of capital structure theory. The saucer-shaped cost of capital curve implied by this theory (Figure 16-9) predicts that managers will add debt to the firm's capital structure when current leverage use is *below* the firm's optimal range of leverage use at the base of the overall cost of capital curve. Conversely, managers will add equity when leverage use is above this optimal range. Under these conditions above, *both* financing activities lower the cost of capital to the firm and increase shareholder wealth.

A 1991 survey of chief financial officers of the top (largest) nonfinancial, nonregulated U.S. firms addressed these predicted activities. Of the 800 firms surveyed, 117 responded, for a response rate of 14.6 percent. These decision makers were asked how their firms would respond if confronted with certain, specific financing situations.

It should be noted that the moderate view does not distinguish between internal equity (retained earnings and depreciation) and external equity (the sale of common stock). The questions posed to the financial managers, however, *do* make this distinction. Based on our financial asset valuation models, common equity is generally considered the most *expensive* source of funds, exceeding the costs of both debt and preferred stock. The cost of external equity exceeds internal equity by the addition of flotation costs. (Recall our discussion in Chapter 12 on these relationships.)

Addressing the downward-sloping portion of the cost of capital curve, managers were asked what their financing choice would be if (1) the firm has internal funds *sufficient* for investment requirements (capital budgeting needs), but (2) the debt ratio is *below* the level

[19] Walsh, *Capital Structures*, 18.

[20] Scanlon, "Bell System Financial Policies," 19.

[21] *Georgia-Pacific 1996 Annual Report*, 15.

FIGURE 16-9 Capital Costs: The Moderate View

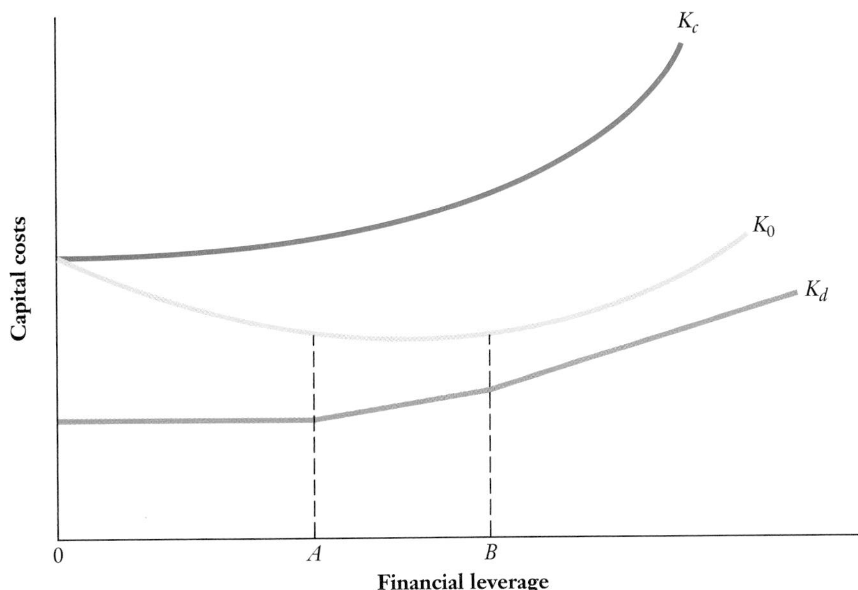

preferred by the firm. The moderate theory predicts that managers will add debt to the firm's capital structure in this situation. However, 81 percent of the respondents said they would use internal equity to finance their investments. Only 17 percent suggested they would use long-term debt, and 11 percent selected short-term debt. In this situation, most managers indicated they would choose to use the more expensive internal equity rather than the (seemingly) less expensive debt for investments.

Similarly, when internal funds are sufficient for new investment and the debt level *exceeds* the firm's optimum range of leverage use, managers again chose to use internal equity in 81 percent of the responses. Seventeen percent would issue new equity if market conditions were favorable. Because the debt level is currently excessive, the moderate theory would predict that external equity would be added to minimize the cost of capital. Instead, most firms preferred to fund investment with the internal funds. This is a prevalent tendency in American industry.

Responses to the preceding questions imply that, if managers follow the financing activity prescribed by the moderate view, it is *only* after internal funds have been exhausted. Because these internal funds are relatively expensive (compared with new debt), their use as the *initial* financing option indicates that either: (1) managers do not view their financing goal to be the minimization of the firm's cost of capital or (2) the explicit and implicit costs of new security issues are understated. If this is actually the case, internal funds may be the *least* expensive source of funds from the perspective of financial managers. This may be a form of the agency problem that we previously discussed in this chapter.

The chief financial officers were also asked what their financing decision would be under these conditions: (1) the firm requires external funds, (2) financial leverage use *exceeds* the desired level, and (3) equity markets are underpricing the firm's stock. Table 16-10 contains the responses to this question.

In this difficult situation, 68 percent of the managers indicated that they would *reduce* their investment plans. That is, capital budgets would shrink. The primary explanations for such investment restriction were (1) that it was in the best interest of current shareholders, and (2) that it controlled risk.

TABLE 16-10 Managers and Theory: Some Responses

QUESTION

Your firm requires external funds to finance the next period's capital investments.
Financial leverage use exceeds that preferred by the firm.
Equity markets are underpricing your securities. Would your firm:

CHOICES	RESPONSES
Reduce your investment plans?	68%
Obtain short-term debt?	28
Attempt to provide the market with adequate information to correctly price your securities before issuing equity?	13
Issue long-term debt?	13
Issue equity anyway?	4
Reduce your dividend payout?	4

Source: Adapted from David F. Scott, Jr., and Nancy Jay, "Financial Managers and Capital Structure Theories," *Working Paper* 9203, Orlando, FL: Dr. Phillips Institute for the Study of American Business Activity, University of Central Florida, March 1992.

The next-favored choice (28 percent) was the use of short-term debt, sometimes combined with investment reduction. This suggests that managers attempt to wait out difficult market conditions by adopting short-term solutions. The timing of security issues with favorable market conditions is a major objective of financial managers and entirely consistent with the optimal capital structure range defined under the moderate theory (Figure 16-9).

Some 4 percent of the respondents indicated that they would issue equity, despite the underpricing of the firm's stock. Thirteen percent of the firms indicated that they would attempt to correct the adverse pricing by providing the market with adequate information before attempting to issue equity. Another 13 percent of the respondents indicated that they would add long-term debt, moving leverage use further beyond the optimal range.

Only 4 percent of the executives responding to this situation stated they would obtain needed funds by *reducing* the cash dividend payout. To managers, the shareholders' cash dividends are quite important. Firms prefer to forgo profitable projects rather than to reallocate the shareholders' expected cash dividends to investment. Dividend policies are discussed extensively in Chapter 17.

You can see that our ability as analysts to *predict* financing choices, as opposed to *prescribing* them, is far from perfect. In many instances, managers appear to react as popular capital structure theories suggest. In other instances, though, managers either are rejecting some aspects of the theories, or the theories need more work. Understanding these aberrations is useful to the analyst.

A thorough grounding in both the theory of financing decisions and in the tools of capital structure management will assist you in making sound choices that maximize shareholder wealth. This combination of theory and practical tools also permits you to ask some very perceptive questions when faced with a decision-making situation.

CONCEPT CHECK

1. Identify several factors that influence target debt ratios in actual business practice.
2. Identify several methods used by executives to make the concept of debt capacity operational.

SUMMARY

This chapter deals with the design of the firm's financing mix, particularly emphasizing manage- **Objective 1** ment of the firm's permanent sources of funds—that is, its capital structure. The objective of capital structure management is to arrange the company's sources of funds so that its common stock price will be maximized, all other factors held constant.

Can the firm affect its composite cost of capital by altering its financing mix? Attempts to **Objective 2** answer this question have comprised a significant portion of capital structure theory for over three decades. Extreme positions show that the firm's stock price is either unaffected or continually affected as the firm increases its reliance on leverage-inducing funds. In the real world, an **Objective 3** operating environment where interest expense is tax deductible and market imperfections operate to restrict the amount of fixed-income obligations a firm can issue, most financial officers and financial academics subscribe to the concept of an optimal capital structure. The optimal capital **Objective 4** structure minimizes the firm's composite cost of capital. Searching for a proper range of financial leverage, then, is an important financial management activity.

Complicating the manager's search for an optimal capital structure are conflicts that lead to agency costs. A natural conflict exists between stockholders and bondholders (the agency costs of debt). To reduce excessive risk taking by management on behalf of stockholders, it may be necessary to include several protective covenants in bond contracts that serve to restrict managerial decision making.

Another type of agency cost is related to "free cash flow." Managers, for example, have an **Objective 5** incentive to hold on to free cash flow and enjoy it, rather than paying it out in the form of higher cash-dividend payments. This conflict between managers and stockholders leads to the concept of the *free cash flow theory of capital structure.* This same theory is also known as the *control hypothesis* and the *threat hypothesis.* The ultimate resolution of these agency costs affects the specific form of the firm's capital structure.

The decision to use senior securities in the firm's capitalization causes two types of financial **Objective 6** leverage effects. The first is the added variability in the earnings-per-share stream that accompanies the use of fixed-charge securities. We explained in Chapter 15 how this could be quantified by use of the degree of financial leverage metric. The second financial leverage effect relates to the level of earnings per share (EPS) at a given EBIT under a specific capital structure. We rely on EBIT–EPS analysis to measure this second effect. Through EBIT–EPS analysis the decision maker can inspect the impact of alternative financing plans on EPS over a full range of EBIT levels.

A second tool of capital structure management is the calculation of comparative leverage ratios. Balance sheet leverage ratios and coverage ratios can be computed according to the contractual stipulations of the proposed financing plans. Comparison of these ratios with industry standards enables the financial officer to determine if the firm's key ratios are materially out of line with accepted practice.

A third tool is the analysis of corporate cash flows. This process involves the preparation of a series of cash budgets that consider different economic conditions and different capital structures. Useful insight into the identification of proper target capital structure ratios can be obtained by analyzing projected cash flow statements that assume adverse operating circumstances.

The euro was introduced as a new currency by the 11 countries comprising the European **Objective 7** Union on January 1, 1999. Swiftly, and by November 2000, the euro had depreciated (weakened) some 38 percent as measured against the U.S. dollar. Such variations in the value of foreign currencies pose huge forecasting problems for the financial executives of multinational firms. Managing currency risk is a daily activity for the finance function of such firms with a significant international presence. Firms with a high exposure to currency value changes might choose to avoid using large relative amounts of corporate debt in their financial structures.

Surveys indicate that most financial officers in large firms believe in the concept of an opti- **Objective 8** mal capital structure. The optimal capital structure is approximated by the identification of target debt ratios. The targets reflect the firm's ability to service fixed financing costs and also consider the business risk to which the firm is exposed.

Survey studies have provided information on who sets or influences the firm's target leverage ratios. The firm's own management group and staff of analysts are the major influence, followed in importance by investment bankers. Studies also show that executives operationalize the concept of debt capacity in many ways. The most popular approach is to define debt capacity in terms of a target long-term debt-to-total-capitalization ratio. Maintaining a specific bond rating (such as Aa or A) is also a popular approach to implementing the debt capacity concept.

Financing policies change in significant ways over time. During the 1980s, for example, most studies confirm that U.S. companies "levered up" when compared with past decades. Specifically, interest coverage ratios deteriorated during the 1980s when compared with the 1970s.

The early 1990s displayed a reversal of this trend. Effective financial managers have a sound understanding of business cycles. The recession that started in July 1990 produced a unique set of financial characteristics that led to relatively high common stock prices. Accordingly, financial managers reversed some of the leverage buildup incurred during the 1980s by bringing substantial amounts of new common stock to the marketplace.

Other studies of managers' financing tendencies suggest that (1) a tremendous preference for the use of internally generated equity to finance investments exists, (2) firms prefer to forgo seemingly profitable projects rather than reduce shareholders' expected cash dividends to finance a greater part of the capital budget, and (3) security issues are timed with favorable market conditions.

KEY TERMS

Go To: www.prenhall.com/keown for downloads and current events associated with this chapter

Capital structure, 552
Debt capacity, 563
EBIT–EPS indifference point, 574
Explicit cost of capital, 558
Financial structure, 552
Financial structure design, 552
Implicit cost of debt, 555
Net income (NI) approach to valuation, 559
Net operating income (NOI) approach to valuation, 557
Optimal capital structure, 553
Optimal range of financial leverage, 563
Sinking fund, 574
Tax shield, 562

STUDY QUESTIONS

16-1. Define the following terms:

a. Financial structure
b. Capital structure
c. Optimal capital structure
d. Debt capacity

16-2. What is the primary weakness of EBIT–EPS analysis as a financing decision tool?

16-3. What is the objective of capital structure management?

16-4. Distinguish between (a) balance sheet leverage ratios and (b) coverage ratios. Give two examples of each and indicate how they would be computed.

16-5. Why might firms whose sales levels change drastically over time choose to use debt only sparingly in their capital structures?

16-6. What condition would cause capital structure management to be a meaningless activity?

16-7. What does the term *independence hypothesis* mean as it applies to capital structure theory?

16-8. Who have been the foremost advocates of the independence hypothesis?

16-9. A financial manager might say that the firm's composite cost of capital is saucer-shaped or U-shaped. What does this mean?

16-10. Define the EBIT–EPS indifference point.

16-11. What is UEPS?

16-12. Explain how industry norms might be used by the financial manager in the design of the company's financing mix.

16-13. Define the term *free cash flow.*

16-14. What is meant by the *free cash flow theory of capital structure?*

16-15. Briefly describe the trend in corporate use of financial leverage during the 1980s.

16-16. Why should the financial manager be familiar with the business cycle?

16-17. In almost every instance, what funds source do managers use first in the financing of their capital budgets?

SELF-TEST PROBLEMS

ST-1. (*Analysis of recessionary cash flows*) The management of Story Enterprises is considering an increase in its use of financial leverage. The proposal on the table is to sell $6 million of bonds that would mature in 20 years. The interest rate on these bonds would be 12 percent. The bond issue would have a sinking fund attached to it requiring that one-twentieth of the principal be retired each year. Most business economists are forecasting a recession that will affect the entire economy in the coming year. Story's management has been saying, "If we can make it through this, we can make it through anything." The firm prefers to carry an operating cash balance of $750,000. Cash collections from sales next year will total $3 million. Miscellaneous cash receipts will be $400,000. Raw material payments will be $700,000. Wage and salary costs will be $1,200,000 on a cash basis. On top of this, Story will experience nondiscretionary cash outlays of $1.2 million, *including* all tax payments. The firm faces a 34 percent tax rate.

a. At present, Story is unlevered. What will be the total fixed financial charges the firm must pay next year?

b. If the bonds are issued, what is your forecast for the firm's expected cash balance at the end of the recessionary year (next year)?

c. As Story's financial consultant, do you recommend that it issue the bonds?

ST-2. (*Assessing leverage use*) Some financial data and the appropriate industry norm for three companies are shown in the following table:

MEASURE	FIRM X	FIRM Y	FIRM Z	INDUSTRY NORM
Total debt to total assets	20%	30%	10%	30%
Times interest and preferred dividend coverage	8 times	16 times	19 times	8 times
Price/earnings ratio	9 times	11 times	9 times	9 times

a. Which firm appears to be employing financial leverage to the most appropriate degree?

b. In this situation, which "financial leverage effect" appears to dominate the market valuation process?

ST-3. (*EBIT–EPS analysis*) Four engineers from Martin-Bowing Company are leaving that firm in order to form their own corporation. The new firm will produce and distribute computer software on a national basis. The software will be aimed at scientific markets and at businesses desiring to install comprehensive information systems. Private investors have been lined up to finance the new company. Two financing proposals are being studied. Both of these plans involve the use of some financial leverage; however, one is much more highly levered than the other. Plan A requires the firm to sell bonds with an effective interest rate of 14 percent. One million dollars would be raised in this manner. In addition, under plan A, $5 million would be raised by selling stock at $50 per common share. Plan B also involves raising $6 million. This would be accomplished by selling $3 million of bonds at an interest rate of 16 percent. The other $3 million would come from selling common stock at $50 per share. In both cases, the use of financial leverage is considered to be a permanent part of the firm's capital structure, so no fixed maturity date is used in the analysis. The firm considers a 50 percent tax rate appropriate for planning purposes.

a. Find the EBIT indifference level associated with the two financing plans, and prepare an EBIT–EPS analysis chart.

b. Prepare an analytical income statement that demonstrates that EPS will be the same regardless of the plan selected. Use the EBIT level found in part (a) above.
c. A detailed financial analysis of the firm's prospects suggests that long-term EBIT will be above $1,188,000 annually. Taking this into consideration, which plan will generate the higher EPS?
d. Suppose that long-term EBIT is forecast to be $1,188,000 per year. Under plan A, a price/earnings ratio of 13 would apply. Under plan B, a price/earnings ratio of 11 would apply. If this set of financial relationships does hold, which financing plan would you recommend be implemented?
e. Again, assume an EBIT level of $1,188,000. What price/earnings ratio applied to the EPS of plan B would provide the same stock price as that projected for plan A? Refer to your data from part (d) above.

STUDY PROBLEMS (SET A)

16-1A. (*Analysis of recessionary cash flows*) The management of Transpacific Inc. is considering an increase in its use of financial leverage to develop several investment projects. The proposal is to sell $15 million of bonds that would mature in 30 years. The interest rate on these bonds would be 18 percent. The bond issue would have a sinking fund attached to it requiring that one-thirtieth of the principal be retired each year. Most business economists are forecasting a recession that will affect the economy in the coming year. Transpacific's management has been maintaining an operating cash balance of $2 million. Cash collections from sales next year are estimated to be $4.5 million. Miscellaneous cash receipts will be $450,000. Raw material payments will be $900,000. Wage and salary cost will total $1.7 million on a cash basis. On top of this, Transpacific will experience nondiscretionary cash outflows of $1.4 million including all tax payments. The firm uses a 50 percent tax rate.

a. At present, Transpacific is unlevered. What will be the total fixed financial charges the firm must pay next year?
b. If the bonds are issued, what is your forecast for the firm's expected cash balance at the end of the recessionary year (next year)?
c. As Transpacific's financial consultant, do you recommend that it issue the bonds?

16-2A. (*Analysis of recessionary cash flows*) Ontherise, Inc. is considering expanding its bagel bakery business with the acquisition of new equipment to be financed entirely with debt. The company does not have any other debt or preferred stock outstanding. The company currently has a cash balance of $200,000, which is the minimum Baruch Chavez, the CFO of Ontherise, believes to be desirable. Baruch has determined that the following relationships exist among the company's various items of cash flow (except as noted, all are expressed as a percentage of cash collections on sales):

Other cash receipts	5%
Cash Disbursements for:	
Payroll	30%
Raw materials	25%
Nondiscretionary expenditures (essentially fixed, thus not percent of sales)	$500,000

The new debt would carry fixed financial charges of $140,000 the first year (interest, $90,000, plus principal–sinking fund, $50,000). To evaluate the sensitivity of the proposed debt plan to economic fluctuations, Baruch would like to determine how low cash collections from sales could be in the next year while ensuring that the cash balance at the end of the year is the minimum he considers necessary.

16-3A. (*EBIT–EPS analysis with sinking fund*) Due to his concern over the effect of the "worst that could happen" if he finances the equipment acquisition only with debt (he believes cash collections on sales could be as low as $1,100,000 in the coming year), Baruch Chavez, the CFO of Ontherise, Inc. (see Problem 16-2A), also has decided to consider a part debt/part equity alternative to the proposed all-debt plan described above. The combination would include 60 percent equity and 40 percent debt. The equity part of the plan would provide $20 per share to the company for 30,000 new shares. The debt portion of this plan would include $400,000 of new debt with fixed financial charges of $52,000 for the first year (interest, $32,000, plus principal–sinking fund, $20,000). The company is in the 35 percent tax bracket. The company currently has 100,000 shares of stock outstanding. Baruch has asked you to determine the EBIT indifference level associated with the two financing alternatives.

16-4A. (*EBIT–EPS analysis*) A group of retired college professors has decided to form a small manufacturing corporation. The company will produce a full line of traditional office furniture. Two financing plans have been proposed by the investors. Plan A is an all-common-equity alternative. Under this agreement, 1 million common shares will be sold to net the firm $20 per share. Plan B involves the use of financial leverage. A debt issue with a 20-year maturity period will be privately placed. The debt issue will carry an interest rate of 10 percent, and the principal borrowed will amount to $6 million. Under this alternative, another $14 million would be raised by selling 700,000 shares of common stock. The corporate tax rate is 50 percent.

- **a.** Find the EBIT indifference level associated with the two financing proposals.
- **b.** Prepare an analytical income statement that proves EPS will be the same regardless of the plan chosen at the EBIT level found in part (a).
- **c.** Prepare an EBIT–EPS analysis chart for this situation.
- **d.** If a detailed financial analysis projects that long-term EBIT will always be close to $2.4 million annually, which plan will provide for the higher EPS?

16-5A. (*Capital structure theory*) Deep End Pools & Supplies has an all-common-equity capital structure. Some financial data for the company are as follows:

Shares of common stock outstanding = 900,000
Common stock price, P_0 = $30 per share
Expected level of EBIT = $5,400,000
Dividend payout ratio = 100 percent

In answering the following questions, assume that corporate income is not taxed.

- **a.** Under the present capital structure, what is the total value of the firm?
- **b.** What is the cost of common equity capital, K_c? What is the composite cost of capital, K_0?
- **c.** Now suppose Deep End sells $1.5 million of long-term debt with an interest rate of 8 percent. The proceeds are used to retire the outstanding common stock. According to the net operating income theory (the independence hypothesis), what will be the firm's cost of common equity after the capital structure change?
  1. What will be the dividend per share flowing to the firm's common shareholders?
  2. By what percentage has the dividend per share changed owing to the capital structure change?
  3. By what percentage has the cost of common equity changed owing to the capital structure change?
  4. What will be the composite cost of capital after the capital structure change?

16-6A. (*EBIT–EPS analysis*) Four recent liberal arts graduates have interested a group of venture capitalists in backing a new business enterprise. The proposed operation would consist of a series of retail outlets to distribute and service a full line of vacuum cleaners and accessories. These stores would be located in Dallas, Houston, and San Antonio. Two financing plans have been proposed by the graduates. Plan A is an all-common-equity structure. Two million dollars would be raised by selling 80,000 shares of common stock. Plan B would involve the use of long-term debt financing. One million dollars would be raised by marketing bonds with an effective interest rate of 12 percent. Under this alternative, another million dollars would be raised by selling 40,000 shares of common stock. With both plans, then, $2 million is needed to launch the new firm's operations. The debt funds raised under plan B are considered to have no fixed maturity date, in that this portion of financial leverage is thought to be a permanent part of the company's capital structure. The fledgling executives have decided to use a 40 percent tax rate in their analysis, and they have hired you on a consulting basis to do the following:

- **a.** Find the EBIT indifference level associated with the two financing proposals.
- **b.** Prepare an analytical income statement that proves EPS will be the same regardless of the plan chosen at the EBIT level found in part (a) above.

16-7A. (*EBIT–EPS analysis*) Three recent graduates of the computer science program at Southern Tennessee Tech are forming a company to write and distribute software for various personal computers. Initially, the corporation will operate in the southern region of Tennessee, Georgia, North Carolina, and South Carolina. Twelve serious prospects for retail outlets have already been identified and committed to the firm. The firm's software products have been tested and displayed at several trade shows and computer fairs in the perceived operating region. All that is lacking is adequate financing to continue with the project. A small group of private investors in the Atlanta, Georgia, area is interested in financing the new company. Two financing proposals are being evaluated. The first (plan A) is an all-common-equity capital structure. Two million dollars would be raised by selling common stock at $20 per common share. Plan B would involve the use of financial leverage. One million dollars would be raised selling bonds with an effective interest rate of 11 percent (per annum). Under this second plan, the remaining $1 million would be raised by selling common stock at the $20 price per share. The use of financial leverage is considered to be a permanent part of the firm's capitalization, so no fixed maturity date is needed for the analysis. A 34 percent tax rate is appropriate for the analysis.

a. Find the EBIT indifference level associated with the two financing plans.

b. A detailed financial analysis of the firm's prospects suggests that the long-term EBIT will be above $300,000 annually. Taking this into consideration, which plan will generate the higher EPS?

c. Suppose long-term EBIT is forecast to be $300,000 per year. Under plan A, a price/earnings ratio of 19 would apply. Under plan B, a price/earnings ratio of 15 would apply. If this set of financial relationships does hold, which financing plan would you recommend?

16-8A. (*EBIT–EPS analysis*) Three recent liberal arts graduates have interested a group of venture capitalists in backing a new business enterprise. The proposed operation would consist of a series of retail outlets to distribute and service a full line of personal computer equipment. These stores would be located in southern New Jersey, New York, and Pennsylvania. Two financing plans have been proposed by the graduates. Plan A is an all-common-equity structure. Three million dollars would be raised by selling 75,000 shares of common stock. Plan B would involve the use of long-term debt financing. One million dollars would be raised by marketing bonds with an effective interest rate of 15 percent. Under this alternative, another $2 million would be raised by selling 50,000 shares of common stock. With both plans, then, $3 million is needed to launch the new firm's operations. The debt funds raised under plan B are considered to have no fixed maturity date, in that this proportion of financial leverage is thought to be a permanent part of the company's capital structure. The fledgling executives have decided to use a 34 percent tax rate in their analysis, and they have hired you on a consulting basis to do the following:

a. Find the EBIT indifference level associated with the two financing proposals.

b. Prepare an analytical income statement that proves EPS will be the same regardless of the plan chosen at the EBIT level found in part (a) above.

16-9A. (*EBIT–EPS analysis*) Two recent graduates of the computer science program at Ohio Tech are forming a company to write, market, and distribute software for various personal computers. Initially, the corporation will operate in Illinois, Indiana, Michigan, and Ohio. Twelve serious prospects for retail outlets in these different states have already been identified and committed to the firm. The firm's software products have been tested and displayed at several trade shows and computer fairs in the perceived operating region. All that is lacking is adequate financing to continue the project. A small group of private investors in the Columbus, Ohio, area is interested in financing the new company. Two financing proposals are being evaluated. The first (plan A) is an all-common-equity capital structure. Four million dollars would be raised by selling stock at $40 per common share. Plan B would involve the use of financial leverage. Two million dollars would be raised by selling bonds with an effective interest rate of 16 percent (per annum). Under this second plan, the remaining $2 million would be raised by selling common stock at the $40 price per share. This use of financial leverage is considered to be a permanent part of the firm's capitalization, so no fixed maturity date is needed for the analysis. A 50 percent tax rate is appropriate for the analysis.

a. Find the EBIT indifference level associated with the two financing plans.

b. Prepare an analytical income statement that proves EPS will be the same regardless of the plan chosen at the EBIT level found in part (a) above.

c. A detailed financial analysis of the firm's prospects suggests that long-term EBIT will be above $800,000 annually. Taking this into consideration, which plan will generate the higher EPS?

d. Suppose that long-term EBIT is forecast to be $800,000 per year. Under plan A, a price/earnings ratio of 12 would apply. Under plan B, a price/earnings ratio of 10 would apply. If this set of financial relationships does hold, which financing plan would you recommend be implemented?

16-10A. (*Analysis of recessionary cash flows*) The management of Idaho Produce is considering an increase in its use of financial leverage. The proposal on the table is to sell $10 million of bonds that would mature in 20 years. The interest rate on these bonds would be 15 percent. The bond issue would have a sinking fund attached to it requiring that one-twentieth of the principal be retired each year. Most business economists are forecasting a recession that will affect the entire economy in the coming year. Idaho's management has been saying, "If we can make it through this, we can make it through anything." The firm prefers to carry an operating cash balance of $1 million. Cash collections from sales next year will total $4 million. Miscellaneous cash receipts will be $300,000. Raw material payments will be $800,000. Wage and salary costs will total $1.4 million on a cash basis. On top of this, Idaho will experience nondiscretionary cash outflows of $1.2 million *including* all tax payments. The firm faces a 50 percent tax rate.

a. At present, Idaho is unlevered. What will be the total fixed financial charges the firm must pay next year?

b. If the bonds are issued, what is your forecast for the firm's expected cash balance at the end of the recessionary year (next year)?

c. As Idaho's financial consultant, do you recommend that it issue the bonds?

16-11A. (*EBIT–EPS analysis*) Four recent business school graduates have interested a group of venture capitalists in backing a small business enterprise. The proposed operation would consist of a series of retail outlets that would distribute and service a full line of energy-conservation equipment. These stores would be located in northern Virginia, western Pennsylvania, and throughout West Virginia. Two financing plans have been proposed by the graduates. Plan A is an all-common-equity capital structure. Three million dollars would be raised by selling 60,000 shares of common stock. Plan B would involve the use of long-term debt financing. One million dollars would be raised by marketing bonds with an interest rate of 10 percent. Under this alternative, another $2 million would be raised by selling 40,000 shares of common stock. With both plans, then, $3 million is needed to launch the new firm's operations. The debt funds raised under plan B are considered to have no fixed maturity date, in that this proportion of financial leverage is thought to be a permanent part of the company's capital structure. The fledgling executives have decided to use a 40 percent tax rate in their analysis.

a. Find the EBIT indifference level associated with the two financing proposals.

b. Prepare an analytical income statement that proves EPS will be the same regardless of the plan chosen at the EBIT level found in part (a).

16-12A. (*EBIT–EPS analysis*) A group of college professors has decided to form a small manufacturing corporation. The company will produce a full line of contemporary furniture. Two financing plans have been proposed by the investors. Plan A is an all-common-equity alternative. Under this arrangement, 1,400,000 common shares will be sold to net the firm $10 per share. Plan B involves the use of financial leverage. A debt issue with a 20-year maturity period will be privately placed. The debt issue will carry an interest rate of 8 percent and the principal borrowed will amount to $4 million. Under this plan, another $10 million would be raised by selling 1 million shares of common stock. The corporate tax rate is 50 percent.

a. Find the EBIT indifference level associated with the two financing proposals.

b. Prepare an analytical income statement that proves EPS will be the same regardless of the plan chosen at the EBIT level found in part (a).

c. Prepare an EBIT–EPS analysis chart for this situation.

d. If a detailed financial analysis projects that long-term EBIT will always be close to $1,800,000 annually, which plan will provide for the higher EPS?

16-13A. (*EBIT–EPS analysis*) The professors discussed in problem 16-12A contacted a financial consultant to provide them with some additional information. They felt that in a few years, the stock of the firm would be publicly traded over the counter, so they were interested in the consultant's opinion as to what the stock price would be under the financing plan outlined in problem 16-12A. The consultant agreed that the projected long-term EBIT level of $1,800,000 was reasonable. He also felt that if plan A were selected, the marketplace would apply a price/earnings ratio of 12 times to the company's stock; for plan B he estimated a price/earnings ratio of 10 times.

a. According to this information, which financing alternative would offer a higher stock price?

b. What price/earnings ratio applied to the EPS related to plan B would provide the same stock price as that projected for plan A?

c. Comment on the results of your analysis of problems 16-12A and 16-13A.

16-14A. (*Analysis of recessionary cash flows*) Cavalier Agriculture Supplies is undertaking a thorough cash flow analysis. It has been proposed by management that the firm expand by raising $5 million in the long-term debt markets. All of this would be immediately invested in new fixed assets. The proposed bond issue would carry an 8 percent interest rate and have a maturity period of 20 years. The bond issue would have a sinking fund provision that one-twentieth of the principal would be retired annually. Next year is expected to be a poor one for Cavalier. The firm's management feels, therefore, that the upcoming year would serve well as a model for the worst possible operating conditions that the firm can be expected to encounter. Cavalier ordinarily carries a $500,000 cash balance. Next year sales collections are forecast to be $3 million. Miscellaneous cash receipts will total $200,000. Wages and salaries will amount to $1 million. Payments for raw materials used in the production process will be $1,400,000. In addition, the firm will pay $500,000 in nondiscretionary expenditures including taxes. The firm faces a 50 percent tax rate.

a. Cavalier currently has no debt or preferred stock outstanding. What will be the total fixed financial charges that the firm must meet next year?

b. What is the expected cash balance at the end of the recessionary period (next year), assuming the debt is issued?

c. Based on this information, should Cavalier issue the proposed bonds?

16-15A. (*Assessing leverage use*) Some financial data for three corporations are as follows:

MEASURE	FIRM A	FIRM B	FIRM C	INDUSTRY NORM
Debt ratio	20%	25%	40%	20%
Times burden covered	8 times	10 times	7 times	9 times
Price/earnings ratio	9 times	11 times	6 times	10 times

a. Which firm appears to be excessively levered?

b. Which firm appears to be employing financial leverage to the most appropriate degree?

c. What explanation can you provide for the higher price/earnings ratio enjoyed by firm B as compared with firm A?

16-16A. (*Assessing leverage use*) Some financial data and the appropriate industry norm are shown in the following table:

MEASURE	FIRM X	FIRM Y	FIRM Z	INDUSTRY NORM
Total debt to total assets	35%	30%	10%	35%
Times interest and preferred dividend coverage	7 times	14 times	16 times	7 times
Price/earnings ratio	8 times	10 times	8 times	8 times

a. Which firm appears to be using financial leverage to the most appropriate degree?

b. In this situation which "financial leverage effect" appears to dominate the market's valuation process?

16-17A. (*Capital structure theory*) Boston Textiles has an all-common-equity capital structure. Pertinent financial characteristics for the company are shown below:

Shares of common stock outstanding = 1,000,000
Common stock price, P_0 = $20 per share
Expected level of EBIT = $5,000,000
Dividend payout ratio = 100 percent

In answering the following questions, assume that corporate income is not taxed.

a. Under the present capital structure, what is the total value of the firm?

b. What is the cost of common equity capital, K_c? What is the composite cost of capital, K_0?

c. Now suppose that Boston Textiles sells $1 million of long-term debt with an interest rate of 8 percent. The proceeds are used to retire outstanding common stock. According to NOI theory (the independence hypothesis), what will be the firm's cost of common equity *after* the capital structure change?

1. What will be the dividend per share flowing to the firm's common shareholders?
2. By what percent has the dividend per share changed owing to the capital structure change?
3. By what percent has the cost of common equity changed owing to the capital structure change?
4. What will be the composite cost of capital after the capital structure change?

16-18A. (*Capital structure theory*) South Bend Auto Parts has an all-common-equity capital structure. Some financial data for the company are as follows:

Shares of common stock outstanding = 600,000
Common stock price, P_0 = \$40 per share
Expected level of EBIT = \$4,200,000
Dividend payout ratio = 100 percent

In answering the following questions, assume that corporate income is not taxed.

a. Under the present capital structure, what is the total value of the firm?

b. What is the cost of common equity capital, K_c? What is the composite cost of capital, K_0?

c. Now, suppose South Bend sells $1 million of long-term debt with an interest rate of 10 percent. The proceeds are used to retire outstanding common stock. According to the net operating income theory (the independence hypothesis), what will be the firm's cost of common equity after the capital structure change?

1. What will be the dividend per share flowing to the firm's common shareholders?
2. By what percentage has the dividend per share changed owing to the capital structure change?
3. By what percentage has the cost of common equity changed owing to the capital structure change?
4. What will be the composite cost of capital after the capital structure change?

16-19A. (*EBIT–EPS analysis*) Albany Golf Equipment is analyzing three different financing plans for a newly formed subsidiary. The plans are described as follows:

PLAN A	PLAN B	PLAN C
Common stock: \$100,000	Bonds at 9%: \$20,000 Common stock: 80,000	Preferred stock at 9%: \$20,000 Common stock: 80,000

In all cases, the common stock will be sold to net Albany \$10 per share. The subsidiary is expected to generate an average EBIT per year of \$22,000. The management of Albany places great emphasis on EPS performance. Income is taxed at a 50 percent rate.

a. Where feasible, find the EBIT indifference levels between the alternatives.

b. Which financing plan do you recommend that Albany pursue?

WEB WORKS

16-1WW. This exercise focuses on capital structure management and its direct relationship to corporate capital costs. We will work with actual relationships from the Coca-Cola Company (ticker symbol KO). Find the 2002 annual report for Coke at **www.reportgallery.com**. In the discussion on "Debt Financing" (see their p. 50), you will find that Coke's long-term debt was rated at Aa by Moody's. Next go to **www.federalreserve.com** to ascertain recent yield levels for Aaa-rated long-term bonds. Recall that you want to access the Fed's H.15 report on "Selected Interest Rates." Finally, go to **www.cnnfn.com** and click on "Markets." The latter site will allow you to do some bond research of your own and find out what the current yield is on bonds rated Aa. Then answer: How many basis points (a basis point is one-hundredth of 1 percent) would Coke financial management gain if its bonds were rated Aaa rather than Aa? Using the sources noted above, how many basis points would the firm give up if its long-term debt rating was lowered to Baa? After these exercises, you should understand the importance of bond ratings to corporate costs of capital.

16-2WW. The Federal Reserve Bank of St. Louis maintains an outstanding Web site at www.stls.frb/org. It is a fertile source for financial and economic time series data. Go to the St. Louis Fed site and click on "Economic Research." Once you get there, click on "Economic-Data-FRED II." The latter acronymn stands for "Federal Reserve Economic Data." Once you have pulled up FRED II, under "Categories" click on the category labeled "Business/Fiscal." This will enable you to find the S&P 500 Composite Total Return (calculated by assuming monthly reinvestment of dividends). Inspect the direction of the index from August 2000 through December 2002. Over the 2001 to 2002 time period, do you think nonfinancial corporate businesses raised more cash by issuing new corporate bonds or by issuing new corporate equities? *Hint:* You can verify your answer by going to any Federal Reserve Web site and searching for the statistical release Z.1, "Flow of Funds Accounts of the United States."

INTEGRATIVE PROBLEM

Several biking enthusiasts recently left their defense industry jobs and grouped together to form a corporation, Freedom Cycle, Inc. (FCI), which will produce a new type of bicycle. These new bicycles are to be constructed using space-age technologies and materials so that they will never need repairs or maintenance. The FCI founders believe there is a need for such a bicycle due to their perception that many people today, especially middle-aged working couples such as themselves, really would like to ride bicycles for transportation as well as for pleasure, but are put off by the perceived high maintenance requirements of most bicycles today.

The founders believe such people would be quite willing to buy a maintenance-free bicycle for themselves as well as for their children, particularly after observing the repair and maintenance needs (for example, keeping spoked wheels trued and derailleurs and brakes adjusted) of the bikes they already have purchased for their children. Accordingly, the FCI group feels certain that their new-age bicycles will meet the needs of this market and will be a tremendous hit.

To assist them with the financial management of the company, the FCI founders have hired Mabra Jordan to be CFO. Mabra has considerable experience with start-up companies such as FCI, and she is well respected in the venture capital community. Indeed, based on the strength of her business plan, Mabra has convinced a local venture capital partnership to provide funding for FCI. Two alternatives have been proposed by the venture capitalists: a high leverage plan primarily using "junk" bonds (HLP), and a low leverage plan (LLP) primarily using equity.

HLP consists of $6 million of bonds carrying a 14 percent interest rate and $4 million of $20-per-share common stock. LLP, however, consists of $2 million of bonds with an interest rate of 11 percent and $8 million of common stock at $20 per share. Under either alternative, FCI is required to use a sinking fund to retire 10 percent of the bonds each year. FCI's tax rate is expected to be 35 percent.

1. Find the EBIT indifference level associated with the two financing alternatives, and prepare an EBIT–EPS analysis graph.
2. Prepare an analytical income statement that demonstrates that EPS will be the same regardless of the alternative selected. Use the EBIT level computed in part 1 above.
3. If an analysis of FCI's long-term prospects indicates that long-term EBIT will be $1,300,000 annually, which financing alternative will generate the higher EPS?
4. If the analysis of FCI's long-term prospects also shows that at a long-term EBIT of $1,300,000 a price/earnings ratio of 18 likely would apply under LLP, and a ratio of 14 would apply under HLP, which of the two financing plans would you recommend and why?
5. At an EBIT level of $1,300,000, what is the price/earnings ratio they would have to obtain under HLP for the EPS of HLP to provide the same stock price as that projected for LLP in part 4 above?

A concern of the venture capitalists, of course, is whether FCI would be able to survive its first year in business if for some reason—such as an economic recession or just an overly optimistic sales projection—the cash flow targets in FCI's business plan were not met. To allay such fears, Mabra included in the FCI business plan a worst-case scenario based on the following pessimistic projections.

Mabra believes FCI should maintain a $500,000 cash balance. Starting initially with zero cash, the company would obtain cash of $10,000,000 from either of the two financing alternatives described above. A total of $9,500,000 of such financing would be used for capital acquisitions; the balance is intended to be available to provide initial working capital. The pessimistic sales forecast indicates cash receipts would be $4 million. Miscellaneous cash receipts (for example, from the sale of scrap titanium and other materials) would be $200,000. Cash payments on raw materials purchases would be $1 million; wage and salary cash outlays would be $1,500,000; nondiscretionary cash costs (not including tax payments) would be $700,000; and estimated tax payments would be $265,000 under LLP and $54,000 under HLP (note that the difference in estimated tax payments is attributable to the variation in taxable income, which reflects the difference in deductible interest expense).

6. What would be the total fixed financial charges under each of the two alternative financing plans being considered by FCI?
7. A significant issue is whether FCI will have a sufficient cash balance at the end of the possible recessionary year. What is your estimate of FCI's cash balance under each of the two financing plans at the end of such a year?
8. In light of the above and your knowledge of FCI's desired cash level, which financing plan, LLP or HLP, would you recommend?

STUDY PROBLEMS (SET B)

16-1B. (*Analysis of recessionary cash flows*) Cappuccino Express, Inc., is considering expanding its cafe business by adding a number of new stores. Strong consideration is being given to financing the expansion entirely with debt. The company does not have any other debt or preferred stock outstanding. The company currently has a cash balance of $400,000, which is the minimum the CFO, Vanessa Jefferson, believes to be desirable. Vanessa has determined that the following relationships exist among the company's various items of cash flow (except as noted, all are expressed as a percentage of cash collections on sales):

Other cash receipts	5%
Cash disbursements for:	
Payroll	40%
Coffee, pastries, and other costs of items sold	20%
Nondiscretionary expenditures (essentially fixed, thus not percent of sales)	$500,000

The new debt would carry fixed financial charges of $300,000 the first year (interest, $200,000, plus principal–sinking fund, $100,000). To evaluate the sensitivity of the proposed debt plan to economic fluctuations, Vanessa would like to determine how low cash collections from sales could be in the next year while ensuring that the cash balance at the end of the year is the minimum she considers necessary.

16-2B. (*EBIT–EPS analysis with sinking fund*) Due to her concern over the effect of the "worst that could happen" if she finances the expansion only with debt (she believes cash collections on sales could be as low as $1,300,000 in the coming year), Vanessa Jefferson, the CFO of Cappuccino Express, Inc. (see Problem 16-1B), also has decided to consider a part debt/part equity alternative to the proposed all-debt plan described above. The combination would include 70 percent equity and 30 percent debt. The equity part of the plan would provide $20 per share to the company for 70,000 new shares. The debt portion of this plan would include $600,000 of new debt with fixed financial charges of $78,000 for the first year (interest, $48,000, plus principal–sinking fund, $30,000). The company is in the 35 percent tax bracket. The company currently has 100,000 shares of stock outstanding. Vanessa has asked you to determine the EBIT indifference level associated with the two financing alternatives.

16-3B. (*EBIT–EPS analysis*) Three recent graduates of the computer science program at Midstate University are forming a company to write and distribute software for various personal computers.

Initially, the corporation will operate in the region of Michigan, Illinois, Indiana, and Ohio. Twelve serious prospects for retail outlets have already been identified and committed to the firm. The firm's software products have been tested and displayed at several trade shows and computer fairs in the perceived operating region. All that is lacking is adequate financing to continue with the project. A small group of private investors in the Chicago, Illinois, area is interested in financing the new company. Two financing proposals are being evaluated. The first (plan A) is an all-common-equity capital structure. Three million dollars would be raised by selling common stock at $20 per common share. Plan B would involve the use of financial leverage. Two million dollars would be raised selling bonds with an effective interest rate of 11 percent (per annum). Under this second plan, the remaining $1 million would be raised by selling common stock at the $20 price per share. The use of financial leverage is considered to be a permanent part of the firm's capitalization, so no fixed maturity date is needed for the analysis. A 34 percent tax rate is appropriate for the analysis.

a. Find the EBIT indifference level associated with the two financing plans.

b. A detailed financial analysis of the firm's prospects suggests that the long-term EBIT will be above $450,000 annually. Taking this into consideration, which plan will generate the higher EPS?

c. Suppose long-term EBIT is forecast to be $450,000 per year. Under plan A, a price/earnings ratio of 19 would apply. Under plan B, a price/earnings ratio of 12.39 would apply. If this set of financial relationships does hold, which financing plan would you recommend?

16-4B. (*EBIT–EPS analysis*) Three recent liberal arts graduates have interested a group of venture capitalists in backing a new business enterprise. The proposed operation would consist of a series of retail outlets to distribute and service a full line of personal computer equipment. These stores would be located in Texas, Arizona, and New Mexico. Two financing plans have been proposed by the graduates. Plan A is an all-common-equity structure. Four million dollars would be raised by selling 80,000 shares of common stock. Plan B would involve the use of long-term debt financing. Two million dollars would be raised by marketing bonds with an effective interest rate of 16 percent. Under this alternative, another $2 million would be raised by selling 50,000 shares of common stock. With both plans, then, $4 million is needed to launch the new firm's operations. The debt funds raised under plan B are considered to have no fixed maturity date, in that this proportion of financial leverage is thought to be a permanent part of the company's capital structure. The fledgling executives have decided to use a 34 percent tax rate in their analysis, and they have hired you on a consulting basis to do the following:

a. Find the EBIT indifference level associated with the two financing proposals.

b. Prepare an analytical income statement that proves EPS will be the same regardless of the plan chosen at the EBIT level found in part (a) above.

16-5B. (*EBIT–EPS analysis*) Two recent graduates of the computer science program at Ohio Tech are forming a company to write, market, and distribute software for various personal computers. Initially, the corporation will operate in Missouri, Iowa, Nebraska, and Kansas. Eight prospects for retail outlets in these different states have already been identified and committed to the firm. The firm's software products have been tested. All that is lacking is adequate financing to continue the project. A small group of private investors are interested in financing the new company. Two financing proposals are being evaluated. The first (plan A) is an all-common-equity capital structure. Three million dollars would be raised by selling stock at $40 per common share. Plan B would involve the use of financial leverage. One million dollars would be raised by selling bonds with an effective interest rate of 14 percent (per annum). Under this second plan, the remaining $2 million would be raised by selling common stock at the $40 price per share. This use of financial leverage is considered to be a permanent part of the firm's capitalization, so no fixed maturity date is needed for the analysis. A 50 percent tax rate is appropriate for the analysis.

a. Find the EBIT indifference level associated with the two financing plans.

b. Prepare an analytical income statement that proves EPS will be the same regardless of the plan chosen at the EBIT level found in part (a) above.

c. A detailed financial analysis of the firm's prospects suggests that long-term EBIT will be above $750,000 annually. Taking this into consideration, which plan will generate the higher EPS?

d. Suppose that long-term EBIT is forecast to be $750,000 per year. Under plan A, a price/earnings ratio of 12 would apply. Under plan B, a price/earnings ratio of 9.836 would apply. If this set of financial relationships does hold, which financing plan would you recommend be implemented?

16-6B. (*Analysis of recessionary cash flows*) The management of Cincinnati Collectibles (CC) is considering an increase in its use of financial leverage. The proposal on the table is to sell $11 million of bonds that would mature in 20 years. The interest rate on these bonds would be 16 percent. The bond issue would have a sinking fund attached to it requiring that one-twentieth of the principal be retired each year. Most business economists are forecasting a recession that will affect the entire economy in the coming year. CC's management has been saying, "If we can make it through this, we can make it through anything." The firm prefers to carry an operating cash balance of $500,000. Cash collections from sales next year will total $3.5 million. Miscellaneous cash receipts will be $300,000. Raw material payments will be $800,000. Wage and salary costs will total $1.5 million on a cash basis. On top of this, CC will experience nondiscretionary cash outflows of $1.3 million *including* all tax payments. The firm faces a 50 percent tax rate.

a. At present, CC is unlevered. What will be the total fixed financial charges the firm must pay next year?

b. If the bonds are issued, what is your forecast for the firm's expected cash balance at the end of the recessionary year (next year)?

c. As CC's financial consultant, do you recommend that it issue the bonds?

16-7B. (*EBIT–EPS analysis*) Four recent business school graduates have interested a group of venture capitalists in backing a small business enterprise. The proposed operation would consist of a series of retail outlets that would distribute and service a full line of energy-conservation equipment. These stores would be located in northern California, western Nevada, and throughout Oregon. Two financing plans have been proposed by the graduates. Plan A is an all-common-equity capital structure. Five million dollars would be raised by selling 75,000 shares of common stock. Plan B would involve the use of long-term debt financing. Two million dollars would be raised by marketing bonds with an interest rate of 12 percent. Under this alternative, another $3 million would be raised by selling 55,000 shares of common stock. With both plans, then, $5 million is needed to launch the new firm's operations. The debt funds raised under plan B are considered to have no fixed maturity date, in that this proportion of financial leverage is thought to be a permanent part of the company's capital structure. The fledgling executives have decided to use a 40 percent tax rate in their analysis.

a. Find the EBIT indifference level associated with the two financing proposals.

b. Prepare an analytical income statement that proves EPS will be the same regardless of the plan chosen at the EBIT level found in part (a).

16-8B. (*EBIT–EPS analysis*) A group of college professors has decided to form a small manufacturing corporation. The company will produce a full line of contemporary furniture. Two financing plans have been proposed by the investors. Plan A is an all-common-equity alternative. Under this arrangement 1,200,000 common shares will be sold to net the firm $10 per share. Plan B involves the use of financial leverage. A debt issue with a 20-year maturity period will be privately placed. The debt issue will carry an interest rate of 9 percent and the principal borrowed will amount to $3.5 million. Under this alternative, another $8.5 million would be raised by selling 850,000 shares of common stock. The corporate tax rate is 50 percent.

a. Find the EBIT indifference level associated with the two financing proposals.

b. Prepare an analytical income statement that proves EPS will be the same regardless of the plan chosen at the EBIT level found in part (a).

c. Prepare an EBIT–EPS analysis chart for this situation.

d. If a detailed financial analysis projects that long-term EBIT will always be close to $1,500,000 annually, which plan will provide for the higher EPS?

16-9B. (*EBIT–EPS analysis*) The professors in problem 16-8B contacted a financial consultant to provide them with some additional information. They felt that in a few years, the stock of the firm would be publicly traded over the counter, so they were interested in the consultant's opinion as to what the stock price would be under the financing plan outlined in problem 16-8B. The consultant agreed that the projected long-term EBIT level of $1,500,000 was reasonable. He also felt that if plan A were selected, the marketplace would apply a price/earnings ratio of 13 times to the company's stock; for plan B he estimated a price/earnings ratio of 11 times.

a. According to this information, which financing alternative would offer a higher stock price?
b. What price/earnings ratio applied to the EPS related to plan B would provide the same stock price as that projected for plan A?
c. Comment upon the results of your analysis of problems 16-8B and 16-9B.

16-10B. (*Analysis of recessionary cash flows*) Seville Cranes, Inc., is undertaking a thorough cash flow analysis. It has been proposed by management that the firm expand by raising \$6 million in the long-term debt markets. All of this would be immediately invested in new fixed assets. The proposed bond issue would carry a 10 percent interest rate and have a maturity period of 20 years. The bond issue would have a sinking fund provision that one-twentieth of the principal would be retired annually. Next year is expected to be a poor one for Seville. The firm's management feels, therefore, that the upcoming year would serve well as a model for the worst possible operating conditions that the firm can be expected to encounter. Seville ordinarily carries a \$750,000 cash balance. Next year sales collections are forecast to be \$3.5 million. Miscellaneous cash receipts will total \$200,000. Wages and salaries will amount to \$1.2 million. Payments for raw materials used in the production process will be \$1,500,000. In addition, the firm will pay \$500,000 in nondiscretionary expenditures including taxes. The firm faces a 50 percent tax rate.

a. Seville currently has no debt or preferred stock outstanding. What will be the total fixed financial charges that the firm must meet next year?
b. What is the expected cash balance at the end of the recessionary period (next year), assuming the debt is issued?
c. Based on this information, should Seville issue the proposed bonds?

16-11B. (*Assessing leverage use*) Some financial data for three corporations are as follows:

MEASURE	FIRM A	FIRM B	FIRM C	INDUSTRY NORM
Debt ratio	15%	20%	35%	25%
Times burden covered	9 times	11 times	6 times	9 times
Price/earnings ratio	10 times	12 times	5 times	10 times

a. Which firm appears to be excessively levered?
b. Which firm appears to be employing financial leverage to the most appropriate degree?
c. What explanation can you provide for the higher price/earnings ratio enjoyed by firm B as compared with firm A?

16-12B. (*Assessing leverage use*) Some financial data and the appropriate industry norm are shown in the following table:

MEASURE	FIRM X	FIRM Y	FIRM Z	INDUSTRY NORM
Total debt to total assets	40%	35%	10%	35%
Times interest and preferred dividend coverage	8 times	13 times	16 times	7 times
Price/earnings ratio	8 times	11 times	8 times	8 times

a. Which firm appears to be using financial leverage to the most appropriate degree?
b. In this situation which "financial leverage effect" appears to dominate the market's valuation process?

16-13B. (*Capital structure theory*) Whittier Optical Labs has an all-common-equity capital structure. Pertinent financial characteristics for the company are as follows:

Shares of common stock outstanding = 1,000,000
Common stock price, P_0 = \$22 per share
Expected level of EBIT = \$4,750,000
Dividend payout ratio = 100 percent

In answering the following questions, assume that corporate income is not taxed.

a. Under the present capital structure, what is the total value of the firm?

b. What is the cost of common equity capital, K_c? What is the composite cost of capital, K_0?

c. Now suppose that Whittier sells $1 million of long-term debt with an interest rate of 9 percent. The proceeds are used to retire outstanding common stock. According to NOI theory (the independence hypothesis), what will be the firm's cost of common equity *after* the capital structure change?

1. What will be the dividend per share flowing to the firm's common shareholders?
2. By what percentage has the dividend per share changed owing to the capital structure change?
3. By what percentage has the cost of common equity changed owing to the capital structure change?
4. What will be the composite cost of capital after the capital structure change?

16-14B. (*Capital structure theory*) Fernando Hotels has an all-common-equity capital structure. Some financial data for the company are as follows:

Shares of common stock outstanding = 575,000
Common stock price, P_0 = $38 per share
Expected level of EBIT = $4,500,000
Dividend payout ratio = 100 percent

In answering the following questions, assume that corporate income is not taxed.

a. Under the present capital structure, what is the total value of the firm?

b. What is the cost of common equity capital, K_c? What is the composite cost of capital, K_0?

c. Now suppose Fernando sells $1.5 million of long-term debt with an interest rate of 11 percent. The proceeds are used to retire outstanding common stock. According to the net operating income theory (the independence hypothesis), what will be the firm's cost of common equity after the capital structure change?

1. What will be the dividend per share flowing to the firm's common shareholders?
2. By what percent has the dividend per share changed owing to the capital structure change?
3. By what percent has the cost of common equity changed owing to the capital structure change?
4. What will be the composite cost of capital after the capital structure change?

16-15B. (*EBIT–EPS analysis*) Mount Rosemead Health Services, Inc., is analyzing three different financing plans for a newly formed subsidiary. The plans are described as follows:

PLAN A	PLAN B	PLAN C
Common stock: $150,000	Bonds at 10%: $ 50,000 Common stock: $100,000	Preferred stock at 10%: $ 50,000 Common stock: $100,000

In all cases, the common stock will be sold to net Mount Rosemead $10 per share. The subsidiary is expected to generate an average EBIT per year of $36,000. The management of Mount Rosemead places great emphasis on EPS performance. Income is taxed at a 50 percent rate.

a. Where feasible, find the EBIT indifference levels between the alternatives.

b. Which financing plan do you recommend that Mount Rosemead pursue?

SELF-TEST SOLUTIONS

ST-1. a.

$$FC = \text{interest} + \text{sinking fund}$$
$$FC = (\$6{,}000{,}000)(.12) + (\$6{,}000{,}000/20)$$
$$FC = \$720{,}000 + \$300{,}000 = \underline{\underline{\$1{,}020{,}000}}$$

b. $CB_r = C_0 + NCF_r - FC$

where $C_0 = \$750{,}000$

$FC = \$1{,}020{,}000$

and

$NCF_r = \$3{,}400{,}000 - \$3{,}100{,}000 = \$300{,}000$

so

$$CB_r = \$750{,}000 + \$300{,}000 - \$1{,}020{,}000$$
$$CB_r = \$30{,}000$$

c. We know that the firm has a preference for maintaining a cash balance of $750,000. The joint impact of the recessionary economic environment and the proposed issue of bonds would put the firm's recessionary cash balance (CB_r) at $30,000. Because the firm desires a minimum cash balance of $750,000 ($C_0$), the data suggest that the proposed bond issue should be postponed.

ST-2. a. Firm Y seems to be using financial leverage to the most appropriate degree. Notice that its price/earnings ratio of 16 times exceeds that of firm X (at 9 times) and firm Z (also at 9 times).

b. The first financial leverage effect refers to the added variability in the earnings per share stream caused by the use of leverage-inducing financial instruments. The second financial leverage effect concerns the level of earnings per share at a specific EBIT associated with a specific capital structure.

Beyond some critical EBIT level, earnings per share will be higher if more leverage is used. Based on the company data provided, the marketplace for financial instruments is weighing the second leverage effect more heavily. Firm Z, therefore, seems to be underlevered (is operating *below* its theoretical leverage capacity).

ST-3. a.

PLAN A		PLAN B
EPS: LESS-LEVERED PLAN		EPS: MORE-LEVERED PLAN
$\frac{(EBIT - I)(1 - t) - P}{S_A}$	=	$\frac{(EBIT - I)(1 - t) - P}{S_B}$
$\frac{(EBIT - \$140{,}000)(1 - 0.5)}{100{,}000 \text{ (shares)}}$	=	$\frac{(EBIT - \$480{,}000)(1 - 0.5)}{60{,}000 \text{ (shares)}}$
$\frac{0.5\,EBIT - \$70{,}000}{10}$	=	$\frac{0.5\,EBIT - \$240{,}000}{6}$
$EBIT = \$990{,}000$		

b. The EBIT–EPS analysis chart for Martin-Bowing is presented in Figure 16-10.

	PLAN A	PLAN B
EBIT	$990,000	$990,000
I	140,000	480,000
EBT	$850,000	$510,000
T(.5)	425,000	255,000
NI	$425,000	$255,000
P	0	0
EAC	$425,000	$255,000
÷ No. of common shares	100,000	60,000
EPS	$ 4.25	$ 4.25

c. Because \$1,188,000 exceeds the calculated indifference level of \$990,000, the more highly levered plan (plan B) will produce the higher EPS.

d. At this stage of the problem, it is necessary to compute EPS under each financing alternative. Then the relevant price/earnings ratio for each plan can be applied to project the common stock price for the plan at a specific EBIT level.

	PLAN A	PLAN B
EBIT	\$1,188,000	\$1,188,000
I	140,000	480,000
EBT	\$1,048,000	\$ 708,000
T(.5)	524,000	354,000
NI	\$ 524,000	\$ 354,000
P	0	0
EAC	\$ 524,000	\$ 354,000
÷ No. of common shares	100,000	60,000
EPS	\$ 5.24	\$ 5.90
× P/E ratio	13	11
= Projected stock price	\$ 68.12	\$ 64.90

Notice that the greater riskiness of plan B results in the market applying a lower price/earnings multiple to the expected EPS. Therefore, the investors would actually enjoy a higher stock price under plan A (\$68.12) than they would under plan B (\$64.90).

e. Here, we want to find the price/earnings ratio that would equate the common stock prices for both plans at an EBIT level of \$1,188,000. All we have to do is take plan B's EPS and relate it to plan A's stock price. Thus:

\$5.90 (P/E) = \$68.12

(P/E) = \$68.12/\$5.90 = 11.546.

A price/earnings ratio of 11.546 when applied to plan B's EPS would give the same stock price as that of plan A (\$68.12).

FIGURE 16-10 EBIT–EPS Analysis Chart for Martin-Bowing Company

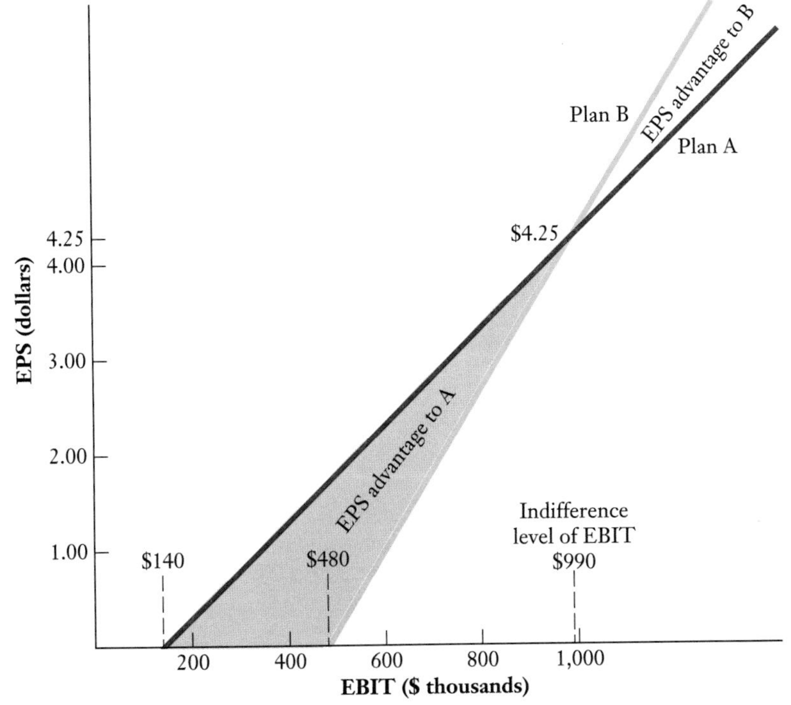

LEARNING OBJECTIVES

After reading this chapter, you should be able to

1. Describe the trade-off between paying dividends and retaining the profits within the company.
2. Explain the relationship between a corporation's dividend policy and the market price of its common stock.
3. Describe practical considerations that may be important to the firm's dividend policy.
4. Distinguish between the types of dividend policy corporations frequently use.
5. Specify the procedures a company follows in administering the dividend payment.
6. Describe why and how a firm might choose to pay noncash dividends (stock dividends and stock splits) instead of cash dividends.
7. Explain the purpose and procedures related to stock repurchases.
8. Understand the relationship between a policy of low dividend payments and international capital-budgeting opportunities that confront the multinational firm.

CHAPTER 17

Dividend Policy and Internal Financing

The corporate choice to pay or not to pay a cash dividend to stockholders and the further choice to increase the dividend, reduce the dividend, or keep it at the same dollar amount represents one of the most challenging and perplexing areas of corporate financial policy. Because stockholder returns only come in two forms: stock price change and cash dividends received, it follows that the dividend decision directly impacts shareholder wealth.

We know that rational investors would rather be more wealthy than less wealthy. Accordingly, corporate boards of directors face a daunting decision every time the question of dividend policy and the possibility of changing the cash dividend is on the agenda.

In the simplest form, increasing the cash dividend simultaneously reduces the stock of internal financial capital (cash) available for capital expenditures. Thus, the firm's stockholders find themselves smack in the middle of **Principle 1: The Risk-Return Trade-Off—We won't take on additional risk unless we expect to be compensated with additional return.** The cash dividend, after all, is there in your hand to be spent today; the proposed capital expenditure is made based on the valuation of its expected incremental net cash flows. Recall **Principle 4.**

The expected net present value of the proposed capital project will be impacted into the firm's stock price. But the arrival of new information over time about the success (or lack of success) of the capital project will be digested by the capital market and subsequently reflected in its stock price. So to be better off in a wealth context, the investor needs the firm to earn a higher rate of return on a dollar that is retained in the firm than that same investor could earn by investing that dollar elsewhere, given all economic considerations, such as having to pay a personal tax on the dollar of cash dividends received now rather than later. It is indeed a perplexing corporate choice.

CHAPTER PREVIEW

The primary goal or objective of the firm should be to maximize the value, or price, of a firm's common stock. The success or failure of management's decisions can be evaluated only in light of their impact on the firm's common stock price. We observed that the company's investment (Chapters 9, 10, and 11) and financing decisions (Chapters 15 and 16) can increase the value of the firm. As we look at the firm's dividend and internal financing policies (*internal financing* means how much of the company's financing comes from cash flows generated internally), we return to the same basic question: "Can management influence the price of the firm's stock, in this case, through its dividend policies?" After addressing this important question, we then look at the practical side of the question, "What are the practices commonly followed by managers in making decisions about paying or not paying a dividend to the firm's stockholders?"

In the development of this chapter, you will be referred to several of the principles that form the basics of business financial management and decision making. These are emphasized: **Principle 1: The Risk-Return Trade-Off—We won't take on additional risk unless we expect to be compensated with additional return; Principle 2: The Time Value of Money—A dollar received today is worth more than a dollar received in the future; Principle 4: Incremental Cash Flows—It's only what changes that counts; Principle 7: The Agency Problem—Managers won't work for owners unless it's in their best interest;** and **Principle 8: Taxes Bias Business Decisions.**

Over the years 1995 through 1999, the total return on the S&P 500 Stock index equaled 37.4, 23.1, 33.4, 28.6, and 21.0 percent, respectively. Not since very precise records have been kept commencing in 1926 did this bellwether index exceed a 20 percent level for five consecutive years. Note that these five years of abnormally high nominal returns followed a run of three consecutive years, 1992 to 1994, in which the total return on this same stock index never exceeded 10 percent. The history of lofty total returns (i.e., 1995 through 1999) on equity investments (which ended in the presidential election year of 2000, by the way, and continued negative through 2002) induced corporate executives and their boards of directors to rein in their dividend payout policies.[1]

For example, in 1997, fewer firms increased their dividends from the previous year than had occurred since 1990. This tendency reflected widespread corporate sentiment that firms could increase shareholder wealth by retaining a larger proportion of earnings per share. Along these same lines, the management of the Coca-Cola Company said, "In 1996, our dividend payout ratio was approximately 36 percent of our net income. To free up additional cash for reinvestment in our high-return beverages business, our Board of Directors intends to gradually reduce our dividend payout ratio to 30 percent over time."[2] From Coca-Cola, above, you have an explicit statement that describes the firm's dividend policy. Another actual example follows.

During periods of strong internal corporate growth, firms tend to maintain modest dividend payout ratios (i.e., cash dividends paid/earnings per share). Harley-Davidson, Inc., provides a sound example of such a financial policy. Over the five-year period from 1995 through 1999, Harley's dividend payout ratio averaged 11.25 percent. Notice that this was considerably less than Coca-Cola's target of 30 percent. But, while Harley-Davidson's payout ratio was quite stable over these five years, the firm did, in fact, increase the absolute amount paid out in cash dividends each year from $.09 per share in 1995 to $.175 per share in 1999.

Harley-Davidson's dividend policy makes sense from the standpoint of its stated and planned capital-expenditure decisions. You will observe in this chapter that the capital-budgeting decision and the dividend decision are as closely linked as is possible within the framework of increasing shareholder wealth and increasing economic value.

Starbucks Corporation has a colorful and useful Website at www.Starbucks.com. The company's financial filings with the Securities and Exchange Commission (e.g., Form 10-K) can be accessed at www.sec.gov. Quarterly financial information is available upon release at www.businesswire.com/cnn/sbux.htm.

In discussing the firm's financial condition and operating results for 1999, Harley-Davidson's management said: "The Company regularly invests in equipment to support and improve its various manufacturing processes. The Company estimates that capital expenditures required in 2000 will be in the range of $150–$170 million. The Company anticipates it will have the ability to fund all capital expenditures with internally generated funds and short-term financing."[3] Thus, the Harley-Davidson's stated policy of financing the major proportion of its capital expenditures with internally generated financial capital means, simultaneously, that fewer dollars will be paid to shareholders in the form of cash dividends. Also notice how similar Harley-Davidson's retention and funding policy, here, is to that of Coca-Cola.

The Starbucks Corporation, the retail coffee giant headquartered in Seattle, Washington, provides a sound example of management clarity concerning its dividend policy. In the firm's 2001 Annual Report (see page 51), management related, "The Company presently intends to retain earnings for use in its business and, therefore, does not anticipate paying a cash dividend in the near future." You cannot get any closer to a straightforward statement concerning a zero dividend payout ratio than that.

You can see that firms have widely divergent views on appropriate dividend policies. Accordingly, dividend policy is the focus of this chapter. You will soon see that arguments and theories abound.

[1] *The Wall Street Journal* (January 3, 1999), R 14, and (January 2, 2003), R 2.

[2] The Coca-Cola Company, *Annual Report* (1996), 42.

[3] Harley-Davidson, Inc., *Annual Report* (1999), 62, 63.

DIVIDEND PAYMENT VERSUS PROFIT RETENTION

Objective 1

Before taking up the particular issues relating to dividend policy, we must understand several key terms and interrelationships.

A firm's dividend policy includes two basic components. First, the **dividend payout ratio** indicates the amount of dividends paid relative to the company's earnings. For instance, if the dividend per share is $2 and the earnings per share is $4, the payout ratio is 50 percent ($2 ÷ $4). The second component is the *stability* of the dividends over time. As will be observed later in the chapter, dividend stability may be almost as important to the investor as the amount of dividends received.

Dividend payout ratio
The amount of dividends relative to the company's net income or earnings per share.

In formulating a dividend policy, the financial manager faces trade-offs. Assuming that management has already decided how much to invest and has chosen its debt-equity mix for financing these investments, the decision to pay a large dividend means simultaneously deciding to retain little, if any, profits; this in turn results in a greater reliance on external equity financing. Conversely, given the firm's investment and financing decisions, a small dividend payment corresponds to high profit retention with less need for externally generated equity funds. These trade-offs, which are fundamental to our discussion, are illustrated in Figure 17-1.

CONCEPT CHECK

1. Can you provide a financial executive a useful definition of the term *dividend payout ratio?*
2. How does the firm's actual dividend policy affect its need for externally generated financial capital?

FIGURE 17-1 Dividend-Retention-Financing Trade-Offs

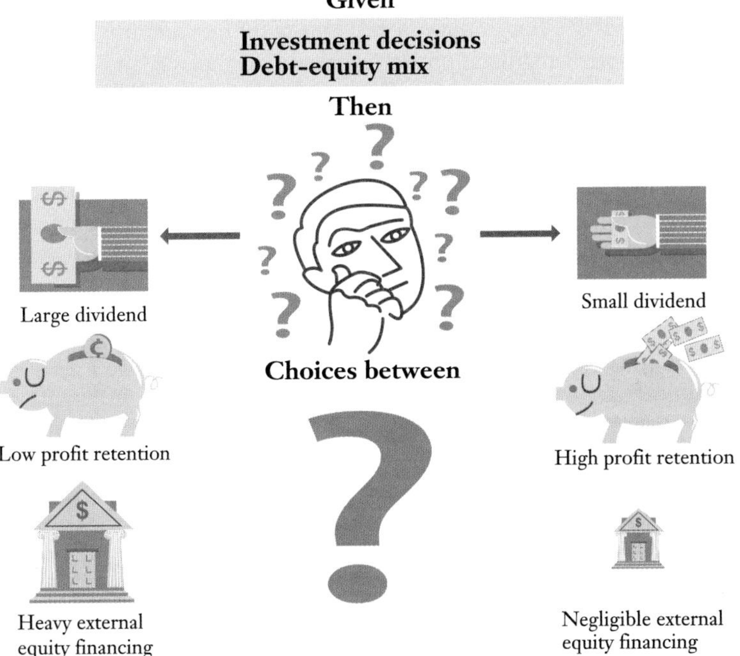

Objective 2

DOES DIVIDEND POLICY AFFECT STOCK PRICE?[4]

The fundamental question to be resolved in our study of the firm's dividend policy may be stated simply: What is a sound rationale or motivation for dividend payments? If we believe our objective should be to maximize the value of the common stock, we may restate the question as follows: Given the firm's capital-budgeting and borrowing decisions, what is the effect of the firm's dividend policies on the stock price? *Does a high dividend payment decrease stock value, increase it, or make no real difference?*

At first glance, we might reasonably conclude that a firm's dividend policy is important. We have already defined the value of a stock to be equal to the present value of future dividends (Chapter 8). How can we now suggest that dividends are not important? Why do so many companies pay dividends, and why is a page in *The Wall Street Journal* devoted to dividend announcements? Based on intuition, we could quickly conclude that dividend policy is important. However, we might be surprised to learn that the dividend question has been a controversial issue for well over three decades. It has even been called the "dividend puzzle."[5]

THREE BASIC VIEWS

Some would argue that the amount of the dividend is irrelevant, and any time spent on the decision is a waste of energy. Others contend that a high dividend will result in a high stock price. Still others take the view that dividends actually hurt the stock value. Let us look at these three views in turn.

VIEW 1: DIVIDEND POLICY IS IRRELEVANT Much of the controversy about the dividend issue is based in the time-honored disagreements between the academic and professional communities. Some experienced practitioners perceive stock price changes resulting from dividend announcements and therefore see dividends as important. Many within the academic community—namely, finance professors—who argue that dividends are irrelevant see the confusion about the matter resulting from not carefully defining what we mean by dividend policy. They would argue that the appearance of a relationship between dividends and stock price may be an illusion.[6]

The position that dividends are not important rests on two preconditions. First, we assume that investment and borrowing decisions have already been made, and that these decisions will not be altered by the amount of any dividend payments. Second, **"perfect" capital markets** are assumed to exist, which means that (1) investors can buy and sell stocks without incurring any transaction costs, such as brokerage commissions; (2) companies can issue stocks without any cost of doing so; (3) there are no corporate or personal taxes; (4) complete information about the firm is readily available; (5) there are no conflicts of interest between management and stockholders; and (6) financial distress and bankruptcy costs are nonexistent.

"Perfect" capital markets Capital markets where (1) investors can buy and sell stock without incurring any transaction costs, such as brokerage commissions; (2) companies can issue stocks without any cost of doing so; (3) there are no corporate or personal taxes; (4) complete information about the firm is readily available; (5) there are no conflicts of interest between management and stockholders; and (6) financial distress and bankruptcy costs are nonexistent.

The first assumption—that we have already made the investment and financing decisions—simply keeps us from confusing the issues. We want to know the effect of div-

[4] The concepts of this section draw heavily from Donald H. Chew, Jr., ed., "Do Dividends Matter? A Discussion of Corporate Dividend Policy," in *Six Roundtable Discussions of Corporate Finance with Joel Stern* (New York: Quorum Books, 1986): 67–101; and a book of readings edited by Joel M. Stern and Donald H. Chew, Jr., *The Revolution in Corporate Finance* (New York: Basil Blackwell, 1986). Specific readings included Merton Miller, "Can Management Use Dividends to Influence the Value of the Firm?" 299–303; Richard Brealey, "Does Dividend Policy Matter?" 304–9; and Michael Rozeff, "How Companies Set Their Dividend Payout Ratios," 320–26.

[5] See Fischer Black, "The Dividend Puzzle," *Journal of Portfolio Management* 2 (Winter 1976): 5–8.

[6] For an excellent presentation of this issue, see Merton Miller, "Can Management Use Dividends to Influence the Value of the Firm?" in Joel M. Stern and Donald H. Chew, Jr., eds., *The Revolution in Corporate Finance* (New York: Basil Blackwell, 1986): 299–305.

idend decisions on a stand-alone basis, without mixing in other decisions. The second assumption, that of perfect markets, also allows us to study the effect of dividend decisions in isolation, much like a physicist studies motion in a vacuum to avoid the influence of friction.

Given these assumptions, the effect of a dividend decision on share price may be stated unequivocally: *There is no relationship between dividend policy and stock value.* One dividend policy is as good as another one. In the aggregate, investors are concerned only with *total* returns from investment decisions; they are indifferent whether these returns come from capital gains or dividend income. They also recognize that the dividend decision, given the investment policy, is really a choice of financing strategy. To finance growth, the firm (1) may choose to issue stock, allowing internally generated funds (profits) to be used to pay dividends; or (2) may use internally generated funds to finance its growth, while paying less in dividends, but not having to issue stock. In the first case, shareholders receive dividend income; in the second case, the value of their stock should increase, providing capital gains. The nature of the return is the only difference; total returns should be about the same. Thus, to argue that paying dividends can make shareholders better off is to argue that paying out cash with one hand and taking it back with the other hand is a worthwhile activity for management.

The firm's dividend payout could affect stock price if the shareholder has no other way to receive income from the investment. However, assuming the capital markets are relatively efficient, a stockholder who needs current income could always sell shares. If the firm pays a dividend, the investor could eliminate any dividend received, in whole or in part, by using the dividend to purchase stock. The investor can thus personally create any desired dividend stream, no matter what dividend policy is in effect.

An Example of Dividend Irrelevance. To demonstrate the argument that dividends may not matter, come to the Land of Ez (pronounced "ease"), where the environment is quite simple. First, the king, being a kind soul, has imposed no income taxes on his subjects. Second, investors can buy and sell securities without paying any sales commissions. In addition, when a company issues new securities (stocks or bonds), there are no flotation costs. Furthermore, the Land of Ez is completely computerized, so that all information about firms is instantaneously available to the public at no cost. Next, all investors realize that the value of a company is a function of its investment opportunities and its financing decisions. Therefore, the dividend policy offers no new information about either the firm's ability to generate earnings or the riskiness of its earnings. Finally, all firms are owned and managed by the same parties; thus, we have no potential conflict between owners and managers.

Within this financial utopia, would a change in a corporation's dividend stream have any effect on the price of the firm's stock? The answer is no. To illustrate, consider Dowell Venture, Inc., a corporation that received a charter at the end of 1998 to conduct business in the Land of Ez. The firm is to be financed by common stock only. Its life is to extend for only two years (1999 and 2000) at which time it will be liquidated.

Table 17-1 presents Dowell Venture's balance sheet at the time of its formation, as well as the projected cash flows from the short-term venture. The anticipated cash flows are based on an expected return on investment of 20 percent, which is exactly what the common shareholders require as a rate of return on their investment in the firm's stock.

At the end of 1999, an additional investment of \$300,000 will be required, which may be financed by (1) retaining \$300,000 of the 1999 profits, (2) issuing new common stock, or (3) some combination of both of these. In fact, two dividend plans for 1999 are under consideration. The investors would receive either \$100,000 or \$250,000 in dividends. If \$250,000 is paid out of 1999's \$400,000 in earnings, the company would be required to issue \$150,000 in new stock to make up the difference in the total \$300,000 needed for reinvestment versus the \$150,000 that is retained. Table 17-2 depicts these two dividend plans and the corresponding new stock issue. Our objective in analyzing the data is to

TABLE 17-1 Dowell Venture, Inc., Financial Data

	DECEMBER 31, 1998
Total assets	$2,000,000
Common stock (100,000 shares)	$2,000,000

	1999	2000
Projected cash available from operations for paying dividends or for reinvesting	$400,000	$460,000

answer this question: Which dividend plan is preferable to the investors? In answering this question, we must take three steps: (1) Calculate the amount and timing of the dividend stream for the *original* investors. (2) Determine the present value of the dividend stream for each dividend plan. (3) Select the dividend alternative providing the higher value to the investors.

Step 1. *Computing the Dividend Streams.* The first step in this process is presented in Table 17-3. The dividends in 1999 (line 1, Table 17-3) are readily apparent from the data in Table 17-2. However, the amount of the dividend to be paid to the present shareholders in 2000 has to be calculated. To do so, we assume that investors receive (1) their original investments (line 2, Table 17-3), (2) any funds retained within the business in 1999 (line 3, Table 17-3), and (3) the profits for 2000 (line 4, Table 17-3). However, if additional stockholders invest in the company, as with plan 2, the dividends to be paid to these investors must be subtracted from the total available dividends (line 6, Table 17-3). The remaining dividends (line 7, Table 17-3) represent the amount current stockholders will receive in 2000. Therefore, the amounts of the dividend may be summarized as follows:

DIVIDEND PLAN	1999	2000
1	$1.00	$27.60
2	$2.50	$25.80

Step 2. *Determining the Present Value of the Cash Flow Streams.* For each of the dividend payment streams, the resulting common stock value is:

$$\text{stock price (plan 1)} = \frac{\$1.00}{(1 + .20)^1} + \frac{\$27.60}{(1 + .20)^2} = \$20$$

$$\text{stock price (plan 2)} = \frac{\$2.50}{(1 + .20)^1} + \frac{\$25.80}{(1 + .20)^2} = \$20$$

TABLE 17-2 Dowell Venture, Inc., 1999 Proposed Dividend Plans

	PLAN 1	PLAN 2
Internally generated cash flow	$400,000	$400,000
Dividend for 1999	100,000	250,000
Cash available for reinvestment	$300,000	$150,000
Amount of investment in 1999	300,000	300,000
Additional external financing required	$ 0	$150,000

TABLE 17-3 Dowell Venture, Inc., Step 1: Measurement of Proposed Dividend Streams

	PLAN 1		PLAN 2	
	TOTAL AMOUNT	AMOUNT PER SHARE[a]	TOTAL AMOUNT	AMOUNT PER SHARE[a]
YEAR 1 (1999)				
(1) Dividend	$ 100,000	$ 1.00	$ 250,000	$ 2.50
YEAR 2 (2000)				
Total dividend consisting of:				
(2) Original investment:				
(a) Old investors	$2,000,000		$2,000,000	
(b) New investors	0		150,000	
(3) Retained earnings from 1999	300,000		150,000	
(4) Profits for 2000	460,000		460,000	
(5) Total dividend to all investors in 2000	$2,760,000		$2,760,000	
(6) Less dividends to new investors:				
(a) Original investment	0		(150,000)	
(b) Profits for new investors (20% of $150,000 investment)	0		(30,000)	
(7) Liquidating dividends available to original investors in 2000	$2,760,000	$27.60	$2,580,000	$25.80

[a]Number of original shares outstanding equals 100,000.

Therefore, the two approaches provide the same end product; that is, the market price of Dowell Venture's common stock is $20 regardless of the dividend policy chosen.

Step 3. *Select the Best Dividend Plan.* If the objective is to maximize the shareholders' wealth, either plan is acceptable. Alternatively, shifting the dividend payments between years by changing the dividend policy does not affect the value of the security. Thus, only if investments are made with expected returns exceeding 20 percent will the value of the stock increase. In other words, the only wealth-creating activity in the Land of Ez, where companies are financed entirely by equity, is management's investment decisions.

VIEW 2: HIGH DIVIDENDS INCREASE STOCK VALUE The belief that a firm's dividend policy is unimportant implicitly assumes that an investor should use the same required rate of return whether income comes through capital gains or through dividends. However, dividends are more predictable than capital gains; management can control dividends, but it cannot dictate the price of the stock. Investors are less certain of receiving income from capital gains than from dividends. The incremental risk associated with capital gains relative to dividend income implies a higher required rate for discounting a dollar of capital gains than for discounting a dollar of dividends. In other words, we would value a dollar of expected dividends more highly than a dollar of expected capital gains. We might, for example, require a 14 percent rate of return for a stock that pays its entire return from dividends, but a 20 percent return for a high-growth stock that pays no dividend. In so doing, we would give a higher value to the dividend income than we would to the capital gains. This view, which says dividends are more certain than capital gains, has been called the **"bird-in-the-hand" dividend theory**.

"Bird-in-the-hand" dividend theory
The belief that dividend income has a higher value to the investor than does capital gains income, because dividends are more certain than capital gains.

The position that dividends are less risky than capital gains, and should therefore be valued differently, is not without its critics. If we hold to our basic decision not to let the firm's dividend policy influence its investment and capital-mix decisions, the company's operating cash flows, both in expected amount and variability, are unaffected by its dividend policy. Because the dividend policy has no impact on the volatility of the company's overall cash flows, it has no impact on the riskiness of the firm.

Increasing a firm's dividend does not reduce the basic riskiness of the stock; rather, if a dividend payment requires management to issue new stock, it only transfers risk *and* ownership from the current owners to new owners. We would have to acknowledge that the current investors who receive the dividend trade an uncertain capital gain for a "safe" asset (the cash dividend). However, if risk reduction is the only goal, the investor could have kept the money in the bank and not bought the stock in the first place.

We might find fault with this "bird-in-the-hand" theory, but there is still a strong perception among many investors and professional investment advisors that dividends are important. They frequently argue their case based on their own personal experience. As expressed by one investment advisor:

> In advising companies on dividend policy, we're absolutely sure on one side that the investors in companies like the utilities and the suburban banks want dividends. We're absolutely sure on the other side that . . . the high-technology companies should have no dividends. For the high earners—the ones that have a high rate of return like 20 percent, or more—we think they should have a low payout ratio. We think a typical industrial company which earns its cost of capital—just earns its cost of capital—probably should be in the average [dividend-payout] range of 40 to 50 percent.[7]

BACK TO THE PRINCIPLES

The preceding discussion that specifies the "bird-in-the-hand" theory between the relationship of stock price and the firm's dividend policy relates directly to ***Principle 2: The Time Value of Money—A dollar received today is worth more than a dollar received in the future.*** *This theory suggests that because the dollar of dividends is received today it should be valued more highly than an uncertain capital gain that might be received in the future. The fundamental premise of this position is that the cash dividend in your hand (placed there today by the firm's payout policy) is more certain (less risky) than a possible capital gain. Many practitioners adhere to this theory; but many also adhere to the theory that is advanced in the next section. If nothing else, because it is controversial, dividend policy is important to the firm and its stockholders. And, in reality, many companies do pay cash dividends. Cash dividends are ubiquitous, so they are discussed in depth.*

VIEW 3: LOW DIVIDENDS INCREASE STOCK VALUE The third view of how dividends affect stock price proposes that dividends actually hurt the investor. This argument has largely been based on the difference in tax treatment for dividend income and capital gains which changes frequently. Unlike the investors in the great Land of Ez, most other investors do pay income taxes. For these taxpayers, the objective is to maximize the *after-tax* return on investment relative to the risk assumed. This objective is realized by *minimizing* the effective tax rate on the income and, whenever possible, by *deferring* the payment of taxes.

[7] From a discussion by John Childs, an investment advisor at Kidder Peabody, in Donald H. Chew, Jr., ed., "Do Dividends Matter? A Discussion of Corporate Dividend Policy," in *Six Roundtable Discussions of Corporate Finance with Joel Stern* (New York: Quorum Books, 1986): 83–84.

Like most tax code complexities, Congress over the years has altered the outcome of whether capital gains are taxed at either (1) a lower or (2) a similar rate as "earned income." Think of a water faucet being randomly turned on and then off. From 1987 through 1992, no federal tax advantage was provided for capital gains income relative to dividend income. A revision in the tax code that took effect beginning in 1993 did provide a preference for capital gains income. Then, the Taxpayer Relief Act of 1997 made the difference (preference) even more favorable for capital gains as opposed to cash dividend income. For some taxpayers, if a minimum holding period has been reached, the tax rate applied to capital gains was reduced to 20 percent from the previous level of 28 percent.

However, in 2003 Congress again felt the need to change the tax code as it pertained to both dividend income and capital gains income. On May 28 President Bush signed into law the "Jobs and Growth Tax Relief Reconciliation Act of 2003." Recall that part of the impetus for this act was the recession that commenced in 2001 and the slow rate of payroll jobs creation that followed that recession.

In a nutshell this 2003 act lowered the top tax rate on dividend income to 15 percent from a previous top rate of 38.6 percent, and also lowered the top rate paid on realized long-term capital gains to the same 15 percent from a previous 20 percent. Thus, you can see that the so-called investment playing field was (mostly) leveled for dividend income relative to qualifying capital gains. This rather dramatic change in the tax code will immediately remind you of **Principle 8: Taxes Bias Business Decisions.** In effect, a major portion of the previous bias against paying cash dividends to investors was mitigated. But, not all of it, as is pointed out next.

Another distinct benefit exists for capital gains vis-a-vis dividend income. Taxes on dividend income are paid when the dividend is received, whereas taxes on price appreciation (capital gains) are deferred until the stock is actually sold. Thus when it comes to tax considerations, most investors prefer the retention of a firm's earnings as opposed to the payment of cash dividends. If earnings are retained within the firm, the stock price increases, but the increase is not taxed until the stock is sold.

Although the majority of investors are subject to taxes, certain investment companies, trusts, and pension plans are exempt on their dividend income. Also, for tax purposes, a corporation may exclude 70 percent of the dividend income received from another corporation. In these cases, investors may prefer dividends over capital gains.

To summarize, when it comes to taxes, we want to maximize our *after-tax* return, as opposed to the *before-tax* return. Investors try to defer taxes whenever possible. Stocks that allow tax deferral (low dividends—high capital gains) will possibly sell at a premium relative to stocks that require current taxation (high dividends—low capital gains). In this way, the two stocks may provide comparable after-tax returns. This suggests that a policy of paying low dividends will result in a higher stock price. That is, high dividends hurt investors, whereas low dividends and high retention help investors. This is the logic of advocates of the low-dividend policy.

Improving Our Thinking

We have now looked at three views on dividend policy. Which is right? The argument that dividends are irrelevant is difficult to refute, given the perfect market assumptions. However, in the real world, it is not always easy to feel comfortable with such an argument. Conversely, the high-dividend philosophy, which measures risk by how we split the firm's cash flows between dividends and retention, is not particularly appealing when studied carefully. The third view, which is essentially a tax argument against high dividends, is persuasive. However, if low dividends are so advantageous and generous dividends are so hurtful, why do companies continue to pay dividends? It is difficult to believe that managers would forgo such an easy opportunity to benefit their stockholders. What are we missing?

The need to find the missing elements in our "dividend puzzle" has not been ignored. When we need to understand better an issue or a phenomenon, we have two options: improving our thinking or gathering more evidence about the topic. Scholars and practitioners have taken both approaches. Although no single definitive answer has yet been found that is acceptable to all, several plausible extensions have been developed. Some of the more popular additions include (1) the residual dividend theory, (2) the clientele effect, (3) information effects, (4) agency costs, and (5) expectations theory.

THE RESIDUAL DIVIDEND THEORY Within the Land of Ez, companies were blessed with professional consultants who were essentially charitable in nature; they did not seek any compensation when they helped a firm through the process of issuing stock. (Even in the Land of Ez, managers needed help from investment bankers, accountants, and attorneys to sell a new issue.) However, in reality, the process is quite expensive and may cost as much as 20 percent of the dollar issue size.[8]

If a company incurs flotation costs, that may have a direct bearing on the dividend decision. Because of these costs, a firm must issue a larger amount of securities in order to receive the amount required for investment. For example, if $300,000 is needed to finance proposed investments, an amount exceeding the $300,000 will have to be issued to offset flotation costs incurred in the sale of the new stock issue. This means, very simply, that new equity capital raised through the sale of common stock will be more expensive than capital raised through the retention of earnings. (Remember what we learned in Chapter 12?)

In effect, flotation costs eliminate our indifference between financing by internal capital and by new common stock. Earlier, the company could pay dividends and issue common stock or retain profits. However, when flotation costs exist, internal financing is preferred. Dividends are paid only if profits are not completely used for investment purposes—that is, only when there are "residual earnings" after the financing of new investments. This policy is called **residual dividend theory**.[9]

Residual dividend theory
A theory asserting that the dividends to be paid should equal capital left over after the financing of profitable investments.

With the assumption of no flotation costs removed, the firm's dividend policy would be as follows:

1. Maintain the optimum debt ratio in financing future investments.
2. Accept an investment if the net present value is positive. That is, the expected rate of return exceeds the cost of capital.
3. Finance the equity portion of new investments first by internally generated funds. Only after this capital is fully utilized should the firm issue new common shares.
4. If any internally generated funds still remain after making all investments, pay dividends to the investors. However, if all internal capital is needed for financing the equity portion of proposed investments, pay no dividend.

In summary, dividend policy is influenced by (1) the company's investment opportunities, (2) the capital structure mix, and (3) the availability of internally generated capital. In the following Krista Corporation example, dividends were paid *only* after all acceptable investments had been financed. This logic, called the residual dividend theory, implies that the dividends to be paid should equal the equity capital *remaining* after financing investments. According to this theory, dividend policy is a passive influence, having by itself no direct influence on the market price of the common stock.

[8] We discussed the costs of issuing securities in Chapter 12.

[9] The residual dividend theory is consistent with the "pecking order" theory of finance as described by Stewart Myers, "The Capital Structure Puzzle," *The Journal of Finance* (July 1984): 575–92.

EXAMPLE: RESIDUAL DIVIDEND THEORY

Assume that the Krista Corporation finances 40 percent of its investments with debt and the remaining 60 percent with common equity. Two million dollars have been generated from operations and may be used to finance the common equity portion of new investments or to pay common dividends. The firm's management is considering five investment opportunities. Figure 17-2 graphs the expected rate of return for these investments, along with the firm's weighted marginal cost of capital curve. From the information contained in the figure, we would accept projects A, B, and C, requiring \$2.5 million in total financing. Therefore, \$1 million in new debt (40% × \$2.5 million) would be needed, with common equity providing \$1.5 million (60% × \$2.5 million). In this instance, the dividend payment decision would be to pay \$500,000 in dividends, which is the residual, or remainder, of the \$2 million internally generated capital.

To illustrate further, consider the dividend decision if project D had also been acceptable. If this investment were added to the firm's portfolio of proposed capital expenditures, then \$4 million in new financing would be needed. Debt financing would constitute \$1.6 million (40% × \$4 million) and common equity would provide the additional \$2.4 million (60% × \$4 million). Because only \$2 million is available internally, \$400,000 in new common stock would be issued. The residual available for dividends would be zero, and no dividend would be paid.

FIGURE 17-2 Krista Corporation Investment Schedule

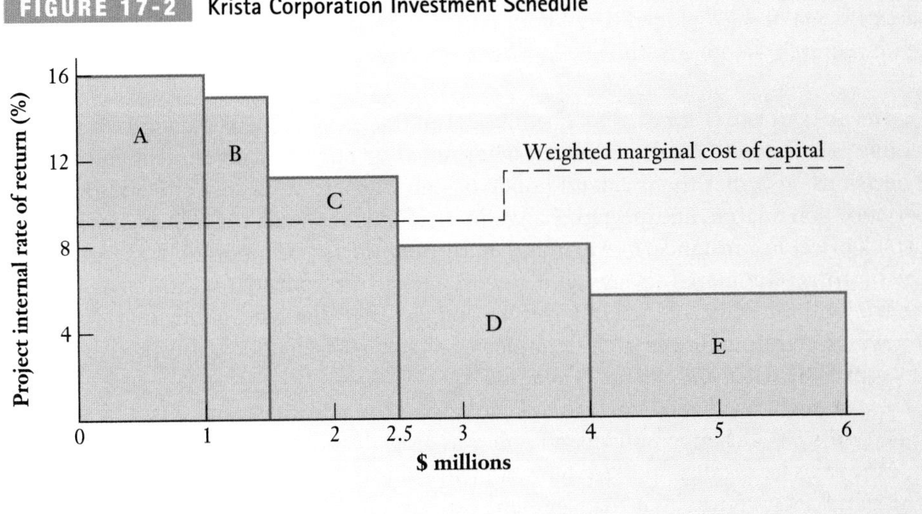

THE CLIENTELE EFFECT What if the investors living in the Land of Ez did not like the dividend policy chosen by Dowell's management? No problem. They could simply satisfy their personal income preferences by purchasing or selling securities when the dividends received did not satisfy their current needs for income. If an investor did not view the dividends received in any given year as sufficient, he or she could simply sell a portion of stock, thereby "creating a dividend." In addition, if the dividend were larger than the investor desired, he or she could purchase stock with the "excess cash" created by the dividend. However, once we leave the Land of Ez, we find that such adjustments in stock ownership are not cost-free. When an investor buys or sells stock, brokerage fees are incurred, ranging from approximately 1 to 10 percent. Even more costly, the investor who buys the stock with cash received from a dividend will have to pay taxes before reinvesting the cash. And when a stock is bought or sold, it must first be reevaluated. Acquisition of the information for decision making also may be time consuming and costly. Finally, aside from the cost of buying or selling part of the stock, some institutional investors, such as university endowment funds, are precluded from selling stock and "spending" the proceeds.

As a result of these considerations, investors may not be too inclined to buy stocks that require them to "create" a dividend stream more suitable to their purposes. Rather, if investors do in fact have a preference between dividends and capital gains, we could expect them to seek firms that have a dividend policy consistent with these preferences. They would, in essence, "sort themselves out" by buying stocks that satisfy their preferences for dividends and capital gains. Individuals and institutions that need current income would be drawn to companies that have high dividend payouts. Other investors, such as wealthy individuals, would much prefer to avoid taxes by holding securities that offer no or small dividend income but deferred large capital gains. In other words, there would be a **clientele effect**: Firms draw a given clientele, given their stated dividend policy.

Clientele effect
The belief that individuals and institutions that need current income will invest in companies that have high dividend payouts. Other investors prefer to avoid taxes by holding securities that offer only small dividend income, but large capital gains as the capital gains are deferred until realized. Thus we have a "clientele" of investors.

The possibility that clienteles of investors exist might lead us to believe that the firm's dividend policy matters. However, unless there is a greater aggregate demand for a particular policy than the market can satisfy, dividend policy is still unimportant; one policy is as good as the other. The clientele effect only warns firms to avoid making capricious changes in their dividend policy. Given that the firm's investment decisions are already made, the level of the dividend is still unimportant. The change in the policy matters only when it requires clientele to shift to another company.

THE INFORMATION EFFECT The investor in the Land of Ez would argue with considerable persuasion that a firm's value is determined strictly by its investment and financing decisions, and that the dividend policy has no impact on value. Yet we know from experience that a large, unexpected change in dividends can have a significant impact on the stock price. For instance, in August 1994, the Continental Corporation, a large insurance company, eliminated its annual dividend of $1. In response, the firm's stock price went from about $18 to $15. How can we suggest that dividend policy matters little, when we can cite numerous such examples of a change in dividend affecting the stock price, especially when the change is negative?

Despite such "evidence," we are not looking at the real cause and effect. It may be that investors use a change in dividend policy as a *signal* about the firm's financial condition, especially its earnings power. Thus, a dividend increase that is larger than expected might signal to investors that management expects significantly higher earnings in the future. Conversely, a dividend decrease, or even a less than expected increase, might signal that management is forecasting less favorable future earnings.

Some would argue that management frequently has inside information about the firm that it cannot make available to investors. This difference in accessibility to information between management and investors, called **information asymmetry**, may result in a lower stock price than would occur under conditions of certainty. This reasoning says that, by regularly increasing dividends, management is making a commitment to continue these cash flows to the stockholders for the foreseeable future. So in a risky marketplace, dividends become a means to minimize any "drag" on the stock price that might come from differences in the level of information available to managers and investors.

Information asymmetry
The difference in accessibility to information between management and investors may result in a lower stock price than would occur under conditions of certainty.

Dividends may therefore be important only as a communication tool; management may have no other credible way to inform investors about future earnings, or at least no convincing way that is less costly.

AGENCY COSTS Let us return again to the Land of Ez. We had avoided any potential conflict between the firm's investors and managers by assuming them to be one and the same. With only a cursory look at the real marketplace, we can see that managers and investors are typically not the same people, and as noted in the preceding section, these two groups do not have the same access to information about the firm. If the two groups are not the same, we must then assume that management is dedicated to maximizing shareholder wealth.[10] That is, we are making a presupposition that the market values of companies with separate owners and managers will not differ from those of owner-managed firms.

BACK TO THE PRINCIPLES

__Principle 7__ warned us there may be a conflict between management and owners, especially in large firms where managers and owners have different incentives. That is: __Managers Won't Work for Owners Unless It's in Their Best Interest.__ As we shall see in this section, the dividend policy may be one way to reduce this problem.

Two possibilities should help managers see things as the equity investors see them: (1) Low market values may attract takeover bids; and (2) a competitive labor market may allow investors to replace uncooperative managers. That is, if management is not sensitive to the need to maximize shareholder wealth, new investors may buy the stock, take control of the firm, and remove management.[11] If current management is being less than supportive of the owners, these owners can always seek other managers who will work in the investors' best interest. If these two market mechanisms worked perfectly without any cost, the potential conflict would be nonexistent. In reality, however, conflicts may still exist, and the stock price of a company owned by investors who are separate from management may be less than the stock value of a closely held firm. The difference in price is the cost of the conflict to the owners, which has come to be called **agency costs.**[12]

Agency costs
The costs, such as a reduced stock price, associated with potential conflict between managers and investors when these two groups are not the same.

Recognizing the possible problem, management, acting independently or at the insistence of the board of directors, frequently takes action to minimize the cost associated with the separation of ownership and management control. Such action, which in itself is costly, includes auditing by independent accountants, assigning supervisory functions to the company's board of directors, creating covenants in lending agreements that restrict management's powers, and providing incentive compensation plans for management that help "bond" the management with the owners.

A firm's dividend policy may be perceived by owners as a tool to minimize agency costs. Assuming that the payment of a dividend requires management to issue stock to finance new investments, new investors may be attracted to the company only if management provides convincing information that the capital will be used profitably. Thus the payment of dividends indirectly results in a closer monitoring of management's investment activities. In this case, dividends may make a meaningful contribution to the value of the firm.

[10] This issue was addressed briefly in Chapter 1.

[11] The "corporate control hypothesis," especially as it relates to companies merging or being acquired, has generated a great amount of interest. For example, see the April 1983 issue of *Journal of Financial Economics.*

[12] See M. C. Jenson and W. H. Meckling, "Theory of the Firm: Managerial Behavior, Agency Costs, and Ownership Structure," *Journal of Financial Economics* (October 1976): 305–60.

EXPECTATIONS THEORY[13] A common thread throughout much of our discussion of dividend policy, particularly as it relates to information effects, is the word *expected.* We should not overlook the significance of this word when we are making any financial decision within the firm. No matter what the decision area, how the market price responds to management's actions is not determined entirely by the action itself; it is also affected by investors' expectations about the ultimate decision to be made by management. This idea is called the **expectations theory**.

Expectations theory
The effect of new information about a company on the firm's stock price depends more on how the new information compares to expectations than on the actual announcement itself.

As the time approaches for management to announce the amount of the next dividend, investors form expectations as to how much that dividend will be. These expectations are based on several factors internal to the firm, such as past dividend decisions, current and expected earnings, investment strategies, and financing decisions. They also consider such things as the condition of the general economy, the strength or weakness of the industry at the time, and possible changes in government policies.

When the actual dividend decision is announced, the investor compares the actual decision with the expected decision. If the amount of the dividend is as expected, even if it represents an increase from prior years, the market price of the stock will remain unchanged. However, if the dividend is higher or lower than expected, investors will reassess their perceptions about the firm. They will question the meaning of the *unexpected* change in the dividend. They may use the unexpected dividend decision as a clue about unexpected changes in earnings; that is, the unexpected dividend change has information content about the firm's earnings and other important factors. In short, management's actual decision about the firm's dividend policy may not be terribly significant, unless it departs from investors' expectations. If there is a difference between actual and expected dividends, we will more than likely see a movement in the stock price.

THE EMPIRICAL EVIDENCE

Our search for an answer to the question of dividend relevance has been less than successful. We have given it our best thinking, but still no single, definitive position has emerged. Maybe we could gather evidence to show the relationship between dividend practices and security prices. We might also inquire into the perceptions of financial managers who make decisions about dividend policies, with the idea that their beliefs affect their decision making. Then we could truly know that dividend policy is important or that it does not matter.

To test the relationship between dividend payments and security prices, we could compare a firm's dividend yield (dividend/stock price) and the stock's total return. The question is: Do stocks that pay high dividends provide higher or lower returns to investors? Such tests have been conducted with the use of highly sophisticated statistical techniques. Despite the use of these extremely powerful analytical tools, which involve intricate and complicated procedures, the results have been mixed.[14] However, over long periods, the results have given a slight advantage to the low-dividend stocks; that is,

[13] Much of the thoughts in this section came from Merton Miller, "Can Management Use Dividends to Influence the Value of the Firm?" in *The Revolution in Corporate Finance*, Joel M. Stern and Donald H. Chew, Jr., eds. (New York: Basil Blackwell, 1986): 299–303.

[14] See F. Black and M. Scholes, "The Effects of Dividend Yield and Dividend Policy on Common Stock Prices and Returns," *Journal of Financial Economics* 1 (May 1974), 1–22; P. Hess, "The Ex-Dividend Behavior of Stock Returns: Further Evidence on Tax Effects," *Journal of Finance* 37 (May 1982), 445–56; R. H. Litzenberger and K. Ramaswamy, "The Effect of Personal Taxes and Dividends on Capital Asset Prices: Theory and Empirical Evidence," *Journal of Financial Economics* 7 (June 1979), 163–95; and M. H. Miller and M. Scholes, "Dividends and Taxes: Some Empirical Evidence," *Journal of Political Economy* 90 (1982): 1118–41.

stocks that pay lower dividends appear to have higher prices. The findings are far from conclusive, however, owing to the relatively large standard errors of the estimates. (The apparent differences may be the result of random sampling error and not real differences.) We simply have been unable to disentangle the effect of dividend policy from other influences.

Several reasons may be given for our inability to arrive at conclusive results. First, to be accurate, we would need to know the amount of dividends investors *expected* to receive. Because these expectations cannot be observed, we can only use historical data, which may or may not relate to current expectations. Second, most empirical studies have assumed a linear relationship between dividend payments and stock prices. The actual relationship may be nonlinear, possibly even discontinuous. Whatever the reasons, the evidence to date is inconclusive and the jury is still out.

Because our statistical prowess does not provide any conclusive evidence, let's turn to our last hope. What do the financial managers of the world believe about the relevance of dividend policy? Although we may not conclude that a manager's opinion is necessarily the "final word on the matter," having these insights is helpful. If financial managers believe that dividends matter and act consistently in accordance with that conviction, they could influence the relationship between stock value and dividend policy.

To help us gain some understanding of managements' perceptions, let's turn to a study by Baker, Farrelly, and Edelman, which surveyed financial executives at 318 firms listed on the New York Stock Exchange.[15] The study conducted in 1983 is summarized in Table 17-4. In looking at the Baker, Farrelly, and Edelman results, the evidence favors the relevance of dividend policy, but not overwhelmingly so. For the most part, managers are divided between believing that dividends are important and having no opinion in the matter.

Regarding the question about the price-dividend relationship, Baker et al. asked the financial managers straight up, "Does the firm's dividend policy affect the price of the common stock?" Slightly more than 60 percent of the responses were affirmative, which is significant, but there were still almost 40 percent who had no opinion or disagreed.

[15] H. Kent Baker, Gail E. Farrelly, and Richard B. Edelman, "A Survey of Management Views on Dividend Policy," *Financial Management* (Autumn 1985): 78–84.

TABLE 17-4 Management Opinion Survey on Dividends

	LEVEL OF MANAGERS' AGREEMENT		
STATEMENT OF MANAGERIAL BELIEFS	**AGREEMENT**	**NO OPINION**	**DISAGREEMENT**
1. A firm's dividend payout ratio affects the price of the common stock.	61%	33%	6%
2. Dividend payments provide a signaling device of future prospects.	52	41	7
3. The market uses dividend announcements as information for assessing security value.	43	51	6
4. Investors have different perceptions of the relative riskiness of dividends and retained earnings.	56	42	2
5. Investors are basically indifferent with regard to returns from dividends versus those from capital gains.	6	30	64
6. A stockholder is attracted to firms that have dividend policies appropriate to the stockholder's particular tax environment.	44	49	7
7. Management should be responsive to its shareholders' preferences regarding dividends.	41	49	10

Source: Adapted from H. Kent Baker, Gail E. Farrelly, and Richard B. Edelman, "A Survey of Management Views on Dividend Policy," *Financial Management* (Autumn 1985): 81.

Thus, we could conclude that most managers think that dividends matter, but they have no mandate. Similarly, when asked if dividends provide informational content about the firm's future (Statements 2 and 3), the managers are basically split between "no opinion" and "agreement." When asked about the trade-off between dividends and capital gains (Statements 4 and 5), almost two-thirds of the managers thought stockholders have a preference for dividend or capital gains, with a lesser number (56 percent) believing that investors perceive the relative riskiness of capital gains and dividends to be different. Interestingly enough, though, almost half of the managers felt no clear responsibility to be responsive to stockholders' preferences. Specifically, 56 percent of the financial executives either had no opinion or did not believe that stockholders are attracted to firms that have dividend policies appropriate to the stockholders' particular tax environment. Finally, Statement 7 suggests that the majority of managers are not true believers in the concept of a clientele effect.

What Are We to Conclude?

We have now looked carefully at the importance of a firm's dividend policy as management seeks to increase the shareholders' wealth. We have gone to great lengths to gain insight and understanding from our best thinking. We have even drawn from the empirical evidence on hand to see what the findings suggest.

A reasonable person cannot reach a definitive conclusion; nevertheless, management is left with no choice. A firm must develop a dividend policy, it is hoped, based on the best available knowledge. Although we can give advice only with some reservations, the following conclusions would appear reasonable:

1. As a firm's investment opportunities increase, the dividend payout ratio should decrease. In other words, an inverse relationship should exist between the amount of investments with an expected rate of return that exceeds the cost of capital and the dividends remitted to investors. Because of flotation costs associated with raising external capital, the retention of internally generated equity financing is preferable to selling stock (in terms of the wealth of the current common shareholders).
2. The firm's dividend policy appears to be important; however, appearances may be deceptive. The real issue may be the firm's *expected* earning power and the riskiness of these earnings. Investors may be using the dividend payment as a source of information about the company's *expected* earnings. Management's actions regarding dividends may carry greater weight than a statement by management that earnings will be increasing.
3. If dividends influence stock price, this is probably based on the investor's desire to minimize and defer taxes and from the role of dividends in minimizing agency costs.
4. If the expectations theory has merit, which we believe it does, management should avoid surprising investors when it comes to the firm's dividend decision. The firm's dividend policy might effectively be treated as a *long-term residual.* Rather than projecting investment requirements for a single year, management could anticipate financing needs for several years. Based upon the expected investment opportunities during the planning horizon, the firm's debt-equity mix, and the funds generated from operations, a *target* dividend payout ratio could be established. If internal funds remained after projection of the necessary equity financing, dividends would be paid. However, the planned dividend stream should distribute residual capital evenly to investors over the planning period. Conversely, if over the long term the entire amount of internally generated capital is needed for reinvestment in the company, then no dividend should be paid.

CONCEPT CHECK

1. Can you summarize the position that dividend policy may be irrelevant with regard to the firm's stock price?
2. What is meant by the bird-in-the-hand dividend theory?
3. Why are cash dividend payments thought to be more certain than prospective capital gains?
4. How might personal taxes affect both the firm's dividend policy and its share price?
5. Distinguish between the residual dividend theory and the clientele effect.

THE DIVIDEND DECISION IN PRACTICE

In setting a firm's dividend policy, financial managers must work in the world of reality with the concepts we have set forth so far in this chapter. Again, although these concepts do not provide an equation that explains the key relationships, they certainly give us a more complete view of the finance world, which can only help us make better decisions. Other considerations of a more practical nature also appear as part of the firm's decision making about its dividend policy.

OTHER PRACTICAL CONSIDERATIONS

Objective 3

Many considerations may influence a firm's decision about its dividends, some of them unique to that company. Some of the more general considerations are given subsequently.

LEGAL RESTRICTIONS Certain legal restrictions may limit the amount of dividends a firm may pay. These legal constraints fall into two categories. First, *statutory restrictions* may prevent a company from paying dividends. Although specific limitations vary by state, generally a corporation may not pay a dividend (1) if the firm's liabilities exceed its assets, (2) if the amount of the dividend exceeds the accumulated profits (retained earnings), and (3) if the dividend is being paid from capital invested in the firm.

The second type of legal restriction is unique to each firm and results from restrictions in debt and preferred stock contracts. To minimize their risk, investors frequently impose restrictive provisions upon management as a condition to their investment in the company. These constraints may include the provision that dividends may not be declared prior to the debt being repaid. Also, the corporation may be required to maintain a given amount of working capital. Preferred stockholders may stipulate that common dividends may not be paid when any preferred dividends are delinquent.

LIQUIDITY POSITION Contrary to common opinion, the mere fact that a company shows a large amount of retained earnings in the balance sheet does not indicate that cash is available for the payment of dividends. The firm's current position in liquid assets, including cash, is basically independent of the retained earnings account. Historically, a company with sizable retained earnings has been successful in generating cash from operations. Yet these funds are typically either reinvested in the company within a short period or used to pay maturing debt. Thus, a firm may be extremely profitable and still be *cash poor*. Because dividends are paid with cash, and not with retained earnings, the firm must have cash available for dividends to be paid. Hence, the firm's liquidity position has a direct bearing on its ability to pay dividends.

ABSENCE OR LACK OF OTHER SOURCES OF FINANCING As already noted, a firm may (1) retain profits for investment purposes, or (2) pay dividends and issue new debt or equity securities to finance investments. For many small or new companies, this second option is not realistic. These firms do not have access to the capital markets, so they must rely more heavily upon internally generated funds. As a consequence, the dividend payout ratio is generally much lower for a small or newly established firm than for a large, publicly owned corporation.

EARNINGS PREDICTABILITY A company's dividend payout ratio depends to some extent on the predictability of a firm's profits over time. If earnings fluctuate significantly, management cannot rely on internally generated funds to meet future needs. When profits are realized, the firm may retain larger amounts to ensure that money is available when needed. Conversely, a firm with a stable earnings trend will typically pay a larger portion of its earnings out in dividends. This company has less concern about the availability of profits to meet future capital requirements.

OWNERSHIP CONTROL For many large corporations, control through the ownership of common stock is not an issue. However, for many small and medium-sized companies, maintaining voting control takes a high priority. If the present common shareholders are unable to participate in a new offering, issuing new stock is unattractive, in that the control of the current stockholders is diluted. The owners might prefer that management finance new investments with debt and through profits rather than by issuing new common stock. This firm's growth is then constrained by the amount of debt capital available and by the company's ability to generate profits.

INFLATION Before the late 1970s, inflationary pressures had not been a significant problem for either consumers or businesses. However, during much of the 1980s, the deterioration of the dollar's purchasing power had a direct impact on the replacement of fixed assets. In a period of inflation, ideally, as fixed assets become worn and obsolete, the funds generated from depreciation are used to finance the replacements. As the cost of equivalent equipment continues to increase, the depreciation funds are insufficient. This requires a greater retention of profits, which implies that dividends have to be adversely affected. In the late 1990s, inflation was not a primary concern.

Objective 4

Constant dividend payout ratio
A dividend payment policy in which the percentage of earnings paid out in dividends is held constant. The dollar amount fluctuates from year to year as profits vary.

Stable dollar dividend per share payout
A dividend policy that maintains a relatively stable dollar dividend per share over time.

Small, regular dividend plus year-end extra dividend payout
A dividend payment policy in which the firm pays a small regular dividend plus an extra dividend only if the firm has experienced a good year.

ALTERNATIVE DIVIDEND POLICIES

Regardless of a firm's long-term dividend policy, most firms choose one of several year-to-year dividend payment patterns:

1. **Constant dividend payout ratio.** In this policy, the percentage of earnings paid out in dividends is held constant. Although the dividend-to-earnings ratio is stable, the dollar amount of the dividend naturally fluctuates from year to year as profits vary.
2. **Stable dollar dividend per share payout.** This policy maintains a relatively stable dollar dividend over time. An increase in the dollar dividend usually does not occur until management is convinced that the higher dividend level can be maintained in the future. Management also will not reduce the dollar dividend until the evidence clearly indicates that a continuation of the present dividend cannot be supported.
3. **Small, regular dividend plus year-end extra dividend payout.** A corporation following this policy pays a small regular dollar dividend plus a year-end *extra dividend* in prosperous years. The extra dividend is declared toward the end of the fiscal year,

when the company's profits for the period can be estimated. Management's objective is to avoid the connotation of a permanent dividend. However, this purpose may be defeated if *recurring* extra dividends come to be expected by investors.

Of the three dividend policies, the stable dollar dividend is by far the most common. In a study by Lintner, corporate managers were found to be reluctant to change the dollar amount of the dividend in response to temporary fluctuations in earnings from year to year. This aversion was particularly evident when it came to decreasing the amount of the dividend from the previous level.[16] In a separate study, Smith explained the tendency for stable dividend in terms of his **"increasing-stream hypothesis of dividend policy."**[17] He proposed that dividend stability is essentially a smoothing of the dividend stream to minimize the effect of other types of company reversals. Thus, corporate managers make every effort to avoid a dividend cut, attempting instead to develop a gradually increasing dividend series over the long-term future. However, if a dividend reduction is absolutely necessary, the cut should be large enough to reduce the probability of future cuts.

"Increasing-stream hypothesis of dividend policy"
A smoothing of the dividend stream in order to minimize the effect of company reversals. Corporate managers make every effort to avoid a dividend cut, attempting instead to develop a gradually increasing dividend series over the long-term future.

EXAMPLE: DIVIDEND POLICY FROM HARLEY-DAVIDSON, INC.

We just discussed several alternative corporate dividend policies. Following are some actual data from Harley-Davidson that provide insight into that firm's payout policy. The table presents Harley's actual reported earnings and dividends per share, along with the calculated dividend payout ratio, which is shown in the last column.

Earnings per Share, Dividends per Share, and the Dividend Payout Ratio. Harley-Davidson, Inc., 1997–2001

YEAR	EARNINGS PER SHARE[a]	DIVIDENDS PER SHARE	PAYOUT RATIO
1997	$.57	$.07	12.3%
1998	.69	.08	11.6
1999	.86	.09	10.5
2000	1.13	.10	8.8
2001	1.43	.12	8.4

[a]This series represents "diluted" earnings.

Source: Basic data from Harley-Davidson, Inc., *Annual Report, 2001*, 41.

Now, which of the alternative dividend policies that we reviewed does the management of Harley seem to follow? Notice two important elements: (1) the payout ratio decreases over the given five-year time frame, but (2) the actual cash dividend paid over time increased each year. Also be aware that the alternative policies we have discussed are not always mutually exclusive. Alternatively stated, the actual data may not *precisely* fit any of the three popular policies.

Hint: Think about the results of the study reported by Dr. K. V. Smith and incorporate that into your analysis.

[16] John Lintner, "Distribution of Income of Corporations Among Dividends, Retained Earnings, and Taxes," *American Economic Review* 46 (May 1956): 97–113.

[17] Keith V. Smith, "Increasing-Stream Hypothesis of Corporate Dividend Policy," *California Management Review* 15 (Fall 1971): 56–64.

TABLE 17-5 Earnings per Share, Dividends per Share, and the Dividend Payout Ratio, W. R. Grace & Co., 1992–1996

YEAR	EARNINGS PER SHARE[a]	DIVIDENDS PER SHARE	PAYOUT RATIO
1992	$1.70	$1.40	82.3%
1993	1.39	1.40	101.0
1994	1.74	1.40	80.5
1995	2.14	1.175	54.9
1996	2.41	0.50	20.7

[a]This series represents earnings from continuing operations, but before special items.

Source: Basic data from W. R. Grace & Co., *Annual Report* (1996), 55.

Home Depot provides a very clear annual report, which can be found at www.homedepot.com. Find the annual report for 2000 and inspect the "10-Year Summary of Financial and Operating Results." You will find that cash dividends per share were $0.01 back in 1991, $0.04 per share in 1995, and $0.16 per share in 2000. In no year over the 1991 to 2000 period did the company not pay a cash dividend or decrease the dividend. Which of the alternative dividend policies that we have studied does Home Depot seem to follow?

Dividend Policy and Corporate Strategy: Things Will Change—Even Dividend Policy

The recessions of 1990 to 1991 and 2001 induced a large number of American corporations to revisit their broadest corporate strategies that directly impact shareholder wealth. Today, the results of that "rethinking" are evident in many aspects of corporate behavior, including adjusted dividend policies.

One firm that altered its dividend policy in response to new strategies was W. R. Grace & Co., headquartered in Columbia, Maryland. The firm's core businesses include packaging, catalysts and silica products, and construction products. Grace & Co. ranked number 271 within the 1997 *Fortune* 500 list of the largest U.S. corporations, with sales of $5.26 billion.

The new corporate plans involved (1) divesting or discontinuing several product lines and (2) initiating a significant repurchase program of its own common stock. Stock repurchase programs are discussed in depth later in this chapter.

As a result, both the firm's payout ratio and actual cash dividend paid per share declined in significant fashion. The change in observed dividend policy is evident in Table 17-5. Notice that over the 1992 to 1994 period, Grace & Co. provided a good example of what we have called a "stable dividend policy." During this period, the firm maintained a stable dollar dividend of $1.40 per share, whereas the payout ratio varied from 80.5 percent to 101.0 percent.

But when company policies changed dramatically, so did the associated dividend variables. The absolute dollar amount of the cash dividend per share was lowered to $0.50 in 1996 and the accompanying payout ratio fell to 20.7 percent. Importantly, the firm's total return to investors was a robust 30.9 percent during 1996, compared to its 10-year average of 16.4 percent. The market liked the change in dividend policy. So, although firms may be reluctant to change their dividend policies, with good planning and proper information dissemination it is possible to convince the financial markets that such a new direction might be good for investors.

CONCEPT CHECK

1. Can you identify some practical considerations that affect a firm's payout policy?
2. Identify and explain three different dividend policies. *Hint:* One of these is a constant dividend payout ratio.
3. What is the increasing-stream hypothesis of dividend policy?

DIVIDEND PAYMENT PROCEDURES

Objective 5

After the firm's dividend policy has been structured, several procedural details must be arranged. For instance, how frequently are dividend payments to be made? If a stockholder sells the shares during the year, who is entitled to the dividend? To answer these questions, we need to understand dividend payment procedures.

Generally, companies pay dividends on a quarterly basis. To illustrate, IBM pays $1 per share in annual dividends. However, the firm actually issues a 25 cent dividend for a total yearly dividend of $1 (25 cents × 4 quarters).

The final approval of a dividend payment comes from the board of directors. As an example, Abbot Labs, on December 12, 1994, announced that holders of record as of January 13, 1995, would receive a 19 cent dividend. The dividend payment was to be made on February 15. December 12 is the **declaration date**—the date when the dividend is formally declared by the board of directors. The **date of record**, January 13, designates when the stock transfer books are to be closed. Investors shown to own stock on this date receive the dividend. If a notification of a transfer is recorded subsequent to January 13, the new owner is not entitled to the dividend. However, a problem could develop if the stock were sold on January 12, one day prior to the record date. Time would not permit the sale to be reflected on the stockholder list by the January 13 date of record. To avoid this problem, stock brokerage companies have uniformly decided to terminate the right of ownership to the dividend two working days prior to the record date. This prior date is the **ex-dividend date**. Therefore, any acquirer of Abbot Labs stock on January 11 or thereafter does not receive the dividend. Finally, the company mails the dividend check to each investor on February 15, the **payment date**. These events may be diagrammed as follows:

Declaration date
The date upon which a dividend is formally declared by the board of directors.

Date of record
Date at which the stock transfer books are to be closed for determining which investor is to receive the next dividend payment.

Ex-dividend date
The date upon which stock brokerage companies have uniformly decided to terminate the right of ownership to the dividend, which is two days prior to the record date.

Payment date
The date on which the company mails a dividend check to each investor.

ANNOUNCEMENT DATE	EX-DIVIDEND DATE	RECORD DATE	PAYMENT DATE
December 12	January 11	January 13	February 15

CONCEPT CHECK

1. What is the typical frequency with which cash dividends are paid to investors?
2. Distinguish among the (a) declaration date, (b) date of record, and (c) ex-dividend date.

STOCK DIVIDENDS AND STOCK SPLITS

Objective 6

An integral part of dividend policy is the use of **stock dividends** and **stock splits**. Both involve issuing new shares of stock on a pro rata basis to the current shareholders, while the firm's assets, its earnings, and the risk assumed and the investor's percentage of ownership in the company remain unchanged. The only *definite* result from either a stock dividend or stock split is the increase in the number of shares of stock outstanding.

Stock dividend
A distribution of shares of up to 25 percent of the number of shares currently outstanding, issued on a pro rata basis to the current stockholders.

Stock split
A stock dividend exceeding 25 percent of the number of shares currently outstanding.

To illustrate the effect of a stock dividend, assume that the Katie Corporation has 100,000 shares outstanding. The firm's after-tax profits are $500,000, or $5 in earnings per share. At present, the company's stock is selling at a price/earnings multiple of 10, or $50 per share. Management is planning to issue a 20 percent stock dividend, so that a stockholder owning 10 shares would receive two additional shares. We might immediately conclude that this investor is being given an asset (two shares of stock) worth $100; consequently, his or her personal worth should increase by $100. This conclusion is erroneous. The firm will be issuing 20,000 new shares (100,000 shares × 20 percent). Because the $500,000 in after-tax profits does not change, the new earnings per share will be $4.167 ($500,000 ÷ 120,000 shares). If the price/earnings multiple remains at 10, the market price of the stock after the dividend should fall to $41.67 ($4.167 earnings per share × 10). The investor now owns 12 shares worth $41.67, which provides a $500 total value; thus, he or she is neither better nor worse off than before the stock dividend.

This example may make us wonder why a corporation would even bother with a stock dividend or stock split if no one benefits. However, before we study the rationale for such distributions, we should understand the differences between a stock split and a stock dividend.

Stock Dividend versus Stock Split

The only difference between a stock dividend and a stock split relates to their respective accounting treatment. Stated differently, *there is absolutely no difference on an economic basis between a stock dividend and a stock split.* Both represent a proportionate distribution of additional shares to the present stockholders. However, *for accounting purposes,* the stock split has been defined as a stock dividend exceeding 25 percent.[18] Thus, a stock dividend is arbitrarily defined as a distribution of shares up to 25 percent of the number of shares currently outstanding.

The accounting treatment for a stock dividend requires the issuing firm to capitalize the "market value" of the dividend. In other words, the dollar amount of the dividend is transferred from retained earnings to the capital accounts (par and paid-in capital). This procedure may best be explained by an example. Assume that the L. Bernard Corporation is preparing to issue a 15 percent stock dividend. Table 17-6 presents the equity portion of the firm's balance sheet prior to the distribution. The market price for the stock has been $14. Thus, the 15 percent stock dividend increases the number of shares by 150,000 (1,000,000 shares × 15 percent). The "market value" of this increase is $2,100,000 (150,000 shares × $14 market price). To record this transaction, $2,100,000 would be transferred from retained earnings, resulting in a $300,000 increase in total par value (150,000 shares × $2 par value) and a $1,800,000 increment to paid-in capital. The $1,800,000 is the residual difference between $2,100,000 and $300,000. Table 17-7 shows the revised balance sheet.

What if the management of L. Bernard Corporation changed the plan and decided to split the stock two for one? In other words, a *100 percent increase* in the number of shares would result. In accounting for the split, the changes to be recorded are (1) the increase

[18] The 25 percent standard applies only to corporations listed on the New York Stock Exchange. The American Institute of Certified Public Accountants states that a stock dividend greater than 20 or 25 percent is for all practical purposes a stock split.

TABLE 17-6 L. Bernard Corporation Balance Sheet Before Stock Dividend

Common stock	
Par value (1,000,000 shares outstanding; $2 par value)	$ 2,000,000
Paid-in capital	8,000,000
Retained earnings	15,000,000
Total equity	$25,000,000

TABLE 17-7 L. Bernard Corporation Balance Sheet After Stock Dividend

Common stock	
Par value (1,150,000 shares outstanding; $2 par value)	$ 2,300,000
Paid-in capital	9,800,000
Retained earnings	12,900,000
Total equity	$25,000,000

TABLE 17-8 L. Bernard Corporation Balance Sheet After Stock Split

Common stock	
Par value (2,000,000 shares outstanding; $1 par value)	$ 2,000,000
Paid-in capital	8,000,000
Retained earnings	15,000,000
Total equity	$25,000,000

in the number of shares and (2) the decrease in the per-share par value from $2 to $1. The dollar amounts of each account do not change. Table 17-8 reveals the new balance sheet.

Thus, for a stock dividend, an amount equal to the market value of the stock dividend is transferred from retained earnings to the capital stock accounts. When stock is split, only the number of shares changes, and the par value of each share is decreased proportionately. Despite this dissimilarity in accounting treatment, remember that no real economic difference exists between a split and a dividend.

RATIONALE FOR A STOCK DIVIDEND OR SPLIT

Although *stock* dividends and splits occur far less frequently than *cash* dividends, a significant number of companies choose to use these share distributions either with or in lieu of cash dividends. Because no economic benefit results, how do corporations justify these distributions?

While a "plain vanilla" stock split merely represents a proportionate distribution of additional shares to current stockholders, more than a few investors believe that stock-split announcements contain useful information. Rightline Power Trading maintains a Web site at www.rightline.net. A proprietary model is used by the firm to identify stock-split candidates. The aim is to uncover "power trading" opportunities. The service is not free, but you can check it out.

Proponents of stock dividends and splits frequently maintain that stockholders receive a key benefit because the price of the stock will not fall precisely in proportion to the share increase. For a two-for-one split, the price of the stock might not decrease a full 50 percent, and the stockholder is left with a higher total value. There are two perceived reasons for this disequilibrium. First, many financial executives believe that an optimal price range exists. Within this range the total market value of the common stockholders is thought to be maximized. As the price exceeds this range, fewer investors can purchase the stock, thereby restraining the demand. Consequently, downward pressure is placed on its price. The second explanation relates to the *information content* of the dividend or split announcement. Stock dividends and splits have generally been associated with companies with growing earnings. The announcement of a stock dividend or split has therefore been perceived as favorable news. The empirical evidence, however, fails to verify these conclusions. Most studies indicate that investors are perceptive in identifying the true meaning of a share distribution. If the stock dividend or split is not accompanied by a positive trend in earnings and increases in cash dividends, price increases surrounding the stock dividend or split are insignificant.[19] Therefore, we should be suspicious of the assertion that a stock dividend or split can help increase the investors' worth.

[19] See James A. Millar and Bruce D. Fielitz, "Stock Split and Stock-Dividend Decisions," *Financial Management* (Winter 1973): 35–45; and Eugene Fama, Lawrence Fisher, Michael Jensen, and Richard Roll, "The Adjustment of Stock Prices to New Information," *International Economic Review* (February 1969): 1–21.

A second reason for stock dividends or splits is the conservation of corporate cash. If a company is encountering cash problems, it may substitute a stock dividend for a cash dividend. However, as before, investors will probably look beyond the dividend to ascertain the underlying reason for conserving cash. If the stock dividend is an effort to conserve cash for attractive investment opportunities, the shareholder may bid up the stock price. If the move to conserve cash relates to financial difficulties within the firm, the market price will most likely react adversely.

CONCEPT CHECK

1. From an economic standpoint, is there any meaningful difference between a stock split and a stock dividend?
2. What managerial logic might lie behind a stock split or a stock dividend?

Objective 7

STOCK REPURCHASES

For well over three decades, corporate managements have been active in repurchasing their own equity securities. For example, on September 14, 2000, the Ford Motor Company announced in a press release that it planned to buy back up to a full $5 billion of its stock. Immediately after the public announcement of this plan, shares of Ford common stock rose by 2.2 percent in the financial markets. Now, a key word in such announcements is the word *plan*. Companies give themselves room across time to execute these buybacks. Ford, at the time, was mired in the midst of a major-league tire quality problem on some of its best-selling vehicles, so not all financial analysts and market-watchers were sure of when the actual repurchases would commence. Several reasons have been given for a firm repurchasing its own stock. Examples of such benefits include:

1. Means for providing an internal investment opportunity
2. Approach for modifying the firm's capital structure
3. Favorable impact on earnings per share
4. Elimination of a minority ownership group of stockholders
5. Minimization of dilution in earnings per share associated with mergers and options
6. Reduction in the firm's costs associated with servicing small stockholders

Stock repurchase (stock buyback) The repurchase of common stock by the issuing firm for any of a variety of reasons resulting in a reduction of shares outstanding.

Also, from the shareholders' perspective, a **stock repurchase**, as opposed to a cash dividend, has a potential tax advantage.

SHARE REPURCHASE AS A DIVIDEND DECISION

Clearly, the payment of a common stock dividend is the conventional method for distributing a firm's profits to its owners. However, it need not be the only way. Another approach is to repurchase the firm's stock. The concept may best be explained by an example.

EXAMPLE: A COMMON STOCK REPURCHASE

Telink, Inc., is planning to pay $4 million ($4 per share) in dividends to its common stockholders. The following earnings and market price information is provided for Telink:

Net income	$7,500,000
Number of shares	1,000,000
Earnings per share	$ 7.50
Price/earnings ratio	8
Expected market price per share after proposed dividend payment	$ 60

In a recent meeting, several board members, who are also major stockholders, questioned the need for a dividend payment. They maintain that they do not need the income, so why not allow the firm to retain the funds for future investments? In response, management contends that the available investments are not sufficiently profitable to justify retention of the income. That is, the investors' required rates of return exceed the expected rates of return that could be earned with the additional $4 million in investments.

Because management opposes the idea of retaining the profits for investment purposes, one of the firm's directors has suggested that the $4 million be used to repurchase the company's stock. In this way, the value of the stock should increase. This result may be demonstrated as follows:

1. Assume that shares are repurchased by the firm at the $60 market price (ex-dividend price) plus the contemplated $4 dividend per share, or for $64 per share.
2. Given a $64 price, 62,500 shares would be repurchased ($4 million ÷ $64 price).
3. If net income is not reduced, but the number of shares declines as a result of the share repurchase, earnings per share would increase from $7.50 to $8, computed as follows:

$$\begin{aligned}
\text{earnings per share} &= \text{net income / outstanding shares} \\
\text{(before repurchase)} &= \$7{,}500{,}000 / 1{,}000{,}000 \\
&= \$7.50 \\
\text{(after repurchase)} &= \$7{,}500{,}000 / (1{,}000{,}000 - 62{,}500) \\
&= \$8.00
\end{aligned}$$

4. Assuming that the price/earnings ratio remains at 8, the new price after the repurchase would be $64, up from $60, where the increase exactly equals the amount of the dividend forgone.

In this example, Telink's stockholders are essentially provided the same value, whether a dividend is paid or stock is repurchased. If management pays a dividend, the investor will have a stock valued at $60 plus $4 received from the dividend. Conversely, if stock is repurchased in lieu of the dividend, the stock will be worth $64. These results were based upon assuming (1) the stock is being repurchased at the exact $64 price, (2) the $7,500,000 net income is unaffected by the repurchase, and (3) the price/earnings ratio of 8 does not change after the repurchase. Given these assumptions, however, the stock repurchase serves as a perfect substitute for the dividend payment to the stockholders.

The Investor's Choice

Given the choice between a stock repurchase and a dividend payment, which would an investor prefer? In perfect markets, where there are no taxes, no commissions when buying and selling stock, and no informational content assigned to a dividend, the investor would be indifferent with regard to the choices. The investor could create a dividend stream by selling stock when income is needed.

Because market imperfections do exist, the investor may have a preference for one of the two methods of distributing the corporate income. First, the firm may have to pay too high a price for the repurchased stock, which is to the detriment of the remaining stockholders. If a relatively large number of shares are being bought, the price may be bid up too high, only to fall after the repurchase operation. Second, as a result of the repurchase, the market may perceive the riskiness of the corporation as increasing, which would lower the price/earnings ratio and the value of the stock.

Financing or Investment Decision

Repurchasing stock when the firm has excess cash may be regarded as a dividend decision. However, a stock repurchase may also be viewed as a financing decision. By issuing debt and then repurchasing stock, a firm can immediately alter its debt-equity mix toward a higher proportion of debt. Rather than choosing how to distribute cash to the stockholders, management is using a stock repurchase as a means to change the corporation's capital structure.

In addition to dividend and financing decisions, many managers consider a stock repurchase an investment decision. When equity prices are depressed in the marketplace, management may view the firm's own stock as being materially undervalued and representing a good investment opportunity. While the firm's management may be wise to repurchase stock at unusually low prices, this decision cannot and should not be viewed in the context of an investment decision. Buying its own stock cannot provide expected returns as other investments do. No company can survive, much less prosper, by investing only in its own stock. See the Finance Matters box, "Many Concerns Use Excess Cash to Repurchase Their Shares.

The Repurchase Procedure

If management intends to repurchase a block of the firm's outstanding shares, it should make this information public. All investors should be given the opportunity to work with complete information. They should be told the purpose of the repurchase, as well as the method to be used to acquire the stock.

Three methods for stock repurchase are available. First, the shares could be bought in the *market*. Here the firm acquires the stock through a stockbroker at the going market price. This approach may place an upward pressure on the stock price until the stock is acquired. Also, commissions must be paid to the stockbrokers as a fee for their services.

Tender offer
The formal offer by the company to buy a specified number of shares at a predetermined and stated price.

The second method is to make a tender offer to the firm's shareholders. A **tender offer** is a formal offer by the company to buy a specified number of shares at a predetermined and stated price. The tender price is set above the current market price in order to attract sellers. A tender offer is best when a relatively large number of shares are to be bought, because the company's intentions are clearly known and each shareholder has the opportunity to sell the stock at the tendered price.

The third and final method for repurchasing stock entails the purchase of the stock from one or more major stockholders. These purchases are made on a *negotiated basis*. Care should be taken to ensure a fair and equitable price. Otherwise, the remaining stockholders may be hurt as a result of the sale.

FINANCE MATTERS

MANY CONCERNS USE EXCESS CASH TO REPURCHASE THEIR SHARES

Stock buybacks are back. Faced with the prospect of only modest economic growth, many companies are using excess cash to buy their own shares rather than build new plants.

Consider the case of Mattel Inc., the El Segundo, California, toy maker. It just announced plans to buy 10 million shares during the next four years, even though its stock, 24 3/8, is selling at a healthly 16.6 times its past 12-month earnings. The reason: Plant capacity is sufficient to handle current sales growth of 10 percent to 12 percent yearly and excess cash is building up at the rate of $200 million a year.

"We don't need the cash to grow so we've decided to give it back," says James Eskridge, Mattel's Chief Financial Officer. Actually, Mattel plans to use about half of the $200 million each year for buybacks and dividends and the rest for growth.

The effect [of a stock repurchase] on individual stocks can be significant, says Robert Giordano, director of economic research at Goldman Sachs & Co. A case in point is General Dynamics Corp., which last summer began selling some divisions and using the proceeds to buy its stock when shares were trading at about $65 each. After nearly $1 billion in buybacks, the stock has gained about 37 percent, closing yesterday at 89 1/2.

"The market reacts positively to purchases, and it appreciates a firm that does not squander excess cash," says Columbia Business School professor Gailen Hite.

Some of the buybacks have come from companies whose stock prices have been hurt. Drug makers, for example, have seen their stocks pummeled by fears that health-care reform will sap profits. As a result, pharmaceutical companies have been big players in the buyback game.

But economists and analysts are much more intrigued by companies that are awash in cash, thanks to improving sales and several years of cost cutting and debt reduction. At this stage of an economic recovery, many such companies would be investing heavily in plant and equipment. Not this time.

"Companies are throwing off more cash than they can ever hope to invest in plant, equipment, or inventories," says Charles Clough, chief investment strategist for Merrill Lynch Capital Markets. Companies already have pared down debt, and now they're turning to equity, he says. His prediction: "He who shrinks his balance sheet the fastest will win in the '90s."

Source: *Wall Street Journal.* Eastern Edition (Staff produced copy only) by Leslie Schism.

CONCEPT CHECK

1. Identify three reasons why a firm might buy back its own common stock shares.
2. What financial relationships must hold for a stock repurchase to be a perfect substitute for a cash dividend payment to stockholders?
3. Within the context of a stock repurchase, what is meant by a tender offer?

THE MULTINATIONAL FIRM: THE CASE OF LOW DIVIDEND PAYMENTS—SO WHERE DO WE INVEST?

Objective 8

Until March of 2001, the U.S. economy continued an outstanding period of aggregate expansion that made it the longest in domestic business cycle history. When such periods of relative prosperity occur, financially strong firms tend to focus their business strategies on growth; as a direct result, corporate dividend yields (i.e., cash dividends divided by common stock price) tend to decline. Firms retain more cash dollars for internal investment opportunities and disgorge less cash to investors. For growth-seeking companies, the capital-budgeting decision takes on greater importance, while the consequence of the dividend decision relative to both firm value and cash outflows shrinks. This might properly remind you of what we called the *residual dividend theory* earlier in this chapter.

TABLE 17-9 U.S. Direct Investment Abroad, 1998, Group of Seven Industrialized Nations

COUNTRY	AMOUNT ($ BILLIONS)	PERCENT OF TOTAL	PERCENT IN MANUFACTURING
Canada	$103.9	24.8%	44.7%
France	39.2	9.4	48.4
Germany	42.9	10.3	51.9
Italy	14.6	3.5	58.5
Japan	38.2	9.2	37.2
United Kingdom	178.6	42.8	26.0
Total	$417.4	100.0%	

Source: *U.S. Net International Position at Yearend, 1998*, U.S. Department of Commerce (June 30, 1999), 10.

During general economic prosperity, the multinational firm logically looks to international markets for prospectively high net present value projects. There are at least two solid reasons for such investing behavior: (1) to spread or dilute country-related economic risks by diversifying geographically and (2) to achieve a cost advantage over competitors. These two reasons for U.S. direct investment abroad should remind you of **Principle 9: All Risk Is Not Equal—Some risk can be diversified away and some cannot;** and **Principle 5: The Curse of Competitive Markets—Why it's hard to find exceptionally profitable projects.**

Table 17-9 identifies those countries, apart from the United States, that make up the so-called "Group of Seven Industrialized Nations." Just think of them as the most advanced economies on the globe. They are referred to in the popular business press as the "G-7" countries. Government finance officials from the G-7 and sometimes their chief executive officers (like the President of the United States) usually meet twice a year to discuss multinational economic policy. In Table 17-9 we can observe the historical dollar amounts in countries where U.S. multinational firms have invested internationally.

Notice that when corporate cash is available, U.S. multinational firms favor (1) the United Kingdom and (2) Canada as domiciles for direct investment. A full 67.6 percent of U.S. firms' investment in other G-7 countries is placed in those two countries. Also notice that the capital projects chosen by U.S. multinational firms tend to be concentrated in various manufacturing industries. For instance, in Italy, a full 58.5 percent of the U.S. investment lies within the manufacturing sector. These relationships and the domi-

FIGURE 17-3 U.S. Direct Investment Abroad, 1998, Group of Seven Industrialized Nations

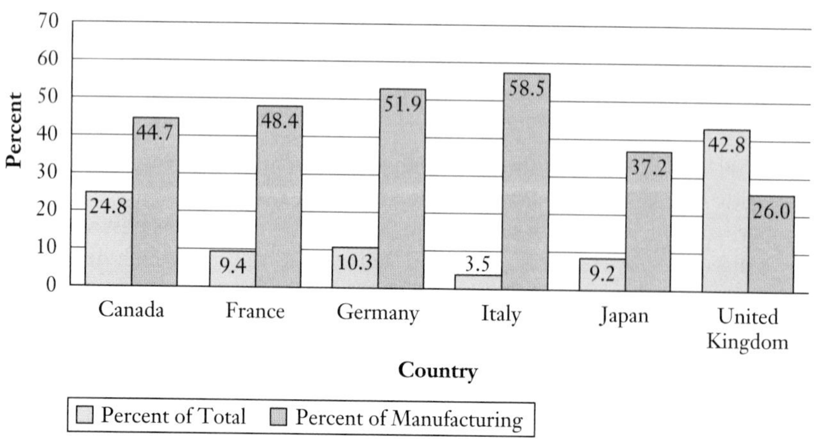

Source: *U.S. Net International Position at Yearend*, 1998. U.S. Department of Commerce (June 30, 1999), 10.

nance of international manufacturing projects are displayed in Figure 17-3. A perceived cost advantage associated with overseas manufacturing, usually related to lower labor costs, explains the bias toward manufacturing-oriented projects by U.S. multinational firms. The competitive nature of a capitalist-based economy induces U.S. firms to seek low-cost labor inputs from their direct international investments.

CONCEPT CHECK

1. Identify two reasons why multinational firms might turn to international markets in search of high net present value projects.
2. Among the Group of Seven countries, which two are most-favored with direct investment by U.S. companies?

HOW FINANCIAL MANAGERS USE THIS MATERIAL

The introduction to this chapter presented a definite statement from the management of Coca-Cola concerning its outlook for the firm's dividend policy that was framed within the concept of its dividend payout ratio. We learned that Coca-Cola plans to gradually reduce its payout ratio.

Coca-Cola management further has said: "We reinvest our operating cash flow principally in three ways: by pumping it back into our own business, by paying dividends, and by buying back our own stock."[20] Note that this latter use of the firm's cash flow relates to our discussion of "stock repurchases" (objective 7) toward the end of the chapter. Again, the differential tax treatment of cash dividends as opposed to capital gains can give investors a potential tax advantage when shares are repurchased, as the capital gains can be deferred. We are reminded once more of **Principle 8: Taxes Bias Business Decisions.**

Another real example is provided by the Walt Disney Company. Recall our discussion of "Alternative Dividend Policies." Disney provides us with a concrete illustration of the stable dollar dividend per share approach in conjunction with an ongoing share repurchase program. Disney management said: "Disney paid out to its shareholders almost $1 billion through dividends and share repurchase in 1997. In January 1997, Disney's Board of Directors voted to increase the company *quarterly* dividend 20 percent from $.11 to $.1325 per share.[21]"

In February 1996, Disney common stock was trading at around $106 per share. This put the firm's annual dividend yield at a tiny 0.5 percent (i.e., $0.53/$106.0). By comparison, the dividend yield on the S&P 500 Index at that same point in time was 1.64 percent or 3.28 times that of Disney. Clearly, Disney management perceives that investors are more interested in expected capital gains than cash dividends, even if they did raise the absolute dollar value of the dividend payout.

SUMMARY

Objective 1

A company's dividend decision has an immediate impact upon the firm's financial mix. If the dividend payment is increased, less funds are available internally for financing investments. Consequently, if additional equity capital is needed, the company has to issue new common stock.

[20] The Coca-Cola Company, *Annual Report* (1996), 27.

[21] The Walt Disney Company, *Annual Report* (1997), 18.

Objective 2

In trying to understand the effect of the dividend policy on a firm's stock price, we must realize the following:

- In perfect markets, the choice between paying or not paying a dividend does not matter. However, when we realize in the real world that there are costs of issuing stock, we have a preference to use internal equity to finance our investment opportunities. Here the dividend decision is simply a residual factor, where the dividend payment should equal the remaining internal capital after financing the equity portion of investments.
- Other market imperfections that may cause a company's dividend policy to affect the firm's stock price include: (1) the tax benefit of capital gains, (2) agency costs, (3) the clientele effect, and (4) the informational content of a given policy.

Objective 3

Other practical considerations that may affect a firm's dividend-payment decision include:

- The firm's liquidity position
- The company's accessibility to capital markets
- Inflation rates
- Legal restrictions
- The stability of earnings
- The desire of investors to maintain control of the company

Objective 4

In practice, managers have generally followed one of three dividend policies:

- Constant dividend payout ratio, where the percentage of dividends to earnings is held constant.
- Stable dollar dividend per share, where a relatively stable dollar dividend is maintained over time.
- Small, regular dividend plus a year-end extra, where the firm pays a small regular dollar dividend plus a year-end extra.

Of the three dividend policies, the stable dollar dividend is by far the most popular.

Objective 5

Generally, companies pay dividends on a quarterly basis. The final approval of a dividend payment comes from the board of directors. The critical dates in this process are as follows:

- Declaration date—the date when the dividend is formally declared by the board of directors.
- Date of record—the date when the stock transfer books are to be closed to determine who owns the stock.
- Ex-dividend date—two working days prior to the record date. After this date, the right to receive the dividend no longer goes with the stock.
- Payment date—the date the dividend check is mailed to the stockholders.

Objective 6

Stock dividends and stock splits have been used by corporations either in lieu of or to supplement cash dividends. At the present, no empirical evidence identifies a relationship between stock dividends and splits and the market price of the stock. Yet a stock dividend or split could conceivably be used to keep the stock price within an optimal trading range. Also, if investors perceive that the stock dividend contained favorable information about the firm's operations, the price of the stock could increase.

Objective 7

As an alternative to paying a dividend, management can repurchase stock. In perfect markets, an investor would be indifferent between receiving a dividend or a share repurchase. The investor could simply create a dividend stream by selling stock when income is needed. If, however, market imperfections exist, the investor may have a preference for one of the two methods of distributing the corporate income. A stock repurchase may also be viewed as a financing decision. By issuing debt and then repurchasing stock, a firm can immediately alter its debt-equity mix toward a higher proportion of debt. Also, many managers consider a stock repurchase an investment decision—buying the stock when they believe it to be undervalued.

Objective 8

During periods of general economic prosperity, financially strong firms tend to focus their business strategies on growth. As a result, dividend yields and cash dividend payments can decline. With internally generated cash to invest, the multinational firm will look to international markets for prospectively high *NPV* projects. This may allow the firm to (1) spread country-related economic risks by diversifying geographically and (2) achieve a cost advantage over competitors.

KEY TERMS

Agency costs, 617
"Bird-in-the-hand" dividend theory, 611
Clientele effect, 616
Constant dividend payout ratio, 622
Date of record, 625
Declaration date, 625
Dividend payout ratio, 607
Ex-dividend date, 625
Expectations theory, 618
"Increasing-stream hypothesis of dividend policy," 623
Information asymmetry, 616
Payment date, 625
"Perfect" capital markets, 608
Residual dividend theory, 614
Small, regular dividend plus year-end extra dividend payout, 622
Stable dollar dividend per share payout, 622
Stock dividend, 625
Stock repurchase (stock buyback), 628
Stock split, 625
Tender offer, 630

STUDY QUESTIONS

17-1. What is meant by the term *dividend payout ratio?*

17-2. Explain the trade-off between retaining internally generated funds and paying cash dividends.

17-3. **a.** What are the assumptions of a perfect market?
b. What effect does dividend policy have on the share price in a perfect market?

17-4. What is the impact of flotation costs on the financing decision?

17-5. **a.** What is the *residual dividend theory?*
b. Why is this theory operational only in the long term?

17-6. Why might investors prefer capital gains to the same amount of dividend income?

17-7. What legal restrictions may limit the amount of dividends to be paid?

17-8. How does a firm's liquidity position affect the payment of dividends?

17-9. How can ownership control constrain the growth of a firm?

17-10. **a.** Why is a stable dollar dividend policy popular from the viewpoint of the corporation?
b. Is it also popular with investors? Why?

17-11. Explain declaration date, date of record, and ex-dividend date.

17-12. What are the advantages of a stock split or dividend over a cash dividend?

17-13. Why would a firm repurchase its own stock?

SELF-TEST PROBLEMS

ST-1. (*Dividend growth rate*) Schutz, Inc., maintains a constant dividend payout ratio of 35 percent. Earnings per share last year were $8.20 and are expected to grow indefinitely at a rate of 12 percent. What will be the dividend per share this year? In five years?

ST-2. (*Residual dividend theory*) Britton Corporation is considering four investment opportunities. The required investment outlays and expected rates of return for these investments are shown below. The firm's cost of capital is 14 percent. The investments are to be financed by 40 percent debt and 60 percent common equity. Internally generated funds totaling $750,000 are available for reinvestment.

a. Which investments should be accepted? According to the residual dividend theory, what amount should be paid out in dividends?
b. How would your answer change if the cost of capital were 10 percent?

INVESTMENT	INVESTMENT COST	INTERNAL RATES OF RETURN
A	$275,000	17.50%
B	325,000	15.72
C	550,000	14.25
D	400,000	11.65

ST-3. (*Stock split*) The debt and equity section of the Robson Corporation balance sheet follows. The current market price of the common shares is $20. Reconstruct the financial statement assuming that (a) a 15 percent stock dividend is issued and (b) a two-for-one stock split is declared.

ROBSON CORPORATION	
Debt	$1,800,000
Common	
Par ($2 par; 100,000 shares)	200,000
Paid-in capital	400,000
Retained earnings	900,000
	$3,300,000

STUDY PROBLEMS (SET A)

17-1A. (*Dividend policies*) The earnings for Harmony Pianos, Inc., have been predicted for the next five years and are listed in the following table. There are 1 million shares outstanding. Determine the yearly dividend per share to be paid if the following policies are enacted:

a. Constant dividend payout ratio of 40 percent.
b. Stable dollar dividend targeted at 40 percent of the earnings over the five-year period.
c. Small, regular dividend of $0.50 per share plus a year-end extra when the profits in any year exceed $1,500,000. The year-end extra dividend will equal 50 percent of profits exceeding $1,500,000.

YEAR	PROFITS AFTER TAXES
1	$1,000,000
2	2,000,000
3	1,600,000
4	900,000
5	3,000,000

17-2A. (*Flotation costs and issue size*) Your firm needs to raise $10 million. Assuming that flotation costs are expected to be $15 per share and that the market price of the stock is $120, how many shares would have to be issued? What is the dollar size of the issue?

17-3A. (*Flotation costs and issue size*) If flotation costs for a common stock issue are 18 percent, how large must the issue be so that the firm will net $5,800,000? If the stock sells for $85 per share, how many shares must be issued?

17-4A. (*Residual dividend theory*) Terra Cotta finances new investments by 40 percent debt and 60 percent equity. The firm needs $640,000 for financing new investments. If retained earnings available for reinvestment equal $400,000, how much money will be available for dividends in accordance with the residual dividend theory?

17-5A. (*Stock dividend*) RCB has 2 million shares of common stock outstanding. Net income is $550,000, and the P/E ratio for the stock is 10. Management is planning a 20 percent stock dividend. What will be the price of the stock after the stock dividend? If an investor owns 100 shares prior to the stock dividend, does the total value of his or her shares change? Explain.

17-6A. (*Dividends in perfect markets*) The management of Harris, Inc., is considering two dividend policies for the years 1996 and 1997, one and two years away. In 1998, the management is planning to liquidate the firm. One plan would pay a dividend of $2.50 in 1996 and 1997 and a liquidating dividend of $45.75 in 1998. The alternative would be to pay out $4.25 in dividends in 1996, $4.75 in dividends in 1997, and a final dividend of $40.66 in 1998. The required rate of return for the common stockholders is 18 percent. Management is concerned about the effect of the two dividend streams on the value of the common stock.

a. Assuming perfect markets, what would be the effect?
b. What factors in the real world might change your conclusion reached in part (a)?

17-7A. (*Long-term residual dividend policy*) Stetson Manufacturing, Inc., has projected its investment opportunities over a five-year planning horizon. The cost of each year's investment and the amount of internal funds available for reinvestment for that year is as follows. The firm's debt-equity mix is 35 percent debt and 65 percent equity. There are currently 100,000 shares of common stock outstanding.

a. What would be the dividend each year if the residual dividend theory were used on a year-to-year basis?
b. What target stable dividend can Stetson establish by using the long-term residual dividend theory over the future planning horizon?
c. Why might a residual dividend policy applied to the five years as opposed to individual years be preferable?

YEAR	COST OF INVESTMENTS	INTERNAL FUNDS AVAILABLE FOR REINVESTMENT OR FOR DIVIDENDS
1	$350,000	$250,000
2	475,000	450,000
3	200,000	600,000
4	980,000	650,000
5	600,000	390,000

17-8A. (*Stock split*) You own 5 percent of the Trexco Corporation's common stock, which recently sold for $98 prior to a planned two-for-one stock split announcement. Before the split there are 25,000 shares of common stock outstanding.

a. Relative to now, what will be your financial position after the stock split? (Assume the stock price falls proportionately.)
b. The executive vice-president in charge of finance believes the price will only fall 40 percent after the split because she feels the price is above the optimal price range. If she is correct, what will be your net gain?

17-9A. (*Dividend policies*) The earnings for Crystal Cargo, Inc., have been predicted for the next five years and follow. There are 1 million shares outstanding. Determine the yearly dividend per share to be paid if the following policies are enacted:

a. Constant dividend payout ratio of 50 percent.
b. Stable dollar dividend targeted at 50 percent of the earnings over the five-year period.
c. Small, regular dividend of $0.50 per share plus a year-end extra when the profits in any year exceed $1,500,000. The year-end extra dividend will equal 50 percent of profits exceeding $1,500,000.

YEAR	PROFITS AFTER TAXES
1	$1,400,000
2	2,000,000
3	1,860,000
4	900,000
5	2,800,000

17-10A. (*Repurchase of stock*) The Dunn Corporation is planning to pay dividends of $500,000. There are 250,000 shares outstanding, with an earnings per share of $5. The stock should sell for $50 after the ex-dividend date. If instead of paying a dividend, management decides to repurchase stock:

- **a.** What should be the repurchase price?
- **b.** How many shares should be repurchased?
- **c.** What if the repurchase price is set below or above your suggested price in part (a)?
- **d.** If you own 100 shares, would you prefer that the company pay the dividend or repurchase stock?

17-11A. (*Flotation costs and issue size*) D. Butler, Inc., needs to raise $14 million. Assuming that the market price of the firm's stock is $95 and flotation costs are 10 percent of the market price, how many shares would have to be issued? What is the dollar size of the issue?

17-12A. (*Residual dividend theory*) Martinez, Inc., finances new acquisitions with 70 percent debt and the rest in equity. The firm needs $1.2 million for a new acquisition. If retained earnings available for reinvestment are $450,000, how much money will be available for dividends according to the residual dividend theory?

17-13A. (*Stock split*) You own 20 percent of Rainy Corp., which recently sold for $86 before a planned two-for-one stock split announcement. Before the split there are 80,000 shares of common stock outstanding.

- **a.** What is your financial position before the split, and what will it be after the stock split? (Assume the stock falls proportionately.)
- **b.** Your stockbroker believes the market will react positively to the split and that the price will fall only 45 percent after the split. If she is correct, what will be your net gain?

WEB WORKS

17-1WW. As was mentioned in this chapter, the "Jobs and Growth Tax Relief Reconciliation Act of 2003" included important changes in the tax code that relate to corporate dividend policy and the preference for investors for capital gains income relative to dividend income. Standard & Poor's provided a very concise, yet useful, three-page summary of these provisions that was provided on the Franklin, Templeton Investments Web site. Visit that site at **www.franklintempleton.com/retail/jsp_cm/corp/articles/common/ma_2003_taxact.jsp**. What specific changes contained in the 2003 Tax Act might shift investors' preferences toward cash dividends and what would you forecast the effect would be on dividend payout ratios?

17-2WW. Stock repurchase plans, as discussed in this chapter, have become a rather common financial policy activity within corporate America. IBM is one well-known firm that has had a long history of a vigorous repurchase program. You can review management's discussion of the IBM repurchase plan at **www.IBM.com** and find the firms' annual report for 2002. Page 55 of that report will give you details, for example, on how much IBM spent on common stock repurchases in the 2002 fourth quarter, and how many fewer shares were left outstanding over the year due to the repurchase program.

INTEGRATIVE PROBLEM

The following article appeared in the July 2, 1995, issue of the *Dallas Morning News*. Scott Burns, the author, argues the case for the importance of dividends.

> Let us now praise the lowly dividend.
>
> Insignificant to some. Small potatoes to others. An irksome sign of tax liability to many. However characterized, dividends are experiencing yet another round of defamation on Wall Street.

Why pay out dividends, the current argument goes, when a dollar of dividend can be retained as a dollar of book value that the market will value at two, three, or four dollars? With the average stock now selling at more than three times book value, investors should prefer companies that retain earnings rather than pay them out, even if they do nothing more with the money than repurchase shares.

The New Wisdom

Instead, the New Wisdom says, the investor should go for companies that retain earnings, reinvest them, and try to maximize shareholder value. Dividends should be avoided in the pursuit of long-term capital gains.

The only problem with this reasoning is that we've heard it before. And always at market tops.

- We heard it in the late 1960s as stock prices soared and dividend yields fell.
- We heard it again in the early 1970s as investors fixated on the "Nifty Fifty" and analysts calmly projected that with growth companies yielding 1 percent or less, the most important part of the return was the certainty of 20 percent annual earnings growth.
- And we're hearing it now, with stock prices hitting new highs each day. The Standard & Poor's 500 Index, for instance, is up 19.7 percent since December 31, the equivalent of more than seven years of dividends at the current yield of 2.6 percent.

Tilting the Yield

Significantly, we didn't hear that dividends were irrelevant in the late 1970s, as stock valuations moved to new lows. At that time, portfolio managers talked about "yield tilt"—running a portfolio with a bias toward dividend return to offset some of the risk of continuing stock market decline. Indeed, many of the best performing funds in the late 1970s were Equity-Income funds, the funds that seek above-average dividend income.

You can understand how much dividends contribute to long-term returns by taking a look at the performance of a major index, with and without dividend reinvestment. If you had invested $10,000 in the S&P's 500 Index in January 1982 and taken all dividends in cash, your original investment would have grown to $37,475 by the end of 1994.

It doesn't get much better than that.

The gain clocks a compound annual return of 10.7 percent, and total gain of $27,475. During the same period you would have collected an additional $14,244 in dividends.

Not a trivial sum, either.

In other words, during one of the biggest bull markets in history, unreinvested dividend income accounted for more than one-third of your total return.

If you had reinvested those dividends in additional stock, the final score would be even better: $60,303. The appreciation of your original investment would have been $27,475 while the growth from reinvested dividends would have been $22,828. Nearly half—45 percent—of your total return came from reinvested dividends. And this happened during a stellar period of rising stock prices.

Now consider the same investment during a period of misery. If you had invested $10,000 in the S&P's Index stocks in January 1968, your investment would have grown to only $14,073 over the next 13 years, a gain of only $4,073. During much of that time, the value of your original investment would have been less than $10,000. Dividends during the period would have totaled $7,088—substantially more than stock appreciation. Reinvested, the same dividends would have grown to $9,705, helping your original investment grow to $23,778.

In a period of major ups and downs that many investors don't like to remember, dividends accounted for 70 percent of total return (see accompanying chart).

We could fiddle with these figures any number of ways. We could reduce the value of dividends by calculating income taxes. We could raise it by starting with the Dow Jones Industrial Average stocks, which tend to have higher dividends. But the point here is very simple: Whether you spend them or reinvest them, dividends are always an important part of the return on common stock.

A Close Look at Dividends in Two Markets

ANATOMY OF THE BULL MARKET OF 1982–1994		
Original investment		$10,000
Gain on original investment		$27,475
Total dividends	$14,244	
Gain on reinvested dividends	$ 8,584	
Total gain from dividends		$22,828
Total		**$60,303**
Compound annualized return equals 14.8%; 45% from dividends		

ANATOMY OF A BEAR MARKET, 1968–1980		
Original investment		$10,000
Gain on original investment		$ 4,073
Total dividends	$ 7,088	
Gain on reinvested dividends	$ 2,617	
Total gain from dividends		$ 9,705
Total		**$23,778**
Compound annualized return equals 6.9%; 70% from dividends.		

Source: Franklin/Templeton Group Hypothetical Illustration Program.

Based on your reading of this chapter, evaluate what Burns is saying. Do you agree or disagree with him? Why?

Source: Reprinted by permission of the *Dallas Morning News*.

STUDY PROBLEMS (SET B)

17-1B. (*Flotation costs and issue size*) Your firm needs to raise $12 million. Assuming that flotation costs are expected to be $17 per share and that the market price of the stock is $115, how many shares would have to be issued? What is the dollar size of the issue?

17-2B. (*Flotation costs and issue size*) If flotation costs for a common stock issue are 14 percent, how large must the issue be so that the firm will net $6,100,000? If the stock sells for $76 per share, how many shares must be issued?

17-3B. (*Residual dividend theory*) Steven Miller finances new investments by 35 percent debt and 65 percent equity. The firm needs $650,000 for financing new investments. If retained earnings available for reinvestment equal $375,000, how much money will be available for dividends in accordance with the residual dividend theory?

17-4B. (*Stock dividend*) DCA has 2.5 million shares of common stock outstanding. Net income is $600,000, and the P/E ratio for the stock is 10. Management is planning an 18 percent stock dividend. What will be the price of the stock after the stock dividend? If an investor owns 120 shares before the stock dividend, does the total value of his or her shares change? Explain.

17-5B. (*Dividends in perfect markets*) The management of Montford, Inc., is considering two dividend policies for the years 1997 and 1998, one and two years away. In 1999, the management is planning to liquidate the firm. One plan would pay a dividend of $2.55 in 1997 and 1998 and a liquidating dividend of $45.60 in 1999. The alternative would be to pay out $4.35 in dividends in 1997, $4.70 in dividends in 1998, and a final dividend of $40.62 in 1999. The required rate of return for the common stockholders is 17 percent. Management is concerned about the effect of the two dividend streams on the value of the common stock.

- **a.** Assuming perfect markets, what would be the effect?
- **b.** What factors in the real world might change your conclusion reached in part (a)?

17-6B. (*Long-term residual dividend policy*) Wells Manufacturing, Inc., has projected its investment opportunities over a five-year planning horizon. The cost of each year's investment and the amount of internal funds available for reinvestment for that year follow. The firm's debt-equity mix is 40 percent debt and 60 percent equity. There are currently 125,000 shares of common stock outstanding.

a. What would be the dividend each year if the residual dividend theory were used on a year-to-year basis?
b. What target stable dividend can Wells establish by using the long-term residual dividend theory over the future planning horizon?
c. Why might a residual dividend policy applied to the five years as opposed to individual years be preferable?

YEAR	COST OF INVESTMENTS	INTERNAL FUNDS AVAILABLE FOR REINVESTMENT OR FOR DIVIDENDS
1	$360,000	$225,000
2	450,000	440,000
3	230,000	600,000
4	890,000	650,000
5	600,000	400,000

17-7B. (*Stock split*) You own 8 percent of the Standlee Corporation's common stock, which most recently sold for $98 before a planned two-for-one stock split announcement. Before the split there are 30,000 shares of common stock outstanding.

a. Relative to now, what will be your financial position after the stock split? (Assume the stock price falls proportionately.)
b. The executive vice-president in charge of finance believes the price will only fall 45 percent after the split because she thinks the price is above the optimal price range. If she is correct, what will be your net gain?

17-8B. (*Dividend policies*) The earnings for Carlson Cargo, Inc., have been predicted for the next five years and are listed in the following table. There are 1 million shares outstanding. Determine the yearly dividend per share to be paid if the following policies are enacted:

a. Constant dividend payout ratio of 40 percent.
b. Stable dollar dividend targeted at 40 percent of the earnings over the five-year period.
c. Small, regular dividend of $0.50 per share plus a year-end extra when the profits in any year exceed $1,500,000. The year-end extra dividend will equal 50 percent of profits exceeding $1,500,000.

YEAR	PROFITS AFTER TAXES
1	$1,500,000
2	2,000,000
3	1,750,000
4	950,000
5	2,500,000

17-9B. (*Repurchase of stock*) The B. Phillips Corporation is planning to pay dividends of $550,000. There are 275,000 shares outstanding, with an earnings per share of $6. The stock should sell for $45 after the ex-dividend date. If instead of paying a dividend, management decides to repurchase stock:

a. What should be the repurchase price?
b. How many shares should be repurchased?
c. What if the repurchase price is set below or above your suggested price in part (a)?
d. If you own 100 shares, would you prefer that the company pay the dividend or repurchase stock?

17-10B. (*Flotation costs and issue size*) D. B. Fool, Inc., needs to raise $16 million. Assuming that the market price of the firm's stock is $100 and flotation costs are 12 percent of the market price, how many shares would have to be issued? What is the dollar size of the issue?

17-11B. (*Residual dividend theory*) Maness, Inc., finances new acquisitions with 35 percent in equity and the rest in debt. The firm needs \$1.5 million for a new acquisition. If retained earnings available for reinvestment are \$525,000, how much money will be available for dividends according to the residual dividend theory?

17-12B. (*Stock split*) You own 25 percent of the Star Corporation, which recently sold for \$90 before a planned two-for-one stock split announcement. Before the split there are 90,000 shares of common stock outstanding.

a. What is your financial position before the split, and what will it be after the stock split? (Assume the stock falls proportionately.)

b. Your stockbroker believes the market will react positively to the split and that the price will fall only 45 percent after the split. If she is correct, what will be your net gain?

SELF-TEST SOLUTIONS

ST-1.
$$\text{Dividend per share} = 35\% \times \$8.20 = \$2.87$$

Dividends:

$$1 \text{ year} = \$2.87(1 + 0.12) = \$3.21$$

$$5 \text{ years} = \$2.87(1 + 0.12)^5 = \$2.87(1.762) = \$5.06$$

ST-2. a. Investments A, B, and C will be accepted, requiring \$1,150,000 in total financing. Therefore, 40 percent of \$1,150,000, or \$460,000, in new debt will be needed, and common equity will have to provide \$690,000. The remainder of the \$750,000 internal funds will be \$60,000, which will be paid out in dividends.

b. Assuming a 10 percent cost of capital, all four investments would be accepted, requiring total financing of \$1,550,000. Equity would provide 60 percent, or \$930,000 of the total, which would not leave any funds to be paid out in dividends. New common would have to be issued.

ST-3. a. If a 15 percent stock dividend is issued, the financial statement would appear as follows:

ROBSON CORPORATION	
Debt	\$1,800,000
Common	
Par (\$2 par; 115,000 shares)	230,000
Paid-in capital	670,000
Retained earnings	\$ 600,000
	\$3,300,000

b. A two-for-one split would result in a 100 percent increase in the number of shares. Because the total par value remains at \$200,000, the new par value per share is \$1 (\$200,000 ÷ 200,000 shares). The new financial statement would be as follows:

ROBSON CORPORATION	
Debt	\$1,800,000
Common	
Par (\$1 par; 200,000 shares)	200,000
Paid-in capital	400,000
Retained earnings	900,000
	\$3,300,000

PART 5

Working-Capital Management and Special Topics in Finance

CHAPTER 18
WORKING-CAPITAL MANAGEMENT AND SHORT-TERM FINANCING

CHAPTER 19
CASH AND MARKETABLE SECURITIES MANAGEMENT

CHAPTER 20
ACCOUNTS RECEIVABLE AND INVENTORY MANAGEMENT

LEARNING OBJECTIVES

After reading this chapter, you should be able to

1. List the determinants of a firm's net working capital and explain the risk-return trade-off involved in managing net working capital.
2. List the advantages and disadvantages of using current liabilities to finance a firm's working-capital requirements.
3. Describe the hedging principle or principle of self-liquidating debt, and the relevance of permanent and temporary sources of financing.
4. Calculate a firm's cash conversion cycle and interpret its component parts.
5. Calculate the effective cost of short-term credit.
6. List and describe the basic sources of short-term credit.
7. Describe the currency exchange risks faced by multinational firms when managing working capital.

CHAPTER 18

Working-Capital Management and Short-Term Financing

U.S. corporations, on average, invest about 15 cents in current assets for each $1 of sales. This is only an average, and pretty dramatic variability exists across firms. For example, Dell Computer Corporation is viewed by many as a master at managing its working capital, yet in 1993 Dell had invested $0.46 per dollar of sales in current assets compared to $0.80 a decade later in 2002. What this comparison fails to reflect is the fact that managing a firm's working capital is about more than managing the firm's current asset accounts. Specifically, working capital management is concerned with the management of the firm's net working capital or the difference in the firm's current assets and current liabilities. When we compare Dell's *net* working capital to sales ratio for 1993 with 2002, the improvement in the firm's management of working capital is reflected in the fact that in 1993 Dell invested roughly $0.22 per dollar of revenues in *net* working capital, and by the end of the decade it was investing only $0.04. American Standard is yet another example of a firm that manages its working capital very well. Facing static sales growth and a high level of interest payments from junk bonds it had issued to stave off a hostile takeover in 1989, the company's chairman, Emmanuel Kampouris, introduced a strategy aimed at reducing the firm's $735 million in net working capital to zero by 1996. The idea was to deliver goods and bill customers more rapidly so that customer payments were sufficient to pay for minimal stocks of inventories. Kampouris sought to accomplish this ambitious goal through implementation of a lean manufacturing system known as demand flow technology. Under this system, plants manufacture products as customers order them. Suppliers deliver straight to the assembly line, thus reducing stocks of parts, and plants ship the products as soon as they are completed. The system dramatically reduces inventories of both parts and finished goods. American Standard has reduced its inventories by more than one-half, down to $326 million, within three years. Thus, American Standard invests

CHAPTER PREVIEW

Chapter 18 is the first of three chapters that address short-term financing problems. Short-term financing decisions relate to the management of current assets, which, by definition, are converted into cash within a period of one year or less and current liabilities, which must be repaid in one year or less. This topic contrasts with capital budgeting, which is a long-term financing issue. We now want to look at short-term investing and financing issues. Short-term financing issues include such things as making sure that the firm has sufficient cash to pay its bills on time, managing the firm's collections of accounts receivable, extending credit to the firm's customers, and determining the proper amount and mix of short-term borrowing. Chapter 18 provides the framework for analyzing how much short-term financing the firm should use and what specific sources of short-term financing the firm should use. In Chapter 19, we discuss the management of cash and marketable securities followed in Chapter 20 by the discussion of managing the firm's investments in accounts receivable and inventories.

This chapter will emphasize these principles: **Principle 1: The Risk-Return Trade-Off—We won't take on additional risk unless we expect to be compensated with additional return; Principle 2: The Time Value of Money—A dollar received today is worth more than a dollar received in the future; Principle 3: Cash—Not Profits—Is King;** and **Principle 4: Incremental Cash Flows—It's only what changes that counts.**

only five cents out of each sales dollar in working capital compared to the norm of 15 cents. By saving interest payments on supplies, the company has increased its cash flow by $60 million a year.

Source: Shawn Tully, "Raiding a Company's Hidden Cash," *Fortune* (August 22, 1994): 82–87.

Objective 1

MANAGING CURRENT ASSETS AND LIABILITIES

Working capital
The firm's total investment in current assets or assets that it expects to be converted into cash within a year or less.

Net working capital
The difference between the firm's current assets and its current liabilities. Frequently when the term *working capital* is used, it is actually intended to mean *net working capital.*

Short-term financing problems arise in the management of a firm's investments in current assets (sometimes referred to as **working capital**) and its use of current liabilities. The firm's **net working capital** (which is the difference in a firm's current assets and its current liabilities) at any particular time provides a very useful summary measure of the firm's short-term financing decisions. As the firm's net working capital decreases, the firm's profitability tends to rise. However, this increase in profitability comes only at the expense of an increased risk of illiquidity. Consequently, short-term financing decisions impact a firm's net working capital and consequently entail a risk-return trade-off.

WORKING-CAPITAL MANAGEMENT AND THE RISK-RETURN TRADE-OFF

Figure 18-1 illustrates the risk-return trade-off that arises in the management of a firm's net working capital. A firm can increase its net working capital by adding to its current assets relative to its current liabilities (for example, holding larger levels of inventories or marketable securities) or by decreasing its current liabilities relative to its current assets (for example, by using long-term sources of finance such as bonds rather than bank loans that must be repaid within the year).

Consider first the effects of increasing a firm's net working capital by holding larger investments in marketable securities and inventories without changing the firm's use of current liabilities. Other things remaining the same, this has the effect of increasing the firm's liquidity. That is, with the additional marketable securities, the firm has a ready source of funds should it experience an unexpected shortfall in its cash flow. In addition, the added inventories reduce the chance of production stoppages, and the loss of sales from inventory shortages. However, because these additional current asset investments earn very low returns, firm profitability is reduced.

Now consider the effects of reducing a firm's net working capital by substituting short-term financing such as notes payable that must be repaid in one year or less for long-term sources such as bonds. This has the net effects pointed out in Figure 18-1. The use of short-term financing increases firm profitability for two reasons. First, short-term financing usually carries a lower rate of interest than does long-term financing. In addition, when short-term sources of financing are used to finance a firm's seasonal needs for

FIGURE 18-1 The Risk-Return Trade-Off in Managing a Firm's Net Working Capital

	Firm Profitability	Firm Liquidity
Investing in additional marketable securities and inventories	Lower	Higher
Increasing the use of short- versus long-term sources of financing	Higher	Lower

financing (such as the buildup of inventories for a retail firm prior to the Christmas season), the firm can repay the funds after the seasonal need has expired, thus requiring the firm to pay interest only during the periods when the funds are needed. If long-term financing is used, the firm will end up holding excess cash during those times of the year when seasonal financing needs are zero, thus incurring additional borrowing costs and reducing overall profitability.

Using short-term financing increases a firm's risk of not being able to pay its bills on time, or the risk of illiquidity. This corresponds to the commonsense notion that short-term financing must be repaid more frequently than long-term financing, thus exposing the firm to additional risk of having the financing come due at a time when its financial condition might make it difficult to repay the loan.

BACK TO THE PRINCIPLES

Working-capital decisions provide a classic example of the risk-return nature of financial decision making. Increasing the firm's net working capital (current assets less current liabilities) reduces the risk that the firm will not be able to pay its bills on time (i.e., the risk of illiquidity) but, at the same time, reduces the overall profitability of the firm. Thus, working-capital decisions involve ***Principle 1: The Risk-Return Trade-Off—We won't take on additional risk unless we expect to be compensated with additional return.***

CONCEPT CHECK

1. What is net working capital and how does it impact firm profitability and liquidity?
2. What are the benefits and costs of increasing net working capital through the addition of current assets?

Objective 2

FINANCING WORKING CAPITAL WITH CURRENT LIABILITIES

ADVANTAGES OF CURRENT LIABILITIES: THE RETURN

Current liabilities offer the firm a more flexible source of financing than do long-term liabilities or equity. They can be used to match the timing of a firm's needs for short-term financing. If, for example, a firm needs funds for a three-month period during each year to finance a seasonal expansion in inventories, then a three-month loan can provide substantial cost savings over a long-term loan (even if the interest rate on short-term financing should be higher). The use of long-term debt in this situation involves borrowing for the entire year rather than for the period when the funds are needed, which increases the amount of interest the firm must pay. This brings us to the second advantage generally associated with the use of short-term financing: interest cost.

In general, interest rates on short-term debt are lower than on long-term debt for a given borrower.

DISADVANTAGES OF CURRENT LIABILITIES: THE RISK

The use of current liabilities, or short-term debt, as opposed to long-term debt subjects the firm to a greater risk of illiquidity for two reasons. First, short-term debt, due to its very nature, must be repaid or rolled over more often, and so it increases the possibility that the firm's financial condition might deteriorate to a point where the needed funds might not be available.[1]

A second disadvantage of short-term debt is the uncertainty of interest costs from year to year. For example, a firm borrowing during a six-month period each year to finance a seasonal expansion in current assets might incur a different rate of interest each year. This rate reflects the current rate of interest at the time of the loan, as well as the lender's perception of the firm's riskiness. If fixed rate long-term debt were used, the interest cost would be known for the entire period of the loan agreement.

CONCEPT CHECK

1. How does investing more heavily in current assets while not increasing the firm's current liabilities decrease both the firm's risk and the expected return on its investments?
2. How does the use of current liabilities enhance firm profitability and also increase the firm's risk of default on its financial obligations?

Objective 3

APPROPRIATE LEVEL OF WORKING CAPITAL

Hedging principle (principle of self-liquidating debt) Financing maturity should follow the cash-flow-producing characteristics of the asset being financed.

Managing the firm's net working capital (its liquidity) has been shown to involve simultaneous and interrelated decisions regarding investment in current assets and use of current liabilities. Fortunately, a guiding principle exists that can be used as a benchmark for the firm's working-capital policies: the **hedging principle**, or **principle of self-liquidating debt**. This principle provides managers with a guide to the maintenance of a level of liquidity sufficient for the firm to meet its maturing obligations on time.[2]

HEDGING PRINCIPLES

Very simply, the hedging principle involves *matching* the cash-flow-generating characteristics of an asset with the maturity of the source of financing used to finance its acquisitions. For example, a seasonal expansion in inventories, according to the hedging principle, should be financed with a short-term loan or current liability. The rationale underlying the rule is straightforward. Funds are needed for a limited period and, when that time has passed, the cash needed to repay the loan will be generated by the sale of the extra inventory items. Obtaining the needed funds from a long-term source (longer than one year) would mean that the firm would still have the funds after the inventories they helped finance had been sold. In this case, the firm would have "excess" liquidity, which it either holds in cash or invests in low-yield marketable securities until the seasonal increase in inventories occurs again and the funds are needed. The result would be an overall lowering of firm profits.

[1] The dangers of such a policy are readily apparent in the experiences of firms that have been forced into bankruptcy. Penn Central, for example, had $80 million in short-term debt that it was unable to refinance (roll over) at the time of its bankruptcy.

[2] A value-maximizing approach to the management of the firm's liquidity involves assessing the value of the benefits derived from increasing the firm's investment in liquid assets and weighing them against the added costs to the firm's owners resulting from investing in low-yield current assets. Unfortunately, the benefits derived from increased liquidity relate to the expected costs of bankruptcy to the firm's owners, and these costs are "unmeasurable" by existing technology. Thus a "valuation" approach to liquidity management exists only in the theoretical realm.

Consider an example in which a firm purchases a new conveyor belt system, which is expected to produce cash savings to the firm by eliminating the need for two laborers and, consequently, their salaries. This amounts to an annual savings of $14,000, whereas the conveyor belt costs $150,000 to install and will last 20 years. If the firm chooses to finance this asset with a one-year note, then it will not be able to repay the loan from the $14,000 cash flow generated by the asset. In accordance with the hedging principle, the firm should finance the asset with a source of financing that more nearly matches the expected life and cash-flow-generating characteristics of the asset. In this case, a 15- to 20-year loan would be more appropriate.

PERMANENT AND TEMPORARY ASSETS

The notion of *maturity matching* in the hedging principle can be most easily understood when we think in terms of the distinction between **permanent** and **temporary asset investments** as opposed to the more traditional fixed and current asset categories. A permanent investment in an asset is an investment that the firm expects to hold for a period longer than one year. Note that we are referring to the period the firm plans to hold an investment, not the useful life of the asset. For example, permanent investments are made in the firm's minimum level of current assets, as well as in its fixed assets. Temporary asset investments, however, are composed of current assets that will be liquidated and not replaced within the current year. Thus, some part of the firm's current assets is permanent and the remainder is temporary. For example, a seasonal increase in inventories is a temporary investment because the buildup in inventories will be eliminated when it is no longer needed.

Permanent asset investment
An investment in an asset that the firm expects to hold for the foreseeable future, whether fixed assets or current assets. For example, the minimum level of inventory the firm plans to hold for the foreseeable future is a permanent investment.

Temporary asset investment
Investments in assets that the firm plans to sell (liquidate) within a period no longer than one year. Although temporary investments can be made in fixed assets, this is not the usual case. Temporary investments generally are made in inventories and receivables.

TEMPORARY, PERMANENT, AND SPONTANEOUS SOURCES OF FINANCING

Because total assets must always equal the sum of temporary, permanent, and spontaneous sources of financing, the hedging approach provides the financial manager with the basis for determining the sources of financing to use at any point.

Now, what constitutes a temporary, permanent, or spontaneous source of financing? **Temporary sources of financing** consist of current liabilities. Short-term notes payable is the most common example of a temporary source of financing. Notes payable include unsecured bank loans, commercial paper, and loans secured by accounts receivable and inventories. **Permanent sources of financing** include intermediate-term loans, long-term debt, preferred stock, and common equity.

Spontaneous sources of financing consist of trade credit and other accounts payable that arise in the firm's day-to-day operations. For example, as the firm acquires materials for its inventories, trade credit is often made available spontaneously or on demand from the firm's suppliers. Trade credit appears on the firm's balance sheet as accounts payable, and the size of the accounts payable balance varies directly with the firm's purchases of inventory items. In turn, inventory purchases are related to anticipated sales. Thus, part of the financing needed by the firm is spontaneously provided in the form of trade credit.

In addition to trade credit, wages, and salaries payable, accrued interest and accrued taxes also provide valuable sources of spontaneous financing. These liabilities accrue throughout the period until they are paid. For example, if a firm has a wage expense of $10,000 a week and pays its employees monthly, then its employees effectively provide financing equal to $10,000 by the end of the first week following a payday, $20,000 by the end of the second week, and so forth. Because these expenses generally arise in direct conjunction with the firm's ongoing operations, they too are referred to as *spontaneous*.

Temporary sources of financing
Another term for current liabilities.

Permanent sources of financing
Sources of financing that do not mature or come due within the year, including intermediate-term debt, long-term debt, preferred stock, and common stock.

Spontaneous sources of financing
Trade credit and other sources of accounts payable that arise in the firm's day-to-day operations.

FIGURE 18-2 Hedging Principle: Financing Strategy

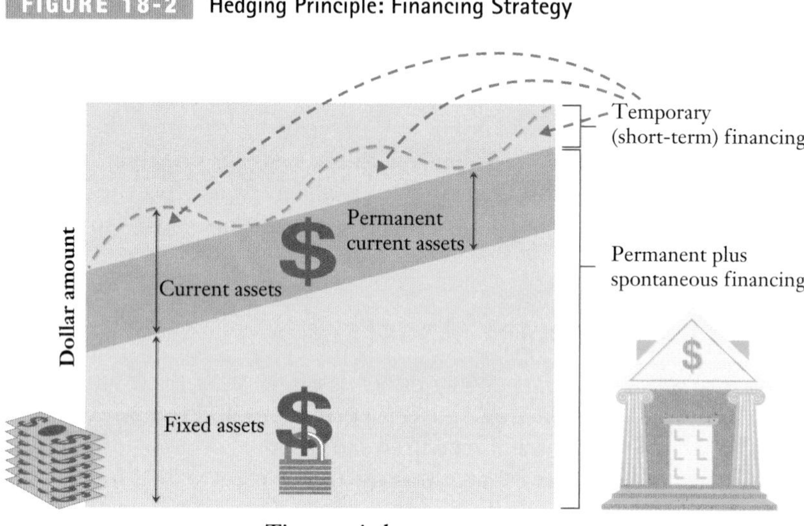

Hedging Principle: Graphic Illustration

The hedging principle can now be stated very succinctly: *Asset needs of the firm not financed by spontaneous sources should be financed in accordance with this rule: Permanent asset investments are financed with permanent sources, and temporary investments are financed with temporary sources.*

The hedging principle is depicted in Figure 18-2. Total assets are broken down into temporary and permanent asset investment categories. The firm's permanent investment in assets is financed by the use of permanent sources of financing (intermediate- and long-term debt, preferred stock, and common equity) or spontaneous sources (trade credit and other accounts payable). For illustration purposes, spontaneous sources of financing are treated as if their amount were fixed. In practice, of course, spontaneous sources of financing fluctuate with the firm's purchases and its expenditures for wages, salaries, taxes, and other items that are paid on a delayed basis. Its temporary investment in assets is financed with temporary (short-term) debt.

To summarize, note that the optimal financing mix involves the use of a combination of short- and long-term sources of financing. The particular mix according to the hedging principle relies on the nature of the firm's needs for financing—that is, whether the need is permanent or temporary.

BACK TO THE PRINCIPLES

Although current liabilities provide financing for periods less than one year, the time value of money is still relevant and should be incorporated into our estimation of their cost. Thus, estimating the cost of short-term credit provides yet another case where we rely on ***Principle 2: The Time Value of Money—A dollar received today is worth more than a dollar received in the future.*** *In addition, as we estimate the cost of credit, we will focus on cash received and paid. So we also rely on* ***Principle 3: Cash—Not Profits—Is King.*** *Finally, we must be careful to consider all the cash flow consequences of the use of a particular source of short-term credit. In particular, we are interested in all the incremental cash inflows and outflows associated with the financing source. This reflects our use of* ***Principle 4: Incremental Cash Flows—It's only what changes that counts.***

CONCEPT CHECK

1. What is the hedging principle, or principle of self-liquidating debt?
2. What are some examples of permanent and temporary investments in current assets?
3. Is trade credit a permanent, temporary, or spontaneous source of financing? Explain.

CASH CONVERSION CYCLE

Objective 4

Because firms vary widely with respect to their ability to manage their net working capital, there exists a need for an overall measure of effectiveness. An increasingly popular method for evaluating a firm's effective management of its working capital takes the approach that the firm's objective should be to minimize working capital subject to the constraint that it has sufficient working capital to support the firm's operations.

Minimizing working capital is accomplished by speeding up the collection of cash from sales, increasing inventory turns, and slowing down the disbursement of cash. We can incorporate all of these factors in a single measure called the *cash conversion cycle.*

MEASURING WORKING CAPITAL EFFICIENCY

The cash conversion cycle, or CCC, is simply the sum of days of sales outstanding and days of sales in inventory less days of payables outstanding:

$$\begin{matrix}\text{cash} \\ \text{conversion (CCC)} \\ \text{cycle}\end{matrix} = \begin{matrix}\text{days of} \\ \text{sales (DSO)} \\ \text{outstanding}\end{matrix} + \begin{matrix}\text{days of} \\ \text{sales in (DSI)} \\ \text{inventory}\end{matrix} - \begin{matrix}\text{days of} \\ \text{payable (DPO)} \\ \text{outstanding}\end{matrix}$$

We calculate days of sales outstanding as follows:

$$\begin{matrix}\text{days of} \\ \text{sales (DSO)} \\ \text{outstanding}\end{matrix} = \frac{\text{accounts receivable}}{\text{sales/365}} \quad \textbf{(18-1)}$$

Recall from Chapter 4 that DSO can also be thought of as the average age of the firm's accounts receivable or the average collection period.

Days of sales in inventory is defined as follows:

$$\begin{matrix}\text{days of} \\ \text{sales in (DSI)} \\ \text{inventory}\end{matrix} = \frac{\text{inventories}}{\text{cost of goods sold/365}} \quad \textbf{(18-2)}$$

We actually calculate cost of goods sold/365 rather than sales/365 since this "per day" amount is compared to inventories, which are carried on the balance sheet at cost.

Note that DSI can also be thought of as the average age of the firm's inventory; that is, the average number of days that a dollar of inventory is held by the firm.

Days of payables outstanding is defined as follows:

$$\begin{matrix}\text{days of} \\ \text{payables (DPO)} \\ \text{outstanding}\end{matrix} = \frac{\text{accounts payable}}{\text{cost of goods sold/365}} \quad \textbf{(18-3)}$$

This ratio indicates the average age, in days, of the firm's accounts payable.

To illustrate the use of the CCC metric, consider Dell Computer Corporation. In 1993 Dell's CCC was 36.74 days (Table 18-1). By 2002, Dell had reduced this number to

TABLE 18-1 Determinants of Dell Computer Corporation's Cash Conversion Cycle for 1993–2002

cash conversion cycle (CCC) = days of sales outstanding (DSO) + days of sales in inventory (DSI) – days of payables outstanding (DPO).

	1993	1994	1995	1996	1997	1998	1999	2000	2001	2002
Days of sales outstanding (DSO)	48.17	49.17	49.14	42.96	37.79	34.88	39.14	36.76	31.46	29.82
Days of sales in inventory (DSI)	50.08	40.28	34.16	31.01	20.25	9.13	6.49	6.01	5.65	4.80
Days of payables outstanding (DPO)	61.51	44.88	57.91	38.73	63.71	62.00	61.16	63.49	60.99	72.22
Cash Conversion Cycle [CCC = DSO + DSI – DPO]	36.74	44.57	25.39	35.24	(5.67)	(17.99)	(15.53)	(20.72)	(23.88)	(37.59)

–37.59 days. How, you might ask, does a firm reduce its CCC below zero? The answer is through very aggressive management of its working capital. As Table 18-1 indicates, Dell achieved this phenomenal reduction in CCC primarily through very effective management of inventories (days of sales in inventories dropped from 50.08 in 1993 to 4.80 in 2002) and more favorable trade credit payment practices (days of payables outstanding increased from 61.51 in 1993 to 72.22 in 2002). Specifically, Dell, a direct marketer of personal computers, does not build a computer until an order is received. It purchases its supplies using trade credit. This business model results in minimal investment in inventories. Dell has obviously improved its working-capital management practices over the 1993–2002 period, as evidenced in Figure 18-3 where we compare Dell with Hewlett-Packard and Apple. The dramatic differences in CCC reflect both differences in business models (direct seller versus the use of more traditional channels of distribution involving resellers such as CompUSA, Best Buy, and Computer City) as well as the relative efficiency of the firm in managing inventories, receivables, and payables. However, it is obvious that Apple has now figured out how to manage its working capital very effectively, too.

CONCEPT CHECK

1. What three actions can a firm take to minimize net working capital?
2. Define *days of sales outstanding, days of sales in inventory,* and *days of payables outstanding.*

FIGURE 18-3 Cash Conversion Cycles for Apple, Dell Computers, and Hewlett-Packard: 1993–2001

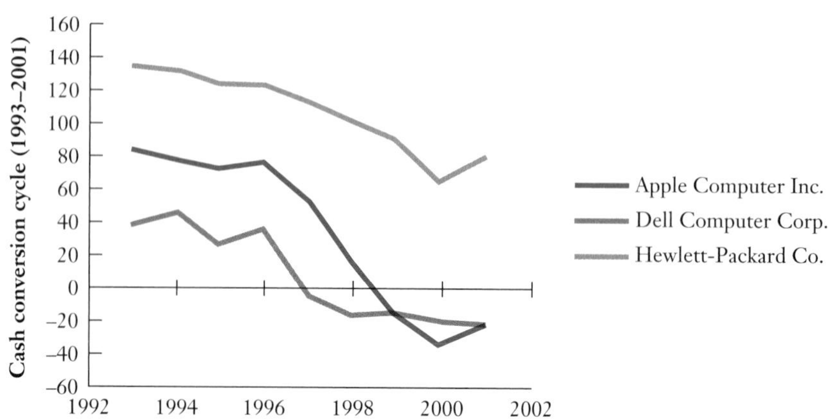

ESTIMATION OF THE COST OF SHORT-TERM CREDIT

Objective 5

There are a myriad of types of short-term financing sources. How is one to choose? A key factor is certainly the cost of credit.

APPROXIMATE COST-OF-CREDIT FORMULA

The procedure for estimating the cost of short-term credit is a very simple one and relies on the basic interest equation:

$$\text{interest} = \text{principal} \times \text{rate} \times \text{time} \quad \textbf{(18-4)}$$

where *interest* is the dollar amount of interest on a *principal* that is borrowed at some annual *rate* for a fraction of a year (represented by *time*). For example, a six-month loan for $1,000 at 8 percent interest would require an interest payment of $40:

$$\text{interest} = \$1{,}000 \times .08 \times 1/2 = \$40$$

We use this basic relationship to solve for the cost of a source of short-term financing, or the annual percentage rate (*APR*), where the interest amount, the principal sum, and the time period for financing are known. Thus, solving the basic interest equation for *APR* produces[3]

$$APR = \frac{\text{interest}}{\text{principal} \times \text{time}} \quad \textbf{(18-5)}$$

or

$$APR = \frac{\text{interest}}{\text{principal}} \times \frac{1}{\text{time}}$$

EXAMPLE: CALCULATING APR FOR A BANK LOAN

The SKC Corporation plans to borrow $1,000 for a 90-day period. At maturity, the firm will repay the $1,000 principal amount plus $30 interest. The effective annual rate of interest for the loan can be estimated using the *APR* equation, as follows:

$$APR = \frac{\$30}{\$1{,}000} \times \frac{1}{90/360}$$

$$= .03 \times \frac{360}{90} = .12 \text{ or } 12\%$$

The effective annual cost of funds provided by the loan is therefore 12 percent.

ANNUAL PERCENTAGE YIELD FORMULA

The simple *APR* calculation does not consider compound interest. To account for the influence of compounding, we can use the following equation:

$$APY = \left(1 + \frac{i}{m}\right)^m - 1 \quad \textbf{(18-6)}$$

[3] For ease of computation, we will assume a 30-day month and 360-day year in this chapter.

where *APY* is the annual percentage yield, *i* is the nominal rate of interest per year (12 percent in the previous example), and *m* is the number of compounding periods within a year [$m = 1/\text{time} = 1 \div (90/360) = 4$ in the preceding example]. Thus, the effective rate of interest on the example problem, considering compounding, is

$$APY = \left(1 + \frac{.12}{4}\right)^4 - 1 = .126 \text{ or } 12.6\%$$

Compounding effectively raises the cost of short-term credit. Because the differences between *APR* and *APY* are usually small, we use the simple interest version or *APR* to compute the cost of short-term credit.

CONCEPT CHECK

1. What is the fundamental interest equation that underlies that calculation of the cost of credit formula?
2. What is the annual percentage yield (*APY*) and why is it preferred to the annual percentage rate (*APR*)?

Objective 

SOURCES OF SHORT-TERM CREDIT

Secured and unsecured loans
Secured loans are backed by the pledge of specific assets as collateral whereas unsecured loans are only backed by the promise of the borrower to honor the loan commitment.

Short-term credit is offered by a wide variety of financial intermediaries in many different forms. For purposes of our review, we will find it useful to categorize them into two basic groups: unsecured and secured. **Unsecured loans** include all those sources that have as their security only the lender's faith in the ability of the borrower to repay the funds when due. Major sources of unsecured short-term credit include accrued wages and taxes, trade credit, unsecured bank loans, and commercial paper. **Secured loans** involve the pledge of specific assets as collateral in the event the borrower defaults in payment of principal or interest. Commercial banks, finance companies, and factors are the primary suppliers of secured credit. The principal sources of collateral are accounts receivable and inventories.

UNSECURED SOURCES: ACCRUED WAGES AND TAXES

Because most businesses pay their employees only periodically (weekly, biweekly, or monthly), firms accrue a wages payable account that is, in essence, a loan from their employees. For example, if the wage expense for the Appleton Manufacturing Company is $450,000 per week and it pays its employees monthly, then by the end of a four-week month, the firm will owe its employees $1.8 million in wages for services they have already performed during the month. Consequently, the employees finance their own efforts through waiting a full month for payment.

Similarly, firms generally make quarterly income tax payments for their estimated quarterly tax liability. This means that the firm has the use of the tax monies it owes based on quarterly profits up through the end of the quarter. In addition, the firm pays sales taxes and withholding (income) taxes for its employees on a deferred basis. The longer the period that the firm holds the tax payments, the greater the amount of financing they provide.

Note that these sources of financing *rise and fall spontaneously* with the level of firm sales. That is, as the firm's sales increase so do its labor expenses, sales taxes collected, and income taxes. Consequently, these accrued expense items provide the firm with automatic or spontaneous sources of financing.

UNSECURED SOURCES: TRADE CREDIT

Trade credit provides one of the most flexible sources of short-term financing available to the firm. We previously noted that trade credit is a primary source of spontaneous, or on-demand, financing. That is, trade credit arises spontaneously with the firm's purchases. To arrange for credit, the firm need only place an order with one of its suppliers. The supplier checks the firm's credit and, if it is good, sends the merchandise. The purchasing firm then pays for the goods in accordance with the supplier's credit terms.

Trade credit
Accounts payable that arise out of the normal course of business when the firm purchases from its suppliers who allow the firm to make payment after the delivery of the merchandise or services.

CREDIT TERMS AND CASH DISCOUNTS Very often the credit terms offered with trade credit involve a cash discount for early payment. For example, a supplier might offer terms of 2/10, net 30, which means that a 2 percent discount is offered for payment within 10 days or the full amount is due in 30 days. Thus, a 2 percent penalty is involved for not paying within 10 days or for delaying payment from the tenth to the thirtieth day (that is, for 20 days). The effective annual cost of not taking the cash discount can be quite severe. Using a $1 invoice amount, the effective cost of passing up the discount period using the preceding credit terms and our *APR* equation can be estimated:

$$APR = \frac{\$.02}{\$.98} \times \frac{1}{20/360} = .3673 \text{ or } 36.73\%$$

Note that the 2 percent cash discount is the *interest* cost of extending the payment period an *additional* 20 days. Note also that the principal amount of the credit is 98 cents. This amount constitutes the full principal amount as of the tenth day of the credit period, after which time the cash discount is lost. The effective cost of passing up the 2 percent discount for 20 days is quite expensive: 36.73 percent. Furthermore, once the discount period has passed, there is no reason to pay before the final due date (the thirtieth day). Table 18-2 lists the effective annual cost of alternative credit terms. Note that the cost of trade credit varies directly with the size of the cash discount and inversely with the length of time between the end of the discount period and the final due date.

STRETCHING OF TRADE CREDIT Some firms that use trade credit engage in a practice called *stretching* trade accounts. This practice involves delaying payments beyond the prescribed credit period. For example, a firm might purchase materials under credit terms of 3/10, net 60; however, when faced with a shortage of cash, the firm might extend payment to the eightieth day. Continued violation of trade terms can eventually lead to a loss of credit. However, for short periods, and at infrequent intervals, stretching may offer the firm an emergency source of short-term credit.

ADVANTAGES OF TRADE CREDIT As a source of short-term financing, trade credit has a number of advantages. First, trade credit is conveniently obtained as a normal part of the firm's operations. Second, no formal agreements are generally involved in extending credit. Furthermore, the amount of credit extended expands and contracts with the needs of the firm; this is why it is classified as a spontaneous, or on-demand, source of financing.

TABLE 18-2 Effective Rates of Interest on Selected Trade Credit Terms

CREDIT TERMS	EFFECTIVE RATE
2/10, net 60	14.69%
2/10, net 90	9.18
3/20, net 60	27.84
6/10, net 90	28.72

UNSECURED SOURCES: BANK CREDIT

Commercial banks provide unsecured short-term credit in two basic forms: lines of credit and transaction loans (notes payable). Maturities of both types of loans are usually one year or less, with rates of interest depending on the creditworthiness of the borrower and the level of interest rates in the economy as a whole.

Line of credit agreement
A line of credit agreement is an agreement between a firm and its banker to provide short-term financing to meet its temporary financing needs.

Revolving credit or revolver
A special type of line of credit agreement in which the line of credit is eventually converted into a term loan that requires periodic payments.

LINE OF CREDIT A **line of credit agreement** is a lending arrangement between a bank and a borrower in which the bank makes available a maximum amount of funds during a specified period of time. The actual borrowing is at the discretion of the borrowing firm and the bank usually requires that the line of credit have a zero balance for some specified period of time such as a month during each year. This requirement is designed to assure that the borrower is using the line of credit to finance working capital and not permanent asset acquisitions such as plant and equipment. **Revolving credit** or a **revolver** is a special type of line of credit agreement in which the line of agreements usually extend from one to five years in duration.

CREDIT TERMS Lines of credit generally do not involve fixed rates of interest; instead, they state that credit will be extended *at 1/2 percent over prime* or some other spread over the bank's prime rate.[4] Furthermore, the agreement usually does not spell out the specific use that will be made of the funds beyond a general statement, such as *for working-capital purposes.*

Lines of credit usually require that the borrower maintain a minimum balance in the bank throughout the loan period, called a *compensating balance.* This required balance (which can be stated as a percent of the line of credit or the loan amount) increases the effective cost of the loan to the borrower, unless a deposit balance equal to or greater than this balance requirement is ordinarily maintained in the bank.

EXAMPLE: CALCULATING APR FOR A LINE OF CREDIT

M&M Beverage Company has a $300,000 line of credit that requires a compensating balance equal to 10 percent of the loan amount. The rate paid on the loan is 12 percent per annum, $200,000 is borrowed for a six-month period, and the firm does not currently have a deposit with the lending bank. The dollar cost of the loan includes the interest expense and, in addition, the opportunity cost of maintaining an idle cash balance equal to the 10 percent compensating balance. To accommodate the cost of the compensating balance requirement, assume that the added funds will have to be borrowed and simply left idle in the firm's checking account. Thus, the amount actually borrowed (B) will be larger than the $200,000 needed. In fact, the needed $200,000 will constitute 90 percent of the total borrowed funds because of the 10 percent compensating balance requirement, hence $.90B = \$200,000$, such that $B = \$222,222$. Thus, interest is paid on a $222,222 loan ($\$222,222 \times .12 \times 1/2 = \$13,333.32$), of which only $200,000 is available for use by the firm.[a] The effective annual cost of credit therefore is

$$APR = \frac{\$13,333.32}{\$200,000} \times \frac{1}{180/360} = 13.33\%$$

[a]The same answer would have been obtained by assuming a total loan of $200,000, of which only 90 percent or $180,000 was available for use by the firm; that is,

$$APR = \frac{\$12,000}{\$180,000} \times \frac{1}{180/360} = 13.33\%$$

Interest is now calculated on the $200,000 loan amount ($\$12,000 = \$200,000 \times .12 \times 1/2$).

[4] The *prime rate of interest* is the rate that a bank charges its most creditworthy borrowers.

In the M&M Beverage Company example, the loan required the payment of principal ($222,222) plus interest ($13,333.32) at the end of the six-month loan period. Frequently, bank loans will be made on a discount basis. That is, the loan interest will be deducted from the loan amount before the funds are transferred to the borrower. Extending the M&M Beverage Company example to consider discounted interest involves reducing the loan proceeds ($200,000) in the previous example by the amount of interest for the full six months ($13,333.32). The effective rate of interest on the loan is now:

$$APR = \frac{\$13{,}333.32}{\$200{,}000 - \$13{,}333.32} \times \frac{1}{180/360}$$
$$= .1429 \text{ or } 14.29\%$$

The effect of discounting interest raises the cost of the loan from 13.33 percent to 14.29 percent. This results from the fact that the firm pays interest on the same amount of funds as before ($222,222); however, this time it gets the use of $13,333.32 less, or $200,000 – $13,333.32 = $186,666.68.

If M&M needs the use of a full $200,000, then it will have to borrow more than $222,222 to cover both the compensating balance requirement *and* the discounted interest. In fact, the firm will have to borrow some amount B such that:

$$B - .10B - (.12 \times 1/2)B = \$200{,}000$$
$$.84B = \$200{,}000$$
$$B = \frac{\$200{,}000}{.84} = \$238{,}095$$
$$\text{and interest} = 0.12 \times \$238{,}095 \times 1/2 = \$14{,}285.70$$

The cost of credit remains the same at 14.29 percent, as follows:

$$APR = \frac{\$14{,}285.70}{\$238{,}095 - \$23{,}810 - \$14{,}285.70} \times \frac{1}{180/360}$$
$$= .1429 \text{ or } 14.29\%$$

Transaction Loans

Still another form of unsecured short-term bank credit can be obtained in the form of *transaction loans*. Here the loan is made for a specific purpose. This is the type of loan that most individuals associate with bank credit and is obtained by signing a promissory note.

Unsecured transaction loans are very similar to a line of credit regarding cost, term to maturity, and compensating balance requirements. In both instances, commercial banks often require that the borrower *clean up* its short-term loans for a 30- to 45-day period during the year. This means, very simply, that the borrower must be free of any bank debt for the stated period. The purpose of such a requirement is to ensure that the borrower is not using short-term bank credit to finance a part of its permanent needs for funds.

Unsecured Sources: Commercial Paper

Commercial paper
Short-term loans by the most creditworthy borrowers that are bought and sold in the market for short-term debt securities.

Only the largest and most creditworthy companies are able to use **commercial paper**, which is simply a short-term *promise to pay* that is sold in the market for short-term debt securities.

The maturity of this credit source is generally six months or less, although some issues carry 270-day maturities. The interest rate on commercial paper is generally slightly lower

(.5 percent to 1 percent) than the prime rate on commercial bank loans. Also, interest is usually discounted, although sometimes interest-bearing commercial paper is available.

New issues of commercial paper are either placed directly (sold by the issuing firm directly to the investing public) or dealer placed. Dealer placement involves the use of a commercial paper dealer, who sells the issue for the issuing firm. Many major finance companies, such as General Motors Acceptance Corporation, place their commercial paper directly. The volume of direct versus dealer placements is roughly 4 to 1 in favor of direct placements. Dealers are used primarily by industrial firms that either make infrequent use of the commercial paper market or, owing to their small size, would have difficulty placing the issue without the help of a dealer.

Several advantages accrue to the user of commercial paper:

1. **Interest rate.** Commercial paper rates are generally lower than rates on bank loans and comparable sources of short-term financing.
2. **Compensating balance requirements.** No minimum balance requirements are associated with commercial paper. However, issuing firms usually find it desirable to maintain lines of credit agreements sufficient to back up their short-term financing needs in the event that a new issue of commercial paper cannot be sold or an outstanding issue cannot be repaid when due.
3. **Amount of credit.** Commercial paper offers the firm with very large credit needs a single source for all its short-term financing. Because of loan restrictions placed on the banks by the regulatory authorities, obtaining the necessary funds from a commercial bank might require dealing with a number of institutions.[5]
4. **Prestige.** Because it is widely recognized that only the most creditworthy borrowers have access to the commercial paper market, its use signifies a firm's credit status.

Using commercial paper for short-term financing, however, involves a very important *risk*. That is, the commercial paper market is highly impersonal and denies even the most creditworthy borrower any flexibility in terms of repayment. When bank credit is used, the borrowing firm has someone with whom it can work out any temporary difficulties that might be encountered in meeting a loan deadline. This flexibility simply does not exist for the user of commercial paper.

The cost of commercial paper can be estimated using the simple effective cost-of-credit equation (*APR*). The key points to remember are that commercial paper interest is usually discounted and that a fee is charged if a dealer is used to place the issue. Even if a dealer is not used, the issuing firm will incur costs associated with preparing and placing the issue, and these costs must be included in estimating the cost of credit.

Example: Calculating APR for Commercial Paper

The EPG Mfg. Company uses commercial paper regularly to support its needs for short-term financing. The firm plans to sell $100 million in 270-day-maturity paper on which it expects to have to pay discounted interest at a rate of 12 percent per annum ($9,000,000). In addition, EPG expects to incur a cost of approximately $100,000 in dealer placement fees and other expenses of issuing the paper. The effective cost of credit to EPG can be calculated as follows:

$$APR = \frac{\$9{,}000{,}000 + \$100{,}000}{\$100{,}000{,}000 - \$100{,}000 - \$9{,}000{,}000} \times \frac{1}{270/360}$$

$$= .1335 \text{ or } 13.35\%$$

[5] Member banks of the Federal Reserve System are limited to 10 percent of their total capital, surplus, and undivided profits when making loans to a single borrower. Thus, when a corporate borrower's needs for financing are very large, it may have to deal with a group of participating banks to raise the needed funds.

where the interest cost is calculated as $100,000,000 × .12 × [270/360] or $9,000,000 plus the $100,000 dealer placement fee. Thus, the effective cost of credit to EPG is 13.35 percent.

SECURED SOURCES: ACCOUNTS RECEIVABLE LOANS

Secured sources of short-term credit have certain assets of the firm pledged as collateral to secure the loan. Upon default of the loan agreement, the lender has first claim to the pledged assets in addition to its claim as a general creditor of the firm. Hence, the secured credit agreement offers an added margin of safety to the lender.

Generally, a firm's receivables are among its most liquid assets. For this reason, they are considered by many lenders to be prime collateral for a secured loan. Two basic procedures can be used in arranging for financing based on receivables: pledging and factoring.

PLEDGING ACCOUNTS RECEIVABLE Under the pledging arrangement, the borrower simply pledges accounts receivable as collateral for a loan obtained from either a commercial bank or a finance company. The amount of the loan is stated as a percent of the face value of the receivables pledged. If the firm provides the lender with a *general line* on its receivables, then all of the borrower's accounts are pledged as security for the loan. This method of pledging is simple and inexpensive. However, because the lender has no control over the quality of the receivables being pledged, it will set the maximum loan at a relatively low percent of the total face value of the accounts, generally ranging downward from a maximum of around 75 percent.

Still another approach to pledging involves the borrower's presenting specific invoices to the lender as collateral for a loan. This method is somewhat more expensive in that the lender must assess the creditworthiness of each individual account pledged; however, given this added knowledge, the lender will be willing to increase the loan as a percent of the face value of the invoices. In this case, the loan might reach as high as 85 percent or 90 percent of the face value of the pledged receivables.

Accounts receivable loans generally carry an interest rate 2 percent to 5 percent higher than the bank's prime lending rate. Finance companies charge an even higher rate. In addition, the lender will usually charge a handling fee stated as a percent of the face value of the receivables processed, which may be as much as 1 percent to 2 percent of the face value.

EXAMPLE: CALCULATING APR FOR OUR ACCOUNTS RECEIVABLE LOAN

The A. B. Good Company sells electrical supplies to building contractors on terms of net 60. The firm's average monthly sales are $100,000; thus, given the firm's two-month credit terms, its average receivables balance is $200,000. The firm pledges all its receivables to a local bank, which in turn advances up to 70 percent of the face value of the receivables at 3 percent over prime and with a 1 percent processing charge on all receivables pledged. A. B. Good follows a practice of borrowing the maximum amount possible, and the current prime rate is 10 percent.

The *APR* of using this source of financing for a full year is computed as follows:

$$APR = \frac{\$18{,}200 + \$12{,}000}{\$140{,}000} \times \frac{1}{360/360} = .2157 \text{ or } 21.57\%$$

(continued)

where the total dollar cost of the loan consists of both the annual interest expense (.13 × .70 × \$200,000 = \$18,200) and the annual processing fee (.01 × \$100,000 × 12 months = \$12,000). The amount extended is .70 × \$200,000 = \$140,000. Note that the processing charge applies to all receivables pledged. Thus, the A. B. Good Company pledges \$100,000 each month, or \$1,200,000 during the year, and a 1 percent fee must be paid, for a total annual charge of \$12,000.

One more point: The lender, in addition to making advances or loans, may be providing certain credit services to the borrower. For example, the lender may provide billing and collection services. The value of these services should be considered in computing the cost of credit. In the preceding example, A. B. Good Company may save credit department expenses of \$10,000 per year by pledging all its accounts and letting the lender provide those services. In this case, the cost of short-term credit is only

$$APR = \frac{\$18{,}200 + \$12{,}000 - \$10{,}000}{\$140{,}000} \times \frac{1}{360/360} = .1443 \text{ or } 14.43\%$$

The primary advantage of pledging as a source of short-term credit is the flexibility it provides the borrower. Financing is available on a continuous basis. The new accounts created through credit sales provide the collateral for the financing of new production. Furthermore, the lender may provide credit services that eliminate or at least reduce the need for similar services within the firm. The primary disadvantage associated with this method of financing is its cost, which can be relatively high compared with other sources of short-term credit, owing to the level of the interest rate charged on loans and the processing fee on pledged accounts.

Factoring
The sale of a firm's accounts receivable to a financial intermediary known as a *factor*.

FACTORING ACCOUNTS RECEIVABLE **Factoring** accounts receivable involves the outright sale of a firm's accounts to a financial institution, called a *factor*. A factor is a firm that acquires the receivables of other firms. The factoring institution may be a commercial finance company that engages solely in factoring receivables (known as an *old-line factor*) or it may be a commercial bank. The factor, in turn, bears the risk of collection and services the accounts for a fee. The fee is stated as a percent of the face value of all receivables factored (usually from 1 percent to 3 percent).

The factor firm typically does not make payment for factored accounts until the accounts have been collected or the credit terms have been met. Should the firm wish to receive immediate payment for factored accounts, it can borrow from the factor, using the factored accounts as collateral. The maximum loan the firm can obtain is equal to the face value of its factored accounts less the factor's fee (1 percent to 3 percent), less a reserve (6 percent to 10 percent), less the interest on the loan. For example, if \$100,000 in receivables is factored, carrying 60-day credit terms, a 2 percent factor's fee, a 6 percent reserve, and interest at 1 percent per month on advances, then the maximum loan or advance the firm can receive is computed as follows:

Face amount of receivables factored	\$100,000
Less: fee (.02 × \$100,000)	(2,000)
reserve (.06 × \$100,000)	(6,000)
interest (.01 × \$92,000 × 2 months)	(1,840)
Maximum advance	\$ 90,160

Note that interest is discounted and calculated based on a maximum amount of funds available for advance ($92,000 = $100,000 – $2,000 – $6,000). Thus, the effective cost of credit can be calculated as follows:

$$APR = \frac{\$1,840 + \$2,000}{\$90,160} \times \frac{1}{60/360}$$

$$= .2555 \text{ or } 25.55\%$$

SECURED SOURCES: INVENTORY LOANS

Inventory loans provide a second source of security for short-term secured credit. The amount of the loan that can be obtained depends on both the marketability and perishability of the inventory. Some items, such as raw materials (grains, oil, lumber, and chemicals), are excellent sources of collateral, because they can easily be liquidated. Other items, such as work-in-process inventories, provide very poor collateral because of their lack of marketability.

Inventory loans
Short-term loans that are secured by the pledge of inventories. The type of pledge or security agreement varies and can include floating liens, chattel mortgage agreements, field warehouse financing agreements, and terminal warehouse agreements.

There are several methods by which inventory can be used to secure short-term financing. These include a *floating* or *blanket lien*, *chattel mortgage*, *field warehouse receipt*, and *terminal warehouse receipt*.

Under a *floating lien* agreement, the borrower gives the lender a lien against all its inventories. This provides the simplest but least secure form of inventory collateral. The borrowing firm maintains full control of the inventories and continues to sell and replace them as it sees fit. Obviously, this lack of control over the collateral greatly dilutes the value of this type of security to the lender.

Under a *chattel mortgage agreement*, the inventory is identified (by serial number or otherwise) in the security agreement and the borrower retains title to the inventory but cannot sell the items without the lender's consent.

Under a *field warehouse financing agreement*, inventories used as collateral are separated from the firm's other inventories and placed under the control of a third-party field warehousing firm.

The *terminal warehouse agreement* differs from the field warehouse agreement in only one respect. Here the inventories pledged as collateral are transported to a public warehouse that is physically removed from the borrower's premises. The lender has an added degree of safety or security because the inventory is totally removed from the borrower's control. Once again, the cost of this type of arrangement is increased because the warehouse firm must be paid by the borrower; in addition, the inventory must be transported to and eventually from the public warehouse.

MULTINATIONAL WORKING-CAPITAL MANAGEMENT

Objective 7

The basic principles of working-capital management are the same for multinational and domestic firms. However, since multinationals spend and receive money in different countries, the exchange rate between the firm's home country and each of the countries in which it does business poses an added source of concern when managing working capital.

Multinational firms, by definition, have assets that are denominated or valued in foreign currencies. This means that the multinational will lose value if that foreign currency declines in value vis-a-vis that of the home currency. Technically, the foreign assets of the firm are exposed to exchange rate risk—the risk that tomorrow's exchange rate will differ from today's rate. However, the possibility of a decline in asset value may be offset by the decline in value of any liability that is also denominated or valued in terms of that foreign currency. Thus, a firm would normally be interested in its net exposed position (exposed assets – exposed liabilities) for each period and in each currency to which the firm has exposure.

If a firm is to manage its foreign exchange risk exposure, it needs good measures. There are three popular measures of foreign exchange risk that can be used: translation exposure, transaction exposure, and economic exposure. Translation exposure arises because the foreign operations of multinational corporations have accounting statements denominated in the local currency of the country in which the operation is located. For U.S. multinational corporations, the reporting currency for its consolidated financial statements is the dollar, so the assets, liabilities, revenues, and expenses of the foreign operations must be translated into dollars. Furthermore, international transactions often require a payment to be made or received in a foreign currency in the future, so these transactions are exposed to exchange rate risk. Economic exposure exists over the long term because the value of the future cash flows in the reporting currency (that is, the dollar) from foreign operations is exposed to exchange rate risk. Indeed, the whole stream of future cash flows is exposed.

CONCEPT CHECK

1. What are some examples of unsecured and secured sources of short-term credit?
2. What is the difference between a line of credit and a revolving credit agreement?
3. What are the types of credit agreements a firm can get that are secured by its accounts receivable as collateral?
4. What are some examples of loans secured by a firm's inventories?

HOW FINANCIAL MANAGERS USE THIS MATERIAL

The very existence of the firm depends upon the ability of its leadership to manage the firm's working capital. Working-capital management involves managing the process of converting investments in inventories and accounts receivable into cash, which the firm can use to pay its bills as investments mature. As such, working-capital management is at the very heart of the firm's day-to-day operating environment.

The firm's management is involved daily in making decisions that will impact this cash flow cycle. New items of inventory are acquired to replace ones that have been sold or to increase the firm's available stock. The inventory may be automatically financed through the creation of accounts payable or it may require that the firm seek out another source. As the firm sells its product or service, it frequently offers credit to its customers, which allows them to pay later. All these decisions impact the firm's financial obligations (debts) and its ability to meet those obligations when due (its liquidity).

The management of the firm's working capital is closely tied to the firm's financial planning process (Chapter 4). Financial planning provides the firm with a means of foreseeing its future cash needs and sources of cash. Thus, the financial planning process provides a tool for preparing for the future working-capital requirements of the firm.

SUMMARY

In this chapter, we studied the determinants of a firm's investment in working capital and the factors underlying the firm's choice among various sources of short-term financing. Working capital constitutes a significant determinant of most firms' total investment, and efforts to manage the level of the firm's investment can have a substantial impact on the firm's overall profitability.

Objective 1

Traditionally, *working capital* is defined as the firm's total investment in current assets. *Net working capital*, however, is the difference between the firm's current assets and its current liabilities.

Net working capital arises out of a firm's investments in current assets and its decisions regarding the use of current liabilities. Investments in current assets are largely determined by the nature of the firm's business (that is, whether it is a manufacturing firm or a retail establishment) and how efficiently the firm is managed. A firm's use of current liabilities is a function of the availability of short-term sources of financing to the firm and management's willingness to expose itself to the risks of insolvency posed by the use of short-term as opposed to long-term or permanent sources of financing.

Managing working capital can be thought of as managing the firm's liquidity, which in turn entails managing the firm's investment in current assets and its use of current liabilities. Each of these decisions involves risk-return trade-offs. Investing in current assets reduces the risk of illiquidity because current assets (generally) can be quickly turned into cash with little loss of value should the need arise. Using short-term sources of financing increases a firm's risk of illiquidity in that these sources of financing must be renegotiated or repaid more frequently than longer-term sources of financing such as bonds and equity.

Objective 2

The principal advantage of using current liabilities for financing working capital is that their repayment term can be matched exactly to the period for which financing is needed. However, should the period for which funding is needed be uncertain, then the firm runs the risk of not having the necessary funds available to retire the short-term financing should it come due while the firm still needs the financing. A further disadvantage of using short-term financing arises when the need for funds extends beyond the term of the financing. This creates uncertainty with respect to the cost of financing. For example, should a firm borrow using a six-month note and discover that it needs financing for a full year, then the firm not only must engage in the renegotiation of the terms of financing (or find a new source of financing), but it also faces the uncertainty as to the cost of credit six months hence. If the firm had borrowed with a one-year maturity, it may have been able to lock in the rate of interest for the full year at the time the loan was taken out.

Objective 3

The hedging principle provides a benchmark for managing a firm's net working capital position. Very simply, the principle involves matching the cash-flow generating characteristics of an asset with the cash flow requirements of the financing source chosen.

Objective 4

The cash conversion cycle is a very useful measure of the overall effectiveness with which a firm is managing its working capital. It is calculated as the sum of the average number of days of sales outstanding in both accounts receivable and inventories less the average number of days of sales represented by the firm's accounts payable. Thus, a cash conversion cycle of 30 implies that the firm has tied up 30 times its average daily sales in accounts receivable and inventories after netting out the firm's use of trade credit or accounts payable.

Objective 5

The effective cost of short-term credit can be calculated using the annual percentage rate (*APR*) formula:

$$APR = \frac{\text{interest}}{\text{principal}} \times \frac{1}{\text{time}}$$

In this formulation, "interest" refers to the dollar amount of interest paid for the use of a sum equal to "principal" for the fraction of a year defined by "time." If interest is compounded, then the appropriate calculation involves computing the annual percentage yield (*APY*) using the following formula:

$$APY = \left(1 + \frac{i}{m}\right)^m - 1$$

where i is the rate of interest per year and m is the number of compounding periods within a year.

Objective 6

Short-term credit can be obtained from a variety of sources and in a wide array of forms. It is helpful to categorize these sources as either secured (repayment is assured by the pledge of specific assets) or unsecured (repayment is assured only by the pledge of the borrower to repay). Unsecured sources consist primarily of accrued expenses (such as wages and taxes) and accounts payable that arise in the normal course of business. Secured sources of short-term financing are generally secured by the pledge of a highly liquid asset. Frequently, the pledged asset is a current asset such as accounts receivable or inventories.

Objective 7

Multinational firms have the additional consideration of exchange rate factors that impact management of its working capital. An asset denominated in terms of foreign currency cash flows will lose value if that foreign currency declines. This decline may be offset by a decline in value of liabilities also denominated in terms of the foreign currency. Thus, a firm is interested in its net exposed position, exposed assets minus exposed liabilities.

KEY TERMS

Go To: www.prenhall.com/keown for downloads and current events associated with this chapter

Commercial paper, 657
Factoring, 660
Hedging principle (principle of self-liquidating debt), 648
Inventory loans, 661
Line of credit agreement, 656
Net working capital, 646
Permanent asset investment, 649
Permanent sources of financing, 649
Revolving credit or revolver, 656
Secured and unsecured loans, 654
Spontaneous sources of financing, 649
Temporary asset investment, 649
Temporary sources of financing, 649
Trade credit, 655
Working capital, 646

STUDY QUESTIONS

18-1. Define and contrast the terms *working capital* and *net working capital.*

18-2. Discuss the risk-return relationship involved in managing the firm's working capital.

18-3. What is the primary advantage and disadvantage associated with the use of short-term debt? Discuss.

18-4. Explain what is meant by the statement, "The use of current liabilities as opposed to long-term debt subjects the firm to a greater risk of illiquidity."

18-5. Define the hedging principle. How can this principle be used in the management of working capital?

18-6. Define the following terms:
- **a.** Permanent asset investments
- **b.** Temporary asset investments
- **c.** Permanent sources of financing
- **d.** Temporary sources of financing
- **e.** Spontaneous sources of financing

18-7. What considerations should be used in selecting a source of short-term credit? Discuss each.

18-8. How can the formula "interest = principal × rate × time" be used to estimate the effective cost of short-term credit?

18-9. How can we accommodate the effects of compounding in our calculation of the effective cost of short-term credit?

18-10. What is meant by the following trade credit terms: 2/10, net 30? 4/20, net 60? 3/15, net 45?

18-11. Define the following:
- **a.** Line of credit
- **b.** Commercial paper
- **c.** Compensating balance
- **d.** Prime rate

18-12. List and discuss four advantages of the use of commercial paper.

18-13. What risk is involved in the firm's use of commercial paper as a source of short-term credit? Discuss.

18-14. List and discuss the distinguishing features of the principal sources of secured credit based on accounts receivable.

SELF-TEST PROBLEMS

ST-1. (*Analyzing the cost of commercial paper*) The Marilyn Sales Company is a wholesale machine tool broker that has gone through a recent expansion of its activities resulting in a doubling of its sales. The company has determined that it needs an additional $200 million in short-term funds to finance peak season sales during roughly six months of the year. Marilyn's treasurer has recommended that the firm use a commercial paper offering to raise the needed funds. Specifically, he has determined that a $200 million offering would require 10 percent interest (paid in advance or discounted) plus a $125,000 placement fee. The paper would carry a six-month (180-day) maturity. What is the effective cost of credit?

ST-2. (*Analyzing the cost of short-term credit*) The treasurer of the Lights-a-Lot Mfg. Company is faced with three alternative bank loans. The firm wishes to select the one that minimizes its cost of credit on a $200,000 note that it plans to issue in the next 10 days. Relevant information for the three loan configurations is as follows:

a. An 18 percent rate of interest with interest paid at the end of the loan period and no compensating balance requirement.

b. A 16 percent rate of interest and a 20 percent compensating balance requirement. This loan also calls for interest to be paid at the end of the loan period.

c. A 14 percent rate of interest that is discounted plus a 20 percent compensating balance requirement.

Analyze the cost of each of these alternatives. You may assume the firm would not normally maintain any bank balance that might be used to meet the 20 percent compensating balance requirements of alternatives (b) and (c). Finally, the loan period is one year.

STUDY PROBLEMS (SET A)

18-1A. (*Liquidity and working-capital policy*) The balance sheets for two firms (A and B) are as follows:

FIRM A

Cash	$ 100,000	Accounts payable	$ 200,000
Accounts receivable	100,000	Notes payable	200,000
Inventories	300,000	Current liabilities	$ 400,000
Net fixed assets	1,500,000	Bonds	600,000
Total	$2,000,000	Common equity	1,000,000
		Total	$2,000,000

FIRM B

Cash	$ 150,000	Accounts payable	$ 400,000
Accounts receivable	50,000	Notes payable	200,000
Inventories	300,000	Current liabilities	$ 600,000
Net fixed assets	1,500,000	Bonds	400,000
Total	$2,000,000	Common equity	1,000,000
		Total	$2,000,000

Which of the two firms follows the most aggressive working-capital policy? Why?

18-2A. (*Cost of trade credit*) Sage Construction Company purchases $480,000 in doors and windows from Crenshaw Doors under credit terms of 1/15, net 45. Assuming that Sage takes advantage of the cash discount by paying on day 15, answer the following questions:

a. What is Sage's average monthly payables balance? You may assume a 360-day year and that the accounts payable balance includes the gross amount owed (that is, no discount has been taken).

b. If Sage were to decide to pass up the cash discount and extend payment until the end of the credit period, what would its payable balance become?

c. What is the opportunity cost of not taking the cash discount?

18-3A. (*Estimating the cost of bank credit*) Paymaster Enterprises has arranged to finance its seasonal working-capital needs with a short-term bank loan. The loan will carry a rate of 12 percent per annum with interest paid in advance (discounted). In addition, Paymaster must maintain a minimum demand deposit with the bank of 10 percent of the loan balance throughout the term of the loan. If Paymaster plans to borrow $100,000 for a period of three months, what is the effective cost of the bank loan?

18-4A. (*Estimating the cost of commercial paper*) On February 3, Burlington Western Company plans a commercial paper issue of $20 million. The firm has never used commercial paper before but has been assured by the firm placing the issue that it will have no difficulty raising the funds. The commercial paper will carry a 270-day maturity and will require interest based on a rate of 11 percent per annum. In addition, the firm will have to pay fees totaling $200,000 in order to bring the issue to market. What is the effective cost of the commercial paper issue to Burlington Western?

18-5A. (*Cost of trade credit*) Calculate the effective cost of the following trade credit terms where payment is made on the net due date, using the annual percentage rate (*APR*) formula.

a. 2/10, net 30
b. 3/15, net 30
c. 3/15, net 45
d. 2/15, net 60

18-6A. (*Annual percentage yield*) Compute the cost of the trade credit terms in problem 18-5A using the compounding formula, or annual percentage yield.

18-7A. (*Cost of short-term financing*) The R. Morin Construction Company needs to borrow $100,000 to help finance a new $150,000 hydraulic crane used in the firm's commercial construction business. The crane will pay for itself in one year. The firm is considering the following alternatives for financing its purchase:

Alternative A—The firm's bank has agreed to lend the $100,000 at a rate of 14 percent. Interest would be discounted, and a 15 percent compensating balance would be required. However, the compensating balance requirement would not be binding on R. Morin because the firm normally maintains a minimum demand deposit (checking account) balance of $25,000 in the bank.

Alternative B—The equipment dealer has agreed to finance the equipment with a one-year loan. The $100,000 loan would require payment of principal and interest totaling $116,300 at year end.

a. Which alternative should R. Morin select?

b. If the bank's compensating balance requirement were to necessitate idle demand deposits equal to 15 percent of the loan, what effect would this have on the cost of the bank loan alternative?

18-8A. (*Cost of short-term bank loan*) The Southwest Forging Corporation recently arranged for a line of credit with the First National Bank of Dallas. The terms of the agreement called for a $100,000 maximum loan with interest set at 1 percent over prime. In addition, the firm has to maintain a 20 percent compensating balance in its demand deposit account throughout the year. The prime rate is currently 12 percent.

a. If Southwest normally maintains a $20,000 to $30,000 balance in its checking account with FNB of Dallas, what is the effective cost of credit through the line-of-credit agreement where the maximum loan amount is used for a full year?

b. Re-compute the effective cost of credit to Southwest if the firm will have to borrow the compensating balance and it borrows the maximum possible under the loan agreement. Again, assume the full amount of the loan is outstanding for a whole year.

18-9A. (*Cost of commercial paper*) Tri-State Enterprises plans to issue commercial paper for the first time in the firm's 35-year history. The firm plans to issue $500,000 in 180-day maturity notes. The paper will carry a 10-1/4 percent rate with discounted interest and will cost Tri-State $12,000 (paid in advance) to issue.

a. What is the cost of credit to Tri-State?

b. What other factors should the company consider in analyzing the use of commercial paper?

18-10A. (*Cost of accounts receivable*) Johnson Enterprises, Inc., is involved in the manufacture and sale of electronic components used in small AM-FM radios. The firm needs $300,000 to finance an anticipated expansion in receivables due to increased sales. Johnson's credit terms are net 60, and its average monthly credit sales are $200,000. In general, the firm's customers pay within the credit period; thus, the firm's average accounts receivable balance is $400,000.

Chuck Idol, Johnson's comptroller, approached the firm's bank with a request for a loan for the $300,000 using the firm's accounts receivable as collateral. The bank offered to make the loan at a rate of 2 percent over prime plus a 1 percent processing charge on all receivables pledged ($200,000 per month). Furthermore, the bank agreed to lend up to 75 percent of the face value of the receivables pledged.

- **a.** Estimate the cost of the receivables loan to Johnson where the firm borrows the $300,000. The prime rate is currently 11 percent.
- **b.** Idol also requested a line of credit for $300,000 from the bank. The bank agreed to grant the necessary line of credit at a rate of 3 percent over prime and required a 15 percent compensating balance. Johnson currently maintains an average demand deposit of $80,000. Estimate the cost of the line of credit to Johnson.
- **c.** Which source of credit should Johnson select? Why?

18-11A. (*Cost of factoring*) MDM, Inc., is considering factoring its receivables. The firm has credit sales of $400,000 per month and has an average receivables balance of $800,000 with 60-day credit terms. The factor has offered to extend credit equal to 90 percent of the receivables factored less interest on the loan at a rate of 1-1/2 percent per month. The 10 percent difference in the advance and the face value of all receivables factored consists of a 1 percent factoring fee plus a 9 percent reserve, which the factor maintains. In addition, if MDM decides to factor its receivables, it will sell them all, so that it can reduce its credit department costs by $1,500 a month.

- **a.** What is the cost of borrowing the maximum amount of credit available to MDM, Inc., through the factoring agreement?
- **b.** What considerations other than cost should be accounted for by MDM, Inc., in determining whether to enter the factoring agreement?

18-12A. (*Cost of secured short-term credit*) The Sean-Janeow Import Co. needs $500,000 for a three-month period. The firm has explored two possible sources of credit:

- **(1)** S-J has arranged with its bank for a $500,000 loan secured by accounts receivable. The bank has agreed to advance S-J 80 percent of the value of its pledged receivables at a rate of 11 percent plus a 1 percent fee based on all receivables pledged. S-J's receivables average a total of $1 million throughout the year.
- **(2)** An insurance company has agreed to lend the $500,000 at a rate of 9 percent per annum, using a loan secured by S-J's inventory of salad oil. A field warehouse agreement would be used, which would cost S-J $2,000 a month.

Which source of credit should S-J select? Explain.

18-13A. (*Cost of short-term financing*) You plan to borrow $20,000 from the bank to pay for a gift shop you have just opened. The bank offers to lend you the money at 10 percent annual interest for the six months the funds will be needed.

- **a.** Calculate the effective rate of interest on the loan.
- **b.** In addition, the bank requires you to maintain a 15 percent compensating balance in the bank. Because you are just opening your business, you do not have a demand deposit account at the bank that can be used to meet the compensating balance requirement. This means that you will have to put 15 percent of the loan amount from your own personal money (which you had planned to use to help finance the business) in a checking account. What is the cost of the loan now?
- **c.** In addition to the compensating balance requirement in (b), you are told that interest will be discounted. What is the effective rate of interest on the loan now?

18-14A. (*Cost of factoring*) A factor has agreed to lend the JVC Corporation funds by factoring $300,000 in receivables. JVC's receivables average $100,000 per month and have a 90-day average collection period. (Note that JVC's credit terms call for payment in 90 days and accounts receivable average $300,000 because of the 90-day average collection period.) The factor will charge 12 percent interest on any advance (1 percent per month paid in advance), will charge a 2 percent factoring fee on all receivables factored, and will maintain a 20 percent reserve. If JVC undertakes the loan, it will reduce its own credit department expenses by $2,000 per month. What is the annual effective rate of interest to JVC on the factoring arrangement? Assume that the maximum advance is taken.

18-15A. (*Cash conversion cycle*) Mega PC, Inc., has been striving for the last five years to improve its management of working capital. Historical data for the firm's sales, accounts receivable, inventories, and accounts payable follow:

	JAN-99	JAN-00	JAN-01	JAN-02	JAN-03
Sales–Net	2,873	3,475	5,296	7,759	12,327
Receivables–Total	411	538	726	903	1,486
Accounts Payable	283	447	466	1,040	1,643
Inventories–Total	220	293	429	251	233

a. Calculate Mega's days of sales outstanding and days of sales in inventory for each of the five years. What has Mega accomplished in its attempts to better manage its investments in accounts receivable and inventory?

b. Calculate Mega's cash conversion cycle for each of the five years. Evaluate Mega's overall management of its working capital.

WEB WORKS

18-1WW. Calculate the cash conversion cycle for Nike using financial statement information found at www.nike.com. How do Nike's operations affect its working capital?

18-2WW. Calculate the cash conversion cycle for Reebok using data found at www.reebok.com. Who has the most aggressive working-capital policy: Nike or Reebok?

STUDY PROBLEMS (SET B)

18-1B. (*Liquidity and working-capital policy*) The balance sheets for two firms (A and B) are as follows:

FIRM A			
Cash	$ 200,000	Accounts payable	$ 400,000
Accounts receivable	200,000	Notes payable	400,000
Inventories	600,000	Bonds	1,200,000
Net fixed assets	3,000,000	Common equity	2,000,000
Total	$4,000,000	Total	$4,000,000

FIRM B			
Cash	$ 200,000	Accounts payable	$ 600,000
Accounts receivable	400,000	Notes payable	400,000
Inventories	400,000	Bonds	500,000
Net fixed assets	3,000,000	Common equity	2,500,000
Total	$4,000,000	Total	$4,000,000

Which of the two firms follows the most aggressive working-capital policy? Why?

18-2B. (*Cost of trade credit*) Clearwater Construction Company purchases $600,000 in parts and supplies under credit terms of 2/30, net 60 every year. Assuming that Clearwater takes advantage of the cash discount by paying on day 30, answer the following questions:

a. What is Clearwater's average monthly payables balance? You may assume a 360-day year and that the accounts payable balance includes the gross amount owed (that is, no discount has been taken).

b. If Clearwater were to decide to pass up the cash discount and extend payment until the end of the credit period, what would its payable balance become?

c. What is the opportunity cost of not taking the cash discount?

18-3B. (*Estimating the cost of bank credit*) Dee's Christmas Trees, Inc., is evaluating options for financing its seasonal working-capital needs. A short-term loan from Liberty Bank would carry a 14 percent annual interest rate, with interest paid in advance (discounted). If this option is chosen, Dee's would also have to maintain a minimum demand deposit equal to 10 percent of the loan balance throughout the term of the loan. If Dee's needs to borrow $125,000 for the upcoming three months before Christmas, what is the effective cost of the loan?

18-4B. (*Estimating the cost of commercial paper*) Duro Auto Parts would like to exploit a production opportunity overseas and is seeking additional capital to finance this expansion. The company plans a commercial paper issue of $15 million. The firm has never issued commercial paper before, but has been assured by the investment banker placing the issue that it will have no difficulty raising the funds, and that this method of financing is the least expensive option, even after the $150,000 placement fee. The issue will carry a 270-day maturity and will require interest based on an annual rate of 12 percent. What is the effective cost of the commercial paper issue to Duro?

18-5B. (*Cost of trade credit*) Calculate the effective cost of the following trade credit terms where payment is made on the net due date.

a. 1/10, net 30
b. 2/15, net 30
c. 2/15, net 45
d. 3/15, net 60

18-6B. (*Annual percentage yield*) Compute the cost of the trade credit terms in problem 18-5B using the compounding formula, or annual percentage yield.

18-7B. (*Cost of short-term financing*) Vitra Glass Company needs to borrow $150,000 to help finance the cost of a new $225,000 kiln to be used in the production of glass bottles. The kiln will pay for itself in one year, and the firm is considering the following alternatives for financing its purchase:

Alternative A—The firm's bank has agreed to lend the $150,000 at a rate of 15 percent. Interest would be discounted, and a 16 percent compensating balance would be required. However, the compensating balance requirement would not be binding on Vitra, because the firm normally maintains a minimum demand deposit (checking account) balance of $25,000 in the bank.

Alternative B—The kiln dealer has agreed to finance the equipment with a one-year loan. The $150,000 loan would require payment of principal and interest totaling $180,000.

a. Which alternative should Vitra select?
b. If the bank's compensating balance requirement were to necessitate idle demand deposits equal to 16 percent of the loan, what effect would this have on the cost of the bank loan alternative?

18-8B. (*Cost of short-term bank loan*) Lola's Ice Cream recently arranged for a line of credit with the Longhorn State Bank of Dallas. The terms of the agreement called for a $100,000 maximum loan with interest set at 2.0 percent over prime. In addition, Lola's must maintain a 15 percent compensating balance in its demand deposit throughout the year. The prime rate is currently 12 percent.

a. If Lola's normally maintains a $15,000 to $25,000 balance in its checking account with LSB of Dallas, what is the effective cost of credit through the line-of-credit agreement where the maximum loan amount is used for a full year?
b. Recompute the effective cost of credit to Lola's Ice Cream if the firm has to borrow the compensating balance and it borrows the maximum possible under the loan agreement. Again, assume the full amount of the loan is outstanding for a whole year.

18-9B. (*Cost of commercial paper*) Luft, Inc., recently acquired production rights to an innovative sailboard design but needs funds to pay for the first production run, which is expected to sell briskly. The firm plans to issue $450,000 in 180-day maturity notes. The paper will carry an 11 percent rate with discounted interest and will cost Luft $13,000 (paid in advance) to issue.

a. What is the effective cost of credit to Luft?
b. What other factors should the company consider in analyzing whether to issue the commercial paper?

18-10B. (*Cost of accounts receivable*) TLC Enterprises, Inc., is a wholesaler of toys and curios. The firm needs $400,000 to finance an anticipated expansion in receivables. TLC's credit terms are net 60, and its average monthly credit sales are $250,000. In general, TLC's customers pay within the credit period; thus, the firm's average accounts receivable balance is $500,000.

Kelly Leaky, TLC's comptroller, approached the firm's bank with a request for a $400,000 loan, using the firm's accounts receivable as collateral. The bank offered to make the loan at a rate of 2 percent over prime plus a 1 percent processing charge on all receivables pledged ($250,000 per month). Furthermore, the bank agreed to lend up to 80 percent of the face value of the receivables pledged.

a. Estimate the cost of the receivables loan to TLC where the firm borrows the $400,000. The prime rate is currently 11 percent.
b. Leaky also requested a line of credit for $400,000 from the bank. The bank agreed to grant the necessary line of credit at a rate of 3 percent over prime and required a 15 percent compensating balance. TLC currently maintains an average demand deposit of $100,000. Estimate the cost of the line of credit.
c. Which source of credit should TLC select? Why?

18-11B. (*Cost of factoring*) To increase profitability, a management consultant has suggested to the Dal Molle Fruit Company that it consider factoring its receivables. The firm has credit sales of $300,000 per month and has an average receivables balance of $600,000 with 60-day credit terms. The factor has offered to extend credit equal to 90 percent of the receivables factored less interest on the loan at a rate of 1-1/2 percent per month. The 10 percent difference in the advance and the face value of all receivables factored consists of a 1 percent factoring fee plus a 9 percent reserve, which the factor maintains. In addition, if Dal Molle decides to factor its receivables, it will sell them all, so that it can reduce its credit department costs by $1,400 a month.

a. What is the cost of borrowing the maximum amount of credit available to Dal Molle, through the factoring agreement?
b. What considerations other than cost should be accounted for by Dal Molle, in determining whether or not to enter the factoring agreement?

18-12B. (*Cost of secured short-term credit*) DST, Inc., a producer of inflatable river rafts, needs $400,000 over the three-month summer season. The firm has explored two possible sources of credit:

a. DST has arranged with its bank for a $400,000 loan secured by accounts receivable. The bank has agreed to advance DST 80 percent of the value of its pledged receivables at a rate of 11 percent plus a 1 percent fee based on all receivables pledged. DST's receivables average a total of $1 million year-round.
b. An insurance company has agreed to lend the $400,000 at a rate of 9 percent per annum, using a loan secured by DST's inventory. A field warehouse agreement would be used, which would cost DST $2,000 a month.

Which source of credit would DST select? Explain.

18-13B. (*Cost of secured short-term financing*) You are considering a loan of $25,000 to finance inventories for a janitorial supply store that you plan to open. The bank offers to lend you the money at 11 percent annual interest for the six months the funds will be needed.

a. Calculate the effective rate of interest on the loan.
b. In addition, the bank requires you to maintain a 15 percent compensating balance in the bank. Because you are just opening your business, you do not have a demand deposit at the bank that can be used to meet the compensating balance requirement. This means that you will have to put 15 percent of the loan amount from your own personal money (which you had planned to use to help finance the business) in a checking account. What is the cost of the loan now?
c. In addition to the compensating balance requirement in (b), you are told that interest will be discounted. What is the effective rate of interest on the loan now?

18-14B. (*Cost of financing*) Tanglewood Roofing Supply, Inc., has agreed to finance its working capital by factoring $450,000 in receivables on the following terms: Tanglewood's receivables average $150,000 per month and have a 90-day average collection period (note that the firm offers 90-day credit terms and its accounts receivable average $450,000 because of the 90-day collection period). The factor will charge 13 percent interest paid in advance, will charge a 2 percent factoring fee on all receivables factored, and will maintain a 15 percent reserve. If Tanglewood undertakes the loan, it will reduce its own credit department expenses by $2,000 per month. What is the annual effective rate of interest to Tanglewood on the factoring agreement? Assume that the maximum advance is taken.

18-15B. Allergan, Inc., has been striving to improve its management of working capital. Historical data for the firm's sales, accounts receivables, inventories, and accounts payable follow:

	JAN-97	JAN-98	JAN-99	JAN-00	JAN-01
Sales–Net	1,149.0	1,296.1	1,452.4	1,562.1	1,685.2
Receivables–Total	187.0	226.1	253.2	268.5	279.4
Accounts Payable	83.3	67.0	80.5	82.9	104.3
Inventories–Total	147.8	123.3	130.7	135.0	120.2

a. Calculate Allergan's days of sales outstanding and days of sales in inventory for each of the five years. What has Allergan accomplished in its attempts to better manage its investments in accounts receivable and inventory?

b. Calculate Allergan's cash conversion cycle for each of the five years. Evaluate Allergan's overall management of its working capital.

	JAN-97	JAN-98	JAN-99	JAN-00	JAN-01
Sales–Net	1,149	1,296.1	1,452.4	1,562.1	1,685.20
Receivables total	187	226.1	253.2	268.5	279.40
Accounts payable	83.3	67	80.5	82.9	104.30
Inventories total	147.8	123.3	130.7	135	120.20
Days of sales outstanding	59.40	63.67	63.63	62.74	60.52
Days of sales in inventory	46.95	34.72	32.85	31.54	26.03
Days of payable outstanding	26.46	18.87	20.23	19.37	22.59
Cash conversion cycle	79.89	79.53	76.25	74.91	63.96

SELF-TEST SOLUTIONS

ST-1. The discounted interest cost of the commercial paper issue is calculated as follows:

$$\text{interest expense} = .10 \times \$200{,}000{,}000 \times 180/360 = \$10{,}000{,}000$$

The effective cost of credit can now be calculated as follows:

$$APR = \frac{\$10{,}000{,}000 + \$125{,}000}{\$200{,}000{,}000 - \$125{,}000 - \$10{,}000{,}000} \times \frac{1}{180/360}$$

$$= .1066 \text{ or } 10.66\%$$

ST-2.

a. $$APR = \frac{.18 \times \$200{,}000}{\$200{,}000} \times \frac{1}{1}$$

$$= .18 \text{ or } 18\%$$

b. $$APR = \frac{.16 \times \$200{,}000}{\$200{,}000 - (.20 \times \$200{,}000)} \times \frac{1}{1}$$

$$= .20 \text{ or } 20\%$$

c. $$APR = \frac{.14 \times \$200{,}000}{\$200{,}000 - (.14 \times \$200{,}000) - (.2 \times \$200{,}000)} \times \frac{1}{1}$$

$$= .2121 \text{ or } 21.21\%$$

Alternative (a) offers the lower cost of financing, although it carries the highest stated rate of interest. The reason for this is that there is no compensating balance requirement, and interest is not discounted for this alternative.

LEARNING OBJECTIVES

After reading this chapter, you should be able to

1. Define *liquid assets.*
2. Understand why a firm holds cash.
3. Explain various cash-management objectives and decisions.
4. Describe and analyze the different mechanisms for managing the firm's cash collection and disbursement procedures.
5. Determine a prudent composition for the firm's marketable securities portfolio.

CHAPTER 19

Cash and Marketable Securities Management

For Harley-Davidson, cash management takes on added importance. After all, it was a cash crisis back in 1985 that left Harley-Davidson only hours away from bankruptcy as one of Harley's largest lenders, Citicorp Industrial Credit, was considering bailing out on its loan.

Today, just as with any large corporation, cash management is an important topic at Harley-Davidson, regardless of how sound the firm is. In fact, at the end of the fiscal year 2001, Harley-Davidson held 14.43 percent of its assets in the form of cash and cash equivalents. During 2001, Harley generated sales revenues of $3.363 billion. Based on a 365-day year, this means that Harley-Davidson "produced" $9.214 million in sales revenues each day.

If the company could have freed up only one day's worth of sales and invested it in a money market account yielding 5 percent, the firm's before-tax profits would have jumped by $460,700. That is a tidy sum and demonstrates why firms like to have efficient treasury management departments in place. Shareholders enjoy the added profits.

Now, if Harley-Davidson's management felt it could bear a little more risk, then the freed-up cash might be invested in a one-year certificate-of-deposit (CD) with a one-year maturity. If one-year maturities were yielding, on average, 6.53 percent, the difference of 153 basis points (i.e., 6.53 – 5.00) may not seem like much, but when put to work on an investment of $9.214 million, it produces a considerable income. In this case, the increased before-tax profits would total $601,674. So by investing the excess cash in CDs rather than money market accounts, Harley-Davidson's before-tax profits could have been $140,974 greater (i.e., $601,674 – $460,700).

Managing the cash and marketable-securities portfolio is an important task for financial executives. This chapter teaches you about sophisticated cash management systems and about prudent places to "park" the firm's excess cash balances so they earn a positive rate of return and are liquid at the same time. We also explore sound management techniques that relate to the other asset components of the firm's working capital—accounts receivable and inventory.

CHAPTER PREVIEW

Chapter 16 introduced the concept of working-capital management. Now we will consider the various elements of the firm's working capital in some depth. This chapter centers on the formulation of financial policies for management of cash and marketable securities. We explore three major areas: (1) techniques available to management for favorably influencing cash receipts and disbursements patterns, (2) sensible investment possibilities that enable the company to productively employ excess cash balances, and (3) some straightforward models that can assist financial officers in deciding on how much cash to hold.

In this chapter, three principles will be relevant to our study: **Principle 1: The Risk-Return Trade-Off—We won't take on additional risk unless we expect to be compensated with additional returns; Principle 2: The Time Value of Money—A dollar received today is worth more than a dollar received in the future;** and **Principle 10: Ethical Behavior Is Doing the Right Thing, and Ethical Dilemmas Are Everywhere in Finance.**

You will see the importance of these principles throughout this chapter.

Objective 1

WHAT ARE LIQUID ASSETS?

Cash
Currency and coin plus demand deposit accounts.

Marketable securities
Security investments (financial assets) the firm can quickly convert to cash balances. Also known as *near cash* or *near-cash assets.*

Liquid assets
The sum of cash and marketable securities.

Before proceeding to our discussion of cash management, it will be helpful to distinguish among several terms. **Cash** is the currency and coin the firm has on hand in petty cash drawers, in cash registers, or in checking or money market accounts. **Marketable securities**, also called *near cash* or *near-cash assets,* are security investments that the firm can quickly convert into cash balances. Generally firms hold marketable securities with very short maturity periods—less than one year. Together, cash and marketable securities are known as **liquid assets**.

Objective 2

WHY A COMPANY HOLDS CASH

A thorough understanding of why and how a firm holds cash requires an accurate conception of how cash flows into and through the enterprise. Figure 19-1 depicts the process of cash generation and disposition in a typical manufacturing setting. The arrows designate the direction of the flow—that is, whether the cash balance increases or decreases.

FIGURE 19-1 The Cash Generation and Disposition Process

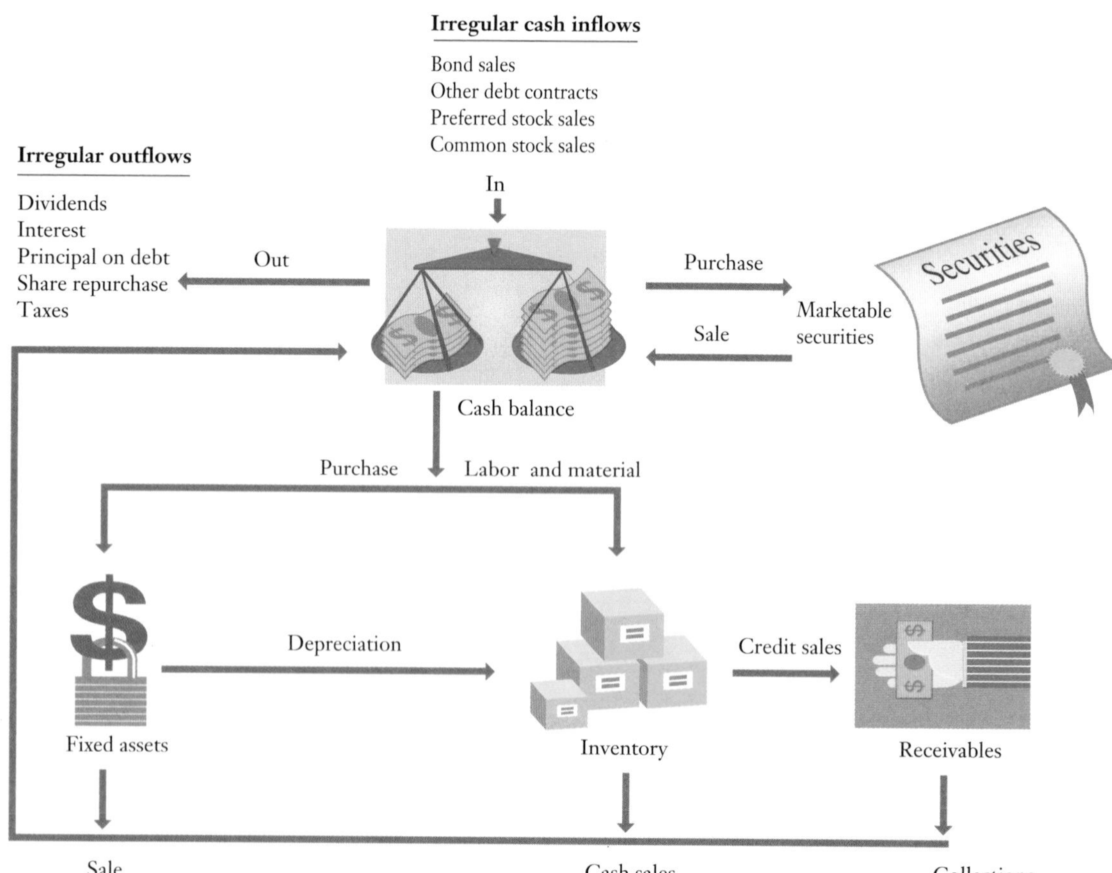

Cash-Flow Process

The firm experiences irregular increases in its cash holdings from several external sources. Funds can be obtained in the financial markets from the sale of securities, such as bonds, preferred stock, and common stock, or the firm can enter into nonmarketable debt contracts with lenders such as commercial banks. These irregular cash inflows do not occur on a daily basis. They tend to be episodic; the financing arrangements that give rise to them are effected at wide intervals. External financing contracts usually involve huge sums of money stemming from a major need identified by the company's management, and these needs do not occur every day. For example, a new product might have moved to the launching stage, or a plant expansion might be required to provide added productive capacity.

In most organizations, the financial officer responsible for cash management also controls the transactions that affect the firm's investment in marketable securities. As excess cash becomes temporarily available, marketable securities are purchased. When cash is in short supply, a portion of the marketable securities portfolio is liquidated.

Whereas the irregular cash inflows are from external sources, the other main sources of cash to the firm arise from internal operations and occur on a more regular basis. Over long periods, the largest receipts come from accounts receivable collections and, to a lesser extent, from direct cash sales of finished goods. Many manufacturing concerns also generate cash on a regular basis through the liquidation of scrap or obsolete inventory. At various times, fixed assets may also be sold, thereby generating some cash inflow. This is not a large source of funds except in unusual situations where, for instance, a complete plant renovation may be taking place.

Apart from the investment of excess cash in near-cash assets, the cash balance experiences reductions for three key reasons. First, on an irregular basis, withdrawals are made to (1) pay cash dividends on preferred and common stock shares; (2) meet interest requirements on debt contracts; (3) repay the principal borrowed from creditors; (4) buy the firm's own shares in the financial markets for use in executive compensation plans, or as an alternative to paying a cash dividend; and (5) pay tax bills. Again, by an *irregular basis*, we mean items *not* occurring on a daily or frequent schedule. Second, the company's capital expenditure program designates that fixed assets be acquired at various intervals. Third, inventories are purchased on a regular basis to ensure a steady flow of finished goods off the production line. Note that the arrow linking the investment in fixed assets with the inventory account is labeled *depreciation*. This indicates that a portion of the cost of fixed assets is charged against the products coming off the assembly line. This cost is subsequently recovered through the sale of the finished goods inventory, because the product selling price will be set by management to cover all the costs of production, including depreciation.

The variety of influences that constantly affect the cash balance held by the firm can be synthesized in terms of the classic motives for holding cash, as identified in the literature of economic theory.

Motives for Holding Cash

In a classic economic treatise, John Maynard Keynes segmented the firm's, or any economic unit's, demand for cash into three categories: (1) the transactions motive, (2) the precautionary motive, and (3) the speculative motive.[1]

TRANSACTIONS MOTIVE Balances held for transactions purposes allow the firm to meet cash needs that arise in the ordinary course of doing business. In Figure 19-1,

[1] John Maynard Keynes, *The General Theory of Employment, Interest, and Money* (New York: Harcourt Brace Jovanovich, 1936).

transactions balances would be used to meet the irregular outflows as well as the planned acquisition of fixed assets and inventories.

The relative amount of cash needed to satisfy transactions requirements is affected by a number of factors, such as the industry in which the firm operates. It is well-known that utilities can forecast cash receipts quite accurately, because of stable demand for their services. Computer software firms, however, have a more difficult time predicting their cash flows. New products are brought to market at a rapid pace, thereby making it difficult to project cash flows and balances very precisely.

THE PRECAUTIONARY MOTIVE Precautionary balances are a buffer stock of liquid assets. This motive for holding cash relates to the maintenance of balances to be used to satisfy possible, but as yet indefinite, needs.

Cash-flow predictability also has a material influence on the firm's demand for cash through the precautionary motive. The airline industry provides a typical illustration. Air passenger carriers are plagued with a high degree of cash-flow uncertainty. The weather, rising fuel costs, and continual strikes by operating personnel make cash forecasting difficult for any airline. The upshot of this problem is that because of all the things that *might* happen, the minimum cash balances desired by the management of the air carriers tend to be large.

In actual business practice, the precautionary motive is met to a large extent by the holding of a portfolio of *liquid assets*, not just cash. Notice in Figure 19-1 the two-way flow of funds between the company's holdings of cash and marketable securities. In large corporate organizations, funds may flow either into or out of the marketable securities portfolio on a daily basis.

THE SPECULATIVE MOTIVE Cash is held for speculative purposes in order to take advantage of potential profit-making situations. Construction firms that build private dwellings will at times accumulate cash in anticipation of a significant drop in lumber costs. If the price of building supplies does drop, the companies that built up their cash balances stand to profit by purchasing materials in large quantities. Generally, the speculative motive is the least important component of a firm's preference for liquidity. The transactions and precautionary motives account for most of the reasons why a company holds cash balances.

CONCEPT CHECK

1. Describe the typical cash-flow cycle for a firm.
2. What are the three primary motives for holding cash?

Objective 3

CASH-MANAGEMENT OBJECTIVES AND DECISIONS

The degree to which a firm invests idle cash into marketable securities will be determined by the amount of insolvency risk the firm is willing to undergo in order to receive additional return on its cash balances. We will see that this trade-off is not easily balanced.

THE RISK-RETURN TRADE-OFF

Insolvency
Situation in which the firm is unable to pay its bills on time.

A company-wide cash-management program must be concerned with minimizing the firm's risk of insolvency. In the context of cash management, the term **insolvency** describes the situation where the firm is unable to pay its bills on time. In such a case, the company is *technically insolvent* in that it lacks the necessary liquidity to make prompt payment on its current debt obligations. A firm could avoid this problem by carrying large cash balances to pay the bills that come due.

The financial manager must strike an acceptable balance between holding too much cash and too little cash. This is the focal point of the risk-return trade-off. A large cash investment minimizes the chances of insolvency, but penalizes company profitability. A small cash investment frees excess balances for investment in both marketable securities and longer-lived assets; this enhances company profitability and the value of the firm's common shares, but increases the chances of running out of cash.

BACK TO THE PRINCIPLES

The dilemma faced by the financial manager is a clear example of the application of ***Principle 1: The Risk-Return Trade-Off—We won't take on additional risk unless we expect to be compensated with additional return.*** *To accept the risk of not having sufficient cash on hand, the firm must be compensated with a return on the cash that is invested. Moreover, the greater the risk of the investment into which the cash is placed, the greater the return that the firm demands.*

The Objectives

The risk-return trade-off can be reduced to two prime objectives for the firm's cash-management system:

1. Enough cash must be on hand to meet the disbursal needs that arise in the course of doing business.
2. Investment in idle cash balances must be reduced to a minimum.

Evaluation of these operational objectives, and a conscious attempt on the part of management to meet them, gives rise to the need for some typical cash-management decisions.

The Decisions

Two conditions or ideals would allow the firm to operate for extended periods with cash balances near or at a level of zero: (1) a completely accurate forecast of net cash flows over the planning horizon and (2) perfect synchronization of cash receipts and disbursements.

Cash-flow forecasting is the initial step in any effective cash-management program. Given that the firm will, as a matter of necessity, invest in some cash balances, certain types of decisions related to the size of those balances dominate the cash-management process. These include decisions that answer the following questions:

1. What can be done to speed up cash collections and slow down or better control cash outflows?
2. What should be the composition of a marketable securities portfolio?

Although the sheer number of cash collection and payment techniques is large, the concepts on which those techniques rest are quite simple. Controlling the cash inflow and outflow is a major theme of treasury management. But, within the confines of ethical management, the cash manager is always thinking (1) "How can I speed up the firm's cash receipts?" and (2) "How can I slow down the firm's cash payments and not irritate too many important constituencies—such as suppliers?"

The critical point is that cash saved becomes available for investment elsewhere in the company's operations, and at a positive rate of return this will increase total profitability. Grasping the elements of cash management requires that you understand the concept of cash "float," to which we now turn.

CONCEPT CHECK

1. Describe the relationship between the firm's cash management program and the firm's risk of insolvency.
2. What are the fundamental decisions that the financial manager must make with respect to cash management?

Objective 

COLLECTION AND DISBURSEMENT PROCEDURES

The efficiency of the firm's cash-management program can be enhanced by knowledge and use of various procedures aimed at (1) accelerating cash receipts and (2) improving the methods used to disburse cash. We will see that greater opportunity for corporate profit improvement lies with the cash receipts side of the funds flow process, although it would be unwise to ignore opportunities for favorably affecting cash-disbursement practices.

MANAGING THE CASH INFLOW[2]

Float
The length of time from when a check is written until the actual recipient can draw upon or use the "good funds."

In order to increase the speed in which we receive cash receipts, it is essential that we understand how to reduce float. **Float** is the length of time from when a check is written until the actual recipient can use the "good funds." Float (or total float) has four elements, as follows:

1. *Mail float* is caused by the time lapse from the moment a customer mails a remittance check until the firm begins to process it.
2. *Processing float* is caused by the time required for the firm to process the customer's remittance checks before they can be deposited in the bank.
3. *Transit float* is caused by the time necessary for a deposited check from a customer to clear through the commercial banking system and become usable funds to the company. Credit is deferred for a maximum of two business days on checks that are cleared through the Federal Reserve System.
4. *Disbursing float* derives from the fact that the customer's funds are available in the company's bank account until the company's payment check has cleared through the banking system. Typically, funds available in the firm's banks *exceed* the balances indicated on its own books (ledgers).

We will use the term *float* to refer to the total of its four elements just described. Float reduction can yield considerable benefits in terms of usable funds that are released for company use and returns produced on such freed-up balances.

THE LOCK-BOX ARRANGEMENT The lock-box system is the most widely used commercial banking service for expediting cash gathering. Banks have offered this service since 1946. Such a system speeds up the conversion of receipts into usable funds by reducing both mail and processing float. Since the Federal Reserve System provides check-clearing facilities for depository institutions, it is possible to reduce transit float if lock boxes are located

[2] The discussions on cash receipt and disbursement procedures draw heavily on materials that were provided by the managements of the Chase Manhattan Bank, Continental Bank, and First National Bank of Chicago.

FIGURE 19-2 Ordinary Cash-Gathering System

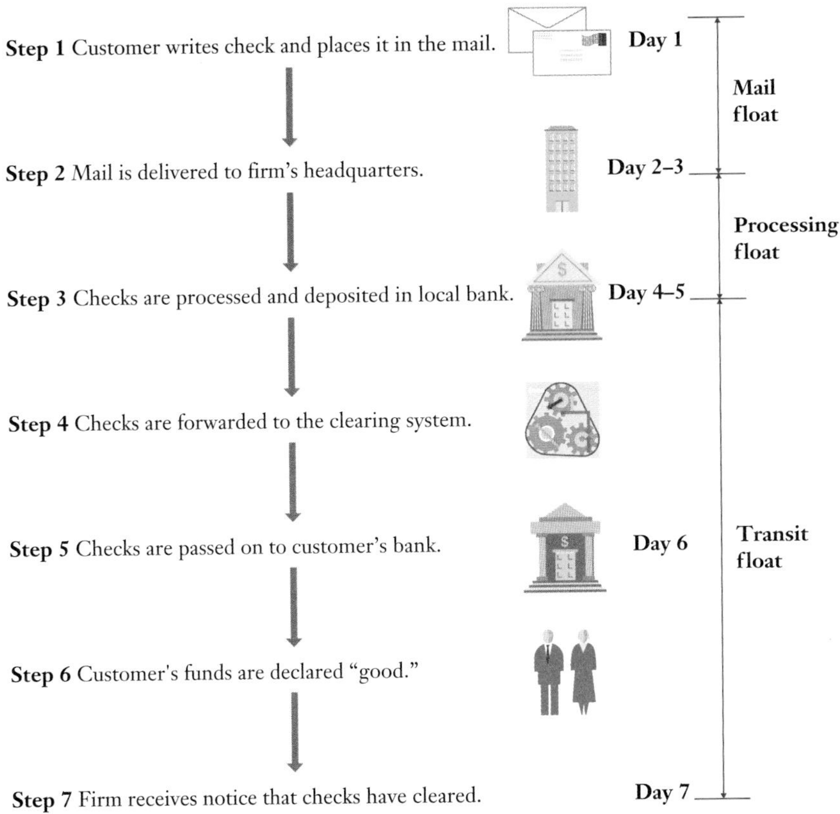

near Federal Reserve Banks and their branches. For large corporations that receive checks from all parts of the country, float reductions of two to four days are not unusual.

Figure 19-2 illustrates an elementary, but typical, cash collection system for a hypothetical firm. It also shows the origin of mail float, processing float, and transit float. In this system, the customer places his or her remittance check in the U.S. mail, which is then delivered to the firm's headquarters. This is mail float. On the check's arrival at the firm's headquarters (or local collection center), general accounting personnel must go through the bookkeeping procedures needed to prepare it for local deposit. The checks are then deposited. This is processing float. The checks are then forwarded for payment through the commercial bank clearing mechanism. The checks will be charged against the customer's own bank account. At this point, the checks are said to be "paid" and become "good funds" available for use by the company that received them. This bank clearing procedure represents transit float and, as we said earlier, can amount to a delay of up to two business days.

A lock-box arrangement is based on a simple procedure. The firm's customers are instructed to mail their remittance checks not to company headquarters or regional offices, but to a numbered Post Office box. This replaces step 2 in Figure 19-2, allowing mail to travel a shorter distance and often cutting the mail float by one day. The bank that is providing the lock-box service is authorized to open the box, collect the mail, process the checks, and deposit the checks directly into the company's account. The bank, eliminating the processing float entirely, now performs step 3 functions and saves an additional two days. Furthermore, transit float (steps 4 to 7) can also be reduced by one day as a result of the lock boxes being located near a Federal Reserve Bank or one of its branches.

Typically, a large bank will collect payments from the lock box at one- to two-hour intervals, 365 days of the year. During peak business hours, the bank may pick up mail every 30 minutes.

Once the mail is received at the bank, the checks will be examined, totaled, photocopied, and scanned. A deposit form is then prepared by the bank, and each batch of processed checks is forwarded to the collection department for clearance. Funds deposited in this manner are usually available for company use in one business day or less.

The same day deposits are made, the bank can notify the firm via some type of telecommunications system as to their amount. At the conclusion of each day, all check photocopies, invoices, deposit slips, and any other documents included with the remittances are mailed to the firm.

Note that the firm that receives checks from all over the country will have to use several lock boxes to take full advantage of a reduction in mail float. The firm's major bank should be able to offer as a service a detailed lock-box study, analyzing the company's receipt patterns to determine the proper number and location of lock-box receiving points.

The installation of the lock-box system can result in funds being credited to the firm's bank account a full four working days *faster* than is possible under the ordinary collection system.

In the chapter opening, we calculated the 2001 sales per day for Harley-Davidson to be $9.214 million and assumed Harley could invest its excess cash in marketable securities yielding 6.53 percent annually. If Harley could speed up its cash collections by four days, the results would be dramatic. The gross annual savings to Harley (apart from operating the lock-box system) would amount to $2.41 million as follows:

$$\text{(sales per day)} \times \text{(days of float reduction)} \times \text{(assumed yield)}$$
$$\$9.214 \text{ million} \times 4 \times .0653 = 2.41 \text{ million}$$

These benefits are not free. Usually, the bank levies a charge for each check processed through the system. The benefits derived from the acceleration of receipts must exceed the incremental costs of the lock-box system, or the firm would be better off without it. Companies that find the average size of their remittances to be quite small, for instance, might avoid a lock-box plan. Later in this chapter, we will illustrate how one calculates the costs and benefits of a specific cash-management service.

PREAUTHORIZED CHECKS (PACS) Whereas the lock-box arrangement can often reduce total float by two to four days, for some firms the use of preauthorized checks (PACs) can be an even more effective way of converting receipts into working cash. A PAC resembles the ordinary check, but it does not contain nor require the signature of the person on whose account it is being drawn. A PAC is created only with the individual's legal authorization.

Concentration banking The selection of a few major banks where the firm maintains significant disbursing accounts.

CONCENTRATION BANKING Both depository transfer checks and wire transfers are used in conjunction with what is known as **concentration banking**. A concentration bank is one in which the firm maintains a major disbursing account.

In an effort to accelerate collections, many companies have established multiple collection centers. Regional lock-box networks are one type of approach to strategically located collection points. Even without lock boxes, firms may have numerous sales outlets throughout the country and collect cash over the counter. This requires many local bank accounts to handle daily deposits. Rather than have funds sitting in these multiple bank accounts in different geographic regions of the country, most firms will regularly transfer the surplus balances to one or more concentration banks.

Depository transfer checks A non-negotiable instrument that provides the firm with a means to move funds from local bank accounts to concentration bank accounts.

Depository transfer checks provide a means for moving funds from local bank accounts to concentration accounts. The depository transfer check itself is an unsigned, non-negotiable instrument. It is payable only to the bank of deposit (the concentration bank) for credit to the firm's specific account. The firm files an authorization form with each bank from which it might withdraw funds. This form instructs the bank to pay the depository transfer checks without any signature.

WIRE TRANSFERS The fastest way to move cash between banks is by use of **wire transfers**, which eliminate transit float. Funds moved in this manner immediately become usable funds or "good funds" to the firm at the receiving bank. The following two major communication facilities are used to accommodate wire transfers:

Wire transfers A method of moving funds electronically between bank accounts in order to eliminate transit float. The wired funds are immediately usable at the receiving bank.

1. *Bank Wire.* Bank Wire is a private wire service used and supported by approximately 250 banks in the United States for transferring funds, exchanging credit information, and effecting securities transactions.
2. *Federal Reserve Wire System.* The Fed Wire is directly accessible to commercial banks that are members of the Federal Reserve System. A commercial bank that is not on the Bank Wire or is not a member of the Federal Reserve System can use the wire transfer through its correspondent bank.

MANAGING THE CASH OUTFLOW

Significant techniques and systems for improving the firm's management of cash disbursements include (1) zero balance accounts, (2) payable-through drafts, and (3) remote disbursing. The first two offer markedly better control over company-wide payments, and as a secondary benefit they *may* increase disbursement float. The last technique, remote disbursing, aims solely to increase disbursement float.

ZERO BALANCE ACCOUNTS Large corporations that operate multiple branches, divisions, or subsidiaries often maintain numerous bank accounts (in different banks) for the purpose of making timely operating disbursements. It does make good business sense for payments for purchased parts that go into, say, an automobile transmission to be made by the Transmission and Chassis Division of the auto manufacturer rather than its central office. The Transmission and Chassis Division originates such purchase orders, receives and inspects the shipment when it arrives at the plant, authorizes payment, and writes the appropriate check. To have the central office involved in these matters would be a waste of company time.

What tends to happen, however, is that with several divisions utilizing their own disbursal accounts, excess cash balances build up in outlying banks and rob the firm of earning assets. Zero balance accounts are used to alleviate this problem. The objectives of a zero balance account system are (1) for the firm to achieve better control over its cash payments, (2) to reduce excess cash balances held in regional banks for disbursing purposes, and (3) to increase disbursing float.

Zero balance accounts A cash-management tool that permits centralized control over cash outflows but also maintains divisional disbursing authority.

Zero balance accounts permit centralized control (at the headquarters level) over cash outflows while maintaining divisional disbursing authority. Under this system, the firm's authorized employees, representing their various divisions, continue to write checks on their individual accounts. Note that the numerous individual disbursing accounts are now *all* located in the same concentration bank. Actually, these separate accounts contain no funds at all, thus their appropriate label, "zero balance." These accounts have all of the other characteristics of regular demand deposit accounts including separate titles, numbers, and statements.

Payable-through drafts A payment mechanism that substitutes for regular checks in that drafts are not drawn on a bank, but instead are drawn on and authorized by the firm against its demand deposit account. The purpose is to maintain control over field-authorized payments.

PAYABLE-THROUGH DRAFTS **Payable-through drafts** are legal instruments that have the physical appearance of ordinary checks but are *not* drawn on a bank. Instead, payable-through drafts are drawn on, and payment is authorized by, the issuing firm against its demand deposit account. Like checks, the drafts are cleared through the banking system and are presented to the issuing firm's bank. The bank serves as a collection point and passes the drafts on to the firm. The corporate issuer usually has to return all drafts it does not wish to cover (pay) by the following business day. Those documents not returned to the bank are automatically paid. The firm inspects the drafts for validity by checking signatures, amounts, and dates. Stop-payment orders can be initiated by the company on any drafts considered inappropriate.

The main purpose of using a payable-through draft system is *to provide for effective control over field payments.* Central office control over payments begun by regional units is provided as the drafts are reviewed in advance of final payment. Payable-through drafts, for example, are used extensively in the insurance industry. The claims agent does not typically have check-signing authority against a corporate disbursement account. This agent can issue a draft, however, for quick settlement of a claim.

Electronic Funds Transfer

In the purest economic sense, "total" float should equal zero days and therefore should be worth zero dollars to any business firm or other economic unit in the society. Float is really a measure of inefficiency of the financial system in an economy. It is a friction of the business environment that stems from the fact that all information arising from business transactions cannot be instantaneously transferred among the parties involved.

Today the extensive use of electronic communication equipment is serving to reduce float. The central concept of electronic funds transfer (EFT) is simple. If firm A owes money to firm B, this situation ought to be immediately reflected on both the books and the bank accounts of these two companies. Instantaneous transfer of funds would eliminate float. Of course, this ideal within the U.S. financial system has not been reached; the trend toward it, however, is readily observable.

Automated teller machines, like those imbedded in the wall of your supermarket or at the airline terminal, are familiar devices to most consumers. Businesses are now beginning to use even more advanced systems, such as terminal-based wire transfers, to move funds within their cash-management systems.

The heart of EFT is the elimination of the check as a method of transferring funds. The elimination of the check may never occur, but certainly a move toward a financial system that uses fewer checks will. Transit, mail, and processing float become less important as EFT becomes more important. Simultaneously, this also implies that disbursing float becomes trivial.

BACK TO THE PRINCIPLES

All of these collection and disbursement procedures are an illustration of what is meant by ***Principle 2: The Time Value of Money—A dollar received today is worth more than a dollar received in the future.*** *The faster the firm can take possession of the money to which it is entitled, the sooner the firm is able to put the money to work generating a return. Similarly, the longer the firm is able to hold onto the liquid assets in its possession, the greater is the return the firm is able to receive on such funds.*

Evaluation of Costs of Cash-Management Services

A form of break-even analysis can help the financial officer decide whether a particular collection or disbursement service will provide an economic benefit to the firm. The evaluation process involves a very basic relationship in microeconomics:

$$\text{added costs} = \text{added benefits} \tag{19-1}$$

If equation 19-1 holds exactly, then the firm is no better or worse off for having adopted the given service. We will illustrate this procedure in terms of the desirability of installing an additional lock box. Equation 19-1 can be restated on a per-unit basis as follows:

$$P = (D)(S)(i) \tag{19-2}$$

where P = increases in per-check processing cost if the new system is adopted
D = days saved in the collection process (float reduction)
S = average check size in dollars
i = the daily, before-tax opportunity cost (rate of return) of carrying cash

Assume now that check processing cost, P, will rise by 18 cents a check if a lock box is used. The firm has determined that the average check size, S, that will be mailed to the lock-box location will be \$900. If funds are freed by use of the lock box, they will be invested in marketable securities to yield an *annual* before-tax return of 6 percent. With these data, it is possible to determine the reduction in check collection time, D, that is required to justify use of the lock box. That level of D is found to be:

$$184 = (D)(\$900)\left(\frac{.06}{365}\right)$$

$$1.217 \text{ days} = D$$

Thus, the lock box is justified if the firm can speed up its collections by *more* than 1.217 days. This same style of analysis can be adapted to analyze the other methods of cash management.

Before moving on to a discussion of the firm's marketable securities portfolio, it will be helpful to draw together the preceding material. Table 19-1 summarizes the key features of the cash-collection and disbursal techniques we have considered here.

TABLE 19-1 Features of Selected Cash-Collection and Disbursal Methods: A Summary

METHOD	OBJECTIVE	HOW ACCOMPLISHED
CASH-COLLECTION METHODS		
1. Lock-box system	Reduce (1) mail float, (2) processing float, and (3) transit float.	Strategic location of lock boxes to reduce mail float and transit float. Firm's commercial bank has access to lock box to reduce processing float.
2. Preauthorized checks	Reduce (1) mail float and (2) processing float.	The firm writes the checks (the PACs) for its customers to be charged against their demand deposit accounts.
3. (Ordinary) Depository transfer checks	Eliminate excess funds in regional banks.	Used in conjunction with concentration banking whereby the firm maintains several collection centers. The transfer check authorizes movement of funds from a local bank to the concentration bank.
4. Automated depository transfer check	Eliminate the mail float associated with the ordinary transfer check.	Telecommunications company transmits deposit data to the firm's concentration bank.
5. Wire transfers	Move funds immediately between banks. This eliminates transit float in that only "good funds" are transferred.	Use of Bank Wire or the Federal Reserve Wire System.
CASH-DISBURSAL METHODS		
1. Zero balance accounts	(1) Achieve better control over cash payments, (2) reduce excess cash balances held in regional banks, and (3) possibly increase disbursing float.	Establish zero balance accounts for all of the firm's disbursing units, but in the same concentration bank. Checks are drawn against these accounts, with the balance in each account never exceeding \$0. Divisional disbursing authority is thereby maintained at the local level of management.
2. Payable-through drafts	Achieve effective central office control over field-authorized payments.	Field office issues drafts rather than checks to settle payables.

CONCEPT CHECK

1. Define *float* and its origins in the cash management process.
2. What is a lock-box arrangement and how does its use reduce float?
3. Describe the use of zero balance accounts and payable-through drafts as methods for managing cash outflow.
4. How would you estimate the financial benefits of using a lock-box system?

Objective 5

COMPOSITION OF MARKETABLE SECURITIES PORTFOLIO

Once the design of the firm's cash receipts and payments system has been determined, the financial manager faces the task of selecting appropriate financial assets for inclusion in the firm's marketable securities portfolio.

GENERAL SELECTION CRITERIA

Certain criteria can provide the financial manager with a useful framework for selecting a proper marketable securities mix. These considerations include evaluation of the (1) financial risk, (2) interest rate risk, (3) liquidity, (4) taxability, and (5) yields among different financial assets. We will briefly delineate these criteria from the investor's viewpoint.

FINANCIAL RISK *Financial risk* refers to the uncertainty of expected returns from a security attributable to possible changes in the financial capacity of the security issuer to make future payments to the security owner. If the chance of default on the terms of the instrument is high (low), then the financial risk is said to be high (low).

In both financial practice and research, when estimates of risk-free returns are desired, the yields available on Treasury securities are consulted and the safety of other financial instruments is weighed against them.

INTEREST RATE RISK *Interest rate risk* refers to the uncertainty of expected returns from a financial instrument attributable to changes in interest rates. Of particular concern to the corporate treasurer is the price volatility associated with instruments that have long, as opposed to short, terms to maturity. An illustration can help clarify this point.

Suppose the financial officer is weighing the merits of investing temporarily available corporate cash in a new offering of U.S. Treasury obligations that will mature in either (1) 90 days or (2) one year from the date of issue. Ninety-day and one-year Treasury bills are issued at a discount from their maturity price of $1,000. The issue price of these bills is found by discounting at 7 percent, compounded daily.

If after 60 days from the date of purchase, prevailing interest rates rise to 9 percent, the market price of these currently outstanding Treasury securities will fall to bring the yields to maturity in line with what investors could obtain by buying a new issue of a given instrument. The market prices of *both* the 90-day and one-year obligations will decline. The price of the one-year instrument will decline by a greater dollar amount, however, than that of the 90-day instrument.

Sixty days from the date of issue, the price obtainable in the marketplace for the original one-year instrument, which now has 305 days until maturity, can be found by computing P as follows:

$$P = \frac{\$1,000}{\left(1 + \frac{.09}{365}\right)^{305}} = \$926.59$$

If interest rates had remained at 7 percent:

$$P = \frac{\$1,000}{\left(1 + \frac{.07}{365}\right)^{305}} = \$943.19$$

Therefore, the rise in interest rates caused the price of the one-year bill to fall by $16.60.

$$\$943.19 - \$926.59 = \$16.60$$

Now, what will happen to the price of the bill that has 30 days remaining to maturity? In a similar manner, we can compute its price, P:

$$P = \frac{\$1,000}{\left(1 + \frac{.09}{365}\right)^{30}} = \$992.63$$

If interest rates had remained at 7 percent:

$$P = \frac{\$1,000}{\left(1 + \frac{.07}{365}\right)^{30}} = \$994.26$$

Therefore, the price of the Treasury bill falls $1.63:

$$\$994.26 - \$992.63 = \$1.63$$

Thus, the market value of the shorter-term security was penalized much less by the given rise in the general level of interest rates.

If we extended the illustration, we would see that, in terms of market price, a one-year security would be affected less than a two-year security, a five-year security less than a 20-year security, and so on. Equity securities would exhibit the largest price changes because of their infinite maturity periods. To hedge against the price volatility caused by interest rate risk, the firm's marketable security portfolio will tend to be composed of instruments that mature over short periods.

LIQUIDITY In the present context of managing the marketable securities portfolio, *liquidity* refers to the ability to transform a security into cash. Should an unforeseen event require that a significant amount of cash be immediately available, then a sizable portion of the portfolio might have to be sold. The financial manager will want the cash *quickly* and will not want to accept a large *price concession* in order to convert the securities. Thus, in the formulation of preferences for the inclusion of particular instruments in the portfolio, the manager must consider (1) the period needed to sell the security and (2) the likelihood that the security can be sold at or near its prevailing market price.

TAXABILITY The tax treatment of the income a firm receives from its security investments does not affect the ultimate mix of the marketable securities portfolio as much as the criteria mentioned earlier. This is because the interest income from most instruments suitable for inclusion in the portfolio is taxable at the federal level. Still, some corporate treasurers seriously evaluate the taxability of interest income and capital gains.

TABLE 19-2 Comparison of After-Tax Yields

	TAX-EXEMPT DEBT ISSUE (6% COUPON)	TAXABLE DEBT ISSUE (8% COUPON)
Interest income	\$ 60.00	\$ 80.00
Income tax (.34)	0.00	27.20
After-tax interest income	60.00	52.80
After-tax yield	$\frac{60.00}{\$1,000.00} = 6\%$	$\frac{52.80}{\$1,000.00} = 5.28\%$

Derivation of equivalent before-tax yield on a taxable debt issue:

$$r = \frac{r^*}{1-t} = \frac{.06}{1-.24} = 9.091\%$$

where

r = equivalent before-tax yield

r^* = after-tax yield on tax-exempt security

t = firm's marginal income tax rate

Proof:

Interest income [\$1,000 × .09091] =	\$90.91
Income tax (.34)	30.91
After-tax interest income	\$60.00

The interest income from only one class of securities escapes the federal income tax. That class of securities is generally referred to as *municipal obligations* or more simply as *municipals*. Because of the tax-exempt feature of interest income from state and local government securities, municipals sell at lower yields to maturity in the market than do securities that pay taxable interest. The after-tax yield on a municipal obligation, however, could be higher than the yield from a non-tax-exempt security. This would depend mainly on the purchasing firm's tax situation.

Consider Table 19-2. A firm is analyzing whether to invest in a one-year tax-free debt issue yielding 6 percent on a \$1,000 outlay or a one-year taxable issue that yields 8 percent on a \$1,000 outlay. The firm pays federal taxes at the rate of 34 percent. The yields quoted in the financial press and in the prospectuses that describe debt issues are *before-tax* returns.

The actual *after-tax* return enjoyed by the firm depends on its tax bracket. Notice that the actual after-tax yield received by the firm is only 5.28 percent on the taxable issue versus 6 percent on the tax-exempt obligation. The lower portion of Table 19-2 shows that the fully taxed bond must yield 9.091 percent to make it comparable with the tax-exempt issue.

YIELDS The final selection criterion that we mention is a significant one—the yields that are available on the different financial assets suitable for inclusion in the near-cash portfolio. By now it is probably obvious that the factors of (1) financial risk, (2) interest rate risk, (3) liquidity, and (4) taxability all influence the available yields on financial instruments. The yield criterion involves an evaluation of the risks and benefits inherent in all of these factors. If a given risk is assumed, such as lack of liquidity, a higher yield may be expected on the nonliquid instrument.

Table 19-3 summarizes our framework for designing the firm's marketable securities portfolio. The four basic considerations are shown to influence the yields available on securities. The financial manager must focus on the risk-return trade-offs identified through analysis. Coming to grips with these trade-offs will enable the financial manager to determine the proper marketable securities mix for the company. Let us look now at the marketable securities prominent in firms' near-cash portfolios.

TABLE 19-3 Designing the Marketable Securities Portfolio

CONSIDERATIONS	→	INFLUENCE	→	FOCUS UPON	→	DETERMINE
Financial risk Interest rate risk Liquidity Taxability		Yields		Risk vs. return preferences mix		Marketable securities

MARKETABLE SECURITY ALTERNATIVES

Based on the forgoing discussion on the criteria to be used in selecting a security investment, let's now look at the investments that are commonly used.

U.S. TREASURY BILLS *U.S. Treasury bills* are the best-known and most popular short-term investment outlets among firms. A Treasury bill is a direct obligation of the U.S. government sold on a regular basis by the U.S. Treasury. New Treasury bills are issued in denominations of $1,000 and up.

At present, bills are regularly offered with maturities of 91, 182, and 365 days. The three-month and six-month bills are auctioned weekly by the Treasury, and the one-year bills are offered every four weeks. Bids (orders to purchase) are accepted by the various Federal Reserve Banks and their branches, which perform the role of agents for the Treasury. Each Monday, bids are received until 1:30 P.M. eastern time; after that time they are opened, tabulated, and forwarded to the Treasury for allocation (filling the purchase orders).

Treasury bills are sold on a discount basis; for that reason, the investor does not receive an actual interest payment. The return is the difference between the purchase price and the face (par) value of the bill.

Of prime importance to the corporate treasurer is the fact that a very active secondary market exists for bills. After a bill has been acquired by the firm, should the need arise to turn it into cash, a group of securities dealers stands ready to purchase it. This highly developed secondary market for bills not only makes them extremely liquid, but also allows the firm to buy bills with maturities of a week or even less.

As bills have the full financial backing of the U.S. government, they are, for all practical purposes, risk-free. This negligible financial risk and high degree of liquidity makes the yields lower than those obtainable on other marketable securities. The income from Treasury bills is subject to federal income taxes, but *not* to state and local government income taxes.

FEDERAL AGENCY SECURITIES *Federal agency securities* are debt obligations of corporations and agencies that have been created to effect the various lending programs of the U.S. government. Five such government-sponsored corporations account for the majority of outstanding agency debt. The "big five" agencies are the Federal National Mortgage Association, the Federal Home Loan Banks, the Federal Land Banks, the Federal Intermediate Credit Banks, and the Banks for Cooperatives.

It is not true that the "big five" federally sponsored agencies are owned by the U.S. government and that the securities they issue are fully guaranteed by the government. The "big five" agencies are now entirely owned by their member associations or the general public. In addition, it is the issuing agency that stands behind its promises to pay, not the federal government.

These agencies sell their securities in a variety of denominations. The entry barrier caused by the absolute dollar size of the smallest available Treasury bill—$10,000—is not as severe in the market for agencies. A wide range of maturities is also available. Obligations can at times be purchased with maturities as short as 30 days or as long as 15 years.

Agency debt usually sells on a coupon basis and pays interest to the owner on a semiannual schedule, although there are exceptions. Some issues have been sold on a discount basis, and some have paid interest only once a year.

The income from agency debt that the investor receives is subject to taxation at the federal level. Of the "big five" agencies, only the income from FNMA issues is taxed at the state and local level.

The yields available on agency obligations will always exceed those of Treasury securities of similar maturity. This yield differential is attributable to lesser marketability and greater default risk. The financial officer might keep in mind, however, that none of these agency issues has ever gone into default.

BANKERS' ACCEPTANCES *Bankers' acceptances* are one of the least understood instruments suitable for inclusion in the firm's marketable securities portfolio. Their part in U.S. commerce today is largely concentrated in the financing of foreign transactions. Generally, an acceptance is a draft (order to pay) drawn on a specific bank by an exporter in order to obtain payment for goods shipped to a customer, who maintains an account with that specific bank.

Because acceptances are used to finance the acquisition of goods by one party, the document is not "issued" in specialized denominations; its dollar size is determined by the cost of the goods being purchased. Usual sizes, however, range from $25,000 to $1 million. The maturities on acceptances run from 30 to 180 days, although longer periods are available from time to time. The most common period is 90 days.

Acceptances, like Treasury bills, are sold on a discount basis and are payable to the holder of the paper. A secondary market for the acceptances of large banks does exist.

The income generated from investing in acceptances is fully taxable at the federal, state, and local levels. Because of their greater financial risk and lesser liquidity, acceptances provide investors a yield advantage over Treasury bills and agency obligations. In fact, the acceptances of major banks are a very safe investment, making the yield advantage over Treasuries worth looking at from the firm's vantage point.

NEGOTIABLE CERTIFICATES OF DEPOSIT A *negotiable certificate of deposit, CD,* is a marketable receipt for funds that have been deposited in a bank for a fixed time period. The deposited funds earn a fixed rate of interest. These are not to be confused with ordinary passbook savings accounts or nonmarketable time deposits offered by all commercial banks. CDs are offered by major money-center banks. We are talking here about "corporate" CDs—not those offered to individuals.

CDs are offered by key banks in a variety of denominations running from $25,000 to $10 million. The popular sizes are $100,000, $500,000, and $1 million. The original maturities on CDs can range from 1 to 18 months.

CDs are offered by banks on a basis differing from Treasury bills; that is, they are not sold at a discount. Rather, when the certificate matures, the owner receives the full amount deposited plus the earned interest.

A secondary market for CDs does exist, the heart of which is found in New York City. Even though the secondary market for CDs of large banks is well organized, it does not operate as smoothly as the aftermarket in Treasuries. CDs are more heterogeneous than Treasury bills. Treasury bills have similar rates, maturity periods, and denominations; more variety is found in CDs. This makes it harder to liquidate large blocks of CDs, because a more specialized investor must be found. The securities dealers who "make" the secondary market in CDs mainly trade in $1 million units. Smaller denominations can be traded but will bring a relatively lower price.

The income received from an investment in CDs is subject to taxation at all government levels. In recent years, CD yields have been above those available on bankers' acceptances.

COMMERCIAL PAPER *Commercial paper* refers to short-term, unsecured promissory notes sold by large businesses to raise cash. These are sometimes described in the popular financial press as short-term corporate IOUs. Because they are unsecured, the issuing side of the market is dominated by large corporations, which typically maintain sound credit ratings. The issuing (borrowing) firm can sell the paper to a dealer who will in turn sell it to the investing public; if the firm's reputation is solid, the paper can be sold directly to the ultimate investor.

The denominations in which commercial paper can be bought vary over a wide range. At times, paper can be obtained in sizes from $5,000 to $5 million, or even more.

Commercial paper can be purchased with maturities that range from 3 to 270 days. Notes with maturities exceeding 270 days are very rare, because they would have to be registered with the Securities and Exchange Commission—a task firms avoid, when possible, because it is time consuming and costly.

These notes are *generally* sold on a discount basis, although sometimes paper that is interest bearing and can be made payable to the order of the investor is available.

The next point is of considerable interest to the financial officer responsible for management of the firm's near-cash portfolio. For practical purposes, there is *no* active trading in a secondary market for commercial paper. This distinguishes commercial paper from all of the previously discussed short-term investment vehicles. On occasion, a dealer or finance company (the borrower) will redeem a note prior to its contract maturity date, but this is not a regular procedure. Thus, when the corporation evaluates commercial paper for possible inclusion in its marketable securities portfolio, it should plan to hold it to maturity.

The return on commercial paper is fully taxable to the investor at all levels of government. Because of its lack of marketability, commercial paper in past years consistently provided a yield advantage over other near-cash assets of comparable maturity. The lifting of interest rate ceilings in 1973 by the Federal Reserve Board on certain large CDs, however, allowed commercial banks to make CD rates fully competitive in the attempt to attract funds. Over any time period, then, CD yields *may* be slightly above the rates available on commercial paper.

REPURCHASE AGREEMENTS *Repurchase agreements (repos)* are legal contracts that involve the actual sale of securities by a *borrower* to the *lender*, with a commitment on the part of the borrower to *repurchase* the securities at the contract price plus a stated interest charge. The securities sold to the lender are U.S. government issues or other instruments of the money market such as those described previously. The borrower is either a major financial institution—most often, a commercial bank—or a dealer in U.S. government securities.

Why might the corporation with excess cash prefer to buy repurchase agreements rather than a given marketable security? There are two major reasons. First, the original maturities of the instruments being sold can, in effect, be adjusted to suit the particular needs of the investing corporation. Funds available for very short time periods, such as one or two days, can be productively employed. The second reason is closely related to the first. The firm could, of course, buy a Treasury bill and then resell it in the market in a few days when cash was required. The drawback here would be the risk involved in liquidating the bill at a price equal to its earlier cost to the firm. The purchase of a repo removes this risk. The contract price of the securities that make up the arrangement is *fixed* for the duration of the transaction. The corporation that buys a repurchase agreement, then, is protected against market price fluctuations throughout the contract period. This makes it a sound alternative investment for funds that are freed up for only very short periods. For example, mutual funds will buy repos as a way to "park" excess cash flows for a few days.

TABLE 19-4 Money Market Funds Asset Composition, Year-End 2001

	AMOUNT ($ MILLIONS)	PERCENT OF TOTAL
U.S. Treasury Bills	$ 93,450.2	4.64
Other Treasury Securities	45,345.7	2.25
U.S. Securities	325,656.1	16.18
Repurchase Agreements	232,186.8	11.54
Certificates of Deposit	195,809.3	9.73
Eurodollar CDs	127,034.9	6.31
Commercial Paper	649,636.4	32.27
Bank Notes	25,342.4	1.26
Bankers' Acceptances	3,850.5	0.19
Corporate Notes	141,353.8	7.02
Cash Reserves and other	4,664.8	.23
Other Assets	168,618.5	8.38

Source: Investment Company Institute (www.ICI.org)

MONEY MARKET MUTUAL FUNDS Money market funds typically invest in a diversified portfolio of short-term, high-grade debt instruments such as those described previously. Some such funds, however, will accept more interest rate risk in their portfolios and acquire some corporate bonds and notes. The portfolio composition of 702 money market funds in 1999 is shown in Table 19-4. We see that commercial paper, repurchase agreements, plus all CDs (both domestic plus Eurodollar) represented 61.1 percent of money fund assets at this point in time. The average maturity period for these same 702 funds stood at 49 days. The interest rate risk contained in this overall portfolio is, therefore, rather small.

The money market funds sell their shares to raise cash, and by pooling the funds of large numbers of small savers, they can build their liquid-asset portfolios. Many of these funds allow the investor to start an account with as little as $1,000. This small initial investment, coupled with the fact that some liquid-asset funds permit subsequent investments in amounts as small as $100, makes this type of outlet for excess cash well suited to the small firm and the individual. Furthermore, the management of a small enterprise may not be highly versed in the details of short-term investments. By purchasing shares in a liquid-asset fund, the investor is also buying managerial expertise.

Money market mutual funds offer the investing firm a high degree of liquidity. By redeeming (selling) shares, the investor can obtain cash quickly. Procedures for liquidation vary among the funds, but shares can usually be redeemed by means of (1) special redemption checks supplied by the fund, (2) telephone instructions, (3) wire instructions, or (4) a letter. When liquidation is ordered by telephone or wire, the mutual fund can remit to the investor by the next business day.

The returns earned from owning shares in a money market fund are taxable at all governmental levels. The yields follow the returns the investor could receive by purchasing the marketable securities directly.

CONCEPT CHECK

1. What are financial and interest rate risk?
2. Describe each of the following: Treasury bills, federal agency securities, bankers' acceptances, negotiable certificates of deposit, commercial paper, repurchase agreements, and money-market mutual funds.
3. What is meant by the yield structure of marketable securities?

THE MULTINATIONAL FIRM: THE USE OF CASH AND MARKETABLE SECURITIES

In terms of principles, not much changes for a multinational firm as opposed to a domestic firm. However, just as with other basic financial principles, everything becomes a bit more complicated. No longer can a firm simply look at the operations of its different units and allow those units to make corporate decisions. In fact, more often than not, the global or centralized financial decisions that a firm makes tend to be superior to decisions made by the different subsidiaries.

As we will see in Chapter 22, International Business Finance, when cash management enters the international arena, we are introduced to delaying collections when the currency being collected is strong, or quickly converting those assets into a relatively stronger currency. The bottom line here is that when we introduce multiple currencies we greatly complicate the process of cash management. Your job may be to manage collections from several countries and to make sure that those collections are maintained in as strong a currency as possible. That will mean transferring funds from country to country.

HOW FINANCIAL MANAGERS USE THIS MATERIAL

Although a company's profitability is important, its ability to manage cash is vital. As a company becomes larger, cash management becomes more difficult and requires sophisticated systems to manage the firm's cash flows. Being effective in managing cash receipts and disbursements can mean thousands of dollars in savings to a larger company over a year's time.

The materials covered in this chapter have addressed many of the techniques used on a daily basis by almost all companies. These include:

- Check clearing mechanisms, electronic funds transfer systems, and float
- Collection (lock box, preauthorized debits), concentration (branch banking, depository transfers), and disbursement (zero balance accounts, remote and controlled disbursements)
- Use of excess funds through short-term investments, which requires written investment policies and guidelines and deciding where to invest excess cash, be it U.S. Treasury bills, CDs, commercial paper, repurchase agreements, bankers' acceptances, money market funds, munis, or other securities
- Information management systems on deposit and balance reporting
- Selecting the right cash management bank

SUMMARY

Objective 1

Liquid assets are the summation of cash and marketable securities. Cash is the currency and coin the firm has on hand in cash drawers, cash registers, or checking accounts. Cash balances earn no return. Near-cash assets, also known as marketable securities, are security investments that earn a rate of return and that the firm can quickly convert into cash balances.

Objective 2

The firm experiences both regular and irregular cash flows. Once cash is obtained, the firm will have three motives for holding cash: to satisfy transactions, precautionary needs for liquidity, and speculative needs for liquidity. To a certain extent, such needs can be satisfied by holding readily marketable securities rather than cash.

Objective 3

The financial manager must (1) ensure that enough cash is on hand to meet the payment needs that arise in the course of doing business and (2) attempt to maximize wealth by reducing the firm's idle cash balances to a minimum.

Objective 4

Float is the length of time from when a check is written until the actual recipient can use the "good funds." To reduce float, the firm can benefit considerably through the use of (1) lock-box arrangements, (2) preauthorized checks, (3) special forms of depository transfer checks, and (4) wire transfers. Lock-box systems and preauthorized checks serve to reduce mail and processing float. Depository transfer checks and wire transfers move funds between banks; they are often used in conjunction with concentration banking. Both the lock-box and preauthorized check systems can be employed as part of the firm's concentration banking setup to speed receipts to regional collection centers.

The firm can delay and favorably affect the control of its cash disbursements through the use of (1) zero balance accounts, (2) payable-through drafts, and (3) remote disbursing. Zero balance accounts allow the company to maintain central-office control over payments while permitting the firm's several divisions to maintain their own disbursing authority. Because key disbursing accounts are located in one major concentration bank, rather than in multiple banks across the country, excess cash balances that tend to build up in the outlying banks are avoided. Payable-through drafts are legal instruments that look like checks but are drawn on and paid by the issuing firm rather than its bank. The bank serves as a collection point for the drafts. Effective central-office control over field-authorized payments is the main reason such a system is used; it is not used as a major vehicle for extending disbursing float.

Before any of these collection and disbursement procedures is initiated by the firm, a careful analysis should be undertaken to see if the expected benefits outweigh the expected costs.

Objective 5

The factors of (1) financial risk, (2) interest rate risk, (3) liquidity, and (4) taxability affect the yields available on marketable securities. By considering these four factors simultaneously with returns desired from the portfolio, the financial manager can design the mix of near-cash assets most suitable for a firm.

We looked at several marketable securities. Treasury bills and federal agency securities are extremely safe investments. Bankers' acceptances, CDs, and commercial paper provide higher yields in exchange for greater risk assumption. Unlike the other instruments, commercial paper enjoys no *developed* secondary market. The firm can hedge against price fluctuations through the use of repurchase agreements. Money market mutual funds, a recent phenomenon of our financial market system, are particularly well suited for the short-term investing needs of small firms.

KEY TERMS

Go To: www.prenhall.com/keown for downloads and current events associated with this chapter

Cash, 674

Concentration banking, 680

Depository transfer checks, 680

Float, 678

Insolvency, 676

Liquid assets, 674

Marketable securities, 674

Payable-through drafts, 681

Wire transfers, 681

Zero balance accounts, 681

STUDY QUESTIONS

19-1. What is meant by the *cash flow process?*

19-2. Identify the principal motives for holding cash and near-cash assets. Explain the purpose of each motive.

19-3. What is concentration banking and how may it be of value to the firm?

19-4. Distinguish between depository transfer checks and automated depository transfer checks (ADTC).

19-5. In general, what type of firm would benefit from the use of a preauthorized check system? What specific types of companies have successfully used this device to accelerate cash receipts?

19-6. What are the two major objectives of the firm's cash-management system?

19-7. What three decisions dominate the cash-management process?

19-8. Within the context of cash management, what are the key elements of (total) float? Briefly define each element.

19-9. Distinguish between financial risk and interest rate risk as these terms are commonly used in discussions of cash management.

19-10. What is meant when we say, "A money market instrument is highly liquid"?

19-11. Which money market instrument is generally conceded to have no secondary market?

19-12. Your firm invests in only three different classes of marketable securities: commercial paper, Treasury bills, and federal agency securities. Recently, yields on these money market instruments of three months' maturity were quoted at 6.10, 6.25, and 5.90 percent. Match the available yields with the types of instruments your firm purchases.

19-13. What two key factors might induce a firm to invest in repurchase agreements rather than a specific security of the money market?

SELF-TEST PROBLEMS

ST-1. (*Costs of services*) Creative Fashion Designs is evaluating a lock-box system as a cash receipts acceleration device. In a typical year, this firm receives remittances totaling $7 million by check. The firm will record and process 4,000 checks over the same time period. Ocala National Bank has informed the management of Creative Fashion Designs that it will process checks and associated documents through the lock-box system for a unit cost of 25 cents per check. Creative Fashion Designs' financial manager has projected that cash freed by adoption of the system can be invested in a portfolio of near-cash assets that will yield an annual before-tax return of 8 percent. Creative Fashion Designs' financial analysts use a 365-day year in their procedures.

- **a.** What reduction in check collection time is necessary for Creative Fashion Designs to be neither better nor worse off for having adopted the proposed system?
- **b.** How would your solution to (a) be affected if Creative Fashion Designs could invest the freed balances only at an expected annual pre-tax return of 5.5 percent?
- **c.** What is the logical explanation for the differences in your answers to (a) and (b)?

ST-2. (*Cash receipts acceleration system*) Artie Kay's Komputer Shops is a large, national distributor and retailer of microcomputers, personal computers, and related software. The company has its central offices in Dearborn, Michigan, not far from the Ford Motor Company executive offices and headquarters. Only recently has Artie Kay's begun to pay serious attention to its cash-management procedures. Last week, the firm received a proposal from the Detroit National Bank. The objective of the proposal is to speed up the firm's cash collections.

Artie Kay's now uses a centralized billing procedure. All checks are mailed to the Dearborn headquarters office for processing and eventual deposit. Remittance checks now take an average of five business days to reach the Dearborn office. The in-house processing at Artie Kay's is quite slow. Once in Dearborn, another three days are needed to process the checks for deposit at Detroit National.

The daily cash remittances of Artie Kay's average $200,000. The average check size is $800. The firm currently earns 10.6 percent on its marketable securities portfolio and expects this rate to continue to be available.

The cash acceleration plan suggested by officers of Detroit National involves both a lock-box system and concentration banking. Detroit National would be the firm's only concentration bank. Lock boxes would be established in (1) Seattle, (2) San Antonio, (3) Chicago, and (4) Detroit. This would reduce mail float by 2.0 days. Processing float would be reduced to a level of 0.5 days. Funds would then be transferred twice each business day by means of automated depository transfer checks from local banks in Seattle, San Antonio, and Chicago to the Detroit National Bank. Each ADTC costs $20. These transfers will occur all 270 business days of the year. Each check processed through the lock-box system will cost Artie Kay's 25 cents.

a. What amount of cash balances will be freed if Artie Kay's adopts the system proposed by Detroit National?
b. What is the opportunity cost of maintaining the current banking arrangement?
c. What is the projected annual cost of operating the proposed system?
d. Should Artie Kay's adopt the new system? Compute the net annual gain or loss associated with adopting the system.

ST-3. (*Buying and selling marketable securities*) Mountaineer Outfitters has $2 million in excess cash that it might invest in marketable securities. In order to buy and sell the securities, however, the firm must pay a transaction fee of $45,000.

a. Would you recommend purchasing the securities if they yield 12 percent annually and are held for:
1. One month?
2. Two months?
3. Three months?
4. Six months?
5. One year?

b. What minimum required yield would the securities have to return for the firm to hold them for three months (what is the break-even yield for a three-month holding period)?

STUDY PROBLEMS (SET A)

19-1A. (*Concentration banking*) Healthy Herbal Beverage, Inc., produces a very healthy herbal beverage in Tupelo, Mississippi, that is distributed to health-food stores primarily along the Gulf Coast, where many health-food aficionados seem to live. Until now, the company has received collections on its accounts receivable at its Tupelo headquarters. Such collections recently have been $40 million at an annual rate and are expected to remain at that level. The company's bank has suggested to Healthy Herbal's CFO, Wanda Jackson, that the bank could establish a concentration banking system for the company that would save the company four days in mail float, three days in processing float, and $35,000 in annual clerical costs. The bank would charge a flat fee per year of $40,000 to operate the system for Healthy Herbal. Wanda believes that the funds freed by such an arrangement could be invested at no transaction cost in the company's money market account and could earn an annual rate of return of 5 percent. Should Wanda accept the bank's proposal? Use a 365-day year in your analysis.

19-2A. (*Buying and selling marketable securities*) An alternative to investing in a no-transaction-fee money market account under consideration by Wanda Jackson, the CFO at Healthy Herbal Beverage, Inc. (see Problem 19-1A), is direct investment in marketable securities. Assume for this problem that Wanda has determined that adoption of a concentration banking system could make $750,000 available for investment in marketable securities, but such direct investing would result in annual transaction fees of $15,000. Would you recommend that Wanda invest the funds in a money market account (at 5 percent per annum) or purchase the marketable securities directly if such securities yield 7.5 percent per annum and the expected holding period is for:

a. One month?
b. Two months?
c. Six months?
d. One year?

19-3A. (*Lock-box system*) The Marino Rug Co. is located on the outskirts of Miramar, Florida. The firm specializes in the manufacture of a wide variety of carpet and tile. All of the firm's output is shipped to 12 warehouses, which are located in the largest metropolitan areas nationwide. National Bank of Miami is Marino Rug's lead bank. National Bank has just completed a study of Marino's cash collection system. Overall, National estimates that it can reduce Marino's total float by three days with the installation of a lock-box arrangement in each of the firm's 12 regions. The lock-box arrangement would cost each region $325 per month. Any funds freed up would be added to the firm's marketable securities portfolio and would yield 9.75 percent on an annual basis. Annual sales average $6,232,375 for each regional office. The firm and the bank use a 365-day year in their analyses. Should Marino's management approve the use of the proposed system?

19-4A. (*Marketable securities portfolio*) Mac's Tennis Racket Manufacturing Company currently pays its employees on a weekly basis. The weekly wage bill is $675,000. This means that, on average, the firm has accrued wages payable of ($675,000 + $0)/2 = $337,500.

Jimmy McEnroe works as the firm's senior financial analyst and reports directly to his uncle, who owns all of the firm's common stock. Jimmy McEnroe wants to move to a monthly wage payment system. Employees would be paid at the end of every fourth week. Jimmy is aware that the labor union representing the company's workers will not permit the monthly payments system to take effect unless the workers are given some type of fringe-benefit compensation.

A plan has been worked out whereby the firm will make a contribution to the cost of life insurance coverage for each employee. This will cost the firm $50,775 annually. Jimmy McEnroe expects the firm to earn 8.5 percent annually on its marketable securities portfolio.

- **a.** Based on the projected information, should Mac's Tennis Racket Manufacturing Company move to the monthly wage payment system?
- **b.** What annual rate of return on the marketable securities portfolio would enable the firm just to break even on this proposal?

19-5A. (*Cash receipts acceleration system*) James Waller Nail Corp. is a buyer and distributor of nails used in the home building industry. The firm has grown very quickly since it was established eight years ago. Waller Nail has managed to increase sales and profits at a rate of about 18 percent annually, despite moderate economic growth at the national level. Until recently, the company paid little attention to cash-management procedures. James Waller, the firm's president, said: "With our growth—who cares?" Bending to the suggestions of several analysts in the firm's finance group, Waller did agree to have a proposal prepared by the Second National Bank in Tampa, Florida. The objective of the proposal is to accelerate the firm's cash collections.

At present, Waller Nail uses a centralized billing procedure. All checks are mailed to the Tampa office headquarters for processing and eventual deposit. Under this arrangement, all customers' remittance checks take an average of five business days to reach the Tampa office. Once in Tampa, another two days are needed to process the checks for deposit at the Second National Bank.

Daily cash remittances at Waller Nail average $750,000. The average check size is $3,750. The firm currently earns 9.2 percent annually on its marketable securities portfolio.

The cash-acceleration plan presented by the officers of Second National Bank involves both a lock-box system and concentration banking. Second National would be the firm's only concentration bank. Lock boxes would be established in (1) Los Angeles, (2) Dallas, (3) Chicago, and (4) Tampa. This would reduce funds tied up in mail float to 3.5 days. Processing float would be totally eliminated. Funds would then be transferred twice each business day by means of automated depository transfer checks from local banks in Los Angeles, Dallas, and Chicago to the Second National Bank. Each ADTC costs $27. These transfers will occur all 270 business days of the year. Each check processed through the lock box will cost Waller Nail 35 cents.

- **a.** What amount of cash balances will be freed if Waller Nail adopts the system proposed by Second National Bank?
- **b.** What is the opportunity cost of maintaining the current banking arrangement?
- **c.** What is the projected annual cost of operating the proposed system?
- **d.** Should Waller Nail Corp. adopt the system? Compute the net annual gain or loss associated with adopting the system.

19-6A. (*Costs of services*) The Mountain Furniture Company of Scranton, Pennsylvania, may install a lock-box system to speed up its cash receipts. On an annual basis, Mountain Furniture receives $40 million in remittances by check. The firm will record and process 15,000 checks over the year. The Third Bank of Scranton will administer the system at a cost of 35 cents per check. Cash that is freed up by use of the system can be invested to yield 9 percent on an annual before-tax basis. A 365-day year is used for analysis purposes. What reduction in check collection time is necessary for Mountain Furniture to be neither better nor worse off for having adopted the proposed system?

19-7A. (*Valuing float reduction*) Griffey Manufacturing Company is forecasting that next year's gross revenues from sales will be $890 million. The senior treasury analyst for the firm expects the marketable securities portfolio to earn 9.60 percent over this same time period. A 365-day year is used in all the firm's financial procedures. What is the value to the company of one day's float reduction?

19-8A. (*Costs of services*) Mustang Ski-Wear, Inc., is investigating the possibility of adopting a lock-box system as a cash receipts acceleration device. In a typical year, this firm receives remittances totaling $12 million by check. The firm will record and process 6,000 checks over this same time period. The Colorado Springs Second National Bank has informed the management of Mustang that it will expedite checks and associated documents through the lock-box system for a unit cost of 20 cents per check. Mustang's financial manager has projected that cash freed by adoption of the system can be invested in a portfolio of near-cash assets that will yield an annual before-tax return of 7 percent. Mustang financial analysts use a 365-day year in their procedures.

a. What reduction in check collection time is necessary for Mustang to be neither better nor worse off for having adopted the proposed system?

b. How would your solution to (a) be affected if Mustang could invest the freed balances only at an expected annual return of 4.5 percent?

c. What is the logical explanation for the difference in your answers to (a) and (b)?

19-9A. (*Valuing float reduction*) The Columbus Tool and Die Works will generate $18 million in credit sales next year. Collections occur at an even rate, and employees work a 270-day year. At the moment, the firm's general accounting department ties up five days' worth of remittance checks. An analysis undertaken by the firm's treasurer indicates that new internal procedures can reduce processing float by two days. If Columbus Tool invests the released funds to earn 8 percent, what will be the annual savings?

19-10A. (*Valuing float reduction*) Montgomery Woodcraft is a large distributor of woodworking tools and accessories to hardware stores, lumber yards, and tradesmen. All its sales are on a credit basis, net 30 days. Sales are evenly distributed over its 12 sales regions throughout the United States. There is no problem with delinquent accounts. The firm is attempting to improve its cash-management procedures. Montgomery recently determined that it took an average of 3.0 days for customers' payments to reach their office from the time they were mailed and another day for processing before payments could be deposited. Annual sales average $5,200,000 for each region, and investment opportunities can be found to return 9 percent per year. What is the opportunity cost to the firm of the funds tied up in mailing and processing? In your calculations, use a 365-day year.

19-11A. (*Accounts payable policy and cash management*) Bradford Construction Supply Company is suffering from a prolonged decline in new construction in its sales area. In an attempt to improve its cash position, the firm is considering changes in its accounts payable policy. After careful study, it has been determined that the only alternative available is to slow disbursements. Purchases for the coming year are expected to be $37.5 million. Sales will be $65 million, which represents about a 20 percent drop from the current year. Currently, Bradford discounts approximately 25 percent of its payments at 3 percent 10 days, net 30, and the balance of accounts are paid in 30 days. If Bradford adopts a policy of payment in 45 days or 60 days, how much can the firm gain if the annual opportunity cost of investment is 12 percent? What will be the result if this action causes Bradford Construction suppliers to increase their prices to the company by 0.5 percent to compensate for the 60-day extended term of payment? In your calculations, use a 365-day year and ignore any compounding effects related to expected returns.

19-12A. (*Interest rate risk*) Two years ago, your corporate treasurer purchased for the firm a 20-year bond at its par value of $1,000. The coupon rate on this security is 8 percent. Interest payments are made to bondholders once a year. Currently, bonds of this particular risk class are yielding investors 9 percent. A cash shortage has forced you to instruct your treasurer to liquidate this bond.

a. At what price will your bond be sold? Assume annual compounding.
b. What will be the amount of your gain or loss over the original purchase price?
c. What would be the amount of your gain or loss had the treasurer originally purchased a bond with a four-year rather than a 20-year maturity? (Assume all characteristics of the bonds are identical except their maturity periods.)
d. What do we call this type of risk assumed by your corporate treasurer?

19-13A. (*Marketable securities portfolio*) Red Raider Feedlots has $4 million in excess cash to invest in a marketable securities portfolio. Its broker will charge $10,000 to invest the entire $4 million. The president of Red Raider wants at least half of the $4 million invested at a maturity period of three months or less; the remainder can be invested in securities with maturities not to exceed six months. The relevant term structure of short-term yields follows:

MATURITY PERIOD	AVAILABLE YIELD (ANNUAL)
1 month	6.2%
2 months	6.4
3 months	6.5
4 months	6.7
5 months	6.9
6 months	7.0

a. What should be the maturity periods of the securities purchased with the excess $4 million to maximize the before-tax income from the added investment? What will be the amount of the income from such an investment?
b. Suppose that the president of Red Raider relaxes his constraint on the maturity structure of the added investment. What would be your profit-maximizing investment recommendation?
c. If one-sixth of the excess cash is invested in each of the preceding maturity categories, what would be the before-tax income generated from such an action?

19-14A. (*Comparison of after-tax yields*) The corporate treasurer of Aggieland Fireworks is considering the purchase of a BBB-rated bond that carries a 9 percent coupon. The BBB-rated security is taxable, and the firm is in the 46 percent marginal tax bracket. The face value of this bond is $1,000. A financial analyst who reports to the corporate treasurer has alerted him to the fact that a municipal obligation is coming to the market with a 5-1/2 percent coupon. The par value of this security is also $1,000.

a. Which one of the two securities do you recommend the firm purchase? Why?
b. What must the fully taxed bond yield before tax to make it comparable with the municipal offering?

WEB WORKS

19-1WW. You can find information on mutual funds at **finance.yahoo.com**. Follow the "Mutual Funds" link and find the "Top Performers." What is the highest return for the three-month, one-year, three-year, and five-year funds?

19-2WW. Use the Federal Reserve Web site at **www.federalreserve.gov/releases/CP/** to find the discount rates for commercial paper and the prime rate of interest. Why do you think these rates are different (holding maturity constant)?

INTEGRATIVE PROBLEM

New Wave Surfing Stuff, Inc., is a manufacturer of surfboards and related gear that sells to exclusive surf shops located in several Atlantic and Pacific mainland coastal towns as well as several Hawaiian locations. The company's headquarters are located in Carlsbad, California, a small

Southern California coastal town. True to form, the company's officers, all veteran surfers, have been somewhat laid back about various critical areas of financial management. With an economic downturn in California adversely affecting their business, however, the officers of the company have decided to focus intently on ways to improve New Wave's cash flows. The CFO, Willy Bonik, has been requested to forgo any more daytime surfing jaunts until he has wrapped up a plan to accelerate New Wave's cash flows.

In an effort to ensure his quick return to the surf, Willy has decided to focus on what he believes is one of the easiest methods of improving New Wave's cash collections—namely, adoption of a cash receipts acceleration system that includes a lock-box system and concentration banking. Willy is well aware that New Wave's current system leaves much room for improvement. The company's accounts receivable system currently requires that remittances from customers be mailed to the headquarters office for processing, then for deposit in the local branch of the Bank of the U.S. Such an arrangement takes a considerable amount of time. The checks take an average of six days to reach the Carlsbad headquarters. Then, depending on the surf conditions, processing within the company takes anywhere from three to five days, with the average from the day of receipt by the company to the day of deposit at the bank being four days.

Willy feels fairly certain that such delays are costly. After all, New Wave's average daily collections are $100,000. The average remittance size is $1,000. If Willy could get these funds into his marketable securities account more quickly, he could earn 6 percent at an annual rate on such funds. In addition, if he could arrange for someone else to do the processing, Willy could save $50,000 per year in costs related to clerical staffing.

New Wave's banker was pleased to provide Willy with a proposal for a combination of a lock-box system and a concentration banking system. Bank of the U.S. would be New Wave's concentration bank. Lock boxes would be established in Honolulu, Newport Beach, and Daytona Beach. Each check processed through the lock-box system would cost New Wave 25 cents. This arrangement, however, would reduce mail float by an average of 3.5 days. The funds so collected would be transferred twice each day, 270 days a year, using automated depository transfer checks from each of the local lock-box banks to Bank of the U.S. Each ADTC would cost $25. The combination of the lock-box system and concentration banking would eliminate the time it takes the company to process cash collections, thereby making the funds available for short-term investment.

1. What would be the average amount of cash made available if New Wave were to adopt the system proposed by Bank of the U.S.?
2. What is the annual opportunity cost of maintaining the current cash collection and deposit system?
3. What is the expected annual cost of the complete system proposed by Bank of the U.S.?
4. What is the net gain or loss that is expected to result from the proposed new system? Should New Wave adopt the new system?

STUDY PROBLEMS (SET B)

19-1B. (*Concentration banking*) Sprightly Step, Inc., produces a line of walking shoes that has become extremely popular with aging baby boomers. The company's recent rapid growth to $80 million in annual credit sales to shoe stores around the country has made consideration of a more advanced billing and collection system worthwhile. Sprightly's bank has proposed a concentration banking system to Sprightly's CFO, Roberto Dylan, that would save the company three days in mail float, two days in processing float, and $50,000 in annual clerical costs. The bank would charge a flat fee per year of $80,000 to operate the system for Sprightly. Roberto believes that the funds freed by such an arrangement could be invested at no transaction cost in the company's money market account and could earn an annual rate of return of 5.5 percent. Should Roberto accept the bank's proposal? Use a 365-day year in your analysis.

19-2B. (*Buying and selling marketable securities*) An alternative to investing in a no-transaction-fee money market account under consideration by Roberto Dylan, the CFO at Sprightly Step,

Inc. (see Problem 19-1B), is direct investment in marketable securities. Assume for this problem that Roberto has determined that adoption of a concentration banking system could make $1,100,000 available for investment in marketable securities, but such direct investing would result in annual transaction fees of $15,000. Would you recommend that Roberto invest the funds in a money market account (at 5.5 percent per annum) or purchase the marketable securities directly if such securities yield 8 percent per annum and the expected holding period is for:

a. One month?
b. Two months?
c. Six months?
d. One year?

19-3B. (*Cash receipts acceleration system*) Kobrin Door & Glass, Inc., is a buyer and distributor of doors used in the home building industry. The firm has grown very quickly since it was established eight years ago. Kobrin Door has managed to increase sales and profits at a rate of about 18 percent annually, despite moderate economic growth at the national level. Until recently, the company paid little attention to cash-management procedures. Charles Kobrin, the firm's president, said: "With our growth—who cares?" Bending to the suggestions of several analysts in the firm's finance group, Kobrin did agree to have a proposal prepared by the First Citizens Bank in Tampa, Florida. The objective of the proposal is to accelerate the firm's cash collections.

At present, Kobrin Door uses a centralized billing procedure. All checks are mailed to the Tampa office headquarters for processing and eventual deposit. Under this arrangement, all customers' remittance checks take an average of five business days to reach the Tampa office. Once in Tampa, another two days are needed to process the checks for deposit at the First Citizens Bank.

Daily cash remittances at Kobrin Door average $800,000. The average check size is $4,000. The firm currently earns 9.5 percent annually on its marketable securities portfolio.

The cash-acceleration plan presented by the officers of First Citizens Bank involves both a lock-box system and concentration banking. First Citizens would be the firm's only concentration bank. Lock boxes would be established in (1) Los Angeles, (2) Dallas, (3) Chicago, and (4) Tampa. This would reduce funds tied up in mail float to 3.5 days. Processing float would be totally eliminated. Funds would then be transferred twice each business day by means of automated depository transfer checks from local banks in Los Angeles, Dallas, and Chicago to the First Citizens Bank. Each depository transfer check (ADTC) costs $30. These transfers will occur all 270 business days of the year. Each check processed through the lock box will cost Kobrin Door 40 cents.

a. What amount of cash balances will be freed if Kobrin Door adopts the system proposed by First Citizens Bank?
b. What is the opportunity cost of maintaining the current banking arrangement?
c. What is the projected annual cost of operating the proposed system?
d. Should Kobrin Door & Glass adopt the system? Compute the net annual gain or loss associated with adopting the system.

19-4B. (*Lock-box system*) Regency Components is located in Nashville, Tennessee. The firm manufactures components used in a variety of electrical devices. All the firm's finished goods are shipped to five regional warehouses across the United States.

Tennessee State Bank of Nashville is Regency Components' lead bank. Tennessee State recently completed a study of Regency's cash-collection system. Tennessee State estimates that it can reduce Regency's total float by 3.0 days with the installation of a lock-box arrangement in each of the firm's five regions.

The lock-box arrangement would cost each region $600 per month. Any funds freed up would be added to the firm's marketable securities portfolio and would yield 11.0 percent on an annual basis. Annual sales average $10,000,000 for each regional office. The firm and the bank use a 365-day year in their analyses. Should Regency Components' management approve the use of the proposed system?

19-5B. (*Costs of services*) The Hallmark Technology Company of Scranton, Pennsylvania, may install a lock-box system in order to speed up its cash receipts. On an annual basis, Hallmark receives $50 million in remittances by check. The firm will record and process 20,000 checks over the year. The Third Bank of Scranton will administer the system at a cost of 37 cents per check. Cash that is freed up by use of the system can be invested to yield 9 percent on an annual before-tax basis. A 365-day year is used for analysis purposes. What reduction in check collection time is necessary for Hallmark to be neither better nor worse off for having adopted the proposed system?

19-6B. (*Valuing float reduction*) Brady Consulting Services is forecasting that next year's gross revenues from sales will be $900 million. The senior treasury analyst for the firm expects the marketable securities portfolio to earn 9.5 percent over this same time period. A 365-day year is used in all the firm's financial procedures. What is the value to the company of one day's float reduction?

19-7B. (*Costs of services*) Colorado Communications is investigating the possibility of adopting a lock-box system as a cash receipts acceleration device. In a typical year, this firm receives remittances totaling $10 million by check. The firm will record and process 7,000 checks over this same time period. The Colorado Springs Second National Bank has informed the management of Colorado Comm that it will expedite checks and associated documents through the lock-box system for a unit cost of 30 cents per check. Colorado Comm's financial manager has projected that cash freed by adoption of the system can be invested in a portfolio of near-cash assets that will yield an annual before-tax return of 7 percent. Colorado Comm's financial analysts use a 365-day year in their procedures.

a. What reduction in check collection time is necessary for Colorado Comm to be neither better nor worse off for having adopted the proposed system?
b. How would your solution to (a) be affected if Colorado Comm could invest the freed balances only at an expected annual return of 4.5 percent?
c. What is the logical explanation for the difference in your answers to (a) and (b)?

19-8B. (*Valuing float reduction*) Campus Restaurants, Inc., will generate $17 million in credit sales next year. Collections occur at an even rate, and employees work a 270-day year. At the moment, the firm's general accounting department ties up four days' worth of remittance checks. An analysis undertaken by the firm's treasurer indicates that new internal procedures can reduce processing float by two days. If Campus invests the released funds to earn 9 percent, what will be the annual savings?

19-9B. (*Marketable securities portfolio*) Katz Jewelers currently pays its employees on a weekly basis. The weekly wage bill is $500,000. This means that, on average, the firm has accrued wages payable of ($500,000 + $0)/2 = $250,000.

Harry Katz works as the firm's senior financial analyst and reports directly to his father, who owns all of the firm's common stock. Harry Katz wants to move to a monthly wage payment system. Employees would be paid at the end of every fourth week. The younger Katz is fully aware that the labor union representing the company's workers will not permit the monthly payments system to take effect unless the workers are given some type of fringe benefit compensation.

A plan has been worked out whereby the firm will make a contribution to the cost of life insurance coverage for each employee. This will cost the firm $40,000 annually. Harry Katz expects the firm to earn 8 percent annually on its marketable securities portfolio.

a. Based on the projected information, should Katz Jewelers move to the monthly wage payment system?
b. What annual rate of return on the marketable securities portfolio would enable the firm to just break even on this proposal?

19-10B. (*Valuing float reduction*) True Locksmith is a large distributor of residential locks to hardware stores, lumber yards, and tradesmen. All its sales are on a credit basis, net 30 days. Sales are distributed over its 10 sales regions throughout the United States. There is no problem with delinquent accounts. The firm is attempting to improve its cash-management procedures. True Locksmith recently determined that it took an average of 3.0 days for customers' payments to reach their office from the time they were mailed, and another day for processing before payments could be deposited. Annual sales average $5,000,000 for each region, and investment opportunities can be found to return 9 percent per year. What is the opportunity cost to the firm of the funds tied up in mailing and processing? In your calculations, use a 365-day year.

19-11B. (*Accounts payable policy and cash management*) Meadowbrook Paving Company is suffering from a prolonged decline in new development in its sales area. In an attempt to improve its cash position, the firm is considering changes in its accounts payable policy. After careful study, it has determined that the only alternative available is to slow disbursements. Purchases for the coming year are expected to be $40 million. Sales will be $65 million, which represents about a 15 percent drop from the current year. Currently, Meadowbrook discounts approximately 25 percent of its payments at 3 percent 10 days, net 30, and the balance of accounts are paid in 30 days. If Meadowbrook adopts a policy of payment in 45 days or 60 days, how much can the firm gain if the annual opportunity cost of investment is 11 percent? What will be the result if this action causes Meadowbrook Paving suppliers to increase their prices to the company by 0.5 percent to compensate for the 60-day extended term of payment? In your calculation, use a 365-day year and ignore any compounding effects related to expected returns.

19-12B. (*Interest rate risk*) Two years ago, your corporate treasurer purchased for the firm a 20-year bond at its par value of $1,000. The coupon rate on this security is 8 percent. Interest payments are made to bondholders once a year. Currently, bonds of this particular risk class are yielding investors 9 percent. A cash shortage has forced you to instruct your treasurer to liquidate his bond.

a. At what price will your bond be sold? Assume annual compounding.
b. What will be the amount of your gain or loss over the original purchase price?
c. What would be the amount of your gain or loss had the treasurer originally purchased a bond with a four-year rather than a 20-year maturity? (Assume all characteristics of the bonds are identical except their maturity periods.)
d. What do we call this type of risk assumed by your corporate treasurer?

19-13B. (*Marketable securities portfolio*) Spencer Pianos has $3.5 million in excess cash to invest in a marketable securities portfolio. Its broker will charge $15,000 to invest the entire $3.5 million. The president of Spencer wants at least half of the $3.5 million invested at a maturity period of three months or less; the remainder can be invested in securities with maturities not to exceed six months. The relevant term structure of short-term yields follows:

MATURITY PERIOD	AVAILABLE YIELD (ANNUAL)
1 month	6.2%
2 months	6.4
3 months	6.5
4 months	6.7
5 months	6.9
6 months	7.0

a. What should be the maturity periods of the securities purchased with the excess $3.5 million in order to maximize the before-tax income from the added investment? What will be the amount of the income from such an investment?
b. Suppose that the president of Spencer relaxes his constraint on the maturity structure of the added investment. What would be your profit-maximizing investment recommendation?
c. If one-sixth of the excess cash is invested in each of the preceding maturity categories, what would be the before-tax income generated from such an action?

19-14B. (*Comparison of after-tax yields*) The corporate treasurer of Ward Grocers is considering the purchase of a BBB-rated bond that carries an 8.0 percent coupon. The BBB-rated security is taxable, and the firm is in the 46 percent marginal tax bracket. The face value of this bond is $1,000. A financial analyst who reports to the corporate treasurer has alerted him to the fact that a municipal obligation is coming to the market with a 5-1/2 percent coupon. The par value of this security is also $1,000.

a. Which one of the two securities do you recommend the firm purchase? Why?
b. What must the fully taxed bond yield before tax to make it comparable with the municipal offering?

SELF-TEST SOLUTIONS

ST-1. **a.** Initially, it is necessary to calculate Creative Fashion's average remittance check amount and the daily opportunity cost of carrying cash. The average check size is

$$\frac{\$7{,}000{,}000}{4{,}000} = \$1{,}750 \text{ per check}$$

The daily opportunity cost of carrying cash is

$$\frac{0.08}{365} = 0.0002192 \text{ per day}$$

Next, the days saved in the collection process can be evaluated according to the general format (see equation 19-1 in the text of this chapter) of

added costs = added benefits

or

$$P = (D)(S)(i) \quad \text{[see equation 19-2]}$$

$$\$0.25 = (D)(\$1{,}750)(.0002192)$$

$$0.6517 \text{ days} = D$$

Creative Fashion Designs therefore will experience a financial gain if it implements the lock-box system and by doing so will speed up its collections by more than 0.6517 days.

b. Here the daily opportunity cost of carrying cash is:

$$\frac{0.055}{365} = 0.0001507 \text{ per day}$$

For Creative Fashion Designs to break even, should it choose to install the lock-box system, cash collections must be accelerated by 0.9480 days, as follows:

$$\$0.25 = (D)(\$1{,}750)(.0001507)$$

$$0.9480 \text{ days} = (D)$$

c. The break-even cash-acceleration period of 0.9480 days is greater than the 0.6517 days found in (a). This is due to the lower yield available on near-cash assets of 5.5 percent annually, versus 8.0 percent. Because the alternative rate of return on the freed-up balances is lower in the second situation, more funds must be invested to cover the costs of operating the lock-box system. The greater cash-acceleration period generates this increased level of required funds.

ST-2. **a.** Reduction in mail float:

(2.0 days)($200,000) = $400,000

+ reduction in processing float:

(2.5 days)($200,000) = $500,000

total float reduction = $900,000

b. The opportunity cost of maintaining the present banking arrangement is

$$\begin{pmatrix}\text{forecast yield on marketable} \\ \text{securities portfolio}\end{pmatrix} \times \begin{pmatrix}\text{total float} \\ \text{reduction}\end{pmatrix}$$

$$(.106)(\$900{,}000) = \$95{,}400$$

c. The average number of checks to be processed each day through the lock-box arrangement is

$$\frac{\text{daily remittances}}{\text{average check size}} = \frac{\$200{,}000}{\$800} = 250 \text{ checks}$$

The resulting cost of the lock-box system on an annual basis is

(250 checks)($0.25)(270 days) = $16,875

Next we must calculate the estimated cost of the ADTC system. Detroit National Bank will *not* contribute to the cost of the ADTC arrangement, because it is the lead concentration bank and thereby receives the transferred data. This means that Artie Kay's Komputer Shops will be charged for six ADTCs (three locations @ two checks each) each business day. Therefore, the ADTC system costs:

(6 daily transfers)($20 per transfer)(270 days) = $32,400

We now have the total cost of the proposed system:

Lock-box cost	$16,875
ADTC cost	32,400
Total cost	$49,275

d. Our analysis suggests that Artie Kay's Komputer Shops should adopt the proposed cash receipts acceleration system. The projected net annual gain is $46,125 as follows:

Projected return on freed balances	$95,400
Less: Total cost of new system	49,275
Net annual gain	$46,125

ST-3. **a.** Here we must calculate the dollar value of the estimated return for each holding period and compare it with the transactions fee to determine if a gain can be made by investing in the securities. Those calculations and the resultant recommendations follow:

					RECOMMENDATION
1. $2,000,000 (.12) (1/12)	=	$ 20,000	<	$45,000	No
2. $2,000,000 (.12) (2/12)	=	$ 40,000	<	$45,000	No
3. $2,000,000 (.12) (3/12)	=	$ 60,000	>	$45,000	Yes
4. $2,000,000 (.12) (6/12)	=	$120,000	>	$45,000	Yes
5. $2,000,000 (.12) (12/12)	=	$240,000	>	$45,000	Yes

b. Let (x) be the required yield. With $2 million to invest for three months we have

$$\begin{aligned} \$200{,}000(x)(3/12) &= \$45{,}000 \\ \$200{,}000(x) &= \$180{,}000 \\ \$200{,}000(x) &= \$180{,}000/2{,}000{,}000 = 9\% \end{aligned}$$

The break-even yield, therefore, is 9 percent.

LEARNING OBJECTIVES

After reading this chapter, you should be able to

1. Discuss the determinants of a firm's investment in accounts receivable and how changes in credit policy are determined.
2. Discuss the reasons for carrying inventory and how inventory management decisions are made.
3. Discuss the changes that TQM and single-sourcing have had on inventory purchasing.

CHAPTER 20

Accounts Receivable and Inventory Management

If you ever visit Harley-Davidson in Milwaukee, you should not miss the opportunity to tour the parts and accessories division. The facilities are state of the art, but, more important, the people who work there take a tremendous pride and ownership for what happens in their part of the business. They are workers *par excellence*. But it was not always this way.

In the early 1990s, the company was experiencing tremendous growth in all segments of the business, including parts and accessories. Having come through a turnaround in the 1980s, the distribution and logistics functions in support of this business growth were strained and in need of a strategic change of direction. In mid-1994, a team was formed to develop and implement a new strategy.

The issues at the time were significant. Harley-Davidson's distribution center was a seven-level facility that was 84 years old. The facility was served by two freight elevators and limited technology support. In addition the facility contained slightly over half the inventory, requiring off-site storage with daily shuttle runs to replenish stock.

Symptoms of the situation included inventory turnover rates that were less than two turns per year; inventory accuracy levels in the 75 to 80 percent range; order cycle times from receipt of order to shipment in the 3 to 10 day range; lost inventory; inventory write-offs in the millions of dollars; and extremely low productivity.

The new strategy was centered on creating a new facility designed around appropriate storage, automation, and technology for each class of inventory to create optimum performance against a comprehensive set of metrics for cost, quality, and timing goals. In addition, a new relationship with employees called "partnering" was instituted throughout the

CHAPTER PREVIEW

In the two previous chapters, we developed a general overview of working-capital management and took an in-depth look at the management of cash and marketable securities. In this chapter, we will focus on the management of two more working-capital items: accounts receivable and inventory. Accounts receivable and inventory make up a large portion of the firm's assets; they actually compose on average 20 and 17 percent, respectively, of a typical firm's assets. Thus, because of their sheer magnitude, any changes in their levels will affect profitability.

In studying the management of these current assets, we first examine accounts receivable management, focusing on its importance, what determines investment in it, what the decision variables are, and how we determine them. Then we turn to inventory management, examine its importance, and discuss order quantity and order point problems, which in combination determine the level of investment in inventory. We also examine the relationship between inventory and total quality management.

As we will see, any changes in levels of accounts receivable and inventory will involve an application of **Principle 1: The Risk-Return Trade-Off—We won't take on additional risk unless we expect to be compensated with additional return**. This chapter will also emphasize **Principle 4: Incremental Cash Flows—It's only what changes that counts,** and **Principle 5: The Curse of Competitive Markets—Why it's hard to find exceptionally profitable projects.**

firm. The partnering program empowered employees and capitalized on their individual and collective knowledge and skills.

The approach for the facility design began with a Pareto analysis that stratified inventory according to velocity, unit-picked versus case-picked items, hazardous materials, and special items that do not lend themselves to automated picking. For each class of inventory a unique storage and picking method was designed into the facility.

All employees were involved in designing the facilities and inventory processes. During the original design of the facility, 16 employee focus teams were engaged in evaluating all major system and process components. This process created a tremendous sense of ownership by the employees, which produced buy-in for the significant changes recommended by the focus teams.

Additionally, there was a tremendous amount of collaboration across functional lines around the need to significantly improve inventory performance enterprise-wide. This activity included the selection and implementation of a major software solution for forecasting demand and planning inventory. Targets included achieving world-class product availability and inventory turnover performance by shortening the supply lead time and by significantly reducing slow-moving and obsolete inventories.

Brian Smith, Director of Distribution and Logistics at Harley-Davidson, describes the improvements as follows:

> This project was implemented in 1997 and the results have been excellent. Inventory accuracy has been improved to the point where it is no longer an issue. Fill rates have improved dramatically and recovery time on stockouts has been substantially improved. Turnover rates have more than doubled and are approaching world-class. Slow-moving and obsolete inventories have been reduced by over 60 percent. Order cycle times to customers have become world-class, with the majority of orders shipped the same day as they are received with very high levels of reliability.

Smith continues his comments:

> The metrics do not tell the entire story, however. One of the most fascinating aspects of the new environment is the role of the employees. Let me give two examples:
>
> - One employee came up with an idea for better utilizing space in the facility. At first he had a difficult time explaining to the engineers how his idea would work. So he arranged to have a small portion of the distribution center reconfigured to show a prototype of the concept. The engineers immediately saw the benefit and worked with the employee to help develop the business case that eventually led to significant savings.
> - Another employee working in the international shipping area asked for a fairly sizable capital budget to modify the shipping conveyors in her work area to enhance the ability to stage inventory bound for international customers. Her idea was approved and implemented with benefits greater than originally envisioned.

Based on our experience, we have learned that employees are typically the masters of the universe in which they work. They know more about the issues and possible solutions than anyone else possibly could. It is the creation of a culture where every employee is encouraged to contribute ideas for improving the work processes and systems and where resources are made available for them to bring their ideas to fruition. In retrospect, it is evident that this culture may be the most important part of the solution.

Objective 1

ACCOUNTS RECEIVABLE MANAGEMENT

All firms by their very nature are involved in selling either goods or services. Although some of these sales will be for cash, a large portion will involve credit. Whenever a sale is made on credit, it increases the firm's accounts receivable. Thus, the importance of how a firm manages its accounts receivable depends on the degree to which the firm sells on

TABLE 20-1 Accounts Receivable as a Percentage of Total Assets for Major Industries

INDUSTRY	ACCOUNTS RECEIVABLE RELATIVE TO TOTAL ASSETS
Total construction	29.16
General merchandising stores—retail	17.27
Automotive dealers and service stations—retail	12.21
Transportation	11.65
Building materials, garden equipment and supplies—retail	11.11
Agriculture, forestry, and fishing	9.74
Air, rail, and water transportation	6.09
Food stores	5.29
Hotels and other lodging places	4.76
All industries	19.26

Source: Internal Revenue Service, U.S. Treasury Department, *Statistics of Income*, 1999, *Corporate Income Tax Returns*, 15–167. www.irs.gov/pub/irs-soi/99co07nr.xls.

credit. Table 20-1 lists, for selected industries, the percentage of total assets made up by accounts receivable. The more that is sold on credit, the higher the proportion of assets that are tied up in accounts receivable. Certainly for firms in the building construction business, managing accounts receivable is important because they make up over 30 percent of a typical firm's assets.

From Table 20-1, we can see that accounts receivable typically comprise about 20 percent of a firm's assets. In effect, when we discuss management of accounts receivable, we are discussing the management of one-fifth of the firm's assets. Moreover, because cash flows from a sale cannot be invested until the account is collected, control of receivables takes on added importance; efficient collection determines both profitability and liquidity of the firm.

SIZE OF INVESTMENT IN ACCOUNTS RECEIVABLE

The size of the investment in accounts receivable is determined by several factors. First, the percentage of credit sales to total sales affects the level of accounts receivable held. Although this factor certainly plays a major role in determining a firm's investment in accounts receivable, it generally is not within the control of the financial manager. The nature of the business tends to determine the blend between credit sales and cash sales. A large grocery store tends to sell exclusively on a cash basis, whereas most construction-lumber supply firms make their sales primarily with credit. Actually, most large grocery stores allow you to use your credit card, but they receive immediate payment from the credit card company. Thus, the nature of the business, and not the decisions of the financial manager, tends to determine the proportion of credit sales.

The level of sales is also a factor in determining the size of the investment in accounts receivable. Very simply, the more sales, the greater accounts receivable. As the firm experiences seasonal and permanent growth in sales, the level of investment in accounts receivable will naturally increase. Thus, although the level of sales affects the size of the investment in accounts receivable, it is not a decision variable for the financial manager.

The final determinants of the level of investment in accounts receivable are the credit and collection policies—more specifically, the *terms of sale*, the *type of customer*, and *collection efforts*. The terms of sale specify both the time period during which the customer must pay and the terms, such as penalties for late payments or discounts for early payments. The type of customer or credit policy also affects the level of investment in accounts receivable. For example, the acceptance of poorer credit risks and their subsequent delinquent payments

FIGURE 20-1 Determinants of Investment in Accounts Receivable

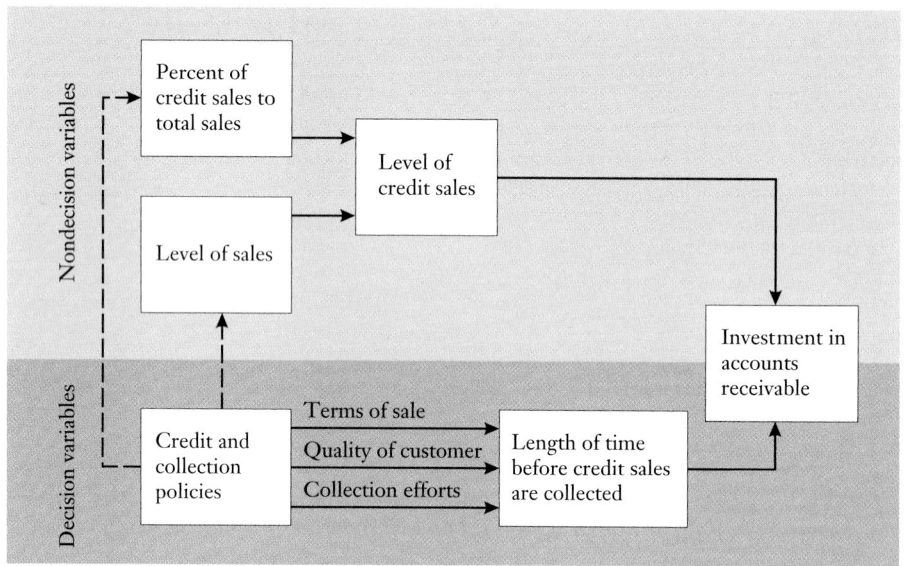

may lead to an increase in accounts receivable. The strength and timing of the collection efforts can affect the period for which past-due accounts remain delinquent, which in turn affects the level of accounts receivable. Collection and credit policy decisions may further affect the level of investment in accounts receivable by causing changes in the sales level and the ratio of credit sales to total sales. However, the three credit and collection policy variables are the only true decision variables under the control of the financial manager. Figure 20-1 shows where the financial manager can—and cannot—make a difference.

To conclude, as we examine the credit decision, try to remember that our goal is not to minimize losses but to maximize profits. Although we will spend a good deal of time trying to sort out those customers with the highest probability of default, this analysis is only an input into a decision based on shareholder wealth maximization. Essentially, a firm with a high profit margin can tolerate a more liberal credit policy than can a firm with a low profit margin.

Terms of sale
The credit terms identifying the possible discount for early payment.

TERMS OF SALE—DECISION VARIABLE The **terms of sale** identify the possible discount for early payment, the discount period, and the total credit period. They are generally stated in the form *a/b*, net *c*, indicating that the customer can deduct *a* percent if the account is paid within *b* days; otherwise, the account must be paid within *c* days. Thus, for example, trade credit terms of 2/10, net 30 indicate that a 2 percent discount can be taken if the account is paid within 10 days; otherwise it must be paid within 30 days. What if the customer decides to forgo the discount and not pay until the final payment date? If such a decision is made, the customer has the use of the money for the time period between the discount date and the final payment date. However, failure to take the discount represents a cost to the customer. For instance, if the terms are 2/10, net 30, the annualized opportunity cost of passing up this 2 percent discount in order to withhold payment for an additional 20 days is 36.73 percent. This is determined as follows:

$$\begin{pmatrix}\text{annualized opportunity cost}\\ \text{of forgoing the discount}\end{pmatrix} = \frac{a}{1-a} \times \frac{360}{c-b} \qquad \textbf{(20-1)}$$

Substituting the values from the example, we get

$$36.73\% = \frac{.02}{1 - .02} \times \frac{360}{30 - 10} \tag{20-2}$$

The typical discount ranges anywhere from one-half percent to 10 percent, whereas the discount period is generally 10 days and the total credit period varies from 30 to 90 days. Although the terms of credit vary radically from industry to industry, they tend to remain relatively uniform within any particular industry. Moreover, the terms tend to remain relatively constant over time, and they do not appear to be used frequently as a decision variable.

TYPE OF CUSTOMER—DECISION VARIABLE A second decision variable involves determining the *type of customer* who is to qualify for trade credit. Several costs always are associated with extending credit to less creditworthy customers (high-risk firms or individuals). First, as the probability of default increases, it becomes more important to identify which of the possible new customers would be a poor risk. When more time is spent investigating the less creditworthy customer, the costs of credit investigation increase.

Default costs also vary directly with the quality of the customer. As the customer's credit rating declines, the chance that the account will not be paid on time increases. In the extreme case, payment never occurs. Thus, taking on less creditworthy customers results in increases in default costs.

Collection costs also increase as the quality of the customer declines. More delinquent accounts force the firm to spend more time and money collecting them. Overall, the decline in customer quality results in increased costs of credit investigation, collection, and default.

In determining whether or not to grant credit to an individual customer, we are primarily interested in the customer's short-run ability and inclination to pay. Thus, liquidity ratios, other obligations, and the overall profitability of the firm become the focal point in this analysis. Credit-rating services, such as Dun & Bradstreet, provide information on the financial status, operations, and payment history for most firms. Other possible sources of information would include credit bureaus, trade associations, Chambers of Commerce, competitors, bank references, public financial statements, and, of course, the customer's past relationship with the firm.

One way in which both individuals and firms are often evaluated as credit risks is through the use of credit scoring. **Credit scoring** involves the numerical evaluation of each applicant. An applicant receives a score based on his or her answers to a simple set of questions. This score is then evaluated according to a predetermined standard, its level relative to the standard determining whether or not credit should be extended. The major advantage of credit scoring is that it is inexpensive and easy to perform. For example, once the standards are set, a computer or clerical worker without any specialized training could easily evaluate any applicant.

Credit scoring
The numerical credit evaluation of each candidate.

The techniques used for constructing credit-scoring indexes range from the simple approach of adding up default rates associated with the answers given to each question, to sophisticated evaluations using multiple discriminant analysis (MDA). MDA is a statistical technique for calculating the appropriate importance to be given to each question used in evaluating the applicant. Figure 20-2 shows a credit "scorecard" used by a large automobile dealer. The weights or scores attached to each answer are based on the auto dealer's past experience with credit sales. For example, the scorecard indicates that individuals with no telephone in their home have a much higher probability of default than those with a telephone. One caveat should be mentioned: Whenever this type of questionnaire is used to evaluate credit applicants, it should be examined carefully to be sure that it does not contain any illegal discriminatory questions.

FIGURE 20-2 Credit "Scorecard"

Telephone — Score

Home	Relative	None				
5	1	0				

Living quarters

Own home no mortgage	Own home mortgage	Rent a house	Live with someone	Rent an apartment	Rent a room	
6	3	2	1	0	0	

Bank accounts

None	1	More than 1				
0	4	6				

Years at present address

Under 1/2	1/2–2	3–7	8 or more			
0	1	3	4			

Size of family including customer

1	2	3–6	7 or more			
2	4	3	0			

Monthly income

Under $1,600	$1,601–$1,900	$1,901–$2,200	$2,201–$2,800	More than $2,800		
0	1	3	6	8		

Length of present employment

Under 1/2 year	1/2–2 years	3–7 years	8 years or more			
0	1	2	4			

Percent of selling price on credit

Under 50	50–69	70–84	85–99			
5	3	1	0			

Interview discretionary points (+5 to –5)

Total

Credit scorecard

(Customer's name)

(Street address)

(City, State, Zip)

(Home/Office telephone)

(Credit scorer)

Credit scorecard evaluation

Dollar amount of loan: $0–$2,000

0–18	19–21	22 or more
Reject	Refer to main credit	Accept

Dollar amount of loan: $2,001–$5,000

0–21	22–24	25 or more
Reject	Refer to main credit	Accept

Dollar amount of loan: more than $5,000

0–23	24–27	28 or more
Reject	Refer to main credit	Accept

If a previous loan customer, were payments received promptly? Yes ☐ No* ☐

Are you willing to take responsibility for authorizing this loan? Yes ☐ No* ☐

*Refer to main credit if answer to either question is No.

Another model that could be used for credit scoring has been provided by Edward Altman, a professor at New York University, who used multiple discriminant analysis to identify businesses that might go bankrupt. In his landmark study, Altman used financial ratios to predict which firms would go bankrupt over a 20-year period. Using multiple discriminant analysis, Altman came up with the following index:

$$Z = 3.3\left(\frac{EBIT}{\text{total assets}}\right) + 1.0\left(\frac{\text{sales}}{\text{total assets}}\right) + .6\left(\frac{\text{market value of equity}}{\text{book value of debt}}\right) + 1.4\left(\frac{\text{retained earnings}}{\text{total assets}}\right) + 1.2\left(\frac{\text{working capital}}{\text{total assets}}\right) \quad \textbf{(20-3)}$$

Altman found that of the firms that went bankrupt over this time period, 94 percent had Z scores of less than 2.7 one year prior to bankruptcy and only 6 percent had scores above 2.7. Conversely, of those firms that did not go bankrupt, only 3 percent had Z scores below 2.7 and 97 percent had scores above 2.7.

Again, the advantages of credit-scoring techniques are low cost and ease of implementation. Simple calculations can easily spot those credit risks that need more screening before credit should be extended to them.

BACK TO THE PRINCIPLES

The credit decision is another application of ***Principle 1: The Risk-Return Trade-Off—We won't take on additional risk unless we expect to be compensated with additional return.*** *The risk is the chance of nonpayment whereas the return stems from additional sales. Although it may be tempting to look at the credit decision as a yes or no decision based on some "black-box" formula, keep in mind that simply looking at the immediate future in making a credit decision may be a mistake. If extending a customer credit means that the customer may become a regular customer in the future, it may be appropriate to take a risk that otherwise would not be prudent. In effect, our goal is to ensure that all cash flows affected by the decision at hand are considered, not simply the most immediate cash flows.*

COLLECTION EFFORTS—DECISION VARIABLE The key to maintaining control over the collection of accounts receivable is the fact that the probability of default increases with the age of the account. Thus, control of accounts receivable focuses on the control and elimination of past-due receivables. One common way of evaluating the current situation is ratio analysis. The financial manager can determine whether or not accounts receivable are under control by examining the average collection period, the ratio of receivables to assets, the ratio of credit sales to receivables (called the *accounts receivable turnover ratio*), and the amount of bad debts relative to sales over time. In addition, the manager can perform what is called an *aging of accounts receivable* to provide a breakdown in both dollars and in percentages of the proportion of receivables that are past due. Comparing the current aging of receivables with past data offers even more control. An example of an *aging account* or *schedule* appears in Table 20-2.

The aging schedule provides you with a listing of how long your accounts receivable have been outstanding. Once the delinquent accounts have been identified, the firm's

TABLE 20-2 Aging Account

AGE OF ACCOUNTS RECEIVABLE (DAYS)	DOLLAR VALUE (00)	PERCENT OF TOTAL
0–30	$2,340	39%
31–60	1,500	25
61–90	1,020	17
91–120	720	12
Over 120	420	7
Total	$6,000	100%

accounts receivable group makes an effort to collect them. For example, a past-due letter, called a *dunning letter*, is sent if payment is not received on time, followed by an additional dunning letter in a more serious tone if the account becomes three weeks past due, followed after six weeks by a telephone call. Finally, if the account becomes 12 weeks past due, it might be turned over to a collection agency. Again, a direct trade-off exists between collection expenses and lost goodwill on one hand and noncollection of accounts on the other, and this trade-off is always part of making the decision.

Thus far, we have discussed the importance and role of accounts receivable in the firm and then examined the determinants of the size of the investment in accounts receivable. We have focused on credit and collection policies, because these are the only discretionary variables for management. In examining these decision variables, we have simply described their traits. These variables are analyzed in a decision-making process called *marginal* or *incremental analysis*.

Credit Policy Changes: The Use of Marginal or Incremental Analysis

Changes in credit policy involve direct trade-offs between costs and benefits. When credit policies are eased, sales and profits from customers increase. Conversely, easing credit policies can also involve an increase in bad debts, additional funds tied up in accounts receivable and inventory, and additional costs from customers taking a cash discount. Given these costs, when is it appropriate for a firm to change its credit policy? The answer is when the increased sales generate enough in the way of new profit to more than offset the increased costs associated with the change. Determining whether this is so is the job of **marginal** or **incremental analysis**. In general, there are three categories of changes in credit policy that a firm can consider: a change in the risk class of the customer, a change in the collection process, or a change in the discount terms. To illustrate, let us follow through an example.

Marginal or incremental analysis
A method of analysis for credit policy changes in which the incremental benefits are compared to the added costs.

BACK TO THE PRINCIPLES

Marginal or incremental analysis is a direct application of ***Principle 4: Incremental Cash Flows—It's only what changes that counts*** *into the credit analysis decision process. What we are really doing in marginal analysis is looking at all the cash flows to the company as a whole with the change in credit policy versus those cash flows without making the credit policy change. Then, if the benefits resulting from the change outweigh the costs, the change should be made.*

EXAMPLE: CHANGING CREDIT POLICY

Assume that Denis Electronics currently has annual sales, all credit, of $8 million and an average collection period of 30 days. The current level of bad debt is $240,000 and the firm's pre-tax opportunity cost or required rate of return is 15 percent. Further assume that the firm produces only one product, with variable costs equaling 75 percent of the selling price. The company is considering a change in the credit terms from the current terms of net 30 to 1/30, net 60. If this change is made, it is expected that half of the customers will take the discount and pay on the thirtieth day, whereas the other half will pass on the discount and pay on the sixtieth day. This will increase the average collection period from 30 days to 45 days. The major reason Denis Electronics is considering this change is that it will generate additional sales of $1,000,000. Although the sales from these new customers will generate new profits, they will also generate more bad debts; however, it is assumed that the level of bad debts on the original sales will remain constant, and that the level of bad debts on the new sales will be 6 percent of those sales. In addition, to service the new sales, it will be necessary to increase the level of average inventory from $1,000,000 to $1,025,000.

Let's see how to evaluate this. Marginal or incremental analysis involves a comparison of the incremental profit contribution from new sales with the incremental costs resulting from the change in credit policy. If the benefits outweigh the costs, the change should be made. If not, the credit policy should remain as is. A four-step procedure for performing marginal or incremental analysis on a change in credit policy is:

Step 1. Estimate the change in profit.
Step 2. Estimate the cost of additional investment in accounts receivable and inventory.
Step 3. Estimate the cost of the discount (if a change in the cash discount is enacted).
Step 4. Compare the incremental revenues with the incremental costs.

Table 20-3 provides a summary of the relevant information concerning Denis's proposed credit change, whereas Table 20-4 provides the results of the incremental analysis.

In Step 1 of the analysis, the additional profits less bad debts from the new sales are calculated to be $190,000. In Step 2, the additional investment in accounts receivable and inventory is determined to be $458,340. Because the pre-tax required rate of return is 15 percent, the company's required return on this investment is $72,501. In Step 3, the cost of introducing a cash discount is determined to be $45,000. Finally, in Step 4, the

TABLE 20-3 Denis Electronics: Relevant Information for Incremental Analysis

New sales level (all credit)	$9,000,000
Original sales level (all credit)	$8,000,000
Contribution margin	25%
Percent bad debt losses on new sales	6%
New average collection period	45 days
Original average collection period	30 days
Additional investment in inventory	$25,000
Pre-tax required rate of return	15%
New percent cash discount	1%
Percent of customers taking the cash discount	50%

TABLE 20-4 Denis Electronics: Incremental Analysis of a Change in Credit Policy

Step 1: **Estimate the change in profit.** This is equal to the increased sales times the profit contribution on those sales less any additional bad debts incurred.

= (increased sales × contribution margin) – (increased sales × percent bad debt losses on new sales)

= ($1,000,000 × .25) – ($1,000,000 × .06)

= $190,000

Step 2: **Estimate the cost of additional investment in accounts receivable and inventory.** This involves first calculating the change in the investment in accounts receivable. The new and original levels of investment in accounts receivable are calculated by multiplying the daily sales level times the average collection period. The additional investment in inventory is added to this, and the sum is then multiplied by the pre-tax required rate of return.

$$= \left(\begin{matrix}\text{additional}\\ \text{accounts}\\ \text{receivable}\end{matrix} + \begin{matrix}\text{additional}\\ \text{inventory}\end{matrix}\right) \times \left(\begin{matrix}\text{pre-tax required}\\ \text{rate of treturn}\end{matrix}\right)$$

First, calculate the additional investment in accounts receivable.

$$\left(\begin{matrix}\text{additional}\\ \text{accounts}\\ \text{receivable}\end{matrix}\right) = \left(\begin{matrix}\text{new level}\\ \text{of daily}\\ \text{sales}\end{matrix}\right) \times \left(\begin{matrix}\text{new average}\\ \text{collection}\\ \text{period}\end{matrix}\right) - \left(\begin{matrix}\text{original level}\\ \text{of daily}\\ \text{sales}\end{matrix}\right) \times \left(\begin{matrix}\text{original average}\\ \text{collection}\\ \text{period}\end{matrix}\right)$$

$$= \left(\frac{\$9{,}000{,}000}{360} \times 45\right) - \left(\frac{\$8{,}000{,}000}{360} \times 30\right)$$

= $458,340

Second, add additional investments in accounts receivable ($458,340) and inventory ($25,000) and multiply this total times the pre-tax required rate of return.

= ($458,340 + $25,000) × .15

= $72,501

Step 3: **Estimate the change in the cost of the cash discount (if a change in the cash discount is enacted).** This is equal to the new level of sales times the new percent cash discount times the percent of customers taking the discount, less the original level of sales times the original percent cash discount times percent of customers taking the discount.

$$= \left(\begin{matrix}\text{new}\\ \text{level}\\ \text{of}\\ \text{sales}\end{matrix}\right) \times \left(\begin{matrix}\text{new}\\ \text{percent}\\ \text{cash}\\ \text{discount}\end{matrix}\right) \times \left(\begin{matrix}\text{percent}\\ \text{customers}\\ \text{taking}\\ \text{discount}\end{matrix}\right) - \left(\begin{matrix}\text{original}\\ \text{level}\\ \text{of}\\ \text{sales}\end{matrix}\right) \times \left(\begin{matrix}\text{original}\\ \text{percent}\\ \text{cash}\\ \text{discount}\end{matrix}\right) \times \left(\begin{matrix}\text{original}\\ \text{percent}\\ \text{taking}\\ \text{discount}\end{matrix}\right)$$

= ($9,000,000 × .01 × .50) – ($8,000,000 × .00 × .00)

= $45,000

Step 4: **Compare the incremental revenues with the incremental costs.**

$$\begin{matrix}\text{net change}\\ \text{in pre-tax}\\ \text{profits}\end{matrix} = \begin{matrix}\text{change}\\ \text{in}\\ \text{profits}\end{matrix} - \left(\begin{matrix}\text{cost of new}\\ \text{investment in}\\ \text{accounts receivable}\\ \text{and inventory}\end{matrix} + \begin{matrix}\text{cost of}\\ \text{change in}\\ \text{cash}\\ \text{discount}\end{matrix}\right)$$

= Step 1 – (Step 2 + Step 3)

= $190,000 – ($72,501 + $45,000)

= $72,499

FIGURE 20-3 Credit Policy Changes and Profits

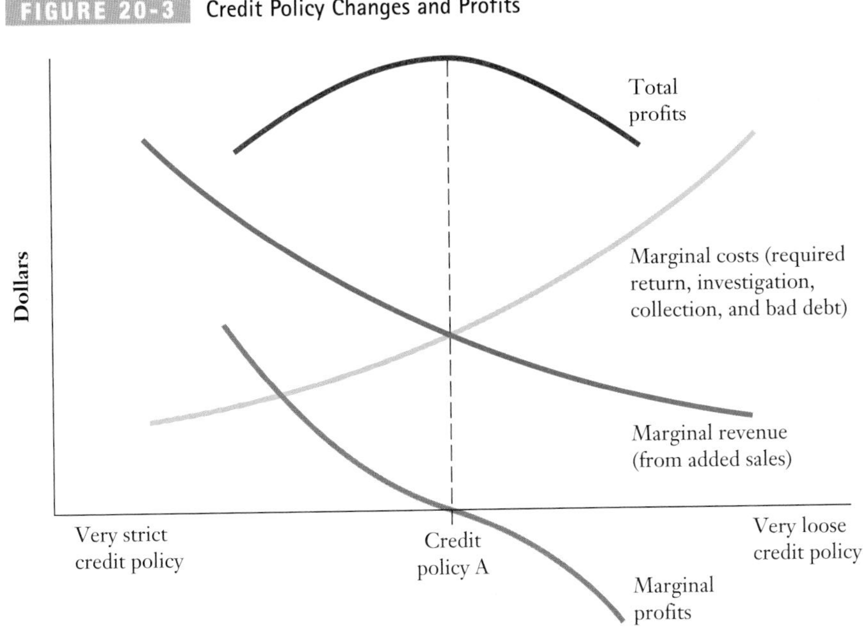

benefits and costs are compared, and the net change in pre-tax profits is determined to be \$72,499. Thus, a change in the present credit policy is warranted.

In summary, the logic behind this approach to credit policy is to examine the incremental or marginal benefits from such a change and compare these with the incremental or marginal costs. If the change promises more benefits than costs, the change should be made. If, however, the incremental costs are greater than the benefits, the proposed change should not be made. Figure 20-3 graphs this process: The point where marginal costs equal marginal benefits occurs at credit policy A.

In summary, the calculations associated with the incremental analysis of a change in credit policy illustrate the changes that occur when credit policy is adjusted. On the positive side, a loosening of credit policy should increase sales. On the negative side, bad debts, investment in accounts receivable and inventory, and costs associated with the cash discount all increase. The decision then boils down to whether the incremental benefits outweigh the incremental costs.

CONCEPT CHECK

1. What factors influence the size of a firm's investment in accounts receivable? Which one(s) of these factors can the financial manager control?
2. What costs are associated with extending credit to high-risk firms or individuals?
3. How can a firm evaluate the credit risk of its customers?
4. Explain the two models of credit scoring. What are the advantages and disadvantages of using these models?
5. Describe the technique of marginal analysis of changing a firm's credit policy.

Objective 2

Inventory management The control of the assets used in the production process or produced to be sold in the normal course of the firm's operations.

INVENTORY MANAGEMENT

Inventory management involves the control of the assets that are used in the production process or produced to be sold in the normal course of the firm's operations. The general categories of inventory include raw materials inventory, work-in-process inventory, and finished goods inventory. The importance of inventory management to the firm depends on the extent of the inventory investment. For an average firm, approximately 16.94 percent of all assets are in the form of inventory. However, the percentage varies widely from industry to industry, as Table 20-5 shows. Thus, the importance of inventory management and control varies from industry to industry also. For example, it is much more important for equipment supply dealers and electronic and appliance stores, where inventories make up 25 percent of total assets, than in the petroleum business, where the average investment in inventory is only 1.22 percent of total assets.

PURPOSES AND TYPES OF INVENTORY

The purpose of carrying inventories is to uncouple the operations of the firm—that is, to make each function of the business independent of each other function—so that delays or shutdowns in one area do not affect the production and sale of the final product. For example, in the auto industry, a strike or shutdown in a parts plant may shut down several assembly plants. Because production shutdowns result in increased costs, and because delays in delivery can lose customers, the management and control of inventory are important duties of the financial manager. To better illustrate the uncoupling function that inventories perform, we will look at several general types of inventories.

BACK TO THE PRINCIPLES

The decision as to how much inventory to keep on hand is a direct application of ***Principle 1: The Risk-Return Trade-Off—We won't take on additional risk unless we expect to be compensated with additional return.*** *The risk is that if the level of inventory is too low, the various functions of business do not operate independently and delays in production and customer delivery can result. The return results because reduced inventory investment saves money. As the size of inventory increases, storage and handling costs as well as the required return on capital invested in inventory rise. Therefore, as the inventory a firm holds is increased, the risk of running out of inventory is lessened, but inventory expenses rise.*

TABLE 20-5 Inventory as a Percentage of Total Assets for Major Industries

INDUSTRY	INVENTORY RELATIVE TO TOTAL ASSETS
Health and personal care stores	25.18%
Building materials, garden equipment, and supply dealers	22.82
Total manufacturing	6.43
Food stores	18.87
Total construction	14.35
Agriculture, forestry, and fishing	10.10
Electronics and appliance stores	25.14
Petroleum and coal products	1.78
Eating and drinking places	2.94
Air, rail, and water transportation	1.12
All industries	2.68

Source: Internal Revenue Service, U.S. Treasury Department, *Statistics of Income*, 1999 *Corporate Income Tax Returns*, www.irs.gov/pub/irs-soi/99co07nr.xls.

RAW MATERIALS INVENTORY **Raw materials inventory** consists of basic materials purchased from other firms to be used in the firm's production operations. These goods may include steel, lumber, petroleum, or manufactured items such as wire, ball bearings, or tires that the firm does not produce itself. Regardless of the specific form of the raw materials inventory, all manufacturing firms by definition maintain a raw materials inventory. Its purpose is to uncouple the production function from the purchasing function—that is, to make these two functions independent of each other, so that delays in shipment of raw materials do not cause production delays. In the event of a delay in shipment, the firm can satisfy its need for raw materials by liquidating its inventory. During the 1991 war with Iraq, many firms that used petroleum as an input in production built up their petroleum inventories in anticipation of a slowdown or possibly a stoppage in the flow of oil from the Middle East. This buildup in raw material inventory would have allowed those firms with adequate inventories to continue production even if the war had severely cut the flow of oil.

Raw materials inventory
This includes the basic materials purchased from other firms to be used in the firm's production operations.

WORK-IN-PROCESS INVENTORY **Work-in-process inventory** consists of partially finished goods requiring additional work before they become finished goods. The more complex and lengthy the production process, the larger the investment in work-in-process inventory. The purpose of work-in-process inventory is to uncouple the various operations in the production process so that machine failures and work stoppages in one operation will not affect the other operations. Assume, for example, there are 10 different production operations, each one involving the piece of work produced in the previous operation. If the machine performing the first production operation breaks down, a firm with no work-in-process inventory will have to shut down all 10 production operations. Yet if a firm has such inventory, the remaining nine operations can continue by drawing the input for the second operation from inventory rather than directly from the output of the first operation.

Work-in-process inventory
Partially finished goods requiring additional work before they become finished goods.

FINISHED-GOODS INVENTORY The **finished-goods inventory** consists of goods on which the production has been completed but that are not yet sold. The purpose of a finished-goods inventory is to uncouple the production and sales functions so that it is not necessary to produce the good before a sale can occur—sales can be made directly out of inventory. In the auto industry, for example, people would not buy from a dealer who made them wait weeks or months, when another dealer could fill the order immediately.

Finished-goods inventory
Goods on which the production has been completed but that are not yet sold.

STOCK OF CASH Although we discussed cash management at some length in Chapter 19, it is worthwhile to mention cash again in the light of inventory management. This is because the *stock of cash* carried by a firm is simply a special type of inventory. In terms of uncoupling the various operations of the firm, the purpose of holding a stock of cash is to make the payment of bills independent of the collection of accounts due. When cash is kept on hand, bills can be paid without prior collection of accounts.

As we examine and develop inventory economic ordering quantity (*EOQ*) models, we will see a striking resemblance between the *EOQ* inventory and *EOQ* cash model; in fact, except for a minor redefinition of terms, they will be exactly the same.

INVENTORY-MANAGEMENT TECHNIQUES

The importance of effective inventory management is directly related to the size of the investment in inventory. Because, on average, approximately 16.94 percent of a firm's assets are tied up in inventory, effective management of these assets is essential to the goal of shareholder wealth maximization. To control the investment in inventory, management must solve two problems: the order quantity problem and the order point problem.

Order quantity problem Determining the optimal order size for an inventory item given its usage, carrying costs, and ordering costs.

ORDER QUANTITY PROBLEM The **order quantity problem** involves determining the optimal order size for an inventory item given its expected usage, carrying costs, and ordering costs. Aside from a change in some of the variable names, it is exactly the same as the inventory model for cash management (*EOQ* model) presented in Chapter 19.

The *EOQ* model attempts to determine the order size that will minimize total inventory costs. It assumes that

$$\text{total inventory costs} = \text{total carrying costs} + \text{total ordering costs} \tag{20-4}$$

Assuming that inventory is allowed to fall to zero and then is immediately replenished (this assumption will be lifted when we discuss the order point problem), the average inventory becomes $Q/2$, where Q is the inventory order size in units. This can be seen graphically in Figure 20-4.

If the average inventory is $Q/2$ and the carrying cost per unit is C, then carrying costs become:

$$\begin{matrix}\text{total}\\ \text{carrying costs}\end{matrix} = \begin{pmatrix}\text{average}\\ \text{inventory}\end{pmatrix}\begin{pmatrix}\text{carrying cost}\\ \text{per unit}\end{pmatrix} \tag{20-5}$$

$$= \left(\frac{Q}{2}\right)C \tag{20-6}$$

where Q = the inventory order size in units
C = carrying cost per unit

The carrying costs on inventory include the required rate of return on investment in inventory, in addition to warehouse or storage costs, wages for those who operate the warehouse, and costs associated with inventory shrinkage. Thus, carrying costs include both real cash flows and opportunity costs associated with having funds tied up in inventory.

FIGURE 20-4 Inventory Level and the Replenishment Cycle

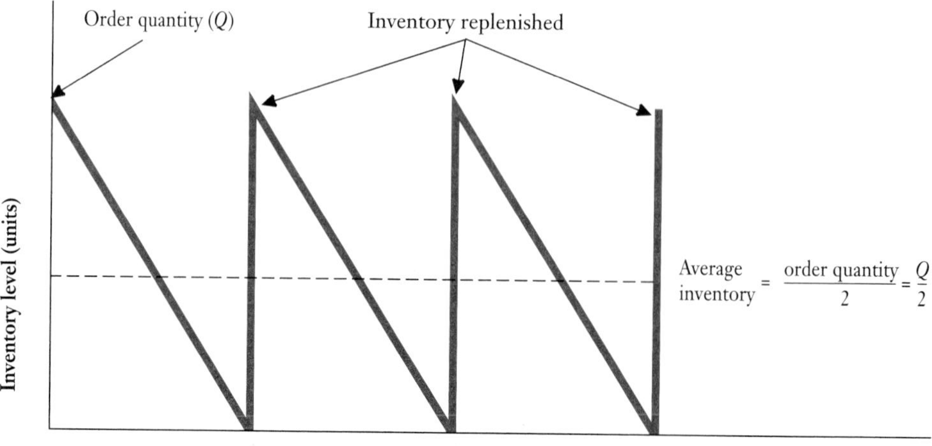

The ordering costs incurred are equal to the ordering costs per order times the number of orders. If we assume total demand over the planning period is S and we order in lot sizes of Q, then S/Q represents the number of orders over the planning period. If the ordering cost per order is O, then

$$\text{total ordering costs} = \binom{\text{number}}{\text{of orders}}\binom{\text{ordering cost}}{\text{per order}} \quad \textbf{(20-7)}$$

$$= \left(\frac{S}{Q}\right)O \quad \textbf{(20-8)}$$

where S = total demand in units over the planning period
O = ordering cost per order

Thus, total costs in equation 20-4 become

$$\text{total costs} = \left(\frac{Q}{2}\right)C + \left(\frac{S}{Q}\right)O \quad \textbf{(20-9)}$$

Figure 20-5 illustrates this equation graphically. As you can see, as the order size increases, so do the carrying costs, because you are holding more inventory. Eventually, the increased carrying costs outweigh the savings in ordering costs from not placing as many orders. At that point, total costs are minimized.

What we are looking for is the ordering size, Q^*, that provides the minimum total costs. By manipulating equation 20-9, we find that the optimal value of Q—that is, the economic ordering quantity (*EOQ*)—is

$$Q^* = \sqrt{\frac{2SO}{C}} \quad \textbf{(20-10)}$$

The use of the *EOQ* model can best be illustrated through an example.

FIGURE 20-5 Total Cost and *EOQ* Determination

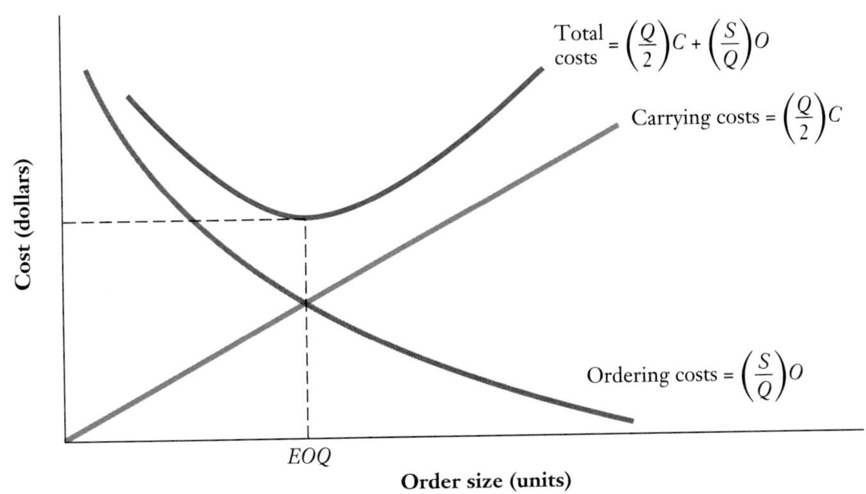

Example: Economic Order Quantity

Suppose a firm expects total demand (S) for its product over the planning period to be 5,000 units, whereas the ordering cost per order (O) is \$200, and the carrying cost per unit (C) is \$2. Substituting these values into equation (20-10) yields

$$Q^* = \sqrt{\frac{2 \times 5{,}000 \times 200}{2}} = \sqrt{1{,}000{,}000} = 1{,}000 \text{ units}$$

Thus, if this firm orders in 1,000-unit lot sizes, it will minimize its total inventory costs.

Despite the fact that the *EOQ* model tends to yield quite good results, there are weaknesses in the *EOQ* model associated with several of its assumptions. When its assumptions have been dramatically violated, the *EOQ* model can generally be modified to accommodate the situation. The model's assumptions are as follows:

Safety stock Inventory held to accommodate any unusually large and unexpected usage during delivery time.

1. **Constant or uniform demand.** Although the *EOQ* model assumes constant demand, demand may vary from day to day. If demand is stochastic—that is, not known in advance—the model must be modified through the inclusion of a **safety stock**, that is, the inventory held to accommodate any unusually large and unexpected usage during the delivery time.
2. **Constant unit price.** The inclusion of variable prices resulting from quantity discounts can be handled quite easily through a modification of the original *EOQ* model, redefining total costs and solving for the optimum order quantity.
3. **Constant carrying costs.** Unit carrying costs may vary substantially as the size of the inventory rises, perhaps decreasing because of economies of scale or storage efficiency or increasing as storage space runs out and new warehouses have to be rented. This situation can be handled through a modification in the original model similar to the one used for variable unit price.
4. **Constant ordering costs.** Although this assumption is generally valid, its violation can be accommodated by modifying the original *EOQ* model in a manner similar to the one used for variable unit price.
5. **Instantaneous delivery.** If delivery is not instantaneous, which is generally the case, the original *EOQ* model must be modified through the inclusion of a safety stock.
6. **Independent orders.** If multiple orders result in cost savings by reducing paperwork and transportation cost, the original *EOQ* model must be further modified. Although this modification is somewhat complicated, special *EOQ* models have been developed to deal with it.

These assumptions illustrate the limitations of the basic *EOQ* model and the ways in which it can be modified to compensate for them. An understanding of the limitations and assumptions of the *EOQ* model provides the financial manager with more of a base for making inventory decisions.

Order Point Problem

Order point problem Determining how low inventory should be depleted before it is reordered.

The two most limiting assumptions—those of constant or uniform demand and instantaneous delivery—are dealt with through the inclusion of safety stock, which is the inventory held to accommodate any unusually large and unexpected usage during delivery time. The decision on how much safety stock to hold is generally referred to as the **order point problem**; that is, how low inventory should be depleted before it is reordered.

FIGURE 20-6 Order Point Determination

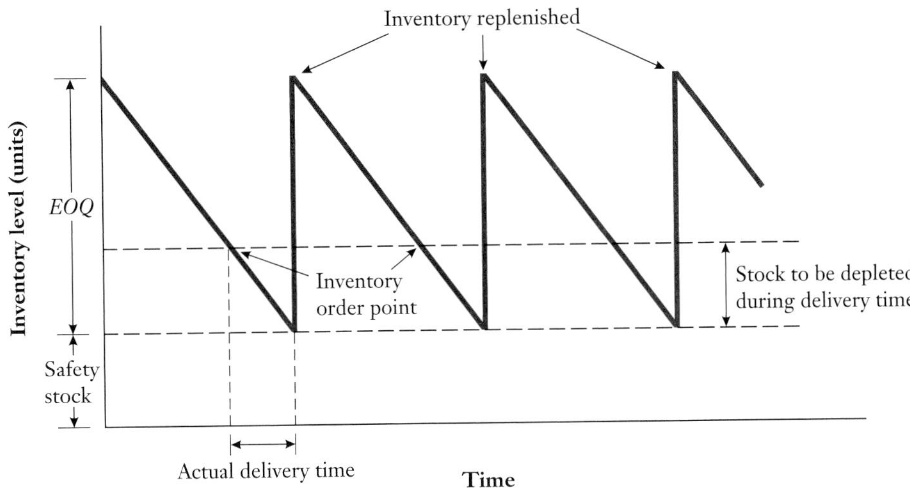

Two factors go into the determination of the appropriate order point: (1) the procurement or delivery-time stock and (2) the safety stock desired. Figure 20-6 graphs the process involved in order point determination. We observe that the order point problem can be decomposed into its two components, the **delivery-time stock**—that is, the inventory needed between the order date and receipt of the inventory ordered—and the safety stock. Thus, the order point is reached when inventory falls to a level equal to the delivery-time stock plus the safety stock.

Delivery-time stock The inventory needed between the order date and the receipt of the inventory ordered.

Inventory order point can be determined as follows:

$$\begin{bmatrix}\text{order new inventory}\\ \text{when the level of}\\ \text{inventory falls to}\\ \text{this level}\end{bmatrix} = \begin{pmatrix}\text{delivery-time}\\ \text{stock}\end{pmatrix} + \begin{pmatrix}\text{safety}\\ \text{stock}\end{pmatrix} \quad \textbf{(20-11)}$$

As a result of constantly carrying safety stock, the average level of inventory increases. Whereas before the inclusion of safety stock the average level of inventory was equal to $EOQ/2$, now it will be

$$\text{average inventory} = \frac{EOQ}{2} + \text{safety stock} \quad \textbf{(20-12)}$$

In general, several factors simultaneously determine how much delivery-time stock and safety stock should be held. First, the efficiency of the replenishment system affects how much delivery-time stock is needed. Because the delivery-time stock is the expected inventory usage between ordering and receiving inventory, efficient replenishment of inventory would reduce the need for delivery-time stock.

The uncertainty surrounding both the delivery time and the demand for the product affects the level of safety stock needed. The more certain the patterns of these inflows and outflows from the inventory, the less safety stock required. In effect, if these inflows and outflows are highly predictable, then there is little chance of any stockout occurring. However, if they are unpredictable, it becomes necessary to carry additional safety stock to prevent unexpected stockouts.

The safety margin desired also affects the level of safety stock held. If it is a costly experience to run out of inventory, the safety stock held will be larger than it would be otherwise. If running out of inventory and the subsequent delay in supplying customers result in strong customer dissatisfaction and the possibility of lost future sales, then additional safety stock is necessary. A final determinant is the cost of carrying additional inventory, in terms of both the handling and storage costs and the opportunity cost associated with the investment in additional inventory. Very simply, the greater the costs, the smaller the safety stock.

The determination of the level of safety stock involves a basic trade-off between the risk of stockout, resulting in possible customer dissatisfaction and lost sales, and the increased costs associated with carrying additional inventory.

INFLATION AND EOQ

Anticipatory buying Buying in anticipation of a price increase to secure goods at a lower cost.

Inflation affects the *EOQ* model in two major ways. First, although the *EOQ* model can be modified to assume constant price increases, often major price increases occur only once or twice a year and are announced ahead of time. If this is the case, the *EOQ* model may lose its applicability and may be replaced with **anticipatory buying**—that is, buying in anticipation of a price increase to secure the goods at a lower cost. Of course, as with most decisions, there are trade-offs. The costs are the added carrying costs associated with the inventory. The benefits, of course, come from buying at a lower price. The second way inflation affects the *EOQ* model is through increased carrying costs. As inflation pushes interest rates up, the cost of carrying inventory increases. In our *EOQ* model, this means that C increases, which results in a decline in Q^*, the optimal economic order quantity:

$$\downarrow Q^* = \sqrt{\frac{2SO}{C\uparrow}} \qquad \textbf{(20-13)}$$

Reluctance to stock large inventories because of high carrying costs became particularly prevalent during the late 1970s and early 1980s, when inflation and interest rates were at high levels.

JUST-IN-TIME INVENTORY CONTROL

Just-in-time inventory control system Keeping inventory to a minimum and relying on suppliers to furnish parts "just in time."

The **just-in-time inventory control system** is more than just an inventory control system; it is a production and management system. Not only is inventory cut down to a minimum, but the time and physical distance between the various production operations are also reduced. In addition, management is willing to trade off costs to develop close relationships with suppliers and promote speedy replenishment of inventory in return for the ability to hold less safety stock.

The just-in-time inventory control system was originally developed in Japan by Taiichi Okno, a vice-president of Toyota. Originally, the system was called the *kanban* system, named after the cards that were placed in the parts bins that were used to call for a new supply. The idea behind the system is that the firm should keep a minimum level of inventory on hand, relying on suppliers to furnish parts "just in time" for them to be assembled. This is in direct contrast to the traditional inventory philosophy of U.S. firms, which is sometimes referred to as a "just-in-case" system, which keeps healthy levels of safety stocks to ensure that production will not be interrupted. Although large inventories may not be a bad idea when interest rates are low, they become very costly when interest rates are high.

Although the just-in-time inventory system is intuitively appealing, it has not proved easy to implement. Long distances from suppliers and plants constructed with too much space for storage and not enough access (doors and loading docks) to receive inventory have limited successful implementation. But many firms have been forced to change their relationships with their suppliers. Because firms rely on suppliers to deliver high-quality parts and materials immediately, they must have a close, long-term relationship with them. Despite the difficulties of implementation, many U.S. firms have moved to cut inventory—in some cases, through the use of a just-in-time inventory system. General Motors and NCR are just two of the many firms that have moved at least some of their operations to a just-in-time system. Dell Computer is a classic example of using a just-in-time inventory system for finished goods inventory. Dell does not carry any finished-goods inventory because it does not assemble any computers until they are ordered. In fact, the average level of inventory relative to total assets for all American corporations has fallen over time, partly because of just-in-time systems.

Although the just-in-time system does not at first appear to bear much of a relationship to the *EOQ* model, it simply alters some of the assumptions of the model with respect to delivery time and ordering costs, and draws out the implications. Actually, it is just a new approach to the *EOQ* model that tries to produce the lowest average level of inventory possible. If we look at the average level of inventory as defined by the *EOQ* model, we find it to be

$$\text{average inventory} = \sqrt{\frac{2SO\downarrow}{C}} + \text{safety stock}\downarrow$$

The just-in-time system attacks this equation in two places. First, by locating inventory supplies in convenient locations, laying out plants in such a way that it is inexpensive and easy to unload new inventory shipments, and computerizing the inventory order system, the cost of ordering new inventory, O, is reduced. Second, by developing a strong relationship with suppliers located in the same geographical area and setting up restocking strategies that cut time, the safety stock is also reduced. The philosophy behind the just-in-time inventory system is that the benefits associated with reducing inventory and delivery time to a bare minimum through adjustment in the *EOQ* model will more than offset the costs associated with the increased possibility of stockouts.

Although just-in-time inventory systems seem to do a great job of reducing inventory costs, if there is ever a breakdown in the supply of inventory to the system, the results can be catastrophic. Take, for example, General Motors, which has saved millions of dollars by going to a just-in-time system. In 1996, General Motors was hit by a strike that involved about 3,000 workers at two of its plants that produced brakes for the cars GM makes. As a result of not having brakes to put in cars, GM was forced to stop production and lay off over 177,000 workers. Moreover, because GM used a just-in-time inventory system, it didn't take long for the shutdown of the brake plant to affect all of GM's other operations.

Now let's take a look at exactly how a just-in-time inventory system works. Ford Motor Company's Avon Lake, Ohio, plant, which produces the Mercury Villager and the Nissan Quest minivans, uses a just-in-time inventory system. In fact, some inventory is limited to a supply of only a few hours, whereas other inventory carries supplies up to several days. To allow for this constant resupply of inventory, Ford built the plant with 65 dock doors placed around the plant so that inventory would arrive as close as possible to the location where it was to be used.

In addition, Ford worked with suppliers so that much of the inventory would arrive partially assembled. For example, tires and wheels came preassembled by Bridgestone. These arrived several times a day delivered in the order in which they were to be used—with each fifth tire delivered being a spare. Seats also arrived hourly, already preassembled, from a supplier located just 25 miles away. In addition, the seats are arranged in the order they are to be used and arrive on the assembly line by conveyors directly from the delivery trucks, ready to use. In effect, the only inventory time for tires and seats is when they are on the delivery truck waiting to be unloaded. Thus, Ford's just-in-time inventory system allows for a dramatically reduced level of investment in inventory by allowing for a continuous flow and resupply of inventory. The end result of all this reduced investment is increased profits.

CONCEPT CHECK

1. Describe the types of inventory a firm holds and the purpose of each type. How is a firm's stock of cash similar to inventory?
2. What is the objective of the order quantity model? What assumptions are made in developing this model?
3. What is the objective of the order point model? Describe the factors that determine the levels of delivery-time stock and safety stock.
4. Explain the just-in-time inventory system. What factors increase the likelihood of successful implementation of a just-in-time system?

Objective 3

TQM AND INVENTORY-PURCHASING MANAGEMENT: THE NEW SUPPLIER RELATIONSHIPS

Total quality management (TQM) A company-wide systems approach to quality.

Out of the concept of **total quality management (TQM)**, which is a company-wide systems approach to quality, has come a new philosophy in inventory management of "love thy supplier." Under this approach, the traditional antagonistic relationship between suppliers and customers, where suppliers are coldly dropped when a cheaper source can be found, is being replaced by a new order in customer-supplier relationships. In effect, what began as an effort to increase quality through closer supplier relations has turned out to have unexpected benefits. Close customer relationships have helped trim costs, in part, by allowing for the production of higher-quality products. This close customer-supplier relationship has allowed the TQM philosophy to be passed across company boundaries to the supplier, enabling the firm to tap the supplier's expertise in designing higher-quality products. In addition, the interdependence between the supplier and customer has also allowed for the development and introduction of new products at a pace much faster than previously possible.

As we have seen, inventory can make up a rather large percentage of a firm's assets. That by itself lends importance to the role of inventory management and, more specifically, purchasing. In terms of manufacturing costs, purchased materials have historically accounted for 50 percent of U.S. and about 70 percent of Japanese manufacturing costs, and most manufacturers purchase more than 50 percent of their parts. Thus, it is hard to overstate the importance of purchasing to the firm.

The traditional purchasing philosophy is to purchase a part or material from a variety of different suppliers, with the suppliers contracting out to a number of different firms. In fact, many companies put an upper limit of 10 or 20 percent on the purchases of any part from a single supplier. The reasoning behind this is that the company can diversify away the effects of poor quality by any one supplier. Thus, if one supplier is unable to meet delivery schedules, delivers a poor quality batch, or even goes out of business, this affects only a small percent of the total parts or material. However, efforts to raise quality have led to a new approach to the customer-supplier relationship called **single-sourcing**.

Single-sourcing Using a single supplier as a source for a particular part or material.

Under single-sourcing, a company uses very few suppliers or, in many cases, a single supplier as a source for a particular part or material. In this way, the company has more direct influence and control over the quality performance of a supplier because the company accounts for a larger proportion of the supplier's volume. The company and supplier can then enter into a partnership, referred to as *partnering*, where the supplier agrees to meet the quality standards of the customer in terms of parts, material, service, and delivery. In this way, the supplier can be brought into the TQM program of the customer. In return, the company enters into a long-term purchasing agreement with the supplier that includes a stable order and delivery schedule. For example, on General Motors' Quad 4 engine (its first new engine in several decades), every part except the engine block is single-sourced, resulting in only 69 total suppliers—half the normal number for a production engine. In return for the suppliers' assurances of top quality and low cost, GM guaranteed the suppliers their jobs for the life of the engine. In the development of its new LH cars, the Chrysler Concorde, the Dodge Intrepid, and the Eagle Vision, Chrysler trimmed its supplier base from 3,000 to less than 1,000 by the mid-1990s. Single-sourcing clearly creates an environment of cooperation between customers and suppliers where both share the common goal of quality.

Although the partnering relationship results in higher-quality parts, it can also improve the quality of the design process by allowing for the involvement of the supplier in production design. For example, the supplier may be given the responsibility of designing a new part or component to meet the quality standards and features outlined by the company. When Guardian Industries of Northville, Michigan, developed an oversized solar glass windshield for Chrysler's LH cars, its engineers met on almost a daily basis with the Chrysler design team to make sure the quality, features, and cost of the windshield met Chrysler standards. To produce the windshields, Guardian opened a new $35 million plant in Ligonier, Indiana. In a similar manner, Bailey Controls and Boise Cascade entered into a pact in which Bailey was the exclusive provider of control systems for 8 of 10 Boise plants. The two worked together, reviewing and modifying the terms of the arrangement to ensure that they reflected the ever-changing business conditions and that the deal remained fair to both parties. In addition, recognizing the long-term nature of the relationship and that Boise's success would also benefit Bailey, Bailey worked with Boise—in fact, using a Boise plant on which to conduct experiments—to improve the software used to operate the Boise plants.

The concept of partnering has radically changed the way inventory is purchased. Moreover, it has turned the customer-supplier relationship from a formerly adversarial one into a cooperative one. The benefits in terms of increased quality of parts, materials, and design are so dramatic that partnering is not likely to fade away, but rather continue to evolve and take on even more importance in the future.

THE FINANCIAL CONSEQUENCES OF QUALITY—THE TRADITIONAL VIEW

Traditionally, the cost of quality has been viewed as being made up of **preventive costs**, **appraisal costs**, and failure costs. The costs the firm incurs in running its quality management program include both preventive and appraisal costs. Preventive costs include those resulting from design and production efforts on the part of the firm to reduce or eliminate defects. Whereas preventive costs deal with the avoidance of defects the first time through, appraisal costs are associated with the detection of defects. Thus, typical appraisal costs would include the costs of testing, measuring, and analyzing materials, parts, and products, as well as the production operations to safeguard against possible defective inventory going unnoticed. Together, preventive and appraisal costs make up much of what a typical total quality management program does.

Preventive costs
Costs resulting from design and production efforts on the part of the firm to reduce or eliminate defects.

Appraisal costs
Costs of testing, measuring, and analyzing to safeguard against possible defects going unnoticed.

Internal failure costs Those costs associated with discovering poor-quality products prior to delivery.

External failure costs Costs resulting from a poor-quality product reaching the customers' hands.

Whereas preventive and appraisal costs deal with the costs associated with achieving good quality, *failure costs* refer to the costs resulting from producing poor-quality products. Failure costs can either occur within the firm, called **internal failure costs**, or once the product has left the firm, referred to as **external failure costs**. Internal failure costs are those costs associated with discovering the poor-quality product prior to delivery to the final customer. Internal failure costs include the costs of reworking the product, downtime costs, the costs of having to discount poorer quality products, and the costs of scrapping the product. External failure costs, however, come as a result of a poor-quality product reaching the customers' hands. Typical external failure costs would include product return costs, warranty costs, product liability costs, customer complaint costs, and lost sales costs.

Traditionally, economists examined the trade-offs between quality and costs looking for the point where costs were minimized. The result of this is that some level of defects should be tolerated. That is because there comes a point when the costs associated with making the product right in the first place are more than the cost of poor quality—the failure costs.

BACK TO THE PRINCIPLES

Principle 5: The Curse of Competitive Markets—Why it's hard to find exceptionally profitable projects *examines how product differentiation can be used as a means of insulating a product from competition, thereby allowing prices to stay sufficiently high to support large profits. Producing a quality product is one of those ways to differentiate products. This strategy has been used effectively by Caterpillar Tractor, Toyota, and Honda Motors in recent years.*

THE FINANCIAL CONSEQUENCES OF QUALITY—THE TQM VIEW

In response to this traditional view, the TQM view argues that the traditional analysis is flawed in that it ignores the fact that increased sales and market share result from better-quality products, and that this increase in sales will more than offset the higher costs associated with increased quality. In effect, the TQM view argues that because lost sales resulting from a poor-quality reputation and increased sales resulting from a reputation for quality are difficult to estimate, they tend to be underestimated or ignored in the traditional approach. In addition, the TQM view argues that the cost of achieving higher quality is less than economists have traditionally estimated. In fact, the benefits from quality improvement programs seem to have spillover effects resulting in increased worker motivation, higher productivity, and improved employee relations. Moreover, large increases in quality have been achieved with very low costs when companies focus on training and educating the production workers.

Thus, the TQM view concludes that traditional analysis underestimates the cost of producing a poor-quality product, while it overestimates the cost of producing a high-quality product. As a result, under this new TQM view of the quality-costs trade-offs, the optimal quality level moves much closer to 100 percent quality.

The adoption of total quality management programs by many firms has borne out this TQM view of the quality-cost relationship. For example, after Xerox Corporation introduced TQM, it experienced a decline of 90 percent in defective items. For Xerox, the end result of this was a 20 percent drop in manufacturing costs over that same period.

CONCEPT CHECK

1. Define single-sourcing. How does this practice impact the firm purchasing goods and services?
2. Describe the components of the cost of quality.
3. Contrast the traditional analysis of the cost of quality with the TQM view.

HOW FINANCIAL MANAGERS USE THIS MATERIAL

Given the fact that the total investment in both accounts receivable and inventory represents approximately one-third of a typical firm's assets, it's no surprise that a good deal of time goes into managing them. This includes deciding who should be able to buy on credit, trying to collect on overdue accounts, managing inventory to make sure you don't run out of any products, and overseeing quality control. But more than just managing these accounts and items, inventory and accounts receivable policies are increasingly used as sales tools. In effect, you sell your product, but you make that sale based upon your accounts receivable policy, your inventory policy, or the quality of your goods.

For example, Mitsubishi has an annual sale on its large-screen projection televisions in which prices are not cut. Instead, the projection televisions are offered at zero percent interest with the first payments not due until the following year. In effect, Mitsubishi uses its accounts receivable policy as a marketing tool. If you're working for Mitsubishi, your job may be to set standards as to who qualifies for this deal or to oversee the collection of those accounts.

Inventory policy is also used as a marketing tool. Having the product available for immediate delivery may be your sales gimmick. Other companies don't keep any inventory on hand and pass the savings that are produced on to the customers. For example, Dell computer does not produce any computers until they are sold, which allows it to keep costs down to a minimum and pass those cost savings on to the customers. In fact, this strategy has proved so profitable that, in late 1997, Apple announced it was also going to start selling over the Internet using the same "build-when-ordered" approach. If you took a job for another firm that sells directly out of inventory, your job might be managing that inventory—making sure you don't run out of anything while keeping your investment in inventory down to a minimum. Is inventory management complicated? The answer is yes. Just look at IBM, which has about 1,000 products currently in service with over 200,000 different inventoried parts supporting those products. To provide customers with prompt service, IBM has developed an inventory system that includes 2 central warehouses, 21 field distribution centers, 64 parts stations, and 15,000 outside locations with over 15,000 customer engineers, not to mention all those involved in managing the inventory.

As for quality control, again, for many firms it is a marketing strategy—"Quality is Job 1" touts Ford Motor Company. ITT Electro-Optical Products Division, which manufactures night vision products including pilot's goggles, aviator's night vision imaging systems, and night goggles, is another company to benefit from a TQM approach to business. Complicating ITT's task is the fact that manufacturing these systems is extremely complex, involving over 200 different chemicals and 400 different processes. This production complexity has led to an industry average production level of good units of only 10 to 40 percent. Prior to implementing a TQM program, which involved continuous process involvement, statistical process control, and employee involvement, only 35 percent of the units ITT produced were good. Implementing the TQM approach raised the percent of good units produced to 75 percent. The savings from reducing the proportion of bad units produced were passed on in lower prices, resulting in a 60-fold increase of the number of units sold over five years. To say the least, there are an awful lot of people inspecting products and working on ways to improve their quality—and that may be your job.

SUMMARY

Objective 1

The size of the investment in accounts receivable depends on three factors: the percentage of credit sales to total sales, the level of sales, and the credit and collection policies. However, only the credit and collection policies are decision variables open to the financial manager. The policies that the financial manager has control over include the terms of sale, the type of customer, and the collection efforts.

Objective 2

Although the typical firm has fewer assets tied up in inventory (16.94 percent) than it does in accounts receivable (20.77 percent), inventory management and control is still an important function of the financial manager. The purpose of holding inventory is to make each function of the business independent of the other functions—that is, to uncouple the firm's operations. Inventory-management techniques primarily involve questions of how much inventory should be ordered and when the order should be placed. The answers directly determine the average level of investment in inventory. The *EOQ* model is employed in answering the first of these questions. This model attempts to calculate the order size that minimizes the sum of the inventory carrying and ordering costs. The order point problem attempts to determine how low inventory can drop before it is reordered. The order point is reached when the inventory falls to a level equal to the delivery-time stock plus the safety stock. Determining the level of safety stock involves a direct trade-off between the risk of running out of inventory and the increased costs associated with carrying additional inventory.

The just-in-time inventory control system lowers inventory by reducing the time and distance between the various production functions. The idea behind the system is that the firm should keep a minimum level of inventory on hand and rely on suppliers to furnish parts "just in time" for them to be assembled.

Objective 3

The TQM philosophy affects the way the purchasing portion of inventory management is handled. The traditional adversarial purchaser-supplier relationship has given way to close customer relationships, which have in turn helped trim costs by allowing for the production of higher-quality products. This close customer-supplier relationship has allowed the TQM philosophy to be passed across company boundaries to the supplier, and has also allowed the firm to tap the supplier's expertise in designing higher-quality products. In addition, this interdependence between the supplier and customer has allowed for the development and introduction of new products much quicker than previously possible. The use of single-sourcing (in which a company uses a very few suppliers or, in many cases, a single supplier as a source for a particular part or material) has helped align the interests of the supplier and customer.

The movement toward a policy of 100 percent quality has been fueled by the realization that quality can be used as a means of differentiating products. The TQM view concludes that traditional quality-cost analysis underestimates the cost of producing a poor quality product, while it overestimates the cost of producing a high quality product. As a result, under this new TQM view of the quality-costs trade-offs, the low point in the total cost curve moves to an optimal quality level of 100 percent quality.

KEY TERMS

Anticipatory buying, 722
Appraisal costs, 725
Credit scoring, 709
Delivery-time stock, 721
External failure costs, 726
Finished-goods inventory, 717
Internal failure costs, 726
Inventory management, 716
Just-in-time inventory control system, 722

http://www

Go To: **www.prenhall.com/keown** for downloads and current events associated with this chapter

STUDY QUESTIONS

20-1. What factors determine the size of the investment a firm makes in accounts receivable? Which of these factors are under the control of the financial manager?

20-2. What do the following trade credit terms mean?

a. 1/20, net 50
b. 2/30, net 60
c. net 30
d. 2/10, 1/30, net 60

20-3. What is the purpose of an aging account in the control of accounts receivable? Can this same function be performed through ratio analysis? Why or why not?

20-4. If a credit manager experienced no bad debt losses over the past year, would this be an indication of proper credit management? Why or why not?

20-5. What is the purpose of credit scoring?

20-6. What are the risk-return trade-offs associated with adopting a more liberal trade credit policy?

20-7. Explain the purpose of marginal analysis.

20-8. What is the purpose of holding inventory? Name several types of inventory and describe their purpose.

20-9. Can cash be considered a special type of inventory? If so, what functions does it attempt to uncouple?

20-10. To control investment in inventory effectively, what two questions must be answered?

20-11. What are the major assumptions made by the *EOQ* model?

20-12. What are the risk-return trade-offs associated with inventory management?

20-13. How might inflation affect the *EOQ* model?

20-14. How do single-sourcing and closer customer-supplier relationships contribute to the firm?

20-15. What does the TQM view of the quality-cost relationship say is misstated by the traditional economic view of trade-offs between quality and cost?

SELF-TEST PROBLEMS

ST-1. (*EOQ calculations*) A local gift shop is attempting to determine how many sets of wine glasses to order. The store feels it will sell approximately 800 sets in the next year at a price of $18 per set. The wholesale price that the store pays per set is $12. Costs for carrying one set of wine glasses are estimated at $1.50 per year whereas ordering costs are estimated at $25.

a. What is the economic order quantity for the sets of wine glasses?
b. What are the annual inventory costs for the firm if it orders in this quantity? (Assume constant demand and instantaneous delivery and thus no safety stock is carried.)

ST-2. (*EOQ calculations*) Given the following inventory information and relationships for the F. Beamer Corporation:

1. Orders can be placed only in multiples of 100 units.
2. Annual unit usage is 300,000. (Assume a 50-week year in your calculations.)

3. The carrying cost is 30 percent of the purchase price of the goods.
4. The purchase price is $10 per unit.
5. The ordering cost is $50 per order.
6. The desired safety stock is 1,000 units. (This does not include delivery-time stock.)
7. Delivery time is two weeks.

Given this information:

a. What is the optimal *EOQ* level?
b. How many orders will be placed annually?
c. At what inventory level should a reorder be made?

STUDY PROBLEMS (SET A)

20-1A. (*Trade credit discounts*) If a firm buys on trade credit terms of 2/10, net 50 and decides to forgo the trade credit discount and pay on the net day, what is the effective annualized cost of forgoing the discount?

20-2A. (*Trade credit discounts*) If a firm buys on trade credit terms of 2/20, net 30 and decides to forgo the trade credit discount and pay on the net day, what is the effective annualized cost of forgoing the discount?

20-3A. (*Trade credit discounts*) Determine the effective annualized cost of forgoing the trade credit discount on the following terms:

a. 1/10, net 20
b. 2/10, net 30
c. 3/10, net 30
d. 3/10, net 60
e. 3/10, net 90
f. 5/10, net 60

20-4A. (*Altman model*) The following ratios were supplied by six loan applicants. Given this information and the credit-scoring model developed by Altman (equation 20-3), which loans have a high probability of defaulting next year?

	EBIT / TOTAL ASSETS	SALES / TOTAL ASSETS	MARKET VALUE OF EQUITY / BOOK VALUE OF DEBT	RETAINED EARNINGS / TOTAL ASSETS	WORKING CAPITAL / TOTAL ASSETS
Applicant 1	.2	.2	1.2	.3	.5
Applicant 2	.2	.8	1.0	.3	.8
Applicant 3	.2	.7	.6	.3	.4
Applicant 4	.1	.4	1.2	.4	.4
Applicant 5	.3	.7	.5	.4	.7
Applicant 6	.2	.5	.5	.4	.4

20-5A. (*Ratio analysis*) Assuming a 360-day year, calculate what the average investment in inventory would be for a firm, given the following information in each case:

a. The firm has sales of $600,000, a gross profit margin of 10 percent, and an inventory turnover ratio of 6.
b. The firm has a cost of goods sold figure of $480,000 and an average age of inventory of 40 days.
c. The firm has a cost of goods sold figure of $1,150,000 and an inventory turnover ratio of 5.
d. The firm has a sales figure of $25 million, a gross profit margin of 14 percent, and an average age of inventory of 45 days.

20-6A. (*Marginal analysis*) The Bandwagonesque Corporation is considering relaxing its current credit policy. Currently, the firm has annual sales (all credit) of $5 million and an average collection period of 60 days (assume a 360-day year). Under the proposed change, the trade credit terms would be changed from net 60 to net 90 days and credit would be extended to a riskier class of customer. It is assumed that bad debt losses on current customers will remain at their current level. Under this change, it is expected that sales will increase to $6 million. Given the following information, should the firm adopt the new policy?

New sales level (all credit)	$6,000,000
Original sales level (all credit)	$5,000,000
Contribution margin	20%
Percent bad debt losses on new sales	8%
New average collection period	90 days
Original average collection period	60 days
Additional investment in inventory	$50,000
Pre-tax required rate of return	15%

20-7A. (*Marginal analysis*) The Foxbase Alpha Corporation is considering a major change in credit policy. Managers are considering extending credit to a riskier class of customer and extending their credit period from net 30 days to net 45 days. They do not expect bad debt losses on their current customers to change. Given the following information, should they go ahead with the change in credit policy?

New sales level (all credit)	$12,500,000
Original sales level (all credit)	$11,000,000
Contribution margin	20%
Percent bad debt losses on new sales	9%
New average collection period	45 days
Original average collection period	30 days
Additional investment in inventory	$75,000
Pre-tax required rate of return	15%

20-8A. (*EOQ calculations*) A downtown comic shop is trying to determine the optimal order quantity for the reprint of a first issue of a popular comic book. It is expected to sell approximately 3,000 copies in the next year at a price of $1.50. The store buys the comic at a wholesale figure of $1. Costs for carrying the comic are estimated at 10 cents a copy per year, and it costs $10 to order more comics.

a. Determine the *EOQ*.
b. What would be the total costs for ordering the comics 1, 4, 5, 10, and 15 times a year?
c. What questionable assumptions are being made by the *EOQ* model?

20-9A. (*EOQ calculations*) The local hamburger fast-food restaurant purchases 20,000 boxes of hamburger rolls every month. Order costs are $50 an order, and it costs 25 cents a box for storage.

a. What is the optimal order quantity of hamburger rolls for this restaurant?
b. What questionable assumptions are being made by the *EOQ* model?

20-10A. (*EOQ calculations*) A local car manufacturing plant has a $75 per-unit per-year carrying cost on a certain item in inventory. This item is used at a rate of 50,000 per year. Ordering costs are $500 per order.

a. What is the *EOQ* for this item?
b. What are the annual inventory costs for this firm if it orders in this quantity? (Assume constant demand and instantaneous delivery.)

20-11A. (*EOQ calculations*) Swank Products is involved in the production of camera parts and has the following inventory, carrying, and storage costs:

1. Orders must be placed in round lots of 200 units.
2. Annual unit usage is 500,000. (Assume a 50-week year in your calculations.)
3. The carrying cost is 20 percent of the purchase price.
4. The purchase price is $2 per unit.
5. The ordering cost is $90 per order.
6. The desired safety stock is 15,000 units. (This does not include delivery-time stock.)
7. The delivery time is one week.

Given the preceding information:

- **a.** Determine the optimal *EOQ* level.
- **b.** How many orders will be placed annually?
- **c.** What is the inventory order point? (That is, at what level of inventory should a new order be placed?)
- **d.** What is the average inventory level?

20-12A. (*EOQ calculations*) Toledo Distributors has determined the following inventory information and relationships:

1. Orders can be placed only in multiples of 200 units.
2. Annual unit usage is 500,000 units. (Assume a 50-week year in your calculations.)
3. The carrying cost is 10 percent of the purchase price of the goods.
4. The purchase price is $5 per unit.
5. The ordering cost is $100 per order.
6. The desired safety stock is 5,000 units. (This does not include delivery time stock.)
7. Delivery time is four weeks.

Given this information:

- **a.** What is the *EOQ* level?
- **b.** How many orders will be placed annually?
- **c.** At what inventory level should a reorder be made?
- **d.** Now assume the carrying costs are 50 percent of the purchase price of the goods and recalculate (a), (b), and (c). Are these the results you anticipated?

INTEGRATIVE PROBLEM

Your first major assignment after your recent promotion at Ice Nine involves overseeing the management of accounts receivable and inventory. The first item that you must attend to involves a proposed change in credit policy that would involve relaxing credit terms from the existing terms of 1/50, net 70 to 2/60, net 90 in hopes of securing new sales. The management at Ice Nine does not expect bad debt losses on its current customers to change under the new credit policy. The following information should aid you in the analysis of this problem.

New sales level (all credit)	$8,000,000
Original sales level (all credit)	$7,000,000
Contribution margin	25%
Percent bad debt losses on new sales	8%
New average collection period	75 days
Original average collection period	60 days
Additional investment in inventory	$50,000
Pre-tax required rate of return	15%
New percent cash discount	2%
Percent of customers taking the new cash discount	50%
Original percent cash discount	1%
Percent of customers taking the old cash discount	50%

To help in your decision on relaxing credit terms, you have been asked to respond to the following questions:

1. What factors determine the size of investment Ice Nine makes in accounts receivable?
2. If a firm currently buys from Ice Nine on trade credit with the present terms of 1/50, net 70 and decides to forgo the trade credit discount and pay on the net day, what is the effective annualized cost to that firm of forgoing the discount?
3. If Ice Nine changes its trade credit terms to 2/60, net 90, what is the effective annualized cost to a firm that buys on credit from Ice Nine and decides to forgo the trade credit discount and pay on the net day?
4. What is the estimated change in profits resulting from the increased sales less any additional bad debts associated with the proposed change in credit policy?

5. Estimate the cost of additional investment in accounts receivable and inventory associated with this change in credit policy.
6. Estimate the change in the cost of the cash discount if the proposed change in credit policy is enacted.
7. Compare the incremental revenues with the incremental costs. Should the proposed change be enacted?

You have also been asked to answer some questions dealing with inventory management at Ice Nine. Presently, Ice Nine is involved in the production of musical products with its German engineered Daedlufetarg music line. Production of this product involves the following inventory, carrying, and storage costs:

a. Orders must be placed in round lots of 100 units.
b. Annual unit usage is 250,000. (Assume a 50-week year in your calculations.)
c. The carrying cost is 10 percent of the purchase price.
d. The purchase price is $10 per unit.
e. The ordering cost is $100 per order.
f. The desired safety stock is 5,000 units. (This does not include delivery-time stock.)
g. The delivery time is one week.

Given the preceding information:

1. Determine the optimal *EOQ* level.
2. How many orders will be placed annually?
3. What is the inventory order point? (That is, at what level of inventory should a new order be placed?)
4. What is the average inventory level?
5. What would happen to the *EOQ* if annual unit sales doubled (all other unit costs and safety stocks remaining constant)? What is the elasticity of *EOQ* with respect to sales? (That is, what is the percent change in *EOQ* divided by the percent change in sales?)
6. If carrying costs double, what would happen to the *EOQ* level? (Assume the original sales level of 250,000 units.) What is the elasticity of *EOQ* with respect to carrying costs?
7. If the ordering costs double, what would happen to the level of *EOQ*? (Again, assume original levels of sales and carrying costs.) What is the elasticity of *EOQ* with respect to ordering costs?
8. If the selling price doubles, what would happen to *EOQ*? What is the elasticity of *EOQ* with respect to selling price?
9. What assumptions are being made by the *EOQ* model that has been used here?
10. How would the results of this model change if carrying cost were to increase, perhaps because of increased inflation?
11. How would an improvement in the relationship that Ice Nine has with its suppliers resulting in a decrease in the average delivery time for replenishment of inventory affect your answer?
12. If Ice Nine could decrease its ordering costs, perhaps by improving its relationship with suppliers, how would this affect your answer?

STUDY PROBLEMS (SET B)

20-1B. (*Trade credit discounts*) If a firm buys on trade credit terms of 2/10, net 60 and decides to forgo the trade credit discount and pay on the net day, what is the effective annualized cost of forgoing the discount?

20-2B. (*Trade credit discounts*) If a firm buys on trade credit terms of 2/20, net 40 and decides to forgo the trade credit discount and pay on the net day, what is the effective annualized cost of forgoing the discount?

20-3B. (*Trade credit discounts*) Determine the effective annualized cost of forgoing the trade credit discount on the following terms:

a. 1/5, net 20
b. 2/20, net 90
c. 1/20, net 100
d. 4/10, net 50
e. 5/20, net 100
f. 5/30, net 50

20-4B. (*Altman model*) The following ratios were supplied by six loan applicants. Given this information and the credit-scoring model developed by Altman (equation 20-3), which loans have a high probability of defaulting next year and thus should be avoided?

	EBIT / TOTAL ASSETS	SALES / TOTAL ASSETS	MARKET VALUE OF EQUITY / BOOK VALUE OF DEBT	RETAINED EARNINGS / TOTAL ASSETS	WORKING CAPITAL / TOTAL ASSETS
Applicant 1	.3	.4	1.2	.3	.5
Applicant 2	.2	.6	1.3	.4	.3
Applicant 3	.2	.7	.6	.3	.2
Applicant 4	.1	.5	1.8	.5	.4
Applicant 5	.5	.7	.5	.4	.6
Applicant 6	.2	.4	.2	.4	.4

20-5B. (*Ratio analysis*) Assuming a 360-day year, calculate what the average investment in inventory would be for a firm, given the following information in each case.

a. The firm has sales of $550,000, a gross profit margin of 10 percent, and an inventory turnover ratio of 5.

b. The firm has a cost of goods sold figure of $480,000 and an average age of inventory of 35 days.

c. The firm has a cost of goods sold figure of $1,250,000 and an inventory turnover ratio of 6.

d. The firm has a sales figure of $25 million, a gross profit margin of 15 percent, and an average age of inventory of 50 days.

20-6B. (*Marginal analysis*) The Hyndford Street Corporation is considering relaxing its current credit policy. Currently the firm has annual sales (all credit) of $6 million and an average collection period of 40 days (assume a 360-day year). Under the proposed change the trade credit terms would be changed from net 40 days to net 90 days and credit would be extended to a riskier class of customer. It is assumed that bad debt losses on current customers will remain at their current level. Under this change, it is expected that sales will increase to $7 million. Given the following information, should the firm adopt the new policy?

New sales level (all credit)	$7,000,000
Original sales level (all credit)	$6,000,000
Contribution margin	20%
Percent bad debt losses on new sales	8%
New average collection period	90 days
Original average collection period	40 days
Additional investment in inventory	$40,000
Pre-tax required rate of return	15%

20-7B. (*Marginal analysis*) The Northern Muse Corporation is considering a major change in credit policy. Managers are considering extending credit to a riskier class of customer and extending their credit period from net 30 days to net 50 days. They do not expect bad debt losses on their current customers to change. Given the following information, should they go ahead with the change in credit policy?

New sales level (all credit)	$18,000,000
Original sales level (all credit)	$17,000,000
Contribution margin	20%
Percent bad debt losses on new sales	8%
New average collection period	50 days
Original average collection period	30 days
Additional investment in inventory	$60,000
Pre-tax required rate of return	15%

20-8B. (*EOQ calculations*) A downtown bookstore is trying to determine the optimal order quantity for a reprint of a first issue of a popular comic book. It is expected to sell approximately 3,500 copies in the next year at a price of $1.50. The store buys the comic at a wholesale figure of $1. Costs for carrying the comic are estimated at 20 cents a copy per year, and it costs $9 to order more comics.

a. Determine the *EOQ*.
b. What would be the total costs for ordering the comics 1, 4, 5, 10, and 15 times a year?
c. What questionable assumptions are being made by the *EOQ* model?

20-9B. (*EOQ calculations*) The local hamburger fast-food restaurant purchases 21,000 boxes of hamburger rolls every month. Order costs are $55 an order, and it costs 20 cents a box for storage.

a. What is the optimal order quantity of hamburger rolls for this restaurant?
b. What questionable assumptions are being made by the *EOQ* model?

20-10B. (*EOQ calculations*) A local car manufacturing plant has a $70 per-unit per-year carrying cost on a certain item in inventory. This item is used at a rate of 55,000 per year. Ordering costs are $500 per order.

a. What is the economic order quantity for this item?
b. What are the annual inventory costs for this firm if it orders in this quantity? (Assume constant demand and instantaneous delivery.)

20-11B. (*EOQ calculations*) Swank Products is involved in the production of camera parts and has the following inventory, carrying, and storage costs:

1. Orders must be placed in round lots of 200 units.
2. Annual unit usage is 600,000. (Assume a 50-week year in your calculations.)
3. The carrying cost is 15 percent of the purchase price.
4. The purchase price is $3 per unit.
5. The ordering cost is $90 per order.
6. The desired safety stock is 15,000 units. (This does not include delivery time stock.)
7. The delivery time is one week.

Given the preceding information:

a. Determine the optimal *EOQ* level.
b. How many orders will be placed annually?
c. What is the inventory order point? (That is, at what level of inventory should a new order be placed?)
d. What is the average inventory level?

20-12B. (*EOQ calculations*) Toledo Distributors has determined the following inventory information and relationships:

1. Orders can be placed only in multiples of 200 units.
2. Annual unit usage is 500,000 units. (Assume a 50-week year in your calculations.)
3. The carrying cost is 9 percent of the purchase price of the goods.
4. The purchase price is $5 per unit.
5. The ordering cost is $75 per order.
6. The desired safety stock is 5,000 units. (This does not include delivery-time stock.)
7. Delivery time is four weeks.

Given this information:

a. What is the *EOQ* level?
b. How many orders will be placed annually?
c. At what inventory level should a reorder be made?
d. Now assume the carrying costs are 50 percent of the purchase price of the goods and recalculate (a), (b), and (c). Are these the results you anticipated?

SELF-TEST SOLUTIONS

ST-1. **a.** The economic order quantity is

$$Q^* = \sqrt{\frac{2SO}{C}}$$

where S = total demand in units over the planning period
O = ordering cost per order
C = carrying costs per unit

Substituting the values given in the self-test problem into the *EOQ* equation we get

$$Q^* = \sqrt{\frac{2 \times 800 \times 25}{1.50}}$$
$$= \sqrt{26{,}667}$$
$$= 163 \text{ units per order}$$

Thus, 163 units should be ordered each time an order is placed. Note that the *EOQ* calculations occur based on several limiting assumptions such as constant demand, constant unit price, and constant carrying costs, which may influence the final decision.

b. Total costs = carrying costs + ordering costs

$$= \left(\frac{Q}{2}\right)C + \left(\frac{S}{Q}\right)O$$
$$= \left(\frac{163}{2}\right)\$1.50 + \left(\frac{800}{163}\right)\$25$$
$$= \$122.25 + \$122.70$$
$$= \$244.95$$

Note that carrying costs and ordering costs are the same (other than a slight difference caused by having to order in whole rather than fractional units). This is because the total costs curve is at its minimum when ordering costs equal carrying costs.

ST-2.

$$Q^* = \sqrt{\frac{2SO}{C}}$$
$$= \sqrt{\frac{2 \times 300{,}000 \times 50}{3}}$$

= 3,162 units, but because orders must be placed in 100-unit lots, the effective *EOQ* becomes 3,200 units

b. $$\frac{\text{Total usage}}{EOQ} = \frac{300{,}000}{3{,}200} = 93.75 \text{ orders per year}$$

c. Inventory order point = delivery-time stock + safety stock

$$= \frac{2}{50} \times 300{,}000 + 1{,}000$$
$$= 12{,}000 + 1{,}000$$
$$= 13{,}000 \text{ units}$$

PART 6

Special Topics in Finance

CHAPTER 21
RISK MANAGEMENT

CHAPTER 22
INTERNATIONAL BUSINESS FINANCE

CHAPTER 23
CORPORATE RESTRUCTURING: COMBINATIONS AND DIVESTITURES

CHAPTER 24
TERM LOANS AND LEASES

LEARNING OBJECTIVES

After reading this chapter, you should be able to

1. Explain the difference between a commodity future and a financial future and how they might be used by a financial manager to control risk.
2. Explain what put and call options are and how they might be used by a financial manager to control risk.
3. Explain what a currency swap is and how it might be used to eliminate exchange rate risk.

CHAPTER 21

Risk Management

This chapter focuses on how financial managers use futures, options, and currency swaps to eliminate risk. Although it looks easy, as many a firm has seen, it is a dangerous undertaking if done incorrectly. It is also an area where understanding is extremely important.

What kinds of risks can a firm control with futures, options, and currency swaps? They can be used to lock in prices of commodities used in production, interest rates if they are going to issue debt, or exchange rates for sales abroad. Let's look at Harley-Davidson. In 2002, about 8.2 percent of its income came from Europe, with another 3.5 percent coming from Japan. In fact, to strengthen its position in the European market Harley acquired its Italian distributor. The new company, Harley-Davidson Italia S.r.l., joins other Harley-Davidson subsidiaries that already exist in Germany, France, the Benelux, and the United Kingdom. In addition, Harley-Davidson also operates a wholly owned subsidiary in Japan. All of that means that Harley sells a lot of motorcycles abroad for Euros, the currency of the European Union, and Japanese Yen. The motorcycles sold in Europe and Japan are made in America, with parts and workers paid in the U.S. dollar. So what happens to profits if the value of the Euro or the yen drops relative to the dollar? That means that Harley will be selling its motorcycles for foreign currency that is worth less and less in terms of dollars. Obviously, this is a risk that Harley would rather not be exposed to. How does it eliminate that risk? It eliminates it through the use of foreign exchange futures. As we will see, foreign exchange futures allow us to lock in an exchange rate ahead of time, thus eliminating the problem of currency fluctuations. Is this a real problem? You bet it is. In fact, during 1999 and 2000, the value of the Euro in terms of U.S. dollars fell by about 28 percent! More recently, the Euro has gone the other way, rising from a rate of \$0.88 per Euro in early 2002 to \$1.16 per Euro in mid-2003! But, as with most other finance tools, the financial manager must have an understanding not only of the proper use of exchange rates, but of their risk potential and limitations.

CHAPTER PREVIEW

In this chapter, we examine two financial instruments that are not created by the firm: futures and options. These financial instruments are commonly referred to as "derivative securities" in that their value or price is determined by, or "derived" from, the price of another asset, exchange rate, commodity price, or interest rate. It is important for us to be familiar with them for two reasons. First, these instruments can be used to reduce the risks associated with interest and exchange rate and commodity price fluctuations. Second, as you will see in future finance courses, an understanding of the pricing of options is extremely valuable because many different financial assets can be viewed as options. In fact, risky bonds, common stock, and the abandonment decision can all be thought of as types of options. We also examine currency swaps that are used to hedge exchange rate risk over longer periods of time.

This chapter will emphasize **Principle 1: The Risk-Return Trade-Off—We won't take on additional risk unless we expect to be compensated with additional return.** Be on the lookout for this concept.

Objective 1

FUTURES

Commodity and financial futures are perhaps the fastest-growing and most exciting new financial instrument today. Financial managers who only a few years ago would not have considered venturing into the futures market are now actively using this market to eliminate risk. As the number of participants in this market has grown, so has the number of items on which future contracts are offered, from the old standbys such as coffee and soybeans, to newer ones such as U.S. Treasury bonds, sorghum, municipal bonds, and diammonium phosphate.

Futures contract
A contract to buy or sell a stated commodity or financial claim at a specified price at some future, specified time.

A **future**, or **futures contract**, is a contract to buy or sell a stated commodity (such as soybeans or corn) or financial claim (such as U.S. Treasury bonds) at a specified price at some future specified time. They are used by the financial manager to lock in future prices of raw materials, interest rates, or exchange rates. As was mentioned in the introduction to this chapter, if not controlled or understood, there are also dangers associated with their use. It is important to note here that this is a contract that *requires* its holder to buy or sell the asset, regardless of what happens to its value during the interim. The importance of a futures contract is that it can be used by financial managers to lock in the price of a commodity or an interest rate and thereby eliminate one source of risk. For example, if a corporation is planning on issuing debt in the near future and is concerned about a possible rise in interest rates between now and when the debt will be issued, it might sell a U.S. Treasury bond futures contract with the same face value as the proposed debt offering and a delivery date the same as when the debt offering is to occur. Alternatively, with the use of a futures contract, Ralston-Purina or Quaker Oats can lock in the future price of corn or oats whenever they wish. Because a futures contract locks in interest rates or commodity prices, the costs associated with any possible rise in interest rates or commodity prices are completely offset by the profits made by writing the futures contract. In effect, futures contracts allow the financial manager to lock in future interest and exchange rates or prices for a number of agricultural commodities such as corn and oats.

As the use of futures contracts becomes more common in the financial management of the firm, it is important for the financial manager to be familiar with the operation and terminology associated with these financial instruments. Although there are many uses for futures, options, and currency swaps, our interest focuses on how financial managers use them to reduce risk. Keep in mind that the financial manager can use them to effectively offset future movements in the price of commodities or interest rates and thereby eliminate risk.

AN INTRODUCTION TO FUTURES MARKETS

The futures markets originated in medieval times. In fact, England, France, and Japan all developed futures markets of their own. Here in the United States, several futures markets sprang up in the early years, but it was not until the establishment of the Chicago Board of Trade (CBT) in 1848 that the futures markets were provided with their true roots. As we will see, although this market has been in operation for 150 years, it was not until the early 1970s—when the futures markets expanded from agricultural commodities to financial futures—that financial managers began to regularly venture into this market.

To develop an understanding of futures markets, let us examine several distinguishing features of futures contracts. A *futures contract* is distinguished by (1) an organized exchange, (2) a standardized contract with limited price changes and margin requirements, (3) a clearinghouse in each futures market, and (4) daily resettlement of contracts. Remember, a futures contract is legally binding. That means you must buy or sell a commodity some time in the future.

THE ORGANIZED EXCHANGE Although the Chicago Board of Trade is the oldest and largest of the futures exchanges, it is certainly not the only exchange. In fact, there are more than 10 different futures exchanges in operation in the United States today. The importance of having organized exchanges associated with the futures market is that they provide a central trading place. If there were no central trading place, then there would be no potential to generate the depth of trading necessary to support a secondary market; in a very circular way, the existence of a secondary market encourages more traders to enter the market and in turn provides additional liquidity.

An organized exchange also encourages confidence in the futures market by allowing for the effective regulation of trading. The various exchanges set and enforce rules and collect and disseminate information on trading activity and the commodities being traded. Together, the liquidity generated by having a central trading place, effective regulation, and the flow of information through the organized exchanges have effectively fostered their development.

STANDARDIZED CONTRACTS To develop a strong secondary market in any security, there must be many identical securities—or in this case, futures contracts—outstanding. In effect, standardization of contracts leads to more frequent trades on that contract, leading to greater liquidity in the secondary market for that contract, which in turn draws more traders into the market. This is why futures contracts are highly standardized and very specific with respect to the description of the goods to be delivered and the time and place of delivery. Let's look at a Chicago Board of Trade oats contract, for example. This contract calls for the delivery of 5,000 bushels of No. 2 heavy or No. 1 grade oats to Chicago or to Minneapolis–St. Paul at a 7.5 cents per bushel discount. In addition, these contracts are written to come due in March, May, July, September, and December. Through this standardization of contracts, trading has built up in enough identical contracts to allow for the development of a strong and highly liquid secondary market.

To encourage investors to participate in the futures market, daily price limits are set on most futures contracts (for some contracts coming due in the next two months, limits are not imposed). Without these limits, it is thought that there would be more price volatility on most futures contracts than many investors would be willing to accept. These daily price limits are set to protect investors, maintain order on the futures exchanges, and encourage the level of trading volume necessary to develop a strong secondary market. For example, the Chicago Board of Trade imposes a 10 cents per bushel ($500 per contract) price movement limit above and below the previous day's settlement price of oats contracts. This limit protects against runaway price movements. These daily price limits do not halt trading once the limit has been reached, but they do provide a boundary within which trading must occur. The price of an oats contract may rise 10 cents very early in the trading day—"up the limit," in futures jargon. This will not stop trading; it only means that no trade can take place above that level. As a result, any dramatic shifts in the market price of a futures contract must take place over a number of days, with the price of the contract going "up the limit" each day.

FUTURES CLEARINGHOUSE The main purpose of the futures clearinghouse is to guarantee that all trades will be honored. This is done by having the clearinghouse interpose itself as the buyer to every seller and the seller to every buyer. Because of this substitution of parties, it is not necessary for the original seller (or buyer) to find the original buyer (or seller) when he or she decides to clear his or her position. As a result, all an individual has to do is make an equal and opposite transaction that will provide a net zero position with the clearinghouse and cancel out that individual's obligation.

Because no trades occur directly between individuals, but between individuals and the clearinghouse, buyers and sellers realizing gains in the market are assured that they will be paid. Because futures contracts are traded with minimal "good faith" money, as we will see in the next section, it is necessary to provide some security to traders so that when money is made, it will be paid. There are other important benefits of a clearinghouse, including providing a mechanism for the delivery of commodities and the settlement of disputed trades, but these benefits also serve to encourage trading in the futures markets and thereby create a highly liquid secondary market.

DAILY RESETTLEMENT OF CONTRACTS Another safeguard of the futures market is a margin requirement. Although margin requirements on futures resemble stock margin requirements in that there is an initial margin and a maintenance margin that comes into play when the value of the contract declines, similarities between futures and stock margins end there.

Before we explore margin requirements on futures, it would be helpful to develop an understanding of the meaning of a margin on futures. The concept of a margin on futures contracts has a meaning that is totally different from its usage in reference to common stocks. The margin on common stocks refers to the amount of equity the investor has invested in the stocks. With a futures contract, no equity has been invested, because nothing has been bought. All that has happened is that a contract has been signed obligating the two parties to a future transaction and defining the terms of that transaction. This is an important thought: There is no actual buying or selling occurring with a futures contract; it is merely an agreement to buy or sell some commodity in the future. As a result, the term **futures margin** refers to "good faith" money the purchaser puts down to ensure that the contract will be carried out.

Futures margin
Good faith money the purchaser puts down to ensure that the contract will be carried out.

The initial margin required for commodities (deposited by both buyer and seller) is much lower than the margin required for common stock, generally amounting to only 3 to 10 percent of the value of the contract. For example, if September oats contracts on the CBT were selling at \$1.65 per bushel, then one contract for 5,000 bushels would be selling for \$1.65 × 5,000 = \$8,250. The initial margin on oats is \$400 per contract, which represents only about 4.85 percent of the contract price. Needless to say, the leverage associated with futures trading is tremendous—both on the up and down sides. Small changes in the price of the underlying commodity result in very large changes in the value of the futures contract, because very little has to be put down to "own" a contract. Moreover, for many futures contracts, if the financial manager can satisfy the broker that he or she is not engaged in trading as a speculator, but as a hedger, the manager can qualify for reduced initial margins. Because of the low level of the initial margin, there is also a *maintenance* or *variation margin* requirement that forces the investor or financial manager to replenish the margin account to a level specified by the exchange after any market loss.

One additional point related to margins deserves mention. The initial margin requirement can be fulfilled by supplying Treasury bills instead of cash. These Treasury bills are valued at 90 percent of their value for margin purposes, so it takes \$100,000 worth of Treasury bills to provide a \$90,000 margin. The advantage of using Treasury bills as margin is that the investor earns money on them, whereas brokerage firms do not pay interest on funds in commodity cash accounts. Moreover, if the financial manager is going to carry Treasury bills anyway, he or she can just deposit the Treasury bills with the broker and purchase the futures contracts with no additional cash outlay.

Suppose you are a financial manager for Ralston-Purina. You are in charge of purchasing raw materials—in particular, oats. Currently, a September futures contract for the delivery of oats has a price of \$1.65 per bushel. You need oats in September, and feel that this is an exceptional price—oats will probably be selling for more than that per bushel in September. Thus, you want to lock in this price, and to do this you purchase one contract for 5,000 bushels at 165 cents or \$1.65 per bushel. On purchasing the September oats contract, the only cash you would have to put up would be the initial margin of $400. Let's further assume that the price of oats futures then falls to a level of 161 cents per bushel the day after you make your purchase. In effect, you have incurred a loss of 4 cents per bushel on 5,000 bushels, for a total loss on your investment of $200.

At this point, the concept of daily resettlement comes into play. What this means is that all futures positions are brought to the market at the end of each trading day and all gains and losses, in this case a loss, are then settled. You have lost $200, which is then subtracted from your margin account, lowering it to $200 ($400 initially, less the $200 loss). Because the margin account has fallen below the maintenance margin on oats, which is $250, you would have to replenish the account back to its initial level of $400. If on the following day the price of September oats contracts fell another cent to 160 cents per bushel, you would have lost another 1 cent on 5,000 bushels for a loss of $50. This would then be subtracted from your margin account during the daily resettlement at the end of the trading day, leaving $350 in the account. Because your margin account would not be below the maintenance margin requirement of $250, you would not have to add any additional funds to the account. Let's carry our example one day further, this time to the upbeat side, and put some profits in. Let's assume that on the third day, the price of September oats contracts is up 5 cents per bushel. This means that you have made 5 cents on 5,000 bushels, for a total profit of $250. This brings your margin account up from $350 to $600, which is $200 above the initial margin of $400. You can withdraw this $200 from your margin account.

Obviously, the purpose of margin requirements is to provide some measure of safety for futures traders; and despite the very small level of margin requirements imposed, they do a reasonable job. They are set in accordance with the historical price volatility of the underlying commodity in such a way that it is extremely unlikely that a trader will ever lose more than is in his or her margin account in any one day.

Commodity Futures

In general, when people talk about commodities, they are referring to nonfinancial futures. This includes agricultural commodities as well as metals, wood products, and fibers. Although there are several new commodity futures contracts now being traded, such as lumber and orange juice, much of the trading in the commodities futures markets involves such traditional favorites as corn and wheat. For the financial manager, these markets provide a means of offsetting the risks associated with future price changes. Here the financial manager is securing a future price for a good that is currently in production, or securing a future price for some commodity that must be purchased in the future. In either case, the manager is using the futures market to eliminate the effects of future price changes on the future purchase or sale of some commodity.

Hedging with Futures

Although there are many different futures contracts available, it's not always possible to find what you're looking for. For example, you may have a manufacturing plant that uses petroleum as its primary raw material. However, there may not be futures contracts available on the specific grade of petroleum that you use. If you want to reduce risk by using the futures market to lock in a future price for petroleum, are you out of luck? Not really. Because all petroleum prices tend to move together, you could hedge away the risk of petroleum price rises using futures contracts on other grades of petroleum.

This use of futures contracts on similar but not identical commodities is referred to as *cross hedging*. With cross hedging, you don't actually want the commodity for which you've entered into a futures contract. What you're trying to do is lock in a price on a commodity whose price moves as close to identically as possible with the commodity you're interested in. As a result, you don't want to hold the futures contract to maturity and actually receive delivery of the commodity. The way you reverse your futures position is by taking an opposite and canceling position. That is, if you had earlier bought a futures contract, you would now sell the same contract and allow the two contracts to cancel each other out.

Is there danger in this? Not if it's done correctly. But that doesn't mean that companies haven't been burned when they thought they were using the futures market to hedge away risks. An example of a billion-dollar mistake is Metallgesellschaft AG, a German firm, that lost over $1 billion in 1993. One of its U.S. subsidiaries had entered into 10-year contracts to supply oil and gasoline at fixed prices. That meant that as long as petroleum prices didn't rise, it would make money, but if petroleum prices rose, it would be in trouble. To eliminate the risk from price rises, it turned to the futures market, buying short-term futures contracts. As it turned out, petroleum prices dropped and the subsidiary suffered enormous losses on these futures contracts. Unfortunately, because Metallgesellschaft AG's petroleum contracts were over 10 years, it was not offsetting gains on them. The result was a billion-dollar loss. It hedged the right product, but it didn't hedge for the right maturity. The bottom line here is that although futures contracts can reduce risk, you've got to make sure you know what you're doing with them.

Financial Futures

Financial futures come in a number of different forms, including futures on Treasury bills, notes and bonds, GMNAs, certificates of deposit, Eurodollars, foreign currencies, and stock indices. These financial newcomers first appeared in 1972, when foreign currencies were introduced; interest rate futures did not appear until 1975. The growth in financial futures has been phenomenal, and today they dominate the futures markets. Our discussion of financial futures will be divided into three sections: (1) interest rate futures, (2) foreign exchange futures, and (3) stock index futures.

INTEREST RATE FUTURES Currently, Treasury bond futures are the most popular of all futures contracts in terms of contracts issued. Although Treasury (or T-bond) futures are just one of several interest rate futures contracts, the fact that they are risk-free, long-term bonds with a maturity of at least 15 years has been the deciding factor in making them the most popular of the interest rate futures.

For the financial manager, interest rate futures provide an excellent means for eliminating the risks associated with interest rate fluctuations. As we learned earlier, there is an inverse relationship between bond prices in the secondary market and yields—that is, when interest rates fall bond prices rise, and when interest rates rise bond prices fall. If you think back to the chapter on valuation, you will recall that this inverse relationship between bond prices and yield is a result of the fact that when bonds are issued, their coupon rate is fixed. However, once the bond is issued, it must compete in the market with other financial instruments. Because new bonds are issued to yield the current interest rate, yields on old bonds must adjust to remain competitive with the newer issues. Thus, when interest rates rise, the price of an older bond with a lower coupon interest rate must decline to increase the yield on the old bond, making it competitive with the return on newly issued bonds.

Interest rate futures offer investors a very inexpensive way of eliminating the risks associated with interest rate fluctuations. For example, banks, pension funds, and insurance companies all make considerable use of the interest rate futures market to avoid paper losses that might otherwise occur when interest rates unexpectedly increase. Corporations also use interest rate futures to lock in interest rates when they are planning to issue debt. If interest rates rise before the corporation has the opportunity to issue the new debt, the profits on the interest rate futures contracts they have sold will offset the increased costs associated with the proposed debt offering.

FOREIGN EXCHANGE FUTURES Of all the financial futures, foreign exchange futures have been around the longest, first appearing in 1972. Foreign exchange futures work in the same way as other futures, but in this case the commodity is the Euro, British pounds, or some other foreign currency. As we will see, the similarities between these futures and the others we have examined are great. Not only do foreign exchange futures work in the same way as other futures, but they also are used by financial managers for the same basic reasons—to hedge away risks, in this case, exchange rate risks. One of the major participants in the foreign exchange futures market is the exporter who will receive foreign currency when its exported goods are finally received and who uses this market to lock in a certain exchange rate. As a result, the exporter is unaffected by any exchange rate fluctuations that might occur before it receives payment. Foreign exchange futures are also used to hedge away possible fluctuations in the value of earnings of foreign subsidiaries.

In the 1990s, fluctuations in exchange rates became common. With exchange rate futures, a financial manager could eliminate the effects—good or bad—of exchange rate fluctuation with a relatively small investment. The extremely high degree of leverage that was available coupled with the dramatic fluctuations in foreign exchange rates encouraged many financial managers to consider entering the exchange rate futures market.

STOCK INDEX FUTURES Stock indexes have been around for many years, but it has only been recently that financial managers and investors have had the opportunity to trade them directly. In fact, despite only first appearing in February 1982, by 1984 they became the second most widely traded futures contract of all, exceeded in trading volume only by T-bond futures contracts.

At this point, after looking at other futures contracts, the workings of stock index futures should be clear. They work basically the same way, with one major exception: Stock index futures contracts allow only for cash settlement. There is no delivery, because what is being traded is the *future price* of the index, not the underlying stocks in the index. Currently there are several stock index futures available, with futures on the S&P 500 Index clearly dominating in terms of volume. However, in mid-1997, futures trading on the Dow Jones Industrial Average (DJIA) was initiated. Given that the DJIA is perhaps the most recognized stock market index, this is almost certain to be a popular stock index future.

Let's examine exactly what an S&P 500 Index futures contract involves. The S&P 500 Index is a broad-based index made up of 400 industrials, 40 utilities, 20 transportations, and 40 financial companies. These companies represent about 80 percent of the value of all issues traded on the NYSE. This is a value-weighted index; the weight each stock takes on in the index is determined by the market value of that stock. The contract size or value of each contract is 500 times the S&P 500 Index, which puts it at about 663,000 in early 2001.

Just as with currency futures, when there is a major fluctuation in the stock market, entire fortunes can be made or lost in the stock index futures market. Take, for example, trading on October 22, 1987, during the week of the great crash. That day one trader, Albert "Bud" Furman III, made \$900,000 in 90 seconds by buying 303 S&P 500 futures contracts at \$196.00 a contract and selling 300 futures contracts 90 seconds later at \$202.00 per contract (500 × \$6/contract × 300 contracts = \$900,000).

After the 1987 crash, a system of shock absorber limits and circuit breakers was introduced to most index futures markets. These serve the same purpose as do daily price limits, but they are not as strict. For example, the New York Futures Exchange has 10-minute,

30-minute, one-hour, and two-hour trading halts that result from wide swings in the stock market. The purpose of these programmed trading halts is to allow investors to rationally appraise the market during periods of large price swings.

To the financial manager, the great popularity of these financial newcomers lies in their ability to reduce or eliminate systematic risk. When we talked about the variability or risk associated with common stock returns, we said that there were two types of risk: systematic and unsystematic risk. Unsystematic risk, although accounting for a large portion of the variability of an individual security's returns, is largely eliminated in large portfolios through random diversification, leaving only systematic or market risk in a portfolio. As a result, we said that a portfolio's returns are basically determined by market movements, as modified by the portfolio's beta. Before the introduction of stock index futures, a portfolio or pension fund manager was forced to adjust the portfolio's beta if he or she anticipated a change in the direction of the market. Stock index futures allow the portfolio or pension fund manager to eliminate or mute the effects of swings in the market without the large transactions costs that would be associated with the trading needed to modify the portfolio's beta. Unfortunately, although stock index futures allow for the elimination of the unwanted effects of market downswings, they also eliminate the effects of market upswings. In other words, they allow the portfolio or pension fund manager to eliminate as much of the effect of the market as he or she wishes from his or her portfolio.

BACK TO THE PRINCIPLES

The area of risk management has grown rapidly over the last decade. In response to volatile interest rates, commodity prices, and exchange rates of the late 1970s through the 1990s, financial managers turned to the futures, options, and swap markets for relief. Once again, the financial markets demonstrated their dynamic and adaptive nature in finding new ways of reducing risk without affecting return. The inspiration for such behavior, of course, finds its roots in ***Principle 1: The Risk-Return Trade-Off—We won't take on additional risk unless we expect to be compensated with additional return.***

CONCEPT CHECK

1. What is a futures contract? What are its distinguishing features?
2. How do you hedge with futures contracts?
3. What is a financial future? Give an example of one.

Objective 2

Option contract
An option contract gives its owner the right to buy or sell a fixed number of shares of stock at a specified price over a limited time period.

OPTIONS

An **option**, or **option contract**, gives its owner the right to buy or sell a fixed number of shares of stock at a specified price over a limited time period. Although trading in option contracts has existed for many years, it was not until the Chicago Board of Exchange (CBOE) began trading in listed options in 1973 that the volume of trading reached any meaningful level. During the time since the CBOE first listed options on 16 stocks, volume has grown at a phenomenal rate, with options on more than 1,332 stocks and 41 indexes traded on the CBOE. Today, the CBOE continues to dominate options trading, accounting for almost half of all listed option trades, with the American Stock Exchange, the Philadelphia Stock Exchange, the Pacific Stock Exchange, and the International Securities Exchange accounting for most of the remaining trades. To give you an idea of how large this market is, consider the fact that on the CBOE alone:

- On a typical day, over $25 billion in contract value is traded.
- Over 1 million option contracts change hands daily.
- It is the second largest listed securities market in the United States, following only the NYSE.

Still, to many financial managers, options remain a mystery, viewed as closer to something one would find in Las Vegas than on Wall Street.

Clearly, there is too much going on in the options markets not to pay attention to them. Financial managers are just beginning to turn to them as an effective way of eliminating risk for a small price. As we will see, they are fascinating, but they are also confusing—with countless variations and a language of their own. Moreover, their use is not limited to speculators; options are also used by the most conservative financial managers to eliminate unwanted risk. In this section, we will discuss the fundamentals of options, their terminology, and how they are used by financial managers.

The Fundamentals of Options

Although the market for options seems to have a language of its own, there are only two basic types of options: puts and calls. Everything else involves some variation. A **call option** gives its owner the right to purchase a given number of shares of stock or some other asset at a specified price over a given period. Thus, if the price of the underlying common stock or asset goes up, a call purchaser makes money. This is essentially the same as a "rain check" or guaranteed price. You have the option to buy something, in this case common stock, at a set price.

Call option
A call option gives its owner the right to purchase a given number of shares of stock or some other asset at a specified price over a given time period.

In effect, a call option gives you the right to buy, but it is not a promise to buy. A **put option**, however, gives its owner the right to sell a given number of shares of common stock or some other asset at a specified price over a given period. A put purchaser is betting that the price of the underlying common stock or asset will drop. Just as with the call, a put option gives its holder the right to sell the common stock at a set price, but it is not a promise to sell. Because these are just options to buy or sell stock or some other asset, they do not represent an ownership position in the underlying corporation, as does common stock. In fact, there is no direct relationship between the underlying corporation and the option. An option is merely a contract between two investors.

Put option
A put option gives its owner the right to sell a given number of shares of common stock or some other asset at a specified price over a given time period.

Because there is no underlying security, a purchaser of an option can be viewed as betting against the seller or *writer* of the option. For this reason, the options markets are often referred to as a *zero sum game*. If someone makes money, then someone must lose money; if profits and losses were added up, the total for all options would equal zero. If commissions are considered, the total becomes negative, and we have a "negative sum" game. As we will see, the options markets are quite complicated and risky. Some experts refer to them as legalized institutions for transferring wealth from the unsophisticated to the sophisticated. However, for the financial manager, they can be tools for eliminating risk.

THE CONTRACT When an option is purchased, it is nothing more than a contract that allows the purchaser to either buy in the case of a call, or sell in the case of a put, the underlying stock or asset at a predetermined price. That is, no asset has changed hands, but the price has been set for a future transaction that will occur *only if and when* the option purchaser wants it to. In this section, we will refer to the process of selling puts and calls as *writing*. Often, selling options is referred to as *shorting* or *taking a short position* in those options, whereas buying an option is referred to as *taking a long position.*

THE EXERCISE OR STRIKING PRICE The **option striking price** is the price at which the stock or asset may be purchased from the writer in the case of a call or sold to the writer in the case of a put.

Option striking price
The price at which the stock or asset may be purchased from the writer in the case of a call, or sold to the writer in the case of a put.

Option premium
The price of the option.

OPTION PREMIUM The **option premium** is merely the price of the option. It is generally stated in terms of dollars per share rather than per option contract, which covers 100 shares. Thus, if a call option premium is $2, then an option contract would cost $200 and allow the purchase of 100 shares of stock at the exercise price.

Option expiration date
The date on which the option expires.

EXPIRATION DATE The **option expiration date** is the date on which the option contract expires. An American option is one that can be exercised any time up to the expiration date. A European option can be exercised only on the expiration date.

COVERED AND NAKED OPTIONS If a call writer owns the underlying stock or asset on which he or she writes a call, the writer is said to have written a *covered call.* Conversely, if the writer writes a call on a stock or asset that he or she does not own, he or she is said to have written a *naked call.* The difference is that if a naked call is exercised, the call writer must deliver stock or assets that he or she does not own.

OPEN INTEREST The term *open interest* refers to the number of option contracts in existence at one point in time. The importance of this concept comes from the fact that open interest provides the investor with some indication of the amount of liquidity associated with that particular option.

IN-, OUT-OF, AND AT-THE-MONEY A call (put) is said to be out-of-the-money if the underlying stock is selling below (above) the exercise price of the option. Alternatively, a call (put) is said to be in-the-money if the underlying stock is selling above (below) the exercise price of the option. If the option is selling at the exercise price, it is said to be selling at-the-money. For example, if Ford Motor's common stock was selling for $22 per share, a call on Ford with an exercise price of $20 would be in-the-money, whereas a call on Ford with an exercise price of $30 would be out-of-the-money.

Option's intrinsic value
The minimum value of the option.

INTRINSIC AND TIME (OR SPECULATIVE) VALUE The term **intrinsic value** refers to the minimum value of the option—that is, the amount by which the stock is in-the-money. Thus, for a call, the intrinsic value is the amount by which the stock price exceeds the exercise price. If the call is out-of-the-money—that is, the exercise price is above the stock price—then its intrinsic value is zero. Intrinsic values can never be negative. For a put, the intrinsic value is again the minimum value the put can sell for, which is the exercise price less the stock price. For example, a Ford April 20 put—that is, a put on Ford stock with an exercise price of $20 that expires in April—when Ford's common stock was selling for $12 per share would have an intrinsic value of $8. If the put was selling for anything less than $8, investors would buy puts and sell the stock until all profits from this strategy were exhausted. Arbitrage, this process of buying and selling like assets for different prices, keeps the price of options at or above their intrinsic value. If an option is selling for its intrinsic value, it is said to be selling at *parity.*

Option's time (or speculative) value
The amount by which the option premium exceeds the intrinsic value of the option.

The **time value**, or **speculative value**, of an option is the amount by which the option premium exceeds the intrinsic value of the option. The time value represents the amount above the intrinsic value of an option that an investor is willing to pay to participate in capital gains from investing in the option. At expiration, the time value of the option falls to zero and the option sells for its intrinsic value, because the chance for future capital gains has been exhausted. These relationships are as follows:

$$\begin{aligned} \text{call intrinsic value} &= \text{stock price} - \text{exercise price} \\ \text{put intrinsic value} &= \text{exercise price} - \text{stock price} \\ \text{call time value} &= \text{call premium} - (\text{stock price} - \text{exercise price}) \\ \text{put time value} &= \text{put premium} - (\text{exercise price} - \text{stock price}) \end{aligned}$$

EXAMPLE: GRAPHING OPTION PRICING RELATIONSHIPS

Perhaps the easiest way to gain an understanding of the pricing of options is to look at them graphically. Figure 21-1 presents a profit and loss graph for the purchase of a call on Ford stock with an exercise price of \$20 that is bought for \$4. This is termed a "Ford 20 call." In Figure 21-1 and all other profit and loss graphs, the vertical axis represents the profits or losses realized on the option's expiration date, and the horizontal axis represents the stock price on the expiration date. Remember that because we are viewing the value of the option at expiration, the option has no time value and therefore it sells for exactly its intrinsic value. To keep things simple, we will also ignore any transaction costs.

For the Ford 20 call shown in Figure 21-1, the call will be worthless at expiration if the value of the stock is less than the exercise or striking price. This is because it would make no sense for an individual to exercise the call option to purchase Ford stock for \$20 per share if he or she could buy the same Ford stock from a broker at a price less than \$20. Although the option will be worthless at expiration, if the stock price is below the exercise price, the most that an investor can lose is the option premium—that is, how much he or she paid for the option, which in this case was \$4. Although this may be the entire investment in the option, it is also generally only a fraction of the stock's price. Once the stock price climbs above the exercise price, the call option takes on a positive value and increases in a linear one-to-one basis as the stock price increases. Moreover, there is no limit on how high the profits can climb. In the case of the Ford 20 call, once the price of Ford stock rises above \$20, the call

FIGURE 21-1 Purchase a Call on Ford Stock with an Exercise Price of \$20 for a Premium of \$4

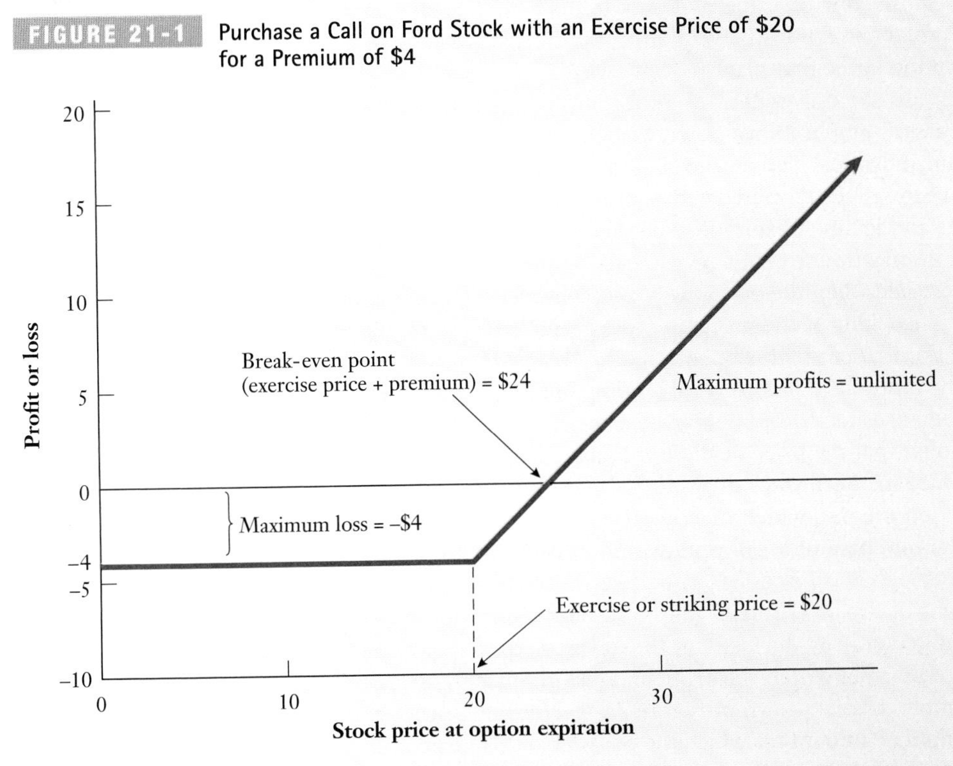

(continued)

FIGURE 21-2 Write a Call on Ford Stock with an Exercise Price of \$20 for a Premium of \$4

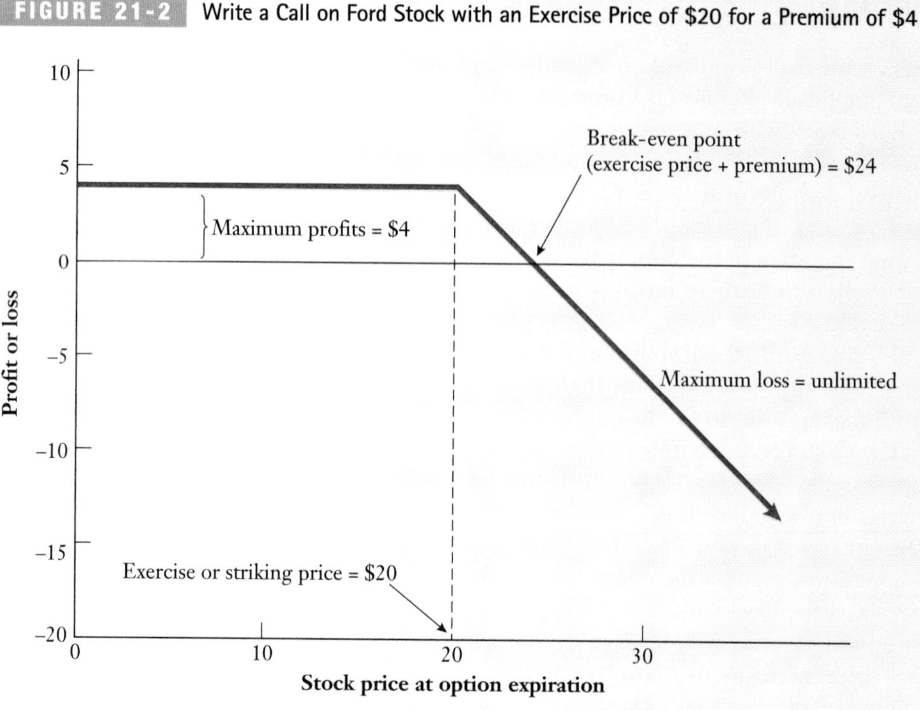

begins taking on value, and once it hits \$24, the investor breaks even. The investor has earned enough in the way of profits to cover the \$4 premium he or she paid for the option in the first place.

To the call writer, the profit and loss graph is the mirror image of the call purchaser's graph. As we noted earlier, the options market is a zero sum game in which one individual gains at the expense of another. Figure 21-2 shows the profits and losses at expiration associated with writing a call option. Once again, we will look at the profits and losses at expiration, because at that point in time options have no time value. The maximum profit to the call writer is the premium, or how much the writer received when the option was sold, whereas the maximum loss is unlimited.

Looking at the profit and loss graph presented in Figure 21-3 for the purchase of a Ford 20 put that is bought for \$3, we see that the lower the price of the Ford stock, the more the put is worth. Here the put only begins to take on value once the price of the Ford stock drops below the exercise price, which in this case is \$20. Then for every dollar that the price of the Ford stock drops, the put increases in value by one dollar. Once the Ford stock drops to \$17 per share, the put purchaser breaks even by making \$3 on the put, which exactly offsets what was initially paid for the put. Here, as with the purchase of a call option, the most an investor can lose is the premium, which although small in dollar value relative to the potential gains, still represents 100 percent of the investment. The maximum gain associated with the purchase of a put is limited only by the fact that the lowest a stock's price can fall to is zero.

To a put writer, the profit and loss graph is the mirror image of the put purchaser's graph. This is shown in Figure 21-4. Here the most a put writer can earn is the premium or amount for which the put was sold. The potential losses for the put writer are limited only by the fact that the stock price cannot fall below zero.

FIGURE 21-3 Purchase a Put on Ford Stock with an Exercise Price of $20 for a Premium of $3

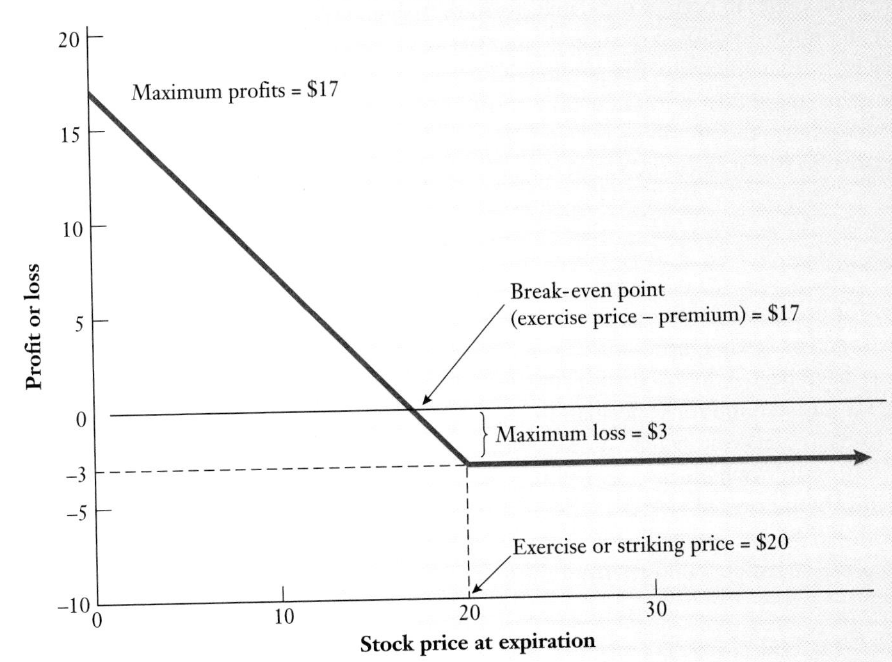

FIGURE 21-4 Write a Put on Ford Stock with an Exercise Price of $20 for a Premium of $3

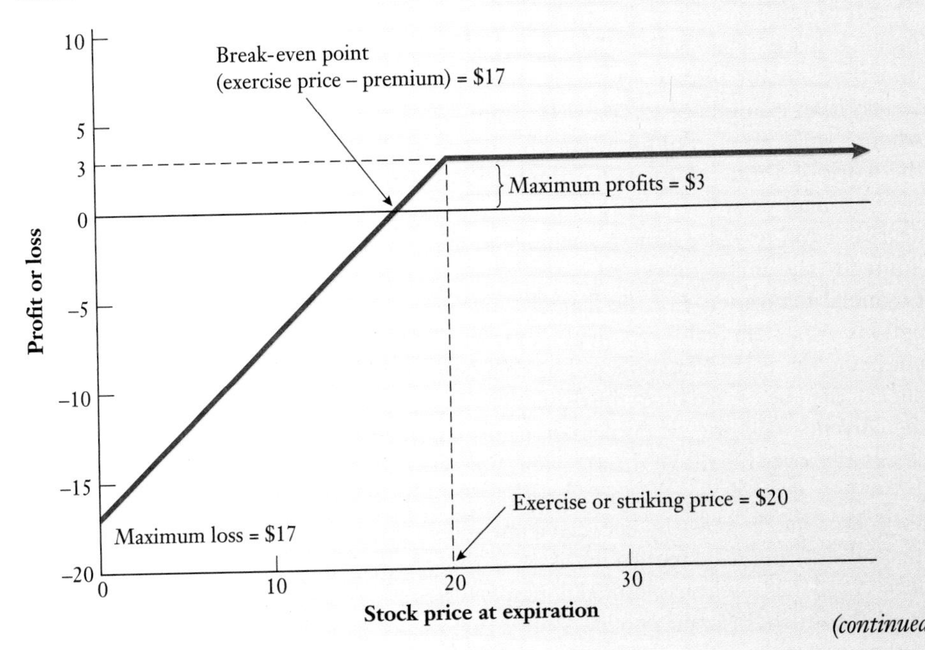

(continued)

All of our graphs have shown the price of the option at expiration. When we reexamine these relationships at a time before expiration, we find that the options now take on some time value. In other words, investors are willing to pay more than the intrinsic value for an option because of the uncertainty of the future stock price. That is, although the stock price may fluctuate, the possible losses on the option are limited, whereas the possible gains are almost unlimited. The most you can ever lose when you purchase a put or call option is the premium, or what you paid for it. Although this may seem rather small relative to the price of the stock, it is still 100 percent of your investment.

This feature in which the potential loss is limited to the amount invested along with unlimited returns is what draws many speculators to options. Although the biggest corporate losses have been associated with futures contracts, in which losses are not limited to the amount invested, options speculation has produced its share of huge losses for corporations. Look at NatWest, which lost £90 million in interest rate options in February 1997, or Dell Computer, which lost $8 million in 1992. No doubt, these companies didn't understand the degree of risk that they had exposed themselves to. Keep in mind that options should be used to reduce risk, but if they aren't fully understood or controlled, they can produce results opposite from those intended.

Characteristics of Options

As we examine options from the viewpoint of the financial manager, we will see that they have some attractive features that help explain their popularity. There are three reasons for the popularity of options:

1. **Leverage.** Calls allow the financial manager the chance for unlimited capital gains with a very small investment. Because a call is only an option to buy, the most a financial manager can lose is what was invested, which is usually a very small percentage of what it would cost to buy the stock itself, whereas the potential for gain is unlimited. As we will see, when a financial manager owns a call, he or she controls or benefits directly from any price increases in the stock. The idea of magnifying the potential return is an example of leverage. It is similar to the concept of leverage in physics, where a small amount of force can lift a heavy load. Here a small investment is doing the work of a much larger investment. Unfortunately, leverage is a double-edged sword: Small price increases can produce a large percentage profit, but small price decreases can produce large percentage losses. With an option, the maximum loss is limited to the amount invested.
2. **Financial insurance.** For the financial manager, this is the most attractive feature of options. A put can be looked on as an insurance policy, with the premium paid for the put being the cost of the policy. The transactions costs associated with exercising the put can then be looked on as the deductible. When a put with an exercise price equal to the current stock price is purchased, it insures the holder against any declines in the stock price over the life of the put. Through the use of a put, a pension fund manager can reduce the risk exposure in a portfolio with little in cost and little change to the portfolio. One dissimilarity between a put and an insurance policy is that with a put an investor does not need to own the asset, in this case the stock, before buying the insurance. A call, because it has limited potential losses associated with it, can also be viewed as an investment insurance policy. With a call, the investor's potential losses are limited to the price of the call, which is quite a bit below the price of the stock itself.

3. **Investment alternative expansion.** From the viewpoint of the investor, the use of puts, calls, and combinations of them can materially increase the set of possible investment alternatives available.

Again, an understanding of the popularity of both puts and calls to the financial manager involves understanding (1) the concept of leverage—in the case of calls unlimited and in the case of puts very large potential gains with limited and relatively small maximum potential losses—and (2) the concept of financial insurance. These two factors combined allow for an expansion of the available investment alternatives. Remember, both puts and calls are merely options to buy or sell the stock at a specified price. The worst that can happen is that the options become worthless and the financial manager loses the investment.

The Chicago Board Options Exchange

Prior to 1973, when the CBOE opened, there was no central marketplace for put and call options. At that time, put and call options transactions took place on the over-the-counter market through what was called the Put and Call Dealers Association, with only about 20 active brokers and dealers in the market. Through a telephone hookup, these dealers acted as middlemen, matching up potential writers and purchasers of options.

Because the specifics of each option were negotiated directly between the writer and the purchaser of the option, very seldom were any two options alike. Generally, every option written had a different expiration date and a different exercise price. As a result, there was little in the way of a secondary market for these individualized options, and the writers and purchasers generally had to hold their position until expiration or until the options were exercised.

With the creation of the CBOE, all this began to change. In 1973, the CBOE began trading listed options on 16 different stocks. Today there are four different exchanges that list and trade options—the CBOE, the AMEX, the Philadelphia, and the Pacific—with over 800 different stocks having listed options. Although the over-the-counter market run by the Put and Call Association is still in operation for stocks that are not listed on the CBOE or any other exchange, it now handles less than 10 percent of all traded options.

This dramatic growth in the trading of options is almost entirely due to the several developments brought on by exchange-listed trading that the CBOE initiated, including the following:

1. **Standardization of the option contracts.** Today, the expiration dates for all options are standardized. As a result, there is only one day per month on which a listed option on any stock can expire. The number of shares that a call allows its owner to purchase, and a put allows its owner to sell, has also been standardized to 100 shares per option contract. In addition, the striking prices have been standardized, generally at five-point intervals, so that there are more identical options. Through this standardization, the number of different option contracts on each stock is severely limited. The result is that more options are identical and the secondary market is made more liquid.
2. **Creation of a regulated central marketplace.** The exchange listing of options provides a central location for continuous trading in options, both newly issued and in the secondary market. The CBOE and the exchanges that followed in listing options also imposed strong surveillance and disclosure requirements.
3. **Creation of the Options Clearinghouse Corporation (OCC).** The OCC bears full responsibility for honoring all options issued on the CBOE. In effect, all options held by individuals have been written by the OCC, and alternatively all options written by individuals are held by the OCC. The purpose of creating a buffer between individual buyers and sellers of options is to provide investors with confidence in the market, in addition to facilitating the clearing and settlement of options. Because of the importance of the OCC, let us look for a moment at its operation.

When an options transaction is agreed upon, the seller writes an option contract to the OCC, which in turn writes an identical option contract to the buyer. If the buyer later wants to exercise the option, he or she gives the OCC the exercise price associated with the option, which in turn provides the buyer with stock. To get the stock to cover the option, the OCC simultaneously exercises a call option it has on this stock. Because of the operation of the OCC and the strong secondary market created by the CBOE, options are not exercised very frequently but are generally sold. Rather than exercise an option, an investor or financial manager usually just sells the option to another investor and realizes the profits in that manner. Writers of options clear their position by buying an option identical to the one they wrote. As a result, the writer has two identical contracts on both sides of the market with the OCC. These positions then cancel each other out.

4. **Trading was made certificateless.** Instead of issuing certificates, the OCC maintains a continuous record of trader's positions. In addition to making the clearing of positions (the canceling out of an option writer's obligation when an identical option is purchased) easier, it has also allowed for an up-to-date record of existing options to be maintained.
5. **Creation of a liquid secondary market with dramatically decreased transactions costs.** There also has been a self-fulfilling generation of volume adding to the liquidity of the secondary market. That is, the innovations created a liquid secondary market for options, and this liquid secondary market attracted more investors into the options market, which in turn created even more liquidity in the secondary market.

Innovations in the Options Market

Recently, five additional variations of the traditional option have appeared: the stock index option, the interest rate option, the foreign currency option, the Treasury bond futures option, and Leaps.

STOCK INDEX OPTIONS The options on stock indexes were first introduced on the CBOE in 1983 and have since proved extremely popular. Although there are a variety of different index options, based on several different broad stock market indexes and also industry indexes such as a computer industry index, it has been the broader stock market indexes that have carried the bulk of the popularity of index options. Although the industry-based index options have received a somewhat mixed reception, stock index options, in particular the S&P 100 Index on the CBOE, have proved to be extremely popular. In fact, more than 80 percent of all stock index options trading involves the S&P 100 Index. Currently it accounts for over half of the volume of all option trading and has made the CBOE the second largest U.S. securities market, with daily trading occasionally reaching nearly 700,000 contracts (remember each contract involves an option on 100 "shares" of the index).

The reason for this popularity is quite simple. These options allow portfolio managers and other investors holding broad portfolios to cheaply and effectively eliminate or adjust the market risk of their portfolios. When we talked about systematic and unsystematic risk, we noted that in a large and well-diversified portfolio, unsystematic risk was effectively diversified away, leaving only systematic risk. Thus, the return on a large and well-diversified portfolio was a result of the portfolio's beta and the movement of the market. As a result, because the movements of the market cannot be controlled, portfolio managers periodically attempt to adjust the beta of the portfolio when they think a change in the market's direction is at hand. Index options allow them to make this change without the massive transaction costs that would otherwise be incurred.

In general, stock index options are used in exactly the same way traditional options are used: for leverage and for investment insurance. However, because of the unusual nature of the "underlying stock," these concepts take on a different meaning. In the case of leverage, the portfolio manager is speculating that the market will head either up or down and is able to cash in on any market volatility with a relatively small investment. In fact, the ability to enjoy the leverage of an option while being concerned with broad market movements has resulted in much of the popularity of stock index options, as small changes in the market can result in very large changes in the price of these options.

In the case of the investment insurance motive for holding index options, the financial manager is really using them to eliminate the effects of a possible downward movement in the market. For example, a portfolio manager who wants to insure the portfolio against a downturn in the market might purchase a put on the S&P 100 or S&P 500 Index. Thus, if the market declines, the put will appreciate in value, offsetting the loss in the investor's portfolio.

In effect, index options can be used in the same way as the more traditional options. The only difference is that here the profits or losses depend on what happens to the value of the index rather than to one stock.

INTEREST RATE OPTIONS Options on 30-year Treasury bonds are also traded on the CBOE. Although the trading appeal of interest rate options is somewhat limited, they do open some very interesting doors to the financial manager. In terms of the insurance and leverage traits, they allow the financial manager to insure against the effects of future changes in interest rates. We know that as interest rates rise, the market value of outstanding bonds falls; thus, through the purchase of an interest rate put, the market value of a portfolio manager's bonds can be protected. Alternatively, a financial manager who is about to raise new capital through a debt offering and who is worried about a possible rise in interest rates before the offering occurs may purchase an interest rate put. This would have the effect of locking in current interest rates at the maximum level that the firm would have to pay.

FOREIGN CURRENCY OPTIONS Foreign currency options are the same as the other options we have examined, except the underlying asset is the Euro, the British pound, the Japanese yen, or some other foreign currency. Although foreign currency options are limited to the Philadelphia Exchange, there is a considerable amount of interest in them largely because of the wide fluctuations foreign currency has had in recent years relative to the dollar. In terms of the insurance and leverage traits, these options allow multinational firms to guard against fluctuations in foreign currencies that might adversely affect their operations. The leverage trait allows investors to speculate in possible future foreign currency fluctuations with a minimum amount of exposure to possible losses.

Let's look at an example of how foreign currency options might be used. As firms trade more and more internationally, the need to protect sales against undesirable currency fluctuations becomes increasingly important. For example, Cessna might use currency options to protect sales on its Citation V aircraft, which are sold in Europe to Swiss customers. Because the Citation V is built in the United States and sold abroad, its costs in labor and materials are based on the dollar. However, as the dollar fluctuates relative to the Swiss franc, so must the sales price in Swiss francs for Cessna to receive the same amount of dollars on each sale in Switzerland.

Problems surface when the value of the Swiss franc falls relative to that of the dollar. For each sale to bring the same amount of dollars back to Cessna, the selling price in Swiss francs would have to be *increased*. Unfortunately, increasing prices may lead to lost sales. To guard against this situation, Cessna may purchase *put options* on the Swiss franc to cover the anticipated Swiss sales. These puts give Cessna the option to sell or convert Swiss francs into dollars at a preset price. If after the put options are purchased, the Swiss franc falls, Cessna could keep its selling prices constant in terms of the Swiss franc and make up for the loss in the currency exchange with the profits on the puts. Conversely, if the value of the Swiss franc rises relative to the value of the dollar, Cessna could lower its Swiss price, sell more aircraft, and still bring home the same dollars per sale—all that would be lost is the price paid for the put options.

OPTIONS ON TREASURY BOND FUTURES Options on Treasury bond futures work the same way as any other option. The only difference between them and other bond options is that they involve the acquisition of a futures position rather than the delivery of actual bonds. To the creative financial manager, they provide a flexible tool to insure against adverse changes in interest rates while retaining the opportunity to benefit from any favorable interest rate movement that might occur. Although a futures contract establishes an obligation for both parties to buy and sell at a specified price, an option only establishes a right. It is therefore exercised only when it is to the option holder's advantage to do so. In effect, a call option on a futures contract does not establish a price obligation, but rather a maximum purchase price. Conversely, a put option on a futures contract is used to establish a minimum selling price. Thus, the buyer of an option on a futures contract can achieve immunization against any unfavorable price movements, whereas the buyer of the futures contract can achieve immunization against any price movements, regardless of whether they are favorable or unfavorable.

In their short history, options on U.S. Treasury bond futures have proved to be extremely popular, with the majority of institutions choosing to trade options on bond futures rather than options on actual bonds. Their extreme popularity can be traced to several important advantages they possess:

1. **Efficient price determination of the underlying instrument.** The U.S. Treasury bond futures contract on the Chicago Board of Trade is the most widely traded futures contract of all. As a result, there is a continuous stream of market-determined price information concerning these contracts. Conversely, price information on most other bonds is generally somewhat sketchy at best, with substantial time between trades and generally a wide gap between existing bid and ask prices.
2. **Unlimited deliverable supply.** Because the Clearinghouse can create as many futures contracts as are needed, the process of exercising an option is made extremely simple. When an option on a futures contract is exercised, the buyer simply assumes a futures position at the exercise price of the option. Because the Clearinghouse can create as many futures contracts as are needed, the market price of these contracts is not affected by the exercise of the options on them. Conversely, if an option holder on an actual bond were to exercise his or her option, he or she would have to take delivery of the underlying bond. Because the supply of any particular bond is limited, a serious price pressure might be placed on that bond, provided the bond does not enjoy sufficient liquidity. Thus, because of the unlimited deliverable supply of futures contracts, the exercise of options on futures does not affect the price of those futures.
3. **Greater flexibility in the event of exercise.** If the option proves to be profitable, the purchaser or writer can settle the transaction in cash by offsetting the futures position acquired by exercise, or do nothing temporarily and assume the futures position and make or take delivery of the actual bonds when the futures contract comes due.
4. **Extremely liquid market.** Because of the other advantages of options on Treasury bond futures, a great number of these options have been created and are traded daily. As a result of the large volume, options on Treasury bond futures have developed a very liquid and active secondary market, which has encouraged other traders to enter this market.

Financial institutions seem to be major participants in the options on the Treasury bond futures market, although there are many potential users of financial futures. They use futures options to alter the risk-return structure of their investment portfolios and actually reduce their exposure to downside risk. A common strategy is to purchase put options and thereby eliminate the possibility of large losses while retaining the possibility of large gains. There is a cost associated with this strategy, because the option premium must be paid regardless of whether or not the option is exercised. An additional return is also generated by those who write call options against a bond portfolio. With this strategy, the premium increases the overall return if bond yields remain stable or rise; however, a maximum return is also established for the portfolio, because it is this tail of the distribution that is sold with the option.

LEAPS—LONG-TERM OPTIONS Long-term Equity Anticipation Securities or "Leaps" are long-term options—both puts and calls—with expiration dates that go out as far as three years in the future. Because they are longer term than traditional options, they can be used to hedge against longer term movements in stocks. Leaps calls allow the investor to benefit from a stock price increase without purchasing the stock, whereas Leaps puts provide a hedge against stock price declines over the long run. As with other options, they expire on the Saturday following the third Friday of the expiration month, with all Leaps expiring in January.

CONCEPT CHECK

1. What is an option? Name and explain two basic types of options.
2. What are three reasons for the popularity of options?
3. What are some recent innovations in the options markets?
4. What is a Leap?

CURRENCY SWAPS

Objective 3

The currency swap is another technique for controlling exchange rate risk. Whereas options and futures contracts generally have a fairly short duration, a currency swap provides the financial manager with the ability to hedge away exchange rate risk over longer periods. It is for that reason that currency swaps have gained in popularity. A **currency swap** is simply an exchange of debt obligations in different currencies. Interest rate swaps are used to provide long-term exchange rate risk hedging. Actually, a currency swap can be quite simple, with two firms agreeing to pay each other's debt obligation.

Currency swap
An exchange of debt obligations in different currencies.

How does this serve to eliminate exchange rate risk? If I am an American firm with much of my income coming from sales in England, I might enter in a currency swap with an English firm. If the value of the British pound depreciates from 1.90 dollars to the pound to 1.70 dollars to the pound, then each dollar of sales in England will bring fewer dollars back to the parent company in the United States. This would be offset by the effects of the currency swap because it costs the U.S. firm fewer dollars to fulfill the English firm's interest obligations. That is, pounds cost less to purchase, and the interest payments owed are in pounds. The nice thing about a currency swap is that it allows the firm to engage in long-term exchange rate risk hedging, because the debt obligation covers a relatively long time period.

Needless to say, there are many variations of the currency swap. One of the more popular is the interest rate currency swap, where the principal is not included in the swap. That is, only interest payment obligations in different currencies are swapped. The key to controlling risk is to get an accurate estimate on the net exposure level to which the firm is subjected. Then the firm must decide whether it feels it is prudent to subject itself to the risk associated with possible exchange rate fluctuations.

These look like great ideas—enter into a contract that reduces risk—but just as with the other derivative securities, they are dangerous if used by those who don't understand

FINANCE MATTERS — ETHICS

THE RISK THAT WON'T GO AWAY

It has been estimated that the derivatives market has been growing at a rate of about 40 percent per year. Examples of losses in this market abound, with Metallgesellschaft (MG), Germany's 14th largest industrial corporation, which we discussed earlier, leading the way with losses. One of MG's subsidiaries, a U.S. marketing organization and part owner of an oil refinery, reported losses approaching $1.3 billion.

To all generally well-informed business people, a few words of semicomfort about financial derivatives: First, if you don't really understand what these are, don't fret. Most of your colleagues, top brass included, are equally baffled. Second, if 10 years from now—despite periodic booster shots from articles like this one—you still can't keep these things in focus, then cheer! That will mean derivatives have not been forcibly brought to your attention by bad, bad news, in which they make headlines as a villain, or even *the* villain, in some financial crisis that sweeps the world.

That possibility must be entertained because derivatives have grown with stunning speed into an enormous, pervasive, and controversial financial force.

Derivatives are contracts whose value is derived—the key word—from the value of some underlying asset, such as currencies, equities, or commodities; from an indicator like interest rates; or from a stock market or other index. The derivative instruments that result—variously called swaps, forwards, futures, puts, calls, swaptions, caps, floors, collars, captions, floortions, spreadtions, lookbacks, and other never-land names—keep bursting into the news as they did recently when the Federal Reserve raised interest rates and share prices sank, costing some traders of derivatives huge amounts that in some cases surely ran into many millions. The "counter-parties" to these contracts customarily use them to hedge some business risk they don't want to bear, such as a jump in interest rates or a fall in the value of a currency.

But transferring such a risk doesn't wipe it away. The risk simply gets passed by the initial contract to a dealer, who in turn may hedge it by a separate contract with still another dealer, who for his part may haul in yet another dealer or maybe a speculator who *wants* the risk. In the words of Roger & Hammerstein's King of Siam: "et cetera, et cetera, et cetera." What results is a tightly wound market of many, many, interconnections—*global* interconnections—that is altogether quite different from anything that has ever existed before.

Most chilling, derivatives hold the possibility of systematic risk—the danger that these contracts might directly or indirectly cause some localized or particularized trouble in the financial markets to spread uncontrollably. An imaginable scenario is some deep crisis at a major dealer that would cause it to default on its contracts and be the instigator of a chain reaction bringing down other institutions and sending paroxysms of fear through a financial market that lives on the expectation of prompt payments. Inevitably, that would put deposit-insurance funds, and the taxpayers behind them, at risk.

Source: Carol J. Loomis, "The Risk That Won't Go Away," *Fortune* (March 7, 1994): 40–57.

their risks. For example, in 1994 Procter & Gamble Corporation lost $157 million on swaps that involved interest rate payments made in German marks and U.S. dollars. How did this happen? Exchange rates and interest rates didn't go the way Procter & Gamble had anticipated and the costs were a lot more than it thought they might ever be. In effect, Procter & Gamble simply got talked into something it didn't understand. The same thing happened to the Australian government in 2002 when they lost over $1 billion in currency swaps. See the Finance Matters box, "The Risk That Won't Go Away."

CONCEPT CHECK

1. What is a currency swap?
2. When might a firm use a currency swap?

THE MULTINATIONAL FIRM AND RISK MANAGEMENT

Over the past 10 years, the use of futures and options by corporations has exploded. The primary way they are used is to hedge away risk in commodity markets, foreign exchange rates, and interest rates. How might you become involved in them? Maybe your first job will be working for McDonald's. To say the least, McDonald's, with operations in 91 countries, gets much of its income from its overseas operations. As a result, currency fluctuations can have a dramatic effect on its profits. With profits from abroad coming in currencies such as the baht (Thailand), the won (Korea), and the ringgit (Malaysia), things got pretty scary in late 1997, when all of these currencies collapsed. How does a company such as McDonald's protect itself and take some of the risk out of its international operations? The answer is, by using futures and options to hedge away the interest rate risk.

Given the risks that globalization brings, futures and options are a great tool to use in reducing those risks. It's important to keep in mind that they can also be used by smaller firms. For example, if you have a small specialty bakery with customers in England, France, and Germany, you could easily eliminate your exchange rate risk with currency options. In addition, you could lock in the future price of your raw materials in the futures markets.

HOW FINANCIAL MANAGERS USE THIS MATERIAL

Most manufacturing firms can use futures to hedge away price fluctuations in their raw materials. For example, Kellogg's may buy futures in rice for Rice Krispies if it feels rice prices are low, and it wants to lock in those prices. USAirways may buy futures on oil to lock in the price of its fuel. In fact, in 2003, when oil prices doubled as war broke out in Iraq, USAirways was able to keep its costs down because it had been an active purchaser of oil futures contracts prior to the jump in oil prices. Your job may be making those purchases, analyzing prices to determine if your company should lock in prices of its raw materials, or it may involve determining how many futures and options you should buy. Unfortunately, some firms use futures and options for speculative purposes rather than to hedge away risk. For example, Sumitomo Bank lost $1.8 billion in June 1996 in copper futures.

SUMMARY

Futures, options, and currency swaps are important for the financial manager due to their ability to reduce risks associated with interest and exchange rate and commodity price fluctuations.

A futures contract is a contract to buy or sell a stated commodity (such as soybeans or corn) or financial claim (such as U.S. Treasury bonds) at a specified price at some future specified time. This contract requires its holder to buy or sell the asset regardless of what happens to its value during the interim. The importance of a futures contract is that it can be used by financial managers to lock in the price of a commodity or an interest rate and thereby eliminate one source of risk. A futures contract is a specialized form of a forward contract distinguished by (1) an organized exchange, (2) a standardized contract with limited price changes and margin requirements, (3) a clearinghouse in each futures market, and (4) daily resettlement of contracts. *Objective 1*

A call option gives its owner the right to purchase a given number of shares of stock at a specified price over a given period. Thus, if the price of the underlying common stock goes up, a call purchaser makes money. A put, conversely, gives its owner the right to sell a given number of shares of common stock at a specified price over a given period. Thus, a put purchaser is betting that the price of the underlying common stock will drop. Because these are just options to buy or sell stock, they do not represent an ownership position in the underlying corporation, as does common stock. *Objective 2*

A currency swap is an exchange of debt obligations in different currencies. Exchange rate variations are offset by the effects of the swap. One major advantage of a currency swap is that it allows for the hedging of exchange rate risk over a long period of time. *Objective 3*

KEY TERMS

Go To: www.prenhall.com/keown for downloads and current events associated with this chapter

call option, 747
currency swap, 757
futures contract, 740
futures margin, 742
option contract, 746
option expiration date, 748
option premium, 748
option striking price, 747
option's intrinsic value, 748
option's time (or speculative) value, 748
put option, 747

STUDY QUESTIONS

21-1. What is the difference between a commodity future and financial future? Give an example of each.

21-2. Describe a situation in which a financial manager might use a commodity future. Assume that during the period following the transaction the price of that commodity went up. Describe what happened. Now assume that the price of that commodity went down. Now what happened?

21-3. Describe a situation in which a financial manager might use an interest rate future. Assume that during the period following the transaction the interest rates went up. Describe what happened. Now assume that interest rates went down following the transaction. Now what happened?

21-4. Define a call option.

21-5. Define a put option.

21-6. What innovative developments were brought on by exchange-listed trading that the CBOE initiated that led to the dramatic growth in the trading of options?

21-7. What is an option on a futures contract? Give an example.

21-8. Compare the two strategies of buying a call and writing a put. What are the differences between the two?

21-9. What is a currency swap and why has it gained so in popularity?

STUDY PROBLEMS (SET A)

21-1A. (*Puts and calls*) Draw a profit or loss graph (similar to Figure 21-1) for the purchase of a call contract with an exercise price of $65 for which a $9 premium is paid. Identify the break-even point, maximum profits, and maximum losses. Now draw the profit or loss graph assuming an exercise price of $70 and a $6 premium.

21-2A. (*Puts and calls*) Repeat problem 21-1A, but this time draw the profit or loss graph (similar to Figure 21-2) for the call writer.

21-3A. (*Puts and calls*) Draw a profit or loss graph (similar to Figure 21-3) for the purchase of a put contract with an exercise price of $45 for which a $5 premium is paid. Identify the break-even point, maximum profits, and maximum losses.

21-4A. (*Puts and calls*) Repeat problem 21-3A, but this time draw the profit or loss graph (similar to Figure 21-4) for the put writer.

WEB WORKS

In his annual letter to his shareholders, Warren Buffett—the Sage of Omaha whose Berkshire Hathaway investment company is a legend among investors—labeled derivatives as "timebombs" and "financial weapons of mass destruction." There's no question there are risks to derivatives; you need only look at the experience of Julian Robertson, whose Tiger Fund lost $2 billion betting against the yen, or former Salomon Brothers vice president John Meriwether who, along with two Nobel laureates and assorted Harvard professors, ran Long-Term Capital Management, which needed a $3.6 billion bailout by the U.S. Federal Reserve to recover from its adventures in derivatives.

Read through Warren Buffett's February 21, 2003, letter to the shareholders of Berkshire Hathaway (**www.berkshirehathaway.com/letters/2002pdf.pdf**) beginning on page 13 and going through page 15. What are his concerns? Why does he think that derivatives are such a danger?

INTEGRATIVE PROBLEM

For your job as the business reporter for a local newspaper, you are given the task of putting together a series of articles on the derivatives markets. Much recent local press coverage has been given to the dangers and the losses that some firms have experienced in those markets. Your editor would like you to address several specific questions in addition to demonstrating the use of futures contracts and options and applying them to several problems.

Please prepare your response to the following memorandum from your editor:

TO: Business Reporter

FROM: Perry White, Editor, Daily Planet

RE: Upcoming Series on the Derivative Securities Market

In your upcoming series on the derivative markets, I would like to make sure you cover several specific points. In addition, before you begin this assignment, I want to make sure we are all reading from the same script, as accuracy has always been the cornerstone of the Daily Planet. As such I'd like a response to the following questions before we proceed:

1. What opportunities do the derivative securities markets (i.e., the futures and options markets) provide to the financial manager?
2. When might a firm become interested in purchasing interest rate futures? Foreign exchange futures? Stock index futures?
3. What can a *firm* do to reduce exchange risk?
4. How would Treasury bond futures and options on Treasury bond futures differ?
5. What is an option on a futures contract? Give an example of one and explain why it exists.
6. Draw a profit or loss graph (similar to Figure 21-1) for the purchase of a call contract with an exercise price of $25 for which a $6 premium is paid. Identify the break-even point, maximum profits, and maximum losses.
7. Repeat question 6, but this time draw the profit or loss graph (similar to Figure 21-2) for the call writer.
8. Draw a profit or loss graph (similar to Figure 21-3) for the purchase of a put contract with an exercise price of $30 for which a $5 premium is paid. Identify the break-even point, maximum profits, and maximum losses.
9. Repeat question 8, but this time draw the profit or loss graph (similar to Figure 21-4) for the put writer.
10. What is a currency swap and who might use one?

STUDY PROBLEMS (SET B)

21-1B. (*Puts and calls*) Draw a profit or loss graph (similar to that in Figure 21-1) for the purchase of a call contract with an exercise price of $50 for which a $5 premium is paid. Identify the break-even point, maximum profits, and maximum losses. Now draw the profit or loss graph assuming an exercise price of $55 and a $6 premium.

21-2B. (*Puts and calls*) Repeat problem 21-1B, but this time draw the profit or loss graph (similar to Figure 21-2) for the call writer.

21-3B. (*Puts and calls*) Draw a profit or loss graph (similar to that in Figure 21-3) for the purchase of a put contract with an exercise price of $60 for which a $4 premium is paid. Identify the break-even point, maximum profits, and maximum losses.

21-4B. (*Puts and calls*) Repeat problem 21-3B, but this time draw the profit or loss graph (similar to that in Figure 21-4) for the put writer.

APPENDIX 21A

Convertible Securities and Warrants

In September of 1997, Costco Companies, Incorporated, issued \$900 million of zero coupon bonds that mature in 2017. What made these bonds interesting is that they were zero coupon convertible bonds; that is, each bond could be traded in for 11.3545 shares of Costco's common stock any time on or prior to maturity. In effect, this financing package put together by Costco looked more like options than normal bonds.

In this appendix, we will examine how convertibles and warrants can be used to raise money. Both of these financing methods contain elements of an option in that they can be exchanged at the owner's discretion for a specified number of shares of common stock. In investigating each financing alternative, we look first at its specific characteristics and purpose; then, we focus on any special considerations that should be examined before the convertible security or the warrant is issued.

CONVERTIBLE SECURITIES

Convertible security
Preferred stock or debentures that can be exchanged for a specified number of shares of common stock at the will of the owner.

A **convertible security** is a preferred stock or a debt issue that can be exchanged for a specified number of shares of common stock at the will of the owner. In effect, it contains elements of an option. It provides the stable income associated with preferred stock and bonds in addition to the possibility of capital gains associated with common stock. This combination of features has led convertibles to be called *hybrid* securities.

When the convertible is initially issued, the firm receives the proceeds from the sale, less flotation costs. This is the only time the firm receives any proceeds from issuing convertibles. The firm then treats this convertible as if it were normal preferred stock or debentures, paying dividends or interest regularly. If the security owner wishes to exercise an option to exchange the convertible for common stock, he or she may do so at any time according to the terms specified at the time of issue. The desire to convert generally follows a rise in the price of the common stock. Once the convertible owner trades the convertibles in for common stock, the owner can never trade the stock back for convertibles. From then on, the owner is treated as any other common stockholder and receives only common stock dividends.

CHARACTERISTICS AND FEATURES OF CONVERTIBLES

Conversion ratio
The number of shares of common stock for which a convertible security can be exchanged.

CONVERSION RATIO The number of shares of common stock for which the convertible security can be exchanged is set out when the convertible is initially issued. On some convertible issues, this **conversion ratio** is stated directly. For example, the convertible may state that it is exchangeable for 15 shares of common stock. Some convertibles give only a **conversion price**, stating, for example, that the security is convertible at \$39 per share. This tells us that for every \$39 of par value of the convertible security, one share of common stock will be received.

$$\text{conversion ratio} = \frac{\text{par value of convertible security}}{\text{conversion price}} \tag{21A-1}$$

For example, Union Carbide has $350 million of convertible debentures outstanding that mature in 2012. These convertibles have a $1,000 par value, a 7-1/2 percent coupon interest rate, and a conversion price of $35.50. Thus, the conversion ratio—the number of shares to be received upon conversion—is $1,000/$35.50 = 28.169 shares. The security owner has the option of holding the 7-1/2 percent convertible debenture or trading it in for 28.169 shares of Union Carbide common stock.

CONVERSION VALUE The **conversion value** of a convertible security is the total market value of the common stock for which it can be exchanged. This can be calculated as follows:

Conversion value
The total market value of the common stock for which it can be exchanged.

$$\text{conversion value} = \begin{pmatrix}\text{conversion}\\ \text{ratio}\end{pmatrix} \times \begin{pmatrix}\text{market value per share}\\ \text{of the common stock}\end{pmatrix} \quad \textbf{(21A-2)}$$

If the Union Carbide common stock were selling for, say, $24 per share, then the conversion value for the Union Carbide convertible would be (28.169)($24.00) = $676.06; that is, the market value of the common stock for which the convertible could be exchanged would be $676.06. Thus, regardless of what this convertible debenture was selling for, it could be converted into $676.06 worth of common stock.

SECURITY VALUE The **security value** (or bond value, as it is sometimes called) of a convertible security is the price the convertible security would sell for in the absence of its conversion feature. This is calculated by determining the required rate of return on a straight (nonconvertible) issue of the same quality and then determining the present value of the interest and principal payments at this rate of return. Thus, regardless of what happens to the value of the firm's common stock, the lowest value to which the convertible can drop should be its value as a straight bond or preferred stock.

Security value
The price the convertible security would sell for in the absence of its conversion feature.

CONVERSION PERIOD On some issues, the time period during which the convertible can be exchanged for common stock is limited. Many times conversion is not allowed until a specified number of years have passed, or it is limited by a terminal conversion date. Still other convertibles may be exchanged at any time during their life. In either case, the **conversion period** is specified when the convertible is originally issued.

Conversion period
The time period during which the convertible can be exchanged for common stock.

CONVERSION PREMIUM The **conversion premium** is the difference between the convertible's market price and the higher of its security value and its conversion value. It can be expressed as an absolute dollar value, in which case it is defined as:

Conversion premium
The difference between the convertible's market price and the higher of its security value and its conversion value.

$$\text{conversion premium} = \begin{pmatrix}\text{market price of}\\ \text{the convertible}\end{pmatrix} - \begin{pmatrix}\text{higher of the security value}\\ \text{and conversion value}\end{pmatrix} \quad \textbf{(21A-3)}$$

In describing convertibles, we have introduced a number of terms. To eliminate confusion, Table 21A-1 summarizes them.

Why Issue Convertibles?

The major reason for choosing to issue convertibles rather than straight debt, preferred stock, or common stock is the fact that interest rates on convertibles are indifferent to the issuing firm's risk level.

While higher risk and uncertainty bring on higher interest costs in straight debt, this is not necessarily the case with convertibles. If we think about a convertible as a package of straight debt and a convertible feature allowing the holder to purchase common stock at a set price, an increase in risk and uncertainty certainly raises the cost of the straight-debt portion of the convertible. However, the convertibility feature benefits from this increase in risk and uncertainty

TABLE 21A-1 Summary of Convertible Terminology

Conversion ratio: The number of shares for which the convertible security can be exchanged.

$$\text{conversion ratio} = \frac{\text{par value of convertible security}}{\text{conversion price}}$$

Conversion value: The total market value of the common stock for which the convertible can be exchanged.

$$\text{conversion value} = \left(\text{conversion ratio}\right) \times \left(\text{market value per share of the common stock}\right)$$

Security value: The price the convertible security would sell for in the absence of its conversion feature.

Conversion period: The time period during which the convertible can be exchanged for common stock.

Conversion premium: The difference between the convertible's market price and the higher of its security value and its conversion value.

$$\text{conversion premium} = \left(\text{market price of the convertible}\right) - \left(\text{higher of the security value and conversion value}\right)$$

and the increase in stock price volatility that follows. In effect, the conversion feature only has value if the stock price rises; otherwise, it has zero value. The more risk and stock price volatility, the greater the likelihood that the conversion feature will be of value at some point before the expiration date. As a result, more risk and uncertainty increase the value of the conversion feature of the convertible. Thus, the negative effect of an increase in risk and uncertainty on the straight-debt portion of a convertible is partially offset by the positive effect on the conversion feature. The result of all this is that the interest rate associated with convertible debt is, to an extent, indifferent to the risk level of the issuing firm. The coupon rates for medium- and high-risk companies issuing convertibles and straight debt might be as follows:

	COMPANY RISK	
	MEDIUM	HIGH
Convertible debt	8%	8.25%
Straight debt	11	13

Thus, convertible debt may allow companies with a high level of risk to raise funds at a relatively favorable rate.

VALUATION OF A CONVERTIBLE

The valuation of a convertible depends primarily upon two factors: the value of the straight debenture or preferred stock and the value of the security if it were converted into common stock. Complicating the valuation is the fact that investors are in general willing to pay a premium for the conversion privilege, which allows them to hedge against the future. If the price of the common stock should rise, the investor would participate in capital gains; if it should decline, the convertible security will fall only to its value as a straight debenture or preferred stock.

In examining the Union Carbide convertible debenture, let us assume that if it were selling as a straight debenture, its price would be $785.46. Thus, regardless of what happens to its common stock, the lowest value the convertible can drop to is $785.46. The conversion value, however, is $676.06, so this convertible is worth more as straight debt than if it were common stock. However, the real question is: Why are investors willing to pay a conversion premium of 16.1 percent over its security or conversion value for this Union Carbide debenture? Quite simply, because investors are willing to pay for the chance for capital gains without the large risk of loss.

Figure 21A-1 graphically depicts the relationship between the value of the convertible and the price of its common stock. The bond value of the convertible serves as a floor for the value of

FIGURE 21A-1 Relationship Between the Market Price of the Common Stock and the Market Price of the Convertible Security

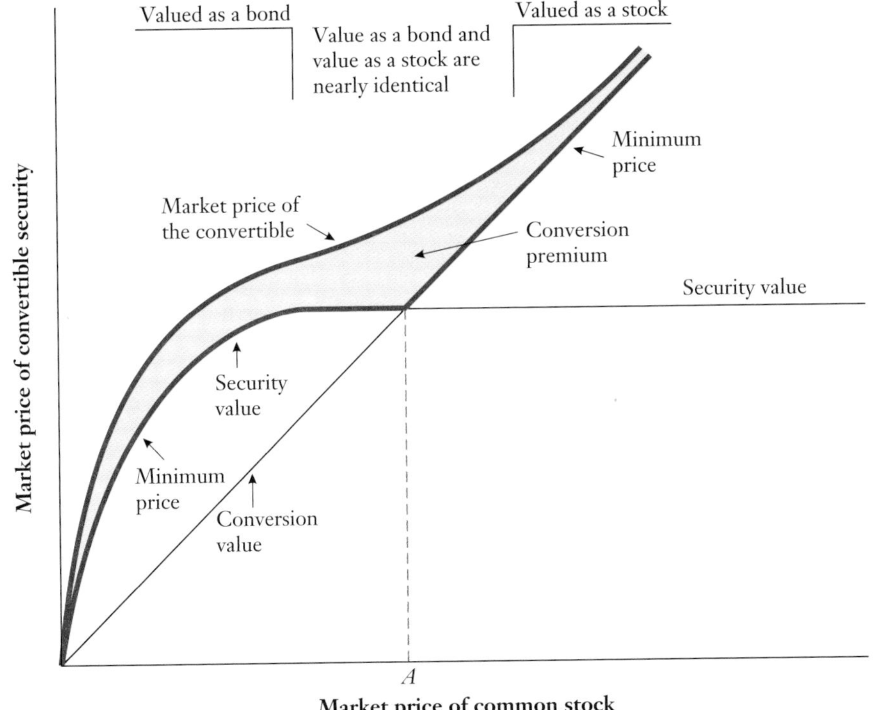

the investment: When the conversion value reaches the convertible's security value (point *A*), the value of the convertible becomes dependent upon its conversion value. In effect, the convertible security is valued as a bond when the price of the common stock is low and as common stock when the price of the common stock rises. Of course, if the firm is doing poorly and in financial distress, both the common stock price and the security value will suffer. In the extreme, when the firm's total value falls to zero both the common stock and any debt that the firm had issued would have no value. Although the minimum price of the convertible is determined by the higher of either the straight bond or preferred stock price or the conversion value, investors also pay a premium for the conversion option. Again, this premium results because convertible securities offer investors stable income from debenture or preferreds—and thus less risk of price decline due to adverse stock conditions—while retaining capital gains prospects from stock price gains. In effect, downside stock price variability is hedged away, whereas upside variability is not.

WARRANTS

Warrant
An option to purchase a fixed number of shares of common stock at a predetermined price during a specified time period.

A **warrant** provides the investor with an option to purchase a fixed number of shares of common stock at a predetermined price during a specified time period. Warrants have been used in the past primarily by weaker firms as sweetener attachments to bonds or preferred stock to improve their marketability. However, in April 1970, when AT&T included them as a part of a major financing package, warrants achieved a new level of respectability.

Only recently have warrants been issued in conjunction with common stock. Their purpose is essentially the same as when they are issued in conjunction with debt or preferred stock—that is, to improve the reception in the market of the new offering or make a tender offer too attractive to turn down.

Although warrants are similar to convertibles in that both provide investors with a chance to participate in capital gains, the mechanics of the two instruments differ greatly. From the standpoint of the issuing firm, there are two major differences. First, when convertibles are exchanged for common stock, debt is eliminated and fixed finance charges are reduced; whereas when warrants are exchanged, fixed charges are not reduced. Second, when convertibles are exchanged, there is no cash inflow into the firm—the exchange is merely one type of security for another. But with warrants, because they are merely an option to buy the stock at a set price, a cash flow accompanies the exchange.

Characteristics and Features of Warrants

Warrant exercise price
The price at which a warrant allows its holder to purchase the firm's common stock.

EXERCISE PRICE The **warrant exercise price** is that price at which the warrant allows its holder to purchase the firm's common stock. The investor trades a warrant plus the exercise price for common stock. Typically, when warrants are issued, the exercise price is set above the current market price of the stock. Thus, if the stock price does not rise above the exercise price, the warrant will never be converted. In addition, there can also be a step-up exercise price, where the warrant's exercise price changes over time.

WARRANT EXPIRATION DATE Although some warrants are issued with no warrant expiration date, most warrants are set to expire after a number of years. In issuing warrants as opposed to convertibles, the firm gives up some control over when the warrants will be exercised. With convertibles, the issuing company can force conversion by calling the issue or using step-up conversion prices, whereas with warrants only the approach of the expiration date or the use of step-up exercise prices can encourage conversion.

DETACHABILITY Most warrants are said to be *detachable* in that they can be sold separately from the security to which they were originally attached. Thus, if an investor purchases a primary issuance of a corporate bond with a warrant attached, he or she has the option of selling the bond alone, selling the warrant alone, or selling the combination intact. *Nondetachable* warrants cannot be sold separately from the security to which they were originally attached. Such a warrant can be separated from the senior security only by being exercised.

Exercise ratio
The number of shares of common stock that can be obtained at the exercise price with one warrant.

EXERCISE RATIO The **exercise ratio** states the number of shares that can be obtained at the exercise price with one warrant. If the exercise ratio on a warrant were 1.5, one warrant would entitle its owner to purchase 1.5 shares of common stock at its exercise price.

Reasons for Issuing Warrants

SWEETENING DEBT Warrants attached to debt offerings provide a feature whereby investors can participate in capital gains while holding debt. The firm can thereby increase the demand for the issue, increase the proceeds, and lower the interest costs. Attaching warrants to long-term debt is a sweetener, performing essentially the same function that the convertibility feature on debt performs—that is, giving investors something they want and thereby increasing the marketability and demand for the bonds.

ADDITIONAL CASH INFLOW If warrants are added to sweeten a debt offering, the firm will receive an eventual cash inflow when and if the warrants are exercised; a convertibility feature would not provide this additional inflow.

VALUATION OF A WARRANT Because the warrant is an option to purchase a specified number of shares of stock at a specified price for a given length of time, the market value of the warrant will be primarily a function of the common stock price. To understand the valuation of warrants, we must define two additional terms, the *minimum price* and the *premium*. Let us look at the Photon Pharmaceutical warrants with an expiration date of December 31, 2004, an exercise ratio of 1.00, and let's assume an exercise price of \$80 through the expiration date. This means that any time until expiration on December 31, 2004, an investor with one warrant can purchase one share of Photon Pharmaceutical stock at \$80 regardless of the market price of that stock. Let's assume these Photon Pharmaceutical warrants were selling at \$5.50, and the Photon Pharmaceutical stock was selling for \$56.75 per share.

MINIMUM PRICE The *minimum price* of a warrant is determined as follows:

$$\text{minimum price} = \left(\begin{matrix}\text{market price of}\\ \text{common stock}\end{matrix}\right) - \left(\begin{matrix}\text{exercise}\\ \text{price}\end{matrix}\right) \times \text{exercise ratio} \tag{21A-4}$$

In the Photon Pharmaceutical example, the exercise price is greater than the price of the common stock (\$80 as opposed to \$56.75). In this case, the minimum price of the warrant is considered to be zero, because things simply do not sell for negative prices [(\$56.75 – \$80) × 1.00 = –\$23.25]. If, for example, the price of the Photon Pharmaceutical common stock rose to \$86 per share, the minimum price on the warrant would become (\$86 – \$80) × 1.00 = \$6. This would tell us that this warrant could not fall below a price of \$6.00, because if it did, investors could realize immediate trading profits by purchasing the warrants and converting them along with the \$80 exercise price into common stock until the price of the warrant was pushed up to the minimum price. This process of simultaneously buying and selling equivalent assets for different prices is called *arbitrage*.

PREMIUM The premium is the amount above the minimum price for which the warrant sells:

$$\text{premium} = \left(\begin{matrix}\text{market price}\\ \text{of warrant}\end{matrix}\right) - \left(\begin{matrix}\text{minimum price}\\ \text{of warrant}\end{matrix}\right)$$

In the case of the Photon Pharmaceutical warrant, the premium is \$5.50 – \$0 = \$5.50. Investors are paying a premium of \$5.50 above the minimum price for the warrant. They are willing to do so because the possible loss is small although the warrant price is only about 9.69 percent of the common stock; in turn, the possible return is large because, if the price of the common stock climbs, the value of the warrant also will climb.

Figure 21A-2 graphs the relationships among the warrant price, the minimum price, and the premium. Point *A* represents the exercise price on the warrant. Once the price of the stock is above the exercise price, the warrant's minimum price takes on positive or nonzero values.

FIGURE 21A-2 Valuation of Warrants

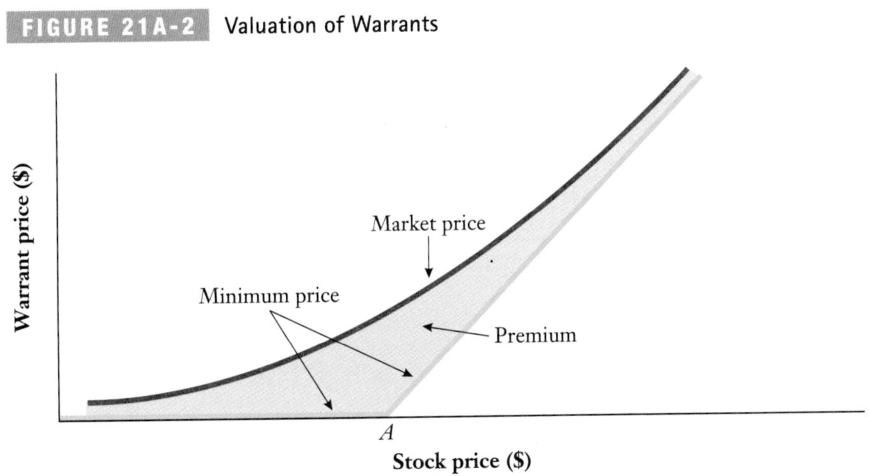

Although the stock price/exercise price ratio is one of the most important factors in determining the size of the premium, several other factors also affect it. One such factor is the time left to the warrant expiration date. As the warrant's expiration date approaches, the size of the premium begins to shrink, approaching zero. A second factor is investors' expectations concerning the capital gains potential of the stock. If they feel favorably about the prospects for price increases in the common stock, a large warrant premium will result, because a stock price increase will affect a warrant price increase. Finally, the degree of price volatility on the underlying common stock affects the size of the warrant premium. The more volatile the common stock price, the higher the warrant premium. As price volatility increases, so does the probability of and potential size of profits.

KEY TERMS

Conversion period, 763
Conversion premium, 763
Conversion ratio, 762
Conversion value, 763
Convertible security, 762
Exercise ratio, 766
Security value, 763
Warrant, 765
Warrant exercise price, 766

STUDY QUESTIONS

21A-1. Define the following terms:

- **a.** Conversion ratio
- **b.** Conversion value
- **c.** Conversion premium

21A-2. What is a reason for issuing convertible securities?

21A-3. Why does a convertible bond sell at a premium above its value as a bond or common stock?

21A-4. Convertible bonds are said to provide the capital gains potential of common stock and the security of bonds. Explain this statement both verbally and graphically. What happens to the graph when interest rates rise? When they fall?

21A-5. Convertible bonds generally carry lower coupon interest rates than do nonconvertible bonds. If this is so, does it mean that the cost of capital on convertible bonds is lower than on nonconvertible? Why or why not?

21A-6. Explain the difference between a convertible security and a warrant.

21A-7. Explain the valuation of warrants both verbally and graphically.

21A-8. What factors affect the size of the warrant premium? How?

SELF-TEST PROBLEMS

ST-1. (*Convertible terminology*) In 2004, Winky's Cow Paste, Inc., issued $10 million of $1,000 par value, 10 percent semiannual convertible debentures that come due in 2024. The conversion price on these convertibles is $16.75 per share. The common stock was selling for $14-3/4 per share on a given date shortly after these convertibles were issued. These convertibles have a B– rating, and straight B– debentures were yielding 14 percent on that date. The market price of the convertible was $970 on that date. Determine the following:

- **a.** Conversion ratio
- **b.** Conversion value
- **c.** Security value
- **d.** Conversion premium

ST-2. (*Warrant terminology*) Petro-Tech, Inc., currently has some warrants outstanding that allow the holder to purchase, with one warrant, one share of common stock at $18.275 per share. If the common stock was selling at $25 per share and the warrants were selling for $9.50, what would be the

a. Minimum price?
b. Warrant premium?

STUDY PROBLEMS (SET A)

21A-1A. (*Convertible terminology*) In 2004, the Andy Fields Corporation of Delaware issued some $1,000 par value, 6 percent convertible debentures that come due in 2024. The conversion price on these convertibles is $40 per share. The price of the common stock is now $27.25 per share. These convertibles have a BBB rating, and straight BBB debentures are now yielding 9 percent. The market price of the convertible is now $840.25. Determine the following (assume bond interest payments are made annually):

a. Conversion ratio
b. Conversion value
c. Security value
d. Conversion premium

21A-2A. (*Convertible terminology*) The L. Padis, Jr., Corporation has an issue of 5 percent convertible preferred stock outstanding. The conversion price on these securities is $27 per share to 9/30/08. The price of the common stock is now $13.25 per share. The preferred stock is selling for $17.75. The par value of the preferred stock is $25 per share. Similar quality preferred stock without the conversion feature is currently yielding 8 percent. Determine the following:

a. Conversion ratio
b. Conversion value
c. Conversion premium

21A-3A. (*Warrant terminology*) The T. Kitchel Corporation has a warrant that allows the purchase of one share of common stock at $30 per share. The warrant is currently selling at $4 and the common stock is priced at $25 per share. Determine the minimum price and the premium of the warrant.

21A-4A. (*Warrant terminology*) Cobra Airlines has some warrants outstanding that allow the purchase of common stock at the rate of one warrant for each share of common stock at $11.71 per share.

a. Given that the warrants were selling for $3 each and the common stock was selling for $10 per share, determine the minimum price and warrant premium as of that date.
b. Given that the warrants were selling for $9.75 each, and the common stock was selling for $16.375 per share, determine the minimum price and warrant premium as of that date.

21A-5A. (*Warrant terminology*) International Corporation has some warrants outstanding that allow the purchase of common stock at the price of $22.94 per share. These warrants are somewhat unusual in that one warrant allows for the purchase of 3.1827 shares of common stock at the exercise price of $22.94 per share. Given that the warrants were selling for $6.25 each, and the common stock was selling for $7.25 per share, determine the minimum price and the warrant premium as of that date.

21A-6A. (*Warrants and their leverage effect*) A month ago, you purchased 100 Bolster Corporation warrants at $3 each. When you made your purchase, the market price of Bolster's common stock was $40 per share. The exercise price on the warrants is $40 per share whereas the exercise ratio is 1.0. Today, the market price of Bolster's common stock has jumped up to $45 per share, whereas the market price of Bolster's warrants has climbed to $7.50 each. Calculate the total dollar gain that you would have received if you had invested the same dollar amount in common stock versus warrants. What is this in terms of return on investment?

STUDY PROBLEMS (SET B)

21A-1B. (*Convertible terminology*) In 2004, the P. Mauney Corporation of Virginia issued some $1,000 par value, 7 percent convertible debentures that come due in 2024. The conversion price on these convertibles is $45 per share. The price of the common stock is now $26 per share. These convertibles have a BBB rating, and straight BBB debentures are now yielding 9 percent. The market price of the convertible is now $840.25. Determine the following (assume bond interest payments are made annually):

- **a.** Conversion ratio
- **b.** Conversion value
- **c.** Security value
- **d.** Conversion premium

21A-2B. (*Convertible terminology*) The Ecotosleptics Corporation has an issue of 6 percent convertible preferred stock outstanding. The conversion price on these securities is $28 per share to 9/30/08. The price of the common stock is now $14 per share. The preferred stock is selling for $20. The par value of the preferred stock is $25 per share. Similar quality preferred stock without the conversion feature is currently yielding 8 percent. Determine the following:

- **a.** Conversion ratio
- **b.** Conversion value
- **c.** Conversion premium

21A-3B. (*Warrant terminology*) The Megacorndoodles Corporation has a warrant that allows the purchase of one share of common stock at $32 per share. The warrant is currently selling at $5 and the common stock is priced at $24 per share. Determine the minimum price and the premium of the warrant.

21A-4B. (*Warrant terminology*) Taco Fever has some warrants outstanding that allow the purchase of common stock at the rate of one warrant for each share of common stock at $11.75 per share.

- **a.** Given that the warrants were selling for $4 each, and the common stock was selling for $9 per share, determine the minimum price and warrant premium as of that date.
- **b.** Given that the warrants were selling for $7 each, and the common stock was selling for $15.375 per share, determine the minimum price and warrant premium as of that date.

21A-5B. (*Warrant terminology*) Fla'vo'phone Corporation has some warrants outstanding that allow the purchase of common stock at the price of $22.94 per share. These warrants are somewhat unusual in that one warrant allows for the purchase of 4.257 shares of common stock at the exercise price of $22.94 per share. Given that the warrants were selling for $6.75 each, and the common stock was selling for $8 per share, determine the minimum price and the warrant premium as of that date.

21A-6B. (*Warrants and their leverage effect*) A month ago, you purchased 100 Annie Kay's Corporation warrants at $2.75 each. When you made your purchase, the market price of Annie Kay's common stock was $35 per share. The exercise price on the warrants is $35 per share whereas the exercise ratio is 1.0. Today, the market price of Annie Kay's common stock has jumped up to $40 per share, whereas the market price of Annie Kay's warrants has climbed to $6.75 each. Calculate the total dollar gain that you would have received if you had invested the same dollar amount in common stock versus warrants. What is this in terms of return on investment?

SELF-TEST SOLUTIONS

ST-1. a.

$$\text{conversion ratio} = \text{par value of convertible security/conversion price}$$
$$= \frac{\$1{,}000}{\$16.75}$$
$$= 59.70 \text{ shares}$$

b.

$$\text{conversion value} = \begin{pmatrix}\text{conversion}\\ \text{ratio}\end{pmatrix} \times \begin{pmatrix}\text{market value per share}\\ \text{of common stock}\end{pmatrix}$$
$$= 59.70 \text{ shares} \times \$14.75/\text{share}$$
$$= \$880.58$$

c.

$$\text{security value} = \sum_{t=1}^{40} \frac{\$50}{(1+.07)^t} + \frac{\$1{,}000}{(1+.07)^{40}}$$
$$= \$50(13.332) + \$1{,}000(.067)$$
$$= \$666.60 + \$67$$
$$= \$733.60$$

(*Note:* Because this debenture pays interest semiannually, $t = 20$ years $\times 2 = 40$ and $i = 14\%/2 = 7\%$ in the calculations.)

d.

$$\text{conversion premium} = \begin{pmatrix}\text{market price of}\\ \text{the convertible}\end{pmatrix} - \begin{pmatrix}\text{higher of the security value}\\ \text{and conversion value}\end{pmatrix}$$
$$= \$970.00 - \$880.58$$
$$= \$89.42$$

ST-2. a.

$$\text{minimum price} = \begin{pmatrix}\text{market price of} & - & \text{exercise}\\ \text{common stock} & & \text{price}\end{pmatrix} \times \begin{pmatrix}\text{exercise}\\ \text{ratio}\end{pmatrix}$$
$$= (\$25.00 - \$18.275) \times (1.0)$$
$$= \$6.725$$

b.

$$\text{warrant premium} = \begin{pmatrix}\text{market price}\\ \text{of warrant}\end{pmatrix} - \begin{pmatrix}\text{minimum price}\\ \text{of warrant}\end{pmatrix}$$
$$= (\$9.50 - \$6.725)$$
$$= \$2.775$$

LEARNING OBJECTIVES

After reading this chapter, you should be able to

1. Discuss the internationalization of business.
2. Explain why foreign exchange rates in two different countries must be in line with each other.
3. Discuss the concept of interest-rate parity.
4. Explain the purchasing-power parity theory and the law of one price.
5. Explain what exchange rate risk is and how it can be controlled.
6. Identify working-capital management techniques that are useful for international businesses to reduce exchange rate risk and potentially increase profits.
7. Explain how the financing sources available to multinational corporations differ from those available to domestic firms.
8. Discuss the risks involved in direct foreign investment.

CHAPTER 22

International Business Finance

Finding new projects doesn't necessarily mean coming up with a new product. It may simply mean taking an existing product and finding a new market. That's what we saw in the introduction to Chapter 9 when we looked at Universal's plans to build a theme park in Shanghai, China. It's also been the direction McDonald's has taken in recent years. Today, McDonald's operates in over 70 countries with more than 20,000 restaurants. One of the biggest is a 700-seat McDonald's in Moscow. Was this an expensive venture? It certainly was. In fact, the food plants that McDonald's built to supply burgers, fries, and everything else sold there cost more than $60 million.

In addition to the costs, McDonald's faces many different and challenging factors as they open outlets outside of the United States. First, in order to keep the quality level identical with what is served at any McDonald's anywhere in the world, they spent six years putting together a supply chain that would provide the necessary raw materials at the quality level McDonald's demands. On top of that, there are risks associated with the Russian economy and its currency that are well beyond the scope of what is experienced in the United States.

These risks all materialized in 1998, when the Russian economy, along with its currency, the ruble, went in the tank. In an attempt to shore up the economy, the Russian government cut the exchange rate from 6,000 rubles for each U.S. dollar to a new rate of 6 rubles per U.S. dollar—in effect, they cut off three zeros. Unfortunately, that wasn't enough to solve the problems the Russian economy faced. In May 1998, the first Russian bank crashed and the value of the ruble started to drop. That summer, the Russian economy lost control, and in August the entire banking system failed.

When it was all over at the end of 1998, the exchange rate had fallen to 23 rubles per dollar, a drop of more than 280 percent. Because McDonald's sells it burgers for rubles, when it came time to trade the rubles for U.S. dollars, the Russian McDonald's sales weren't worth nearly as much as they were the year before. In spite of all this, the Moscow McDonald's has proven to be enormously successful since it opened. In fact, by 2003, McDonald's had 71 stores in 22 Russian cities, representing an investment of more than $215 million. It all goes to show that not all capital budgeting projects have to be new products; they can be existing domestic products that are introduced into international markets.

CHAPTER PREVIEW

This chapter highlights the complications that an international business faces when it deals in multiple currencies. Effective strategies for the reduction of foreign exchange risk are discussed. Working-capital management and capital structure decisions in the international context are also covered. For the international firm, direct foreign investment is a capital-budgeting decision—with some additional complexities.

As you study this chapter on international business finance, you will be reminded of two of the principles that tie this entire text together: **Principle 1: The Risk-Return Trade-Off—We won't take on additional risk unless we expect to be compensated with additional return;** and **Principle 3: Cash—Not Profits—Is King.** Look for them as you work through the several discussions.

Objective 1

THE GLOBALIZATION OF PRODUCT AND FINANCIAL MARKETS

Today, there is no ducking the global markets. In fact, it has been estimated that the United States exports about one-fifth of its industrial production and that about 70 percent of all U.S. goods compete directly with foreign goods.

There has also been a rise in the global level of international portfolio and direct investment. Both direct and portfolio investment in the United States have been increasing faster than U.S. investment overseas. Direct investment occurs when the **multinational corporation (MNC)**, a corporation with holdings and/or operations in more than one country, has control over the investment, such as when it builds an offshore manufacturing facility. Portfolio investment involves financial assets with maturities greater than one year, such as the purchase of foreign stocks and bonds. Total foreign investment in the United States now exceeds such U.S. investment overseas.

Multinational corporation (MNC)
A corporation with holdings and/or operations in one or more countries.

A major reason for long-run overseas investments of U.S. companies is the high rates of return obtainable from these investments. The amount of U.S. *direct foreign investment* (*DFI*) abroad is large and growing. Significant amounts of the total assets, sales, and profits of American MNCs are attributable to foreign investments and foreign operations. Direct foreign investment is not limited to American firms. Many European and Japanese firms have operations abroad, too. During the last decade, these firms have been increasing their sales and setting up production facilities abroad, especially in the United States.

Capital flows between countries for international financial investment purposes have also been increasing. Many firms, investment companies, and individuals invest in the capital markets in foreign countries. The motivation is twofold: to obtain returns higher than those obtainable in the domestic capital markets and to reduce portfolio risk through international diversification. The increase in world trade and investment activity is reflected in the recent globalization of financial markets. The Eurodollar market is larger than any domestic financial market. U.S. companies are increasingly turning to this market for funds. Even companies and public entities that have no overseas presence are beginning to rely on this market for financing.

In addition, most national financial markets are becoming more integrated with global markets because of the rapid increase in the volume of interest rate and currency swaps. Because of the widespread availability of these swaps, the currency denomination and the source country of financing for many globally integrated companies are dictated by accessibility and relative cost considerations regardless of the currency ultimately needed by the firm.

The foreign exchange markets have also grown rapidly, and the weekly trading volume in these globally integrated markets (between $4 and $7 trillion) exceeds the annual trading volume on the world's securities markets. Even a purely domestic firm that buys all its inputs and sells all its output in its home country is not immune to foreign competition, nor can it totally ignore the workings of the international financial markets.

CONCEPT CHECK

1. Why do U.S. companies invest overseas?
2. What kinds of risks are introduced when a firm invests overseas?

Objective 2

EXCHANGE RATES

Recent History of Exchange Rates

Between 1949 and 1970, the exchange rates between the major currencies were fixed. All countries were required to set a specific *parity rate* for their currency vis-à-vis the U.S. dollar. For example, consider the German currency, the deutsche mark (DM). In 1949, the parity rate was set at DM 4.0 per dollar (DM 4.0/$). The actual exchange rate prevailing on any day was allowed to lie within a narrow band around the parity rate. The DM was allowed to fluctuate between DM 4.04 and DM 3.96/$. A country could effect a major adjustment in the exchange rate by changing its parity rate with respect to the dollar. When the currency was made cheaper with respect to the dollar, this adjustment was called a *devaluation*. A *revaluation* resulted when a currency became more expensive with respect to the dollar. In 1969, the DM parity rate was adjusted to DM 3.66/$. This adjustment was a revaluation of the DM parity by 9.3 percent. The new bands around the parity were DM 3.7010 and DM 3.6188/$. The DM strengthened against the dollar because fewer DM were needed to buy a dollar.

Since 1973, a **floating-rate international currency system**, a system in which exchange rates between different national currencies are allowed to fluctuate with supply and demand conditions, has been operating. For most currencies, there are no parity rates and no bands within which the currencies fluctuate.[1] Most major currencies, including the U.S. dollar, fluctuate freely, depending upon their values as perceived by the traders in foreign exchange markets. The country's relative economic strengths, its level of exports and imports, the level of monetary activity, and the deficits or surpluses in its balance of payments (BOP) are all important factors in the determination of exchange rates.[2] Short-term, day-to-day fluctuations in exchange rates are caused by changing supply and demand conditions in the foreign exchange market.

Floating-rate international currency system
An international currency system in which exchange rates between different national currencies are allowed to fluctuate with supply and demand conditions. This contrasts with a fixed rate system in which exchange rates are pegged for extended periods of time and adjusted infrequently.

Introduction of the Euro

In July of 2002 the national currencies of 11 countries of the European Union, often referred to as Euroland, including Germany, France, Italy, Spain, Portugal, Belgium, the Netherlands, Luxembourg, Ireland, Finland, and Austria, were replaced with the Euro. Without question, Germany and France are the big players, accounting for over 50 percent of Euroland's output.

Why did the European Union go to a single currency? For several reasons: First, it made it easier for goods, people, and services to travel across national borders. As a result, the economies of the European Union flourished. A common currency eliminated the exchange costs that occur when trading German marks for French francs. It also eliminated the uncertainty associated with exchange rate fluctuations. It, for example, also helped to eliminate cost differences for goods in different countries. For example, just before the Euro was introduced, "The Classics" Swatch watch was selling for 39.2 Euros ($45.97) in Belgium and only 25.7 Euros ($30.14) in Italy. The introduction of the Euro made it easier to compare prices and eliminate the discrepancies.

What did all this mean for the United States? It meant several things: First, it meant the competition from abroad was stronger. It also made the exchange rate between the Euro and the U.S. dollar a very important exchange rate. If the Euro is strong, it helps

[1] The system of floating rates is referred to as the "floating-rate regime."

[2] The balance of payments for the United States reflects the difference between the import and export of goods (the trade balance) and services. Capital inflows and outflows are tabulated in the capital account.

AN ENTREPRENEUR'S PERSPECTIVE

"SHIP THOSE BOXES, CHECK THE EURO!"—HOW A TINY FIRM RIDES FOREIGN-EXCHANGE WAVES

Plymouth Meeting, Pa.—THE FIRST THING Kim Reynolds, president of Markel Corp., does each morning is meet with his top factory-floor managers to see if all is well on the production line. The second thing he does is scan the latest intelligence from global currency markets to see if all's well on his bottom line.

Markel, whose Teflon-like tubing and insulated lead wire is used in the automotive, appliance, and water-purification industries, expects 40 percent of its $26 million in sales this year will be overseas, mostly in Europe. "We use a fixed [currency-price] conversion when we quote prices, and we assume the currency loss or gain," says Cheryl Jolly, Markel's export manager, as she supervises the weighing of boxes bound for Germany.

To protect himself and his company Mr. Reynolds has forged a business strategy that allows it to survive, and perhaps even prosper, when a key element of his profitability is far beyond his control. Markel's is a four-part approach: charge customers relatively stable prices in their own currencies to build overseas market share; tap "forward" currency markets to provide revenue stability over the next few months; improve efficiency to make it through the times when currency trading turns ugly; and roll the dice and hope things get better.

Markel signs contracts that lead to the delivery of wads of Euros months or even years down the road, when the value of those Euros in dollars may be much less than it was at signing. To minimize the uncertainty over the span of a few months, Markel's Chief Financial Officer, James A. Hoban, buys forward contracts through PNC Financial Services Group in Pittsburgh. Markel promises the bank, say, 50,000 Euros in four months, and the bank guarantees a certain number of dollars no matter what happens to the exchange rate.

When he thinks the dollar is on its way up, Mr. Hoban might hedge his entire expected Euro revenue stream with a forward contract. When he thinks the dollar is heading down, he will hedge perhaps 50 percent and take a chance that he will make more dollars by remaining exposed to currency swings.

He doesn't always guess right. Sometime this month, for instance, Markel will have to provide PNC with 50,000 Euros from a contract the company bought in early January. The bank will pay $1.05 per Euro, or $52,500. Had Mr. Hoban waited, Markel could have sold at the going rate, $1.08, and made an additional $1,500. To make matters worse, Markel cut the supply deal with Germany's Kuster in 1998 and set the sales price assuming the Euro would be at $1.18 by now, just a tad stronger than it traded at when introduced officially at the beginning of 1999. "Dumb us," Mr. Reynolds says. "At the time it was introduced, nobody thought it would immediately plunge."

In fact, the Euro sank like a rock, bottoming out near 82 cents on Oct. 26, 2000, and that meant each Euro Markel received for its products was worth far less in dollars than the company had expected. In 2001 and 2002 combined, Markel identified more than $625,000 in currency losses, and the company posted overall losses in both years.

Most of Markel's current deals were written assuming that the Euro would be valued between 90 cents and 95 cents. But at the current $1.08, helped by worries about the U.S. trade deficit, jittery U.S. financial markets, and a possible war in Iraq, it has been a currency windfall for Markel. Company executives figure that if the Euro remains between $1.05 and $1.07, and the British pound remains at about $1.60, Markel will post $400,000 to $500,000 in currency gains this year.

Source: Michael M. Phillips, "'Ship Those Boxes, Check the Euro!'—How a Tiny Firm Rides Foreign-Exchange Waves," *The Wall Street Journal*, excerpt, February 7, 2003, page C1.

U.S. exports by making them cheaper. However, if the Euro is weak, U.S. exports may suffer. Fortunately, many U.S. multinational firms appear to be in good shape to cash in on any economic surge that may hit Euroland. For example, look at Wal-Mart, which has 21 stores in Germany. In Germany, Wal-Mart is doing just what it does here in the United States: It is wiping out the competition. For the Germans, this is their first sight of wide aisles—bigger than some of the local streets—and discount shopping. The Euro will allow Wal-Mart to offer even more bargains from all over Euroland, and it will allow Wal-Mart to provide a much more diverse selection of goods. That's because in Europe, because of all the exchange rate uncertainties, most goods are regional in nature. That's the bottom line—the Euro should introduce greater choice and greater competition—both good for the consumer. See the An Entrepreneur's Perspective box, " 'Ship Those Boxes, Check the Euro!'—How a Tiny Firm Rides Foreign-Exchange Waves."

THE FOREIGN EXCHANGE MARKET

The foreign exchange market provides a mechanism for the transfer of purchasing power from one currency to another. This market is not a physical entity such as the New York Stock Exchange; it is a network of telephone and computer connections among banks, foreign exchange dealers, and brokers. The market operates simultaneously at three levels. At the first level, customers buy and sell foreign exchange (that is, foreign currency) through their banks. At the second level, banks buy and sell foreign exchange from other banks in the same commercial center. At the last level, banks buy and sell foreign exchange from banks in commercial centers in other countries. Some important commercial centers for foreign exchange trading are New York, London, Zurich, Frankfurt, Hong Kong, Singapore, and Tokyo.

An example will illustrate this multilevel trading. A trader in Texas may buy foreign exchange (pounds) from a bank in Houston for payment to a British supplier against some purchase made. The Houston bank, in turn, may purchase the foreign currency (pounds) from a New York bank. The New York bank may buy the pounds from another bank in New York or from a bank in London.

Because this market provides transactions in a continuous manner for a very large volume of sales and purchases, the currency markets are efficient: In other words, it is difficult to make a profit by shopping around from one bank to another. Minute differences in the quotes from different banks are quickly eliminated. Because of the arbitrage mechanism, simultaneous quotes to different buyers in London and New York are likely to be the same.

Two major types of transactions are carried out in the foreign exchange markets: spot and forward transactions.

SPOT EXCHANGE RATES

A typical spot transaction involves an American firm buying foreign currency from its bank and paying for it in dollars. The price of foreign currency in terms of the domestic currency is the **exchange rate**. Another type of spot transaction occurs when an American firm receives foreign currency from abroad. The firm typically would sell the foreign currency to its bank for dollars. These are both **spot transactions** because one currency is traded for another currency today. The actual exchange rate quotes are expressed in several different ways, as discussed later. To allow time for the transfer of funds, the *value date* when the currencies are actually exchanged is two days after the spot transaction occurs. Four banks could easily be involved in the transactions: the local banks of the buyer and seller of the foreign exchange, and the money-center banks that handle the purchase and sale in the interbank market. Perhaps the buyer or seller will have to move the funds from one of its local banks to another, bringing even more banks into the transaction. A forward transaction entails an agreement today to deliver a specified number of units of a currency on a future date in return for a specified number of units of another currency.

Exchange rate
The price of foreign currency stated in terms of the domestic or home currency.

Spot transaction
A transaction made immediately in the marketplace at the market price.

On the spot exchange market, contrasted with the over-the-counter market, the quoted exchange rate is typically called a direct quote. A **direct quote** indicates the number of units of the home currency required to buy one unit of the foreign currency. That is, in New York the typical exchange-rate quote indicates the number of dollars needed to buy one unit of a foreign currency: dollars per pound, dollars per mark, and so on. The spot rates in Table 22-1 are the direct exchange quotes taken from *The Wall Street Journal*. Thus, according to Table 22-1, to buy 1 British pound (£1), $1.6229 was needed. To buy Japanese Yen and Euros, $0.008623, and $1.1574 were needed, respectively.

An **indirect quote** indicates the number of units of foreign currency that can be bought for one unit of the home currency. This reads as Euros per dollar, pecos per dollar, and so forth. An indirect quote is the general method used in the over-the-counter

Direct quote
The exchange rate that indicates the number of units of the home currency required to buy one unit of foreign currency.

Indirect quote
The exchange rate that expresses the required number of units of foreign currency to buy one unit of home currency.

TABLE 22-1 Foreign Exchange Rates Reported on May 16, 2003

KEY CURRENCY CROSS RATES — LATE NEW YORK TRADING, FRIDAY, MAY 16, 2003

	DOLLAR	EURO	POUND	SFRANC	PESO	YEN	CDNDIR
Canada	1.3648	1.5796	2.2150	1.0441	.13239	.01177	–
Japan	115.97	134.22	188.21	88.716	11.249	–	84.970
Mexico	10.3093	11.9320	16.731	7.8866	–	0.8890	7.5536
Switzerland	1.3072	1.5129	2.1214	–	.12680	.01127	.9578
U.K.	.61620	.7132	–	.4714	.05977	.00531	.45148
Euro	.86400	–	1.4022	.66096	.08381	.00745	.63306
U.S.	–	1.1574	1.6229	.76500	.09700	.00862	.73270

Source: Reuters.

EXCHANGE RATES

The foreign exchange mid-range rates below apply to trading among banks in amounts of $1 million and more, as quoted at 4 p.m. Eastern time by Reuters and other sources. Retail transactions provide fewer units of foreign currency per dollar.

COUNTRY	U.S. $ EQUIVALENT	CURRENCY PER U.S. $
Argentina (Peso)-y	.3407	2.9351
Australia (Dollar)	.6527	1.5321
Brazil (Real)	.3398	2.9429
Canada (Dollar)	.7327	1.3648
1-month forward	.7315	1.3671
3-months foward	.7288	1.3721
6-months forward	.7245	1.3803
China (Renminbi)	.1208	8.2781
Czech. Rep. (Koruna)		
Commerical rate	.03700	27.027
Denmark (Krone)	.1558	6.4185
Hong Kong (Dollar)	.1282	7.8003
Hungary (Forint)	.004719	211.91
India (Rupee)	.02124	47.081
Indonesia (Rupiah)	.0001182	8460
Israel (Shekel)	.2230	4.4843
Japan (Yen)	.008623	115.97
1-month forward	.008633	115.83
3-months forward	.008651	115.59
6-months forward	.008675	115.27
Kuwait (Dinar)	3.3526	.2983
Malaysia (Ringgit)-b	.2632	3.7994
Mexico (Peso)		
Floating rate	.0970	10.3093
New Zealand (Dollar)	.5810	1.7212
Russia (Ruble)-a	.03238	30.883
Saudi Arabia (Riyal)	.2667	3.7495
South Africa (Rand)	.1297	7.7101
South Korea (Won)	.0008334	1199.90
Sweden (Krona)	.1253	7.9177
Switzerland (Franc)	.7650	1.3072
1-month forward	.7654	1.3065
3-months forward	.7665	1.3046
6-months forward	.7680	1.3021
Taiwan (Dollar)	.02890	34.602
Thailand (Baht)	.02374	42.123
Turkey (Lira)	.00000067	1492537
U.K. (Pound)	1.6229	.6162
1-month forward	1.6197	.6174
3-months forward	1.6134	.6198
6-months forward	1.6040	.6234
Venezuela (Bolivar)	.000626	1597.44
SDR	1.4066	.7109
Euro	1.1574	.8640

Special Drawings Rights (SDR) are based on exchange rates for the U.S., British, and Japanese currencies. Source: International Monetary Fund.

a-Russian Central Bank rate. b-Government rate. y-Floating rate.

Source: *The Wall Street Journal*, May 19, 2003, page C11.

market. Exceptions to this rule include British pounds, Irish punts, Australian dollars, and New Zealand dollars, which are quoted via direct quote for historical reasons. Indirect quotes are given in the last column of Table 22-1.

In summary, a direct quote is the dollar/foreign currency rate ($/FC), and an indirect quote is the foreign currency/dollar (FC/$). Therefore, an indirect quote is the reciprocal of a direct quote and vice versa. The following example illustrates the computation of an indirect quote from a given direct quote.

EXAMPLE: INDIRECT QUOTE

Suppose you want to compute the indirect quote from the direct quote of spot rates for pounds given in column 1 of Table 22-1. The direct quote for the pound is $1.6229. The related indirect quotes are calculated as the *reciprocal* of the direct quote as follows:

$$\text{indirect quote} = \frac{1}{\text{direct quote}}$$

Thus,

$$\text{pounds} \frac{1}{\$1.6229/\pounds} = \pounds.6162$$

Notice that this quote and indirect quote are identical to those shown in the second column of Table 22-1.

Direct and indirect quotes are useful in conducting international transactions, as the following examples show.

EXAMPLE: CONVERTING EUROS TO DOLLARS

An American business must pay 1,000 Euros to a German firm on May 16, 2003. How many dollars will be required for this transaction?

$$\$1.1574/€ \times €1,000 = \$1,157.42$$

EXAMPLE: CONVERTING DOLLARS TO POUNDS

An American business must pay $2,000 to a British resident on May 16, 2003. How many pounds will the British resident receive?

$$\pounds.6162/\$ \times \$2,000 = \pounds1,232.40$$

EXCHANGE RATES AND ARBITRAGE

The foreign exchange quotes in two different countries must be in line with each other. The direct quote for U.S. dollars in London is given in pounds per dollar. Because the foreign exchange markets are efficient, the direct quotes for the per U.S. dollar rate in London on May 16, 2003, must be very close to the indirect rate prevailing in New York on that date.

If the exchange-rate quotations between the London and New York spot exchange markets were out of line, then an enterprising trader could make a profit by buying in the market where the currency was cheaper and selling it in the other. Such a buy-and-sell strategy would involve a zero net investment of funds and no risk bearing yet would provide a sure profit. Such a person is called an **arbitrageur**, and the process of buying and selling in more than one market to make a riskless profit is called *arbitrage*. Spot exchange markets are efficient in the sense that arbitrage opportunities do not persist for any length of time. That is, the exchange rates between two different markets are quickly brought in line, aided by the arbitrage process. **Simple arbitrage** eliminates exchange rate differentials across the markets for a single currency, as in the preceding example for the New York and London quotes. **Triangular arbitrage** does the same across the markets for all currencies. **Covered-interest arbitrage** eliminates differentials across currency and interest rate markets.

Arbitrageur
A person involved in the process of buying and selling in more than one market to make riskless profits.

Simple arbitrage
Trading to eliminate exchange rate differentials across the markets for a single currency, for example, for the New York and London markets.

Triangular arbitrage
Arbitrage across the markets for all currencies.

Covered-interest arbitrage
Arbitrage designed to eliminate differentials across currency and interest rate markets.

Suppose that London quotes £.6300/$ instead of £.6162/$. If you simultaneously bought a pound in New York for £.6162/$ and sold a pound in London for £.6300/$, you would have (1) taken a zero net investment position since you bought £1 and sold £1, (2) locked in a sure profit of £.0138/$ no matter which way the pound subsequently moves, and (3) set in motion the forces that will eliminate the different quotes in New York and London. As others in the marketplace learn of your transaction, they will attempt to make the same transaction. The increased demand to buy pounds in New York will lead to a higher quote there and the increased supply of pounds will lead to a lower quote in London. The workings of the market will produce a new spot rate that lies between £.6162/$ and £.6300/$ and is the same in New York and in London.

Asked and Bid Rates

Two types of rates are quoted in the spot exchange market: the asked and the bid rates. The **asked rate** is the rate the bank or the foreign exchange trader "asks" the customer to pay in home currency for foreign currency when the bank is selling and the customer is buying. The asked rate is also known as the **selling rate** or the *offer rate*. The **bid rate** is the rate at which the bank buys the foreign currency from the customer by paying in home currency. The bid rate is also known as the **buying rate**. Note that Table 22-1 contains only the selling, offer, or asked rates, and not the buying rate.

Asked rate
The rate a bank or foreign exchange trader "asks" the customer to pay in home currency for foreign currency when the bank is selling and the customer is buying.

Selling rate
Same as the asked rate.

Bid rate
The rate at which the bank buys the foreign currency from the customer by paying in home currency.

Buying rate
The bid rate in a currency transaction.

Bid-asked spread
The difference between the asked quote and the bid quote.

The bank sells a unit of foreign currency for more than it pays for it. Therefore, the direct asked quote ($/FC) is greater than the direct bid quote. The difference between the asked quote and the bid quote is known as the **bid-asked spread**. When there is a large volume of transactions and the trading is continuous, the spread is small and can be less than –1 percent (.01) for the major currencies. The spread is much higher for infrequently traded currencies. The spread exists to compensate the banks for holding the risky foreign currency and for providing the service of converting currencies.

Cross Rates

A **cross rate** is the computation of an exchange rate for a currency from the exchange rates of two other currencies. These are given at the top of Table 22-1. The following example illustrates how this works.

Cross rate
The computation of an exchange rate for a currency from the exchange rates of two other currencies.

Example: Cross Rates

Taking the dollar/pound and the Euro/dollar rates from columns 1 and 2 of Table 22-1, determine the Euro/pound and pound/Euro exchange rates. We see that

$$(\$/£) \times (€/\$) = (€/£)$$

or

$$1.6229 \times .8640 = €1.4022/£$$

Thus, the pound/Euro exchange rate is

$$1/1.4022 = £.7132/€$$

Cross-rate computations make it possible to use quotations in New York to compute the exchange rate between pounds, dollars, and Euros. Arbitrage conditions hold in cross rates, too. For example, the pound exchange rate in London (the direct quote Euros/pound) must be 1.4022 as shown in the example. The Euro exchange rate in London must be .7132 Euros/mark. If the rates prevailing in Frankfurt and London were different from the computed cross rates, using quotes from New York, a trader could use three different currencies to lock in arbitrage profits through a process called *triangular arbitrage*.

FORWARD EXCHANGE RATES

A **forward exchange contract** requires delivery, at a specified future date, of one currency for a specified amount of another currency. The exchange rate for the forward transaction is agreed on today; the actual payment of one currency and the receipt of another currency take place at the future date. For example, a 30-day contract on March 1 is for delivery on March 31. Note that the forward rate is not the same as the spot rate that will prevail in the future. The actual spot rate that will prevail is not known today; only the forward rate is known. The actual spot rate will depend on the market conditions at that time; it may be more or less than today's forward rate. **Exchange rate risk** is the risk that tomorrow's exchange rate will differ from today's rate.

Forward exchange contract
A contract that requires delivery on a specified future date of one currency in return for a specified amount of another currency.

Exchange rate risk
The risk that tomorrow's exchange rate will differ from today's.

As indicated earlier, it is extremely unlikely that the future spot rate will be exactly the same as the forward rate quoted today. Assume that you are going to receive a payment denominated in pounds from a British customer in 30 days. If you wait for 30 days and exchange the pounds at the spot rate, you will receive a dollar amount reflecting the exchange rate 30 days hence (that is, the future spot rate). As of today, you have no way of knowing the exact dollar value of your future pound receipts. Consequently, you cannot make precise plans about the use of these dollars. If, conversely, you buy a future contract, then you know the exact dollar value of your future receipts, and you can make precise plans concerning their use. The forward contract, therefore, can reduce your uncertainty about the future, and the major advantage of the forward market is that of risk reduction.

Forward contracts are usually quoted for periods of 30, 90, and 180 days. A contract for any intermediate date can be obtained, usually with the payment of a small premium. Forward contracts for periods longer than 180 days can be obtained by special negotiations with banks. Contracts for periods greater than one year can be costly.

Forward rates, like spot rates, are quoted in both direct and indirect form. The direct quotes for the 30-day and 90-day forward contracts on pounds, francs, and marks are given in column 1 of Table 22-1. The indirect quotes for forward contracts, like spot rates, are reciprocals of the direct quotes. The indirect quotes are indicated in column 2 of Table 22-1. The direct quotes are the dollar/foreign currency rate, and the indirect quotes are the foreign currency/dollar rate similar to the spot exchange quotes.

In Table 22-1, the 30-day forward quote for pounds is \$1.6197 per pound. This means that the bank is contractually bound to deliver £1 at this price, and the buyer of the contract is legally obligated to buy it at this price. Therefore, this is the price the customer must pay regardless of the actual spot rate prevailing in 30 days. If the spot price of the pound is less than $1.6197, then the customer pays *more* than the spot price. If the spot price is greater than $1.6197 then the customer pays *less* than the spot price.

The forward rate is often quoted at a premium to or discount from the existing spot rate. For example, the 30-day forward rate for the pound may be quoted as .0032 discount (1.6197 forward rate – 1.6229 spot rate). If the British pound is more expensive in the future than it is today, it is said to be selling at a premium relative to the dollar, and the dollar is said to be selling at a discount to the British pound. Notice in Table 22-1 that while the British pound and Canadian dollar are selling at a discount relative to the dollar, both the Swiss franc and Japanese yen are selling at a premium to the dollar. This premium or discount is also called the **forward-spot differential**.

Forward-spot differential
The premium or discount between forward and spot currency exchange rates.

Notationally, the relationship may be written:

$$F - S = \text{premium } (F > S) \text{ or discount } (S > F) \tag{22-1}$$

where F = the forward rate, direct quote
S = the spot rate, direct quote

The premium or discount can also be expressed as an annual percentage rate, computed as follows:

$$\frac{F - S}{S} \times \frac{12}{n} \times 100 = \text{annualized percentage premium } (F > S) \text{ or discount } (S > F) \tag{22-2}$$

where n = the number of months of the forward contract

Example: Computing the Percent-per-annum Premium

Compute the percent-per-annum premium on the 30-day pound.

Step 1. Identify F, S, and n.

$F = 1.6197$, $S = 1.6229$, $n = 1$ month

Step 2. Because S is greater than F, we compute the annualized percentage discount:

$$D = \frac{1.6197 - 1.6229}{1.6229} \times \frac{12 \text{ months}}{1 \text{ month}} \times 100$$
$$= -2.37\%$$

The percent-per-annum discount on the 30-day pound is –2.37 percent. The percent-per-annum discount on the 30-day and 90-day Canadian dollar, Swiss franc, and Japanese yen contracts are computed similarly with the exception that a 90-day contract is annualized by dividing 12 months by 3 months rather than 1 month. The results for pounds and Swiss francs are:

	30-Day	90-Day
British pound	–2.37%	–2.34%
Swiss francs	+0.627%	+0.784%

Examples of Exchange Rate Risk

The concept of exchange rate risk applies to all types of international businesses. The measurement of these risks, and the type of risk, may differ among businesses. Let us see how exchange risk affects international trade contracts, international portfolio investments, and direct foreign investments.

EXCHANGE RATE RISK IN INTERNATIONAL TRADE CONTRACTS The idea of exchange rate risk in trade contracts is illustrated in the following situations.

Case I. An American automobile distributor agrees to buy a car from the manufacturer in Detroit. The distributor agrees to pay \$15,000 on delivery of the car, which is expected to be 30 days from today. The car is delivered on the thirtieth day and the distributor pays \$15,000. Notice that from the day this contract was written until the day the car was delivered, the buyer knew the exact dollar amount of the liability. There was, in other words, no uncertainty about the value of the contract.

Case II. An American automobile distributor enters into a contract with a British supplier to buy a car from Great Britain for £8,800. The amount is payable on the delivery of the car, 30 days from today. From Figure 22-1, we see the range of spot rates that we believe can occur on the date the contract is consummated. On the thirtieth day, the American importer will pay some amount in the range of \$13,699.84 (8,800 × 1.5568) to \$15,087.60 (8,800 × 1.7145) for the car. Today, the American firm is not certain what its future dollar outflow will be 30 days hence. That is, the dollar value of the contract is uncertain.

These two examples help illustrate the idea of foreign exchange risk in international trade contracts. In the domestic trade contract (Case I), the exact dollar amount of the future dollar payment is known today with certainty. In the case of the international trade contract (Case II), where the contract is written in the foreign currency, the exact dollar amount of the contract is not known. The variability of the exchange rate induces variability in the future cash flow.

FIGURE 22-1 A Subjective Probability Distribution of the Pound Exchange Rate, 30 Days in the Future

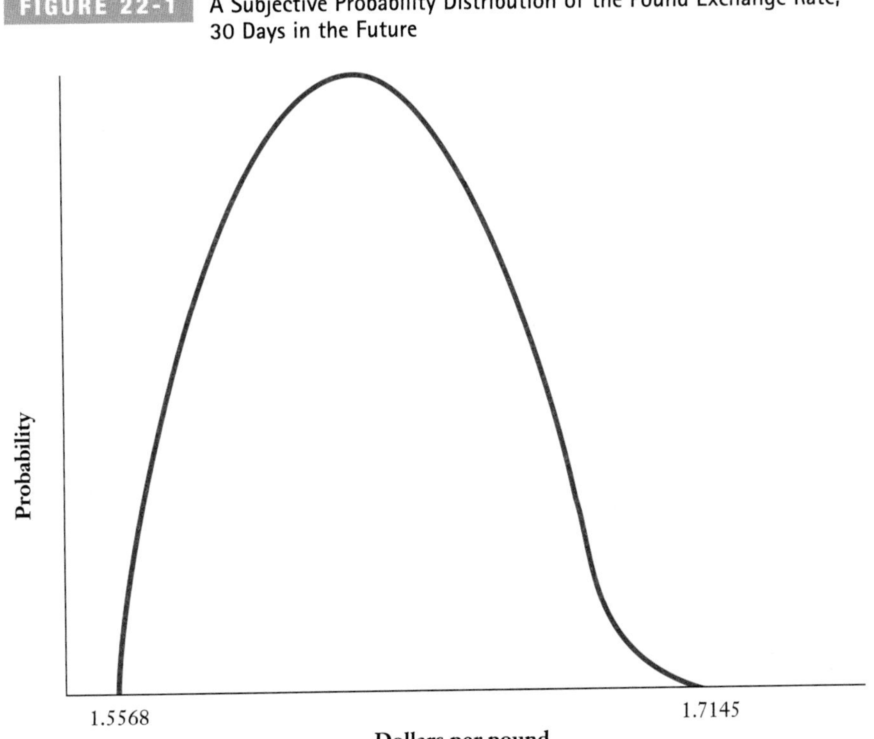

Exchange rate risk exists when the contract is written in terms of the foreign currency or *denominated* in foreign currency. There is no direct exchange risk if the international trade contract is written in terms of the domestic currency. That is, in Case II, if the contract were written in dollars, the American importer would face no direct exchange risk. With the contract written in dollars, the British exporter would bear all the exchange rate risk because the British exporter's future pound receipts would be uncertain. That is, the British exporter would receive payment in dollars, which would have to be converted into pounds at an unknown (as of today) pound/dollar exchange rate. In international trade contracts of the type discussed here, at least one of the two parties to the contract always bears the exchange rate risk.

Certain types of international trade contracts are denominated in a third currency, different from either the importer's or the exporter's domestic currency. In Case II, the contract might have been denominated in, say, the deutsche mark. With a mark contract, both importer and exporter would be subject to exchange rate risk.

Exchange rate risk is not limited to the two-party trade contracts; it exists also in foreign portfolio investments and direct foreign investments.

EXCHANGE RATE RISK IN FOREIGN PORTFOLIO INVESTMENTS Let us look at an example of exchange rate risk in the context of portfolio investments. An American investor buys a New Zealand security in denominated New Zealand dollars (NZD). The exact return on the investment in the security is unknown. Thus, the security is a risky investment. The investment return in the holding period of, say, three months stated in marks could be anything from –2 to +8 percent. In addition, the NZD/US dollar exchange rate may depreciate by 4 percent or appreciate by 6 percent in the three-month period during which the investment is held. The return to the American investor, in dollars, will therefore be in the range of –6 to +14 percent.[3] Notice that the return to a New Zealand investor, in euros, is in the range of –2 to +8 percent. Clearly, for the American investor, the exchange factor induces a greater variability in the dollar rate of return. Hence, the exchange rate fluctuations may increase the riskiness of the investments.

EXCHANGE RATE RISK IN DIRECT FOREIGN INVESTMENT The exchange rate risk of a direct foreign investment (DFI) is more complicated. In a DFI, the parent company invests in assets denominated in a foreign currency. That is, the balance sheet and the income statement of the subsidiary are written in terms of the foreign currency. The parent company receives the repatriated profit stream in dollars. Thus, the exchange rate risk concept applies to fluctuations in the dollar value of the assets located abroad as well as to the fluctuations in the home currency-denominated profit stream. Exchange risk not only affects immediate profits, but it may affect the future profit stream as well.

Although exchange rate risk can be a serious complication in international business activity, remember the principle of the risk-return trade-off: Traders and corporations find numerous reasons that the returns from international transactions outweigh the risks.

[3] Example: Assume the spot exchange rate is \$.50/NZD. In three months, the exchange rate would be .50 × (1 – .04) = .48 to .50 × (1 + .06) = .53. A \$50 investment today is equivalent to an NZD 100 investment. The NZD 100 investment would return NZD 98 to € 108 in three months. The return, in the worst case, is NZD 98 × .48 = \$47.04. The return, in the best case, is NZD 108 × .53 = \$57.24. The holding-period return, on the \$50 investment, will be between –6 percent (\$47.04 – \$50)/\$50 and +14 percent (\$57.24 – \$50)/\$50.

BACK TO THE PRINCIPLES

In international transactions, just as in domestic transactions, the key to value is the timing and amounts of cash flow spent and received. However, economic transactions across international borders add an element of risk because cash flows are denominated in the currency of the country in which business is being transacted. Consequently, the dollar value of the cash flows will depend on the exchange rate that exists at the time the cash changes hands. The fact remains, however, that it's cash spent and received that matters. This is the point of ***Principle 3: Cash—Not Profits—Is King.***

CONCEPT CHECK

1. What is a spot transaction? What is a direct quote? An indirect quote?
2. What is an arbitrageur? How does an arbitrageur make money?
3. What is a forward exchange rate?
4. Describe exchange rate risk in direct foreign investment.

Objective 3

INTEREST-RATE PARITY THEORY

Forward rates generally entail a premium or a discount relative to current spot rates. However, these forward premiums and discounts differ between currencies and maturities as we saw with the British pound and Swiss franc. These differences depend solely on the difference in the level of interest rates between the two countries, called the *interest-rate differential.* The value of the premium or discount can be theoretically computed from the **interest-rate parity (IRP) theory**. This theory states that (except for the effects of small transaction costs) the forward premium or discount should be equal and opposite in size to the difference in the national interest rates for securities of the same maturity.

Interest-rate parity (IRP) theory
States that (except for the effects of small transaction costs) the forward premium or discount should be equal and opposite in size to the differences in the national interest rates for securities of the same maturity.

Stated very simply, what does all this mean? It means that because of arbitrage, the interest-rate differential between two countries must be equal to the difference between the forward and spot exchange rates. If this were not true, arbitrageurs would buy in the forward market and sell in the spot market (or vice versa) until prices were back in line and there were no profits left to be made. For example, if prices in the forward market were too low, arbitrageurs would enter the market, increase the demand for the forward foreign currency, and drive up the prices in the forward market until those prices obeyed the interest-rate parity theory.

CONCEPT CHECK

1. In simple terms, what does the interest-rate parity theory mean?

Objective 4

PURCHASING-POWER PARITY

Long-run changes in exchange rates are influenced by international differences in inflation rates and the purchasing power of each nation's currency. Exchange rates of countries with high rates of inflation will tend to decline. According to the **purchasing-power parity**

Purchasing-power parity (PPP) theory
In the long run, exchange rates adjust so that the purchasing power of each currency tends to remain the same. Thus, exchange rate changes tend to reflect international differences in inflation rates. Countries with high rates of inflation tend to experience declines in the value of their currency.

(PPP) theory, in the long run, exchange rates adjust so that the purchasing power of each currency tends to be the same. Thus, exchange rate changes tend to reflect international differences in inflation rates. Countries with high rates of inflation tend to experience declines in the value of their currency. Thus, if Great Britain experiences a 10 percent rate of inflation in a year that Switzerland experiences only a 6 percent rate, the UK currency (the pound) will be expected to decline in value approximately by 3.77 percent (1.10/1.06) against the Swiss currency (the Swiss franc). More accurately, according to the PPP:

$$\text{expected spot rate} = \text{current spot rate} \times \text{expected difference in inflation rate}$$

$$\begin{array}{c}\text{expected spot rate}\\\text{(domestic currency}\\\text{per unit of foreign}\\\text{currency)}\end{array} = \begin{array}{c}\text{current spot rate}\\\text{(domestic currency}\\\text{per unit of foreign}\\\text{currency)}\end{array} \times \frac{(1 + \text{expected domestic inflation rate})}{(1 + \text{expected foreign inflation rate})}$$

Thus, if the beginning value of the Swiss franc were £.40, with a 6 percent inflation rate in Switzerland and a 10 percent inflation rate in Great Britain, according to the PPP, the expected value of the Swiss franc at the end of that year will be £.40 × [1.10/1.06], or £.4151.

Stated very simply, what does this mean? It means that a dollar should have the same purchasing power anywhere in the world—well, at least on average. Obviously, this is not quite true. However, what the purchasing-power parity theory tells us is that we should expect, on average, that differences in inflation rates between two countries should be reflected in changes in the exchange rates. In effect, the best forecast of the difference in inflation rates between two countries should also be the best forecast of the change in the spot rate of exchange.

THE LAW OF ONE PRICE

Law of one price
The proposition that in competitive markets the same goods should sell for the same price where prices are stated in terms of a single currency.

Underlying the PPP relationship is the **law of one price**. This law is actually a proposition that in competitive markets where there are no transportation costs or barriers to trade, the same goods sold in different countries sell for the same price if all the different prices are expressed in terms of the same currency. The idea is that the worth, in terms of marginal utility, of a good does not depend on where it is bought or sold. Because inflation will erode the purchasing power of any currency, its exchange rate must adhere to the PPP relationship if the law of one price is to hold over time.

There are enough obvious exceptions to the concept of purchasing-power parity that it may, at first glance, seem difficult to accept. For example, recently, a Big Mac cost \$2.36 in the United States, and given the then existing exchange rates, it cost an equivalent of \$2.02 in Mexico, \$2.70 in Japan, and \$3.22 in Germany. On the surface this might appear to violate the purchasing-power parity theory and the law of one price; however, we must remember that this theory is based upon the concept of arbitrage. In the case of a Big Mac, it's pretty hard to imagine buying Big Macs in Mexico for \$2.02, shipping them to Germany, and reselling them for \$3.22. But for commodities such as gold and other items that are relatively inexpensive to ship and do not have to be consumed immediately, the law of one price holds much better.

INTERNATIONAL FISHER EFFECT

According to the domestic Fisher effect (FE) (remember our discussion in Chapter 6), nominal interest rates reflect the expected inflation rate and a real rate of return. In other words,

$$\begin{array}{c}\text{nominal}\\\text{interest rate}\end{array} = \begin{array}{c}\text{expected}\\\text{inflation rate}\end{array} + \begin{array}{c}\text{real rate}\\\text{of interest}\end{array}$$

Although there is mixed empirical support for the international Fisher effect (IFE), it is widely thought that, for the major industrial countries, the real rate of interest is about 3 percent when a long-term period is considered. In such a case, with the previous assumption regarding inflation rates, interest rates in Great Britain and Switzerland would be (.10 + .03 + .003) or 13.3 percent and (.06 + .03 + .0018) or 9.18 percent, respectively.

In effect, the IFE states that the real interest rate should be the same all over the world, with the difference in nominal or stated interest rates simply resulting from the difference in expected inflation rates. As we look at interest rates around the world, this tells us that we should not necessarily send our money to a bank account in the country with the highest interest rates. That course of action might only result in sending our money to a bank in the country with the highest expected level of inflation.

CONCEPT CHECK

1. What does the law of one price say?
2. What is the international Fisher effect?

EXPOSURE TO EXCHANGE RATE RISK

Objective 5

An asset denominated or valued in terms of foreign-currency cash flows will lose value if that foreign currency declines in value. It can be said that such an asset is exposed to exchange rate risk. However, this possible decline in asset value may be offset by the decline in value of any liability that is also denominated or valued in terms of that foreign currency. Thus, a firm would normally be interested in its net exposed position (exposed assets—exposed liabilities) for each period in each currency.

Although expected changes in exchange rates can often be included in the cost-benefit analysis relating to such transactions, in most cases, there is an unexpected component in exchange rate changes and often the cost-benefit analysis for such transactions does not fully capture even the expected change in the exchange rate. For example, price increases for the foreign operations of many MNCs often have to be less than those necessary to fully offset exchange rate changes, owing to the competitive pressures generated by local businesses.

Three measures of foreign exchange exposure are translation exposure, transaction exposure, and economic exposure. Translation exposure arises because the foreign operations of MNCs have accounting statements denominated in the local currency of the country in which the operation is located. For U.S. MNCs, the *reporting currency* for its consolidated financial statements is the dollar, so the assets, liabilities, revenues, and expenses of the foreign operations must be translated into dollars. International transactions often require a payment to be made or received in a foreign currency in the future, so these transactions are exposed to exchange rate risk. Economic exposure exists over the long term because the value of future cash flows in the reporting currency (that is, the dollar) from foreign operations is exposed to exchange rate risk. Indeed, the whole stream of future cash flows is exposed. The Japanese automaker situation highlights the effect of economic exposure on an MNC's revenue stream. The three measures of exposure now are examined more closely.

TRANSLATION EXPOSURE

Foreign currency assets and liabilities are considered exposed if their foreign currency value for accounting purposes is to be translated into the domestic currency using the currency exchange rate—the exchange rate in effect on the balance sheet date. Other assets and liabilities and equity amounts that are translated at the historic exchange rate—the rate in effect when these items were first recognized in the company's accounts—are not considered to be exposed. The rate (current or historic) used to translate various accounts depends on the translation procedure used.

Although transaction exposure can result in exchange rate change-related losses and gains that are realized and have an impact on both reported and taxable income, translation exposure results in exchange rate losses and gains that are reflected in the company's accounting books, but are unrealized and have little or no impact on taxable income. Thus, if financial markets are efficient and managerial goals are consistent with owner wealth maximization, a firm should not have to waste real resources hedging against possible paper losses caused by translation exposure. However, if there are significant agency or information costs or if markets are not efficient, a firm may indeed find it economical to hedge against translation losses or gains.

Transaction Exposure

Transaction exposure
The net contracted foreign currency transactions for which the settlement amounts are subject to changing exchange rates.

Receivables, payables, and fixed-price sales or purchase contracts are examples of foreign currency transactions whose monetary value was fixed at a time different from the time when these transactions are actually completed. **Transaction exposure** is a term that describes the net contracted foreign currency transactions for which the settlement amounts are subject to changing exchange rates. A company normally must set up an additional reporting system to track transaction exposure, because several of these amounts are not recognized in the accounting books of the firm.

Exchange rate risk may be neutralized or hedged by a change in the asset and liability position in the foreign currency. An exposed asset position (such as an account receivable) can be hedged or covered by creating a liability of the same amount and maturity denominated in the foreign currency (such as a forward contract to sell the foreign currency). An exposed liability position (such as an account payable) can be covered by acquiring assets of the same amount and maturity in the foreign currency (such as a forward contract to buy the foreign currency). The objective is to have a zero net asset position in the foreign currency. This eliminates exchange rate risk, because the loss (gain) in the liability (asset) is exactly offset by the gain (loss) in the value of the asset (liability) when the foreign currency appreciates (depreciates). Two popular forms of hedge are the money-market hedge and the exchange-market or forward-market hedge. In both types of hedge, the amount and the duration of the asset (liability) positions are matched. Note as you read the next two subsections how IRP theory assures that each hedge provides the same cover.

MONEY-MARKET HEDGE In a money-market hedge, the exposed position in a foreign currency is offset by borrowing or lending in the money market. Consider the case of the American firm with a net liability position (that is, the amount it owes) of £3,000. The firm knows the exact amount of its pound liability in 30 days, but it does not know the liability in dollars. Assume that the 30-day money-market rates in both the United States and Great Britain are, respectively, 1 percent for lending and 1.5 percent for borrowing. The American business can take the following steps:

Step 1. Calculate the present value of the foreign currency liability (£3,000) that is due in 30 days. Use the money-market rate applicable for the foreign country (1 percent in the United Kingdom). The present value of £3,000 is £2,970.30, computed as follows: 3,000/(1 + .01).

Step 2. Exchange dollars on today's spot market to obtain the £2,970.30. The dollar amount needed today is $4,820.50 (2,970.30 × 1.6229).

Step 3. Invest £2,970.30 in a United Kingdom one-month money-market instrument. This investment will compound to exactly £3,000 in one month. The future liability of £3,000 is covered by the £2,970.30 investment.[4]

Note: If the American business does not own this amount today, it can borrow $4,820.50 from the U.S. money market at the going rate of 1.5 percent. In 30 days, the American business will need to repay $4,892.81 [$4,820.50 × (1 + .015)].

Assuming that the American business borrows the money, its management may base its calculations on the knowledge that the British goods, on delivery in 30 days, will cost it $4,892.81. The British business will receive £3,000. The American business need not wait for the future spot exchange rate to be revealed. On today's date, the future dollar payment of the contract is known with certainty. This certainty helps the American business in making its pricing and financing decisions.

Many businesses hedge in the money market. The firm needs to borrow (creating a liability) in one market, lend or invest in the other money market, and use the spot exchange market on today's date. The mechanics of covering a net asset position in the foreign currency are the exact reverse of the mechanics of covering the liability position. With a net asset position in pounds: Borrow in the United Kingdom money market in pounds, convert to dollars on the spot exchange market, invest in the U.S. money market. When the net assets are converted into pounds (i.e., when the firm receives what it is owed), pay off the loan and the interest. The cost of hedging in the money market is the cost of doing business in three different markets. Information about the three markets is needed, and analytical calculations of the type indicated here must be made.

Many small and infrequent traders find the cost of the money-market hedge prohibitive, owing especially to the need for information about the market. These traders use the exchange-market or the forward-market hedge, which has very similar hedging benefits.

THE FORWARD-MARKET HEDGE The forward market provides a second possible hedging mechanism. It works as follows: A net asset (liability) position is covered by a liability (asset) in the forward market. Consider again the case of the American firm with a liability of £3,000 that must be paid in 30 days. The firm may take the following steps to cover its liability position:

Step 1. Buy a forward contract today to purchase £3,000 in 30 days. The 30-day forward rate is $1.6197/£.

Step 2. On the thirtieth day pay the banker $4,859.10 (3,000 × $1.6197) and collect £3,000. Pay these pounds to the British supplier.

By the use of the forward contract the American business knows the exact worth of the future payment in dollars ($4,859.10). The exchange rate risk in pounds is totally eliminated by the net asset position in the forward pounds. In the case of a net asset exposure, the steps open to the American firm are the exact opposite: Sell the pounds forward, and on the future day receive and deliver the pounds to collect the agreed-on dollar amount.

The use of the forward market as a hedge against exchange rate risk is simple and direct. That is, match the liability or asset position against an offsetting position in the forward market. The forward-market hedge is relatively easy to implement. The firm directs its banker that it needs to buy or sell a foreign currency on a future date, and the banker gives a forward quote.

The forward-market hedge and the money-market hedge give an identical future dollar payment (or receipt) if the forward contracts are priced according to the interest-rate parity theory. The alert student may have noticed that the dollar payments in the money-market hedge and the forward-market hedge examples were, respectively, $4,820.50 and $4,859.10.

[4] Observe that £2,970.30 × (1 + .01) = £3,000.

A FOCUS ON HARLEY-DAVIDSON ROAD RULES

MANAGING FOREIGN EXCHANGE RISK EXPOSURE AT HARLEY-DAVIDSON—THE EURO EXPERIENCE

Harley-Davidson is one of those companies that focus on the long-run growth, and one of the markets that it looks to for future growth is Europe. The potential there for Harley is tremendous. In fact, according to Jim Brostowitz, the Vice President Controller/Treasurer at Harley-Davidson, the number of heavyweight motorcycles registered in Europe is only slightly less than in the United States, with Harley controlling about 6.6 percent of that market. As a result, Harley has set its sights on Europe and has set the seeds for a bright future. It has done that by developing dealer networks, H.O.G. (Harley Owners Group) events, and Harley-Davidson events just like the ones that have been so successful in the United States. Things looked bright in Europe.

When the Euro was first introduced in January 1999, it looked like that might make managing exchange risk much easier, but that was not the case. In the next two years the bottom fell out of the Euro as the exchange rate dropped from \$1.17/€ to \$0.84/€. Then, by the summer of 2003, the exchange rate was back up to \$1.17/€. To say the least, this was a financial nightmare.

At Harley-Davidson, the job of overseeing this nightmare has fallen in the lap of Jim Brostowitz. One of the problems Harley faces is the fact that virtually all of its motorcycles sold in Europe are made in the United States, and its workers and suppliers are paid in U.S. dollars. However, when Harleys are sold in Europe, the payment comes in the form of Euros. What happens if the Euro falls by 28 percent between the time the motorcycle is built and payment is received? In that case, Harley receives the purchase price in Euros, but they are worth 28 percent less than expected.

How does Jim Brostowitz go about protecting Harley's bottom line against this exchange rate fluctuation risk? He does it with a combination of hedging in the forward markets, a topic we cover in Chapter 22, and price adjustments. As Brostowitz notes with respect to the drop in the dollar in 2000, "Motorcycle prices are set with the introduction of new models, just like car prices are set, and there generally aren't any mid-year price increases. To eliminate short-term exchange rate risk we hedge forward contracts, going out about 6 months. This gives us short-term stability. In the longer-term, you've got to adjust prices. For example, for the 2001 model year, which was introduced in July 2000, the general U.S. price increase was about 1.5 percent, but in Europe, the price increase was between 5 and 10 percent depending on the model." As Harley is well aware, risks from economic and currency problems abroad can be devastating. For that reason, it prepares ahead of time for those risks.

Recall from our previous discussions that, in efficient markets, the forward contracts do indeed conform to IRP theory. However, the numbers in our example are not identical because the forward rate used in the forward-market hedge is not exactly equal to the interest rates in the money-market hedge. See the Focus on Harley-Davidson box.

CURRENCY-FUTURES CONTRACTS AND OPTIONS The forward-market hedge is not adequate for some types of exposure. If the foreign currency asset or liability position occurs on a date for which forward quotes are not available, the forward-market hedge cannot be accomplished. In certain cases, the forward-market hedge may cost more than the money-market hedge. In these cases, a corporation with a large amount of exposure may prefer the money-market hedge. In addition to forward-market and money-market hedges, a company can also hedge its exposure by buying (or selling) some relatively new instruments—foreign currency futures contracts and foreign currency options. Although futures contracts are similar to forward contracts in that they provide fixed prices for the required delivery of foreign currency at maturity, exchange traded options permit fixed (strike) price foreign currency transactions anytime before maturity. Futures contracts and options differ from forward contracts in that, unlike forward contracts, which are customized regarding amount and maturity date, futures and options are traded in standard amounts with standard maturity dates. In addition, although forward contracts are written by banks, futures and options are traded on organized exchanges, and individual traders deal with the exchange-based clearing organization rather than with each other. The purchase of futures requires the fulfillment of margin requirements (about 5 to 10 percent of the face amount), whereas the purchase of forward contracts requires only good credit standing with a bank. The purchase of options requires an immediate outlay that reflects a premium above the strike price and an outlay equal to the strike price when and if the option is executed.

ECONOMIC EXPOSURE

The economic value of a company can vary in response to exchange rate changes. This change in value may be caused by a rate change-induced decline in the level of expected cash flows and/or by an increase in the riskiness of these cash flows. *Economic exposure* refers to the overall impact of exchange rate changes on the value of the firm and includes not only the strategic impact of changes in competitive relationships that arise from exchange rate changes, but also the economic impact of transactions exposure, and if any, translation exposure.

Economic exposure to exchange rate changes depends on the competitive structure of the markets for a firm's inputs and outputs and how these markets are influenced by changes in exchange rates. This influence, in turn, depends on several economic factors, including price elasticities of the products, the degree of competition from foreign markets and direct (through prices) and indirect (through incomes) impact of exchange rate changes on these markets. Assessing the economic exposure faced by a particular firm thus depends on the ability to understand and model the structure of the markets for its major inputs (purchases) and outputs (sales).

A company need not engage in any cross-border business activity to be exposed to exchange rate changes, because product and financial markets in most countries are related and influenced to a large extent by the same global forces. The output of a company engaged in business activity only within one country may be competing with imported products, or it may be competing for its inputs with other domestic and foreign purchasers. For example, a Canadian chemical company that did no cross-border business nevertheless found that its profit margins depended directly on the U.S. dollar/Japanese yen exchange rate. The company used coal as an input in its production process, and the Canadian price of coal was heavily influenced by the extent to which the Japanese bought U.S. coal, which in turn depended on the dollar/yen exchange rate.

Although translation exposure need not be managed, it might be useful for a firm to manage its transaction and economic exposures because they affect firm value directly. In most companies, transaction exposure is generally tracked and managed by the office of the corporate treasurer. Economic exposure is difficult to define in operating terms, and very few companies manage it actively. In most companies, economic exposure is generally considered part of the strategic planning process, rather than a treasurer's or finance function.

CONCEPT CHECK

1. Give a simple explanation of translation exposure.
2. Give a simple explanation of transaction exposure.
3. Give a simple explanation of economic exposure.

MULTINATIONAL WORKING-CAPITAL MANAGEMENT

Objective 6

The basic principles of working-capital management for a multinational corporation are similar to those for a domestic firm. However, tax and exchange rate factors are additional considerations for the MNC. For an MNC with subsidiaries in many countries, the optimal decisions in the management of working capital are made by considering the market as a whole. The global or centralized financial decisions for an MNC are superior to the set of independent optimal decisions for the subsidiaries. This is the control problem of the MNC. If the individual subsidiaries make decisions that are best for them individually, the consolidation of such decisions may not be best for the MNC as a whole. To effect global management, sophisticated computerized models—incorporating many variables for each subsidiary—are solved to provide the best overall decision for the MNC.

Before considering the components of working-capital management, we examine two techniques that are useful in the management of a wide variety of working-capital components.

Leading and Lagging

Two important risk-reduction techniques for many working-capital problems are called *leading* and *lagging*. Often, forward-market and money-market hedges are not available to eliminate exchange risk. Under such circumstances, leading and lagging may be used to reduce exchange risk.

Recall that a net asset (long) position is not desirable in a weak or potentially depreciating currency. If a firm has a net asset position in such a currency, it should expedite the disposal of the asset. The firm should get rid of the asset earlier than it otherwise would have, or *lead*, and convert the funds into assets in a relatively stronger currency. By the same reasoning, the firm should *lag*, or delay the collection against a net asset position in a strong currency. If the firm has a net liability (short) position in the weak currency, then it should delay the payment against the liability, or lag, until the currency depreciates. In the case of an appreciating or strong foreign currency and a net liability position, the firm should lead the payments—that is, reduce the liabilities earlier than it would otherwise have.

These principles are useful in the management of working capital of an MNC. They cannot, however, eliminate the foreign exchange risk. When exchange rates change continuously, it is almost impossible to guess whether or when the currency will depreciate or appreciate. This is why the risk of exchange rate changes cannot be eliminated. Nevertheless, the reduction of risk, or the increased gain from exchange rate changes, via the lead and lag is useful for cash management, accounts-receivable management, and short-term liability management.

Cash Management and Positioning of Funds

Positioning of funds takes on an added importance in the international context. Funds may be transferred from a subsidiary of the MNC in country A to another subsidiary in country B such that the foreign exchange exposure and the tax liability of the MNC as a whole are minimized. It bears repeating that, owing to the global strategy of the MNC, the tax liability of the subsidiary in country A may be greater than it would otherwise have been, but the overall tax payment for all units of the MNC is minimized.

The transfer of funds among subsidiaries and the parent company is done by royalties, fees, and transfer pricing. A **transfer price** is the price a subsidiary or a parent company charges other companies that are part of the MNC for its goods or services. A parent that wishes to transfer funds from a subsidiary in a depreciating-currency country may charge a higher price on the goods and services sold to this subsidiary by the parent or by subsidiaries from strong-currency countries.

Transfer price
The price a subsidiary or a parent company charges other companies that are part of the same MNC for its goods or services.

CONCEPT CHECK

1. Describe the risk-reduction techniques of leading and lagging.
2. How can a parent company use the concept of transfer pricing to move funds from a subsidiary in a depreciating currency country to a strong currency country?

Objective 7

INTERNATIONAL FINANCING AND CAPITAL-STRUCTURE DECISIONS

An MNC has access to many more financing sources than does a domestic firm. It can tap not only the financing sources in its home country that are available to its domestic counterparts, but also sources in the foreign countries in which it operates. Host countries often provide access to low-cost subsidized financing to attract foreign investment.

In addition, the MNC may enjoy preferential credit standards because of its size and investor preference for its home currency. An MNC may be able to access third-country capital markets—countries in which it does not operate but that may have large, well-functioning capital markets. Finally, an MNC can also access external currency markets: Eurodollar, Eurocurrency, or Asian dollar markets. These external markets are unregulated and, because of their lower spread, can offer very attractive rates for financing *and* for investments. With the increasing availability of interest rate and currency swaps, a firm can raise funds in the lowest-cost maturities and currencies and swap them into funds with the maturity and currency denomination it requires. Because of its ability to tap a larger number of financial markets, the MNC may have a lower cost of capital, and because it may be better able to avoid the problems or limitations of any one financial market, it may have a more continuous access to external finance compared to a domestic company.

Access to national financial markets is regulated by governments. For example, in the United States, access to capital markets is governed by SEC regulations. Access to Japanese capital markets is governed by regulations issued by the Ministry of Finance. Some countries have extensive regulations; other countries have relatively open markets. These regulations may differ depending on the legal residency terms of the company raising funds. A company that cannot use its local subsidiary to raise funds in a given market will be treated as foreign. In order to increase their visibility in a foreign capital market, a number of MNCs are now listing their equities on the stock exchanges of many of these countries.

The external currency markets are predominantly centered in Europe, and about 80 percent of their value is denominated in terms of the U.S. dollar. Thus, most external currency markets can be characterized as Eurodollar markets. Such markets consist of an active short-term money market and an intermediate-term capital market with maturities ranging up to 15 years and averaging about 7 to 9 years. The intermediate-term market consists of the Eurobond and the Syndicated Eurocredit markets. Eurobonds are usually issued as unregistered bearer bonds and generally tend to have higher flotation costs but lower coupon rates compared to similar bonds issued in the United States. A Syndicated Eurocredit loan is simply a large-term loan that involves contributions by a number of lending banks.

In arriving at its capital-structure decisions, an MNC has to consider a number of factors. First, the capital structure of its local affiliates is influenced by local norms regarding capital structure in that industry and in that country. Local norms for companies in the same industry can differ considerably from country to country. Second, the local affiliate capital structure must also reflect corporate attitudes toward exchange rate and political risk in that country, which would normally lead to higher levels of local debt and other local capital. Third, local affiliate capital structure must reflect home country requirements with regard to the company's consolidated capital structure. Finally, the optimal MNC capital structure should reflect its wider access to financial markets, its ability to diversify economic and political risks, and its other advantages over domestic companies.

BACK TO THE PRINCIPLES

Investment across international boundaries gives rise to special risks not encountered when investing domestically. Specifically, political risks and exchange rate risk are unique to international investing. Once again, ***Principle 1: The Risk-Return Trade-Off—We won't take on additional risk unless we expect to be compensated with additional return*** *provides a rationale for evaluating these considerations. Where added risks are present, added rewards are necessary to induce investment.*

CONCEPT CHECK

1. What factors might an MNC consider in making a capital-structure decision?

Objective 8

DIRECT FOREIGN INVESTMENT

An MNC often makes direct foreign investments abroad in the form of plants and equipment. The decision process for this type of investment is very similar to the capital-budgeting decision in the domestic context—with some additional twists. Most real-world capital-budgeting decisions are made with uncertain future outcomes. Recall that a capital-budgeting decision has three major components: the estimation of the future cash flows (including the initial cost of the proposed investment), the estimation of the risk in these cash flows, and the choice of the proper discount rate. We will assume that the *NPV* criterion is appropriate as we examine (1) the risks associated with direct foreign investment, and (2) factors to be considered in making the investment decision that may be unique to the international scene.

RISKS IN DIRECT FOREIGN INVESTMENTS

Risks in domestic capital budgeting arise from two sources: business risk and financial risk. The international capital-budgeting problem incorporates these risks as well as political risk and exchange risk.

BUSINESS RISK AND FINANCIAL RISK International business risk is due to the response of business to economic conditions in the foreign country. Thus, the U.S. MNC needs to be aware of the business climate in both the United States and the foreign country. Additional business risk is due to competition from other MNCs, local businesses, and imported goods. *Financial risk* refers to the risks introduced in the profit stream by the firm's financial structure. The financial risks of foreign operations are not very different from those of domestic operations.

POLITICAL RISK Political risk arises because the foreign subsidiary conducts its business in a political system different from that of the home country. Many foreign governments, especially those in the Third World, are less stable than the U.S. government. A change in a country's political setup frequently brings a change in policies with respect to businesses—and especially with respect to foreign businesses. An extreme change in policy might involve nationalization or even outright expropriation of certain businesses. These are the political risks of conducting business abroad. A business with no investment in plant and equipment is less susceptible to these risks. Some examples of political risk are as follows:

1. Expropriation of plants and equipment without compensation.
2. Expropriation with minimal compensation that is below actual market value.
3. Nonconvertibility of the subsidiary's foreign earnings into the parent's currency—the problem of *blocked funds*.
4. Substantial changes in the laws governing taxation.
5. Governmental controls in the foreign country regarding the sale price of the products, wages, and compensation to personnel, hiring of personnel, making of transfer payments to the parent, and local borrowing.
6. Some governments require certain amounts of local equity participation in the business. Some require that the majority of the equity participation belong to their country.

All of these controls and governmental actions introduce risks in the cash flows of the investment to the parent company. These risks must be considered before making the foreign investment decision. The MNC may decide against investing in countries with risks of types 1 and 2. Other risks can be borne—provided that the returns from the foreign investments are high enough to compensate for them. Insurance against some types of political risks may be purchased from private insurance companies or from the U.S. government Overseas Private Investment Corporation. It should be noted that although an MNC cannot protect itself against all foreign political risks, political risks are also present in domestic business.

EXCHANGE RATE RISK The exposure of the fixed assets is best measured by the effects of the exchange rate changes on the firm's future earnings stream: that being economic exposure rather than translation exposure. For instance, changes in the exchange rate may adversely affect sales by making competing imported goods cheaper. Changes in the cost of goods sold may result if some components are imported and their price in the foreign currency changes because of exchange rate fluctuations. The thrust of these examples is that the effect of exchange rate changes on income statement items should be properly measured to evaluate exchange risk. Finally, exchange rate risk affects the dollar-denominated profit stream of the parent company, whether or not it affects the foreign-currency profits.

CONCEPT CHECK

1. What are some of the risks associated with direct foreign investments?

HOW FINANCIAL MANAGERS USE THIS MATERIAL

As the magnitude of international trade has expanded over the past two decades, so has the role of the multinational corporation. Firms routinely report their operating results by breaking out revenues *both* from major product lines *and* country-of-origin where direct foreign investment has taken place.

The expanded U.S. multinational presence has made financial executives acutely aware of the problems associated with foreign exchange rate risk. Management of the Walt Disney Company has said: "The Company's objective in managing the exposure to foreign currency fluctuations is to reduce earnings and cash flow volatility associated with foreign exchange rate changes to allow management to focus its attention on its core business issues and challenges."

The preponderance of multinational corporations do indeed focus on their main lines of business and do not, therefore, voluntarily enter into either foreign currency transactions or interest rate transactions for purposes of speculation on possible profit-making opportunities.

International markets have also been fertile grounds for finding new products. In fact, for many firms, finding new projects doesn't necessarily mean coming up with a new product; it may mean taking an existing product and applying it to a new market. That's certainly been the direction that McDonald's has taken in recent years. Today, McDonald's operates in over 70 countries with more than 20,000 restaurants. One of the biggest is a 700-seat McDonald's in Moscow. Was this an expensive venture? It certainly was. In fact, the food plant that McDonald's built to supply burgers, buns, fries, and everything else sold there cost over $60 million. In addition to the costs, there are a number of other factors that make opening an outlet outside of the United States both different and challenging. First, in order to keep the quality of what McDonald's sells identical with what is served at any McDonald's anywhere in the world, McDonald's spent six years putting together a supply chain that would provide the necessary raw materials at the quality level McDonald's demands. On top of that, there are the risks associated with the Russian economy and its currency that are well beyond the scope of what is experienced in the United States.

These risks all materialized in 1998 when the Russian economy, along with its currency, the ruble, went in the tank. In an attempt to shore up its economy, the Russian government cut its exchange rate from 6,000 rubles for each U.S. dollar to a new rate of 6 rubles per U.S. dollar—in effect, it cut off three zeros. Unfortunately, that didn't solve the problems the Russian economy faced. In May of 1998, the first Russian bank crashed and the value of the ruble started to drop. Then, in the summer of 1998, the Russian economy lost control and, finally, in August the entire banking system failed. When it was all over by the end of 1998, the exchange rate had fallen to 23 rubles per dollar, a drop of over 280 percent. McDonald's sells its burgers for rubles, so when it comes time to trade the rubles in for U.S. dollars, McDonald's won't be worth nearly as much as it was a year prior. In spite of all of this, since it opened, the Moscow McDonald's has proven to be enormously successful. It all goes to show that not all capital-budgeting projects have to be new products—they can be existing domestic products that are introduced into the international markets.

SUMMARY

Objective 1

The growth of our global economy, the increasing number of multinational corporations, and the increase in foreign trade itself underscore the importance of the study of international finance.

Exchange rate mechanics are discussed in the context of the prevailing floating rates. Under this system, exchange rates between currencies vary in an apparently random fashion in accordance with the supply and demand conditions in the exchange market. Important economic factors affecting the level of exchange rates include the relative economic strengths of the countries involved, the balance-of-payments mechanism, and the countries' monetary policies. Several important exchange rate terms are introduced. These include the asked and the bid rates, which represent the selling and buying rates of currencies. The direct quote is the units of home currency per unit of foreign currency, and the indirect quote is the reciprocal of the direct quote. Cross-rate computations reflect the exchange rate between two foreign currencies. *Objective* 2

The forward exchange market provides a valuable service by quoting rates for the delivery of foreign currencies in the future. The foreign currency is said to sell at a discount (premium) forward from the spot rate when the forward rate is greater (less) than the spot rate, in direct quotation. In addition, the influences of purchasing-power parity (PPP) and the international Fisher effect (IFE) in determining the exchange rate are discussed. In rational and efficient markets, forward rates are unbiased forecasts of future spot rates that are consistent with the PPP. *Objective* 3 *Objective* 4

Exchange rate risk exists because the exact spot rate that prevails on a future date is not known with certainty today. The concept of exchange rate risk is applicable to a wide variety of businesses, including export-import firms and firms involved in making direct foreign investments or international investments in securities. Exchange exposure is a measure of exchange rate risk. There are different ways of measuring the foreign exposure, including the net asset (net liability) measurement. Different strategies are open to businesses to counter the exposure to this risk, including the money-market hedge, the forward-market hedge, futures contracts, and options. Each involves different costs. *Objective* 5

In discussing working-capital management in an international environment, we find leading and lagging techniques useful in minimizing exchange rate risks and increasing profitability. In addition, funds positioning is a useful tool for reducing exchange rate risk exposure. The MNC may have a lower cost of capital because it has access to a larger set of financial markets than does a domestic company. In addition to the home, host, and third-country financial markets, the MNC can tap the rapidly growing external currency markets. In making capital-structure decisions, the MNC must consider political and exchange rate risks and host and home country capital structure norms. *Objective* 6

The complexities encountered in the direct foreign investment decision include the usual sources of risk—business and financial—and additional risks associated with fluctuating exchange rates and political factors. Political risk is due to differences in political climates, institutions, and processes between the home country and abroad. Under these conditions, the estimation of future cash flows and the choice of the proper discount rates are more complicated than for the domestic investment situation. *Objective* 7 *Objective* 8

KEY TERMS

Arbitrageur, 780
Asked rate, 780
Bid rate, 780
Bid-asked spread, 780
Buying rate, 780
Covered-interest arbitrage, 780
Cross rate, 780
Direct quote, 777
Exchange rate, 777
Exchange rate risk, 781
Floating-rate international currency system, 775
Forward exchange contract, 781
Forward-spot differential, 782
Indirect quote, 777
Interest-rate parity (IRP) theory, 785
Law of one price, 786
Multinational corporation (MNC), 774
Purchasing-power parity (PPP) theory, 785
Selling rate, 780
Simple arbitrage, 780
Spot transaction, 777
Transaction exposure, 788
Transfer price, 792
Triangular arbitrage, 780

Go To: www.prenhall.com/keown for downloads and current events associated with this chapter

STUDY QUESTIONS

22-1. What additional factors are encountered in international as compared with domestic financial management? Discuss each briefly.

22-2. What different types of businesses operate in the international environment? Why are the techniques and strategies available to these firms different?

22-3. What is meant by *arbitrage profits?*

22-4. What are the markets and mechanics involved in generating (a) simple arbitrage profits, and (b) triangular arbitrage profits?

22-5. How do the purchasing power parity, interest rate parity, and the Fisher effect explain the relationships between the current spot rate, the future spot rate, and the forward rate?

22-6. What is meant by (a) exchange risk, and (b) political risk?

22-7. How can exchange risk be measured?

22-8. What are the differences among transaction, translation, and economic exposures? Should all of them be ideally reduced to zero?

22-9. What steps can a firm take to reduce exchange risk? Indicate at least two different techniques.

22-10. How are the forward market and the money-market hedges affected? What are the major differences between these two types of hedges?

22-11. In the New York exchange market, the forward rate for the Indian currency, the rupee, is not quoted. If you were exposed to exchange risk in rupees, how could you cover your position?

22-12. Compare and contrast the use of forward contracts, futures contracts, and options to reduce foreign exchange exposure. When is each instrument most appropriate?

22-13. Indicate two working-capital management techniques that are useful for international businesses to reduce exchange risk and potentially increase profits.

22-14. How do the financing sources available to an MNC differ from those available to a domestic firm? What do these differences mean for the company's cost of capital?

22-15. What risks are associated with direct foreign investment? How do these risks differ from those encountered in domestic investment?

22-16. How is the direct foreign investment decision made? What are the inputs to this decision process? Are the inputs more complicated than those to the domestic investment problem? If so, why?

22-17. A corporation desires to enter a particular foreign market. The DFI analysis indicates that a direct investment in the plant in the foreign country is not profitable. What other course of action can the company take to enter the foreign market? What are the important considerations?

22-18. What are the reasons for the acceptance of a sales office or licensing arrangement when the DFI itself is not profitable?

SELF-TEST PROBLEMS

The data for Self-Test Problem ST-1 are given in the following table:

Selling Quotes for the Saudi Riyal in New York

COUNTRY-CURRENCY	CONTRACT	$/FOREIGN CURRENCY
Saudi–riyal	Spot	.3893
	30-day	.3910
	90-day	.3958

ST-1. You own \$10,000. The dollar rate on the Saudi riyal is 2.5823 riyal/\$. The Saudi riyal rate is given in the preceding table. Are arbitrage profits possible? Set up an arbitrage scheme with your capital. What is the gain (loss) in dollars?

STUDY PROBLEMS (SET A)

The data for Study Problems 22-1A through 22-6A are given in the following table:

Selling Quotes for Foreign Currencies in New York

COUNTRY-CURRENCY	CONTRACT	\$/FOREIGN CURRENCY
Canada—dollar	Spot	.8437
	30-day	.8417
	90-day	.8395
Japan—yen	Spot	.004684
	30-day	.004717
	90-day	.004781
Switzerland—franc	Spot	.5139
	30-day	.5169
	90-day	.5315

22-1A. (*Converting currencies*) An American business needs to pay (a) 10,000 Canadian dollars, (b) 2 million yen, and (c) 50,000 Swiss francs to businesses abroad. What are the dollar payments to the respective countries?

22-2A. (*Converting currencies*) An American business pays \$10,000, \$15,000, and \$20,000 to suppliers in, respectively, Japan, Switzerland, and Canada. How much, in local currencies, do the suppliers receive?

22-3A. (*Indirect quotes*) Compute the indirect quote for the spot and forward Canadian dollar, yen, and Swiss franc contracts.

22-4A. (*Bid, spot, and forward rates*) The spreads on the contracts as a percent of the asked rates are 2 percent for yen, 3 percent for Canadian dollars, and 5 percent for Swiss francs. Show, in a table similar to the preceding one, the bid rates for the different spot and forward rates.

22-5A. (*Foreign exchange arbitrage*) You own \$10,000. The dollar rate in Tokyo is 216.6743£. The yen rate in New York is given in the previous table. Are arbitrage profits possible? Set up an arbitrage scheme with your capital. What is the gain (loss) in dollars?

22-6A. (*Spot rates*) Compute the Canadian dollar/yen and the yen/Swiss franc spot rate from the data in the preceding table.

WEB WORKS

If you ever need to convert money from one currency to another, the Web is the place to go. There are a number of different currency converters available that are easy to use.

First take a look at the FX Converter (**www.oanda.com/convert/classic**). Use it to convert 100 Fiji dollars into U.S. dollars. How much are the 100 Fiji dollars worth in U.S. dollars?

Now use the Bank of Canada currency converter (**www.bankofcanada.ca/en/exchform.htm**) to convert 100 Croatian kunas to U.S. dollars. How much are they worth?

Now try the Yahoo! Finance currency calculator (**finance.yahoo.com/m3?u**) to convert 100 U.S. dollars into Euros. How many Euros would you get for \$100?

Now, use whatever currency calculator you'd like and move 100 U.S. dollars to Euros, then convert those Euros to Japanese yen, then convert those Japanese yen into U.S. dollars. How many U.S. dollars do you have?

INTEGRATIVE PROBLEM

For your job as the business reporter for a local newspaper, you are given the assignment of putting together a series of articles on the multinational finance and the international currency markets for your readers. Much recent local press coverage has been given to losses in the foreign exchange markets by JGAR, a local firm that is the subsidiary of Daedlufetarg, a large German manufacturing firm. Your editor would like you to address several specific questions dealing with multinational finance. Prepare a response to the following memorandum from your editor:

TO: Business Reporter

FROM: Perry White, Editor, *Daily Planet*

RE: Upcoming Series on Multinational Finance

In your upcoming series on multinational finance, I would like to make sure you cover several specific points. In addition, before you begin this assignment, I want to make sure we are all reading from the same script, as accuracy has always been the cornerstone of the *Daily Planet.* I'd like a response to the following questions before we proceed:

1. What new problems and factors are encountered in international as opposed to domestic financial management?
2. What does the term *arbitrage profits* mean?
3. What can a firm do to reduce exchange risk?
4. What are the differences between a forward contract, a futures contract, and options?

Use the following data in your response to the remaining questions:

Selling Quotes for Foreign Currencies in New York

COUNTRY-CURRENCY	CONTRACT	$/FOREIGN
Canada—dollar	Spot	.8450
	30-day	.8415
	90-day	.8390
Japan—yen	Spot	.004700
	30-day	.004750
	90-day	.004820
Switzerland—franc	Spot	.5150
	30-day	.5182
	90-day	.5328

5. An American business needs to pay (a) 15,000 Canadian dollars, (b) 1.5 million yen, and (c) 55,000 Swiss francs to businesses abroad. What are the dollar payments to the respective countries?
6. An American business pays $20,000, $5,000, and $15,000 to suppliers in, respectively, Japan, Switzerland, and Canada. How much, in local currencies, do the suppliers receive?
7. Compute the indirect quote for the spot and forward Canadian dollar contract.
8. You own $10,000. The dollar rate in Tokyo is 216.6752. The yen rate in New York is given in the preceding table. Are arbitrage profits possible? Set up an arbitrage scheme with your capital. What is the gain (loss) in dollars?
9. Compute the Canadian dollar/yen spot rate from the data in the preceding table.

STUDY PROBLEMS (SET B)

The data for Study Problems 22-1B through 22-6B are given in the following table:

Selling Quotes for Foreign Currencies in New York

COUNTRY-CURRENCY	CONTRACT	$/FOREIGN CURRENCY
Canada—dollar	Spot	.8439
	30-day	.8410
	90-day	.8390
Japan—yen	Spot	.004680
	30-day	.004720
	90-day	.004787
Switzerland—franc	Spot	.5140
	30-day	.5179
	90-day	.5335

22-1B. (*Converting currencies*) An American business needs to pay (a) 15,000 Canadian dollars, (b) 1.5 million yen, and (c) 55,000 Swiss francs to businesses abroad. What are the dollar payments to the respective countries?

22-2B. (*Converting currencies*) An American business pays $20,000, $5,000, and $15,000 to suppliers in, respectively, Japan, Switzerland, and Canada. How much, in local currencies, do the suppliers receive?

22-3B. (*Indirect quotes*) Compute the indirect quote for the spot and forward Canadian dollar, yen, and Swiss franc contracts.

22-4B. (*Bid, ask, and forward rates*) The spreads on the contracts as a percent of the asked rates are 4 percent for yen, 3 percent for Canadian dollars, and 6 percent for Swiss francs. Show, in a table similar to the previous one, the bid rates for the different spot and forward rates.

22-5B. (*Foreign exchange arbitrage*) You own $10,000. The dollar rate in Tokyo is 216.6752£. The yen rate in New York is given in the previous table. Are arbitrage profits possible? Set up an arbitrage scheme with your capital. What is the gain (loss) in dollars?

22-6B. (*Spot rates*) Compute the Canadian dollar/yen and the yen/Swiss franc spot rate from the data in the preceding table.

SELF-TEST SOLUTIONS

ST-1. The Saudi rate is 2.5823 riyals/$1, while the (indirect) New York rate is 1/.3893 = 2.5687 riyals/$.

Assuming no transaction costs, the rates between Saudi Arabia and New York are out of line. Thus, arbitrage profits are possible.

Step 1. Because the riyal is cheaper in Saudi Arabia, buy $10,000 worth of riyals in Saudi Arabia. The number of riyals purchased would be $10,000 × 2.5823 = 25,823 riyals.

Step 2. Simultaneously sell the riyals in New York at the prevailing rate. The amount received upon the sale of the riyals would be:

25,823 riyals × $.3893/riyals = $10,052.89
net gain is $10,052.89 – $10,000 = $52.89

APPENDIX A

USING A CALCULATOR

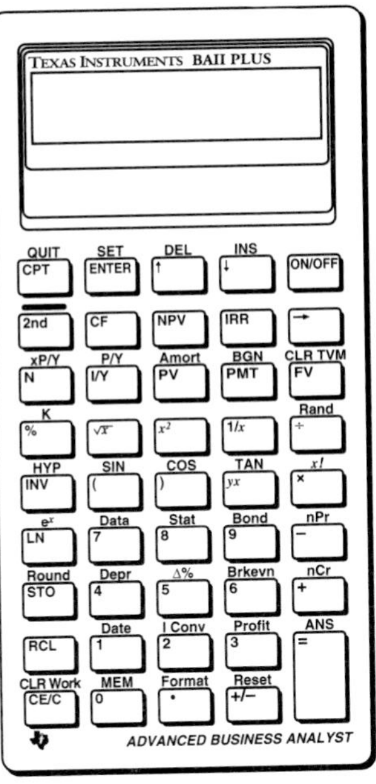

As you prepare for a career in business, the ability to use a financial calculator is essential, whether you are in the finance division or the marketing department. For most positions, it will be assumed that you can use a calculator in making computations that at one time were simply not possible without extensive time and effort. The following examples let us see what is possible, but they represent only the beginning of using the calculator in finance.

With just a little time and effort, you will be surprised at how much you can do with the calculator, such as calculating a stock's beta, or determining the value of a bond on a specific day given the exact date of maturity, or finding net present values and internal rates of return, or calculating the standard deviation. The list is almost endless.

In demonstrating how calculators may make our work easier, we must first decide which calculator to use. The options are numerous and largely depend on personal preference. We have chosen the Texas Instruments BAII Plus.

We will limit our discussion to the following issues:

I. Introductory Comments
II. An Important Starting Point
III. Calculating Table Values for:
   A. Appendix B (Compound sum of $1)
   B. Appendix C (Present value of $1)
   C. Appendix D (Sum on an annuity of $1 for *n* periods)
   D. Appendix E (Present value of an annuity for $1 for *n* periods)
IV. Calculating Present Values
V. Calculating Future Values (Compound sum)
VI. Calculating the Number of Payments or Receipts
VII. Calculating the Payment Amount
VIII. Calculating the Interest Rate
IX. Bond Value
   A. Computing the value of a bond
   B. Calculating the yield to maturity on a bond
X. Computing the Net Present Value and Internal Rate of Return
   A. Where future cash flows are equal amounts in each period (annuity)
   B. Where future cash flows are unequal amounts in each period.

I. INTRODUCTORY COMMENTS

In the examples that follow, you are told (1) which keystrokes to use, (2) the resulting appearance of the calculator display, and (3) a supporting explanation.

The keystrokes column tells you which keys to press. The keystrokes shown in an unshaded box tell you to use one of the calculator's dedicated or "hard" keys. For example, if +/– is shown in the keystrokes instruction column, press that key on the keyboard of the calculator. To use a function printed in gray lettering above a dedicated key, always press the gray key 2nd first, then the function key.

II. AN IMPORTANT STARTING POINT

Example: You want to display four numbers to the right of the decimal.

Keystrokes	Display	Explanation
2nd		
Format	Dec =	
4 Enter	DEC = 4.0000	Sets display to show four numbers to the right of the decimal
CE/C CE/C	0.0000	Clears display

Example: You want to display two payments per year to be paid at the end of each period.

Keystrokes	Display	Explanation
2nd		
P/Y	P/Y =	
2 Enter	P/Y = 2.0000	Sets number of payments per year at 2
2nd		
BGN	END	Sets timing of payment at the end of each period
CE/C CE/C	0.0000	Clears display

III. CALCULATING TABLE VALUES

A. The compound sum of $1 (Appendix B)

Example: What is the table value for the compound sum of $1 for 5 years at a 12 percent annual interest rate?

Keystrokes	Display	Explanation
2nd		
P/Y	P/Y =	
1 Enter	P/Y = 1.0000	Sets number of payments per year at 1
2nd		
BGN	END	Sets timing of payment at the end of each period
CE/C CE/C	0.0000	Clears display
2nd		
CLR TVM	0.0000	Clears TVM variables
1 +/–	PV = –1.0000	Stores initial $1 as a negative present value
PV		Otherwise, the answer will appear as a negative
5 N	N = 5.0000	Stores number of periods
12 I/Y	I/Y = 12.0000	Stores interest rate
CPT FV	FV = 1.7623	Table value

III. CALCULATING TABLE VALUES (CONTINUED)

B. The present value of $1 (Appendix C)

Example: What is the table value for the present value of $1 for 8 years at a 10 percent annual interest rate?

Keystrokes	Display	Explanation
2nd		
P/Y	P/Y =	
1 Enter	P/Y = 1.0000	Sets number of payments per year at 1
2nd		
BGN	END	Sets timing of payment at the end of each period
CE/C CE/C	0.0000	Clears display
2nd		
CLR TVM	0.0000	Clears TVM variables
1 +/−	FV = −1.0000	Stores future amount as negative value
FV		
8 N	N = 8.0000	Stores number of periods
10 I/Y	I/Y = 10.0000	Stores interest rate
CPT PV	PV = 0.4665	Table value

C. The sum of an annuity of $1 for *n* periods (Appendix D)

Example: What is the table value for the compound sum of an annuity of $1 for 6 years at a 14 percent annual interest rate?

Keystrokes	Display	Explanation
2nd		
P/Y	P/Y =	
1 Enter	P/Y = 1.0000	Sets number of payments per year at 1
2nd		
BGN	END	Sets timing of payment at the end of each period
CE/C CE/C	0.0000	Clears display
2nd		
CLR TVM	0.0000	Clears TVM variables
1 +/−	PMT = −1.0000	Stores annual payment (annuity) as a negative number. Otherwise, the answer will appear as a negative.
PMT		
6 N	N = 6.0000	Stores number of periods
14 I/Y	I/Y = 14.0000	Stores interest rate
CPT FV	PV = 8.5355	Table value

III. CALCULATING TABLE VALUES (CONTINUED)

D. The present value of an annuity of $1 for *n* periods (Appendix E)

Example: What is the table value for the present value of an annuity of $1 for 12 years at 9 percent annual interest rate?

Keystrokes	Display	Explanation
2nd		
P/Y	P/Y =	
1 Enter	P/Y = 1.0000	Sets number of payments per year at 1
2nd		
BGN	END	Sets timing of payment at the end of each period
CE/C CE/C	0.0000	Clears display
2nd		
CLR TVM	0.0000	Clears TVM variables
1 +/– PMT	PMT = –1.0000	Stores annual payment (annuity) as a negative number. Otherwise, the answer will appear as a negative.
12 N	N = 12.0000	Stores number of periods
9 I/Y	I/Y = 9.0000	Stores interest rate
CPT FV	PV = 7.1607	Table value

IV. CALCULATING PRESENT VALUES

Example: You are considering the purchase of a franchise of quick oil-change locations, which you believe will provide an annual cash flow of $50,000. At the end of 10 years, you believe that you will be able to sell the franchise for an estimated $900,000. Calculate the maximum amount you should pay for the franchise (present value) in order to realize at least an 18 percent annual yield.

Keystrokes	Display	Explanation
2nd		
BGN	END	Sets timing of payment at the end of each period
CE/C CE/C	0.0000	Clears display
2nd		
CLR TVM	0.0000	Clears TVM variables
10 N	N = 10.0000	Stores *n*, the holding period
18 I/Y	I/Y = 18.0000	Stores *i*, the required rate of return
50,000 PMT	PMT = 50,000,000	Stores PMT, the annual cash flow to be received
900,000 FV	FV = 900,000.000	Stores FV, the cash flow to be received at the end of the project
CPT PV	PV = –396,662.3350	The present value, given a required rate of reutrn of 18 percent. (Note: The present value is displayed with a minus sign because it represents cash paid out.)

V. CALCULATING FUTURE VALUES (COMPOUND SUM)

Example: If you deposit $300 a month (at the beginning of each month) into a new account that pays 6.25% annual interest compounded monthly, how much will you have in the account after 5 years?

Keystrokes	Display	Explanation
2nd		
BGN	END	Sets timing of payment at the end of each period
2nd		
SET	BGN	Sets timing of payment at the end of each period
2nd		
P/Y	PY =	
12 Enter	P/Y = 12.0000	Sets 12 payments per year
CE/C CE/C	0.0000	Clears display
2nd		
CLR TVM	0.0000	Clears TVM variables
60 N	N = 60.0000	Stores *n,* the number of months for the investment
6.25 I/Y	I/Y = 6.2500	Stores *i,* the annual rate
300 +/– PMT	PMT = –300.0000	Stores PMT, the monthly amount invested (with a minus sign for cash paid out)
CPT FV	FV = 21,175.7613	The future value after 5 years

VI. CALCULATING THE NUMBER OF PAYMENTS OR RECEIPTS

Example: If you wish to retire with $500,000 saved, and can only afford payments of $500 each month, how long will you have to contribute toward your retirement if you can earn a 10 percent return on your contributions?

Keystrokes	Display	Explanation
2nd		
BGN	BGN	Verifies timing of payment at the beginning of each period
2nd		
P/Y	P/Y = 12.0000	
12 Enter	P/Y = 12.0000	Sets 12 payments per year
CE/C CE/C	0.0000	Clears display
2nd		
CLR TVM	0.0000	Clears TVM variables
10 I/Y	I/Y = 10.0000	Stores *i,* the interest rate
500 +/– PMT	PMT = –500.0000	Stores PMT, the monthly amount invested (with a minus sign for cash paid out)
50,000 FV	FV = 500,000.000	The value we want to achieve
CPT N	N = 268.2539	Number of months (because we considered monthly payments) required to achieve our goal

VII. CALCULATING THE PAYMENT AMOUNT

Example: Suppose your retirement needs were $750,000. If you are currently 25 years old and plan to retire at age 65, how much will you have to contribute each month for retirement if you can earn 12.5% on your savings?

Keystrokes	Display	Explanation
2nd		
BGN	BGN	Verifies timing of payment at the beginning of each period
2nd		
P/Y	P/Y = 12.0000	
12 Enter	P/Y = 12.0000	Sets 12 payments per year
CE/C CE/C	0.0000	Clears display
2nd		
CLR TVM	0.0000	Clears TVM variables
12.5 I/Y	I/Y = 12.5000	Stores *i*, the interest rate
480 N	N = 480.0000	Stores *n*, the number of periods until we stop contributing (40 years × 12 months/years = 480 months)
750,000 FV	FV = 750,000.000	The value we want to achieve
CPT PMT	PMT = –53.8347	Monthly contribution required to achieve our ultimate goal (shown as negative because it represents cash paid out)

VIII. CALCULATING THE INTEREST RATE

Example: If you invest $300 at the end of each month for 6 years (72 months) for a promised $30,000 return at the end, what interest rate are you earning on your investment?

Keystrokes	Display	Explanation
2nd		
BGN	BGN	Sets timing of payments to beginning of each period
2nd		
SET	END	Sets timing of payments to end of each period
2nd		
P/Y	P/Y = 12.0000	
12 Enter	P/Y = 12.0000	Sets 12 payments per year
CE/C CE/C	0.0000	Clears display
2nd		
CLR TVM	0.0000	Clears TVM variables
72 N	N = 72.0000	Stores N, the number of deposits (investments)
300 +/– PMT	PMT = –300.0000	Stores PMT, the monthly amount invested (with a minus sign for cash paid out)
30,000 FV	FV = 30,000.000	Stores the future value to be received in 6 years
CPT I/Y	I/Y= 10.5892	The annual interest rate earned on the investment

IX. BOND VALUATION

A. Computing the value of a bond

Example: Assume the current date is January 1, 1993, and that you want to know the value of a bond that matures in 10 years and has a coupon rate of 9 percent (4.5% semiannually). Your required rate of return is 12 percent.

Keystrokes	Display	Explanation
2nd		
BGN	END	Verifies timing of payment at the beginning of each period
2nd		
P/Y	P/Y = 12.0000	
2 Enter	P/Y = 2.0000	Sets 2 payments per year; end mode (END) assumes cash flows are at the end of each 6-month period
CE/C CE/C	0.0000	Clears display
2nd		
CLR TVM	0.0000	Clears TVM variables
20 N	N = 20.0000	Stores the number of semiannual periods (10 years × 2)
12 I/Y	I/Y = 12.0000	Stores annual rate of return
45 PMT	PMT = 45.0000	Stores the semiannual interest payment
1,000 FV	FV = 1,000.0000	Stores the bond's maturity or par value
CPT PV	PV = –827.9512	Value of the bond, expressed as a negative number

Solution using the bond feature:

CE/C CE/C	0.0000	Clears display
2nd		
BOND	STD = 1-01-1970	(This will be the last date entered)
2nd		
CLR WORK	STD = 1-01-1970	Clears BOND variables
1.01.93 Enter	STD = 1-01-1993	Stores the current date (month, day, year)
↓	CPN = 0.0000	
9 Enter	CPN = 9.0000	Stores the coupon interest rate
↓	RDT = 12-31-1990	(This will be the last date entered)
1.01.03 Enter	RDT = 1-01-2003	Stores the maturity date in 10 years
↓	RV = 100.0000	Verifies bonds maturity or par value
↓	ACT	
2nd		
SET	360	Sets calculations to be based on 360-day year
↓	2/Y	Verifies semiannual compounding rate
↓	YLD = 0.0000	
12 Enter	YLD = 12.0000	Stores the investor's required rate of return
↓	PRI = 0.0000	
CPT	PRI = 82.7951	Value of bond as % of par value; i.e., value of bond is $827.95

IX. BOND VALUATION

B. Computing the yield to maturity on a bond

Example: Assume the current date is January 1, 1994, and that you want to know your yield to maturity on a bond that matures in 8 years and has a coupon rate of 12% (6% semiannually). The bond is selling for $1,100.

Keystrokes	Display	Explanation
2nd		
BGN	END	Verifies timing of payment at the beginning of each period
2nd		
P/Y	P/Y = 12.0000	
2 Enter	P/Y = 2.0000	Sets 2 payments per year; end mode (END) assumes cash flows are at the end of each 6-month period
CE/C CE/C	0.0000	Clears display
2nd		
CLR TVM	0.0000	Clears TVM variables
16 N	N = 16.0000	Stores the number of semiannual periods (8 years × 2)
1100 +/–		
PV	PV = –1,100.0000	Value of the bond, expressed as a negative number
60 PMT	PMT = 60.0000	Stores the semiannual interest payment
1,000 FV	FV = 1,000.0000	Stores the bond's maturity or par value
CPT I/Y	I/Y = 10.1451	The yield to maturity, expressed on an annual basis

Solution using the bond feature:

CE/C CE/C	0.0000	Clears display
2nd		
BOND	SDT = 1-01-1993	(This will be the last date entered)
2nd		
CLR WORK	SDT = 1-01-1993	Clears BOND variables
1.03.94 Enter	SDT = 1-03-1994	Stores the current date (month, day, year)
↓	CPN = 0.0000	
12 Enter	CPN = 12.0000	Stores the coupon interest rate
↓	RDT = 1-01-2003	(This will be the last date entered)
1.03.02 Enter	RDT = 1-03-2002	Stores the maturity date in 8 years
↓	RV = 100.0000	Verifies bonds maturity or par value
↓	360	
2nd		
SET	ACT	Sets calculations to be based on 360-day year
↓	2/Y	Verifies semiannual compounding rate
↓	YLD = 0.0000	
↓	PRI = 0.0000	
110 Enter	PRI = 110.0000	Stores the bond value as a percentage of par value
↑	YLD = 0.0000	
CPT	YLD = 10.1451	Bond's yield to maturity

X. COMPUTING THE NET PRESENT VALUE AND INTERNAL RATE OF RETURN

A. Where future cash flows are equal amounts in each period (annuity)

Example: The firm is considering a capital project that would cost \$80,000. The firm's cost of capital is 12 percent. The project life is 10 years, during which time the firm expects to receive \$15,000 per year. Calculate the NPV and the IRR.

Keystrokes	Display	Explanation
2nd		
BGN	END	Verifies timing of payment at the beginning of each period
2nd P/Y 1 Enter	P/Y = 21.0000	Sets 1 payment per year; end mode (END) assumes cash flows are at the end of each year
CE/C CE/C	0.0000	Clears display
2nd		
CLR TVM	0.0000	Clears TVM variables
15,000 PMT	PMT = 15.0000	Stores the annual cash flows at \$15,000
10 N	N = 10.0000	Stores the life of the project
12 I/Y	I/Y = 12.0000	Stores the cost of capital
CPT PV	PV = –84,753.3454	Calculates present value
+/–	PV = 84,753.3454	Changes PV to positive
–80,000 =	4,753.3454	Calculates net present value by subtracting the cost of the project
80,000 +/–	–80,000.0000	
PV	PV = –80,000.0000	
CPT I/Y	I/Y = 13.4344	Calculates the IRR

B. Where future cash flows are unequal amounts in each period

Example: The firm is considering a capital project that would cost \$110,000. The firm's cost of capital is 15 percent. The project life is 5 years, with the following expected cash flows: \$ – 25,000, \$50,000, \$60,000, \$60,000, and \$70,000. In addition, you expect to receive \$30,000 in the last year from the salvage value of the equipment. Calculate the NPV and IRR.

Keystrokes	Display	Explanation
CE/C CE/C	0.0000	Clears display
CF	CF_0 = 0.0000	
2nd		
CLR WORK	CF_0 = 0.0000	Clears cash flow variables
110,000 +/– Enter	CF_0 = 110,000.0000	Stores CF_0, the initial investment (with a minus sign for a negative cash flow)
↓	C01 = 0.0000	Stores CF_1, the first year's cash flow (with a minus sign for a negative cash flow)
25,000 +/–	C01 = –25,000.0000	
Enter		
↓	F01 = 1.0000	Stores the number of years CF_1 is repeated (in this case, 1 year only)
Enter		
↓	C02 = 0.0000	
50,000	C02 = 50,000.0000	Stores CF_2
Enter		
↓	FO_2 = 1.0000	

X. COMPUTING THE NET PRESENT VALUE AND INTERNAL RATE OF RETURN (CONTINUED)

Enter	F02 = 1.0000	Store the number of years CF_2 is repeated
↓	C03 = 0.0000	
60,000	C03 = 60,000.0000	Stores CF_3
Enter		
↓ 2 Enter	F03 = 2.0000	Stores the number of years CF_3 is repeated (here, 2 years, so our response is 2 to the FO_3 prompt)
↓	C04 = 0.0000	
100,000	C04 = 100,000.0000	Stores CF_4, \$70,000 plus expected \$30,000
Enter		
↓	F04 = 1.0000	Stores the number CF_4 is repeated
Enter		
2nd QUIT	0.0000	Ends storage of individual cash flows
NPV	I = 0.0000	
15 Enter	I = 15.0000	Stores interest rate
↓	NPV = 0.0000	
CPT	NPV = 25,541.8951	Calculates the project's NPV at the stated interest rate
IRR	IRR = 0.0000	
CPT	IRR = 22.9533	Calculates the project's IRR

APPENDIX B

COMPOUND SUM OF $1

n	1%	2%	3%	4%	5%	6%	7%	8%	9%	10%
1	1.010	1.020	1.030	1.040	1.050	1.060	1.070	1.080	1.090	1.100
2	1.020	1.040	1.061	1.082	1.102	1.124	1.145	1.166	1.188	1.210
3	1.030	1.061	1.093	1.125	1.158	1.191	1.225	1.260	1.295	1.331
4	1.041	1.082	1.126	1.170	1.216	1.262	1.311	1.360	1.412	1.464
5	1.051	1.104	1.159	1.217	1.276	1.338	1.403	1.469	1.539	1.611
6	1.062	1.126	1.194	1.265	1.340	1.419	1.501	1.587	1.677	1.772
7	1.072	1.149	1.230	1.316	1.407	1.504	1.606	1.714	1.828	1.949
8	1.083	1.172	1.267	1.369	1.477	1.594	1.718	1.851	1.993	2.144
9	1.094	1.195	1.305	1.423	1.551	1.689	1.838	1.999	2.172	2.358
10	1.105	1.219	1.344	1.480	1.629	1.791	1.967	2.159	2.367	2.594
11	1.116	1.243	1.384	1.539	1.710	1.898	2.105	2.332	2.580	2.853
12	1.127	1.268	1.426	1.601	1.796	2.012	2.252	2.518	2.813	3.138
13	1.138	1.294	1.469	1.665	1.886	2.133	2.410	2.720	3.066	3.452
14	1.149	1.319	1.513	1.732	1.980	2.261	2.579	2.937	3.342	3.797
15	1.161	1.346	1.558	1.801	2.079	2.397	2.759	3.172	3.642	4.177
16	1.173	1.373	1.605	1.873	2.183	2.540	2.952	3.426	3.970	4.595
17	1.184	1.400	1.653	1.948	2.292	2.693	3.159	3.700	4.328	5.054
18	1.196	1.428	1.702	2.026	2.407	2.854	3.380	3.996	4.717	5.560
19	1.208	1.457	1.753	2.107	2.527	3.026	3.616	4.316	5.142	6.116
20	1.220	1.486	1.806	2.191	2.653	3.207	3.870	4.661	5.604	6.727
21	1.232	1.516	1.860	2.279	2.786	3.399	4.140	5.034	6.109	7.400
22	1.245	1.546	1.916	2.370	2.925	3.603	4.430	5.436	6.658	8.140
23	1.257	1.577	1.974	2.465	3.071	3.820	4.740	5.871	7.258	8.954
24	1.270	1.608	2.033	2.563	3.225	4.049	5.072	6.341	7.911	9.850
25	1.282	1.641	2.094	2.666	3.386	4.292	5.427	6.848	8.623	10.834
30	1.348	1.811	2.427	3.243	4.322	5.743	7.612	10.062	13.267	17.449
40	1.489	2.208	3.262	4.801	7.040	10.285	14.974	21.724	31.408	45.258
50	1.645	2.691	4.384	7.106	11.467	18.419	29.456	46.900	74.354	117.386

n	11%	12%	13%	14%	15%	16%	17%	18%	19%	20%
1	1.110	1.120	1.130	1.140	1.150	1.160	1.170	1.180	1.190	1.200
2	1.232	1.254	1.277	1.300	1.322	1.346	1.369	1.392	1.416	1.440
3	1.368	1.405	1.443	1.482	1.521	1.561	1.602	1.643	1.685	1.728
4	1.518	1.574	1.630	1.689	1.749	1.811	1.874	1.939	2.005	2.074
5	1.685	1.762	1.842	1.925	2.011	2.100	2.192	2.288	2.386	2.488
6	1.870	1.974	2.082	2.195	2.313	2.436	2.565	2.700	2.840	2.986
7	2.076	2.211	2.353	2.502	2.660	2.826	3.001	3.185	3.379	3.583
8	2.305	2.476	2.658	2.853	3.059	3.278	3.511	3.759	4.021	4.300
9	2.558	2.773	3.004	3.252	3.518	3.803	4.108	4.435	4.785	5.160
10	2.839	3.106	3.395	3.707	4.046	4.411	4.807	5.234	5.695	6.192
11	3.152	3.479	3.836	4.226	4.652	5.117	5.624	6.176	6.777	7.430
12	3.498	3.896	4.334	4.818	5.350	5.936	6.580	7.288	8.064	8.916
13	3.883	4.363	4.898	5.492	6.153	6.886	7.699	8.599	9.596	10.699
14	4.310	4.887	5.535	6.261	7.076	7.987	9.007	10.147	11.420	12.839
15	4.785	5.474	6.254	7.138	8.137	9.265	10.539	11.974	13.589	15.407
16	5.311	6.130	7.067	8.137	9.358	10.748	12.330	14.129	16.171	18.488
17	5.895	6.866	7.986	9.276	10.761	12.468	14.426	16.672	19.244	22.186
18	6.543	7.690	9.024	10.575	12.375	14.462	16.879	19.673	22.900	26.623
19	7.263	8.613	10.197	12.055	14.232	16.776	19.748	23.214	27.251	31.948
20	8.062	9.646	11.523	13.743	16.366	19.461	23.105	27.393	32.429	38.337
21	8.949	10.804	13.021	15.667	18.821	22.574	27.033	32.323	38.591	46.005
22	9.933	12.100	14.713	17.861	21.644	26.186	31.629	38.141	45.923	55.205
23	11.026	13.552	16.626	20.361	24.891	30.376	37.005	45.007	54.648	66.247
24	12.239	15.178	18.788	23.212	28.625	35.236	43.296	53.108	65.031	79.496
25	13.585	17.000	21.230	26.461	32.918	40.874	50.656	62.667	77.387	95.395
30	22.892	29.960	39.115	50.949	66.210	85.849	111.061	143.367	184.672	237.373
40	64.999	93.049	132.776	188.876	267.856	378.715	533.846	750.353	1051.642	1469.740
50	184.559	288.996	450.711	700.197	1083.619	1670.669	2566.080	3927.189	5988.730	9100.191

COMPOUND SUM OF $1 (CONTINUED)

n	21%	22%	23%	24%	25%	26%	27%	28%	29%	30%
1	1.210	1.220	1.230	1.240	1.250	1.260	1.270	1.280	1.290	1.300
2	1.464	1.488	1.513	1.538	1.562	1.588	1.613	1.638	1.664	1.690
3	1.772	1.816	1.861	1.907	1.953	2.000	2.048	2.097	2.147	2.197
4	2.144	2.215	2.289	2.364	2.441	2.520	2.601	2.684	2.769	2.856
5	2.594	2.703	2.815	2.932	3.052	3.176	3.304	3.436	3.572	3.713
6	3.138	3.297	3.463	3.635	3.815	4.001	4.196	4.398	4.608	4.827
7	3.797	4.023	4.259	4.508	4.768	5.042	5.329	5.629	5.945	6.275
8	4.595	4.908	5.239	5.589	5.960	6.353	6.767	7.206	7.669	8.157
9	5.560	5.987	6.444	6.931	7.451	8.004	8.595	9.223	9.893	10.604
10	6.727	7.305	7.926	8.594	9.313	10.086	10.915	11.806	12.761	13.786
11	8.140	8.912	9.749	10.657	11.642	12.708	13.862	15.112	16.462	17.921
12	9.850	10.872	11.991	13.215	14.552	16.012	17.605	19.343	21.236	23.298
13	11.918	13.264	14.749	16.386	18.190	20.175	22.359	24.759	27.395	30.287
14	14.421	16.182	18.141	20.319	22.737	25.420	28.395	31.691	35.339	39.373
15	17.449	19.742	22.314	25.195	28.422	32.030	36.062	40.565	45.587	51.185
16	21.113	24.085	27.446	31.242	35.527	40.357	45.799	51.923	58.808	66.541
17	25.547	29.384	33.758	38.740	44.409	50.850	58.165	66.461	75.862	86.503
18	30.912	35.848	41.523	48.038	55.511	64.071	73.869	85.070	97.862	112.454
19	37.404	43.735	51.073	59.567	69.389	80.730	93.813	108.890	126.242	146.190
20	45.258	53.357	62.820	73.863	86.736	101.720	119.143	139.379	162.852	190.047
21	54.762	65.095	77.268	91.591	108.420	128.167	151.312	178.405	210.079	247.061
22	66.262	79.416	95.040	113.572	135.525	161.490	192.165	228.358	271.002	321.178
23	80.178	96.887	116.899	140.829	169.407	203.477	244.050	292.298	349.592	417.531
24	97.015	118.203	143.786	174.628	211.758	256.381	309.943	374.141	450.974	542.791
25	117.388	144.207	176.857	216.539	264.698	323.040	393.628	478.901	581.756	705.627
30	304.471	389.748	497.904	634.810	807.793	1025.904	1300.477	1645.488	2078.208	2619.936
40	2048.309	2846.941	3946.340	5455.797	7523.156	10346.879	14195.051	19426.418	26520.723	36117.754
50	13779.844	20795.680	31278.301	46889.207	70064.812	104354.562	154942.687	229345.875	338440.000	497910.125

n	31%	32%	33%	34%	35%	36%	37%	38%	39%	40%
1	1.310	1.320	1.330	1.340	1.350	1.360	1.370	1.380	1.390	1.400
2	1.716	1.742	1.769	1.796	1.822	1.850	1.877	1.904	1.932	1.960
3	2.248	2.300	2.353	2.406	2.460	2.515	2.571	2.628	2.686	2.744
4	2.945	3.036	3.129	3.224	3.321	3.421	3.523	3.627	3.733	3.842
5	3.858	4.007	4.162	4.320	4.484	4.653	4.826	5.005	5.189	5.378
6	5.054	5.290	5.535	5.789	6.053	6.328	6.612	6.907	7.213	7.530
7	6.621	6.983	7.361	7.758	8.172	8.605	9.058	9.531	10.025	10.541
8	8.673	9.217	9.791	10.395	11.032	11.703	12.410	13.153	13.935	14.758
9	11.362	12.166	13.022	13.930	14.894	15.917	17.001	18.151	19.370	20.661
10	14.884	16.060	17.319	18.666	20.106	21.646	23.292	25.049	26.924	28.925
11	19.498	21.199	23.034	25.012	27.144	29.439	31.910	34.567	37.425	40.495
12	25.542	27.982	30.635	33.516	36.644	40.037	43.716	47.703	52.020	56.694
13	33.460	36.937	40.745	44.912	49.469	54.451	59.892	65.830	72.308	79.371
14	43.832	49.756	54.190	60.181	66.784	74.053	82.051	90.845	100.509	111.120
15	57.420	64.358	72.073	80.643	90.158	100.712	112.410	125.366	139.707	155.567
16	75.220	84.953	95.857	108.061	121.713	136.968	154.002	173.005	194.192	217.793
17	98.539	112.138	127.490	144.802	164.312	186.277	210.983	238.747	269.927	304.911
18	129.086	148.022	169.561	194.035	221.822	253.337	289.046	329.471	375.198	426.875
19	169.102	195.389	225.517	260.006	299.459	344.537	395.993	454.669	521.525	597.625
20	221.523	257.913	299.937	348.408	404.270	468.571	542.511	627.443	724.919	836.674
21	290.196	340.446	398.916	466.867	545.764	637.256	743.240	865.871	1007.637	1171.343
22	380.156	449.388	530.558	625.601	736.781	865.668	1018.238	1194.900	1400.615	1639.878
23	498.004	593.192	705.642	838.305	994.653	1178.668	1394.986	1648.961	1946.854	2295.829
24	652.385	783.013	938.504	1123.328	1342.781	1602.988	1911.129	2275.564	2706.125	3214.158
25	854.623	1033.577	1248.210	1505.258	1812.754	2180.063	2618.245	3140.275	3761.511	4499.816
30	3297.081	4142.008	5194.516	6503.285	8128.426	10142.914	12636.086	15716.703	19517.969	24201.043
40	49072.621	66519.313	89962.188	121388.437	163433.875	219558.625	294317.937	393684.687	525508.312	700022.688

APPENDIX C

PRESENT VALUE OF $1

n	1%	2%	3%	4%	5%	6%	7%	8%	9%	10%
1	.990	.980	.971	.962	.952	.943	.935	.926	.917	.909
2	.980	.961	.943	.925	.907	.890	.873	.857	.842	.826
3	.971	.942	.915	.889	.864	.840	.816	.794	.772	.751
4	.961	.924	.888	.855	.823	.792	.763	.735	.708	.683
5	.951	.906	.863	.822	.784	.747	.713	.681	.650	.621
6	.942	.888	.837	.790	.746	.705	.666	.630	.596	.564
7	.933	.871	.813	.760	.711	.665	.623	.583	.547	.513
8	.923	.853	.789	.731	.677	.627	.582	.540	.502	.467
9	.914	.837	.766	.703	.645	.592	.544	.500	.460	.424
10	.905	.820	.744	.676	.614	.558	.508	.463	.422	.386
11	.896	.804	.722	.650	.585	.527	.475	.429	.388	.350
12	.887	.789	.701	.625	.557	.497	.444	.397	.356	.319
13	.879	.773	.681	.601	.530	.469	.415	.368	.326	.290
14	.870	.758	.661	.577	.505	.442	.388	.340	.299	.263
15	.861	.743	.642	.555	.481	.417	.362	.315	.275	.239
16	.853	.728	.623	.534	.458	.394	.339	.292	.252	.218
17	.844	.714	.605	.513	.436	.371	.317	.270	.231	.198
18	.836	.700	.587	.494	.416	.350	.296	.250	.212	.180
19	.828	.686	.570	.475	.396	.331	.277	.232	.194	.164
20	.820	.673	.554	.456	.377	.312	.258	.215	.178	.149
21	.811	.660	.538	.439	.359	.294	.242	.199	.164	.135
22	.803	.647	.522	.422	.342	.278	.226	.184	.150	.123
23	.795	.634	.507	.406	.326	.262	.211	.170	.138	.112
24	.788	.622	.492	.390	.310	.247	.197	.158	.126	.102
25	.780	.610	.478	.375	.295	.233	.184	.146	.116	.092
30	.742	.552	.412	.308	.231	.174	.131	.099	.075	.057
40	.672	.453	.307	.208	.142	.097	.067	.046	.032	.022
50	.608	.372	.228	.141	.087	.054	.034	.021	.013	.009

n	11%	12%	13%	14%	15%	16%	17%	18%	19%	20%
1	.901	.893	.885	.877	.870	.862	.855	.847	.840	.833
2	.812	.797	.783	.769	.756	.743	.731	.718	.706	.694
3	.731	.712	.693	.675	.658	.641	.624	.609	.593	.579
4	.659	.636	.613	.592	.572	.552	.534	.516	.499	.482
5	.593	.567	.543	.519	.497	.476	.456	.437	.419	.402
6	.535	.507	.480	.456	.432	.410	.390	.370	.352	.335
7	.482	.452	.425	.400	.376	.354	.333	.314	.296	.279
8	.434	.404	.376	.351	.327	.305	.285	.266	.249	.233
9	.391	.361	.333	.308	.284	.263	.243	.225	.209	.194
10	.352	.322	.295	.270	.247	.227	.208	.191	.176	.162
11	.317	.287	.261	.237	.215	.195	.178	.162	.148	.135
12	.286	.257	.231	.208	.187	.168	.152	.137	.124	.112
13	.258	.229	.204	.182	.163	.145	.130	.116	.104	.093
14	.232	.205	.181	.160	.141	.125	.111	.099	.088	.078
15	.209	.183	.160	.140	.123	.108	.095	.084	.074	.065
16	.188	.163	.141	.123	.107	.093	.081	.071	.062	.054
17	.170	.146	.125	.108	.093	.080	.069	.060	.052	.045
18	.153	.130	.111	.095	.081	.069	.059	.051	.044	.038
19	.138	.116	.098	.083	.070	.060	.051	.043	.037	.031
20	.124	.104	.087	.073	.061	.051	.043	.037	.031	.026
21	.112	.093	.077	.064	.053	.044	.037	.031	.026	.022
22	.101	.083	.068	.056	.046	.038	.032	.026	.022	.018
23	.091	.074	.060	.049	.040	.033	.027	.022	.018	.015
24	.082	.066	.053	.043	.035	.028	.023	.019	.015	.013
25	.074	.059	.047	.038	.030	.024	.020	.016	.013	.010
30	.044	.033	.026	.020	.015	.012	.009	.007	.005	.004
40	.015	.011	.008	.005	.004	.003	.002	.001	.001	.001
50	.005	.003	.002	.001	.001	.001	.000	.000	.000	.000

PRESENT VALUE OF $1 (CONTINUED)

n	21%	22%	23%	24%	25%	26%	27%	28%	29%	30%
1	.826	.820	.813	.806	.800	.794	.787	.781	.775	.769
2	.683	.672	.661	.650	.640	.630	.620	.610	.601	.592
3	.564	.551	.537	.524	.512	.500	.488	.477	.466	.455
4	.467	.451	.437	.423	.410	.397	.384	.373	.361	.350
5	.386	.370	.355	.341	.328	.315	.303	.291	.280	.269
6	.319	.303	.289	.275	.262	.250	.238	.227	.217	.207
7	.263	.249	.235	.222	.210	.198	.188	.178	.168	.159
8	.218	.204	.191	.179	.168	.157	.148	.139	.130	.123
9	.180	.167	.155	.144	.134	.125	.116	.108	.101	.094
10	.149	.137	.126	.116	.107	.099	.092	.085	.078	.073
11	.123	.112	.103	.094	.086	.079	.072	.066	.061	.056
12	.102	.092	.083	.076	.069	.062	.057	.052	.047	.043
13	.084	.075	.068	.061	.055	.050	.045	.040	.037	.033
14	.069	.062	.055	.049	.044	.039	.035	.032	.028	.025
15	.057	.051	.045	.040	.035	.031	.028	.025	.022	.020
16	.047	.042	.036	.032	.028	.025	.022	.019	.017	.015
17	.039	.034	.030	.026	.023	.020	.017	.015	.013	.012
18	.032	.028	.024	.021	.018	.016	.014	.012	.010	.009
19	.027	.023	.020	.017	.014	.012	.011	.009	.008	.007
20	.022	.019	.016	.014	.012	.010	.008	.007	.006	.005
21	.018	.015	.013	.011	.009	.008	.007	.006	.005	.004
22	.015	.013	.011	.009	.007	.006	.005	.004	.004	.003
23	.012	.010	.009	.007	.006	.005	.004	.003	.003	.002
24	.010	.008	.007	.006	.005	.004	.003	.003	.002	.002
25	.009	.007	.006	.005	.004	.003	.003	.002	.002	.001
30	.003	.003	.002	.002	.001	.001	.001	.001	.000	.000
40	.000	.000	.000	.000	.000	.000	.000	.000	.000	.000
50	.000	.000	.000	.000	.000	.000	.000	.000	.000	.000

n	31%	32%	33%	34%	35%	36%	37%	38%	39%	40%
1	.763	.758	.752	.746	.741	.735	.730	.725	.719	.714
2	.583	.574	.565	.557	.549	.541	.533	.525	.518	.510
3	.445	.435	.425	.416	.406	.398	.389	.381	.372	.364
4	.340	.329	.320	.310	.301	.292	.284	.276	.268	.260
5	.259	.250	.240	.231	.223	.215	.207	.200	.193	.186
6	.198	.189	.181	.173	.165	.158	.151	.145	.139	.133
7	.151	.143	.136	.129	.122	.116	.110	.105	.100	.095
8	.115	.108	.102	.096	.091	.085	.081	.076	.072	.068
9	.088	.082	.077	.072	.067	.063	.059	.055	.052	.048
10	.067	.062	.058	.054	.050	.046	.043	.040	.037	.035
11	.051	.047	.043	.040	.037	.034	.031	.029	.027	.025
12	.039	.036	.033	.030	.027	.025	.023	.021	.019	.018
13	.030	.027	.025	.022	.020	.018	.017	.015	.014	.013
14	.023	.021	.018	.017	.015	.014	.012	.011	.010	.009
15	.017	.016	.014	.012	.011	.010	.009	.008	.007	.006
16	.013	.012	.010	.009	.008	.007	.006	.006	.005	.005
17	.010	.009	.008	.007	.006	.005	.005	.004	.004	.003
18	.008	.007	.006	.005	.005	.004	.003	.003	.003	.002
19	.006	.005	.004	.004	.003	.003	.003	.002	.002	.002
20	.005	.004	.003	.003	.002	.002	.002	.002	.001	.001
21	.003	.003	.003	.002	.002	.002	.001	.001	.001	.001
22	.003	.002	.002	.002	.001	.001	.001	.001	.001	.001
23	.002	.002	.001	.001	.001	.001	.001	.001	.001	.000
24	.002	.001	.001	.001	.001	.001	.001	.000	.000	.000
25	.001	.001	.001	.001	.001	.000	.000	.000	.000	.000
30	.000	.000	.000	.000	.000	.000	.000	.000	.000	.000
40	.000	.000	.000	.000	.000	.000	.000	.000	.000	.000

APPENDIX D

SUM OF AN ANNUITY OF $1 FOR *n* PERIODS

n	1%	2%	3%	4%	5%	6%	7%	8%	9%	10%
1	1.000	1.000	1.000	1.000	1.000	1.000	1.000	1.000	1.000	1.000
2	2.010	2.020	2.030	2.040	2.050	2.060	2.070	2.080	2.090	2.100
3	3.030	3.060	3.091	3.122	3.152	3.184	3.215	3.246	3.278	3.310
4	4.060	4.122	4.184	4.246	4.310	4.375	4.440	4.506	4.573	4.641
5	5.101	5.204	5.309	5.416	5.526	5.637	5.751	5.867	5.985	6.105
6	6.152	6.308	6.468	6.633	6.802	6.975	7.153	7.336	7.523	7.716
7	7.214	7.434	7.662	7.898	8.142	8.394	8.654	8.923	9.200	9.487
8	8.286	8.583	8.892	9.214	9.549	9.897	10.260	10.637	11.028	11.436
9	9.368	9.755	10.159	10.583	11.027	11.491	11.978	12.488	13.021	13.579
10	10.462	10.950	11.464	12.006	12.578	13.181	13.816	14.487	15.193	15.937
11	11.567	12.169	12.808	13.486	14.207	14.972	15.784	16.645	17.560	18.531
12	12.682	13.412	14.192	15.026	15.917	16.870	17.888	18.977	20.141	21.384
13	13.809	14.680	15.618	16.627	17.713	18.882	20.141	21.495	22.953	24.523
14	14.947	15.974	17.086	18.292	19.598	21.015	22.550	24.215	26.019	27.975
15	16.097	17.293	18.599	20.023	21.578	23.276	25.129	27.152	29.361	31.772
16	17.258	18.639	20.157	21.824	23.657	25.672	27.888	30.324	33.003	35.949
17	18.430	20.012	21.761	23.697	25.840	28.213	30.840	33.750	36.973	40.544
18	19.614	21.412	23.414	25.645	28.132	30.905	33.999	37.450	41.301	45.599
19	20.811	22.840	25.117	27.671	30.539	33.760	37.379	41.446	46.018	51.158
20	22.019	24.297	26.870	29.778	33.066	36.785	40.995	45.762	51.159	57.274
21	23.239	25.783	28.676	31.969	35.719	39.992	44.865	50.422	56.764	64.002
22	24.471	27.299	30.536	34.248	38.505	43.392	49.005	55.456	62.872	71.402
23	25.716	28.845	32.452	36.618	41.430	46.995	53.435	60.893	69.531	79.542
24	26.973	30.421	34.426	39.082	44.501	50.815	58.176	66.764	76.789	88.496
25	28.243	32.030	36.459	41.645	47.726	54.864	63.248	73.105	84.699	98.346
30	34.784	40.567	47.575	56.084	66.438	79.057	94.459	113.282	136.305	164.491
40	48.885	60.401	75.400	95.024	120.797	154.758	199.630	295.052	337.872	442.580
50	64.461	84.577	112.794	152.664	209.341	290.325	406.516	573.756	815.051	1163.865

n	11%	12%	13%	14%	15%	16%	17%	18%	19%	20%
1	1.000	1.000	1.000	1.000	1.000	1.000	1.000	1.000	1.000	1.000
2	2.110	2.120	2.130	2.140	2.150	2.160	2.170	2.180	2.190	2.200
3	3.342	3.374	3.407	3.440	3.472	3.506	3.539	3.572	3.606	3.640
4	4.710	4.779	4.850	4.921	4.993	5.066	5.141	5.215	5.291	5.368
5	6.228	6.353	6.480	6.610	6.742	6.877	7.014	7.154	7.297	7.442
6	7.913	8.115	8.323	8.535	8.754	8.977	9.207	9.442	9.683	9.930
7	9.783	10.089	10.405	10.730	11.067	11.414	11.772	12.141	12.523	12.916
8	11.859	12.300	12.757	13.233	13.727	14.240	14.773	15.327	15.902	16.499
9	14.164	14.776	15.416	16.085	16.786	17.518	18.285	19.086	19.923	20.799
10	16.722	17.549	18.420	19.337	20.304	21.321	22.393	23.521	24.709	25.959
11	19.561	20.655	21.814	23.044	24.349	25.733	27.200	28.755	30.403	32.150
12	22.713	24.133	25.650	27.271	29.001	30.850	32.824	34.931	37.180	39.580
13	26.211	28.029	29.984	32.088	34.352	36.786	39.404	42.218	45.244	48.496
14	30.095	32.392	34.882	37.581	40.504	43.672	47.102	50.818	54.841	59.196
15	34.405	37.280	40.417	43.842	47.580	51.659	56.109	60.965	66.260	72.035
16	39.190	42.753	46.671	50.980	55.717	60.925	66.648	72.938	79.850	87.442
17	44.500	48.883	53.738	59.117	65.075	71.673	78.978	87.067	96.021	105.930
18	50.396	55.749	61.724	68.393	75.836	84.140	93.404	103.739	115.265	128.116
19	56.939	63.439	70.748	78.968	88.211	98.603	110.283	123.412	138.165	154.739
20	64.202	72.052	80.946	91.024	102.443	115.379	130.031	146.626	165.417	186.687
21	72.264	81.698	92.468	104.767	118.809	134.840	153.136	174.019	197.846	225.024
22	81.213	92.502	105.489	120.434	137.630	157.414	180.169	206.342	236.436	271.028
23	91.147	104.602	120.203	138.295	159.274	183.600	211.798	244.483	282.359	326.234
24	102.173	118.154	136.829	158.656	184.166	213.976	248.803	289.490	337.007	392.480
25	114.412	133.333	155.616	181.867	212.790	249.212	292.099	342.598	402.038	471.976
30	199.018	241.330	293.192	356.778	434.738	530.306	647.423	790.932	966.698	1181.865
40	581.812	767.080	1013.667	1341.979	1779.048	2360.724	3134.412	4163.094	5529.711	7343.715
50	1668.723	2399.975	3459.344	4994.301	7217.488	10435.449	15088.805	21812.273	31514.492	45496.094

SUM OF AN ANNUITY OF $1 FOR *n* PERIODS (CONTINUED)

n	21%	22%	23%	24%	25%	26%	27%	28%	29%	30%
1	1.000	1.000	1.000	1.000	1.000	1.000	1.000	1.000	1.000	1.000
2	2.210	2.220	2.230	2.240	2.250	2.260	2.270	2.280	2.290	2.300
3	3.674	3.708	3.743	3.778	3.813	3.848	3.883	3.918	3.954	3.990
4	5.446	5.524	5.604	5.684	5.766	5.848	5.931	6.016	6.101	6.187
5	7.589	7.740	7.893	8.048	8.207	8.368	8.533	8.700	8.870	9.043
6	10.183	10.442	10.708	10.980	11.259	11.544	11.837	12.136	12.442	12.756
7	13.321	13.740	14.171	14.615	15.073	15.546	16.032	16.534	17.051	17.583
8	17.119	17.762	18.430	19.123	19.842	20.588	21.361	22.163	22.995	23.858
9	21.714	22.670	23.669	24.712	25.802	26.940	28.129	29.369	30.664	32.015
10	27.274	28.657	20.113	31.643	33.253	34.945	36.723	38.592	40.556	42.619
11	34.001	35.962	38.039	40.238	42.566	45.030	47.639	50.398	53.318	56.405
12	42.141	44.873	47.787	50.895	54.208	57.738	61.501	65.510	69.780	74.326
13	51.991	55.745	59.778	64.109	68.760	73.750	79.106	84.853	91.016	97.624
14	63.909	69.009	74.528	80.496	86.949	93.925	101.465	109.611	118.411	127.912
15	78.330	85.191	92.669	100.815	109.687	119.346	129.860	141.302	153.750	167.285
16	95.779	104.933	114.983	126.010	138.109	151.375	165.922	181.867	199.337	218.470
17	116.892	129.019	142.428	157.252	173.636	191.733	211.721	233.790	258.145	285.011
18	142.439	158.403	176.187	195.993	218.045	242.583	269.885	300.250	334.006	371.514
19	173.351	194.251	217.710	244.031	273.556	306.654	343.754	385.321	431.868	483.968
20	210.755	237.986	268.783	303.598	342.945	387.384	437.568	494.210	558.110	630.157
21	256.013	291.343	331.603	377.461	429.681	489.104	556.710	633.589	720.962	820.204
22	310.775	356.438	408.871	469.052	538.101	617.270	708.022	811.993	931.040	1067.265
23	377.038	435.854	503.911	582.624	673.626	778.760	900.187	1040.351	1202.042	1388.443
24	457.215	532.741	620.810	723.453	843.032	982.237	1144.237	1332.649	1551.634	1805.975
25	554.230	650.944	764.596	898.082	1054.791	1238.617	1454.180	1706.790	2002.608	2348.765
30	1445.111	1767.044	2160.459	2640.881	3227.172	3941.953	4812.891	5873.172	7162.785	8729.805
40	9749.141	12936.141	17153.691	22728.367	30088.621	39791.957	52570.707	69376.562	91447.375	120389.375

n	31%	32%	33%	34%	35%	36%	37%	38%	39%	40%
1	1.000	1.000	1.000	1.000	1.000	1.000	1.000	1.000	1.000	1.000
2	2.310	2.320	2.330	2.340	2.350	2.360	2.370	2.380	2.390	2.400
3	4.026	4.062	4.099	4.136	4.172	4.210	4.247	4.284	4.322	4.360
4	6.274	6.362	6.452	6.542	6.633	6.725	6.818	6.912	7.008	7.104
5	9.219	9.398	9.581	9.766	9.954	10.146	10.341	10.539	10.741	10.946
6	13.077	13.406	13.742	14.086	14.438	14.799	15.167	15.544	15.930	16.324
7	18.131	18.696	19.277	19.876	20.492	21.126	21.779	22.451	23.142	23.853
8	24.752	25.678	26.638	27.633	28.664	29.732	30.837	31.982	33.167	34.395
9	33.425	34.895	36.429	38.028	39.696	41.435	43.247	45.135	47.103	49.152
10	44.786	47.062	49.451	51.958	54.590	57.351	60.248	63.287	66.473	69.813
11	59.670	63.121	66.769	70.624	74.696	78.998	83.540	88.335	93.397	98.739
12	79.167	84.320	89.803	95.636	101.840	108.437	115.450	122.903	130.822	139.234
13	104.709	112.302	120.438	129.152	138.484	148.474	159.166	170.606	182.842	195.928
14	138.169	149.239	161.183	174.063	187.953	202.925	219.058	236.435	255.151	275.299
15	182.001	197.996	215.373	234.245	254.737	276.978	301.109	327.281	355.659	386.418
16	239.421	262.354	287.446	314.888	344.895	377.690	413.520	452.647	495.366	541.985
17	314.642	347.307	383.303	422.949	466.608	514.658	567.521	625.652	689.558	759.778
18	413.180	459.445	510.792	567.751	630.920	700.935	778.504	864.399	959.485	1064.689
19	542.266	607.467	680.354	761.786	852.741	954.271	1067.551	1193.870	1334.683	1491.563
20	711.368	802.856	905.870	1021.792	1152.200	1298.809	1463.544	1648.539	1856.208	2089.188
21	932.891	1060.769	1205.807	1370.201	1556.470	1767.380	2006.055	2275.982	2581.128	2925.862
22	1223.087	1401.215	1604.724	1837.068	2102.234	2404.636	2749.294	3141.852	3588.765	4097.203
23	1603.243	1850.603	2135.282	2462.669	2839.014	3271.304	3767.532	4336.750	4989.379	5737.078
24	2101.247	2443.795	2840.924	3300.974	3833.667	4449.969	5162.516	5985.711	6936.230	8032.906
25	2753.631	3226.808	3779.428	4424.301	5176.445	6052.957	7073.645	8261.273	9642.352	11247.062
30	10632.543	12940.672	15737.945	19124.434	23221.258	28172.016	34148.906	41357.227	50043.625	60500.207

APPENDIX E

PRESENT VALUE OF AN ANNUITY OF $1 FOR *n* PERIODS

n	1%	2%	3%	4%	5%	6%	7%	8%	9%	10%
1	.990	.980	.971	.962	.952	.943	.935	.926	.917	.909
2	1.970	1.942	1.913	1.886	1.859	1.833	1.808	1.783	1.759	1.736
3	2.941	2.884	2.829	2.775	2.723	2.673	2.624	2.577	2.531	2.487
4	3.902	3.808	3.717	3.630	3.546	3.465	3.387	3.312	3.240	3.170
5	4.853	4.713	4.580	4.452	4.329	4.212	4.100	3.993	3.890	3.791
6	5.795	5.601	5.417	5.242	5.076	4.917	4.767	4.623	4.486	4.355
7	6.728	6.472	6.230	6.002	5.786	5.582	5.389	5.206	5.033	4.868
8	7.652	7.326	7.020	6.733	6.463	6.210	5.971	5.747	5.535	5.335
9	8.566	8.162	7.786	7.435	7.108	6.802	6.515	6.247	5.995	5.759
10	9.471	8.983	8.530	8.111	7.722	7.360	7.024	6.710	6.418	6.145
11	10.368	9.787	9.253	8.760	8.306	7.887	7.499	7.139	6.805	6.495
12	11.255	10.575	9.954	9.385	8.863	8.384	7.943	7.536	7.161	6.814
13	12.134	11.348	10.635	9.986	9.394	8.853	8.358	7.904	7.487	7.103
14	13.004	12.106	11.296	10.563	9.899	9.295	8.746	8.244	7.786	7.367
15	13.865	12.849	11.938	11.118	10.380	9.712	9.108	8.560	8.061	7.606
16	14.718	13.578	12.561	11.652	10.838	10.106	9.447	8.851	8.313	7.824
17	15.562	14.292	13.166	12.166	11.274	10.477	9.763	9.122	8.544	8.022
18	16.398	14.992	13.754	12.659	11.690	10.828	10.059	9.372	8.756	8.201
19	17.226	15.679	14.324	13.134	12.085	11.158	10.336	9.604	8.950	8.365
20	18.046	16.352	14.878	13.590	12.462	11.470	10.594	9.818	9.129	8.514
21	18.857	17.011	15.415	14.029	12.821	11.764	10.836	10.017	9.292	8.649
22	19.661	17.658	15.937	14.451	13.163	12.042	11.061	10.201	9.442	8.772
23	20.456	18.292	16.444	14.857	13.489	12.303	11.272	10.371	9.580	8.883
24	21.244	18.914	16.936	15.247	13.799	12.550	11.469	10.529	9.707	8.985
25	22.023	19.524	17.413	15.622	14.094	12.783	11.654	10.675	9.823	9.077
30	25.808	22.397	19.601	17.292	15.373	13.765	12.409	11.258	10.274	9.427
40	32.835	27.356	23.115	19.793	17.159	15.046	13.332	11.925	10.757	9.779
50	39.197	31.424	25.730	21.482	18.256	15.762	13.801	12.234	10.962	9.915

n	11%	12%	13%	14%	15%	16%	17%	18%	19%	20%
1	.901	.893	.885	.877	.870	.862	.855	.847	.840	.833
2	1.713	1.690	1.668	1.647	1.626	1.605	1.585	1.566	1.547	1.528
3	2.444	2.402	2.361	2.322	2.283	2.246	2.210	2.174	2.140	2.106
4	3.102	3.037	2.974	2.914	2.855	2.798	2.743	2.690	2.639	2.589
5	3.696	3.605	3.517	3.433	3.352	3.274	3.199	3.127	3.058	2.991
6	4.231	4.111	3.998	3.889	3.784	3.685	3.589	3.498	3.410	3.326
7	4.712	4.564	4.423	4.288	4.160	4.039	3.922	3.812	3.706	3.605
8	5.146	4.968	4.799	4.639	4.487	4.344	4.207	4.078	3.954	3.837
9	5.537	5.328	5.132	4.946	4.772	4.607	4.451	4.303	4.163	4.031
10	5.889	5.650	5.426	5.216	5.019	4.833	4.659	4.494	4.339	4.192
11	6.207	5.938	5.687	5.453	5.234	5.029	4.836	4.656	4.487	4.327
12	6.492	6.194	5.918	5.660	5.421	5.197	4.988	4.793	4.611	4.439
13	6.750	6.424	6.122	5.842	5.583	5.342	5.118	4.910	4.715	4.533
14	6.982	6.628	6.303	6.002	5.724	5.468	5.229	5.008	4.802	4.611
15	7.191	6.811	6.462	6.142	5.847	5.575	5.324	5.092	4.876	4.675
16	7.379	6.974	6.604	6.265	5.954	5.669	5.405	5.162	4.938	4.730
17	7.549	7.120	6.729	6.373	6.047	5.749	5.475	5.222	4.990	4.775
18	7.702	7.250	6.840	6.467	6.128	5.818	5.534	5.273	5.033	4.812
19	7.839	7.366	6.938	6.550	6.198	5.877	5.585	5.316	5.070	4.843
20	7.963	7,469	7.025	6.623	6.259	5.929	5.628	5.353	5.101	4.870
21	8.075	7.562	7.102	6.687	6.312	5.973	5.665	5.384	5.127	4.891
22	8.176	7.645	7.170	6.743	6.359	6.011	5.696	5.410	5.149	4.909
23	8.266	7.718	7.230	6.792	6.399	6.044	5.723	5.432	5.167	4.925
24	8.348	7.784	7.283	6.835	6.434	6.073	5.747	5.451	5.182	4.937
25	8.442	7.843	7.330	6.873	6.464	6.097	5.766	5.467	5.195	4.948
30	8.694	8.055	7.496	7.003	6.566	6.177	5.829	5.517	5.235	4.979
40	8.951	8.244	7.634	7.105	6.642	6.233	5.871	5.548	5.258	4.997
50	9.042	8.305	7.675	7.133	6.661	6.246	5.880	5.554	5.262	4.999

PRESENT VALUE OF AN ANNUITY OF $1 FOR *n* PERIODS (CONTINUED)

n	21%	22%	23%	24%	25%	26%	27%	28%	29%	30%
1	.826	.820	.813	.806	.800	.794	.787	.781	.775	.769
2	1.509	1.492	1.474	1.457	1.440	1.424	1.407	1.392	1.376	1.361
3	2.074	2.042	2.011	1.981	1.952	1.923	1.896	1.868	1.842	1.816
4	2.540	2.494	2.448	2.404	2.362	2.320	2.280	2.241	2.203	2.166
5	2.926	2.864	2.803	2.745	2.689	2.635	2.583	2.532	2.483	2.436
6	3.245	3.167	3.092	3.020	2.951	2.885	2.821	2.759	2.700	2.643
7	3.508	3.416	3.327	3.242	3.161	3.083	3.009	2.937	2.868	2.802
8	3.726	3.619	3.518	3.421	3.329	3.241	3.156	3.076	2.999	2.925
9	3.905	3.786	3.673	3.566	3.463	3.366	3.273	3.184	3.100	3.019
10	4.054	3.923	3.799	3.682	3.570	3.465	3.364	3.269	3.178	3.092
11	4.177	4.035	3.902	3.776	3.656	3.544	3.437	3.335	3.239	3.147
12	4.278	4.127	3.985	3.851	3.725	3.606	3.493	3.387	3.286	3.190
13	4.362	4.203	4.053	3.912	3.780	3.656	3.538	3.427	3.322	3.223
14	4.432	4.265	4.108	3.962	3.824	3.695	3.573	3.459	3.351	3.249
15	4.489	4.315	4.153	4.001	3.859	3.726	3.601	3.483	3.373	3.268
16	4.536	4.357	4.189	4.033	3.887	3.751	3.623	3.503	3.390	3.283
17	4.576	4.391	4.219	4.059	3.910	3.771	3.640	3.518	3.403	3.295
18	4.608	4.419	4.243	4.080	3.928	3.786	3.654	3.529	3.413	3.304
19	4.635	4.442	4.263	4.097	3.942	3.799	3.664	3.539	3.421	3.311
20	4.657	4.460	4.279	4.110	3.954	3.808	3.673	3.546	3.427	3.316
21	4.675	4.476	4.292	4.121	3.963	3.816	3.679	3.551	3.432	3.320
22	4.690	4.488	4.302	4.130	3.970	3.822	3.684	3.556	3.436	3.323
23	4.703	4.499	4.311	4.137	3.976	3.827	3.689	3.559	3.438	3.325
24	4.713	4.507	4.318	4.143	3.981	3.831	3.692	3.562	3.441	3.327
25	4.721	4.514	4.323	4.147	3.985	3.834	3.694	3.564	3.442	3.329
30	4.746	4.534	4.339	4.160	3.995	3.842	3.701	3.569	3.447	3.332
40	4.760	4.544	4.347	4.166	3.999	3.846	3.703	3.571	3.448	3.333
50	4.762	4.545	4.348	4.167	4.000	3.846	3.704	3.571	3.448	3.333

n	31%	32%	33%	34%	35%	36%	37%	38%	39%	40%
1	.763	.758	.752	.746	.741	.735	.730	.725	.719	.714
2	1.346	1.331	1.317	1.303	1.289	1.276	1.263	1.250	1.237	1.224
3	1.791	1.766	1.742	1.719	1.696	1.673	1.652	1.630	1.609	1.589
4	2.130	2.096	2.062	2.029	1.997	1.966	1.935	1.906	1.877	1.849
5	2.390	2.345	2.302	2.260	2.220	2.181	2.143	2.106	2.070	2.035
6	2.588	2.534	2.483	2.433	2.385	2.339	2.294	2.251	2.209	2.168
7	2.739	2.677	2.619	2.562	2.508	2.455	2.404	2.355	2.308	2.263
8	2.854	2.786	2.721	2.658	2.598	2.540	2.485	2.432	2.380	2.331
9	2.942	2.868	2.798	2.730	2.665	2.603	2.544	2.487	2.432	2.379
10	3.009	2.930	2.855	2.784	2.715	2.649	2.587	2.527	2.469	2.414
11	3.060	2.978	2.899	2.824	2.752	2.683	2.618	2.555	2.496	2.438
12	3.100	3.013	2.931	2.853	2.779	2.708	2.641	2.576	2.515	2.456
13	3.129	3.040	2.956	2.876	2.799	2.727	2.658	2.592	2.529	2.469
14	3.152	3.061	2.974	2.892	2.814	2.740	2.670	2.603	2.539	2.477
15	3.170	3.076	2.988	2.905	2.825	2.750	2.679	2.611	2.546	2.484
16	3.183	3.088	2.999	2.914	2.834	2.757	2.685	2.616	2.551	2.489
17	3.193	3.097	3.007	2.921	2.840	2.763	2.690	2.621	2.555	2.492
18	3.201	3.104	3.012	2.926	2.844	2.767	2.693	2.624	2.557	2.494
19	3.207	3.109	3.017	2.930	2.848	2.770	2.696	2.626	2.559	2.496
20	3.211	3.113	3.020	2.933	2.850	2.772	2.698	2.627	2.561	2.497
21	3.215	3.116	3.023	2.935	2.852	2.773	2.699	2.629	2.562	2.498
22	3.217	3.118	3.025	2.936	2.853	2.775	2.700	2.629	2.562	2.498
23	3.219	3.120	3.026	2.938	2.854	2.775	2.701	2.630	2.563	2.499
24	3.221	3.121	3.027	2.939	2.855	2.776	2.701	2.630	2.563	2.499
25	3.222	3.122	3.028	2.939	2.856	2.776	2.702	2.631	2.563	2.499
30	3.225	2.124	3.030	2.941	2.857	2.777	2.702	2.631	2.564	2.500
40	3.226	3.125	3.030	2.941	2.857	2.778	2.703	2.632	2.564	2.500
50	3.226	3.125	3.030	2.941	2.857	2.778	2.703	2.632	2.564	2.500

APPENDIX F

SOLUTIONS FOR SELECTED END-OF-CHAPTER PROBLEMS

CHAPTER 1

no solutions provided

CHAPTER 2

2-1A. Total assets $120,650
Net income $3,360
2-3A. Taxes $469,000
2-5A. Free cash flow ($10,000)
2-7A. Free cash flow ($14,000)

CHAPTER 3

3-1A. Cash $201,875
Accounts receivable $175,000
Long-term debt $320,000

3-3A. Current ratio 1.75
Operating profit margin 21%
Operating income return on investment 21%
Debt ratio 50%
Return on equity 20%

3-5A. a. Average collection period 30 days
b. Accounts receivable $369,863
c. Inventory $700,000

3-7A. a. Total asset turnover 2.25
Operating profit margin 11.1%
Operating income return on investment 25%
b. 19.5%
c. 14.5%

3-9A. Current ratio 2.51
OIROI 23.2%
Debt ratio 0.26
Return on equity 22.4%

CHAPTER 4

4-1A. Discretionary Financing Needed = ($0.5 million)
4-3A. Total Assets = $1.8 million
4-5A. Total Assets = $2 million
4-9A. a. Notes Payable = $1.11 million
b. Current Ratio = 2x and 1.12x

4-11A.

	January	February	March
Net Monthly Change	$65,500	(1,000)	(127,500)
Cumulative Borrowing	$–0–	–0–	61,000

4-13A. a. Debt to Assets = 61.1%, 61.9%, 59.4%, 50.4%, 44.4%

CHAPTER 5

5-1A. a. $12,970
c. $3,019.40
5-2A. a. n = 15 years
5-3A. b. 5%
c. 9%
5-4A. b. PV = $235.20
5-5A. a. $6,289
c. $302.89
5-6A. c. $1,562.96
5-7A. a. FV_1 = $10,600
FV_5 = $13,380
FV_{15} = $23,970
5-9A. a. $6,690
b. Semiannual: $6,720
Bimonthly: $6,740
5-11A. Year 1: 18,000 books
Year 2: 21,600 books
Year 3: 25,920 books
5-13A. $6,108.11
5-15A. 8%
5-17A. $658,197.85
5-21A. b. $8,333.33
5-26A. $6,509
5-28A. 22%
5-29A. $6,934.81
5-32A. a. $1,989.73
5-35A. $15,912

CHAPTER 6

6-3A. $\bar{k}$ = 9.1%: σ = 3.06%
6-5A. Security A: $\bar{k}$ = 16.7%; σ = 10.12%
Security B: $\bar{k}$ = 9.2%; σ = 3.57%
6-7A. About 0.5

6-11A.

Time	Asman Return
2	20.0%

6-13A. a. 15.8%
b. 0.95
6-14A. S&P 500: $\bar{k}$ = 0.71%
σ = 4.52%
Intel: $\bar{k}$ = 6.07%
σ = 9.69%

CHAPTER 7

7-1A. $752.52
7-5A. 5.28%
7-7A. a. $863.78
b. Market Value $707.63 when required rate of return is 15%;
Market Value $1,171.19 when required rate of return is 8%
7-9A. a. $1,182.57
b. (i) $925.31; (ii) $1,573.50
7-11A. a. 7.14
b. $1,107.79
7-13A. I. 3.68 years
II. 4.08 years

CHAPTER 8

8-1A. $50
8-3A. $116.67
8-5A. a. 8.5%
b. $42.50
8-7A. a. 18.9%
b. $28.57
8-9A. 7.2%
8-11A. $39.96
8-13A. a. 10.91%
b. $36
8-17A. a. 18%
b. $32.14
8-19A. a. 5.1%

CHAPTER 9

9-1A. a. IRR = 7%

b. IRR = 17%
9-3A. a. IRR = approximately 19%
9-5A. a. Payback Period = $80,000/$20,000 = 4 years
Discounted Payback Period = 5.0 + 4,200/11,280 = 5.37 years.
c. PI = 1.0888
9-7A. Project C:
Payback Period = 3.5 years
Discounted Payback Period = 4.0 + 397/1,242 = 4.32 years
9-9A. Project C: IRR = 16%

CHAPTER 10

10-1A. a. $6,800
b. $3,400
c. No taxes
d. $1,020 refund
10-3A. $404,500
10-9A. a. $110,000
b. $33,600
10-11A. a. $230,000
10-15A. b. NPV_B = $12,100
10-17A. a. EAA_A = $9,729

CHAPTER 11

11-1A. b. NPV_A = $8,025
NPV_B = $10,112
11-3A. NPV_A = $726,380
11-5A. NPV_A = $24,780

CHAPTER 12

12-1A. a. After-tax cost of debt = 7.49%
b. k_{nc} = 14.37%
c. k_c = 15.14%
d. k_{ps} = 8.77%
12-3A. k_{pc} = 12.06%
12-5A. k_{ps} = 7.69%
12-7A. k_{ps} = 14.29%
12-9A. a. k_{cb} = 17.59%
b. k_{ac} = 18.25%
12-11A. a. V_b = $1,063.80
b. NP_o = $952.10
c. 525 bonds
12-13A. K_d = 6.4%

CHAPTER 13

13-1A. Stock price = $14.23
13-3A. a. EVA (year 1) = $2,181.82
b. ROI (year 1) = 34.22%
c. Firm value = $30,730.95
Present value of EVAs = $20,912.76

CHAPTER 14

no solutions provided

CHAPTER 15

15-2A. Breakeven point = 40,000 bottles.
15-4A. a. Jake's EBIT = $154,067.40
Sarasota = 480,000
Jefferson = 28,970
b. Jake's = 8.232
Sarasota = 1.789
Jefferson = 8.310
c. Jake's = 1.78 times
Sarasota = 2.77 times
Jefferson = 4.09 times
d. Jefferson Wholesale would suffer the largest decline in profitability.
15-6A. a. 6,296 pairs of shoes
b. $534,591.19
c. At 7,000, EBIT = $19,000
At 9,000, EBIT = $73,000
At 15,000, EBIT = $235,000
d. 9.95 times; 3.33 times; 1.72 times
15-7A. a. 9,000 units
b. $1,620,000
15-9A. a. $85,416.67
b. 7,030 units; $189,815
15-11A. a. 1.94 times
15-13A. a. 10,000 units
b. $1,800,000
15-15A. a. F = $173,333.33
b. 14,444 units; S^* = $288,888.88
15-21. a. 5,000 units
b. $125,000
c. –$10,000; $10,000; $30,000
15-23A. 5 times
15-25A. 1,400,000 units
15-27A. a. 3 times
b. 1.25 times
c. 3.75 times
d. $8 million

CHAPTER 16

16-2A. Cash collection from sales = $1,280,000
16-4A. a. EBIT = $2,000,000
b. EPS will be $1.00 for each plan.
d. Plan B
16-6A. a. EBIT = $240,000
b. EPS will be $1.80 for each plan.
16-7. a. EBIT = $220,000
b. Plan B.
16-9A. a. $640,000
b. EPS = $3.20
16-11A. a. $300,000
b. EPS = $3.00
16-13A. a. Plan A = $7.68
b. 10.378
16-17A. a. $20,000,000
b. k_c = 25%; k_o = 25%
16-19A. a. Plan A vs. Plan B = $9,000
Plan A. vs. Plan C = $18,000

CHAPTER 17

17-2A. 95,238 shares
17-4A. Dividend = $16,000
17-6A. Value of stock both plans = $31.76
17-8A. b. Net gain = $24,500
17-10A. b. 9,615 shares
17-12A. Dividend = $90,000

CHAPTER 18

18-1A.

	Firm A	Firm B
Working Capital	$500,000	$550,000
Current Ratio	1.25x	.917x

18-3A. APR = 13.79%
18-5A. a. 36.73%
b. 74.23%
c. 37.11%
d. 16.33%

18-7A. a. APR = 16.3%
b. APR = 19.7%
18-9A. a. APR = 16.27%
18-11A. a. APR = 22.85%
18-13A. a. APR = 10%
b. APR = 11.75%
c. APR = 12.5%

CHAPTER 19

19-1A. Yes, the projected net annual gain from using the new system is $33,356.
19-4A. a. Yes, the firm will generate $35,288 in net annual savings.
b. 5.01%
19-5A. a. $2,625,000
b. $241,500
19-6A. .5322 days
19-9A. $10,667

CHAPTER 20

20-1A. 18.37%
20-3A. a. 36.36%
b. 36.73%
20-5A. a. $90,000
b. $53,333
20-7A. $56,875
20-8A. a. 775 units
20-10A. a. 816 units
b. $61,237
20-12A. b. 35.2 orders per year

CHAPTER 21

no solutions provided

CHAPTER 22

22-1A. a. $8,437
b. $9,368
c. $25,695
22-3A. Canada: 1,1853; 1,1881; 1,912
Japan: 213,4927; 211,9992; 209,1613
Switzerland: 1,9459, 1,9346: 1,8815
22-5A. Net gain = $149.02

CHAPTER 23*

Web site 23-1A. Average theoretical value = $12,433
Web site 23-3A. Net present value = $14.87

CHAPTER 24*

Web site 24-1A. Balloon = $268,160.75
Web site 24-3A. Payment = $31,977.78
Web site 24-5A. a. 15%
b. Payment = $76,359.19
c. 9%
Web site 24-7A. a. NPV(P) = −$2,271
b. NAL = −$874

*Chapters 23 and 24 can be found at **www.prenhall.com/keown**

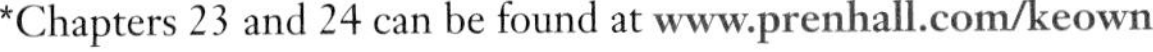

GLOSSARY

Accounting book value The value of an asset as shown on a firm's balance sheet. It represents the historical cost of the asset rather than its current market value or replacement cost.

Accounts payable Liability of the firm for goods purchased from suppliers on credit.

Accounts receivable A promise to receive cash from customers who purchased goods from the firm on credit.

Accounts receivable turnover ratio Accounts receivable turnover ratio indicates how rapidly the firm is collecting its credit, as measured by the number of times its accounts receivable are collected or "rolled over" during the year.

Accrued expenses Expenses that have been incurred but not yet paid in cash.

Acid-test (quick) ratio Acid-test ratio indicates a firm's liquidity, as measured by its liquid assets, excluding inventories, relative to its current liabilities.

Adjustable rate preferred stock Preferred stock intended to provide investors with some protection against wide swings in the stock value that occur when interest rates move up and down. The dividend rate changes along with prevailing interest rates.

Agency costs The costs, such as a reduced stock price, associated with potential conflict between managers and investors when these two groups are not the same.

Agency problem Problem resulting from conflicts of interest between the manager (the stockholder's agent) and the stockholders.

Amortized loan A loan paid off in equal installments.

Analytical income statement A financial statement used by internal analysts that differs in composition from audited or published financial statements.

Annual percentage yield (APY) or effective annual rate (EAR) The annual compound rate that produces the same return as the nominal or quoted rate.

Annuity A series of equal dollar payments for a specified number of years.

Annuity due An annuity in which the payments occur at the beginning of each period.

Anticipatory buying Buying in anticipation of a price increase to secure goods at a lower cost.

Appraisal costs Costs of testing, measuring, and analyzing to safeguard against possible defects going unnoticed.

Appraisal value The worth of a company as determined by an independent appraiser. Appraisers use a variety of methods to determine the value of a firm; however, replacement value of the firm's assets is often the basis for the appraisal value.

Arbitrageur A person involved in the process of buying and selling in more than one market to make riskless profits.

Asked rate The rate a bank or foreign exchange trader "asks" the customer to pay in home currency for foreign currency when the bank is selling and the customer is buying.

Asset allocation Identifying and selecting the asset classes appropriate for a specific investment portfolio and determining the proportions of these assets within the given portfolio.

Auction rate preferred stock Variable rate preferred stock in which the dividend rate is set by an auction process.

Average collection period Average collection period indicates how rapidly a firm is collecting its credit, as measured by the average number of days it takes to collect its accounts receivable.

Average tax rate Taxes owed by the firm divided by the firm's taxable income.

Balance sheet A statement of financial position at a particular date. The form of the statement follows the balance sheet equation: total assets = total liabilities + owners' equity.

Base pay Fixed amount of compensation paid to an employee.

Beta A measure of the relationship between an investment's returns and the market's returns. This is a measure of the investment's non-diversifiable risk.

Bid rate The rate at which the bank buys the foreign currency from the customer by paying in home currency.

Bid-asked spread The difference between the asked quote and the bid quote.

"Bird-in-the-hand" dividend theory The belief that dividend income has a higher value to the investor than does capital gains income, because dividends are more certain than capital gains.

Bond A type of debt or a long-term promissory note, issued by the borrower, promising to pay its holder a predetermined and fixed amount of interest each year.

Bonus payment Compensation paid to an employee that is dependent upon the firm's performance compared to predetermined targets.

Book value The value of an asset as shown on a firm's balance sheet. It represents the historical cost of the asset rather than its current market value or replacement cost.

Bounded incentive pay programs Incentive pay programs that place upper and lower limits on the levels of firm performance for which incentive compensation will be awarded to employees.

Business risk The potential variability in a firm's earnings before interest and taxes resulting from the nature of the firm's business endeavors.

Buying rate The bid rate in a currency transaction.

Call option A call option gives its owner the right to purchase a given number of shares of stock or some other asset at a specified price over a given time period.

Call provision Lets the company buy its preferred stock back from the investor, usually at a premium price above the stock's par value.

Capital asset pricing model (CAPM) An equation stating that the expected rate of return on an investment is a function of (1) the risk-free rate, (2) the investment's systematic risk, and (3) the expected risk premium for the market portfolio of all risky securities.

Capital budgeting The decision-making process with respect to investment in fixed assets.

Capital charge The firm's invested capital at the beginning of the period multiplied by the firm's weighted average cost of capital. This value is deducted from the firm's net operating profit after taxes (NOPAT) to estimate EVA.

Capital market All institutions and procedures that facilitate transactions in long-term financial instruments.

Capital rationing The placing of a limit by the firm on the dollar size of the capital budget.

Capital structure The mix of long-term sources of funds used by the firm.

Cash Currency and coin plus demand deposit accounts.

Cash break-even analysis A variation from traditional break-even analysis that removes (deducts) noncash expenses from the cost items.

Cash budget A detailed plan of future cash receipts and disbursements.

Certainty equivalent The amount of cash a person would require with certainty to make him or her indifferent between this certain sum and a particular risky or uncertain sum.

Certainty equivalent approach A method for incorporating risk into the capital-budgeting decision in which the decision maker substitutes a set of equivalent riskless cash flows for the expected cash flows and then discounts these cash flows back to the present.

Characteristic line The line of "best fit" through a series of returns for a firm's stock relative to the market returns. The slope of the line, frequently called beta, represents the average movement of the firm's stock returns in response to a movement in the market's returns.

Chop-shop or break-up value Firm value is estimated by determining the value of the different business segments of the firm. Segment value is computed by applying average valuation ratios of pure-play companies to the various business segments of the firm. Firm value is then calculated as the sum of the segment values.

Clientele effect The belief that individuals and institutions that need current income will invest in companies that have high dividend payouts. Other investors prefer to avoid taxes by holding securities that offer only small dividend income, but large capital gains as the capital gains are deferred until realized. Thus we have a "clientele" of investors.

Commercial paper Short-term loans by the most creditworthy borrowers that are bought and sold in the market for short-term debt securities.

Common stock Common stock shares represent the ownership in a corporation.

Common stockholders Investors who own the firm's common stock. Common stockholders are the residual owners of the firm.

Compound annuity Depositing an equal sum of money at the end of each year for a certain number of years and allowing it to grow.

Compound interest Interest that occurs when interest paid on the investment during the first period is added to the principal; then, during the second period, interest is earned on this new sum.

Concentration banking The selection of a few major banks where the firm maintains significant disbursing accounts.

Constant dividend payout ratio A dividend payment policy in which the percentage of earnings paid out in dividends is held constant. The dollar amount fluctuates from year to year as profits vary.

Contribution margin Unit sales price minus unit variable cost.

Conversion period The time period during which the convertible can be exchanged for common stock.

Conversion premium The difference between the convertible's market price and the higher of its security value and its conversion value.

Conversion ratio The number of shares of common stock for which a convertible security can be exchanged.

Conversion value The total market value of the common stock for which it can be exchanged.

Convertible preferred stock Convertible preferred stock allows the preferred stockholder to convert the preferred stock into a predetermined number of shares of common stock, if he or she so chooses.

Convertible security Preferred stock or debentures that can be exchanged for a specified number of shares of common stock at the will of the owner.

Corporation An entity that 'legally' functions separate and apart from its owners.

Coupon interest rate A bond's coupon interest rate indicates what percentage of the par value of the bond will be paid out annually in the form of interest.

Covered-interest arbitrage Arbitrage designed to eliminate differentials across currency and interest rate markets.

Credit scoring The numerical credit evaluation of each candidate.

Cross rate The computation of an exchange rate for a currency from the exchange rates of two other currencies.

Cumulative preferred stock Requires all past unpaid preferred stock dividends to be paid before any common stock dividends are declared.

Cumulative voting Each share of stock allows the shareholder a number of votes equal to the number of directors being elected. The shareholder can then cast all of his or her votes for a single candidate or split them among the various candidates.

Currency swap An exchange of debt obligations in different currencies.

Current assets (gross working capital) Current assets are assets that are expected to be converted into cash within a year, consisting primarily of cash, marketable securities, accounts receivable, inventories, and prepaid expenses.

Current debt Debt due to be paid within 1 year.

Current ratio Current ratio indicates a firm's liquidity, as measured by its liquid assets (current assets) relative to its liquid debt (short-term or current liabilities).

Current yield The ratio of the annual interest payment to the bond's market price.

Date of record Date at which the stock transfer books are to be closed for determining which investor is to receive the next dividend payment.

Debenture Any unsecured long-term debt.

Debt Consists of such sources as credit extended by suppliers or a loan from a bank.

Debt capacity The maximum proportion of debt that the firm can include in its capital structure and still maintain its lowest composite cost of capital.

Debt capital Funds provided to the firm by a creditor.

Debt ratio Debt ratio indicates how much debt is used to finance a firm's assets.

Declaration date The date upon which a dividend is formally declared by the board of directors.

Delivery-time stock The inventory needed between the order date and the receipt of the inventory ordered.

Depository transfer checks A non-negotiable instrument that provides the firm with a means to move funds from local bank accounts to concentration bank accounts.

Direct quote The exchange rate that indicates the number of units of the home currency required to buy one unit of foreign currency.

Direct sale The sale of securities by the corporation to the investing public without the services of an investment banking firm.

Direct securities The pure financial claims issued by economic units to savers. These can later be transformed into indirect securities.

Discount bond A bond that is selling below its par value.

Discounted payback period A variation of the payback period decision criterion defined as the number of years required to recover the initial cash outlay from the discounted net cash flows.

Discretionary financing Sources of financing that require an explicit decision on the part of the firm's management every time funds are raised.

Dividend payout ratio The amount of dividends relative to the company's net income or earnings per share.

DuPont analysis The DuPont analysis is an approach to evaluate a firm's profitability and return on equity.

Duration A measure of how responsive a bond's price is to changing interest rates. Also, it is a weighted average time to maturity in which the weight attached to each year is the present value of the cash flow for that year.

Earnings before interest, taxes, depreciation, and amortization (EBITDA) Operating income plus depreciation and amortization expenses.

Earnings before taxes Operating income minus interest expense.

EBIT-EPS indifference point The level of earnings before interest and taxes (EBIT) that will equate earnings per share (EPS) between two different financing plans.

Economic value added The difference in a firm's net operating profit after taxes (NOPAT) and the capital charge for the period (i.e., the product of the firm's cost of capital and its invested capital at the beginning of the period).

Efficient market A market in which the values of securities at any instant in time fully reflect all available information, which results in the market value and the intrinsic value being the same.

Equity Stockholders' investment in the firm and the cumulative profits retained in the business up to the date of the balance sheet.

Equivalent annual annuity (EAA) An annual cash flow that yields the same present value as the project's *NPV*. It is calculated by dividing the project's *NPV* by the appropriate $PVIFA_{i,n}$.

Eurobonds Bonds issued in a country different from the one in whose currency the bond is denominated—for instance, a bond issued in Europe or in Asia by an American company that pays interest and principal to the lender in U.S. dollars.

Eurodollar loans Intermediate-term loans made by major international banks to businesses based on foreign deposits that are denominated in dollars.

Exchange rate The price of foreign currency stated in terms of the domestic or home currency.

Exchange rate risk The risk that tomorrow's exchange rate will differ from today's.

Ex-dividend date The date upon which stock brokerage companies have uniformly decided to terminate the right of ownership to the dividend, which is two days prior to the record date.

Exercise ratio The number of shares of common stock that can be obtained at the exercise price with one warrant.

Expectations theory The effect of new information about a company on the firm's stock price depends more on how the new information compares to expectations than on the actual announcement itself.

Expected rate of return The weighted average of all possible returns where the returns are weighted by the probability that each will occur.

Explicit cost of capital The cost of capital for any funds source considered in isolation from other funds sources.

External failure costs Costs resulting from a poor-quality product reaching the customers' hands.

Factoring The sale of a firm's accounts receivable to a financial intermediary known as a factor.

Financial assets Claims for future payment by one economic unit on another.

Financial lease A noncancelable contractual commitment on the part of the firm leasing the asset (the lessee) to make a series of payments to the firm that actually owns the asset (the lessor) for use of the asset.

Financial leverage Financing a portion of the firm's assets with securities bearing a fixed or limited rate of return.

Financial markets Those institutions and procedures that facilitate transactions in all types of financial claims (securities).

Financial policy The firm's policies regarding the sources of financing and the particular mix in which they will be used.

Financial ratios Restating the accounting data in relative terms to identify some of the financial strengths and weaknesses of a company.

Financial risk The added variability in earnings available to a firm's shareholders and the additional risk of insolvency caused by the use of financing sources that require a fixed return.

Financial structure The mix of all funds sources that appear on the right side of the balance sheet.

Financial structure design The management activity of seeking the proper mix of all financing components in order to minimize the cost of raising a given amount of funds.

Financing cash flows Financing free cash flows the firm pays to or receives from the investors (lenders and shareholders).

Finished-goods inventory Goods on which the production has been completed but that are not yet sold.

Firm-specific risk or company-unique risk (diversifiable risk or unsystematic risk) The portion of the variation in investment returns that can be eliminated through investor diversification. This diversifiable risk is the result of factors that are unique to the particular firm.

Fixed assets Assets comprising equipment, buildings, and land.

Fixed costs (indirect costs) Costs that do not vary in total dollar amount as sales volume or quantity of output changes.

Float The length of time from when a check is written until the actual recipient can draw upon or use the "good funds."

Floating-rate international currency system An international currency system in which exchange rates between different national currencies are allowed to fluctuate with supply and demand conditions. This contrasts with a fixed rate system in which exchange rates are pegged for extended periods of time and adjusted infrequently.

Flotation costs The underwriter's spread and issuing costs associated with the issuance and marketing of new securities.

Forward exchange contract A contract that requires delivery on a specified future date of one currency in return for a specified amount of another currency.

Forward-spot differential The premium or discount between forward and spot currency exchange rates.

Free cash flows Amount of cash available from operations after paying for investments in net operating working capital and fixed assets. This cash is available to distribute to the firm's creditors and owners.

Free cash-flow model Method of valuing a firm by calculating the present value of all future free cash flows.

Futures contract A contract to buy or sell a stated commodity or financial claim at a specified price at some future, specified time.

Futures margin Good faith money the purchaser puts down to ensure that the contract will be carried out.

Future-value interest factor ($FVIF_{i,n}$) The value $(1 + i)^n$ used as a multiplier to calculate an amount's future value.

Future-value interest factor for an annuity ($FVIFA_{i,n}$) The value used as a multiplier to calculate the future value of an annuity.

Hedging principle (principle of self-liquidating debt) Financing maturity should follow the cash-flow-producing characteristics of the asset being financed.

Implicit cost of debt The change in the cost of common equity caused by the choice to use additional debt.

Incentive (performance-based) compensation Compensation such as bonus and long-term compensation that is designed to motivate the employee to align employee actions with shareholder wealth creation.

Income statement The statement of profit or loss for the period, comprised of revenues less expenses for the period.

"Increasing-stream hypothesis of dividend policy" A smoothing of the dividend stream in order to minimize the effect of company reversals. Corporate managers make every effort to avoid a dividend cut, attempting instead to develop a gradually increasing dividend series over the long-term future.

Indenture The legal agreement or contract between the firm issuing the bonds and the bond trustee who represents the bondholders.

Indirect quote The exchange rate that expresses the required number of units of foreign currency to buy one unit of home currency.

Indirect securities The unique financial claims issued by financial intermediaries. Mutual fund shares are an example.

Information asymmetry The difference in accessibility to information between management and investors may result in a lower stock price than would occur under conditions of certainty.

Initial outlay The immediate cash outflow necessary to purchase the asset and put it in operating order.

Initial public offering (IPO) The first time the company's stock is sold to the public.

Insolvency Situation in which the firm is unable to pay its bills on time.

Interest expense Interest paid on a firm's outstanding debt. A firm's interest expense is tax deductible.

Interest-rate parity (IRP) theory States that (except for the effects of small transaction costs) the forward premium or discount should be equal and opposite in size to the differences in the national interest rates for securities of the same maturity.

Interest-rate risk The variability in a bond's value (risk) caused by changing interest rates.

Internal failure costs Those costs associated with discovering poor-quality products prior to delivery.

Internal rate of return (IRR) A capital-budgeting decision criterion that reflects the rate of return a project earns.

Mathematically, it is the discount rate that equates the present value of the inflows with the present value of the outflows.

Intrinsic or economic value The present value of the asset's expected future cash flows. This value is the amount the investor considers to be a fair value, given the amount, timing, and riskiness of future cash flows.

Inventory Raw materials, work-in-progress, and finished goods held by the firm for eventual sale.

Inventory loans Short-term loans that are secured by the pledge of inventories. The type of pledge or security agreement varies and can include floating liens, chattel mortgage agreements, field warehouse financing agreements, and terminal warehouse agreements.

Inventory management The control of the assets used in the production process or produced to be sold in the normal course of the firm's operations.

Inventory turnover ratio Inventory turnover indicates the relative liquidity of inventories, as measured by the number of times a firm's inventories are replaced during the year.

Invested capital Total amount of funds invested in a firm.

Investment banker A financial specialist who underwrites and distributes new securities and advises corporate clients about raising external financial capital.

Investor's required rate of return The minimum rate of return necessary to attract an investor to purchase or hold a security.

Joint probability The probability of two different sequential outcomes occurring.

Junk or high-yield bonds Bonds rated BB or below.

Just-in-time inventory control system Keeping inventory to a minimum and relying on suppliers to furnish parts "just in time."

Law of one price The proposition that in competitive markets the same goods should sell for the same price where prices are stated in terms of a single currency.

Lease A contract between a lessee, who acquires the services of a leased asset by making a series of rental payments to the lessor, who is the owner of the asset.

Lessee and lessor The user of the leased asset, who agrees to make periodic lease or rental payments to the lessor, who owns the asset.

Limited liability company (LLC) An organizational form that is a cross between a partnership and a corporation.

Line of credit agreement A line of credit agreement is an agreement between a firm and its banker to provide short-term financing to meet its temporary financing needs.

Liquid assets The sum of cash and marketable securities.

Liquidation value The amount that could be realized if an asset were sold individually and not as a part of a going concern.

Liquidity The ability of a firm to pay its bills on time, and how quickly a firm converts its liquid assets (accounts receivables and inventories) into cash.

Loan amortization schedule A breakdown of loan payments into interest and principal payments.

Long-term compensation Compensation paid to the employee as an incentive to align the employee's actions to the firm's goal of maximizing shareholder wealth. The most common form of long-term compensation is stock options.

Long-term debt Loans from banks or other sources that lend money for longer than 12 months.

Majority voting Each share of stock allows the shareholder one vote, and each position on the board of directors is voted on separately. As a result, a majority of shares has the power to elect the entire board of directors.

Marginal or incremental analysis A method of analysis for credit policy changes in which the incremental benefits are compared to the added costs.

Marginal tax rate The tax rate that would be applied to the next dollar of taxable income.

Market value The observed value for the asset in the marketplace.

Market value added (*MVA*) The difference in the market value of the firm and the capital that has been invested in it.

Marketable securities Security investments (financial assets) the firm can quickly convert to cash balances. Also known as near cash or near-cash assets.

Market-related risk (nondiversifiable risk or systematic risk) The portion of variations in investment returns that cannot be eliminated through investor diversification. This variation results from factors that affect all stocks.

Maturity The length of time until the bond issuer returns the par value to the bondholder and terminates the bond.

Modified internal rate of return (*MIRR*) A variation of the IRR capital-budgeting decision criterion defined as the discount rate that equates the present value of the project's annual cash outlays with the present value of the project's terminal value, where the terminal value is defined as the sum of the future value of the project's free cash flows compounded to the project's termination at the project's required rate of return.

Money market All institutions and procedures that facilitate transactions in short-term credit instruments.

Mortgage bond A bond secured by a lien on real property.

Multinational corporation (MNC) A corporation with holdings and/or operations in one or more countries.

Mutually exclusive projects A set of projects that perform essentially the same task, so that acceptance of one will necessarily mean rejection of the others.

Net and net-net leases In a net lease agreement, the lessee assumes the risk and burden of ownership over the term of the lease. This means that the lessee must pay insurance and taxes on the asset as well as maintain the operating condition of the asset. In a net-net lease, the lessee must, in addition to the requirements of a net lease, return the asset to the lessor at the end of the lease while still worth a preestablished value.

Net income A figure representing the firm's profit or loss for the period. It also represents the earnings available to the firm's common stockholders.

Net income (NI) approach to valuation The concept from financial theory that suggests the firm's capital structure has a direct impact upon and can increase its market valuation.

Net operating income (NOI) approach to valuation The concept from financial theory that suggests the firm's capital structure has no impact on its market valuation.

Net present value (NPV) A capital-budgeting decision criterion defined as the present value of the free cash flows after tax less the project's initial outlay.

Net present value profile A graph showing how a project's net present value changes as the discount rate changes.

Net profit margin Net profit margin measures the net income of a firm as a percent of sales.

Net working capital The difference between the firm's current assets and its current liabilities. When the term 'working capital' is used, it is frequently intended to mean net working capital.

Nominal or quoted interest rate The stated rate of interest on the contract.

Noninterest-bearing current liabilities Current liabilities other than short-term debt.

Operating income (earnings before interest and taxes) Profit from sales minus total operating expenses.

Operating income return on investment Operating income return on investment indicates the effectiveness of management at generating operating profits on the firm's assets, as measured by operating profits relative to the total assets.

Operating lease A lease agreement (see financial lease) in which the lessee can cancel the agreement at any time by giving proper notice to the lessor.

Operating leverage The incurrence of fixed operating costs in the firm's income stream.

Operating profit margin Operating profit margin indicates management's effectiveness in managing the firm's income statement, as measured by operating profits relative to sales.

Opportunity cost of funds The next best rate of return available to the investor for a given level of risk.

Optimal capital structure The unique capital structure that minimizes the firm's composite cost of long-term capital.

Optimal range of financial leverage The range of various financial structure combinations that generate the lowest composite cost of capital for the firm.

Option contract An option contract gives its owner the right to buy or sell a fixed number of shares of stock at a specified price over a limited time period.

Option expiration date The date on which the option expires.

Option premium The price of the option.

Option striking price The price at which the stock or asset may be purchased from the writer in the case of a call, or sold to the writer in the case of a put.

Option's intrinsic value The minimum value of the option.

Option's time (or speculative) value The amount by which the option premium exceeds the intrinsic value of the option.

Order point problem Determining how low inventory should be depleted before it is reordered.

Order quantity problem Determining the optimal order size for an inventory item given its usage, carrying costs, and ordering costs.

Ordinary annuity An annuity in which the payments occur at the end of each period.

Organized security exchanges Formal organizations involved in the trading of securities. They are tangible entities that conduct auction markets in listing securities.

Other assets Assets not included in current assets or fixed assets.

Other payables Interest payable and income taxes payable that are to be paid within 1 year.

Over-the-counter markets All security markets except the organized exchanges.

Par value and paid-in capital The amount the firm receives from selling stock to investors.

Par value of a bond The bond's face value that is returned to the bondholder at maturity, usually $1,000.

Participating preferred stock Allows the preferred stockholder to participate in earnings beyond the payment of the stated dividend.

Partnership An association of two or more individuals joining together as co-owners to operate a business for profit.

Payable-through drafts A payment mechanism that substitutes for regular checks in that drafts are not drawn on a bank, but instead are drawn on and authorized by the firm against its demand deposit account. The purpose is to maintain control over field-authorized payments.

Payback period A capital-budgeting criterion defined as the number of years required to recover the initial cash investment.

Payment date The date on which the company mails a dividend check to each investor.

Percent of sales method Estimating the level of an expense, asset, or liability for a future period as a percent of the sales forecast.

"Perfect" capital markets Capital markets where (1) investors can buy and sell stock without incurring any transaction costs, such as brokerage commissions;
(2) companies can issue stocks without any cost of doing so; (3) there are no corporate or personal taxes; (4) complete information about the firm is readily available; (5) there are no conflicts of interest between management and stockholders; and (6) financial distress and bankruptcy costs are nonexistent.

Permanent asset investment An investment in an asset that the firm expects to hold for the foreseeable future, whether fixed assets or current assets. For example, the minimum level of inventory the firm plans to hold for the foreseeable future is a permanent investment.

Permanent sources of financing Sources of financing that do not mature or come due within the year, including intermediate-term debt, long-term debt, preferred stock, and common stock.

Perpetuity An annuity that continues forever.

PIK preferred stock Investors receive no dividends initially; they merely get more preferred stock, which in turn pays dividends in even more preferred stock.

Plowback ratio The percent of a firm's earnings that are reinvested in the firm.

Portfolio beta The relationship between a portfolio's returns and the market's different returns. It is a measure of the portfolio's nondiversifiable risk.

Preemptive rights The right of a common shareholder to maintain a proportionate share of ownership in the firm. When new shares are issued, common shareholders have the first right of refusal.

Preferred stock A hybrid security with characteristics of both common stock and bonds. It is similar to common stock because it has no fixed maturity date, the nonpayment of dividends does not bring on bankruptcy, and dividends are not deductible for tax purposes. Preferred stock is similar to bonds in that dividends are limited in amount.

Preferred stockholders Investors who own the firm's preferred stock.

Premium bond A bond that is selling above its par value.

Prepaid expenses Expenses that have been paid in advance. These assets are recorded on the balance sheet and expensed on the income statement as they are used.

Present value The current value of a future sum.

Present-value interest factor ($PVIF_{i,n}$) The value $[1/(1 + i)^n]$ used as a multiplier to calculate an amount's present value.

Present-value interest factor for an annuity ($PVIFA_{i,n}$) The value used as a multiplier to calculate the present value of an annuity.

Preventive costs Costs resulting from design and production efforts on the part of the firm to reduce or eliminate defects.

Primary market A market in which new, as opposed to previously issued, securities are traded.

Primary markets Transactions in securities offered for the first time to potential investors.

Private placement (direct placement) A security offering limited to a small number of potential investors.

Privileged subscription The process of marketing a new security issue to a select group of investors.

Probability tree A schematic representation of a problem in which all possible outcomes are graphically displayed.

Profitability index (PI) (or Benefit/Cost Ratio) A capital-budgeting decision criterion defined as the ratio of the present value of the future free cash flows to the initial outlay.

Project standing alone risk The risk of a project standing alone is measured by the variability of the asset's expected returns. That is, it is the risk of a project ignoring the fact that it is only one of many projects within the firm, and the firm's stock is but one of many stocks within a stockholder's portfolio.

Project's contribution-to-firm risk The amount of risk that a project contributes to the firm as a whole. That is, it is a project's risk considering the effects of diversification among different projects within the firm, but ignoring the effects of shareholder diversification within the portfolio.

Protective provisions Provisions for preferred stock that are included in the terms of the issue to protect the investor's interest.

Proxy A proxy gives a designated party the temporary power of attorney to vote for the signee at the corporation's annual meeting.

Proxy fights When rival groups compete for proxy votes in order to control the decisions made in a stockholder meeting.

Public offering A security offering where all investors have the opportunity to acquire a portion of the financial claims being sold.

Purchasing-power parity (PPP) theory In the long run, exchange rates adjust so that the purchasing power of each currency tends to remain the same. Thus, exchange rate changes tend to reflect international differences in inflation rates. Countries with high rates of inflation tend to experience declines in the value of their currency.

Pure play method A method of estimating a project's beta that attempts to identify a publicly traded firm that is engaged solely in the same business as the project, and uses that beta as a proxy for the project's beta.

Put option A put option gives its owner the right to sell a given number of shares of common stock or some other asset at a specified price over a given time period.

Raw materials inventory This includes the basic materials purchased from other firms to be used in the firm's production operations.

Real assets Tangible assets such as houses, equipment, and inventories.

Real rate of interest The nominal rate of interest less the expected rate of inflation over the maturity of the fixed-income security. This represents the expected increase in actual purchasing power to the investor.

Residual dividend theory A theory asserting that the dividends to be paid should equal capital left over after the financing of profitable investments.

Retained earnings The cumulative earnings that have been retained and reinvested in the firm over its life (cumulative earnings – cumulative dividends).

Return on assets Return on assets determines the amount of net income produced on a firm's assets by relating net income to total assets.

Return on common equity Return on common equity indicates the accounting rate of return on the stockholders' investment, as measured by net income relative to common equity.

Return on invested capital The ratio of net operating income after tax for the period divided by the firm's invested capital at the end of the previous period.

Revolving credit or revolver A special type of line of credit agreement in which the line of credit is eventually converted into a term loan that requires periodic payments.

Rights Certificates issued to shareholders giving them an option to purchase a stated number of new shares of stock at a specified price during a 2- to 10-week period.

Risk The likely variability associated with expected revenue or income streams.

Risk premium The additional rate of return we expect to earn above the risk-free rate for assuming risk.

Risk-adjusted discount rate A method for incorporating the project's level of risk into the capital-budgeting process, in which the discount rate is adjusted upward to compensate for higher than normal risk or downward to adjust for lower than normal risk.

Risk-free or riskless rate of return The rate of return on risk-free investments. The interest rate on short-term U.S. government securities is commonly used to measure this rate.

Safety stock Inventory held to accommodate any unusually large and unexpected usage during delivery time.

Sale and leaseback arrangement An arrangement arising when a firm sells land, buildings, or equipment that it already owns and simultaneously enters into an agreement to lease the property back for a specified period under specific terms.

Scenario analysis Simulation analysis that focuses on an examination of the range of possible outcomes.

Seasoned new issue Stock offerings by companies that already have common stock traded.

Secondary market The market in which stock previously issued by the firm trades.

Secondary markets Transactions in currently outstanding securities.

Secured and unsecured loans Secured loans are backed by the pledge of specific assets as collateral whereas unsecured loans are only backed by the promise of the borrower to honor the loan commitment.

Security market line The return line that reflects the attitudes of investors regarding the minimal acceptable return for a given level of systematic risk.

Security value The price the convertible security would sell for in the absence of its conversion feature.

Selling rate Same as the asked rate.

Sell-off The sale of a subsidary, division, or product line by one firm to another.

Semivariable costs (semifixed costs) Costs that exhibit the joint characteristics of both fixed and variable costs over different ranges of output.

Sensitivity analysis The process of determining how the distribution of possible returns for a particular project is affected by a change in one particular input variable.

Shelf registration (shelf offering) A procedure for issuing new securities where the firm obtains a master registration statement approved by the SEC.

Short-term notes Amounts borrowed from a creditor that are due within 1 year.

Simple arbitrage Trading to eliminate exchange rate differentials across the markets for a single currency, for example, for the New York and London markets.

Simulation The process of imitating the performance of an investment project under evaluation using a computer. This is done by randomly selecting observations from each of the distributions that affect the outcome of the project, combining those observations to determine the final output of the project, and continuing with this process until a representative record of the project's probable outcome is assembled.

Single-sourcing Using a single supplier as a source for a particular part or material.

Sinking fund A cash reserve used for the orderly and early retirement of the principal amount of a bond issue. Payments into the fund are known as sinking fund payments.

Small, regular dividend plus year-end extra dividend payout A dividend payment policy in which the firm pays a small regular dividend plus an extra dividend only if the firm has experienced a good year.

Sole proprietorship A business owned by a single individual.

Spin-off The separation of a subsidary from its parent, with no change in the equity ownership. The management of the parent company gives up operating control over the assets involved in the spin-off but the stockholders retain ownership, albeit through shares of the newly created spin-off company.

Spontaneous sources of financing Sources of financing that arise naturally during the course of business. Accounts payable is a primary example.

Spot transaction A transaction made immediately in the marketplace at the market price.

Stable dollar dividend per share payout A dividend policy that maintains a relatively stable dollar dividend per share over time.

Standard deviation A measure of the spread or dispersion about the mean of a probability distribution. We calculate it by squaring the difference between each outcome and its expected value, weighting each squared difference by its associated probability, summing over all possible outcomes, and taking the square root of this sum.

Stock dividend A distribution of shares of up to 25 percent of the number of shares currently outstanding, issued on a pro rata basis to the current stockholders.

Stock repurchase (stock buyback) The repurchase of common stock by the issuing firm for any of a variety of reasons resulting in a reduction of shares outstanding.

Stock split A stock dividend exceeding 25 percent of the number of shares currently outstanding.

Subordinated debenture A debenture that is subordinated to other debentures in being paid in the case of insolvency.

Sustainable rate of growth The maximum rate of growth in sales that the firm can sustain while maintaining its present capital structure (debt and equity mix) and without having to sell new common stock.

Syndicate A group of investment bankers who contractually assist in the buying of a new security issue.

Systematic risk The risk of a project measured from the point of view of a well-diversified shareholder. That is, it is a project's risk taking into account the fact that this project is only one of many projects within the firm, and the firm's stock is but one of many stocks within a stockholder's portfolio.

Target capital structure proportions The mix of financing sources that the firm plans to maintain through time.

Tax shield The element from the federal tax code that permits interest costs to be deductible when computing the firm's tax bill. The dollar difference (the shield) flows to the firm's security holders.

Temporary asset investment Investments in assets that the firm plans to sell (liquidate) within a period no longer than one year. Although temporary investments can be made in fixed assets, this is not the usual case. Temporary investments generally are made in inventories and receivables.

Temporary sources of financing Another term for current liabilities.

Tender offer The formal offer by the company to buy a specified number of shares at a predetermined and stated price.

Term loans Loans that have maturities of 1 to 10 years and are repaid in periodic installments over the life of the loan; usually secured by a chattel mortgage on equipment or a mortgage on real property.

Term structure of interest rates (yield to maturity) Relationship between a debt security's rate of return and the length of time until the debt matures.

Terminal value The estimated value of the firm at the end of the planning period or the present value of the firm's free cash flows to be received after the end of the planning period.

Terms of sale The credit terms identifying the possible discount for early payment.

Times interest earned Times interest earned indicates a firm's ability to cover its interest expense, as measured by its earnings before interest and taxes relative to the interest expense.

Total asset turnover Total asset turnover indicates management's effectiveness at managing a firm balance sheet—its assets—as indicated by the amount of sales generated per one dollar of assets.

Total quality management (TQM) A company-wide systems approach to quality.

Total revenue Total sales dollars.

Trade credit Accounts payable that arise out of the normal course of business when the firm purchases from its suppliers who allow the firm to make payment after the delivery of the merchandise or services.

Transaction exposure The net contracted foreign currency transactions for which the settlement amounts are subject to changing exchange rates.

Transfer price The price a subsidiary or a parent company charges other companies that are part of the same MNC for its goods or services.

Treasury stock The firm's stock that has been issued and reacquired by the firm.

Triangular arbitrage Arbitrage across the markets for all currencies.

Unbounded incentive compensation plan An incentive program that has no minimum or maximum performance targets that limit the payment of incentive pay.

Underwriting The purchase and subsequent resale of a new security issue. The risk of selling the new issue at a profitable price is assumed (underwritten) by an investment banker.

Value drivers Variables that affect firm value and can be controlled or influenced by the firm's management.

Variable costs (direct costs) Costs that are fixed per unit of output but vary in total as output changes.

Volume of output The firm's level of operations expressed either in sales dollars or as units of output.

Warrant An option to purchase a fixed number of shares of common stock at a predetermined price during a specified time period.

Warrant exercise price The price at which a warrant allows its holder to purchase the firm's common stock.

Weighted average cost of capital The average of the after-tax costs of each of the sources of capital used by a firm to finance a project. The weights reflect the proportion of the total financing raised from each source.

Wire transfers A method of moving funds electronically between bank accounts in order to eliminate transit float. The wired funds are immediately usable at the receiving bank.

Working capital The firm's total investment in current assets or assets that it expects to be converted into cash within a year or less.

Work-in-process inventory Partially finished goods requiring additional work before they become finished goods.

Yield to maturity The same as the expected rate of return.

Zero and very low coupon bonds Bonds issued at a substantial discount from their $1,000 face value that pay no or little interest.

Zero balance accounts A cash-management tool that permits centralized control over cash outflows but also maintains divisional disbursing authority.

ORGANIZATION INDEX

Double-numbered entries refer to Web site chapters.

L

M

N

O

P

Q

R

S

T

U

V

W

X

SUBJECT INDEX

Double-numbered entries refer to Web site chapters.

D

J

K

L

T

U

V

W

Y

Z